The Compleat
WHO'S
WHO
in the
BIBLE

The Compleat
WHO'S
WHO
in the
BIBLE

David Mandel

Bridge-Logos

Gainesville, Florida 32614 USA

The Compleat Who's Who in the Bible
by David Mandel
Copyright ©2004 by Bridge-Logos Publishers
All Rights Reserved
Printed in the United States of America
Library of Congress Catalog Card Number: Pending
International Standard Book Number: 0882709720

Scripture quotations are from the Holy Bible, King James Version.

Published by:

Bridge-Logos
Gainesville, FL 32614
www.bridgelogos.com

Introduction

The Bible is today, and has been since two thousand years ago, the cardinal text for Judaism and Christianity. Its stories and characters have greatly influenced Western culture and civilization.

Many of the elements of a specific biography are widely separated in the Bible, distributed across great stretches of the text. This book brings together in a narrative format all the information and references about each character, which are scattered in the different Bible books, and presents the biography of each person as a coherent and continuous story. For the purposes of the book, it is not important if each person in the Bible really existed in historical fact, or only in folk mythology, or as fictional characters in tales written for moral purposes.

Unavoidably, there is some redundancy in the narrations, because many of the biographies share the same events. The author has strived in each case to present the events from the point of view of the specific individual, so that, ideally, each biography should stand independently on its own.

The Compleat Who's Who in the Bible differs from comparable volumes in having only the Bible text as its source. The book is based solely on the biblical text as it is commonly understood, without extra-biblical legends, theological interpretations, or other additions.

The book does not have a theological approach to the Bible. It is based on a literal reading of the biblical text, treating the text as a historical document. However, the author considers that many of the biographies, long or short, of the three thousand persons who inhabit the biblical text, convey the profound truths of the Bible. It is his hope that the user should find these biographies instructive, enjoyable, and interesting to read and, at the same time, gain new insights, as a study of

characters to be learned from, as examples to be emulated or avoided.

The Compleat Who's Who in the Bible is an authoritative and comprehensive reference for a wide audience, including scholars and general readers; students and teachers in high school, religious institutions, colleges, and seminaries; rabbis, ministers, and religious educators; and participants in religious education and Bible study programs. It can be read by people of all ages for information and enjoyment, and at the same time, it can be used as an indispensable reference by Bible students, scholars, researchers, teachers, and clergy persons.

Method of presentation

The biographical entries are arranged alphabetically by name. If more than one person shares the same name, the entries are ordered and numbered according to their first appearance in the Bible.

The name of the person is shown in the first line of each entry, accompanied by information about the origin of the name and its meaning.

On the second line appears the first mention (book-chapter-verse) of the specific personality in the biblical text, and, next to it, the century where he/she lived. The date format is according to B.C. (Before Christ).

The speeches and dialogues of the characters in the text are either translations by the author or paraphrases of their Bible quotations.

Chronology of Biblical Events

The dates mentioned in the entries are a great help in giving context and reality to the biographies, but they should be considered an approximation, not an exact figure. Also, in many cases, persons were born in one century and died in the next one, but, for the sake of simplicity, only one century is mentioned.

The dates, until the division of the kingdom, are based on the internal biblical chronology (e.g. Exodus 12:40) and on estimates—some of them approximations—made by archaeologists and scholars.

After the division of the kingdom, the number of years that each king reigned, as reported by the Bible, does not always coincide with the internal chronology, due to the fact that, in many cases, the heir to the throne, before becoming king on his own, was coregent with his father. The years that the Bible mentions that a king ruled might include years when the heir was not yet officially king, but only co-ruler with his father.

Names in the Bible

A great percentage of biblical names are theophanic; that is, they are compounded with the name of the God of Israel in its different forms, such as *El, Jo, Jah,* or *Jahu,* or some pagan god, such as *Baal.* For example, Abiel, *God is my father*; Jonathan, *God gave*; Malchijah, *God is my king*; Jerubbaal, *Baal will contend.*

Many of the proper names in the Bible times tell important events related to that character. For example, the changing of Abram's name, *Exalted father*, to Abraham, *Father of multitude*, symbolizes God's promise; Leah's naming her firstborn Reuben, *See a son*, shows Leah's effort to gain the love of Jacob, her husband; or Naomi, *Pleasant,* returning to her native town a widow, bereft of her sons, asked to be called Mara, *Bitter.*

A number of names are descriptive, such as Laban, *White*; Dibri, *Wordy*; Edom, *Red*; Doeg, *Worrier*; Er, *Watchful*; Geber, *Man*; Ham, *Hot*; Haran, *Mountaineer*; Hariph, *Sharp*; Heresh, *Deaf*; Ibri, *Hebrew*; Matri, *Rainy*; Kareah, *Bald*; Naarah, *Young girl.*

In many cases, people were given the names of animals, such as Caleb, *Dog*; Nahash, *Snake*; Shaphan, *Rabbit*; Huldah, *Weasel*; Arad, *Wild donkey*; Zippor, *Bird*; Deborah, *Bee*; Hamor, *Donkey.*

The translation of the names has been done by consulting biblical Hebrew dictionaries and Hebrew encyclopedias. The phrase *Hebrew origin* next to the name does not necessarily mean that the name can be accurately and exactly translated to English. In many cases, the name derives from an unused or primitive root, and its meaning can be applied only figuratively or by implication. In frequent cases, the nuances of the meaning are debatable. For example, Hananiah can be understood as *God has favored* or as *God will favor.* The name Bani can be translated as *Built* and also as *My son.* Barzillai can be *Iron maker* or *Man of Iron.* Beeliada can be translated as *Baal knows* and also as *One who knows Baal.*

Chronology of Biblical events

The dates below, until the division of the kingdom, are based on the internal biblical chronology, (e.g. Exodus 12:40) and on estimates, - some of them approximations, - made by archaeologists and scholars.

The number of years that each king reigned, as reported by the Bible, does not always coincide with the internal chronology, due to the fact that in many cases the heir to the throne, before becoming king on his own, was co-regent with his father. The years that the Bible mentions that a king ruled might include years when the heir was not yet officially king, but only co-ruler with his father.

NOTE: The minus sign - before the number refers to the calendar years before the Christian era.

PART 1. From the Patriarchs to the death of King Solomon

20th Century B.C.
−1950 Abraham is born in Ur of the Chaldeans (situated in today's Iraq).

19th Century B.C.
−1875 Abraham emigrates with his wife Sarah and his nephew Lot from Haran, (situated in today's Turkey), to Canaan, (today's Israel), at the age of 75.

−1850 Isaac is born.

−1810 Isaac at the age of 40 marries Rebekah.

18th Century B.C.
−1790 Jacob is born.

−1750 Hyksos, (possibly a Canaanite people) invade Egypt and seize control.

17th Century B.C.
−1660 Jacob with his family settles in Egypt.

−1643 Death of Jacob in Egypt.

−1600 Alphabet writing is developed probably in Canaan.

16th Century B.C.
−1570 Ahmose I expels the Hyksos and restores native Egyptian control to Egypt.

13th Century B.C.
−1230 Exodus of the people of Israel from Egypt, after having been 430 years in Egypt, (Exodus 12:40), led by Moses.

12th Century B.C.
−1190 After wandering forty years in the desert of Sinai, the Hebrew tribes enter Canaan, under the command of Joshua, defeat and destroy a number of Canaanite cities.

−1150 The Peoples from the Sea invade Egypt but are turned back. Part of them, the Philistines, settle in the southern coast of Canaan, where they set up a network of five cities, Ashdod, Ashkelon, Ekron, Gaza, and Gath.

−1120 The northern tribes of Israel, under the leadership of Deborah, defeat Sisera.

−1100 Gideon is judge over Israel. After his death, his son Abimelech destroys the city of Shechem.

11th Century B.C.

−1075 The city of Geba is destroyed during an intertribal war against the tribe of Benjamin.

−1050 The Philistines destroy Shiloh and capture the Ark of God. Samuel becomes judge over Israel.

−1020 Saul is anointed by Samuel as the first king of Israel. He unites the tribes which until then had formed a loose confederation.

−1005 Saul is defeated by the Philistines and dies. David is chosen king of Judah in Hebron at the age of thirty.

10th Century B.C.

−998 After reigning seven years over Judah in Hebron, David becomes king of all   t h e   tribes, when the northern Israelite tribes join Judah in recognizing David as king.

−990 David conquers Jerusalem from the Jebusites and makes it the capital of his kingdom.

−970 Absalom attempts to overthrow his father David.

−965 David dies at the age of seventy, after reigning for forty years, seven over Judah in Hebron, and thirty three in Jerusalem over the united country. He is succeeded by his son Solomon.

−961 Solomon starts the building of the Temple.

−954 King Solomon finishes the Temple, a project which took seven years.

−928 Rehoboam succeeds Solomon. The northern tribes secede and choose Jeroboam as king of Israel, while Rehoboam remains King of Judah.

PART 2. From the division of the Kingdom to the fall of Israel

10th Century B.C.

−923 The Egyptian pharaoh Sheshonk I (called Shishak in the Bible) invades Israel, takes away all the treasures of the Temple and the palace in Jerusalem and destroys several cities in both Judah and Israel.

−922 Jeroboam moves his capital from Shechem to Tirzah, and establishes two shrines at both ends of his kingdom, Bethel and Dan.

−913 Abijah succeeds Rehoboam in Judah, and reigns for three years.

−908 Asa succeeds Abijah in Judah, and reigns for forty-one years.

−907 Nadab succeeds his father Jeroboam in Israel, and reigns for one year.

−906 Nadab is killed by one of his officers, Baasha, who usurps the throne of Israel, and reigns for twenty-three years.

9th Century B.C.

−886 King Asa asks King Ben Hadad of Damascus for help against Baasha, who is trying to seize the territory just north of Jerusalem.

−883 Baasha of Israel is succeeded by his son Elah, who reigns one year.

−882 Elah, king of Israel, is killed by Zimri, one of his army commanders, who reigned for only seven days, until Omri, acclaimed king by the people, takes Tirzah, the capital city, and Zimri seeing that he is lost, find refuge in the palace, burns it, and dies in the flames. Tibni challenges Omri for the Kingdom, but Omri prevails, and Tibni dies.

| –871 | Omri of Israel dies, after reigning the first years in the old capital of Tirzah, and his final years in Samaria, which he founded and made his capital. His son Ahab succeeds him, and reigns for twenty-one years. |

–871 Omri of Israel dies, after reigning the first years in the old capital of Tirzah, and his final years in Samaria, which he founded and made his capital. His son Ahab succeeds him, and reigns for twenty-one years.

–867 Asa, king of Judah, dies, and is succeeded by his son Jehoshaphat, who reigns for twenty-one years.

–853 The Assyrian record of Shalmaneser III mentions that king Ahab took part in the battle of Qarqar with 2,000 chariots and 10,000 soldiers. This event is not mentioned in the Bible.

–850 Ahab, king of Israel, is mortally wounded in battle. His son Ahaziah succeeds him. During Ahab's reign, his wife Jezebel, a Sidonian princess, introduces in Israel the worship of the Phoenician god Baal against the protest and resistance of the prophet Elijah.

–848 Elisha succeeds Elijah as the leading prophet. Ahaziah, the king of Israel, dies of his injury resulting from falling from his balcony, and his succeeded by his brother Jehoram.

–846 Jehoshaphat of Judah dies, and is succeeded by his son Jehoram.

–843 Jehoram, King of Judah, and is succeeded by his son Ahaziah.

–842 King Jehoram of Israel and King Ahaziah of Judah are killed in a revolt by Jehu, who becomes king, and kills all the members of the royal house of Israel, together with members of the royal family of Judah. Athaliah, Judah's queen mother, liquidates the surviving members of the royal house of Judah, with the exception of Jehoash, who is hidden by the high priest.

–836 Athaliah is killed in a palace revolt, and Jehoash is proclaimed king in Judah.

–814 Jehu, King of Israel, dies and is succeeded by his son Jehoahaz.

–800 Jehoahaz, King of Israel, dies and is succeeded by his son Jehoash, during whose reign the prophet Elisha became very ill and died.

8th Century B.C.

–798 Jehoash of Judah is killed by palace conspirators. His son, Amaziah, succeeds him.

–784 King Jehoash of Israel dies and is succeeded by his son Jeroboam II, during whose rule the prophet Amos is active.

–769 King Amaziah of Judah is murdered by conspirators, and his son Uzziah reigns in his place.

–748 King Jeroboam II of Israel dies and is succeeded by his son Zechariah. He rules six months and is murdered by Shallum, who, after being king for only one month, is himself murdered by Menahem, who becomes king.

–739 Uzziah of Judah dies and is succeeded by his son Jotham.

–737 Menahem of Israel, who had become a tributary of Assyria, dies and is succeeded by his son Pekahiah.

–735 King Pekahiah of Israel is killed by Pekah, one of his commanders, who succeeds him as king.

–733 Tiglathpileser, king of Assyria, invades Israel, captures a number of cities and exiles many inhabitants.

–732 Hoshea plots against Pekah, king of Israel, assassinates him, and succeeds him as king, with Israel becoming a vassal kingdom of the Assyrian empire. Jotham, the king of Judah, dies and is succeeded by his son Ahaz.

–725 Hoshea revolts against Assyria. King Shalmaneser of Assyria invades Israel, and besieges Samaria. Micah prophesies the fall of the city.

–721   Sargon II, king of Assyria, sacks Samaria, and exiles a large segment of the population. The kingdom of Israel comes to an end. The deported Israelites – the legendary 10 lost tribes – did not survive as a community; they assimilated into their new localities and disappeared from history. Esarhaddon, king of Assyria, and after him his son Ashurbanipal, brought foreigners (whose descendants were later known as Samaritans) to settle in the abandoned cities of Israel.

PART 3. From the fall of Israel to the fall of Judah

8th Century B.C.

–727   Jotham of Judah dies and is succeeded by his son Ahaz.

–716   King Ahaz of Judah dies and is succeeded by his son Hezekiah, who encourages the immigration of the Northerners who escaped exile.

–701   The Assyrians, under Sennacherib, lay siege to Jerusalem, but King Hezekiah, with the moral encouragement of the prophet Isaiah, does not surrender, and the Assyrians retire without taking the city.

7th Century B.C.

–688   King Hezekiah of Judah dies and is succeeded by his son Manasseh, who becomes an Assyrian vassal and promotes foreign cults in Judah.

–642   King Manasseh of Judah dies and is succeeded by his son Amon.

–640   Amon is murdered by his officers in the palace. The people of Judah kill the assassins and make his son Josiah king of Judah, during whose kingdom the prophets Zephaniah, Jeremiah and Nahum are active.

–609   Josiah, while trying to stop an expedition force of Pharaoh Necho, is killed in battle, and succeeded by his son Jehoahaz, who is dethroned after three months by Pharaoh Necho, and succeeded by another of Josiah's sons, Jehoiakim, who becomes an Egyptian vassal.

–605   Pharaoh Necho is defeated by Nebuchadnezzar, who makes Jehoiakim a vassal of Babylon.

6th Century B.C.

–598   Jehoiakim dies, and is succeeded by his son Jehoiachin.

–597   Nebuchadnezzar lays siege to Jerusalem, the king surrenders and is taken prisoner to Babylon, together with the treasures in the Temple. Zedekiah, uncle of the deposed king Jehoiachin, is named king by the Babylonians and governs as a puppet, until a few years later he revolts.

–586   After two years of siege the Babylonians breach the walls of Jerusalem. King Zedekiah escapes but is caught, blinded, after seeing his sons get killed, put in chains and taken to Babylon. Nebuzaradan, commander of the Babylonian army, burns down the Temple, the palace, and most of the city, and exiles the people to Babylon.

PART 4. From the fall of Judah to the return to Zion

6th Century B.C.

−585   Gedaliah, appointed governor of Judah by Babylon, is murdered by Judean national-ists who considered him a Babylonian collaborator. Other Babylonian supporters flee to Egypt taking the prophet Jeremiah with them.

−561   Upon the death of Nebuchadnezzar, Evil-Merodach, the new king of Babylon, releases Jehoiachin from prison and lets him stay in the Babylonian court.

−550   Cyrus the Persian gains control of the Median Empire.

−539   Cyrus, king of Persia, conquers Babylon.

−538   Cyrus authorizes the exiles to return to their land. A number of them do, led by Sheshbazzar, a member of the Judean royal family.

−522   Zerubbabel, a descendant of the royal family, is made governor of Judea, which is now a Persian province.

−520   The reconstruction of the Temple begins.

−515   The Temple is completed.

5th Century B.C.

−486   Xerxes 1 succeeds his late father Darius as king of Persia. Most scholars identify him as King Ahasuerus in the book of Esther.

−450   The book of Malachi is written.

−445   A Jewish official of the Persian court, Nehemiah, is appointed governor of Judea, and is sent to Jerusalem, where he rebuilds the walls of the city.

−437   The Jerusalem walls are completed.

−433   Nehemiah returns to Babylon. Eliashib, the high priest, allows Tobiah, governor of the Persian province of Transjordan and bitter enemy of Nehemiah, to stay in the Temple.

−431   Nehemiah is reappointed to Jerusalem. Upon his arrival he expels Tobiah and enforces observance of the Sabbath and the ban on intermarriage.

−428   The priest-scribe Ezra arrives in Judah, authorized by the Persian government to teach the Jews the laws of Moses. He forces those who had married foreign women to divorce them and to commit themselves to the exact observance of the religious laws.

PART 5. From the return to Zion to the birth of Jesus

4th Century B.C.

−330   Alexander the Great conquers Persia, and the whole Middle East including the land of Israel.

−323   Alexander the Great dies of malaria in Babylon. His generals divide the empire between them. Ptolemy gets control of Egypt. Seleucus controls Babylonia.

−301   Ptolemy I of Egypt conquers the land of Israel.

3rd Century B.C.

- *–250*   The Hebrew Bible is translated to Greek in Alexandria.
- *–217*   Antiochus III of Syria conquers the land of Israel, but Ptolemy IV defeats him and recovers it.

2nd Century B.C.

- *–198*   The Seleucids conquer the land of Israel.
- *–175*   Antiochus IV Epiphanes, descendant of Seleucus, becomes king.
- *–169*   Antiochus IV plunders the Temple treasuries.
- *–167*   Antiochus bans Jewish religious practices, and desecrates the Temple.
- *–166*   The Hasmonean family of priests in the Judean town of Modiin leads a rebellion against the Hellenistic priests in Jerusalem and against the regime of Antiochus. The revolt begins when the Hasmonean patriarch slays a Jew making a sacrifice ordained by Antiochus.
- *–164*   Judah Maccabee, leader of the rebellion, is victorious over the Syrian armies, captures Jerusalem and rededicates the Temple.
- *–160*   Judah Maccabee dies in battle. His brother Jonathan assumes the leadership.
- *–142*   Jonathan is murdered. His brother Simeon assumes leadership; the independence of Judea is recognized by the Syrians; Judea signs a treaty with Rome.
- *–134*   Simeon is assassinated. John Hyrcanus assumes the leadership.

1st Century B.C.

- *–67*   Civil war starts between Hyrcanus II and his brother Aristobulus II.
- *–63*   Pompey captures Jerusalem, brings Palestine under Roman rule and appoints Hyrcanus II high priest.
- *–44*   Julius Caesar is assassinated by Brutus, Cassius and others.
- *–40*   The Parthians invade Palestine; help Antigonus, son of Aristobulus II, to seize control. The Senate in Rome proclaims Herod, son of the Idumean Antipater, king of the Jews.
- *–37*   Jerusalem is captured by Herod, who starts his reign.
- *–31*   Octavius defeats Mark Anthony, and becomes master of the Roman world.
- *–27*   Octavius is proclaimed emperor under the name Augustus (the Exalted).
- *–22*   Herod begins the construction of the Roman port of Caesarea in the Mediterranean.

PART 6 . From the birth of Jesus to the death of Paul

1st Century B.C.

- *–7*   Birth of Jesus in Bethlehem. (Although the traditional date for the birth of Jesus is the year zero, many archeologists and scholars believe that it was some years before the beginning of the Era).
- *–4*   Death of Herod. The Romans divide his kingdom among his three sons, Judea, Samaria and Idumea to Archelaus, Galilee to Herod Antipas, and the Lebanon districts to Philip.

1st Century a.d.

6   Augustus deposes Archelaus and puts Judea under the direct control of a Roman governor.

14   Tiberius succeeds Augustus as Roman emperor.

26   Pontius Pilate becomes governor of Judea.

28   John begins baptizing in the fifteenth year of the reign of Tiberius.

30   Crucifixion of Jesus.

33   Paul is converted.

37   Caligula succeeds Tiberius as Roman emperor.

41   Claudius succeeds Caligula. Herod Agrippa I, appointed king of Judea, executes James, and imprisons Peter.

44   Herod Agrippa dies, and Judea reverts to direct Roman government under a procurator.

47   Paul, accompanied by Barnabas, begins his first missionary journey to Cyprus.

48   Paul confers with leaders of the church in Jerusalem and wins approval of his mission to the Gentiles. He begins his second missionary journey, accompanied this time by Silas, going overland through Asia Minor and crossing to Macedonia.

50   Paul arrives in Corinth, and meets Aquila and Priscilla.

53   Paul arrives at Ephesus on his third missionary journey.

54   Nero succeeds Claudius as Roman emperor.

57   Paul visits Jerusalem, is arrested, and sent to the procurator Felix at Caesarea.

59   Festus replaces Felix as procurator. Paul appeals to the emperor, and is sent to Rome.

60   Paul arrives in Rome, and is imprisoned there.

64   A fire destroys much of Rome. Christians are blamed and persecuted. It is probable that Peter and Paul were among the martyrs.

66   The Jews revolt against Rome.

70   Titus takes Jerusalem and burns down the Temple.

73   Masada, the last Jewish fortress, falls to the Romans. Hundreds of defenders commit suicide, choosing to die before becoming slaves.

75   The book of Mark is written.

85   The book of Matthew is written

90   The books of Luke and Acts are written

92   The letters of Paul are collected and circulated together.

2nd Century A.D.

110   The letters of John are written.

Aaron

(Hebrew origin: Uncertain meaning)

(Exodus 4:14). 13th century B.C. Aaron was the founder of the priesthood in Israel and the first High Priest

His mother, Jochebed, the Egyptian-born daughter of Levi, married her nephew Amram, son of Kohath, and gave birth to three children: Miriam, the eldest; Aaron; and Moses, the youngest, who was born when Aaron was three years old.

The Bible does not tell us anything about Aaron's birth, his early life, or his upbringing. It states that he married Elisheba, daughter of Amminadab, of the tribe of Judah, with whom he had four sons: Nadab, Abihu, Eleazar, and Ithamar. His brother-in-law, Nahshon, was a direct ancestor of King David.

The first mention of Aaron in the Bible is when God, angry that Moses was reluctant to accept the mission to free the Israelites from the Egyptian oppression, told him that Aaron was a good speaker, and that he would be Moses' spokesman.

Aaron's eloquent speech to Pharaoh was reinforced by the miracles that his walking stick performed, changing at one time into a serpent and, at another, breaking into blossoms and almonds. Also, by stretching out his walking stick at the request of Moses, he brought on the first three plagues: blood, frogs, and lice; and, in cooperation with Moses, he produced the sixth plague, boils, and the eighth plague, locusts.

It is significant that, when he performed his wonders, it was not by virtue of any innate ability or individual initiative, but only by divine command, mediated through Moses. When Pharaoh finally yielded and let the Israelites go, the two brothers were already old men: Aaron was eighty-three years old, and Moses was eighty.

After the march out of Egypt, Aaron is no longer a central figure in the events, but only a secondary player at Moses' side. He didn't play any important part in the crossing of the Red Sea, the songs of victory hymns, or the water crisis at Marah. He reappeared again in connection with the incident of the manna.

When the Israelites fought a battle against the Amalekites, Aaron, together with Hur, supported Moses' hands stretched upward to assure victory. Later, again with Hur, he deputized for Moses, when his brother climbed Mount Sinai to receive the two stone tablets of the Law.

During Moses' prolonged absence on the mountain, Aaron yielded to the pressure of the people and made them a golden calf that became a cause of apostasy. Despite his involvement in this incident, he was neither punished nor disqualified from the priesthood. The people, on the other hand, were harshly punished, when the Levites killed about three thousand of the idol worshippers, by order of Moses.

Although Aaron did not take any part in the construction of the portable sanctuary, he and his sons were appointed priests and consecrated into that office by Moses. During the consecration ceremonies, two of his sons, Nadab and Abihu, died, when they burned forbidden incense before the Lord, a tragic loss that Aaron bore in silent resignation.

Once a year, on the Day of Atonement, Aaron was allowed to come into the Sacred Sanctuary, the holiest part of the Tent of Testimony, bringing his offering.

The Bible records one incident of friction between the brothers, when Aaron sided with his sister, Miriam, against Moses' preeminence, using as a pretext Moses' Cushite wife. God punished Miriam by making her skin leprous, white as snow. She was shut out of the camp for seven days, until her skin healed. Aaron again was not punished.

Aaron and Moses were the target of a serious revolt led by their cousin, the Levite Korah, who claimed that all the members of the congregation were equally holy. The earth split open and swallowed Korah and his followers.

To demonstrate the special status of the priesthood and the Levites, Moses placed a stick from each of the tribes overnight in the Tent of Testimony, and the following day, the stick representing the tribe of Levi, which had Aaron's name inscribed on it, was the only one sprouting blossoms and almonds.

On one occasion, the people complained that there was no water and that they would die of thirst. God told Moses to take the stick that was in front of the Ark, assemble the community, and, in front of them, speak to a rock. Water would flow from it. Moses and Aaron assembled the whole community in front of the rock. But this time, Moses could not control his anger and his frustration with the constantly complaining Israelites. He lost his patience and shouted, "Listen, you rebels! Shall we get water for you out of this rock?" Then, he raised the stick and struck the rock twice with it. Out came a great stream of water, and the people and the animals drank their fill. God reproved Moses and Aaron, saying, "Because you did not believe in me enough to affirm my sanctity in the eyes of the Israelites, you will not bring this congregation into the land, which I have given them".

Thus, Aaron never lived to see the Promised Land. He died at the age of one hundred and twenty-three on Mount Hor, near the southern end of the Dead Sea. The Israelites mourned him for thirty days, the same number of days that the Israelites mourned, when Moses died.

Aaron was succeeded as High Priest by his son Eleazar. (Please read the entry on Moses for more detailed information on the Exodus from Egypt.)

Abaddon

(Hebrew origin: *Destruction*)

(Revelation 9:11). Abaddon is depicted in the book of Revelation as the king of monstrous scorpion-like locusts, an angel of destruction residing in the bottomless pit. His name in Greek is Apollyon, which means *Destroyer*.

Abagtha

(Persian origin: Uncertain meaning)

(Esther 1:10). 5th century B.C. Abagtha was one of the seven eunuchs, who served in the court of Ahasuerus, the king of Persia, usually identified by historians as King Xerxes I of Persia, son and successor of Darius I.

The other six eunuchs who served the king were Harbona, Mehuman, Biztha, Bigtha, Zethar, and Carcas.

In the third year of his reign, the king gave a banquet for all his princes and administrators to show off his wealth. The great celebration lasted one hundred and eighty days.

When the festivities for the nobles ended, the king gave a banquet in the garden of his palace for the common people of Shushan. During seven days, everybody, rich and poor, drank as much as he wanted. At the same time, Vashti, his queen, gave a banquet for the women inside the palace.

On the seventh day of the celebration, the drunken Ahasuerus ordered Abagtha and the other six eunuchs who served the king to fetch Queen Vashti, and to make sure that she was wearing her royal crown. She was a beautiful woman, and the king wanted everybody to see her. The eunuchs returned and told the king that the queen refused to come.

Abda

(Hebrew origin: *Servitude*)

1. (1 Kings 4:6). 11th century B.C. Abda was the father of Adoniram—also called Adoram and Hadoram—the official in charge of levying the forced labor, necessary for the royal building programs, during the reigns of David, Solomon, and Rehoboam.
2. (Nehemiah 11:17). 5th century B.C. Abda, son of Shammua, grandson of Galal, a Levite descendant of Jeduthun, settled in the land of Judah, after the return from the Babylonian Exile, and was one of the two hundred and eighty-four Levites residing in Jerusalem, during the days of Nehemiah. Abda is also called Obadiah, son of Shemaiah (1 Chronicles 9:16).

Abdeel

(Hebrew origin: *Servant of God*)

(Jeremiah 36:26). 7th century B.C. Abdeel was the father of Shelemiah, a palace official in the court of King Jehoiakim.

The king ordered Shelemiah and two other officials—Jerahmeel, son of Hammelech, and Seraiah, son of Azriel—to arrest the prophet Jeremiah and his trusted companion Baruch. The three men failed in their mission, because Jeremiah and Baruch had gone into hiding.

Abdi

(Hebrew origin: *My servant*)

1. (1 Chronicles 6:44). 11th century B.C. Abdi, son of Malluch, was a descendant of Merari. His grandson Ethan was one of the Levites appointed by King David to be in charge of the singers in the House of the Lord.
2. (2 Chronicles 29:12). 8th century B.C. Abdi was a descendant of Merari. His son Kish was one of the Levites who assembled all the other Levites to make themselves ritually clean and to purify the Temple, during the reign of King Hezekiah of Judah.
3. (Ezra 10:26). 5th century B.C. Abdi, a descendant of Elam, divorced his foreign wife, during the days of Ezra.

Abdiel

(Hebrew origin: *Servant of God*)

(1 Chronicles 5:15). 8th century B.C. Abdiel, son of Guni, was the father of Ahi, the head of a family who lived in Gilead, during the reign of King Jeroboam II of Israel.

Abdon

(Hebrew origin: *Servant*)

1. (Judges 12:13). 12th century B.C. Abdon, son of Hillel, judged Israel eight years. He had a large family and was very wealthy for his time and day: "He had forty sons and thirty nephews who rode on seventy donkeys".

Note: In the book of Judges, a judge is a ruler or governor of territory or a military leader in pre-monarchical Israel. Later, during the monarchy, the king served in this role and judges were more like the judicial officers that we know today.

2. (1 Chronicles 8:23). Unspecified date. Abdon, son of Shashak, was the leader of a clan of the tribe of Benjamin who lived in Jerusalem.
3. (1 Chronicles 8:30). 11th century B.C. Abdon, a Benjamite, was the firstborn son of Jehiel, the founder of Gibeon, and Maachah.
4. (2 Chronicles 34:20). 7th century B.C. Abdon, son of Micah, was an official in the court of King Josiah. The king sent Abdon and two other officials to consult with Huldah, the prophetess, concerning the Book of the Law that had been found in the Temple, during repair work. He is also called Achbor, son of Michaiah (2 Kings 22:12).

Abednego

(Babylonian origin: *Servant of the god Nego, a Babylonian deity*)

(Daniel 1:7). 6th century B.C. Abednego was the Babylonian name given by the chief of the eunuchs of King Nebuchadnezzar to Azariah, a young boy from a noble Jewish family.

Azariah and three other young Jewish boys—Daniel, Hananiah, and Mishael—were chosen to receive an education that would allow them to become officials of the king's court.

Years later, after ending their studies, the king, at the request of Daniel, appointed Azariah and his friends, Hananiah and Mishael, to be in charge over the affairs of the province of Babylon.

The king set up a golden idol and decreed that everybody in the kingdom should worship it. When the king was informed that Azariah, Hananiah, and Mishael refused to worship the golden idol and did not serve the Babylonian gods, he gave orders to throw them into a burning furnace.

The three men were saved, by an angel, and survived, without even one hair of their heads being singed. Nebuchadnezzar was so impressed by their miraculous survival that he blessed God and decreed that, from that moment on, anyone in the Babylonian Empire who would dare speak against God would be cut in pieces, and his house would be turned into a dunghill.

Abel

(Hebrew origin: *Emptiness; vanity; vapor*)

(Genesis 4:2). Antediluvian. Abel, the second son of Adam and Eve, was a shepherd. His older brother, Cain, was a tiller of the soil.

One day, both brothers wished to bring each one an offering to God. Cain brought from the fruit of the soil, while Abel brought the choicest of the firstlings of his flock. The Lord accepted Abel's offering but rejected that of Cain. When God saw that Cain was much distressed, he advised him to control himself and do right.

Cain, instead of following God's advice, asked Abel to go with him to the field, and there, angry and jealous, he killed his brother. When the Lord asked Cain for Abel's whereabouts, Cain pretended that he didn't know and insolently asked God whether he was his brother's keeper. God cursed him and condemned him to failure as a farmer, and to ceaselessly wander on earth.

Abi

(Hebrew origin: *My father*)

(2 Kings 18:2). 8th century B.C. Abi, daughter of Zechariah, was the wife of King Ahaz of Judah and the mother of his successor, King Hezekiah. She is also called Abijah (2 Chronicles 29:1).

Abia

(Hebrew origin: *God is my father*)

(1 Chronicles 3:10). 10th century B.C. Abia, the second king of Judah, after the partition of the United Monarchy, was the son of

King Rehoboam and his wife Maachah.

This is the only verse in the Bible where his name appears as Abia. In all the other verses that mention him, he is called Abijah or Abijam.

Abiah

(Hebrew origin: *God is my father*)

1. (1 Samuel 8:2). 11th century B.C. Abiah was the second-born son of the prophet Samuel. He and his brother Joel—also called Vashni (1 Chronicles 6:28)—were corrupt judges in Beersheba, who took bribes and perverted judgment. The behavior of the two brothers caused the elders of Israel to request a king, rather than let the sons of Samuel rule over Israel.

2. (1 Chronicles 2:24). Unspecified date. Abiah, daughter of Machir, was the wife of Hezron. Her sons were Segub and Ashur, the second of whom was born after her husband died.

3. (1 Chronicles 7:8). 16th century B.C. Abiah, the son of Becher and the grandson of Benjamin, was a member of a family of heads of the tribe and brave warriors. His brothers were Zemira, Joash, Eliezer, Elioenai, Omri, Jerimoth, Anathoth, and Alameth.

Abialbon

(Hebrew origin: *Father of strength*)

(2 Samuel 23:31). 10th century B.C. Abialbon, the Arbathite, was one of "The Thirty", an elite group of warriors in King David's army. He is also called Abiel (1 Chronicles 11:32).

Abiasaph

(Hebrew origin: *My father gathered*)

(Exodus 6:24). 13th century B.C. Abiasaph was one of the three sons of Korah, the man who led a rebellion against Moses. The sons did not take any part in their father's rebellion and, therefore, were not punished, when Korah and his followers were swallowed by the earth.

Abiasaph became the ancestor of a clan of Levites. His descendant Shallum, son of Kore, was in charge of the gatekeepers of the Tabernacle, during the reign of King David.

Another of his descendants, Heman, was one of the Levites appointed by King David, to be in charge of the singers in the House of the Lord, as the ancestor of a clan of Levites.

Abiathar

(Hebrew origin: *Father of excellence*)

(1 Samuel 22:20). 11th century B.C. Abiathar, son of the priest Ahimelech, survived King Saul's slaughter of his father and of all the other priests of Nob. He managed to escape and join David's band in the wilderness. David, feeling that he was the cause of the death of Abiathar's father, asked him to remain with him.

During David's reign, Abiathar and Zadok, the son of Ahitub, brought the Ark of the Covenant to Jerusalem and were, both of them, appointed High Priests.

When Absalom rebelled against David, Abiathar stayed in Jerusalem and used his son Jonathan as a messenger to transmit Hushai's reports to David. Abiathar's son, named Ahimelech, was High Priest, together with Zadok, during the reign of King David (2 Samuel 8:17).

When David fled from Jerusalem, during the rebellion of Absalom, Abiathar and Zadok, assisted by a number of Levites, accompanied the king carrying the Ark of the Covenant. King David ordered them to return the Ark to Jerusalem and to take back with them Ahimaaz, the son of Zadok, and Jonathan, the son of Abiathar.

During Absalom's stay in Jerusalem, Zadok and Abiathar used their sons as messengers and sent through them to King David all the information that Hushai, David's secret agent, was able to gather. After the defeat of Absalom, Zadok and Abiathar were sent by David to the elders of Judah to ask them why they, belonging to the same tribe as David, were the last ones to call him back.

When David was old and his sons were

maneuvering for the succession, Abiathar made the grievous mistake of supporting Adonijah's failed bid to succeed King David. Solomon did not forget where Abiathar's loyalties had been placed. When he became king, Solomon spared Abiathar's life, only because he had carried the Ark of the Covenant before David, but expelled him from the priesthood, and exiled him from Jerusalem to his estate in Anathoth. Solomon named Zadok as sole High Priest and gave his son Azariah a high position in his court.

Abida

(Hebrew origin: *Father of knowledge*)

(1 Chronicles 1:33). 18th century B.C. Abida, a son of Midian, was a grandson of Abraham and Keturah, the woman whom Abraham married, after Sarah died. Abida's brothers were Ephah, Epher, Hanoch, and Eldaah. His name is also spelled Abidah (Genesis 25:4).

Abidah

(Hebrew origin: *Father of knowledge*)

(Genesis 25:4). 18th century B.C. Abidah is an alternative spelling for Abida (1 Chronicles 1:33), a son of Midian.

Abidan

(Hebrew origin: *Father of judgment*)

(Numbers 1:11). 13th century B.C. Abidan, son of Gideoni, of the tribe of Benjamin, commanded the army of his tribe, during the march in the wilderness. He was one of the twelve Israelite leaders, who donated gifts of silver and gold, bulls, rams, goats, and lambs for the dedication of the altar.

Abiel

(Hebrew origin: *God is my father*)

1. (1 Samuel 9:1). 12th century B.C. Abiel, son of Zeror of the tribe of Benjamin, was the father of Kish, the father of King Saul, and of Ner, the father of Abner, the

commander of the king's army. Abiel, who was also called Jehiel (1 Chronicles 9:35), lived in Gibeon with his wife Maachah.

2. (1 Chronicles 11:32). 10th century B.C. Abiel the Arbathite was one of "The Thirty", an elite group in King David's army. He is also called Abialbon (2 Samuel 23:31).

Abiezer

(Hebrew origin: *Father of help*)

1. (Joshua 17:2). Unspecified date. Abiezer, a descendant of Manasseh, was the ancestor of the clan of the Jeezerites to whom land was assigned, during the days of Joshua. The clan fought with Gideon against the Midianites (Judges 6:34). Abiezer was called Jeezer in the book of Numbers (Numbers 26:30).

2. (2 Samuel 23:27). 10th century B.C. Abiezer, from Anathoth in the territory of the tribe of Benjamin, was one of "The Thirty", an elite army group of warriors in King David's army. He served as a captain of the army, during the ninth month of each year, commanding a division of twenty-four thousand soldiers.

3. (1 Chronicles 7:18). Unspecified date. Abiezer was one of the three sons of Hammoleketh, the sister of Gilead; the other two were Ishod and Mahalah.

Abigail

(Hebrew origin: *Father of joy*)

1. (1 Samuel 25:3). 11th century B.C. Abigail, a beautiful and intelligent woman, married David, after the death of her first husband. She had been married to Nabal, a wealthy but churlish man.

At that time, David was the head of a band of outcasts, living from contributions that he requested and received from wealthy men, who lived in the surrounding towns. Hearing that Nabal was sheering his sheep, he sent ten men to ask for a contribution.

Nabal treated them rudely and refused to give them anything. Abigail realized that

David would come to punish Nabal for his insulting behavior. She loaded several asses with food and wine and, without telling her husband, went to intercept David.

Abigail met David and his men on the way. She apologized to David for her husband's bad manners and convinced him not to take revenge against Nabal.

Abigail returned home and found Nabal drunk. She waited to the next morning to tell him what she had done. When Nabal heard of his close escape, he suffered a stroke and died ten days later.

David, when told that Nabal had died, asked Abigail to marry him, and she agreed. Later, to escape Saul's persecution, David fled to Gath with his wives, Abigail and Ahinoam, and his six hundred men, and found employment with the Philistines as a mercenary. Achish, the king of Gath, allowed David, his men, and their families to settle in the town of Ziklag.

When the Philistines marched against Saul, David, who was accompanying Achish, was sent back to Philistia by the distrustful Philistine commanders. He arrived back at Ziklag and found that the Amalekites, taking advantage of his absence, had attacked the town, burned it, and taken all the women and children with them, including Ahinoam and Abigail. David pursued the raiders, rescued the prisoners, and recovered the booty that the Amalekites had taken.

After the death of Saul, David moved to Hebron, taking Ahinoam and Abigail with him. There, she gave birth to Chileab, David's second son, who was also called Daniel (1 Chronicles 3:1), and who apparently died in his infancy, because the Bible does not mention him again.

2. (2 Samuel 17:25). 11th century B.C. Abigail, one of David's sisters, was the wife of an Israelite called Ithra—although the first book of Chronicles states that her husband was called Jether the Ishmaelite (1 Chronicles 2:17).

She was the mother of Amasa, commander of Absalom's army. Her sister was Zeruiah, the mother of Joab, commander of David's army.

The first book of Chronicles (1 Chronicles 2:16) states that both women were David's sisters, but the second book of Samuel (2 Samuel 17:25) says that Abigail's father was called Nahash, in which case, David and his sister had the same mother, but not the same father. The only Nahash mentioned in the Bible is the king of Ammon, which would explain Nahash's friendliness toward David, and the support that Shobi, one of the sons of Nahash, gave to David, during his flight from Absalom.

Abihail

(Hebrew origin: *Father of might*)

1. (Numbers 3:35). 14th century B.C. Abihail was the father of Zuriel, the chief of the Levite clan of Merari, during the days of Moses. The clan was commanded to camp on the northern side of the Tabernacle and was in charge of the boards of the Tabernacle, its bars, pillars, and sockets.
2. (1 Chronicles 2:29). Unspecified date. Abihail was the wife of Abishur, the son of Shammai, with whom she had two sons: Ahban and Molid.
3. (1 Chronicles 5:14). Unspecified date. Abihail, son of Huri, of the tribe of Gad, lived in Gilead in Bashan, east of the Jordan River.
4. (2 Chronicles 11:18). 10th century B.C. Abihail, the daughter of Eliab, David's eldest brother, married her cousin Jerimoth, a son of David. Their daughter Mahalath was one of the eighteen wives of King Rehoboam.
5. (Esther 2:15). 5th century B.C. Abihail, the uncle of Mordecai, was the father of Hadassah, the future Queen Esther.

Abihu

(Hebrew origin: *He is my father*)

(Exodus 6:23). 13th century B.C. Abihu was the second son of the High Priest Aaron

and his wife Elisheba. He and Nadab, his older brother, accompanied Moses, and seventy elders, up Mount Sinai, where they saw God standing on a pavement of sapphire stone, clear as heaven.

Nadab and Abihu were burned to death by a fire sent by God, in punishment for having burned forbidden incense before the Lord. Moses forbade Aaron and his two youngest sons, Eleazar and Ithamar, to uncover their heads and rend their clothes, which were the traditional signs of mourning.

The priestly line was continued through Eleazar and Ithamar, because Nadab and Abihu died childless.

Abihud

(Hebrew origin: *Father of magnificence*)

(1 Chronicles 8:3). 16th century B.C. Abihud was the son of Belah and grandson of Benjamin.

Abijah

(Hebrew origin: *God is my father*)

1. (1 Kings 14:1). 10th century B.C. Abijah was a young son of Jeroboam I, king of Israel. When the boy fell mortally sick, Jeroboam's wife went in disguise to the prophet Ahijah, who was old and blind, to ask whether the child would recover.

   Despite his blindness and the queen's disguise, the old prophet recognized her and told her that the sick child would die, as soon as she would arrive back to her city, as God's punishment for having worshipped idols.
2. (1 Chronicles 24:10). 10th century B.C. During the reign of King David, the priestly service in the Tabernacle was divided by lot into twenty-four turns. Abijah was in charge of the eighth turn.
3. (2 Chronicles 11:20). 10th century B.C. Abijah—also called Abia (1 Chronicles 3:10), and Abijam (1 Kings 14:31)—was the second king of Judah, after the partition of the United Monarchy. He was the son and successor of King Rehoboam and the

grandson of Absalom, through his mother, Maachah.

During his short reign of only three years, Abijah was constantly in war against King Jeroboam of Israel. He succeeded in expanding the territory of Judah, by conquering several cities, including Bethel.

The Bible mentions that he married fourteen wives and had thirty-eight children. When he died, he was buried in the royal tombs in the City of David. He was succeeded by Asa.

The prophet Iddo wrote the biography of King Abijah, which has not survived to our days.

Note: Although the Bible states (1 Kings 15:8) that King Asa was King Abijah's son, some scholars—based on the mention of Abishalom, as the common grandfather of both kings, and of Maachah, as their common mother—believe that Abijah and Asa were brothers.

4. (2 Chronicles 29:1). 8th century B.C. Abijah, daughter of Zechariah and wife of King Ahaz of Judah, was the mother of King Hezekiah. She is also called Abi (2 Kings 18:2).

5. (Nehemiah 10:7). 5th century B.C. He was one of the priests who signed with Nehemiah a solemn agreement to separate themselves from the foreigners living in the land, to refrain from intermarrying with them, and to dedicate their firstborn to God, among other obligations.

6. (Nehemiah 12:4). 6th century B.C. He was one of the priests who returned from the Babylonian Exile with Zerubbabel. He was the ancestor of a clan of priests that—during the days of the High Priest Joiakim, son of Jeshua—was led by Zichri.

Abijam

(Hebrew origin: *Father of the sea*)

(1 Kings 14:31). 10th century B.C. Abijam—also called Abia (1 Chronicles 3:10), and Abijah (2 Chronicles 11:20)—was the second king of Judah, after the partition of the United Monarchy.

He was the son and successor of King Rehoboam and the grandson of Absalom, through his mother Maachah.

During his short reign of only three years, Abijam was constantly in war against King Jeroboam of Israel, a war, during which, he succeeded in expanding the territory of Judah, by conquering several cities, including Bethel.

The Bible mentions that he married fourteen wives and had thirty-eight children. When he died, he was buried in the royal tombs in the City of David. He was succeeded by Asa.

The prophet Iddo wrote his biography, which has not survived to our days.

Note: Although the Bible states (1 Kings 15:8) that King Asa was King Abijam's son, some scholars—based on the mention of Abishalom, as the common grandfather of both kings, and of Maachah, as their common mother—believe that Abijah and Asa were brothers.

Abimael

(Hebrew origin: *Father of Mael*)

(Genesis 10:28). Unspecified date. Abimael, son of Joktan, descended from Noah through Shem, Noah's second son. His brothers were Almodad, Sheleph, Hazarmaveth, Jerah, Hadoram, Uzal, Diklah, Obal, Sheba, Ophir, Havilah, and Jobab.

Abimelech

(Hebrew origin: *My father is king*)

1. (Genesis 20:2). 19th century B.C. Abimelech was king of Gerar, a region in the Negev, south of Gaza.

When Abimelech was told by Abraham that Sarah was his sister, he, admiring her beauty, had her brought to his harem. That night, God warned him in a dream not to touch Sarah. That vision, and the realization that God had closed the wombs of the women in his house because of Sarah, made him return her to Abraham, accompanied by gifts of sheep, oxen, and servants. He also allowed Abraham to live anywhere in his kingdom. Abraham, in gratitude, prayed to God, and God healed Abimelech's wife, and she gave birth to children.

Later, Abraham met with Abimelech and Phichol, the commander of Abimelech's army, and complained that Abimelech's servants had taken, by force, a well of water. Abimelech protested his innocence and made a peace treaty with Abraham at Beersheba.

Years later, Isaac, who was living at that time in Gerar, feared that men would kill him to possess his wife. Remembering his father's subterfuge, he also told the same King Abimelech—or a descendant by the same name—that Rebekah was his sister.

When Abimelech, looking through a window, saw Isaac and Rebekah making love, the king reproached Isaac and told him that his deception could have caused people to sin with Rebekah. Abimelech forbade his people to take any action against Isaac or Rebekah, under penalty of death.

Isaac remained in Gerar and prospered. His wealth made him the target of envy by the people of Gerar, who fought with Isaac's herdsmen for the wells of water.

Isaac moved back to Beersheba, where Abimelech visited him and signed a peace treaty with him.

Note: Abimelech's title, "King of the Philistines", was considered by historians in the past as anachronistic, because the Sea People's invasion of Egypt and Canaan took place, during the 12th century B.C., about five hundred years after Abraham's and Isaac's times. Today, many scholars believe that Abimelech was indeed the ruler of a small colony of Sea People, established in the Gerar area, who were forerunners of the main Philistine invasion, centuries later.

2. (Judges 8:31). 12th century B.C. Abimelech was the son of Gideon, the judge, and a woman from Shechem.

After his father died, Abimelech went to Shechem and asked his mother's brothers for political and financial support. They gave him seventy pieces of silver from their Temple's treasury. Abimelech used this money to hire mercenaries to murder his seventy brothers in order to eliminate them as rivals.

Jotham, the only son of Gideon who survived the massacre, went to the top of Mount Gerizim and gazed down at the plain of the pillar in Shechem. He saw that the men of the city were crowning Abimelech as king and shouted at them a parable of the trees, whose elected king consumed them by his fire. Jotham prophesied that the parable would come true, and that, one day, the men of Shechem and Abimelech would destroy each other.

During the fourth year of Abimelech's rule, a man called Gaal, son of Ebed, incited the men of Shechem to rebel against Abimelech, saying, "Who is Abimelech that we should serve him? If I would rule the city, I would get rid of him".

Zebul, the governor of Shechem, sent a secret message to Abimelech informing him of the gravity of the situation. He advised him to come immediately and to attack at dawn. Abimelech brought his army to Shechem, during the night, and waited hidden in the fields outside the city.

Early the next morning, Gaal went out and stood outside the gate to the city. From there, he saw Abimelech and his men approaching, did not recognize them, and asked Zebul, "I see men coming down from the hills".

Zebul answered, "You are confusing the shadows of the hills with men".

Gaal insisted, "See, there are people coming down the hills, and another group is approaching by the plain of Meonenim".

Zebul then said to him, "Where is your mouth now? You asked, 'Who is Abimelech that we should serve him?' This is the army that you despised. Go now and fight them!"

Gaal and his supporters went out to fight against Abimelech, but were defeated, and ran away. Zebul expelled him and his rebels from the city.

Abimelech attacked Shechem, slew the people, and destroyed the city completely. About a thousand men and women found refuge in the tower of the city, but Abimelech set fire to the fortress, killing everyone in it. He then marched against the neighboring town of Thebez.

During the siege of the tower of Thebez, which he was trying to burn with fire, he was wounded by a millstone thrown down on him by a woman. Fatally injured, he asked his armor bearer to kill him, rather than having the people say that he had died disgracefully at the hand of a woman.

3. (1 Chronicles 18:16). 10th century B.C. Abimelech, son of Abiathar and grandson of Ahimelech, the Nob priest killed by Saul's orders, served as High Priest, during King David's reign, sharing this position with Zadok. He was called Ahimelech in the second book of Samuel (2 Samuel 8:17). His brother Jonathan served as King David's messenger and spy in Jerusalem, during Absalom's revolt, transmitting Hushai's messages to David.

4. (Psalm 34:1). 11th century B.C. Abimelech is the name, by which, the book of Psalms calls Achish (1 Samuel 21:10), king of Gath, the city to which David fled, while escaping from Saul's persecution.

Abinadab

(Hebrew origin: *Father of generosity*)

1. (1 Samuel 7:1). 11th century B.C. Abinadab kept the Ark of the Covenant, in his house on a hill near the town of Kirjathjearim, during many years. The story of how the Ark came to be in his house is the following:

The Ark of the Covenant, captured by the Philistines in a battle, was brought by them to the Temple of Dagon in Ashdod and placed in front of the statue of the god. The next morning, the statue was found fallen on the ground, with its head and hand cut off.

This incident, plus a plague of hemorrhoids, convinced the Philistines to send the Ark back to Israel in a cart pulled by two cows, carrying also five golden mice and five golden figures, representing the hemorrhoids.

When the cart came to a stop, in the field of a man named Joshua, the Israelites used the wood of the cart to light a fire, where they sacrificed the cows to God. Unfortunately for them, they couldn't resist the temptation and looked inside the Ark.

God sent a plague to punish them. Thousands of men died. The scared survivors sent the Ark to the house of Abinadab, who sanctified his son Eleazar to take care of it.

Many years later, during the reign of King David, Abinadab's sons, Uzzah and Ahio, took the Ark in a cart to Jerusalem, but Uzzah died on the road, because he accidentally touched the Ark.

2. (1 Samuel 16:8). 11th century B.C. Abinadab, David's brother, was the second eldest son of Jesse. He, together with his brothers Eliab and Shammah, joined Saul's army to fight against the Philistines.

3. (1 Samuel 31:2). 11th century B.C. Abinadab, son of King Saul, fought with his father against the Philistines in the battle of Mount Gilboa and was killed together with his brothers, Jonathan and Melchishua. He is called Ishui elsewhere in the first book of Samuel (1 Samuel 14:49).

4. (1 Kings 4:11). 10th century B.C. Abinadab was the father of a man—his name is not specified by the Bible—who married Taphath, one of King Solomon's daughters, and was appointed by the king to be one of the twelve district governors, responsible for providing food from his district, the territory of Dor, for the king and the royal household, for one month out of each year.

Abinoam

(Hebrew origin: *Father of pleasantness*)

(Judges 4:6). 12th century B.C. Abinoam was the father of Barak, the commander of the tribes of Naphtali and Zebulun who defeated the troops of Sisera at Mount Tabor.

Abiram

(Hebrew origin: *My father is elevated*)

1. (Numbers 16:1). 13th century B.C. Abiram and Dathan, of the tribe of Reuben, sons of Eliab, were two of the leaders of Korah's rebellion against Moses. Their brother Nemuel did not participate in the rebellion.

Korah, Dathan, Abiram, and On, son of Peleth, at the head of a group of two hundred fifty renowned men, accused Moses and Aaron of raising themselves over the rest of the people.

Moses threw himself on the ground and said to the rebels, "Tomorrow, the Lord will show us who belongs to him, who can come close to him. Take your fire pans, you Korah, and all your followers, and put incense and fire in it, and present them to the Lord tomorrow, and we will see who will the Lord choose to make holy. You have gone too far, sons of Levi! It seems that it is not enough for you that God has set you apart from the community to serve him, and brought you near him. You also want the priesthood? You are not standing against Aaron, you have banded against the Lord!"

Moses called Dathan and Abiram to talk with them, but they refused to come, saying, "Isn't it enough that you took us out of Egypt, a land that flowed with milk and honey, to kill us in the wilderness, that you also want to lord it over us? Even if you had brought us to a land of milk and honey, and given us possession of fields and vineyards, should you gouge out those men's eyes? We will not come!"

Moses became very angry and said to God, "Don't accept their offerings. I have never hurt any of them, nor have I taken even one of their donkeys!"

The next day, the rebels, with their fire pans, stood in the door of the Tabernacle, with Moses and Aaron, surrounded by the people.

The Presence of God appeared to the whole community, and God said to Moses and Aaron, "Stand apart from this community that I may annihilate them immediately".

Moses and Aaron threw themselves to the ground and said, "O God, do not be angry with the whole community because of the sins of one man".

God said to them, "Tell the community to get away from the tents of Korah, Dathan, and Abiram".

Moses got up and went toward the tents of Dathan and Abiram, followed by the leaders of the people. He then asked the people to stay away from the tents of the rebels, so that they should not also be destroyed.

Dathan and Abiram came out and stood at the entrance of their tents, with their wives, sons, and small children.

Moses then spoke, "This is how you will know that God has sent me to do all these things. They are not done by my own choice. If these men will die of a natural death, then I have not been sent by God, but if God does something never before seen, so that the earth will open and swallow them up with all they own, this will prove that the rebels have offended God".

As soon as he finished speaking, the earth opened, and Korah, Dathan, Abiram, and their followers, with their tents and all their possessions, fell inside. The earth closed upon them, and they all perished.

Eleazar, the priest, took the fire pans of the rebels and made with them broad plates for the covering of the altar, to remind the people that only the descendants of Aaron could offer incense to God.

2. (1 Kings 16:34). 9th century B.C. Abiram, son of Hiel the Bethelite, and his brother Segub lost their lives, when their father rebuilt Jericho, during the reign of Ahab, thus, fulfilling Joshua's curse (Joshua 6:26).

Abishag

(Hebrew origin: *Father of error*)

(1 Kings 1:3). 10th century B.C. King David, in his old age, felt constantly cold, even

when his servants covered him with clothes, and the room was heated up.

The officials of the court brought him Abishag, a beautiful Shunammite virgin girl, to warm him in his bed, and to be his nurse.

After King David's death, Adonijah, King Solomon's half brother, asked Bathsheba to intercede with Solomon, to receive his permission to marry Abishag.

Solomon considered that Adonijah's request was a subtle attempt to claim the throne. He did not hesitate and immediately ordered Benaiah to kill his older brother.

Abishai

(Hebrew origin: *Father of gift*)

(1 Samuel 26:6). 10th century B.C. Abishai was one of the three leading commanders in David's army. His bravery was legendary, and he was credited with killing single-handed three hundred enemies. He was devoted to David and saved his life, during a battle against the Philistines, by killing the giant Ishbibenob.

Abishai, one of the three sons of Zeruiah, King David's sister, was thus a nephew of David. His brothers were Joab and Asahel. Joab was the commander of the king's army and, probably, the second most powerful man in the country. Asahel was the officer in charge of the army, during the fourth month, with twenty-four thousand men under him.

During the time when David was an outlaw, Abishai was a member of his band. On one occasion, he stood, with David, right next to the sleeping, defenseless King Saul. Abishai wanted to kill him, but David wouldn't allow it.

Abishai and his brother Joab murdered Abner, in revenge for the death of their brother Asahel, without taking into account that Abner had been forced to kill him in self-defense. Abishai also took part, under the command of Joab, in the war against the Ammonites, who had insulted and maltreated King David's ambassadors.

Abishai was with David, when the king fled from Absalom's rebellion. Shimei, the son of Gera, a relative of King Saul, met them on the road, cursed David, and threw stones at him,

shouting, "Get out, get out! You are a bloody man, a criminal! You usurped Saul's kingdom, and God is punishing for murdering Saul's family! God has given the kingdom to your son Absalom because you are a bloody man!"

Abishai, who was standing nearby with his brother Joab, said to David, "Why should this dog curse my lord, the king? Please let me go over and take off his head!"

David said, "What have I to do with you, you sons of Zeruiah? Let him curse, because God has said to him, 'Curse David'. Who has the right to ask why he does it? My own son is trying to kill me, so don't be surprised at this Benjamite. Leave him alone, let him curse. Perhaps, God will see my affliction and will repay this cursing with blessings".

David and his men continued on their way, with Shimei walking on the hillside, cursing him and throwing stones.

In the counterattack against Absalom, Abishai commanded a third of David's army. After Absalom's defeat and death, Shimei, accompanied by a thousand men of Benjamin, hurried to meet David, who was on the other side of the river Jordan. They crossed the river, and when Shimei was in front of the king, he threw himself down and begged for forgiveness.

Abishai said, "Shimei should be put to death for having cursed God's anointed".

David said, "What have I to do with you, you sons of Zeruiah? I am the king of Israel now, and no Israelite will be put to death today".

Abishai helped Joab to put down the rebellion of Sheba, son of Bichri. He defeated the Edomites, set garrisons in Edom, and made its inhabitants subjects to King David.

Abishalom

(Hebrew origin: *Father of peace*)

(1 Kings 15:2). 10th century B.C. Abishalom, the father of Maachah, King Rehoboam's favorite wife, was the grandfather of King Abijam—also called Abijah—and King Asa.

It is very likely that Abishalom and Absalom, King David's rebellious son, was the same person. Evidence for this is that Abishalom's daughter, Maachah, had the same name as King David's wife, Absalom's mother (1 Chronicles 3:2).

Although the first book of Kings (1 Kings 15:8) states that King Asa was King Abijam's son, some scholars—based on the mention of Abishalom, as the common grandfather of both kings, and Maachah, as their common mother—believe that these two kings were brothers.

Note: The second book of Chronicles (2 Chronicles 13:2) states that King Abijah's mother was Michaiah, and that his grandfather's name was Uriel.

Abishua

(Hebrew origin: *Father of abundance*)
1. (1 Chronicles 6:4). 12th century B.C. Abishua, son of Phinehas and grandson of Eleazar, was an ancestor of Ezra (Ezra 7:5).
2. (1 Chronicles 8:4). 16th century B.C. Abishua was the son of Belah and grandson of Benjamin.

Abishur

(Hebrew origin: *Father of protection*)
(1 Chronicles 2:28). Unspecified date. Abishur, son of Shammai, brother of Nadab, was married to Abihail, with whom he had two sons: Ahban and Molid.

Abital

(Hebrew origin: *Father of dew*)
(2 Samuel 3:4). 10th century B.C. Abital, one of King David's wives, was the mother of Shephatiah, one of the six sons born to David in Hebron.

Abitub

(Hebrew origin: *Father of goodness*)
(1 Chronicles 8:11). Unspecified date. Abitub, of the tribe of Benjamin, was the son of Shaharaim and his wife Hushim. Abitub's brother was Elpaal.

Abiud

(Hebrew origin: *Father of magnificence*)
(Matthew 1:13). 6th century B.C. Abiud, an ancestor of Christ, was a son of Zerubbabel.

Abner

(Hebrew origin: *Father of light*)
(1 Samuel 14:50). 11th century B.C. Abner, the son of Ner, Saul's uncle, was the commander of the army of his cousin King Saul and the power behind the throne, during the short reign of Ishbosheth.

He introduced David to Saul, after David had killed Goliath. At court, Abner occupied the seat of honor next to Saul. He accompanied Saul in his pursuit of David, who taunted him for not guarding his master properly.

After Saul and three of his sons died in the battle of Mount Gilboa, Abner made Ishbosheth, Saul's only surviving son, king over Israel, with his capital at Mahanaim, on the other side of the Jordan, while the people of Judah seceded and elected David as their king in Hebron.

During the subsequent warfare between Israel and Judah, David's army, commanded by Joab, met Abner and his army, by the pool of Gibeon. Abner suggested to Joab that twelve men of each side should fight to the death.

After the twenty-four men died killing each other, both armies engaged in battle. Abner's army was defeated. Abner, pursued by Asahel, Joab's brother, begged him not to run after him, saying that he could not face Joab, if he was forced to kill Asahel. Asahel refused to stop, and Abner killed him with a backward thrust of his spear.

Joab and his brother Abishai continued to pursue Abner, until Abner's soldiers rallied behind him on top of a hill, and he called on Joab to stop the bloodshed. Joab stopped the fighting and allowed Abner and his army to retreat to the other side of the Jordan.

Ishbosheth, without foreseeing the consequences, made the fatal error of accusing Abner of having made love to Rizpah, a woman who had been one of King Saul's concubines. Making love to the present or past concubine of a king was interpreted, in ancient Israel, as a symbolic attempt to usurp power, reminiscent of the episode, when Absalom made love to the ten concubines, whom David, in his flight from Jerusalem, had left behind to take care of the palace.

Abner became very angry and said, "Am I a dog's head? I have served loyally the house of Saul your father, and have not betrayed you into the hands of David! And you are accusing me over this woman! May God punish Abner if I don't make David king over Israel and Judah!" Ishbosheth remained speechless, because he feared Abner.

Abner, furious at Ishbosheth, decided to transfer his loyalties to David. He contacted David and told him that he could convince the heads of the tribes to recognize him as king.

David told Abner that he was willing to receive him, on condition that Michal, Saul's daughter, who had been his first wife, should be returned to him. She was forcefully taken away from her husband, Phaltiel, who walked with her as far as Bahurim, weeping as he followed her, until Abner ordered him to turn back.

Abner spoke on behalf of David to the elders of Israel and to the tribe of Benjamin, King Saul's own tribe. Then, he came to Hebron accompanied by twenty men. David received him warmly and celebrated his visit with a feast for his guests. The two men came to an agreement, by which Abner promised that he would rally the entire nation to David's side. David gave Abner a guarantee of safety and sent him on his way.

Joab, who had been away fighting, was told on his return to Hebron that Abner had come to visit the king. Immediately, Joab went to David and warned him that Abner had come to spy. Then, without David's knowledge, he managed to lure Abner back to Hebron, and while pretending to speak privately with him, he stabbed Abner in the stomach and killed him, in vengeance for the death of his brother Asahel.

Shocked by this treacherous murder, David buried Abner in Hebron with full honors. He walked behind the bier weeping, eulogized

him, and fasted the whole day, to show that he had no part in the murder of Abner. The people noticed David's behavior and approved of it. Nobody blamed him for the death of Abner.

David cursed Joab and his house for his bloody deed, but he did not punish him. It was only many years later that David, in his deathbed, instructed his son Solomon to have Joab killed for this and other crimes.

After Ishbosheth himself was murdered by two of his captains, the elders of Israel came to Hebron and anointed David king over a united Israel. The head of the unfortunate son of Saul was buried in Abner's sepulcher.

Years later, David designated Jaasiel, Abner's son, to be in charge of the tribe of Benjamin.

Abraham

(Hebrew origin: *Father of multitude*)

(Genesis 17:5). 19th century B.C. Abraham—whose original name was Abram, until God changed his name—is the earliest biblical character whose biographical data can place him, to a limited extent, within world history. He was the first patriarch, the traditional ancestor of the Hebrews, the Arabs, and many other nations. His story is told in the book of Genesis, from chapter 11 to chapter 25.

Abraham was a man of many facets. He was respected and honored by kings, who treated him as an equal. His talent for business transactions—as shown in his purchase of the Machpelah burial cave—brought him great wealth.

He loved his wife and would usually give in to her demands, but he was also a brave warrior, if the occasion demanded it—as he proved in his pursuit and defeat of the coalition of the four kings and the liberation of his nephew Lot.

His perfect faith in God made him accept in silence the divine command to sacrifice Isaac, his beloved son, but it did not prevent him from arguing and bargaining with God for the life of the inhabitants of Sodom, although they were complete strangers to him.

Abram, as he was called until he was 95 years old, was born in Ur of the Chaldeans, a Sumerian city in the Euphrates valley, near the head of the Persian Gulf, in an area which today lies in Iraq. He was the tenth generation from Noah, through the line of Shem. His father was Terah, and his brothers were Nahor and Haran.

While the family was still living in Ur, Abram married Sarai—whose name God later changed to Sarah—and Nahor married his niece Milcah, daughter of Haran, their brother.

When Haran died, Terah took his son Abram, Sarai, and his grandson Lot, the son of Haran, and traveled to the city of Haran, which is situated between the Euphrates and the Tigris in northern Aram, in today's Turkey, near its frontier with Syria.

Abram, who was at the time seventy-five years old, received the divine call and a promise of nationhood, in response to which he proceeded, together with his wife and nephew Lot, to the land of Canaan, which God told him would be given to him and his descendants.

Abram's first stop in Canaan was near the city of Shechem—today's Nablus—where he built an altar to the Lord. God again appeared to him and reiterated his promise to give the land to the descendants of Abram.

From Shechem, Abram went to Bethel, where he pitched his tent near the city and built an altar. After a short stay, he traveled toward the Negev in the south, where a famine in the land forced him to go to Egypt.

When they were close to Egypt, Abram, fearing that the Egyptians might kill him for his wife, instructed Sarai to say that she was not his wife but his sister. The Egyptians who saw her admired her beauty and praised her to Pharaoh. He had her brought to the palace and gave to her "brother" a generous gift of sheep, oxen, asses, camels, and slaves.

Pharaoh found out that he had been deceived, when God punished him and his house with plagues and sickness, for having brought Abram's wife to his harem. Pharaoh ordered that Abram should be brought to his presence, returned Sarai to him, and expelled them from Egypt.

Abram returned to Canaan, with his wife and his nephew Lot, and settled near Bethel. He was now a prosperous man, rich in cattle, silver, and gold.

Lot—by this time also a wealthy man owning flocks, herds, and tents—continued to live with his uncle Abram. Their proximity caused problem between their respective herdsmen, who started arguing and fighting over the limited grazing area that was available for their animals.

Abram, trying to find a solution to this problem, proposed to Lot that they should separate amicably, and Lot, given first choice by Abram, settled in the well-watered valley of the Jordan, near the cities of Sodom and Gomorrah, while Abram went to live in the plain of Mamre, near Hebron, and built there an altar to God, who again promised to give all the land that Abram could see to him and his descendants.

Chedorlaomer, king of Elam, was the overlord of several kingdoms. Bera, king of Sodom, was one of his vassals. After serving him for twelve years, Bera and four other kings— Shinab, king of Admah; Shemeber, king of Zeboiim; Birsha, king of Gomorrah; and the king of Bela—rebelled and formed an alliance. Chedorlaomer and his allies—King Amraphel of Shinar, King Arioch of Ellasar, and King Tidal—fought against them in the valley of Sidim, in the region of the Dead Sea, and defeated them.

Bera and Birsha ran away from the battle and fell into the tar pits of the valley. Shinab and the other two kings managed to escape to the mountains.

The victors took a number of prisoners, including Lot, and departed back to their countries, loaded with all the goods from Sodom and Gomorrah that they could carry.

A man, who managed to escape from Chedorlaomer, came to Abram and told him that his nephew Lot had been captured, and was being taken away. Abram armed three hundred and eighteen of his servants and— with his allies Aner, Eshcol, and Mamre—pursued the four kings, until he caught up with them in Daniel. There, he divided his men in groups, attacked the enemy that night, and defeated them, chasing them back as far as Hobah, near Damascus. He succeeded in recovering all the stolen loot, liberated Lot, and brought him to Sodom with all his possessions, together with the women who had been captured, and other prisoners.

The king of Sodom came out of the city to receive him, accompanied by Melchizedek, who was the king of Salem and also a priest of God. Melchizedek brought bread and wine and blessed Abram, who gave him a tenth of all the booty that he had recovered. The king of Sodom told Abram that he could keep all the recovered loot for himself, but Abram refused, saying that he did not want to give him a pretext to say that he had made Abram rich. Abram only accepted what his men had used, but he told the king of Sodom to let Abram's allies take their share.

God again appeared to Abram, who mentioned that he had no children and that his servant Eliezer of Damascus was his only heir. God reassured him that his descendants would be as numerous as the stars in the sky, that they would be strangers in a land not their own and would be afflicted, during four hundred years, but afterward, they would come out with great wealth.

Sarai, Abram's wife who was still barren, owned a slave, an Egyptian girl named Hagar. She decided to give Hagar to Abram as a concubine, so that she could have Abram's child through her maid.

Her plan did not work out exactly as she had hoped. Hagar did get pregnant, but this made her feel so proud that she forgot her place, in the household, and started behaving toward her mistress Sarai with great insolence. Sarai complained to Abram, who told her that Hagar was her slave, and that, therefore, she could do with her whatever she wanted.

Sarai treated Hagar so cruelly that she ran away. An angel met Hagar at a spring in the desert and told her to return to Sarai, prophesying that her descendants would be without number, and that she would have a son whom she would name Ishmael. Hagar returned and, in due course, gave birth to Ishmael. Abram was eighty-six years old at the time.

Thirteen years later, when Abram was ninety-nine years old, God again appeared to Abram, saying that his name would no longer be Abram but Abraham, because he would be the father of many nations.

God made a covenant with Abraham, promising the land of Canaan to him and his descendants. Abraham, on his part, as a sign of the covenant, would circumcise himself, and from then on, every male child born in his house, or bought from any stranger, would be circumcised, when the baby would be eight days old.

God added that Sarai, from then on, would be called Sarah, and that she would have a son. Abraham bowed down and laughed, when he thought, "How can a child be born to one who is one hundred years old, and how can Sarah have a child at ninety?" He mentioned to God that he already had a son, Ishmael. God answered that Ishmael would also be blessed, and would become the father of twelve princes, and the ancestor of a great nation; but it would be with Isaac, Sarah's future son, that God would establish an everlasting covenant.

On that same day, Abraham circumcised his son Ishmael and all the other males in his household, including the slaves.

One hot day, Abraham was sitting at the entrance of his tent, when he looked up and saw three men standing. He ran to them and offered to bring them water, to refresh their feet, and some food. They accepted, and Abraham ran back to the tent and asked Sarah to bake some cakes. Then, he ran to the herd, chose a calf that was tender and fat, and ordered a servant to prepare it. Then, he took butter, milk, and the meat, and he set the food before the men and served it, and they ate.

The men asked him about the whereabouts of Sarah, and Abraham told them that she was inside the tent. One of them said, "I will return to you at this season, and your wife Sarah will have a son". Sarah, who was standing behind the tent door, heard this and laughed to herself, because she considered that they were too old to have a child.

The men rose, accompanied by Abraham, and went to a place, from where they could see Sodom in the distance. There, God told Abraham that the sins of Sodom and Gomorrah were too great to be forgiven. The two men continued on their way toward Sodom, but God remained with Abraham, who argued and bargained, trying to convince him not to destroy the city, even if not more than a few innocent people could be found there. God promised to Abraham that he would not destroy Sodom, if there were ten innocent men in the city. None were found, and the city was completely destroyed. Only Lot, his wife, and their two daughters managed to escape.

Abraham moved from the Hebron area to the Negev, between Kadesh and Shur, near Gerar, a Philistine city south of Gaza, outside the frontiers of the Promised Land.

Abraham remembered that, years ago, when he went to Egypt, he had been in danger of being killed because of Sarah. So, when he met Abimelech, the king of Gerar, he again presented Sarah as his sister. Abimelech, struck by her beauty, ordered his officials to take her to his harem.

God punished Abimelech, by closing the wombs of all the women in his household, and appeared to the king in a dream, warning him not to touch Sarah. Abimelech immediately returned Sarah to Abraham, gave him gifts of sheep, oxen, and servants, and allowed him to live anywhere in his kingdom. Abraham, in gratitude, prayed to God on behalf of Abimelech. God then healed the women, and Abimelech's wife bore him children.

Sarah became pregnant and gave birth to a son, whom Abraham called Isaac. The baby was circumcised eight days later. Abraham, at the time, was one hundred years old.

Time went by, and Isaac grew up. One day, Sarah saw Ishmael, the son of Hagar, mocking, and demanded from Abraham that he should send away the slave girl and her son, and that Isaac should become his sole heir. Abraham, who loved Ishmael, did not want to yield to Sarah's demand, until God told him to do what she said, reassuring him that his descendants through Ishmael would also be a great nation. Abraham rose early next morning, gave Hagar some bread and water, and sent her away with the boy. Hagar and her son survived their ordeal; Ishmael grew up to become an archer and married an Egyptian girl.

Sometime later, the servants of Abimelech, king of Gerar, violently took possession of one of Abraham's wells of water. Abraham complained to Abimelech, who was with Phichol, his army commander. When Abimelech denied having knowledge of the incident, Abraham gave him seven lambs as witness that it was he, Abraham, who had dug the well. Both men swore a pact of friendship, which is why Abraham called that place Beersheba, *Well of the swearing*.

God decided to test Abraham and told him to take Isaac to the land of Moriah, and there sacrifice his son on a mountaintop. Abraham did not question God's order; he set out on his donkey, taking with him Isaac, two young servants, and some firewood.

After traveling for three days, they arrived at Moriah. Abraham told the servants to wait for them with the donkey and gave the wood to Isaac to carry, and he himself carried a knife and live coals to start the sacrificial fire.

As they walked along together, Isaac asked his father, "Where is the lamb for the sacrifice?"

Abraham answered, "God will provide one". They continued walking in silence.

When they came to the place that God had told him, Abraham built an altar and carefully arranged the wood on it. He tied up Isaac and placed him on the altar, on top of the wood. Then, he raised the knife to kill the boy, when, suddenly, an angel called him from heaven, "Abraham, Abraham". He answered, "Here I am". The angel said, "Do not lay your hand upon the lad, and do not do anything to him, for now I know that you fear God, seeing that you have not kept your son, your only son, from him".

Abraham looked around, and seeing a ram caught in a bush by its horns, he went to it, got it, and sacrificed it, instead of his son. The angel spoke to Abraham a second time, "By myself have I sworn, said God, because you have not withheld your son, that I will bless you, and that you will have as many descendants as there are stars in the sky or grains of sand in the seashore. Your descendants will conquer their enemies, and all nations will be blessed through them, because you have obeyed my command". Abraham and Isaac went back to their servants, and they all returned to Beersheba.

Sarah lived to be one hundred and twenty-seven years old. She died in Hebron, and Abraham mourned her death. Abraham bought the cave of Machpelah, in the outskirts of Hebron, as a family sepulcher, from Ephron the Hittite, for four hundred shekels of silver, and there, he buried Sarah.

Abraham, now a very old man, decided that the time had come to find a wife for his son Isaac, who was now forty years old. He told Eliezer, his trusted servant, to solemnly swear that he would not get a Canaanite woman for Isaac, and then sent him to his relatives in Haran with instructions to bring from there a bride for Isaac. The servant returned with Rebekah, daughter of Bethuel and granddaughter of Nahor, Abraham's brother. Isaac married her, and she became a great comfort to him.

Abraham himself remarried. His new wife, a woman named Keturah, gave birth to six children: Zimran, Jokshan, Medan, Midian, Ishbak, and Shuah; but Isaac remained his sole heir.

Abraham passed away at the age of one hundred and seventy-five. His sons Isaac and Ishmael buried him next to Sarah, in the cave of Machpelah, in Hebron.

Abram

(Hebrew origin: *Exalted father*)

(Genesis 11:26). 19th century B.C. This was the name of the first patriarch, before God changed it to Abraham. This form, Abram, appears in Genesis, from 11:26 to 17:5, and only in two other places in the rest of the Bible: Nehemiah 9:7 and 1 Chronicles 1:27. (Please see the entry for Abraham [Genesis 17:5].)

Absalom

(Hebrew origin: *Father of peace*)

(2 Samuel 3:3). 10th century B.C. Absalom, the third son of King David, was born in Hebron. He was the only son of David who was of royal blood: his mother was Maacah, daughter of Talmai, king of Geshur, a kingdom situated northeast of the Sea of Galilee.

Absalom's sister, Tamar, was raped and then cast aside by their half brother Amnon, David's firstborn son. She put dust on her head, tore the ornamented tunic she was wearing, and walked away, screaming loudly as she went. Absalom met her and asked her, "Was it your brother Amnon who did this to you? For the present, sister, keep quiet about it; he is your brother. Don't brood over this matter". Absalom gave her refuge in his house. When King David heard about all this, he was greatly upset, but he did not rebuke Amnon. Absalom, on his side, didn't utter a word to Amnon, but silently hated him, and waited patiently for an opportunity to revenge his sister.

Two years later, Absalom saw his opportunity. He invited his father, King David, to a sheep-shearing celebration. The king did not accept the invitation, but, when Absalom insisted, he allowed Amnon and his other sons to attend the party. During the feast, Absalom had his servants kill Amnon to avenge his sister's rape. The first report that King David received was that Absalom had killed all his sons, but then, he was informed by his nephew Jonadab that only Amnon was dead. Absalom fled to Geshur and stayed there with his maternal relatives.

After three years had gone by, Joab, David's army commander, considered that the time had come for Absalom to return to Jerusalem. Knowing that David refused to talk about Absalom, Joab organized a charade by getting a woman of Tekoah to tell David a tale, which was, in all essential points, Absalom's tale, and pointed to the need for forgiveness. This convinced King David to send Joab to Geshur and bring Absalom back. Absalom returned to his house in Jerusalem, but he was not allowed to come into the king's presence.

Two years later, Absalom decided that he had waited long enough and decided that he wanted to see his father now. Knowing how close Joab and his father were, he wanted Joab to speak to David on his behalf. Absalom sent for him, but Joab refused to come. He sent for him a second time, again with no results. Absalom then ordered his servants to burn the fields of Joab.

This drastic step produced the expected result. Joab came immediately to Absalom's house and demanded to know why he had given orders to set fire to his fields.

Absalom answered, "I ordered my servants to burn your fields because you wouldn't come to me, when I called you. I want you to go to the king and arrange for me to see him".

Joab went to David and convinced him to receive his son. Absalom came to the palace, was taken to the presence of the king, and bowed down to the ground in front of him. When David saw his son, he welcomed him warmly and kissed him.

Absalom, the third-born son of David, was now the eldest surviving son of the king, after the death of Amnon, David's firstborn, and the probable death at a young age—the Bible does not mention him again—of Chileab, David's second son. As such, he was the obvious successor to the throne. Considering this, it is not easy to understand why, after his reconciliation with his father, Absalom started preparing, carefully and patiently, the groundwork for his attempt to depose David and become king. It is possible that Absalom was afraid that David, under the influence of Bathsheba, his favorite wife, would make Solomon, her son, his successor, which is what eventually happened.

Absalom, though strong headed and willful, knew how to bide his time in order to achieve his purpose, and how to work for that end. As a first step, he dedicated himself to win the love of the people. He would stand at the city gates, intercept inhabitants bringing their disputes for judgment, and pay them flattering attention. He became very popular, and the most admired man in the kingdom, famous for his beauty, and for his luxurious head of hair that he would cut only once a year.

He carefully planned his plot, and when he judged that the time had come, Absalom went to Hebron, with two hundred men, and proclaimed himself king. Ahithophel, David's most respected counselor, joined him there.

David, upon hearing of the revolt, abandoned Jerusalem and retreated with his bodyguard, his foreign mercenaries—the Kerethites and Pelethites—and six hundred Gittites, to the other side of the Jordan River. The king left in Jerusalem ten of his concubines to take care of the palace.

Ittai the Gittite, one of the commanders of David's army, was told by David that he, as a foreigner, should go back and stay with the new king. Ittai refused to leave David and accompanied him in his flight, saying that, in life or death, he would remain with the king.

The people along the road wept as the troops marched by. The priests Zadok and Abiathar, accompanied by Levites, came carrying the Ark of the Covenant.

The king said to Zadok, "Take the Ark back to the city. If I find favor with the Lord, he will bring me back and let me see it and its abode. But if he says, 'I find no delight in you', I am ready; let him do with me as he pleases".

Zadok and his son Ahimaaz, and Abiathar and his son Jonathan, returned to Jerusalem. David, and all the people who were with him, went up, barefooted, the slope of the Mount of Olives, weeping, with covered heads. David, who was told that his wise counselor Ahithophel had joined the conspiracy, prayed, "O Lord, please thwart the advice of Ahithophel!"

Hushai the Archite, a loyal friend and adviser of King David, wanted to join David in his flight from Absalom. David refused, saying that Hushai would only be a burden to the fleeing army, but that he could be most useful to his cause if he would go to Absalom, pretend that he had transferred his loyalties to him, and do his utmost to defeat the counsel of Ahithophel. Whatever he learned in the rebel's camp, he should report back to David, sending this information by two messengers: Ahimaaz, son of Zadok the Priest, and Jonathan, son of Abiathar the Priest.

Absalom entered Jerusalem with his army and took possession of the royal palace. Hushai came to Absalom and greeted him, saying, "Long live the king! Long live the king!" Absalom said to Hushai, "Is this your loyalty to your friend? Why didn't you go with him?" Hushai replied, "I am for the one whom the Lord and this people and all the men of Israel have chosen, and I will stay with him. As I was in your father's service, so I will be in yours".

Absalom then asked Ahithophel for his advice. Ahithophel told him to make clear to the Jerusalemites who was now in charge, by having sexual relations with the concubines whom David had left in the palace.

Ahithophel asked Absalom to allow him to pick twelve thousand men and set out that same night in pursuit of David, saying, "I will come upon him, when he is weak and disheartened, and when all the troops with him flee, I will kill the king alone". Absalom was pleased with the advice, but he wanted to hear what Hushai had to say about it. Hushai came, and after being told what Ahithophel had advised, he said, "This time Ahithophel's advice is not good. You know that your father and his men are courageous fighters. Your father is an experienced soldier and he will not spend the night with his troops; he will be hiding in one of the pits. My advice to you is to call all the men of Israel, from Dan to Beersheba, and that you march at their head into battle. No one will survive, neither he nor any of the men with him". Absalom and his council accepted Hushai's advice as better than Ahithophel's.

Hushai met secretly with the priests Zadok and Abiathar and told them that Absalom had agreed to do what he had suggested. He instructed them to send, at once, messengers to David, telling him not to delay, and to cross over the river at once; otherwise, the king and all his men would be annihilated.

Ahithophel, knowing that Absalom's rejection of his advice would result in a catastrophic defeat, saddled his donkey and went home to his native town. He set his affairs in order, and then, he hanged himself.

David reached Mahanaim, when Absalom and his army, under the command of Amasa, crossed the Jordan. David divided his army in three regiments—one under the command of Joab, the other under Abishai, and the third under Ittai the Gittite—and told them that he personally would lead them, but the troops told him that it would be better if he would stay in town. The king gave orders to his commanders to deal gently with Absalom.

In the subsequent battle in the woods of Ephraim, Absalom's army was utterly defeated. Absalom fled, riding on a mule, but his hair was caught in the branches of a thick tree, and was killed on Joab's orders, against the express command of David to spare his life. The king's bitter mourning for his son almost cost him the support of his loyal troops.

His name was remembered, in Jerusalem, by a pillar called Absalom's monument that he erected, at a time when he did not yet have any sons; eventually, he had three sons and two daughters. One of his daughters was called Tamar, in memory of his unfortunate sister. The other daughter was called Maachah, in memory of his mother. Maachah, years later, married King Rehoboam and gave birth to his successor King Abijah.

He was called Abishalom in the first book of Kings (1 Kings 15:2).

Achaicus

(Greek origin: *From Achaia, a Roman province*)

(1 Corinthians 16:17). A.D. 1st century. Achaicus was one of the three Corinthians—the other two were Stephanas and Fortunatus—whose visit to Paul, in Ephesus, made the apostle very glad.

Achan

(Hebrew origin: *Troublesome*)

(Joshua 7:1). 12th century B.C. Achan—called Achar in the first book of Chronicles (1 Chronicles 2:7)—son of Carmi, of the tribe of Judah, transgressed sacrilegiously, by stealing some of the booty taken by Joshua in Jericho, which Joshua had expressly forbidden the people to touch.

This trespass caused God to punish the Israelites, by allowing them to be defeated by the men of Ai, with thirty-six men dying in the battle. When Joshua appealed to God to tell him what he had done wrong, God answered that Israel had sinned, by stealing the devoted things. Joshua then assembled the twelve tribes, and lots were cast to find out the guilty.

The tribe of Judah was singled out, and Joshua went through them, family by family, until he came to Achan, who confessed to Joshua that he had stolen a garment, gold, and silver from the booty, which he had buried in the ground under his tent. Joshua sent men to retrieve the stolen goods, which were brought back and displayed publicly.

Achan, his family, and all his possessions were taken to the valley of Achor, where they were stoned to death and burned. A huge mound of stones was raised over him. The assault on Ai was renewed, and this time, it succeeded.

Achar

(Hebrew origin: *Troublesome*)

(1 Chronicles 2:7). 12th century B.C. Achar is an alternative name for Achan (Joshua 7:1), son of Carmi, of the tribe of Judah, who transgressed sacrilegiously, by stealing some of the booty taken by Joshua in Jericho.

Achaz

(Hebrew origin: *Possessor*)

(Matthew 1:9). 8th century B.C. Achaz is an alternative spelling for Ahaz #1 (2 Kings 15:38), father of Ezekias, ancestor of Jesus, in the genealogy of Matthew.

Achbor

(Hebrew origin: *Mouse*)

1. (Genesis 36:38). Unspecified date. Achbor was the father of Baalhanan, one of the first kings of Edom.
2. (2 Kings 22:12). 7th century B.C. Achbor, son of Michaiah, was an official in the court of King Josiah. The king sent him, and two other officials, to consult with

Huldah, the prophetess, concerning the Book of the Law that had been found in the Temple, while it was being repaired.

His son Elnathan was sent to Egypt by King Jehoiakim to bring back the fugitive prophet Urijah (Jeremiah 26:22). Achbor is called Abdon, son of Micah, in the second book of Chronicles (2 Chronicles 34:20).

Achim

(Hebrew origin: *God will raise*)

(Matthew 1:14). Unspecified date. Achim, son of Sadoc, was the father of Eliud, an ancestor of Jesus, according to the genealogy of Matthew.

Achish

(Philistine origin: Uncertain meaning)

(1 Samuel 21:10). 11th century B.C. Achish, son of Maoch, was king of Gath, the Philistine city to which David fled, while escaping from Saul's persecution.

Achish's courtiers recognized David, as one of King Saul's commanders, and remembered those songs that were sung in Israel about his feats in his battles against the Philistines. David, to save his life, feigned madness, and Achish let him go away.

Later, when David was the leader of a band of six hundred outlaws, he again sought refuge, with Achish in Gath. This time, Achish allowed him to stay, in the land of the Philistines, and settle in the town of Ziklag.

David used Ziklag as a base, from which, to make raids against the Amalekites and other inhabitants of the southern Negev. He would falsely report to Achish that his raids had been directed against the Israelites, thus, making Achish believe that David was making himself hateful to his own people.

When the Philistines decided to go to war against Israel, King Achish, absolutely convinced of David's loyalty, made him his bodyguard. However, the other Philistine leaders suspected David, of being a potential fifth columnist, and told Achish to send him back to Ziklag, which the king did reluctantly and apologetically.

Many years later, when Solomon was king of Israel, and Achish was already a very old man, two of the slaves of Shimei ran away to Gath and tried to find refuge, with the Philistine king. The slaves were pursued by Shimei, who, thus, broke Solomon's order that he should never leave Jerusalem, under penalty of death. When Shimei returned to Jerusalem, King Solomon carried out the suspended death sentence.

Achish is called Abimelech in the book of Psalms (Psalm 34:1). His father Maoch was called Maachah in the first book of Kings (1 Kings 2:39).

Achsa

(Hebrew origin: *Anklet*)

(1 Chronicles 2:49). 12th century B.C. Achsa—spelled Achsah in the book of Joshua (Joshua 15:16)—was the daughter of Caleb.

Her father gave her in marriage to her cousin Othniel, as his reward for having taken Kirjathsepher, during the conquest of Canaan. She convinced her father to give her springs of water, complaining that he had given her away as Negev-land, "dry land"—i.e. without dowry.

Achsah

(Hebrew origin: *Anklet*)

(Joshua 15:16). 12th century B.C. Achsah is an alternative spelling for Achsa (1 Chronicles 2:49), the daughter of Caleb.

Adah

(Hebrew origin: *Ornament*)

1. (Genesis 4:19). Antediluvian. Adah was one of Lamech's two wives. She had two sons: Jabal, the first man to live in tents and raise cattle; and Jubal, the first man to play musical instruments. Her husband Lamech, son of Methusael, boasted to her and to Zillah, his other wife, that he had killed two men who had wounded him. He added that, if Cain would be avenged sevenfold, he, Lamech, would be avenged seventy-sevenfold.

2. (Genesis 36:2). 18th century B.C. Adah, the daughter of Elon the Hittite, was one of Esau's wives. She was the mother of Eliphaz and the grandmother of Amalek. Adah was also called Bashemath #1 (Genesis 26:34).

Adaiah

(Hebrew origin: *Witness of God*)

1. (2 Kings 22:1). 8th century B.C. Adaiah was the grandfather of King Josiah, through his daughter Jedidah, the wife of King Amon of Judah.

2. (1 Chronicles 6:41). Unspecified date. Adaiah was the son of Ethan, of the clan of the Kohathites. His descendant Asaph was one of the Levites appointed by King David to be in charge of the singing in the House of the Lord.

3. (1 Chronicles 8:21). Unspecified date. Adaiah, son of Shimhi, was a leader of the tribe of Benjamin who lived in Jerusalem.

4. (1 Chronicles 9:12). 5th century B.C. Adaiah, son of Jeroham and grandson of Pashur, was a priest who served in the Temple, after the return from the Babylonian Exile.

5. (2 Chronicles 23:1). 9th century B.C. Adaiah was the father of Maaseiah, one of the army commanders who conspired with the priest Jehoiada to overthrow Queen Athaliah and crown Joash, the legitimate heir to the throne of Judah.

6. (Ezra 10:29). 5th century B.C. Adaiah, descendant of Bani, divorced his foreign wife, during the time of Ezra.

7. (Ezra 10:39). 5th century B.C. Adaiah, as his namesake above, divorced his foreign wife, during the time of Ezra.

8. (Nehemiah 11:5). Unspecified date. Adaiah, son of Joiarib, was an ancestor of Maaseiah, one of the Israelites who settled in Jerusalem, after the return from the Babylonian Exile.

9. (Nehemiah 11:12). 5th century B.C. Adaiah, son of Jeroham and grandson of Pelaliah, was one of the priests serving in the Temple, after the return from the Babylonian Exile.

Adalia

(Persian origin: Uncertain meaning)

(Esther 9:8). 5th century B.C. Adalia was one of the ten sons of Haman, the vizier of Persia who wanted to kill all the Jews in the kingdom.

His brothers were Parshandatha, Arisai, Dalphon, Poratha, Aspatha, Aridatha, Parmashta, Aridai, and Vajezatha. All of them were executed, when Haman's plot against the Jews backfired.

Adam

(Hebrew origin: *Man*)

(Genesis 2:19). Antediluvian. Adam was the first human being and the progenitor of the human race. The first chapter of Genesis states that God made man in the sixth day of the creation, fashioning him in His own image and giving him dominion over the rest of creation.

The second chapter of Genesis tells the creation of man in more detail. God created man, from the dust of the ground, and breathed into his nostrils the breath of life, placing him in the Garden of Eden to cultivate it and keep it.

God told the man that he could eat from every tree in the garden, except from the tree of the knowledge of good and evil, under penalty of death.

God brought all the animals and birds to Adam, who gave them their respective names, but Adam could not find among the animals a suitable helpmate. God then put the man to sleep, extracted one of his ribs, and fashioned with it the first woman, whom Adam called Eve because she was the mother of all living.

The man and the woman were naked and felt no shame, until the serpent convinced the woman to eat the fruit of the forbidden tree. After Eve shared the fruit with Adam, the couple became aware of their nakedness. They covered themselves, with fig leaves, and hid from God in embarrassment.

God asked Adam, "How did you know that you were naked? You have eaten the forbidden fruit".

Adam blamed Eve, and Eve blamed the serpent. As punishment for this transgression, God condemned the serpent to crawl on its belly and eat dust. He told the woman that she would suffer pain in childbirth, would crave for her husband, and be subject to him.

To the man, God said, "Because you listened to the woman and violated the prohibition, you are destined to work hard all the days of your life, and to gain your bread by the sweat of your brow".

God then made garments of skin and clothed the man and the woman. To prevent them from eating the fruit of the tree of life, and, thus, becoming immortal, God expelled them from the Garden of Eden.

After being driven out of the Garden of Eden, Eve conceived and gave birth to Cain and, later, to Abel. After the death of Abel, who was murdered by his jealous brother Cain, Eve gave birth to her third son, Seth, when Adam was a hundred and thirty years old. There is no further mention of Eve in the Bible, and it is not known how old she was, when she died.

Though Adam lived on for many years, dying at the age of nine hundred and thirty, the Bible gives no account of how he adapted himself to life, outside the Garden of Eden, except to mention that he fathered sons and daughters.

Note: The etymology of the word "Adam" connects this name with Adamah, *Ground* or *Soil*, and also with Adom, *Red*. This suggests that Adam was formed from red soil or clay.

Adbeel

(Hebrew origin: *Disciplined of God*)

(Genesis 25:13). 18th century B.C. Adbeel, a grandson of Abraham and his Egyptian concubine Hagar, was one of the twelve sons of Ishmael.

Adbeel's brothers were Nebajoth, Hadad, Mibsam, Mishma, Dumah, Massa, Jetur, Tema, Kedar, Naphish, and Kedemah, all of them ancestors of great nations. His sister Mahalath—also called Bashemath—married Esau, the son of Isaac.

Addar

(Hebrew origin: *Magnificent*)

(1 Chronicles 8:3). 16th century B.C. Addar, son of Belah and grandson of Benjamin, was the ancestor of the clan of the Ardites. He is also called Ard (Numbers 26:40).

Addi

(Probably from Hebrew origin: *Magnificent*)

(Luke 3:28). Unspecified date. Addi was the son of Cosam and father of Melchi, ancestor of Jesus, in the genealogy of Luke.

Ader

(Hebrew origin: *Arrangement of animals, flock, drove*)

(1 Chronicles 8:15). Unspecified date. Ader, an inhabitant of Jerusalem, was the head of a Benjamite clan.

Adiel

(Hebrew origin: *Ornament of God*)

1. (1 Chronicles 4:36). 8th century B.C. Adiel was one of the leaders of the tribe of Simeon who went to the fertile valley of Gedor in search of pasture for their flocks, during the reign of Hezekiah, king of Judah.

   The Simeonites destroyed the tents of the people—descendants of Ham—who lived there, wiped them out forever, and settled in their place.
2. (1 Chronicles 9:12). 5th century B.C. Adiel, son of Jahzerah, was the father of Maasiai, a priest who served in the Temple, after the return from the Babylonian Exile.
3. (1 Chronicles 27:25). 11th century B.C. Adiel was the father of Azmaveth, the court official in charge of King David's treasures.

Adin

(Hebrew origin: *Delicate*)

1. (Ezra 2:15). Unspecified date. Adin was the ancestor of a family of Judah who returned with Zerubbabel from Babylon.

2. (Nehemiah 10:16). 5th century B.C. Adin was one of the leaders who signed Nehemiah's solemn agreement to separate themselves from the foreigners living in the land, to refrain from intermarrying with them, and to dedicate their firstborn to God, among other obligations.

Adina

(Hebrew origin: *Delicate*)

(1 Chronicles 11:42). 10th century B.C. Adina, son of Shiza, was one of King David's brave warriors and a captain of the Reubenites.

Adino

(Hebrew origin: *Delicate*)

(2 Samuel 23:8). 10th century B.C. Adino the Eznite was one of King David's bravest warriors, famous for killing eight hundred men on one occasion.

Adlai

(Hebrew origin: Uncertain meaning)

(1 Chronicles 27:29). 11th century B.C. Adlai's son Shaphat was the official in charge of the cattle in the valleys, during the reign of King David.

Admatha

(Persian origin: Uncertain meaning)

(Esther 1:14). 5th century B.C. Admatha was one of the seven high officials of Persia and Media—the others were Shethar, Carshena, Tarshish, Meres, Marsena, and Memucan—whom King Ahasuerus consulted about the punishment to be imposed on Queen Vashti for disobeying his command to appear before him.

Adna

(Hebrew origin: *Pleasure*)

1. (Ezra 10:30). 5th century B.C. Adna, a descendant of Pahathmoab, divorced his foreign wife, during the days of Ezra.

2. (Nehemiah 12:15). 5th century B.C. Adna was the head of a priestly clan, descended from Harim, when Joiakim was High Priest, during the time of Nehemiah.

Adnah

(Hebrew origin: *Pleasure*)

1. (1 Chronicles 12:20). 11th century B.C. Adnah, from the tribe of Manasseh, deserted Saul's army with his men, joined David at Ziklag, and became a captain of his army.
2. (2 Chronicles 17:14). 9th century B.C. Adnah was the commander of one of King Jehoshaphat's largest armies, with three hundred thousand warriors under his command.

Adonibezek

(Hebrew origin: *Lord of lightning*)

(Judges 1:5). 12th century B.C. Adonibezek, ruler of Canaanites and Perizzites, was defeated at Bezek by the tribes of Judah and Shimeon, after Joshua's death.

Adonibezek fled, but was captured, and had his thumbs and great toes cut off. He was stoic about it, stating that God had repaid him for having done the same to seventy kings. He was brought to Jerusalem, and there, he died.

Adonijah

(Hebrew origin: *God is my Lord*)

1. (2 Samuel 3:4). 10th century B.C. Adonijah, the son of King David and his wife Haggith, was born in Hebron. He grew up to be a very handsome man, whom David, his father, had never disciplined (1 Kings 1:6).

He was the fourth-born son of the king, but the death of his older brothers—Amnon, Chileab, and Absalom—made him the eldest surviving son of David, and, thus, the apparent heir to the throne.

Adonijah behaved boastfully and made no secret of his ambition to be king one day. He provided himself with chariots, horses, and fifty men to run before him.

Joab, the army's commander, and Abiathar, the High Priest, supported him in his bid for the throne, but other influential people in the court opposed him, among them Zadok, the other High Priest, and Nathan, the prophet, who sided with Solomon.

When Adonijah invited the leaders of the tribe of Judah, and all his brothers, except Solomon, to a sacrificial feast, Nathan told Bathsheba to go to King David, tell him what Adonijah was doing, and mention to the old king that he had promised the throne to Solomon.

While Bathsheba was still talking with David, Nathan came in and confirmed her words. Convinced by Nathan to act without delay, David ordered that Zadok and Nathan should immediately anoint Solomon king in Gihon.

When this was done the people shouted, "Long live King Solomon", and rejoiced with great joy. Jonathan, the son of Abiathar, rushed to Adonijah's feast with the news that Solomon had been proclaimed king. All the guests of Adonijah hurriedly left in fear.

Adonijah himself sought sanctuary at the altar. King Solomon took no action at that moment against his older brother and allowed him to go in peace to his house.

After the death of King David, Adonijah went to see Bathsheba and told her that he wished to marry Abishag, the beautiful Shunammite girl who had been brought to King David in his old age to be his nurse and warm his bed. Adonijah asked Bathsheba to intercede on his behalf with her son, King Solomon, and persuade him to give his approval to the marriage.

Solomon was angered by this request, which he interpreted as a poorly disguised bid for the throne, and ordered Benaiah to kill Adonijah that same day.

2. (2 Chronicles 17:8). 9th century B.C. Adonijah, a Levite, was sent by King Jehoshaphat in the third year of his reign, to teach the laws of God in the cities of Judah.

Adonijah was accompanied in his mission by other Levites, by two priests—Elishama and Jehoram—and by several officials of the court.

3. (Nehemiah 10:16). 5th century B.C. He was one of the leaders of Judah who signed Nehemiah's solemn agreement to separate themselves from the foreigners living in the land, to refrain from intermarrying with them, and to dedicate their firstborn to God, among other obligations.

Adonikam

(Hebrew origin: *My Lord has raised*)

(Ezra 2:13). Unspecified date. Adonikam was the ancestor of six hundred and sixty-six men who returned with Zerubbabel. Years later, three of his descendants—Eliphelet, Jeiel, and Shemaiah—returned with Ezra from the Babylonian Exile, at the head of a group of sixty males.

Adoniram

(Hebrew origin: *My Lord is exalted*)

(1 Kings 4:6). 10th century B.C. Adoniram, son of Abda, was an important court official, during the reigns of David, Solomon, and Rehoboam.

Adoniram is mentioned in a list from the later years of David's reign, as the official in charge of levying the forced labor, necessary for the royal building programs.

During the reign of Solomon, Adoniram continued in the same office and was in charge of the levy of all Israel sent to Lebanon to cut lumber.

At the beginning of Rehoboam's reign, Adoniram was sent to face the discontented and rebellious assembly at Shechem and died by the hand of the mob, stoned to death by the people.

He was called Adoram in the books of Second Samuel (2 Samuel 20:24) and First Kings (1 Kings 12:18), and Hadoram in the second book of Chronicles (2 Chronicles 10:18).

Adonizedek

(Hebrew origin: *Lord of justice*)

(Joshua 10:1). 12th century B.C. Adonizedek, king of Jerusalem, heard that Joshua had taken Ai and destroyed it, and that the inhabitants of Gibeon had become Joshua's allies.

He made a military alliance—with Hoham, king of Hebron; Piram, king of Jarmuth; Japhia, king of Lachish; and Debir, king of Eglon—to attack the town of Gibeon for having made peace with the people of Israel. The people of Gibeon appealed to Joshua for help.

Joshua—after ordering the sun to stand still, over Gibeon, and the moon, over the valley of Ajalon—fought against the five kings and defeated them. Their armies ran away, during a storm of hailstones, which killed many of their soldiers, even more than those who had been killed in the fighting. The five kings fled and hid in a cave at Makkedah, where they were trapped.

After Joshua had liquidated all the surviving enemies, he ordered that the kings should be taken out from the cave. Adonizedek, Debir, Hoham, Japhia, and Piram, after being humiliated, were killed and hanged on five trees, until the evening. At sunset, their corpses were taken down and thrown into the cave, where they had been hiding, and large stones were placed over the entrance to the cave.

Adoram

(Hebrew origin: *The Lord is exalted*)

(2 Samuel 20:24). 10th century B.C. Adoram, son of Abda, was an important court official, during the reigns of David, Solomon, and Rehoboam.

Adoram is mentioned in a list from the later years of David's reign, as the official in charge of levying the forced labor, necessary for the royal building programs.

During the reign of Solomon, Adoram continued in the same office and was in charge of the levy of all Israel sent to Lebanon to cut lumber.

At the beginning of Rehoboam's reign, Adoram was sent to face the discontented and rebellious assembly at Shechem and died by the hand of the mob, stoned to death by the people.

He was called Adoniram in the first book of Kings (1 Kings 4:6), and Hadoram in the second book of Chronicles (2 Chronicles 10:18).

Adrammelech

(Hebrew origin: *Splendor of the king*)

1. (2 Kings 17:31). Adrammelech was one of the gods of the Sepharvites, a tribe that the Assyrians settled in Samaria, after they destroyed the kingdom of Israel in 722 B.C. The cult of Adrammelech and Anammelech, another god, was accompanied by the sacrifice of children.

2. (2 Kings 19:37). 8th century B.C. Adrammelech and his brother Sharezer murdered their father Sennacherib, king of Assyria, while the king was worshipping in the Temple of his god Nisroch. The two patricides escaped to Armenia, and their brother Esarhaddon became king of Assyria.

Adriel

(Hebrew origin: *Flock of God*)

(1 Samuel 18:19). 11th century B.C. Adriel, the son of Barzillai the Meholathite, married Merab, the eldest daughter of King Saul, with whom he had five sons.

Merab's hand had been previously promised to David, as part of Saul's plan to get rid of him by offering him his daughter in marriage, if he would fight against the Philistines. Saul, who by that time envied and hated David, hoped that he would die in battle.

Saul was so sure that David would be killed that, without waiting to see how the battle would turn out, he married Merab to Adriel.

David returned from the battle, victorious and unhurt, and claimed Merab's hand. Saul, then, had no choice but to give him Michal, his youngest daughter, instead of Merab.

Many years later, when David was already the king of Israel, he handed over the five sons of Adriel and Merab—together with Mephibosheth and Armoni, the sons of King Saul, and his concubine Rizpah—to the Gibeonites, who hanged them on a hill, in revenge for the massacre that Saul had perpetrated against them.

Aeneas

(Uncertain origin and meaning)

(Acts of the Apostles 9:33). A.D. 1st century. Aeneas, an Israelite who lived in Lydda, was a paralytic who had been confined to his bed for eight years. Peter, in the name of Jesus, cured him.

Agabus

(Hebrew origin: *Locust*)

(Acts of the Apostles 11:28). A.D. 1st century. Agabus, a prophet, traveled from Jerusalem to Antioch. There, he prophesied that a severe famine would come over all the earth. This prediction came to pass, during the reign of Emperor Claudius.

Years later, Agabus came to the house of Philip the evangelist in Caesarea, where Paul was staying, and prophesied that Paul would be arrested in Jerusalem (Acts of the Apostles 21:10).

Agag

(Hebrew origin: Uncertain meaning)

1. (Numbers 24:7). 13th century B.C. Balaam, in one of his oracles, prophesied that the king of Israel would be "higher than Agag". It is not clear if the "Agag" here mentioned refers to the specific name of an Amalekite king, or is the generic title of the kings of Amalek.

2. (1 Samuel 15:8). 11th century B.C. Agag, king of the Amalekites, was defeated by King Saul, who spared his life. God, angry by Saul's misplaced compassion, told Samuel that he regretted having made Saul king.

Samuel went to Gilgal and demanded from Saul that Agag should be brought to him. The Amalekite king was brought to Samuel, who reproached him, for having made so many women childless with his sword, and told him, "So shall your mother be childless among women". After saying this, the prophet cut Agag in pieces.

This incident caused a complete rupture between Samuel and Saul, and they never saw each other again.

Note: The book of Esther mentions that Haman, the man who wished to exterminate the Persian Jews, was a descendant of Agag (Esther 9:24).

Agee

(Hebrew origin: Uncertain meaning)

(2 Samuel 23:11). 11th century B.C. Agee was the father of Shammah, a brave warrior in King David's army, who heroically stood his ground, when all others fled, during a battle with the Philistines, and turned a rout into a great victory.

Agrippa

(Greek origin: *Wild-horse tamer*)

(Acts of the Apostles 25:13). A.D. 1st century. King Agrippa—Herod Agrippa II— was the great grandson of Herod I the Great, and the last of the Herodian dynasty.

Agrippa, who was raised and educated at the imperial court in Rome, became king of Chalcis, in southern Lebanon, in A.D. 50, when he was twenty-three years old.

In A.D. 53, he became tetrarch of Batanea and Trachonitis in south Syria. Around that time, his sister Bernice came to live with him, a situation that caused a scandal and alienated the Jews.

When the new Roman Governor Porcius Festus came to Judea, King Agrippa came to Caesarea with Bernice to pay him a courtesy visit. After several days of official festivities, Festus consulted with the king the case of Paul, who had been jailed by Felix, the previous governor, but had not been charged with any crime.

"There is a man left in jail by Felix", he said, "against whom the chief priests and the elders of the Jews brought charges, during my visit to Jerusalem, and asked me to condemn him. I told them that it was not the custom of the Romans to hand over any accused man, before he had met his accusers face to face and had the opportunity to defend himself. When they came here, I didn't waste any time, and the next day, I sat in the Judgment Hall and ordered the man to be brought in. The accusers stood up but did not bring any charge of evil doings, they just argued certain points about their own religion and about a man named Jesus, who is dead, but whom Paul claims that he is alive. Not being sure of how to proceed, I asked Paul if he would be willing to go to Jerusalem and be tried there on these charges. He asked to be kept in custody for the decision of the emperor, so I gave orders to be held, until I could send him to the emperor".

Agrippa said, "I would like to hear this man myself".

"Tomorrow you will hear him", answered Festus.

The next morning, King Agrippa and Bernice came to the Governor's Palace with great pomp, accompanied by military commanders and the leading citizens of the city. When Paul was brought in, Festus spoke to the gathering, "King Agrippa, and all men who are present here, the Jews who live here and in Jerusalem have asked me to put to death the man that you see here. I have not found guilty of any charge deserving death, but as he appealed to the emperor, I decided to send him. But I have nothing specific to write to my lord about him. Therefore, I have brought him before this assembly, and especially before you, King Agrippa, so that, after we have interrogated him, I may have something to write. It doesn't seem reasonable to me to send a prisoner without specifying the charges against him".

King Agrippa said to Paul, "You have permission to speak for yourself". Paul stretched out his hand and spoke to the assembly.

"I am fortunate, King Agrippa, that today I am able to defend myself before you against all the accusations of the Jews, because you are an expert regarding all the customs and disputes of the Jews. Please listen to me with patience.

"The events of my life, during my youth, among my own nation and at Jerusalem, are known to all the Jews. Those who knew me then, can testify, if they are willing, that I was a Pharisee, a member of the strictest sect of our religion. I stand now on trial for having hope in the promise that God made to our ancestors, for which our twelve tribes pray to God, day and night. Why should it be incredible to you that God can raise the dead?

"I was very active in Jerusalem against the believers in Jesus. I put many of them in prison, and voted for their death penalty. I punished them many times in the synagogues, and tried to make them blaspheme. I was so angry against them that I even went to foreign cities to persecute them.

"That is why I went to Damascus with the full knowledge and authorization of the chief priests. At midday, I saw a light from heaven, brighter than the sun, shining around me and my companions. And when we had fallen to the ground, I heard a voice saying to me in Hebrew, 'Saul, Saul, why do you persecute me?' I asked, 'Who are you, Lord?' And the voice answered, 'I am Jesus whom you are persecuting. Rise and stand on your feet. I have appeared to you to appoint you to serve me, and to testify of what you have seen, and what I will show you in the future. I will rescue you from the Jews and from the Gentiles, to whom I am now sending you. Open their eyes and turn them from darkness to light, from the power of Satan to God, so that they may have their sins forgiven and find their place among those who are sanctified through their faith in me'.

"King Agrippa, I didn't disobey the vision from heaven. First in Damascus and in Jerusalem, and then in the whole country of Judea and among the Gentiles, I preached that they must repent and turn to God, and perform deeds proving their repentance.

"It is for this reason that the Jews seized me in the Temple and tried to kill me. I continue to this day, with God's help, to testify to small and great, saying nothing but what the prophets and Moses said would come to pass. That Christ would suffer, that he would be the first to rise from the dead, and proclaim light to the Jews and to the Gentiles".

Festus interrupted him, shouting, "Paul, you are crazy. Too much learning has made you mad". Paul said, "I am not mad, most noble Festus. I am speaking the sober truth. The king understands these things, and to him, I speak freely. I am convinced that none of these things has escaped his notice, because all this has not happened away in a corner".

Addressing himself to the king, Paul asked, "King Agrippa, do you believe in the prophets? I know you do".

Agrippa answered, "You think that you can convert me in such a short time?"

Paul replied, "I wish that not only you but all those that hear me today might become as I am, except for these chains, of course".

The king rose up and brought the proceedings to an end. Festus and Agrippa agreed that Paul was innocent, but they were powerless to help him, because, once the apostle had appealed to Rome for a ruling, the case was out of their jurisdiction.

Paul was handed to a centurion of the Augustus regiment named Julius and, a short time later, was put in a ship bound for Rome.

During the Jewish revolt against Rome, between the years of A.D. 66 to A.D. 70, Agrippa fought on the side of the Romans against the Jewish rebels. He died childless, in A.D. 93, ending the Herodian dynasty.

Agur

(Hebrew origin: *Gathered*)

(Proverbs 30:1). Unspecified date. Agur, son of Jakeh, spoke a series of proverbs, which appear in chapter 30 of the book of Proverbs.

Ahab

(Hebrew origin: *Father's brother* [i.e. *Father's friend*])

1. (1 Kings 16:28). 9th century B.C. Ahab, the seventh king of the northern kingdom of Israel, after the partition of the United

Monarchy, reigned for twenty-two years in the capital Samaria, the city founded by his father King Omri.

Ahab continued the foreign policies of his father: peaceful and friendly relations with the kingdom of Judah in the south, cemented by marrying his sister Athaliah to Jehoram, the crown prince of Judah; economic cooperation with the Phoenicians in the north, to whom he was related by marriage; and, in the northeast, resisting the military pressure of Benhadad, king of Aram-Damascus, who was intent in making Ahab his vassal.

He beautified Samaria, where he built for himself a palace decorated with ivory. He fortified cities and rebuilt Jericho.

His Phoenician wife, Jezebel, the daughter of Ethbaal, king of Sidon, had a strong influence over him. He gave her unlimited administrative authority and did not oppose the Phoenician cult of the god Baal that she introduced in the country. On the contrary, he cooperated with his wife by building a Temple for Baal in Samaria, and erecting an ashera or sacred post.

The prophet Elijah bitterly opposed the worship of Baal, and after telling the king that God would punish the country by withholding rain, he left the country to avoid Jezebel's harassment.

There was a severe famine in Samaria, which lasted three years. In the third year, King Ahab arranged with Obadiah, the governor of the royal palace, that they would both travel through the land—one in one direction, the other in another direction— searching for places where there would be grass to feed the horses and the mules.

Obadiah, a God-fearing man, had risked his life protecting a hundred prophets of the Lord from Jezebel's murderous persecution, by hiding them in a cave. When he found Elijah, the prophet told him to announce to the king that Elijah was back in Israel. Obadiah, although he was afraid that Ahab would kill him, went to the king and informed him that the prophet had returned.

Ahab went to meet Elijah and, when he saw him, accused him of troublemaking. Elijah retorted that Ahab and his father were the real troublemakers for forsaking the true God and worshiping the idols of Baal.

Elijah requested an encounter with the several hundred prophets of Baal who were under Queen Jezebel's protection and who ate at her table. King Ahab consented.

The contest took place in Mount Carmel, and the result was that the foreign priests were confounded and put to death by Elijah.

The drought, which had lasted three years, broke in a great storm. Ahab drove back in his chariot through the heavy rain, with the prophet Elijah running in front of the king all the way to Jezreel.

The queen, furious that Elijah had killed her prophets, sent a messenger to Elijah, threatening to kill him, but the prophet escaped to Beersheba.

King Benhadad of Aram—today's Syria—gathered his whole army and, with a coalition of thirty-two kings, invaded Israel, and laid siege to the city of Samaria. His insulting demands to Ahab—to deliver all his gold, silver, wives, and children— were so harsh that Ahab, who previously had considered surrendering, was advised by the elders of the land to reject Benhadad's demands, and fight back.

The Aramean king and his men were drinking and celebrating what they considered their soon-to-be victory, over Israel, when the Israelite army attacked them by surprise. Benhadad managed to escape and rode, on his horse, back to his country. He reorganized his army and, about a year later, again invaded Israel. Benhadad believed that the reason for his previous defeat was that he had fought in the hills against the Israelites. He changed his tactics and attacked in the plains.

The battle took place at Aphek, and Benhadad again was badly defeated, and this time, he was taken prisoner. Brought to the presence of Ahab, he was treated with respect and honor. The two kings signed a peace agreement, by which Benhadad promised to return to Ahab the Israelite cities, which had been captured by his father, and to allow Israelite merchants to open businesses in Damascus.

When Ahab returned to Samaria, a prophet, standing on the road, rebuked him for letting Benhadad go free and prophesied that, for this grave error, Ahab would be defeated and killed.

Sometime afterward, Ahab decided that a vineyard, adjacent to the palace, would be most useful as a vegetable garden. Ahab spoke to Naboth the Jezreelite, owner of the plot of land, and offered to pay him for the land or to exchange it for an equivalent piece of land somewhere else.

Naboth refused to give up his family inheritance, and the king went back to the palace depressed and angry. When his wife Jezebel asked him why he was depressed and why he refused to eat, he told her it was because Naboth had refused to sell him his land.

Jezebel told him to be cheerful and to leave the matters in her hands. The queen arranged to have Naboth falsely accused of insulting God. Naboth was tried and executed, and Ahab took possession of the property.

The prophet Elijah went to Naboth's vineyard, confronted the king, and accused him of murdering the man and taking over his property. The prophet told the king that God would punish him for his evil deeds; that dogs would lick his blood in the very place that dogs licked up Naboth's blood; that his family would come to the same bad end as the descendants of King Jeroboam and King Baasha; and that dogs would eat the body of his wife Jezebel.

When Elijah finished speaking, Ahab tore his clothes, took them off, and put on sackcloth. He fasted, slept in the sackcloth, and walked around gloomy and depressed. Ahab's humble behavior made God relent and postpone the prophesied disaster after Ahab's death, in his son's lifetime.

There was a three-year period of peace between Israel and Aram. During the third year, King Jehoshaphat of Judah came to see King Ahab, who wanted to recover Ramoth in Gilead from the hands of the king of Aram and asked Jehoshaphat if he would join him in attacking Ramoth.

Jehoshaphat answered that he was willing, but first, he wanted to consult God. Ahab gathered about four hundred prophets and asked them if he should attack Ramoth or not, and they all answered in one voice, "Attack, the Lord will give you victory".

Jehoshaphat, still doubtful, asked if there was another prophet of God through whom they could inquire. Ahab answered that there was one more, Micaiah, the son of Imlah, whom he hated because he never prophesied anything good for the king, only misfortune. King Jehoshaphat replied that Ahab shouldn't say that.

A court official was sent to bring Micaiah to the presence of the two kings, who, dressed in their royal robes, were sitting on their thrones at the threshing place at the entrance of the gate of Samaria.

All the prophets were in front of the kings, predicting victory. One of them, Zedekiah, the son of Chenaanah, had iron horns with him and told Ahab that, with those horns, the king would defeat the Arameans.

The court official, who was bringing Micaiah, told him that all the other prophets had prophesied victory, and that Micaiah should better do the same.

Micaiah answered that he would only speak what God would tell him. When the prophet was in front of Ahab, the king asked him if they should march against Ramoth or not.

The prophet readily answered, "Go and triumph, for the Lord will deliver it into your hands". Ahab felt the sarcasm in the prophet's answer and said, "How many times must I ask you to tell me nothing but the truth in the name of the Lord?"

The prophet replied that he could see

the army of Israel scattered over the hills like sheep without a shepherd.

Ahab, on an aside, told Jehoshaphat, "Didn't I tell you that he would not prophesy anything good for me, but only misfortune?"

The prophet continued, "I saw God seated upon his throne with all the angels standing around him. And God asked, 'Who will convince Ahab so that he will go and be killed at Ramoth?' A spirit stepped forward and said that he would entice Ahab by making his prophets tell lies, and God told him to go and deceive him". And Micaiah concluded, "God has made your prophets lie to you, for He has decreed disaster upon you".

Then, the prophet Zedekiah went to Micaiah, slapped his face, and asked, "Which way did the Spirit of the Lord pass from me to speak to you?"

Micaiah answered, "You will find out on the day when you try to hide into some back room".

The king ordered his guards to put Micaiah in prison, under the supervision of Amon, the governor of the city, and Prince Joash, and to give him only bread and water, until the king would return safely.

Micaiah's parting words were, "If you return safely, then God has not spoken through me!"

King Ahab and King Jehoshaphat went to attack the city of Ramoth in Gilead. King Ahab told Jehoshaphat that he would go disguised into battle but that the king of Judah should wear his royal clothing.

The king of Aram had commanded his thirty-two chariot commanders to attack no one else except the king of Israel. So, when they saw Jehoshaphat, they thought that he was the king of Israel and turned to attack him.

Jehoshaphat cried out, his attackers realized that he was not the king of Israel, and ceased to pursue him.

By chance, a man shot an arrow, which struck King Ahab between the joints of his armor. The wounded king said to the driver

of his chariot, "Take me outside the battle, for I am injured!" While the battle raged on, King Ahab remained propped up in his chariot, facing the Arameans. The blood from his wound ran down and covered the bottom of the chariot, and at evening, he died.

Near sunset the order went out through the Israelite army: "Every man go back to his own country and city". The king's body was brought to Samaria and buried. The blood-stained chariot was washed in the pool of Samaria, where dogs licked up his blood, and prostitutes washed themselves, in accordance to the word that the Lord had spoken.

His son Ahaziah succeeded him to the throne.

2. (Jeremiah 29:21). 6th century B.C. Ahab, son of Kolaiah, and Zedekiah, son of Maaseiah, were two false prophets who lived in Babylon, during the days of Jeremiah. They were accused by the prophet Jeremiah of doing vile things, committing adultery and prophesying falsehoods. Jeremiah predicted that their death, by burning at Nebuchadnezzar's command, would be mentioned as a curse by the exiled Judean community in Babylon.

Aharah

(Hebrew origin: *After his brother*)

(1 Chronicles 8:1). 17th century B.C. Aharah, one of the five sons of Benjamin, was the ancestor of the clan of the Ahiramites. In the book of Numbers (Numbers 26:38), he is called Ahiram.

In the book of Genesis (Genesis 46:21), where he is called Ehi, he is mentioned as being one of the ten sons of Benjamin, who were counted among the seventy Israelites, who immigrated to Egypt.

Aharhel

(Hebrew origin: *Behind the entrenchment* or *Rachel's brother*)

(1 Chronicles 4:8). Unspecified date. Aharhel, son of Harum, belonged to the tribe of Judah.

Ahasai

(Hebrew origin: *Seizer*)

(Nehemiah 11:13). Unspecified date. Ahasai, son of Meshillemoth, was the grandfather of Amashai, a priest who settled in Jerusalem, after the return from the Babylonian Exile.

Ahasbai

(Hebrew origin: Uncertain meaning)

(2 Samuel 23:34). 11th century B.C. Ahasbai's son Eliphelet was one of the warriors in King David's elite army group known as The Thirty. He is called Ur in the first book of Chronicles (1 Chronicles 11:35), where his son's name is given as Eliphal.

Ahasuerus

(Persian origin: Title of a Persian king)

1. (Ezra 4:6). 5th century B.C. The name Ahasuerus, according to scholars, was a title of the Persian kings, rather than a personal name.

   In the mention of Ahasuerus in the book of Ezra, he is identified as Artaxerxes (Ezra 4:7), the Persian king to whom the enemies of the returning exiles wrote a letter accusing the Jews of rebuilding Jerusalem for purposes of rebellion. The result of the letter was that the work on the Temple ceased, until the second year of the reign of Darius, king of Persia (Ezra 4:24).

2. (Esther 1:1). 5th century B.C. Ahasuerus, king of Persia, is usually identified by historians as King Xerxes I of Persia, the son and successor of Darius I. The Bible states that he was king of an empire, which extended from India to Cush in Africa, ruling over one hundred and twenty-seven provinces from his capital Shushan.

   In the third year of his reign, Ahasuerus gave a banquet for all his princes and administrators to show off his wealth. The great celebration lasted one hundred and eighty days.

   When the festivities for the nobles ended, the king gave a banquet in the garden of his palace for the common people of Shushan. During seven days, everybody, rich and poor, drank as much as he wanted. At the same time, Vashti, his queen, gave a banquet for the women inside the palace.

On the seventh day of the celebration, the drunken Ahasuerus ordered the seven eunuchs, who were his personal servants, to fetch Queen Vashti, and to make sure that she was wearing her royal crown. She was a beautiful woman, and the king wanted everybody to see her. The eunuchs returned and told the king that the queen refused to come.

The king, barely able to contain his fury, consulted with his law experts about what he should do with Vashti, for having refused to obey the king's command.

Memucan, one of his chief advisers, declared, "Queen Vashti has offended not only the king, but also all his officials, and all the people in the empire. Her bad example will make all the wives in the empire despise their husbands. The king should issue a royal decree and make it into a law, so that it could never be changed, that Vashti shall never again appear before the king. Another worthier woman should be made queen instead. The women in the empire will then surely treat their husbands with respect!" The proposal was approved by the king and his ministers.

Sometime later, after the king had calmed down, he kept thinking about Vashti, what she had done, and what had been decreed against her. His advisers suggested that beautiful virgins from every province should be brought to the harem in Shushan, to be placed under the care of Hege, the eunuch in charge of the women. The girls would be given a beauty treatment, and the one that the king would like best should be made queen, instead of Vashti. The king liked the proposal and put it into effect.

Maidens from all corners of the empire, Esther among them, were brought to the harem. Each girl would undergo a beauty treatment that lasted a whole year. Then, she would be brought to the king, to spend the night with him. The next morning, she would be taken to the second harem, where the women, who had already spent one night with the king, were kept under the supervision of the eunuch Shaashgaz. These women remained in the harem and never saw the king again, except when he specifically summoned one of them by her name.

One of the girls who were brought to the harem was Esther—whose Hebrew name was Hadassah, *Myrtle*—the daughter of Abihail, a descendant of King Saul, who had been exiled by the Babylonians from Jerusalem together with King Jeconiah of Judah. She had been orphaned at an early age and had been brought up by her cousin Mordecai.

During the seventh year of King Ahasuerus' reign, Esther's turn came to be brought to the king. He liked her more than any other girl and made her his queen. The king gave a great banquet in her honor, for all his officials and courtiers, where he proclaimed a tax amnesty, and distributed gifts. Esther, advised by Mordecai, didn't let it be known that she was Jewish.

One day, Mordecai, sitting in the palace gate, overheard two of Ahasuerus' guards plotting against the king's life. Mordecai told it to Esther, who reported it to the king in Mordecai's name. The matter was investigated and verified, and the two men were executed. The king ordered to write an account of this event in the official records of the empire.

Sometime later, the king promoted a man, named Haman, to the position of vizier of the empire, and ordered all the officials in his service to show him respect by kneeling and bowing to him. Everybody complied with the king's order except Mordecai.

Mordecai refused to kneel or bow to Haman, saying that he was a Jew, and that Jews only kneeled and bowed to God. Haman, angry and offended, decided that punishing Mordecai alone was not enough. All the Jews in the empire should be exterminated!

Haman went to the king and denounced that the Jews were a people with different customs who did not obey the king's laws. He added that, if the king would issue the death decree against the Jews, Haman would pay ten thousand talents of silver to the royal treasury.

The king took off his ring and gave it to Haman, saying, "The silver and the people are yours to do with them as you see fit".

Haman chose the month of Adar as an appropriate month for the genocide by casting lots, "Pur" in Hebrew. The king's scribes were called, and Haman dictated letters proclaiming that all the Jews, young and old, women and children, would be killed on the thirteenth day of the month of Adar. These letters, sealed with the king's ring, were sent to all the governors of the provinces. Having taken care of this business, the king and Haman sat down to drink.

When Mordecai learned of the death decree, he tore his clothes, dressed in sackcloth, covered his head with ashes, and walked through the city, bitterly crying out in a loud voice, until he reached the gates of the palace. He couldn't enter, because this was forbidden for people wearing sackcloth. In the provinces, the Jews fasted, wept, wailed, and put on sackcloth.

Queen Esther's maids and eunuchs informed her that Mordecai was outside the gates of the palace, dressed in sackcloth, crying and shouting. The queen became very agitated and worried about the mental health of her cousin. She sent somebody to the palace gates, with clothing for Mordecai, so that he could wear them, instead of his sackcloth. Mordecai refused to receive the clothing.

The queen sent Hatach, one of the eunuchs who served her, to Mordecai to find out the reason for his strange and disturbing behavior. Mordecai told Hatach that Haman had promised to give money to the king's treasuries for being allowed to exterminate the Jews. He gave the eunuch a copy of the decree and told him to show it to Esther, so that she would know the danger and go to the king to plead for her people.

Esther received the message and sent a note back to Mordecai saying that, according to the law, if she would go to the king without being summoned, she would be put to death, unless the king would extend his golden scepter to her.

Mordecai replied that Esther should not feel safer than any other Jew, just because she was in the palace. Esther answered that the Jews in Shushan should fast on her behalf for three days. She would also fast, and then she would go to the king, even if she had to die for doing so.

On the third day of her fast, Esther put on her royal dress and stood in the inner court of the king's palace, facing the throne room, in front of the king, who was sitting on his throne, holding a golden scepter in his hand.

When the king saw her, she won his favor. He extended to Esther his scepter; Esther approached and touched the tip of the scepter.

"What do you wish, Queen Esther?" the king asked. "Tell me and you shall have it, even if it is half my empire".

"If it pleases Your Majesty", Esther replied, "let Your Majesty and Haman come today to the feast that I have prepared for him".

That night, the king and Haman went to the queen's chambers. During the wine feast, the king again asked Esther, "What is your wish? And what is your request? I will grant it even if it is half my empire". Esther replied that she would like the king and Haman to be again her guests the next day at another banquet.

Haman left the banquet in a good mood. His happiness was marred, when he went through the palace gate and saw that Mordecai did not show him any signs of respect. Haman was filled with rage, but he made an effort to control himself and went home.

He invited his friends and his wife to join him. He boasted to them about his great wealth, his many sons, his high position in court, and how he, besides the king, was the only guest in a banquet offered by Queen Esther.

"However", he lamented, "all of that meant nothing to me, when I saw the insolent Jew Mordecai, sitting in the palace gate".

His wife and friends advised him to build a gallows, and to ask the king to allow him to hang Mordecai from it. Haman liked the idea, and he had the gallows built.

That night, the king, suffering of insomnia, asked that the official records of the empire should be brought and read to him. He heard the account of how Mordecai had uncovered a plot to assassinate the king and inquired if the man had been honored and rewarded for his deed. His servants answered that nothing had been done for him.

The king then asked if any of his officials were in the palace. Haman, who had come that night to ask the king for permission to hang Mordecai, had just entered the courtyard. The king's servants brought Haman to the royal chambers.

The king asked him, "What should be done for a man whom the king wishes to honor?"

Haman, assuming that the king was referring to him, answered, "The man whom the king wishes to honor should be dressed in royal robes and set upon the king's horse. One of the empire's noblest courtiers should lead the horse through the city square, proclaiming, 'See how the king rewards a man he wishes to honor'".

"Hurry", said the king to Haman. "Get the robes and the horse as you have said, and do this to Mordecai the Jew. Omit nothing of all you have proposed".

Haman did what he was told. Afterward, Mordecai returned to his usual place at the king's gate, and Haman hurried home, his head covered in mourning. There, Haman told his wife and friends all that had happened to him. They predicted that Mordecai would defeat him. While they were still talking, the palace eunuchs arrived and took Haman in a hurry to Esther's banquet.

Over the wine, the king asked Esther once more, "What is your wish, Queen Esther? I'll even give you half the empire".

Esther answered, "My wish is that I and my people may live, because we are about to be destroyed and exterminated".

"Who dares to do such a thing? Where is this man?" asked Ahasuerus.

Esther answered, "Our enemy, our persecutor, is this evil Haman!" Haman cringed in terror. The king got up in a fury, left the room, and went outside to the palace gardens to calm down. Haman stayed in the dining room to beg Queen Esther for his life. He threw himself down on Esther's couch and implored for mercy. At that moment, the king came back and saw Haman on the queen's couch.

"Is this man going to rape the queen right here in front of me, in my own palace?" shouted the king.

The eunuchs held Haman's face down. One of them, named Harbonah, said that Haman had build a gallows at his house to hang Mordecai. The king immediately ordered, "Hang Haman on it!"

Haman was hanged, and the king calmed down. That same day, King Ahasuerus gave Haman's property to Esther. When the queen told Ahasuerus that Mordecai was her relative, the king took off the ring, which he had taken back from Haman, and gave it to Mordecai, and he named him vizier, second in rank only to the king. From then on, Mordecai wore royal robes of blue and white, a cloak of fine purple linen, and a magnificent crown of gold.

Esther fell weeping at the king's feet and asked him to stop the evil plot that Haman had made against the Jews. The king extended the golden scepter to Esther; she stood up and said, "Please issue a proclamation revoking the orders that Haman gave for the destruction of the Jews in the empire".

The king told Esther and Mordecai that proclamations issued in the king's name and stamped with the royal seal could not be revoked, but that they could write to the Jews whatever they liked, in the king's name, and stamp it with the royal seal.

Mordecai dictated letters in the name of King Ahasuerus, stamped them with the royal seal, and sent them to all the provinces by couriers, mounted on fast horses from the royal stables. These letters stated that the Jews were authorized by the king to organize for self-defense, fight back if attacked, destroy their enemies with their wives and children, and plunder their possessions.

On the thirteenth day of the month of Adar, the day, on which, the enemies of the Jews had planned to destroy them, the Jews attacked them with swords and slaughtered them. When the number of those killed in Shushan was reported to the king, Ahasuerus said to Esther, "In Shushan alone, the Jews have killed five hundred people. What then must they have done in the provinces?! What do you want now? You shall have it".

Esther answered, "Let the Jews in Shushan be allowed to do again tomorrow what they were allowed to do today; and let Haman's ten sons hang in the gallows". The king ordered this to be done. The bodies of Haman's ten sons were publicly displayed, and the next day, the Jews of Shushan killed three hundred more of their enemies.

Esther and Mordecai wrote a letter to all the Jews, wishing them peace and security, and directing them and their descendants to celebrate every year a festival to be called Purim, because Haman had chosen the date of the genocide by casting lots, "Pur" in Hebrew.

3. (Daniel 9:1). 6th century B.C. The father of King Darius, the Mede, is called Ahasuerus in the book of Daniel.

Ahaz

(Hebrew origin: *Possessor*)

1. (2 Kings 15:38). 8th century B.C. Ahaz, son of King Jotham, was the eleventh king of Judah, after the partition of the United Monarchy. He succeeded to the throne, at the age of twenty, and ruled for sixteen years. His name is spelled Achaz, in Matthew's genealogy of Jesus (Matthew 1:9).

   In contrast to his father and grandfather, who were faithful to God, Ahaz reverted to idolatry and even sacrificed one of his sons to pagan gods.

   His reign was a succession of military defeats. Rezin, king of Aram, and Pekah, king of Israel, invaded Judah and besieged Jerusalem. The two kings were unable to capture the city, but Rezin succeeded in taking Elath away from Judah. Their objective was to depose Ahaz, and install a certain son of Tabeal in his place (Isaiah 7:6). The prophet Isaiah, accompanied by his son Shearjashub, met with King Ahaz and told him not to fear, because the invaders would not succeed.

   The Edomites raided the kingdom, around that time, and took many prisoners (2 Chronicles 28:17), while the Philistines captured several cities and settled there permanently.

   Ahaz asked Tiglathpileser, the king of Assyria, to help him against Aram and Israel, and sent him, as a tribute, the treasuries of the Temple and the palace. The king of Assyria attacked Damascus, captured it, and killed King Rezin.

   Ahaz went to Damascus to pay homage to the victor. There, in one of the temples of the city, he saw an altar that he liked very much. He wrote to Urijah, the High Priest, instructing him to introduce Aramean cults into the Temple of Jerusalem, and sent him the plans to build an exact copy of the Damascus altar.

   As soon as Ahaz returned to Jerusalem, he went to the Temple and was very pleased to see that the new altar had been finished. He sacrificed on it to the gods of Damascus (2 Chronicles 28:23), installed a sundial in the Temple, made changes in the Temple ritual, and set up pagan altars in many cities.

   When he died, he was buried in Jerusalem, but not in the royal tombs. His son Hezekiah reigned in his place.

2. (1 Chronicles 8:35). Unspecified date. Ahaz, son of Micah, of the tribe of Benjamin, a descendant of King Saul, was the father of Jehoadah, also called Jarah. His brothers were Pithon, Melech, and Tarea.

Ahaziah

(Hebrew origin: *God holds firm*)

1. (1 Kings 22:40). 9th century B.C. Ahaziah, the son of Ahab and Jezebel, was the eighth king of Israel, after the partition of the United Monarchy.

   His reign, which lasted less than two years, was a sad succession of failures and misfortunes. He encouraged the worship of Baal, a cult introduced by his Phoenician mother, Jezebel. During his reign, Moab, a vassal state of Israel, during the reign of Ahab, rebelled and recovered its independence.

   A maritime project that he had planned was a nonstarter, when King Jehoshaphat rebuffed his proposal to allow Israelites to sail in the Judean ships (1 Kings 22:49). The second book of Chronicles (2 Chronicles 20:36) mentions that the two kings were partners in a ship building venture in Ezion Geber, but the ships were wrecked and never got to Tarshish.

   Ahaziah was severely injured, when he fell from the window of an upper story of his palace. He sent messengers to inquire from Baalzebub, the god of the Philistine city of Ekron, whether he would recover.

   The prophet Elijah reproved him for his idolatry and prophesied that he would die. The king sent fifty soldiers to seize the prophet, but they were consumed by a fire that came down from heaven. The same thing happened to a second company of soldiers. The third company of soldiers, sent by the king, succeeded in bringing Elijah to the palace, where the prophet repeated his terrible prophecy to the king.

Ahaziah died shortly afterward, childless, and was succeeded in the throne by his brother Jehoram.

2. (2 Kings 8:24). 9th century B.C. Ahaziah, the son of Jehoram and Athaliah, the daughter of King Omri, was the sixth king of Judah, after the partition of the United Monarchy. He is called Azariah in a verse in Second Chronicles (2 Chronicles 22:6) and Jehoahaz in another verse in Second Chronicles (2 Chronicles 21:17).

Ahaziah, the youngest son of King Jehoram, became the heir to the throne, when nomad raiders killed all his older brothers (2 Chronicles 22:1). He succeeded to the throne, at the age of twenty-two, and ruled for only one year, during which the real power behind the throne was his mother, Athaliah.

Ahaziah went to Jezreel to visit his relative Jehoram, king of Israel, who was convalescing from the injuries that he had received in a battle against the Arameans. The kings met at the field of Naboth, where Jehu, the commander of the army of Israel, found them.

Jehoram asked Jehu if all was well. Jehu answered, "How could all be well as long as Jezebel, your mother, carries on harlotries and sorceries".

Jehoram turned his chariot around and fled, crying out to Ahaziah, "Treason, Ahaziah!" Jehu drew his bow and hit Jehoram between the shoulders. The arrow pierced his heart, and he died.

Ahaziah tried to escape in his chariot, but he was wounded. He managed to go to Megiddo and died there, according to the second book of Kings (2 Kings 9:27).

The second book of Chronicles (2 Chronicles 22:9) has a different version of the death of Ahaziah; it states that Ahaziah was caught in Samaria, where he was hiding, brought to the presence of Jehu, and killed.

Ahban

(Hebrew origin: *Brother of understanding*)

(1 Chronicles 2:29). Unspecified date. Ahban, a descendant of Judah, was the son of Abishur and Abihail. His brother was called Molid.

Aher

(Hebrew origin: *Other*)

(1 Chronicles 7:12). Unspecified date. Aher, a descendant of Benjamin, was the ancestor of the clan of Hushim.

Ahi

(Hebrew origin: *My brother*)

1. (1 Chronicles 5:15). 8th century B.C. Ahi, son of Abdiel, was the leader of a clan of the tribe of Gad, in the region of Gilead, in the land of Bashan, east of the Jordan River. The genealogy of his clan was registered, during the days of Jotham, king of Judah, and Jeroboam II, king of Israel.

2. (1 Chronicles 7:34). Unspecified date. Ahi, son of Shamer, was the leader of a clan of the tribe of Asher. His brothers were Rohgah, Jehubbah, and Aram.

Ahiah

(Hebrew origin: *My brother is God*)

1. (1 Samuel 14:3). 11th century B.C. Ahiah—also called Ahimelech (1 Samuel 21:2)—son of Ahitub, a descendant of Eli, the priest in Shiloh, was the High Priest in charge of the Ark of the Covenant, during the days of King Saul.

David fled from Saul and came to Nob, the town where Ahimelech lived. Ahimelech thought that it was very odd that David was alone and asked him why he didn't bring any men with him.

David answered that he was on a secret mission on behalf of King Saul, and that he would be meeting his men in such and such a place. He asked for bread, and Ahimelech answered that the only bread that he had available was consecrated bread, which

David's men could eat only if they had kept themselves away from women. When David assured him that this was so, and that the utensils of his young men were consecrated, Ahimelech gave him the consecrated bread.

David, who had brought no weapons with him, asked Ahimelech for a sword or a spear, and Ahimelech gave him the sword of Goliath, the Philistine, that had been under his care, since the day that David had killed him. David, received the food and the weapon, and fled to the Philistine city of Gath.

Unfortunately, David's meeting with Ahimelech was witnessed by Doeg the Edomite, King Saul's chief herdsman. Doeg rushed back to Saul's court and reported that he had seen David in Nob with Ahimelech.

The king ordered that Ahimelech, and all the other priests of Nob, should be brought to his presence. Saul accused them of conspiring with David, and encouraging him to rebel against the king, by giving him food and a weapon.

Ahimelech denied any wrongdoing. He said in his defense that everybody knew that David was the king's son-in-law, and was faithful to the king. Saul refused to listen to any explanations and condemned him to die. The king ordered his guards to kill the priests, and when the men refused to carry out the order, Saul told Doeg to kill the priests. Eighty-five priests were massacred that day. Then, Doeg killed all the people in Nob, including women and children, and even their animals.

Abiathar, the son of Ahimelech, survived the slaughter of the priests of Nob. He managed to escape and told David about the terrible events. David, feeling that he had caused unwittingly the death of Abiathar's father, asked him to remain with him. Years later, Abiathar became one of King David's High Priests.

2. (1 Kings 4:3). 10th century B.C. Ahiah and his brother Elihoreph were scribes in the court of King Solomon. They followed in the footsteps of their father Seraiah, who was the scribe in the court of King David (2 Samuel 8:17).

3. (1 Chronicles 8:7). Unspecified date. Ahiah, a descendant of Ehud, was the leader of a clan of the tribe of Benjamin that was expelled from Geba to Manahath.

Ahiam

(Hebrew origin: *Brother of the mother*)

(2 Samuel 23:33). 10th century B.C. Ahiam, son of Sharar the Hararite, was one of "The Thirty", an elite army group of warriors in King David's army. The first book of Chronicles (1 Chronicles 11:35) gives his father's name as Sacar.

Ahian

(Hebrew origin: *Younger brother*)

(1 Chronicles 7:19). Unspecified date. Ahian was the son of Shemida, of the tribe of Manasseh.

Ahiezer

(Hebrew origin: *Brother of help*)

1. (Numbers 1:12). 13th century B.C. Ahiezer, son of Ammishaddai, was the head of the tribe of Dan, and one of the men who helped Moses and Aaron to take a census of the whole Israelite community. He was also the commander of his tribe's army, and one of the twelve Israelite leaders, who donated gifts of silver and gold, bulls, rams, goats, and lambs for the dedication of the altar.

2. (1 Chronicles 12:3). 11th century B.C. Ahiezer, son of Shemaah the Gibeathite, was the commander of a group of Benjamites—his brother Joash was one of them—who deserted King Saul's army and joined David's band at Ziklag. Ahiezer and his men could use both their right and left hands to shoot arrows and sling stones.

Ahihud

(Hebrew origin: *Brother of renown*)

1. (Numbers 34:27). 13th century B.C. Ahihud, son of Shelomi, was a leader of the tribe of Asher, chosen to help apportion the land of Canaan among the Hebrew tribes.
2. (1 Chronicles 8:7). Unspecified date. Ahihud was a Benjamite, son of Gera and brother of Uzza.

Ahijah

(Hebrew origin: *Brother of God*)

1. (1 Kings 11:29). 10th century B.C. Ahijah, a priest and prophet, served in the sanctuary of Shiloh, in the territory of Ephraim, during the reign of King Solomon.

   Ahijah met Jeroboam, in an isolated road outside of Jerusalem, and prophesied that he would become king over ten tribes. To symbolize his prophecy, Ahijah tore his garment into twelve pieces and gave ten to Jeroboam.

   Years later, when Jeroboam was already the king of the northern kingdom of Israel, his young child became very ill. Jeroboam's wife went in disguise to the house of the prophet Ahijah, who had become blind in his old age, to ask whether the child would recover.

   Despite his blindness and the queen's disguise, the old prophet, forewarned by God, recognized her. He told the queen that, because Jeroboam had worshipped idols, God would bring evil upon his dynasty, and that the sick child would die, as soon as she would arrive back in her city.
2. (1 Kings 15:27). 10th century B.C. Ahijah, of the tribe of Issachar, was the father of Baasha, the man who killed King Nadab of Israel, and usurped the throne.
3. (1 Chronicles 2:25). Unspecified date. Ahijah was the son of Jerahmeel, of the clan of the Hezronites, of the tribe of Judah. His brothers were Ram, Bunah, Oren, and Ozem.
4. (1 Chronicles 11:36). 10th century B.C. Ahijah, the Pelonite, was one of King David's brave warriors.
5. (1 Chronicles 26:20). 10th century B.C. Ahijah was a Levite in charge of the treasures of the House of God and consecrated articles, during the reign of King David.
6. (Nehemiah 10:26). 5th century B.C. Ahijah was one of the leaders who signed Nehemiah's solemn agreement to separate themselves from the foreigners living in the land, to refrain from intermarrying with them, and to dedicate their firstborn to God, among other obligations.

Ahikam

(Hebrew origin: *My brother has risen*)

(2 Kings 22:12). 7th century B.C. Ahikam, son of Shaphan, belonged to one of the most prominent and influential noble families in the kingdom of Judah. The members of the family, known for their policy of moderation and submission to Babylon, played important roles in the historical events of their times, during the reigns of King Josiah and his sons.

Ahikam, his father Shaphan, and other court officials were sent by King Josiah to consult with Huldah, the prophetess, concerning the Book of the Law that had been found in the Temple, while it was being repaired.

Later, during the reign of King Jehoiakim, Ahikam protected the life of the prophet Jeremiah (Jeremiah 26:24).

His father Shaphan held the position of scribe in the court of King Josiah. His son Gedaliah is a tragic figure in the history of the Jewish people, who, even today, observe the anniversary of his death as a day of fasting and mourning. Gedaliah had been appointed governor of Judah by the Babylonian King Nebuchadnezzar. A few months later, he was murdered by Ishmael, son of Nethaniah, who probably hoped to start an uprise against the Babylonians by his bloody act.

Ahilud

(Hebrew origin: *Brother of one born*)

(2 Samuel 8:16). 11th century B.C. Ahilud was the father of Jehoshaphat, court recorder

for both King David and King Solomon, and Baana, one of King Solomon's twelve district governors, in charge of a district that included the region from Megiddo to Beth-Shean.

Ahimaaz

(Hebrew origin: *Brother of anger*)

1. (1 Samuel 14:50). 11th century B.C. Ahimaaz was the father of Ahinoam, the wife of King Saul.
2. (2 Samuel 15:27). 10th century B.C. Ahimaaz was the son of the High Priest Zadok. He and Jonathan, the son of the High Priest Abiathar, served as King David's messengers and spies in Jerusalem, during Absalom's revolt, transmitting Hushai's messages to David, at a great risk to their lives. On one occasion, the two young men, pursued by Absalom's soldiers, had to hide down in a well. King David considered Ahimaaz a good man (2 Samuel 18:27).

   Ahimaaz was sent by Joab to David, to bring him news of the victory against Absalom, but diplomatically evaded answering him about Absalom's death.

   Years later, he married Basmath, one of King Solomon's daughters (1 Kings 4:15), and was appointed one of the twelve district governors, responsible for providing food from his district, the territory of Naphtali, for the king and the royal household, for one month out of each year. His great grandson Azariah became High Priest (1 Chronicles 6:10).

Ahiman

(Hebrew origin: *My brother is a gift*)

1. (Numbers 13:22). 13th century B.C. Ahiman, Talmai, and Sheshai were three brothers, sons of Anak, and grandsons of Arba, the founder of the city of Hebron. Their gigantic height made the spies, sent by Moses, feel like grasshoppers.

   The three brothers were expelled from Hebron by Caleb, the son of Jephunneh, during the Israelite conquest of Canaan, and were later killed by the tribe of Judah.

2. (1 Chronicles 9:17). 10th century B.C. Ahiman, a Levite, was one of the gate-keepers—the others were Akkub and Talmon—in charge of the East Gate of the Tabernacle, under the supervision of Shallum, during the reign of King David.

Ahimelech

(Hebrew origin: *My brother is king*)

1. (1 Samuel 21:1). 11th century B.C. Ahimelech—called Ahiah in another verse in the first book of Samuel (1 Samuel 14:3)—son of Ahitub, a descendant of Eli, the priest in Shiloh, was the High Priest in charge of the Ark of the Covenant, during the days of King Saul.

   David fled from Saul and came to Nob, the town where Ahimelech lived. Ahimelech thought that it was very odd that David was alone and asked him why he didn't bring any men with him.

   David answered that he was on a secret mission on behalf of King Saul, and that he would be meeting his men in such and such a place. He asked for bread, and Ahimelech answered that the only bread that he had available was consecrated bread, which David's men could eat only if they had kept themselves away from women. When David assured him that this was so, and that the utensils of his young men were consecrated, Ahimelech gave him the consecrated bread.

   David, who had brought no weapons with him, asked Ahimelech for a sword or a spear, and Ahimelech gave him the sword of Goliath, the Philistine, that had been under his care, since the day that David had killed him. David, received the food and the weapon, and fled to the Philistine city of Gath.

   Unfortunately, David's meeting with Ahimelech was witnessed by Doeg the Edomite, King Saul's chief herdsman. Doeg rushed back to Saul's court and reported that he had seen David in Nob with Ahimelech.

   The king ordered that Ahimelech, and all the other priests of Nob, should be brought to his presence. Saul accused them of conspiring with David, and encouraging him to rebel against the king, by giving him food and a weapon.

Ahimelech denied any wrongdoing. He said in his defense that everybody knew that David was the king's son-in-law, and was faithful to the king. Saul refused to listen to any explanations and condemned him to die. The king ordered his guards to kill the priests, and when the men refused to carry out the order, Saul told Doeg to kill the priests. Eighty-five priests were massacred that day. Then, Doeg killed all the people in Nob, including women and children, and even their animals.

Abiathar, the son of Ahimelech, survived the slaughter of the priests of Nob. He managed to escape and told David about the terrible events. David, feeling that he had caused unwittingly the death of Abiathar's father, asked him to remain with him. Years later, Abiathar became one of King David's High Priests.

2. (1 Samuel 26:6). 11th century B.C. Ahimelech, the Hittite, was a member of David's band of outlaws. On one occasion, when Saul was pursuing them, Ahimelech was asked, by David, to go with him and Abishai, Joab's brother, to the camp, where King Saul was sleeping. Apparently, he did not go, because only Abishai is mentioned in the Bible as the one accompanying David in this adventure.

3. (2 Samuel 8:17). 10th century B.C. Ahimelech, son of Abiathar and grandson of Ahimelech, the Nob priest killed by Saul's orders, served as High Priest, together with Zadok, son of Ahitub, during the reign of David.

Ahimelech descended from Aaron's son Ithamar, while Zadok descended from Aaron's son Eleazar (1 Chronicles 24:3). His brother Jonathan served as King David's messenger and spy in Jerusalem, during Absalom's revolt, transmitting Hushai's messages to David. He was called Abimelech in the first book of Chronicles (1 Chronicles 18:16).

Ahimoth

(Hebrew origin: *Brother of death* or *Brother of Moth, Canaanite god*)

(1 Chronicles 6:25). Unspecified date. Ahimoth, a Levite, was the son of Elkanah, descendant of Kohath, Levi's second son.

Ahinadab

(Hebrew origin: *Brother of generosity*)

(1 Kings 4:14). 10th century B.C. Ahinadab, son of Iddo, was one of King Solomon's twelve district governors, responsible for providing food from his district, the territory of Mahanaim, for the king and the royal household, for one month out of each year.

Ahinoam

(Hebrew origin: *Brother of pleasantness*)

1. (1 Samuel 14:50). 11th century B.C. Ahinoam, daughter of Ahimaaz, was King Saul's wife.

2. (1 Samuel 25:43). 11th century B.C. Ahinoam, from Jezreel, was the mother of Amnon, David's firstborn son.

David, escaping from Saul's persecution, fled to Gath with his wives, Ahinoam and Abigail, and his six hundred men, and found employment with the Philistines as a mercenary. Achish, the king of Gath, allowed David, his men, and their families to settle in the town of Ziklag.

When the Philistines marched against Saul, David, who was accompanying Achish, was sent back to Philistia by the distrustful Philistine commanders. He arrived back at Ziklag and found that, taking advantage of his absence, the Amalekites had attacked the town, burned it, and taken all the women and children with them, including Ahinoam and Abigail. David pursued the raiders, rescued the prisoners, and recovered the booty that the Amalekites had taken.

After the death of Saul, David moved to Hebron, taking Ahinoam and Abigail with him. There, she gave birth to Amnon.

Ahio

(Hebrew origin: *God's brother*)

1. (2 Samuel 6:3). 10th century B.C. Ahio and his brother Uzzah, sons of Abinadab, drove the cart carrying the Ark of the Covenant from Gibeah, where it had been kept for many years in their father's house, toward Jerusalem.

    King David and all Israel accompanied them, singing and playing musical instruments. When God struck down Uzzah, for touching the Ark, David decided that this was not the appropriate moment to take the Ark to Jerusalem and left it for an indefinite time in the house of Obededom the Gittite.
2. (1 Chronicles 8:14). Unspecified date. Ahio, son of Elpaal, was a leader of a clan of the tribe of Benjamin.
3. (1 Chronicles 8:31). 11th century B.C. Ahio, a Benjamite, was a brother of an ancestor of King Saul. His parents were Jehiel, the founder of Gibeon, and his wife Maachah.

Ahira

(Hebrew origin: *My brother is bad* or *My brother is Ra, an Egyptian god*)

(Numbers 1:15). 13th century B.C. Ahira, son of Enan, of the tribe of Naphtali, was the leader of his tribe, during the march in the wilderness, and commander of its army. He was one of the twelve Israelite leaders who donated gifts of silver and gold, bulls, rams, goats, and lambs for the dedication of the altar.

Ahiram

(Hebrew origin: *My brother is elevated*)

(Numbers 26:38). 17th century B.C. Ahiram, one of the five sons of Benjamin, according to the list in Numbers, was the ancestor of the clan of the Ahiramites.

In the first book of Chronicles (1 Chronicles 8:1), he is called Aharah. In the book of Genesis (Genesis 46:21), where he is called Ehi, he is mentioned as one of the ten sons of Benjamin and is counted among the seventy Israelites who immigrated to Egypt.

Ahisamach

(Hebrew origin: *My brother supports*)

(Exodus 31:6). 14th century B.C. Ahisamach, of the tribe of Dan, was the father of Aholiab, an engraver and skillful craftsman, who helped Bezaleel to construct and decorate the Tabernacle in the wilderness.

Ahishahar

(Hebrew origin: *Brother of the dawn* or *Brother of Shahar, a Canaanite god*)

(1 Chronicles 7:10). Unspecified date. Ahishahar, a brave warrior and leader of a clan of Benjamites, was a son of Bilhan. His brothers were Jeush, Benjamin, Ehud, Zethan, Tharshish, and Chenaanah.

Ahishar

(Hebrew origin: *My brother sang*)

(1 Kings 4:6). 10th century B.C. Ahishar was the court official in charge of the king's household, during the reign of King Solomon.

Ahithophel

(Hebrew origin: *Brother of folly*)

(2 Samuel 15:12). 10th century B.C. Ahithophel, born in Giloh, was the grandfather of Bathsheba through his son Eliam—also called Ammiel (1 Chronicles 3:5).

Ahithophel, one of King David's top advisers, was known for his wise advice, which King David respected almost as if it were the word of God.

When Absalom rebelled against his father, King David, Ahithophel joined the rebellion. The Bible does not mention his reason for doing so, but a plausible explanation is that he secretly resented King David for having seduced his granddaughter Bathsheba, and arranged the death of her first husband, Uriah.

To counter Ahithophel's sagacious advice to Absalom, King David instructed his loyal friend Hushai to pretend that he had also switched his loyalties to Absalom, win the confidence of the young man, learn of the rebels' plans, and report them to David.

When King David fled from Jerusalem, and Absalom entered the city, Ahithophel advised him to show his contempt for David by appropriating his father's concubines.

He strongly advised Absalom to let him choose an army of twelve thousand men and start immediately in pursuit of David, taking advantage of the fact that the king would be tired and weak handed.

However, fortunately for David, Hushai succeeded in convincing Absalom that this time Ahithophel's advice was not practical, and that it should be rejected. First, suggested Hushai, Absalom should raise a much larger army, and only then, he should go after David. This delay gave time to David to cross to the other side of the Jordan River, and there regroup his army.

When Ahithophel saw that his advice had been rejected, he realized that Absalom was making a fatal mistake, and that the rebellion would be defeated. He went home, put his household in order, and hanged himself.

Ahitub

(Hebrew origin: *My brother is good*)

1. (1 Samuel 14:3). 11th century B.C. Ahitub was the son of Phinehas and the brother of Ichabod. His father, Phinehas, was killed in a battle with the Philistines. His grandfather, Eli, the priest in Shiloh, who was ninety years old, fell from his seat, upon hearing the terrible news, and broke his neck.

   Ahitub's son Ahimelech—also called Ahiah—served as High Priest, during the reign of Saul, until he innocently got involved in the conflict between King Saul and David and paid with his life.

2. (2 Samuel 8:17). 11th century B.C. Ahitub, son of Amariah, was the father of King David's High Priest Zadok (Ezra 7:2).

3. (1 Chronicles 9:11). Unspecified date. Ahitub was the father of Meraioth. His descendant Azariah—also called Seraiah—served as High Priest, after the return from Babylonian Exile.

Ahlai

(Hebrew origin: *I wish*)

1. (1 Chronicles 2:31). Unspecified date. The Bible mentions that Ahlai was the son of Sheshan, of the tribe of Judah. A few verses later, it says that Sheshan gave one of his daughters in marriage to his Egyptian servant Jarha, because he didn't have any sons (1 Chronicles 2:34). This apparent contradiction can be solved if we assumed that Ahlai either died young, or that he was born after one of his sisters had married Jarha.

2. (1 Chronicles 11:41). 11th century B.C. His son Zabad was one of King David's brave warriors.

Ahoah

(Hebrew origin: *Brotherly*)

(1 Chronicles 8:4). 16th century B.C. Ahoah, son of Belah and grandson of Benjamin, was the ancestor of the clan of the Ahohites. Several members of this clan, such as Eleazar, the son of Dodo the Ahohite, fought bravely in David's army (2 Samuel 23:9).

Aholah

(Hebrew origin: *Her tent*)

(Ezekiel 23:4). This is a symbolic name given to Samaria by the prophet Ezekiel. The prophet accused Samaria of promiscuous behavior with the Assyrians. God punished Samaria by delivering her into the hand of the Assyrians, who took her sons and daughters and slew her with the sword.

Aholiab

(Hebrew origin: *Tent of the father*)

(Exodus 31:6). 13th century B.C. Aholiab, son of Ahisamach, of the tribe of Dan, was an engraver, embroider, and skillful craftsman, who helped Bezaleel to build and decorate the Tabernacle in the wilderness.

Aholibah

(Hebrew origin: *My tent is in her*)

(Ezekiel 23:4). This is a symbolic name given to Jerusalem by the prophet Ezekiel. The prophet said that, although Aholibah had seen how God had punished her sister, Aholah—i.e. Samaria—for her promiscuous behavior with the Assyrians, she was even more corrupt than her sister, and God would make of her a horror and a spoil.

Aholibamah

(Hebrew origin: *My tent is high*)

1. (Genesis 36:2). 18th century B.C. Aholibamah, sister to Dishon, daughter of Anah, and granddaughter of Zibeon the Hivite, was one of Esau's wives. Her sons Jeush, Jaalam, and Korah were born in Canaan, before the family moved to Edom, where they became heads of clans.
2. (Genesis 36:41). Unspecified date. Aholibamah was a chief of an Edomite clan.

Ahumai

(Hebrew origin: *Brother of water*)

(1 Chronicles 4:2). Unspecified date. Ahumai, of the clan of the Zorathites, of the tribe of Judah, was one of the two sons of Jahath. His brother was called Lahad.

Ahuzam

(Hebrew origin: *Possession*)

(1 Chronicles 4:6). Unspecified date. Ahuzam, Temeni, Haahashtari, and Hepher, of the tribe of Judah, were the sons of Ashur, the founder of Tekoa, and his wife Naarah. Their father's other wife, Helah, was the mother of Zereth, Zohar, and Ethnan.

Ahuzzath

(Hebrew origin: *Possession*)

(Genesis 26:26). 19th century B.C. Ahuzzath was a friend of Abimelech, the Philistine king of Gerar. He and Phichol,

captain of the Abimelech's army, were present, when the king met Isaac and made a peace covenant with him.

Aiah

(Hebrew origin: *Hawk*)

1. (2 Samuel 3:7). 11th century B.C. Aiah was the father of Rizpah, one of King Saul's concubines. His grandchildren, Mephibosheth and Armoni, the sons of King Saul and Rizpah, were hanged by the Gibeonites in revenge for the massacre that Saul had perpetrated against them.
2. (1 Chronicles 1:40). Unspecified date. Aiah, brother of Anah, was a son of Zibeon, a descendant of Seir the Horite, who lived in the land of Edom. An alternative spelling is Ajah (Genesis 36:24).

Ajah

(Hebrew origin: *Hawk*)

(Genesis 36:24). Unspecified date. Ajah is an alternative spelling for Aiah (1 Chronicles 1:40), brother of Anah.

Akan

(Hebrew origin: *Tortuous*)

(Genesis 36:27). Unspecified date. Akan, son of Ezer, a descendant of Seir, was the leader of a clan of Horites, in the land of Edom. His brothers were Bilhan and Zaavan. Alternative spellings are Jakan (1 Chronicles 1:42) and Jaakan (Deuteronomy 10:6).

Akkub

(Hebrew origin: *Insidious*)

1. (1 Chronicles 3:24). Unspecified date. Akkub, son of Elioenai, was a descendant of Jeconiah—also called Jehoiachin—the king of Judah, who was taken to captivity in Babylon. Akkub's brothers were Eliashib, Pelaiah, Anani, Johanan, Dalaiah, and Hodaiah.
2. (1 Chronicles 9:17). 10th century B.C. Akkub, a Levite, was one of the gate-

keepers—the others were Talmon and Ahiman—in charge of the East Gate of the Tabernacle, under the supervision of Shallum, during the reign of King David. He was the ancestor of a clan of gatekeepers (Ezra 2:42), and a clan of Temple servants (Ezra 2:45), who returned with Zerubbabel from the Babylonian Exile.

3. (Nehemiah 8:7). 5th century B.C. Akkub was one of the Levites who explained the Law to the people in Jerusalem, after Ezra the Scribe had read it, while standing on a wooden platform, in front of the open space, before the Water Gate.

4. (Nehemiah 11:19). 5th century B.C. Akkub was a gatekeeper in the days of Nehemiah.

Alameth

(Hebrew origin: *Covering*)

(1 Chronicles 7:8). 16th century B.C. Alameth was the son of Becher and grandson of Benjamin, member of a family of heads of the tribe and brave warriors. His brothers were Zemira, Joash, Eliezer, Elioenai, Omri, Jerimoth, Anathoth, and Abiah.

Alemeth

(Hebrew origin: *Covering*)

(1 Chronicles 8:36). Unspecified date. Alemeth, a Benjamite, was a descendant of King Saul. His brothers were Azmaveth and Zimri. His father Jehoadah was called Jarah in First Chronicles (1 Chronicles 9:42).

Alexander

(Greek origin: *Man defender*)

1. (Mark 15:21). A.D. 1st century. Alexander and Rufus were the sons of Simon, a Cyrenian who was compelled by the Roman soldiers to carry Jesus' cross on his way to Calvary. It is likely that the family converted to Christianity, if we assume that the Rufus mentioned in the letter to the Romans (Romans 16:13) was, as some scholars believe, the son of Simon.

2. (Acts of the Apostles 4:6). A.D. 1st century.

Alexander, a relative of Annas, the High Priest, was present, when the Jewish Council interrogated Peter and John about their healing and preaching and warned them not to preach anymore in the name of Jesus.

3. (Acts of the Apostles 19:33). A.D. 1st century. Alexander, a convert to Christianity, attempted to calm the crowd, during a riot in Ephesus, when silversmiths and followers of the goddess Diana protested against the missionary activities of Paul and his companions. Alexander was shouted down, when he was recognized as a Jew.

Later, he became an apostate, together with a certain Hymenaeus, giving cause to Paul to write in his first letter to Timothy (1 Timothy 1:20) that he "had delivered them unto Satan, that they may learn not to blaspheme".

Years later, Paul, still bitter about Alexander's defection, wrote in his second letter to Timothy (2 Timothy 4:14), "Alexander the coppersmith did me much evil; the Lord reward him according to his works".

Aliah

(Hebrew origin: *Iniquity*)

(1 Chronicles 1:51). Unspecified date. Aliah, a descendant of Esau, was the leader of an Edomite clan. An alternative spelling is Alvah (Genesis 36:40).

Alian

(Hebrew origin: *Lofty*)

(1 Chronicles 1:40). Unspecified date. Alian was the son of Shobal, a descendant of Seir. An alternative spelling is Alvan (Genesis 36:23).

Allon

(Hebrew origin: *Oak*)

(1 Chronicles 4:37). Unspecified date. Allon, the son of Jedaiah, was the father of

Shiphi. His descendant Ziza was one of the leaders of the tribe of Simeon who, in search of pasture for their flocks, went to the fertile valley of Gedor, during the reign of Hezekiah, king of Judah, destroyed the tents of the people—descendants of Ham—who lived there, wiped them out forever, and settled in their place.

Almodad

(Hebrew origin: Uncertain meaning)

(Genesis 10:26). Unspecified date. Almodad was the son of Joktan, a descendant of Shem. His brothers were Sheleph, Hazarmaveth, Jerah, Hadoram, Uzal, Diklah, Ebal, Abimael, Sheba, Ophir, Havilah, and Jobab.

Alphaeus

(Hebrew origin: *Thousand*)

1. (Matthew 10:3). A.D. 1st century. Alphaeus was the father of the apostle James.
2. (Mark 2:14). A.D. 1st century. Alphaeus was the father of Levi, the tax collector, later known as the apostle Matthew. It is possible that this Alphaeus and the one in the entry above were the same person, in which case, this would mean that James and Matthew were brothers.

Alvah

(Hebrew origin: *Iniquity*)

(Genesis 36:40). Unspecified date. Alvah, a descendant of Esau, was the leader of an Edomite clan. An alternative spelling is Aliah (1 Chronicles 1:51).

Alvan

(Hebrew origin: *Lofty*)

(Genesis 36:23). Unspecified date. Alvan was the son of Shobal, a descendant of Seir. An alternative spelling is Alian (1 Chronicles 1:40). His brothers were Manahath, Ebal, Shephi, and Onam.

Amal

(Hebrew origin: *Toil*)

(1 Chronicles 7:35). Unspecified date. Amal, a clan chief of the tribe of Asher, was the son of Helem. His brothers were Zophah, Imna, and Shelesh. His father was called Hotham in First Chronicles (1 Chronicles 7:32).

Amalek

(Hebrew origin: Uncertain meaning)

(Genesis 36:12). 17th century B.C. Amalek, grandson of Esau, was the son of Eliphaz and his concubine Timna. Amalek was the ancestor of the Amalekites, Israel's first and worst enemy, about whom God swore that there would be war with them in each generation (Exodus 17:16).

The last surviving Amalekites were killed, during the reign of King Hezekiah, by a force of five hundred men of the tribe of Simeon, in Mount Seir, southeast of the Dead Sea (1 Chronicles 4:43).

Amariah

(Hebrew origin: *God said*)

1. (1 Chronicles 6:7). 11th century B.C. Amariah was the son of the priest Meraioth and grandfather of Zadok, King David's High Priest.
2. (1 Chronicles 6:11). Unspecified date. Amariah was the son of Azariah. His descendant Jehozadak was the High Priest exiled by Nebuchadnezzar with the rest of Judah and Jerusalem.
3. (1 Chronicles 23:19). Unspecified date. Amariah was a Levite descendant of Hebron, the son of Kohath.
4. (2 Chronicles 19:11). 9th century B.C. The High Priest Amariah was in charge of all religious matters, during the reign of King Jehoshaphat, while Zebadiah, son of Ishmael, was in charge of all the king's matters.
5. (2 Chronicles 31:15). 8th century B.C. Amariah was a Levite who, during the days of King Hezekiah, worked under Kore, assisting him in registering the priests and

the Levites, and distributing among the other Levites the gifts offered by the people to God.

6. (Ezra 7:3). Unspecified date. Amariah, son of Azariah and father of Ahitub, was a descendant of Aaron, and an ancestor of Ezra the Scribe.

7. (Ezra 10:42). 5th century B.C. Amariah was one of the men who divorced his foreign wife in the time of Ezra.

8. (Nehemiah 10:3). 5th century B.C. He was one of the priests who signed Nehemiah's solemn agreement to separate themselves from the foreigners living in the land, to refrain from intermarrying with them, and to dedicate their firstborn to God, among other obligations.

9. (Nehemiah 11:4). Unspecified date. Amariah, the son of Shephatiah, was the father of Zechariah, of the clan of Perez, of the tribe of Judah. His descendant Athaiah was one of the people of Judah who settled in Jerusalem, after the Exile.

10. (Nehemiah 12:2). 6th century B.C. Amariah was one of the priests who returned from the Babylonian Exile, with Zerubbabel and the High Priest Jeshua. He was the ancestor of a priestly clan that was headed by Jehohanan, when Joiakim was High Priest, during the time of Nehemiah.

11. (Zephaniah 1:1). Unspecified date. Amariah, the son of Hizkiah—probably an alternative spelling for King Hezekiah—was an ancestor of the prophet Zephaniah.

Amasa

(Hebrew origin: *Burden*)

1. (2 Samuel 17:25). 10th century B.C. Amasa was the son of Abigail, King David's sister. His father was either Jether, an Ishmaelite (1 Chronicles 2:17), or Ithra, an Israelite (2 Samuel 17:25).

Although Amasa had been the commander of Absalom's rebel army, David, after the defeat and death of Absalom, made him the new commander in chief of the kingdom's army, replacing Joab. The king's magnanimous appointment was done for the sake of national reconciliation, but the inevitable result of that unfortunate decision was the same as if he would have signed Amasa's death warrant. Joab's implacable jealousy was aroused, and he waited for the opportunity to kill Amasa.

Shortly afterward, a Benjamite called Sheba, son of Bichri, rebelled against the king. David considered that this insurrection could be even more dangerous than the rebellion of Absalom. He urged Amasa to organize an army in three days.

When Amasa did not report back in the allotted time, the king sent Abishai to pursue the rebels. Amasa met Abishai and Joab near Gibeon. Joab saluted Amasa saying, "How are you, brother?" While he was speaking, he took hold of Amasa's beard with his right hand, as if to kiss him, and with his left hand, drove his sword into Amasa's belly, and spilled his bowels to the ground. Joab and Abishai left Amasa, lying in a puddle of blood in the middle of the road, and went after Sheba. The soldiers were stunned and didn't follow Joab, until one of the officers pushed Amasa's body to the field, on the side of the road, and covered the corpse with a cloth.

The king not only did not punish Joab, but also appointed him again commander of the army. Many years later, David, in his dying bed, gave instructions to Solomon to kill Joab for the murders of Abner and Amasa.

2. (2 Chronicles 28:12). 8th century B.C. During the war of King Pekah of Israel against King Ahaz of Judah, the Israelite army defeated Judah and returned to Samaria, with tens of thousands of prisoners of war, with the intention of making them slaves.

Amasa, son of Hadlai, was one of the leaders of the tribe of Ephraim who supported the prophet Oded in his demand to free the captives and return them to Judah. Amasa and his companions gave clothing, shoes, food, and drink to the captives and returned them to the city of Jericho in Judah.

Amasai

(Hebrew origin: *Burdensome*)

1. (1 Chronicles 6:25). Unspecified date. Amasai, son of Elkanah and father of Mahath, was an ancestor of Elkanah, the father of Samuel. His descendant Heman, of the clan of the Kohathites, was one of the Levites appointed by King David to be in charge of the singers in the House of the Lord.
2. (1 Chronicles 12:18). 11th century B.C. Amasai was the leader of a group of men from Benjamin and Judah who deserted King Saul's army and joined David's forces at Ziklag.
3. (1 Chronicles 15:24). 10th century B.C. Amasai was one of the priests who blew the trumpets, during the joyful procession led by King David that brought the Ark of the Covenant to Jerusalem.
4. (2 Chronicles 29:12). 8th century B.C. Amasai, a Levite, was the son of Elkanah, descendant of Kohath, Levi's second son. His son Mahath was one of the Levites who gathered to make themselves ritually clean, and to purify the Temple, during the reign of King Hezekiah of Judah.

Amashai

(Hebrew origin: *Burdensome*)

(Nehemiah 11:13). 5th century B.C. Amashai, son of Azareel, was one of the priests who settled in Jerusalem, after the return from the Babylonian Exile.

Amasiah

(Hebrew origin: *God has burdened*)

(2 Chronicles 17:16). 9th century B.C. Amasiah, son of Zichri, commanded a force of two hundred thousand men in the army of King Jehoshaphat of Judah.

Amaziah

(Hebrew origin: *Strength of God*)

1. (2 Kings 12:21). 8th century B.C. Amaziah was the eighth king of Judah, after the partition of the United Monarchy. His mother was Jehoaddan from Jerusalem.

Amaziah ascended to the throne at the age of twenty-five, after his father, King Joash, was murdered by two of his court officials. One of Amaziah's first acts, after he felt that he was firmly in power, was to kill the conspirators who had murdered his father. He reigned for twenty-nine years and died, at the age of fifty-four, at the hand of assassins, like his father before him.

He raised an army of three hundred thousand soldiers and hired another one hundred thousand mercenaries from the northern kingdom of Israel, paying them one hundred talents of silver. A prophet came to him and told him that he should let go the Israelite soldiers, because "the Lord was not with Israel". Amaziah, worried about the money that he had paid them in advance, asked, "But what shall we do about the hundred talents, which I have given to the army of Israel?" The prophet reassured him that God would pay him back much more. Amaziah discharged the Israelite army, and they returned to their country in great anger.

With his own army, he attacked the Valley of Salt, in Edom, and killed ten thousand men of Seir. He captured another ten thousand men, brought them up to the top of the rock, and threw them down to their death.

He returned victorious to Jerusalem, bringing back with him the Edomite idols. He prostrated himself before them and sacrificed to them. A prophet came to him and asked, "Why are you worshipping gods that could not save their people from you?" Amaziah, furious, asked him, "Has somebody appointed you to be a counselor to the king? Stop right now or you will be killed!" The prophet answered, "I see that God wants your destruction, since you act this way and disregard my counsel".

Amaziah's victory over the Edomites made him overconfident. He challenged Jehoash, the king of Israel, to a confrontation. Jehoash scornfully advised him not to make trouble for his kingdom and himself.

Amaziah, undeterred, went to war against Israel, but he was defeated and captured in a battle at Bethshemesh, and then he was taken by King Jehoash to Jerusalem. The Israelite king tore down a large section of the city walls and returned to Samaria, carrying with him all the treasuries of the Temple and the royal palace, and a number of hostages.

Years later, a number of men, who were upset by his idolatry, conspired against his life. Amaziah fled to the city of Lachish, but his enemies sent men after him, who killed him there. His body was brought back on horses, to Jerusalem, and was buried in the royal tombs of his ancestors. His sixteen-year-old son Azariah, called Uzziah, succeeded him on the throne.

2. (1 Chronicles 4:34). 8th century B.C. His son Joshah was one of the leaders of the tribe of Simeon who went to the fertile valley of Gedor in search of pasture for their flocks, during the reign of Hezekiah, king of Judah. The Simeonites destroyed the tents of the people—descendants of Ham—who lived there, wiped them out forever, and settled in their place.

3. (1 Chronicles 6:45). Unspecified date. Amaziah, son of Hilkiah, was a descendant of Merari. His descendant Ethan was one of the Levites appointed by King David to be in charge of the singers in the House of the Lord.

4. (Amos 7:10). 8th century B.C. Amaziah, the priest of the royal sanctuary at Bethel, accused the prophet Amos of conspiring against King Jeroboam II of Israel. Amos, undaunted, said that the king would die by the sword, and that Israel would be exiled from its land. Amaziah told the prophet to flee to the land of Judah, and never again return to prophesy in Bethel.

Ami

(Hebrew origin: *Reliable; trustworthy*)

(Ezra 2:57). 10th century B.C. Ami, a servant of King Solomon, was the ancestor of a family that returned with Zerubbabel from the Babylonian Exile. He is called Amon in the book of Nehemiah (Nehemiah 7:59).

Aminadab

(Hebrew origin: *Generous people*)

(Matthew 1:4). 13th century B.C. Aminadab is an alternative spelling for Amminadab (Exodus 6:23), the father of Nahshon and Elisheba.

Amittai

(Hebrew origin: *Truthful*)

(2 Kings 14:25). 8th century B.C. Amittai was the father of the prophet Jonah.

Ammi

(Hebrew origin: *My people*)

(Hosea 2:1). 8th century B.C. The complete name is Loammi, *Not my People,* the name given by the prophet Hosea to his second son to symbolize that Israel was no longer God's people.

Later, the prophet said that, when, one day, Judah and Israel would be reunited, he would call his son Ammi, *My people.*

Ammiel

(Hebrew origin: *People of God*)

1. (Numbers 13:12) 13th century B.C. Ammiel, son of Gemalli, of the tribe of Dan, was one of the twelve spies sent by Moses to Canaan, to scout the land, its cities, and its inhabitants; to find out if they were strong or weak, few or many; and to bring back the fruit of the land. The spies came back, frightened and disheartened, and told the Israelites that the Canaanites were too big and too strong to be defeated.

Two of the spies—Joshua, the son of Nun, and Caleb, the son of Jephunneh—disagreed and told the people not to fear.

The Israelites refused to listen to the encouraging words of Joshua and Caleb, and they started to wail and cry. God punished their cowardice by condemning them to wander forty years in the wilderness, one year for each day that the spies scouted the land. All those who complained against God, including Ammiel, died in the wilderness, except Caleb and Joshua.

(For more detailed information about the twelve spies, please see the entry for Joshua [Exodus 17:9].)

2. (2 Samuel 9:4). 10th century B.C. Ammiel was the father of Machir, a good-hearted man who gave shelter in his house to Mephibosheth, the lame son of Jonathan. When David fled from Absalom, Machir and some other men brought beds, utensils, and food to David and his weary and hungry companions.

3. (1 Chronicles 3:5). 11th century B.C. Ammiel—called Eliam in Second Samuel (2 Samuel 11:3)—was the son of Ahithophel and the father of Bathsheba—called Bathshua in First Chronicles (1 Chronicles 3:5)—King David's wife and mother of King Solomon.

4. (1 Chronicles 26:5). 10th century B.C. Ammiel, the sixth son of Obededom, was, like his father and seven brothers, a gatekeeper of the Tabernacle, during the reign of King David. His brothers were Shemaiah, Jehozabad, Joah, Sacar, Nethaneel, Issachar, and Peulthai.

Ammihud

(Hebrew origin: *People of splendor*)

1. (Numbers 1:10). 14th century B.C. Ammihud, son of Laadan (1 Chronicles 7:26), was the father of Elishama, the leader of the tribe of Ephraim, commander of his tribe's army, during the march in the wilderness. His son was one of the twelve Israelite leaders who donated gifts of silver and gold, bulls, rams, goats, and lambs for the dedication of the altar.

2. (Numbers 34:20). 14th century B.C. Ammihud was the father of Shemuel, the leader of the tribe of Simeon. His son was one of the men appointed by Moses to apportion the land of Canaan among the tribes.

3. (Numbers 34:28). 14th century B.C. His son Pedahel of the tribe of Naphtali was among those appointed by Moses to divide out the land of Canaan among the tribes.

4. (2 Samuel 13:37). 11th century B.C. His son Talmai was the king of Geshur, a kingdom situated northeast of the Sea of Galilee. His granddaughter Maachah married David and was the mother of Absalom and Tamar.

5. (1 Chronicles 9:4). 6th century B.C. Ammihud was the son of Omri, of the tribe of Judah. His son Uthai was among the first persons who returned from the Babylonian Exile to live in Jerusalem. In the book of Nehemiah (Nehemiah 11:4), Ammihud is called Uzziah, and his son is called Athaiah.

Amminadab

(Hebrew origin: *Generous people*)

1. (Exodus 6:23). 14th century B.C. Amminadab, son of Ram, of the tribe of Judah, was the father of two distinguished persons: Nahshon and Elisheba. Nahshon, a direct ancestor of King David, was the commander of his tribe's army, during the march in the wilderness, and one of the twelve Israelite leaders who donated gifts of silver and gold, bulls, rams, goats, and lambs for the dedication of the altar. Elisheba, Amminadab's daughter, was the wife of Aaron, the brother of Moses.

2. (1 Chronicles 6:22). 14th century B.C. Amminadab—called Izhar in the book of Exodus (Exodus 6:18), and Izehar in the book of Numbers (Numbers 3:19)—was a Levite, son of Kohath, and the ancestor of the Levite clan of Izeharites. His brothers were Hebron, Uzziel, and Amram, the father of Miriam, Aaron, and Moses. His sons were Korah—who led a rebellion against Moses and Aaron—Nepheg and Zichri.

3. (1 Chronicles 15:10). 10th century B.C. Amminadab, a leader of a clan descendant from Uzziel, was one of the Levites chosen by King David to carry upon their shoulders the Ark of the Covenant to Jerusalem, accompanied by singers and musicians.

Amminadib

(Hebrew origin: *My people are generous*)

(Song of Songs 6:12). Unspecified date. He is mentioned in the Song of Songs as the owner of beautiful chariots.

Ammishaddai

(Hebrew origin: *People of the Almighty*)

(Numbers 1:12). 14th century B.C. Ammishaddai was the father of Ahiezer, a leader of the tribe of Dan. His son helped Moses and Aaron to take a census of the whole Israelite community and was one of the twelve Israelite leaders who donated gifts of silver and gold, bulls, rams, goats, and lambs for the dedication of the altar.

Ammizabad

(Hebrew origin: *People of endowment*)

(1 Chronicles 27:6). 10th century B.C. Ammizabad, son of Benaiah and grandson of the priest Jehoiada, served in King David's army. His commanding officer was his father Benaiah, who, during the reign of King David, was the leader of an elite army group known as The Thirty, and, later, during the reign of King Solomon, was promoted to be the commander of the whole army.

Ammon

(Hebrew origin: *Tribal, inbred*)

(Numbers 21:24). 19th century B.C. Ammon, called Benammi by his mother, was born from the incestuous union of Lot and his younger daughter (Genesis 19:38). He was the ancestor of the Ammonites, constant enemies of the Israelites. Their capital, Rabbath Ammon, is called today Amman, the capital of Jordan.

Amnon

(Hebrew origin: *Trustworthy*)

1. (2 Samuel 3:2). 10th century B.C. Amnon, born in Hebron, was King David's firstborn son. His mother was Ahinoam the Jezreelitess.

He developed a passion for Tamar, his half sister, and, following the advice of his shrewd cousin Jonadab, convinced his father that he was sick, and that he wished that Tamar should bring him food to his house.

David sent Tamar to Amnon's house, where she baked cakes for him. Amnon told his men to go out and leave Tamar alone with him. After raping her, he couldn't stand her sight and had her thrown out of his house.

Tamar put dust on her head, tore the ornamented tunic she was wearing, and walked away, screaming loudly as she went. Absalom met her and asked her, "Was it your brother Amnon who did this to you? For the present, sister, keep quiet about it; he is your brother. Don't brood over this matter". Absalom gave her refuge in his house.

When King David heard about the rape, he was greatly upset but did not rebuke Amnon. Absalom also didn't utter a word to Amnon. He hated him in silence and waited patiently for the right moment to revenge his sister.

Two years later, Absalom saw his opportunity. He invited his father, King David, to a sheep-shearing celebration. The king did not accept the invitation, but, when Absalom insisted, he allowed Amnon and his other sons to attend the party.

During the feast, Absalom had his servants kill Amnon to avenge his sister's rape. Absalom fled to Geshur and stayed there with his maternal relatives for three years, until David allowed him to return to Jerusalem.

2. (1 Chronicles 4:20). Unspecified date. Amnon, son of Shimon, was a descendant of Judah. His brothers were Rinnah, Ben-Hanan, and Tilon.

Amok

(Hebrew origin: *Deep*)

(Nehemiah 12:7). 6th century B.C. Amok was the leader of a family of priests who returned with Zerubbabel from the Babylonian Exile, when Jeshua was the High Priest. He was the ancestor of a clan of priests that was led by Eber, during the days of the High Priest Joiakim (Nehemiah 12:20)

Amon

(Hebrew origin: *Skilled; faithful, reliable, steadfast; multitude*)

1. (1 Kings 22:26). 9th century B.C. Amon was the governor of the city of Samaria, during the reign of King Ahab. The king ordered him to put the prophet Micaiah in prison, and to give him only bread and water, till he would return in peace from the war against the Arameans.

2. (2 Kings 21:18). 7th century B.C. Amon, the son of Manasseh and Meshullemeth, was twenty-two years old, when he became the fourteenth king of Judah, after the partition of the United Monarchy. His wife's name was Jedidah, daughter of Adaiah of Boscath. Amon continued the idolatrous practices introduced by his father Manasseh. After reigning two years, he was murdered in his palace by conspirators, who were later caught and put to death by the people. Amon was buried, as his father had been, in the garden of the palace. His eight-year-old son Josiah succeeded him.

3. (Nehemiah 7:59). 10th century B.C. Amon, a servant of King Solomon, was the ancestor of a family that returned with Zerubbabel from the Babylonian Exile. He is called Ami in the book of Ezra (Ezra 2:57).

4. (Jeremiah 46:25). Amon was the tutelary deity of the Egyptian city of Thebes, which was called No in the Bible.

Amos

(Hebrew origin: *Burdensome*)

1. (Amos 1:1). 8th century B.C. The prophet Amos was born in the town of Tekoa, in the kingdom of Judah. He was a herdsman and a gatherer of sycamore fruit, not a member of a professional prophetic guild.

Amos received the divine call to go and preach to the people of the northern kingdom of Israel, during the days of Uzziah, king of Judah, and Jeroboam II, king of Israel. Although the historical period, during which Amos lived, was apparently a time of great economic prosperity, religious piety, and security, the prophet felt that it was all false. Prosperity was limited to the wealthy, and it was based on injustice, and on the oppression of the poor. Religious observance was insincere, and security was more apparent than real.

Amaziah, the priest of the royal sanctuary at Bethel, accused the prophet Amos of conspiring against King Jeroboam II of Israel. Amos, undaunted, said that the king would die by the sword, and that Israel would be exiled from its land. Amaziah told the prophet to flee to the land of Judah, and never again return to prophesy in Bethel. Amos answered that it was God who had sent him to prophesy to Israel.

Three other prophets preached, during that same period, the latter half of the 8th century B.C.—Isaiah, Hosea, and Micah—but there is no evidence in the Bible that any of them knew in person any of the others.

Amos and Isaiah share the same lines of thought, with the main difference being that Amos addressed the northern kingdom of Israel, while Isaiah preached in Judah.

The book of Amos, a collection of individual sayings and reports of visions, is basically a message of doom. The prophet accused Israel that it had defected from the worship of God to the worship of Canaanite idols. He attacked the rich for their self-indulgence, their injustice, and their oppression of the poor. He preached that God would punish the nation with exile, but he ended his book with a prophecy of comfort for Israel.

The book of Amos is one of the twelve books that make up the Minor Prophets—also called the Twelve—a collection of the books of twelve prophets: Hosea, Joel, Amos, Obadiah, Jonah, Micah, Nahum,

Habakkuk, Zephaniah, Haggai, Zechariah, and Malachi.

Note: The phrase "Minor Prophets" does not mean that these prophets are less important than Isaiah, Jeremiah, and Ezekiel; it refers only to the fact that the books of these twelve prophets are much shorter than the books of the other three prophets.

2. (Luke 3:25). Unspecified date. Amos, son of Naum and father of Mattathias, was an ancestor of Jesus, according to Luke's genealogy.

Amoz

(Hebrew origin: *Strong*)

(2 Kings 19:2). 8th century B.C. Amoz was the father of the prophet Isaiah.

Amplias

(Latin origin: contraction of *Ampliatus* [*Enlarged*])

(Romans 16:8). A.D. 1st century. Amplias was one of the Christian residents in Rome to whom Paul, in his letter to the Romans, sent warm regards, calling him "my beloved in the Lord".

Amram

(Hebrew origin: *Exalted people*)

1. (Exodus 6:18). 14th century B.C. Amram was the son of Kohath and the grandson of Levi. He married his aunt Jochebed, with whom he had three children: Miriam, Aaron, and Moses. Amram died at the age of one hundred and thirty-seven.

2. (1 Chronicles 1:41). 18th century B.C. Amram was the son of Dishon and nephew of Aholibamah, Esau's wife. He is called Hemdan in Genesis (Genesis 36:26). His brothers were Eshban, Ithran, and Cheran.

Note: The Hebrew spelling of Amram in this entry is different from the entry above.

3. (Ezra 10:34). 5th century B.C. Amram, a descendant of Bani, divorced his foreign wife, during the days of Ezra.

Amraphel

(Hebrew origin: Uncertain meaning)

(Genesis 14:1). 19th century B.C. Amraphel, king of Shinar, allied himself to Arioch, king of Ellasar; Chedorlaomer, king of Elam; and Tidal, king of nations; and they went to war in the valley of Siddim against five Canaanite kings of the Dead Sea region: Bera, king of Sodom; Birsha, king of Gomorrah; Shinab, king of Admah; Shemeber, king of Zeboiim; and the king of Bela.

Amraphel and his allies defeated their five enemies, took a number of prisoners, including Lot, Abram's nephew, and departed back to their countries, loaded with all the booty that they could carry.

A man, who managed to escape from the battle, came to Abram and told him that his nephew Lot had been captured, and was being taken away. Abram armed three hundred and eighteen of his servants and—with his allies Aner, Eshcol, and Mamre—pursued the four kings, until he caught up with them in Daniel. There, he divided his men in groups, attacked the enemy that night, and defeated them, chasing them back as far as Hobah, near Damascus. He succeeded in recovering the stolen loot, liberated Lot, and brought him to Sodom with all his possessions, together with the women who had been captured, and other prisoners.

Amzi

(Hebrew origin: *Strong*)

1. (1 Chronicles 6:46). Unspecified date. Amzi, son of Bani, was a descendant of Merari. His descendant, Ethan, was one of the Levites appointed by King David to be in charge of the singers in the House of the Lord.

2. (Nehemiah 11:12). Unspecified date. Amzi, a priest, son of Zechariah, was the father of Pelaliah. His descendant Adaiah was a Temple priest, during the days of Nehemiah.

Anah

(Hebrew origin: *Responded*)

1. (Genesis 36:2). 19th century B.C. According to this verse, Anah was the daughter of Zibeon the Hivite, and the mother of Aholibamah, one of the Canaanite wives of Esau. However, according to another verse (Genesis 36:24), Anah was a son of Zibeon, who found mules—an alternative translation for this uncertain Hebrew word is "hot springs"—in the wilderness, while pasturing the asses of his father Zibeon. He/she was the nephew/niece of Anah #2.
2. (Genesis 36:20). Unspecified date. Anah was one of the sons of Seir the Horite, ancestor of the clans that settled in the land of Edom. His brothers were Lotan, Shobal, Zibeon, Dishon, Ezer, and Dishan. His children were Dishon and Aholibamah. He was the uncle of Anah #1.

Anaiah

(Hebrew origin: *God has answered*)

(Nehemiah 8:4). 5th century B.C. Anaiah was one of the leaders who stood next to Ezra, upon a pulpit of wood, when the scribe read the Law of Moses to the people in the marketplace. He was also one of the leaders who signed Nehemiah's solemn agreement to separate themselves from the foreigners living in the land, to refrain from intermarrying with them, to dedicate their firstborn to God, and other obligations (Nehemiah 10:22).

Anak

(Hebrew origin: *Giant, necklace*)

(Numbers 13:22). 14th century B.C. Anak, son of Arba, the founder of the city of Hebron, was the father of Ahiman, Sheshai, and Talmai. His three sons' gigantic height made the spies sent by Moses feel like grasshoppers. Caleb, the son of Jephunneh, expelled the three brothers from Hebron, during the conquest of Canaan. They were later killed by the tribe of Judah.

Anamim

(Egyptian origin: Uncertain meaning)

(Genesis 10:13). Unspecified date. Anamim was the son of Mizraim—Hebrew for Egypt—and grandson of Ham.

Anammelech

(Hebrew origin: *The king has answered*)

(2 Kings 17:31). Anammelech and Adrammelech were the gods of the Sepharvites, a tribe that the Assyrians settled in Samaria, after they conquered and destroyed the city in 722 B.C. The cult of these gods was accompanied by the sacrifice of children.

Anan

(Hebrew origin: *Cloud*)

(Nehemiah 10:26). 5th century B.C. Anan was one of the leaders who signed Nehemiah's solemn agreement to separate themselves from the foreigners living in the land, to refrain from intermarrying with them, and to dedicate their firstborn son to God, among other obligations.

Anani

(Hebrew origin: *My cloud*)

(1 Chronicles 3:24). Unspecified date. Anani, son of Elioenai, was a descendant of Jeconiah—also called Jehoiachin—the king of Judah, who was taken to captivity in Babylon. Anani's brothers were Eliashib, Pelaiah, Akkub, Johanan, Dalaiah, and Hodaiah.

Ananiah

(Hebrew origin: *Cloud of God*)

(Nehemiah 3:23). 6th century B.C. His grandson Azariah, son of his son Maaseiah, helped to repair the walls of Jerusalem in the stretch next to his house, during the days of Nehemiah.

Ananias

(Hebrew origin: *God has favored*)

1. (Acts of the Apostles 5:1). A.D. 1st century. Ananias was a convert to Christianity who lived in Jerusalem. At that time, it was the custom in the community of believers to own all their belongings in common. The members of the community, who had owned fields or houses, sold their possessions and gave the money to the apostles, who distributed it to each one according to his or her need.

One couple, Ananias and his wife Sapphira, behaved differently, motivated by greed. They sold their property but, instead of turning all the money over to the apostles, connived to keep part of it for themselves.

Peter, who was told of their unchristian behavior, went to Ananias' house and said to him, "Ananias, why did you let Satan fill your heart and make you lie to the Holy Spirit by keeping part of the money you received for the property? The property, before you sold it, belonged to you, but after you sold it, the money was ours. You have not lied to men; you have lied to God!"

Ananias, upon hearing these words, fell down and died. Several young men of the congregation came in, carried the body out, and buried him.

Three hours later Sapphira, who had been out, returned to her home, not yet knowing what had happened to her husband. She was confronted by Peter, who showed her the money and asked, "Is this the full amount you and your husband received for your property?" "Yes", she answered, "It is the full amount".

Peter asked her, "Why did you and your husband put the Spirit of the Lord to the test? The men who buried your husband are outside the door, and they will carry you out too!" And, at that moment, Sapphira fell down at his feet and died.

The young men came in, carried her out, and buried her next to her husband. The believers and all others who heard of this were terrified.

2. (Acts of the Apostles 9:10). A.D. 1st century. Ananias, a Christian who lived in Damascus, was instructed by God in a vision to go to the house of a man called Judas, which was located in the street called Straight. There, he would find, immersed in prayer, the blind Saul.

Ananias protested to God that he had heard of Saul's reputation as a persecutor of Christians. God told him that he had chosen Saul to spread the divine message to Gentiles, kings, and Jews.

Ananias went to Saul, told him that Jesus had sent him, and touched him. Saul—who had seen in a vision that he would recover his sight, when Ananias would come in and touch him—immediately recovered his eyesight. He arose and was baptized.

Years later, at his trial in Jerusalem, Paul recounted the story of his conversion and baptism, calling Ananias, "a devout man according to the law, having a good report of all the Jews, which dwelt there".

3. (Acts of the Apostles 23:2). A.D. 1st century. The High Priest Ananias was the head of the council that interrogated Paul in Jerusalem, after he had been arrested by the Roman soldiers.

When Paul attempted to defend himself, Ananias instructed those who were close to Paul to strike him on the mouth. Paul, furious, called him a "whitewashed wall" and protested that his order to strike him was against the law. Those around Paul were scandalized and reproached him for daring to insult the High Priest

Paul apologized, "The Scriptures forbid speaking evil of the rulers of the people, but I didn't know that he was the High Priest".

Claudius Lysias, the commander of the Antonia fortress, sent the apostle to Caesarea to be judged by Felix, the Roman governor. Five days later, Ananias, with several elders, came himself to Caesarea, bringing with him a spokesman called Tertullus, to present to the governor the charges against Paul. These accusations included sedition, incitement, and profanation of the Temple.

Felix, after hearing Paul eloquently deny the charges, decided to await for the arrival of Claudius Lysias to receive from him more detailed information about Paul's activities in Jerusalem. In the meantime, he gave limited liberty to Paul under the supervision of a centurion.

Two years later, when Porcius Festus, the new governor, arrived to replace him, Felix, wishing to ingratiate himself with Paul's enemies, had him bound.

Anath

(Hebrew origin: derived from *Answer*)

(Judges 3:31). 12th century B.C. His son Shamgar judged Israel, after Ehud and before Deborah.

Note: In the book of Judges, a judge is a ruler or governor of territory or a military leader in pre-monarchical Israel. Later, during the monarchy, the king served in this role and judges were more like the judicial officers that we know today.

Anathoth

(Hebrew origin: derived from *Answers*)

1. (1 Chronicles 7:8). 16th century B.C. Anathoth, the son of Becher and grandson of Benjamin, was a member of a family of leaders of the tribe and brave warriors. His brothers were Zemira, Joash, Eliezer, Elioenai, Omri, Jerimoth, Abiah, and Alameth.
2. (Nehemiah 10:19). 5th century B.C. Anathoth was one of the leaders who signed Nehemiah's solemn agreement to separate themselves from the foreigners living in the land, to refrain from inter-marrying with them, and to dedicate their firstborn to God, among other obligations.

Andrew

(Greek origin: *Manly*)

(Matthew 4:18). A.D. 1st century. Andrew, the first man chosen by Jesus to be his disciple,

was born in Bethsaida. He had previously been a disciple of John the Baptist.

Andrew and his brother Simon, whom Jesus renamed Peter, were fishing in the Sea of Galilee, when Jesus called them to follow him and become "fishers of men".

Andrew and the apostles—Peter, James, and John—were contemplating the Temple, from the Mount of Olives, when Jesus foretold its destruction.

On another occasion, he brought to Jesus' attention a little boy who had five barley loaves and two small fishes, with which Jesus miracu-lously fed five thousand men.

Andrew was the disciple whom people approached to express their desire to meet Jesus, as was the case with a group of Greek pilgrims, after Jesus' triumphal entry in Jerusalem on Palm Sunday.

The Bible's last mention of Andrew shows him to be with his brother Peter and other apostles, praying in an upper room, together with Mary, the mother of Jesus, and other women.

Andronicus

(Greek origin: *Man of victory*)

(Romans 16:7). A.D. 1st century. Andronicus was a Christian residing in Rome, to whom Paul sent greetings in his epistle to the Romans. Paul mentioned him in the same sentence with Junia, calling them his "kinsmen" and his "fellow prisoners". Paul added that they had become Christians, before he did.

Note: Junia is a woman's name, but in some texts, the name appears in its masculine form as "Junias". If Junia was indeed a woman, it is possible that she was the wife of Andronicus.

Aner

(Hebrew origin: derived from *Young man*)

(Genesis 14:13). 19th century B.C. Aner, Mamre, and Eshcol were three Amorite brothers who joined Abram in his pursuit of the kings who had taken Lot captive. Abram overtook the kings, defeated them, and brought back the captives and the stolen booty.

The king of Sodom offered to reward him, but he declined, suggesting instead that the reward should be given to Aner and his brothers.

Aniam

(Hebrew origin: *Lament of the people* or *I am people*)

(1 Chronicles 7:19). Unspecified date. Aniam was the son of Shemidah, a descendant of Manasseh. His brothers were Ahian, Shechem, and Likhi.

Anna

(Greek derived from Hebrew origin: *Grace*)

(Luke 2:36). A.D. 1st century. Anna, an old woman eighty-four years old, was the daughter of Phanuel, of the tribe of Aser—alternative transliteration for Asher. Her husband died, after seven years of marriage, and she had never remarried.

She spent all her time in the Temple, fasting and praying, day and night. Many people considered her to be a prophetess.

Anna and Simeon, a devout man, were present, when Joseph and Mary brought the child Jesus to the Temple to sacrifice on his behalf, according to the custom for firstborn male children.

Anna thanked God for having given her the opportunity of seeing Jesus and spoke of him to all the pilgrims who came to Jerusalem seeking redemption.

Annas

(Greek derived from Hebrew origin: *God has favored*)

(Luke 3:2). A.D. 1st century. Annas was the High Priest, during the time when John the Baptist started to preach. His successor as High Priest was his son-in-law Caiaphas.

When Jesus was taken prisoner, he was first brought to the house of Annas, who, after interrogating him, sent him tied up to Caiaphas.

The last mention of Annas in the New Testament places him in the court of the Jewish Council, where he, together with Caiaphas, and other leaders, asked the apostles by what power and by what name were they preaching and healing people. Peter answered that the healing was done in the name of Jesus Christ of Nazareth. The court acquitted the apostles without punishment.

Antipas

(Greek composite word: *Instead of father*)

(Revelation 2:13). A.D. 1st century. Antipas was a Christian martyr, slain in Pergamos, an event, which is mentioned by John in Revelation.

Antothijah

(Hebrew origin: derived from *Answers of God*)

(1 Chronicles 8:24). Unspecified date. Antothijah, son of Shashak, was a leader of the tribe of Benjamin who lived in Jerusalem.

Anub

(Hebrew origin: *Has borne fruit*)

(1 Chronicles 4:8). Unspecified date. Anub, a descendant of Judah, was the son of Coz.

Apelles

(Name of Latin origin or Greek abbreviation for *Apollonius*).

(Romans 16:10). A.D. 1st century. Apelles was a Christian resident of Rome. Paul sent him regards in his letter to the Christian community in Rome, calling him "approved in Christ".

Aphiah

(Hebrew origin: *Breeze*)

(1 Samuel 9:1). Unspecified date. Aphiah, a Benjamite, was the father of Bechorath, and an ancestor of King Saul.

Aphses

(Hebrew origin: *The dispersive)*

(1 Chronicles 24:15). 10th century B.C. During the reign of King David, the priestly service in the Tabernacle was divided by lot into twenty-four turns. Aphses was in charge of the eighteenth turn.

Apollos

(Greek origin: *Destroyer or The pagan god Apollos [i.e. the sun])*

(Acts of the Apostles 18:24). A.D. 1st century. Apollos, an Alexandrian Jew, was an eloquent scholar, well versed in the Hebrew Scriptures, but less so in Christian doctrine, about, which he knew only about the baptism of John.

Aquila and Priscilla, a couple living in Ephesus, heard him preach about Jesus in the synagogue. They were impressed by his eloquence and enthusiasm, but they realized that his knowledge of Christianity was very limited. The couple took Apollos under their wing, taught him the Way of God, and sent him to Corinth, carrying letters exhorting the local Christian community to receive him.

In Corinth, Apollos proved to be a convincing and effective Christian preacher. He succeeded in converting many Jews by proving, by quoting the appropriate Hebrew Scriptures, that Jesus was the Messiah.

He became so popular and respected among the Corinthian Christians that at one point there was a real danger that the congregation would become divided into three separate groups: the followers of Paul, the followers of Apollos, and the followers of Cephas, as Peter was called. This prompted Paul to write to the Corinthians that he had planted, and Apollos had watered, but both were servants of God, and that it was God alone who produced the results (1 Corinthians 3:6).

Later, in his letter addressed to Titus, Paul stated that he wanted Apollos, accompanied by the lawyer Zenas, to go on a mission to Nicopolis, a town situated on the Adriatic coast of Greece.

Apollyon

(Greek origin: *Destroyer).*

(Revelation 9:11). Apollyon, king of monstrous scorpion-like locusts, is an angel of destruction, Satan, residing in the bottomless pit. His name in Hebrew is Abaddon.

Appaim

(Hebrew origin: *Two nostrils*)

(1 Chronicles 2:30). Unspecified date. Appaim, of the tribe of Judah, was a descendant of Jerahmeel and his wife Atarah. Appaim's father was Nadab, and his son was Ishi.

Apphia

(Greek word of foreign derivation)

(Philemon 1:2). A.D. 1st century. Apphia was a Christian woman, living in Colossae. Although it is not expressly mentioned in the Bible, it is likely that she was the wife of Philemon—a prominent Christian who hosted the town's Christian congregation in his house—and the mother of Archippus.

Paul wrote a short letter to Philemon about Onesimus, an escaped slave whom Paul had met in prison and converted to Christianity. In this letter, Paul sends greetings to Philemon, Apphia, and Archippus and appeals to Philemon to be reconciled to his slave, whom Paul is sending back to him, and to welcome him not only as a forgiven slave but as a brother in Christ.

Aquila

(Latin origin: *Eagle)*

(Acts of the Apostles 18:2). A.D. 1st century. Aquila, a Jew born in Pontus—a city situated in Asia Minor—was married to Priscilla. The couple, who had been residing in Rome, moved to Corinth, when the emperor Claudius expelled all the Jews from Rome.

In Corinth, they made their living by making tents, which was also Paul's trade. Paul, during his stay in Corinth, was lodged in the house of Aquila and Priscilla, and he probably assisted them in their work. When Paul departed from Corinth, he took the couple with him and, on his way to Antioch, left them in Ephesus.

Aquila and Priscilla heard Apollos, an Alexandrian Jew, well versed in Hebrew Scripture, give a lecture about Jesus in the Ephesus synagogue. They were impressed by his eloquence but realized that his knowledge of Christianity was very limited. They took Apollos under their wing, taught him the Way of God, and sent him to Corinth, carrying letters exhorting the local Christian community to receive him.

Later, after Claudius' death, when the imperial edict, expelling the Jews, was no longer being enforced, the couple returned to Rome. Paul, in his letter to the Romans, sent them greetings, adding that they had risked their necks to save his life.

It seems—according to the greetings that Paul sent them, in his second letter to Timothy, where he calls Priscilla "Prisca"—that the couple returned to Ephesus.

Ara

(Hebrew origin: derived from *Lion*)

(1 Chronicles 7:38). Unspecified date. Ara, son of Jether, was a brave warrior and the leader of a clan of the tribe of Asher. His brothers were Jephunneh and Pispah.

Arad

(Hebrew origin: *Wild donkey*)

1. (Numbers 21:1). 13th century B.C. Arad was the ruler of a Canaanite city of the same name, situated in the Negev desert. When he heard that the Israelites were coming, he attacked them and took some of them captive.

   The Israelites vowed to God that, if He would deliver the Canaanites into their hands, they would utterly destroy their towns. The destruction was carried out to such an extent that, from then on, the city of Arad was called Hormah, which in Hebrew means *complete ruin* or *Destruction*.

2. (1 Chronicles 8:15). Unspecified date. Arad, son of Beriah, was a Benjamite, leader of a clan, who lived in Jerusalem.

Arah

(Hebrew origin: *Traveler*)

1. (1 Chronicles 7:39). Unspecified date. Arah, son of Ulla, was a brave warrior, leader of a clan of the tribe of Asher. His brothers were Haniel and Rezia.

2. (Ezra 2.5). Unspecified date. Arah was an ancestor of a family that returned to Judah from the Babylonian Exile.

3. (Nehemiah 6:18). 5th century B.C. His son Shechaniah was the father-in-law of Tobiah, Nehemiah's enemy.

Aram

(Hebrew origin: *Highland*)

1. (Genesis 10:22). Unspecified date. Aram, son of Shem and grandson of Noah, was the ancestor of the Arameans, a people who lived in what today is Syria. According to the book of Genesis, he was the father of Uz, Hul, Gether, and Mash. However, according to the first book of Chronicles, he was their brother, not their father (1 Chronicles 1:17).

2. (Genesis 22:21). 19th century B.C. Aram was the son of Kemuel and grandson of Nahor, Abraham's brother.

3. (1 Chronicles 7:34). Unspecified date. Aram was the son of Shamer, a leader of the tribe of Asher. His brothers were Ahi, Rohgah, and Jehubbah.

4. (Matthew 1:3). Unspecified date. Aram, son of Esrom and father of Aminadab, was an ancestor of Jesus in the genealogies of Matthew and Luke.

Aran

(Hebrew origin: *Strident*)

(Genesis 36:28). Unspecified date. Aran, son of Dishan and brother of Uz, was a descendant of Seir the Horite. Aran was the leader of a clan that lived in the land of Edom, south of the Dead Sea.

Araunah

(Jebusite title, meaning *The Lord*)

(2 Samuel 24:16). 10th century B.C. Araunah the Jebusite—called Ornan in First Chronicles (1 Chronicles 21:15)—owned a threshing floor on Mount Moriah, on the outskirts of the City of David.

Scholars believe that Araunah might have been the last Jebusite king of the conquered Jerusalem, based on a verse in the second book of Samuel (2 Samuel 24:23), where Araunah is called king.

God, speaking through the prophet Gad, told David to build an altar in Araunah's threshing floor, in expiation for having taken a forbidden census, a transgression that the Lord had punished by sending a plague that killed seventy thousand people.

Araunah was threshing wheat, when he saw the king and his courtiers approaching. He bowed to the ground and asked to what he owed the great honor. David answered that he had come to buy his threshing floor, which he needed for the altar that he planned to build to stop the plague.

Araunah answered that the king should take the threshing floor, and sacrifice there whatever he would see fit, adding that he would be pleased to provide also the oxen and the wood for the sacrifice.

David refused his offer, and saying that he could not sacrifice to God, if it did not cost him anything, he paid Araunah fifty shekels of silver—elsewhere it is reported that the amount paid was six hundred shekels of gold (1 Chronicles 21:25)—for the threshing floor and the oxen.

The king built an altar, on the piece of land, and sacrificed the oxen. God heard his plea and stopped the plague. Years later, King Solomon built the Temple in this site.

Arba

(Hebrew origin: *Four*)

(Joshua 14:15). Unspecified date. Arba was the founder of the city of Hebron, originally called Kirjatharba—the city of Arba—in his honor. His son Anak and his grandsons were so tall that they made the spies sent by Moses feel like grasshoppers. Caleb, the son of Jephunneh, received Hebron as his share of the conquered Canaan, and expelled the descendants of Arba from the city.

Archelaus

(Greek origin: *People ruling*)

(Matthew 2:22). A.D. 1st century. Archelaus, a son of Herod, was the king of Judea,er when Joseph, Mary, and Jesus returned from Egypt.

Joseph, fearful of Herod's son, went to the Galilee, where the family settled in the town of Nazareth.

Archippus

(Greek origin: *Horse ruler*)

(Colossians 4:17). A.D. 1st century. Archippus was a Christian leader in Colossae, to whom Paul sent regards in his letter to the Colossians. He is also mentioned in Paul's letter to Philemon, where the apostle calls him "a fellow soldier".

Although it is not expressly mentioned in the Bible, it is likely that Archippus was the son of Apphia and her husband, Philemon, a prominent Christian who hosted the town's Christian congregation in his house

Ard

(Hebrew origin: *Wanderer*)

1. (Genesis 46:21). 17th century B.C. Ard, son of Benjamin and grandson of Jacob, was one of the seventy Israelites who immigrated to Egypt. His brothers, according to a list in the book of Genesis, were Becher, Ashbel, Gera, Naaman, Ehi, Rosh, Muppim, Huppim, and Belah. Ard is not mentioned in any of the other three lists of the sons of Benjamin: Numbers 26:38, 1 Chronicles 7:6, and 1 Chronicles 8:1.

2. (Numbers 26:40). 16th century B.C. Ard, son of Bela—alternative spelling Belah—and grandson of Benjamin, was the ancestor of the clan of the Ardites. His

brother was Naaman. Ard is called Addar in the first book of Chronicles (1 Chronicles 8:3).

Ardon

(Hebrew origin: *Roaming*)

(1 Chronicles 2:18). Unspecified date. Ardon, son of Caleb and grandson of Hezron, was a descendant of Judah. His mother was Azubah. His brothers were Jesher and Shobab.

Areli

(Hebrew origin: *Lion of God*)

(Genesis 46:16). 17th century B.C. Areli, son of Gad and grandson of Jacob and Zilpah, Leah's maid, was one of the seventy Israelites who immigrated to Egypt.

Areli's brothers were Ziphion, Haggi, Shuni, Ezbon, Arodi, and Eri. Areli was the ancestor of the clan of Arelites.

Aretas

(Nabatean origin: Uncertain meaning)

(2 Corinthians 11:32). A.D. 1st century. Aretas, the king of the Nabatean kingdom, controlled Damascus, during the period when Paul was in that city.

The governor of the city tried to arrest the apostle, but Paul was able to escape by being let down the walls of the city inside a basket.

Aridai

(Persian origin: Uncertain meaning)

(Esther 9:9). 5th century B.C. Aridai was one of the ten sons of Haman, the vizier of Persia who wanted to kill all the Jews in the kingdom.

His brothers were Parshandatha, Arisai, Dalphon, Poratha, Aspatha, Aridatha, Parmashta, Adalia, and Vajezatha. All of them were executed, when Haman's plot against the Jews backfired.

Aridatha

(Persian origin: Uncertain meaning)

(Esther 9:8). 5th century B.C. Aridatha was one of the ten sons of Haman, the vizier of Persia who wanted to kill all the Jews in the kingdom.

His brothers were Parshandatha, Arisai, Dalphon, Poratha, Aspatha, Aridai, Parmashta, Adalia, and Vajezatha. All of them were executed, when Haman's plot against the Jews backfired.

Ariel

(Hebrew origin: *Lion of God*)

(Ezra 8:16). 5th century B.C. Ariel was one of the leaders of Judah who was sent by Ezra to Casiphia to speak to Iddo, and request from him to send Levites to serve in the Temple in Jerusalem.

Arioch

(Babylonian origin: Uncertain meaning)

1. (Genesis 14:1). 19th century B.C. Arioch, king of Ellasar, allied himself to Amraphel, king of Shinar; Chedorlaomer, king of Elam; and Tidal, king of nations; and went to war in the valley of Siddim against five Canaanite kings of the Dead Sea region: Bera, king of Sodom; Birsha, king of Gomorrah; Shinab, king of Admah; Shemeber, king of Zeboiim; and the king of Bela.

   Arioch and his allies defeated their five enemies, took a number of prisoners, including Lot, Abram's nephew, and departed back to their countries, loaded with all the booty that they could carry.

   A man, who managed to escape from the battle, came to Abram and told him that his nephew Lot had been captured, and was being taken away. Abram armed three hundred and eighteen of his servants and—with his allies Aner, Eshcol, and Mamre—pursued the four kings, until he caught up with them in Daniel. There, he divided his men in groups, attacked the enemy that night, and defeated them, chasing them back as far as Hobah, near

Damascus. He succeeded in recovering the stolen loot, liberated Lot, and brought him to Sodom with all his possessions, together with the women who had been captured, and other prisoners.

2. (Daniel 2:14). 6th century B.C. Arioch was the captain of King Nebuchadnezzar's guard. The king commanded him to kill all the wise men of Babylon who had failed to interpret the king's dream. Daniel and his friends were included in the decree. Daniel, after asking Arioch for an explanation of the decree, went to the king and requested an extension of time to give him the interpretation of the dream.

Arisai

(Persian origin: *Uncertain meaning*)

(Esther 9:9). 5th century B.C. Arisai was one of the ten sons of Haman, the vizier of Persia who wanted to kill all the Jews in the kingdom.

His brothers were Parshandatha, Dalphon, Aspatha, Poratha, Adalia, Aridatha, Parmashta, Aridai, and Vajezatha. All of them were executed, when Haman's plot against the Jews backfired.

Aristarchus

(Greek origin: *Best ruling*)

(Acts of the Apostles 19:29). A.D. 1st century. Aristarchus, a Macedonian Christian from Thessalonica, was a faithful and long-time companion of Paul, with whom he shared many difficult experiences, beatings, imprisonment, and shipwreck.

Aristarchus is first mentioned in the book of Acts of the Apostles, when he and Gaius, a fellow Macedonian, were caught by a mob in Ephesus that was violently demonstrating in favor of the goddess Diana, whose cult was threatened by the teachings of Paul. The two Macedonians were dragged inside a theatre.

Paul attempted to enter the theatre, but, to save his life, his disciples stopped him from doing so. Aristarchus and Gaius were lucky to escape unhurt. They later accompanied Paul in

his final trip from Greece to Jerusalem, together with some other people, including Secundus, a fellow Macedonian, Sopater of Berea, Timotheus, Tychicus and Trophimus.

Aristarchus also sailed with Paul in his final voyage from Caesarea to Rome, during which they were shipwrecked.

Paul, in his letter to the Colossians, mentioned that Aristarchus was a fellow prisoner in Rome. In his letter to Philemon, Paul called Aristarchus a fellow worker.

Aristobulus

(Greek origin: *Best counseling*)

(Romans 16:10). A.D. 1st century. Paul sent greetings to this man's family in his letter to the Romans.

Armoni

(Hebrew origin: *Palatial*)

(2 Samuel 21:8). 10th century B.C. Armoni was the son of King Saul and his concubine Rizpah. He, his brother Mephibosheth, and their five nephews were delivered by King David to the Gibeonites, who hanged them in a hill, to avenge Saul's massacre.

His mother Rizpah placed sackcloth on a rock and sat on it to guard the bodies against the birds and the beasts of the field, from the beginning of the harvest season, until the rains came, months later.

Arnan

(Hebrew origin: *Happy shout*)

(1 Chronicles 3:21). 5th century B.C. Arnan, son of Rephaiah and father of Obadiah, descended from King David through Zerubbabel.

Arod

(Hebrew origin: *Fugitive*)

(Numbers 26:17). 17th century B.C. Arod—also called Arodi (Genesis 46:16)—was the son of Gad and grandson of Jacob and Zilpah. (Please see the entry for Arodi.)

Arodi

(Hebrew origin: *Descendant of Arod* or *Habitant of the city Arvad*)

(Genesis 46:16). 17th century B.C. Arodi—also called Arod (Numbers 26:17)—son of Gad and grandson of Jacob and Zilpah, Leah's maid, was one of the seventy Israelites who immigrated to Egypt.

Arodi's brothers were Ziphion, Haggi, Shuni, Ezbon, Areli, and Eri. Arodi was the ancestor of the clan of Arodites.

Arphaxad

(Hebrew origin: Uncertain meaning)

(Genesis 10:22). Unspecified date. Arphaxad, a son of Shem and grandson of Noah, was born two years after the flood, when his father was one hundred years old. He was thirty-five years old, when his son Salah was born. After that, he lived for another four hundred and three years and fathered other sons and daughters. His son Salah is called Sala in Luke (Luke 3:35), and Shelah in First Chronicles (1 Chronicles 1:18).

Artaxerxes

(Persian origin: Title of several Persian kings)

(Ezra 4:7). 5th century B.C. Artaxerxes was king of Persia, during the 5th century B.C. The foreign settlers of Samaria sent a letter—written in Aramaic by Rehum, the Persian commissioner, and Shimshai the Scribe—to the king, accusing the Jews of rebuilding the walls of Jerusalem with the intention to rebel.

The king, who was persuaded that the rebuilding constituted a threat to his authority, ordered the work to stop and decreed that the city should not be rebuild unless explicitly allowed by him.

Later, in the seventh year of his reign, he had a change of heart and allowed Ezra the Scribe, and anybody else who wanted to return to Jerusalem, to do so, giving him silver and gold for the service of the Temple. Some scholars disagree with this interpretation and date Ezra's mission to the reign of Artaxerxes II, 404 B.C. to 359 B.C.

During the twentieth year of his reign, Artaxerxes sent Nehemiah his cupbearer on a visit to Jerusalem and then made him governor of the province of Judea.

Artemas

(Greek origin: *Gift of Artemis*)

(Titus 3:12). A.D. 1st century. Artemas was a companion of Paul, mentioned by the apostle in his letter to Titus. Paul wrote that he intended to send either Artemas or Tychicus to Crete, probably to substitute for Titus, whom the apostle wanted to come and spend the winter with him at Nicopolis.

Arza

(Hebrew origin: *Earthiness*)

(1 Kings 16:9). 9th century B.C. Arza was the steward of the royal palace in Tirzah, the capital of the kingdom of Israel, during the short reign of King Elah. The king came to visit Arza in his house and got himself to a drunken stupor.

Zimri, commander of half the chariots in the army, entered the house and murdered the inebriated Elah. He also killed all the other members of the royal family and then proclaimed himself king. One week later, Zimri committed suicide, when Omri fought against him.

Asa

(Hebrew origin: Uncertain meaning)

1. (1 Kings 15:8). 9th century B.C. King Asa of Judah was the third king of Judah, after the division of the kingdom. He succeeded his father Abijah in the twentieth year of the reign of Jeroboam, king of Israel.

   During his long reign of forty-one years, Asa distinguished himself for his military prowess and religious fervor. He was in constant war against Baasha, king of Israel, who had built Ramah, north of Jerusalem, to blockade the southern kingdom. The blockade compelled Asa to send the silver and gold treasures from the

Temple and the royal palace to Benhadad, king of Syria, to pay him to attack Baasha. Asa took advantage of Benhadad's war against Baasha to take Ramah and destroy it, using its stones and timber, to rebuild the cities of Geba and Mizpah.

Years later, when Zerah the Ethiopian invaded Judah, with a huge army of foot soldiers and three hundred chariots, Asa fought against him in the valley of Zephathah at Mareshah. He inflicted a great defeat on the Ethiopians, who fled back to their own country.

Asa's domestic policy was to fight against the foreign idolatrous cults that had become popular in the kingdom. Encouraged by the prophet Oded, Asa destroyed all the idols that were to be found in the kingdom of Judah and in the cities of Israel, which he had annexed, including the idol made by the queen mother, Maachah, who, for this reason, he stripped from her position.

Although the Bible praises him for doing what was "right in the eyes of the Lord", it also disapproves of his pragmatism, accusing Asa of relying more on his doctors' treatment, than on prayers to God, when at the end of his life, he suffered from a serious disease in his legs.

The Bible also mentions that sometimes he oppressed the people, and would imprison those who did not agree with his policies. He did that to Hanani, the seer, who had reproved him for asking Benhadad for help against the kingdom of Israel, instead of relying on God.

When Asa died, he was buried in the royal tombs, in the City of David, and was succeeded by his son Jehoshaphat.

2. (1 Chronicles 9:16). 6th century B.C. Asa, a Levite son of Elkanah, was the father of Berechiah, who was one of the first Israelites to settle in the land of Judah, after the return from the Babylonian Exile.

Asahel

(Hebrew origin: *God has made*)

1. (2 Samuel 2:18). 10th century B.C. Asahel,

Joab, and Abishai were the sons of Zeruiah, King David's sister. The three brothers served in the army, in an elite army group of brave warriors known as The Thirty. Asahel was the officer in charge of the army, during the fourth month of every year, with twenty-four thousand men under him.

During the warfare between Israel and Judah, the armies of the two countries met by the pool of Gibeon. Abner suggested to Joab that twelve men of each side should fight to the death. After the twenty-four men died killing each other, both armies engaged in battle. Abner's army was defeated.

Abner, who was pursued by Asahel, begged him not to run after him, saying that he was forced to kill him, and he would not be able to face Joab. Asahel refused to stop, and Abner killed him with a backward thrust of his spear.

Sometime later, Abner decided to switch his loyalties, from Ishbosheth to David, and came to Hebron to meet with the king. Joab took advantage of the opportunity and murdered him at the gate in revenge for the killing of his brother Asahel.

Shocked by this treacherous murder, David buried Abner in Hebron with full honors, mourning him publicly and eulogizing him. David cursed Joab and his house for his bloody deed, but he did not punish him. It was only, many years later, that David, in his deathbed, instructed his son Solomon to have Joab killed for this and other crimes.

2. (2 Chronicles 17:8). 9th century B.C. Asahel, a Levite, was sent by King Jehoshaphat in the third year of his reign, to teach the laws of God in the cities of Judah. Asahel was accompanied in his mission by other Levites, by two priests— Elishama and Jehoram—and by several officials of the court.

3. (2 Chronicles 31:13). 8th century B.C. Asahel was one of the Levites who were named by King Hezekiah to serve under Cononiah and Shimei, as supervisors of the

gifts, tithes, and offerings, brought by the people to the Temple.

4. (Ezra 10:15). 5th century B.C. His son Jonathan was one of the two leaders of Judah—the other was Jahaziah, the son of Tikvah—who remained in Jerusalem, to represent the people, when Ezra deliberated on the matter of the marriages to foreign women.

Asahiah

(Hebrew origin: *God has made*)

(2 Kings 22:12). 7th century B.C. Asahiah, an official in the court of King Josiah, was sent by the king to consult with the prophetess Huldah about the Book of God's Law found by the High Priest in the Temple.

He was accompanied in his mission by Hilkiah the High Priest; Shaphan the Scribe; Ahikam, Shaphan's son; and Achbor, the son of Michaiah. An alternative spelling is Asaiah, in the second book of Chronicles (2 Chronicles 34:20).

Asaiah

(Hebrew origin: *God has made*)

1. (1 Chronicles 4:36). 8th century B.C. Asaiah was one of the leaders of the tribe of Simeon who went to the fertile valley of Gedor in search of pasture for their flocks, during the reign of Hezekiah, king of Judah. The Simeonites destroyed the tents of the people—descendants of Ham—who lived there, wiped them out forever, and settled in their place.

2. (1 Chronicles 6:30). 10th century B.C. Asaiah, son of Haggiah, a member of a clan descendant from Merari, was one of the Levites chosen by King David to carry the Ark of the Covenant to Jerusalem, by means of poles upon their shoulders, accompanied by singers and musicians.

Later, he was appointed by King David to be in charge of the singers in the House of the Lord, from the time that the Ark came to rest in Jerusalem.

3. (1 Chronicles 9:5). Unspecified date.

Asaiah was the head of the clan of Shilonites that settled in Jerusalem, after they returned from the Babylonian Exile.

4. (2 Chronicles 34:20). 7th century B.C. Asaiah, an official in the court of King Josiah, was sent by the king to consult with the prophetess Huldah about the Book of God's Law, found by the High Priest in the Temple. He was accompanied in his mission by Hilkiah the High Priest; Shaphan the Scribe; and others. Alternative spelling is Asahiah (2 Kings 22:12).

Asaph

(Hebrew origin: *Collector*)

1. (2 Kings 18:18). 8th century B.C. His son Joah, a high official in the palace of King Hezekiah, was a member of a three-man delegation sent by the king to talk to the commanders of the Assyrian army laying siege to Jerusalem. The men returned to the king with their clothes torn to show the failure of their negotiations.

2. (1 Chronicles 6:39). 10th century B.C. Asaph, son of Berachiah, of the clan of the Kohathites, played the brass cymbal in the procession of the Levites who accompanied the Ark from the house of Obededom to its resting place in Jerusalem, singing and playing musical instruments.

When the Ark arrived in Jerusalem, Asaph was appointed by King David to be in charge of the singers in the House of the Lord, assisted by his sons Zaccur, Joseph, Nethaniah, and Asarelah.

The Bible calls him a seer and attributes to him the authorship of songs, including twelve psalms. In later centuries, the singers and musicians in the Temple considered him their ancestor.

During the reign of King Hezekiah of Judah, his descendants, Zechariah and Mattaniah, were among the Levites who assembled other Levites to make themselves ritually clean, and to purify the Temple.

Two of Asaph's descendants were among the Levites who returned from the Babylonian Exile: one, called Mattaniah, was among the first to settle in the land of Judah; and the other, also called Zechariah, played the trumpet, during the days of Nehemiah.

3. (1 Chronicles 9:15). Unspecified date. Asaph, father of Zichri—called Zabdi in the book of Nehemiah (Nehemiah 11:17)—was an ancestor of Mattaniah, a Levite who settled in Jerusalem, after he returned from the Babylonian Exile, and led the thanksgiving prayers, during the days of Nehemiah.

4. (Nehemiah 2:8). 5th century B.C. Asaph was the court official in charge of the Persian royal forest, to whom Nehemiah asked the king to write a letter requesting timber for beams to be used in the reconstruction of the walls of Jerusalem, the palace, and the residence of Nehemiah himself.

Asareel

(Hebrew origin: *Right of God*)

(1 Chronicles 4:16). Unspecified date. Asareel, son of Jehaleleel, a descendant of Judah, was the brother of Ziph, Ziphah, and Tiria.

Asarelah

(Hebrew origin: *Straight toward God*)

(1 Chronicles 25:2). 10th century B.C. Asarelah was the son of Asaph, the Levite appointed by King David to be in charge of the singers in the House of the Lord.

Asarelah and his brothers—Zaccur, Joseph, and Nethaniah—assisted Asaph in his work, with Asarelah taking the seventh turn of service. He is called Jesharelah in First Chronicles (1 Chronicles 25:14).

Asenath

(Egyptian origin: Uncertain meaning)

(Genesis 41:45). 17th century B.C. Asenath, an Egyptian woman, daughter of Potipherah, priest of On, was given by Pharaoh in marriage to Joseph. Their two sons, Manasseh and Ephraim, were ancestors of Israelite tribes.

Aser

(Hebrew origin: *Happy*)

(Luke 2:36). 17th century B.C. Aser was the son of Jacob and ancestor of the tribe that was called by his name. His descendant Phanuel was the father of the prophetess Anna. Alternative spelling is Asher.

Ashbel

(Hebrew origin: *Flowing*)

(Genesis 46:21). 17th century B.C. Ashbel, a son of Benjamin, was one of the seventy Israelites who immigrated to Egypt.

In the Genesis' list of the sons of Benjamin, Ashbel is the third of ten sons. In the Numbers' list, he is the second of five sons (Numbers 26:38). In the first book of Chronicles, there are two different lists, but his name is mentioned in only one of them as the second of five sons (1 Chronicles 8:1). He was the ancestor of the clan of the Ashbelites.

Ashchenaz

(Hebrew origin: Uncertain meaning)

(1 Chronicles 1:6). Unspecified date. Ashchenaz was the son of Gomer and a grandson of Japheth. His brothers were Riphath and Togarmah. Alternative spelling is Ashkenaz (Genesis 10:3).

Asher

(Hebrew origin: *Happy*)

(Genesis 30:13). 17th century B.C. Asher, the ancestor of the tribe of Asher, was the eighth son of Jacob and the second son of his concubine Zilpah, Leah's maid. He was born in Paddan-Aram, while Jacob was working for his father-in-law Laban. Leah gave him the name Asher, because, she said, "I am very happy, and the women will call me blessed".

Asher was the full brother of Gad. His half brothers were Judah, Reuben, Levi, Simeon, Issachar, and Zebulun, sons of Leah; Joseph and Benjamin, sons of Rachel; and Dan and Naphtali, sons of Bilhah. His half sister was Dinah, daughter of Leah.

Asher and his brothers were involved in the events that led to Joseph being taken as a slave to Egypt. (For the detailed story of Joseph and his brothers, please see the entry for Joseph.)

Years later, when there was a famine in the land, he and his brothers were sent, by Jacob, to Egypt to buy corn. Joseph, who was now the second most powerful man in the country, recognized them, forgave them, and invited them to settle in Egypt.

Asher, his daughter Serah, his sons Jimnah—also spelled Jimna—Ishuah, Isui, Beriah, and his grandsons, Heber and Malchiel, sons of Beriah, were among the seventy Israelites who immigrated to Egypt.

Jacob, on his deathbed blessings to his sons, said about Asher, "his bread shall be fat, and he shall yield royal dainties".

Centuries later, Moses blessed the tribes in his farewell speech. Of Asher, he said, "Let Asher be blessed with children; let him be acceptable to his brothers, and let him dip his foot in oil. Your shoes shall be iron and brass; and as your days, so shall your strength be".

When Joshua conquered Canaan, the tribe of Asher was allotted the coastal area of western Galilee, an area that extends from today's city of Haifa on Mount Carmel in northern Israel to the city of Zidon in southern Lebanon.

Alternative spelling is Aser in the gospel according to Luke (Luke 2:36).

Ashima

(Hittite origin: Uncertain meaning)

(2 Kings 17:30). Ashima was an idol worshipped by the men of Hamath, a foreign tribe that the Assyrians settled in Samaria, after they destroyed it in the 8th century B.C.

Ashkenaz

(Hebrew origin: Uncertain meaning)

(Genesis 10:3). Unspecified date. Ashkenaz was the son of Gomer and a grandson of Japheth. His brothers were Riphath and Togarmah. Alternative spelling is Ashchenaz (1 Chronicles 1:6).

Ashpenaz

(Persian origin: Uncertain meaning)

(Daniel 1:3). 6th century B.C. Ashpenaz, the chief of the eunuchs of Nebuchadnezzar, king of Babylon, was commanded by the king to choose several good-looking and intelligent Israelite children of royal descent and of the nobility, and teach them the Chaldean language and writings. The king allotted daily rations to them from the king's food and from the wine that he drank. The young boys were to be educated for three years, at the end of which, they would enter the king's service.

Among these children were Daniel, Hananiah, Mishael, and Azariah, to whom Ashpenaz gave Babylonian names. When Daniel refused to eat the ritually impure food, the chief of the eunuchs worried that this could affect Daniel's health and appearance, and, if that would be the case, the displeased king would hold him responsible and punish him.

Daniel asked Ashpenaz to bring him and his companions vegetables and water, and to compare them, after ten days, with other youths who ate of the king's food. When the ten days were over, the Israelite children looked better and healthier than the other youths did.

When the three years of schooling was over, Ashpenaz brought Daniel and his companions to Nebuchadnezzar, who was very pleased, and put them in his service.

Ashriel

(Hebrew origin: *Right of God*)

(1 Chronicles 7:14). 17th century B.C. Ashriel and Machir were the two sons of Manasseh and his Aramean concubine. Ashriel was the ancestor of the clan of the Asrielites. Alternative name is Asriel (Numbers 26:31).

Ashtaroth

(Hebrew origin: *Phoenician goddess*)

(Judges 2:13). This is the Hebrew plural form for the Canaanite goddess Astarte, female companion of the god Baal. (Please see the entry for Ashtoreth [1 Kings 11:5].)

Ashtoreth

(Hebrew origin: *Phoenician goddess*)

(1 Kings 11:5). This is the Hebrew word for the Canaanite goddess Astarte, companion of the god Baal. These pagan gods were worshipped by the Israelites, during the periods when they forsook God. Even Solomon, in his old age, who was influenced by his foreign wives, built her a shrine in the outskirts of Jerusalem. This shrine was destroyed centuries later by King Josiah, and desecrated with human bones. Elsewhere in the Bible—e.g. (Judges 2:13)—she is called Ashtaroth.

Ashur

(Hebrew origin: *Successful*)

(1 Chronicles 2:24). Unspecified date. Ashur, founder of Tekoa, was a descendant of Judah. His mother Abiah gave birth to him, after his father Hezron had died. Ashur had seven sons from his two wives, Helah and Naarah.

Ashvath

(Hebrew origin: *Bright*)

(1 Chronicles 7:33). Unspecified date. Ashvath, son of Japhlet, a leader of the tribe of Asher, was the brother of Pasach and Bimhal.

Asiel

(Hebrew origin: *Made by God*)

(1 Chronicles 4:35). Unspecified date. His descendant Jehu was one of the leaders of the tribe of Simeon who went to the fertile valley of Gedor in search of pasture for their flocks, during the reign of Hezekiah, king of Judah. The Simeonites destroyed the tents of the people—descendants of Ham—who lived there, wiped them out forever, and settled in their place.

Asnah

(Hebrew origin: *Thorn bush*)

(Ezra 2:50). Unspecified date. Asnah was an ancestor of a clan of Temple servants that returned with Zerubbabel from the Babylonian Exile.

Asnapper

(Assyrian origin: Uncertain meaning)

(Ezra 4:10). 8th century B.C. King Asnapper of Assyria, known by historians as Ashurbanipal, was the son of King Esarhaddon. Asnapper continued the policy of his father and settled foreign tribes in Samaria, to replace the Israelites who had been deported, when the kingdom of Israel was conquered by the Assyrians.

Aspatha

(Persian origin: Uncertain meaning)

(Esther 9:7). 5th century B.C. Aspatha was one of the ten sons of Haman, the vizier of Persia who wanted to kill all the Jews in the kingdom. His brothers were Parshandatha, Arisai, Dalphon, Poratha, Adalia, Aridatha, Parmashta, Aridai, and Vajezatha. All of them were executed, when Haman's plot against the Jews backfired.

Asriel

(Hebrew origin: *Right of God*)

(Numbers 26:31). 17th century B.C. Asriel and Machir were the two sons of Manasseh and his Aramean concubine. Asriel was the ancestor of the clan of the Asrielites. Alternative name is Ashriel in First Chronicles (1 Chronicles 7:14).

Asshur

(Hebrew origin: *To be straight*)

(Genesis 10:11). Unspecified date. Asshur was the son of Shem and grandson of Noah. Asshur was the founder of Nineveh and the ancestor of the Assyrians. His brothers were Elam, Arphaxad, Lud, Aram, Uz, Hul, Gether, and Meshech.

Asshurim

(Hebrew origin: Uncertain meaning)

(Genesis 25:3). Unspecified date. Asshurim, son of Dedan, was a descendant of Abraham and Keturah, the woman whom Abraham married, after Sarah died. Asshurim's brothers were Letushim and Leummim.

Assir

(Hebrew origin: *Captive*)

1. (Exodus 6:24). 13th century B.C. Assir was one of the sons of Korah, the Levite who led the rebellion against Moses in the wilderness. The sons of Korah were not punished, when their father was swallowed by the earth, in punishment for his rebellion against Moses.
2. (1 Chronicles 3:17). 6th century B.C. Assir—meaning *Captive* in Hebrew—is not a proper name in this case. The word refers to the king Jeconiah, whom the Babylonians took captive.
3. (1 Chronicles 6:23). 13th century B.C. Assir, son of Ebiasaph, was the father of Tahath. His descendant Heman, of the clan of the Kohathites, was one of the Levites appointed by King David to be in charge of the singers in the House of the Lord.

Asyncritus

(Greek origin: *Incomparable*)

(Romans 16:14). A.D. 1st century. Asyncritus was a Christian to whom Paul sent greetings in his letter to the Christians in Rome.

The apostle mentioned him in the same verse with four other men—Phlegon, Hermas, Patrobas, and Hermes—and "the brothers who were with them", which gives grounds to think that Asyncritus and his companions formed a small separate group within the larger Christian community of Rome.

Atarah

(Hebrew origin: *Crown*)

(1 Chronicles 2:26). Unspecified date. Atarah was the second wife of Jerahmeel, of the tribe of Judah. She was the mother of Onam and the grandmother of Shammai and Jada.

Ater

(Hebrew origin: *Maimed*)

1. (Ezra 2:16). Unspecified date. Ater was an ancestor of a family who returned with Zerubbabel from the Babylonian Exile.
2. (Ezra 2:42). Unspecified date. Ater was an ancestor of a clan of gatekeepers who returned with Zerubbabel from the Babylonian Exile.
3. (Nehemiah 10:17). 5th century B.C. Ater was one of the leaders who signed Nehemiah's solemn agreement to separate themselves from the foreigners living in the land, to refrain from intermarrying with them, and to dedicate their firstborn to God, among other obligations.

Athaiah

(Hebrew origin: *God has helped*)

(Nehemiah 11:4). 6th century B.C. Athaiah, son of Uzziah, of the tribe of Judah, was the leader of a clan that settled in Jerusalem, after they returned from the Babylonian Exile. The first book of Chronicles (1 Chronicles 9:4) calls him Uthai, son of Ammihud.

Athaliah

(Hebrew origin: *God has constrained*)

1. (2 Kings 8:26). 9th century B.C. Athaliah was the only sovereign of Judah, who did not descend from King David, and the only female monarch that the kingdoms of Judah and Israel ever had.

She was the daughter of King Omri of Israel and the sister of King Ahab—some historians say that she was the daughter of King Ahab—whose marriage to Jehoram—also spelled Joram—crown prince of Judah, sealed the alliance between Israel and Judah.

Her husband Jehoram, who ruled for eight years, died at the age of forty. He was succeeded by his twenty-two-year-old son Ahaziah, who died one year later, killed by Jehu in the course of the anti-Omride revolt in the northern kingdom of Israel.

When Athaliah, the queen mother, heard that her son, the king, had died, she decided to grab power for herself and gave orders to kill all the members of the royal family. Only Joash, an infant son of Ahaziah, survived, hidden in a chamber of the Temple by his aunt Jehosheba, a sister of Ahaziah and the wife of the High Priest Jehoiada.

During her six years rule, Athaliah promoted the cult of the Phoenician god Baal. This provoked the hate of the priesthood and the people, who saw in her a foreign usurper and the murderer of the royal Davidic line.

When Joash was seven years old, the High Priest Jehoiada conspired with several army officers to dethrone Athaliah. Jehoiada proclaimed publicly in the Temple that Jehoash was the legitimate king, placed a crown on the boy's head, and anointed him.

Athaliah heard the crowd shouting, "God save the king", and rushed to the Temple, screaming, "Treason! Treason!" The guards seized her and killed her at the Horse Gate of the palace. The crowd assaulted the Temple of Baal, killed Mattan, the pagan High Priest, and destroyed the building and the idols.

2. (1 Chronicles 8:26). Unspecified date. Athaliah, son of Jeroham, was a leader of the tribe of Benjamin who lived in Jerusalem.

3. (Ezra 8:7). 5th century B.C. His son Jeshaiah, of the clan of Elam, returned with Ezra from Babylon, at the head of seventy males of his clan.

Athlai

(Hebrew origin: *God has constrained*)

(Ezra 10:28). 5th century B.C. Athlai, descendant of Bebai, was one of the men who had married foreign women, during the time of Ezra, and who gave his word that he would divorce her.

Attai

(Hebrew origin: *Timely*)

1. (1 Chronicles 2:35). Unspecified date. Attai was the son of an Egyptian called Jarha, who had married the daughter of his master Sheshan, a leader of the tribe of Judah. Attai's son was called Nathan.

2. (1 Chronicle 12:11). 11th century B.C. Attai was a Gadite warrior who joined David at Ziklag, while he was still hiding from King Saul.

3. (2 Chronicles 11:20). 10th century B.C. Attai was one of the sons of King Rehoboam and his favorite wife Maachah, the daughter of Absalom. His brothers were Abijah, who succeeded King Rehoboam, Ziza, and Shelomith.

Augustus

(Latin origin: *Title of the Roman emperors*)

(Luke 2:1). A.D. 1st century. The name Augustus was the title given in 27 B.C. to Octavian, the first Roman emperor, and one of the great administrative geniuses of history.

Octavian, who was born in 63 B.C., was the grand nephew of Julius Caesar, who had adopted him and made him his heir. In the power struggle that followed Caesar's assassination, he overcame his rivals and became, in 31 B.C., the ruler of the Greek-Roman world, which he governed, until his death in A.D. 14. He was succeeded by his stepson, Tiberius.

Although Luke mentions that Augustus decreed the census, which required the presence of Joseph and Mary in Bethlehem, it is more likely that this census was ordered by King Herod, who was the effective ruler of Judea at that time. Judea came under direct Roman rule only, after the death of Herod.

Azaliah

(Hebrew origin: *God has reserved*)

(2 Kings 22:3). 7th century B.C. Azaliah, son of Meshullam, was the father of Shaphan, King Josiah's scribe.

His great grandson, Gedaliah, the son of Ahikam, is a tragic figure in the history of the

Jewish people, who, even today, observe the anniversary of his death as a day of fasting and mourning.

Due to his family's well-known policy of moderation and submission to Babylon, Gedaliah was appointed governor of Judah by the Babylonian King Nebuchadnezzar. A few months later, he was murdered by Ishmael, son of Nethaniah, who probably hoped to start an uprise against the Babylonians by his bloody act.

Azaniah

(Hebrew origin: *God heard*)

(Nehemiah 10:9). 5th century B.C. His son Jeshua was one of the Levites who signed Nehemiah's solemn agreement to separate themselves from the foreigners living in the land, to refrain from intermarrying with them, and to dedicate their firstborn to God, among other obligations.

Azarael

(Hebrew origin: *God has helped*)

(Nehemiah 12:36). 5th century B.C. Azarael was one of the priests who played musical instruments, marching behind Ezra the Scribe, in the joyful procession, which celebrated the dedication of the rebuilt walls of Jerusalem, during the days of Nehemiah.

Azareel

(Hebrew *God has helped*)

1. (1 Chronicles 12:6). 11th century B.C. Azareel, a Korhite, was one of the men who deserted King Saul's army and joined David's band at Ziklag. These men were skilled warriors who could use both their right and left hands to shoot arrows and sling stones.

2. (1 Chronicles 25:18). 10th century B.C. Azareel—also called Uzziel (1 Chronicles 25:4)—a Levite, member of a family of musicians, was in charge of the eleventh turn of service that played musical instruments—cymbals, psalteries, and harps—in the House of God, during the reign of

David. (For more detailed information, please see the entry for Uzziel.)

3. (1 Chronicles 27:22). 10th century B.C. Azareel, son of Jeroham, was the leader of the tribe of Dan, during the reign of King David.

4. (Ezra 10:41). 5th century B.C. This man divorced his foreign wife, during the days of Ezra.

5. (Nehemiah 11:13). 6th century B.C. Azareel, son of Ahasai, was the father of Amashai, one of the priests who settled in Jerusalem, after the return from the Babylonian Exile.

Azariah

(Hebrew origin: *God has helped*)

1. (1 Kings 4:2). 10th century B.C. Azariah, son of the High Priest Zadok, was a court official in the court of King Solomon.

2. (1 Kings 4:5). 10th century B.C. Azariah, son of the prophet Nathan, was one of the top administrators in the court of King Solomon. He was in charge of the twelve officials of the king who provided the food for the king and the royal household, each one of them for one month out of each year. His brother Zabud, another of Solomon's principal officials, is called the king's friend.

3. (2 Kings 14:21). 8th century B.C. Azariah—also called Uzziah—the ninth king of Judah, after the partition of the United Monarchy, ruled the kingdom of Judah, for fifty-two years, a period that included the years when he was coregent with his father Amaziah, during his youth, and with his son Jotham, during his old age, when he suffered of leprosy.

His mother was Jecholiah from Jerusalem. His wife was Jerushah, daughter of Zadok. Azariah succeeded to the throne at the age of sixteen, after his father was murdered by conspirators in the city of Lachish.

His reign was one of the most successful in the history of Judah. He defeated the Philistines, completed the conquest of

Edom, including the harbor of Elath, subjugated the Arab tribes in the border, and received tribute from the Ammonites.

Azariah undertook a vast construction program of fortifications, dug many water wells, and greatly expanded agriculture. He paid special attention to the army, reorganized it, increased its size to over three hundred thousand men, and equipped it with new weapons.

The preaching of the prophets Isaiah, Hosea, Amos, and Zechariah, during Azariah's reign, allowed the nation to achieve great spiritual heights.

A great earthquake, which was mentioned by the prophets Amos and Zechariah, caused much damage, during his reign.

The king got into conflict with the priesthood, when he tried to perform the religious ritual of burning incense in the Temple. He became a leper and had to be isolated for the remainder of his life. His son and successor, Jotham, became regent and governed the country under his father's direction, until Azariah died at the age of sixty-eight.

4. (1 Chronicles 2:8). Unspecified date. Azariah, son of Ethan and grandson of Zerah, was a leader of the tribe of Judah.

5. (1 Chronicles 2:38). Unspecified date. Azariah, son of Jehu and grandson of Obed, of the tribe of Judah, was a descendant of Jarha, an Egyptian servant who married the daughter of his master Sheshan. Azariah's son was called Helez.

6. (1 Chronicles 6:9). 11th century B.C. Azariah, son of Ahimaaz and father of Johanan, was the grandfather of his namesake Azariah (Please see the next entry.), the High Priest, during the reign of Solomon.

7. (1 Chronicles 6:10). 10th century B.C. Azariah, son of Johanan, was the High Priest, during the reign of Solomon. He was the father of Amariah and an ancestor of Ezra the Scribe. He was the grandson of his namesake Azariah (Please see the previous entry.).

8. (1 Chronicles 6:13). 7th century B.C. Azariah, son of Hilkiah and father of

Seraiah, was the grandfather of Jehozadak, the High Priest who was sent into captivity, by Nebuchadnezzar, when the Babylonians conquered the kingdom of Judah. Azariah's son Seraiah was taken to the presence of Nebuchadnezzar, who had him beaten and put to death.

9. (1 Chronicles 6:36). Unspecified date. Azariah, a Levite, father of Joel, was the son of Zephaniah and the grandson of Tahath, a descendant of Kohath. His descendant Heman, of the clan of the Kohathites, was one of the Levites appointed by King David to be in charge of the singers in the House of the Lord.

10. (1 Chronicles 9:11). 5th century B.C. Azariah, son of Hilkiah, a descendant of Ahitub, was the priest in charge of the Temple in the days of Nehemiah. He is called Seraiah in the book of Nehemiah (Nehemiah 11:11).

11. (2 Chronicles 15:1). 9th century B.C. Azariah, son of Oded, prophesied to King Asa, when he returned victorious over Zerah the Ethiopian, that God would be with him, as long as the king would not forsake God.

12. (2 Chronicles 21:2). 9th century B.C. Azariah was the name of two princes, sons of King Jehoshaphat, who received from their father great gifts of gold, silver, and fenced cities. When Jehoshaphat died, his firstborn son Jehoram ascended to the throne and killed all his brothers.

13. (2 Chronicles 22:6). 9th century B.C. King Ahaziah of Judah, son of King Jehoram, is called Azariah in this verse. (Please see the entry for Ahaziah [2 Kings 8:24].)

14. (2 Chronicles 23:1). 9th century B.C. Azariah was the name of two army commanders: one was the son of Jehoram, and the other was the son of Obed. The two men joined the conspiracy, headed by Jehoiada the Priest, that overthrew Queen Athaliah and crowned Joash as king of Judah.

15. (2 Chronicles 26:17). 8th century B.C. Azariah, the High Priest, at the head of eighty priests, confronted King Azariah—

also called Uzziah—for daring to try to perform religious rituals—the king wanted to burn incense upon the altar of incense in the Temple—that only the priests descendants of Aaron were allowed to do. The king angrily wanted to proceed with the incense burning but was struck by leprosy and expelled from the Temple.

16. (2 Chronicles 28:12). 8th century B.C. During the war of King Pekah of Israel against King Ahaz of Judah, the Israelite army defeated Judah and brought tens of thousands of prisoners back to Samaria with the intention of making them slaves.

Azariah, the son of Johanan, was one of the leaders of the tribe of Ephraim who supported the prophet Oded in his demand to free the captives and return them to Judah. Azariah and his companions took charge of the prisoners, gave them clothing and shoes, food and drink, and took them back to the city of Jericho in Judah.

17. (2 Chronicles 29:12). 8th century B.C. His son Joel, a descendant of Kohath, was one of the Levites who assembled all the other Levites to make themselves ritually clean, and to purify the Temple, during the reign of King Hezekiah of Judah.

18. (2 Chronicles 29:12). 8th century B.C. Azariah, son of Jehalelel, a descendant of Merari, was one of the Levites who assembled all the other Levites to make themselves ritually clean, and to purify the Temple, during the reign of King Hezekiah of Judah.

19. (2 Chronicles 31:10). 8th century B.C. Azariah, who held the position of High Priest, during the reign of Hezekiah, told the king that the priests had more than enough to eat, because the people were bringing offerings to the Temple. The king, after hearing Azariah's report, commanded him to prepare chambers in the Temple to store the offerings and tithes.

20. (Ezra 7:1). 6th century B.C. Azariah was the son of Hilkiah and descendant of Aaron. His son Seraiah was the father of Ezra the Scribe.

21. (Ezra 7:3). Unspecified date. Azariah was the son of Meraioth and father of Amariah. He was a descendant of Aaron and an ancestor of Ezra the Scribe.

22. (Nehemiah 3:23). 5th century B.C. Azariah, son of Maaseiah, repaired the part of the walls of Jerusalem that was opposite his house in the days of Nehemiah.

23. (Nehemiah 7:7). 6th century B.C. Azariah was one of the men who returned with Zerubbabel from the Babylonian captivity. He is called Seraiah in the book of Ezra (Ezra 2:2).

24. (Nehemiah 8:7). 5th century B.C. Azariah was one of the Levites who explained the Law to the people, after Ezra the Scribe had read it, while standing on a wooden platform, in front of the open space, before the Water Gate.

25. (Nehemiah 10:2). 5th century B.C. Azariah was one of the priests who signed Nehemiah's solemn agreement to separate themselves from the foreigners living in the land, to refrain from intermarrying with them, and to dedicate their firstborn to God, among other obligations.

26. (Nehemiah 12:33). 5th century B.C. Azariah was one of the leaders of the people who marched in the joyful procession, which celebrated the dedication of the rebuilt walls of Jerusalem, during the days of Nehemiah.

27. (Jeremiah 43:2). 6th century B.C. Azariah, son of Hoshaiah; his brother Jezaniah; and Johanan, son of Kareah, were leaders of the defeated army of Judah. Azariah accused Jeremiah of lying, when the prophet said that God wanted the survivors to stay in Judah and not flee to Egypt.

28. (Daniel 1:6). 6th century B.C. Azariah was a young boy from a noble Jewish family in Babylon, who was chosen, together with his companions Daniel, Hananiah, and Mishael, to receive an education that would prepare them to become officials of the king's court.

Azariah was given the Babylonian name of Abednego by the chief of the eunuchs of King Nebuchadnezzar.

In order not to transgress by eating and drinking ritually forbidden food and wine, the boys received permission from Melzar, the man who had been placed in charge of them, to eat only legumes and drink only water. Melzar feared that this diet could endanger their health, but they asked him to let them try it for ten days.

When the ten days were over, the four Jewish boys looked better and healthier than the boys who had eaten of the king's food.

During the three following years, the four boys acquired knowledge and skill, and Daniel learned to interpret the significance of visions and dreams. The king examined them and found them to be ten times better than all the magicians and astrologers in the kingdom.

Years later, at the request of Daniel, the king appointed Mishael, Hananiah and Azariah to be in charge over the affairs of the province of Babylon.

When the three men refused to serve the Babylonian gods or worship the golden idol that the king had set up, they were thrown into a burning furnace but were saved by an angel.

Nebuchadnezzar was so impressed that the three men were able to survive the fire without even one hair of their heads being singed, that he blessed God and decreed that, from then on, anyone who would dare speak against God would be cut in pieces, and his house would be turned into a dunghill.

Azaz

(Hebrew origin: *Strong*)

(1 Chronicles 5:8). Unspecified date. Azaz, son of Shema, of the tribe of Reuben, was the father of Bela.

Azaziah

(Hebrew origin: *God has strengthened*)

1. (1 Chronicles 15:21). 10th century B.C. Azaziah was one of the Levites who accom-

panied the Ark from the house of Obededom to its resting place in Jerusalem, singing and playing harps.

2. (1 Chronicles 27:20). 10th century B.C. Azaziah was the father of Hoshea, a leader of the tribe of Ephraim, during the reign of King David.

3. (2 Chronicles 31:13). 8th century B.C. Azaziah was one of the Levites named by King Hezekiah to serve under Cononiah and Shimei, as supervisors of the gifts, tithes, and offerings, brought by the people to the Temple.

Azbuk

(Hebrew origin: *Stern depopulator*)

(Nehemiah 3:16). 5th century B.C. His son Nehemiah ruled half the district of Beth-Zur and helped to repair the walls of Jerusalem, during the days of Nehemiah, the governor of Jerusalem.

Azel

(Hebrew origin: *Noble*)

(1 Chronicles 8:37). Unspecified date. Azel, son of Eleasah, of the tribe of Benjamin, a descendant of King Saul, was the father of six sons: Azrikam, Bocheru, Ishmael, Sheariah, Obadiah, and Hanan.

Azgad

(Hebrew origin: *Stern troop*)

1. (Ezra 2:12). Unspecified date. Azgad was an ancestor of a large family that returned with Zerubbabel from the Babylonian Exile. His descendant Johanan, son of Hakkatan, returned with Ezra to Judah, with another hundred and ten men (Ezra 8:12).

2. (Nehemiah 10:15). 5th century B.C. He was one of the leaders who signed Nehemiah's solemn agreement to separate themselves from the foreigners living in the land, to refrain from intermarrying with them, and to dedicate their firstborn to God, among other obligations.

Aziel

(Hebrew origin: *Strengthened by God*)

(1 Chronicles 15:20). 10th century B.C. Aziel, a Levite of the second rank—called Jaaziel in First Chronicles (1 Chronicles 15:18)—was chosen by the chief of the Levites to sing and play musical instruments in front of the Ark of the Covenant, when, by King David's order, it was carried from the house of Obededom to its resting place in Jerusalem.

Aziza

(Hebrew origin: *Strengthfulness*)

(Ezra 10:27). 5th century B.C. Aziza, descendant of Zattu, divorced his foreign wife, during the days of Ezra.

Azmaveth

(Hebrew origin: *Strong as death*)

1. (2 Samuel 23:31) 11th century B.C. Azmaveth the Barhumite was one of King David's mighty warriors. His sons Jeziel and Pelet joined David's band in Ziklag.
2. (1 Chronicles 8:36). Unspecified date. Azmaveth, a son of Jehoadah, of the tribe of Benjamin, was a descendant of King Saul. His brothers were Alemeth and Zimri. His father Jehoadah is called Jarah in First Chronicles (1 Chronicles 9:42).
3. (1 Chronicles 27:25). 10th century B.C. Azmaveth, son of Adiel, was King David's treasurer.

Azor

(Hebrew origin: *Helper*)

(Matthew 1:13). Unspecified date. Azor, a descendant of Zorobabel—alternative spelling for Zerubbabel—was an ancestor of Jesus, in Matthew's genealogy.

Azriel

(Hebrew origin: *God helped me*)

1. (1 Chronicles 5:24). Unspecified date. Azriel, a member of the half tribe of Manasseh that had settled east of the Jordan River, was a mighty warrior and leader of his clan.

    His tribe was deported from their land by the Assyrians and forcibly settled in the region of the river Gozan, where it eventually assimilated into the local population and disappeared from history, being remembered today as one of the "ten lost tribes".
2. (1 Chronicles 27:19). 10th century B.C. His son Jerimoth was the leader of the tribe of Naphtali, during the reign of King David.
3. (Jeremiah 36:26). 7th century B.C. His son Seraiah, a court official of King Jehoiakim, was one of the men ordered by the king to arrest Jeremiah and Baruch, the prophet's trusted companion. They failed in their mission, because Jeremiah and Baruch had gone into hiding.

Azrikam

(Hebrew origin: *My help has arisen*)

1. (1 Chronicles 3:23). Unspecified date. Azrikam, son of Neariah, was a descendant of Jeconiah—also called Jehoiachin—the king of Judah, who was taken to captivity in Babylon. Azrikam's brothers were Elioenai and Hezekiah.
2. (1 Chronicles 8:38). Unspecified date. Azrikam was one of the six sons of Azel, son of Eleasah, of the tribe of Benjamin, a descendant of King Saul. His brothers were Bocheru, Ishmael, Sheariah, Obadiah, and Hanan.
3. (1 Chronicles 9:14). 6th century B.C. Azrikam, son of Hashabiah, descendant of Merari, was the father of Hashub. His grandson Shemaiah was one of the first Levites to settle in Jerusalem, after the return from the Babylonian Exile.
4. (2 Chronicles 28:7). 8th century B.C. Azrikam, governor of the palace of King Ahaz of Judah, was killed in battle by Zichri, a commander of King Pekah's army, during a war between the two countries.

Azubah

(Hebrew origin: *Forsaken*)

1. (1 Kings 22:42). 9th century B.C. Azubah, daughter of Shilhi, wife of Asa, was the mother of Jehoshaphat, king of Judah.

2. (1 Chronicles 2:18). Unspecified date. Azubah was one of the two wives of Caleb, the son of Hezron, a descendant of Judah. After her death, Caleb married Ephrath. Azubah's sons were Jesher, Shobab, and Ardon.

Azur

(Hebrew origin: *Helpful*)

1. (Jeremiah 28:1). 7th century B.C. Azur was the father of Hananiah, the Gibeonite, a false prophet who predicted the immediate defeat of Babylon and the return of the captives, together with the vessels that Nebuchadnezzar had taken away from the Temple. Jeremiah told Hananiah that, in punishment for his lies, he would die within a year.

2. (Ezekiel 11:1). 6th century B.C. Azur was the father of Jaazaniah, a leader of the people, whom the prophet Ezekiel, in a vision, saw at the gate of the Temple, falsely telling the people that the city would not be destroyed.

Azzan

(Hebrew origin: *Strong one*)

(Numbers 34:26). 14th century B.C. His son Phaltiel was the leader of the tribe of Issachar, chosen by Moses, to help apportion the land of Canaan among the tribes.

Azzur

(Hebrew origin: *Helpful*)

(Nehemiah 10:17). 5th century B.C. Azzur was one of the leaders who signed Nehemiah's solemn agreement to separate themselves from the foreigners living in the land, to refrain from intermarrying with them, and to dedicate their firstborn to God, among other obligations.

Baal

(Hebrew origin: *Canaanite god; master; possessor; husband*)

1. (Numbers 22:41). Baal was the god of the Canaanites and the Phoenicians. The cult of Baal remained widespread, throughout the period of the First Temple, and was aggressively denounced by the prophets. Through the influence of Queen Jezebel, a Phoenician princess, it became the court religion, during the reign of King Ahab.

   The worship of Baal was bitterly opposed by the prophet Elijah, who, on one opportunity, confronted four hundred and fifty priests of Baal on Mount Carmel, and had them slain. Later, King Jehu, after taking over the throne, massacred the followers of Baal.
2. (1 Chronicles 5:5). 8th century B.C. Baal, son of Reaia, was the father of Beerah, a leader of the tribe of Reuben who was carried away captive by Tilgathpilneser, king of Assyria.
3. (1 Chronicles 8:30). 11th century B.C. Baal, of the tribe of Benjamin, was the son of Jehiel, the founder of Gibeon, who was married to Maachah.

Baalberith

(Hebrew origin: *Lord of the Covenant*)

(Judges 8:33). Baalberith was a Canaanite god worshipped in Shechem, during the days of Abimelech, son of Gideon. Abimelech's uncles gave him silver from Baalberith's Temple, which he used to hire mercenaries.

Baalhanan

(Hebrew origin: *Possessor of grace* or *Baal was merciful*)

1. (Genesis 36:38). Unspecified date. Baalhanan, son of Achbor, succeeded Saul, of Rehoboth by the river, as king of Edom,

and was himself succeeded by Hadar.
2. (1 Chronicles 27:28). 10th century B.C. Baalhanan, the Gederite, was the official in charge of the olive trees and the sycamore trees that were in the low plains, during the reign of King David.

Baalis

(Hebrew origin: *In exultation* or *Son of delight*)

(Jeremiah 40:14). 6th century B.C. Baalis was the king of the Ammonites, during the days of the prophet Jeremiah. He sent Ishmael, son of Nethaniah, to assassinate Gedaliah, the Jewish governor of Judah under the Babylonian occupation.

Baalpeor

(Hebrew origin: *Lord of the opening* or *Baal of Mount Peor*)

(Numbers 25:3). Baalpeor was a Canaanite god, who was worshipped by the Midianites on the mountain of the same name. The Israelites in the desert worshipped this deity and ate the sacrifices of the dead (Psalm 106:28). God sent a plague to punish them for their immoral behavior with the daughters of Moab and their sacrifices to the pagan god Baalpeor. The plague ceased, when Phinehas killed Zimri and Cozbi, a Midianite woman, whom Zimri had brought to his tent.

Baalzebub

(Hebrew origin: *God of the flies*)

(2 Kings 1:2). Baalzebub was the god of the Philistine city of Ekron. When King Ahaziah of Israel fell from a second floor and was seriously hurt, he sent messengers to Ekron to inquire of Baalzebub if he would recover.

The prophet Elijah intercepted the messengers and asked them, "Is there not a God in Israel that you must go to Ekron and inquire from their god?" The prophet added that the king would die.

Baal is called Beelzebub, "the Prince of the Devils", in the New Testament (Matthew 12:24), another name for Satan.

Baana

(Hebrew origin: *In affliction*)

1. (1 Kings 4:12). 10th century B.C. Baana was the son of Ahilud and brother of Jehoshaphat. As one of King Solomon's twelve district governors, in charge of a district that included the region from Megiddo to Beth-Shean, he was responsible for providing food from his district for the king and the royal household for one month each year.

   His brother Jehoshaphat was the court recorder for King David and, later, held the same position under King Solomon.

2. (Nehemiah 3:4). 5th century B.C. His son Zadok helped to rebuild the walls of Jerusalem, during the days of Nehemiah.

Baanah

(Hebrew origin: *In affliction*)

1. (2 Samuel 4:2). 11th century B.C. Baanah and his brother Rechab, of the tribe of Benjamin, sons of Rimmon from Beeroth, were captains in the army of King Ishbosheth, the son and heir of King Saul.

   The two brothers came to the royal palace at noontime, found Ishbosheth lying on his bed, beheaded him, and brought his head to David in Hebron, expecting to be rewarded.

   David's reaction was not what the two murderers had expected. He said to them, "The man who told me that Saul was dead thought that he was bringing me good news. Instead of rewarding him, I had him killed. How much more then, when wicked men have killed a blameless man in bed in his own house?! I will avenge his blood on you, and I will rid the earth of you!"

   The king ordered his men to kill the murderers, cut off their hands and feet, and hang them up by the pool in Hebron. The head of Ishbosheth was buried in the sepulcher of Abner in Hebron.

2. (2 Samuel 23:29). 11th century B.C. Baanah, a Netophathite, was the father of Heleb—also called Heled (1 Chronicles 11:30). His son was one of "The Thirty", an elite army group of warriors in King David's army.

3. (1 Kings 4:16). 10th century B.C. Baanah was the son of Hushai, King David's loyal friend and advisor. As one of King Solomon's twelve district governors, in charge of the territories of Asher and Aloth, he was responsible for providing food from his district for the king and the royal household for one month each year.

4. (Ezra 2:2). 6th century B.C. Baanah was one of the men who returned with Zerubbabel from the Babylonian Exile.

5. (Nehemiah 10:27). 5th century B.C. Baanah was one of the leaders of the people who signed with Nehemiah a solemn agreement to separate themselves from the foreigners living in the land, to refrain from intermarrying with them, and to dedicate their firstborn to God, among other obligations.

Baara

(Hebrew origin: *Brutish* or contraction of *Baal sees*)

(1 Chronicles 8:8). Unspecified date. Baara was the wife of Shaharaim, a descendant of Benjamin. Her husband Shaharaim sent her and Hushim, his other wife, away. He then settled in the land of Moab, east of the river Jordan, and married Hodesh with whom he had seven children, Jobab, Zibia, Mesha, Malcham, Jeuz, Shachia, and Mirma.

Baaseiah

(Hebrew origin: *Work of God*)

(1 Chronicles 6:40). Unspecified date. Baaseiah, of the clan of the Kohathites, was the son of Malchiah and the father of Michael. His descendant Asaph was one of the Levites appointed by King David, to be in charge of the singers, in the House of the Lord, from the time when the Ark came to rest in Jerusalem.

Baasha

(Hebrew origin: *Offensiveness*)

(1 Kings 15:16). 10th century B.C. Baasha,

son of Ahijah, of the tribe of Issachar, was the third king of Israel, after the division of the kingdom. He conspired against King Nadab who had succeeded his father Jeroboam only two years before.

Baasha killed Nadab, liquidated all the other descendants of Jeroboam, and took over the throne. Israel, during his reign, was in constant war with Judah. Baasha fortified Ramah in order to blockade Judah. Asa of Judah took all the silver and gold that were left in the treasures of the Temple and sent them to Benhadad, king of Syria, begging him for help against Baasha. Baasha retreated, and Asa used the construction materials, which Baasha had left in Ramah to build Geba and Mizpah.

Baasha's capital was Tirzah, where he was buried, after having reigned twenty-four years. His son Elah, a drunkard, succeeded him and reigned for only two years, until Zimri, the commander of the army, murdered him.

Bakbakkar

(Hebrew origin: *Searcher*)

(1 Chronicles 9:15). 6th century B.C. Bakbakkar was one of the first Levites to settle in the land of Judah, after the return from the Babylonian Exile.

Bakbuk

(Hebrew origin: *Bottle*)

(Ezra 2:51). Unspecified date. Bakbuk was the ancestor of a clan of Temple servants that returned with Zerubbabel from the Babylonian Exile.

Bakbukiah

(Hebrew origin: *God's bottle*)

1. (Nehemiah 11:17). 5th century B.C. Bakbukiah, a Levite, lived in Jerusalem, during the days of Nehemiah. He was the second in command to Mattaniah, the Levite who led the thanksgiving prayers. Both Bakbukiah and Mattaniah were gate-keepers (Nehemiah 12:25).

2. (Nehemiah 12:9). 6th century B.C. Bakbukiah was a Levite who returned with Zerubbabel from the exile in Babylon.

Balaam

(Hebrew origin: *Not of the people* or *Foreigner*)

(Numbers 22:5). 13th century B.C. Balaam, son of Beor, was a seer from Aram, internationally famous for the effectiveness of his blessings and curses. Balak, king of Moab, afraid of the invading Israelites who vastly outnumbered Moab, asked Balaam to come and curse the people of Israel.

God told Balaam, in a vision, that he should not go with Balak's emissaries, but, after further urging from the messengers, God allowed him to go. Balaam mounted his female donkey and left with the messengers.

An angel, sent by the Lord, stood on the road with a drawn sword. The donkey saw the angel and swerved aside, refusing to continue, even when Balaam hit her with his stick. The donkey, granted by God the power to speak, complained to Balaam against his ill-treatment. Balaam's eyes were then opened, and he saw the angel, who told him that he could proceed with the men, but he was allowed to say only what the angel would tell him.

Balak, the king of Moab, came out to meet Balaam and reproached him for his reluctance to come. Balaam answered that he could only utter the words that God would put in his mouth.

The next day, Balak went up with Balaam to a high mountain, from where they could see the camp of the people of Israel. On Balaam's instructions, seven altars were built, and a bull and a ram were sacrificed in each of them.

Then, Balaam spoke. To Balak's surprise, Balaam uttered blessings for Israel, instead of curses. This same turn of events happened two more times: once on the top of Pisgah, and the other on the peak of Peor.

Balak, angry and disappointed, told Balaam to flee back to his land. Balaam's last words to Balak were a prophecy that Israel, one day, would triumph over Moab.

Balaam, instead of returning to his country,

stayed in the area and became involved with the Midianites. He suggested that the way to defeat Israel was to encourage the Israelites to be immoral and promiscuous. He paid with his life, when the Israelites defeated the Midianites in battle.

Balac

(Hebrew origin: *Waster*)

(Revelation 2:14). 13th century B.C. Balac is an alternative spelling for the name of Balak, the king of Moab who hired Balaam to curse the people of Israel.

Balak, son of Zippor, king of Moab, in the days of Moses, was terrified that the people of Israel, which had recently defeated the Amorites, would do the same to Moab.

Seeing that the people of Israel vastly outnumbered Moab, Balak asked the seer Balaam to come from his home in Aram, and curse the people of Israel. God told Balaam in a vision not to go with Balak's emissaries, but, after further urging, and with God's permission, he went with them.

Balak, the king of Moab, came out to meet Balaam and reproached him for his reluctance to come. Balaam answered that he could only utter the words that God would put in his mouth.

The next day, Balak went up with Balaam to a high mountain, from where they could see the camp of the people of Israel. On Balaam's instructions, seven altars were built, and a bull and a ram were sacrificed in each of them.

Then, Balaam spoke. To Balak's surprise, Balaam uttered blessings for Israel, instead of curses. This same turn of events happened two more times: once on the top of Pisgah, and the other on the peak of Peor.

Balak, angry and disappointed, told Balaam to flee back to his land. Balaam's last words to Balak were a prophecy that Israel, one day, would triumph over Moab.

Baladan

(Akkadian origin: *The god Bel is lord*)

(2 Kings 20:12). 8th century B.C. His son, King Berodachbaladan of Babylon—called

Merodachbaladan in the book of Isaiah (Isaiah 39:1)—sent presents to King Hezekiah of Judah, when he heard that Hezekiah was sick.

Hezekiah gave the Babylonian emissaries a royal welcome. Proudly, but naively, he showed them all his treasures, thinking that Babylon, such a far away country, could never become a possible threat to Judah.

The prophet Isaiah berated him, saying that, one day, everything in the palace would be carried off to Babylon.

Balak

(Hebrew origin: *Waster* or *God opened the mother's womb*)

(Numbers 22:2). 13th century B.C. Balak, son of Zippor, king of Moab, in the days of Moses, was terrified that the people of Israel, who had recently defeated the Amorites, would do the same to Moab.

Seeing that the people of Israel vastly outnumbered Moab, Balak asked the seer Balaam to come from his home in Aram, and curse the people of Israel. God told Balaam in a vision not to go with Balak's emissaries, but, after further urging, and with God's permission, he went with them.

Balak, the king of Moab, came out to meet Balaam and reproached him for his reluctance to come. Balaam answered that he could only utter the words that God would put in his mouth.

The next day, Balak went up with Balaam to a high mountain, from where they could see the camp of the people of Israel. On Balaam's instructions, seven altars were built, and a bull and a ram were sacrificed in each of them.

Then, Balaam spoke. To Balak's surprise, Balaam uttered blessings for Israel, instead of curses. This same turn of events happened two more times: once on the top of Pisgah, and the other on the peak of Peor.

Balak, angry and disappointed, told Balaam to flee back to his land. Balaam's last words to Balak were a prophecy that Israel, one day, would triumph over Moab.

An alternative spelling is Balac (Revelation 2:14).

Bani

(Hebrew origin: *Built* or *My son*)

1. (2 Samuel 23:36).10th century B.C. Bani the Gadite was one of "The Thirty", an elite army group in King David's army.

2. (1 Chronicles 6:46). Unspecified date. Bani, son of Shamer, was a descendant of Merari. His descendant Ethan was one of the Levites appointed by King David, to be in charge of the singers, in the House of the Lord, from the time when the Ark came to rest in Jerusalem.

3. (1 Chronicles 9:4). Unspecified date. His descendant Uthai was the leader of a clan that settled in Jerusalem, after they returned from the Babylonian Exile.

4. (Ezra 2:10). Unspecified date. Bani was the ancestor of a clan of Israelites who returned with Zerubbabel from Babylon. Several of his descendants divorced their foreign wives, during the days of Ezra. He is called Binnui in the book of Nehemiah (Nehemiah 7:15).

5. (Ezra 10:38). 5th century B.C. Bani divorced his foreign wife, during the days of Ezra.

6. (Nehemiah 3:17). 5th century B.C. His son Rehum was one of the Levites who helped to repair the walls of Jerusalem, during the days of Nehemiah.

7. (Nehemiah 8:7). 5th century B.C. Bani was one of the Levites who explained the Law to the people, after Ezra the Scribe had read it, while standing on a wooden platform, in front of the open space, before the Water Gate.

He also was one of the Levites who led the public worship, during the days of Nehemiah (Nehemiah 9:4).

Bani signed Nehemiah's solemn agreement where the people promised to separate themselves from the foreigners living in the land, to refrain from intermarrying with them, to dedicate their firstborn to God, and other obligations (Nehemiah 10:13).

8. (Nehemiah 10:14). 5th century B.C. Bani was one of the leaders who signed Nehemiah's solemn agreement where the people promised to separate themselves from the foreigners living in the land, to refrain from intermarrying with them, and to dedicate their firstborn to God, among other obligations.

9. (Nehemiah 11:22). 5th century B.C. Bani, son of Hashabiah, was the father of Uzzi, the overseer of the Levites in Jerusalem, during the days of Nehemiah.

Barabbas

(Hebrew origin: *Son of the father*)

(Matthew 27:16). A.D. 1st century. Barabbas, a notorious rebel, robber, and murderer, was a prisoner of the Romans, at the time when Jesus was arrested.

It was customary to release a prisoner to the crowds in honor of the Passover Festival. The Roman governor Pontius Pilate told the mob that he was willing to release either Barabbas or Jesus. The mob, persuaded by the chief priests and the elders, told Pilate to free Barabbas and crucify Jesus. Pilate reluctantly agreed to the crowd's request: Barabbas was freed, and Jesus was crucified.

Barachel

(Hebrew origin: *God will bless*)

(Job 32:2). Unspecified date. Barachel the Buzite was the father of Elihu, the youngest of Job's friends.

Barachias

(Derived from Hebrew origin: *God blessed*)

(Matthew 23:35). Unspecified date. His son, the prophet Zacharias, was murdered between the Temple and the altar, according to the words of Jesus.

Note: If Jesus refers to the post-Exilic prophet Zechariah, son of Berechiah and grandson of the prophet Iddo, this murder is not mentioned elsewhere in the Bible. The Old Testament does mention that a man called Zechariah, son of the priest Jehoiada, was stoned to death in the court of the Temple by the command of King Joash (2 Chronicles 24:20).

Barak

(Hebrew origin: *Lightning*)

(Judges 4:6). 12th century B.C. Barak, son of Abinoam, lived in the town of Kedesh in the Naphtali region.

The judge and prophetess Deborah ordered Barak to take ten thousand men from the tribes of Naphtali and Zebulun, and go to Mount Tabor to fight against Sisera, the commander of the army of King Jabin of Hazor.

Barak agreed with the condition that Deborah should go with him. Although Sisera had nine hundred iron chariots, Barak defeated him and utterly destroyed the Canaanite army.

Sisera fled on foot to the tent of Heber the Kenite, where he was killed in his sleep by Jael, Heber's wife.

Bariah

(Hebrew origin: *A bolt; fugitive*)

(1 Chronicles 3:22). Unspecified date. Bariah, son of Shemaiah, was the brother of Hattush, Igeal, Neariah, and Shaphat. Their ancestor, King Jehoiachin of Judah, was taken to captivity in Babylon, after reigning for only three months.

Barjesus

(Hebrew origin: *Son of Jesus*)

(Acts of the Apostles 13:6). A.D. 1st century. Barjesus—also called Elymas (Acts of the Apostles 13:8)—was a sorcerer and false prophet who lived in the city of Paphos in the island of Cyprus.

Sergius Paulus, the Roman proconsul of Cyprus, having learned that Paul was in the island, invited him to his quarters so that he could hear the word of God from his mouth. Barjesus, who was present in the meeting, attempted to refute Paul's arguments. The apostle turned to him, cursed him, and told him that he wouldn't be able to see the sun for a season. Barjesus immediately became blind and had to be lead outside by his hand.

This event so impressed the proconsul that he became a Christian believer.

Barjona

(Hebrew origin: *Son of Jona*)

(Matthew 16:17). A.D. 1st century. The original name of the apostle Peter was Simon Barjona, before Jesus called him Peter.

Barkos

(Hebrew origin: Uncertain meaning)

(Ezra 2:53). Unspecified date. Barkos was the ancestor of a clan of Temple servants that returned with Zerubbabel from the Babylonian Exile.

Barnabas

(Greek form of the Hebrew origin: *Son of prophecy*)

(Acts of the Apostles 4:36). A.D. 1st century. Barnabas—a name given by the apostles to Joses—a Jewish convert and Levite, "a good man, full of the Holy Ghost and faith", resided in the island of Cyprus.

The strength of his belief caused him to sell his land and give the money to the apostles. He eventually became Paul's most loyal helper and travel companion.

It was Barnabas who convinced the fearful and suspicious Jerusalem believers of the truth and sincerity of Paul's vision and conversion. He testified that Saul had seen the Lord in the road to Damascus, and that, during his stay in that city, he had preached courageously in the name of Jesus.

Barnabas was sent by the Jerusalem church to preach in Antioch. From there, he traveled to Tarsus and brought Paul back with him to Antioch, where they stayed for one year, preaching the word of God, and organizing the church. It was in Antioch that the believers in Jesus were first called Christians.

A prophet named Agabus, who recently arrived from Jerusalem, predicted that a severe famine was about to come over the entire world. The Antioch congregation decided that each of the believers would send as much as he could, to help their brothers in Judea, and gave the money that was collected to Barnabas and Paul, to take to Jerusalem.

Having accomplished their mission, Barnabas and Paul returned to Antioch, bringing with them a young man called John, whose surname was Mark.

After a short stay in Antioch, the leaders of the Christian community sent them off to preach the word of God in other lands.

The men went to Seleucia and sailed from there to the island of Cyprus. They arrived in Salamis and preached the word of God in the synagogues. They went all the way across the island to Paphos, where they met a sorcerer and false prophet named Barjesus—also called Elymas. This man tried to prevent Sergius Paulus, the Roman proconsul in the island, from hearing the preaching of Paul, and lost his sight, when the apostle cursed him and wished him to be blind. This event so impressed the proconsul that he became a Christian believer.

From Paphos, the three men sailed to the town of Perga in Pamphylia—in today's Anatolia, Turkey. There, John Mark left his companions and returned to Jerusalem. Paul and Barnabas continued to Antioch in Pisidia.

On the Sabbath, they went to the synagogue and sat down. After the public reading of the Law and the prophets, the rulers of the synagogue invited them to speak to the people. Paul stood up and gave a speech, summarizing the history of the people of Israel, from the time that God had freed them from slavery in Egypt, until the death and resurrection of Jesus. He told them that it was through Jesus that sins were forgiven.

When Paul finished speaking, the people invited them to come back the next Sabbath and tell them more. When the services were over, many Jews and Gentiles, who had been converted to Judaism, followed Paul and Barnabas, who spoke to them and encouraged them to continue in the grace of God.

The next Sabbath, the whole town came to the synagogue to hear the word of God. The Jews saw the multitude and were filled with jealousy. They argued with Paul and insulted him. Paul and Barnabas told them that, because they rejected the word of God, they would no longer preach in their synagogue, but they would go to the Gentiles.

The Gentiles, hearing this, were very happy and praised the word of God. The word of God spread throughout the region, and many converted. After the Jews incited the city authorities to persecute Paul and Barnabas and expel them from their region, Paul and Barnabas left the city and went to Iconium.

In Iconium, Paul and Barnabas went to the synagogue, preached, and made many Jewish and Gentile converts. The Jews who did not convert stirred up the Gentiles and turned them against the believers. Some of the people of the city were on the side of the Jews, others on the side of the apostles.

When the apostles heard that they were threatened with stoning, they fled to the Lycaonian cities of Lystra and Derbe, where they preached the gospel.

During the stay of Paul and Barnabas in Lystra, Paul noticed a cripple who had never walked in his life. He told the poor man, "Stand upright on your feet". The man jumped up and started walking around. This miracle so impressed the pagans in the city that they shouted in their local Lycaonian language, "The gods have come down to us in the shape of men", and excitedly exclaimed that Barnabas was Jupiter, and Paul, Mercurius. The priest of Jupiter brought oxen to sacrifice in front of them. Paul and Barnabas cried out that they were not gods but men and that the people of the city should turn away from idols and believe in the living God.

Some Jews from Antioch and Iconium, present at that moment, aroused the crowd, who stoned Paul, and dragged him out of the city, thinking that he was dead. The believers gathered around him and were relieved to see him get up and return to the town.

The next day, Barnabas and Paul went to Derbe, where they preached the gospel and made many new converts. Afterward, they again visited Lystra, Iconium, and Antioch on Pisidia, founding a congregation in each town. From Pisidia, they went to Pamphylia, Perga, and Attalia, and then they sailed to Antioch, where they stayed for a long time, converting the Gentiles.

Some men, who came from Judea, told the

believers that they could not be saved if previously they had not been circumcised according to the Law of Moses. Paul and Barnabas disagreed and fiercely argued with them. It was then decided that Paul, Barnabas, and some of the other leaders of the Antiochian church, including Titus, an uncircumcised Greek convert, should go to Jerusalem and consult with the apostles and the elders about this matter. Paul refused to circumcise Titus, who, thus, became a symbol of the apostle's determination to receive Gentiles into the church.

Back in Jerusalem, they were welcomed by the church, the apostles, and the elders, to whom they gave a full report of all their activities. Some believers, who belonged to the party of the Pharisees, stood up and stated that the Gentiles should be circumcised, and instructed to obey the Law of Moses.

After much discussion Peter stood up and said, "Brothers, you know that a long time ago God chose me from among you to preach the gospel to the Gentiles, so that they should hear and believe. God has given the Holy Spirit to the Gentiles as he had to us. There is no difference between them and us. Why put God to the test by imposing a burden on the backs of the believers, which neither we nor our ancestors were able to carry? We believe that we shall be saved through the grace of the Lord Jesus, just as they are".

The assembly kept silent, while Paul and Barnabas reported all the miracles and wonders that God had performed through them among the Gentiles. When they finished speaking, James stood and said, "Brothers, listen to me! Simon has explained how God showed his care for the Gentiles by taking out of them a people for his name. This agrees with the words of the prophets. Therefore, I suggest that we should not trouble the Gentiles. Instead, we should write to them that they should not eat food that has been offered to idols, that they should avoid sexual promiscuity, and not eat any animal that has been strangled, or any blood".

The apostles, elders, and the whole congregation chose two men—Judas, also called Barsabas, and Silas—to accompany Paul and Barnabas to Antioch, carrying a letter from the Jerusalem church to the Gentile believers in Antioch, Syria, and Cilicia, exonerating them of the need for circumcision, and asking them to abstain from food offered to idols, from blood, from eating strangled animals, and from sexual immorality. In Antioch, they gathered the congregation and read the letter, and Barsabas and Silas, who were themselves prophets, spoke a long time with the believers and gave them encouragement. Barsabas then returned to Jerusalem, but Silas stayed on for a while.

After sometime, Paul told Barnabas that they should visit all the cities where they had founded churches to see how they were doing. Barnabas wanted to take John Mark with them, but Paul opposed the idea. They could not agree and decided to separate. Barnabas and John Mark sailed to Cyprus, while Paul took Silas with him and left Antioch.

Barnabas and Paul parted their ways but continued to be in friendly relations, and Paul in his letters spoke very highly of Barnabas.

Barsabas

(Greek form of the Hebrew origin: *Son of Sabas* or *Son of the Sabbath*)

1. (Acts of the Apostles 1:23). A.D. 1st century. Joseph Barsabas, also called Justus, was one of the two candidates to replace Judas as the twelfth apostle. The apostles chose by lot Matthias, the other candidate.

2. (Acts of the Apostles 15:22). A.D. 1st century. Judas Barsabas and Silas, two prophets, were sent by the Jerusalem church, together with Paul and Barnabas, to Antioch, carrying a letter from the Jerusalem church to the Gentile believers in Antioch, Syria, and Cilicia, exonerating them of the need for circumcision, and asking them to abstain from food offered to idols, from blood, from eating strangled animals, and from sexual immorality.

   In Antioch, they gathered the congregation and read the letter. Barsabas and Silas spoke a long time with the believers and gave them encouragement. Barsabas then returned to Jerusalem, but Silas stayed in Antioch for a while.

Bartholomew

(Greek form of the Hebrew origin: *Son of Tolmai*)

(Matthew 10:3). A.D. 1st century. Scholars identify the apostles Nathanael and Bartholomew as being the same person, stating that the name Bartholomew was Nathanael's patronymic—i.e. a name derived from the name of a person's father or paternal ancestor. The complete name of the apostle would be, in this case, Nathanael, son of Tolmai. (Please see the entry for Nathanael [John 1:45].)

Bartimaeus

(Greek form of the Hebrew phrase: *Son of Timaeus*)

(Mark 10:46). A.D. 1st century. Bartimaeus, a blind pauper, was begging by the road to Jericho, when he was told that Jesus was passing by. He cried out, "Jesus, son of David, have mercy on me".

The people around tried to quiet him, but the blind wretch persisted in his cries. Jesus called Bartimaeus to his side and asked him what he wanted from him. The blind man asked to receive his sight back.

Jesus told him that his faith had made him whole. Bartimaeus immediately recovered his sight and followed Jesus.

Baruch

(Hebrew origin: *Blessed*)

1. (Nehemiah 3:20). 5th century B.C. Baruch, son of Zabbai, repaired a section of the walls of Jerusalem, from the place where the walls turned, until the door of the house of Eliashib the High Priest

2. (Nehemiah 10:6). 5th century B.C. Baruch was one of the priests who signed Nehemiah's solemn agreement to separate themselves from the foreigners living in the land, to refrain from intermarrying with them, and to dedicate their firstborn to God, among other obligations.

3. (Nehemiah 11:5). 5th century B.C. Baruch, son of Colhozeh, was a descendant of Perez of the tribe of Judah. His son Maaseiah

lived in Jerusalem, during the days of Nehemiah. His brother Shallun, the ruler of part of the district of Mizpah, during the days of Nehemiah, repaired the Gate of the Fountain, including the doors, locks, and bars of the gate, and the wall of the pool of Siloah.

4. (Jeremiah 32:12). 6th century B.C. Baruch, son of Neriah and grandson of Maaseiah, scribe and trusted companion of Jeremiah, wrote down the oracles of the prophet and was probably the author of the biographical narrative about Jeremiah.

His brother Seraiah, a high official of the court under King Zedekiah, accompanied the king on a royal visit to Babylon and, after the Babylonian destruction of Jerusalem, was sent to the Babylonian Exile.

During the reign of King Jehoiakim, Jeremiah dictated his prophecies to Baruch, who wrote them in a scroll. Jeremiah, who had been forbidden to go to the Temple, instructed Baruch to go to the House of God on a fast day, and read aloud the scroll, hoping that the listeners would repent from their evil ways.

Michaiah, son of Gemariah, heard Baruch's reading and reported it to an official of the court. Jehudi, son of Nethaniah, was ordered to bring Baruch to the palace. When Baruch arrived, he was told to sit and read the scroll. Disturbed by Jeremiah's prophecies, the officials decided to tell the king, and, knowing how Jehoiakim would react, they advised Baruch that he and Jeremiah should hide.

The scroll was read to King Jehoiakim, who burned it and commanded three of his officers to arrest Jeremiah and Baruch, but they could not find them. When Jeremiah heard that the king had burned the scroll, he again dictated his prophecies to Baruch, adding even more.

During the tenth year of King Zedekiah's reign, when Jerusalem was under siege by the Babylonians, Jeremiah, wishing to demonstrate his faith in the future of Israel, purchased a plot of land from his cousin Hanameel. Baruch witnessed the transaction and was given the Deed of Transfer to guard in an earthen vessel.

After the fall of Jerusalem to the Babylonians in 587 B.C., Jeremiah and Baruch were protected by the Babylonian commanders, who did not send them into exile. The two men found refuge in the city of Mizpah where Gedaliah, the Babylonian appointed governor of Judea, resided.

After Gedaliah was murdered, the remnant of the population, which had not been exiled, consulted Jeremiah whether they should stay in the land or escape to Egypt. Jeremiah advised them to stay.

The survivors suspected the prophet of giving this advice under Baruch's instigation, who, they believed, hated them and planned to place them at the mercy of the Babylonians. They fled to Egypt and forced Jeremiah and Baruch to go with them, against their will. It is likely that Baruch and Jeremiah lived their remaining days in Egypt and died there.

Barzillai

(Hebrew origin: *Iron maker* or *Man of iron*)
1. (2 Samuel 17:27). 10th century B.C. Barzillai, the Gileadite of Rogelim, was one of the men who showed kindness to David, when the king was fleeing from Absalom, bringing him utensils and food.

After King David's army had defeated the rebellion, the king invited Barzillai to come with him to Jerusalem. Barzillai, who was eighty years old, declined the offer, saying that he was an old man, and that all he wanted at that stage of his life was to die in his own city and be buried near the graves of his parents. Instead, he proposed that his son Chimham should go with the king.

The king gladly accepted, kissed Barzillai, blessed him, and returned to Jerusalem, taking Chimham with him.

Years later, in his dying bed, King David asked his son Solomon to show kindness to the sons of Barzillai, and to include them in his court.

During the days of Zerubbabel, the members of a clan who descended from one of the daughters of Barzillai were rejected as priests, because no proof of their claim was found in the records of the genealogy.

2. (2 Samuel 21:8). 11th century B.C. Barzillai, the Meholathite, was the father of Adriel, the man who married Merab, the daughter of King Saul.

The five sons of the couple were delivered, many years later, by King David to the Gibeonites, together with two other descendants of King Saul, to be hanged in revenge for King Saul's attempt to exterminate the people of Gibeon.

Bashemath

(Hebrew origin: *Fragrance*)
1. (Genesis 26:34). 18th century B.C. Bashemath, daughter of Elon, was one of the two Hittite women—the other one was Judith—whom Esau married, when he was forty years old. Both women made miserable the lives of Isaac and Rebekah. Bashemath—also called Adah in Genesis (Genesis 36:2)—was the mother of Eliphaz and grandmother of Amalek.

2. (Genesis 36:3). 18th century B.C. Bashemath, one of Esau's wives, was the daughter of Ishmael and the mother of Reuel. She is also called Mahalath (Genesis 28:9). Bashemath had twelve brothers: Nebajoth, Kedar, Mibsam, Mishma, Dumah, Massa, Hadad, Tema, Jetur, Naphish, Adbeel, and Kedemah, all of them ancestors of great nations.

Basmath

(Hebrew origin: *Fragrance*)
(1 Kings 4:15). 10th century B.C. Basmath, daughter of King Solomon, was married to Ahimaaz, one of the twelve officials in charge of providing food one month in the year for the king and the royal household.

Bathsheba

(Hebrew origin: *Daughter of an oath* or *Daughter of seven*)

(2 Samuel 11:3). 10th century B.C. Bathsheba was King David's favorite wife. Her first baby died in infancy, but her second son Solomon grew up to become a great and wise king. Her other sons were Shimea—also called Shammuah—Shobab, and Nathan. Her father was Eliam, the son of Ahithophel the Gilonite. The first book of Chronicles (1 Chronicles 3:5) calls her Bathshua, daughter of Ammiel.

She was married to Uriah the Hittite, a loyal officer in the army of King David. One warm evening, while the army was in campaign against the Ammonites, King David, who had stayed in Jerusalem, went up to the rooftop of his palace and saw, in one of the neighboring houses, a beautiful woman washing herself. He made some inquiries and was told that the woman was Bathsheba, Uriah's wife. David had her brought to the palace, made love to her, and then sent her back to her house.

Sometime later, the king was informed that she was pregnant. David, in order to prevent a scandal, ordered that Uriah should return immediately to Jerusalem, ostensibly to report about the war, but in reality to spend a night with his wife.

Uriah came to Jerusalem and was received by the king in the palace. After hearing Uriah's report about the state of the army, the king told him to go to his house and rest there. Uriah did not go to his wife. Instead, he spent that night, and the following night, sleeping at the entrance of the king's palace with the guards.

David, hiding his annoyance, asked him, "Why didn't you go to your house?"

Uriah answered, "While my army comrades are in the front lines, and sleeping in tents, I will not sleep in my own home and be with my wife".

David came to the conclusion that the only solution to avoid the scandal was the death of Uriah. He wrote a letter to Joab, sealed it, and gave it to Uriah, ordering Joab to arrange that Uriah should be sent to the forefront of the battle, and there, he should be abandoned by his fellow soldiers to make sure that he would be killed.

Joab carried David's orders and notified David that Uriah was dead. The king married Bathsheba, as soon as her days of mourning were over. When her time was due, she gave birth to a baby boy.

The prophet Nathan came to David and told him a parable of a rich man, who owned many sheep but, instead of sacrificing one of his, took a poor man's lamb, and cooked it to honor a traveler. David, not understanding the allusion, became outraged and threatened to punish the rich man for his lack of pity. Nathan exclaimed, "You are that man". David expressed remorse and recognized that he had sinned. Nathan told him that he would not die, but the baby would. So it happened, the baby fell sick and died.

Later, Bathsheba gave birth to four more sons: Solomon, Shimea—also called Shammuah—Shobab, and Nathan.

Years later, when David was an old man, Bathsheba, together with the prophet Nathan, convinced David to make Solomon his heir, instead of Adonijah, who was Solomon's older half brother.

When Solomon became king, after the death of David, Bathsheba, as the king's mother, continued to be powerful and influential. When Adonijah asked her to ask Solomon on his behalf for permission to marry Abishag, the Shunammite girl who had warmed King David's bed in his old age, Bathsheba went to the king, who angrily refused Adonijah's request, interpreting it as a bid for the throne. Solomon, taking no chances, gave immediate orders to kill Adonijah.

Bathshua

(Hebrew origin: *Daughter of wealth*)

1. (1 Chronicles 3:5). 10th century B.C. Bathshua, daughter of Ammiel—also called Eliam—is better known as Bathsheba, King David's favorite wife and the mother of King Solomon. (Please read the entry for Bathsheba [2 Samuel 11:3].)

2. (1 Chronicles 2:3). 17th century. Bathshua, *Daughter of Shua*, was the Canaanitess wife of Judah. (Please see the entry for Shua [1 Chronicles 2:3].)

Bavai

(Persian origin: **Uncertain meaning**)

(Nehemiah 3:18). 5th century B.C. Bavai, ruler of half the district of Keilah, helped to repair the walls of Jerusalem, during the days of Nehemiah. His father was Henadad.

Bazlith

(Hebrew origin: *Onion-like*)

(Nehemiah 7:54). Unspecified date. Bazlith was the ancestor of a clan of Temple servants that returned with Zerubbabel from the Babylonian Exile. An alternative spelling in the book of Ezra is Bazluth (Ezra 2:52).

Bazluth

(Hebrew origin: *Onion-like*)

(Ezra 2:52). Unspecified date. Bazluth was the ancestor of a clan of Temple servants that returned with Zerubbabel from the Babylonian Exile. An alternative spelling in the book of Nehemiah is Bazlith (Nehemiah 7:54).

Bealiah

(Hebrew origin: *The Lord is God*)

(1 Chronicles 12:5). 11th century B.C. Bealiah was one of the Benjamites who deserted King Saul's army and joined David's band at Ziklag. These Benjamites were skilled warriors who could use both their right and left hands to shoot arrows and sling stones.

Bebai

(Hebrew origin: Uncertain meaning)

1. (Ezra 2:11). Unspecified date. Bebai was the ancestor of a large family that returned with Zerubbabel from the Babylonian Exile.

Years later, his descendant Zechariah, leading twenty-eight males, returned from the Babylonian Exile with Ezra.

Four of his descendants—Jehohanan, Hananiah, Zabbai, and Athlai—were among the men who, during the time of Ezra, had married foreign women and gave their word that they would divorce them.

2. (Nehemiah 10:15). 5th century B.C. Bebai was one of the leaders of Judah who signed Nehemiah's solemn agreement to separate themselves from the foreigners living in the land, to refrain from intermarrying with them, and to dedicate their firstborn to God, among other obligations.

Becher

(Hebrew origin: *Young camel* or *Firstborn*)

1. (Genesis 46:21). 17th century B.C. Becher, son of Benjamin and grandson of Jacob, was one of the seventy Israelites who immigrated to Egypt. His sons were Zemira, Joash, Eliezer, Elioenai, Omri, Jerimoth, Abiah, Anathoth, and Alameth.

According to the list in Genesis, he had nine brothers: Belah, Ashbel, Gera, Naaman, Ehi, Rosh, Muppim, Huppim, and Ard.

Another list, in the first book of Chronicles, states that he only had two brothers: Bela and Jediael (1 Chronicles 7:6). In two other lists, he is not mentioned among the sons of Benjamin (Numbers 26:38 and 1 Chronicles 8:1).

2. (Numbers 26:35). 16th century B.C. Becher, son of Ephraim and grandson of Joseph, was the ancestor of the clan of the Bachrites. He is called Bered in First Chronicles (1 Chronicles 7:20).

Bechorath

(Hebrew origin: *Primogeniture*)

(1 Samuel 9:1). 12th century B.C. Bechorath, a Benjamite, son of Aphiah and father of Zeror, was an ancestor of King Saul.

Bedad

(Hebrew origin: *Solitary*)

(Genesis 36:35). Unspecified date. His son Hadad was an Edomite king, who reigned at a time before Israel had become a kingdom. Hadad, whose capital was Avith, defeated Midian in the fields of Moab.

Bedan

(Hebrew origin: *Servile*)

1. (1 Samuel 12:11). Unspecified date. Bedan was a judge of Israel, who, according to the prophet Samuel, was sent by God, after Gideon and before Jephthah, to save the Israelites from their enemies.

   Note: In the book of Judges, a judge is a ruler or governor of territory or a military leader in pre-monarchical Israel. Later, during the monarchy, the king served in this role and judges were more like the judicial officers that we know today.

2. (1 Chronicles 7:17). Unspecified date. Bedan was the son of Ulam, descendant of Machir, of the tribe of Manasseh

Bedeiah

(B*ranch of God*)

(Ezra 10:35). 5th century B.C. Bedeiah was one of the men who married foreign women, during the days of Ezra.

Beeliada

(Hebrew origin: *Baal knows* or *Who knows Baal*)

(1 Chronicles 14:7). 10th century B.C. Beeliada was one of the sons of King David who was born in Jerusalem. In the second book of Samuel, he is called Eliada (2 Samuel 5:16).

Beelzebub

(Hebrew origin: *God of the flies*)

(Matthew 10:25). In the New Testament, Beelzebub, "the Prince of Devils", is another name for Satan. In the Old Testament, where he is called Baalzebub (2 Kings 1:2), he is the god of the Philistine city of Ekron.

When King Ahaziah of Israel fell from a second floor, he sent messengers to Ekron to inquire of Baalzebub if he would recover. The prophet Elijah intercepted them on their way and angrily asked, "Is there not a God in Israel that you go to Ekron to inquire from their god?" and then he prophesied that the king would die.

In the gospel according to Matthew, the Pharisees denied that Jesus cast out demons and attributed this deed to Beelzebub (Matthew 12:24). Jesus answered that their accusation lacked logic and common sense, because "if Satan cast out Satan, he is divided against himself, how then could he stand?"

Beera

(Hebrew origin: *A well*)

(1 Chronicles 7:37). Unspecified date. Beera, son of Zophah, was a brave warrior, leader of a clan of the tribe of Asher.

Beerah

(Hebrew origin: *A well*)

(1 Chronicles 5:6). 8th century B.C. Beerah, son of Baal, leader of the tribe of Reuben, was carried away captive with his tribe by Tilgathpilneser, king of Assyria.

Beeri

(Hebrew origin: *My well*)

1. (Genesis 26:34). 18th century B.C. Beeri was the father of Judith, one of the two Hittite women—the other one was Bashemath—whom Esau married, when he was forty years old. Both women made miserable the lives of Isaac and Rebekah.

2. (Hosea 1:1). 8th century B.C. Beeri was the father of the prophet Hosea.

Behemoth

(Hebrew origin: *A monstrous animal*)

(Job 40:15). Behemoth—actually, the

Hebrew plural for Behemah, *Dumb beast*—is described in the book of Job as an animal that eats grass like an ox, lies under thorny bushes, and is surrounded by the willows of a brook. Some scholars believe that this refers to a hippopotamus.

Bel

(Babylonian origin: *Lord*)

(Isaiah 46:1). Bel was one of the gods of Babylon.

Bela

(Hebrew origin: *Destroying*)

1. (Genesis 36:32). Unspecified date. Bela, the son of Beor, reigned in Edom, at a time before there were kings in Israel. The capital of his kingdom was Dinhabah. When he died, he was succeeded by Jobab, son of Zerah.

2. (Numbers 26:38). 17th century B.C. Bela—also spelled Belah (Genesis 46:21)—the eldest son of Benjamin and grandson of Jacob, was one of the seventy Israelites who immigrated to Egypt. Bela was the ancestor of the clan of the Belaites. His name is the only one that appears in all the four lists of the sons of Benjamin.

The Genesis' list mentions that he had nine brothers: Becher, Ashbel, Gera, Naaman, Ehi, Rosh, Muppim, Huppim, and Ard (Genesis 46:21).

In the Numbers' list, he had four brothers: Ashbel, Ahiram, Shupham, and Hupham (Numbers 26:38).

In one of the lists in the first book of Chronicles, he only had two brothers: Becher and Jediael (1 Chronicles 7:6).

In the other list of First Chronicles, he had four brothers: Ashbel, Aharah, Nohah, and Rapha (1 Chronicles 8:1).

His sons, according to the book of Numbers, were Ard, ancestor of the clan of the Ardites, and Naaman, ancestor of the clan of the Naamites (Numbers 26:40).

According to the first book of Chronicles (1 Chronicles 7:7), Bela's sons were Ezbon, Uzzi, Uzziel, Jerimoth, and Iri, all of them brave leaders of their clans.

Elsewhere in the first book of Chronicles (1 Chronicles 8:3), Bela had a different set of sons: Addar, Gera, Abihud, Abishua, Naaman, Ahoah, Gera, Shephuphan, and Huram.

3. (1 Chronicles 5:8). Unspecified date. Bela, son of Azaz, was the leader of a clan of Reubenites who lived in the region east of Gilead. The clan raised cattle and, during the days of King Saul, made war against the descendants of Hagar.

Belah

(Hebrew origin: *Destroying*)

(Genesis 46:21). 17th century B.C. Belah is an alternative spelling for Bela (Numbers 26:38), the son of Benjamin and grandson of Jacob. (Please see the entry for Bela.)

Belial

(Hebrew origin: *Worthlessness*)

(Deuteronomy 13:13). Belial is a term of scorn used in the Hebrew Bible to characterize wicked and dissolute people, despicable liars, and perverts. The term was usually applied to men, but it could also be said of women, as for example, Hannah asks the priest Eli not to take her for a daughter of Belial (1 Samuel 1:16). In the New Testament, the term was used as the antithesis of Christ (2 Corinthians 6:15).

Belshazzar

(Babylonian origin: *god Bel protects the king*)

(Daniel 5:1). 6th century B.C. Belshazzar, according to the book of Daniel, was the last king of Babylon, the son and successor of Nebuchadnezzar.

Historians believe that Belshazzar was not a king, nor was he related to Nebuchadnezzar, but that he was the son of Nabonidus, the last king of Babylon. Belshazzar, the crown prince and regent of the kingdom, invited a thousand guests to a great banquet, where he and his wives drank from the gold and silver utensils, which Nebuchadnezzar had taken from the Temple, when Jerusalem was conquered.

While the men and women at the feast were getting drunk and praying to idols, a hand wrote a mysterious message on the wall. None of the king's astrologers and counselors was able to read or understand the writing on the wall. Daniel was brought to the palace at the queen's suggestion and was promised gifts and a high position in the royal court if he could succeed in interpreting the cryptic writing.

Daniel refused the rewards and explained the message: "*Mene, mene*—God has numbered your kingdom and finished it—*tekel*—you have been weighed in the balances and found wanting—*peres*—your kingdom is divided and given to the Medes and the Persians".

The king gave the promised gifts to Daniel. Later that night, Belshazzar was slain, and Darius the Median took over the kingdom of Babylon.

Belteshazzar

(Babylonian origin: derived from the name of the god *Bel*)

(Daniel 1:7). 6th century B.C. Belteshazzar was the Babylonian name given by the chief of the king's eunuchs to Daniel, a bright Jewish youth who was chosen, with three other boys, to be educated in the Babylonian court. (Please see the entry for Daniel [Daniel 1:6].)

Ben

(Hebrew origin: *Son*)

(1 Chronicles 15:18). 10th century B.C. Ben, a Levite of the second rank, was one of the men chosen, by the chief of the Levites, to sing and play musical instruments in front of the Ark of the Covenant, when it was carried from the house of Obededom to its resting place in Jerusalem, as commanded by David.

Benaiah

(Hebrew origin: *God has built* or *God will make him understand*)

1. (2 Samuel 8:18). 10th century B.C. Benaiah, son of the High Priest Jehoiada,

from the town of Kabzeel, was one of the most distinguished military commanders of King David, and the leader of "The Thirty", an elite army group composed of the bravest men in the army.

His many heroic deeds included the slaying of two lion-like men of Moab, the killing of a lion in the midst of a pit, and his fight with an armed Egyptian. Benaiah, who was unarmed except for a staff in his hand, plucked the spear from the Egyptian's hand and killed him with his own weapon.

Benaiah was in charge of the Cherethite and Pelethite mercenary divisions in the army of King David. Later, he commanded a division of twenty-four thousand men, where one of his soldiers was his son Ammizabad. Benaiah was in charge of everything related to the army, during the third month of each year.

Politically, he made the right choice, when he, together with Nathan, the prophet, and Zadok the Priest, supported Solomon as heir of the throne against Adonijah. When Solomon ascended to the throne, Benaiah carried out personally the king's orders to execute Adonijah, Joab, and Shimei. Solomon rewarded his loyalty by making him head of the army, replacing Joab.

2. (2 Samuel 23:30). 10th century B.C. Benaiah the Pirathonite, of the tribe of Ephraim, was one of "The Thirty", an elite group in King David's army. He commanded a division of twenty-four thousand men and was in charge of every-thing related to the army, during the eleventh month of each year.

3. (1 Chronicles 4:36). 8th century B.C. Benaiah was one of the leaders of the tribe of Simeon who went to the fertile valley of Gedor in search of pasture for their flocks, during the reign of Hezekiah, king of Judah. The Simeonites destroyed the tents of the people—descendants of Ham—who lived there, wiped them out forever, and settled in their place.

4. (1 Chronicles 15:18). 10th century B.C. Benaiah, a Levite of the second rank, was

chosen, by the chief of the Levites, to sing and play musical instruments in front of the Ark of the Covenant, when it was carried from the house of Obededom to its resting place in Jerusalem, as commanded by David. Later, he was one of the Levites appointed by King David, to minister before the Ark.

5. (1 Chronicles 15:24). 10th century B.C. Benaiah was one of the priests who blew the trumpets in front of the Ark of the Covenant, when it was carried from the house of Obededom to its resting place in Jerusalem. Later, he, with Jahaziel, another priest, played the trumpet continually, before the Ark of the Covenant, together with other priests, who played harps, lyres, and cymbals.

6. (1 Chronicles 27:34). 11th century B.C. Benaiah was the father of Jehoiada, a counselor of King David, who became the chief advisor to the king, after the suicide of Ahithophel.

7. (2 Chronicles 20:14). 9th century B.C. Benaiah was a Levite descendant of Asaph. His grandson Jahaziel prophesied victory for King Jehoshaphat of Judah in his war against the armies of Ammon and Moab.

8. (2 Chronicles 31:13). 8th century B.C. Benaiah was one of the Levites named by King Hezekiah to serve under Cononiah and Shimei, as a supervisor of the gifts, tithes, and offerings, brought by the people to the Temple.

9. (Ezra 10:25). 5th century B.C. Benaiah, a descendant of Parosh, divorced his foreign wife, during the days of Ezra.

10. (Ezra 10:30). 5th century B.C. Benaiah, a descendant of Pahathmoab, divorced his foreign wife, during the days of Ezra.

11. (Ezra 10:35). 5th century B.C. Benaiah, a descendant of Bani, divorced his foreign wife, during the days of Ezra.

12. (Ezra 10:43). 5th century B.C. Benaiah, a descendant of Nebo, divorced his foreign wife, during the days of Ezra.

13. (Ezekiel 11:1). 6th century B.C. Benaiah was the father of Pelatiah, a leader of the people and false prophet. In one of his visions, the prophet Ezekiel saw Pelatiah, standing at the east gate of the Temple, falsely telling the people that Jerusalem would not be destroyed, when suddenly he died.

Benammi

(Hebrew origin: *Tribal, inbred*)

(Genesis 19:38). 19th century B.C. Benammi, born from the incestuous union of Lot and his younger daughter, was the ancestor of the Ammonites, constant enemies of the Israelites. Their capital, Rabbath Ammon, is called today Amman, the capital of Jordan.

Benhadad

(Hebrew origin: *Son of the god Hadad*)

1. (1 Kings 15:18). 9th century B.C. Benhadad I, son of Tabrimon and grandson of Hezion, was the king of Aram—today's Syria—when King Asa reigned in Judah.

   Asa's enemy, Baasha, king of Israel, fortified the frontier town of Ramah in order to blockade Judah. Asa took all the silver and gold that were left in the treasures of the Temple and sent it to Damascus, to Benhadad, begging him to help him against Baasha.

   Benhadad invaded Israel and captured several towns in the north of the country. Baasha retreated from Ramah, leaving behind a lot of building materials, which Asa then used to build Geba and Mizpah.

2. (1 Kings 20:1). 9th century B.C. King Benhadad II of Aram—today's Syria—gathered his whole army, and, with a coalition of thirty-two kings, they invaded Israel and laid siege to the city of Samaria. His insulting demands to Ahab, to deliver all his gold, silver, wives, and children, were so harsh that Ahab, who previously had considered surrendering, was advised by the elders of the land to reject Benhadad's demands and fight back.

   The Aramean king and his men were drinking and celebrating what they considered their soon-to-be victory, over Israel, when the Israelite army attacked them by surprise. Benhadad managed to escape and rode on his horse, back to his country. He reorganized his army and, about a year later, again invaded Israel.

Benhadad believed that the reason for his previous defeat was that he had fought in the hills against the Israelites. He changed his tactics and attacked in the plains.

The battle took place at Aphek, and Benhadad again was badly defeated, and this time, he was taken prisoner. When brought to the presence of Ahab, he was treated with respect and honor. The two kings signed a peace agreement, by which Benhadad promised to return to Ahab the Israelite cities, which had been captured by his father, and to allow Israelite merchants to open businesses in Damascus.

When Ahab returned to Samaria, a prophet, standing on the road, rebuked him for letting Benhadad go free and prophesied that, for this grave error, Ahab would be defeated and killed.

After three years of peace, Ahab decided to recuperate the town of Ramothgilead that was in the hands of the Arameans. He made an alliance with King Jehoshaphat of Judah, and went to war against Benhadad.

During the battle, a stray arrow, shot by an Aramean soldier, wounded King Ahab and caused his death, several hours later.

Shortly after Jehu's accession to the throne of Israel, Benhadad became very ill and instructed his army commander Hazael to take a present to the prophet Elisha, who had come to Damascus, and to inquire from the holy man if the king would recover his health. Hazael loaded forty camels with gifts and went to see Elisha.

The prophet told him that, although the king would recover from his illness, he would nevertheless die. Hazael returned to the ailing king and told him that Elisha had said that he would recover. Early the next morning, he went to Benhadad's bedroom, smothered him with a wet cloth, and proclaimed himself king.

3. (2 Kings 13:24). 8th century B.C. Ben-Hadad III, king of Syria, the son of the regicide and throne usurper Hazael, fought three wars against King Jehoash of Israel, who defeated him and took back the Israelite cities, which Hazael had captured.

Benhail

(Hebrew origin: *Son of valor*)

(2 Chronicles 17:7). 9th century B.C. Benhail was an official in the court of King Jehoshaphat. During the third year of his reign, the king sent Benhail, with some other officials, Levites and priests, to teach the laws of God in the cities of Judah.

Benhanan

(Hebrew origin: *Son of grace*)

(1 Chronicles 4:20). Unspecified date. Benhanan, son of Shimon, was a descendant of Judah. His brothers were Rinnah, Amnon, and Tilon.

Beninu

(Hebrew origin: *Our son*)

(Nehemiah 10:13). 5th century B.C. Beninu was one of the Levites who signed Nehemiah's solemn agreement to separate themselves from the foreigners living in the land, to refrain from intermarrying with them, and to dedicate their firstborn to God, among other obligations.

Benjamin

(Hebrew origin: *Son of the right hand* or *Son of the south*)

1. (Genesis 35:18). 17th century B.C. Benjamin, the youngest son of Jacob by his wife Rachel, was the ancestor of the tribe of Benjamin.

Rachel, his mother, who died when he was born, gave him the name Benoni, *Son of my suffering*, but Jacob called him Benjamin, *Son of the south*, probably because he was the only one of Jacob's sons who was born in the south, that is, in Canaan; all his brothers—including Joseph, his full brother—were born in Aram-Naharaim.

Benjamin was the full brother of Joseph. His half brothers were Judah, Reuben, Levi, Simeon, Issachar, and Zebulun, sons of Leah; Gad and Asher, sons of Zilpah; and Dan and Naphtali, sons of Bilhah. His half sister was Dinah, daughter of Leah.

Benjamin, too young at the time, was not involved in the incident when his brothers sold Joseph to a caravan of Ishmaelites who took him to Egypt. (For the detailed story about Joseph and his brothers, please see the entry for Joseph.)

Many years went by, Joseph, after having been the trusted servant in the home of an important Egyptian official, spent years in jail, because of the trumped-up charges of his master's wife, and had now become, in an astonishing turn of events, the most powerful man in Egypt after Pharaoh.

There was a great famine in Egypt, but Joseph, having foreseen that this would happen, had taken care of storing in warehouses the abundant crops that had been produced in the previous seven years.

The famine in Canaan was also severe. When Jacob heard that it was possible to buy grain in Egypt, he sent there all his sons, except for young Benjamin, because his father was afraid that something would happen to him.

The brothers arrived in Egypt and were brought to the presence of Joseph, who was personally in charge of selling the grain. They didn't recognize that the powerful Egyptian vizier in front of them was the young brother whom they had last seen over twenty years before, but Joseph recognized them immediately and remembered his dreams, in which his family bowed to him. He decided to act as if he didn't know them and accused them of being spies. The brothers denied this, saying that they were all sons of the same man, and that they had a younger brother at home.

Joseph confined them in prison for three days. On the third day, he told them that they could return to their families with the grain bought in Egypt, but one of them would have to stay in prison to make sure that they would return with their younger brother.

When the brothers came back to Canaan, they told their father every word that the Egyptian vizier had said to them, and his demand that they should bring Benjamin to Egypt. This, Jacob absolutely refused to allow.

Reuben tried to change his father's mind and said, "I authorize you to kill my two sons if I don't bring Benjamin back to you! Give him to my care, and I will bring him back!" Not surprisingly, Jacob was not convinced by this senseless offer to have two of his grandsons killed.

The famine got worse, and, soon enough, the grain that the brothers had brought from Egypt was finished. Judah asked his father to let Benjamin go with them to Egypt and assured him that he would be personally responsible for his young brother's safe return to Canaan. Jacob, seeing that he had no choice, reluctantly allowed Benjamin to go with his brothers to Egypt.

When Benjamin was brought to his presence, Joseph, unable to control his emotion, went into another room and wept there. Returning to his brothers, he invited them to dinner, but still he did not make himself known to them. To his servant, he gave instructions that Benjamin should receive extra portions.

When the time came for the brothers to return to Canaan, Joseph's steward, on the orders of his master, concealed a silver cup in Benjamin's bag, and, later, he overtook the brothers on their way home, accused Benjamin of theft, and brought them all back.

The brothers interceded for Benjamin, and Judah declared that he would remain as a prisoner in exchange for Benjamin's release, in order to spare the grief that his father would feel if Benjamin failed to return.

Joseph could not contain himself anymore and disclosed his identity to them. He embraced Benjamin, and they both wept. He kissed all his brothers and wept upon them.

Pharaoh, when told that Joseph's brothers had come, was very pleased with the news. He said to Joseph, "Tell your brothers to load their donkeys, and go immediately to Canaan. They should bring your father and their families, and I will give them the best land in Egypt. Tell them to take wagons from Egypt for their wives and children. Also, they shouldn't worry about their belongings, because the best of the land of Egypt will be theirs".

Joseph gave his brothers wagons and provisions for the journey. To each of them, he gave a change of clothing, but to Benjamin, he gave five changes of clothing and three hundred pieces of silver. To his father, he sent ten male donkeys loaded with the best things of Egypt, and ten female donkeys loaded with grain, bread, and provisions for his father on the journey. As he sent his brothers off on their way, he admonished them not to quarrel among them.

Jacob immigrated to Egypt with his entire family, which included the ten sons of Benjamin: Belah, Becher, Ashbel, Gera, Naaman, Ehi, Rosh, Muppim, Huppim, and Ard.

Jacob, in his deathbed blessings, said that Benjamin was like a wolf, killing and devouring, morning and evening.

Centuries later, Moses blessed the tribes in his farewell speech. About Benjamin, he said, "This is the tribe that God protects and loves. He guards them all day long, and dwells in their midst".

Note: There are four differing lists of the sons of Benjamin. The book of Genesis gives a list of ten sons: Belah, Becher, Ashbel, Gera, Naaman, Ehi, Rosh, Muppim, Huppim, and Ard (Genesis 46:21).

The book of Numbers gives a list of five sons: Bela, Ashbel, Ahiram, Shupham, and Hupham (Numbers 26:38).

The first book of Chronicles gives two different lists; the first has three sons: Bela, Becher, and Jediael (1 Chronicles 7:6); and the second list has five sons: Bela, Ashbel, Aharah, Nohah, and Rapha (1 Chronicles 8:1).

2. (1 Chronicles 7:10). Unspecified date. Benjamin, a brave warrior and leader of a clan of Benjamites, was the son of Bilhan and the brother of Jeush, Ahishahar, Ehud, Zethan, Tharshish, and Chenaanah.

3. (Ezra 10:32). 5th century B.C. Benjamin, a descendant of Harim, divorced his foreign wife, during the days of Ezra.

4. (Nehemiah 3:23). 5th century B.C. Benjamin was one of the leaders of the people who helped to repair the walls of Jerusalem, during the days of Nehemiah. Later, he marched in the joyful procession, which celebrated the dedication of the rebuilt walls of Jerusalem.

Beno

(Hebrew origin: *His son*)

(1 Chronicles 24:26). 10th century B.C. Beno, a Levite, was the son of Jaaziah, a descendant of Merari, who served in the Tabernacle, during the reign of David together with his brothers Shoham, Zaccur, and Ibri.

Benoni

(Hebrew origin: *Son of my suffering*)

(Genesis 35:18). 17th century B.C. Benoni, *Son of my suffering*, was the name that Rachel, on her deathbed gave to Benjamin, her second child. (Please see the entry for Benjamin [Genesis 35:18].)

Benzoheth

(Hebrew origin: *Son of Zoheth*).

(1 Chronicles 4:20). Unspecified date. Benzoheth, a descendant of Judah, was the son of Ishi. His brother was Zoheth.

Beor

(Hebrew origin: *Burning* or *Torch*)

1. (Genesis 36:32). Unspecified date. Beor was the father of Bela. His son reigned in Edom, at a time before there were kings in Israel.
2. (Numbers 22:5). 14th century B.C. Beor was the father of Balaam. His son, internationally famous for the effectiveness of his blessings and curses, was asked by Balak, king of Moab, to curse the people of Israel, but God made him utter blessings, instead of curses. Beor is called Bosor in the New Testament.

Bera

(Hebrew origin: *Son of evil*)

(Genesis 14:2). 19th century B.C. Bera, king of Sodom, was one of the vassals of Chedorlaomer, king of Elam. After serving him for twelve years, Bera and four other kings—Shinab, king of Admah; Shemeber, king of Zeboiim; Birsha, king of Gomorrah; and the king of Bela—rebelled, formed an alliance, and joined forces in the valley of Siddim, which is now the Dead Sea.

Chedorlaomer and his allies—King Amraphel of Shinar, King Arioch of Ellasar, and King Tidal—defeated them in battle.

Bera and Birsha ran away from the battle and fell into the tar pits of the valley. Shinab, Shemeber, and the king of Bela managed to escape to the mountains.

Berachah

(Hebrew origin: *Blessing*)

(1 Chronicles 12:3). 11th century B.C. Berachah was one of a group of Benjamite fighters, commanded by Ahiezer, who deserted King Saul's army and joined David's band at Ziklag. They were skilled warriors who could use both their right and left hands to shoot arrows and sling stones.

Berachiah

(Hebrew origin: *God will bless*)

(1 Chronicles 6:39). 10th century B.C. Berachiah, son of Shimea, of the clan of the Kohathites, was the father of Asaph, a leading musician, during the reign of King David. His name is spelled Berechiah in the first book of Chronicles (1 Chronicles 15:17).

Beraiah

(Hebrew origin: *The Lord has created*)

(1 Chronicles 8:21). Unspecified date. Beraiah, son of Shimhi, was a leader of the tribe of Benjamin who lived in Jerusalem.

Berechiah

(Hebrew origin: *God will bless*)

1. (1 Chronicles 3:20). 6th century B.C. Berechiah was a descendant of the royal family of Judah. His father Zerubbabel was the leader of the first group of captives who returned from the Babylonian Exile.
2. (1 Chronicles 9:16). 5th century B.C. Berechiah, a Levite son of Asa, was one of the first to settle in the land of Judah, after the return from the Babylonian Exile.
3. (1 Chronicles 15:17). 10th century B.C. Berechiah, son of Shimea, of the clan of the Kohathites, was the father of Asaph, a leading musician, during the reign of King David. His name is also spelled Berachiah in the first book of Chronicles (1 Chronicles 6:39).
4. (1 Chronicles 15:23). 10th century B.C. Berechiah was a doorkeeper in the Tabernacle, during the reign of King David.
5. (2 Chronicles 28:12). 8th century B.C. During the war of King Pekah of Israel against King Ahaz of Judah, the Israelite army defeated Judah and brought tens of thousands of captives back to Samaria with the intention of making them slaves. Berechiah, son of Meshillemoth, was one of the leaders of the tribe of Ephraim who supported the prophet Oded in his successful demand to free the captives and return them to Judah.
6. (Nehemiah 3:4). 5th century B.C. Berechiah, son of Meshezabeel, was the father of Meshullam. His son, who was

related by marriage to Tobiah, Nehemiah's enemy, helped to repair the walls of Jerusalem.

7. (Zechariah 1:1). 6th century B.C. Berechiah, son of the prophet Iddo, was the father of the prophet Zechariah.

Bered

(Hebrew origin: *Hail*)

(1 Chronicles 7:20). 16th century B.C. Bered, son of Ephraim, was the grandson of Joseph. He is called Becher in the book of Numbers (Numbers 26:35).

Beri

(Hebrew origin: *Healthy*)

(1 Chronicles 7:36). Unspecified date. Beri, the son of Zophah, was a brave warrior, leader of a clan of the tribe of Asher.

Beriah

(Hebrew origin: *In trouble*)

1. (Genesis 46:17). 17th century B.C. Beriah, the son of Asher, was a grandson of Jacob. He and his two sons, Heber and Malchiel, were among the seventy Israelites who immigrated to Egypt. Beriah was the ancestor of the clan of the Berites.
2. (1 Chronicles 7:23). 17th century B.C. Beriah, a son of Ephraim, was born after his brothers had been killed by the men of Gath, while attempting to take away their cattle.
3. (1 Chronicles 8:13). Unspecified date. Beriah was the leader of a clan of Benjamites who lived in Aijalon and had driven away the inhabitants of Gath.
4. (1 Chronicles 23:10). 10th century B.C. Beriah, a Levite, descendant of Shimei, served in the Tabernacle, during the reign of King David. His brothers were Jeush, Zina and Jahath. Because Beriah did not have many children, the census of the Levites considered him and his brother Jeush as members of a single clan.

Berith

(Hebrew origin: *Covenant*)

(Judges 9:46). Berith was the god of the city of Shechem, during the period of the Judges. When Abimelech captured the city, the men of Shechem closed themselves, in the Temple of Berith, and were burned alive, when Abimelech set fire to the Temple.

Bernice

(Greek origin: *Victorious*)

(Acts of the Apostles 25:13). A.D. 1st century. Bernice, the daughter of Herod Agrippa I, was the sister of King Agrippa—Herod Agrippa II—and the great granddaughter of Herod the Great. She lived with her brother, an arrangement that caused a great deal of gossip and alienated the Jews.

Bernice went with her brother to Caesarea to visit Festus, the Roman procurator, who was holding Paul prisoner. Festus consulted with Agrippa in the presence of Bernice concerning the apostle's case. They agreed that Paul was innocent, but they were powerless to help him, because the apostle had appealed to Rome for a ruling, which took the case out of their jurisdiction.

Berodachbaladan

(Babylonian origin: Uncertain meaning)

(2 Kings 20:12). 8th century B.C. Berodachbaladan, son of Baladan, was the king of Babylon, during the reign of Hezekiah. He was called Merodachbaladan in the book of Isaiah (Isaiah 39:1).

When Berodachbaladan heard that Hezekiah was sick, he sent ambassadors to Judah to wish the king a speedy and complete recovery, carrying with them letters and presents. Hezekiah gave the Babylonians a royal welcome and naively showed them all his treasures.

The prophet Isaiah, upon learning who the men were, prophesied that the day would come when all the treasures of Jerusalem would be carried off to Babylon.

Besai

(Hebrew origin: *Domineering*)

(Ezra 2:49). Unspecified date. Besai was an ancestor of a clan of Temple servants that returned with Zerubbabel from the Babylonian Exile.

Besodeiah

(Hebrew origin: *God's secret*)

(Nehemiah 3:6). 5th century B.C. His son Meshullam repaired the Old Gate of Jerusalem, during the days of Nehemiah.

Bethrapha

(Hebrew origin: *House of the giant*)

(1 Chronicles 4:12). Unspecified date. Bethrapha, a descendant of Judah, was the son of Eshton. His brothers were Paseah and Tehinnah

Bethuel

(Hebrew origin: *God's house*)

(Genesis 22:22). 19th century B.C. Bethuel was the youngest of the eight children born to Milcah, the wife of Nahor, Abraham's brother. His daughter Rebekah married Isaac, Abraham's son. Through his son Laban, he was the grandfather of Leah and Rachel, who married Jacob, Isaac's son. His brothers were Huz, Jidlaph, Kemuel, Buz, Hazo, Pildash, and Chesed.

Beulah

(Hebrew origin: *Espoused*)

(Isaiah 62:4). This is the name, by which, according to the prophet Isaiah, God would call the land of Israel.

Bezai

(Hebrew origin: *Domineering*)

1. (Ezra 2:17). Unspecified date. Bezai was the ancestor of a clan that returned with Zerubbabel from the Babylonian Exile.

2. (Nehemiah 10:18). 5th century B.C. Bezai was one of the leaders who signed Nehemiah's solemn agreement to separate themselves from the foreigners living in the land, to refrain from intermarrying with them, and to dedicate their firstborn to God, among other obligations.

Bezaleel

(Hebrew origin: *In God's shadow*)

1. (Exodus 31:2). 13th century B.C. Bezaleel, the son of Uri, of the tribe of Judah, was a gifted craftsman, expert in working in gold, silver, brass, wood, and embroidering. God told Moses that Bezaleel was chosen to design and carry out the work for the sacred Tent, the Ark, the furniture, and the altar, helped by Aholiab, the son of Ahisamach, of the tribe of Dan.

2. (Ezra 10:30). 5th century B.C. Bezaleel, a descendant of Pahathmoab, divorced his foreign wife, during the days of Ezra.

Bezer

(Hebrew origin: *Fortification*)

(1 Chronicles 7:37). Unspecified date. Bezer, son of Zophah, was a brave warrior and the leader of a clan of the tribe of Asher.

Bichri

(Hebrew origin: *My firstborn*)

(2 Samuel 20:1). 10th century B.C. His son Sheba, a Benjamite, led a failed insurrection against King David, after the death of Absalom.

Bidkar

(Hebrew origin: *Stabber*)

(2 Kings 9:25). 9th century B.C. Bidkar was a captain in the army of Israel under the command of Jehu. After Jehu rebelled and killed King Jehoram, he ordered Bidkar to throw the body into the field of the murdered Naboth.

Bigtha

(Persian origin: *Gift of God*)

(Esther 1:10). 5th century B.C. Bigtha was one of the seven eunuchs who served in the court of Ahasuerus, the king of Persia, usually identified by historians as King Xerxes I of Persia, son and successor of Darius I.

The other six eunuchs who served the king were Harbona, Abagtha, Biztha, Mehuman, Zethar, and Carcas.

In the third year of his reign, the king gave a banquet for all his princes and administrators to show off his wealth. The great celebration lasted one hundred and eighty days.

When the festivities for the nobles ended, the king gave a banquet in the garden of his palace for the common people of Shushan. During seven days, everybody, rich and poor, drank as much as he wanted. At the same time, Vashti, his queen, gave a banquet for the women inside the palace.

On the seventh day of the celebration, the drunken Ahasuerus ordered Bigtha and the other six eunuchs who served the king to fetch Queen Vashti, and to make sure that she was wearing her royal crown. She was a beautiful woman, and the king wanted everybody to see her. The eunuchs returned and told the king that the queen refused to come.

Bigthan

(Persian origin: *Gift of God*)

(Esther 2:21). 5th century B.C. Bigthan—also spelled Bigthana (Esther 6:2)—was a gatekeeper in the palace of King Ahasuerus, in the city of Shushan. He conspired with Teresh, another gatekeeper, to kill the king. Mordecai learned of the plot and told it to Queen Esther, who reported it to the king.

An investigation found the two conspirators guilty, and they were hanged from a tree.

Bigthana

(Persian origin: *Gift of God*)

(Esther 6:2). 5th century B.C. Bigthana—also spelled Bigthan (Esther 2:21)—was a gatekeeper in the palace of King Ahasuerus, in the city of Shushan. He conspired with Teresh, another gatekeeper, to kill the king.

Mordecai learned of the plot and told it to Queen Esther, who reported it to the king. An investigation found the two conspirators guilty, and they were hanged from a tree.

Bigvai

(Uncertain origin and meaning)

1. (Ezra 2:2). 6th century B.C. Bigvai was one of the men who returned with Zerubbabel from the Babylonian Exile.

2. (Ezra 2:14). Unspecified date. Bigvai was the ancestor of a clan who returned with Zerubbabel from the Babylonian Exile. Other members of the family returned years later with Ezra (Ezra 8:14).

3. (Nehemiah 10:16). 5th century B.C. He was one of the leaders who signed Nehemiah's solemn agreement to separate themselves from the foreigners living in the land, to refrain from intermarrying with them, and to dedicate their firstborn to God, among other obligations.

Bildad

(Uncertain origin and meaning)

(Job 2:11). Unspecified date. Bildad the Shuhite was one of the three friends of Job who came to comfort him.

They sat down with him for seven days and nights without speaking a word, not wishing to disturb Job in his grief.

After Job broke his silence with a bitter diatribe against his life, his friends were surprised. They had come to commiserate and console, not to participate in a rebellion against God's judgment, and so they turned from comforters to scolders. Bildad in his speeches ascribed the death of Job's children to their sins.

Bilgah

(Hebrew origin: *Self restrained*)

1. (1 Chronicles 24:14). 10th century B.C. During the reign of King David, the priestly service in the Tabernacle was divided by lot into twenty-four turns. Bilgah was in charge of the fifteenth turn.

2. (Nehemiah 12:5). 6th century B.C. Bilgah was one of the leading priests who returned with Zerubbabel from the Babylonian. He was the ancestor of a clan of priests that was led by Shammua, during the days of the High Priest Joiakim (Nehemiah 12:18).

Bilgai

(Hebrew origin: *Self restrained*)

(Nehemiah 10:8). 5th century B.C. Bilgai was one of the priests who signed Nehemiah's solemn agreement to separate themselves from the foreigners living in the land, to refrain from intermarrying with them, and to dedicate their firstborn to God, among other obligations.

Bilhah

(Hebrew origin: *Timid*)

(Genesis 29:29). 18th century B.C. Bilhah was the maid whom Laban gave to his daughter Rachel, as a wedding gift, when she married Jacob.

Years later, Rachel childless at the time, told Jacob to take Bilhah as a concubine, so that, according to the custom of the time, any children that would be born from her maid would be considered Rachel's. Bilhah gave birth to two sons: Dan and Naphtali.

Bilhan

(Hebrew origin: *Timid*)

1. (Genesis 36:27). Unspecified date. Bilhan, son of Ezer, a descendant of Esau, was the leader of a clan of Horites in the land of Edom. His brothers were Zaavan and Akan.

2. (1 Chronicles 7:10). 16th century B.C. Bilhan, a leader of a clan of Benjamites, was the son of Jediael and the grandson of Benjamin. His sons were Jeush, Benjamin, Ehud, Chenaanah, Zethan, Tharshish, and Ahishahar.

Bilshan

(Hebrew origin: *Eloquent*)

(Ezra 2:2). 6th century B.C. Bilshan was one of the men who returned with Zerubbabel from the Babylonian Exile.

Bimhal

(Hebrew origin: *With pruning*)

(1 Chronicles 7:33). Unspecified date. His father Japhlet was a leader of the tribe of Asher. Bimhal's brothers were Pasach and Ashvath.

Binea

(Uncertain origin and meaning)

(1 Chronicles 8:37). Unspecified date. Binea, son of Moza, a Benjamite, was a descendant of Jonathan, King Saul's son. His son was called Rapha, also spelled Rephaiah (1 Chronicles 9:43).

Binnui

(Hebrew origin: *Built*)

1. (Ezra 8:33). 5th century B.C. His son Noadiah, a Levite, was one of the men who helped the priest Meremoth, son of Uriah, to weigh the silver and gold vessels of the Temple, brought to Jerusalem by Ezra from the Babylonian Exile.

2. (Ezra 10:30). 5th century B.C. Binnui, a descendant of Pahathmoab, divorced his foreign wife, during the days of Ezra.

3. (Ezra 10:38). 5th century B.C. Binnui, an Israelite, divorced his foreign wife, during the days of Ezra.

4. (Nehemiah 3:24). 5th century B.C. Binnui, a Levite son of Henadad, helped to repair the walls of Jerusalem, during the days of Nehemiah. He was one of the Levites who signed Nehemiah's solemn agreement to separate themselves from the foreigners living in the land, to refrain from intermar-

rying with them, to dedicate their firstborn to God, and other obligations (Nehemiah 10:9).

5. (Nehemiah 7:15). Unspecified date. Binnui was the ancestor of a clan of Israelites who returned with Zerubbabel from Babylon. He was also called Bani (Ezra 2:10).

6. (Nehemiah 12:8). 6th century B.C. Binnui, a Levite, returned with Zerubbabel from the Babylonian Exile.

Birsha

(Hebrew origin: *With wickedness*)

(Genesis 14:2). 19th century B.C. Birsha, king of Gomorrah, was one of the vassals of Chedorlaomer, king of Elam.

After serving him for twelve years, Birsha and four other kings—Shinab, king of Admah; Shemeber, king of Zeboiim; Bera, king of Sodom; and the king of Bela—rebelled, formed an alliance, and joined their forces in the valley of Siddim, which is now the Dead Sea.

Chedorlaomer and his allies—King Amraphel of Shinar, King Arioch of Ellasar, and King Tidal—defeated them in battle.

Birsha and Bera ran away from the battle and fell into the tar pits of the valley. Shinab, Shemeber, and the king of Bela managed to escape to the mountains.

Birzavith

(Hebrew origin: *Holes*)

(1 Chronicles 7:31). Unspecified date. His father Malchiel was a leader of the tribe of Asher.

Bishlam

(Hebrew origin: *In peace*)

(Ezra 4:7). 6th century B.C. Bishlam, Tabeel, and Mithredath, the non-Jews who lived in the land of Israel, offered to help the returnees from Babylon in the reconstruction of the Temple. When their offer was rejected, they became offended and angry. As an act of revenge, they wrote a letter in Syrian to Artaxerxes, king of Persia, asking the king to stop the work in the Temple.

Bithiah

(Hebrew origin: *Daughter of God*)

(1 Chronicles 4:18). Unspecified date. Bithiah, daughter of the Pharaoh, was the wife of Mered, a descendant of Judah.

Biztha

(Persian origin: Uncertain meaning)

(Esther 1:10). 5th century B.C. Biztha was one of the seven eunuchs who served in the court of Ahasuerus, the king of Persia, usually identified by historians as King Xerxes I of Persia, son and successor of Darius I.

The other six eunuchs who served the king were Harbona, Abagtha, Mehuman, Bigtha, Zethar, and Carcas.

In the third year of his reign, the king gave a banquet for all his princes and administrators to show off his wealth. The great celebration lasted one hundred and eighty days.

When the festivities for the nobles ended, the king gave a banquet in the garden of his palace for the common people of Shushan. During seven days, everybody, rich and poor, drank as much as he wanted. At the same time, Vashti, his queen, gave a banquet for the women inside the palace.

On the seventh day of the celebration, the drunken Ahasuerus ordered Biztha and the other six eunuchs who served the king to fetch Queen Vashti, and to make sure that she was wearing her royal crown. She was a beautiful woman, and the king wanted everybody to see her. The eunuchs returned and told the king that the queen refused to come.

Blastus

(Greek origin: *To germinate*)

(Acts of the Apostles 12:20). A.D. 1st century. Blastus, the chamberlain of King Herod Agrippa I, arranged a meeting at Caesarea between the king and the people of Tyre and Sidon, who, being dependent on the Galilee region for their food supply, desired peaceful relations with Herod Agrippa.

Boanerges

(Aramaic origin: *Sons of thunder* **or** *Sons of commotion*)

(Mark 3:17). A.D. 1st century. This nickname, given by Jesus to the two brothers—apostles James and John, sons of Zebedee—most likely referred to their irate temperaments.

Boaz

(Hebrew origin: *Strength in him*)

(Ruth 2:1). 12th century B.C. Boaz, son of Salmon, a descendant of Nahshon—the leader of the tribe of Judah, during the wanderings in the desert—was a wealthy landowner who lived in Bethlehem, during the time of the Judges.

One day, during the barley harvest, he went to his field and noticed a young woman, walking behind his workers and gleaning the scattered ears left behind by the reapers. He inquired about her and was told that she was Ruth, widow of Mahlon, the son of his late relative Elimelech, and that she had recently arrived from her native land of Moab with her widowed mother-in-law Naomi.

Boaz spoke to Ruth and told her that he greatly appreciated her kindness and devotion to Naomi. At the end of the harvest, Boaz, who was spending the night on the winnowing floor, woke up in the middle of the night, surprised to find Ruth, lying at his feet, dressed in her best clothes.

The following morning, Boaz spoke to a kinsman whose family relationship to Elimelech was closer than his. With the elders of the town as witnesses, Boaz asked the other man if he wanted to buy from Naomi the land that had belonged to Elimelech, which implied marrying Ruth.

When the relative politely refused, Boaz declared publicly that he would buy the land and marry Ruth. Their son Obed was King David's grandfather. Boaz is called Booz in the New Testament (Matthew 1:5 and Luke 3:32).

Bocheru

(Hebrew origin: *His firstborn*)

(1 Chronicles 8:38). Unspecified date. Bocheru was one of the six sons of Azel, son of Eleasah of the tribe of Benjamin, a descendant of King Saul. His brothers were Azrikam, Ishmael, Sheariah, Obadiah, and Hanan.

Bohan

(Hebrew origin: *Thumb*)

(Joshua 15:6). Unspecified date. Bohan was a son of Reuben. The stone that marked the boundary between the territories of the tribes of Benjamin and Judah was named after him.

Booz

(Hebrew origin: Uncertain meaning)

(Matthew 1:5). 12th century B.C. Booz is an alternative spelling for Boaz, a wealthy landowner who lived in Bethlehem, married Ruth, and was an ancestor of King David. (Please see the entry for Boaz [Ruth 2:1].)

Bosor

(Hebrew origin: Uncertain meaning)

(2 Peter 2:15). 14th century B.C. His son Balaam, a seer famous for the effectiveness of his blessings and curses, was asked by Balak, king of Moab, to curse the people of Israel, but God made him utter blessings, instead of curses.

Bosor is called Beor in the Old Testament (Numbers 22:5).

Bukki

(Hebrew origin: *Wasteful*)

1. (Numbers 34:22). 13th century B.C. Bukki, son of Jogli, leader of the tribe of Dan, was one of the men appointed by Moses to apportion the land of Canaan among the tribes.
2. (1 Chronicles 6:5). Unspecified date. Bukki was the son of Abishua, a descendant of Aaron. Bukki's son was Uzzi, an ancestor of Ezra the Scribe.

Bukkiah

(Hebrew origin: *Wasting of God*)

(1 Chronicles 25:4). 10th century B.C. Bukkiah, a Levite, member of a family of musicians, was in charge of the sixth turn of service that played musical instruments—cymbals, psalteries, and harps—in the House of God, during the reign of David.

He had thirteen brothers and three sisters, all of them trained as skillful musicians by their father Heman, one of the leading musicians of the period.

Bunah

(Hebrew origin: *Discretion*)

(1 Chronicles 2:25). Unspecified date. Bunah was the son of Jerahmeel, of the clan of the Hezronites, of the tribe of Judah. His brothers were Ram, Ahijah, Oren, and Ozem.

Bunni

(Hebrew origin: *Built*)

1. (Nehemiah 9:4). 5th century B.C. Bunni, a Levite, stood with other Levites on a raised platform and prayed to God in a loud voice in a solemn assembly, on a day of confession and public fast, during the days of Ezra.
2. (Nehemiah 10:15). 5th century B.C. Bunni was one of the leaders who signed Nehemiah's solemn agreement to separate themselves from the foreigners living in the land, to refrain from intermarrying with them, and to dedicate their firstborn to God, among other obligations.
3. (Nehemiah 11:15). Unspecified date. Bunni was a Levite descendant of Merari. His descendant Shemaiah was one of the first Levites to settle in Jerusalem, after the return from the Babylonian Exile.

Buz

(Hebrew origin: *Disrespect*)

1. (Genesis 22:21). 19th century B.C. Buz was the second eldest of the eight children born to Milcah, the wife of Nahor, Abraham's brother. His brothers were Huz, Jidlaph, Kemuel, Chesed, Hazo, Pildash, and Bethuel.

   Buz was the ancestor of the Buzites, a tribe mentioned in the book of Job.
2. (1 Chronicles 5:14). Unspecified date. Buz, of the tribe of Gad, was the father of Jahdo. His descendants lived in Gilead, on the eastern side of the Jordan River.

Buzi

(Hebrew origin: *Descendant of Buz*)

(Ezekiel 1:3). 6th century B.C. Buzi was the father of the prophet Ezekiel.

Caesar

(Latin origin: *Title of the Roman emperors*)

(Matthew 22:17). This was the title of the Roman emperors from the reign of Augustus—born 63 B.C., died A.D. 14—until the A.D. 3rd century. The word is used in the New Testament to mean "the ruling power", rather than the particular occupant of the throne.

The name Caesar was originally that of an important Roman family whose most famous member was Julius Caesar—100 B.C. to 44 B.C.—one of the greatest generals in history, and the man who laid the foundations of the Roman imperial state.

The Caesars who reigned, during the lifetimes of Jesus and the apostles, were Augustus, during whose reign Jesus was born, and in whose honor Herod named the city of Caesarea; Tiberius, during whose reign Jesus was crucified, and Paul was converted, and in whose honor Herod named the city of Tiberias; Caligula; Claudius; and Nero, during whose reign Peter and Paul were martyred.

Caiaphas

(Chaldean origin: *The Dell*)

(Matthew 26:3). A.D. 1st century. The High Priest Caiaphas, son-in-law of Annas, the previous High Priest, conspired with the chief priests, the scribes, and the elders of the people to arrest Jesus, accuse him of blasphemy, and have him crucified by the Roman authorities in Jerusalem. It was to Caiaphas' house that Jesus was brought, after his arrest there.

Caiaphas, years later, took part in the interrogation of Peter and John, when they were arrested, for their preaching and healing activities in the Temple. The apostles were acquitted without receiving any punishment.

Cain

(Hebrew origin: *Spear*)

(Genesis 4:1). Antediluvian. Cain, the eldest son of Adam and Eve, was a tiller of the soil. His brother Abel was a shepherd. One day, when the brothers wished to bring an offering to God, Cain brought the fruit of the soil, while Abel brought the choicest of the firstlings of his flock.

The Lord accepted Abel's offering but rejected that of Cain. God saw that Cain was much distressed and advised him to control himself, and to do what was right. Cain, instead of following God's advice, asked Abel to go with him to the field, and, once there, he killed his brother.

The Lord asked Cain for Abel's whereabouts. Cain pretended that he didn't know and asked God if he was his brother's keeper. God cursed him and condemned him to fail as a farmer, and to ceaselessly wander the earth. Cain protested that, as a wanderer, anybody who met him would try to kill him. God, to prevent this from happening, put a mark on him.

Cain traveled to the land of Nod, east of Eden, where he settled down, married, and had a son, called Enoch, whose name he also gave to a city that he founded.

Cainan

(Hebrew origin: derived from *Nest*)

1. (Genesis 5:9). Antediluvian. Cainan, son of Enos, was the grandson of Seth, Adam's third son. He was seventy years old, when his son Mahalaleel was born. Cainan died at the age of nine hundred and ten, after having had more sons and daughters. In the first book of Chronicles (1 Chronicles 1:2), he is called Kenan, son of Enosh.
2. (Luke 3:36). Unspecified date. Cainan, son of Arphaxad and grandson of Sem, Noe's son, was the father of Sala, called Salah in Genesis (Genesis 10:24).

Calcol

(Hebrew origin: *Sustenance, nourishment*)

(1 Chronicles 2:6). Unspecified date. Calcol, one of the five sons of Zerah, the son of Judah, was a leader of the tribe of Judah. His brothers were Ethan, Heman, Zimri, and Dara.

Caleb

(Hebrew origin: *Dog*)

1. (Numbers 13:6). 13th century B.C. Caleb, son of Jephunneh, of the tribe of Judah, was one of the twelve men sent by Moses to spy the land of Canaan and report back about its cities and its inhabitants; to find out if they were strong or weak, few or many; and to bring back the fruit of the land.

   The spies went and scouted the land, from the wilderness of Zin to Rehob, near the entrance to Hamath. Forty days later, they returned back to the camp, carrying pomegranates, figs, and a branch, which had a bunch of grapes, so heavy that it took two men to carry it on a pole between them.

   Their report turned out to be disheartening and defeatist. "We came to the land, and it flows with milk and honey, and here is the fruit that we have brought. But the inhabitants are strong; their cities are walled and very large. The Amalekites dwell in the south; the Hittites, the Jebusites, and the Amorites live in the hill country; and the Canaanites dwell by the sea and along the Jordan River. We are not able to go against them. They are too strong for us. That land devours its inhabitants. All the men that we saw are of great stature, and we even saw giants, the sons of Anak. We felt like grasshoppers, and we must have looked like that to them too".

   Only Caleb, who was forty years old at the time, and Joshua, the son of Nun, disagreed. They said, "The land that we scouted is an excellent land. If God is pleased with us, he will take us there, and deliver to us a land flowing with milk and honey. Do not rebel against the Lord, and don't be afraid of the people who live there, because we can conquer them easily. God is with us; do not fear them!"

   The Israelites refused to listen to the encouraging words of Joshua and Caleb, and they started to wail and cry. God punished their cowardice by condemning them to wander forty years in the wilderness, one year for each day that the spies scouted the land, with the exception of Caleb and Joshua, whose bravery was rewarded by being allowed to come into the Promised Land and possess it.

   Caleb gave Achsah, his daughter, in marriage to her cousin Othniel—son of Kenaz, Caleb's younger brother—as a reward to Othniel for having taken Kirjathsepher, during the conquest of Canaan.

   Achsah convinced her father to give her springs of water, complaining that he had given her away as "dry land"—i.e. without dowry.

   Caleb had three sons: Iru, Elah, and Naam.

   Some scholars believe that Caleb, son of Jephunneh, and Caleb, son of Hezron (see the entry below), are the same person.

2. (1 Chronicles 2:18). Unspecified date. Caleb, son of Hezron and brother of Ram and Jerahmeel, of the tribe of Judah, was married to Azubah and to Jerioth.

   Azubah gave him three sons: Jesher, Shobab, and Ardon. When she died, Caleb married Ephrath, with whom he had a son called Hur. He also had two concubines: Ephah, the mother of Haran, Moza, and Gazez; and Maachah, who gave birth to Sheber, Tirhanah, and Shaaph. The first book of Chronicles (1 Chronicles 2:42) mentions that Caleb had another son called Mesha.

   In the first book of Chronicles (1 Chronicles 2:9), Caleb is called Chelubai. Some scholars believe that Caleb, son of Hezron, and Caleb, son of Jephunneh (see the entry above), are the same person.

Canaan

(Hebrew origin: *Trader, merchant*)

(Genesis 9:18). Unspecified date. Canaan was the son of Ham, the youngest son of Noah. Canaan was cursed, by Noah, and condemned to be a servant to the descendants of his father's brothers, because his father Ham had treated Noah disrespectfully, by seeing Noah's nakedness, when he was drunk.

Canaan's brothers were Cush, *Ethiopia*; Mizraim, *Egypt*; and Phut, also called Put; all of them were ancestors of the nations that were called by their names. Canaan's first son was Sidon.

Candace

(Ethiopian origin: Uncertain meaning)

(Acts of the Apostles 8:27). A.D. 1st century. Candace, the queen of Ethiopia, had a eunuch, a powerful and influential official of her court, who served as the treasurer of her kingdom. This man went on a pilgrimage to Jerusalem. On his way back, he stopped on the road from Jerusalem to Gaza and read the words of the prophet Isaiah, sitting in his chariot.

Philip, the evangelist, was told by the Spirit to go to the chariot, where the man was reading the book of Isaiah in a loud voice, "Although he was oppressed, and afflicted, he did not open his mouth; he was brought as a lamb to the slaughter, and, as a sheep is dumb in front of its shearers, he did not open his mouth". (Isaiah 53:7)

Philip asked him, "Do you understand what you are reading?" The man answered that he didn't, and he asked Philip to sit with him and explain the meaning of the verse. "Was the prophet speaking about himself, or about some other man?"

Philip explained to the eunuch that the verse referred to Jesus. They continued on their way, and when they approached a body of water, the eunuch said, "Here is water. Does anything prevent me from being baptized?" Philip answered, "If you believe with all your heart, you may be baptized". The eunuch replied, "I believe that Jesus Christ is the Son of God".

He ordered to stop the chariot. Both men went to the water, and Philip baptized him. Philip left, and the eunuch continued in his way, full of joy.

Caphthorim

(Hebrew origin: *Buttons*)

(Genesis 10:14). Unspecified date. Caphtorim was the son of Mizraim, *Egypt*, and the grandson of Ham. His descendants lived in Caphtor, the native land of the Philistines.

Carcas

(Persian origin: Uncertain meaning)

(Esther 1:10). 5th century B.C. Carcas was one of the seven eunuchs who served in the court of Ahasuerus, the king of Persia, usually identified by historians as King Xerxes I of Persia, son and successor of Darius I.

The other six eunuchs who served the king were Harbona, Abagtha, Biztha, Mehuman, Bigtha, and Zethar.

In the third year of his reign, the king gave a banquet for all his princes and administrators to show off his wealth. The great celebration lasted one hundred and eighty days.

When the festivities for the nobles ended, the king gave a banquet in the garden of his palace for the common people of Shushan. During seven days, everybody, rich and poor, drank as much as he wanted. At the same time, Vashti, his queen, gave a banquet for the women inside the palace.

On the seventh day of the celebration, the drunken Ahasuerus ordered Carcas and the other six eunuchs who served the king to fetch Queen Vashti, and to make sure that she was wearing her royal crown. She was a beautiful woman, and the king wanted everybody to see her. The eunuchs returned and told the king that the queen refused to come.

Careah

(Hebrew origin: *Bald*)

(2 Kings 25:23). 6th century B.C. His sons Johanan and Jonathan were officers of the

defeated army of Judah. The two men, and other captains, went to Mizpah to speak with Gedaliah, the Babylonian appointed governor of Judah.

Gedaliah told them that all would go well if they would serve the king of Babylon. This statement caused that some of his visitors considered him a Babylonian collaborator and, sometime later, murdered him. Careah's name is spelled Kareah by Jeremiah (Jeremiah 40:8).

Carmi
(Hebrew origin: *Vine dresser*)

1. (Genesis 46:9). 17th century B.C. Carmi, son of Reuben and grandson of Jacob, was one of the seventy Israelites who immigrated to Egypt. Carmi's brothers were Hanoch, Phallu, and Hezron. He was the ancestor of the clan of the Carmites.
2. (Joshua 7:1). 13th century B.C. Carmi, of the tribe of Judah, was the father of Achan, called Achar in First Chronicles (1 Chronicles 2:7). His son transgressed sacrilegiously, by stealing some of the booty taken by the Israelites in Jericho, which Joshua had forbidden the people to touch.

   This trespass caused God's punishment: the Israelites were defeated by the men of Ai, and thirty-six men died in the battle.

   After Achan was found guilty, he, his family, and all his possessions were taken to the valley of Achor, where they were stoned to death and burned.
3. (1 Chronicles 4:1). 17th century B.C. Carmi was the son of Judah and grandson of Jacob.

Carpus
(Greek origin: *Fruit*)

(2 Timothy 4:13). A.D. 1st century. Carpus, a Christian, kept a cloak, books, and parchments that Paul, during his stay in the town of Troas, had left with him.

Years later, Paul, imprisoned in Rome, wrote to Timothy, asking him to bring him the articles that he had left with Carpus, especially the parchments.

Carshena
(Persian origin: Uncertain meaning)

(Esther 1:14). 5th century B.C. Carshena was one of the seven high officials of Persia and Media; the others were Shethar, Admatha, Tarshish, Meres, Marsena, and Memucan.

King Ahasuerus consulted with Carshena and his colleagues about the punishment to be imposed on Queen Vashti for disobeying his command to appear before him.

Casluhim
(Uncertain origin and meaning)

(Genesis 10:14). Unspecified date. Casluhim, son of Mizraim and grandson of Ham, was the ancestor of the Philistines.

Castor
(Latin origin: Uncertain origin and meaning)

(Acts of the Apostles 28:11). Castor and his twin Roman deity, Pollux, were depicted on a sign on the Alexandrian ship, which took the apostle Paul from the island of Melita—today called Malta—to Syracuse.

The Romans used to offer sacrifices to the two deities, asking for favorable winds, and help for shipwrecked sailors.

Centurion
(Latin origin: *Hundred*)

Centurion was the rank of the officer in the Roman army in charge of a hundred soldiers. Several centurions are mentioned in the Bible, but only two of them are called by their names: Cornelius (Acts of the Apostles 10:1) and Julius (Acts of the Apostles 27:1).

1. (Matthew 8:5). A.D. 1st century. A centurion came to Jesus in Capernaum and told him that his servant was very sick. Jesus offered to go to the centurion's house and heal the servant.

   The centurion humbly answered that he was not worthy of Jesus' visit, and that a word of Jesus would suffice to heal the servant. Jesus praised his faith and told him to go. The servant was healed at that same hour.

2. (Matthew 27:54). A.D. 1st century. A centurion, present at Jesus' death, witnessed the earthquake and other wonders. Full of fear, he recognized that Jesus was a righteous man, and truly the Son of God.

3. (Acts of the Apostles 10:1). A.D. 1st century. Cornelius, a centurion of the Italian regiment stationed in Caesarea, was a just, devout, and charitable man. One night, in a vision, an angel told him to send men to Joppa, and fetch Peter who was staying there in the house of Simon the tanner.

Cornelius sent two of his servants to Joppa, accompanied by a soldier. That night, Peter had a vision where God told him that he was allowed to eat anything, including food that was ritually forbidden to Jews.

The envoys arrived to the house and inquired if Peter was lodged there. At that moment, the apostle was being told by the Spirit that three men were seeking him, and that he should go with them.

The next day, Peter, together with some of his Joppa followers, went to Caesarea. Cornelius was waiting for him with his relatives and friends. Seeing Peter, he fell down at his feet. Peter told him to stand up, and that he was a man like all others. Then, Peter understood that the meaning of his night vision was that God had told him that no man was unclean, even if he belonged to a different nation.

Cornelius told the apostle what he had seen in his own vision, and then he and his friends started to speak in tongues and magnify God. Peter, seeing this, immediately baptized them in the name of the Lord. Cornelius, thus, became the first Roman baptized by Peter

4. (Acts of the Apostles 22:25). A.D. 1st century. Paul, during a visit to Jerusalem, was taken by the Romans into the Antonia fortress to protect him from the mob who wanted to kill him, incited by some Jews from the Roman province of Asia who were visiting Jerusalem.

The commander, called Claudius Lysias, ordered that Paul should be interrogated under the lash to find out why the mob hated him. While he was being bound, Paul asked the centurion in charge, "Is it lawful to scourge a Roman citizen who has not been condemned?"

The centurion immediately went to his superior officer and told him that Paul was a Roman citizen. The officer, after verifying this with Paul, arranged to send the apostle the next day to the chief priests' council.

5. (Acts of the Apostles 23:17). A.D. 1st century. Paul's nephew heard the priests conspiring to kill Paul. He went to the Antonia fortress where Paul was being held and told Paul. The apostle asked a centurion to take the young man to the officer in charge so that he could report the plot.

6. (Acts of the Apostles 24:23). A.D. 1st century. Felix, the Roman governor, after listening to Paul, who had been brought to him at Caesarea, ordered a centurion to free the apostle.

7. (Acts of the Apostles 27:1). A.D. 1st century. Julius, a centurion of the Augustus regiment, was in charge of Paul, and other prisoners who were being sent from Caesarea to Rome. When the ship made a stopover in Sidon, Julius kindly allowed Paul to go ashore.

Later, when the ship was in Crete, the centurion disregarded the peril warnings of Paul and was convinced, by the captain and the owner of the ship, to continue with the trip.

A fierce storm threatened to sink the ship, and eventually the ship ran aground in the island of Melita—today's Malta. The soldiers wanted to kill the prisoners to foil their escape. Julius prevented this and instructed all who could swim to jump into the sea and swim to the land. Others followed on planks and broken pieces of the ship. All were saved. When they finally arrived in Rome, Julius delivered the prisoners to the captain of the guard.

Cephas

(Chaldean: *Rock*)

(John 1:42). A.D. 1st century. This was one of the names, by which, Jesus called Peter. It is mentioned several times in the first epistle to the Corinthians, and once in Galatians. (Please see the entry for Peter [Matthew 4:18].)

Chalcol

(Hebrew origin: *Sustenance, nourishment*)

(1 Kings 4:31). Unspecified date. Chalcol, Heman, and Darda were three brothers, sons of Mahol. They, together with Ethan the Ezrahite, were famous for their wisdom, which was surpassed only by King Solomon.

Chedorlaomer

(Uncertain origin and meaning)

(Genesis 14:1). 19th century B.C. Chedorlaomer, king of Elam—a kingdom in what today is Iran—had been for twelve years the overlord of several kingdoms situated in the Dead Sea region. On the thirteenth year, these kingdoms rebelled.

Chedorlaomer, with his allies—Amraphel, king of Shinar; Arioch, king of Ellasar; and Tidal, king of nations—went to war in the valley of Siddim against five Canaanite kings: Bera, king of Sodom; Birsha, king of Gomorrah; Shinab, king of Admah; Shemeber, king of Zeboiim; and the king of Bela.

Chedorlaomer and his allies defeated the five kings and carried away booty and a number of captives, including Lot, Abraham's nephew. Abraham pursued them as far as Hobah, near Damascus, rescued the captives, and recuperated the booty.

Chelal

(Hebrew origin: *Complete*)

(Ezra 10:30). 5th century B.C. Chelal, a descendant of Pahathmoab, divorced his foreign wife, during the days of Ezra.

Chelluh

(Hebrew origin: *Completed*)

(Ezra 10:35). 5th century B.C. Chelluh was one of the men who divorced his foreign wife, during the days of Ezra.

Chelub

(Hebrew origin: *Basket, cage*)

1. (1 Chronicles 4:11). Unspecified date. Chelub, a descendant of Judah, was the brother of Shuah and the father of Mehir.
2. (1 Chronicles 27:26). 11th century B.C. His son Ezri was in charge of the workers who tilled the fields, during the reign of King David.

Chelubai

(Hebrew origin: derived from *Dog*)

(1 Chronicles 2:9). Unspecified date. Chelubai, called Caleb elsewhere in the Bible, was the son of Hezron and the brother of Jerahmeel, of the tribe of Judah. The history of the conquest of Canaan mentions a Caleb that was the son of Jephunneh, but it is most likely that the references are to the same person.

Chelubai had three sons—Jesher, Shobab, and Ardon—from his wife Azubah. After her death, he married Ephrath, with whom he had a son called Hur. The first book of Chronicles (1 Chronicles 2:42) mentions another son Mesha.

Chemosh

(Hebrew origin: *Subduer*)

(Numbers 21:29). Chemosh was the god of the Moabites, one of the pagan gods for whom King Solomon, influenced by his foreign wives, built a shrine in the outskirts of Jerusalem. This shrine was destroyed centuries later by King Josiah, who desecrated it with human bones.

The king of Moab—facing defeat in a battle against Jehoram, king of Israel, and Jehoshaphat, king of Judah—sacrificed his eldest son, the successor to the throne, to his god Chemosh. This human sacrifice so shocked the Israelite armies that they left Moab and returned to their country.

Chenaanah

(Hebrew origin: feminine of *Canaan* [*Merchant*])

1. (1 Kings 22:11). 9th century B.C. His son Zedekiah, a false prophet, told King Ahab that he would be victorious in his war against the Arameans. The Israelites were defeated, and King Ahab was killed in the battle.
2. (1 Chronicles 7:10). Unspecified date. Chenaanah, a brave warrior and leader of a clan of Benjamites, was the son of Bilhan and the brother of Jeush, Benjamin, Ehud, Zethan, Tharshish, and Ahishahar.

Chenani

(Hebrew origin: *Planted*)

(Nehemiah 9:4). 5th century B.C. Chenani was one of the Levites who led the public worship, during the days of Nehemiah.

Chenaniah

(Hebrew origin: *God is merciful*)

1. (1 Chronicles 15:22). 10th century B.C. Chenaniah was the Levite in charge of the singers who accompanied the Ark from the house of Obededom to its resting place in Jerusalem, dressed in robes of fine linen, and singing and playing musical instruments, during the reign of King David.
2. (1 Chronicles 26:29). 10th century B.C. Chenaniah was a Levite descendant from Izhar. He and his sons were responsible for supervising the judges and the public officials, during the reign of King David.

Cheran

(Uncertain origin and meaning)

(Genesis 36:26). Unspecified date. Cheran, a descendant of Seir the Horite, lived in the land of Edom. His father was Dishon. His

brothers were Hemdan—called Amram in First Chronicles (1 Chronicles 1:41)—Eshban, and Ithran.

Chesed

(Uncertain origin and meaning)

(Genesis 22:22). 19th century B.C. Chesed was one of the eight sons, born to Milcah, the wife of Nahor, Abraham's brother. His brothers were Huz, Jidlaph, Kemuel, Buz, Hazo, Pildash, and Bethuel.

Chidon

(Hebrew origin: *Dart*)

(1 Chronicles 13:9). 10th century B.C. Chidon—also called Nachon (2 Samuel 6:6)—was the owner of the threshing floor where Uzza died, when he accidentally touched the Ark, while it was being brought to Jerusalem.

Chileab

(Hebrew origin: *Like the father*)

(2 Samuel 3:3). 10th century B.C. Chileab, born in Hebron, was King David's second son. His mother was Abigail, the widow of Nabal the Carmelite. He is called Daniel in the book of First Chronicles (1 Chronicles 3:1). Chileab probably died in childhood as the Bible does not mention him again.

Chilion

(Hebrew origin: *Sickly*)

(Ruth 1:2). 12th century B.C. Chilion and Mahlon, from the town of Bethlehem, immigrated to Moab with their parents, Elimelech and Naomi, because of a famine. After the death of their father, the brothers married two Moabite girls: Orpah and Ruth.

Ten years later, both men died childless. Orpah, Chilion's widow, remained in Moab, while Ruth went to Bethlehem with Naomi.

Chimham

(Hebrew origin: *Pining*)

(2 Samuel 19:37). 10th century B.C. Chimham was the son of Barzillai, the Gileadite of Rogelim. His father showed kindness to David, when the king was fleeing from Absalom, bringing him utensils and food.

After King David's army had defeated the rebellion, the king invited Barzillai to come with him to Jerusalem. Barzillai, who was eighty years old, declined the offer, pleading his old age, and said that all he wanted at that stage of his life was to die in his own city and be buried near the graves of his parents.

However, Barzillai proposed that his son Chimham should go with the king. The king gladly accepted, kissed Barzillai, blessed him, and returned to Jerusalem, taking Chimham with him. Years later, in his dying bed, King David asked his son Solomon to show kindness to the sons of Barzillai, and to include them in his court.

Chislon

(Hebrew origin: *Hopeful*)

(Numbers 34:21). 14th century B.C. His son Elidad, a leader of the tribe of Benjamin, was appointed by Moses to apportion the land of Canaan among the tribes.

Chiun

(Hebrew origin: *Statue*)

(Amos 5:26). Chiun was a heathen idol—called Remphan in the book of Acts of the Apostles (Acts of the Apostles 7:43)—worshipped by the foreign settlers of Samaria.

Chloe

(Greek origin: *Green*)

(1 Corinthians 1:11). A.D. 1st century. Chloe was a woman who lived in Corinth. The members of her household, either her relatives or her slaves, informed Paul that there was contention within the Christian church at Corinth, with different groups considering themselves followers of Paul, Apollos, Cephas, or Christ.

Christ

(Greek origin: *Anointed* or *Messiah*)

(Matthew 1:1). A.D. 1st century. This title of Jesus refers to his divine nature as Savior and Redeemer. The word "Christ", from the Greek word "Christos", is a translation from the Hebrew word "Mashiah", transliterated to English as *Messiah*. The word means "anointed" or "consecrated to an office", denoting a person with a special mission from God.

In the Old Testament, this title may apply to priests (Exodus 29:29), prophets (Isaiah 61:1), and kings (1 Samuel 2:10). It can refer to an Israelite, such as David, who is called the Lord's anointed (1 Samuel 16:6), or to a non-Israelite, as in the case of the Persian King Cyrus, who is also called the Lord's anointed (Isaiah 45:1).

In Judaism, the word came to mean the ultimate redeemer, and expected king of the Davidic line. The Messiah's mission in Judaism is to deliver Israel from foreign bondage, to bring back all the Jews to the Holy Land, and to inaugurate a utopian era of the world.

In Christianity, the nationalistic and political implications of the word "Messiah" are not present. The term is used exclusively for Jesus, who is considered the promised "Anointed One" of the Lord, and descendant of David. Christians expect the Second Coming of Christ, in power and glory, to judge the living and the dead.

Chushanrishathaim

(Hebrew origin: *Chushan, a region of Arabia, of double wickedness*)

(Judges 3:8). 12th century B.C. Chushanrishathaim, king of Mesopotamia, oppressed the Israelites, during eight years, until Othniel, the son of Kenaz, Caleb's younger brother, fought against the foreign tyrant and freed the Israelites.

Chuza

(Uncertain origin and meaning)

(Luke 8:3). A.D. 1st century. Chuza was the steward of Herod Antipas. His wife Joanna, together with Mary Magdalene, Susanna, and other women, accompanied Jesus and the twelve disciples in his teaching tour of Galilean cities and villages, providing for them out of their means.

Cis

(Hebrew origin: alternative spelling for *Kish* [*a bow*])

(Acts of the Apostles 13:21). 11th century B.C. Cis is an alternative spelling for Kish (1 Samuel 9:1), father of King Saul.

Claudia

(Latin origin: feminine form of the Roman name *Claudius*)

(2 Timothy 4:21). a.d. 1st century. She was one of the four persons—the others were Eubulus, Pudens, and Linus—who sent greetings to Timothy in the last letter written by Paul.

Claudius

(Latin origin: a Roman name)

1. (Acts of the Apostles 11:28). A.D. 1st century. Claudius was an emperor of Rome. During his reign, there was a great famine in the land of Israel, prophesied by Agabus. The relief that was donated by Christians in other provinces was brought to Jerusalem by Barnabas and Paul. The book of Acts of the Apostles (Acts of the Apostles 18:2) mentions that Claudius expelled all the Jews from Rome.
2. (Acts of the Apostles 23:26). A.D. 1st century. Claudius Lysias was the commander of the Antonia fortress, which was the headquarters of the Roman army in Jerusalem.

   Paul, during his last visit to Jerusalem, was arrested by the Romans, and taken into the Antonia fortress to protect him from a violent mob that wanted to kill him.

Later, Claudius Lysias, having been told by Paul's nephew that there was a plot to ambush Paul and kill him, sent Paul, with an armed escort, to Felix, the governor in Caesarea, with a written report, where he shrewdly put himself in a good light by stating that he had rescued Paul from the mob, because he realized that Paul was a Roman.

(For more detailed information, please see the entry for Lysias [Acts of the Apostles 23:26].)

Clement

(Latin origin: *Merciful*)

(Philippians 4:3). A.D. 1st century. Clement was a Philippian Christian who, during Paul's stay in Philippi, assisted the apostle in his mission, greatly helped by two women, Euodias and Syntyche.

Cleopas

(Greek origin: contraction of *Cleopatros* [*Father of glory*])

(Luke 24:18). A.D. 1st century. Cleopas was walking with another man toward the village of Emmaus, near Jerusalem, discussing the recent events, surrounding the death of Jesus, three days before, when they met Jesus but did not recognize him.

Jesus asked them the reason for their sadness. They told him about the death and crucifixion of Jesus of Nazareth and mentioned that the women, who visited the sepulcher and found it empty, had been informed by angels that Jesus was alive.

Jesus expounded to them the Scriptures. When they arrived at the village, they invited Jesus to eat with them, still not recognizing him. Jesus sat with them, took bread, blessed it, broke it, and gave it to them. Their eyes were then opened, and they recognized Jesus, but he vanished out of their sight.

Cleopas and his companion returned to Jerusalem and reported to the disciples that Jesus had risen, and, while they spoke, Jesus himself appeared and made himself known to them.

Cleophas

(Uncertain origin and meaning)

(John 19:25). A.D. 1st century. Cleophas was the husband of a woman named Mary, mother of Joses and James the Younger. Mary was one of the women named who witnessed Jesus' crucifixion.

Colhozeh

(Hebrew origin: *Sees everything*)

(Nehemiah 3:15). 5th century B.C. Colhozeh, son of Hazaiah, a descendant of Perez of the tribe of Judah, had two sons: Shallun and Baruch.

Shallun, the ruler of part of the district of Mizpah, during the days of Nehemiah, repaired the Gate of the Fountain, including the doors, locks, and bars of the gate, and the wall of the pool of Siloah.

Colhozeh's other son, Baruch, was the father of Maaseiah who lived in Jerusalem, during the days of Nehemiah.

Conaniah

(Hebrew origin: *God has sustained*)

(2 Chronicles 35:9). 7th century B.C. Conaniah was one of the Levites who, during the reign of King Josiah, gave to the priests the cattle and oxen, which had been donated by the princes of the kingdom for the Passover offerings.

Coniah

(Hebrew origin: *God will establish*)

(Jeremiah 22:24). 6th century B.C. Coniah, the son of King Jehoiakim and Nehushta, reigned under the name of Jehoiachin (2 Kings 24:6).

Cononiah

(Hebrew origin: *God has sustained*)

(2 Chronicles 31:12). 8th century B.C. Cononiah, a Levite, was appointed by King Hezekiah to supervise the gifts, tithes, and offerings, brought by the people to the Temple.

His brother Shimei served as his second in command, with a number of Levites under them, working as overseers.

Cornelius

(Latin origin: *Horn*)

(Acts of the Apostles 10:1). A.D. 1st century. Cornelius, a centurion of the Italian regiment stationed in Caesarea, was a just, devout, and charitable man.

One night, in a vision, an angel told him to send men to Joppa and fetch Peter who was staying there in the house of Simon the tanner. Cornelius sent two of his servants to Joppa, accompanied by a soldier.

That night, Peter had a vision where God told him that he was allowed to eat anything, including food that was ritually forbidden to Jews. The envoys arrived at the house and inquired if Peter was lodged there. At that moment, the apostle was being told by the Spirit that three men were seeking him, and that he should go with them.

The next day, Peter, together with some of his Joppa followers, went to Caesarea. Cornelius was waiting for him with his relatives and friends. Seeing Peter, he fell down at his feet. Peter told him to stand up, and that he was a man like all others. Then, Peter understood that the meaning of his night vision was that God had told him that no man was unclean, even if he belonged to a different nation.

Cornelius told the apostle what he had seen in his own vision, and then he and his friends started to speak in tongues and magnify God. Peter, seeing this, immediately baptized them in the name of the Lord. Cornelius, thus, became the first Roman baptized by Peter

Cosam

(Hebrew origin: *Oracle*)

(Luke 3:28). Unspecified date. Cosam was the son of Elmodam and father of Addi, ancestor of Jesus, in the genealogy of Luke.

Coz

(Hebrew origin: *Thorn*)

(1 Chronicles 4:8). Unspecified date. Coz, a descendant of Judah, was the father of Anub and Zobebah.

Cozbi

(Hebrew origin: *False*)

(Numbers 25:15). 13th century B.C. Cozbi, daughter of a Midianite prince called Zur, was taken by Zimri, son of Salu, of the tribe of Simeon, into his tent, while the people were suffering from a plague sent by God to punish them for their immoral behavior with the daughters of Moab, and their sacrifices to the pagan god Baalpeor.

Phinehas, the grandson of Aaron the Priest, saw Zimri and Cozbi going into the tent, took a javelin in his hand, went inside, and killed the couple. God was appeased by Phinehas' act and lifted the plague.

Crescens

(Latin origin: *Growing*)

(2 Timothy 4:10). A.D. 1st century. Crescens, a companion of Paul in Rome, left him to go to Galatia.

Crispus

(Latin origin: *Crisp*)

(Acts of the Apostles 18:8). A.D. 1st century. Crispus, head of the synagogue in Corinth, converted to Christianity and was baptized by Paul.

Cush

(Hebrew origin: *Black, a name for the people and land of Ethiopia*)

1. (Genesis 10:6). Unspecified date. Cush was the son of Ham; his brothers were Mizraim, *Egypt*; Phut, also called Put; and Canaan. His son Nimrod was called mighty upon the earth.
2. (Psalm 7:1). 11th century B.C. Cush the Benjamite is the subject of a psalm written by David about a pursuing enemy.

Cushi

(Hebrew origin: *Black, Ethiopian, descendant of Cush*)

1. (2 Samuel 18:21). 10th century B.C. Cushi, a soldier in David's army, was sent by the commander Joab to inform the king about the defeat and death of Absalom. Cushi was overran by Ahimaaz, the son of Zadok the High Priest, who brought news of the victory against Absalom, but diplomatically evaded answering the king's questions about Absalom's fate. Cushi, upon his arrival, told David that his son was dead.
2. (Jeremiah 36:14). 7th century B.C. Cushi, the father of Shelemiah, was an ancestor of Jehudi, the court official who was sent to bring Baruch, the trusted companion of Jeremiah, to the palace, to read Jeremiah's scroll.
3. (Zephaniah 1:1). 7th century B.C. Cushi, the son of Gedaliah, a descendant of Hizkiah—an alternative transliteration for the name of King Hezekiah—was the father of the prophet Zephaniah.

Cyrenius

(Latin name)

(Luke 2:2). A.D. 1st century. Cyrenius was the governor of the Roman province of Syria, at the time when the census that brought Joseph and Mary to Bethlehem was decreed.

Cyrus

(Persian name)

(2 Chronicles 36:22). 6th century B.C. Cyrus, the king of Persia and conqueror of Babylon, issued a decree authorizing the exiled Jews to return to their land.

He also gave back the utensils of the Temple, which Nebuchadnezzar had brought to Babylon, to Sheshbazzar, the leader of the returning captives, and allowed the Jews to rebuild the Temple. These actions caused the prophet Isaiah to call him God's shepherd and God's anointed.

Dagon

(Hebrew origin: *Grain*)

(Judges 16:23). Dagon was the Syrian and Canaanite god of seed, vegetation, and crops. The Philistines, after they settled in Canaan, adopted Dagon as their god and set up temples to him in Gaza and Ashdod.

The Temple of Dagon in Gaza was brought down by Samson, killing himself and thousands of Philistine worshippers.

The Ark of the Covenant, captured by the Philistines, was brought to the Temple of Dagon in Ashdod and placed in front of the statue of the god. The next morning, the statue was found fallen on the ground, with its head and hand cut off.

This incident, plus a plague of hemorrhoids, convinced the Philistines to send the Ark back to Israel in a cart pulled by two cows, carrying also five golden statuettes of mice and five golden figures representing the hemorrhoids.

Years later, when the Philistines defeated the Israelites in the battle at Mount Gilboa, they fastened the head of Saul in the Temple of Dagon.

Dalaiah

(Hebrew origin: *God has delivered*)

(1 Chronicles 3:24). Unspecified date. Dalaiah, son of Elioenai, was a descendant of Jeconiah—also called Jehoiachin—the king of Judah, who was taken into captivity in Babylon. Dalaiah's brothers were Eliashib, Pelaiah, Akkub, Johanan, Hodaiah, and Anani.

Dalphon

(Persian origin: Uncertain meaning)

(Esther 9:7). 5th century B.C. Dalphon was one of the ten sons of Haman, the vizier of Persia who wanted to kill all the Jews in the kingdom.

His brothers were Parshandatha, Arisai, Aspatha, Poratha, Adalia, Aridatha, Parmashta, Aridai, and Vajezatha. All of them were executed, when Haman's plot against the Jews backfired.

Damaris

(Greek origin: Uncertain meaning, perhaps *Gentle*)

(Acts of the Apostles 17:34). A.D. 1st century. Damaris, an Athenian woman, became a believer, after hearing Paul explain his doctrine in front of the Areopagus, the Athenian High Council, which met on Mars Hill to debate philosophical issues and legal cases.

Another convert, mentioned in the same verse, was a member of the Areopagus, named Dionysius, who, some scholars believe, was Damaris' husband.

Dan

(Hebrew origin: *Judge*)

(Genesis 30:6). 17th century B.C. Dan, the ancestor of the tribe of Dan, was the eldest of the two sons—the other was Naphtali—whom Bilhah, Rachel's maid, had with Jacob. His mother had been given, as a wedding gift, by Laban to his daughter Rachel, when she married Jacob.

Rachel, unable to get pregnant, gave Bilhah to Jacob, so that, according to the custom of the time, any children who would be born from her maid would be considered Rachel's. Dan was born in Paddan-Aram where Jacob was working for his father-in-law Laban.

Rachel gave him the name Dan, because, she said, "God has judged me, has also heard my voice, and has given me a son".

Dan was the full brother of Naphtali. His half brothers were Judah, Reuben, Levi, Simeon, Issachar, and Zebulun, sons of Leah; Gad and Asher, sons of Zilpah; and Benjamin and Joseph, sons of Rachel. His half sister was Dinah, daughter of Leah.

Dan and his brothers were involved in the events that led to Joseph being taken as a slave to Egypt. (For the detailed story of Joseph and his brothers, please see the entry for Joseph.)

Years later, when there was a famine in the land, he and his brothers were sent, by Jacob, to Egypt to buy corn. Joseph, now the second most powerful man in the country, recognized them, forgave them, and invited them to settle in Egypt.

Dan and his son Hushim were among the seventy Israelites who immigrated to Egypt. They arrived in Goshen, and Joseph came to them in his chariot. He greeted his father, embraced him, and wept for a long time.

Seventeen years later, Jacob, feeling that he would soon die, called his sons to bless them and tell them what would happen to them in the future. He said, "Dan is a serpent by the road that would bite the heels of a horse, so that the rider will be thrown backward".

Jacob's last words were to ask them to bury him in the cave of Machpelah, where Abraham, Sarah, Isaac, Rebekah, and Leah were buried. Jacob's body was accompanied in his last trip by his sons, their children, flocks and herds, all the officials of Pharaoh and members of his court, chariots and horsemen. Before crossing the Jordan, the funeral procession made a stop and mourned Jacob for seven days. Then, Judah and his brothers took him to Canaan and buried him in the cave of Machpelah.

After burying their father, they all returned to Canaan. Joseph's brothers feared that, with Jacob now dead, Joseph would pay them back for the wrong that they had done to him.

They sent a message to Joseph, saying that Jacob, before his death, had told them to urge Joseph to forgive them. Judah and his brothers came to Joseph, flung themselves before him, and told him that they were prepared to be his slaves.

Joseph answered kindly, "Do not fear! Although you intended me harm, God intended it all for good, to assure the survival of many people. Don't worry; I will take care of you and your children".

Centuries later, Moses blessed the tribes in his farewell speech and called Dan a lion's whelp.

During the conquest of Canaan the tribe of Dan conquered the city of Leshem in the northern frontier of the country and changed its name to Dan in honor of their ancestor. It became a common saying, during the days of the Bible, to describe the extent of the country as "from Dan to Beersheba".

Years later, after the division of the kingdom, the city of Dan became an important religious center, when King Jeroboam installed golden calves in the cities of Dan and Bethel, so that his people would not turn to Jerusalem as the center of their religious life.

Daniel

(Hebrew origin: *God is my judge*)

1. (1 Chronicles 3:1). 10th century B.C. Daniel, born in Hebron, was King David's second son. His mother was Abigail, the widow of Nabal the Carmelite. He is called Chileab in the second book of Samuel. The Bible never mentions him again, which probably means that he died in childhood.

2. (Ezra 8:2). 5th century B.C. Daniel, a priest descendant from Ithamar, returned with Ezra from the Babylonian Exile.

   Later, he was one of the priests who signed Nehemiah's solemn agreement to separate themselves from the foreigners living in the land, to refrain from intermarrying with them, and to dedicate their firstborn to God, among other obligations.

3. (Daniel 1:6). 6th century B.C. Daniel, a prophet, visionary, and interpreter of dreams, was a high official in the Babylonian administration and, according to the prophet Ezekiel, was one of the three righteous men—the other two were Noah and Job.

   Daniel, a young man from a noble Jewish family that lived in exile in Babylon, was selected with three other boys—Hananiah, Mishael, and Azariah—by order of King Nebuchadnezzar, to take a three year instruction course that would prepare them to serve in the Babylonian administration. Daniel was given the Babylonian name Belteshazzar.

In order not to transgress the Law of Moses by eating and drinking ritually forbidden food and wine, Daniel asked permission from Melzar, the man who had been placed in charge of the boys, to eat only legumes, and drink only water. Melzar feared that this diet might endanger their health, but Daniel asked him to let them try it for ten days. When the ten days were over, the four Jewish boys looked better and healthier than the boys who had eaten the regular food.

During the three following years, the four boys acquired knowledge and skill, and Daniel learned to interpret the significance of visions and dreams. When their instruction ended, the king examined them and found them to be ten times better than all the magicians and astrologers in the kingdom.

Sometime later, the king had a disturbing dream, but he could not recall it. He summoned the magicians to his presence and ordered them to tell him the dream that he had dreamt, and its interpretation. The magicians replied that it was impossible to comply with his request. The king flew into a rage and gave orders to Arioch, the captain of the king's guard, to kill all the wise men of Babylon.

When Arioch came to kill him, Daniel asked for an explanation, and, when he heard the king's demand, he asked to be given some time to study the matter. That night, the king's dream was revealed to Daniel in a vision.

The next morning, he spoke to Arioch and asked him to take him to the king's presence, so that he could interpret the dream for the king. Daniel told the king that he had dreamt of a great statue, its head made of gold, its breast and arms of silver, its thighs of brass, its legs of iron, and its feet partly of iron and partly of clay. A thrown stone, which broke the statue in small pieces blown away by the wind, grew into a great mountain that filled the whole earth.

Daniel explained that the head of gold was Nebuchadnezzar himself, and that the rest of the statue, made of different materials, represented successive kingdoms, which would be swept away by the Kingdom of God that would last forever.

The astonished king acknowledged the supremacy of God and appointed Daniel governor of the province of Babylon and head of all the wise men in the kingdom.

Daniel also had visions of his own, where he saw grotesque creatures, which symbolized different successive kingdoms, signifying that, one day, the Kingdom of God would be established and last forever.

Sometime later, the king made a large idol of gold and invited all the princes, governors, and leading personalities of the kingdom to come to the dedication of the image. A herald proclaimed that all should fall down and worship the statue upon hearing the sound of musical instruments. Shadrach, Meshach, and Abednego refused to worship the golden idol.

Nebuchadnezzar had the three men brought to him and threatened that, if they would continue in their refusal to worship the idol, he would have them thrown into a burning fiery furnace. The three men refused and were thrown into the furnace, which was so hot that it burned to death the men who pushed them in. An angel came and protected the three men from injury.

The amazed king told them to come out, recognized the supremacy of God, and decreed that nobody should dare speak against God.

The king dreamt of a tree of great height with beautiful foliage and abundant fruit, which a holy man ordered to cut down and leave just the stump of the roots. Daniel, when called to interpret the dream, told Nebuchadnezzar that the king was the tree, and that God would make him eat grass as an animal and live with the beasts of the field.

A year later, while the king was boasting of his power, a voice from heaven told him that the kingdom had departed from him, and that he would dwell with the beasts of the field and eat grass as oxen do.

Later, when the king had recovered his sanity, he praised God and was restored to his former exalted position.

Years later, Belshazzar, who was by then the ruler in Babylon, invited a thousand guests to a great banquet, where he and his wives drank from the gold and silver utensils, which Nebuchadnezzar had taken from the Temple, when Jerusalem was conquered.

While the men and women at the feast were praying to idols and getting drunk, a hand wrote a mysterious message on the wall, which the king's astrologers and counselors were unable to read or understand.

At the queen's suggestion, Daniel was brought to the palace and was promised gifts and a high position in the royal court if he could interpret the writing in the wall.

Daniel refused the rewards and explained the message: "*Mene, mene*—God has numbered your kingdom and finished it—*tekel*—you have been weighed in the balances and found wanting—*peres*—your kingdom is divided and given to the Medes and the Persians".

The king gave the promised gifts to Daniel. Later that night, Belshazzar was slain and Darius the Median took over the kingdom of Babylon. Daniel was named one of the three top ministers of the new king.

Some officials were jealous and envious of Daniel but could not find a valid cause to discredit him. They managed to persuade the new ruler to decree the death punishment for anybody who, during the next thirty days, would make any petition from God or man, except from the king.

When Daniel was observed praying to God, his enemies did not waste any time in reporting it to the king. The reluctant king, unable to change the decree, had Daniel thrown into a lion's den.

The next morning, the king, who had fasted the whole night, rushed to the lion's den and was very happy to see Daniel coming out unhurt. He ordered that the accusers should be thrown to the lions, and that everybody in the kingdom should revere God.

Dara

(Hebrew origin: **contraction of** *Darda* [*Pearl of knowledge*])

(1 Chronicles 2:6). Unspecified date. Dara, son of Zerah, was a leader of the tribe of Judah. His brothers were Zimri, Ethan, Heman, and Calcol.

Darda

(Hebrew origin: *Pearl of knowledge*)

(1 Kings 4:31). Unspecified date. Darda, Heman, and Chalcol were sons of Mahol. The three brothers and Ethan the Ezrahite were famous for their wisdom, which was surpassed only by that of King Solomon.

Darius

(Persian origin: Title of several kings)

1. (Ezra 4:5). 6th century B.C. Darius I the Great, king of Persia, received a letter from Tatnai, the governor of Judea, Shetharboznai, and other Persian court officials, informing him that the Jews were rebuilding the Temple.

   The governor asked the king to have a search made in the records in order to verify if King Cyrus had allowed the rebuilding work to be done. The governor concluded his letter by requesting instructions on how to deal with this matter.

   A search was made, and a scroll was found in a palace in Achmetha, in the province of the Medes, which showed that Cyrus had given his full approval to the rebuilding of the Temple, with specific architectural instructions and orders that the work should be paid from the royal treasury.

   The king wrote back, ordering Tatnai to allow the work to proceed, to help the Jews to rebuild, and to refrain from interfering with the construction.

   Tatnai and his officials fully and speedily complied with the king's commands.

2. (Nehemiah 12:22). 5th century B.C. Darius II was a king of Persia mentioned in the book of Nehemiah.

3. (Daniel 5:31). 6th century B.C. Darius the Mede, according to the book of Daniel, was the conqueror of Babylon who appointed Daniel as one of the three top ministers of the kingdom.

Some officials were jealous and envious of Daniel but could not find a valid cause to discredit him. They managed to persuade the new ruler to decree the death punishment for anybody who, during the next thirty days, would make any petition from God or man, except from the king.

When Daniel was observed praying to God, his enemies did not waste any time in reporting it to the king. The reluctant king, unable to change the decree, had Daniel thrown into a lion's den.

The next morning, the king, who had fasted the whole night, rushed to the lion's den and was very happy to see Daniel coming out unhurt. He ordered that the accusers should be thrown to the lions, and that everybody in the kingdom should revere God.

Darkon

(Hebrew origin: Uncertain meaning)

(Ezra 2:56). 10th century B.C. Darkon, a servant of Solomon, was the ancestor of a family that returned with Zerubbabel from the Babylonian Exile.

Dathan

(Hebrew origin: Uncertain meaning)

(Numbers 16:1). 13th century B.C. Dathan and Abiram, sons of Eliab, of the tribe of Reuben, were two of the leaders of Korah's rebellion against Moses. Their brother Nemuel did not participate in the rebellion.

Korah, Dathan, Abiram, and On, son of Peleth, at the head of a group of two hundred fifty renowned men, accused Moses and Aaron of raising themselves over the rest of the people.

Moses threw himself on the ground and said to the rebels, "Tomorrow, the Lord will show us who belongs to him, who can come close to him. Take your fire pans, you Korah, and all your followers, and put incense and fire in it, and present them to the Lord tomorrow, and we will see who will the Lord choose to make holy. You have gone too far, sons of Levi! It seems that it is not enough for you that God has set you apart from the community to serve him, and brought you near him. You also want the priesthood? You are not standing against Aaron, you have banded against the Lord!"

Moses called Dathan and Abiram to talk with them, but they refused to come, saying, "Isn't it enough that you took us out of Egypt, a land that flowed with milk and honey, to kill us in the wilderness, that you also want to lord it over us? Even if you had brought us to a land of milk and honey, and given us possession of fields and vineyards, should you gouge out those men's eyes? We will not come!"

Moses became very angry and said to God, "Don't accept their offerings. I have never hurt any of them, nor have I taken even one of their donkeys!"

The next day, the rebels, with their fire pans, stood in the door of the Tabernacle, with Moses and Aaron, surrounded by the people.

The Presence of God appeared to the whole community, and God said to Moses and Aaron, "Stand apart from this community that I may annihilate them immediately".

Moses and Aaron threw themselves to the ground, and said, "O God, do not be angry with the whole community because of the sins of one man".

God said to them, "Tell the community to get away from the tents of Korah, Dathan, and Abiram".

Moses got up and went toward the tents of Dathan and Abiram, followed by the leaders of the people. He then asked the people to stay away from the tents of the rebels so that they should not also be destroyed.

Dathan and Abiram came out and stood at the entrance of their tents, with their wives, sons, and small children.

Moses then spoke, "This is how you will know that God has sent me to do all these things. They are not done by my own choice. If these men will die of a natural death, then I have not been sent by God, but if God does something never before seen, so that the earth will open and swallow them up with all they own, this will prove that the rebels have offended God".

As soon as he finished speaking, the earth opened, and Korah, Dathan, Abiram, and their followers, with their tents and all their possessions, fell inside. The earth closed upon them, and they all perished.

Eleazar the Priest took the fire pans of the rebels and made with them broad plates for the covering of the altar, to remind the people that only the descendants of Aaron could offer incense to God.

David

(Hebrew origin: *Beloved, loving*)

(Ruth 4:17). 10th century B.C. David, the second king of Israel, reigned forty years, from about 1005 B.C. to 965 B.C.: the first seven years, as king of the Judah tribe in Hebron, and the following thirty-three years, over a united Israel, ruling from Jerusalem.

David was one of the most remarkable personalities in the Bible, vividly depicted with all his virtues and all his faults. He established a United Monarchy with Jerusalem as its capital, founded a dynasty that lasted four hundred years, and created a national Jewish identity that has survived till today.

Never again, under any other king, was the Hebrew nation so strong and powerful. David controlled an extensive empire, which reached from the river Euphrates to the frontier with Egypt. He became in the Jewish tradition the ideal king around whose figure and reign cluster messianic expectations of the restoration of the city and the people of Israel. In Christianity, the writers of the New Testament emphasized that Jesus was a descendant of David, since he was a symbol of fulfillment in the future. In the Hebrew Scriptures, his importance is second only to Moses.

He was a brilliant and complex man with protean talents, a brave warrior, a wily politician, a gifted musician, and a sensitive poet. In his private life, he was a ladies' man, and the indulgent father of a dysfunctional family.

The Bible describes David as a good-looking man, redhead, and with beautiful eyes. It was also said of him that he was "skillful in playing music, a fine warrior, a man of war, prudent in speech, and handsome".

David, the eighth and youngest son of Jesse, a well-to-do farmer, was born in the town of Bethlehem. His father was the grandson of Ruth the Moabitess and Boaz, of the clan of Perez of the tribe of Judah. From an early age, David, while guarding his father's sheep, had occasion to show his bravery by slaying a lion and a bear that had taken a lamb from the flock.

The prophet Samuel, who had become disillusioned with King Saul, was sent by God to Bethlehem. The elders of the town asked him in alarm, "Have you come in peace?" "Yes", he replied, "I have come to sacrifice to the Lord. Purify yourselves, and come with me to the sacrifice". He also instructed Jesse and his sons to purify themselves and to attend the sacrifice.

Samuel saw the sons of Jesse and said to himself about Eliab, the eldest one, "Surely he must be the one that will be anointed". But God said to Samuel, "Don't pay attention to his appearance or stature, because I have not chosen him. God sees not as man sees; man sees the outward appearance, but God looks into the heart".

After Jesse had made seven of his sons pass in front of Samuel, the prophet said to Jesse, "The Lord has not chosen any of these boys. Are these all your children?" Jesse answered, "There is one more, the youngest. He is out, taking care of the sheep". Samuel told him, "Send somebody to bring him here, because I will not sit down till he arrives". David, a ruddy and handsome boy, was brought in from the field. God said, "Arise and anoint him, because this is the one". Samuel took the horn of oil and anointed him in the presence of his brothers. And then, he returned to Ramah.

King Saul, after his final break with Samuel, became increasingly subject to fits of depression. His worried servants felt that music might make the king feel better. Somebody recommended David as a skilled musician, and the king asked that David be brought to him.

David came to the palace at Gibeah, carrying the gifts of bread, wine, and a young goat that his father Jesse had sent to the king. Saul was charmed by David, and from then on, whenever Saul would fall into one of his black moods, David would play music to him with his harp.

Sometime later, the Philistines gathered for battle on a hill, and the Israelites, led by Saul, lined on another hill, with a valley between the two armies. A nine feet tall giant, called Goliath, wearing heavy bronze armor, came out from the Philistine camp everyday and shouted a challenge to the Israelite army, saying that he was ready to fight any of them. Goliath did this every morning and evening for forty days.

David was in Bethlehem at that time, helping his father Jesse take care of the sheep. His three eldest brothers—Eliab, Abinadab, and Shammah—served in King Saul's army. Jesse, wanting to know how his sons were getting along, sent David to the army camp to find out, carrying with him ten loaves of bread for his brothers, and a gift of ten cheeses for their commanding officer.

David's arrival at the camp coincided with the moment when Goliath came forward to challenge the Israelites. David heard from the terrified soldiers that King Saul had promised great rewards to the man who would kill the giant. The king would give his daughter in marriage to this man and would free his family from the obligation of paying taxes.

Eliab, David's eldest brother, heard the young boy talking to the men and became angry with him. He asked him, "Why did you come here? With whom did you leave the sheep? I know your impudence and your impertinence. You came here to watch the fighting!" David answered, "What have I done now? I was only asking". He turned away to talk to other soldiers and asked them, "Who is that uncircumcised Philistine that he dares defy the ranks of the living God?"

David's words were overheard and were reported to Saul, who had him brought to his presence. David told Saul, "Your servant will go and fight that Philistine!" When the king expressed his doubts that he, a mere boy, could fight against the experienced Philistine warrior, David assured him that he had killed lions and bears. "God, who saved me from lion and bear, will also save me from that Philistine", said David. "Then, go", Saul said to David. "And may the Lord be with you!"

Saul gave him his armor to wear, but David, not used to it, took it off, picked up five smooth stones, and, with his sling ready in his hand, went to meet Goliath. The giant, seeing a young boy coming against him, called down curses on him. David told him, "You come against me with sword, spear, and javelin, but I come against you in the name of the Lord".

Goliath started walking ponderously toward David, who ran quickly toward the Philistine, took out a stone from his bag, and slung it at Goliath. The stone hit the giant on the forehead and made him fall to the ground. Goliath tried to get up but was unable to do so.

David ran to him, stood over the fallen giant, took his sword, and cut off his head. The Philistines, in shock, ran away, and the Israelites pursued them all the way up to the gates of their cities.

Saul appointed David as an officer in the army and did not allow him to go back to his father's home in Bethlehem. From that day on, the king kept David next to him. And Jonathan, Saul's son, became David's best friend.

David was successful in all his military missions and became very popular with the people. The women sang, "Saul has killed thousands, but David has killed tens of thousands". Saul became jealous and angry, and, suffering of depressive paranoia, he started to suspect that David planned to seize the throne. During one of his fits of depression, Saul tried to kill David with his spear but missed.

Saul considered that God was now with

David and became afraid of him. He removed David from his daily sight, by appointing him captain of a company of a thousand soldiers, and devised a plan to get rid of him by offering him his eldest daughter Merab in marriage, if he would fight against the Philistines, secretly hoping that David would be killed in battle.

When the time came to fulfill his promise, Saul, instead of giving Merab to David, married her to Adriel, the son of Barzillai the Meholathite. However, Michal, Saul's youngest daughter, loved David, which pleased Saul, as he saw a way to use her as a snare. He sent a message to David offering him his daughter in marriage and asked for a peculiar dowry, the foreskins of a hundred Philistines, still hoping that David would be killed by them.

David went and slew not one hundred Philistines but two hundred, and he brought their foreskins to the king. Saul, this time, did as he had promised and gave him Michal, his daughter, for a wife.

Saul grew more and more afraid of David. He even asked Jonathan, David's devoted friend, to kill him, but Jonathan advised David to hide, while he tried to convince his father not to kill him.

Saul listened to Jonathan's good words about David and agreed that he would not try to kill him, or hurt him. This did not last long, and, soon afterward, while David was playing the harp for him, Saul once more attempted to kill David with his spear. The weapon struck the wall, and David fled to his house.

That same night, helped by his wife Michal, David escaped through a window. Saul's envoys brought Michal to the palace, where her father asked her, "Why did you help my enemy to escape?"

Michal answered, "I did it only because David had threatened to kill me".

Saul, having heard that David had found refuge with Samuel in the town of Naioth in Ramah, sent soldiers to capture him. The men came to the town, but, instead of arresting David, they joined a company of prophets, and started to prophesy. Twice again, Saul sent men to Naioth, both times with the same result. Finally, the king decided to go himself in search of David, but, when he came to Naioth, he took off his clothes, lay down naked on the ground, all that day and all that night, and prophesied.

David fled from Naioth and went to see Jonathan, to find out from him why Saul hated him with such a murderous rage. He arrived the day before a banquet that Saul was giving in honor of the New Moon Festival. David told Jonathan that he would not take the risk of attending the king's banquet, and that Jonathan should explain his absence from the celebrations, by saying that David had gone to Bethlehem for the yearly family sacrifice. David instructed Jonathan to watch for Saul's reaction.

The two friends arranged that David should go away for three days, and then return and hide in a field. Jonathan would come to that place, under the pretext of shooting arrows, but in truth to inform David, by a prearranged code, whether it was safe to return to the royal court or not.

The next day, during the banquet, Saul noticed David's absence, but he attributed it to a possible illness. The following day, noticing that David was still absent, Saul asked Jonathan why David was not present. Jonathan answered that David was in Bethlehem for a family sacrifice. Saul, furious, screamed that Jonathan was a fool, and that, as long as David was alive, Jonathan would never be king. Jonathan asked him, "Why should he be killed? What has he done?" His father, losing all control, raised his spear to strike him. Jonathan arose from the table and left the hall, angry and humiliated. The next day, Jonathan went to the field where he had arranged to meet David. They embraced and wept, and David fled to Nob.

David arrived in the priestly town of Nob and went to see Ahimelech the Priest, who, thinking that it was very odd that David had come alone, asked him why he didn't bring any men with him. David told him a false story of being in a secret mission on behalf of King Saul, and that he was going to meet his men in such and such a place. He asked for bread, and Ahimelech answered that the only bread that he had available was consecrated bread, which David's men could eat only if they had kept themselves away from women. When David assured him that this was so, and that the utensils of the young men were consecrated, Ahimelech gave him the consecrated bread.

David, who had brought no weapons with him, asked Ahimelech for a sword or a spear, and the priest gave him the sword of Goliath the Philistine that had been entrusted to his care. David, carrying the weapon and the bread, fled to the Philistine city of Gath, which was ruled by King Achish.

The king's officials recognized David as the man about whom the Israelites had sang songs celebrating the killing of tens of thousands. David, afraid for his life, pretended to be insane, acted like a madman, scribbled on the city's gates, and let spit drool down his beard. Achish was convinced that David was truly crazy and allowed him to flee unharmed from the city.

David found refuge in the desert of Judah, in a cave near the town of Adullam. Men who were oppressed, dissatisfied, or in debt, came to him, and soon, David found himself leading a band of more than four hundred outlaws.

David, worried about the safety of his parents, went to Mizpeh of Moab to ask permission from the king of Moab to let his father and mother stay, under his royal protection, in the land of Jesse's grandmother, Ruth.

Unbeknownst to David, his meeting with Ahimelech had been witnessed by Doeg the Edomite, the head of the king's herdsmen. Doeg rushed back to Saul and reported what he had seen. The king had Ahimelech and all the other priests of Nob brought to his presence and accused them of conspiring with David against him and encouraging him to rebel against the king, by giving him food and a weapon.

Ahimelech denied any wrongdoing, saying that David, the king's son-in-law, was known to be a faithful servant to the king. Saul would not accept any explanations and condemned him to die. The king ordered the soldiers who were guarding the priests to kill them. Appalled, the servants did not move, and the king ordered Doeg to slay them, which he readily did, killing that day eighty-five priests. Then, he massacred all the people in Nob, including the women and the children, and even their animals. Abiathar, son of Ahimelech, the only survivor of King Saul's slaughter, managed to escape, and told David about the mass murder. David, feeling that he was the cause of the death of Abiathar's father, asked him to remain with him.

David was told that the Philistines were raiding the town of Keilah and plundering the threshing floors. David consulted the oracle of the Lord, if he should go and attack the Philistines, and was told to go at once to Keilah, and God would deliver the Philistines into his hands. David and his band, which by now had six hundred men, went to Keilah, fought against the Philistines, and defeated them.

Saul was told that David had come to Keilah and rejoiced, thinking that David had shut himself in by entering a town with gates and bars. He summoned his army, to go to Keilah, and besiege David and his men. David again consulted the oracle of God, through the ephod that the priest Abiathar had brought with him, "Saul intends to come to Keilah and destroy the town because of me. Will the citizens of the town deliver me into his hands?" God, through the oracle, answered, "They will". David and his men left Keilah immediately, and Saul desisted from his intention to besiege the town.

David returned to the desert, moving from place to place, constantly pursued by Saul. Once, while David was in Horesh in the wilderness of Ziph, Jonathan came to him in secret and told him, "Do not be afraid. You are going to be king over Israel, and I shall be second to you; and even my father Saul knows this is so". They never saw each other again.

David went from there and stayed in the wilderness of Engedi, near the Dead Sea. Saul took three thousand men and went in search of David and his men. There was a cave, and Saul went in to relieve himself. David and his men were hiding in the back of the cave. His men told him, "God has delivered your enemy into your hands; you can do with him as you please". David went and surreptitiously cut off the corner of Saul's cloak. He went back to his men and told them, "God forbid that I should raise my hand against the Lord's anointed". Later, he even felt remorse for cutting off a piece of Saul's cloak.

Saul left the cave and started back to his army's camp. Then, David went out of the cave and called after Saul, "My lord king!" Saul turned around, and David bowed low in homage, with his face to the ground, and said, "Why do you listen to people who say that I wish to do you harm? You can see for yourself that the Lord had delivered you into my hands in the cave today. Though I was urged to kill you, I did not raise a hand against you, because you are the Lord's anointed. My father, look at this piece of your cloak in my hand. When I cut it, I did not kill you. You can see that I have not done anything evil or rebellious. My hand will never touch you. Against whom has the king of Israel come out? A dead dog? A single flea?"

Saul asked, "Is that your voice, my son David?" The king broke down, wept, and said, "You are right, not I. I now know that you will become king. So swear to me by the Lord that you will not destroy my descendants or wipe out my name from my father's house". David swore to Saul. The king went home, and David and his men went up to the strongholds.

David and his band made their living from the contributions that he requested and received from the rich men who lived in the surrounding area. He sent ten of his men to Nabal, one of the wealthiest men in the region, to ask for his support. Nabal answered with contempt and refused to give them anything.

Abigail, the beautiful and intelligent wife of Nabal, realized David would come to punish Nabal for his insulting refusal. To prevent this, she loaded several asses with food and wine and, without telling her husband, went to intercept David. She apologized to David for her husband's bad manners and convinced him not to take revenge against Nabal. Abigail returned home and, because Nabal was drunk, only told him the next morning what she had done. Nabal, on hearing of his close escape,

suffered a stroke and died ten days later. David, hearing that Nabal had died, asked Abigail to marry him, and she agreed.

Saul, when told that David was hiding in the wilderness of Ziph, took with him three thousand chosen men and went in search of David. David came to the place where Saul and his army commander, Abner, lay asleep, with troops around them. David asked Ahimelech the Hittite and Abishai, the brother of Joab, to go with him to the king's camp. Abishai answered, "I will go with you". The two men approached the camp by night and found Saul asleep, his spear stuck in the ground near his head, and Abner and the troops sleeping around him. Abishai whispered to David, "God has delivered your enemy into your hands. Let me pin him to the ground with a single thrust of his spear. I will not have to strike him twice!" David rebuked him, "Don't kill him! No one can lay hands on the Lord's anointed with impunity. God himself will strike him down, or his time will come, and he will die, or he will fight in a battle and be killed. Just take the spear and the water jar at his head, and let's get out!" They left without being noticed, or waking anybody up.

David crossed over to the other side, stood on top of a hill, quite a distance away from the king's camp, and started shouting, "Abner, aren't you going to answer?" Abner shouted back, "Who are you to shout at the king?" David answered, "Aren't you a brave man? There is nobody like you in Israel. So why didn't you watch over your lord, the king? One of my men came to kill your master. You failed in your duty! You deserve to die for not protecting your master, the Lord's anointed. Look around, where are the king's spear and the water jar that were right by his head?"

Saul recognized David's voice and said, "Is this your voice, David, my son?" David replied, "It is, my lord king. Why does my lord continue to pursue his servant? What have I done? Of what wrong am I guilty? If God has incited you against me, I will make an offering to him, but if men have turned you against me, God should curse them, for they have driven me out of God's land to a foreign country and told me to worship foreign gods. Don't let me be killed away from the presence of the Lord. The king of Israel has come out to seek a single flea, as if he were hunting a partridge in the hills".

Saul answered, "I am wrong. Come back, David, my son. I will do no more harm to you, because you have spared my life tonight. I have been a fool, and I have made so many mistakes!" David said, "Here is the king's spear. Let one of the young men come over and get it. Today, I spared your life. May the Lord do the same to me and free me from all my troubles!" Saul said to David, "God bless you, my son! You will succeed in everything you do!" David then went his way, and Saul returned home.

David knew that Saul would not keep his promise, and would soon again try to capture and kill him. So he went with his wives, Abigail and Ahinoam, and his six hundred men to the Philistine city of Gath. Saul, when informed that David had fled to Gath, stopped pursuing him. Achish, the king of Gath, allowed David, his men, and their families to settle in the town of Ziklag, where they stayed for sixteen months.

David and his band became mercenary troops for the king of Gath. David would report to Achish that he had attacked and plundered Israelite towns, when in reality, he had raided the lands of the neighboring tribes and killed all the inhabitants to prevent Achish from learning the truth.

Achish trusted implicitly in David, having convinced himself that David's supposed acts against his own people had given cause to the Israelites to hate him so much that there was no going back for David, and he had now no choice but to serve him all his life. As an expression of his complete confidence in David, he made him his bodyguard.

The Philistines gathered a great army and marched against Israel, with Achish, David, and his men marching at the rear. The Philistine commanders asked, "Who are these Hebrews?" "That is David, King Saul's servant", answered Achish. "He has been with me for a year or more, and I have found no fault in him". The Philistine commanders, who did not share Achish's trust in David, were angry with him and said, "Send this man back. He will not march with us to the battle, or else he will turn against us, during the fight". Achish summoned David and said to him, "You are an honest man, but you are not acceptable to the other commanders. So, go back in peace tomorrow morning, as soon as it is light".

David and his men arrived back at Ziklag on the third day and found that, in their absence, Amalekites marauders had attacked the town, burned it, and taken all the women and children with them, including David's two wives, Ahinoam and Abigail. David pursued the raiders, rescued the captives, and recovered everything that the Amalekites had taken. When he reached Ziklag, he sent some of the goods that he had seized from the Amalekites to the elders of Judah in several towns, with a message, saying, "This is a present for you from the booty that we took from the enemies of the Lord".

Saul felt himself in need of guidance for the upcoming battle against the large Philistine army. He went to a medium in Endor, hoping to summon the spirit of Samuel. The prophet appeared and predicted the defeat of Israel and the death of Saul and his sons.

The next day, the armies engaged in battle. The Philistines slaughtered the Israelites and put them to flight. Three sons of Saul, including Jonathan, were among the slain. The king himself was badly wounded by an arrow and begged his armor bearer to kill him, rather than let him fall into the hands of the enemy. When the armor bearer, terrified, refused to do so, Saul fell on his own sword and died. The armor bearer, seeing that his master was dead, also committed suicide.

The Philistines cut off Saul's head and hang his body and those of his sons on the wall of the city of Beth-Shean. When the men of Jabesh-Gilead—the town that Saul had saved at the beginning of his reign—heard what the Philistines had done to Saul's body, they traveled all night, recovered the bodies, brought them to their city, cremated them, and buried their bones under a tree.

Three days after the return of David from his victory over the Amalekites, a young Amalekite arrived at Ziklag and told David that the Philistines had defeated the Israelites, and that Saul and Jonathan were dead.

David asked, "How do you know that they are dead?"

The Amalekite answered, "I was at Mount Gilboa and saw Saul leaning on his spear. He asked me to finish him off, because he was mortally wounded. This, I did. Then, I took the crown from his head, and the armlet from his arm, and I have brought them here to my lord".

David tore his clothes in sorrow and ordered his men to kill the bearer of the bad news for having dared to kill the Lord's chosen king. David was full with grief. Though Saul had persecuted him, he had raised the young David from obscurity to fame. Jonathan had been his beloved friend. His pain inspired him to compose one of the most beautiful laments in literature: "How Have the Mighty Fallen".

David consulted with God's oracle, if he should go to one of the cities of Judah, and was told to go to Hebron. He went there with his two wives and his men. The elders of the tribe came to him and crowned him king of Judah. David was thirty years old.

Abner, Saul's army commander, fled to the other side of the river Jordan with Saul's forty-year-old son, Ishbosheth, and made him king. During Ishbosheth's reign, which only lasted two years, there was sporadic fighting between the men of Abner and the men of David. In one of those battles, Abner's army was defeated, and Abner, while escaping, was forced to kill Asahel, the brother of Joab, commander of David's army.

Ishbosheth, without foreseeing the consequences, accused Abner of sleeping with Rizpah, Saul's concubine. Abner, furious at the accusation, transferred his support to David and promised to use his influence to help rally Israel to his side.

David told Abner that he was willing to receive him, on condition that Michal, Saul's daughter who once loved him, and who had been his first wife, should be returned to him. She was forcefully taken away from her husband, Phaltiel, who walked with her as far as Bahurim, weeping as he followed her, until Abner ordered him to turn back.

Abner spoke on behalf of David to the elders of Israel and to the tribe of Benjamin, King Saul's own tribe. Then, he came to Hebron, accompanied by twenty men. David received him warmly and celebrated his visit with a feast for his guests. The two men came to an agreement, by which Abner promised that he would rally the entire nation to David's side. David gave Abner a guarantee of safety and sent him on his way.

Joab, who had been away fighting, was told on his return to Hebron that Abner had come to visit the king. Immediately, Joab went to David and warned him that Abner had come to spy. Then, without David's knowledge, he managed to lure Abner back to Hebron, and while pretending to speak privately with him, Joab stabbed Abner in the stomach and killed him, in vengeance for the death of his brother Asahel.

Shocked by this treacherous murder, David buried Abner in Hebron with full honors. He walked behind the bier weeping, eulogized him, and fasted the whole day, to show that he had no part in the murder of Abner. The people noticed David's behavior and approved of it. Nobody blamed him for the death of Abner.

David cursed Joab and his house for his bloody deed, but he did not punish him. It was only many years later that David, on his deathbed, instructed his son Solomon to have Joab killed for this and other crimes.

A short time afterward, Ishbosheth was murdered in his sleep by two of his officers. They cut off his head and brought it to David at Hebron, expecting a reward. Instead, David ordered them killed for murdering an innocent man in his sleep. Their hands and feet were cut off, and they were hung by the pool in Hebron. The head of Ishbosheth was buried in the grave of Abner at Hebron. Finding themselves leaderless, the elders of Israel came to Hebron and acclaimed David king of Israel.

Jerusalem, at that time, was a Jebusite city, strongly fortified, outside of the control of the Israelite tribes. David decided to conquer it and besieged the city. Its overconfident inhabitants taunted him, shouting from the walls that even the blind and the cripple could defend the city against him. David promised to reward whoever would go up through the water tunnel and attack the Jebusites. Joab climbed and the city was taken.

David moved from Hebron to Jerusalem, called it David's City and made it his capital. The Philistines heard that David had been anointed king over Israel and sent an army against David, but they were defeated and pushed back all the way to Gezer.

David decided to make Jerusalem, not only the political center of the nation, but also its religious focus, by bringing into it the sacred Ark of the Covenant, which had been kept for many years by Abinadab in his house on a hill, near the town of Kirjathjearim, after the Philistines had returned it to the Israelites.

Uzzah, son of Abinadab, together with his brother Ahio, drove the cart carrying the Ark of the Covenant, from Gibeah, where it had been kept in their father's house, during twenty years, to Jerusalem. King David and the people of Israel accompanied the cart playing music and singing.

When the cart arrived to the threshing floor of Nachon, the oxen stumbled, and the Ark would have fallen if Uzzah had not steadied it with his hand. Immediately, he fell to the floor and died.

David, afraid that the Lord had stricken Uzzah for having touched the Ark with his hand, left the Ark in the house of Obededom the Gittite.

After three months, when David saw that Obededom had been blessed by God, he decided to have the Ark brought to Jerusalem. This was done with a great celebration, shouts of joy and the sounds of trumpets, with David dancing in front of the Ark with all his might to honor the Lord.

Michal, Saul's daughter, looking out from a window of the palace, saw David dancing and jumping, and she was disgusted with him.

When the king returned to greet his household, Michal came out to him and said, "How glorious was the king of Israel today, showing off himself in the sight of the slave girls of his servants, as one of the rabble might do!"

David replied, "It was before the Lord who chose me, instead of your father and all his family, and appointed me ruler over his people Israel! I will dance before the Lord, and disgrace myself even more, and be low in my own sight, but among the slave girls that you speak of I will be honored!" He never again came near Michal, and she, the only woman reported by the Bible as being in love with a man, died unloved, childless, and full of hate and contempt toward David, the love of her youth.

The Ark was placed in a tent, and David consulted with the prophet Nathan about building a Temple for the Ark. That night, the word of God told Nathan to say to David that his dynasty would be established forever, and that the building of the Temple would be done by his successor.

David made war against his neighbors and expanded the territories under his control. He defeated the Philistines and the Moabites. The Arameans and the Edomites became his vassals, and he stationed garrisons in Damascus and Edom. The river Euphrates became his northern frontier.

King David summoned Ziba, Saul's servant, to the court, and asked him if anybody was left of Saul's family. Ziba informed David that there was one survivor, Mephibosheth, a cripple, who lived in the house of Machir in Lodebar. King David had him brought to his presence. When Mephibosheth saw David, he flung himself on his face and prostrated himself. David told him not to be afraid, that his grandfather's land would be returned to him, for the sake of Jonathan's memory, and that he would always eat at the king's table. The king told Ziba that he was giving to Mephibosheth everything that had belonged to Saul, and that he, Ziba, his fifteen sons, and his twenty servants would farm the land for Mephibosheth to provide food for his master's grandson. Mephibosheth stayed in Jerusalem with his young son, Micha.

Nahash, king of Ammon, died and was succeeded by his son Hanun. David, grateful for the kindness that Nahash had always shown him, sent a delegation to offer his condolences to Hanun. This gesture was misinterpreted by Hanun's advisors, who told him that the Israelite ambassadors where not comforters but spies. Hanun seized the Israelites, shaved off half their beards, cut their garments up to their buttocks, and expelled them from his country.

The men, ashamed and embarrassed, were told by David to stay in Jericho, and not return to Jerusalem, until their beards had grown back.

Hanun belatedly realized that David would not let this insult go unpunished, so he hired an army of Aramean mercenaries to defend his kingdom. David sent his army under the command of Joab, who defeated the Arameans. The Ammonites, when they saw that the Arameans had fled, withdrew into their city. Joab broke off the attack and returned to Jerusalem.

At the turn of the year, David again sent Joab and the army to fight against the Ammonites and to besiege their city, while David remained in Jerusalem. One day, late in the afternoon, while walking on the roof of his palace, the king saw a beautiful woman bathing in her house. He made inquiries and was told that the woman's name was Bathsheba, and that she was the wife of Uriah the Hittite, a member of an elite army group known as The Thirty who served in the army under Joab. He had her brought to the palace and spent the night with her. The woman conceived and sent word to David, informing him that she was pregnant.

David sent a message to Joab, commander of the army, telling him to send Uriah home. Uriah, upon his arrival to Jerusalem, went straight to the king's palace to give his report. After hearing from Uriah about the state of the army, the king told him to go home. Uriah, instead of going home, stayed at the palace gate and slept next to the king's guards, because, as he explained to David, while his fellow soldiers were in the field, he would not go home, eat, drink, or sleep with his wife. David told him to stay in Jerusalem for one more day.

The next day, David invited him to dinner and got him drunk, but in the evening, Uriah again refused to go home. The next morning, David wrote a letter to Joab, which was carried by Uriah to the army camp. The letter stated, "Place Uriah in the front line where the fighting is the heaviest, then have the other soldiers retreat so that he may be killed".

Joab stationed Uriah and several other warriors close to the besieged city walls. The men of the city came out and killed several of the Israelite officers, Uriah among them. Joab sent a messenger to David to report the battle and the casualties. He told the messenger that, when the king would hear that several of his officers had been killed, he would be angry and would ask why they took the risk of coming so close to the city walls, and the messenger should answer, "Your servant Uriah the Hittite was among those killed".

The conversation between the messenger and David went exactly as Joab had expected. When David heard that Uriah was dead, he breathed a silent sigh of relief and said, "Tell Joab not to be distressed about this matter, because the sword may kill anyone. Press your attack on the city and destroy it. Encourage him!"

King David married Bathsheba, as soon as her days of mourning were over. After she gave birth to the baby, the prophet Nathan came to David and told him a parable of a rich man with many sheep who took a poor man's lamb and cooked it to honor a traveler. David, not understanding the allusion, became very angry and threatened to punish the rich man for his lack of pity. Nathan told him, "You are that man". David expressed remorse and recognized that he had sinned. Nathan told him that he would not die, but the baby would.

Bathsheba's baby fell critically ill. David prayed to God to heal the boy. He fasted and spent the night, lying on the ground. His courtiers tried to induce him to get up, and eat something, but he refused. On the seventh day, the baby died. His servants were afraid to tell him that the baby was dead, saying, "While the boy was still alive, he would not listen to us. How will he react if we tell him that the child has died?" When David saw his servants talking in whispers, he asked them, "Is the child dead?" "Yes", they replied.

David rose from the ground, bathed, anointed himself, and changed his clothing. He went to the House of the Lord and prayed. Then, he came back to the palace, asked for food, and ate. His courtiers were bewildered and asked him, "While the child was alive, you fasted and wept; but now that the child is dead, you rise and eat?"

David answered, "While the child was still alive, I fasted and wept, because I thought that God may have pity on me, and let the child live. But now that he is dead, why should I fast? Can I bring him back? I shall go to him, but he will never come back to me". David went to Bathsheba and consoled her. She had a baby who was named Solomon, although the prophet Nathan called him Jedidiah.

David had nineteen sons, not counting the sons of his concubines, and one daughter. Six sons were born in Hebron: Amnon, his first-born, the son of Ahinoam the Jezreelitess; Chileab—also called Daniel—the son of Abigail the Carmelitess; Absalom, the son of Maacah, the daughter of Talmai, king of Geshur; Adonijah, the son of Haggith; Shephatiah, the son of Abital; and Ithream, the son of Eglah.

Another thirteen sons were born in Jerusalem. Four of them were the sons of Bathsheba: Shimea—also called Shammuah—Shobab, Nathan, and Solomon. The other nine were Ibhar, Nogah, Nepheg, Japhia, Eliada, two boys called Elishama, and two boys called Eliphelet. His daughter Tamar, Absalom's sister, was also born in Jerusalem.

Joab sent messengers to David, saying, "I have captured the water supply of Rabbah, the capital city of the Ammonites. Come with the rest of the army, and capture the city. Otherwise, I will capture it myself, and call it after my name". David gathered his troops, came over, and took the city. The king of Ammon's heavy gold crown, adorned with precious stones, was placed on David's head. He set the people to do forced labor, and, carrying off a vast amount of booty from the

city, he and the army returned to Jerusalem.

Amnon, King David's firstborn son, developed a passion for Tamar, his half sister. Following the advice of his shrewd cousin Jonadab, he convinced his father that he was sick, and that he wished that Tamar should bring him food to his house. David sent Tamar to Amnon's house, where she baked cakes for him. Amnon told his men to go out and leave Tamar alone with him. After raping her, he couldn't stand her sight and had her thrown out of his house. Tamar put dust on her head, tore the ornamented tunic she was wearing, and walked away, screaming loudly as she went. Absalom met her and asked her, "Was it your brother Amnon who did this to you? For the present, sister, keep quiet about it; he is your brother. Don't brood over this matter". Absalom gave her refuge in his house.

When King David heard about the rape, he was greatly upset, but he did not rebuke Amnon. Absalom also didn't utter a word to Amnon. He hated him in silence and waited patiently for the right moment to revenge his sister. Two years later, Absalom saw his opportunity. He invited his father, King David, to a sheep-shearing celebration. The king did not accept the invitation, but, when Absalom insisted, he allowed Amnon and his other sons to attend the party. During the feast Absalom had his servants kill Amnon to avenge his sister's rape. The first report that King David received was that Absalom had killed all his brothers, but then, the news came that only Amnon had died. Absalom fled to Geshur and stayed there with his maternal relatives for three years.

Joab noticed that David longed for Absalom, but his stubbornness didn't allow him to call him back. Therefore, Joab organized a charade by getting a woman from Tekoah to tell David a tale, which was in all its essential points Absalom's tale, and pointed to the need for forgiveness. David asked her, "Has Joab instructed you to do this?" She confessed that, yes, Joab had told her what to say.

The king told Joab, "Go and bring Absalom back". Joab flung himself to the ground and thanked the king for granting him his request. Joab went to Geshur and brought Absalom back. However, King David refused to see him, and Absalom went directly to his house in Jerusalem.

Two years passed, after his return, and Absalom had not yet seen the king. He sent for Joab to ask him to speak to the king on his behalf, but Joab would not come. Again Absalom sent for him, and again Joab refused to come. Absalom then forced Joab to come to him by having his servants burn Joab's field. Joab went to Absalom's house and demanded to know why Absalom's servants had set fire to his field. Absalom answered that it was because Joab had not come, when he had sent for him, and that he wanted Joab to arrange for Absalom to see the king. Joab went to King David and told him what Absalom had said. The king sent for Absalom, who went to him and bowed down to the ground in front of him. The king welcomed him with a kiss.

Absalom, after the death of Amnon, as the eldest surviving son of David, was the obvious successor to the throne. Considering this, it is not easy to understand why, after the reconciliation with his father, Absalom started preparing, carefully and patiently, the groundwork for an attempt to depose David and make himself king. It is possible that Absalom was afraid that David, under the influence of Bathsheba, his favorite wife, would make Solomon, his successor, which indeed is what eventually happened.

Absalom, though strong headed and willful, was a patient man, who knew how to bide his time in order to achieve his purpose, and how to work for that end. His first step was to win the love of the people. He would stand at the city gates, intercept the travelers who were bringing their disputes for judgment, and pay them flattering attention. He provided himself with a chariot, horses, and fifty runners. Absalom soon became very popular, and the most admired man in the kingdom, famous for his beauty, and for his luxurious head of hair that he would cut only once a year.

The conspiracy to dethrone David was carefully planned. When Absalom judged that the time had come, he went to Hebron with two hundred men and proclaimed himself king. Ahithophel, David's most respected counselor, joined Absalom in Hebron. The Bible does not explain why Ahithophel supported Absalom's rebellion, but the fact that he was the grandfather of Bathsheba, through his son Eliam, suggests that Ahithophel might have been angry with David for causing the death of Uriah, and then marrying his widow.

David, upon hearing of the revolt, abandoned Jerusalem and retreated with his bodyguards, his foreign mercenaries—the Kerethites and Pelethites—and six hundred Gittites, to the other side of the Jordan River. The king left in Jerusalem ten of his concubines to take care of the palace.

Ittai the Gittite, one of the commanders of David's army, was told by David that he, as a foreigner, should go back and stay with the new king. Ittai refused to leave David and accompanied him in his flight, saying that, in life or death, he would remain with the king.

The people along the road wept as the troops marched by. The priests Zadok and Abiathar, accompanied by Levites, came carrying the Ark of the Covenant. The king said to Zadok, "Take the Ark back to the city. If I find favor with the Lord, he will bring me back and let me see it and its abode. But if he says, 'I find no delight in you', I am ready; let him do with me as he pleases". Zadok and his son Ahimaaz, and Abiathar and his son Jonathan, returned to Jerusalem.

David, and all the people who were with him, went up, barefooted, the slope of the Mount of Olives, weeping, with covered heads. David, when told that his wise counselor Ahithophel had joined the conspiracy, prayed, "O Lord, please thwart the advice of Ahithophel!"

Hushai the Archite, a loyal friend and adviser of King David, wanted to join David in his flight from Absalom. David refused, saying that Hushai would only be a burden to the fleeing army, but that he could be most useful to his cause if he would go to Absalom, pretend that he had transferred his loyalties to him, and do his utmost to defeat the counsel of Ahithophel. Whatever he learned in the rebel's camp, he should report back to David, sending this information by two messengers: Ahimaaz, son of Zadok the Priest, and Jonathan, son of Abiathar the Priest.

After they had passed the summit of the Mount of Olives, Ziba, the servant of Mephibosheth, came to him with two asses, carrying two hundred loaves of bread, a hundred bunches of raisins, a hundred summer fruits, and a bottle of wine, and told the king that the asses were for the king's family, the food for his attendants, and the wine for those who were exhausted.

The king asked him about the whereabouts of Mephibosheth, and Ziba told him that he had stayed behind in Jerusalem, hoping that the people of Israel would crown him king. David told Ziba that everything that had belonged to Mephibosheth was now his. Ziba bowed low and thanked him.

As King David was approaching Bahurim, a member of Saul's clan, a man named Shimei, the son of Gera, met David and his men on the road, cursed David, and threw stones at him, shouting, "Get out, get out! You are a bloody man, a criminal! You usurped Saul's kingdom, and God is punishing for murdering Saul's family! God has given the kingdom to your son Absalom because you are a bloody man!"

Abishai, King David's nephew, who was standing nearby with his brother Joab, said to David, "Why should this dog curse my lord, the king? Please let me go over and take off his head!" David said, "What have I to do with you, you sons of Zeruiah? Let him curse, because God has said to him, 'Curse David'. Who has the right to ask why he does it? My own son is trying to kill me, so don't be surprised at this Benjamite. Leave him alone, let him curse. Perhaps, God will see my affliction and will repay this cursing with blessings".

David and his men continued on their way, with Shimei walking on the hillside, cursing him and throwing stones.

Absalom came to Jerusalem with all his people, including Ahithophel. Hushai met Absalom and exclaimed, "Long live the king!

Long live the king!" Absalom, surprised, asked him, "Is this your loyalty to your friend? Why didn't you go with him?" Hushai answered, "I am on the side of the one that the Lord, and the people of Israel have chosen".

Absalom then asked Ahithophel, "What do you advise me to do now?" Ahithophel advised Absalom to have sexual relations with the concubines whom David had left in the palace, so as to make clear to the people who was now in charge. A tent was pitched for Absalom on the roof of the palace, and Absalom and the concubines went in there.

The rebels held a council attended by Absalom, Ahithophel, and the elders of Israel. Ahithophel said to Absalom, "Let me pick twelve thousand men and set out tonight in pursuit of David. I will come upon him, while he is still tired and weak. His troops will flee, and I will kill only the king. I will bring back his men to you, and the people will be at peace".

Absalom and the elders liked the advice, but Absalom said, "Let's hear what Hushai has to say about this". Hushai came to Absalom and heard what Ahithophel had advised. He said to Absalom, "This time Ahithophel's advice is not good. Your father and his men are brave fighters and would fight with all the courage of their desperation. Your father is an experienced soldier. He will not be with his troops, but probably hiding somewhere. I advise you to call all the men in the kingdom to your army, and then march against your father, with you personally leading them. No one will survive, not your father, and not his men". Absalom and the elders considered Hushai's advice better than Ahithophel's.

When Ahithophel saw that his advice had been rejected, he saw clearly that Absalom was making a fatal mistake, and that the rebellion would be defeated. He went home, put his household in order, and hanged himself.

Hushai told the priests Zadok and Abiathar that he had succeeded in convincing Absalom, that this time Ahithophel's advice was not practical, and that it should be rejected. He told them to send their sons at once to David, and tell him to cross immediately to the other side of the Jordan River, to avoid being annihilated.

David had reached Mahanaim and had managed to regroup his army, when Absalom and his army, commanded by Amasa, crossed the Jordan. Shobi—the son of King Nahash of Ammon—Machir, and Barzillai came to Mahanaim, bringing beds, basins, vessels, and food for David and his men.

David divided his army and placed one-third under the command of Joab, one-third under the command of Abishai, Joab's brother, and one-third under the command of Ittai the Gittite. The king told the troops that he would lead them, but the soldiers replied that it would be better if he would support them from the town. The king stood beside the gate of the city, as the army marched out. David gave orders to the three commanders to deal gently with his son. These orders were heard by all the soldiers.

The battle between the two armies took place in the woods of Ephraim. The rebels were routed by David's army and suffered over twenty thousand casualties. Absalom, fleeing the scene of his defeat, was caught by the hair on his head in the branches of a thick tree and was left dangling in the air, while his mule kept going. One of the men saw him and told Joab, "I have just seen Absalom hanging from a tree". Joab exclaimed, "You saw him, and you didn't kill him? I would have given you ten shekels of silver and a girdle". The man replied, "Even for a thousand shekels, I wouldn't have done it. The king gave orders not to hurt Absalom". Joab said, "I will not wait for you". He took three darts in his hand and drove them into Absalom's chest. Ten of Joab's soldiers closed in and struck Absalom, until he died.

Ahimaaz, the son of Zadok, asked Joab to let him run to the king, and report the victory to him. Joab said to him, "You will not bring him news this day, because his son has died". Joab told a soldier called Cushi, "Go tell the king what you have seen". Cushi bowed and ran off. Ahimaaz insisted, "Let me run too". Joab asked him, "Why should you run, when you have no news worth telling?" Ahimaaz

replied, "I will run, anyway". "Then, run", said Joab.

David was sitting between the inner and outer gate of the city. The watchman on the roof of the gate looked up, saw a man running alone, and told David.

David said, "If he is alone, he is bringing news".

Then, the watchman announced that he saw a second man running, and the king said, "He is also bringing news".

The watchman said, "I think that the first runner is Ahimaaz, the son of Zadok".

The king said, "He is a good man and comes with good news".

Ahimaaz called out and said to the king, "All is well". He bowed low to the king and said, "Blessed be the Lord, your God, who has delivered the men who lifted their hand against my lord, the king".

The king asked, "Is the young man Absalom safe?" Ahimaaz answered, "When Joab, the king's servant, was sending me off, I saw a great commotion, but I don't know what it was about".

The king told him, "Step aside and stand over there".

Cushi arrived and said, "News, my lord, the king. The Lord has avenged you this day against all those who rebelled against you". The king asked, "Is the young man Absalom safe?"

Cushi replied, "May all the enemies of my lord, the king, and all who rise against you to harm you, fare like that young man".

The king was much shaken. He went up to the chamber over the gate and wept, repeating again and again, "O my son Absalom, my son, my son Absalom! If only I had died, instead of you! O Absalom, my son, my son!"

Joab was told that the king was weeping and mourning for Absalom. The troops heard that the king was grieving for his son, and their victory that day turned into mourning. Joab went to see David and told him bluntly, "Today, you have humiliated all your followers, who this day saved your life, and the lives of your sons and daughters, and the lives of your wives and concubines, by showing love to those who hate you, and hate to those who love you. You have made it very clear that you do not care about your officers and your men. I am sure that, if Absalom today was alive, and the rest of us dead, you would have been glad. Now, arise, come out, and reassure your men. I swear by the Lord that, if you don't come out, not even one soldier will remain with you overnight, and that would be the worst thing that you will have suffered in your whole life".

The king got up and sat by the gate, and the troops gathered around him.

A short time later, David named Amasa, who had been the commander of Absalom's army, as the new commander in chief of the army, replacing Joab, for the sake of national reconciliation. Amasa spoke to the elders of Judah, and they sent a message to David, asking him to return to Jerusalem with his followers.

The king started back, and, before crossing the Jordan, he was met by the men of Judah. Shimei, the son of Gera, accompanied by a thousand men of Benjamin, also hurried to meet David, who was still on the other side of the river Jordan. Shimei crossed the river, and when he was in front of the king, he threw himself down and begged for forgiveness. Abishai said, "Shimei should be put to death for having cursed God's anointed". David said, "What have I to do with you, you sons of Zeruiah? I am the king of Israel now, and no Israelite will be put to death today". And to Shimei he said, "I swear to you that you will not be put to death".

Mephibosheth, Saul's grandson, also came down to meet the king. He had not pared his toenails, or trimmed his beard, nor did he wash his clothes from the day that the king had departed.

The king asked him, "Why didn't you come with me?"

Mephibosheth told David that he had intended to saddle his donkey and join the king, but Ziba had deceived him and slandered him. He added that he was grateful to David, and that he had no right to appeal to him. The king told him that there was no need to explain anymore, and that the property would be divided between him and Ziba. Mephibosheth answered that Ziba should take it all as long as King David had returned home safe.

Barzillai, the Gileadite of Rogelim, one of the men who had brought utensils and food to David, during his stay in Mahanaim, came to greet the king. The king invited Barzillai to come with him to Jerusalem. Barzillai declined the offer, saying that he was already an old man—he was eighty years old at the time—and that all he wanted at that stage of his life was to die in his own city and be buried near the graves of his parents. Instead, he proposed that his son Chimham should go with the king. The king gladly accepted, kissed Barzillai, blessed him, and returned to Jerusalem, taking Chimham with him.

Sheba, son of Bichri, a Benjamite, rebelled against the king and was followed by the men of Israel, but the men of Judah accompanied David to Jerusalem. David went to his palace and placed the ten concubines, whom he had left to take care of the palace, under guard. He never went close to them again. They lived in seclusion, living in widowhood, until the day they died.

David, believing that Sheba's insurrection could be even more dangerous than the rebellion of Absalom, urged Amasa to organize an army in three days. When Amasa did not report back in the allotted time, the king sent Abishai to pursue the rebels. Amasa met Abishai and Joab near Gibeon. Joab saluted Amasa, saying, "How are you, brother?" While he was speaking, he took hold of Amasa's beard with his right hand, as if to kiss him, and, with his left hand, drove his sword into Amasa's belly, killing him. Joab then proceeded to pursue Sheba who found refuge in the town of Abel. When the troops started to batter down the walls of the city, the inhabitants cut off Sheba's head and threw it down to Joab. Joab and his army returned to Jerusalem, and Joab was again named commander of the army.

There was a famine in the land, which lasted for three years. David consulted the oracle of God and was told that the famine was caused by the guilt of Saul and his family for having put some Gibeonites to death. The Gibeonites were a remnant of the Amorite people, whom the Israelites had promised to protect, but Saul had tried to exterminate in his zeal for the people of Israel and Judah.

David called the Gibeonites and asked them, "How can I make expiation for Saul's crime?" They replied, "This cannot be solved with a payment of silver or gold, nor do we wish for the death of any Israelite. Give us seven of Saul's male descendants and we will hang them in Gibeah, Saul's city". David answered, "I will give them to you".

The king spared Jonathan's son Mephibosheth, the grandson of Saul, because of the oath that he and Jonathan had sworn to each other. He took Armoni and Mephibosheth, the sons of Rizpah, Saul's concubine, and the five sons whom Merab, the daughter of Saul, had borne to Adriel, the son of Barzillai the Meholathite, and he handed them over to the Gibeonites.

The seven men were hanged on a hill. Rizpah took sackcloth, sat on it upon a rock, and guarded the bodies against the birds and the beasts of the field, from the beginning of the harvest season until, months later, the rains came.

David gathered the bones of Saul and Jonathan from the men of Jabesh-Gilead—the town that Saul had saved at the beginning of his reign—and the bones of the seven men, who had been hanged by the Gibeonites, and reburied them in the tomb of Kish, Saul's father.

David decided to take a census of the people and put Joab in charge of carrying it out. It took Joab and his men nine months and twenty days to count the people and report to the king that there were eight hundred thousand men capable of military service in Israel and five hundred thousand in Judah.

David repented of having taken the census, which had not been authorized by God, and asked forgiveness for his sin. The prophet Gad, sent by God, allowed David to choose one of three alternative punishments: seven years of famine, three months fleeing from his enemies, or three days of pestilence in the land. David chose the third alternative, and over seventy thousand people died.

God, speaking through the prophet Gad, told David to build an altar in Araunah's threshing floor, in expiation for his sin. Araunah was threshing wheat, when he saw the king and his courtiers approaching.

Araunah bowed to the ground and asked, "To what do I owe this great honor?"

David answered, "I have come to buy your threshing floor, which I need for the altar that I want to build to stop the plague".

Araunah replied, "Please take the threshing floor, and sacrifice there whatever you may see fit. I will be pleased to provide also the oxen and the wood for the sacrifice".

David refused his offer and said that he could not sacrifice to God if it did not cost him anything. He paid Araunah fifty shekels of silver—elsewhere it is reported that the amount paid was six hundred shekels of gold (1 Chronicles 21:25)—for the threshing floor and the oxen.

The king built an altar on the piece of land and sacrificed the oxen. God heard his plea and stopped the plague. Years later, King Solomon built the Temple in this site.

David grew old, and when he was almost killed, during a battle against the Philistines, his soldiers asked him not to go with them into battle anymore. In his old age, he shivered with cold, and his servants brought to him a beautiful girl, Abishag, who became his nurse and took care of him.

Adonijah, the fourth son of King David—his mother was Haggith—was next in line as heir to the kingdom and behaved accordingly, boasting that he would be king and providing himself with chariots and horses, and fifty men to run before him. Joab, the army's commander, and Abiathar, the High Priest, supported him in his bid for the throne, but other influential people in the court opposed him, among them Zadok, the other High Priest, and Nathan, the prophet, who sided with Solomon, the son of Bathsheba.

Adonijah invited all his brothers, except Solomon, and the leaders of the tribe of Judah to a sacrificial feast. Nathan asked Bathsheba to go to King David, tell him what Adonijah was doing, and remind the old king that he had promised the throne to Solomon. While Bathsheba was still talking to the king, Nathan came in and confirmed the story. Under Nathan's influence, David ordered that Solomon should immediately be anointed king in Gihon by the priest Zadok and the prophet Nathan. When this was done the people shouted, "Long live King Solomon", and rejoiced with great joy.

Jonathan, the son of Abiathar, came to Adonijah's feast with the news that Solomon had been proclaimed king. All the guests who were with Adonijah hurriedly left in fear. Adonijah himself sought sanctuary at the altar. Solomon, at that moment, took no action against his brother and allowed him to go to his house, but, after the death of David, he had him killed, when he interpreted Adonijah's desire to marry Abishag, the beautiful Shunammite girl, who had warmed King David in his old age, as a bid for the throne.

On his deathbed, David told Solomon to follow the Lord's commandments, to show special kindness to the children of Barzillai, who had been kind to David, when he was fleeing from Absalom, and to punish Joab for having murdered the two commanders of Israel's army: Abner and Amasa. Interestingly enough, David did not include, in the list of Joab's murders, the killing of Absalom, which Joab had carried out against his specific instructions.

David also told Solomon that he should not let Shimei go unpunished, for having cursed the king, during his darkest hours.

David died at the age of seventy, after having been king for forty years: seven in Hebron and thirty-three in Jerusalem. He was buried in the City of David and was succeeded by his son Solomon.

Debir

(Hebrew origin: *Oracle*)

(Joshua 10:3). 12th century B.C. Debir, the king of Eglon, was asked by Adonizedek, the king of Jerusalem, to join him and several other kings—Hoham, the king of Hebron; Japhia, the king of Lachish; and Piram, the king of Jarmuth—in a military alliance against the city of Gibeon to punish the Gibeonites for having made peace with the people of Israel. The people of Gibeon appealed to Joshua for help.

Joshua—after ordering the sun to stand still over Gibeon, and the moon over the valley of Ajalon—fought against the five kings and defeated them. Their armies ran away, during a storm of hailstones, which killed many of their soldiers, even more than those who had been killed in the fighting. The five kings fled and hid in a cave at Makkedah, where they were trapped.

After Joshua had liquidated all the surviving enemies, he ordered that the kings should be taken out from the cave. Debir, Adonizedek, Hoham, Japhia, and Piram, after being humiliated, were killed and hanged on five trees, until the evening. At sunset, their corpses were taken down and thrown into the cave, where they had been hiding, and large stones were placed over the entrance to the cave.

Deborah

(Hebrew origin: *Bee*)

1. (Genesis 35:8). 19th century B.C. Deborah, Rebekah's nurse, who had raised the girl from childhood, accompanied Rebekah to Canaan, when the young woman went to marry Isaac. She remained with Rebekah, for many years, until her death. Deborah was buried in Bethel under an oak tree.

2. (Judges 4:4). 12th century B.C. Deborah, the wife of a man named Lapidoth, was a prophetess and judge of Israel. The Israelites would come to Deborah's home, situated between Ramah and Bethel, where she, sitting under a palm tree, would settle their disputes.

At that time, the Israelites were oppressed by Jabin, the king of Hazor—a city kingdom situated in the northern part of the Galilee—whose powerful army included nine hundred iron chariots.

Deborah summoned Barak, son of Abinoam, and told him to go to Mount

Tabor with an army of ten thousand men, drawn from the tribes of Naphtali and Zebulun, and fight against Sisera, the commander of Jabin's army. Barak accepted with the condition that she would also come.

She said, "I will go with you, but the honor of the victory will not be yours, because God will deliver Sisera into the hands of a woman".

Barak defeated the army of Hazor. Sisera lighted down from his chariot and fled by foot to the tent of Heber the Kenite, whom he thought was neutral in the war between Hazor and the Israelites. There, he was killed in his sleep by Jael, Heber's wife.

The power of King Jabin over the Israelites was thus broken. Deborah, in her victory song, mentioned that, although she had also called other tribes to join them in the fight against Sisera, the tribes of Dan, Reuben, and Asher did not respond to her call.

Note: In the book of Judges, a judge is a ruler or governor of territory or a military leader in pre-monarchical Israel. Later, during the monarchy, the king served in this role and judges were more like the judicial officers that we know today.

Dedan

(Hebrew origin: Uncertain meaning)

1. (Genesis 10:7). Unspecified date. Dedan and Sheba were the sons of Raamah, a descendant of Noah through his son Ham.
2. (Genesis 25:3). 18th century B.C. Dedan and Sheba were the sons of Jokshan and grandsons of Abraham and Keturah, the woman whom Abraham married, after Sarah died. The sons of Dedan were Asshurim, Letushim, and Leummim.

Dekar

(Hebrew origin: *Stabber* or *Piercer*)

(1 Kings 4:9). 10th century B.C. Dekar was the father of one of King Solomon's twelve district governors—whose name is not speci-

fied by the Bible—responsible for providing food from his district for the king and the royal household for one month out of each year.

Delaiah

(Hebrew origin: *God has delivered*)

1. (1 Chronicles 24:18). 10th century B.C. During the reign of King David, the priestly service in the Tabernacle was divided by lot into twenty-four turns. Delaiah was in charge of the twenty-third turn.
2. (Ezra 2:60). Unspecified date. Delaiah was the ancestor of a family that returned with Zerubbabel from the Babylonian Exile. The members of this family were dismissed from the priesthood, because they could not prove their genealogy.
3. (Nehemiah 6:10). 5th century B.C. Delaiah, son of Mehetabeel, was the father of Shemaiah, the man who was hired by Tobiah and Sanballat, Nehemiah's enemies, to try to convince Nehemiah that he should hide in the Temple. Shemaiah failed, because Nehemiah realized that his enemies were setting a trap for him to induce him to sin, and would then report it.
4. (Jeremiah 36:12). 7th century B.C. Delaiah, son of Shemaiah, was an official in the court of King Jehoiakim, sympathetic to Jeremiah and Baruch. Baruch was brought to the palace and was asked to read aloud the scroll, on which he had written Jeremiah's words.

When Baruch finished reading, the officials, terrified at what they had heard, told Baruch that he and Jeremiah should hide.

Baruch's scroll was brought to King Jehoiakim and was read to him. As soon as a couple of leaves of the scroll had been read, the king would cut them off with a knife and throw them into the fireplace, although his officers—Gemariah, Delaiah, and Elnathan—tried unsuccessfully to convince the king not to burn the scroll.

Delilah

(Hebrew origin: *Languishing*)

(Judges 16:4). 12th century B.C. Delilah, a Philistine woman who lived in the valley of Sorek, was loved by Samson.

Several Philistine leaders offered her the sum of eleven hundred pieces of silver each, if she would find out the secret of Samson's great strength. Three times she asked Samson, and three times he gave her a wrong explanation. Eventually, her daily insistence broke him down, and he revealed to her that the real cause of his strength was that never had a razor cut his hair.

When Delilah heard this, she called the Philistines leaders, who paid her the promised sum for her betrayal. That night, she made Samson sleep upon her knees and had a man cut the seven locks of his head. Samson, having lost his strength, was easily overpowered by the Philistines. His eyes were put out, and he was thrown in prison in Gaza.

Demas

(Greek origin: probably a contraction of *Demetrius*)

(Colossians 4:14). A.D. 1st century. Demas, one of the companions of Paul in the Roman prison, is mentioned by the apostle as sending greetings in two of his letters: Colossians and Philemon.

In a third letter—Second Timothy—Paul expresses disappointment with Demas for having forsaken him due to "his love for this present world".

Demetrius

(Greek origin: *Belonging to Demeter, Greek goddess of agriculture*)

1. (Acts of the Apostles 19:24). A.D. 1st century. Demetrius, a silversmith in the city of Ephesus, earned his living making and selling silver statuettes of the goddess Diana. He felt that the missionary activities of Paul were sharply reducing the demand for idols, and, thus, threatening his livelihood.

Demetrius instigated a riot against Paul and his companions, but he was told by the town official that, if he had any complaints against Paul, he should follow the legal procedure and bring the matter to court.

2. (3 John 1:12). A.D. 1st century. Demetrius was the bearer of the third letter of John the Elder, which was addressed to Gaius.

Deuel

(Hebrew origin: *Known by God*)

(Numbers 1:14). 14th century B.C. His son Eliasaph was the leader of the tribe of Gad, during the Exodus from Egypt. His name is spelled Reuel in the book of Numbers (Numbers 2:14).

Devil

(Greek origin: *Slanderer*)

(Matthew 4:1). Devil is an evil angel, also called Beelzebub and Satan. The New Testament tells his attempts to tempt Jesus in the desert and describes several cases of the devil possessing a person, and being expelled by Jesus. (See the entry for Satan [1 Chronicles 21:1].)

Diana

(Name of a pagan goddess)

(Acts of the Apostles 19:24). Diana—called Artemis in Greek—the goddess of fertility, was represented in her statues as a multiple breasted woman. Her Temple in Ephesus was one of the most important centers of pilgrimage in antiquity.

Her followers, instigated by Demetrius, a silversmith, rioted against Paul, accusing him of threatening the tourism to their city, and, thus, their income, by deriding her worship.

(Please see the entry for Demetrius [Acts of the Apostles 19:24].)

Diblaim

(Hebrew origin: *Two cakes*)

(Hosea 1:3). 8th century B.C. Diblaim was the father of Gomer, a woman of ill repute, whom the prophet Hosea married to symbolize the faithlessness of Israel to God. She had three children: two boys, Jezreel and Loammi, and a girl, Loruhamah.

Dibri

(Hebrew origin: *Wordy*)

(Leviticus 24:11). 14th century B.C. His grandson, son of his daughter Shelomith and an Egyptian, was stoned to death for having blasphemed the name of the Lord.

Didymus

(Greek origin: *Twin*)

(John 11:16). A.D. 1st century. This Greek word is not a surname but a translation of the apostle's name Thomas, which means *Twin* in Hebrew. It might be that both "Thomas" and "Didymus" are nicknames of an apostle whose real name is not known.

Thomas was loyal to Jesus to the point that he was ready to die for him and with him (John 11:16), but he did not hesitate to interrupt Jesus by asking him questions if he thought that something was not clear (John 14:5).

Thomas was a practical man who preferred to believe the evidence of his own eyes. When he heard that the other disciples had seen Jesus resurrected, he refused to believe them, until Jesus appeared to them and showed them his wounds (John 20:27).

He was together with Peter and other disciples at the sea of Tiberias during the third and last time that Jesus appeared to them, after he had risen from the dead.

Thomas is last mentioned in the New Testament (Acts of the Apostles 1:13), when the disciples got together, in the Upper Room, to choose a replacement for Judas.

Diklah

(Hebrew origin: *Palm tree*)

(Genesis 10:27). Unspecified date. Diklah was the son of Joktan, a descendant of Noah and Shem. His brothers were Sheleph, Hazarmaveth, Jerah, Hadoram, Uzal, Almodad, Obal, Abimael, Sheba, Ophir, Havilah, and Jobab.

Dinah

(Hebrew origin: *Judgment*)

(Genesis 30:21). 17th century B.C. Dinah, the daughter of Jacob and Leah, was born after her mother had given birth to six sons.

Dinah's full brothers were Zebulun, Issachar, Reuben, Levi, Judah, and Simeon, sons of Leah. Her half brothers were Gad and Asher, sons of Zilpah; Dan and Naphtali, sons of Bilhah; and Benjamin and Joseph, sons of Rachel.

She was raped by Shechem, son of the ruler of the city of Shechem, who fell in love with her and asked his father Hamor to speak to Jacob, on his behalf, and ask for Dinah's hand.

The sons of Jacob took charge of the negotiations and deceitfully agreed to Hamor's request on condition that Hamor, Shechem, and all the men in their city would be circumcised. Hamor and his son agreed to this condition, and they, together with all the men in the city, were circumcised.

Simeon and Levy, brothers of Dinah, took advantage of the weakened condition of the circumcised men to revenge their sister's lost honor. They slaughtered all the men in the city of Shechem, including Hamor and Shechem, took their sheep, oxen, and other possessions, and brought Dinah back home.

Jacob told them that their actions could provoke the Canaanites to attack them and slay them. The brothers answered, "Should he treat our sister as a harlot?"

Dionysius

(Greek origin: *Reveler*)

(Acts of the Apostles 17:34). A.D. 1st century. Dionysius was a member of the Areopagus, the High Council of Athens, which met on Mars Hill to debate philosophical issues and legal cases.

Dionysius became a believer, after hearing Paul explain his doctrine in front of the

Areopagus. Another convert, mentioned in the same verse, was a woman named Damaris, who some scholars believe to have been Dionysius' wife.

Diotrephes

(Greek origin: *Nourished by Zeus*)

(3 John 1:9). A.D. 1st century. Diotrephes was the church leader accused by John the Elder in his third letter, which was addressed to Gaius, of being domineering, refusing to receive his messengers, and spreading malicious gossip against John.

Dishan

(Hebrew origin: *Antelope*)

(Genesis 36:21). Unspecified date. Dishan was one of the sons of Seir the Horite, ancestor of the clans that settled in the land of Edom. His sons were Uz and Aran. His brothers were Lotan, Shobal, Zibeon, Dishon, Ezer, and Anah.

Dishon

(Hebrew origin: *Antelope*)

1. (Genesis 36:21). Unspecified date. Dishon was one of the sons of Seir the Horite, ancestor of the clans that settled in the land of Edom. His sons were Hemdan, Eshban, Ithran, and Cheran. His brothers were Lotan, Shobal, Zibeon, Dishan, Ezer, and Anah.
2. (Genesis 36:25). 18th century B.C. Dishon was the son of Anah and grandson of Seir the Horite. His sister was Aholibamah, one of the wives of Esau. His sons were Hemdan—also called Amram (1 Chronicles 1:41)—Eshban, Ithran, and Cheran.

Dodai

(Hebrew origin: *Loving*)

(1 Chronicles 27:4). 10th century B.C. Dodai the Ahohite was one of the twelve commanders of King David's army. He had twenty-four thousand men in his division and was responsible for the service, during the second month of the year. His chief officer was called Mikloth.

Dodanim

(Hebrew origin: Uncertain meaning)

(Genesis 10:4). Unspecified date. Dodanim was the son of Javan and grandson of Japheth. His brothers were Elishah, Tarshish, and Kittim. According to the Hebrew text in First Chronicles, the correct transliteration of the Hebrew name should be Rodanim (1 Chronicles 1:7).

Dodavah

(Hebrew origin: *Love of God*)

(2 Chronicles 20:37). 9th century B.C. Dodavah of Mareshah was the father of the prophet Eliezer. His son prophesied to King Jehoshaphat that, because he had allied himself to King Ahaziah of Israel, his ships would be broken, and they would not be able to go to Tarshish.

Dodo

(Hebrew origin: *Loving*)

1. (Judges 10:1). Unspecified date. Dodo, of the tribe of Issachar, was the father of Puah. His grandson Tola judged Israel, after the death of Abimelech.
2. (2 Samuel 23:9). 11th century B.C. Dodo, the Ahohite, was the father of Eleazar, one of the three top commanders of King David's army.
3. (2 Samuel 23:24). 11th century B.C. Dodo of Bethlehem was the father of Elhanan, one of the warriors in King David's elite army group known as The Thirty.

Doeg

(Hebrew origin: *Worrier*)

(1 Samuel 21:7). 11th century B.C. Doeg, an Edomite, chief of King Saul's herdsmen, was present, when Ahimelech, the priest of Nob, gave David food and the sword of Goliath the Philistine.

Doeg rushed back to Saul's court and reported that he had seen David in Nob with Ahimelech.

The king ordered that Ahimelech, and all the other priests of Nob, should be brought to his presence. Saul accused them of conspiring with David and encouraging him to rebel against the king, by giving him food and a weapon.

Ahimelech denied any wrongdoing and defended himself saying that everybody knew that David was the king's son-in-law and was faithful to the king. Saul refused to listen to any explanations and condemned him to die. The king ordered his guards to kill the priests, and, when the men refused to carry out the order, Saul told Doeg to kill the priests. Eighty-five priests were massacred that day. Then, Doeg killed all the people in Nob, including women and children, and even their animals.

Dorcas

(Greek origin: *Gazelle*)

(Acts of the Apostles 9:36). A.D. 1st century. Dorcas—Tabitha in Chaldean—was a Christian convert, known for her charity and good deeds, who lived in Joppa.

When Dorcas got sick and died, Peter, who was staying in the neighboring town of Lydda, was asked to come to Joppa. As soon as he arrived, he was taken to Dorcas' room in the upper floor, where there were several women, crying and wailing. Peter asked the women to leave the room. He then knelt and prayed, and he said, "Tabitha, arise". Dorcas came back to life.

Drusilla

(Roman name, feminine diminutive of *Drusus*)

(Acts of the Apostles 24:24). A.D. 1st century. Drusilla was the Jewish wife of Felix, the Roman procurator. She was present, when her husband sent for Paul, and heard him explain his faith in Jesus.

Dumah

(Hebrew origin: *Silence*)

(Genesis 25:14). 18th century B.C. Dumah, grandson of Abraham and his Egyptian concubine Hagar, was one of the twelve sons of Ishmael. Dumah's brothers were Nebajoth, Hadad, Mibsam, Mishma, Jetur, Massa, Adbeel, Tema, Kedar, Naphish, and Kedemah, all of them ancestors of great nations. His sister, Mahalath—also called Bashemath—married Esau, the son of Isaac.

Ebal

(Hebrew origin: *Bare*)

1. (Genesis 36:23). Unspecified date. Ebal was the son of Shobal, a descendant of Seir the Horite. His brothers were Alian, Manahath, Shephi, and Onam.
2. (1 Chronicles 1:22). Unspecified date. Ebal—also called Obal (Genesis 10:28)—was a son of Joktan, a descendant of Noah and Shem. His brothers were Sheleph, Hazarmaveth, Jerah, Hadoram, Uzal, Diklah, Almodad, Abimael, Sheba, Ophir, Havilah, and Jobab.

Ebed

(Hebrew origin: *Servant*)

1. (Judges 9:26). 12th century B.C. His son Gaal led an unsuccessful rebellion against Abimelech in Shechem.
2. (Ezra 8:6). 5th century B.C. Ebed, son of Jonathan, descendant of Adin, was the head of a group of fifty men who returned with Ezra from the Babylonian Exile.

Ebedmelech

(Hebrew origin: *Servant of the king*)

(Jeremiah 38:7). 6th century B.C. Ebedmelech, an Ethiopian eunuch in the service of King Zedekiah, was a friend and protector of the prophet Jeremiah.

He told the king that Jeremiah had been wrongly accused, and that the prophet was in danger of dying of hunger in the dungeon where he had been imprisoned. The king authorized him to pull Jeremiah out.

The prophet told Ebedmelech that he would not die, when the Babylonians conquered Jerusalem, as a reward for his kind words and actions.

Eber

(Hebrew origin: *Across*)

1. (Genesis 10:21). Unspecified date. Eber, son of Salah—called Shelah in the first book of Chronicles—was a descendant of Shem and an ancestor of Abraham. He was the father of Peleg, who was born when Eber was thirty-four years old, and Joktan.
2. (1 Chronicles 8:12). Unspecified date. Eber was a Benjamite, son of Elpaal, leader of a clan that lived in Jerusalem.
3. (Nehemiah 12:20). 5th century B.C. Eber was the head of a priestly clan, descendent from Amok, when Joiakim was the High Priest, in the days of Nehemiah.

Ebiasaph

(Hebrew origin: *My father gathered*)

(1 Chronicles 6:23). Unspecified date. Ebiasaph, a descendant of Kohath, was the son of Elkanah and the father of Assir.

Eden

(Hebrew origin: *Delight*)

(2 Chronicles 29:12). 8th century B.C. Eden—called Iddo in the first book of Chronicles (1 Chronicles 6:21)—was the son of Joah and the father of Zerah.

He and his father Joah were among the Levites who gathered to make themselves ritually clean, and to purify the Temple, during the reign of King Hezekiah of Judah.

Eden also helped to distribute among the priests the offerings that the people brought to the Temple.

Eder

(Hebrew origin: *Herd*)

(1 Chronicles 23:23). Unspecified date. Eder, son of Mushi and grandson of Merari, was the brother of Mahli and Jeremoth.

Edom

(Hebrew origin: *Red*)

(Genesis 25:30). This is an alternative name for Esau, Jacob's twin brother. He was thus called because he was born red and hairy.

His descendants, the Edomites, lived in a region situated between the Dead Sea and the Gulf of Aqabah. The Edomite nation was very often in war against the Israelites, until they were converted to Judaism, during the period of the Second Temple. Herod the Great was a descendant of an Edomite family.

Eglah

(Hebrew origin: *Heifer*)

(2 Samuel 3:5). 10th century B.C. Eglah was one of the wives of King David, mother of his sixth son, Ithream, born in Hebron.

Eglon

(Hebrew origin: *Calf-like*)

(Judges 3:12). 12th century B.C. Eglon, king of Moab, allied to the Ammonites and Amalekites, invaded the land of Israel, conquered Jericho, and exacted tribute from the Israelites.

After eighteen years of oppression, the Israelites could not take it anymore and decided to get rid of Eglon. For that purpose, they sent Ehud, son of Gera, a Benjamite, to Jericho, ostensibly to deliver the tribute, but in reality to kill the king.

Ehud, a left-handed man, hid a two-edged dagger on his right thigh, under his clothing. When he finished presenting the tribute to Eglon, he sent away the men who had accompanied him and asked the king for a private audience, saying that he had a secret message for him.

The king, an obese man, shouted, "Silence!" Everybody left the room, and, once they were alone, Ehud approached him and said, "I have a message for you from God". Reaching with his left hand, Ehud drew the dagger from his right side and drove it into the king's fat belly, leaving it there.

Ehud stepped out of the room, closed the doors, and locked them. After he left, the officials of the court returned, but seeing that the door to the king's chamber was closed, they assumed that the king was answering a call of nature.

They waited a long time, and when Eglon did not open the door, they got a key and opened it, and they were shocked to see their master, lying dead, on the floor.

Ehud escaped, rallied the Israelites, and defeated the Moabites, killing over ten thousand men, thus, freeing the Israelites.

Egypt

Please see the entry for Mizraim, the Hebrew name for Egypt (Genesis 10:6).

Ehi

(Hebrew origin: *Brotherly*)

(Genesis 46:21). 17th century B.C. Ehi, son of Benjamin and grandson of Jacob, was one of the seventy Israelites who immigrated to Egypt, and the ancestor of the clan of the Ahiramites.

The book of Genesis mentions that he had nine brothers, but the book of Numbers, where he is called Ahiram (Numbers 26:38), and the first book of Chronicles, where he is called Aharah (1 Chronicles 8:1), state that he only had four brothers.

He is not mentioned in the other list of First Chronicles (1 Chronicles 7:6).

Ehud

(Hebrew origin: *United*)

1. (Judges 3:15). 12th century B.C. King Eglon of Moab had been oppressing the Israelites for eighteen years, until the Israelites could not take it anymore and decided to get rid of him.

    The Israelites sent Ehud, son of Gera, a Benjamite, to Jericho, ostensibly to deliver the tribute to King Eglon of Moab, but in reality to kill him.

    Ehud, a left-handed man, hid a two-edged dagger on his right thigh, under his clothing. When he finished presenting the tribute, he sent away the men who had accompanied him and asked the king for a private audience, saying that he had a secret message for him.

The king, an obese man, shouted, "Silence!" Everybody left the room, and, once they were alone, Ehud approached him and said, "I have a message for you from God". Reaching with his left hand, Ehud drew the dagger from his right side and drove it into the king's fat belly, leaving it there.

Ehud stepped out of the room, closed the doors, and locked them. After he left, the officials of the court returned, but seeing that the door to the king's chamber was closed, they assumed that the king was answering a call of nature.

They waited a long time, and when Eglon did not open the door, they got a key and opened it, and they were shocked to see their master, lying dead, on the floor.

Ehud escaped, rallied the Israelites, and defeated the Moabites, killing over ten thousand men, thus, freeing the Israelites.

2. (1 Chronicles 7:10). Unspecified date. Ehud, a brave warrior and leader of a clan of Benjamites, was the son of Bilhan and brother of Jeush, Benjamin, Chenaanah, Zethan, Tharshish, and Ahishahar.

Eker

(Hebrew origin: *Plucked up, transplanted*)

(1 Chronicles 2:27). Unspecified date. Eker was the son of Ram and grandson of Jerahmeel, of the tribe of Judah. His brothers were Jamin and Maaz.

Eladah

(Hebrew origin: *God has decked*)

(1 Chronicles 7:20). Unspecified date. Eladah was an Ephraimite whose father and son were both called Tahath.

Elah

(Hebrew origin: *Oak tree*)

1. (Genesis 36:41). Unspecified date. Elah was the head of an Edomite clan, descendant of Esau.

2. (1 Kings 4:18). 10th century B.C. His son Shimei was one of the twelve district governors of King Solomon responsible, during one month of the year, for the provision of food for the king and the royal household.

3. (1 Kings 16:6). 9th century B.C. King Elah, the fourth king of Israel, after the partition of the United Monarchy, succeeded his father Baasha on the throne of Israel. He had reigned for only two years, when, one day, he went to visit Arza, the steward of the royal palace in Tirzah, the capital of the kingdom of Israel.

During the visit, the king got himself to a drunken stupor. Zimri, commander of half the chariots in the army, entered the house and murdered the inebriated Elah.

The regicide proclaimed himself king and killed all the other members of the royal family. A week later, Zimri committed suicide, when Omri, another army commander, rose against him.

4. (2 Kings 15:30). 8th century B.C. His son Hoshea, the last king of Israel, ascended to the throne, by killing King Pekah.

Shalmaneser, the king of the Assyrians, made him his vassal and forced him to pay a yearly tribute. Hoshea decided to stop paying the tribute, and he sent messengers to King So of Egypt, asking for his help.

King Shalmaneser attacked Samaria and, after a siege, which lasted three years, took Hoshea prisoner and destroyed Samaria. This final defeat marked the end of the northern kingdom of Israel, which had been in existence for over two hundred years.

5. (1 Chronicles 4:15). 12th century B.C. Elah was one of the sons of Caleb, son of Jephunneh, a descendant of Judah. His son was called Kenaz. Elah's brothers were Iru and Naam.

6. (1 Chronicles 9:8). Unspecified date. Elah, the son of Uzzi, was the leader of a Benjamite clan that lived in Jerusalem.

Elam

(Hebrew origin: *Hidden, distant, concealed from view*)

1. (Genesis 10:22). Unspecified date. Elam was the son of Shem and a grandson of Noah.
2. (1 Chronicles 8:24). Unspecified date. Elam, son of Shashak, was a leader of the tribe of Benjamin who lived in Jerusalem.
3. (1 Chronicles 26:3). 10th century B.C. Elam, son of Meshelemiah, was one of the gatekeepers of the Tabernacle, during the reign of King David. His brothers were Jathniel, Jediael, Zebadiah, Zechariah, Jehohanan, and Elioenai. His father Meshelemiah was called Shallum in the first book of Chronicles (1 Chronicles 9:17).
4. (Ezra 2:7). Unspecified date. Elam was the ancestor of a large group of Israelites who returned with Zerubbabel from the Babylonian Exile.

   Another group, with seventy of his descendants, returned years later with Ezra from the Babylonian Exile (Ezra 8:7).

   His descendant Shechaniah was one of the leaders who signed Nehemiah's solemn agreement to separate themselves from the foreigners living in the land, to refrain from intermarrying with them, and to dedicate their firstborn to God, among other obligations.

   Several of his descendants were forced to divorce their foreign wives, during the days of Ezra (Ezra 10:26).
5. (Ezra 2:31). Unspecified date. Elam, called the other Elam by the Bible, was the ancestor of a large group of Israelites who returned with Zerubbabel from the Babylonian Exile.
6. (Nehemiah 10:14). 5th century B.C. Elam was one of the leaders who signed Nehemiah's solemn agreement to separate themselves from the foreigners living in the land, to refrain from intermarrying with them, and to dedicate their firstborn to God, among other obligations.
7. (Nehemiah 12:42). 5th century B.C. Elam was one of the priests led by Jezrahiah, their overseer, who marched, singing at the top of their voices, in the joyful procession, which celebrated the dedication of the rebuilt walls of Jerusalem, during the days of Nehemiah.

Elasah

(Hebrew origin: *God made*)

1. (Ezra 10:22). 5th century B.C. Elasah, a priest descendant of Pashur, divorced his foreign wife, during the days of Ezra.
2. (Jeremiah 29:3). 6th century B.C. Elasah was one of the four sons of Shaphan, a member of one of the most prominent and influential noble families in the kingdom, during the reigns of King Josiah and his sons.

   His father Shaphan and his nephew Gedaliah played important roles in the historical events of their times.

   Elasah, accompanied by Gemariah, son of Hilkiah, was sent by King Zedekiah—the last king of Judah—in a mission to King Nebuchadnezzar, carrying a letter by Jeremiah to the captives in Babylon. The letter encouraged them to live a normal life in Babylon—build their homes, plant gardens, marry, and have children—and promised them that, after seventy years, they would return from the Babylonian Exile.

Eldaah

(Hebrew origin: *God of knowledge*)

(Genesis 25:4). 18th century B.C. Eldaah was a son of Midian and a grandson of Abraham and Keturah, the woman whom Abraham married, after the death of Sarah.

His brothers were Ephah, Epher, Hanoch, and Abidah.

Eldad

(Hebrew origin: *God has loved*)

(Numbers 11:26). 13th century B.C. Eldad and Medad were two of the elders to whom God gave some of the spirit of Moses, so that they could help him by sharing his leadership tasks.

Moses, overwhelmed by his responsibilities, had spoken to God in his distress, "Why have you treated me so badly, laying the burden of this people on me? Did I conceive them? Did I bring them to birth? I cannot be responsible for all these people by myself; it is too much for me. If you deal, thus, with me, I prefer that you kill me, and let me see no more of my misery".

God answered, "Bring seventy elders of the people that you know are respected leaders to the Tent, and let them stand next to you. I will come down and speak with you there, and I will take from the spirit, which is on you, and will put it on them, and they will share your burden".

Moses brought the elders to the Tent and placed them around it. God came down in a cloud, spoke to Moses, took from his spirit, and gave it to the elders, who started to prophesy.

Two of the elders, Eldad and Medad, had remained in the camp, but they also received the spirit and prophesied inside the camp.

A young man came running and complained to Moses, "Eldad and Medad are acting like prophets in the camp".

Joshua heard this and said, "My lord Moses, forbid them!"

Moses answered, "Are you worried about me? I wish that the Lord would give his Spirit to all his people, and make all of them prophets!"

Elead

(Hebrew origin: *God has testified*)

(1 Chronicles 7:21). Unspecified date. Elead was a descendant of Ephraim. He and his brothers were killed by the men of Gath, while trying to steal their cattle.

Eleasah

(Hebrew origin: *God has made*)

1. (1 Chronicles 2:39). Unspecified date. Eleasah, son of Helez, and father of Sisamai, of the tribe of Judah, was a descendant of Jarha, an Egyptian servant who married the daughter of his master Sheshan.

2. (1 Chronicles 8:37). Unspecified date. Eleasah, a leader of the tribe of Benjamin, was the son of Rapha—also called Rephaiah—and the father of Azel.

Eleazar

(Hebrew origin: *God helped*)

1. (Exodus 6:23). 13th century B.C. Eleazar was the third son of Aaron, the High Priest, and his wife Elisheba. His older brothers, Nadab and Abihu, were burned to death by a fire sent by God, in punishment for having burned forbidden incense before the Lord. As they both died childless, the priestly line was continued through Eleazar and Ithamar.

Eleazar became High Priest, when Aaron died, and was the ancestor of the main priestly line. His younger brother Ithamar was also the ancestor of a line of priests, but it was smaller than the line descended from Eleazar.

Eleazar married one of the daughters of Putiel, with whom he had a son, Phinehas, who was the High Priest in the days of Joshua.

When he died, Eleazar was buried in Canaan, in a hill that belonged to his son Phinehas, in the region of Ephraim.

2. (1 Samuel 7:1). 11th century B.C. Eleazar, the son of Abinadab, was appointed to guard over the Ark of the Covenant that the men of Kirjathjearim had brought to his father's house.

3. (2 Samuel 23:9). 10th century B.C. Eleazar, the son of Dodo the Ahohite, was one of the three bravest men in David's army.

4. (1 Chronicles 23:21). Unspecified date. Eleazar, the son of Mahli, was a descendant of Merari, the son of Levi. He did not have any sons, and, after he died, his daughters married their cousins, the sons of his brother Kish, so that the property would remain in the family.

5. (Ezra 8:33). 5th century B.C. Eleazar, the son of Phinehas, helped Meremoth, son of the priest Uriah, to count and weigh the silver and gold utensils of the Temple, which Ezra had brought back from the Babylonian Exile.

6. (Ezra 10:25). 5th century B.C. Eleazar, a descendant of Parosh, divorced his foreign wife, during the days of Ezra.

7. (Nehemiah 12:42). 5th century B.C. Eleazar was one of the priests led by Jezrahiah, their overseer, who marched, singing at the top of their voices, in the joyful procession, which celebrated the dedication of the rebuilt walls of Jerusalem, during the days of Nehemiah.

8. (Matthew 1:15). Unspecified date. Eleazar was the son of Eliud and father of Matthan, in Matthew's genealogy of Jesus.

Elhanan

(Hebrew origin: *God is gracious*)

1. (2 Samuel 21:19). 10th century B.C. Elhanan, a Bethlehemite, killed Lahmi, the brother of Goliath, the Philistine giant, in the battle of Gob, during the reign of King David. Elhanan's father, Jaareoregim, was also called Jair.

2. (2 Samuel 23:24). 10th century B.C. Elhanan, son of Dodo, a Bethlehemite, was one of "The Thirty", an elite group in King David's army.

Eli

(Hebrew origin: *Lofty*)

(1 Samuel 1:3). 11th century B.C. Eli was the priest in Shiloh, a center of worship and pilgrimage, during the time before there was a king in Israel.

A man named Elkanah came every year with his family to Shiloh to worship and sacrifice to the Lord. In one of the family's yearly pilgrimages, Hannah, one of the two wives of Elkanah, prayed to God, silently and bitterly, for a son.

Eli saw that her lips moved but heard no sound. Thinking that she was drunk, he advised her to stop drinking.

Hannah explained to Eli that she had not drunk wine but was expressing her grief to God. Eli told her to go away in peace and promised that God would grant her wish.

The family returned home, and Hannah, in due time, gave birth to a baby, whom she called Samuel. When the boy was weaned, she brought him to Shiloh and left him with Eli, who brought him up.

Eli's own sons, Hophni and Phinehas, were wicked and corrupt. A man of God came to Eli and accused him that he honored his sons more than he honored God, and that his punishment would be that his two sons would both die on the same day, that his descendants would no longer be the leading priestly family, and that his survivors would be reduced to beg the new High Priest for money and food.

There was constant war at that time between the Philistines and the Israelites. In a battle, at Aphek, the Philistines inflicted a heavy defeat to the Israelites and killed over thirty thousand men, including the sons of Eli. The Philistines captured the Ark of the Covenant and carried it away.

When Eli was told about the tragic news, he fell from his seat and broke his neck. He was ninety-eight years old and had judged Israel, during forty years. Samuel succeeded him as judge.

Eli's descendant, Ahiah, was the High Priest in Shiloh, during the reign of King Saul.

Note: In the book of Judges, a judge is a ruler or governor of territory or a military leader in pre-monarchical Israel. Later, during the monarchy, the king served in this role and judges were more like the judicial officers that we know today.

Eliab

(Hebrew origin: *My God is father*)

1. (Numbers 1:9). 13th century B.C. Eliab, the son of Helon, was the leader of the tribe of Zebulun in the days of Moses.

2. (Numbers 16:1). 14th century B.C. Eliab, son of Peleth, of the tribe of Reuben, was the father of Nemuel, Dathan, and Abiram. Dathan and Abiram, leaders of the rebel-

lion led by Korah against Moses and Aaron, were punished by being swallowed by the earth, together with their families and all their possessions.

3. (1 Samuel 16:6). 11th century B.C. Eliab—also called Elihu (1 Chronicles 27:18)—son of Jesse, was the eldest brother of David. He and his brothers, Abinadab and Shammah, served in King Saul's army.

Their father Jesse, wanting to know how his sons were getting along, sent David to the army camp. The boy carried with him ten loaves of bread for his brothers and a gift of ten cheeses for their commanding officer.

Eliab heard the young boy talking to the men and became annoyed with him, as many older brothers do with their younger siblings.

He asked David, "Why did you come here? With whom did you leave the sheep? I know your impudence and your impertinence. You came here to watch the fighting!"

David answered, "What have I done now? I was only asking".

An hour or two later David killed Goliath.

Evidently, David did not bear a grudge against Eliab, because, when he became king, he named him leader of the tribe of Judah.

Eliab's daughter, Abihail, married Jerimoth, a son of David, and was the mother of daughter Mahalath, one of the eighteen wives of King Rehoboam.

4. (1 Chronicles 6:27). 12th century B.C. Eliab—also called Elihu (1 Samuel 1:1), and Eliel (1 Chronicles 6:34)—was the son of Nahath, an ancestor of Samuel. His descendants served in the Tabernacle, during the reign of King David. His father Nahath was also called Toah (1 Chronicles 6:34) and Tohu (1 Samuel 1:1).

5. (1 Chronicles 12:9). 11th century B.C. Eliab, a Gadite, was one of the men who joined David's band, when he was hiding from Saul.

6. (1 Chronicles 15:18). 10th century B.C. Eliab, a Levite of the second rank, was one of the Levites chosen, by their chief, to sing and play musical instruments in front of the Ark of the Covenant, when it was carried from the house of Obededom to its resting place in Jerusalem, during the reign of King David.

Eliada

(Hebrew origin: *God knows* or *One who knows God*)

1. (2 Samuel 5:16). 10th century B.C. Eliada was one of the sons of King David who was born in Jerusalem. The first book of Chronicles calls him Beeliada (1 Chronicles 14:7).

2. (2 Chronicles 17:17). 9th century B.C. Eliada, from the tribe of Benjamin, commanded an army of two hundred thousand men, armed with bows and shields, during the reign of King Jehoshaphat.

Eliadah

(Hebrew origin: *God knows*)

(1 Kings 11:23). 10th century B.C. His son Rezon was an officer in the army of Hadadezer, king of Zobah. When David conquered Zobah, Rezon and a band of his soldiers fled to Damascus and settled there.

Eventually, he was able to take over the country and proclaimed himself king of Syria. Rezon remained a bitter enemy of Israel, during all the days of Solomon.

Eliah

(Hebrew origin: *God is Jehovah*)

1. (1 Chronicles 8:27). Unspecified date. Eliah, son of Jeroham, was a leader of the tribe of Benjamin who lived in Jerusalem. His brothers were Jaresiah and Zichri.

2. (Ezra 10:26). 5th century B.C. Eliah, a descendant of Elam, was one of the men who divorced their foreign wives, during the days of Ezra.

Eliahba

(Hebrew origin: *God has hidden*)

(2 Samuel 23:32). 10th century B.C. Eliahba the Shaalbonite was one of "The Thirty", an elite group in King David's army.

Eliakim

(Hebrew origin: *God will raise*)

1. (2 Kings 18:18). 8th century B.C. Eliakim, son of Hilkiah, was appointed as supervisor of the royal palace, during the reign of King Hezekiah. He replaced Shebna, the previous overseer, who had been criticized by the prophet Isaiah for having prepared for himself a tomb high on a cliff.

   The prophet Isaiah prophesied that Eliakim would be in charge of the government and would be "a father to the inhabitants of Jerusalem and to the house of Judah" (Isaiah 22:20).

   Eliakim was sent by the king, together with Joah and Shebna, to talk to the commanders of the Assyrian army, laying siege to Jerusalem.

   Rabshakeh, one of the top Assyrian officers, met the delegation outside the walls of the city and spoke to them in Hebrew in a loud voice. Eliakim and his companions asked the Assyrian to please speak to them in Aramaic, as they did not wish that the people on the wall should hear his threats. Rabshakeh paid no attention to their request and continued shouting at them in Hebrew.

   The men remained silent and returned to the king, with their clothes torn, to report the failure of the negotiations.

   Hezekiah, after hearing them, sent Eliakim and Shebna, accompanied by the elders of the priests, all of them covered with sackcloth, to speak to the prophet Isaiah. The king then tore his clothes, covered himself with sackcloth, and went to the Temple.

   Isaiah told the king's men that they should not be afraid, of what Rabshakeh had said, and assured them that the Assyrian army would withdraw without taking Jerusalem.

2. (2 Kings 23:34). 7th century B.C. Eliakim, son of King Josiah and Zebudah, was the older brother of King Jehoahaz.

   Pharaoh Necho deposed Jehoahaz and set Eliakim, who was twenty-five years old at the time, on the throne, changing his name to Jehoiakim and making him his vassal.

   When Necho was defeated in the battle of Carchemish, by the river Euphrates, Eliakim became a vassal of Babylon. Three years later, Eliakim rebelled, against the advice of the prophet Jeremiah.

   Urijah son of Shemaiah, a prophet who had spoken against the king, fled to Egypt to save his life. Eliakim sent a group of men, led by Elnathan, son of Achbor, to Egypt to bring Urijah back to Jerusalem. The prophet was brought to the presence of the king, who killed him with his sword.

   Sometime later, the prophet Jeremiah dictated his prophecies to his trusted companion Baruch, who wrote them on a scroll. The scroll was brought to the palace of Eliakim and was read to him. The king burned the scroll and commanded three of his officials—Jerahmeel, Seraiah, and Shelemiah—to arrest Jeremiah and Baruch, but the men were not able to find them.

   Jeremiah criticized Eliakim bitterly for building a luxurious palace for himself, instead of following his father Josiah's example of caring for his people (Jeremiah 22:15).

   Eliakim reigned eleven years and died at the age of thirty-six. He was succeeded by his son Jehoiachin.

3. (Nehemiah 12:41). 5th century B.C. Eliakim was one of the priests who played the trumpet in the joyful procession, which celebrated the dedication of the rebuilt walls of Jerusalem, during the days of Nehemiah.

4. (Matthew 1:13). Unspecified date. Eliakim, son of Abiud, was the grandson of Zorobabel and an ancestor of Jesus, according to Matthew's genealogy.

5. (Luke 3:30). Unspecified date. Eliakim, son of Melea, was an ancestor of Jesus, according to Luke's genealogy.

Eliam

(Hebrew origin: *God of the people*)

(2 Samuel 11:3). 11th century B.C. Eliam, the son of Ahithophel, was the father of Bathsheba, King David's favorite wife, and the grandfather of King Solomon. He was also called Ammiel (1 Chronicles 3:5).

Elias

(Hebrew origin: *The Lord is my God*)

(Matthew 11:14). 9th century B.C. This is the spelling used, in the New Testament, for the prophet Elijah, who appeared together with Moses, when Jesus was transfigured. At that time, there were some people who believed that Jesus was the reincarnation of Elijah. (Please see the entry for Elijah [1 Kings 17:1].)

Eliasaph

(Hebrew origin: *God increased* or *God has gathered*)

1. (Numbers 1:14). 13th century B.C. Eliasaph, the son of Deuel—also called Reuel—was the leader of the tribe of Gad, during the Exodus from Egypt.
2. (Numbers 3:24). 13th century B.C. Eliasaph, the son of Lael, was the head of the Gershonite clan of the Levites. The clan was responsible for the Tabernacle, the tent, its covering, and the screen for the entrance.

Eliashib

(Hebrew origin: *God will restore*)

1. (1 Chronicles 3:24). Unspecified date. Eliashib, son of Elioenai, was a descendant of Jeconiah—also called Jehoiachin—the king of Judah, who was taken to captivity in Babylon. Eliashib's brothers were Hodaiah, Pelaiah, Akkub, Johanan, Dalaiah, and Anani.
2. (1 Chronicles 24:12). 10th century B.C. During the reign of King David, the priestly service in the Tabernacle was divided by lot into twenty-four turns. Eliashib was in charge of the eleventh turn.

3. (Ezra 10:6). 5th century B.C. He was the father of Johanan, in whose chamber Ezra fasted for the sins of the people.
4. (Ezra 10:24). 5th century B.C. Eliashib, a Levite Temple singer, divorced his foreign wife, during the days of Ezra.
5. (Ezra 10:27). 5th century B.C. Eliashib, a descendant of Zattu, divorced his foreign wife, during the days of Ezra.
6. (Ezra 10:36). 5th century B.C. Eliashib, a descendant of Bani, divorced his foreign wife, during the days of Ezra.
7. (Nehemiah 3:1). 5th century B.C. Eliashib, the son of Joiakim and the father of Joiada, was the High Priest, during the days of Nehemiah. He helped to repair the Sheep Gate in the walls of Jerusalem.

Eliashib permitted Tobiah, the enemy of Nehemiah, to have a chamber in the courts of the Temple. Through one of his grandsons, he was related by marriage to Sanballat, another of Nehemiah's enemies.

Eliathah

(Hebrew origin: *God of his consent*)

(1 Chronicles 25:4). 10th century B.C. Eliathah, a Levite, member of a family of musicians, was in charge of the twentieth turn of service that played musical instruments—cymbals, psalteries, and harps—in the House of God, during the reign of David.

He had thirteen brothers and three sisters, all of them trained as skillful musicians by their father, Heman, one of King David's three leading musicians; the other two were Asaph and Jeduthun.

Elidad

(Hebrew origin: *God's beloved*)

(Numbers 34:21). 13th century B.C. Elidad, son of Chislon, leader of the tribe of Benjamin, was one of the men appointed by Moses to apportion the land of Canaan among the tribes.

Eliel

(Hebrew origin: *My God is God*)

1. (1 Chronicles 5:24). Unspecified date. Eliel, of the half tribe of Manasseh that had settled east of the Jordan River, was a mighty warrior and leader of his clan.

   His tribe was deported from their land by the Assyrians and forcibly settled in the region of the river Gozan, where it eventually assimilated into the local population and disappeared from history, being remembered today as one of the "ten lost tribes".

2. (1 Chronicles 6:34). 12th century B.C. Eliel, the son of Toah—also called Tohu and Nahath—was an ancestor of the prophet Samuel. He is also called Eliab (1 Chronicles 6:27) and Elihu (1 Samuel 1:1). His descendant Heman, of the clan of the Kohathites, was one of the Levites appointed by King David to be in charge of the singers in the House of the Lord.

3. (2 Chronicles 8:20). Unspecified date. Eliel, a descendant of Shimhi, was a leader of the tribe of Benjamin who lived in Jerusalem.

4. (1 Chronicles 8:22). Unspecified date. Eliel, descendant of Shashak, was a leader of the tribe of Benjamin who lived in Jerusalem.

5. (1 Chronicles 11:46). 10th century B.C. Eliel the Mahavite was one of the brave soldiers in King David's army.

6. (1 Chronicles 11:47). 10th century B.C. Eliel was one of the brave soldiers in King David's army.

7. (1 Chronicles 12:11). 11th century B.C. Eliel was a Gadite warrior who joined David at Ziklag, while he was hiding from King Saul.

8. (1 Chronicles 15:9). 10th century B.C. Eliel, leader of a clan, descendant from Hebron, was one of the Levites chosen to carry the Ark of the Covenant to Jerusalem by means of poles upon their shoulders, accompanied by singers and musicians, during the reign of King David.

9. (2 Chronicles 31:13). 8th century B.C. Eliel was one of the Levites named by King Hezekiah to serve under Cononiah and Shimei, as supervisors of the gifts, tithes, and offerings, brought by the people to the Temple.

Elienai

(Hebrew origin: *God is my eyes*)

(1 Chronicles 8:20). Unspecified date. Elienai, a descendant of Shimhi, was a leader of the tribe of Benjamin who lived in Jerusalem.

Eliezer

(Hebrew origin: *God helps*)

1. (Genesis 15:2). 19th century B.C. Eliezer of Damascus was the steward of Abraham's house and his presumed heir, before the birth of Isaac.

   When Isaac was forty years old and still unmarried, Abraham, who did not want his son to marry any of the local Canaanite girls, sent his trusted servant Eliezer to his relatives in Haran, Mesopotamia, with instructions to bring back a bride for Isaac.

   Eliezer took with him ten loaded camels and set out for the city of Nahor. When he arrived to the town, he made the camels kneel down by the well outside the city. He said to himself, "If a girl comes to whom I will say, 'Please, lower your jar that I may drink', and she replies, 'Drink and I will also water your camels', she will be the one that God has chosen for Isaac".

   He had scarcely finished speaking his thoughts aloud, when Rebekah came, carrying a jar on her shoulder. She descended to the spring, filled her jar, and climbed back up. Eliezer ran to her and asked her if he could drink a little water from her jar.

   "Drink, my lord", she said.

   After he had drunk, she said "I will also bring water for your camels, until they finish drinking".

   Eliezer gazed at her silently, while she gave water to the camels. When she finished, he gave her a gold earring and two gold bracelets and asked her, "Whose daughter are you? Is there room in your father's house for us to stay?"

She replied, "I am the daughter of Bethuel. There is plenty of straw and feed at home, and also room to spend the night".

The man bowed low and blessed the Lord for having guided him to the house of his master's kinsmen. Rebekah ran to her mother's house and told her relatives what had happened. Her brother Laban saw the earring and the bracelets on his sister's hands and ran to the well to invite the man to come to the house.

Eliezer entered the house, while his camels were unloaded and given straw. Water was brought to bathe Eliezer's feet and the feet of the men with him.

When food was set before him, he refused to eat, until he told them how Abraham had send him to find a bride for his son and heir, and how he had realized that Rebekah was the intended one.

Laban and Bethuel answered, "The matter was decreed by God; we cannot speak to you bad or good. Here is Rebekah, take her with you and go, and let her be a wife to your master's son, as the Lord has spoken".

When Eliezer heard these words, he bowed low to the ground before God. Then, he took out more objects of silver and gold, and clothing, and gave them to Rebekah. He also gave presents to Laban and to his mother. Eliezer and his men ate and drank, and they spent the night.

Early next morning, they announced that they would depart. Rebekah's mother and Laban asked if Rebekah could stay with them for another ten days. Eliezer answered, "Please do not delay our departure".

They called Rebekah and asked her, "Will you go with this man?"

Rebekah answered, "I will".

Then, Rebekah, her nurse Deborah, and her maids arose, mounted the camels, and followed Eliezer, while her relatives blessed her.

2. (Exodus 18:4). 13th century B.C. Eliezer was the second son of Moses and Zipporah and the brother of Gershom. His only son, Rehabiah, gave him many grandsons.

Eliezer's descendant Shelomith was in charge of the gifts donated to the Tabernacle by King David and the captains of his army from the spoils of the wars.

3. (1 Chronicles 7:8). 16th century B.C. Eliezer was the son of Becher and a grandson of Benjamin. He was a member of a family of tribe leaders and brave warriors.

4. (1 Chronicles 15:24). 10th century B.C. Eliezer was one of the priests who blew the trumpets, during the joyful procession led by King David that brought the Ark of the Covenant to Jerusalem.

5. (1 Chronicles 27:16). 10th century B.C. Eliezer the son of Zichri was the leader of the tribe of Reuben, during the days of King David.

6. (2 Chronicles 20:37). 9th century B.C. Eliezer, the son of Dodavah of Mareshah, prophesied against King Jehoshaphat, saying that, because he had allied himself to King Ahaziah of Israel, his ships would be broken and he would not be able to go to Tarshish.

7. (Ezra 8:16). 5th century B.C. Eliezer was one of the leaders of Judah who was sent by Ezra to Casiphia to speak to Iddo, and to request from him a number of Levites to serve in the Temple in Jerusalem.

8. (Ezra 10:18). 5th century B.C. Eliezer, son of Jozadak, was a priest who divorced his foreign wife, during the days of Ezra, and offered a ram from the flock to expiate his transgression. His brothers Jeshua, Maaseiah, Gedaliah, and Jarib did the same.

9. (Ezra 10:23). 5th century B.C. Eliezer was a Levite who divorced his foreign wife, during the days of Ezra.

10. (Ezra 10:31). 5th century B.C. Eliezer, a descendant of Harim, divorced his foreign wife, during the days of Ezra.

11. (Luke 3:29). Unspecified date. Eliezer was the son of Jorim and father of Jose, in the genealogy of Jesus, according to Luke.

Elihoenai

(Hebrew origin: *My eyes are toward God*)

(Ezra 8:4). 5th century B.C. Elihoenai, the son of Zerahiah, a descendant of Pahathmoab, returned with Ezra from Babylon, leading two hundred men.

Elihoreph

(Hebrew origin: *God of winter*)

(1 Kings 4:3). 10th century B.C. Elihoreph and his brother Ahijah were scribes in the court of King Solomon. They followed in the footsteps of their father Shisha, who was the scribe in the court of King David.

Note: Shisha was also called Sheva (2 Samuel 20:25), Shavsha (1 Chronicles 18:16), and Seraiah (2 Samuel 8:17).

Elihu

(Hebrew origin: *He is my God*)

1. (1 Samuel 1:1) 12th century B.C. Elihu—also called Eliab (1 Chronicles 6:27), and Eliel (1 Chronicles 6:34)—the son of Tohu, was an ancestor of the prophet Samuel.

   His descendants served in the Tabernacle, during the reign of King David. His father Tohu was also called Toah (1 Chronicles 6:34) and Nahath (1 Chronicles 6:26).

2. (1 Chronicles 12:20). 11th century B.C. Elihu, from the tribe of Manasseh, deserted Saul's army with his men, joined David at Ziklag, and became a captain of his army.

3. (1 Chronicles 26:7). 10th century B.C. Elihu, son of Shemaiah and grandson of Obededom, was one of the gatekeepers of the Tabernacle in Jerusalem, during the reign of King David.

   His brothers—all of them brave men and leaders of their clan—were Othni, Rephael, Obed, Elzabad, and Semachiah.

4. (1 Chronicles 27:18). 11th century B.C. Elihu, also called Eliab, was the eldest brother of David. (Please see the entry for Eliab #3 [1 Samuel 16:6].)

5. (Job 32:2). Unspecified date. Elihu, son of Barachel the Buzite, was the youngest of Job's friends and did not speak, until the others had their say. He told Job that God punished the bad people, and that, if Job would repent of his sins, God would forgive him.

Elijah

(Hebrew origin: *My God is Jehovah*)

1. (1 Kings 17:1). 9th century B.C. Elijah the Tishbite, from the region of Gilead, was one of the two men in the Hebrew Scriptures who did not die but was taken by God; the other was Enoch (Genesis 5:24).

   Elijah prophesied, during the reign of King Ahab of Israel. He performed his first miracles in the town of Zarephath, near Sidon, in the house of a poor widow, where he converted a handful of meal and a little oil into an endless supply, and brought back to life the dead child of the widow.

   Jezebel, the wife of King Ahab, was a Phoenician princess, daughter of Ethbaal, king of Sidon. She exerted a strong influence over the king, who granted her unlimited administrative authority. She introduced in Israel the Phoenician pagan cult of the god Baal, a development, which was bitterly opposed by the prophet Elijah.

   Ahab did not only tolerate the foreign cult introduced by his wife, but also cooperated with her by building a Temple for Baal in Samaria and erecting a sacred post. Elijah told the king that God would withhold rain to punish him and left the country.

   There was a severe food shortage in Samaria, which lasted three years. In the third year of the famine, King Ahab arranged with Obadiah, the governor of the royal palace, that they would both travel through the land—the king in one direction, and the palace governor in another—searching for places where there would be grass to feed the horses and the mules.

   Obadiah was a God-fearing man who had risked his life by protecting a hundred prophets of the Lord from Jezebel's murderous persecution, and hiding them in a cave.

He met Elijah on the road and was told by the prophet to tell the king that he was back in Israel. Obadiah, although afraid that Ahab would kill him for bringing news of Elijah, informed the king that Elijah had returned to the kingdom.

Ahab went to meet Elijah and, when he saw him, accused the prophet of being a troublemaker. Elijah retorted that it was Ahab and his father who were the real troublemakers, because they had forsaken the true God and worshipped the idols of Baal.

Elijah requested an encounter with the several hundred prophets of Baal who were under Queen Jezebel's protection and who ate at her table. King Ahab consented.

Elijah confronted four hundred and fifty of the priests of Baal in Mount Carmel and challenged them to prove who was the true God, the Lord or Baal, by having fire from heaven come down and consume the sacrifice.

The priests of Baal prayed for hours without any results, while Elijah mocked them. When it was Elijah's turn to pray to God, fire came down on the altar and consumed the sacrifice. Elijah then had the priests of Baal seized and killed.

The drought, which had lasted three years, broke in a great storm. Ahab drove back to his capital in his chariot through the heavy rain, with the prophet Elijah running in front of the king all the way to Jezreel.

When Ahab told Jezebel that Elijah had killed her prophets, the queen was furious and sent a messenger to Elijah, threatening to kill him. The prophet escaped to the desert in the south. There, he found Elisha, the son of Shaphat, who was plowing with oxen, when Elijah placed his cloak upon him, thus, symbolizing that he had chosen him as a disciple. Elisha slaughtered two oxen, used the plough for firewood, gave the meat to his people, and left to follow Elijah.

Sometime afterward, Ahab coveted the vineyard of his neighbor Naboth the Jezreelite. The king's intention was to use that land, which was adjacent to the palace, for a vegetable garden. He offered to pay Naboth for the land, or to exchange it for an equivalent piece of land. Naboth refused to give up his family inheritance, and the king went back to the palace depressed and angry.

His wife Jezebel asked him why he was depressed, and why he refused to eat. The king replied that it was because Naboth had refused to sell him his land. Jezebel told him to be cheerful, and to leave the matters in her hands.

Jezebel arranged to have Naboth accused falsely of insulting God. Naboth was tried for blasphemy and was executed. Ahab then took possession of the property.

The prophet Elijah went to Naboth's vineyard, where Ahab was at that moment, confronted the king, and accused him of murdering the man, and taking over his property. The prophet told the king that God would punish him for his evil deeds, that dogs would lick his blood in the very place that dogs had licked up Naboth's blood, that his family would come to the same bad end as King Jeroboam and King Baasha, and that dogs would eat the body of his wife Jezebel.

When Elijah finished speaking, Ahab tore his clothes, took them off, and put on sackcloth. He fasted, slept in the sackcloth, and walked about gloomy and depressed. The king's humble behavior made God relent and postpone the prophesied disaster to the lifetime of Ahab's son, after Ahab's death.

Ahab died fighting against the Arameans, and his son Ahaziah succeeded to the throne. Shortly afterward, the new king severely injured himself, when he fell from the window of an upper story of his palace.

Ahaziah sent messengers to inquire from Baalzebub, the god of the Philistine city of Ekron, whether he would recover.

Elijah reproved him for this act and prophesied that he would die.

When the king heard what Elijah had prophesied, he sent a company of fifty soldiers to seize the prophet, but the troops were killed by fire from heaven. The same thing happened to a second company of soldiers. A third company of soldiers was sent, which this time succeeded in bringing Elijah to the palace. Elijah, once in the presence of the king, repeated his prophecy. The king died soon afterward.

Elijah knew that his own end was near. Together with his disciple Elisha, who refused to leave him, he went to the river Jordan, divided the waters by hitting them with his mantle, and crossed over on dry ground.

Elijah asked Elisha, "What can I do for you before I am taken away?"

Elisha answered, "I wish to receive a double portion of your spirit".

While they were talking, a chariot, pulled by horses of fire, appeared and took Elijah by a whirlwind into heaven.

During the lifetime of Jesus, Elijah appeared with Moses on the top of a high mountain, where the apostles—Peter, James, and John—witnessed the transfiguration of Jesus.

Elijah was called Elias in the New Testament (Matthew 11:14).

2. (Ezra 10:21). 5th century B.C. This man, a priest descendant of Harim, divorced his foreign wife, during the days of Ezra.

Elika

(Hebrew origin: *God of rejection*)

(2 Samuel 23:25). 10th century B.C. Elika the Harodite was one of "The Thirty", an elite group in King David's army.

Elimelech

(Hebrew origin: *God is king*)

(Ruth 1:2). 12th century B.C. Elimelech, a Bethlehemite, immigrated with his wife Naomi and his two sons to Moab, during a famine in the land of Israel.

His sons, Mahlon and Chilion, married two Moabite girls named Ruth and Orpah. After the deaths of Elimelech and the two young men, Naomi and Ruth, both of them now widows, left Moab and went to Bethlehem.

There, their relative Boaz bought from Naomi all the properties that had been owned by Elimelech and his sons and married Ruth. Obed, the son of Boaz and Ruth, was the grandfather of King David.

Elioenai

(Hebrew origin: *My eyes are toward God*)

1. (1 Chronicles 3:23). Unspecified date. Elioenai, son of Neariah, was a descendant of Jeconiah—also called Jehoiachin—the king of Judah, who was taken to captivity in Babylon. Elioenai's brothers were Hezekiah and Azrikam, and his sons were Hodaiah, Eliashib, Pelaiah, Akkub, Johanan, Dalaiah, and Anani.

2. (1 Chronicles 4:36). 8th century B.C. Elioenai was one of the leaders of the tribe of Simeon who went to the fertile valley of Gedor in search of pasture for their flocks, during the reign of Hezekiah, king of Judah.

   The Simeonites destroyed the tents of the people—descendants of Ham—who lived there, wiped them out forever, and settled in their place.

3. (1 Chronicles 7:8). 16th century B.C. Elioenai, a son of Becher and a grandson of Benjamin, was a member of a family of brave warriors and heads of their tribe. His brothers were Zemira, Joash, Eliezer, Abiah, Omri, Jerimoth, Anathoth, and Alameth.

4. (1 Chronicles 26:3). 10th century B.C. Elioenai, son of Meshelemiah, was one of the gatekeepers of the Tabernacle, during the reign of King David. His brothers were Jathniel, Jediael, Zebadiah, Zechariah, Elam, and Jehohanan. His father Meshelemiah was called Shallum in the first book of Chronicles (1 Chronicles 9:17).

5. (Ezra 10:22). 5th century B.C. Elioenai was a priest, descendant of Pashur, who divorced his foreign wife, during the days of Ezra.

6. (Ezra 10:27). 5th century B.C. This man, descendant of Zattu, divorced his foreign wife, during the days of Ezra.

7. (Nehemiah 12:41). 5th century B.C. Elioenai was one of the priests who played the trumpet in the joyful procession, which celebrated the dedication of the rebuilt walls of Jerusalem, during the days of Nehemiah.

Eliphal

(Hebrew origin: *God of judgment*)

(1 Chronicles 11:35). 10th century B.C. Eliphal, son of Ur, was one of "The Thirty", an elite group in King David's army. The second book of Samuel calls him Eliphelet, son of Ahasbai (2 Samuel 23:34).

Eliphalet

(Hebrew origin: *God of deliverance*)

(2 Samuel 5:16). 10th century B.C. Eliphalet was one of the sons of King David, born to him in Jerusalem. The first book of Chronicles spells his name Eliphelet (1 Chronicles 3:8).

Eliphaz

(Hebrew origin: *God of gold*)

1. (Genesis 36:4). 17th century B.C. Eliphaz, born in Canaan, was the son of Esau and his wife Adah, the daughter of Elon the Hittite. The sons of Eliphaz were Teman, Omar, Zepho, Gatam, and Kenaz. Eliphaz' concubine Timna was the mother of his son Amalek.

2. (Job 2:11). Unspecified date. Eliphaz the Temanite, having heard of the tragedies that had struck his friend Job, came to visit him with two other men, Bildad and Zophar, to mourn with Job, and to comfort him.

When the friends saw Job and were not able to recognize him, they wailed and wept, rented their mantles, and sprinkled dust upon their heads. Then, they sat with Job for seven days and seven nights without speaking a word, not wanting to disturb Job whose grief was so great.

After Job broke his silence with a bitter diatribe against his life, his friends were surprised. They had come to commiserate and console, not to participate in a rebellion against God's judgment, and so they turned from comforters to scolds.

Eliphaz told Job that he must have sinned, as there was no other way to explain God's treatment.

In the end, God vindicated Job and gave him back his health and fortune. Then, the Lord turned to Eliphaz, rebuked him and his two friends for their presumptuous words, and ordered them to go to Job, make a sacrifice, and ask Job to pray for them, so that God would not punish them.

Elipheleh

(Hebrew origin: *God of his distinction*)

(1 Chronicles 15:18). 10th century B.C. Elipheleh, a Levite of the second rank, was one of the musicians chosen, by the chief of the Levites, to sing and play musical instruments in front of the Ark of the Covenant, when it was carried from the house of Obededom to its resting place in Jerusalem, during the reign of King David.

Eliphelet

(Hebrew origin: *God of deliverance*)

1. (2 Samuel 23:34). 10th century B.C. Eliphelet, son of Ahasbai, was one of "The Thirty", an elite group in King David's army. The first book of Chronicles (1 Chronicles 11:35) calls him Eliphal, son of Ur.

2. (1 Chronicles 3:6). 10th century B.C. Eliphelet was one of the two sons of King David born in Jerusalem, who had the same name. His name was also spelled Elpalet (1 Chronicles 14:5). The name of the other

Eliphelet is spelled Eliphalet in the second book of Samuel (2 S2 Samuel 5:16).

3. (1 Chronicles 3:8). 10th century B.C. Eliphelet was one of the two sons of King David born in Jerusalem, who had the same name. His name was also spelled Eliphalet in the second book of Samuel (2 Samuel 5:16). The name of the other Eliphelet is spelled Elpalet in the first book of Chronicles (1 Chronicles 14:5).

4. (1 Chronicles 8:39). Unspecified date. Eliphelet, the third son of Eshek of the tribe of Benjamin, was a descendant of Jonathan, the son of King Saul. His brothers were Ulam and Jehush.

5. (Ezra 8:13). 5th century B.C. Eliphelet, a descendant of Adonikam, returned with Ezra to Jerusalem from the Babylonian Exile, together with his brothers Jeiel and Shemaiah and another sixty males, during the reign of King Artaxerxes of Persia.

6. (Ezra 10:33). 5th century B.C. Eliphelet, a descendant of Hashum, divorced his foreign wife, during the days of Ezra.

Elisabeth

(Hebrew origin: *God of the oath*)

(Luke 1:5). 1st century B.C. Elisabeth, a descendant of the High Priest Aaron, was married to a priest named Zacharias. The elderly couple, who had no children, lived in a town, today identified as Ein Kerem, near Jerusalem, in the hill country of Judah.

One day, Zacharias went to the Temple to burn incense, and an angel appeared to him, standing next to the altar of incense. The angel told him not to fear, his prayers had been heard, and Elisabeth would give birth to a son, whom they should call John. Zacharias, overwhelmed by his vision, became a deaf mute.

When Elisabeth was in her sixth month of pregnancy, the angel Gabriel appeared to Mary in Nazareth and announced that she would become pregnant and give birth to a son. The angel informed her that her old cousin Elisabeth was six months pregnant. After the angel had departed, Mary arose and went to visit her cousin.

When Elisabeth saw Mary, she blessed her and the fruit of her womb. Mary stayed with her relatives for three months and then returned to her own house.

In due course, Elisabeth's baby was born. On his eighth day, the neighbors came to circumcise the child, wanting to name him Zacharias, in honor of his father. Elisabeth insisted that he should be called John. The neighbors argued that no relative of the couple was called by that name. They turned to Zacharias and, by signs, asked him how the child should be called. Zacharias wrote, "His name is John". As soon as he finished writing, he immediately recovered the power of speech, praised God, and prophesied that his son would be called the prophet of the Highest.

Eliseus

(Hebrew origin: *God of salvation*)

(Luke 4:27). 9th century B.C. Eliseus is an alternative spelling of the prophet Elisha's name. (Please see the entry for Elisha [1 Kings 19:16].)

Elisha

(Hebrew origin: *God of salvation*)

(1 Kings 19:16). 9th century B.C. Elisha—called Eliseus by Luke—son of Shaphat of Abelmeholah, was chosen by the prophet Elijah, to be his disciple, by God's command. Elisha was plowing with oxen, when Elijah placed his cloak upon him. Elisha slaughtered two oxen, used the plough for firewood, gave the meat to his people, and left to follow Elijah.

Some years later, Elijah knew that his own end was near. Together with Elisha, who refused to leave him, he went to the river Jordan, divided the waters by hitting them with his mantle, and crossed over on dry ground. Elijah asked Elisha, "What can I do for you before I am taken away?"

Elisha replied, "I wish to receive a double portion of your spirit".

While they talked, a chariot and horses of fire appeared and took Elijah by a whirlwind into heaven. Elisha saw this, tore his clothes in two, and put on the mantle of Elijah that had fallen from him. Elisha hit the waters of the Jordan with the mantle, the waters parted, and he passed to the other bank of the river.

A group of prophets came to meet him, bowed to the ground, and asked permission to send fifty men to search for Elijah in the surrounding mountains and valleys. Initially, Elisha refused, but when they urged him, he agreed to the search. After three days, the men, not having found Elijah, gave up the search.

The men of Jericho came to him, complaining that the water of the city was polluted. Elisha went to the water spring, threw salt in it, and purified the water. Elisha proceeded to go to Bethel. While approaching the city, a group of children came and made fun of his baldness. Elisha cursed them, and two female bears came out of the forest and mangled forty-two of the children.

King Jehoram of Israel, the son of Ahab, made an alliance with Jehoshaphat, king of Judah, and the king of Edom to go and fight against Moab, a vassal kingdom of Judah, which wanted to be independent. The allied army marched for seven days, until there was no water left for the soldiers and their cattle. Elisha was called, and, upon his arrival, he told the king of Israel that he would not even look at him if the king of Judah had not been also present. Elisha asked them to bring a musician, and while the musician played, he told them that God commanded them to dig ditches. The next morning, water came rushing from Edom and turned the ditches into pools. Early the next day, the Moabites, seeing the red reflection of the rising sun on the pools, thought that it was the blood of the kings' armies who had fought between themselves. They attacked the Israelite camp, but they were repulsed and defeated.

A poor widow came to Elisha and complained that her creditor wanted to take her two sons because of her debts. When asked by Elisha what she had in her house, she answered that only a pot of oil. Elisha told her to borrow empty jars from her neighbors. All the jars were filled from her pot of oil. She sold the oil and had more than enough to pay her debt.

Elisha, in his trips, would stop to eat bread in the house of a wealthy woman. She convinced her husband to prepare a furnished room in their house where Elisha could stay whenever he would come to their town. Grateful, Elisha consulted with his servant Gehazi on how he could repay her. Gehazi pointed out that she had no children and that her husband was old. Elisha told him to call her and prophesied to her that she would have a son. She conceived, and the baby was born according to Elisha's prediction.

Years later, the child, already a young boy, went to the field to see his father who was with the reapers. When the boy complained of a terrible headache, his father instructed his servants to take the boy home to his mother. The woman sat with her son, until he died, then she laid the body in Elisha's room, shut the door, saddled a donkey, and went to Mount Carmel in search for Elisha. The prophet recognized the woman from far away. After she had told him what had happened to her son, Elisha gave his staff to Gehazi and instructed him to go before them, and try to bring the boy back to life by placing his staff upon the face of the child. When Elisha arrived at the Shunammite's house, Gehazi told him that the boy had not awakened. Elisha went up to his room, closed the door behind him, prayed to God, placed his mouth against the dead boy's mouth, and breathed in it, until the boy came back to life.

Elisha made many miracles. During a famine, Elisha took a poisoned pot of pottage and made it eatable. On another occasion, he fed a hundred men with only twenty loaves of barley bread.

Naaman, the commander of the Syrian army, was a leper. Somebody told the king of Syria that a captured Israelite girl was saying that the prophet in Samaria could cure Naaman of his leprosy. The king wrote a letter to the king of Israel, informing him that he was sending Naaman to Israel, and that he expected the king of Israel to cure his commander. The only explanation that the king of Israel found to this unprecedented request was that it was a pretext to declare war, and he rented his clothes. When Elisha heard about it, he sent a message to the king of Israel to tell Naaman to come to him. Naaman came to the prophet's house. Elisha did not come out to meet him but sent him a messenger who told Naaman that, if he would bathe seven times in the Jordan River, he would be cured. Naaman was angry and offended that Elisha had not spoken personally to him, and he went away, saying that the rivers in Syria were just as good, if not better than the Jordan, and he could bathe in them. However, when his servants convinced him that he should try Elisha's suggestion, Naaman went to the Jordan, bathed seven times, and was cured.

Naaman went back to Elisha's house to thank the prophet and offered him a gift in appreciation, which Elisha refused to receive. Naaman told Elisha that he now recognized that God was the true God and asked God to pardon him in advance, if he, in the future, would bow to the idol Rimmon, when he visited its Temple, accompanying the Syrian king.

Gehazi, seeing that Elisha had refused the reward offered by Naaman, decided that he should get something and ran after him. Naaman saw him, alighted from his chariot, and asked him if everything was well. Gehazi told him that Elisha had sent him, with a request for two changes of clothing, and a talent of silver for two young prophets who had come to visit him. Naaman gave him the two changes of clothing and two talents of silver. Gehazi returned to his master, and Elisha asked him, "Where have you been?"

Gehazi answered that he had not gone out. Elisha told him that he knew that he had received money from Naaman, and that, in punishment, Naaman's leprosy would cling to him and his posterity forever.

Elisha's disciples told him that the house where they lived with him was too small for all of them. They invited Elisha to come with them to the Jordan where they would build a larger place. Elisha went with them. While one of them was cutting down a tree, his borrowed ax fell into the water and sunk below the surface. Elisha made it float so that the workers were able to pick it up from the water.

Elisha, through his prophetic powers, learned about the movements of the Syrian army and reported them to the king of Israel. The Syrian king initially suspected that there was an Israelite spy among his officers, but then, he was told that the prophet Elisha reported to the king of Israel every word that he spoke, even those uttered in the intimacy of his bedroom.

The king of Syria heard that Elisha was in Dothan and sent an army of horsemen and chariots to capture the prophet. Early next morning, the servant of Elisha woke up to find that soldiers had surrounded the city. Alarmed, he asked his master, "What shall we do?"

Elisha calmed him by saying that they outnumbered the enemy. The prophet prayed to God to open the eyes of the young man, and the servant saw that all the hills around them were covered with horses and chariots of fire. When the Syrians came to him, Elisha asked God to strike them with blindness. He then told the soldiers that they were in the wrong city and offered to take them to the man whom they wanted to capture. Instead, he led them to Samaria, where God restored their sight. The king of Israel asked the prophet if he should kill them. The prophet said that, to the contrary, he should give them food and water and free them to return to Syria.

After sometime, Benhadad, the king of Syria, marched upon Samaria and besieged it. There was a great famine in the city, and the hunger was such that some of the starving people ate their own children. The king, furious with Elisha, swore that he would cut the prophet's head off, and he sent a man to Elisha's house. When the messenger arrived, Elisha prophesied that, the next day, food would be so abundant that a measure of fine flour would be sold for only a shekel. A high court officer, on whose hand the king leaned, mockingly said that he doubted that this would happen even if God opened the windows of heaven. The prophet replied, "You will see it with your own eyes, but you will not eat of it".

During the night, the Syrians heard noises of chariots, horses, and great armies, and thinking that the kings of the Hittites and the Egyptians were coming to the aid of Israel, fled in panic, abandoning their tents and horses. Early next morning, four lepers, who had decided they had nothing to lose, went to the Syrian camp and found it empty. They ate and drank, looted whatever gold and silver they found, and hid it. Then, they, realizing that this news should be reported to the king as soon as possible, went to the gatekeeper of the city and told him that the Syrians had left, leaving their tents, horses, and asses. The king was told but suspected that it was a trap. His officials convinced him to send a small party to follow the fleeing Syrians. The men returned and reported to the king that they had followed them as far as the Jordan and found the entire road full of clothing and gear, which the Syrians in their panic had thrown away. The people of the city rushed to the camp to plunder it. The multitude, in its desperate haste, trampled to death the man whom the king had placed in charge of the gate of the city, who was that same high court officer who had mocked the prophet.

Elisha advised the Shunammite woman, whose son he had brought back to life, that she and her family should leave the country for seven years, because there would be a famine. The woman followed the prophet's advice. After seven years, she returned and went to the king to request that her house and land should be restored to her. Gehazi, Elisha's servant, was at that moment in the palace, telling the king all the great deeds that the prophet had done. Seeing the woman, Gehazi told the king that she was the mother of the boy whom Elisha had brought back to life. The woman confirmed the story, and the king gave instructions to restore all her property, including all the revenue from her farm, from the time that she left the country.

Benhadad, the king of Syria, who was very sick, heard that the prophet Elisha had come to Damascus. He ordered Hazael to take presents to the prophet and inquire from him if he would recover from his illness. The prophet told Hazael to tell the king that he would recover, although God had told him that the king would die. The prophet remained expressionless for a while and then started to cry. Hazael asked him, "Why are you weeping?"

Elisha answered, "God showed me that you will be king of Syria, and will do great harm to my people".

Hazael returned to his king and told him that he would surely recover. The next day, he came to the king's room, suffocated Benhadad to death, and proclaimed himself the new king of Syria.

King Joram of Israel, allied to his cousin King Ahaziah of Judah, went to battle against Hazael, was wounded, and returned to Jezreel, where Ahaziah came to visit him in his sick bed. Elisha called one of the disciples of the prophets, gave him a flask of oil, and told him to go to Ramothgilead, and anoint the army commander Jehu, king over Israel.

Many years later, when Elisha was very old and mortally ill, King Joash of Israel, grandson of King Jehu, came to visit him and cried, when he saw how sick the prophet was. Elisha told the king to take a bow and arrows, to open the window toward the east, and to shoot an arrow. This arrow, explained the prophet, meant that the king would defeat the Syrians in Aphek. Then, Elisha told the king to take the arrows and strike the ground with them. The king struck three times and stopped. The prophet angrily told him, "If only you had struck five or six times, you would have annihilated Syria; as it is, you shall defeat them only three times".

Even after his death, Elisha performed a miracle. The body of a dead man was thrown into the sepulcher of the prophet, and when it touched the bones of Elisha, the man came back to life.

Elishah

(Uncertain origin and meaning)

(Genesis 10:4). Unspecified date. Elishah, the son of Javan, was the brother of Tarshish, Kittim, and Dodanim.

Elishama

(Hebrew origin: *God heard*)

1. (Numbers 1:10). 13th century B.C. Elishama, son of Ammihud son of Laadan, was a leader of the tribe of Ephraim. He commanded his tribe's army, during the march in the wilderness, and was one of the twelve Israelite leaders who donated gifts of silver and gold, bulls, rams, goats, and lambs for the dedication of the altar.

2. (2 Samuel 5:16). 10th century B.C. Elishama, one of the two sons of the same name of King David, was born in Jerusalem. The other son of the same name was Elishama #5.

3. (2 Kings 25:25). 6th century B.C. Elishama, a descendant of the royal family, was the grandfather of Ishmael, the assassin who killed Gedaliah, the Babylonian appointed governor of Judah.

4. (1 Chronicles 2:41). Unspecified date. Elishama was the son of Jekamiah and the grandson of Shallum.

5. (1 Chronicles 3:6). 10th century B.C. Elishama, one of the two sons of the same name of King David, was born in Jerusalem. He is called Elishua in the second book of Samuel (2 Samuel 5:15). The other son of the same name was Elishama #2.

6. (2 Chronicles 17:8). 9th century B.C. Elishama, a priest, was sent by King Jehoshaphat in the third year of his reign, to teach the laws of God in the cities of Judah. Elishama was accompanied in his mission by a priest called Jehoram, several officials of the court, and a number of Levites.

7. (Jeremiah 36:12). 7th century B.C. Elishama was the scribe in the court of King Jehoiakim. The roll where Baruch had written Jeremiah's dictations was kept in Elishama's room, until the king ordered that it should be brought to him.

Elishaphat

(Hebrew origin: *My God judged*)

(2 Chronicles 23:1). 9th century B.C. Elishaphat, the son of Zichri, was one of the five army commanders who conspired with the priest Jehoiada to overthrow Queen Athaliah and crown Joash, the legitimate heir to the throne of Judah.

Elisheba

(Hebrew origin: *My God is her oath*)

(Exodus 6:23). 13th century B.C. Elisheba, daughter of Amminadab of the tribe of Judah and sister of Naashon, married Aaron, the High Priest. The couple had four sons: Nadab, Abihu, Eleazar, and Ithamar.

Elishua

(Hebrew origin: *God of wealth*)

(2 Samuel 5:15). 10th century B.C. Elishua was one of the sons of King David born in Jerusalem. He is called Elishama in the first book of Chronicles (1 Chronicles 3:6). (Please see the entry for Elishama #5.)

Eliud

(Hebrew origin: *God of majesty*)

(Matthew 1:14). Unspecified date. Eliud, son of Achim and father of Eleazar, was one of the ancestors of Jesus, according to Matthew's genealogy.

Elizaphan

(Hebrew origin: *God of treasure*)

1. (Numbers 3:30). 13th century B.C. Elizaphan—also called Elzaphan (Exodus 6:22)—son of Uzziel and brother of Mishael and Zithri, was a first cousin of Moses and Aaron.

He was the head of the Levite clan of Kohathites that was in charge of the Ark, the table, the candlesticks, the altars, and the vessels of the sanctuary, during the wanderings of the Israelites in the wilderness.

When Abihu and Nadab, the sons of Aaron, burned forbidden incense and were killed by a fire from the Lord, Moses told Elizaphan and Mishael to take out the two bodies from the sanctuary and to carry them to a place outside the camp.

His descendant Shemaiah, during the reign of David, helped to bring the Ark to Jerusalem (1 Chronicles 15:8).

During the reign of King Hezekiah of Judah, his descendants Shimri and Jeiel were among the Levites who assembled all the other Levites to make themselves ritually clean, and to purify the Temple (2 Chronicles 29:13).

2. (Numbers 34:25). 13th century B.C. Elizaphan, son of Parnach, was the leader of the tribe of Zebulun, chosen by Moses to help apportion the land of Canaan among the tribes.

Elizur

(Hebrew origin: *My God is a rock*)

(Numbers 1:5). 13th century B.C. Elizur, son of Shedeur, of the tribe of Reuben, commanded his tribe's army, during the march in the wilderness.

He was one of the twelve Israelite leaders who donated gifts of silver and gold, bulls, rams, goats, and lambs for the dedication of the altar.

Elkanah

(Hebrew origin: *God provided*)

1. (Exodus 6:24). 13th century B.C. Elkanah was a son of Korah, the Levite who led the rebellion against Moses in the wilderness. He and his brothers, Assir and Abiasaph, were not punished, when their father was swallowed by the earth, in punishment for his rebellion against Moses.

2. (1 Samuel 1:1). 11th century B.C. Elkanah, son of Jeroham—of the tribe of Ephraim, according to the first book of Samuel, but a descendant of Levi, according to chapter 6 of the first book of Chronicles—lived in Ramathaimzophim with his two wives: Peninnah, who had several children, and Hannah, who was barren.

Hannah was desperate to have a child, and Elkanah tried to console her by asking her if he was not better to her than ten sons.

In one of the family's yearly trips to Shiloh to worship and sacrifice to the Lord, Hannah prayed silently and bitterly asking God for a son.

Eli, the Shiloh priest, thought that she was drunk. When Hannah explained that she was pouring her grief to God, Eli told her to go in peace and that God would grant her wish.

Hannah, in due time, gave birth to Samuel. When the boy was weaned, she brought him to Shiloh and left him with the priest Eli who brought him up.

After Samuel's birth, Elkanah and Hannah had five more children: three boys and two girls. Samuel grew up to be the last of the judges and the anointer of King Saul and King David.

Elkanah was an ancestor of Heman, one of King David's leading musicians. His descendants, Jehiel and Shimei, during the reign of King Hezekiah of Judah, were among the Levites who gathered to make themselves ritually clean, and to purify the Temple.

3. (1 Chronicles 6:23). Unspecified date. Elkanah, the son of Assir, a descendant of Kohath, was the grandson of Korah, the man who led the rebellion against Moses. His son was called Ebiasaph.

4. (1 Chronicles 6:26). Unspecified date. Elkanah, the son of Mahath, a descendant of Kohath, was the father of Zophai—also called Zuph (1 Chronicles 6:35)—and an ancestor of the judge Samuel.

5. (1 Chronicles 6:36). Unspecified date. Elkanah was the father of Amasai and the son of Joel.

6. (1 Chronicles 9:16). 6th century B.C. Elkanah, father of Asa, was the grandfather of Berechiah, a Levite who was one of the first to settle in the land of Judah, after the return from the Babylonian Exile.

7. (1 Chronicles 12:6). 11th century B.C. Elkanah, a Korhite, was one of the men who deserted King Saul's army and joined David's band at Ziklag. These men were

skilled warriors who could use both their right and left hands to shoot arrows and sling stones.

8. (1 Chronicles 15:23). 10th century B.C. Elkanah was one of the doorkeepers of the Ark—the other was Berechiah—during the reign of King David.

9. (2 Chronicles 28:7). 8th century B.C. Elkanah, an official in the court of King Ahaz of Judah, was killed in battle together with Azrikam, governor of the royal palace, by Zichri, a commander of King Pekah's army, during a war between the two countries.

Elmodam

(Uncertain origin and meaning)

(Luke 3:28). Unspecified date. Elmodam was the son of Er and father of Cosam, ancestor of Jesus, in the genealogy of Luke.

Elnaam

(Hebrew origin: *God is my delight*)

(1 Chronicles 11:46). 11th century B.C. His sons Jeribai and Joshaviah were brave soldiers in King David's army.

Elnathan

(Hebrew origin: *God gave*)

1. (2 Kings 24:8). 8th century B.C. Elnathan, who lived in Jerusalem, was the father of Nehushta, mother of Jehoiachin, the young king of Judah, who only reigned for three months, until Nebuchadnezzar, king of Babylon, brought him prisoner to Babylon, together with his mother, his wives, and the nobles of his court.

2. (Ezra 8:16). 5th century B.C. Elnathan was the name of three men, members of a delegation that was sent by Ezra to Casiphia to speak to Iddo and request from him to send Levites to serve in the Temple in Jerusalem.

3. (Jeremiah 26:22). 7th century B.C. Elnathan, son of Achbor, was sent by King Jehoiakim to Egypt with a group of men to capture the prophet Urijah, son of Shemaiah.

The prophet had displeased the king, by uttering prophesies similar to the words of Jeremiah, and, to save his life, fled to Egypt.

Elnathan brought Urijah back to Judah, where he was killed by the king with his sword and his body thrown into a common grave.

Elnathan, who was sympathetic to Jeremiah and Baruch, tried unsuccessfully, together with Delaiah and Gemariah, two other officials of the court, to convince King Jehoiakim not to burn the roll where Baruch had written Jeremiah's dictations.

Elon

(Hebrew origin: *Oak tree*)

1. (Genesis 26:34). 18th century B.C. Elon the Hittite was the father of Bashemath—also called Adah—one of the wives of Esau who embittered the lives of Isaac and Rebekah.

2. (Genesis 46:14). 17th century B.C. Elon, son of Zebulun, was the grandson of Jacob and Leah. His brothers were Sered and Jahleel. Elon, the ancestor of the clan of the Elonites (Numbers 26:26), was one of the seventy Israelites who immigrated to Egypt.

3. (Judges 12:11). 12th century B.C. Elon of the tribe of Zebulun judged Israel, during ten years after the death of the judge Ibzan. When Elon died, he was buried in Aijalon in the country of Zebulun. Abdon the son of Hillel became judge after him.

Note: In the book of Judges, a judge is a ruler or governor of territory or a military leader in pre-monarchical Israel. Later, during the monarchy, the king served in this role and judges were more like the judicial officers that we know today.

Elpaal

(Hebrew origin: *God acted*)

(1 Chronicles 8:11). Unspecified date. Elpaal, of the tribe of Benjamin, was the son of Shaharaim and his wife Hushim. His brother was Abitub.

Elpaal's mother Hushim and Baara, the other wife of his father, were sent away by

Shaharaim, who then settled in the land of Moab, east of the river Jordan, and married Hodesh with whom he had seven children: Jobab, Zibia, Mesha, Malcham, Jeuz, Shachia, and Mirma.

Elpalet

(Hebrew origin: *God of deliverance*)

(1 Chronicles 14:5). 10th century B.C. Elpalet was one of the sons of King David born in Jerusalem. Elsewhere in the Bible, his name is spelled Eliphelet (1 Chronicles 3:8).

Eluzai

(Hebrew origin: *God is my defense*)

(1 Chronicles 12:5). 11th century B.C. Eluzai was one of the Benjamites who deserted King Saul's army and joined David's band at Ziklag.

These men were skilled warriors who could use both their right and left hands to shoot arrows and sling stones.

Elymas

(Uncertain origin and meaning)

(Acts of the Apostles 13:8). A.D. 1st century. Elymas was a sorcerer and false prophet, whom Paul met in the city of Paphos in the island of Cyprus.

He tried to prevent Sergius Paulus, the Roman proconsul in the island, from hearing the preaching of Paul, and lost his sight, when the apostle cursed him and wished him to be blind. This event so impressed the proconsul that he became a Christian believer. Elymas was also called Barjesus (Acts of the Apostles 13:6).

Elzabad

(Hebrew origin: *God has bestowed*)

1. (1 Chronicles 12:12). 11th century B.C. Elzabad was a Gadite warrior who joined David at Ziklag, while he was still hiding from King Saul.
2. (1 Chronicles 26:7). 10th century B.C. Elzabad, son of Shemaiah and grandson of

Obededom, was one of the gatekeepers of the Tabernacle, during the reign of King David. His brothers—all of them brave men and leaders of their clan—were Othni, Rephael, Elihu, Obed, and Semachiah.

Elzaphan

(Hebrew origin: *God of treasure*)

(Exodus 6:22). 13th century B.C. Elzaphan, son of Uzziel, and brother of Mishael and Zithri, was a first cousin of Moses and Aaron. He was the head of the Levite clan of Kohathites that was in charge of the Ark, the table, the candlesticks, the altars, and the vessels of the sanctuary, during the wanderings of the Israelites in the wilderness.

When Abihu and Nadab, the sons of Aaron, burned forbidden incense and were killed by a fire from the Lord, Moses told Elzaphan and Mishael to take out the two bodies from the sanctuary and to carry them to a place outside the camp.

His descendant Shemaiah, during the reign of David, helped to bring the Ark to Jerusalem (1 Chronicles 15:8). During the reign of King Hezekiah of Judah, his descendants, the Levites Shimri and Jehiel, helped to assemble all the other Levites to make themselves ritually clean, and to purify the Temple (2 Chronicles 29:13). He is also called Elizaphan (Numbers 3:30).

Emmanuel

(Hebrew origin: *God is with us*)

(Matthew 1:23). A.D. 1st century. This is the spelling, which appears in Matthew for Immanuel, the child whose birth was prophesied by Isaiah (Isaiah 7:14).

Emmor

(Uncertain origin and meaning)

(Acts of the Apostles 7:16). 18th century B.C. According to the martyr Stephen, Emmor—called Hamor in the Old Testament—was the ancestor of the people who sold a sepulcher to Abraham in Sychem, i.e. Shechem.

Note: Genesis states that it was Ephron the Hittite who sold a sepulcher to Abraham in Mamre, near Hebron. Jacob did buy a piece of land near Shechem from the children of Hamor, but he used it to build an altar on it.

Enan
(Hebrew origin: *Having eyes*)

(Numbers 1:15). 14th century B.C. His son Ahira, of the tribe of Naphtali, was the commander of his tribe's army, during the march in the wilderness, and one of the twelve Israelite leaders who donated gifts of silver and gold, bulls, rams, goats, and lambs for the dedication of the altar.

Enoch
(Hebrew origin: *Initiated*)

1. (Genesis 4:17). Antediluvian. Enoch was the son of Cain, born in the land of Nod, on the east of Eden. The city that Cain founded was called Enoch in his honor. Enoch was the father of Irad.
2. (Genesis 5:18). Antediluvian. Enoch—also spelled Henoch (1 Chronicles 1:3)—was the son of Jared—also spelled Jered. Enoch was sixty-five years old, when his first son, Methuselah, was born.

   The Bible says that "Enoch walked with God". When he was three hundred and sixty-five years old, God took him. He shares with the prophet Elijah the singular distinction of being taken by God, and not dying.

Enos
(Hebrew origin: *Mortal, human, man*)

(Genesis 4:26). Antediluvian. Enos, son of Seth, the third son of Adam and Eve, was born when his father Seth was one hundred and five years old.

Enos became the father of Cainan, at the age of ninety, and died many years later, at the age of nine hundred and five.

The first book of Chronicles spells his name as Enosh (1 Chronicles 1:1), the name

of his father as Sheth, and the name of his son as Kenan.

Enosh
(Hebrew origin: *Mortal, human, man*)

(1 Chronicles 1:1). Antediluvian. Enosh, son of Sheth, the third son of Adam and Eve, was born, when his father was one hundred and five years old.

Enosh became the father of Kenan, at the age of ninety, and died many years later, at the age of nine hundred and five.

The book of Genesis spells his name as Enos (Genesis 4:26), the name of his father as Seth, and the name of his son as Cainan.

Epaenetus
(Greek origin: *Praised*)

(Romans 16:5). A.D. 1st century. Epaenetus was a Christian to whom Paul sent greetings in his letter to the Christians in Rome.

Paul called him his "well beloved" and mentioned that Epaenetus was one of the first converts to Christianity in Achaia, which is on today's mainland Greece.

Note: Some manuscripts, instead of Achaia, write Asia, which is in today's Turkey.

Epaphras
(Greek origin: contraction of *Epaphroditus* [*Devoted to Aphrodite*])

(Colossians 1:7). A.D. 1st century. Epaphras was a Christian who evangelized Colossae and other cities. Paul called him "fellow servant" and "faithful minister of Christ".

Epaphras was in prison, in Rome, with Paul, when the apostle wrote his letter to Philemon.

Epaphroditus
(Greek origin: *Devoted to the goddess Venus* [i.e. *Aphrodite*])

(Philippians 2:25). A.D. 1st century. Epaphroditus, a Christian whom Paul called "my brother" and "companion in labor and fellow soldier", traveled from Philippi to Rome, bringing messages to Paul. There, he became very ill and almost died.

When Epaphroditus recovered, he longed to return to Philippi, and Paul sent him back from Rome to his native city.

In his letter to the Philippians, the apostle wrote, "Receive him in the Lord with joy, and honor him, because he risked his life and nearly died for the work of Christ, to complete your service to me".

Ephah

(Hebrew origin: *Darkness*)

1. (Genesis 25:4). 18th century B.C. Ephah was a son of Midian and grandson of Abraham and Keturah, the woman whom Abraham married, after the death of Sarah.

   Ephah's brothers were Epher, Eldaah, Hanoch and Abidah; the names of the two last ones are spelled Henoch and Abida in the first book of Chronicles (1 Chronicles 1:33).
2. (1 Chronicles 2:46). Unspecified date. Ephah was a concubine of Caleb, the son of Hezron and brother of Jerahmeel, of the tribe of Judah. She and Caleb had three sons: Haran, Moza, and Gazez.
3. (1 Chronicles 2:47). Unspecified date. Ephah was the son of Jahdai of the tribe of Judah. His brothers were Regem, Jotham, Gesham, Pelet, and Shaaph.

Ephai

(Hebrew origin: *Gloomy*)

(Jeremiah 40:8). 7th century B.C. Ephai, the Netophathite, was the father of some men from the defeated army of Judah, who went with Ishmael and others to Mizpah to speak with Gedaliah, the Babylonian appointed governor of the land of Judah.

Gedaliah told them that they should cooperate with the Babylonians and serve the king of Babylon.

Epher

(Hebrew origin: *Calf*)

1. (Genesis 25:4). 18th century B.C. Epher was a son of Midian and grandson of Abraham and Keturah, the woman whom Abraham married, after the death of Sarah.

   Epher's brothers were Ephah, Eldaah, Hanoch and Abidah; the names of the two last ones are spelled Henoch and Abida in the first book of Chronicles (1 Chronicles 1:33).
2. (1 Chronicles 4:17). Unspecified date. Epher, son of a man called Ezra, a descendant of Judah, was the brother of Jether, Jalon, and Mered, the last of which married Bithiah, the daughter of the Pharaoh of Egypt.
3. (1 Chronicles 5:24). Unspecified date. Epher, of the half tribe of Manasseh that had settled east of the Jordan River, was a mighty warrior and leader of his clan.

   His tribe was deported from their land by the Assyrians and forcibly settled in the region of the river Gozan, where it eventually assimilated into the local population and disappeared from history, being remembered today as one of the "ten lost tribes".

Ephlal

(Hebrew origin: *Judgment*)

(1 Chronicles 2:37). Unspecified date. Ephlal was the son of Zabad and father of Obed. His ancestor Jarha was an Egyptian servant who had married the daughter of his master Sheshan, a leader of the tribe of Judah.

Ephod

(Hebrew origin: *Girdle of the High Priest*)

(Numbers 34:23). 14th century B.C. His son Hanniel, leader of the tribe of Manasseh, was one of the men appointed by Moses to apportion the land of Canaan among the tribes.

Ephraim

(Hebrew origin: *Fruitfulness*)

(Genesis 41:52). 17th century B.C. Ephraim, ancestor of the tribe of Ephraim, was the second son of Joseph and Asenath, his Egyptian wife. He was born in Egypt like his older brother Manasseh.

Years later, after Joseph's brother and father had settled in Egypt, Joseph was informed that his father Jacob was dying. He took with him his two sons, Manasseh and Ephraim, to be blessed by his father, who told him that he was adopting the two boys.

Joseph placed Ephraim on the left side of his father, and Manasseh on the right side. Jacob placed his right hand on Ephraim, the younger son, and his left hand on Manasseh. Joseph tried to remove Jacob's hand from Ephraim's head and place it on Manasseh's head, telling his father that Manasseh was the firstborn. Jacob refused, saying that both brothers would be the ancestors of tribes, but the younger brother's descendants would be more numerous.

Ephraim's sons were Shuthelah, ancestor of the clan of the Shuthalhites; Becher, ancestor of the clan of the Bachrites; Tahan, ancestor of the clan of the Tahanites (Numbers 26:35).

Some of his descendants were killed by the men of Gath, when they tried to take away their cattle. Ephraim mourned them, many days, until his wife gave birth to his son Beriah.

Ephratah

(Hebrew origin: *Fruitfulness*)

(1 Chronicles 2:50). Unspecified date. Ephratah married Caleb, son of Hezron, after the death of Azubah, Caleb's wife. Hur, her firstborn son, founded Bethlehem, which was also called Ephratah, in her honor.

An alternative spelling of her name is Ephrath (1 Chronicles 2:19).

Ephrath

(Hebrew origin: *Fruitfulness*)

(1 Chronicles 2:19). Unspecified date. Ephrath married Caleb, son of Hezron, after the death of Azubah, Caleb's wife. Hur, her firstborn son, founded Bethlehem, which was also called Ephratah, in her honor.

An alternative spelling is Ephratah (1 Chronicles 2:50).

Ephron

(Hebrew origin: *Fawn-like*)

(Genesis 23:8). 19th century B.C. Ephron, the son of Zohar the Hittite, owned a field in Mamre, in the outskirts of Hebron. The land included the cave of Machpelah that Abraham, whose wife Sarah had just died, wished to buy and use for a family burial place.

Was Ephron acquainted with Abraham's negotiating talents? Did he perhaps know that Abraham had debated with God and succeeded in persuading him to lower the minimum number of righteous people expected to be found in Sodom from fifty to ten?

Expecting to be faced with some hard bargaining, Ephron's opening rhetorical gambit—still very much in use in the markets of Middle East countries—was an offer to give Abraham the field and the cave as a free gift!

Abraham didn't want any doubt to ever arise in the future about the legality of his ownership of the cave. And for that, he needed a clear title to the property. He refused Ephron's phony offer and insisted that he wanted to pay.

Ephron then went on to the second stage of his usual bargaining: he quoted Abraham a price of four hundred shekels of silver, an exorbitant amount of money in those days, and added, "What is that amount between you and me?"

He was, of course, sure that Abraham would make a counter offer. How happily surprised he must have been, when Abraham paid him, on the spot, the high sum that he had quoted!

Abraham buried Sarah, in the cave of Machpelah. When he himself died, his sons Isaac and Ishmael buried him there, and many years later, Isaac, Rebekah, Leah, and Jacob were also buried in the same cave.

The cave of Machpelah, covered by a beautiful edifice built by Herod the Great, is today occupied by a mosque and a synagogue, where the descendants of Ishmael and Isaac pray under one roof.

Er

(Hebrew origin: *Watchful*)

1. (Genesis 38:3). 17th century B.C. Er, a grandson of Jacob, was the son of Judah and a Canaanite woman, daughter of a man named Shuah. His brothers were Onan and Shelah. Er, whose father had married him to Tamar, died young and childless.
2. (1 Chronicles 4:21). 17th century B.C. Er, one of the sons—the others were Laadah, Jokim, Joash, and Saraph—of Shelah, Judah's youngest son, was the founder of Lecah.
3. (Luke 3:28). Unspecified date. Er was the son of Jose and father of Elmodam, ancestor of Jesus, in the genealogy of Luke.

Eran

(Hebrew origin: *Watchful*)

(Numbers 26:36). 17th century B.C. Eran, the son of Shuthelah and grandson of Ephraim, was the ancestor of the clan of the Eranites.

Erastus

(Greek origin: *Beloved*)

(Acts of the Apostles 19:22). A.D. 1st century. Erastus, a helper of Paul in the Roman province of Asia—today's Anatolia, in Turkey—was sent by the apostle to Macedonia, together with Timotheus. Paul joined them there, after he left Ephesus, where he was almost lynched by the followers of the goddess Diana.

Paul, in his letter to the Roman church, mentioned that Erastus, who had become the chamberlain of the city of Corinth, and two other Christians, Gaius and Quartus, sent greetings to the church in Rome (Romans 16:23).

In his second letter to Timothy—probably the last letter that the apostle wrote from his prison in Rome—Paul mentioned that Erastus stayed at Corinth (2 Timothy 4:20).

Note: Some scholars believe that these three separate mentions of Erastus in the Bible might not refer to the same person but to two or three different persons of the same name.

Eri

(Hebrew origin: *Watchful*)

(Genesis 46:16). 17th century B.C. Eri, son of Gad and grandson of Jacob and Zilpah, Leah's maid, was one of the seventy Israelites who immigrated to Egypt.

Eri was the ancestor of the clan of Erites. His brothers were Ziphion, Haggi, Shuni, Ezbon, Arodi, and Areli.

Esaias

(Hebrew origin: *God has saved*)

(Matthew 3:3). 7th century B.C. Esaias is an alternative spelling for the name of the prophet Isaiah. (Please see the entry for Isaiah [2 Kings 19:2].)

Esarhaddon

(Assyrian origin: *Ashur has given me a brother*)

(2 Kings 19:37). 7th century B.C. Esarhaddon ascended to the throne of Assyria, after his brothers Adrammelech and Sharezer murdered their father, Sennacherib, while the king was worshipping in the Temple of his god Nisroch.

He settled foreign tribes in Samaria, to replace the Israelites who had been deported, when the kingdom of Israel was conquered.

On his death, Esarhaddon was succeeded by his son Ashurbanipal, called Asnapper in the Bible, who continued his policy of settling foreigners in conquered territories.

Esau

(Hebrew origin: *Rough*)

(Genesis 25:25). 18th century B.C. Esau

was the ancestor of the Edomites, a people who lived in the region of Seir, between the Dead Sea and the Gulf of Aqabah. The Edomite nation was very often in war against the Israelites, until they were converted to Judaism, during the period of the Second Temple.

Esau and his twin brother, Jacob, were born after their parents, Isaac and Rebekah, had been childless for twenty years.

During Rebekah's pregnancy, she felt the babies struggling in her womb and was told by the Lord that each of the boys would become the progenitor of a nation, but that the older would serve the younger. Esau was born first, red and hairy, and moments later, Jacob came out holding Esau's heel.

Esau, his father's favorite, grew up to be a skilled hunter, a simple fellow, an outdoor man, impetuous, impatient, and easily manipulated by his shrewd brother.

Jacob, his mother's favorite, was completely his opposite: a patient, thoughtful, stay-at-home type.

One day, Esau returned famished from the field and saw that Jacob was cooking a soup of red lentils. He said to Jacob, "I am starving! Give me some of that red stuff!"

Jacob said, "First, sell me your birthright".

"I am at the point of death, so what use is my birthright to me?" replied Esau.

"Swear to me first", said Jacob. Esau swore and sold his birthright to his brother. Jacob then gave him bread and lentil soup. Esau ate and drank, and then, he went away.

Esau married at the age of forty, the same age of his father, Isaac, when he married Rebekah. His wives, two Hittite women called Judith and Bashemath, did all they could to make life miserable for Isaac and Rebekah.

Years went by, Isaac, now grown old and blind, decided to bless his eldest son, but first, he would eat. He called Esau and told him, "I am old, and I may die any day. Take your weapons, bow and arrows, go out to the fields, and hunt me some venison. Then, prepare it the way I like it, and bring it to me to eat, so that I may give you my soul's blessing, before I die".

Rebekah overheard the conversation and devised a plan, by which Jacob would receive Isaac's blessing. She instructed Jacob to disguise himself as Esau, by putting on his brother's clothing and covering his arms and neck with the skin of a goat to simulate Esau's hairiness. She prepared a savory dish of meat and sent Jacob with it to his father. Jacob succeeded in convincing his father that he was Esau, and the deceived old man bestowed his blessing on Jacob.

Esau returned from his hunt. He too prepared a delicious meal, brought it to his father, and said, "Let my father sit up and eat of his son's venison, so that your soul may bless me". Isaac, bewildered, asked him, "Who are you?"

"I am your son Esau, your firstborn".

Isaac was seized with a violent trembling. "Who was it then", he asked, "that brought me the venison dish? I ate all of it, before you came, and I blessed him. He will remain blessed".

Esau burst into uncontrolled sobbing and said, "Bless me too, Father!" Isaac answered, "Your brother came with deviousness and took away your blessing".

"How rightly was he named Jacob?! He has now supplanted me two times, the first time when he took away my birthright, and now he has taken away my blessing. Don't you have another blessing for me?"

Isaac said, "I have made him master over you and have given him grain and wine. What, then, can I still do for you, my son?"

"Do you only have one blessing, my father? Bless me too, Father!" said Esau in a loud voice and wept.

His father said to him, "Your dwelling shall be the fatness of the earth, and the dew of heaven above. You shall live by your sword, and you shall serve your brother, but one day, you shall break his yoke from your neck".

Furious at Jacob's trickery, Esau vowed to kill Jacob, as soon as Isaac passed away. Rebekah, to protect Jacob from Esau's revenge, decided to send him away to her brother Laban in Haran. She went to Isaac and complained that she was weary of her life because of the

Hittite wives of Esau, and if Jacob would also marry one of the local girls, she had no wish to continue living.

Isaac called Jacob, blessed him, and said, "You shall not marry any Canaanite girl. Go to Paddan-Aram, to the house of Bethuel, your mother's father, and marry one of the daughters of your uncle Laban".

When Esau learned that Canaanite women displeased his parents, he went to the house of his uncle Ishmael and married his cousin Mahalath, the daughter of Ishmael.

Twenty years went by, Jacob, who had become a very wealthy man, decided to return to Canaan, with his wives Leah and Rachel, his two concubines, and his children. He sent messengers to his brother Esau, who now lived in the region of Seir, in the country of Edom, announcing his return. The messengers came back and told Jacob that Esau was coming to meet him with four hundred men.

Jacob feared that Esau was bringing so many men with him to exact his revenge for the blessing that Jacob had received, under false pretenses, from their father Isaac. To assuage the anger and the hate that, he thought, his brother felt, he sent him a great number of goats, ewes, rams, camels, and donkeys, as a gift.

Esau approached with his troop of four hundred men. Jacob saw him and bowed to the ground seven times. Esau ran to him and embraced him, and both brothers wept.

After Jacob had presented his family to his brother, Esau asked him, "Why did you send me all those animals?"

"To gain my lord's favor", answered Jacob.

"I have enough, my brother; keep what is yours", said Esau.

"No, please! If I have found favor in your eyes, receive my gift; for to see your face is like seeing the face of God, and you have received me with friendship. Please accept my present, because God has favored me, and I have enough".

Jacob urged him, and Esau accepted and said, "And now let's start on our journey".

Jacob answered, "My lord knows that the children are very young, and the flocks and herds are nursing their young. If we would drive them hard for even one day, they would die. Let my lord go on ahead of his servant. I will follow slowly, at the pace of the children and the cattle, until I arrive in Seir".

Esau said, "Let me leave some of my men with you". Jacob answered, "Thank you, but that is not necessary". Esau went back to Seir, and Jacob continued on his journey to Succoth.

The next and last time that the two brothers met was when they buried their father Isaac in the cave of Machpelah (Genesis 35:29).

The sons whom Esau had with his wives—Adah, Aholibamah, and Bashemath—were Eliphaz, Reuel, Jeush, Jaalam, and Korah. Esau, through his son Eliphaz, was the grandfather of Amalek, Israel's eternal enemy.

Eshbaal

(Hebrew origin: *Man of the Canaanite god Baal*)

(1 Chronicles 8:33). 11th century B.C. Eshbaal, also called Ishbosheth, was the fourth son of King Saul and the last member of his family to reign in Israel. (Please see the entry for Ishbosheth [2 Samuel 2:8].)

Note: The word "Baal", which means *Master* or *Lord* in Hebrew, was originally a title of dignity. Eventually, it became associated to a Canaanite god, causing the ancient Hebrew editors of the Bible to substitute the word "Bosheth", meaning *Shame,* for "Baal".

Eshban

(Hebrew origin: *Vigorous*)

(Genesis 36:26). Unspecified date. Eshban, son of Dishon, a descendant of Seir the Horite, lived in the land of Edom.

His brothers were Hemdan—called Amram in First Chronicles (1 Chronicles 1:41)—Cheran, and Ithran.

Eshcol

(Hebrew origin: *Cluster of grapes*)

(Genesis 14:13). 19th century B.C. Eshcol, Aner, and Mamre were three Amorite brothers who joined Abraham in his pursuit of the kings who had taken Lot captive.

Abram overtook the kings, defeated them, and brought back the captives and the stolen booty. The king of Sodom offered to reward him, but he declined, suggesting instead that the reward should be given to Eshcol and his brothers.

Eshek

(Hebrew origin: *Oppression*)

(1 Chronicles 8:39). Unspecified date. Eshek, of the tribe of Benjamin, was a descendant of Jonathan, the son of King Saul. His sons were Ulam, Jehush, and Eliphelet.

Eshtemoa

(Hebrew origin: *Hear obediently*)

(1 Chronicles 4:19). Unspecified date. Eshtemoa the Maachathite was the grandson of Hodiah, Naham's sister.

Eshton

(Hebrew origin: *Restful*)

(1 Chronicles 4:11). Unspecified date. Eshton was the son of Mehir, a descendant of Judah. His sons were Bethrapha, Paseah, and Tehinnah.

Esli

(Uncertain origin and meaning)

(Luke 3:25). Unspecified date. Esli, son of Nagge and father of Naum, was an ancestor of Jesus, in the genealogy of Luke.

Esrom

(Hebrew origin: *Courtyard*)

(Matthew 1:3). Unspecified date. Esrom, son of Phares and father of Aram, was an ancestor of Jesus in the genealogies of Matthew and Luke.

Esther

(Persian origin: *Star*)

(Esther 2:7). 5th century B.C. Esther—whose Hebrew name was Hadassah, *Myrtle*—was the daughter of Abihail, a descendant of King Saul, who had been exiled by the Babylonians from Jerusalem together with King Jeconiah of Judah.

Esther, orphaned at an early age, was brought up by her cousin Mordecai in Shushan, the capital of the Persian Empire, during the reign of Ahasuerus, king of Persia.

In the third year of his reign, Ahasuerus—usually identified by historians as King Xerxes I of Persia, son and successor of Darius I—gave a banquet for all his princes and administrators to show off his wealth. The great celebration lasted one hundred and eighty days.

When the festivities for the nobles ended, the king gave a banquet in the garden of his palace for the common people of Shushan. During seven days, everybody, rich and poor, drank as much as he wanted. At the same time, Vashti, his queen, gave a banquet for the women inside the palace.

On the seventh day of the celebration, the drunken Ahasuerus ordered the seven eunuchs, who were his personal servants, to fetch Queen Vashti, and to make sure that she was wearing her royal crown. She was a beautiful woman, and the king wanted everybody to see her. The eunuchs returned and told the king that the queen refused to come.

The king, barely able to contain his fury, consulted with his law experts about what he should do with Vashti, for having refused to obey the king's command.

Memucan, one of his chief advisers, declared, "Queen Vashti has offended not only the king, but also all his officials, and all the people in the empire. Her bad example will make all the wives in the empire despise their husbands. The king should issue a royal decree and make it into a law, so that it could never be changed, that Vashti shall never again appear before the king. Another, worthier, woman should be made queen instead. The women in the empire will then surely treat their husbands with respect!" The proposal was approved by the king and his ministers.

Sometime later, after the king had calmed down, he kept thinking about Vashti, what she had done, and what had been decreed against her. His advisers suggested that beautiful virgins from every province should be brought to the harem in Shushan, to be placed under the care of Hege, the eunuch in charge of the women. The girls would be given a beauty treatment, and the one that the king would like best should be made queen, instead of Vashti. The king liked the proposal and put it into effect.

Maidens from all corners of the empire, Esther among them, were brought to the harem. Each girl would undergo a beauty treatment that lasted a whole year. Then, she would be brought to the king, to spend the night with him. The next morning, she would be taken to the second harem, where the women, who had already spent one night with the king, were kept under the supervision of the eunuch Shaashgaz. These women remained in the harem and never saw the king again, except when he specifically summoned one of them by her name.

During the seventh year of King Ahasuerus' reign, Esther's turn came to be brought to the king. He liked her more than any other girl and made her his queen. The king gave a great banquet in her honor for all his officials and courtiers, where he proclaimed a tax amnesty, and distributed gifts. Esther, advised by Mordecai, didn't let it be known that she was Jewish.

One day, Mordecai, sitting in the palace gate, overheard two of Ahasuerus' guards plotting against the king's life. Mordecai told it to Esther, who reported it to the king in Mordecai's name. The matter was investigated and verified, and the two men were executed. The king ordered to write an account of this event in the official records of the empire.

Sometime later, the king promoted a man named Haman to the position of vizier of the empire and ordered all the officials in his service to show him respect by kneeling and bowing to him. Everybody complied with the king's order except Mordecai.

Mordecai refused to kneel or bow to Haman, saying that he was a Jew, and that Jews only kneeled and bowed to God. Haman, angry and offended, decided that punishing Mordecai alone was not enough. All the Jews in the empire should be exterminated!

Haman went to the king and denounced that the Jews were a people with different customs who did not obey the king's laws. He added that, if the king would issue the death decree against the Jews, Haman would pay ten thousand talents of silver to the royal treasury.

The king took off his ring and gave it to Haman, saying, "The silver and the people are yours to do with them as you see fit".

Haman chose the month of Adar as an appropriate month for the genocide by casting lots, "Pur" in Hebrew. The king's scribes were called, and Haman dictated letters proclaiming that all the Jews, young and old, women and children, would be killed on the thirteenth day of the month of Adar. These letters, sealed with the king's ring, were sent to all the governors of the provinces. Having taken care of this business, the king and Haman sat down to drink.

When Mordecai learned of the death decree, he tore his clothes, dressed in sackcloth, covered his head with ashes, and walked through the city, bitterly crying out in a loud voice, until he reached the gates of the palace. He couldn't enter, because this was forbidden for people wearing sackcloth. In the provinces, the Jews fasted, wept, wailed, and put on sackcloth.

Queen Esther's maids and eunuchs informed her that Mordecai was outside the gates of the palace, dressed in sackcloth, crying and shouting. The queen became very agitated and worried about the mental health of her cousin. She sent somebody to the palace gates, with clothing for Mordecai, so that he could wear them, instead of his sackcloth. Mordecai refused to receive the clothing.

The queen sent Hatach, one of the eunuchs who served her, to Mordecai to find out the reason for his strange and disturbing behavior. Mordecai told Hatach that Haman had promised to give money to the king's treasuries for being allowed to exterminate the Jews. He gave the eunuch a copy of the decree and told him to show it to Esther, so that she would know the danger and go to the king to plead for her people.

Esther received the message and sent a note back to Mordecai, saying that, according to the law, if she would go to the king without being summoned, she would be put to death, unless the king would extend his golden scepter to her.

Mordecai replied that Esther should not feel safer than any other Jew, just because she was in the palace. Esther answered that the Jews in Shushan should fast on her behalf for three days. She would also fast, and then she would go to the king, even if she had to die for doing so.

On the third day of her fast, Esther put on her royal dress and stood in the inner court of the king's palace, facing the throne room, in front of the king, who was sitting on his throne, holding a golden scepter in his hand.

When the king saw her, she won his favor. He extended to Esther his scepter; Esther approached and touched the tip of the scepter.

"What do you wish, Queen Esther?" the king asked. "Tell me and you shall have it, even if it is half my empire".

"If it pleases Your Majesty", Esther replied, "let Your Majesty and Haman come today to the feast that I have prepared for him".

That night, the king and Haman went to the queen's chambers. During the wine feast, the king again asked Esther, "What is your wish? And what is your request? I will grant it even if it is half my empire". Esther replied that she would like the king and Haman to be again her guests the next day at another banquet.

Haman left the banquet in a good mood. His happiness was marred, when he went through the palace gate and saw that Mordecai did not show him any signs of respect. Haman was filled with rage, but he made an effort to control himself and went home.

He invited his friends and his wife to join him. He boasted to them about his great wealth, his many sons, his high position in court, and how he, besides the king, was the only guest in a banquet offered by Queen Esther. "However", he lamented, "all that

meant nothing to me, when I saw that insolent Jew Mordecai, sitting in the palace gate".

His wife and friends advised him to build a gallows, and to ask the king to allow him to hang Mordecai from it. Haman liked the idea, and he had the gallows built.

That night, the king, suffering of insomnia, asked that the official records of the empire should be brought and read to him. He heard the account of how Mordecai had uncovered a plot to assassinate the king and inquired if the man had been honored and rewarded for his deed. His servants answered that nothing had been done for him.

The king then asked if any of his officials were in the palace. It so happened that Haman, who had come that night to ask the king for permission to hang Mordecai, had just entered the courtyard. The king's servants brought Haman to the royal chambers.

The king asked him, "What should be done for a man whom the king wishes to honor?"

Haman, assuming that the king was referring to him, answered, "The man whom the king wishes to honor should be dressed in royal robes and set upon the king's horse. One of the empire's noblest courtiers should lead the horse through the city square, proclaiming: 'See how the king rewards a man he wishes to honor'".

"Hurry", said the king to Haman. "Get the robes and the horse as you have said, and do this to Mordecai the Jew. Omit nothing of all you have proposed".

Haman did what he was told. Afterward, Mordecai returned to his usual place at the king's gate, and Haman hurried home, his head covered in mourning. There, Haman told his wife and friends all that had happened to him. They predicted that Mordecai would defeat him. While they were still talking, the palace eunuchs arrived and took Haman in a hurry to Esther's banquet.

Over the wine, the king asked Esther once more, "What is your wish, Queen Esther? I'll even give you half the empire".

Esther answered, "My wish is that I and my people may live, because we are about to be destroyed and exterminated".

"Who dares to do such a thing? Where is this man?" asked Ahasuerus.

Esther answered, "Our enemy, our persecutor, is this evil Haman!" Haman cringed in terror. The king got up in a fury, left the room, and went outside to the palace gardens to calm down. Haman stayed in the dining room to beg Queen Esther for his life. He threw himself down on Esther's couch and implored for mercy. At that moment, the king came back and saw Haman on the queen's couch.

"Is this man going to rape the queen right here in front of me, in my own palace?" shouted the king.

The eunuchs held Haman's face down. One of them, named Harbonah, said that Haman had build a gallows at his house to hang Mordecai. The king immediately ordered, "Hang Haman on it!"

Haman was hanged, and the king calmed down. That same day, King Ahasuerus gave Haman's property to Esther. When the queen told Ahasuerus that Mordecai was her relative, the king took off the ring, which he had taken back from Haman, gave it to Mordecai, and named him vizier, second in rank only to the king. From then on, Mordecai wore royal robes of blue and white, a cloak of fine purple linen, and a magnificent crown of gold.

Esther fell weeping at the king's feet and asked him to stop the evil plot that Haman had made against the Jews. The king extended the golden scepter to Esther; she stood up and said, "Please issue a proclamation revoking the orders that Haman gave for the destruction of the Jews in the empire".

The king told Esther and Mordecai that proclamations issued in the king's name and stamped with the royal seal could not be revoked, but that they could write to the Jews whatever they liked, in the king's name, and stamp it with the royal seal.

Mordecai dictated letters in the name of King Ahasuerus, stamped them with the royal seal, and sent them to all the provinces by couriers, mounted on fast horses from the royal stables. These letters stated that the Jews were authorized by the king to organize for self-defense, fight back if attacked, destroy their enemies with their wives and children, and plunder their possessions.

On the thirteenth day of the month of Adar, the day on which the enemies of the Jews had planned to destroy them, the Jews attacked them with swords and slaughtered them. When the number of those killed in Shushan was reported to the king, Ahasuerus said to Esther, "In Shushan alone, the Jews have killed five hundred people. What then must they have done in the provinces?! What do you want now? You shall have it".

Esther answered, "Let the Jews in Shushan be allowed to do again tomorrow what they were allowed to do today; and let Haman's ten sons hang in the gallows". The king ordered this to be done. The bodies of Haman's ten sons were publicly displayed, and the next day, the Jews of Shushan killed three hundred more of their enemies.

Esther and Mordecai wrote a letter to all the Jews, wishing them peace and security, and directing them and their descendants to celebrate every year a festival to be called Purim, because Haman had chosen the date of the genocide by casting lots, "Pur" in Hebrew.

Ethan

(Hebrew origin: *Permanent*)

1. (1 Kings 4:31). Unspecified date. Ethan the Ezrahite and the three sons of Mahol—Chalcol, Heman, and Darda—were famous for their wisdom, which was surpassed only by that of King Solomon. Ethan was the author of the Eighty-ninth Psalm.

2. (1 Chronicles 2:6). 16th century B.C. Ethan, the son of Zerah, was the grandson of Judah and Tamar. His brothers were Zimri, Heman, Calcol and Dara. His son was Azariah.

3. (1 Chronicles 6:42). Unspecified date. Ethan, son of Zimmah, of the clan of the Kohathites, was the father of Adaiah.
   His descendant Asaph was one of the Levites appointed by King David to be musicians in the House of the Lord.

4. (1 Chronicles 6:44). 10th century B.C. Ethan, son of Kishi—also called Kushaiah—

a descendant of Merari, was one of the Levites appointed by King David to be musicians in the House of the Lord. Ethan played the trumpets and the cymbals of brass.

Some scholars believe that this Ethan is the same person as Jeduthun (1 Chronicles 16:41).

Ethbaal

(Hebrew origin: *With Baal*)

(1 Kings 16:31). 9th century B.C. Ethbaal was the king of Sidon, an important Phoenician city kingdom. His daughter Jezebel married King Ahab and introduced the cult of Baal in Israel.

Ethnan

(Hebrew origin: *Reward*)

(1 Chronicles 4:7). Unspecified date. Ethnan, a descendant of Judah, was the son of Ashur and his wife Helah. His brothers were Zereth and Jezoar.

Ethni

(Hebrew origin: *Gift*)

(1 Chronicles 6:41). Unspecified date. Ethni, son of Zerah, of the clan of the Kohathites, was the father of Malchiah.

His descendant Asaph was one of the Levites appointed by King David to be in charge of the musicians in the House of the Lord.

Eubulus

(Greek origin: *Good-willer*)

(2 Timothy 4:21). A.D. 1st century. Eubulus was one of the four persons—the others were Claudia, Pudens, and Linus—who sent greetings to Timothy in the last letter written by Paul.

Eunice

(Greek origin: *Victorious*)

(2 Timothy 1:5). A.D. 1st century. Eunice, a Jewish woman married to a Greek, lived in Lystra. She, her mother Lois, and her son Timothy were Christians, probably converted by Paul in his previous visit to Lystra. Timothy became Paul's constant companion, his invaluable helper, and messenger.

Euodias

(Greek origin: *Successful journey*)

(Philippians 4:2). A.D. 1st century. Euodias, a Christian woman living in Philippi, was involved in a disagreement with another Christian woman called Syntyche.

Paul, who was grateful to both women for having helped him and Clement, a fellow worker, to spread the word of God, beseeched them in his letter to the Philippians to put aside their quarrel.

Eutychus

(Greek origin: *Fortunate*)

(Acts of the Apostles 20:9). A.D. 1st century. Eutychus, a young man, attended a sermon preached by Paul, whose ship was making a stopover in Troas.

The apostle, who planned to continue his voyage the next day, spoke for hours, until midnight. Eutychus, sitting in a window in the third floor, fell soundly asleep, fell out of the window, and lost consciousness.

People thought that he was dead, but Paul rushed downstairs, checked the boy and, to everybody's relief, pronounced him alive. Paul then went back upstairs, ate a piece of bread, and resumed his sermon, before leaving in the early hours of the morning.

Eve

(Hebrew origin: *Life giver*)

(Genesis 3:20). Antediluvian. Eve was created by God, from one of Adam's ribs, when Adam could not find, among the animals, a suitable helpmate. God put the man to sleep, extracted one of his ribs, and fashioned with it the first woman, whom Adam called Eve because she was the mother of all living.

The man and the woman were naked and felt no shame, until the serpent convinced the woman to eat the fruit of the forbidden tree. After Eve shared the fruit with Adam, the couple became aware of their nakedness. They covered themselves with fig leaves and hid from God in embarrassment.

God asked Adam, "How did you know that you were naked? You have eaten the forbidden fruit!"

Adam blamed Eve, and Eve blamed the serpent. As punishment for this transgression, God condemned the serpent to crawl on its belly and eat dust. He told the woman that she would suffer pain in childbirth, would crave for her husband, and be subject to him.

To the man, God said, "Because you listened to the woman and violated the prohibition, you are destined to work hard all the days of your life, and to gain your bread by the sweat of your brow."

God then made garments of skin and clothed the man and the woman. To prevent them from eating the fruit of the tree of life and, thus, becoming immortal, God expelled them from the Garden of Eden.

After being driven out of the Garden of Eden, Eve conceived and gave birth to Cain and, later, to Abel. After the death of Abel, who was murdered by his jealous brother Cain, Eve gave birth to her third son, Seth, when Adam was a hundred and thirty years old. There is no further mention of Eve in the Bible, and it is not known how old she was, when she died.

Though Adam lived on for many years, dying at the age of nine hundred and thirty, the Bible gives no account of how he adapted himself to life outside the Garden of Eden, except for mentioning that he fathered sons and daughters.

Evi

(Hebrew origin: *Desirous*)

(Numbers 31:8). 13th century B.C. Evi was one of the five kings of Midian—the others were Rekem, Zur, Hur, and Reba—who were killed in battle by the Israelites under the command of Phinehas, the son of Eleazar the Priest.

Sihon, king of the Amorites, and Balaam, the seer, were also killed in the same battle.

Evilmerodach

(Chaldean: *Soldier of the god Merodach*)

(2 Kings 25:27). 6th century B.C. Evilmerodach, when he became king of Babylonia, freed Jehoiachin, changed his prison garments, and gave him a place of honor in his court. The deposed king of Judah had languished in prison, during thirty-seven years.

Ezar

(Hebrew origin: *Help*)

(1 Chronicles 1:38). Unspecified date. Ezar is an alternative spelling for Ezer (Genesis 36:21), one of the sons of Seir the Horite, ancestor of the clans that settled in the land of Edom. His brothers were Lotan, Shobal, Zibeon, Dishon, Anah, and Dishan.

Ezbai

(Hebrew origin: *Hyssop-like*)

(1 Chronicles 11:37). 11th century B.C. Ezbai was the father of Naarai, one of the soldiers in King David's army.

Ezbon

(Hebrew origin: *Finger*)

1. (Genesis 46:16). 17th century B.C. Ezbon, son of Gad and grandson of Jacob, was one of the seventy Israelites who immigrated to Egypt. His brothers were Ziphion, Haggi, Shuni, Eri, Arodi, and Areli. He is called Ozni in the book of Numbers (Numbers 26:16).

2. (1 Chronicles 7:7). 16th century B.C. Ezbon was a son of Bela, the eldest son of Benjamin. His brothers were Uzzi, Uzziel, Jerimoth, and Iri, all of them brave leaders of their clans.

Note: Elsewhere in the first book of Chronicles (1 Chronicles 8:3), Bela has a different list of sons: Addar, Gera, Abihud, Abishua, Naaman, Ahoah, Gera, Shephuphan, and Huram.

Ezekias

(Hebrew origin: *Strengthened by God*)

(Matthew 1:9). 8th century B.C. Ezekias is an alternative spelling for Hezekiah, king of Judah, and ancestor of Jesus. (See the entry for Hezekiah [2 Kings 16:20].)

Ezekiel

(Hebrew origin: *Strength of God*)

(Ezekiel 1:3). 6th century B.C. The prophet Ezekiel, son of Buzi, was a man of passionate faith and great imagination, a unique seer who saw the future in his visions.

In the year of 597 B.C., the Babylonians laid siege to Jerusalem, captured the city, and deported King Jehoiachin to Babylon, together with many nobles and prominent people. Among them was Ezekiel, a priest whose wife had died, during the siege.

Ten years later, the Babylonians under Nebuchadnezzar returned, destroyed the Temple, and brought to an end the kingdom of Judah, exiling most of the population.

Ezekiel, who was living in Babylon in a place called Telabib by the Chebar River, had a vision of the throne chariot of God. His prophetic message, directed both to the exiles in Babylon, and to the survivors, who remained in Jerusalem, sought to awaken their hopes for the restoration of the nation. He prophesied that the exiles would return to the land of Israel, and that the Temple would be rebuilt.

Ezekiel's prophesies were expressed in strange visions and vivid symbolic actions. In one of his visions, he saw himself transported to the future Temple in Jerusalem, guided by an angel who gave him a detailed tour.

His symbolic actions included the building of a model of the siege of Jerusalem; eating a scroll, on which words of prophecy were written; lying motionless on his side, consuming scant rations of grain and water; using excrement to bake a cake; and shaving his head.

Ezer

(Hebrew origin: *Treasure* or [with a different spelling in Hebrew] *Help*)

1. (Genesis 36:21). Unspecified date. Ezer and his brothers—Lotan, Shobal, Zibeon, Dishan, Dishon, and Anah—sons of Seir the Horite, were ancestors of the clans that settled in the land of Edom. Ezer's sons were Bilhan, Zaavan, and Akan, called Jakan in the first book of Chronicles (1 Chronicles 1:42). His name was spelled Ezar in the first book of Chronicles (1 Chronicles 1:38).

2. (1 Chronicles 4:4). Unspecified date. Ezer, the son of Hur, of the tribe of Judah, was the brother of Penuel and the founder of Hushah.

3. (1 Chronicles 7:21). Unspecified date. Ezer was a descendant of Ephraim. He and his brothers were killed by the men of Gath, while trying to steal their cattle.

4. (1 Chronicles 12:9). 11th century B.C. Ezer commanded a group of Gadite fighters, who joined David's band in Ziklag, when he was hiding from Saul. These men were lion-faced skilled warriors, who could easily handle shield and buckler, and who were as swift as deer upon the mountains.

5. (Nehemiah 3:19). 5th century B.C. Ezer, the son of Jeshua, ruler of Mizpah, was a Levite who helped to repair the walls of Jerusalem, during the days of Nehemiah.

6. (Nehemiah 12:42). 5th century B.C. Ezer was one of the priests led by Jezrahiah, their overseer, who marched, singing in a loud voice, in the joyful procession, which celebrated the dedication of the rebuilt walls of Jerusalem, during the days of Nehemiah.

Ezra

(Hebrew origin: *Help*)

1. (1 Chronicles 4:17). Unspecified date. Ezra, a descendant of Judah, was the father of Jether, Mered, Epher, and Jalon. His son Mered married Bithiah, daughter of the Pharaoh of Egypt.

2. (Ezra 7:1). 5th century B.C. Ezra, a priest, scribe, and scholar, knowledgeable in the

Law of Moses, was one of the most influential religious leaders in the history of the Jewish people. His father was Seraiah, a descendant of Eleazar, the son of Aaron.

In the seventh year of the reign of Artaxerxes, king of Persia, Ezra asked the king for permission to return to Jerusalem together with any other exile who also wished to do so.

The king gave his whole-hearted approval to Ezra's mission. Not only did he give Ezra a written authorization, but he also donated gold and silver to be offered to the God of Israel in Jerusalem, ordered all the governors of his provinces to render full cooperation to Ezra, and forbade them to demand any toll, tax or custom duties from him.

In addition, the king gave authority to Ezra to set magistrates and judges in Jerusalem. Artaxerxes would have gladly provided an armed escort, but Ezra was ashamed to ask for it, because he had assured the king that God would protect them.

Ezra left Persia with a few thousand men. On the way, he realized that there were no Levites with him and sent messengers to Iddo, the leader of a place called Casiphia, requesting him to send Levites to serve in the Temple in Jerusalem.

After traveling for five months, the returnees arrived in Jerusalem. Ezra was shocked to find that the people had been intermarrying with foreigners. He assembled all the people, under threat of confiscating the possessions of anybody who would not come to the assembly, and forced them to promise to divorce their foreign wives, a process which took about three months.

Thirteen years later, Nehemiah, named governor of Jerusalem, came and rebuilt the walls of the city. After the work was finished, the entire population of Jerusalem assembled in the square, before the Water Gate, and Ezra, standing on a wooden pulpit, read to the people the Book of the Law of Moses, from sunrise till noon. The priests and the Levites explained the teachings to the people, who cried and wept, until the Levites told them to rejoice and not to be sad, for this was a holy day.

On the next day, the leaders of the people, the priests, and the Levites met with Ezra to study the books of Moses. They read that God had commanded the Israelites to celebrate the Feast of Booths, which had not been done since the days of Joshua. The people immediately went to the fields, brought back branches of trees and built booths on their roofs, in their courtyards and in many public places.

When Nehemiah finished the reconstruction of the walls of Jerusalem, Ezra, followed by priests who played musical instruments, led the joyful procession, which celebrated the completion of the walls.

3. (Nehemiah 12:1) 6th century B.C. Ezra was one of the priests who returned with Zerubbabel from the Babylonian Exile. He was the ancestor of a priestly clan, headed by Meshullam, when Joiakim was High Priest, during the time of Nehemiah.

4. (Nehemiah 12:33). 5th century B.C. Ezra was one of the leaders of the people who marched in the joyful procession, which celebrated the dedication of the rebuilt walls of Jerusalem, during the days of Nehemiah.

Ezri

(Hebrew origin: *My help*)

(1 Chronicles 27:26). 10th century B.C. Ezri, son of Chelub, was in charge of the workers who tilled the fields, during the reign of King David.

Felix

(Latin origin: *Happy*)

(Acts of the Apostles 23:24). A.D. 1st century. Felix, the governor of Judea, lived in Caesarea, the administrative center of the Roman rule in Judea. His wife was a Jewish woman called Drusilla.

Claudius Lysias, the commander of the Antonia fortress, headquarters of the Roman army in Jerusalem, had written to Felix a self-serving letter, where he shrewdly showed himself in a good light. He wrote:

Claudius Lysias sends greetings to His Excellency, Governor Felix: This man was seized by the Jews who would have killed him if I, having learned that he was a Roman citizen, hadn't come with my soldiers and rescued him.

Wishing to know the accusations against him, I brought him to their council. I found out that the accusations merely referred to questions about their own religious law, and that the man had done nothing deserving of death or jail.

When I was informed that the Jews were planning to ambush him, I sent him to you at once.

I have told his accusers to personally bring to you their charges against him.

The troop departed the fortress of Antonia, taking Paul with them. That night, they got as far as Antipatris. The next morning, the foot soldiers returned to Jerusalem, and the horsemen proceeded on. They arrived in Caesarea, delivered Claudius Lysias' letter to Felix, and turned Paul over to him.

Felix read the letter and, after finding out from Paul that he was from Cilicia, told him, "I will give you a hearing when your accusers arrive". Then, he gave orders that, in the meantime, Paul should be kept in Herod's Judgment Hall.

Five days later, the High Priest Ananias came to Caesarea, accompanied by several elders and a spokesman called Tertullus, to present to the governor the charges against Paul.

Tertullus stood up, before Felix, and said, "First of all, we wish to thank you, Governor Felix, for the peace that we are enjoying, and for the excellent reforms that you have carried out for the good of our country. But I do not wish to take too much of your time; I will be brief. I beg you to be kind and hear my account. This is a pestilent man, he incites the Jews all over the world to riot, and is one of the ringleaders of the Nazarene sect. We caught him, when he attempted to defile the Temple, and would have judged him according to our Law if the commander Lysias, by violent means, had not taken him away from us, and commanded us to bring charges against him before you. If you examine him yourself, you will verify our accusations". The Jews joined in the accusation and said that all the charges were true.

The governor then motioned to Paul to speak in his own defense. Paul said, "I am glad to defend myself in front of you, because I know that you have been a judge over this nation for many years. As you can easily find out, it was only twelve days ago that I went to Jerusalem to worship. They did not find me in the Temple arguing with any man, or inciting them to riot, either in the synagogues or anywhere else in the city. They cannot prove the charges that they have brought against me. But I confess to you that, although I worship the God of my ancestors, and fully believe in the Law and the prophets, I do so following the Way, which they consider heretical. I share their hope that all people, both the good and the bad, will resurrect from death. My conscience before God and man is clear. After many years abroad, I have returned bringing donations to my people, and to offer sacrifices. Some Jews from the region of Asia saw me in the Temple, when I had completed the ceremony of purification. It is not true that there was a crowd with me, nor was there a riot. They themselves should be here before you and accuse me if they have anything against me. The real reason why I am being tried by you today is for believing in the resurrection of the dead".

Felix, who was well informed of the Way, declined to make a decision and said, "I will wait for the Commander Lysias to come here and give me a full report". He ordered a centurion to place Paul under guard, but to give him some freedom, and allow his friends to attend to his needs.

A few days later, Felix, with his wife Drusilla, had Paul brought to his residence. The apostle explained his faith in Jesus to the couple. Felix became very uneasy, when Paul started talking about justice, self-control, and the Judgment Day. He cut short the meeting, telling Paul to go away, and that he would call him, when he had the opportunity.

This was the first of many similar conversations that Felix had with Paul, during the next two years. Actually, the Roman's interest was not purely theological; he hoped that Paul would give him some money.

Two years later, when Porcius Festus, the new governor, arrived to replace him, Felix, wishing to ingratiate himself with Paul's enemies, had him put in jail.

Festus

(Latin origin: *Festive*).

(Acts of the Apostles 24:27). A.D. 1st century. Porcius Festus replaced Felix as the Roman governor of Judea. Upon his arrival in Caesarea, he found that Felix had put Paul in jail, although he had not been convicted of any crime.

Three days after his arrival, Festus went to Jerusalem to meet with the High Priest and the leaders of the people. They presented their accusations against Paul and asked Festus to do them the favor of having the apostle brought to Jerusalem, with the secret intention of killing him in the way. Festus refused their request and, instead, asked them to come to Caesarea with him, and repeat their charges there.

After staying eight or ten days in Jerusalem, Festus returned to Caesarea. The next day, he ordered that Paul should be brought to the Judgment Hall. When he arrived, the Jews who had come from Jerusalem made serious charges against him, but they were not able to prove them.

Paul rejected all the charges and declared himself innocent. When Festus, trying to ingratiate himself with the Jews, asked him if he was willing to go to Jerusalem and be judged by him there, Paul answered, "If I had broken the law and deserved to die, I would not try to evade my punishment. But if there is no truth in their charges, no one can deliver me to them". Exercising his rights as a Roman citizen, he added, "I appeal to the emperor!"

Festus, after consulting with his advisers, decreed, "You have appealed to the emperor, so to the emperor you will go".

Sometime later, King Agrippa—Herod Agrippa II—the great grandson of Herod the Great, came to Caesarea with his sister Bernice to visit Festus. After several days of official festivities, Festus consulted the case of Paul with the king.

"There is a man left in jail by Felix", he said, "against whom the chief priests and the elders of the Jews brought charges, during my visit to Jerusalem, and asked me to condemn him. I told them that it was not the custom of the Romans to hand over any accused man, before he had met his accusers face to face and had the opportunity to defend himself. When they came here, I didn't waste any time, and the next day, I sat in the Judgment Hall and ordered the man to be brought in. The accusers stood up but did not bring any charge of evil doings, they just argued certain points about their own religion and about a man named Jesus, who is dead, but whom Paul claims that he is alive. Not being sure of how to proceed, I asked Paul if he would be willing to go to Jerusalem and be tried there on these charges. He asked to be kept in custody for the decision of the emperor, so I gave orders to be held, until I could send him to the emperor".

Agrippa said to Festus, "I would like to hear this man myself". Festus answered, "Tomorrow you will hear him".

The next morning, King Agrippa and Bernice came to the Governor's Palace with great pomp, accompanied by military commanders and the leading citizens of the city. When Paul was brought in, Festus spoke to the gathering, "King Agrippa, and all men who are present here, the Jews who live here and in Jerusalem have asked me to put to death the man that you see here. I have not found him guilty of any charge deserving death, but as he appealed to the emperor, I decided to send him. But I have nothing specific to write to my lord about him. Therefore, I have brought him before this assembly, and especially before you, King Agrippa, so that, after we have interrogated him, I may have something to write. It doesn't seem reasonable to me to send a prisoner without specifying the charges against him".

King Agrippa said to Paul, "You have permission to speak for yourself". Paul stretched out his hand and spoke to the assembly.

"I am fortunate, King Agrippa, that today I am able to defend myself before you against all the accusations of the Jews, because you are an expert regarding all the customs and disputes of the Jews. Please listen to me with patience.

"The events of my life, during my youth, among my own nation and at Jerusalem, are known to all the Jews. Those who knew me then can testify, if they are willing, that I was a Pharisee, a member of the strictest sect of our religion. I stand now on trial for having hope in the promise that God made to our ancestors, for which our twelve tribes pray to God, day and night. Why should it be incredible to you that God can raise the dead?

"I was very active in Jerusalem against the believers in Jesus. I put many of them in prison and voted for their death penalty. I punished them many times in the synagogues and tried to make them blaspheme. I was so angry against them that I even went to foreign cities to persecute them.

"That is why I went to Damascus with the full knowledge and authorization of the chief priests. At midday, I saw a light from heaven, brighter than the sun, shining around me and my companions. And when we had fallen to the ground, I heard a voice saying to me in Hebrew, 'Saul, Saul, why do you persecute me?' I asked, 'Who are you, Lord?' And the voice answered, 'I am Jesus whom you are persecuting. Rise and stand on your feet. I have appeared to you to appoint you to serve me, and to testify of what you have seen, and what I will show you in the future. I will rescue you from the Jews and from the Gentiles, to whom I am now sending you. Open their eyes and turn them from darkness to light, from the power of Satan to God, so that they may have their sins forgiven and find their place among those who are sanctified through their faith in me'.

"King Agrippa, I didn't disobey the vision from heaven. First in Damascus and in Jerusalem, and then in the whole country of Judea and among the Gentiles, I preached that they must repent and turn to God, and perform deeds proving their repentance.

"It is for this reason that the Jews seized me in the Temple and tried to kill me. I continue to this day, with God's help, to testify to small and great, saying nothing but what the prophets and Moses said would come to pass. That Christ would suffer, that he would be the first to rise from the dead, and proclaim light to the Jews and to the Gentiles".

Festus interrupted him, shouting, "Paul, you are crazy. Too much learning has made you mad". Paul said, "I am not mad, most noble Festus. I am speaking the sober truth. The king understands these things, and to him, I speak freely. I am convinced that none of these things has escaped his notice, because all this has not happened away in a corner".

Addressing himself to the king, Paul asked, "King Agrippa, do you believe in the prophets? I know you do".

Agrippa answered, "You think that you can convert me in such a short time?"

Paul replied, "I wish that not only you but all those that hear me today might become as I am, except for these chains, of course".

The king rose up and brought the proceedings to an end. Festus and Agrippa agreed that Paul was innocent, but they were powerless to help him, because, once the apostle had appealed to Rome for a ruling, the case was out of their jurisdiction.

Paul was handed to a centurion of the Augustus regiment named Julius and, a short time later, was put on a ship bound for Rome.

Fortunatus

(Latin origin: *Fortunate*).

(1 Corinthians 16:17). A.D. 1st century. Fortunatus was one of the three Corinthians—the other two were Stephanas and Achaicus—whose visit to Paul, in Ephesus, made the apostle very glad.

Gaal

(Hebrew origin: *Contempt*)

(Judges 9:26). 12th century B.C. Gaal, son of Ebed, led the men of Shechem in a revolt against Abimelech, the son of Gideon, during the fourth year of his reign in Shechem.

Gaal incited the mob, saying, "Who is Abimelech that we should serve him? If I would rule the city, I would get rid of him".

Zebul, governor of the town, sent a secret message to Abimelech, informing of the situation, and advised him to come immediately, and to attack at dawn.

Abimelech, who lived outside the city, in Arumah, brought his army to Shechem, during the night, and waited hidden in the fields outside the city.

Early the next morning, Gaal went out and stood at the entrance to the city. From there, he could see Abimelech and his men approaching, but he did not recognize them. He told Zebul, "I see men coming down from the hills".

Zebul answered, "You are confusing the shadows of the hills with men".

"See, there are people coming down the hills, and another group is approaching by the plain of Meonenim", insisted Gaal.

Zebul then said to him, "Where is your mouth now? You asked, 'Who is Abimelech that we should serve him?' This is the army that you despised. Go fight them now!"

Gaal and his supporters went to fight against Abimelech, but they were defeated and ran away. Zebul expelled him and his rebels from the city. Abimelech attacked Shechem, slew the people, and destroyed the city completely.

Gabbai

(Hebrew origin: *Collective*)

(Nehemiah 11:8). 5th century B.C. Gabbai, of the tribe of Benjamin, was one of the men who settled in Jerusalem, after the return from the Babylonian Exile.

Gabriel

(Hebrew origin: *Man of God*)

(Daniel 8:16). Gabriel, an angel of the Lord, was sent by God to Daniel to help him understand his vision.

Centuries later, Gabriel appeared to the priest Zacharias in the Temple and announced to him that his wife Elisabeth would give birth to a son, who would be called John. Shortly afterward, Gabriel also appeared to Mary in Nazareth and announced that she would give birth to Jesus.

Gad

(Hebrew origin: *Fortune*)

1. (Genesis 30:11). 17th century B.C. Gad, the ancestor of the tribe of Gad, was the seventh son of Jacob and the second son of his concubine Zilpah, Leah's maid. He was born in Paddan-Aram where Jacob was working for his father-in-law Laban.

   Gad was the full brother of Asher; his half brothers were Judah, Reuben, Levi, Simeon, Issachar, and Zebulun, sons of Leah; Dan and Naphtali, sons of Bilhah; and Benjamin and Joseph, sons of Rachel. His half sister was Dinah, daughter of Leah.

   Gad and his brothers were involved in the events that led to Joseph being taken as a slave to Egypt. (For the detailed story of Joseph and his brothers, please see the entry for Joseph.)

   Years later, when there was a famine in the land, he and his brothers were sent, by Jacob, to Egypt to buy corn. Joseph, now the second most powerful man in the country, recognized them, forgave them, and invited them to settle in Egypt.

   Gad and his sons—Ziphion, Haggi, Shuni, Ezbon, Eri, Arodi, and Areli—were among the seventy Israelites who immigrated to Egypt. They arrived in Goshen, and Joseph came to them in his chariot. He greeted his father, embraced him, and wept for a long time.

Seventeen years later, Jacob, feeling that he would soon die, called his sons to bless them and tell them what would happen to them in the future. He said, "A troop shall overcome Gad, but he shall overcome at last".

Jacob's last words were to ask them to bury him in the cave of Machpelah, where Abraham, Sarah, Isaac, Rebekah and Leah were buried. Jacob's body was accompanied in his last trip by his sons, their children, flocks and herds, all the officials of Pharaoh and members of his court, chariots and horsemen. Before crossing the Jordan, the funeral procession made a stop and mourned Jacob for seven days. Then, Judah and his brothers took him to Canaan and buried him in the cave of Machpelah.

After burying their father, they all returned to Canaan. Joseph's brothers feared that, with Jacob now dead, Joseph would pay them back for the wrong that they had done to him.

They sent a message to Joseph, saying that Jacob, before his death, had told them to urge Joseph to forgive them. Judah and his brothers came to Joseph, flung themselves before him, and told him that they were prepared to be his slaves.

Joseph answered kindly, "Do not fear! Although you intended me harm, God intended it all for good, to assure the survival of many people. Don't worry; I will take care of you and your children".

Centuries later, Moses in his farewell speech blessed the tribe of Gad, saying, "Blessed be he that enlarges Gad, he dwells as a lion, and tears the arm with the crown of the head".

When Joshua conquered Canaan, the tribe of Gad settled in Gilead, on the east side of the Jordan, a land which was appropriate for their cattle. The Assyrians exiled them in the 8th century B.C., and they disappeared from history, being known since then as one of the "ten lost tribes".

2. (1 Samuel 22:5). 10th century B.C. The prophet Gad was David's seer and advisor, from the days when David was hiding from Saul's persecution. At that time, he told David to abandon his stronghold, near the frontier with Moab, and go to the land of Judah.

Many years later, when David has displeased God, by conducting an unauthorized census of the people, Gad, who was sent by God, told David to choose one among three alternative punishments: seven years of famine, three months fleeing from his enemies, or three days of pestilence in the land.

David chose the third alternative, and over seventy thousand people died. When the epidemic ran its course, Gad told David to build an altar to God in the threshing floor of Araunah the Jebusite, the place where years later King Solomon built the Temple.

Gad wrote a book about David, which unfortunately has not survived to our days.

Gaddi

(Hebrew origin: *My fortune*)

(Numbers 13:11). 13th century B.C. Gaddi, son of Susi, of the tribe of Manasseh, was one of the twelve spies sent by Moses to Canaan, to scout the land, its cities, and its inhabitants; to find out if they were strong or weak, few or many; and to bring back the fruit of the land. The spies came back, frightened and disheartened, and told the Israelites that the Canaanites were too big and too strong to be defeated.

Two of the spies—Joshua, the son of Nun, and Caleb, the son of Jephunneh—disagreed and told the people not to fear.

The Israelites refused to listen to the encouraging words of Joshua and Caleb, and they started to wail and cry. God punished their cowardice by condemning them to wander forty years in the wilderness, one year for each day that the spies scouted the land. All those who complained against God, including Gaddi, died in the wilderness, except Caleb and Joshua.

(For more detailed information about the twelve spies, please see the entry for Joshua.)

Gaddiel

(Hebrew origin: *God is my fortune*)

(Numbers 13:10). 13th century B.C. Gaddiel, son of Sodi, of the tribe of Zebulun, was one of the twelve spies sent by Moses to Canaan, to scout the land, its cities, and its inhabitants; to find out if they were strong or weak, few or many; and to bring back the fruit of the land. The spies came, back frightened and disheartened, and told the Israelites that the Canaanites were too big and too strong to be defeated.

Two of the spies—Joshua, the son of Nun, and Caleb, the son of Jephunneh—disagreed and told the people not to fear.

The Israelites refused to listen to the encouraging words of Joshua and Caleb, and they started to wail and cry. God punished their cowardice by condemning them to wander forty years in the wilderness, one year for each day that the spies scouted the land. All those who complained against God, including Gaddiel, died in the wilderness, except Caleb and Joshua.

(For more detailed information about the twelve spies, please see the entry for Joshua.)

Gadi

(Hebrew origin: *My fortune*)

(2 Kings 15:14). 8th century B.C. His son Menahem, after killing Shallum, who had assassinated King Zachariah, proclaimed himself king of the northern kingdom of Israel and reigned ten years.

Gaham

(Hebrew origin: *Flame*)

(Genesis 22:24). 19th century B.C. Gaham, a nephew of Abraham, was one of the sons of Nahor, Abraham's brother, and his concubine Reumah. His brothers were Tebah, Thahash, and Maachah.

Gahar

(Hebrew origin: *Lurker*)

(Ezra 2:47). Unspecified date. Gahar was the ancestor of a clan of Temple servants that returned with Zerubbabel from the Babylonian Exile.

Gaius

(Latin origin)

1. (Acts of the Apostles 19:29). A.D. 1st century. Gaius and Aristarchus were two Macedonians who accompanied Paul in his travels. During their stay in Ephesus, a mob violently demonstrated in favor of the goddess Diana, whose cult was threatened by the teachings of Paul.

   The multitude dragged the two men inside a theatre. When Paul attempted to enter the theatre, his disciples, to save his life, stopped him from doing so. Fortunately, Aristarchus and Gaius managed to escape unhurt.

2. (Acts of the Apostles 20:4). A.D. 1st century. Gaius, a Galatian born in Derbe, was one of the companions of Paul, during his stay in Greece, who traveled with the apostle back to Asia.

3. (Romans 16:23). A.D. 1st century. Gaius was one of the few people personally baptized by Paul in Corinth (1 Corinthians 1:14), where he hosted Paul in his house.

   The apostle, in his letter to the Roman church, mentioned that Gaius, his host, together with Quartus and Erastus, chamberlain of the city of Corinth, sent greetings to the Christian community in Rome.

4. (3 John 1:1). A.D. 1st century. Gaius was the addressee of the third and last letter written by John the Elder, who praised him highly.

Galal

(Hebrew origin: *Rolled*)

1. (1 Chronicles 9:15). 6th century B.C. Galal, a Levite, was one of the first to settle in the land of Judah, after the return from the Babylonian Exile.

2. (1 Chronicles 9:16). 7th century B.C. Galal, son of Jeduthun, was the father of Shemaiah. His grandson Obadiah, a Levite, was one of the first to settle in the land of Judah, after the return from the Babylonian Exile.

Note: In the book of Nehemiah, Shemaiah and Obadiah are called respectively Shammua and Abda (Nehemiah 11:17).

Gallio

(Latin origin)

(Acts of the Apostles 18:12). A.D. 1st century. Gallio was the Roman proconsul of Achaia, during Paul's stay in Corinth.

Sosthenes, the head of the synagogue, and other leaders of the Corinthian synagogue brought Paul to Gallio's presence, accusing him of persuading the people to worship God in a manner contrary to the law.

Before Paul could open his mouth to defend himself, Gallio dismissed the case, saying that he was not qualified to judge in matters of words, names, and Jewish religious law. The Greeks then seized Sosthenes and beat him in the presence of Gallio, who made no effort to stop the whipping.

Gamaliel

(Hebrew origin: *God's reward*)

1. (Numbers 1:10). 13th century B.C. Gamaliel, son of Pedahzur, was a leader of the tribe of Manasseh. He commanded his tribe's army, during the march in the wilderness, and was one of the twelve Israelite leaders who donated gifts of silver and gold, bulls, rams, goats, and lambs for the dedication of the altar.

2. (Acts of the Apostles 5:34). A.D. 1st century. Gamaliel, a Pharisee doctor of the law, enjoyed great renown among the people. Paul had been one of his students, before his conversion.

When Peter and other apostles were put in prison for healing the people and preaching in the Temple, after the High Priest had forbidden them to do so, they were brought to the council and threatened with the death penalty. Gamaliel was the only member of the council who rose and argued against killing them, saying that, if the acts of the accused were not directed by God, they had no meaning, but if they were directed by God, opposing them would mean fighting against God. The council members were persuaded by Gamaliel's arguments, and they contented themselves with having the apostles beaten.

Gamul

(Hebrew origin: *Rewarded*)

(1 Chronicles 24:17). 10th century B.C. During the reign of King David, the priestly service in the Tabernacle was divided by lot into twenty-four turns. Gamul was in charge of the twenty-second turn.

Gareb

(Hebrew origin: *Scabby*)

(2 Samuel 23:38). 10th century B.C. Gareb the Ithrite was one of "The Thirty", an elite group in King David's army.

Gashmu

(Hebrew origin: *Rain*)

(Nehemiah 6:6). 5th century B.C. Gashmu—also called Geshem—an Arab, was an ally of Sanballat, the Horonite, and Tobiah, the Ammonite, who were enemies of Nehemiah. (Please see the entry for Geshem [Nehemiah 2:19].)

Gatam

(Hebrew origin: Uncertain meaning)

(Genesis 36:11). 16th century B.C. Gatam, the ancestor of an Edomite clan, was the son of Eliphaz and the grandson of Esau and his wife Adah, the daughter of Elon the Hittite. His brothers were Teman, Omar, Zepho, Kenaz, and Amalek.

Gazez

(Hebrew origin: *Shearer*)

1. (1 Chronicles 2:46). Unspecified date. Gazez, of the tribe of Judah, was the son of Caleb and his concubine Ephah. His brothers were Haran and Moza. His nephew, the son of Haran, was also called Gazez.

2. (1 Chronicles 2:46). Unspecified date. Gazez, of the tribe of Judah, was the son of Haran and the grandson of Caleb and his concubine Ephah. His uncles were Gazez and Moza.

Gazzam

(Hebrew origin: *Wood cutter*)

(Ezra 2:48). Unspecified date. Gazzam was an ancestor of a clan of Temple servants that returned with Zerubbabel from the Babylonian Exile.

Geber

(Hebrew origin: *Man*)

1. (1 Kings 4:13). 11th century B.C. Geber was the father of one of King Solomon's twelve district governors—his name is not mentioned in the Bible—responsible for providing food from his district, which included the towns of Jair in the territory of Gilead and the region of Argob in Bashan, for the king and the royal household for one month out of each year.

2. (1 Kings 4:19). 10th century B.C. Geber, son of Uri, was one of King Solomon's twelve district governors, responsible for providing food from his district for the king and the royal household for one month out of each year.

He ruled over the territories of Gilead and Bashan that had once belonged to Sihon, king of the Amorites, and Og, king of Bashan. His district had over sixty large towns, fortified with walls and bronze bars on the gates.

Gedaliah

(Hebrew origin: *God is great*)

1. (2 Kings 25:22). 6th century B.C. Gedaliah, son of Ahikam, is a tragic figure in the history of the Jewish people, who, even in our days, observe the anniversary of his death as a day of fasting and mourning.

He was a member of one of the most prominent and influential noble families in the kingdom, during the reigns of King Josiah and his sons. His father Ahikam, a high court official, and his grandfather Shaphan, the scribe in the court of King Josiah, played important roles in the historical events of their times.

Due to his family's well-known policy of moderation and submission to Babylon, Gedaliah was appointed governor of Judah by the Babylonian King Nebuchadnezzar, ruling from the city of Mizpah, where he was joined by the prophet Jeremiah, and other survivors who had not been sent to exile.

Gedaliah told the commanders of the defeated army that all would go well if they would serve the king of Babylon. This gave cause to some of them to consider him a Babylonian collaborator, and to plot against his life.

Johanan, the son of Kareah, came to Mizpah and told Gedaliah that Baalis, the king of the Ammonites, had instructed Ishmael, the son of Nethaniah, to kill him. Johanan volunteered to kill Ishmael, but Gedaliah refused to believe him and accused him of lying.

Two months later, what Johanan had warned came to pass. Ishmael, the son of Nethaniah, a member of the deposed royal family, came to Mizpah with ten men. During dinner, Ishmael murdered Gedaliah and all the Jews and Babylonians who were with him, apparently with the hope of overthrowing Babylonian rule.

The surviving Jews, fearing Babylonian vengeance, fled to Egypt, taking the prophet Jeremiah with them.

2. (1 Chronicles 25:3). 10th century B.C. Gedaliah, son of Jeduthun, was in charge of the second turn of service that played musical instruments in the House of God, during the reign of David.

His father Jeduthun, a Levite, was one of David's three leading musicians; the other two were Asaph and Heman.

3. (Ezra 10:18). 5th century B.C. The brothers—Gedaliah, Jeshua, Maaseiah, Eliezer, and Jarib—all priests and sons of Jozadak, divorced their foreign wives, during the days of Ezra, and offered a ram from the flock to expiate their transgression.

4. (Jeremiah 38:1). 6th century B.C. Gedaliah, son of Pashur, was an official in the court of King Zedekiah. He—together with his father Pashur; Jucal, son of Shelemiah; and Shephatiah, son of Mattan—asked the king to put Jeremiah to death for preaching surrender and undermining the courage of the soldiers.

When King Zedekiah told them that they could do with Jeremiah whatever they wanted, Gedaliah and his fellow court officials cast the prophet into the dungeon of Malchiah, which was in the court of the prison.

Ebedmelech, an Ethiopian eunuch in the service of the king, told the king that Jeremiah might die of hunger in the dungeon. Zedekiah instructed Ebedmelech to pull Jeremiah out of the dungeon.

5. (Zephaniah 1:1). 7th century B.C. Gedaliah, son of Amariah and grandson of Hizkiah—alternative transliteration for the name of King Hezekiah—was the father of Cushi and the grandfather of the prophet Zephaniah.

Gedeon

(Hebrew origin: *Warrior*)

(Hebrews 11:32). 12th century B.C. Gedeon is an alternative spelling for Gideon. (See the entry for Gideon [Judges 6:11].)

Gedor

(Hebrew origin: *Wall*)

(1 Chronicles 8:31). Unspecified date. Gedor, a Benjamite, was one of the sons of Jehiel, the founder of Gibeon, and his wife Maachah.

Gehazi

(Hebrew origin: *Valley of vision*)

(2 Kings 4:12). 9th century B.C. Gehazi was the servant of the prophet Elisha. When Elisha, grateful to the Shunammite woman for her hospitality, asked what he could do for her, Gehazi mentioned that she was childless and that her husband was old. The prophet then announced to her that the next year she would give birth to a son.

A few years later, when Elisha was on his way to her house, the woman came to him and, in despair, grabbed the feet of the prophet. Gehazi tried to push her away, but the prophet, realizing that her son must be very ill, told him to leave her alone. Elisha gave his staff to Gehazi and told him to hurry to the child, without wasting time in any conversation on the way, and try to bring the boy back to life, by placing his staff upon the face of the child. When Elisha arrived at the Shunammite's house, Gehazi told him that the boy had not awakened. Elisha went up to his room, closed the door behind him, prayed to God, placed his mouth against the dead boy's mouth, and breathed in it, until the boy came back to life.

Gehazi had the opportunity, years later, of telling this miraculous cure to the king, and of presenting the child's mother to him.

On another occasion, Naaman, the commander of the Syrian army, came to Elisha and asked to be cured of his leprosy. Elisha did not come out to meet him but sent him a messenger who told Naaman that, if he would bathe seven times in the Jordan River, he would be cured. Naaman was angry and offended that Elisha had not spoken personally to him, and he went away, saying that the rivers in Syria were just as good, if not better than the Jordan, and he could bathe in them. However, when his servants convinced him that he should try Elisha's suggestion, Naaman went to the Jordan, bathed seven times, and was cured.

Naaman went back to Elisha's house to thank the prophet and offered him a gift in appreciation, which Elisha refused to receive. Gehazi, seeing that Elisha had refused the reward offered by Naaman, decided that he should get something, and he ran after him. Naaman saw him, alighted from his chariot, and asked him if everything was well. Gehazi told him that Elisha had sent him, with a request for two changes of clothing and a talent of silver for two young prophets who had come to visit him. Naaman gave him the two changes of clothing and two talents of silver. Gehazi returned to his master, and Elisha asked him where he had been. Gehazi answered that he had not gone out. Elisha told him he knew that he had received money from Naaman, and that, in punishment, Naaman's leprosy would cling to him and his posterity forever.

Gemalli

(Hebrew origin: *I was rewarded*)

(Numbers 13:12) 14th century B.C. His son Ammiel, of the tribe of Dan, was one of the twelve men sent by Moses to spy the land of Canaan and report back about its cities and its inhabitants, if they were strong or weak, few or many, and to bring back the fruit of the land. The spies returned and gave a report, which was disheartening and defeatist.

Only two of the spies—Joshua, the son of Nun, and Caleb, the son of Jephunneh—disagreed and told the people that they should not fear the inhabitants of Canaan.

The Israelites refused to listen to the words of Joshua and Caleb, and they started to wail and cry. God punished their cowardice by condemning them to wander forty years in the wilderness, one year for each day that the spies scouted the land.

Gemariah

(Hebrew origin: *Perfected by God*)

1. (Jeremiah 29:3). 6th century B.C.

Gemariah, the son of the High Priest Hilkiah, was sent by King Zedekiah, together with Elasah, son of Shaphan, to speak with Nebuchadnezzar, king of Babylon.

He carried with him a letter by Jeremiah to the captives. The letter encouraged them to live a normal life in Babylon, build their homes, plant gardens, marry, and have children. It ended in a prophecy that said that, after seventy years, they would return from the Babylonian Exile.

Gemariah's father, the High Priest Hilkiah, discovered the Book of the Law in the Temple, during the reign of King Josiah.

2. (Jeremiah 36:10). 7th century B.C. Gemariah, son of Shaphan the Scribe, was the occupant of the chamber in the Temple where Baruch, Jeremiah's trusted companion, read aloud the prophet's words.

Gemariah's son Michaiah went to the king's palace and reported to Gemariah and to the other assembled officials what Baruch had read. Baruch was brought to the palace and was asked to read aloud the scroll where he had written Jeremiah's words.

When Baruch finished, the officials, terrified at what they had heard, told Baruch that he and Jeremiah should hide. Baruch's scroll was brought to King Jehoiakim and was read to him. As soon as a couple of leaves of the scroll had been read, the king would cut them with a knife and throw them into the fireplace. Gemariah, Delaiah—son of Shemaiah—and Elnathan tried unsuccessfully to convince the king not to burn the scroll.

Genubath

(Hebrew origin: *Theft*)

(1 Kings 11:20). 10th century B.C. Genubath was the son of Hadad, an Edomite refugee of royal blood who lived in Egypt under the protection of Pharaoh. His mother was the sister-in-law of the Pharaoh of Egypt.

He grew up in the royal palace of Egypt, with the sons of Pharaoh.

Gera

(Hebrew origin: *Stranger*)

1. (Genesis 46:21). 17th century B.C. Gera, a son of Benjamin and grandson of Jacob, was one of the seventy Israelites who immigrated to Egypt.

   His nine brothers were Becher, Ashbel, Belah, Naaman, Ehi, Rosh, Muppim, Huppim, and Ard.

   Gera's name does not appear in other lists of the sons of Benjamin: Numbers 26:38, 1 Chronicles 7:6, and 1 Chronicles 8:1.

2. (Judges 3:15). 12th century B.C. Gera, a Benjamite, was the father of Ehud, a leader of Israel, during the period of the judges. His son killed Eglon, the king of Moab who had been oppressing Israel.

3. (2 Samuel 16:5). 11th century B.C. His son Shimei, of the tribe of Benjamin, a relative of King Saul, insulted King David and threw stones at him, when David was fleeing from Absalom.

   Although David didn't take any action against Shimei at that moment, many years later, when the king was in his deathbed, he instructed Solomon to find a way to have Shimei killed.

4. (1 Chronicles 8:3). 17th century B.C. Gera was one of the sons of Bela, Benjamin's firstborn.

5. (1 Chronicles 8:5). 17th century B.C. Gera was another son of Bela (of the same name as the previous entry).

Gershom

(Hebrew origin: *Exiled*)

1. (Exodus 2:22). 13th century B.C. Gershom—also spelled Gershon (Genesis 46:11)—was the firstborn son of Moses and Zipporah. He and his brother Eliezer were both born in Midian.

   After all the men in Egypt who had sought the death of Moses had died, God commanded Moses to return to Egypt. On the road, Moses, his wife, and his two children stayed in an inn. There, Zipporah circumcised Gershom to prevent Moses from being killed by God. After that event, Moses sent Zipporah and the children back to her father Jethro in Midian.

   After Moses succeeded in taking the Israelites out of Egypt, Jethro came to the Hebrew camp in the wilderness, bringing with him Zipporah and the children.

   Gershom's descendant, Shebuel, was in charge of the treasuries of the Tabernacle, during the reign of King David.

2. (Judges 18:30). 12th century B.C. Gershom, son of Manasseh, was the father of Jonathan, the man who served as a priest to the tribe of Dan's graven image.

   Some Hebrew manuscripts have the letter *nun* in Manasseh, suspended above, which would indicate an earlier reading of "Moses", in which case, this Gershom is the same person as the above entry.

3. (1 Chronicles 6:16). 17th century B.C. Gershom was one of the three sons of Levi. His brothers were Kohath and Merari. Through his sons Libni and Shimei, he was the ancestor of two clans of Levites: the Libnites and the Shimites. Gershom was one of the seventy Israelites who immigrated to Egypt.

   His descendant, Asaph, was one of the Levites appointed by King David to be in charge of the singers in the House of the Lord.

   Alternative spelling in Genesis is Gershon (Genesis 46:11).

4. (Ezra 8:2). 5th century B.C. Gershom, a descendant of Phinehas, returned with Ezra from the Babylonian Exile.

Gershon

(Hebrew origin: *Exiled*)

(Genesis 46:11). 17th century B.C. Gershon is an alternative spelling for Gershom, one of the three sons of Levi. (Please see the entry for Gershom [1 Chronicles 6:16].)

Gesham

(Hebrew origin: *Lumpish*)

(1 Chronicles 2:47). Unspecified date. Gesham was the son of Jahdai of the tribe of Judah. His brothers were Ephah, Regem, Jotham, Pelet, and Shaaph.

Geshem

(Hebrew origin: *Rain*)

(Nehemiah 2:19). 5th century B.C. Geshem—also called Gashmu (Nehemiah 6:6)—an Arab, was an ally of Sanballat, the Horonite, and Tobiah, the Ammonite, who were enemies of Nehemiah.

The three men scorned Nehemiah and the Jews, for trying to rebuild the walls of Jerusalem, but when they saw that the walls had been built, they asked Nehemiah repeatedly to meet with them, in one of the villages in the plain of Ono, with the secret purpose of killing him.

Nehemiah suspected that they meant him harm and refused each time, giving the excuse that he could not afford to leave his work.

Finally, Sanballat came to Nehemiah with an open letter, where Geshem was quoted, as saying that Nehemiah was rebuilding the walls of Jerusalem, in order to lead a rebellion against the king of Persia.

Nehemiah rejected the charge and accused Sanballat of making spurious accusations.

Gether

(Hebrew origin: Uncertain meaning)

(Genesis 10:23). Unspecified date. Gether was the son of Aram and grandson of Shem, the son of Noah. His brothers were Uz, Hul, Gether and Mash. According to the first book of Chronicles, Gether and his brothers were not the grandsons of Shem, but his sons, and, thus, brothers of Aram (1 Chronicles 1:17).

Geuel

(Hebrew origin: *Majesty of God*)

(Numbers 13:15) 13th century B.C. Geuel, son of Machi, of the tribe of Gad, was one of the twelve spies sent by Moses to Canaan, to scout the land, its cities, and its inhabitants; to find out if they were strong or weak, few or many; and to bring back the fruit of the land. The spies came back, frightened and disheartened, and told the Israelites that the Canaanites were too big and too strong to be defeated.

Two of the spies—Joshua, the son of Nun, and Caleb, the son of Jephunneh—disagreed and told the people not to fear.

The Israelites refused to listen to the encouraging words of Joshua and Caleb, and they started to wail and cry. God punished their cowardice by condemning them to wander forty years in the wilderness, one year for each day that the spies scouted the land. All those who complained against God, including Geuel, died in the wilderness, except Caleb and Joshua.

(For more detailed information about the twelve spies, please see the entry for Joshua.)

Giddalti

(Hebrew origin: *I have made great*)

(1 Chronicles 25:4). 10th century B.C. Giddalti, a Levite, member of a family of musicians, was in charge of the twenty-second turn of service that played musical instruments— cymbals, psalteries, and harps—in the House of God, during the reign of David.

He had thirteen brothers and three sisters, all of them trained as skillful musicians by their father, Heman, one of the three leading musicians—the other two were Asaph and Jeduthun—of the period.

Giddel

(Hebrew origin: *Increased*)

1. (Ezra 2:47). Unspecified date. Giddel was the ancestor of a clan of Temple servants that returned with Zerubbabel from the Babylonian Exile.
2. (Ezra 2:56). 10th century B.C. Giddel, a servant of Solomon, was the ancestor of a family that returned with Zerubbabel from the Babylonian Exile.

Gideon

(Hebrew origin: *Warrior*)

(Judges 6:11). 12th century B.C. Gideon, the youngest son of Joash of the clan of Abiezer, of the tribe of Manasseh, was a judge and military commander who defeated a large army of Midianites and Amalekites, who had been oppressing the Israelites.

(Note: In the book of Judges, a judge is a ruler or governor of territory or a military leader in pre-monarchical Israel. Later, during the monarchy, the king served in this role and judges were more like the judicial officers that we know today.)

An angel appeared to Gideon, while he was threshing wheat by the winepress to hide it from the Midianites, and announced that Gideon would save Israel from the Midianites.

Gideon demanded a sign as proof that the announcement was true. He was told by the angel to place some meat and unleavened cakes on a rock. When the angel touched the food with the end of his staff, fire rose from the rock and consumed the meat and the cakes. Gideon, now convinced that the message was true, built an altar to God on that spot.

That same night, God told Gideon to destroy his father's altar to Baal, and to cut down the sacred grove next to it. Gideon, afraid that his father's servants and the men of the city would see him destroying the idols, took ten of his servants under the cover of the night's darkness, destroyed the pagan altar, and sacrificed a bull to God on the altar that he had built the day before.

When the men of the city found out that Gideon had destroyed their pagan altar and the grove, they demanded that Joash should deliver his son to them to be killed for what he had done.

Joash refused and told them that, if Baal was a god, he should plead for himself, and that anybody that would plead for Baal would die. Since that day, Gideon was also called Jerubbaal, which means *Let Baal contend with him*.

The Midianites, joined by the Amalekites and other tribes from the east, crossed the Jordan River and encamped in the valley of Jezreel. Gideon sounded the horn and rallied behind him his own clan of Abiezer, the whole tribe of Manasseh, together with the tribes of Asher, Zebulun, and Naphtali.

Gideon asked God for a sign that would prove to him that he would succeed in his fight to save Israel. He placed a fleece of wool on the floor and said that, if dew would fall only on the fleece, but the ground around it would remain dry, this would be the proof that he needed. Next morning, he saw that the ground was dry, but that the fleece was so wet that he was able to squeeze from it a bowl full of water.

Gideon, still not convinced, asked God for a new sign. This time the fleece should remain dry, while the ground would be wet. And so it happened, and Gideon was reassured.

Gideon, with thirty-two thousand men under him, encamped by the spring of Harod, across the valley from the Midianites, who were on the hill of Moreh. God, not wanting the Israelites to feel that victory would be won only because they were so many, instructed Gideon to release all those who were fearful and afraid. Twenty thousand men went away.

God thought that the ten thousand men that had remained with Gideon were still too many, and he told Gideon to bring his men down to the water. Gideon was to keep with him only those who would lap the water as dogs do, and to release all the others who got down on their knees to drink.

Gideon released most of the troops and kept only three hundred men with him. That night, Gideon and his servant Phurah approached stealthily the camp of the Midianites and Amalekites, and they heard one of the enemy soldiers tell a dream where a cake of bread fell into their camp and destroyed a tent. The other soldier interpreted the dream as meaning that Gideon would defeat Midian.

Gideon, encouraged by the defeatism of the Midianites, returned to his troops and divided them into three companies; he gave a trumpet and an empty pitcher with a lamp inside the pitcher to each man. He told his men to follow him, to blow the trumpets, and to shout, "The sword of the Lord and of Gideon". The men did so, and the enemy fled in panic, pursued by the Israelites. Over one hundred twenty thousand Midianites perished in the battle.

The men of Ephraim captured and killed Oreb and Zeeb, two Midianite princes. They cut their heads and brought them to Gideon. The Ephraimites complained that Gideon had not called them to fight at his side against the Midianites. Gideon, to assuage them, said that whatever he had done was nothing compared to their capture of Oreb and Zeeb.

The two kings of Midian, Zalmunna and Zebah, fled with their remaining army of fifteen thousand soldiers to the other side of the river Jordan, pursued by Gideon and his three hundred men, who, by now, were tired and exhausted.

Gideon asked the men of Succoth to give loaves of bread to his famished men, but they refused and mocked him, saying, "Are Zebah and Zalmunna already in your power that we should give bread to your army?" Gideon said to them, "When the Lord hands me Zebah and Zalmunna, I will tear your flesh with thorns and briers from the desert".

Gideon continued on his way and made the same request of the people of Penuel. They also refused and gave the same answer as the men of Succoth. Gideon swore that he would destroy their tower, after he returned from capturing the Midianites.

Zebah and Zalmunna camped at Karkor with their army. Gideon attacked them and captured the two kings.

On his way back from the battle, Gideon seized a young man from Succoth and questioned him. The boy gave him a list of the names of seventy-seven of the most prominent men of Succoth. Gideon went to the town and told them, "You refused to give food to my men, because Zebah and Zalmunna were not in my hands. Well, here are Zebah and Zalmunna now". He then took thorns and briers and punished the leaders of the town. He also tore down the tower of Penuel and killed the men of the town.

Zebah and Zalmunna confessed to Gideon that they had killed his brothers in Tabor. Gideon ordered his eldest son, Jether, to kill them, but the boy, who was young and timid, hesitated and did not draw his sword. The two Midianites said to Gideon, "Kill us yourself! It's a man's job!" Gideon killed the two Midianites and took the ornaments that were on their camels' necks.

The men of Israel asked Gideon to rule over them, and his son after him, but Gideon refused, saying that only God would rule over them, but he requested that they should give him the golden earrings of the Midianites that they had received as booty. The men willingly agreed. The weight of the golden earrings that they gave to Gideon was a thousand and seven hundred shekels of gold. Gideon used the gold to make an ephod, which he placed in his city of Ophrah, and which became an object of idol worship for the people of Israel.

Gideon died at a ripe old age and was buried in the tomb of his father, Joash, in the city of Ophrah. He was survived by the seventy sons whom his many wives had given him, and by another son, called Abimelech, who had been born to his concubine in Shechem.

Gideoni

(Hebrew origin: *Warlike*)

(Numbers 1:11). 13th century B.C. Gideoni was a member of the tribe of Benjamin. His son Abidan, commander of his tribe's army, during the march in the wilderness, was one of the twelve Israelite leaders who donated gifts of silver and gold, bulls, rams, goats, and lambs for the dedication of the altar.

Gilalai

(Hebrew origin: *Dungy*)

(Nehemiah 12:36). 5th century B.C. Gilalai was one of the priests who marched behind Ezra the Scribe, playing musical instruments, in the joyful procession, which celebrated the dedication of the rebuilt walls of Jerusalem, during the days of Nehemiah.

Gilead

(Hebrew origin: *Hilly*)

1. (Numbers 26:29). 16th century B.C. Gilead, son of Machir and grandson of

Manasseh, was the ancestor of the clan of the Gileadites.

2. (Judges 11:1). 12th century B.C. Gilead was the father of the judge Jephthah, who was born from the relationship that he had with a prostitute.

   After Gilead died, the sons that he had with his legitimate wife expelled Jephthah from their ancestral house, fearing that he would try to share their inheritance.

3. (1 Chronicles 5:14). Unspecified date. Gilead, son of Michael, was the father of Jaroah, of the tribe of Gad. His descendants lived in the region of Gilead, on the eastern side of the Jordan River.

Ginath

(Hebrew origin: *Garden*)

(1 Kings 16:21). 10th century B.C. His son Tibni challenged Omri for the throne of Israel, after the suicide of the usurper Zimri, but he was defeated and killed.

Ginnetho

(Hebrew origin: *Gardener*)

(Nehemiah 12:4). 6th century B.C. Ginnetho—also called Ginnethon (Nehemiah 12:16)—was one of the priests who returned from the Babylonian Exile with Zerubbabel.

Ginnetho was the ancestor of a priestly clan that was headed by Meshullam, when Joiakim was High Priest, during the time of Nehemiah.

Ginnethon

(Hebrew origin: *Gardener*)

1. (Nehemiah 10:6). 5th century B.C. Ginnethon was one of the priests who signed Nehemiah's solemn agreement to separate themselves from the foreigners living in the land, to refrain from intermarrying with them, and to dedicate their firstborn to God, among other obligations.

2. (Nehemiah 12:16). 6th century B.C. Ginnethon is an alternative spelling for Ginnetho (Nehemiah 12:4). (Please see the entry for Ginnetho.)

Gispa

(Hebrew origin: Uncertain meaning)

(Nehemiah 11:21). 5th century B.C. Gispa and Ziha were leaders of a clan of Temple servants that, during the days of Nehemiah, dwelt in the Jerusalem neighborhood known as Ophel.

Gog

(Hebrew origin: Uncertain meaning)

1. (1 Chronicles 5:4). Unspecified date. Gog, son of Shemaiah and father of Shimei, was an ancestor of Beerah, a leader of the tribe of Reuben who was carried away captive by Tilgathpilneser, king of Assyria.

2. (Ezekiel 38:2). Unspecified date. Gog was the chief prince of Meshech and Tubal, about whom God instructed Ezekiel to prophesy that, one day, he would lead an alliance against Israel and would be utterly destroyed in battle.

   The book of Revelation (Revelation 20:8) states that Gog, together with Magog and Satan, will go to battle against God's people and will be destroyed by fire from heaven.

Goliath

(Philistine: Uncertain meaning)

(1 Samuel 17:4) 11th century B.C. Goliath of Gath, a leader of the Philistine forces arrayed against Saul's army, was a giant over nine feet tall.

He came out from the Philistine camp everyday, wearing heavy bronze armor, and shouted a challenge to the Israelites, saying that he was ready to fight any of them. He did this every morning and evening for forty days.

One day, young David, was told by his father Jesse to take ten loaves of bread to his older brothers, who were serving in the Israelite army, and a gift of ten cheeses to their commanding officer.

David arrived at the camp, at the moment when Goliath came forward to challenge the Israelites as he had done for the last forty days, and heard his challenge. He spoke to the terrified Israelite soldiers, who told him that King Saul had promised great rewards to the man who would kill the giant. The king would give him his daughter in marriage and would free his family from the obligation of paying taxes.

David was brought to Saul's presence and assured the king that he could fight the experienced Philistine warrior, because, while taking care of his sheep, he had killed lions and bears. Saul gave him his armor to wear, but David, not used to it, took it off.

The young man picked up five smooth stones and, with his sling in his hand, went to meet Goliath. The giant saw that David was just a boy and called down curses on him. David told him, "You come against me with sword, spear, and javelin, but I come against you in the name of the Lord".

Goliath started walking toward David, who ran quickly toward the Philistine, took out a stone from his bag, and slung it at Goliath. The stone hit the giant on the forehead and made him fall on the ground. David ran to him, took Goliath's sword, and cut off his head.

The Philistines, seeing this, ran away, with the Israelites pursuing them all the way up to the gates of their cities.

Goliath had a brother called Lahmi, also a giant, who was killed in battle by Elhanan, son of Jair.

Goliath's sword was kept in the priestly town of Nob, until the priest Ahimelech gave it to David, who had brought no weapons with him, when he fled from Saul.

Gomer

(Hebrew origin: *Completion*)

1. (Genesis 10:2). Unspecified date. Gomer, son of Japheth and grandson of Noah, was the brother of Magog, Madai, Javan, Tubal, Meshech, and Tiras. His sons were Ashkenaz, Riphath, and Togarmah.

2. (Hosea 1:3). 8th century B.C. Gomer, daughter of Diblaim, was the unfaithful wife of the prophet Hosea. She gave birth to three children—all of whom were given symbolic names by the prophet—Jezreel, Loruhamah, and Loammi. Hosea mentioned his marital woes in his prophecies as an allegory for the relationship between God and Israel.

Guni

(Hebrew origin: *Protected*)

1. (Genesis 46:24). 17th century B.C. Guni, son of Naphtali and grandson of Jacob and Bilhah, was one of the seventy Israelites who immigrated to Egypt. His brothers were Jahzeel, Jezer, and Shillem. Guni was the ancestor of the clan of the Gunites.

2. (1 Chronicles 5:15). 9th century B.C. Guni, the father of Abdiel, was the grandfather of Ahi, the head of a family that lived in Gilead, during the reign of King Jeroboam II of Israel.

Haahashtari

(Probably of Persian origin: *The courier*)

(1 Chronicles 4:6). Unspecified date. Haahashtari, of the tribe of Judah, was a son of Ashur, the founder of Tekoa. His mother was Naarah, one of the two wives of his father. His brothers were Temeni, Hepher, and Ahuzam.

Note: The prefix "Ha" is the Hebrew article equivalent to the English "The"; therefore, this word should be considered as a designation, rather than a name: Ha-Ahashtari, *The courier*.

Habaiah

(Hebrew origin: *God has hidden*)

(Ezra 2:61). Unspecified date. Habaiah was the ancestor of a family, whose members, during the days of Zerubbabel, were rejected as priests, because no proof of their claim was found in the records of the genealogy.

Habakkuk

(Hebrew origin: *Embrace*)

(Habakkuk 1:1). 7th century B.C. Habakkuk prophesied at a time when the Babylonians, having defeated the Egyptians at Carchemish, had become the dominant regional power. Habakkuk was deeply disturbed, by the fact that cruelty, violence, and inhumanity prevailed in the world.

The problem of injustice in the world is one of the greatest problems in biblical thought, also dealt with in the books of Jeremiah and Job. Habakkuk's approach differs from the other books by offering a prophetic answer that the wicked eventually shall fail, but the righteous shall live by their faith.

The book of Habakkuk consists of only three chapters, totaling fifty-six verses. The first two chapters are considered narrative. In the first chapter, Habakkuk complains to God about injustice, and God answers that he will take action at the proper time. Chapter two is

a prophecy of doom against the unrighteous. The third chapter is a prayer, which celebrates the greatness of God, and expresses the undying faith of the prophet.

The book of Habakkuk is one of the twelve books that make up the Minor Prophets—also called the Twelve—a collection of the books of twelve prophets: Hosea, Joel, Amos, Obadiah, Jonah, Micah, Nahum, Habakkuk, Zephaniah, Haggai, Zechariah, and Malachi.

Note: The phrase "Minor Prophets" does not mean that these prophets are less important than Isaiah, Jeremiah, and Ezekiel. It refers only to the fact that the books of these twelve prophets are much shorter than the books of the other three prophets.

Habaziniah

(Hebrew origin: Uncertain meaning)

(Jeremiah 35:3). 7th century B.C. Habaziniah was the grandfather of Jaazaniah, a leader of the Rechabite sect.

The prophet Jeremiah brought Jaazaniah and the other members of his sect to one of the chambers of the Temple and offered them wine. They refused, because their ancestor Jonadab, son of Rechab, had forbidden them to drink alcoholic beverages. Jeremiah, greatly impressed by their refusal, praised the Rechabites to the men of Jerusalem as an example to follow of people who kept their commandments and principles.

Hachaliah

(Hebrew origin: *Waits for God*)

(Nehemiah 1:1). 5th century B.C. Hachaliah was the father of Nehemiah, the Jewish court official who was named governor of the province of Judea by the king of Persia.

Hachmoni

(Hebrew origin: *Wise*)

(1 Chronicles 27:32). 10th century B.C. Hachmoni was the father of Jehiel, the official in charge of the royal princes in King David's court.

Hadad

(Hebrew origin: *Sharp*)

1. (Genesis 25:15). 18th century B.C. Hadad, a grandson of Abraham and his Egyptian concubine Hagar, was one of the twelve sons of Ishmael. Hadad had eleven brothers: Nebajoth, Kedar, Mibsam, Mishma, Dumah, Massa, Adbeel, Tema, Jetur, Naphish, and Kedemah, all of them ancestors of great nations. His sister, Mahalath—also called Bashemath—married Esau, the son of Isaac.

2. (Genesis 36:35). Unspecified date. Hadad, son of Bedad, succeeded Husham as king of Edom and was himself succeeded by Samlah of Masrekah. Hadad defeated the Midianites in the field of Moab. His capital city was Avith.

3. (1 Kings 11:14). 10th century B.C. Hadad, an Edomite of royal blood, was taken as a child to Egypt by the Edomites who had survived Joab's massacre of the Edomite males.

    The Pharaoh of Egypt received him warmly and gave him land and a house. When Hadad grew up, Pharaoh married him to his wife Tahpenes' sister.

    The couple had a son, Genubath, who was raised by Queen Tahpenes in the palace together with her own sons.

    Years later, Hadad, having heard that his enemies, David and Joab, had died, requested permission from Pharaoh to return to Edom, which Pharaoh reluctantly granted. Back in Edom, he became an adversary to Israel, during the reign of King Solomon.

4. (1 Chronicles 1:30). 18th century B.C. Hadad was one of the sons of Ishmael, the son of Abraham.

5. (1 Chronicles 1:50). Unspecified date. Hadad, who succeeded Baalhanan as king of Edom, reigned in the city of Pai.

    His wife's name was Mehetabel, daughter of Matred, the daughter of Mezahab.

    In the book of Genesis, he is called Hadar (Genesis 36:39), and his city is called Pau.

Hadadezer

(Hebrew origin: *The god Hadad is his help*)

(2 Samuel 8:3). 10th century B.C. Hadadezer—also spelled Hadarezer (2 Samuel 10:16)—son of Rehob, was the king of Zobah, a Syrian kingdom situated near the river Euphrates.

King David defeated him and captured a thousand chariots, seven hundred horsemen, and twenty thousand footmen, which he brought back to Jerusalem, together with much gold and brass from Hadadezer's cities. The Syrians of Damascus came to the help of Hadadezer but were also defeated by David. Years later, King Solomon used the gold and the brass taken from Hadadezer to decorate the Temple.

Hadadezer didn't give up, and, some years later, he sent an army under the command of his captain Shobach—called Shophach in the first book of Chronicles (1 Chronicles 19:16)—to fight against Israel. David defeated them at Helam, and Shobach died in the battle. Hadadezer then became a vassal of David.

Hadar

(Hebrew origin: *Grandeur*)

(Genesis 36:39). Unspecified date. Hadar—called Hadad in the first book of Chronicles (1 Chronicles 1:50)—succeeded Baalhanan as king of Edom and reigned in the city of Pai. His wife's name was Mehetabel, daughter of Matred, the daughter of Mezahab.

Hadarezer

(Hebrew origin: *The god Hadar is his help*)

(2 Samuel 10:16). 10th century B.C. Hadarezer—also spelled Hadadezer (2 Samuel 8:3)—son of Rehob, was the king of Zobah, a Syrian kingdom situated near the river Euphrates. (Please see the entry for Hadadezer.)

Hadassah

(Hebrew origin: *Myrtle*)

(Esther 2:7). 5th century B.C. Hadassah was

the Hebrew name of Esther, the Jewish queen of Persia who thwarted the genocidal designs of the evil minister Haman to kill all the Jews in the kingdom. (Please see the entry for Esther.)

Hadlai

(Hebrew origin: *Idle*)

(2 Chronicles 28:12). 8th century B.C. His son Amasa, one of the leaders of the tribe of Ephraim, protested against King Pekah for having brought to Israel the prisoners whom he had captured in a battle against King Ahaz of Judah.

Amasa and his companions took the captives, gave them clothing and shoes, food and drink, and brought them back to the city of Jericho in Judah.

Hadoram

(Hebrew origin: Uncertain meaning)

1. (Genesis 10:27). Unspecified date. Hadoram was the son of Joktan, a descendant of Noah and Shem. His brothers were Sheleph, Hazarmaveth, Jerah, Almodad, Uzal, Diklah, Obal, Abimael, Sheba, Ophir, Havilah, and Jobab.
2. (1 Chronicles 18:10). 10th century B.C. Hadoram, son of Tou, king of Hamath, was sent by his father, with gifts of gold, silver, and bronze, to congratulate King David on his victory against Hadadezer, king of Zobah, who was also King Tou's enemy. In the second book of Samuel, he is called Joram, son of Toi (2 Samuel 8:10).
3. (2 Chronicles 10:18). 10th century B.C. Hadoram—called Adoram in the books of Second Samuel and First Kings, and Adoniram in the first book of Kings—was in charge of levying the forced labor, necessary for the royal building programs, under three consecutive kings: David, Solomon, and Rehoboam.

His name first appears in a list of King David's officials from the later years of David's reign (2 Samuel 20:24).

During the reign of Solomon, Hadoram

was in charge of the levy of the Israelites who were sent to Lebanon to cut lumber (1 Kings 5:14).

Rehoboam, as soon as he became king, sent Hadoram to confront the discontented and rebellious assembly at Shechem. He died there, stoned to death by the rebellious mob.

Hagab

(Hebrew origin: *Locust*)

(Ezra 2:46). Unspecified date. Hagab—also spelled Hagaba (Nehemiah 7:48)—was the ancestor of a clan of Temple servants that returned with Zerubbabel from the Babylonian Exile.

Hagaba

(Hebrew origin: *Locust*)

(Nehemiah 7:48). Unspecified date. Hagaba—also spelled Hagab (Ezra 2:46)—was the ancestor of a clan of Temple servants that returned with Zerubbabel from the Babylonian Exile.

Hagabah

(Hebrew origin: *Locust*)

(Ezra 2:45). Unspecified date. Hagabah was the ancestor of a clan of Temple servants that returned with Zerubbabel from the Babylonian Exile.

Hagar

(Hebrew origin: Uncertain meaning)

(Genesis 16:1). 19th century B.C. Hagar, an Egyptian girl, was the handmaid of Sarai, Abram's wife.

The childless Sarai gave Hagar to eighty-five-year-old Abram as a concubine, so that she could have her husband's child through her maid.

When Hagar got pregnant, she treated Sarai with insolence. Sarai complained to Abram, who told her that Hagar was her slave, and, therefore, she could do with her whatever she wanted. Sarai then treated Hagar so harshly that the maid ran away to the desert

An angel met Hagar at a spring and told her to return to Sarai, prophesying that she would have a son whom she would name Ishmael, and that her descendants would be without number. Hagar returned and, in due course, gave birth to Ishmael.

Fourteen years later, when Abraham was one hundred years old, Sarah gave birth to a son, who was named Isaac.

One day, Sarah, seeing Ishmael, the son of Hagar, mocking, demanded from Abraham that he should send away the slave girl and her son, and that he should declare Isaac as his sole heir.

Abraham, who loved Ishmael, did not want to yield to Sarah's demand, but God told him to do what she said and reassured him that his descendants through Ishmael would also become a great nation. Abraham rose early in the morning, gave Hagar some bread and water, and sent her away with the boy.

Hagar and Ishmael wandered in the wilderness of Beersheba. After they had finished drinking all the water in the bottle, Hagar, not wanting to see her son die of thirst, placed him under a shrub. Then, she moved some distance away, crying and lamenting.

God heard her cries and sent an angel, who told her not to fear, and that her son would grow up to be the ancestor of a great nation. God opened her eyes, and she saw a well of water nearby. She filled the water bottle and gave the lad a drink.

Ishmael grew in the wilderness, became a skilled archer, and married an Egyptian girl whom Hagar chose for him.

Some scholars identify Hagar with Keturah, the woman whom Abraham married, after the death of Sarah, and who gave him six sons: Zimran, Jokshan, Medan, Midian, Ishbak, and Shuah.

Haggai

(Hebrew origin: *Festive*)

(Ezra 5:1). 6th century B.C. The prophet Haggai, a contemporary of the prophet Zechariah, lived and preached in Jerusalem, during the days of Zerubbabel, the man who was appointed governor of Judah by Darius I, king of Persia.

Haggai's prophecies dealt mainly with the construction of the Temple. He encouraged the people not to postpone the work, but to begin immediately, promising that the nation would experience great events in the future as a result of it.

The book of Haggai consists of two short chapters written in simple prose. It is one of the twelve books that make up the Minor Prophets—also called the Twelve—a collection of the books of twelve prophets: Hosea, Joel, Amos, Obadiah, Jonah, Micah, Nahum, Habakkuk, Zephaniah, Haggai, Zechariah, and Malachi.

Note: The phrase "Minor Prophets" does not mean that these prophets are less important than Isaiah, Jeremiah, and Ezekiel. It refers only to the fact that the books of these twelve prophets are much shorter than the books of the other three prophets.

Haggeri

(Hebrew origin: *Descendant of Hagar*)

(1 Chronicles 11:38). 11th century B.C. Haggeri was the father of Mibhar, one of King David's brave soldiers.

Haggi

(Hebrew origin: *Festive*)

(Genesis 46:16). 17th century B.C. Haggi, son of Gad and grandson of Jacob and Zilpah, Leah's maid, was one of the seventy Israelites who immigrated to Egypt. His brothers were Ziphion, Areli, Shuni, Ezbon, Arodi, and Eri. Haggi was the ancestor of the clan of Haggites.

Haggiah

(Hebrew origin: *Feast of the Lord*)

(1 Chronicles 6:30). 11th century B.C. Haggiah, son of Shimea, was the father of Asaiah, a Levite descendant of Merari who was appointed by King David to be in charge of the singers in the House of the Lord.

Haggith

(Hebrew origin: *Festive*)

(2 Samuel 3:4). 10th century B.C. Haggith was the mother of Adonijah, the fourth son of David, who was born in Hebron.

Adonijah became the presumptive heir to the throne, after the death of his older brothers—Amnon, Chileab, and Absalom—but he failed in his efforts to succeed his father, David, and was later put to death by his half brother King Solomon.

Hakkatan

(Hebrew origin: *The Small One*)

(Ezra 8:12). 5th century B.C. Hakkatan was the father of Johanan, a descendant of Azgad, who, together with other hundred and ten men, returned with Ezra from the Babylonian Exile.

Note: The prefix "Ha" is the Hebrew article equivalent to the English "The"; therefore, this word should be considered as a designation, rather than a name: Ha-kkatan, *The Small One.*

Hakkoz

(Hebrew origin: *The Thorn*)

(1 Chronicles 24:10). 10th century B.C. Hakkoz was the priest in charge of the seventh turn, out of a total of twenty-four turns, of the priestly service in the Tabernacle, during the reign of King David.

Note: The prefix "Ha" is the Hebrew article equivalent to the English "The"; therefore, this word should be considered as a designation, rather than a name: Ha-kkoz, *The Thorn.*

Hakupha

(Hebrew origin: *Bended*)

(Ezra 2:51). Unspecified date. Hakupha was the ancestor of a clan of Temple servants that returned with Zerubbabel from the Babylonian Exile.

Hallohesh

(Hebrew origin: *The Enchanter*)

(Nehemiah 10:24). 5th century B.C. Hallohesh—also spelled Halohesh—was one of the leaders who signed Nehemiah's solemn agreement to separate themselves from the foreigners living in the land, to refrain from intermarrying with them, and to dedicate their firstborn to God, among other obligations.

His son Shallum, chief of half the district of Jerusalem, helped to repair the walls of Jerusalem, during the days of Nehemiah, assisted by his daughters.

Note: The prefix "Ha" is the Hebrew article equivalent to the English "The"; therefore, this word should be considered as a designation, rather than a name: Ha-llohesh, *The Enchanter.*

Halohesh

(Hebrew origin: *The Enchanter*)

(Nehemiah 3:12). 5th century B.C. Halohesh is an alternative spelling for Hallohesh (Nehemiah 10:24).

Ham

(Hebrew origin: *Hot*)

(Genesis 5:32). Unspecified date. Ham was one of the three sons of Noah. He, his brothers Shem and Japheth, and their wives survived the flood, together with their parents, in the Ark built by Noah.

After the flood, Noah planted a vineyard, drank from its wine, and became drunk. Ham entered his father's tent and saw him lying there, naked and drunk. Instead of decently covering him, Ham went out and told his brothers, who, averting their eyes, entered Noah's tent and covered his nakedness.

When Noah woke up and found that his son Ham had not treated him with respect, he cursed Canaan, the son of Ham, and prophesied that he would be a servant to Japheth and Shem.

The other sons of Ham were Cush, ancestor of the Ethiopians; Mizraim, ancestor of the Egyptians; and Phut.

Haman

(Persian origin: Uncertain meaning)

(Esther 3:1). 5th century B.C. Haman, son of Hammedatha, was a high official in the court of the Persian King Ahasuerus, in the city of Shushan. He was a descendant of Agag, the king of Amalek who was defeated by King Saul and killed by the prophet Samuel.

The king promoted Haman to the position of vizier of the kingdom and ordered all the officials in his service to show him respect by kneeling and bowing to him. Everybody complied with the king's order except Mordecai, a Jew who sat in the palace's gate, who, unknown to everybody, was the cousin of the queen.

Mordecai refused to kneel or bow to Haman, saying that he was a Jew, and that Jews only kneeled and bowed to God. Haman, angry and offended, decided that punishing Mordecai alone was not enough. All the Jews in the empire should be exterminated!

Haman went to the king and denounced that the Jews were a people with different customs who did not obey the king's law's. He added that, if the king would issue the death decree against the Jews, Haman would pay ten thousand talents of silver to the royal treasury.

The king took off his ring and gave it to Haman, saying, "The silver and the people are yours to do with them as you see fit".

Haman chose the month of Adar as an appropriate month for the genocide by casting lots, "Pur" in Hebrew. The king's scribes were called, and Haman dictated letters proclaiming that all the Jews, young and old, women and children, would be killed on the thirteenth day of the month of Adar. These letters, sealed with the king's ring, were sent to all the governors of the provinces. Having taken care of this business, the king and Haman sat down to drink.

When Mordecai learned of the death decree, he tore his clothes, dressed in sackcloth, covered his head with ashes, and walked through the city, bitterly crying out in a loud voice, until he reached the gates of the palace. He couldn't enter, because this was forbidden for people wearing sackcloth. In the provinces the Jews fasted, wept, wailed, and put on sackcloth.

Queen Esther's maids and eunuchs informed her that Mordecai was outside the gates of the palace, dressed in sackcloth, crying and shouting. The queen became very agitated and worried about the mental health of her cousin. She sent somebody to the palace gates, with clothing for Mordecai, so that he could wear them, instead of his sackcloth. Mordecai refused to receive the clothing.

The queen sent Hatach, one of the eunuchs who served her, to Mordecai to find out the reason for his strange and disturbing behavior. Mordecai told Hatach that Haman had promised to give money to the king's treasuries for being allowed to exterminate the Jews. He gave the eunuch a copy of the decree and told him to show it to Esther, so that she would know the danger, and go to the king to plead for her people.

Esther received the message and sent a note back to Mordecai, saying that, according to the law, if she would go to the king without being summoned, she would be put to death, unless the king would extend his golden scepter to her.

Mordecai replied that Esther should not feel safer than any other Jew, just because she was in the palace. Esther answered that the Jews in Shushan should fast on her behalf for three days. She would also fast, and then she would go to the king, even if she had to die for doing so.

On the third day of her fast, Esther put on her royal dress and stood in the inner court of the king's palace, facing the throne room, in front of the king who was sitting on his throne, holding a golden scepter in his hand.

When the king saw her, she won his favor. He extended to Esther his scepter; Esther approached and touched the tip of the scepter.

"What do you wish, Queen Esther?" the king asked. "Tell me and you shall have it, even if it is half my empire".

"If it pleases Your Majesty", Esther replied, "let Your Majesty and Haman come today to the feast that I have prepared for him".

That night, the king and Haman went to the queen's chambers.

During the wine feast, the king again asked Esther, "What is your wish? And what is your request? I will grant it even if it is half my empire".

Esther replied that she would like the king and Haman to be again her guests the next day at another banquet.

Haman left the banquet in a good mood. His happiness was marred, when he went through the palace gate and saw that Mordecai did not show him any signs of respect. Haman was filled with rage, but he made an effort to control himself and went home.

He invited his friends and his wife to join him. He boasted to them about his great wealth, his many sons, his high position in court, and how he, besides the king, was the only guest in a banquet offered by Queen Esther. "However", he lamented, "All of that meant nothing to me, when I saw that insolent Jew Mordecai, sitting in the palace gate".

His wife and friends advised him to build a gallows, and to ask the king to allow him to hang Mordecai from it. Haman liked the idea, and he had the gallows built.

That night, the king, suffering of insomnia, asked that the official records of the empire should be brought and read to him. He heard the account of how Mordecai had uncovered a plot to assassinate the king, and he inquired if the man had been honored and rewarded for his deed. His servants answered that nothing had been done for him.

The king then asked if any of his officials were in the palace. It so happened that Haman, who had come that night to ask the king for permission to hang Mordecai, had just entered the courtyard. The king's servants brought Haman to the royal chambers.

The king asked him, "What should be done for a man whom the king wishes to honor?"

Haman, assuming that the king was referring to him, answered, "The man whom the king wishes to honor should be dressed in royal robes and set upon the king's horse. One of the empire's noblest courtiers should lead the horse through the city square, proclaiming, 'See how the king rewards a man he wishes to honor'".

"Hurry", said the king to Haman. "Get the robes and the horse as you have said, and do this to Mordecai the Jew. Omit nothing of all you have proposed".

Haman did what he was told. Afterward, Mordecai returned to his usual place at the king's gate, and Haman hurried home, his head covered in mourning. There, Haman told his wife and friends all that had happened to him. They predicted that Mordecai would defeat him. While they were still talking, the palace eunuchs arrived and took Haman in a hurry to Esther's banquet.

Over the wine, the king asked Esther once more, "What is your wish, Queen Esther? I'll even give you half the empire".

Esther answered, "My wish is that I and my people may live, because we are about to be destroyed and exterminated".

"Who dares to do such a thing? Where is this man?" asked Ahasuerus.

Esther answered, "Our enemy, our persecutor, is this evil Haman!" Haman cringed in terror. The king got up in a fury, left the room, and went outside to the palace gardens to calm down. Haman stayed in the dining room to beg Queen Esther for his life. He threw himself down on Esther's couch and implored for mercy. At that moment, the king came back and saw Haman on the queen's couch.

"Is this man going to rape the queen right here in front of me, in my own palace?" shouted the king.

The eunuchs held Haman's head down. One of them, named Harbonah, said that Haman had build a gallows at his house to hang Mordecai. The king immediately ordered, "Hang Haman on it!"

Haman was hanged, and the king calmed down. That same day, King Ahasuerus gave Haman's property to Esther. When the queen told Ahasuerus that Mordecai was her relative, the king took off the ring, which he had taken back from Haman, gave it to Mordecai, and named him vizier, second in rank only to the king. From then on, Mordecai wore royal robes of blue and white, a cloak of fine purple linen, and a magnificent crown of gold.

Esther fell weeping at the king's feet and asked him to stop the evil plot that Haman had made against the Jews. The king extended the golden scepter to Esther; she stood up and said, "Please issue a proclamation revoking the orders that Haman gave for the destruction of the Jews in the empire".

The king told Esther and Mordecai that proclamations issued in the king's name and stamped with the royal seal could not be revoked, but that they could write to the Jews whatever they liked, in the king's name, and stamp it with the royal seal.

Mordecai dictated letters in the name of King Ahasuerus, stamped them with the royal seal, and sent them to all the provinces by couriers, mounted on fast horses from the royal stables. These letters stated that the Jews were authorized by the king to organize for self-defense, fight back if attacked, destroy their enemies with their wives and children, and plunder their possessions.

On the thirteenth day of the month of Adar, the day, on which, the enemies of the Jews had planned to destroy them, the Jews attacked them with swords and slaughtered them. When the number of those killed in Shushan was reported to the king, Ahasuerus said to Esther, "In Shushan alone, the Jews have killed five hundred people. What then must they have done in the provinces?! What do you want now? You shall have it".

Esther answered, "Let the Jews in Shushan be allowed to do again tomorrow what they were allowed to do today; and let Haman's ten sons hang in the gallows". The king ordered this to be done. The bodies of Haman's ten sons—Parshandatha, Adalia, Arisai, Dalphon, Poratha, Aspatha, Aridatha, Parmashta, Aridai, and Vajezatha—were publicly displayed. The next day, the Jews of Shushan killed three hundred more of their enemies.

Esther and Mordecai wrote a letter to all the Jews, wishing them peace and security, and directing them and their descendants to celebrate every year a festival to be called Purim, because Haman had chosen the date of the genocide by casting lots, "Pur" in Hebrew.

Hammedatha

(Persian origin: Uncertain meaning)

(Esther 3:1). 5th century B.C.

Hammedatha, a descendant of Agag, the Amalekite king, was the father of Haman, the Persian vizier whose intention to exterminate the Jews ended in failure, and in the death and dishonor of Haman and his sons.

Hammelech

(Hebrew origin: *The King*)

(Jeremiah 36:26). 7th century B.C. Hammelech was the father of two men: Jerahmeel and Malchiah.

Jerahmeel, an official of King Jehoiakim, was ordered by the king to arrest the prophet Jeremiah and Baruch, his trusted companion, but was not able to find them.

Malchiah, Hammelech's other son, was the owner of a dungeon, situated in the court of the prison, where Jeremiah was cast.

Note: Some scholars believe that Hammelech is not a given name but a title, "The King", in which case, Jerahmeel and Malchiah were royal princes, sons of a king, either King Josiah or King Jehoiakim.

Hammoleketh

(Hebrew origin: *She who reigns*)

(1 Chronicles 7:18). Unspecified date. Hammoleketh, the sister of Gilead, a descendant of Manasseh, was the mother of Ishod, Abiezer, and Mahalah.

Hamor

(Hebrew origin: *Donkey*)

(Genesis 33:19). 17th century B.C. Hamor, the Hivite, was the ruler of the city of Shechem, during the days of Jacob. The patriarch bought for one hundred pieces of silver a parcel of land from him, to pitch his tent. Years later, the bones of Joseph, which the Israelites had brought with them from Egypt, were buried there.

Shechem, the son of Hamor, raped Dinah, the daughter of Jacob and Leah, and, having fallen in love with her, asked his father to ask Jacob for Dinah's hand.

The sons of Jacob took charge of the negotiations and deceitfully agreed to Hamor's request on condition that Hamor, Shechem, and all the men in their city should be circumcised. Hamor and his son agreed to this condition, and they, together with all the men in the city, were circumcised.

Simeon and Levy, brothers of Dinah, took advantage of the weakened condition of the circumcised men to revenge their sister's lost honor. They slaughtered all the men, including Hamor and Shechem, took their sheep, oxen, and other possessions, and brought Dinah back to their home.

Jacob told his sons that their actions could provoke the Canaanites to attack them and slay them. The brothers answered, "Should he treat our sister as a harlot?"

In the book of Acts of the Apostles, Hamor is called Emmor, and his son is called Sychem.

Hamuel

(Hebrew origin: *Anger of God*)

(1 Chronicles 4:26). Unspecified date. Hamuel, of the tribe of Simeon, was the son of Mishma and the father of Zacchur. His grandson Shimei had a very large family, sixteen sons and six daughters, which was unusual for the members of his tribe.

Hamul

(Hebrew origin: *Pitied*)

(Genesis 46:12). 17th century B.C. Hamul, the son of Pharez and a grandson of Judah, was one of the seventy Israelites who immigrated to Egypt. His brother was Hezron.

Hamutal

(Hebrew origin: *Father-in-law of dew*)

(2 Kings 23:31). 7th century B.C. Hamutal, daughter of Jeremiah of Libnah and wife of King Josiah, was the mother of two kings: King Jehoahaz, who reigned for only three months; and King Zedekiah, who reigned for eleven years, and was the last king of Judah.

Hanameel

(Hebrew origin: *God has favored*)

(Jeremiah 32:7). 6th century B.C. Hanameel, son of Shallum, was a cousin of the prophet Jeremiah. He visited Jeremiah in his prison and sold him his field in Anathoth for seventeen pieces of silver. This transaction symbolized to Jeremiah that fields and vineyards would again be owned in Israel.

Hanan

(Hebrew origin: *Merciful*)

1. (1 Chronicles 8:23). Unspecified date. Hanan, son of Shashak, was a leader of the tribe of Benjamin who lived in Jerusalem.

2. (1 Chronicles 8:38). Unspecified date. Hanan, son of Azel and grandson of Eleasah of the tribe of Benjamin, a descendant of King Saul, was the brother of Azrikam, Bocheru, Ishmael, Sheariah, and Obadiah.

3. (1 Chronicles 11:43). 10th century B.C. Hanan, son of Maachah, was one of the brave soldiers in the army of King David.

4. (Ezra 2:46). Unspecified date. Hanan was the ancestor of a clan of Temple servants that returned with Zerubbabel from the Babylonian Exile.

5. (Nehemiah 8:7). 5th century B.C. Hanan was one of the Levites who explained the Law to the people in Jerusalem, after Ezra the Scribe had read it, while standing on a wooden platform, in front of the open space, before the Water Gate.

He was also one of the Levites who signed Nehemiah's solemn agreement to separate themselves from the foreigners living in the land, to refrain from intermarrying with them, to dedicate their firstborn to God, and other obligations (Nehemiah 10:10).

6. (Nehemiah 10:22 and Nehemiah 10:26). 5th century B.C. They were two leaders of the same name who signed Nehemiah's solemn agreement to separate themselves from the foreigners living in the land, to refrain from intermarrying with them, and to dedicate their firstborn to God, among other obligations.

7. (Nehemiah 13:13). 5th century B.C. Hanan, son of Zaccur and grandson of Mattaniah, was one of the four persons designated by Nehemiah to supervise the treasuries of the Temple, and to distribute the offerings among the Levites and the priests. The other three were Shelemiah the Priest, Zadok the Scribe, and Pedaiah the Levite.

8. (Jeremiah 35:4). 6th century B.C. Hanan, son of Igdaliah, was a man of God. His sons had a chamber in the Temple, above the chamber of Maaseiah, son of Shallum, where Jeremiah brought the Rechabites and invited them to drink wine, which they refused.

Hanani

(Hebrew origin: *Gracious*)

1. (1 Kings 16:1). 9th century B.C. Hanani, the seer, told King Asa of Judah that he had behaved like a fool for asking King Benhadad of Syria to help him in his war against Baasha, king of Israel, instead of relying on God (2 Chronicles 16:7).

The seer added that, because of this, the Syrian army had slipped out of his hands, and that, from then on, the king would know only war. Furious, Asa put Hanani in prison.

Hanani's son, Jehu, wrote a book about King Jehoshaphat and prophesied against King Baasha of Israel, saying that his dynasty would come to an end, and that his descendants would be eaten by dogs and birds.

2. (1 Chronicles 25:4). 10th century B.C. Hanani, a Levite, member of a family of musicians, was in charge of the eighteenth turn of service that played musical instruments—cymbals, psalteries, and harps—in the House of God, during the reign of David.

He had thirteen brothers and three sisters, all of them trained as skillful musicians by their father, Heman, one of the three leading musicians—the other two were Asaph and Jeduthun—of the period.

3. (Ezra 10:20). 5th century B.C. Hanani, a descendant of Immer, was a priest who divorced his foreign wife, during the days of Ezra.

4. (Nehemiah 1:2). 5th century B.C. Hanani came to the royal palace in Shushan, together with some men from Judah, to tell his brother Nehemiah, the cupbearer of Artaxerxes, about the dire problems of the survivors in Jerusalem. This report so moved Nehemiah that he asked the king to send him to Judah.

Later, when the walls of Jerusalem had been rebuilt, Nehemiah placed Hanani in charge of Jerusalem, together with Hananiah, the ruler of the fortress, giving them detailed instructions about when to open and close the gates of the city.

5. (Nehemiah 12:36). 5th century B.C. Hanani was one of the priests who marched behind Ezra the Scribe, playing musical instruments in the joyful procession, which celebrated the dedication of the rebuilt walls of Jerusalem, during the days of Nehemiah.

Hananiah

(Hebrew origin: *God has favored*)

1. (1 Chronicles 3:19). 6th century B.C. Hananiah was the son of Zerubbabel and the father of Pelatiah and Jesaiah. His father, a descendant of the kings of Judah, was the leader of the first group of captives who returned from the Babylonian Exile.

2. (1 Chronicles 8:24). Unspecified date. Hananiah, son of Shashak, was a leader of the tribe of Benjamin who lived in Jerusalem.

3. (1 Chronicles 25:4). 10th century B.C. Hananiah, a Levite, member of a family of musicians, was in charge of the sixteenth turn of service that played musical instruments—cymbals, psalteries, and harps—in the House of God, during the reign of David.

He had thirteen brothers and three sisters, all of them trained as skillful musicians by their father, Heman, one of the three leading musicians—the other two were Asaph and Jeduthun—of the period.

4. (2 Chronicles 26:11). 8th century B.C. Hananiah was one of the commanders of King Uzziah's army.

5. (Ezra 10:28). 5th century B.C. Hananiah, a descendant of Bebai, divorced his foreign wife, during the days of Ezra.

6. (Nehemiah 3:8). 5th century B.C. Hananiah, the son of an apothecary, was one of the men who repaired the walls of Jerusalem, during the days of Nehemiah.

7. (Nehemiah 3:30). 5th century B.C. Hananiah, the son of Shelemiah, was one of the men who repaired the walls of Jerusalem, during the days of Nehemiah.

8. (Nehemiah 7:2). 5th century B.C. Hananiah, the ruler of the fortress in Jerusalem, was placed by Nehemiah, together with Hanani, Nehemiah's brother, in charge of Jerusalem, receiving detailed instructions from Nehemiah about when to open and close the gates of the city.

9. (Nehemiah 10:23). 5th century B.C. He was one of the leaders who signed Nehemiah's solemn agreement to separate themselves from the foreigners living in the land, to refrain from intermarrying with them, and to dedicate their firstborn to God, among other obligations.

10. (Nehemiah 12:12). 5th century B.C. Hananiah was the head of a priestly clan, descended from Jeremiah, during the days of the High Priest Joiakim.

11. (Nehemiah 12:41). 5th century B.C. Hananiah was one of the priests who played the trumpet in the joyful procession, which celebrated the dedication of the rebuilt walls of Jerusalem, during the days of Nehemiah.

12. (Jeremiah 28:1). 6th century B.C. Hananiah, the son of Azur, a native of Gibeon, prophesied that the Babylonian Exile would last for only two years, and then all the exiles would return to Judah.

He broke the yoke that Jeremiah was wearing in his neck as a symbol of the captivity, saying that, thus, would God break the yoke of Nebuchadnezzar, king of Babylon, from the neck of all the nations.

Jeremiah told Hananiah that he was misleading the people, and that God would put an iron yoke upon the neck of all the nations, to replace the wooden yoke broken by Hananiah, and that they may serve Nebuchadnezzar. And as for Hananiah, he would die within the year, punished by God for inciting rebellion against the Lord. Hananiah died seven months later.

13. (Jeremiah 36:12). 7th century B.C. His son Zedekiah was one of the officials of the court to whom Baruch, Jeremiah's trusted companion, read the scroll, which the prophet had dictated to him. After hearing Baruch, the officials told him that they would have to report the matter to the king, and that Baruch and Jeremiah would be well advised to hide.

14. (Jeremiah 37:13). 7th century B.C. Hananiah, father of Shelemiah, was the grandfather of Irijah, the gate guard who accused Jeremiah of trying to defect to the Babylonians.

15. (Daniel 1:6). 6th century B.C. Hananiah, a young boy from a noble Jewish family in Babylon, was chosen—together with his companions Daniel, Azariah, and Mishael—to receive an education that would allow them to become officials of the king's court.

Hananiah was given the Babylonian name of Shadrach by the chief of the eunuchs of King Nebuchadnezzar.

The boys asked permission to eat only vegetables and drink only water in order not to transgress by eating and drinking ritually forbidden food and wine. Melzar, the man who had been placed in charge of them, feared that this diet might endanger their health, but he allowed them to try it for ten days. When the ten days were over, the four Jewish boys looked better and healthier than the boys who had eaten of the king's food.

During the three following years, the four boys acquired knowledge and skill, and Daniel learned to interpret the significance of visions and dreams.

Years later, after ending their studies, the king, at the request of Daniel, appointed Hananiah and his companions Azariah and Mishael to be in charge over the affairs of the province of Babylon.

The king set up a golden idol and decreed that everybody in the kingdom should worship it. When the king was informed that Hananiah, Azariah, and Mishael refused to worship the golden idol and did not serve the Babylonian gods, he gave orders to throw them into a burning furnace.

The three men were saved by an angel and survived, without even one hair of their heads being singed. Nebuchadnezzar was so impressed by their miraculous survival that he blessed God and decreed that, from that moment on, anyone in the Babylonian Empire who would dare speak against God would be cut in pieces, and his house would be turned into a dunghill.

Haniel

(Hebrew origin: *God's favor*)

(1 Chronicles 7:39). Unspecified date. Haniel, son of Ulla, was a brave warrior, leader of a clan of the tribe of Asher. His brothers were Arah and Rezia.

Hannah

(Hebrew origin: *Favored*)

(1 Samuel 1:2). 11th century B.C. Hannah was one of the two wives of a man named Elkanah, who lived in Ramathaimzophim.

Hannah, barren and desperate to have a child, was constantly provoked by Elkanah's other wife, Peninnah, who had several children. Hannah would weep and fast, and Elkanah, who loved her very much, would try to console her by telling her that he was better to her than ten sons.

In one of the family's yearly pilgrimages to Shiloh to worship and sacrifice to the Lord, Hannah prayed silently and bitterly to God, asking for a son.

Eli, the Shiloh priest, saw that her lips moved but heard no sound. He thought that she was drunk and advised her to stop drinking.

Hannah said, "Oh no, my lord! I have not drunk wine. I am a very unhappy woman, and have been pouring my heart to God".

"Go away in peace. God will grant your wish", said Eli.

The family returned home, and Hannah conceived and, in due time, gave birth to Samuel. When the boy was weaned, she brought him to Shiloh and left him with the priest Eli who brought him up to follow in his footsteps.

Every year, Hannah made a coat for Samuel and brought it to him, during the family's annual pilgrimages to Shiloh.

Eli would bless her and her husband, saying, "May God grant you children by this woman to replace the loan she has made to the Lord". Elkanah and Hannah had five more children: three boys and two girls.

Samuel, her firstborn, grew up to be a prophet, a seer, the last and greatest of the judges, and the anointer of King Saul and King David.

Hanniel

(Hebrew origin: *God's favor*)

(Numbers 34:23). 13th century B.C. Hanniel, son of Ephod, was the leader of the tribe of Manasseh and one of the men appointed by Moses to apportion the land of Canaan among the tribes.

Hanoch

(Hebrew origin: *Initiated*)

1. (Genesis 25:4). 18th century B.C. Hanoch, son of Midian, was a grandson of Abraham and Keturah, the woman whom Abraham married, after Sarah died. His brothers were Ephah, Epher, Abidah, and Eldaah. His name is also spelled Henoch (1 Chronicles 1:33).

2. (Genesis 46:9). 17th century B.C. Hanoch, son of Reuben and grandson of Jacob, was one of the seventy Israelites who immigrated to Egypt. His brothers were Phallu—also spelled Pallu—Hezron, and Carmi, each one of them ancestors of their respective clans.

Hanun

(Hebrew origin: *Favored*)

1. (2 Samuel 10:1). 10th century B.C. Hanun, son of King Nahash, succeeded to the throne of Ammon, when his father died.

    David, grateful for the kindnesses shown to him by the late king, sent a delegation to offer his condolences to Hanun. This gesture was misinterpreted by Hanun's advisors, who told him that the visiting Israelites were not comforters but spies.

    Hanun, after humiliating the Israelite delegates by shaving half their beards and cutting their garments up to their buttocks, expelled them from his country. David advised his shamed ambassadors to stay in Jericho, and not to return to Jerusalem, until their beards had grown back.

    Hanun, belatedly realizing that David would not let his insult go unpunished, hired an army of Syrian mercenaries to defend his kingdom. David sent his army under the command of Joab, who defeated the Syrians and the Ammonites, and besieged their capital city Rabbah.

2. (Nehemiah 3:13). 5th century B.C. Hanun was one of the men who repaired the Valley Gate of the walls of Jerusalem, including the doors, locks, and bars, during the days of Nehemiah.

3. (Nehemiah 3:30). 5th century B.C. Hanun, son of Zalaph, helped to repair the walls of Jerusalem, during the days of Nehemiah.

Haran

(Hebrew origin: *Mountaineer*)

1. (Genesis 11:26). 20th century B.C. Haran, son of Terah, was the brother of Abram and Nahor and the father of Lot, Iscah, and

Milcah. Haran died in his native city Ur, while his father was still alive.

2. (1 Chronicles 2:46). Unspecified date. Haran, of the tribe of Judah, a descendant of Hezron, was the son of Caleb and his concubine Ephah. His brothers were Moza and Gazez. His son was called Gazez.

3. (1 Chronicles 23:9). 10th century B.C. Haran, son of Shimei, a Levite descendant of Gershon, worked in the House of the Lord, during the reigns of David and Solomon.

Harbona

(Persian origin: Uncertain meaning)

(Esther 1:10). 5th century B.C. Harbona—also spelled Harbonah—was one of the seven eunuchs who served in the court of Ahasuerus, the king of Persia, usually identified by historians as King Xerxes I of Persia, son and successor of Darius I.

The other six eunuchs who served the king were Abagtha, Mehuman, Biztha, Bigtha, Zethar, and Carcas.

In the third year of his reign, the king gave a banquet for all his princes and administrators to show off his wealth. The great celebration lasted one hundred and eighty days.

When the festivities for the nobles ended, the king gave a banquet in the garden of his palace for the common people of Shushan. During seven days, everybody, rich and poor, drank as much as he wanted. At the same time, Vashti, his queen, gave a banquet for the women inside the palace.

On the seventh day of the celebration, the drunken Ahasuerus ordered Harbona and the other six eunuchs who served the king to fetch Queen Vashti, and to make sure that she was wearing her royal crown. She was a beautiful woman, and the king wanted everybody to see her. The eunuchs returned and told the king that the queen refused to come.

Harbona and other eunuchs were present at the banquet where Esther accused Haman of plotting to exterminate the Jews. When the king shouted that the vizier was trying to rape the queen, they held Haman's head down.

Harbona said, "Haman built a gallows fifty cubits high in his house to hang Mordecai, who saved Your Majesty's life".

"Hang him on it!" commanded the king immediately.

Harbonah

(Persian origin: Uncertain meaning)

(Esther 7:9). 5th century B.C. Harbonah is an alternative spelling for Harbona (Esther 1:10).

Hareph

(Hebrew origin: *Reproachful*)

(1 Chronicles 2:51). Unspecified date. Hareph, son of Hur, was the founder of the town of Bethgader.

Harhaiah

(Hebrew origin: *God fearing*)

(Nehemiah 3:8). 5th century B.C. His son Uzziel, of the Guild of the Goldsmiths, was one of the men who repaired the walls of Jerusalem, during the days of Nehemiah.

Harhas

(Hebrew origin: *Shining*)

(2 Kings 22:14). 7th century B.C. His grandson Shallum, keeper of the wardrobe, during the reign of King Josiah, was the husband of the prophetess Huldah. Harhas is also called Hasrah (2 Chronicles 34:22).

Harhur

(Hebrew origin: *Inflammation*)

(Ezra 2:51). Unspecified date. Harhur was the ancestor of a clan of Temple servants that returned with Zerubbabel from the Babylonian Exile.

Harim

(Hebrew origin: *Consecrated*)

1. (1 Chronicles 24:8). 10th century B.C. During the reign of King David, the priestly service in the Tabernacle was divided by lot into twenty-four turns. Harim was in charge of the third turn.

A clan of priests, who descended from Harim, returned from the Babylonian Exile, with Zerubbabel (Ezra 2:32). Several priests of this clan divorced their foreign wives, during the days of Ezra.

His descendant Adna was the head of the clan, when Joiakim was High Priest, during the time of Nehemiah (Nehemiah 12:15).

2. (Nehemiah 3:11). 5th century B.C. His son Malchijah, together with Hashub, the son of Pahathmoab, repaired a sector of the walls of Jerusalem and the tower of the furnaces, during the days of Nehemiah.

3. (Nehemiah 10:5). 5th century B.C. Harim was one of the priests who signed Nehemiah's solemn agreement to separate themselves from the foreigners living in the land, to refrain from intermarrying with them, and to dedicate their firstborn to God, among other obligations.

4. (Nehemiah 10:27). 5th century B.C. Harim was one of the leaders who signed Nehemiah's solemn agreement to separate themselves from the foreigners living in the land, to refrain from intermarrying with them, and to dedicate their firstborn to God, among other obligations.

Hariph

(Hebrew origin: *Sharp*)

1. (Nehemiah 7:24). Unspecified date. Hariph was the ancestor of a family that returned with Zerubbabel from the Babylonian Exile.

2. (Nehemiah 10:19). 5th century B.C. Hariph was one of the leaders who signed Nehemiah's solemn agreement to separate themselves from the foreigners living in the land, to refrain from intermarrying with them, and to dedicate their firstborn to God, among other obligations.

Harnepher

(Hebrew origin: Uncertain meaning)

(1 Chronicles 7:36). Unspecified date. Harnepher, son of Zophah, of the tribe of Asher, was a brave warrior and leader of his clan.

Haroeh

(Hebrew origin: *Seer*)

(1 Chronicles 2:52). Unspecified date. Haroeh was a descendant of Shobal, the founder of Kirjathjearim.

Harsha

(Hebrew origin: *Magician*)

(Ezra 2:52). Unspecified date. Harsha was the ancestor of a clan of Temple servants that returned with Zerubbabel from the Babylonian Exile.

Harum

(Hebrew origin: *High*)

(1 Chronicles 4:8). Unspecified date. Harum, father of Aharhel, was a descendant of Coz, of the tribe of Judah.

Harumaph

(Hebrew origin: *Snub nosed*)

(Nehemiah 3:10). 5th century B.C. Harumaph was the father of Jedaiah, one of the men who helped to repair the walls of Jerusalem, during the days of Nehemiah.

Haruz

(Hebrew origin: *Incisive*)

(2 Kings 21:19). 7th century B.C. Haruz, of the town of Jotbah, was the father of Meshullemeth, King Manasseh's wife and the mother of King Amon.

Hasadiah

(Hebrew origin: *God has favored*)

(1 Chronicles 3:20). 6th century B.C. His father Zerubbabel, a descendant of the royal family of Judah, was the leader of the first group of captives who returned from the Babylonian Exile.

Hasenuah

(Hebrew origin: *The pointed*)

(1 Chronicles 9:7). Unspecified date. Hasenuah, of the tribe of Benjamin, was the father of Hodaviah. His descendant Sallu was one of the first captives who returned from the Babylonian Exile and settled in Jerusalem.

Note: The prefix "Ha" is the Hebrew article equivalent to the English "The"; therefore, this word should be considered as a designation, rather than a name: Ha-Senuah, *The Pointed.*

Hashabiah

(Hebrew origin: *God has regarded*)

1. (1 Chronicles 6:45). Unspecified date. Hashabiah, son of Amaziah and father of Malluch, was a descendant of Merari. His descendant Ethan was one of the Levites appointed by King David to be in charge of the singers in the House of the Lord.
2. (1 Chronicles 9:14). Unspecified date. Hashabiah, son of Bunni (Nehemiah 11:15), and father of Azrikam, was an ancestor of Shemaiah, a Levite descendant of Merari, who was one of the first to settle in Jerusalem, after the return from the Babylonian Exile.
3. (1 Chronicles 25:3). 10th century B.C. Hashabiah was one of the sons of Jeduthun, a Levite who was one of the three leading musicians—the other two were Asaph and Heman—during the reign of David.

   Hashabiah was in charge of the twelfth turn of service to play musical instruments in the House of God.
4. (1 Chronicles 26:30). 10th century B.C. Hashabiah, with one thousand seven hundred Hebronites under his orders, supervised the Israelites on the west side of the Jordan, during the reign of King David.
5. (1 Chronicles 27:17). 10th century B.C. Hashabiah, son of Kemuel, was in charge of the Levites, during the reign of King David.

6. (2 Chronicles 35:9). 7th century B.C. Hashabiah was one of the Levites who donated cattle and oxen for the Passover offerings, during the reign of King Josiah.

7. (Ezra 8:19). 5th century B.C. Hashabiah, a Levite of the clan of Merari, was sent by Iddo, the leader of Casiphia, to join Ezra on his trip to Jerusalem, in response to Ezra's request for Levites to serve God in the Temple.

Hashabiah went with two other Levites, Jeshaiah and Sherebiah, and a group of their relatives. Ezra made him, Sherebiah, and ten others, responsible for taking care, during the journey, of the precious vessels of the Temple, which were to be delivered to the priests in Jerusalem.

8. (Nehemiah 3:17). 5th century B.C. Hashabiah, a Levite and the ruler of half of the district of Keilah, helped to repair the walls of the city, during the days of Nehemiah.

He was one of the Levites who signed Nehemiah's solemn agreement to separate themselves from the foreigners living in the land, to refrain from intermarrying with them, and to dedicate their firstborn to God, among other obligations.

9. (Nehemiah 11:22). 5th century B.C. Hashabiah, son of Mattaniah and father of Bani, was the grandfather of Uzzi, the overseer of the Levites in Jerusalem, during the days of Nehemiah.

10. (Nehemiah 12:21). Hashabiah was the head of the priestly clan, descended from Hilkiah, when Joiakim was the High Priest, during the days of Nehemiah.

Hashabnah

(Hebrew origin: *Inventiveness*)

(Nehemiah 10:25). 5th century B.C. Hashabnah was one of the leaders who signed Nehemiah's solemn agreement to separate themselves from the foreigners living in the land, to refrain from intermarrying with them, and to dedicate their firstborn to God, among other obligations.

Hashabniah

(Hebrew origin: *God has thought of me*)

1. (Nehemiah 3:10). 5th century B.C. His son Hattush helped to repair the walls of Jerusalem, during the days of Nehemiah.

2. (Nehemiah 9:5). 5th century B.C. Hashabniah was one of the Levites who led the public worship, during the days of Nehemiah.

Hashbadana

(Hebrew origin: *Considerate judge*)

(Nehemiah 8:4). 5th century B.C. Hashbadana was one of the leaders who stood upon a pulpit of wood, next to Ezra, when the scribe read the Law of Moses to the people in the marketplace.

Hashem

(Hebrew origin: *The name*)

(1 Chronicles 11:34). Unspecified date. Hashem was the ancestor of valiant warriors in King David's army. He is also called Jashen (2 Samuel 23:32).

Hashub

(Hebrew origin: *Important*)

1. (Nehemiah 3:11). 5th century B.C. Hashub, son of Pahathmoab, together with Malchijah, son of Harim, repaired a sector of the walls of Jerusalem and the tower of the furnaces, during the days of Nehemiah. He also repaired the section of the city wall in front of his house (Nehemiah 3:23).

2. (Nehemiah 10:23). 5th century B.C. He was one of the leaders who signed Nehemiah's solemn agreement to separate themselves from the foreigners living in the land, to refrain from intermarrying with them, and to dedicate their firstborn to God, among other obligations.

3. (Nehemiah 11:15). 6th century B.C. Hashub, a Levite descendant of Merari, was the son of Azrikam. His son Shemaiah was one of the first Levites to settle in Jerusalem, after the return from the

Babylonian Exile. Alternative spelling is Hasshub (1 Chronicles 9:14).

Hashubah
(Hebrew origin: *Estimation*)

(1 Chronicles 3:20). 6th century B.C. His father Zerubbabel, a descendant of the royal family of Judah, was the leader of the first group of captives who returned from the Babylonian Exile.

Hashum
(Hebrew origin: *Enriched*)

1. (Ezra 2:19). Unspecified date. Hashum was the ancestor of a family that returned with Zerubbabel from the Babylonian Exile. Some of his descendants divorced their foreign wives, during the days of Ezra (Ezra 10:33).
2. (Nehemiah 8:4). 5th century B.C. Hashum was one of the leaders who stood upon a pulpit of wood, next to Ezra, when the scribe read the Law of Moses to the people in the marketplace.
3. (Nehemiah 10:18). 5th century B.C. Hashum was one of the leaders who signed Nehemiah's solemn agreement to separate themselves from the foreigners living in the land, to refrain from intermarrying with them, and to dedicate their firstborn to God, among other obligations.

Hashupha
(Hebrew origin: *Nakedness*)

(Nehemiah 7:46). Unspecified date. Hashupha—also spelled Hasupha (Ezra 2:43)—was the ancestor of a clan of Temple servants that returned with Zerubbabel from the Babylonian Exile.

Hasrah
(Hebrew origin: *Lacks*)

(2 Chronicles 34:22). 7th century B.C. His grandson Shallum, keeper of the wardrobe, during the reign of King Josiah, was the

husband of the prophetess Huldah. Hasrah is also called Harhas (2 Kings 22:14).

Hassenaah
(Hebrew origin: *The Thorny*)

(Nehemiah 3:3). Unspecified date. Hassenaah was the ancestor of a family that returned with Zerubbabel from the Babylonian Exile.

The members of the family reconstructed the Fish Gate of the walls of Jerusalem, including its doors, locks, and bars, during the days of Nehemiah.

Note: The prefix "Ha" is the Hebrew article equivalent to the English "The"; therefore, this word should be considered as a designation, rather than a name: Ha-ssenaah, *The Thorny*. He is also called Senaah (Ezra 2:35).

Hasshub
(Hebrew origin: *Important*)

(1 Chronicles 9:14). 6th century B.C. Hasshub, a Levite descendant of Merari, was the son of Azrikam. His son Shemaiah was one of the first Levites to settle in Jerusalem, after the return from the Babylonian Exile. Alternative spelling is Hashub (Nehemiah 11:15).

Hasupha
(Hebrew origin: *Nakedness*)

(Ezra 2:43). Unspecified date. Hasupha—also spelled Hashupha (Nehemiah 7:46)—was the ancestor of a clan of Temple servants that returned with Zerubbabel from the Babylonian Exile.

Hatach
(Uncertain origin and meaning)

(Esther 4:5). 5th century B.C. Hatach, a eunuch, servant of Queen Esther, carried messages between the queen and Mordecai.

Hathath

(Hebrew origin: *Fear*)

(1 Chronicles 4:13). Unspecified date. Hathath, son of Othniel, was a descendant of Judah.

Hatipha

(Hebrew origin: *Captive*)

(Ezra 2:54). Unspecified date. Hatipha was the ancestor of a clan of Temple servants that returned with Zerubbabel from the Babylonian Exile.

Hatita

(Hebrew origin: *Explorer*)

(Ezra 2:42). Unspecified date. Hatita was the ancestor of a clan of Temple gatekeepers who returned with Zerubbabel from the Babylonian Exile.

Hattil

(Hebrew origin: *Fluctuating*)

(Ezra 2:57). 10th century B.C. Hattil, a servant of Solomon, was the ancestor of a family that returned with Zerubbabel from the Babylonian Exile.

Hattush

(Hebrew origin: Uncertain meaning)

1. (1 Chronicles 3:22). 5th century B.C. Hattush, son of Shemaiah, a descendant of King Jehoiachin, returned with Ezra from the Babylonian Exile (Ezra 8:2). His brothers were Igeal, Bariah, Neariah, and Shaphat.
2. (Nehemiah 3:10). 5th century B.C. Hattush, son of Hashabniah, was one of the men who helped to repair the walls of Jerusalem, during the days of Nehemiah.
3. (Nehemiah 10:4). 5th century B.C. Hattush was one of the priests who signed Nehemiah's solemn agreement to separate themselves from the foreigners living in the land, to refrain from intermarrying with them, and to dedicate their firstborn to God, among other obligations.

4. (Nehemiah 12:2). 6th century B.C. Hattush was a priest who returned with Zerubbabel from the Babylonian Exile.

Havilah

(Hebrew origin: *Circular*)

1. (Genesis 10:7). Unspecified date. Havilah was the son of Cush and grandson of Ham. His brothers were Seba, Raamah, Sabtah, and Sabtechah.

    Later, his father Cush had another son, Nimrod, a powerful man and a mighty hunter, who established a kingdom in the land of Shinar and founded Nineveh and other cities.
2. (Genesis 10:29). Unspecified date. Havilah was the son of Joktan, a descendant of Shem. His brothers were Almodad, Sheleph, Hazarmaveth, Jerah, Hadoram, Uzal, Diklah, Obal, Abimael, Sheba, Ophir, and Jobab.

Hazael

(Hebrew origin: *God sees*)

(1 Kings 19:15). 9th century B.C. Hazael, commander of the Syrian army, was instructed by his sick King Benhadad to take a present to the prophet Elisha, who had come to Damascus, and to inquire from the holy man if the king would recover his health.

Hazael loaded forty camels with presents and went to see Elisha. The prophet told him that, although the king would recover from his illness, he would nevertheless die. Then, Elisha wept bitterly.

Hazael asked him, "Why do you cry?"

The prophet answered, "I foresee that you will become king of Syria, and will inflict great suffering to the Israelites".

Hazael returned to his ailing king and told him that Elisha had said that he would recover. Early the next morning, he went to the king's bedroom, smothered him with a wet cloth, and proclaimed himself king.

Some years later, King Joram of Israel and his cousin Ahaziah, king of Judah, went to war against Hazael to defend Ramothgilead, which was under Syrian attack. King Joram was wounded in the battle and, shortly after, was killed by Jehu, the commander of his army.

Hazael defeated the Israelites, occupied the territory, east of the Jordan River, and threatened to take Jerusalem. King Jehoash of Judah took all the treasures of the Temple and the palace, and he sent them as a tribute to Hazael.

After the death of Hazael, his son Benhadad reigned in his place. He was not as successful in war as his father, and he lost to King Jehoash of Israel all the cities that Hazael had captured.

Hazaiah

(Hebrew origin: *God has seen*)

(Nehemiah 11:5). Unspecified date. Hazaiah, son of Adaiah, was an ancestor of Maaseiah, one of the persons who settled in Jerusalem, after the return from the Babylonian Exile.

Hazarmaveth

(Hebrew origin: *Village of death*)

(Genesis 10:26). Unspecified date. Hazarmaveth was the son of Joktan, a descendant of Noah and Shem. His brothers were Sheleph, Almodad, Jerah, Hadoram, Uzal, Diklah, Ebal, Abimael, Sheba, Ophir, Havilah, and Jobab.

Hazelelponi

(Hebrew origin: *Shade facing*)

(1 Chronicles 4:3). Unspecified date. Hazelelponi, a descendant of Judah, was the daughter of the founder of Etam. Her brothers were Jezreel, Ishma, and Idbash.

Haziel

(Hebrew origin: *Vision of God*)

(1 Chronicles 23:9). 10th century B.C. Haziel, son of Shimei, a Levite descendant of Gershon, worked in the House of the Lord, during the reigns of David and Solomon.

Hazo

(Hebrew origin: *Seer*)

(Genesis 22:22). 19th century B.C. Hazo was one of the eight children born to Milcah, the wife of Nahor, Abraham's brother. His brothers were Huz, Chesed, Kemuel, Buz, Jidlaph, Pildash, and Bethuel.

Heber

(Hebrew origin: *Alliance*)

1. (Genesis 46:17). 16th century B.C. Heber was the son of Beriah and the grandson of Asher. He and his brother Malchiel were among the seventy Israelites who immigrated to Egypt. Heber was the ancestor of the clan of the Heberites.

2. (Judges 4:11). 12th century B.C. Heber, a member of the Kenite tribe, descendant of Hobab, Moses' father-in-law, left his tribe's territory and settled in the plain of Zaanaim near Kedesh, with his wife Jael. He enjoyed peaceful relationships with the Israelites, and also with their enemy Jabin, king of Hazor.

   When Sisera, the commander of the army of Hazor, fled from his defeat at the hands of the Israelites, he sought refuge in the tent of Jael, trusting her husband's friendship with King Jabin. Jael killed him, while he was sleeping.

3. (1 Chronicles 4:18). Unspecified date. Heber, a descendant of Judah, was the son of Jehudijah. He was the founder of Socho and the brother of Jered and Jekuthiel.

4. (1 Chronicles 5:13). Unspecified date. Heber was a leader of the tribe of Gad who lived in the land of Bashan. His brothers were Michael, Meshullam, Sheba, Jorai, Zia, and Jachan.

5. (1 Chronicles 7:31). Unspecified date. Heber, of the tribe of Asher, was the son of Beriah and the father of Japhlet, Shomer, Hotham, and Shua, their sister.

6. (1 Chronicles 8:17). Unspecified date. Heber, son of Elpaal, a Benjamite, was the leader of a clan that lived in Jerusalem.

7. (1 Chronicles 8:22). Unspecified date. Heber, son of Shashak, was a leader of the

tribe of Benjamin who lived in Jerusalem.

8. (Luke 3:35). Unspecified date. In the genealogy according to Luke, Heber, the son of Sala, was an ancestor of Abraham, David, and Jesus.

Hebron

(Hebrew origin: *Association*)

1. (Exodus 6:18). 14th century B.C. Hebron, son of Kohath, was the ancestor of a clan of Levites. His brother Amram was the father of Moses.

2. (1 Chronicles 2:42). Unspecified date. Hebron, son of Mareshah, of the tribe of Judah, was the father of Korah, Tappuah, Rekem, and Shema.

Hegai

(Persian origin: Uncertain meaning)

(Esther 2:8). 5th century B.C. Hegai—also spelled Hege (Esther 2:3)—was the eunuch in charge of the maidens who were brought to King Ahasuerus' harem. He liked Esther and treated her with special favor.

Hege

(Persian origin: Uncertain meaning)

(Esther 2:3). 5th century B.C. Hege is an alternative spelling for Hegai (Esther 2:8).

Helah

(Hebrew origin: *Disease*)

(1 Chronicles 4:5). Unspecified date. Helah was one of the two wives—the other one was Naarah—of Ashur, the founder of Tekoa. She had three sons: Zereth, Jezoar, and Ethnan.

Heldai

(Hebrew origin: *Worldliness*)

1. (1 Chronicles 27:15). 10th century B.C. Heldai the Netophathite, a descendant of Othniel, commanded a division of twenty-four thousand men, during the reign of King David. He was in charge of everything related to the army, during the eleventh month of each year.

2. (Zechariah 6:10). 6th century B.C. Heldai—also called Helem (Zechariah 6:14)—a returnee from the Babylonian Exile, was taken by the prophet Zechariah, together with Tobijah and Jedaiah, to the house of Josiah, son of Zephaniah, where they made crowns of gold and silver and placed them on the head of the High Priest, Joshua, son of Josedech. The crowns remained in the Temple as a memorial to the three donors.

Heleb

(Hebrew origin: *Fatness*)

(2 Samuel 23:29). 10th century B.C. Heleb, son of Baanah, a Netophathite, was one of "The Thirty", an elite group in King David's army. He is called Heled in First Chronicles (1 Chronicles 11:30).

Heled

(Hebrew origin: *Transient*)

(1 Chronicles 11:30). 10th century B.C. Heled, the son of Baanah, a Netophathite, was one of "The Thirty", an elite group in King David's army. He is called Heber in the second book of Samuel (2 Samuel 23:29).

Helek

(Hebrew origin: *Portion*)

(Numbers 26:30). Unspecified date. Helek, a descendant of Gilead, of the tribe of Manasseh, was the ancestor of the clan of the Helekites.

Helem

(Hebrew origin: *Dreamy*)

1. (1 Chronicles 7:35). Unspecified date. Helem—also called Hotham (1 Chronicles 7:32)—the chief of a clan of the tribe of Asher, was the son of Heber. His brothers were Japhlet and Shomer. His sister was

Shua. His sons were Zophah, Imna, Shelesh, and Amal.

2. (Zechariah 6:14). 6th century B.C. Helem—also called Heldai (Zechariah 6:10)—a returnee from the Babylonian Exile, was taken by the prophet Zechariah, together with Tobijah and Jedaiah, to the house of Josiah, son of Zephaniah, where they made crowns of gold and silver and placed them on the head of the High Priest, Joshua, son of Josedech. The crowns remained in the Temple as a memorial to the three donors.

Helez

(Hebrew origin: *Strength*)

1. (2 Samuel 23:26). 10th century B.C. Helez the Paltite—or, according to the first book of Chronicles, Helez the Pelonite—of the tribe of Ephraim, was one of "The Thirty", an elite group in King David's army.

   Helez commanded a division of twenty-four thousand men and was in charge of everything related to the army, during the seventh month of each year.

2. (1 Chronicles 2:39). Unspecified date. Helez, son of Azariah, of the tribe of Judah, was a descendant of Jarha, an Egyptian servant who married the daughter of his master Sheshan. He was the father of Eleasah.

Heli

(Hebrew origin: derived from the Hebrew *Eli* [*Lofty*])

(Luke 3:23). 1st century B.C. Heli, son of Matthat, was the father of Joseph the carpenter, father of Jesus, in Luke's genealogy.

Helkai

(Hebrew origin: *My portions*)

(Nehemiah 12:15). 5th century B.C. Helkai was the head of a priestly clan, descended from Meraioth, when Joiakim was High Priest, during the time of Nehemiah.

Helon

(Hebrew origin: *Strong*)

(Numbers 1:9). 14th century B.C. Helon was the father of Eliab, the leader of the tribe of Zebulun in the days of Moses.

Hemam

(Hebrew origin: *Raging*)

(Genesis 36:22). Unspecified date. Hemam, son of Lotan, brother of Hori, nephew of Timna, and grandson of Seir the Horite, was the leader of a clan of Horites that lived in Edom. In the first book of Chronicles, he is called Homam (1 Chronicles 1:39).

Heman

(Hebrew origin: *Faithful*)

1. (1 Kings 4:31). Unspecified date. Heman—son of Mahol—his two brothers, Chalcol and Darda, and Ethan the Ezrahite, were famous for their wisdom, which was surpassed only by that of King Solomon.

2. (1 Chronicles 2:6). Unspecified date. Heman, son of Zerah, was a leader of the tribe of Judah. His brothers were Ethan, Zimri, Calcol, and Dara.

3. (1 Chronicles 6:33). 10th century B.C. Heman, son of Joel, of the clan of the Kohathites, was one of the Levites appointed by King David to be in charge of the singers in the House of the Lord.

   He had fourteen sons, who also played musical instruments—cymbals, psalteries, and harps—in the House of the Lord, and three daughters.

   His descendants, Jehiel and Shimei, were among the Levites who gathered to make themselves ritually clean, and to purify the Temple, during the reign of King Hezekiah of Judah.

Hemdan

(Hebrew origin: *Pleasant*)

(Genesis 36:26). 18th century B.C. Hemdan—called Amram in the first book of

Chronicles (1 Chronicles 1:41)—was the son of Dishon and the nephew of Aholibamah, Esau's wife. His brothers were Eshban, Ithran, and Cheran.

Hen

(Hebrew origin: *Grace*)

(Zechariah 6:14). 6th century B.C. Hen, son of Zephaniah, was memorialized in the Temple by the crowns of gold and silver that three returnees from the Babylonian Exile—Helem, Tobijah, and Jedaiah—had placed on the head of the High Priest, Joshua, son of Josedech, and donated to the Temple, as instructed by the prophet Zechariah.

Hen was probably the brother of Josiah, son of Zephaniah, in whose house the crowns had been made.

Henadad

(Hebrew origin: *Favor of Hadad*)

1. (Ezra 3:9). Unspecified date. Henadad was the ancestor of a family of Levites that helped to repair the walls of Jerusalem, during the days of Nehemiah.
2. (Nehemiah 3:18). 5th century B.C. Henadad was the father of Bavai and Binnui. His sons helped to repair the walls of Jerusalem, during the days of Nehemiah.

Henoch

(Hebrew origin: *Initiated*)

1. (1 Chronicles 1:3). Antediluvian. Henoch—also spelled Enoch—an ancestor of Noah, was the son of Jered. (Please see the entry for Enoch [Genesis 5:18].)
2. (1 Chronicles 1:33). 18th century B.C. Henoch—also spelled Hanoch (Genesis 25:4)—a son of Midian, was the grandson of Abraham and Keturah, the woman whom Abraham married, after Sarah died. His brothers were Ephah, Epher, Abidah, and Eldaah.

Hepher

(Hebrew origin: *Pit*)

1. (Numbers 26:32). Unspecified date. Hepher, ancestor of the clan of the Hepherites, was the son of Gilead and a descendant of Manasseh. His granddaughters—Mahlah, Noah, Hoglah, Milcah, and Tirzah—claimed the family's inheritance, when their father, Zelophehad, passed away.
2. (1 Chronicles 4:6). Unspecified date. Hepher was a son of Ashur and Naarah. His brothers were Temeni, Haahashtari, and Ahuzam. His father, Ashur, of the tribe of Judah, was the founder of Tekoa.
3. (1 Chronicles 11:36). 10th century B.C. Hepher the Mecherathite was one of "The Thirty", an elite group in King David's army.

Hephzibah

(Hebrew origin: *My delight is in her*)

1. (2 Kings 21:1). 8th century B.C. Hephzibah was the wife of King Hezekiah of Judah and the mother of King Manasseh.
2. (Isaiah 62:4). This is the name, by which, God would call the people of Israel, according to the prophet Isaiah.

Heresh

(Hebrew origin: *Deaf*)

(1 Chronicles 9:15). 5th century B.C. Heresh, a Levite, was one of the first to settle in the land of Judah, after the return from the Babylonian Exile.

Hermas

(Greek origin: Name of a Greek god)

(Romans 16:14). A.D. 1st century. Hermas was a Christian to whom Paul sent greetings in his letter to the Christians in Rome.

The apostle mentioned him in the same verse with four other men—Phlegon, Asyncritus, Patrobas, and Hermes—and "the brothers who were with them". This mention gives ground to think that Hermas and his companions formed a small separate group within the larger Christian community of Rome.

Hermes

(Greek origin: Name of a Greek god)

(Romans 16:14). A.D. 1st century. Hermes was a Christian to whom Paul sent greetings in his letter to the Christians in Rome. The apostle mentioned him in the same verse with four other men—Phlegon, Hermas, Patrobas, and Asyncritus—and "the brothers who were with them". This mention gives ground to think that Hermes and his companions formed a small separate group within the larger Christian community of Rome.

Hermogenes

(Greek origin: *Born of Hermes*)

(2 Timothy 1:15). A.D. 1st century. Hermogenes, an apostate Christian, lived in Asia. He, together with Phygellus and others, turned against the apostle Paul.

Herod

(Greek origin: *Hero shaped*)

1. (Matthew 2:1). 1st century B.C. Herod, called the Great, was king of Judea, when Jesus was born. Herod heard that three wise men, from the east, had arrived in Jerusalem and were inquiring about a newly born king of the Jews, whose star they had seen in the sky.

He questioned them, and when he heard that they were seeking a baby born in Bethlehem, the king told them to go there and to report back to him as soon as they found the baby.

The three men found the baby, worshipped him, and gave him gifts of gold, frankincense, and myrrh. They departed to their own country by another way, because God warned them in a dream that they should not return to Herod.

Joseph, also warned in a dream by an angel of the Lord that Herod was seeking the child to destroy him, fled with Jesus and Mary to Egypt.

Herod realized that the three wise men had deceived him, and he gave orders to kill all the children in Bethlehem who were two years old and younger.

Joseph and his family stayed in Egypt, until the angel of the Lord appeared to Joseph in a dream and told him that it was safe to return to the land of Israel, because Herod had died.

Joseph, fearful of Archelaus, the son of Herod who was the new king, avoided Judea and went to the Galilee, where he settled with his wife and son in Nazareth.

2. (Matthew 14:1). A.D. 1st century. Herod the Tetrarch, second son of Herod the Great, had married Herodias, his brother Philip's wife. John the Baptist denounced this act and was imprisoned by Herod.

During a feast honoring Herod's birthday, the daughter of Herodias danced before the king, who, pleased with her dancing, promised to give her whatever she would ask. The girl asked for John's head in a platter. The king, reluctantly, gave instructions to behead John. The head of the slain man was brought and given to the girl, who gave it to her mother.

Jesus, hearing of the death of John, departed by ship to a desert place. When sometime later, Herod heard about Jesus' teachings and miracles, he thought that he was John, returning from the dead.

Herod met Jesus, when he visited Jerusalem, at the time when Jesus had been taken prisoner. Pilate, learning that Jesus was from the Galilee, a region under the jurisdiction of Herod, sent him to the tetrarch. Herod was glad to finally meet Jesus about whom he had heard so much, and he hoped to see him perform a miracle. The tetrarch questioned him, at length, but when Jesus remained silent, Herod and his men mocked him, dressed him in a gorgeous robe, and sent him back to Pilate. This act ingratiated him to Pilate, with whom he had been, till then, on unfriendly terms.

3. (Acts of the Apostles 12:1). A.D. 1st century. Herod Agrippa I was a grandson of Herod the Great. Luke, in the Acts of the Apostles, accuses him of being the initiator of the first persecution of the Christians, and of personally killing the apostle James, brother of John, with the sword.

When Peter miraculously escaped from prison, Herod had his guards put to death. He died suddenly in Caesarea, during a reception for the ambassadors of Tyre and Sidon.

4. (Acts of the Apostles 23:35). A.D. 1st century. Herod Agrippa II was the son of Herod Agrippa I. (Please see the entry for Agrippa [Acts of the Apostles 25:13].)

Herodias

(Greek origin: derived from *Herodes*, name of four Jewish rulers)

(Matthew 14:3). A.D. 1st century. Herodias, previously the wife of Philip, the youngest son of Herod the Great, married her brother-in-law, Herod the Tetrarch, the second son of Herod the Great.

John the Baptist denounced this act as adultery, and he was imprisoned by Herod. During a feast honoring Herod's birthday, the daughter of Herodias danced before the king, who, pleased with her dancing, promised to give her whatever she would ask.

The girl asked for John's head on a platter. The king, reluctantly, gave instructions to behead John. The head of the slain man was brought and given to the girl, who gave it to her mother.

Herodion

(Greek origin: derived from *Herodes*, name of four Jewish rulers)

(Romans 16:11). A.D. 1st century. Herodion was a Christian to whom Paul sent greetings in his letter to the Christians in Rome, calling him his "kinsman".

Hesed

(Hebrew origin: *Kindness*)

(1 Kings 4:10). 10th century B.C. Hesed was the father of one of King Solomon's twelve district governors.

His son, whose name is not specified by the Bible, was responsible for providing food from his district, a territory that included Aruboth, Sochoh, and the land of Hepher, for the king and the royal household for one month out of the year.

Heth

(Hebrew origin: *Terror*)

(Genesis 10:15). Unspecified date. Heth was the second son of Canaan and brother of Sidon. His descendants, the Hittites, allowed Abraham to buy the cave of Machpelah and use it as a sepulcher for Sarah.

Hezeki

(Hebrew origin: *Strong*)

(1 Chronicles 8:17). Unspecified date. Hezeki, son of Elpaal, a Benjamite, was the leader of a clan that lived in Jerusalem.

Hezekiah

(Hebrew origin: *Strength of God*)

1. (2 Kings 16:20). 8th century B.C. Hezekiah, one of the greatest Judean kings, succeeded his father Ahaz in the throne, at the age of twenty-five, and reigned, as the twelfth king of Judah, after the partition of the United Monarchy, for twenty-nine years, dying at the age of fifty-four. His mother was Abi, the daughter of Zachariah. His wife was Hephzibah. Judah, at the time, was a shrunken state, vassal to Assyria.

Hezekiah's first act was to reopen the gates of the Temple and to have them repaired. He asked the priests and the Levites to purify the Temple, and after they had done so, the king assembled the leaders of the people and brought animals to the Temple, to have them sacrificed by the priests.

He reformed the cult in the Temple, reorganized the priests and the Levites, and eradicated idolatry throughout the country.

It was during his reign, in 722 B.C., that Assyria conquered the kingdom of Israel and deported most of its inhabitants. Hezekiah invited the remnants who had stayed in the territories of the former kingdom of Israel to come to Jerusalem for Passover. The object of this invitation was probably to intensify the consciousness of national unity of the survivors of the northern tribes, as a first step in the territorial and political restoration of the kingdom of David and Solomon.

To achieve political independence from Assyria, he assured the supply of water to Jerusalem by closing off the outlet of the Gihon spring, which was outside the walls of the city, and diverting the spring waters by means of a tunnel to the pool of Siloam, which was inside the city walls.

The Assyrians attacked Judah, took the city of Lachish, and besieged Jerusalem, demanding unconditional surrender. During the siege, the king received powerful backing from the great prophet-statesman Isaiah. A plague on the Assyrian camp wiped out the invaders, and Jerusalem was thus saved, but the result of the war was that Judah reverted to its vassal status and continued to pay tribute.

Not long after that, the king became seriously ill. Isaiah came to him and told the king that he would die. Hezekiah prayed to God, and God granted him another fifteen years of life. Isaiah placed a lump of figs on the king's boil, and the king recovered. Hezekiah, unconvinced, asked Isaiah that, as a sign that God would heal him, the prophet should make the shadow in the dial of Ahaz to go back ten degrees. Isaiah prayed to God, and the miracle was done.

The king of Babylonia sent envoys with letters and gifts to wish him a speedy recovery. Hezekiah gave them a tour of the palace and the treasure house. When Isaiah heard about this, he predicted that, one day, the Babylonians would destroy Judah.

The remaining years of Hezekiah's reign were uneventful. The Bible mentions that, during his reign, the proverbs of Solomon were compiled and copied.

Hezekiah died loved and honored by the people, and he was succeeded by his son Manasseh.

The Bible mentions him—under the alternative transliteration of Hizkiah—as the father of Amariah, an ancestor of the prophet Zephaniah.

2. (1 Chronicles 3:23). Unspecified date. Hezekiah, son of Neariah, was a descendant of Jeconiah—also called Jehoiachin—the king of Judah, who was taken to captivity in Babylon. Hezekiah's brothers were Elioenai and Azrikam.

3. (Ezra 2:16). Unspecified date. Hezekiah was the ancestor of a group of men who returned with Zerubbabel from the Babylonian Exile.

Hezion

(Hebrew origin: *Vision*)

(1 Kings 15:18). 10th century B.C. Hezion, the father of Tabrimon, was the grandfather of King Benhadad, who reigned in Syria, when King Asa reigned in Judah.

Hezir

(Hebrew origin: *Boar*)

1. (1 Chronicles 24:15). 10th century B.C. During the reign of King David, the priestly service in the Tabernacle was divided by lot into twenty-four turns. Hezir was in charge of the seventeenth turn.

2. (Nehemiah 10:20). 5th century B.C. He was one of the leaders who signed Nehemiah's solemn agreement to separate themselves from the foreigners living in the land, to refrain from intermarrying with them, and to dedicate their firstborn to God, among other obligations.

Hezrai

(Hebrew origin: *Courtyard*)

(2 Samuel 23:35). 10th century B.C. Hezrai the Carmelite was one of "The Thirty", an elite group in King David's army. He is called Hezro in the first book of Chronicles (1 Chronicles 11:37).

Hezro

(Hebrew origin: *Courtyard*)

(1 Chronicles 11:37). 10th century B.C. Hezro the Carmelite was one of "The Thirty", an elite group in King David's army. He is called Hezrai in the second book of Samuel (2 Samuel 23:35).

Hezron

(Hebrew origin: *Courtyard*)

1. (Genesis 46:9). 17th century B.C. Hezron, son of Reuben and grandson of Jacob, was one of the seventy Israelites who immigrated to Egypt. His brothers were Hanoch, Phallu, and Carmi.
2. (Genesis 46:12). 17th century B.C. Hezron was the son of Pharez and a grandson of Judah—although the first book of Chronicles (1 Chronicles 4:1) mentions him as brother of Pharez.

   Hezron, one of the seventy Israelites who immigrated to Egypt, was the ancestor of the clan of the Hezronites. His brother was Hamul. His sons were Jerahmeel, Chelubai—also called Caleb—and Ram, an ancestor of King David.

   When Hezron was sixty years old, he married Abiah, the daughter of Machir, who gave birth to Segub and, after his death, to Ashur, the founder of Tekoa.

   The history of the conquest of Canaan mentions a Caleb, son of Jephunneh (Numbers 13:6). If the references are to the same person, then Hezron was also called Jephunneh.

Hiddai

(Hebrew origin: Uncertain meaning)

(2 Samuel 23:30). 10th century B.C. Hiddai of Gaash was one of "The Thirty", an elite group in King David's army. In the first book of Chronicles, he is called Hurai (1 Chronicles 11:32).

Hiel

(Hebrew origin: *God lives*)

(1 Kings 16:34). 9th century B.C. Hiel of Bethel rebuilt the city of Jericho, during the reign of King Ahab of Israel. His sons Abiram and Segub died because of this, thus, fulfilling Joshua's curse (Joshua 6:26).

Hilkiah

(Hebrew origin: *God's portion*)

1. (2 Kings 18:18). 8th century B.C. Hilkiah was the father of Eliakim, the official in charge of the palace, during the reign of King Hezekiah, who, in the words of the prophet Isaiah, was "a father to the inhabitants of Jerusalem and to the house of Judah" (Isaiah 22:21).
2. (2 Kings 22:4). 7th century B.C. Hilkiah, son of Shallum—called Meshullam in the first book of Chronicles—the High Priest, during the reign of King Josiah, was among those who donated lambs, goats, and bulls to the priests for the Passover sacrifices (2 Chronicles 35:8).

   While supervising the repair work that was being done in the Temple, Hilkiah found a Book of the Law. He gave it to Shaphan the Scribe who took the book to the king and read it to him.

   Josiah realized with dread that the laws of the Lord were not being carried out, rented his clothes, and sent Hilkiah, accompanied by Ahikam, the son of Shaphan, and Achbor, the son of Michaiah, to consult with Huldah, the prophetess.

   She predicted that God would punish the nation for having forsaken him, but that King Josiah, having humbled himself, would be spared the sight of this evil and would go to his grave, before the collective punishment.

The king instructed Hilkiah to take out from the Temple all the utensils made for Baal and other idols, to burn them in the fields of Kidron and to carry the ashes to Bethel.

Hilkiah's son Azariah, the grandfather of Ezra (Ezra 7:1), succeeded him as High Priest

His other son, Gemariah, was sent by King Zedekiah, together with Elasah, son of Shaphan, to King Nebuchadnezzar of Babylon, carrying a letter by Jeremiah to the captives in Babylon (Jeremiah 29:3). The letter encouraged them to live a normal life in Babylon, build their homes, plant gardens, marry, and have children. Jeremiah's letter ended in a prophecy that, after seventy years, they would return from the Babylonian Exile.

His descendant, Jehozadak, son of Seraiah, was sent to exile by the Babylonians.

3. (1 Chronicles 6:45). Unspecified date. Hilkiah, son of Amzi, descendant of Merari, was an ancestor of Ethan, who was one of the Levites appointed by King David to be in charge of the singers in the House of the Lord.

4. (1 Chronicles 26:11). 10th century B.C. Hilkiah, son of Hosah, a Levite descendant of Merari, was one of the gatekeepers of the Tabernacle, during the reign of King David.

His brothers were Simri, Tebaliah, and Zechariah. His father Hosah was posted on the western side of the Tabernacle, near the Shallecheth Gate.

5. (Nehemiah 8:4). 5th century B.C. He was one of the leaders who stood next to Ezra, upon a pulpit of wood, when the scribe read the Law of Moses to the people in the marketplace of Jerusalem.

6. (Nehemiah 11:11). 5th century B.C. His son Seraiah was a priest in the Temple, during the days of Nehemiah.

7. (Nehemiah 12:7). 6th century B.C. Hilkiah was the head of a family of priests that returned with Zerubbabel from the Babylonian Exile, when Jeshua was the High Priest. His descendant Hashabiah was the leader of the clan, when Joiakim was the High Priest, during the days of Nehemiah (Nehemiah 12:21).

8. (Jeremiah 1:1). 7th century B.C. Hilkiah, a priest in Anathoth in the land of Benjamin, was the father of the prophet Jeremiah.

Hillel

(Hebrew origin: *Praise*)

(Judges 12:13). 12th century B.C. Hillel was the father of Abdon, the man who judged Israel, during eight years, and had forty sons and thirty nephews who rode on seventy donkeys.

Hinnom

(Hebrew origin: Uncertain meaning)

(Joshua 15:8). Unspecified date. Hinnom was an unknown person, probably a Jebusite, who gave his name to the valley, which surrounded the city of Jerusalem to the west and south. This is the valley where child sacrifices were sometimes offered to pagan gods.

Hirah

(Hebrew origin: *Splendor*)

(Genesis 38:1). 17th century B.C. Hirah the Adullamite, a good friend of Judah, was sent by him with a young goat to exchange for the personal articles that Judah had left as a pledge with Tamar, in payment for her sexual services.

Hiram

(Hebrew origin: *Noble*)

1. (2 Samuel 5:11). 10th century B.C. Hiram—called Huram in the second book of Chronicles (2 Chronicles 2:3)—king of Tyre, was a close ally of both David and Solomon.

He sent cedar trees, carpenters, and masons to Jerusalem for the building of David's palace. Later, when Solomon ascended to the throne, Hiram sent him cedar trees and workers to help build the Temple.

King Solomon, in exchange, sent him wheat and olive oil for his household, and he also transferred to him twenty cities in the Galilee, which were a disappointment to Hiram.

The two kings had a commercial joint venture whereby they used Hiram's ships to import gold, exotic trees, and precious stones from Ophir, and precious metals, ivory, apes, and peacocks from Tarshish.

2. (1 Kings 7:13). 10th century B.C. Hiram— called Huram in the second book of Chronicles (2 Chronicles 2:13)—of Tyre, son of a man of Tyre, was renowned as an expert metal worker. King Solomon brought him from Tyre to Jerusalem to make the brass pillars and other decorations for the Temple.

Hiram's mother, according to the first book of Kings (1 Kings 7:14), was a widowed woman of the tribe of Naphtali, but according to the second book of Chronicles (2 Chronicles 2:14), she was a woman of the tribe of Dan.

Hizkiah

(Hebrew origin: *Strength of God*)

(Zephaniah 1:1). Unspecified date. Hizkiah—an alternative transliteration for the name of King Hezekiah—was the father of Amariah and the ancestor of the prophet Zephaniah.

Hizkijah

(Hebrew origin: *Strength of God*)

(Nehemiah 10:17). 5th century B.C. Hizkijah was one of the leaders who signed Nehemiah's solemn agreement to separate themselves from the foreigners living in the land, to refrain from intermarrying with them, and to dedicate their firstborn to God, among other obligations.

Note: Hizkijah is an alternative transliteration for Hezekiah.

Hobab

(Hebrew origin: *Cherished*)

(Numbers 10:29). 13th century B.C. Hobab, according to the book of Numbers, was Moses' brother-in-law—i.e. the son of Jethro, the father-in-law of Moses.

However, the book of Judges mentions Hobab as being the father-in-law of Moses (Judges 4:11), which would mean that Hobab was another name for Jethro himself.

Moses told Hobab that they were journeying to a land promised by God to the Israelites, and he invited him to come along. Hobab refused saying that he would go back to his own land and to his kindred. Moses insisted, "Please do not leave us, as you know where we should camp in the wilderness and can be our guide".

One of the descendants of Hobab was Heber the Kenite, the husband of Jael.

(Please see the entry for Jethro [Exodus 3:1].)

Hod

(Hebrew origin: *Grandeur*)

(1 Chronicles 7:37). Unspecified date. Hod, son of Zophah, was a brave warrior and leader of a clan of the tribe of Asher.

Hodaiah

(Hebrew origin: *Grandeur of God*)

(1 Chronicles 3:24). Unspecified date. Hodaiah, son of Elioenai, was a descendant of Jeconiah, the king of Judah, who was taken to captivity in Babylon. Hodaiah's brothers were Eliashib, Pelaiah, Akkub, Johanan, Dalaiah, and Anani.

Hodaviah

(Hebrew origin: *Grandeur of God*)

1. (1 Chronicles 5:24). Unspecified date. Hodaviah, of the half tribe of Manasseh that had settled east of the Jordan River, was a mighty warrior and leader of his clan.

His tribe was deported from their land by the Assyrians and forcibly settled in the region of the river Gozan, where it eventually assimilated into the local population and disappeared from history, being remembered today as one of the "ten lost tribes".

2. (1 Chronicles 9:7). Unspecified date. Hodaviah, son of Hasenuah, of the tribe of Benjamin, was the father of Meshullam. His descendant Sallu was one of the first captives who returned from the Babylonian Exile and settled in Jerusalem.

3. (Ezra 2:40). Unspecified date. Hodaviah was the ancestor of a clan of Levites who returned with Zerubbabel from the Babylonian Exile. He is called Hodevah in the book of Nehemiah (Nehemiah 7:43).

Hodesh

(Hebrew origin: *New Moon*)

(1 Chronicles 8:9). Unspecified date. Hodesh was one of the wives—the others were Hushim and Baara—of Shaharaim, a descendant of Benjamin. Hodesh had seven sons: Jobab, Zibia, Mesha, Malcham, Jeuz, Shachia, and Mirma.

Hodevah

(Hebrew origin: *Grandeur of God*)

(Nehemiah 7:43). Unspecified date. Hodevah was the ancestor of a clan of Levites who returned with Zerubbabel from the Babylonian Exile. He is called Hodaviah in the book of Ezra (Ezra 2:40).

Hodiah

(Hebrew origin: *Grandeur of God*)

(1 Chronicles 4:19). Unspecified date. Hodiah was the sister of a man named Naham. Her sons were the fathers of Eshtemoa the Maachathite and Keilah the Garmite.

Hodijah

(Hebrew origin: *Grandeur of God*)

1. (Nehemiah 8:7). 5th century B.C. Hodijah was one of the Levites who explained the

Law to the people in Jerusalem, after Ezra the Scribe had read it, while standing on a wooden platform, in front of the open space, before the Water Gate.

He also was one of the Levites who led the public worship, during the days of Nehemiah. Later, he was one of the Levites who signed Nehemiah's solemn agreement to separate themselves from the foreigners living in the land, to refrain from intermarrying with them, and to dedicate their firstborn to God, among other obligations.

2. (Nehemiah 10:13). 5th century B.C. He was another Levite of the same name who signed Nehemiah's solemn agreement to separate themselves from the foreigners living in the land, to refrain from intermarrying with them, and to dedicate their firstborn to God, among other obligations.

3. (Nehemiah 10:18). 5th century B.C. He was one of the leaders who signed Nehemiah's solemn agreement to separate themselves from the foreigners living in the land, to refrain from intermarrying with them, and to dedicate their firstborn to God, among other obligations.

Hoglah

(Hebrew origin: *Partridge*)

(Numbers 26:33). 13th century B.C. Hoglah was one of the five daughters of Zelophehad, the son of Hepher, of the tribe of Manasseh.

When Zelophehad died, Hoglah and her sisters—Mahlah, Noah, Milcah, and Tirzah—came to Moses and Eleazar the High Priest, asking to inherit from their father, who had died in the wilderness without sons.

Moses, after consulting with God, modified the law to entitle a daughter to inherit from her father if he did not have any sons, but with the condition that she had to marry within the clan, in order that her inheritance would remain in her tribe.

After the death of Moses, the sisters came to Joshua and demanded, as their right, to receive a portion of the conquered territories, which had been given to the tribe of Manasseh.

Hoham

(Hebrew origin: Uncertain meaning)

(Joshua 10:3). 12th century B.C. Hoham, the king of Hebron, was asked by Adonizedek, the king of Jerusalem, to join him and several other kings—Debir, the king of Eglon; Japhia, the king of Lachish; and Piram, the king of Jarmuth—in a military alliance against the city of Gibeon to punish the Gibeonites for having made peace with the people of Israel. The people of Gibeon appealed to Joshua for help.

Joshua—after ordering the sun to stand still over Gibeon, and the moon over the valley of Ajalon—fought against the five kings and defeated them. Their armies ran away, during a storm of hailstones, which killed many of their soldiers, even more than those who had been killed in the fighting. The five kings fled and hid in a cave at Makkedah, where they were trapped.

After Joshua had liquidated all the surviving enemies, he ordered that the kings should be taken out from the cave. Hoham, Debir, Adonizedek, Japhia, and Piram, after being humiliated, were killed and hanged on five trees, until the evening.

At sunset, their corpses were taken down and thrown into the cave, where they had been hiding, and large stones were placed over the entrance to the cave.

Homam

(Hebrew origin: *Raging*)

(1 Chronicles 1:39). Unspecified date. Homam, brother of Hori, son of Lotan, nephew of Timna, and grandson of Seir the Horite, was the leader of a clan of Horites who lived in Edom. (In the book of Genesis, he is called Hemam [Genesis 36:22].)

Hophni

(Hebrew origin: *Pugilist*)

(1 Samuel 1:3). 11th century B.C. Hophni and his brother Phinehas were the two wicked and corrupt sons of Eli the Shiloh Priest

A man of God came to Eli and charged him with honoring his sons more than he honored

God, and that his punishment would be that his two sons would both die on the same day, that his descendants would no longer be the leading priestly family, and that his survivors would be reduced to beg the new head priest for money and food.

During a battle with the Philistines, the Israelites suffered a heavy defeat, the Ark of the Covenant was captured, and over thirty thousand men, including the sons of Eli, were killed. When Eli, who was ninety-eight years old, was told about the news, he fell from his seat and broke his neck.

Hophra

(Egypt origin: Unknown meaning)

(Jeremiah 44:30). 6th century B.C. Pharaoh Hophra of Egypt was a contemporary of King Zedekiah of Judah. Jeremiah prophesied his defeat and death at the hand of his enemies.

Horam

(Hebrew origin: *High*)

(Joshua 10:33). 12th century B.C. Horam, king of Gezer, came to the help of the town of Lachish, which was being attacked by Joshua, and was defeated.

Hori

(Hebrew origin: *Cave dweller*)

1. (Genesis 36:22). Unspecified date. Hori, brother of Hemam, son of Lotan, nephew of Timna, and grandson of Seir the Horite, was the leader of a clan of Horites, who lived in Edom.

2. (Numbers 13:5) 14th century B.C. His son Shaphat, of the tribe of Simeon, was one of the twelve men sent by Moses to spy the land of Canaan and report back about its cities and its inhabitants, if they were strong or weak, few or many, and to bring back the fruit of the land. The spies returned and gave a report, which was disheartening and defeatist.

Only two of the spies—Joshua, the son of Nun, and Caleb, the son of

Jephunneh—disagreed and told the people that they should not fear the inhabitants of Canaan.

The Israelites refused to listen to the words of Joshua and Caleb, and they started to wail and cry. God punished their cowardice by condemning them to wander forty years in the wilderness, one year for each day that the spies scouted the land.

Hosah

(Hebrew origin: *Refuge*)

(1 Chronicles 16:38). 10th century B.C. Hosah, a Levite descendant of Merari, was one of the gatekeepers of the Tabernacle, during the reign of King David.

He and Shuppim were posted on the western side, near the Shallecheth Gate. His sons were Simri, Hilkiah, Tebaliah, and Zechariah.

Hosea

(Hebrew origin: *Deliverer*)

(Hosea 1:1). 8th century B.C. Hosea, the son of Beeri, preached in the northern kingdom of Israel, during the reign of King Jeroboam II, until almost the fall of Samaria in 721 B.C.

He married Gomer, daughter of Diblaim, who gave birth to three children—all of whom were given symbolic names by the prophet—Jezreel, Loruhamah, and Loammi.

Gomer was unfaithful to Hosea who mentioned his marital situation in his prophecies to illustrate the relationship between God and Israel.

The dominant theme of his preaching is God's love and compassion for Israel, despite the idolatry of the people, and their "playing the harlot" with Canaanite religions and practices. God would punish Israel for her infidelity, in the same way as a cheated husband would punish his unfaithful wife, by casting her out of her home. This meant that the people would go into exile. In spite of all this, God's love for Israel will never cease, and eventually He will welcome Israel like a forgiving husband who takes back his unfaithful wife.

Three other prophets preached, during that same period, the latter half of the 8th century B.C.—Amos, Isaiah, and Micah—but there is no evidence in the Bible that any of them knew in person any of the others.

The book of Hosea is the first of the twelve books that make up the Minor Prophets—also called the Twelve—a collection of the books of twelve prophets: Hosea, Joel, Amos, Obadiah, Jonah, Micah, Nahum, Habakkuk, Zephaniah, Haggai, Zechariah, and Malachi.

Note: The phrase "Minor Prophets" does not mean that these prophets are less important than Isaiah, Jeremiah, and Ezekiel. It refers only to the fact that the books of these twelve prophets are much shorter than the books of the other three prophets.

Hoshaiah

(Hebrew origin: *God has saved*)

1. (Nehemiah 12:32). 5th century B.C. Hoshaiah was one of the leaders of the people who marched in the joyful procession, which celebrated the dedication of the rebuilt walls of Jerusalem, during the days of Nehemiah.

2. (Jeremiah 42:1). 7th century B.C. Hoshaiah, the Maachathite, was the father of Jezaniah—also spelled Jaazaniah—and Azariah, who were among the leaders of the Judean survivors, after Jerusalem had fallen to Babylon.

Hoshama

(Hebrew origin: *God has heard*)

(1 Chronicles 3:18). 6th century B.C. Hoshama was one of the seven sons of Jehoiachin, the king of Judah, who was deposed by the Babylonians and taken to captivity in Babylon.

Hoshama's brothers were Salathiel, Malchiram, Pedaiah, Shenazar, Jecamiah, and Nedabiah.

Hoshea

(Hebrew origin: *Salvation*)

1. (Deuteronomy 32:44). 13th century B.C. Hoshea was the original name of Joshua, son of Nun, until Moses changed it. In the book of Numbers, his name is spelled Oshea (Numbers 13:16). (Please see the entry for Joshua [Exodus 17:9].)

2. (2 Kings 15:30). 8th century B.C. Hoshea, son of Elah, was the nineteenth and last king of the northern kingdom. In the time-honored way of many of his predecessors, he ascended to the throne, after conspiring against King Pekah of Israel and killing him.

   Shalmaneser, the king of the Assyrians, made him his vassal and forced him to pay a yearly tribute. Hoshea decided to stop paying the tribute, and he sent messengers to King So of Egypt, asking for his help.

   King Shalmaneser attacked Samaria, and, after a siege, which lasted three years, he took Hoshea prisoner and destroyed Samaria. This final defeat marked the end of the northern kingdom of Israel, which had been in existence for over two hundred years.

   The Assyrians deported most of the inhabitants and forcefully settled them in other regions of their empire. They eventually assimilated into the local population and disappeared from history, being remembered today as the "ten lost tribes".

   The Assyrians settled the abandoned cities of Israel with foreigners, who adopted the Hebrew religion to their beliefs, and eventually became the people known today as the Samaritans.

3. (1 Chronicles 27:20). 10th century B.C. Hoshea, son of Azaziah, was the leader of the tribe of Ephraim, during the reign of King David.

4. (Nehemiah 10:23). 5th century B.C. Hoshea was one of the leaders of Judea who signed Nehemiah's solemn agreement to separate themselves from the foreigners living in the land, to refrain from intermarrying with them, and to dedicate their firstborn to God, among other obligations.

Hotham

(Hebrew origin: *Seal*)

(1 Chronicles 7:32). Unspecified date. Hotham, the chief of a clan of the tribe of Asher, was the son of Heber. His brothers were Japhlet and Shomer. His sister was Shua. His sons were Zophah, Imna, Shelesh, and Amal. He was called Helem in another verse (1Chronicles 7:35).

Hothan

(Hebrew origin: *Seal*)

(1 Chronicles 11:44). 11th century B.C. Hothan the Aroerite was the father of Shama and Jehiel, two of King David's brave warriors.

Hothir

(Hebrew origin: *He has caused to remain*)

(1 Chronicles 25:4). 10th century B.C. Hothir, a Levite, member of a family of musicians, was in charge of the twenty-first turn of service that played musical instruments—cymbals, psalteries, and harps—in the House of God, during the reign of David.

He had thirteen brothers and three sisters, all of them trained as skillful musicians by their father, Heman, one of the three leading musicians—the other two were Asaph and Jeduthun—of the period.

Hul

(Hebrew origin: *Circle*)

(Genesis 10:23). Unspecified date. Hul was the son of Aram and grandson of Shem, the son of Noah. His brothers were Uz, Gether, Gether and Mash.

According to the first book of Chronicles, Hul and his brothers were the sons of Shem, and, thus, brothers of Aram (1 Chronicles 1:17).

Huldah

(Hebrew origin: *Weasel*)

(2 Kings 22:14). 7th century B.C. Huldah, a prophetess, was married to Shallum, keeper of the royal wardrobe, during the reign of King Josiah.

While supervising the repair work that was being done in the Temple, the High Priest Hilkiah found a Book of the Law. He gave it to Shaphan the Scribe, who took the book to the king and read it to him.

King Josiah realized with dread that the laws of the Lord were not being carried out. He rented his clothes and sent Hilkiah, accompanied by Ahikam, the son of Shaphan, and Achbor, the son of Michaiah, to consult with Huldah, the prophetess.

She predicted that God would punish the nation for having forsaken him, but that King Josiah, having humbled himself, would be spared the sight of this evil and would go to his grave, before the collective punishment

Hupham

(Hebrew origin: *Protection*)

(Numbers 26:39). 17th century B.C. Hupham, one of the five sons of Benjamin according to the list in Numbers, was the ancestor of the clan of the Huphamites.

In the book of Genesis, he is mentioned, under the name Huppim (Genesis 46:21), as one of the ten sons of Benjamin, who were among the seventy Israelites, who immigrated to Egypt.

The two lists of the sons of Benjamin, which are both found in First Chronicles, do not mention him (1 Chronicles 7:6 and 1 Chronicles 8:1).

Huppah

(Hebrew origin: *Canopy*)

(1 Chronicles 24:13). 10th century B.C. During the reign of King David, the priestly service in the Tabernacle was divided by lot into twenty-four turns. Huppah was in charge of the thirteenth turn.

Huppim

(Hebrew origin: *Protection*)

1. (Genesis 46:21). 17th century B.C. Huppim, son of Benjamin and grandson of Jacob, was one of the seventy Israelites who immigrated to Egypt. According to the list in Genesis, he had nine brothers: Becher, Ashbel, Gera, Naaman, Ehi, Rosh, Muppim, Belah, and Ard.

In the book of Numbers, he is mentioned under the name Hupham as one of the five sons of Benjamin (Numbers 26:39).

In the two lists of the sons of Benjamin, which both appear in the first book of Chronicles, he is not mentioned (1 Chronicles 7:6 and 1 Chronicles 8:1).

2. (1 Chronicles 7:12). Unspecified date. Huppim was the son of Ir, descendant of Benjamin, brother of Shuppim, and leader of his clan. His sister Maachah married Machir.

Hur

(Hebrew origin: *White linen*)

1. (Exodus 17:10). 13th century B.C. During the battle with Amalek, Hur, together with Aaron, held up the hands of Moses to encourage the Israelites to fight. Later, when Moses ascended Mount Sinai, he and Aaron were left in charge of the camp.

2. (Exodus 31:2). 14th century B.C. Hur, son of Caleb and Ephrath, of the tribe of Judah, was the father of Uri.

His grandson Bezaleel was a gifted craftsman, expert in working in gold, silver, brass, wood, and embroidering, chosen by God to design and carry out the work for the Tabernacle, the Ark, the furniture, and the altar.

3. (Numbers 31:8). 13th century B.C. Hur was one of the five kings of Midian—the others were Reba, Zur, Rekem, and Evi—who were killed in battle by the Israelites under the command of Phinehas, the son of Eleazar the Priest

Sihon, king of the Amorites, and Balaam were also killed in the same battle.

4. (1 Kings 4:8). 10th century B.C. Hur was the father of one of King Solomon's twelve district governors, whose name is not specified in the Bible. His son was responsible for providing food from his district, the

territory of Mount Ephraim, for the king and the royal household for one month out of each year.

5. (1 Chronicles 4:1). 17th century B.C. Hur was a son of Judah and grandson of Jacob.

6. (Nehemiah 3:9). 5th century B.C. His son Rephaiah, ruler of half of Jerusalem, helped to repair the walls of the city, during the days of Nehemiah.

Hurai

(Hebrew origin: *Linen worker*)

(1 Chronicles 11:32).10th century B.C. Hurai of Gaash was one of "The Thirty", an elite group in King David's army. In the second book of Samuel, he is called Hiddai (2 Samuel 23:30).

Huram

(Hebrew origin: *Noble*)

1. (1 Chronicles 8:5). 17th century B.C. Huram was one of the sons of Bela, the firstborn of Benjamin.

2. (2 Chronicles 2:3). 10th century B.C. Huram—called Hiram in the second book of Samuel—king of Tyre, was a close ally of both David and Solomon. (Please see the entry for Hiram [2 Samuel 5.11].)

3. (2 Chronicles 2:13). 10th century B.C. Huram—called Hiram in the first book of Kings—of Tyre, was an expert metal worker who made brass decorations for King Solomon's Temple. (Please see the entry for Hiram [1 Kings 7:13].)

Huri

(Hebrew origin: *Linen worker*)

(1 Chronicles 5:14). Unspecified date. Huri, son of Jaroah, of the tribe of Gad, was the father of Abihail, leader of a clan that lived in Gilead, in Bashan, east of the Jordan River.

Hushah

(Hebrew origin: *Haste*)

(1 Chronicles 4:4). Unspecified date.

Hushah, the son of Ezer, was a descendant of Hur, of the tribe of Judah.

Hushai

(Hebrew origin: *Hasty*)

(2 Samuel 15:32). 10th century B.C. Hushai the Archite was a loyal friend and adviser of King David. He wanted to join David in his flight from Absalom. David refused, saying that Hushai would only be a burden to the fleeing army, but that he could be most useful to his cause if he would go to Absalom, pretend that he had transferred his loyalties to him, do his utmost to defeat the counsel of Ahithophel, and report back to David whatever he learned in the rebel's camp. Hushai should send this information to David by two messengers: Ahimaaz, son of Zadok the Priest, and Jonathan, son of Abiathar the Priest.

Absalom entered Jerusalem with his army and took possession of the royal palace. Hushai came to Absalom and greeted him, saying, "Long live the king! Long live the king!" Absalom said to Hushai, "Is this your loyalty to your friend? Why didn't you go with him?" Hushai replied, "I am for the one whom the Lord and this people and all the men of Israel have chosen, and I will stay with him. As I was in your father's service, so I will be in yours".

Absalom then asked Ahithophel for his advice. Ahithophel told him to make clear to the Jerusalemites who was now in charge, by having sexual relations with the concubines whom David had left in the palace.

Ahithophel asked Absalom to allow him to pick twelve thousand men and set out that same night in pursuit of David, saying, "I will come upon him, when he is weak and disheartened, and when all the troops with him flee, I will kill the king alone". Absalom was pleased with the advice, but he wanted to hear what Hushai had to say about it. Hushai came, and after being told what Ahithophel had advised, he said "This time Ahithophel's advice is not good. You know that your father and his men are courageous fighters. Your father is an experienced soldier and he will not spend the night with his troops; he will be hiding in one of the pits. My advice to you is to call all the men of Israel, from Dan to Beersheba, and that you march at their head into battle. No one will survive, neither he nor any of the men with him". Absalom and his council accepted Hushai's advice as better than Ahithophel's.

Hushai met secretly with the priests Zadok and Abiathar and told them that Absalom had agreed to do what he had suggested. He instructed them to send, at once, messengers to David, telling him not to delay, and to cross over the river at once; otherwise, the king and all his men would be annihilated.

Ahithophel, knowing that Absalom's rejection of his advice would result in a catastrophic defeat, saddled his donkey and went home to his native town. He set his affairs in order, and then, he hanged himself.

The fact that Hushai is not mentioned again in the Bible makes it likely that he was killed by Absalom.

His son Baanah, appointed by King Solomon to be one of the twelve district governors, was responsible for providing food from his district, the territories of Asher and Aloth, for the king and the royal household for one month out of each year.

Husham

(Hebrew origin: *Hastily*)

(Genesis 36:34). Unspecified date. Husham, of the land of Temani, succeeded Jobab as king of Edom. When he died, Hadad, son of Bedad, reigned in his stead.

Hushim

(Hebrew origin: *Hasters*)

1. (Genesis 46:23). 17th century B.C. Hushim, son of Dan and grandson of Jacob, was one of the seventy Israelites who immigrated to Egypt. He is called Shuham in the book of Numbers (Numbers 26:42), and he was the ancestor of the clan of Shuhamites.

2. (1 Chronicles 7:12). Unspecified date. Hushim was a Benjamite, leader of his clan, son of Aher.

3. (1 Chronicles 8:8). Unspecified date. Hushim, the mother of Abitub and Elpaal, was one of the wives of Shaharaim, a descendant of Benjamin.

She and Baara, the other wife, were sent away by Shaharaim, who then settled in the land of Moab, east of the river Jordan, and married Hodesh, with whom he had seven children: Jobab, Zibia, Mesha, Malcham, Jeuz, Shachia, and Mirma.

Huz

(Hebrew origin: *Consultation*)

(Genesis 22:21). 19th century B.C. Huz was the eldest of the eight children born to Milcah, the wife of Nahor, Abraham's brother. His brothers were Jidlaph, Buz, Kemuel, Chesed, Hazo, Pildash, and Bethuel.

Hymenaeus

(Greek origin: derived from the *God of weddings*)

(1 Timothy 1:20). A.D. 1st century. Hymenaeus was an apostate, who, together with Alexander, the coppersmith, gave cause to Paul to write that he "had delivered them unto Satan that they may learn not to blaspheme".

Years later, Paul complained in Second Timothy (2 Timothy 2:17) about the false teachings of Hymenaeus and Philetus concerning the Resurrection.

the monarchy, the king served in this role and judges were more like the judicial officers that we know today.

Ibhar

(Hebrew origin: *He will choose*).

(2 Samuel 5:15). 10th century B.C. Ibhar was one of the sons of King David who were born in Jerusalem.

Ibneiah

(Hebrew origin: *God builds*)

(1 Chronicles 9:8). Unspecified date. Ibneiah, the son of Jeroham, was the head of a Benjamite clan that lived in Jerusalem.

Ibnijah

(Hebrew origin: *God builds*)

(1 Chronicles 9:8). Unspecified date. Ibnijah was the father of Reuel. His descendant Meshullam was the head of a Benjamite clan that lived in Jerusalem.

Ibri

(Hebrew origin: *Hebrew*)

(1 Chronicles 24:27). 10th century B.C. Ibri, son of Jaaziah, a Levite descendant of Merari, served in the Tabernacle, during the reign of David. His brothers were Shoham, Zaccur, and Beno.

Ibzan

(Hebrew origin: *Splendid*)

(Judges 12:8). 12th century B.C. Ibzan of Bethlehem judged Israel, after the death of Jephthah the Gileadite. He had thirty sons, for whom he brought thirty wives from abroad, and thirty daughters whom he sent abroad.

After judging Israel, during seven years, he died and was buried in Bethlehem. Elon, a Zebulonite, succeeded him as judge.

Note: In the book of Judges, a judge is a ruler or governor of territory or a military leader in pre-monarchical Israel. Later, during

Ichabod

(Hebrew origin: *Without honor*)

(1 Samuel 4:21). 11th century B.C. Ichabod was the youngest son of Phinehas, the corrupt son of Eli the Priest. His older brother was called Ahitub.

During a battle with the Philistines, the Israelites suffered a heavy defeat. The Ark of the Covenant was captured, and over thirty thousand men, including the sons of Eli, were killed. When Eli, who was ninety-eight years old, was told about the news, he fell from his seat and broke his neck.

Phinehas' wife was at that time in a very advanced stage of pregnancy. When she heard that the Ark of the Covenant had been captured, and that her father-in-law and her husband were dead, she was seized with labor pains and gave birth. As she lay dying, the woman, attending her, said, "Do not be afraid, for you have borne a son". When Phinehas' wife did not respond, the woman named the boy Ichabod, saying, "The glory of God has departed".

Idbash

(Hebrew origin: *Honeyed*)

(1 Chronicles 4:3). Unspecified date. Idbash, a descendant of Judah, was the son of the founder of Etam and the brother of Jezreel, Ishma, and their sister Hazelelponi.

Iddo

(Hebrew origin: *Timely*)

1. (1 Kings 4:14). 10th century B.C. His son Ahinadab, one of King Solomon's twelve district governors, was responsible for providing food from his district, the territory of Mahanaim, for the king and the royal household for one month out of each year.

2. (1 Chronicles 6:21). 8th century B.C. Iddo—called Eden in the second book of

Chronicles (2 Chronicles 29:12)—son of Joah and father of Zerah, was a Levite, descendant of Gershom.

He and his father Joah were among the Levites who gathered to make themselves ritually clean, and to purify the Temple, during the reign of King Hezekiah of Judah.

Iddo also helped to distribute among the priests the offerings that the people brought to the Temple.

3. (1 Chronicles 27:21). 10th century B.C. Iddo, son of Zechariah, was a leader of half the tribe of Manasseh in Gilead, during the reign of King David. Joel, son of Pedaiah, was the leader of the other half of the tribe.

4. (2 Chronicles 9:29). 10th century B.C. Iddo, the seer, had visions concerning Jeroboam, son of Nebat, the first ruler of the northern kingdom of Israel. He wrote a book, now lost, about the acts of the kings: Solomon, Rehoboam, and Abijah.

5. (Ezra 5:1). 7th century B.C. According to the book of Ezra, Iddo was the father of the prophet Zechariah, who, together with the prophet Haggai, prophesied in Jerusalem, during the days of Zerubbabel.

However, according to the book of Zechariah, Iddo's son was Berechiah, the father of Zechariah, which means that Iddo was the grandfather of the prophet, and not his father (Zechariah 1:1).

6. (Ezra 8:17). 5th century B.C. Iddo was the chief of a place called Casiphia, to whom Ezra sent a delegation, requesting him to send Levites to serve in the Temple in Jerusalem.

7. (Nehemiah 12:4) 6th century B.C. Iddo was one of the priests who returned from the Babylonian Exile with Zerubbabel.

He was the ancestor of a priestly clan that was headed by Zechariah, when Joiakim was the High Priest, during the time of Nehemiah.

Igal

(Hebrew origin: *Redeemer*)

1. (Numbers 13:7) 13th century B.C. Igal, son of Joseph, of the tribe of Issachar, was one of the twelve spies sent by Moses to Canaan, to scout the land, its cities, and its inhabitants; to find out if they were strong or weak, few or many; and to bring back the fruit of the land. The spies came back, frightened and disheartened, and told the Israelites that the Canaanites were too big and too strong to be defeated.

Two of the spies—Joshua, the son of Nun, and Caleb, the son of Jephunneh—disagreed and told the people not to fear.

The Israelites refused to listen to the encouraging words of Joshua and Caleb, and they started to wail and cry. God punished their cowardice by condemning them to wander forty years in the wilderness, one year for each day that the spies scouted the land. All those who complained against God, including Igal, died in the wilderness, except Caleb and Joshua.

(For more detailed information about the twelve spies, please see the entry for Joshua.)

2. (2 Samuel 23:36). 10th century B.C. Igal, the son of Nathan of Zobah, was one of "The Thirty", an elite group in King David's army.

Igdaliah

(Hebrew origin: *God will be glorified*)

(Jeremiah 35:4). 6th century B.C. Igdaliah was the father of Hanan, who was called a Man of God by the prophet Jeremiah. His grandsons had a chamber in the Temple, where Jeremiah offered wine to the Rechabites, which they refused.

Igeal

(Hebrew origin: *Redeemer*)

(1 Chronicles 3:22). Unspecified date. Igeal, son of Shemaiah, was a descendant of King Jehoiachin, the king of Judah, who was taken to captivity in Babylon. Igeal's brothers were Hattush, Bariah, Neariah, and Shaphat.

Ikkesh

(Hebrew origin: *Perverse*)

(2 Samuel 23:26). 10th century B.C. Ikkesh the Tekoite was the father of Ira, a member of King David's elite army group known as The Thirty who commanded a division of twenty-four thousand men and was in charge of everything related to the army, during the sixth month of each year.

Ilai

(Hebrew origin: *Elevated*)

(1 Chronicles 11:29). 10th century B.C. Ilai the Ahohite was one of "The Thirty", an elite group in King David's army. In the second book of Samuel, he is called Zalmon (2 Samuel 23:28).

Imla

(Hebrew origin: *Fullness*)

(2 Chronicles 18:7). 10th century B.C. Imla—also called Imlah (1 Kings 22:8)—was the father of Micaiah, the prophet who told Ahab, king of Israel, and Jehoshaphat, king of Judah, that they would be defeated in their war against the Syrians.

Imlah

(Hebrew origin: *Fullness*)

(1 Kings 22:8). 10th century B.C. Imlah is an alternative spelling for Imla (2 Chronicles 18:7), father of the prophet Micaiah.

Immanuel

(Hebrew origin: *God is with us*)

(Isaiah 7:14). Immanuel is a symbolic name given by the prophet Isaiah to a child who would be born to the royal house of David, and who would reject evil and choose good. Christian theologians consider that this verse predicts the birth of Jesus.

Immer

(Hebrew origin: *Talkative*)

1. (1 Chronicles 9:12). 10th century B.C. During the reign of King David, the priestly service in the Tabernacle was divided by lot into twenty-four turns. Immer was in charge of the sixteenth turn (1 Chronicles 24:14).

   Immer was the ancestor of a clan of priests who returned with Zerubbabel from the Babylonian Exile (Ezra 2:37).

2. (Nehemiah 3:29). 5th century B.C. His son Zadok helped to repair the walls of Jerusalem, during the days of Nehemiah.

3. (Nehemiah 11:13). Unspecified date. Immer, father of Meshillemoth—also called Meshillemith (1 Chronicles 9:12)—was an ancestor of Amashai, son of Azareel, and Maasiai, son of Adiel, two priests who settled in Jerusalem, after the return from the Babylonian Exile.

4. (Jeremiah 20:1). 6th century B.C. Immer was the father of Pashur, the priest in charge of the Temple who had Jeremiah flogged and jailed for preaching "defeatism".

Imna

(Hebrew origin: *He will restrain*)

(1 Chronicles 7:35). Unspecified date. Imna, a clan chief of the tribe of Asher, was the son of Helem, who was called Hotham in First Chronicles (1 Chronicles 7:32). His brothers were Zophah, Amal, and Shelesh.

Imnah

(Hebrew origin: *Right hand*)

1. (1 Chronicles 7:30). 17th century B.C. Imnah—also called Jimnah (Genesis 46:17), and Jimna (Numbers 26:44)—was one of the sons of Asher. He, his father, his sister Serah, and his brothers—Ishuah, Isui, and Beriah—were among the seventy Israelites who immigrated to Egypt. Imnah was the ancestor of the clan of the Jimnites.

2. (2 Chronicles 31:14). 8th century B.C. His son Kore was one of the Levites named by

King Hezekiah to distribute the gifts, tithes, and offerings, brought by the people to the Temple.

Imrah

(Hebrew origin: *Interchange*)

(1 Chronicles 7:36). Unspecified date. Imrah, son of Zophah, of the tribe of Asher, was a brave warrior and leader of his clan.

Imri

(Hebrew origin: *Wordy*)

1. (1 Chronicles 9:4). Unspecified date. Imri, son of Bani, of the tribe of Judah, was the father of Omri and an ancestor of Uthai, the leader of a clan that settled in Jerusalem, after they returned from the Babylonian Exile.
2. (Nehemiah 3:2). 5th century B.C. His son Zaccur helped to rebuild the walls of Jerusalem, during the days of Nehemiah.

Iphedeiah

(Hebrew origin: *God will liberate*)

(1 Chronicles 8:25). Unspecified date. Iphedeiah, son of Shashak, was a leader of the tribe of Benjamin who lived in Jerusalem.

Ir

(Hebrew origin: *City*)

(1 Chronicles 7:12). Unspecified date. Ir, a descendant of Benjamin, was the father of Shuppim and Huppim. His daughter Maachah married Machir (1 Chronicles 7:15).

Ira

(Hebrew origin: *Wakefulness*)

1. (2 Samuel 20:26). 10th century B.C. Ira the Jairite was a priest in the court of King David.
2. (2 Samuel 23:26). 10th century B.C. Ira, the son of Ikkesh the Tekoite, was one of "The Thirty", an elite group in King David's army. Ira commanded a division of

twenty-four thousand men and was in charge of everything related to the army, during the sixth month of each year.

3. (2 Samuel 23:38). 10th century B.C. Ira the Ithrite was one of "The Thirty", an elite group in King David's army.

Irad

(Hebrew origin: *Fugitive*)

(Genesis 4:18). Antediluvian. Irad, son of Enoch, was the grandson of Cain and the father of Mehujael.

Iram

(Hebrew origin: *City wise*)

(Genesis 36:43). Unspecified date. Iram, a ruler of Edom, was a descendant of Esau.

Iri

(Hebrew origin: *Urbane*)

(1 Chronicles 7:7). 16th century B.C. Iri, son of Bela and grandson of Benjamin, was a brave leader of his clan. His brothers were Ezbon, Uzzi, Uzziel, and Jerimoth.

Note: Elsewhere in the first book of Chronicles (1 Chronicles 8:3), Bela has a different list of sons: Addar, Gera, Abihud, Abishua, Naaman, Ahoah, Gera, Shephuphan, and Huram.

Irijah

(Hebrew origin: *God fearing*)

(Jeremiah 37:13). 6th century B.C. Irijah, son of Shelemiah, was a gatekeeper, in charge of the Benjamin Gate, during the reign of King Zedekiah.

During the siege of Jerusalem, Jeremiah wanted to leave the city and go to the territory of Benjamin.

When the prophet arrived at the gate, Irijah accused him of intending to defect to the Babylonians. Jeremiah answered that he had no such intention. Irijah refused to listen, arrested Jeremiah, and took him to the authorities. The officials angrily beat the prophet and imprisoned him in the house of Jonathan the Scribe.

Iru

(Hebrew origin: *Citizen*)

(1 Chronicles 4:15). 12th century B.C. Iru was one of the sons of Caleb, son of Jephunneh, a descendant of Judah.

Isaac

(Hebrew origin: *He will laugh*)

(Genesis 17:19). 19th century B.C. Isaac, the son of Abraham and Sarah, was born to them, in their old age, when they had given up hope that Sarah would, one day, have children. God announced to Abraham that Sarah would have a son, with whom He would establish an everlasting covenant and with his seed after him. Sarah became pregnant and gave birth to a son, whom Abraham called Isaac and circumcised when the baby was eight days old, Abraham being one hundred years old at the time.

The boy was given the name Isaac, because Sarah said, "God made me laugh, so that all that hear will laugh with me".

When Isaac was a lad, God decided to test Abraham by telling him to take the boy to the land of Moriah and sacrifice him there upon one of the mountains. Abraham did not question God's order; he set out on his donkey, taking with him Isaac, two young servants, and some firewood.

After traveling three days, they came near the place. Abraham told the servants to wait there with the donkey and gave the wood to Isaac to carry, and he himself carried live coals, for starting the fire, and a knife. As they walked along together, Isaac asked his father about the lamb for the sacrifice. Abraham answered that God would provide one.

When they came to the place that God had told him, Abraham built an altar and arranged the wood on it. He tied up his son and placed him on the altar, on top of the wood. Then, when he picked up the knife to kill the boy, an angel called to him from heaven, "Abraham,

Abraham". He answered, "Here I am".

The angel said, "Don't hurt the boy. Now, I know that you fear God because you have not kept your only son from him".

Abraham looked around and saw a ram caught in a bush by its horns. He went to it, got it and sacrificed it, instead of his son. Abraham named that place Adonai Yireh, *God sees.*

The angel spoke to Abraham a second time, "By myself have I sworn, said God, because you have not withhold your son, that I will bless you, and that you will have as many descendants as there are stars in the sky or grains of sand in the seashore. Your descendants will conquer their enemies, and all nations will be blessed through them, because you have obeyed my command".

Abraham went back to his servants, and they returned together to Beersheba, where he settled.

Isaac's mother, Sarah, died in Kirjatharba, Hebron, at the age of one hundred and twenty-seven, when Isaac was thirty-six years old. His father Abraham bought the cave of Machpelah, in the outskirts of Hebron, as a family sepulcher, from Ephron the Hittite, for four hundred shekels of silver, and there, he buried Sarah.

Isaac was already forty years old, when his father, not wanting him to marry any of the local Canaanite girls, sent Eliezer, his trusted servant, to his relatives in Haran, with instructions to bring, from there, a bride for Isaac. The servant returned with Rebekah, the granddaughter of Nahor, Abraham's brother.

Isaac was strolling in the field toward evening, when, looking up, he saw camels approaching. Raising her eyes, Rebekah saw Isaac. She alighted from the camel and asked Eliezer, "Who is that man walking in the field toward us?"

Eliezer answered, "That's my master".

Rebekah took her veil and covered herself. Isaac brought her into the tent of his mother Sarah. When they married, Rebekah became a great comfort to Isaac, after the death of his mother, whom he mourned and missed for many years.

Abraham married a woman called Keturah, with whom he had six more sons: Abida, Ephah, Epher, Hanoch, and Eldaah. Shortly before he died, he made Isaac his sole heir, and, in order to avoid trouble, he donated gifts to the sons of his second marriage and sent them away. Abraham died at the age of one hundred and seventy-five and was buried by his sons Ishmael and Isaac in the cave of Machpelah, next to Sarah.

There was a famine in the land, and Isaac went to live in Gerar, a city ruled by Abimelech, king of the Philistines. As Abraham, his father, had done many years ago in similar circumstances, Isaac passed Rebekah as his sister, because he was afraid that, if the men of Gerar would know that he was her husband, they would kill him to get rid of him.

When Abimelech, looking through a window, saw Isaac and Rebekah making love, the king reproached Isaac and told him that his deception could have caused people to sin with Rebekah. Abimelech forbade his people to take any action against Isaac or Rebekah, under penalty of death.

Isaac stayed in Gerar and became so rich and powerful that Abimelech asked him to leave his kingdom.

Isaac's herdsmen fought with the herdsmen of Gerar, disputing the ownership of a water well, but in a meeting with Abimelech, they reached a peace agreement between them.

For twenty years, Rebekah was not able to conceive, until Isaac, then sixty years old, prayed to God on her behalf. During Rebekah's pregnancy, she felt the babies struggling in her womb and was told by the Lord that each of the boys would become the progenitor of a nation, and that the older would serve the younger. Esau was born first, red and hairy. Moments later, Jacob came out, holding Esau's heel.

Esau, his father's favorite, grew up to be a skilled hunter, a simple fellow, an outdoor man, impetuous, impatient, and easily manipulated by his shrewd brother. Jacob, his mother's favorite, was completely his opposite: a patient, thoughtful, stay-at-home type.

Esau married at the age of forty, the same age as his father, Isaac, when he married Rebekah. His wives, two Hittite women called Judith and Bashemath, did all they could to make life miserable for Isaac and Rebekah.

Years went by, Isaac, now grown old and blind, decided to bless his eldest son, but first, he would eat. He called Esau and told him, "I am old, and I may die any day. Take your weapons, bow and arrows, go out to the fields, and hunt me some venison. Then, prepare it the way I like it, and bring it to me to eat, so that I may give you my soul's blessing, before I die".

Rebekah overheard the conversation and devised a plan, by which Jacob would receive Isaac's blessing. She instructed Jacob to disguise himself as Esau, by putting on his brother's clothing and covering his arms and neck with the skin of a goat to simulate Esau's hairiness. She prepared a savory dish of meat and sent Jacob with it to his father. Jacob succeeded in convincing his father that he was Esau, and the deceived old man bestowed his blessing on Jacob.

Esau returned from his hunt. He too prepared a delicious meal, brought it to his father, and said, "Let my father sit up and eat of his son's venison, so that your soul may bless me". Isaac, bewildered, asked him, "Who are you?"

"I am your son Esau, your firstborn".

Isaac was seized with a violent trembling. "Who was it then", he asked, "that brought me the venison dish? I ate all of it, before you came, and I blessed him. He will remain blessed".

Esau burst into uncontrolled sobbing and said, "Bless me too, Father!" Isaac answered, "Your brother came with deviousness and took away your blessing".

"How rightly was he named Jacob?! He has now supplanted me two times, the first time when he took away my birthright, and now he has taken away my blessing. Don't you have another blessing for me?"

Isaac said, "I have made him master over you and have given him grain and wine. What, then, can I still do for you, my son?"

"Do you only have one blessing, my father? Bless me too, Father!" said Esau in a loud voice and wept.

Isaac said to him, "Your dwelling shall be the fatness of the earth, and the dew of heaven above. You shall live by your sword, and you shall serve your brother, but one day, you shall break his yoke from your neck".

Furious at Jacob's trickery, Esau made a vow to kill Jacob, as soon as Isaac passed away. Rebekah, to protect Jacob from Esau's revenge, decided to send him away to her brother Laban in Haran. She went to Isaac and complained that she was weary of her life because of the Hittite wives of Esau, and if Jacob would also marry one of the local girls, she had no wish to continue living.

Isaac called Jacob, blessed him, and said, "You shall not marry any Canaanite girl. Go to Paddan-Aram, to the house of Bethuel, your mother's father, and marry one of the daughters of your uncle Laban".

Isaac died at the age of one hundred and eighty. His sons Esau and Jacob buried him in the cave of Machpelah where his parents and his wife Rebekah were also buried.

Isaiah

(Hebrew origin: *God has saved*)

(2 Kings 19:2). The book of Isaiah covers two different historical periods: The first half—chapters 1 to 39 of the book of Isaiah—relates events in Jerusalem in the 8th century B.C., between the years 740 B.C. and 700 B.C. The second half—chapters 40 to 66—tells of events in Babylonia around the year 540 B.C. The idea of rebuke is prominent in the first part of the book, while in the second half, the major idea is consolation.

These historical eras, separated by two hundred years, plus the great difference in styles between the two halves of the book, provide grounds for a scholarly theory that states that the book of Isaiah should be considered the work of two different authors: the first part by Isaiah himself, and the second part by an unknown prophet, whom they call Deutero-Isaiah—i.e. Second Isaiah.

Some scholars refute this theory and state that the second half of the book of Isaiah, dealing with matters taking place two hundred

years later than the first half, is based on the prophet's ability to envision the distant future.

Isaiah, son of Amoz, is considered the greatest of all the Hebrew prophets. He lived in Jerusalem and had two sons with a woman whom he called the prophetess.

It is likely that he was a member of the nobility, perhaps even related to the royal family. According to a rabbinical tradition, Isaiah was a nephew of King Amaziah of Judah. Although Isaiah freely moved in the court and advised kings, his sympathies did not lie with the aristocrats, the upper classes, or the rich, but with the poor, the oppressed, the widows, the orphans, the victims of injustice and exploitation.

According to chapter 6 of the book of Isaiah (Isaiah 6:1), the prophet's call started the year that King Uzziah died, approximately in the year 633 B.C., when, having a vision of God sitting upon a throne, Isaiah cried that he was unworthy, "a man of unclean lips". Seraphim flew to him and purified his mouth with a burning coal. Isaiah heard the voice of God asking, "Whom shall I send?" and he answered, "Here I am, send me".

Isaiah's ministry began, at a time of prosperity in Judah, when comfort and luxury were accompanied by corruption, injustice, exploitation of the poor, evil doing, and idolatry. Politically, the country was threatened by the powerful Assyrian army, but the prophet considered that the real threat to Judah was not the might of Assyria, but the nation's sins, disobedience toward God, and lack of trust in him.

During the reign of King Ahaz of Judah, Rezin, king of Aram, and Pekah, king of Israel, invaded Judah and besieged Jerusalem, but they could not capture the city. Rezin and Pekah wanted to depose the king and install a certain son of Tabeal in his place (Isaiah 7:6). The prophet Isaiah went with his son Shearjashub to meet King Ahaz, and he told him not to fear, and that the invaders would not succeed.

During the reign of King Hezekiah, son of King Ahaz, the Assyrians attacked Judah, took the city of Lachish, and besieged Jerusalem, demanding unconditional surrender. During the siege, the king received powerful moral support from Isaiah. A plague on the Assyrian camp wiped out the invaders, and Jerusalem was thus saved, but the result of the war was that Judah reverted to its vassal status and continued to pay tribute to Assyria.

Not long after that, Hezekiah became seriously ill. Isaiah came to him and told the king that he would die. Hezekiah prayed to God, and God granted him another fifteen years of life. Isaiah placed a lump of figs on the king's boil, and the king recovered.

Hezekiah, unconvinced that he had recovered, asked Isaiah that, as a sign that God would heal him, the prophet should make the shadow in the dial of Ahaz to go back ten degrees. Isaiah prayed to God, and the miracle was done.

Berodachbaladan, king of Babylon, hearing that the king of Judah was very sick, sent messengers to Jerusalem with letters and gifts to King Hezekiah, to wish him a speedy recovery. Hezekiah naively gave the Babylonian ambassadors a tour of his palace and the treasure house, and he showed them all his treasures. He disregarded the Babylonians as a possible threat, because to him, Babylon was a far-away country.

The prophet Isaiah berated him, saying that, one day, the Babylonians would destroy Judah, and everything in the palace would be carried off to Babylon.

Isaiah taught by words, such as giving his sons the symbolic names Shearjashub, *A remnant will return*, and Mahershalalhashbaz, *Speed-spoil-hasten-plunder*, and by deeds, such as going naked and barefoot for three years to symbolize what the Assyrians would do to Egypt.

A rabbinical tradition states that Isaiah was killed by King Manasseh.

The essential doctrines of Isaiah are an emphasis on the holiness of God; a total reliance on God, rejecting human schemes, as the means of working out the destiny of Israel; faith in Jerusalem, as the city of God, and its proclamation, as the site of the future universal acceptance of God by the nations; a belief that a messianic king would bring a reign of justice and peace; a remnant of Israel would survive from the doom, brought by God's punishment; and ritual religious observance without justice and ethical morality becomes an abomination in the eyes of God.

His message said that God would come in fierce anger to punish Israel and the nations, and only a remnant would survive, war would be abolished, and the nations would turn to peace. A messiah, descendant of David, will come to defend the poor against their oppressors and establish a reign of righteousness and truth, where even the beasts will coexist in peace and gentleness.

Immanuel—a symbolic name given by the prophet Isaiah to a child who would be born to the royal house of David, and who would reject evil and choose good—is considered by Christian theologians as a prophecy concerning the birth of Jesus, based on the Greek rendering of the Hebrew word "alma", which means *young woman*, as "parthenos", which means *virgin.*

Three other prophets preached, during that same period, the latter half of the 8th century B.C.—Amos, Hosea, and Micah—but there is no evidence in the Bible that any of them knew in person any of the others. Although they were apart and alone, Isaiah and Amos share the same lines of thought, with the main difference being that Amos addressed the northern kingdom of Israel, while Isaiah preached in Judah.

The second Isaiah—or Deutero-Isaiah, chapters 40 to 66—was, according to the scholarly theory, an unnamed prophet, who lived, during the time of Cyrus, and whose prophecies reflect the experience and events of the Babylonian Exile. According to some scholars, these chapters are the expression of Isaiah's prophetic visions of the distant future.

Iscah

(Hebrew origin: *Who watches*)

(Genesis 11:29). 19th century B.C. Iscah was a daughter of Haran, the brother of Abram and Nahor. Her brother was Lot, and her sister was Milcah.

Iscariot

(Hebrew origin: *Inhabitant of Kerioth*)

(Matthew 10:4). A.D. 1st century. Iscariot was the surname of Judas, the disciple who betrayed Jesus. (Please see the entry for Judas #2.)

Ishbah

(Hebrew origin: *He will praise*)

(1 Chronicles 4:17). Unspecified date. Ishbah, a descendant of Judah, was the founder of Eshtemoa.

Ishbak

(Hebrew origin: *He will leave*)

(Genesis 25:2). 19th century B.C. Ishbak was one of the six sons of Keturah, the woman whom Abraham married, after the death of Sarah. His brothers were Zimran, Jokshan, Medan, Midian, and Shuah.

Shortly before Abraham died, he made Isaac his sole heir, and, in order to avoid trouble, he donated gifts to the sons of his second marriage and sent them away to the east.

Ishbibenob

(Hebrew origin: *Resides in Nob*)

(2 Samuel 21:16). 10th century B.C. Ishbibenob was a giant Philistine who, during a battle, tried to kill David with a new sword. Abishai killed the giant and saved the king's life. Because of his close brush with death, David's men told him that he should not go out to battle anymore.

Ishbosheth

(Hebrew origin: *Man of shame*)

(2 Samuel 2:8). 11th century B.C. Ishbosheth was the fourth son of King Saul and the last member of his family to reign in Israel.

His real name was Eshbaal (1 Chronicles 8:33), *Man of Baal*. The word "Baal", which means *Master* or *Lord* in Hebrew, was origi-

nally a title of dignity. Eventually, it became associated to a Canaanite god, causing the ancient Hebrew editors of the Bible to substitute the word "Bosheth", meaning *Shame* for "Baal".

Ishbosheth's three brothers—Jonathan, Malchishua, and Abinadab—died in Mount Gilboa, fighting with their father against the Philistines.

Abner, the commander of the army and the real ruler of the country, after the death of Saul, brought the forty-year-old Ishbosheth to Mahanaim and made him king over all the tribes with the exception of the tribe of Judah, who recognized David as its ruler.

Ishbosheth made the fatal error of accusing Abner of having made love to Rizpah, a woman who had been one of King Saul's concubines. Making love to the present or past concubine of a king was interpreted, in ancient Israel, as a symbolic attempt to usurp power, reminiscent of the episode, when Absalom made love to the ten concubines, whom David, in his flight from Jerusalem, had left behind to take care of the palace.

Abner became very angry and said, "Am I a dog's head? I have served loyally the House of Saul your father, and have not betrayed you into the hands of David! And you are accusing me over this woman! May God punish Abner if I don't make David king over Israel and Judah!" Ishbosheth remained speechless, because he feared Abner.

Abner went with twenty men to speak with David in Hebron. During their meeting, Abner promised that he would rally the entire nation around David. Joab murdered him at the city's gate in revenge for the death of his brother Asahel, who had been killed by Abner.

The death of Abner weakened the position of Ishbosheth. Two of his captains—Baanah and his brother Rechab, sons of Rimmon from Beeroth—came to the king's palace at noontime, found Ishbosheth lying on his bed, beheaded him, and brought his head to David in Hebron, expecting to be rewarded.

David's reaction was not what the two murderers had expected. He said to them, "The man who told me that Saul was dead thought that he was bringing me good news. Instead of rewarding him, I had him killed. How much more then, when wicked men have killed a blameless man in bed in his own house?! I will avenge his blood on you, and I will rid the earth of you!"

He ordered his men to kill the murderers, cut off their hands and feet, and hang them up by the pool in Hebron. The head of Ishbosheth was buried in the sepulcher of Abner in Hebron.

Ishi

(Hebrew origin: *Saving*)

1. (1 Chronicles 2:31). Unspecified date. Ishi, a descendant of Judah, was the son of Appaim and the father of Sheshan.
2. (1 Chronicles 4:20). Unspecified date. Ishi, a descendant of Judah, was the father of Zoheth and Benzoheth.
3. (1 Chronicles 4:42). 8th century B.C. Ishi, a descendant of Simeon, was the father of Pelatiah, Neariah, Rephaiah, and Uzziel. His sons, during the reign of Hezekiah, king of Judah, went to Mount Seir, southeast of the Dead Sea, with a force of five hundred men, destroyed the remnant of the Amalekites, and settled there.
4. (1 Chronicles 5:24). 8th century B.C. Ishi, of the half tribe of Manasseh, who had settled east of the Jordan River, was a mighty warrior and leader of his clan.

   His tribe was deported from their land by the Assyrians and forcibly settled in the region of the river Gozan, where it eventually assimilated into the local population and disappeared from history, being remembered today as one of the "ten lost tribes".

Ishiah

(Hebrew origin: *God will lend*)

(1 Chronicles 7:3). Unspecified date. Ishiah, son of Izrahiah, a descendant of Tola, was the leader of a clan of the tribe of Issachar. His brothers were Michael, Obadiah, and Joel.

Ishijah

(Hebrew origin: *God will lend*)

(Ezra 10:31). 5th century B.C. Ishijah, a descendant of Harim, divorced his foreign wife, during the days of Ezra.

Ishma

(Hebrew origin: *Desolate*)

(1 Chronicles 4:3). Unspecified date. Ishma, a descendant of Judah, was the son of the founder of Etam and the brother of Jezreel, Idbash, and their sister Hazelelponi.

Ishmael

(Hebrew origin: *God hears*)

1. (Genesis 16:11). 19th century B.C. Ishmael was the son of Abraham and his Egyptian concubine Hagar, Sarah's maid.

   When Hagar became pregnant, she behaved insolently toward Sarah, who in return treated her harshly. Hagar fled into the desert where an angel appeared to her and announced that she would have a son to be called Ishmael, because God had heard her affliction, who would grow to be a wild man, his hand against every man, and the hand of every man against him. Hagar returned to her mistress and, in due course, gave birth to Ishmael, Abraham being eighty-six years old at that time.

   Thirteen years later, God appeared to Abraham and announced that Sarah would have a son, with whom God would establish an everlasting covenant, and that Ishmael would also be blessed and would be the ancestor of a great nation. God commanded Abraham to circumcise himself, Ishmael, and all the males in his household.

   A year later, Sarah gave birth to a son, who was named Isaac. One day, Sarah, seeing Ishmael, the son of Hagar, mocking, demanded from Abraham that he should send away the slave girl and her son, and that he should declare Isaac as his sole heir.

   Abraham, who loved Ishmael, did not want to yield to Sarah's demand, but God told him to do what she said, reassuring him that his descendants through Ishmael would also become a great nation. Abraham rose early in the morning, gave Hagar some bread and water, and sent her away with the boy.

Hagar and Ishmael wandered in the wilderness of Beersheba. After they had finished all the water in the bottle, Hagar, not wanting to see her son die of thirst, placed him under a shrub and moved some distance away, crying and lamenting. God heard her cries and sent an angel, who told her not to fear, and that her son would grow up to be the ancestor of a great nation. God opened her eyes, and she saw a well of water nearby. She filled the water bottle and gave the lad a drink.

Ishmael grew in the wilderness, became a skilled archer, and married an Egyptian girl whom Hagar chose for him.

When his father Abraham died at the age of one hundred and seventy-five, he and his half brother Isaac buried him in the cave of Machpelah, next to Sarah.

Ishmael had twelve sons: Nebajoth, Kedar, Adbeel, Mibsam, Mishma, Dumah, Massa, Hadad, Tema, Jetur, Naphish, and Kedemah, all of them ancestors of great nations. His daughter Mahalath—also called Bashemath—married Esau, the son of Isaac.

Ishmael died at the age of one hundred and thirty-seven.

2. (2 Kings 25:23). 6th century B.C. Ishmael, a member of the royal family of Judah, son of Nethaniah and grandson of Elishama, was a captain of the Judean army, defeated by the Babylonians.

He and a group of other commanders and their men went to the city of Mizpah to meet with Gedaliah, son of Ahikam, who had been appointed governor of Judah by the Babylonians. Gedaliah told them that everything would be well with them if they would serve the king of Babylon.

Baalis, king of the Ammonites, plotted with Ishmael to assassinate Gedaliah, whom they considered a Babylonian collaborator. Johanan, the son of Kareah,

heard of this plot and went to Mizpah, to warn Gedaliah that Ishmael wanted to kill him, and he volunteered to kill Ishmael first. Gedaliah did not believe him and accused him of lying.

Two months later, what Johanan had warned came to pass. Ishmael came to Mizpah with ten men and, during dinner, murdered Gedaliah and all the Jews and Babylonians who were with the governor.

The next day, a group of eighty pilgrims from Shechem, Shiloh, and Samaria came with their beards shaven, their clothes torn, bleeding from cuts that they had inflicted themselves, carrying offerings and incense for the Temple. Ishmael came out of the city to meet them, weeping as he went. When he met them, he asked them to come to Gedaliah. As soon as they arrived into the city, Ishmael murdered them and threw the bodies into a pit. He spared only ten men who promised him stores of wheat, barley, oil, and honey.

Ishmael forced the people, who were left in Mizpah, including the royal princesses, to depart with him to Ammon. Johanan, the son of Kareah, who was horrified when he heard what Ishmael had done, pursued him, until he caught up with him at the pool of Gibeon. As soon as the prisoners saw Johanan, they broke free and joined him.

Ishmael and eight of his men managed to escape and found refuge with the Ammonites. Johanan, fearing Babylonian vengeance, fled to Egypt with the surviving Jews and took the prophet Jeremiah with him.

3. (1 Chronicles 8:38). Unspecified date. Ishmael was one of the six sons of Azel, son of Eleasah of the tribe of Benjamin, a descendant of King Saul. His brothers were Bocheru, Azrikam, Sheariah, Obadiah, and Hanan.

4. (2 Chronicles 19:11). 9th century B.C. His son Zebadiah was the top official in the royal court, during the reign of King Jehoshaphat, in charge of the "king's matters".

5. (2 Chronicles 23:1). 9th century B.C. Ishmael, son of Jehohanan, was one of the five army commanders who joined the conspiracy, headed by Jehoiada the Priest, to overthrow Queen Athaliah and crown Joash as king of Judah.

6. (Ezra 10:22). 5th century B.C. Ishmael, a priest, was a descendant of Pashur, who divorced his foreign wife, during the days of Ezra.

Ishmaiah

(Hebrew origin: *God will hear*)

(1 Chronicles 27:19). 10th century B.C. Ishmaiah, son of Obadiah, was the leader of the tribe of Zebulun, during the reign of King David.

Ishmerai

(Hebrew origin: *God guards*)

(1 Chronicles 8:18). Unspecified date. Ishmerai, son of Elpaal, was a Benjamite, leader of a clan that lived in Jerusalem.

Ishod

(Hebrew origin: *Man of renown*)

(1 Chronicles 7:18). Unspecified date. Ishod, a descendant of Manasseh, was the brother of Abiezer and Mahalah. His mother was Hammoleketh, the sister of Gilead.

Ishpan

(Hebrew origin: *He will hide*)

(1 Chronicles 8:22). Unspecified date. Ishpan, son of Shashak, was a leader of the tribe of Benjamin who lived in Jerusalem.

Ishuah

(Hebrew origin: *Level*)

(Genesis 46:17). 17th century B.C. Ishuah, son of Asher and grandson of Jacob, was among the seventy Israelites who immigrated to Egypt, together with his sister Serah; his brothers Jimnah, Isui, and Beriah; and his nephews, Heber and Malchiel, sons of Beriah. His name is spelled Isuah in the first book of Chronicles (1 Chronicles 7:30).

Ishuai

(Hebrew origin: *Level*)

(1 Chronicles 7:30). 17th century B.C. Ishuai, son of Asher and grandson of Jacob, was among the seventy Israelites who immigrated to Egypt, together with his sister Serah; his brothers Jimnah, Isuah, and Beriah; and his nephews, Heber and Malchiel, sons of Beriah. His name is spelled Isui in the book of Genesis (Genesis 46:17).

Ishui

(Hebrew origin: *Level*)

(1 Samuel 14:49). 11th century B.C. Ishui—also called Abinadab (1 Samuel 31:2)—the second son of King Saul, died together with his brothers Jonathan and Melchishua, fighting in Mount Gilboa against the Philistines.

Ismachiah

(Hebrew origin: *God will sustain*)

(2 Chronicles 31:13). 8th century B.C. Ismachiah was one of the Levites who were named by King Hezekiah to serve under Cononiah and Shimei, as supervisors of the gifts, tithes, and offerings, brought by the people to the Temple.

Ismaiah

(Hebrew origin: *God will hear*)

(1 Chronicles 12:4). 11th century B.C. Ismaiah, the Gibeonite, was the leader of a group of thirty Benjamite warriors who deserted King Saul's army and joined David's band at Ziklag. They were skilled fighters who could use both their right and left hands to shoot arrows and sling stones.

Ispah

(Hebrew origin: *He will scratch*)

(1 Chronicles 8:16). Unspecified date. Ispah, son of Beriah, was a Benjamite, leader of a clan, who lived in Jerusalem.

Israel

(Hebrew origin: *Prevails with God*)

(Genesis 32:28). 18th century B.C. This is the name that a mysterious man or angel gave to Jacob, after wrestling with him, during the night.

As the dawn broke, the man asked Jacob to let him go. Jacob refused, unless the man would bless him. The man told him that, from then on, his name would be Israel, because he had fought with God and men, and he had prevailed. Since then, Israel is the name, by which, Jacob's descendants are known. (Please see the entry for Jacob [Genesis 25:26].)

Issachar

(Hebrew origin: *He will bring a reward*)

1. (Genesis 30:18). 17th century B.C. Issachar, the ancestor of the tribe of Issachar, was the ninth son of Jacob and the fifth son of Leah.

   Issachar was the full brother of Judah, Reuben, Levi, Simeon, and Zebulun, sons of Leah. His half brothers were Gad and Asher, sons of Zilpah; Dan and Naphtali, sons of Bilhah; and Benjamin and Joseph, sons of Rachel. His sister was Dinah, daughter of Leah.

   Before his birth, Leah, convinced that she was no longer capable of having children, had given her maid Zilpah to Jacob as a concubine, so that she could have a child by her. One day, Reuben, Leah's eldest son, brought some mandrakes from the field and gave them to his mother. Rachel saw the mandrakes and said to Leah, "Please give me some of your son's mandrakes".

   Leah answered, "Is it not enough that you have taken my husband? You must also take my son's mandrakes?"

   Rachel replied, "He will lie with you tonight, in return for your son's mandrakes".

That evening, when Jacob returned from working in the field, Leah told him, "You are to come with me tonight, because I have hired you with my son's mandrakes". That night, Leah conceived, and, when the time came, she gave birth to Issachar, calling him by that name, because, she said, "God had rewarded me for having given my maid to my husband".

Gad and his brothers were involved in the events that led to Joseph being taken as a slave to Egypt. (For the detailed story of Joseph and his brothers, please see the entry for Joseph.)

Years later, when there was a famine in the land, he and his brothers were sent, by Jacob, to Egypt to buy corn. Joseph, now the second most powerful man in the country, recognized them, forgave them, and invited them to settle in Egypt.

Issachar and his sons—Tola, Phuvah, Job, and Shimron—were among the seventy Israelites who immigrated to Egypt. They arrived in Goshen, and Joseph came to them in his chariot. He greeted his father, embraced him, and wept for a long time.

Seventeen years later, Jacob, feeling that he would soon die, called his sons to bless them and tell them what would happen to them in the future. He said, "Issachar is a strong donkey, couching down between two burdens".

Jacob's last words were to ask them to bury him in the cave of Machpelah, where Abraham, Sarah, Isaac, Rebekah, and Leah were buried. Jacob's body was accompanied in his last trip by his sons, their children, flocks and herds, all the officials of Pharaoh and members of his court, chariots and horsemen. Before crossing the Jordan, the funeral procession made a stop and mourned Jacob for seven days. Then, Judah and his brothers took him to Canaan and buried him in the cave of Machpelah.

After burying their father, they all returned to Canaan. Joseph's brothers feared that, with Jacob now dead, Joseph would pay them back for the wrong that they had done to him.

They sent a message to Joseph, saying that Jacob, before his death, had told them to urge Joseph to forgive them. Judah and his brothers came to Joseph, flung themselves before him, and told him that they were prepared to be his slaves.

Joseph answered kindly, "Do not fear! Although you intended me harm, God intended it all for good, to assure the survival of many people. Don't worry; I will take care of you and your children".

Centuries later, when Moses blessed the tribes in his farewell speech, he said, "Rejoice Issachar in thy tents".

When Joshua conquered Canaan, the tribe of Issachar settled in the valley of Jezreel and the surrounding regions.

During the 10th century B.C. one of Issachar's descendants, Baasha, son of Ahijah, killed King Nadab of Israel and reigned in his place.

The tribe of Issachar was among the Israelites exiled by the Assyrians in the 8th century B.C. They assimilated into the local populations and disappeared from history as one of the "ten lost tribes".

2. (1 Chronicles 26:5). 10th century B.C. Issachar, the seventh son of Obededom, was, like his father and brothers, a gatekeeper of the Tabernacle, during the reign of King David. His brothers were Ammiel, Shemaiah, Jehozabad, Joah, Sacar, Nethaneel, and Peulthai.

Isshiah

(Hebrew origin: *God will lend*)

(1 Chronicles 24:21). 10th century B.C. Isshiah, a descendant of Rehabiah and father of Zechariah, was a Levite in the service of the Tabernacle, during the reign of King David. His brother was called Michah.

Isuah

(Hebrew origin: *Level*)

(1 Chronicles 7:30). 17th century B.C. Isuah, son of Asher and grandson of Jacob, was one of the seventy Israelites who immigrated to Egypt, together with his sister Serah; his brothers Jimnah, Isui, and Beriah; and his nephews, Heber and Malchiel, sons of Beriah. His name is spelled Ishuah in the book of Genesis (Genesis 46:17).

Isui

(Hebrew origin: *Level*)

(Genesis 46:17).17th century B.C. Isui, son of Asher and grandson of Jacob, was one of the seventy Israelites who immigrated to Egypt, together with his sister Serah; his brothers Jimnah, Isuah, and Beriah; and his nephews, Heber and Malchiel, sons of Beriah. His name is spelled Ishuai in the first book of Chronicles (1 Chronicles 7:30).

Ithai

(Hebrew origin: *God is with me*)

(1 Chronicles 11:31). 10th century B.C. Ithai, a Benjamite, the son of Ribai of Gibeah, was one of "The Thirty", an elite group in King David's army. He is called Ittai in the second book of Samuel (2 Samuel 23:29).

Ithamar

(Hebrew origin: *Island of the palm tree*)

(Exodus 6:23). 13th century B.C. Ithamar, the fourth son of Aaron and Elisheba, was in charge of recording the gifts brought for the erection of the Tabernacle.

Nadab and Abihu, the two eldest brothers, died childless, before their father. Eleazar, the third brother, was named High Priest, when Aaron died, and became the ancestor of the main priestly line.

Ithamar was also the ancestor of a line of priests, but it was smaller than the line descended from Eleazar. The last descendant of Ithamar mentioned in the Bible was a priest named Daniel, who returned with Ezra from the Babylonian Exile.

Ithiel

(Hebrew origin: *God is with me*)

1. (Nehemiah 11:7). Unspecified date. Ithiel, son of Jesaiah and father of Maaseiah, was an ancestor of Sallu, a Benjamite who settled in Jerusalem, after his return from the Babylonian Exile.
2. (Proverbs 30:1). Unspecified date. Ithiel was one of the two men—the other was Ucal—to whom Agur, the son of Jakeh, spoke his proverbs.

Ithmah

(Hebrew origin: *Orphanage*)

(1 Chronicles 11:46). 10th century B.C. Ithmah, a Moabite, was one of the brave warriors in King David's army.

Ithra

(Hebrew origin: *Wealth*)

(2 Samuel 17:25). 11th century B.C. Ithra, an Israelite—called Jether, the Ishmaelite, in the first book of Chronicles (1 Chronicles 2:17)—was married to Abigail, King David's sister. Their son was Amasa, the commander of Absalom's army, who died at the hands of Joab.

Ithran

(Hebrew origin: *Excellent*)

1. (Genesis 36:26). 18th century B.C. Ithran was the son of Dishon and nephew of Aholibamah, Esau's wife. His brothers were Eshban, Cheran, and Hemdan—called Amram in the first book of Chronicles (1 Chronicles 1:41).
2. (1 Chronicles 7:37). Unspecified date. Ithran, son of Zophah, was a brave warrior, leader of a clan of the tribe of Asher.

Ithream

(Hebrew origin: *Excellent people*)

(2 Samuel 3:5). 10th century B.C. Ithream, who was born in Hebron, was King David's sixth son. His mother was Eglah. He probably died in childhood, as his birth is the only fact that the Bible mentions about him.

Ittai

(Hebrew origin: *God is with me*)

1. (2 Samuel 15:19). 10th century B.C. Ittai the Gittite was one of the commanders of David's army. Although he was a foreigner, a Philistine, his loyalty to David was exemplary. During Absalom's rebellion, David told him that he, as a foreigner and an exile, could go back to Jerusalem. Ittai refused to leave David, declaring that, in life or death, he would remain with the king.

   The king placed him in charge of one-third of the army—the other two commanders were Joab and Abishai—in the battle that defeated the forces of Absalom

2. (2 Samuel 23:29). 10th century B.C. Ittai, a Benjamite, the son of Ribai of Gibeah, was one of "The Thirty", an elite group in King David's army. In the first book of Chronicles, he is called Ithai (1 Chronicles 11:31).

Izehar

(Hebrew origin: *Oil*)

(Numbers 3:19). 14th century B.C. Izehar, son of Kohath and grandson of Levi, was the ancestor of the Levite clan of Izeharites. His brothers were Hebron, Uzziel, and Amram, the father of Miriam, Aaron, and Moses. His sons were Nepheg, Zichri, and Korah, who led a rebellion against Moses and Aaron.

He is called Izhar in the book of Exodus (Exodus 6:18), and Amminadab in the first book of Chronicles (1 Chronicles 6:22).

Izhar

(Hebrew origin: *Oil*)

(Exodus 6:18). 14th century B.C. Izhar, son of Kohath and grandson of Levi, was the ancestor of the Levite clan of Izharites. His brothers were Hebron, Uzziel, and Amram, the father of Miriam, Aaron, and Moses. His sons were Korah—who led a rebellion against Moses and Aaron—Nepheg, and Zichri.

He is called Izehar in the book of Numbers (Numbers 3:19), and Amminadab in the first book of Chronicles (1 Chronicles 6:22).

Izrahiah

(Hebrew origin: *God will shine*)

(1 Chronicles 7:3). Unspecified date. Izrahiah, the son of Uzzi and grandson of Tola, was the father of Michael, Obadiah, Ishiah, and Joel. He and his sons were leaders of the tribe of Issachar.

Izri

(Hebrew origin: *Form*)

(1 Chronicles 25:11). 10th century B.C. Izri—called Zeri in the first book of Chronicles (1 Chronicles 25:3)—was in charge of the fourth turn of service to play musical instruments in the House of God.

His father Jeduthun, a Levite, was one of the three leading musicians—the other two were Asaph and Heman—during the reign of David.

Aholibamah, one of Esau's wives, in Canaan, before the family moved to Edom, where the brothers became heads of clans.

Jaakan

(Hebrew origin: *Tortuous*)

(Deuteronomy 10:6). Unspecified date. Jaakan was the son of Ezer, leader of a clan of Horites, descendant of Seir, who lived in the land of Edom. Alternative spellings are Akan (Genesis 36:27) and Jakan (1 Chronicles 1:42).

Jaakobah

(Hebrew origin: *Heel catcher*)

(1 Chronicles 4:36). 8th century B.C. Jaakobah was one of the leaders from the tribe of Simeon who, during the reign of Hezekiah, king of Judah, went to the fertile valley of Gedor, destroyed the tents of the people—descendants of Ham—who lived there, wiped them out forever, and settled in their place, because there was pasture there for their flocks.

Jaala

(Hebrew origin: *Wild goat*)

(Nehemiah 7:58). 10th century B.C. Jaala, a servant of Solomon, was the ancestor of a family that returned with Zerubbabel from the Babylonian Exile. His name is spelled Jaalah in the book of Ezra (Ezra 2:56).

Jaalah

(Hebrew origin: *Wild goat*)

(Ezra 2:56). 10th century B.C. Jaalah, a servant of Solomon, was the ancestor of a family that returned with Zerubbabel from the Babylonian Exile. His name is spelled Jaala in the book of Nehemiah (Nehemiah 7:58).

Jaalam

(Hebrew origin: *Occult*)

(Genesis 36:5). 18th century B.C. Jaalam, Jeush, and Korah were the three sons born to

Jaanai

(Hebrew origin: *Responsive*)

(1 Chronicles 5:12). Unspecified date. Jaanai was a leader of the tribe of Gad who lived in the region of Bashan, in the other side of the river Jordan.

Jaareoregim

(Hebrew origin: *Wood of weavers*)

(2 Samuel 21:19). 10th century B.C. Jaareoregim was the father of Elhanan, a Bethlehemite who killed Lahmi, the brother of Goliath, the Philistine giant, in the battle of Gob. The first book of Chronicles calls him Jair (1 Chronicles 20:5).

Jaasau

(Hebrew origin: *They will do*)

(Ezra 10:37). 5th century B.C. Jaasau, a descendant of Bani, divorced his foreign wife, during the days of Ezra.

Jaasiel

(Hebrew origin: *Made by God*)

(1 Chronicles 27:21). 10th century B.C. Jaasiel, son of Abner, the commander of Saul's army, was a leader of the tribe of Benjamin, during the reign of King David.

Jaazaniah

(Hebrew origin: *May God hear*)

1. (2 Kings 25:23). 6th century B.C. Jaazaniah—called Jezaniah in the book of Jeremiah (Jeremiah 40:8)—son of Hoshaiah, was an officer of the defeated Judean army. He came with a group of other commanders and their men to the city of Mizpah to meet with Gedaliah, son of Ahikam, who had been appointed governor of Judah by the Babylonians.

Gedaliah told them that everything would be well with them if they would serve the king of Babylon.

Sometime later, Ishmael murdered Gedaliah. Afraid of the Babylonians' revenge, Jaazaniah and Johanan, the son of Kareah, asked Jeremiah to pray to God on behalf of the survivors, and to ask him where they should go and what they should do.

After ten days, Jeremiah told them that God wanted them to remain in the land of Israel, and to be unafraid of the Babylonians. The people led by the officials, including Azariah, Jaazaniah's brother, screamed at the prophet that he was lying and forced him to go with them to Egypt.

2. (Jeremiah 35:3). 6th century B.C. Jaazaniah was the son of a man called Jeremiah and the grandson of Habaziniah. He and other members of the clan of the Rechabites were brought by the prophet Jeremiah to one of the chambers of the Temple, where he offered them wine.

They refused to drink, because their ancestor, Jonadab, son of Rechab, had forbidden them to drink wine. Jeremiah praised the Rechabites to the men of Jerusalem as an example to follow of people who keep their commandments and principles.

3. (Ezekiel 8:11). 6th century B.C. Jaazaniah, son of Shaphan, was one of the seventy elders seen in a vision, by the prophet Ezekiel, committing abominations, because they believed that God did not see them, and that God had forsaken the earth.

4. (Ezekiel 11:1). 6th century B.C. Jaazaniah, son of Azur, was a leader of the people and a false prophet. Jaazaniah was seen in a vision by the prophet Ezekiel, standing at the east gate of the Temple, falsely telling the people that Jerusalem would not be destroyed.

Jaaziah
(Hebrew origin: *May God strengthen*)

(1 Chronicles 24:26). 10th century B.C. Jaaziah, a Levite, was a descendant of Merari. His

sons—Beno, Shoham, Zaccur, and Ibri—served in the Tabernacle, during the reign of David.

Jaaziel
(Hebrew origin: *May God strengthen*)

(1 Chronicles 15:18). 10th century B.C. Jaaziel, a Levite of the second rank, was one of those chosen by the chief of the Levites to sing and play musical instruments in front of the Ark of the Covenant, during the reign of King David. He is also called Aziel (1 Chronicles 15:20).

Jabal
(Hebrew origin: *Stream*)

(Genesis 4:20). Antediluvian. Jabal, son of Lamech and Adah, was the ancestor of the tribes that lived in tents and raised cattle. His brother Jubal was the ancestor of the musicians who played the harp and the organ.

Jabesh
(Hebrew origin: *Dry*)

(2 Kings 15:10). 8th century B.C. His son Shallum murdered King Zachariah of Israel, thus, putting an end to the hundred-year-old Jehu dynasty. After reigning for only one month, Shallum was murdered and succeeded by Menahem.

Jabez
(Hebrew origin: *Sorrowful*)

(1 Chronicles 4:9). Unspecified date. Jabez, of the tribe of Judah, is described by the Bible as being more honorable than his brothers. His mother gave him the name of Jabez, because, she said, "I bore him with sorrow". Jabez prayed to God to bless him and keep him from evil, and God granted him his wish.

Jabin
(Hebrew origin: *Understands*)

1. (Joshua 11:1). 12th century B.C. Jabin, king of Hazor, the most powerful

Canaanite city kingdom, organized a confederation of armies to fight against the Israelites, led by Joshua.

The battle took place by the waters of Meron and resulted in a complete defeat for the confederated armies. Joshua then took Hazor, killed the king, and burned the city down.

2. (Judges 4:2). 12th century B.C. Jabin, king of Hazor, a namesake of the previous entry and probably his descendant, sent his army under the command of Sisera to fight against the Israelites. Sisera was defeated by Deborah and Barak and was later killed by Jael, the wife of Heber the Kenite.

Jachan

(Hebrew origin: *Troublesome*)

(1 Chronicles 5:13). Unspecified date. Jachan was a leader of the tribe of Gad who lived in the land of Bashan. His brothers were Michael, Meshullam, Sheba, Jorai, Zia, and Heber.

Jachin

(Hebrew origin: *Established*)

1. (Genesis 46:10). 17th century B.C. Jachin, fourth son of Simeon and grandson of Jacob, was one of the seventy Israelites who immigrated to Egypt. In the first book of Chronicles, he is called Jarib (1 Chronicles 4:24). Jachin was the ancestor of the clan of the Jachinites. His brothers were Jemuel, Jamin, Ohad, Zohar, and Shaul.
2. (1 Chronicles 9:10). 10th century B.C. During the reign of King David, the priestly service in the Tabernacle was divided by lot into twenty-four turns. Jachin was in charge of the twenty-first turn (1 Chronicles 24:17).
3. (Nehemiah 11:10). 5th century B.C. Jachin was a priest, living in Jerusalem, during the days of Nehemiah.

Jacob

(Hebrew origin: *Supplanter*)

(Genesis 25:26). 18th century B.C. Jacob, also called Israel, son of Isaac and Rebekah and grandson of Abraham, was the third Hebrew patriarch and the traditional ancestor of the people of Israel.

During Rebekah's pregnancy, she felt the babies struggling in her womb, and she was told by the Lord that each of the boys would become the progenitor of a nation, but that the older would serve the younger. Esau was born first, red and hairy, and, moments later, Jacob came out, holding Esau's heel.

Esau, his father's favorite, grew up to be a skilled hunter, a simple fellow, an outdoor man, impetuous, impatient, and easily manipulated by his shrewd brother. Jacob, his mother's favorite, was completely his opposite: a patient, thoughtful, stay-at-home type.

One day, Esau returned famished from the field and saw that Jacob was cooking a soup of red lentils. He said to Jacob, "I am starving! Give me some of that red stuff!"

Jacob said, "First, sell me your birthright".

"I am at the point of death, so what use is my birthright to me?" replied Esau.

"Swear to me first", said Jacob. Esau swore and sold his birthright to his brother. Jacob then gave him bread and lentil soup. Esau ate and drank, and then, he went away.

Esau married at the age of forty, the same age of his father, Isaac, when he married Rebekah. His wives, two Hittite women called Judith and Bashemath, did all they could to make life miserable for Isaac and Rebekah.

Years went by, Isaac, now grown old and blind, decided to bless his eldest son, but first, he would eat. He called Esau and told him, "I am old, and I may die any day. Take your weapons, bow and arrows, go out to the fields, and hunt me some venison. Then, prepare it the way I like it, and bring it to me to eat, so that I may give you my soul's blessing, before I die".

Rebekah overheard the conversation and devised a plan, by which Jacob would receive Isaac's blessing.

She said to Jacob, "Bring me two young goats from the flock and I will prepare a delicious meal for your father. You will take it to your father, he will eat it, and he will bless you, before he dies".

Jacob said, "But Esau, my brother, is a hairy man, and I am smooth skinned. My father might touch me, and when he realizes that I am deceiving him, he will curse me, not bless me!"

Rebekah tried to calm him, "Your curse will be upon me, my son. Just go, fetch the goats, and do what I say".

Jacob went to the flock, picked up two goats, and brought them back to his mother. She cooked them the way Isaac liked.

Rebekah took the best clothes of her older son Esau, and Jacob put them on. She took the skin of the goats and put them on his hands and neck. Then, she gave him the dish and the bread that she had prepared. Jacob took them to his father and said, "Father".

Isaac answered, "I am here. Which of my sons are you?"

"I am Esau, your firstborn. I have done as you told me. Please sit up and eat of my venison, that you may bless me".

"How did you find it so quickly, my son?" asked Isaac.

"Because the Lord, your God, brought it to me", answered Jacob.

"Please come closer so that I may feel you, my son, whether you really are my son Esau, or not".

Jacob drew close to his father, and Isaac touched his hands, which were covered with the goat's skin, and felt as hairy as Esau's.

Feeling confused, Isaac said, "The voice is Jacob's but the hands are the hands of Esau".

"Are you really my son Esau?"

"I am", answered Jacob.

"Come close to me, and I will eat my son's venison, and I will bless him".

Jacob gave the dish and wine to his father, who ate and drank with delight. Isaac said to him, "Come near now, and kiss me, my son". He smelled Jacob's clothing and said, "The smell of my son is like the smell of the fields that God has blessed".

And Isaac blessed Jacob, saying, "God shall give you the dew of heaven, and the fat of the earth, abundance of grain and wine. People

will sever you and nations will bow to you. You will be master over your brothers, and they will bow to you. Cursed is he that curses you, and blessed he that blesses you".

Jacob left his father's presence, and a few minutes later, Esau came in, back from his hunting. He also had cooked a delicious meal, which he brought to his father, and said, "Let my father sit up and eat of his son's venison, so that your soul may bless me". Isaac, bewildered, asked him, "Who are you?"

"I am your son Esau, your firstborn".

Isaac was seized with a violent trembling. "Who was it then", he asked, "that brought me the venison dish? I ate all of it, before you came, and I blessed him. He will remain blessed".

Esau burst into uncontrolled sobbing and said, "Bless me too, Father!" Isaac answered, "Your brother came with deviousness and took away your blessing".

"How rightly was he named Jacob?! He has now supplanted me two times, the first time when he took away my birthright, and now he has taken away my blessing. Don't you have another blessing for me?"

Isaac said, "I have made him master over you and have given him grain and wine. What, then, can I still do for you, my son?"

"Do you only have one blessing, my father? Bless me too, Father!" said Esau in a loud voice and wept.

His father said to him, "Your dwelling shall be the fatness of the earth, and the dew of heaven above. You shall live by your sword, and you shall serve your brother, but one day, you shall break his yoke from your neck".

Furious at Jacob's trickery, Esau made a vow to kill Jacob, as soon as Isaac passed away. Rebekah, to protect Jacob from Esau's revenge, decided to send him away to her brother Laban in Haran.

She went to Isaac and complained, "The Hittite wives of Esau have made my life miserable. If Jacob would also marry a local girl, I wouldn't wish to continue living!"

Isaac called Jacob, blessed him, and said, "You shall not marry any Canaanite girl. Go to Paddan-Aram, to the house of Bethuel, your mother's father, and marry one of the daughters of your uncle Laban".

When Esau learned that Canaanite women displeased his parents, he went to the house of his uncle Ishmael and married his cousin Mahalath, the daughter of Ishmael.

Jacob left Beersheba and set out for Haran. One night, during the long trip from Beersheba to Haran, Jacob went to sleep, using a stone as a pillow. He dreamed that there was a ladder rising up to heaven, with angels going up and down on it. God, standing next to him, said, "I am the Lord, your God, the God of your father Abraham and the God of Isaac. I am giving the land, on which you are lying, to you and your descendants, which will be as numerous as the dust of the earth. All the families in the earth shall bless themselves for you and your descendants. I am with you, I will protect you, wherever you go, and will bring you back to this land".

The next morning, Jacob rose early in the morning, poured oil on the stone that had served him as a pillow, and named the place where he had seen his vision Bethel, *House of God*. He promised that whatever he would receive in the future, he would give a tenth to God.

Upon arriving to Haran, Jacob saw shepherds next to a well and asked them if they knew Laban. They answered that they did, and they added that Rachel, Laban's daughter, was approaching with her father's sheep. Jacob went to the well, rolled the stone from its opening, watered the sheep, kissed Rachel, and wept, when he told her that he was her relative. She ran home and told her father, who came out to see Jacob, embraced him, and brought him to his house.

Four weeks later, during which time Jacob had fallen in love with his beautiful cousin Rachel, Laban said to Jacob, "You are my relative, but you should not work for me for nothing! What shall your wages be?"

Jacob answered, "I will serve you seven years for your younger daughter Rachel".

"It is better that I should give her to you than to an outsider. Stay with me", said Laban.

The seven years that Jacob worked for Laban seemed to him like only a few days, so great was his love for her. When the seven years were over, Jacob told Laban, "Give me Rachel now, because my time has been fulfilled".

Laban made a wedding feast and invited all the people of the place. After the wedding night, Jacob woke up to find that the woman next to him was not Rachel but her older sister Leah. When he complained that he had been deceived, Laban explained that it was the custom of the land that the elder daughter should be married before the younger, but that he would allow Rachel to marry him, a week later, with the condition that Jacob should work another seven years for Laban.

Leah, although unloved by Jacob, became the mother of four boys: Reuben, Simeon, Levi, and Judah. Rachel became envious of her sister and said to Jacob, "Give me children, or I shall die". Jacob was angry and answered, "Can I take the place of God, who has denied you the fruit of your womb?"

Rachel said, "Take my maid Bilhah as a concubine, so that through her, I too may have children". Bilhah had two children, Dan and Naphtali, whom Rachel considered hers.

When Leah saw that she had stopped bearing children, she followed her sister's example and gave her maid Zilpah to Jacob as a concubine. Zilpah gave birth to Gad and Asher, both of whom were born in Paddan-Aram.

One day, Reuben, Leah's oldest son, brought her some mandrakes from the field. Rachel said to Leah, "Please give me some of your son's mandrakes". Leah replied, "Is it not enough for you to take my husband away that you also want my son's mandrakes?"

Rachel answered, "If you give me those mandrakes, I promise that Jacob will spend the night with you". When Jacob came home from the field that evening, Leah went out to meet him and said, "You are to sleep with me, because I have hired you with my son's mandrakes". That night, Leah conceived, and when the time came, she gave birth to Issachar. Later, she gave birth to another son, Zebulun, and a daughter, Dinah.

Much to her surprise, Rachel also got pregnant and gave birth to a son, whom she named Joseph.

When the second seven years period was over, Jacob told Laban, "I wish to return to my own homeland with my wives and children, for whom I have served you".

"I know that God has blessed me for your sake. Name your wages and I will give them to you", said Laban.

"You know how I have served you. You had a small flock, before I came to you, and it has grown tremendously under my care. Now, I have to look out for my own interests", said Jacob.

"What shall I pay you?"

"You don't have to pay me anything. If you agree to my proposal, I will continue to take care of your flock. I will go through all your flock today and remove every speckled, spotted, and brown lamb, and every spotted and speckled goat. That is all the pay I want. In the future, you will easily see if I have been honest. When you come to check my wages, any goat that is not speckled and spotted, and any sheep, which is not brown, you will know that it has been stolen".

"It's a deal", answered Laban. That same day, he removed all the goats that were speckled, spotted, or that had some white in them, and all the brown sheep, and gave them to his sons. He then went away from Jacob as far as he could travel in three days. Jacob took care of the rest of Laban's flock.

Jacob took some green branches of poplar, hazel, and chestnut trees, and stripped off some of the bark, so that the branches had white stripes on them. He placed these branches in front of the flocks, at their drinking troughs, so that they would look at them when they mated, when they came to drink. All the young animals that were born were streaked, speckled, and spotted. In this way, he built up his own flock and became a very wealthy man.

After six years, Jacob, who now owned much cattle, slaves, camels, and donkeys, felt that Laban's sons were jealous of his wealth, and that Laban himself looked at him differently than before.

He called his wives, Leah and Rachel, and said to them, "Your father is not as friendly to me as he used to be. You know that I have worked for your father with all my strength, but he has cheated me and changed my wages ten times. But God was on my side. Whenever Laban said, 'The speckled goats shall be your wages' all the flocks produced speckled young. God told me in a dream that all the male goats that were mating were streaked, speckled, and spotted, because He had seen what Laban was doing to me, and he said, 'Now, get ready and return to the land where you were born'".

Leah and Rachel answered, "There is nothing left for us to inherit from our father. He treats us like strangers. He sold us and has spent all our money. All this wealth that God has taken from our father belongs to us and to our children. Do whatever God has told you".

Jacob gathered all his possessions and his flocks, put his sons and his wives on the camels, and left Paddan-Aram. Rachel secretly took her father's idols, taking advantage that Laban had gone to shear his sheep.

When Laban discovered that Jacob was gone, he and his men set out in pursuit and caught up with Jacob and his family seven days later, near the hills of Gilead. Laban reproached Jacob for taking away his daughters in secret, without letting him say goodbye, or kiss his grandchildren.

"I understand", he said, "that you wish to return to your home, but why did you have to steal my household gods?"

"I was afraid that you might take your daughters away from me. If you find that anyone here has your gods, that person will be put to death", answered Jacob, not knowing that Rachel had stolen the idols. Laban searched the tents but did not find the idols, because Rachel was sitting upon them.

Jacob and Laban made a covenant between them, which they celebrated by gathering stones into a heap, making a sacrifice, and eating. Then, they parted in peace: Laban returned home, and Jacob continued his voyage to Canaan.

On the way, Jacob had a vision of angels welcoming him, and he called the place Mahanaim. He sent messengers to his brother Esau, who was living in Edom, announcing that he was returning from his long sojourn with Laban. The messengers returned, saying that Esau was coming to meet him with four hundred men.

Fearing that Esau wanted to revenge himself, Jacob sent servants to Esau with gifts of goats, rams, camels, bulls, asses, and foals. He made his wives, concubines, and children cross to the other side of the Jabbok River, and stayed behind alone. That night, Jacob wrestled with a mysterious stranger, until, at daybreak, the other tried to get away. Jacob would not let the stranger go, until he received his blessing. The stranger told Jacob that, from then on, he would be called Israel, because he had fought with God and men and had prevailed. And he blessed him. Jacob called the place Peniel, for there, he had seen God face to face. Limping, because the stranger had damaged his hip, Jacob went to join his family.

Esau approached with his troop of four hundred men. Jacob saw him and bowed to the ground seven times. Esau ran to him and embraced him, and both brothers wept.

After Jacob had presented his family to his brother, Esau asked him, "Why did you send me all those animals?"

"To gain my lord's favor", answered Jacob.

"I have enough, my brother; keep what is yours", said Esau.

"No, please! If I have found favor in your eyes, receive my gift; for to see your face is like seeing the face of God, and you have received me with friendship. Please accept my present, because God has favored me, and I have enough".

Jacob urged him, and Esau accepted and said, "And now let's start on our journey".

Jacob answered, "My lord knows that the children are very young, and the flocks and herds are nursing their young. If we would drive them hard for even one day, they would die. Let my lord go on ahead of his servant. I will follow slowly, at the pace of the children and the cattle, until I arrive in Seir".

Esau said, "Let me leave some of my men with you". Jacob answered, "Thank you, but that is not necessary". Esau went back to Seir, and Jacob continued on his journey to Succoth.

Jacob and his family settled near Shechem. Dinah, the daughter of Jacob and Leah, went to the city to visit some Canaanite women. Shechem, son of Hamor, the ruler of the city, saw her, took her, and raped her. He then fell in love with her and spoke to her tenderly.

Jacob heard what had happened to his daughter, but, as his sons were out in the field with their cattle, he didn't react. When they returned and heard of their sister's disgrace, they became very angry.

Shechem went to his father and asked him to get Dinah for his wife. Hamor and Shechem came to speak with Jacob. Shechem said, "Let me find favor in your eyes, and whatever you say to me, I will give dowry and gifts, but give me Dinah as a wife".

The sons of Jacob agreed deceitfully to allow Dinah to marry Shechem, but they set the condition that every male in the city of Shechem would have to be circumcised. Hamor and Shechem were very pleased. The young man, who was greatly respected in the city, wanted to do this immediately, because he loved Jacob's daughter.

Hamor and his son went to the gate of the city and said to the men of the city, "These people have peaceful intentions; let them settle among us, for the land is large enough for them. We will marry their daughters, and they will marry ours. But they have set the condition that our men should be circumcised as they are. If we do so, their cattle and possessions will be ours".

The men of the city were convinced by these arguments, and they were all circumcised, including Hamor and Shechem. On the third day, when they were still weak and in pain, two of the sons of Jacob—Simeon and Levi, full brothers of Dinah—came to the city, armed with swords, and killed all the males. They took Dinah away from Shechem's house and went away. The other sons of Jacob came upon the slain and plundered the city. They seized their flocks, herds, and asses, and all their wealth; they took their wives and children as captives. Jacob told them that the Canaanites would surely want revenge. The brothers answered, "Should he treat our sister as a harlot?" Jacob, fearing that the actions of his sons had placed them all in great danger, moved the family to Hebron.

On the way to Hebron, near Ephrath, Rachel, Jacob's favorite wife, died, while giving birth to Benjamin.

Years later, Isaac died at the age of one hundred and eighty. The two brothers Esau and Jacob buried him (Genesis 35:29), in the cave of Machpelah where Abraham, Sarah and Rebekah were also buried. This was the last time that Jacob saw Esau.

Jacob loved Joseph, the first son of his beloved Rachel, more than his other sons, and he gave him a coat of many colors as a gift, which caused Joseph's brothers to be jealous and envious. It did not help that Joseph would report to Jacob whatever they did. The brothers became angrier, when Joseph claimed that, in his dreams, he had seen his parents and brothers bowing to him.

One day, when Joseph was seventeen years old, Jacob sent him to seek his brothers, who were pasturing their sheep near Nablus, and to bring back a report of their doings. Joseph found them further north in Dothan. When his brothers saw Joseph coming, they decided to get rid of him and sold him to a caravan of Midianites who took him to Egypt, where the boy was sold as a slave.

The brothers dipped Joseph's coat of many colors in goat's blood and showed it to Jacob, who assumed that Joseph had been killed by a wild animal and mourned his son for a long time.

Many years passed, during which, unbeknownst to his father and brothers, Joseph had become the second most important man in Egypt. The famine in Canaan was severe. When Jacob heard that it was possible to buy grain in Egypt, he said to his sons, "Why do you just sit there looking at each other? Go to Egypt and buy grain. If not, we will die".

Jacob sent his sons to Egypt, except for young Benjamin, because he was afraid that something would happen to him. The brothers were taken to Joseph, but they did not recognize him, although he did.

Joseph accused them of being spies and locked them up for three days. Then, he allowed them to go back to Canaan with the food that they had bought, but with the condition that they would return to Egypt bringing with them their youngest brother as proof that their story was true. Simeon was kept in Egypt as a hostage.

When they came back to Canaan, they said to Jacob, "The lord of Egypt spoke harshly to us and accused us of being spies. We told him that we are honest men, not spies. That we are twelve brothers, sons of the same father; the youngest stayed in Canaan with our father and one is no more. The lord told us that we had to prove our honesty by leaving one of us there, take grain to our hungry families, and then return to Egypt with our youngest brother".

They opened their bags, found their money inside, and were dismayed.

Jacob said to them, "You have made me lose my children. Joseph is no more, Simeon is gone, and you want to take Benjamin away? All these things are against me!"

Reuben said to his father, "I authorize you to kill my two sons if I don't bring him back to you! Give him to my care, and I will bring him back!"

Jacob answered, "My son will not go to Egypt with you. His brother is dead, and he is left alone. If something would happen to him on the way, the sorrow would kill me".

The famine got worse, and after sometime, the family finished all the grain that they had brought from Egypt.

Jacob said to his sons, "Go again to Egypt, and buy a small quantity of grain for us".

Judah answered, "The man swore that we would not see his face if we didn't bring our brother with us. If you will send our brother with us, we will go to Egypt and buy grain for you. But, if you don't send him with us, there is no point in us going there, because the man will refuse to see us".

Jacob complained to them, "Why did you cause me so much trouble by telling the man that you had another brother?"

They answered, "The man asked us directly about our family. 'Is your father alive?' he asked. 'Do you have another brother?' How could we guess that he would ask to bring our brother to Egypt?"

Judah said to his father, "Send the boy with me, and we will go immediately. That is the only way that we will live, and not die, all of us—we, you, our children. I will personally guarantee his safety. If I don't bring him back to you, I will assume the blame forever. If we hadn't stayed, we could have been back twice already".

Jacob said to them, "Well, if we have no choice, take with you the best fruits of the land in your packs, and bring the man a gift, a little balm, a little honey, spices, myrrh, nuts, and almonds. This time, take twice as much money as the last time, and carry in your hand the money that you found returned in your bags, because it might have been a mistake. Take your brother, get up, and go to the man. Let God Almighty make the man merciful toward you, so that he may release your other brother and Benjamin. If I have to lose my children, so be it".

The men took the gift, the money, and their young brother Benjamin, and returned to Egypt.

This time Joseph made himself known to his brothers, forgave them, and told them to bring Jacob and their families to Egypt and settle in the fertile land of Goshen.

Joseph gave his brothers wagons and provisions for the journey. To each of them, he gave a change of clothing, but to Benjamin, he gave five changes of clothing and three hundred pieces of silver. To his father, he sent ten male donkeys loaded with the best things of Egypt, and ten female donkeys loaded with grain, bread, and provisions for his father on the journey. As he sent his brothers off on their way, he admonished them not to quarrel among themselves.

The brothers returned to their father, Jacob, in the land of Canaan, and told him, "Joseph lives, and he is the ruler of Egypt!"

At first, Jacob could not believe them, but when he saw the wagons that Joseph had sent to transport him, he exclaimed, "My son Joseph is alive! I must go and see him, before I die!"

The brothers placed their father, Jacob, their children, and their wives in the wagons, took along their livestock and their possessions, and went to the land of Goshen in Egypt. On their way, they stopped in Beersheba, where Jacob offered sacrifices to the God of his father, Isaac.

That night, God appeared to Jacob in a vision and said to him, "I am God, the God of your father. Do not fear going to Egypt, because there, I will make you into a great nation. I will go with you to Egypt, and I will bring you out too. Joseph's hand shall close your eyes".

The total number of the Israelites who came to Egypt was seventy. The number included Jacob, Joseph, and the two sons of Joseph who were born in Egypt. The number did not include the wives of Jacob's sons.

They arrived in Goshen, and Joseph came to them in his chariot. He greeted his father, embraced him, and wept for a long time.

Jacob told him, "Now that I have seen your face, and know that you live, I can die".

Joseph then said to his brothers, "I will go now to Pharaoh and tell him that you have arrived. When Pharaoh calls you and asks, 'What is your occupation?' tell him that you are shepherds and breeders of livestock. This way, you will be able to stay in Goshen, because shepherds are repulsive to Egyptians".

Joseph came to Pharaoh with five of his brothers, and their conversation went as Joseph had predicted. Pharaoh allowed them to settle in Goshen and shepherd their sheep. Joseph then introduced his father Jacob to Pharaoh.

Pharaoh asked Jacob, "How old are you?"

Jacob answered, "One hundred and thirty are the years of my pilgrimage. They have been few and hard, shorter than the life spans of my ancestors". He blessed Pharaoh and departed.

Joseph settled his family in the region of Rameses, as Pharaoh had commanded, and he took care that they were all provided with bread.

Seventeen years later, Jacob, feeling that he would soon die, called Joseph and asked him to promise that he would not be buried in Egypt, but in the cave of Machpelah with Abraham and Isaac. Joseph swore that he would do so.

Shortly afterward, Joseph was told that his father was very ill. He went to see him with his two sons, Manasseh and Ephraim, to be blessed by Jacob. Jacob told him that he was adopting the two boys. He then looked at them and asked who they were.

Joseph answered, "These are my sons, whom God has given me here". He brought them closer to his father's bed, and Jacob kissed them and embraced them.

Jacob said to Joseph, "I never expected to see you again, and here, God has let me see your children as well".

Joseph placed Manasseh, his firstborn, on the right side of his father, and Ephraim on the left side of his father. Jacob placed his left hand on Manasseh. He stretched his right hand and placed it on Ephraim's head.

Joseph said to Jacob, "Not so, Father. The other one is the firstborn". He tried to remove Jacob's hand from Ephraim's head and place it on Manasseh's head.

Jacob answered, "I know, my son, he also shall become a great people, but his younger brother shall be greater than he", and he blessed the two boys.

The dying Jacob called his sons to bless them and tell them what would happen to them in the future. His last words were to ask them to bury him in the cave of Machpelah, where Abraham, Sarah, Isaac, Rebekah, and Leah were buried. Joseph flung himself over his father's body, and he wept over him and kissed him.

Jacob died at the age of one hundred and forty-seven. Joseph ordered the Egyptian physicians to embalm his father, a process which took forty days. When the seventy days' period of mourning was over, Joseph asked permission from the Pharaoh to allow him to go to Canaan and bury his father there. Pharaoh gave him permission to go and bury Jacob as he had promised.

Jacob's body was accompanied in his last trip by his sons, their children, flocks and herds, all the officials of Pharaoh and members of his court, chariots and horsemen. Before crossing the Jordan, the funeral procession made a stop and mourned Jacob for seven days. Then, Jacob's sons took him to Canaan and buried him in the cave of Machpelah.

Jada

(Hebrew origin: *Knowing*)

(1 Chronicles 2:28). Unspecified date. Jada, of the tribe of Judah, was the son of Onam and the brother of Shammai. His sons were Jether and Jonathan.

Jadau

(Hebrew origin: *Praised*)

(Ezra 10:43). 5th century B.C. Jadau, a descendant of Nebo, divorced his foreign wife, during the days of Ezra.

Jaddua

(Hebrew origin: *Known*)

1. (Nehemiah 10:21). 5th century B.C. Jaddua was one of the leaders who signed Nehemiah's solemn agreement to separate themselves from the foreigners living in the land, to refrain from intermarrying with them, and to dedicate their firstborn to God, among other obligations.
2. (Nehemiah 12:11). 5th century B.C. Jaddua, son of Jonathan, was a descendant of Jeshua, the High Priest who returned with Zerubbabel from the Babylonian Exile.

Jadon

(Hebrew origin: *Praised*)

(Nehemiah 3:7). 5th century B.C. Jadon the Meronothite helped to repair the walls of Jerusalem, during the days of Nehemiah.

Jael

(Hebrew origin: *Ibex*)

(Judges 4:17). 12th century B.C. Jael was the wife of Heber, a member of the Kenite tribe descendant of Hobab, Moses' father-in-law.

Jael and her husband Heber left their tribe's territory and settled in the plain of Zaanaim, near Kedesh. They enjoyed peaceful relationships with the Israelites, and also with Jabin, the king of Hazor, largest of the Canaanite cities.

There was a battle between the army of Israel, commanded by Barak, and the army of Hazor, commanded by Sisera. Hazor was defeated, and Sisera fled from his defeat at the hands of the Israelites.

Sisera sought refuge in the tent of Jael, trusting in her husband's friendship with King Jabin. Jael invited him to come into the tent, covered him with a mantle, and brought him some milk. As soon as Sisera fell asleep, Jael killed him by hammering a nail in his head.

When Barak, the commander of the Israelite army, approached the tent, Jael came out to meet him and told him that the man that he was pursuing was dead.

Deborah, who had prophesied that Sisera would be killed by a woman, sang her praises.

Jah

(Hebrew origin: *God*)

(Psalm 68:4). This is a contraction of the Hebrew sacred name of God.

Jahath

(Hebrew origin: *Unity*)

1. (1 Chronicles 4:2). Unspecified date. Jahath, a descendant of Judah, was the son of Reaiah and the father of Ahumai and Lahad, of the clan of the Zorathites.
2. (1 Chronicles 6:20). Unspecified date. Jahath, son of Libni and grandson of Gershom, was the father of Zimmah. His descendant Asaph was one of the Levites appointed by King David to be in charge of the singers in the House of the Lord.
3. (1 Chronicles 23:10). 10th century B.C. Jahath, a Levite, descendant of Shimei, served in the Tabernacle, during the reign of King David. The census of the Levites considered him as leader of a clan. His brothers were Beriah, Zina, and Jeush.
4. (1 Chronicles 24:22). 10th century B.C. Jahath, a Levite son of Shelomoth, served

in the Tabernacle, together with his father, during the reign of David.

5. (2 Chronicles 34:12). 7th century B.C. Jahath, a Levite descendant of Merari, was one of the four overseers of the repairs done in the Temple, during the reign of King Josiah. The other overseers were Obadiah—a descendant of Merari—Zechariah, and Meshullam, of the clan of the Kohathites.

Jahaziah

(Hebrew origin: *God will behold*)

(Ezra 10:15). 5th century B.C. Jahaziah, the son of Tikvah, and Jonathan, the son of Asahel, were the two leaders of Judah, who remained in Jerusalem to represent the people, when Ezra deliberated on the matter of the marriages to foreign women. They were helped by two Levites: Meshullam and Shabbethai.

Jahaziel

(Hebrew origin: *God will behold*)

1. (1 Chronicles 12:4). 11th century B.C. Jahaziel was one of the Benjamites who deserted King Saul's army and joined David's band at Ziklag. They were skilled warriors who could use both their right and left hands to shoot arrows and sling stones.
2. (1 Chronicles 16:6). 10th century B.C. Jahaziel was one of the priests appointed by King David to minister and play the trumpet before the Ark. He, together with another priest called Benaiah, played the trumpet, accompanied by other priests who played harps, lyres, and cymbals.
3. (1 Chronicles 23:19). Unspecified date. Jahaziel was a Levite descendant of Hebron, the son of Kohath and grandson of Levi.
4. (2 Chronicles 20:14). 9th century B.C. Jahaziel, a Levite son of Zechariah and a descendant of Asaph, prophesied to King Jehoshaphat that he would not have to fight against a great army of Moabites and Ammonites who were coming against him, because God would win the battle. The prophecy came true, when the invaders

fought among themselves and annihilated each other.

5. Ezra 8:5). 6th century B.C. Jahaziel, a descendant of Shechaniah, was the father of a man who returned with Ezra from Babylon to Jerusalem leading a group of three hundred men.

Jahdai

(Hebrew origin: *Judaistic*)

(1 Chronicles 2:47). Unspecified date. Jahdai, of the tribe of Judah, was the father of Ephah, Regem, Jotham, Gesham, Pelet, and Shaaph.

Jahdiel

(Hebrew origin: *Together with God*)

(1 Chronicles 5:24). 8th century B.C. Jahdiel, of the half tribe of Manasseh that had settled east of the Jordan River, was a mighty warrior and leader of his clan.

His tribe was deported from their land by the Assyrians and forcibly settled in the region of the river Gozan, where it eventually assimilated into the local population and disappeared from history, being remembered today as one of the "ten lost tribes".

Jahdo

(Hebrew origin: *Together with him*)

(1 Chronicles 5:14). Unspecified date. Jahdo, of the tribe of Gad, was the father of Jeshishai and the son of Buz. His descendants lived in Gilead, on the eastern side of the Jordan River.

Jahleel

(Hebrew origin: *Waiting for God*).

(Genesis 46:14). 17th century B.C. Jahleel, son of Zebulun, was the grandson of Jacob and Leah. His brothers were Sered and Elon.

Jahleel, the ancestor of the clan of the Jahleelites (Numbers 26:26), was one of the seventy Israelites who immigrated to Egypt.

Jahmai

(Hebrew origin: *Hot*)

(1 Chronicles 7:2). Unspecified date. Jahmai, son of Tola, and his brothers—Uzzi, Rephaiah, Jeriel, Jibsam, and Shemuel—were leaders of the tribe of Issachar.

Jahzeel

(Hebrew origin: *May God grant a portion*)

(Genesis 46:24). 17th century B.C. Jahzeel, son of Naphtali and grandson of Jacob and Bilhah, was one of the seventy Israelites who immigrated to Egypt. His brothers were Guni, Jezer, and Shillem. Jahzeel was the ancestor of the clan of the Jahzeelites. In the first book of Chronicles, his name is spelled Jahziel (1 Chronicles 7:13).

Jahzerah

(Hebrew origin: *Enclosed*)

(1 Chronicles 9:12). 6th century B.C. Jahzerah, son of Meshullam, was the grandfather of Maasiai, a priest who served in the Temple, after the return from the Babylonian Exile.

Jahziel

(Hebrew origin: *May God grant a portion*)

(1 Chronicles 7:13). 17th century B.C. Jahziel is an alternative spelling for Jahzeel, son of Naphtali and grandson of Jacob and Bilhah. (Please see the entry for Jahzeel [Genesis 46:24].)

Jair

(Hebrew origin: *Enlightener*)

1. (Numbers 32:41). 12th century B.C. Jair, of the tribe of Manasseh, conquered several small towns in the region of Gilead and called them, after his name, Havothjair.
2. (Judges 10:3). 11th century B.C. Jair, a Gileadite, became judge over Israel after Tola. He judged Israel, during twenty-two years. His thirty sons rode on donkey colts and controlled thirty cities, called

Havothjair, in the region of Gilead. When Jair died, he was buried in Camon.

Note: In the book of Judges, a judge is a ruler or governor of territory or a military leader in pre-monarchical Israel. Later, during the monarchy, the king served in this role and judges were more like the judicial officers that we know today.

3. (1 Chronicles 2:22). Unspecified date. Jair, the son of Segub, a descendant of Hezron of the tribe of Judah, had twenty-three cities in the land of Gilead.

4. (1 Chronicles 20:5). 10th century B.C. Jair was the father of Elhanan, a Bethlehemite who killed the Philistine Lahmi, the brother of the giant Goliath, in the battle of Gob. The second book of Samuel calls him Jaareoregim (2 Samuel 21:19).

5. (Esther 2:5). 5th century B.C. Jair, the son of Shimei, of the tribe of Benjamin, was the father of Mordecai. His brother Abihail was the father of Esther, the Jewish maiden who married King Ahasuerus and became the queen of Persia.

Jairus

(Hebrew origin: *Enlightener*)

(Mark 5:22). A.D. 1st century. Jairus was one of the leaders of the synagogue in Capernaum. His only child, a girl of twelve years old, was mortally ill.

Jairus prostrated himself at the feet of Jesus and begged him to come to his house and cure his daughter. On the way to the house, a woman, suffering from hemorrhage, touched the hem of Jesus' garment and was cured.

A man came to them from Jairus' house and said that the girl had died, and that Jairus should not trouble Jesus anymore. Jesus heard this and said to Jairus, "Do not fear, believe, and she will be made whole".

Arriving to the house, Jesus allowed no one to enter except for his disciples—Peter, James, and John—and the parents of the girl. Jesus took the girl's hand and told her to arise. The girl came back to life. Her parents were astonished, but Jesus instructed them to tell no man what he had done.

Jakan

(Hebrew origin: *Tortuous*)

(1 Chronicles 1:42). Unspecified date. Jakan, son of Ezer, a descendant of Seir, was the leader of a clan of Horites who lived in the land of Edom. His brothers were Bilhan and Zavan. Alternative spellings are Akan (Genesis 36:27) and Jaakan (Deuteronomy 10:6).

Jakeh

(Hebrew origin: *Obedient*)

(Proverbs 30:1). Unspecified date. His son Agur was the author of a series of proverbs, which appear in chapter 30 of the book of Proverbs.

Jakim

(Hebrew origin: *Will raise*)

1. (1 Chronicles 8:19). Unspecified date. Jakim, a descendant of Shimhi, was a leader of the tribe of Benjamin who lived in Jerusalem.

2. (1 Chronicles 24:12). 10th century B.C. During the reign of King David, the priestly service in the Tabernacle was divided by lot into twenty-four turns. Jakim was in charge of the twelfth turn.

Jalon

(Hebrew origin: *Lodging*)

(1 Chronicles 4:17). Unspecified date. Jalon, son of Ezra, a descendant of Judah, was the brother of Jether, Mered, and Epher. His brother Mered married Bithiah, daughter of the Pharaoh of Egypt.

Jambres

(Egyptian origin: Uncertain meaning)

(2 Timothy 3:8). 13th century B.C. Jambres, according to Paul's second letter to Timothy, was one of the two Egyptian magicians—the other one was Jannes—who reproduced the miracle performed by Moses and Aaron of converting their rods to serpents in front of Pharaoh (Exodus 7:11).

Timothy mentioned Jambres and Jannes as examples of men of corrupt minds, who resisted the truth, but whose folly would be a manifest to all men.

James

(Greek origin: derived from the Hebrew *Jacob* [*Supplanter*])

1. (Matthew 4:21). A.D. 1st century. James and his brother John, sons of Zebedee, were fishermen in the Sea of Galilee, in partnership with Simon Peter.

   One day, the two brothers and their father Zebedee were mending their nets in their ship, when Jesus, walking by the shore of the Sea of Galilee, called them. The two brothers immediately left their father and their ship and followed him. They became, together with Peter, the favorite disciples of Jesus.

   The two brothers—whom Jesus surnamed Boanerges, which means *The sons of thunder,* because of their irate temperament—wanted in one occasion to call down fire from heaven and destroy a Samaritan village, which had not been hospitable to them. Jesus rebuked them, saying that the Son of man had not come to destroy lives but to save them.

   The brothers were witnesses to the miraculous cure of Peter's sick mother, and to the resurrection of the dead daughter of Jairus. They also accompanied Jesus on the top of a high mountain, where they, together with Peter, witnessed his transfiguration and saw Moses and Elias appear and talk with Jesus.

   One day, their mother came with them to Jesus and asked that her sons be allowed to sit next to Jesus in his glory: one on his right side, and the other on his left side. Jesus replied that it was not in his power to grant her wish, as those places belonged to those for whom God had prepared them.

   The other disciples, when they heard the request, were very upset with the two brothers. Jesus called the disciples and told them that, if anyone of them wanted to be

great, he would have to be the servant of the rest, and that the Son of man did not come to be served but to serve, and to give his life for the redemption of the people.

James, John, and Peter heard Jesus say, in the Garden of Gethsemane, how sorrowful his soul was. James was the first of the apostles to suffer martyrdom, when King Herod Agrippa I, grandson of Herod the Great, killed him with the sword.

He was called "James the Greater" to distinguish him from James, the son of Cleophas, who was called the Lesser—i.e. the Younger.

2. (Matthew 10:3). A.D. 1st century. James, son of Alphaeus, was one of the twelve apostles. It is possible that his father was the same Alphaeus who was the father of the apostle Matthew, in which case, this would mean that James and Matthew were brothers.

3. (Matthew 13:55). A.D. 1st century. James was one of the four brothers of Jesus mentioned by the people of Nazareth, when they expressed their surprise and anger against Jesus for preaching in their synagogue. The other brothers were Judas, Joses, and Simon.

   After the death of Jesus, James, now the leader of the church in Jerusalem, allowed Paul to preach to the Gentiles, and to limit their obligations to comply with the Law of Moses. The Gentiles, from then on, would only be required to abstain from eating food, which had been offered to idols, blood or animals, which had been strangled, and were forbidden to engage in sexual promiscuity.

   When Paul returned to Jerusalem, James reproached him for teaching the Jews to forsake Moses and the Jewish laws, and he told him to purify himself for seven days in the Temple.

   James wrote the letter named after him, where he lists over fifty commandments, or instructions, written in a straight and forceful style to all of God's people, regarding practical wisdom and guidance for Christian attitudes and conduct, emphasizing the importance of actions along with faith in the practice of the Christian religion.

Note: Some scholars believe that Joses, James, Simon, and Judas were Joseph's children from a previous marriage. Others say that the terms "brothers" and "sisters", in these verses, refer to cousins or other close relatives.

4. (Matthew 27:56). A.D. 1st century. James was the brother of Joses. His mother, Mary, the wife of Cleophas, was one of the women who witnessed the crucifixion of Jesus. He was called the Lesser—i.e. the Younger— to distinguish him from the apostle James, called "James the Greater".

5. (Luke 6:16). A.D. 1st century. James was the father of the apostle Judas, also called Thaddaeus (Matthew 10:3), Mark (Mark 3:18), and Lebbaeus (Matthew 10:3).

Jamin

(Hebrew origin: *South* or *Right hand*)

1. (Genesis 46:10). 17th century B.C. Jamin, a son of Simeon and grandson of Jacob, was one of the seventy Israelites who immigrated to Egypt. His brothers were Jemuel, Ohad, Jachin, Zohar, and Saul, the son of a Canaanite woman. Jamin was the ancestor of the clan of the Jaminites.

In the first book of Chronicles, Jemuel, Jachin, and Zohar are called respectively: Nemuel, Jarib, and Zerah (1 Chronicles 4:24). Ohad is not listed in the first book of Chronicles.

2. (1 Chronicles 2:27). Unspecified date. Jamin was the son of Ram and grandson of Jerahmeel, of the tribe of Judah. His brothers were Eker and Maaz.

3. (Nehemiah 8:7). 5th century B.C. Jamin was one of the Levites who explained the Law to the people, after Ezra the Scribe had read it, while standing on a wooden platform, in front of the open space, before the Water Gate.

Jamlech

(Hebrew origin: *He will make king*)

(1 Chronicles 4:34). 8th century B.C. Jamlech was one of the leaders of the tribe of Simeon who went to the fertile valley of Gedor in search of pasture for their flocks, during the reign of Hezekiah, king of Judah.

The Simeonites destroyed the tents of the people—descendants of Ham—who lived there, wiped them out forever, and settled in their place.

Janna

(Greek derived from Hebrew origin: *To be violent*)

(Luke 3:24). Unspecified date. Janna was the son of Joseph and father of Melchi, ancestor of Jesus, in the genealogy of Luke.

Jannes

(Egyptian origin: Uncertain meaning)

(2 Timothy 3:8). 13th century B.C. Jannes, according to Paul's second letter to Timothy, was one of the two Egyptian magicians—the other one was Jambres—who reproduced the miracle performed by Moses and Aaron of converting their rods to serpents in front of Pharaoh (Exodus 7:11).

Timothy mentioned Jambres and Jannes as examples of men of corrupt minds, who resisted the truth, but whose folly would be a manifest to all men.

Japheth

(Hebrew origin: *Expansion*)

(Genesis 5:32). Unspecified date. Japheth, one of the three sons of Noah—the other two were Shem and Ham—went into the Ark with his wife, parents, brothers, and the wives of his brothers.

When Ham shamed his father Noah by seeing his nakedness, Japheth and Shem took a garment, walked backward, and covered Noah. Noah awoke from his drunken sleep and heard what Ham had done. He cursed Canaan and blessed Japheth and Shem.

Japheth was the father of Gomer, Magog, Madai, Javan, Tubal, Meshech, and Tiras.

Japhia

(Hebrew origin: *Bright*)

1. (Joshua 10:3). 12th century B.C. Japhia, king of Lachish, was asked by Adonizedek, the king of Jerusalem, to join him and several other kings—Hoham, the king of Hebron; Debir, the king of Eglon; and Piram, the king of Jarmuth—in a military alliance against the city of Gibeon to punish the Gibeonites for having made peace with the people of Israel.

   The people of Gibeon appealed to Joshua for help. Joshua—after ordering the sun to stand still over Gibeon, and the moon over the valley of Ajalon—fought against the five kings and defeated them. Their armies ran away, during a storm of hailstones, which killed many of their soldiers, even more than those who had been killed in the fighting. The five kings fled and hid in a cave at Makkedah, where they were trapped.

   After Joshua had liquidated all the surviving enemies, he ordered that the kings should be taken out from the cave. Japhia, Debir, Adonizedek, Hoham, and Piram, after being humiliated, were killed and hanged on five trees, until the evening. At sunset, their corpses were taken down and thrown into the cave, where they had been hiding, and large stones were placed over the entrance to the cave.

2. (2 Samuel 5:15). 10th century B.C. Japhia, born in Jerusalem, was a son of King David.

Japhlet

(Hebrew origin: *He will deliver*)

(1 Chronicles 7:32). Unspecified date. Japhlet, the chief of a clan of the tribe of Asher, was the son of Heber. His brothers were Hotham and Shomer. His sister was Shua. Japhlet was the father of Pasach, Bimhal, and Ashvath.

Jarah

(Hebrew origin: *Forest*)

(1 Chronicles 9:42). Unspecified date. Jarah, a Benjamite, son of Ahaz, was a descendant of King Saul. His sons were Alemeth, Azmaveth, and Zimri. Jarah is called Jehoadah in another verse (1 Chronicles 8:36).

Jareb

(Hebrew origin: *He will contend*)

(Hosea 5:13). 8th century B.C. Jareb is a symbolic name given by the prophet Hosea to the king of Assyria.

Jared

(Hebrew origin: *Descent*)

(Genesis 5:15). Antediluvian. Jared, son of Mahalaleel, had a son named Enoch, at the age of one hundred and sixty-two. After the birth of Enoch, Jared lived for another eight hundred years and had more sons and daughters. He was the grandfather of Methuselah and the ancestor of Noah.

His name is also spelled Jered (1 Chronicles 1:2).

Jaresiah

(Hebrew origin: Uncertain meaning)

(1 Chronicles 8:27). Unspecified date. Jaresiah, son of Jeroham, was a leader of the tribe of Benjamin who lived in Jerusalem. His brothers were Eliah and Zichri.

Jarha

(Egyptian origin: Meaning unknown)

(1 Chronicles 2:34). Unspecified date. Jarha, an Egyptian, worked for a man called Sheshan, who didn't have any sons, only daughters. Jarha married one of the daughters of his master and had a son called Attai.

Jarib

(Hebrew origin: *Opponent*)

1. (1 Chronicles 4:24). 17th century B.C.

Jarib—called Jachin in the book of Genesis (Genesis 46:10)—was a grandson of Jacob and one of the seventy Israelites who immigrated to Egypt.

According to the first book of Chronicles, Jarib was the third son of Simeon. However, according to the book of Genesis, he was the fourth son of Simeon, because of the inclusion of Ohad in the Genesis' list.

According to Genesis, his brothers were Jemuel—called Nemuel in the book of Numbers (Numbers 26:12)—Jamin, Ohad—not mentioned in the list in First Chronicles—Zerah—called Zohar in the book of Genesis—and Shaul.

2. (Ezra 8:16). 5th century B.C. Jarib was one of the leaders of Judah sent by Ezra to Casiphia to speak to Iddo and request from him to send Levites to serve in the Temple in Jerusalem.

3. (Ezra 10:18). 5th century B.C. Jarib and his brothers, sons of Jozadak, were priests who divorced their foreign wives, during the days of Ezra, and offered a ram from the flock to expiate their transgression.

Jaroah

(Hebrew origin: *New Moon*)

(1 Chronicles 5:14). Unspecified date. Jaroah, son of Gilead and father of Huri, of the tribe of Gad, was an ancestor of a clan that lived in Gilead in Bashan, east of the Jordan River.

Jashen

(Hebrew origin: *Sleepy*)

(2 Samuel 23:32). Unspecified date. Jashen was the ancestor of valiant warriors in King David's army. He is also called Hashem (1 Chronicles 11:34).

Jashobeam

(Hebrew origin: *People will return*)

1. (1 Chronicles 11:11). 10th century B.C. Jashobeam, son of Hachmoni, was one of the top commanders of David's army. As a

brave man, he once killed three hundred Philistines with his spear in one battle.

2. (1 Chronicles 12:6). 11th century B.C. Jashobeam, a Korhite, was one of the men who deserted King Saul's army and joined David's band at Ziklag. These men were skilled warriors who could use both their right and left hands to shoot arrows and sling stones.

3. (1 Chronicles 27:2). 10th century B.C. Jashobeam, son of Zabdiel, descendant of Perez, was one of the twelve commanders of King David's army, with twenty-four thousand men in his division, and was responsible for the service, during the first month of the year.

Jashub

(Hebrew origin: *He will return*)

1. (Numbers 26:24). 17th century B.C. Jashub—called Job in the book of Genesis (Genesis 46:13)—was the third son of Issachar and one of the seventy Israelites who immigrated to Egypt. His brothers were Tola, Pua—called Phuvah in the book of Genesis, and Puah in First Chronicles—and Shimrom—called Shimron in Genesis.

Jashub was the ancestor of the clan of the Jashubites.

2. (Ezra 10:29). 5th century B.C. Jashub, descendant of Bani, divorced his foreign wife, during the time of Ezra.

Jasiel

(Hebrew origin: *Made by God*)

(1 Chronicles 11:47). 10th century B.C. Jasiel, the Mesobaite, was one of King David's brave warriors.

Jason

(Greek origin: *Healer*)

1. (Acts of the Apostles 17:5). A.D. 1st century. Jason was a Christian who lived in Thessalonica. Paul and his companion Silas stayed in his house, during the weeks that Paul preached in the synagogue.

Some of the members of the synagogue, upset with Paul's teachings, gathered a mob and assaulted the house of Jason, searching for Paul and Silas. Not finding them in the house, they grabbed Jason and other Christians and took them to the rulers of the city, accusing them of saying that Jesus was their king, instead of Caesar. The authorities made Jason and the others deposit security and let them go.

It is likely that he was the same person as the Jason mentioned by Paul in his epistle to the Romans (see below).

2. (Romans 16:21). 1st century A.D. Jason was a Christian mentioned by Paul, in his epistle to the Romans, as being a kinsman who sent his regards. It is likely that he was the same person as the Jason who lived in Thessalonica (see above).

Jathniel

(Hebrew origin: *Continued by God*)

(1 Chronicles 26:2). 10th century B.C. Jathniel, son of Meshelemiah, was one of the gatekeepers of the Tabernacle, during the reign of King David.

His brothers were Zechariah—the first-born—Jediael, Zebadiah, Elam, Jehohanan, and Elioenai. His father Meshelemiah was called Shallum in the first book of Chronicles (1 Chronicles 9:17).

Javan

(Hebrew origin: *Ionians* [i.e. *Greece*])

(Genesis 10:2). Unspecified date. Javan was a son of Japheth and grandson of Noah. His brothers were Gomer, Magog, Madai, Tubal, Meshech, and Tiras. The sons of Javan were Elishah, Tarshish, Kittim, and Dodanim.

Jaziz

(Hebrew origin: *He will make prominent*)

(1 Chronicles 27:31). 10th century B.C. Jaziz the Hagerite was in charge of the royal flocks, during the reign of King David.

Jeaterai

(Hebrew origin: *He will make prominent*)

(1 Chronicles 6:21). 7th century B.C. Jeaterai, son of Zerah, was a Levite descendant of Gershom.

Jeberechiah

(Hebrew origin: *God will bless*)

(Isaiah 8:2). 8th century B.C. His son Zechariah was one of the two witnesses—Uriah the Priest was the other—to the prophecies written by Isaiah concerning the conquests of the king of Assyria.

Jecamiah

(Hebrew origin: *God will rise*)

(1 Chronicles 3:18). 6th century B.C. Jecamiah was one of the seven sons of Jehoiachin, the king of Judah, who was deposed by the Babylonians and taken to captivity in Babylon, after reigning for only three months.

Jecamiah's brothers were Salathiel, Malchiram, Pedaiah, Shenazar, Hoshama, and Nedabiah.

Jecholiah

(Hebrew origin: *God can*)

(2 Kings 15:2). 8th century B.C. Jecholiah, born in Jerusalem, was the wife of King Amaziah of Judah who was murdered by conspirators.

Her son Azariah, also called Uzziah, succeeded to the throne at the age of sixteen. She is called Jecoliah in the second book of Chronicles (2 Chronicles 26:3).

Jechonias

(Hebrew origin: *God will establish*)

(Matthew 1:11). 6th century B.C. Jechonias is an alternative spelling of the name of Jeconiah—also called Jehoiachin and Coniah—king of Judah. According to Matthew, Jechonias' son Salathiel was the father of Zorobabel, ancestor of Joseph, the husband of Mary, the mother of Jesus. (Please see the entry for Jehoiachin [2 Kings 24:6].)

Jecoliah

(Hebrew origin: *God can*)

(2 Chronicles 26:3). 8th century B.C. Jecoliah is an alternative spelling for Jecholiah, wife of the murdered King Amaziah of Judah. (Please see the entry for Jecholiah [2 Kings 15:2].)

Jeconiah

(Hebrew origin: *God will establish*)

(1 Chronicles 3:16). 6th century B.C. Jeconiah, the son of King Jehoiakim and Nehushta, reigned under the name of Jehoiachin (2 Kings 24:6).

Jedaiah

(Hebrew origin: *God knows*)

1. (1 Chronicles 4:37). Unspecified date. Jedaiah was the son of Shimri and the father of Allon. His descendant Ziza was one of the leaders of the tribe of Simeon who went to the fertile valley of Gedor in search of pasture for their flocks, during the reign of Hezekiah, king of Judah.

   The Simeonites destroyed the tents of the people—descendants of Ham—who lived there, wiped them out forever, and settled in their place.

2. (1 Chronicles 24:7). 10th century B.C. During the reign of King David, the priestly service in the Tabernacle was divided by lot into twenty-four turns. Jedaiah was in charge of the second turn. A number of his descendants returned with Zerubbabel from the Babylonian Exile (Ezra 2:36).

3. (Nehemiah 3:10). 5th century B.C. Jedaiah, son of Harumaph, repaired part of the walls of Jerusalem, opposite his house, in the days of Nehemiah.

4. (Nehemiah 11:10). 5th century B.C. Jedaiah, son of Joiarib, was a priest living in Jerusalem, during the days of Nehemiah.

5. (Nehemiah 12:6). 6th century B.C. Jedaiah was one of the leading priests who returned to Jerusalem with Zerubbabel from the Babylonian Exile, when the High Priest was Joshua.

Jedaiah was the ancestor of a clan of priests, led by Uzzi, during the days of Nehemiah, when Joiakim was the High Priest (Nehemiah 12:19).

6. (Nehemiah 12:7). 6th century B.C. Jedaiah was one of the leading priests who returned to Jerusalem with Zerubbabel from the Babylonian Exile, when the High Priest was Joshua.

   He was taken by the prophet Zechariah, together with Tobijah and Heldai (Zechariah 6:10), to the house of Josiah, son of Zephaniah, where they made crowns of gold and silver, and they placed them on the head of the High Priest, Joshua, son of Josedech. The crowns remained in the Temple as a memorial to the three donors.

   Jedaiah was the ancestor of a clan of priests, led by Nethaneel, during the days of Nehemiah, when Joiakim was the High Priest (Nehemiah 12:21).

Jediael

(Hebrew origin: *Knowing God*)

1. (1 Chronicles 7:6). 17th century B.C. Jediael, according to the list in the first book of Chronicles, was one of the three sons of Benjamin. He was the father of Bilhan and was one of the leaders of his tribe.

   The other three lists of the sons of Benjamin—Genesis 46:21, Numbers 26:38, and 1 Chronicles 8:1—do not mention him.

2. (1 Chronicles 11:45). 10th century B.C. Jediael and his brother Joha, sons of Shimri, were two of King David's brave warriors.

3. (1 Chronicles 12:20). 11th century B.C. Jediael, from the tribe of Manasseh, deserted from Saul's army with his men, joined David at Ziklag, and became a captain of his army.

4. (1 Chronicles 26:2). 10th century B.C. Jediael, son of Meshelemiah, was one of the gatekeepers of the Tabernacle, during the reign of King David.

His brothers were Zechariah—the first-born—Jathniel, Zebadiah, Elam, Jehohanan, and Elioenai. His father Meshelemiah was called Shallum in the first book of Chronicles (1 Chronicles 9:17).

Jedidah

(Hebrew origin: *Beloved*)

(2 Kings 22:1). 7th century B.C. Jedidah, the daughter of Adaiah of Boscath, was the wife of King Amon of Judah and the mother of King Josiah.

Her husband was murdered by conspirators at the age of twenty-two, after having reigned two years. Her eight-year-old son Josiah succeeded to the throne.

Jedidiah

(Hebrew origin: *Beloved of God*)

(2 Samuel 12:25). 10th century B.C. This was the name given by the prophet Nathan to Solomon, the son who was born to David and Bathsheba, after their first baby had died in his infancy. (Please read the entry for Solomon [2 Samuel 5:14].)

Jeduthun

(Hebrew origin: *Laudatory*)

(1 Chronicles 9:16). 10th century B.C. Jeduthun, a Levite, was one of King David's three leading musicians; the other two were Asaph and Heman. He prophesied with the harp and was called the seer of the king. David appreciated him so much that he even dedicated some of his psalms to him.

Six of the sons of Jeduthun were also musicians: Gedaliah, Zeri, Jeshaiah, Hashabiah, and Mattithiah. His son Obededom was one of the gatekeepers of the Tabernacle. His descendant Obadiah was one of the first to settle in the land of Judah, after the return from the Babylonian Exile. His descendants Shemaiah

and Uzziel were among the Levites who gathered to make themselves ritually clean, and to purify the Temple, during the reign of King Hezekiah of Judah.

Some scholars believe that Jeduthun was the same person as Ethan (1 Chronicles 6:44)—one of the Levites appointed by King David to play the trumpets and the cymbals of brass in the House of the Lord—son of Kishi or Kushaiah.

Jeezer

(Hebrew origin: *Helpless*)

(Numbers 26:30). Unspecified date. Jeezer—called Abiezer in the book of Joshua (Joshua 17:2)—a descendant of Gilead, of the tribe of Manasseh, was the ancestor of the clan of the Jeezerites.

The clan was assigned land, during the days of Joshua, and later fought with Gideon against the Midianites (Judges 6:34).

Jehaleleel

(Hebrew origin: *Praising God*)

(1 Chronicles 4:16). Unspecified date. Jehaleleel, of the tribe of Judah, was the father of Ziph, Ziphah, Tiria, and Asareel.

Jehalelel

(Hebrew origin: *Praising God*)

(2 Chronicles 29:12). 8th century B.C. Jehalelel was a Levite descendant of Merari. His son Azariah was one of the Levites who assembled all the other Levites to make themselves ritually clean, and to purify the Temple, during the reign of King Hezekiah of Judah.

Jehdeiah

(Hebrew origin: *United with God*)

1. (1 Chronicles 24:20). 10th century B.C. Jehdeiah, a Levite, was the son of Shubael, who served in the Tabernacle, during the reign of King David.

2. (1 Chronicles 27:30). 10th century B.C. Jehdeiah the Meronothite was in charge of King David's asses.

Jehezekel

(Hebrew origin: *God will strengthen*)

(1 Chronicles 24:16). 10th century B.C. During the reign of King David, the priestly service in the Tabernacle was divided by lot into twenty-four turns. Jehezekel was in charge of the twentieth turn.

Jehiah

(Hebrew origin: *God will live*)

(1 Chronicles 15:24). 10th century B.C. Jehiah—also called Jeiel (1 Chronicles 15:18)—a Levite of the second rank, was one of the two gatekeepers of the Tabernacle—the other was Obededom—during the reign of King David.

Jehiah was among those chosen, by the chief of the Levites, to sing and play musical instruments in front of the Ark of the Covenant, when it was carried from the house of Obededom to its resting place in Jerusalem.

Jehiel

(Hebrew origin: *Carried away of God* or [with a different spelling in Hebrew] *God lives*)

1. (1 Chronicles 9:35). 12th century B.C. Jehiel, of the tribe of Benjamin, was married to Maachah and lived in Gibeon.

   He was the father of Ner, King Saul's grandfather. In the first book of Samuel (1 Samuel 9:1), he is called Abiel, son of Zeror, and he is mentioned as the father of two sons: Kish, the father of King Saul, and Ner, the father of Abner, the commander of the king's army.

2. (1 Chronicles 11:44). 10th century B.C. Jehiel and his brother Shama, sons of Hothan the Aroerite, were two of King David's brave warriors.

3. (1 Chronicles 15:18). 10th century B.C. Jehiel, a Levite of the second rank, was among those chosen, by the chief of the Levites, to sing and play musical instruments in front of the Ark of the Covenant, when it was carried from the house of Obededom to its resting place in Jerusalem, during the reign of King David.

4. (1 Chronicles 23:8). 10th century B.C. Jehiel, Joel, and Zetham, descendants of Laadan of the clan of the Gershonites, were Levites who worked in the Tabernacle, during the reign of David.

   Jehiel was in charge of receiving the gifts of precious stones for the house of the Lord. He is also called Jehieli (1 Chronicles 26:21).

5. (1 Chronicles 27:32). 10th century B.C. Jehiel, the son of Hachmoni, was responsible for the royal princes in the court of King David.

6. (2 Chronicles 21:2). 9th century B.C. Jehiel, a son of King Jehoshaphat, received from his father great gifts of gold, silver, and fenced cities.

   When Jehoshaphat died, his firstborn son Jehoram ascended to the throne and killed Jehiel and all his other brothers.

7. (2 Chronicles 29:14). 8th century B.C. Jehiel—a descendant of Heman, King David's leading musician—was one of the Levites who gathered to make themselves ritually clean, and to purify the Temple, during the reign of King Hezekiah of Judah.

   King Hezekiah appointed him as one of the supervisors serving under Cononiah and Shimei, who were responsible for the gifts, tithes, and offerings, brought by the people to the Temple (2 Chronicles 31:13).

8. (2 Chronicles 35:8). 7th century B.C. During the reign of King Josiah, the king and the princes of the kingdom donated thousands of cattle and oxen to be used for the Passover offerings. Jehiel, one of the rulers of the Temple, was among those who donated lambs, goats, and bulls to the priests for the Passover sacrifices.

9. (Ezra 8:9). 5th century B.C. His son Obadiah, a descendant of Joab, returned with Ezra from Babylon, leading two hundred and eighteen males of his clan

10. (Ezra 10:2). 5th century B.C. His son Shechaniah, a descendant of Elam, after hearing Ezra's public prayer of confession, declared that the people had sinned against God and had taken foreign wives.

He proposed that a covenant should be made with God to put away all the foreign wives and the children who had been born to these women.

11. (Ezra 10:21). 5th century B.C. Jehiel, a priest descendant of Harim, divorced his foreign wife, during the days of Ezra.

12. (Ezra 10:26). 5th century B.C. This man, a descendant of Elam, divorced his foreign wife, during the days of Ezra.

Jehieli

(Hebrew origin: *God lives*)

(1 Chronicles 26:21). 10th century B.C. Jehieli—also called Jehiel (1 Chronicles 23:8)—a Levite descendant of Laadan, of the clan of the Gershonites, worked in the Tabernacle, during the reign of David. Jehieli was in charge of receiving the gifts of precious stones for the house of the Lord.

Jehizkiah

(Hebrew origin: *Strengthened by God*)

(2 Chronicles 28:12). 8th century B.C. King Pekah of Israel made war against King Ahaz of Judah and defeated him. Pekah brought tens of thousands of captives back to Samaria with the intention of making them slaves.

Jehizkiah, the son of Shallum, was one of the leaders of the tribe of Ephraim who supported the prophet Oded in his demand to free the captives and return them to Judah. He and his companions gave clothing, shoes, food, and drink to the captives, and returned them to the city of Jericho in Judah.

Jehoadah

(Hebrew origin: *God adorned*)

(1 Chronicles 8:36). Unspecified date. Jehoadah—also called Jarah (1 Chronicles 9:42)—a Benjamite descendant of King Saul, was the son of Ahaz and the father of Alemeth, Azmaveth, and Zimri.

Jehoaddan

(Hebrew origin: *God pleased*)

(2 Kings 14:2). 9th century B.C. Jehoaddan of Jerusalem was the wife of King Joash of Judah and the mother of King Amaziah.

Jehoahaz

(Hebrew origin: *God possessed*)

1. (2 Kings 10:35). 9th century B.C. Jehoahaz, the eleventh king of Israel, after the partition of the United Monarchy, was the son of King Jehu, the man who destroyed the Omrite dynasty.

The reign of Jehoahaz lasted seventeen years, a period, during which, the kingdom declined, and the Israelite army shrunk to the point that it only had fifty horsemen, ten chariots, and ten thousand footmen. Hazael, king of Syria, took advantage of Jehoahaz' weakness to make him his vassal, and to incorporate several Israelite cities to his kingdom.

During a war with Aram-Damascus, the Syrians laid siege to Samaria and tried to starve the inhabitants into surrendering, but they retreated without obtaining their purpose. Eventually, the pressure of the Assyria's campaigns in Syria liberated Israel from the Aramean oppressor.

Jehoahaz died and was buried in Samaria. His son Jehoash succeeded him.

2. (2 Kings 23:30). 7th century B.C. Jehoahaz—also called Shallum (1 Chronicles 3:15 and Jeremiah 22:11)— was the sixteenth king of Judah, after the partition of the United Monarchy. His parents were King Josiah and Hamutal. His brothers were Johanan, the firstborn; Eliakim; and Mattaniah, who later became King Zedekiah.

Pharaoh Necho crowned him king of Judah, after the Egyptian had mortally wounded King Josiah in a battle at Megiddo. Three months later, Pharaoh Necho summoned the young king—who was twenty-three years old at the time—to his headquarters at Riblah in the land of Hamath, Syria. When Jehoahaz arrived,

Necho arrested him, put him in chains, and deported him to Egypt. He died there, as Jeremiah had prophesied. Necho then made Jehoahaz' older brother Eliakim the puppet king of Israel and changed his name to Jehoiakim.

3. (2 Chronicles 21:17). 9th century B.C. Jehoahaz is called Ahaziah in all the other biblical verses, which mention him (2 Kings 8:24), and Azariah in a verse in Second Chronicles (2 Chronicles 22:6). Jehoahaz, the son of Jehoram and Athaliah, the daughter of King Omri, was the sixth king of Judah, after the partition of the United Monarchy.

Jehoahaz, the youngest son of King Jehoram, became the heir to the throne, when nomad raiders killed all his older brothers (2 Chronicles 22:1). He succeeded to the throne at the age of twenty-two and ruled for only one year, during which the real power behind the throne was his mother Athaliah.

Jehoahaz went to Jezreel to visit his relative Jehoram, king of Israel, who was convalescing from the injuries that he had received in a battle against the Arameans. The kings met at the field of Naboth, where Jehu, the commander of the army of Israel, found them.

Jehoram asked Jehu if all was well. Jehu answered, "How could all be well as long as Jezebel, your mother, carries on harlotries and sorceries".

Jehoram turned his chariot around and fled, crying out to Jehoahaz, "Treason, Ahaziah!" Jehu drew his bow and hit Jehoram between the shoulders. The arrow pierced his heart, and he died.

Jehoahaz tried to escape in his chariot, but he was wounded. He managed to go to Megiddo and died there, according to the second book of Kings (2 Kings 9:27).

The second book of Chronicles (2 Chronicles 22:9) has a different version of the events; it states that Jehoahaz was caught in Samaria, where he was hiding, was brought to the presence of Jehu, and killed.

His mother Athaliah took advantage of his death to get rid of the other members of the royal family and seize the throne of Judah.

Jehoash

(Hebrew origin: *Fire of God*)

1. (2 Kings 11:21). 9th century B.C. Jehoash—also called Joash—the seventh king of Judah, after the partition of the United Monarchy, was the son of King Ahaziah of Judah. (Please see the entry for Joash [2 Kings 11:2].)

2. (2 Kings 13:10). 8th century B.C. Jehoash—also called Joash—the twelfth king of Israel, after the partition of the United Monarchy, succeeded his father Jehoahaz and reigned sixteen years.

When the prophet Elisha was very old and mortally ill, Jehoash went to visit him and cried, when he saw how sick the prophet was. Elisha told the king to take a bow and arrows, to open the window toward the east, and to shoot an arrow from it. This arrow, explained the prophet, meant that the king would defeat the Syrians in Aphek.

Then, Elisha told the king to take the arrows and strike the ground with them. The king struck three times and stopped.

The prophet angrily told him, "If only you had struck five or six times, you would have annihilated Syria; as it is you shall defeat them only three times".

Jehoash fought three times successfully against the Syrians and recovered the towns that his father had lost.

Amaziah, the king of Judah, whose triumph in a war over the Edomites had gone to his head, challenged Jehoash but was scornfully told not to make trouble for his kingdom and himself. Amaziah, undeterred, went to war against Israel. Jehoash defeated and captured Amaziah in a battle at Bethshemesh. The Israelite king came to Jerusalem, tore down a large section of the city walls, and returned to Samaria, carrying with him all the treasuries of the

Temple and the royal palace, and a number of hostages.

Jehoash was succeeded by his son Jeroboam II.

Jehohanan

(Hebrew origin: *Favored by God*)

1. (1 Chronicles 26:3). 10th century B.C. Jehohanan, son of Meshelemiah, was one of the gatekeepers of the Tabernacle, during the reign of King David.

    His brothers were Jathniel, Jediael, Zebadiah, Zechariah, Elam, and Elioenai. His father Meshelemiah was called Shallum in the first book of Chronicles (1 Chronicles 9:17).

2. (2 Chronicles 17:15). 9th century B.C. Jehohanan commanded a force of two hundred and sixty thousand men in the army of King Jehoshaphat of Judah.

3. (2 Chronicles 23:1). 9th century B.C. His son Ishmael, together with four other army commanders, joined the conspiracy headed by Jehoiada the Priest, which succeeded in overthrowing Queen Athaliah and crowned Joash as king of Judah.

4. (Ezra 10:28). 5th century B.C. Jehohanan, descendant of Bebai, was one of the men who had married foreign women, during the time of Ezra, and who gave his word that he would divorce her.

5. (Nehemiah 12:13). 5th century B.C. Jehohanan, of the Amariah clan, was one of the chief priests in Jerusalem under the High Priest Joiakim, in the days of Nehemiah.

    He was one of the priests led by Jezrahiah, their overseer, who marched, singing at the top of their voices, in the joyful procession, which celebrated the dedication of the rebuilt walls of Jerusalem, during the days of Nehemiah.

Jehoiachin

(Hebrew origin: *God will establish*)

(2 Kings 24:6). 6th century B.C. Jehoiachin—called Jechonias by Matthew,

Coniah by Jeremiah, and elsewhere Jeconiah—the eighteenth king of Judah, after the partition of the United Monarchy, was the son of King Jehoiakim and Nehushta.

He was eighteen years old, when his father died, and he ascended to the throne. After reigning for only three months, he surrendered to Nebuchadnezzar, king of Babylon, who had laid siege to Jerusalem.

Jehoiachin, his mother, his family, officials, princes, soldiers, leading citizens, craftsmen, and smiths were taken to captivity in Babylon, together with the Temple treasures. Only the poorest people remained in the land.

His uncle Mattaniah was made king by Nebuchadnezzar, who changed his name to Zedekiah. Jehoiachin was kept in a Babylonian prison for thirty-seven years, until Evilmerodach, the new king of Babylon, in the first year of his reign, set him free, changed his prison garments to fine clothing, and gave him a place of honor in the Babylonian court.

Jehoiada

(Hebrew origin: *God knows*)

1. (2 Samuel 8:18). 10th century B.C. Jehoiada, son of Benaiah, a descendant of Aaron, deserted King Saul's army, at the head of a troop of three thousand and seven hundred men, and joined David's army in Hebron. Later, he became High Priest (1 Chronicles 27:5), and one of the main advisors of King David (1 Chronicles 27:34).

    His son Benaiah, named after Jehoiada's father, was one of the bravest and most distinguished military commanders of King David and, later, became head of the army under King Solomon.

2. (2 Kings 11:4). 9th century B.C. Jehoiada, the High Priest, during the reign of King Ahaziah, was related by marriage to the royal family; his wife Jehosheba was the sister of Ahaziah and the aunt of Jehoash, the infant son of Ahaziah.

    When Ahaziah was killed by Jehu, the rebel commander of the Israelite army, Athaliah, the queen mother, decided to grab power for herself and gave orders to kill all the members of the royal family. Only Jehoash, who was still a baby, survived, hidden by Jehosheba in a chamber of the Temple.

During her rule, Athaliah promoted the cult of the Phoenician god Baal. This provoked the hate of the priesthood and the people, who saw in Athaliah a foreign usurper and the murderer of the royal Davidic line.

When Jehoash was seven years old, Jehoiada conspired with a number of army officers to make Jehoash king. On the appointed day of the coup, the priest gave to the officers the spears and shields of King David, which had been kept in the Temple.

Jehoiada brought out the boy and proclaimed publicly in the Temple that Jehoash was the legitimate king. The priest placed the crown on the boy's head and anointed him, while everybody shouted, "God save the king".

Athaliah heard the shouts of the crowd and rushed to the Temple, screaming, "Treason! Treason!" The guards seized her and killed her at the Horse Gate of the palace. The crowd assaulted the Temple of Baal, destroyed the building and the idols, and killed Mattan, the High Priest of Baal.

Jehoash became king at the age of seven and reigned for forty years. Jehoiada became his closest and most trusted adviser, and he even chose the two wives whom the king married.

The king noticed that the money donated by the people was not being used to repair the Temple, and he gave instructions that the money should no longer be kept by the priests. Jehoiada took a chest, made a hole on its lid, converting it into a collection box, which he placed beside the altar. The priests were ordered to put in it all the money that was brought to the Temple. Periodically, the king's scribe and Jehoiada would together open the chest, count the money, and put it in bags. The money was given directly to the supervisors of the work done in the Temple to pay the carpenters, builders, masons, and stonecutters, and also to buy the timber, stones, and all the other materials needed. None of the money was used to make utensils of silver or gold for the House of God. Jehoiada did not request an accounting from the men to whom he gave the money, as he considered them to be completely honest.

Thus, the Temple was repaired by means of contributions solicited from the nation and restored to its former glory. Jehoiada died at a very old age and was buried in the royal tombs of the City of David, in recognition of the service that he had given to the Temple and to the king. His son Zechariah succeeded him as High Priest

After Jehoiada's death, the people stopped worshipping in the Temple and reverted to idolatry. Zechariah told the people that they were bringing disaster upon themselves for disobeying God's commands. The king, in his anger at Zechariah, forgot everything that he owed to Jehoiada and gave orders to stone him to death in the courtyard of the Temple. Years later, conspirators killed Jehoash to avenge the death of Zechariah.

3. (1 Chronicles 27:34). 10th century B.C. Jehoiada, son of Benaiah, was one of the main advisors of King David.

4. (Jeremiah 29:26). 7th century B.C. Jehoiada was the High Priest, during the days of Jeremiah. He was succeeded by Zephaniah, son of Maaseiah.

Jehoiakim

(Hebrew origin: *God will raise*)

(2 Kings 23:34). 7th century B.C. Eliakim, the son of King Josiah and Zebudah, was crowned as the seventeenth king of Judah by Pharaoh Necho, who gave him the name of Jehoiakim. He was twenty-five years old at the time.

Eliakim had one older brother, Johanan, the firstborn; and two younger ones: Mattaniah, who later became King Zedekiah; and Shallum, who reigned under the name Jehoahaz.

Pharaoh Necho deposed King Jehoahaz and placed Jehoiakim on the throne, as his vassal. Four years later, Necho was defeated by Nebuchadrezzar, king of Babylon, in the battle of Carchemish, by the river Euphrates.

Jehoiakim became a vassal of Babylon. Three years later, disregarding the advice of the prophet Jeremiah, he rebelled against Babylon.

A prophet, Urijah, son of Shemaiah, fled for his life to Egypt to escape the murderous wrath of the king, for having dared to speak against him. Jehoiakim sent a group of men to Egypt, led by Elnathan, son of Achbor, to capture Urijah and bring him back to Jerusalem. The prophet was brought to the presence of the king, who killed him with his sword.

Sometime later, the prophet Jeremiah dictated his prophecies to his trusted companion Baruch, who wrote them in a scroll. The scroll was brought to the royal palace and was read aloud to the king, who listened to it, while warming himself with a fire burning in a brazier next to him. After listening to three or four columns, the king would cut that segment with a knife and throw it into the fire, until the entire scroll was consumed by the fire.

After he burned the scroll, the king commanded three of his officials—Jerahmeel, Seraiah, and Shelemiah—to arrest Jeremiah and Baruch, but they could not find them.

Jeremiah criticized King Jehoiakim bitterly, accusing him of building for himself a luxurious palace, instead of following his father Josiah's example of caring for his people (Jeremiah 22:15). When he died, he was succeeded by his son Jehoiachin.

Jehoiarib

(Hebrew origin: *God will contend*)

1. (1 Chronicles 9:10). 6th century B.C. Jehoiarib—called Joiarib in the book of Nehemiah (Nehemiah 11:10)—father of Jedaiah, was one of the priests who returned to Jerusalem with Zerubbabel and served under the High Priest Jeshua.

Jehoiarib was the ancestor of a priestly clan that was led by Mattenai, when Joiakim was the High Priest, during the days of Nehemiah (Nehemiah 12:19).

2. (1 Chronicles 24:7). 10th century B.C. During the reign of King David, the priestly service in the Tabernacle was divided by lot into twenty-four turns. Jehoiarib was in charge of the first turn.

Jehonadab

(Hebrew origin: *Generosity of God*)

(2 Kings 10:15). 9th century B.C. Jehonadab—called Jonadab in the book of Jeremiah (Jeremiah 35:6)—son of Rechab, was the leader of an ascetic sect, who abstained from wine, did not sow seeds nor plant vineyards, and did not build houses but lived in tents.

Jehonadab assisted Jehu, the commander of King Joram's army, to seize the throne of Israel and exterminate the entire house of Omri, and the followers of Baal.

Centuries later, the prophet Jeremiah praised the sect to the men of Jerusalem as an example to follow of people who kept their commandments and principles.

Jehonathan

(Hebrew origin: *God gave*)

1. (1 Chronicles 27:25). 10th century B.C. Jehonathan, son of Uzziah, was in charge of the warehouses in the fields, cities, villages, and citadels, during the reign of King David.

2. (2 Chronicles 17:8). 9th century B.C. Jehonathan, a Levite, was sent by King Jehoshaphat in the third year of his reign, to teach the laws of God in the cities of Judah. Jehonathan was accompanied in his mission by other Levites, by two priests—Elishama and Jehoram—and by several officials of the court.

3. (Nehemiah 12:18). 5th century B.C. Jehonathan was the head of a priestly clan, descended from Shemaiah, when Joiakim was the High Priest, in the days of Nehemiah.

Jehoram

(Hebrew origin: *God raised*)

1. (1 Kings 22:50). 9th century B.C. Jehoram—also called Joram—the fifth king of Judah, after the partition of the United Monarchy, was thirty-two years old, when his father Jehoshaphat died, and he ascended to the throne. His brothers had received from their father Jehoshaphat generous gifts of gold, silver, and fenced cities.

When Jehoram ascended to the throne, he killed all his brothers and some high officials of the kingdom.

His wife Athaliah, daughter of Omri, king of Israel, introduced the worship of Baal, a foreign pagan cult, in the kingdom.

During Jehoram's reign, the vassal nation of Edom broke away and declared itself an independent kingdom. Jehoram led a military expedition against the Edomites but was defeated.

Also, during this time—while the king and the army were probably away from Jerusalem—Philistines and Arabs raided the city, looted the royal palace, and absconded with all the king's wives and sons, except for Ahaziah, Jehoram's youngest son. The raiders killed the captured princes.

Due to these unfortunate events and to the idolatrous activities of his wife Athaliah, Jehoram was not popular with the people. After ruling for eight years, he died, after a long and painful illness, and nobody mourned him. He was buried in the City of David, but not in the royal tombs. His son Ahaziah succeeded him.

2. (2 Kings 1:17). 9th century B.C. Jehoram—also called Joram—ninth king of Israel, after the partition of the United Monarchy, was the son of Ahab and Jezebel, and he succeeded to the throne, after the death of his brother Ahaziah. (Please see the entry for Joram [2 Kings 8:16].)

3. (2 Chronicles 17:8). 9th century B.C. Jehoram, a priest, was sent by King Jehoshaphat, in the third year of his reign, to teach the laws of God in the cities of Judah. Jehoram was accompanied in his mission by a priest called Elishama, several officials of the court, and a number of Levites.

Jehoshabeath

(Hebrew origin: *God's oath*)

(2 Chronicles 22:11). 9th century B.C. Jehoshabeath—also called Jehosheba (2 Kings 11:2)—was the daughter of King Jehoram of Judah, the sister of King Ahaziah, and the wife of Jehoiada, the High Priest

When Ahaziah was killed by Jehu, the rebel commander of the Israelite army, Athaliah, the queen mother, decided to grab power for herself and gave orders to kill all the members of the royal family. Only Jehoash, who was still a baby, survived, hidden by Jehoshabeath in a chamber of the Temple.

During her rule, Athaliah promoted the cult of the Phoenician god Baal. This provoked the hate of the priesthood and the people, who saw in Athaliah a foreign usurper and the murderer of the royal Davidic line. When Jehoash was seven years old, Jehoshabeath's husband, the priest Jehoiada, headed a successful conspiracy, which killed Athaliah and proclaimed Jehoash as king.

Jehoshaphat

(Hebrew origin: *God judged*)

1. (2 Samuel 8:16). 10th century B.C. Jehoshaphat, son of Ahilud, was the court recorder under King David and King Solomon. His brother, Baana, one of King Solomon's twelve district governors, was in charge of a district that included the cities of Megiddo and Bethshean.

2. (1 Kings 4:17). 10th century B.C. Jehoshaphat, son of Paruah, was one of

King Solomon's twelve district governors, responsible for providing food from his district, the territory of Issachar, for the king and the royal household for one month out of each year.

3. (1 Kings 15:24). 9th century B.C. Jehoshaphat, son of King Asa and Azubah, was the fourth king of Judah, after the partition of the United Monarchy. He ascended to the throne at the age of thirty-five and ruled for twenty-five years.

Jehoshaphat was the most capable king that Judah ever had, and, during his reign, the kingdom enjoyed peace and prosperity. His accomplishments were wide ranging. He reorganized the judicial system, appointing both local judges and a central judicial body in Jerusalem. He continued the religious policies of his father, destroyed many of the local altars, and restored the central authority of the Temple in Jerusalem, with Amariah, the High Priest, being in charge of all religious matters. He sent a group of priests, Levites, and officials of the court to teach the laws of God in the cities of the kingdom. He fortified towns and fortresses and expanded the army, which grew to over one million soldiers. To achieve a stable peace with the kingdom of Israel, he married his son and heir Jehoram to the princess Athaliah, daughter of King Omri.

His control over Edom, through a governor whom he appointed, allowed him to use the port of Ezion-Geber, near today's Eilat in the Red Sea. He intended to renew foreign commerce and built a fleet, which, unfortunately, sank, before it could sail, realizing the prophecy of Eliezer who had said that, as a punishment for Jehoshaphat having entered into an alliance with King Ahaziah of Israel, his ships would be broken, and he would not be able to go to Tarshish.

During a visit that Jehoshaphat made to King Ahab, the son of King Omri, he was asked by Ahab to help him recover Ramothgilead from the hands of the king of Aram. Jehoshaphat answered that he was willing, but first, he wanted to consult God. Ahab gathered about four hundred prophets and asked them if he should attack Ramoth or not, and they all answered in one voice, "Attack, the Lord will give you victory".

Jehoshaphat, still not convinced, asked if there was another prophet of God through whom they could inquire. Ahab answered that there was one more, Micaiah, the son of Imlah, whom he hated because he never prophesied anything good for the king, only misfortune, but King Jehoshaphat replied that Ahab shouldn't say that.

An official was sent to bring Micaiah to the presence of the two kings, who, dressed in their royal robes, were sitting on their thrones at the threshing place at the entrance of the gate of Samaria.

All the prophets were in front of the kings, predicting victory. One of them, Zedekiah, the son of Chenaanah, had iron horns with him and told Ahab that with those horns, the king would defeat the Arameans.

The official sent to bring Micaiah to the kings' presence told the prophet that all the other prophets had predicted victory, and that Micaiah should better do the same. Micaiah answered that he would only speak what God would tell him.

When he came before the king, the king asked him if they should march against Ramoth or not. The prophet answered, "Go and triumph, for the Lord will deliver it into your hands". Ahab sensed sarcasm in the prophet's answer and said, "How many times must I ask you to tell me nothing but the truth in the name of the Lord?"

The prophet replied that he could see the army of Israel scattered over the hills like sheep without a shepherd. Ahab, on an aside, told Jehoshaphat, "Didn't I tell you that he would not prophesy anything good for me, but only misfortune?" The prophet continued, "I saw God seated upon his throne with all the angels standing around him. And God asked, 'Who will convince

Ahab so that he will go and be killed at Ramoth?' A spirit stepped forward and said that he would entice Ahab by making the prophets tell lies, and God told him to go forth and deceive him". Micaiah concluded, "God has made your prophets lie to you, for He has decreed disaster upon you".

The prophet Zedekiah went to Micaiah, slapped his face, and asked, "Which way did the Spirit of the Lord pass from me to speak to you?" And Micaiah replied, "You will find out on the day when you try to hide into some back room".

The king ordered his guards to put Micaiah in prison, under the supervision of Amon, the governor of the city, and Prince Joash, and to give him only bread and water, until the king would return safely. Micaiah's parting words were, "If you return safely then God has not spoken through me!"

King Ahab and King Jehoshaphat went to attack the city of Ramothgilead. King Ahab told Jehoshaphat that he would go disguised into battle, but that the king of Judah should wear his royal clothing.

The king of Aram had commanded his thirty-two chariot commanders to attack no one else except the king of Israel. The Arameans saw Jehoshaphat and, thinking that he was Ahab, attacked him. Jehoshaphat cried out, and the Arameans realized that he was not the king of Israel, and they turned back from pursuing him. Ahab was wounded by a chance arrow, and that evening, he died.

When Jehoram, after the death of his brother Ahaziah, ascended to the throne of Israel, he asked Jehoshaphat to join him and to recruit also his vassal, the king of Edom, in a war against Moab, a vassal kingdom of Israel who wanted to be independent.

The armies of Judah, Israel, and Edom traveled for seven days, until there was no water left for the soldiers and their cattle. The prophet Elisha was called, and upon his arrival, he told the king of Israel that he

would not deign to even look at him if the king of Judah had not been also present. Elisha asked them to bring a musician, and, while the musician played, he told them that God commanded them to dig ditches. The next morning, water came rushing down from the heights of Edom and turned the ditches into pools.

Early the next morning, the Moabites, thinking that the red reflection of the rising sun on the pools was blood, and convinced that the kings' armies had fought between themselves, attacked the allied camp but were repulsed and defeated. When the king of Moab saw that the battle was lost, he sacrificed his heir, the successor to the throne, to his god. The shocked allied army left Moab and returned home.

Sometime later, the Moabites, this time allied to the Ammonites, came to Judah with a great army. Jahaziel, a Levite, prophesied to King Jehoshaphat that he would not have to fight against the invading army, because God would win the battle. The prophecy came true, when the invaders fought among themselves and annihilated each other.

Jehoshaphat designated his son Jehoram as heir to the throne, and, to compensate his other sons, he gave them gifts of gold, silver, and fenced cities. Jehoshaphat died at the age of sixty and was buried in the royal tombs in the City of David. Jehoram succeeded him, and, as soon as he felt secure in the throne, he had all his brothers killed with the sword.

4. (2 Kings 9:2). 9th century B.C. Jehoshaphat, son of Nimshi, was the father of Jehu, the commander of the army who rebelled against King Jehoram, killed him, and seized the throne.

Jehosheba

(Hebrew origin: *God's oath*)

(2 Kings 11:2). 9th century B.C. Jehosheba—also called Jehoshabeath—was the daughter of King Jehoram of Judah, the sister of King Ahaziah, and the wife of Jehoiada, the

High Priest. (Please see the entry for Jehoshabeath [2 Chronicles 22:11].)

Jehoshua

(Hebrew origin: *God saved*)

(Numbers 13:16). 13th century B.C. Jehoshua is an alternative spelling for Joshua, the leader of the Hebrews, during the conquest of Canaan. (Please see the entry for Joshua [Exodus 17:9].)

Jehoshuah

(Hebrew origin: *God saved*)

(1 Chronicles 7:27). 13th century B.C. Jehoshuah is an alternative spelling for Joshua, the leader of the Hebrews, during the conquest of Canaan. (Please see the entry for Joshua [Exodus 17:9].)

Jehovah

(Hebrew origin: *The Eternal*)

(Exodus 6:3). This is a transliteration of the four Hebrew letters—Tetragrammaton—YHWH or JHVH, the biblical proper name for God. In today's Judaism, when the Tetragrammaton is read aloud from the Scriptures or the prayer books, it is rendered as Adonai, *The Lord*, because only the High Priest was allowed to pronounce it correctly.

Jehozabad

(Hebrew origin: *God endowed*)

1. (2 Kings 12:21). 8th century B.C. Jehozabad was an official in the court of King Jehoash. His father was Shomer, and his mother was a Moabitess called Shimrith (2 Chronicles 24:26).

   After the death of the priest Jehoiada, the people stopped worshipping in the Temple and reverted to idolatry. Zechariah, son of the priest Jehoiada, protested, and the king had him killed.

   Jehozabad and another of the king's officials, Jozachar, son of Shimeath, decided to avenge the death of Zechariah

and killed Jehoash who was lying in bed, recuperating from injuries received in a battle against the king of Aram.

Amaziah succeeded his father to the throne and put the two murderers to death.

2. (1 Chronicles 26:4). 10th century B.C. Jehozabad, the second son of Obededom, was, like his father and seven brothers, a gatekeeper of the Tabernacle, during the reign of King David. His brothers were Ammiel, Shemaiah, Joah, Sacar, Nethaneel, Issachar, and Peulthai.

3. (2 Chronicles 17:18). 9th century B.C. Jehozabad commanded a force of one hundred and eighty thousand men in the army of King Jehoshaphat of Judah.

Jehozadak

(Hebrew origin: *God is righteous*)

(1 Chronicles 6:14). 6th century B.C. The priest Jehozadak—called Jozadak in the book of Ezra (Ezra 3:2), and Josedech in the books of Haggai and Zechariah—son of Seraiah, was carried into captivity, by Nebuchadnezzar, when the Babylonians conquered the kingdom of Judah. His son, the High Priest Jeshua—also called Joshua—returned with Zerubbabel from the Babylonian Exile.

Jehu

(Hebrew origin: *God is He*)

1. (1 Kings 16:1). 9th century B.C. Jehu, son of Hanani, the seer, prophesied against King Baasha of Israel, announcing that his dynasty would come to an end and his descendants would be eaten by dogs and birds, because the king had induced the people of Israel to sin. Jehu wrote a book about King Jehoshaphat, which has not come down to us.

2. (1 Kings 19:16). 9th century B.C. Jehu, the commander of King Joram's army, exterminated the entire house of Omri and made himself the tenth king of Israel, after the partition of the United Monarchy. The dynasty that he established ruled Israel for almost one hundred years.

The prophet Elijah was commanded by God to anoint Hazael to be king over Syria, and Jehu to be king over Israel. He sent one of his disciples with a box of oil to the army camp in Ramothgilead. The young man found Jehu, who was accompanied by other officers, and asked to talk to him in private. When they were alone, he poured the oil on Jehu's head and announced that God had anointed him to be king of Israel, and it was his task to kill the house of Ahab and to avenge the blood of the prophets killed by Jezebel. Having said this, the disciple opened the door and fled.

Jehu went back to his companions and told him that he had been anointed king of Israel. The officers blew the trumpets and proclaimed Jehu as king.

Jehu, after instructing them not to let anybody out of the city, rode his chariot to Jezreel where King Joram was recuperating from the wounds, which he had received in the battle against the Syrians. A watchman on the tower in Jezreel saw the chariot approaching from a distance and told the king that the driver was Jehu because of his distinctive furious driving.

Joram, king of Israel, and Ahaziah, king of Judah, each in his chariot, drove toward Jehu and met him in the property of the murdered Naboth the Jezreelite. Joram asked Jehu if all was well. Jehu answered, "How could all be well as long as Jezebel, your mother, carries on harlotries and sorceries". Joram turned his chariot around and fled, crying out to Ahaziah, "Treason, Ahaziah!" Jehu drew his bow and hit Jehoram between the shoulders. The arrow pierced his heart, and he died. Jehu told Bidkar, his officer, to throw the body in the property of Naboth, to avenge the blood of the murdered Naboth, whose death was due to the greed of King Ahab.

Ahaziah, the king of Judah, saw this and fled, by the way of the garden house. Jehu followed him and had him shot with arrows. Ahaziah, mortally wounded, fled to Megiddo and died there.

Jehu went to the palace, where Jezebel, having heard what had happened, painted her face and looked out from the window. She saw Jehu and greeted him sarcastically as "Zimri, the regicide". Jehu lifted his face to the window and told the eunuchs who were with the queen to throw her down. Her blood sprinkled on the wall, and Jehu trampled her with his horse.

Jehu wrote to the elders of Samaria, challenging them to choose as king one of the seventy sons of Ahab who lived in the city, and to fight against him. The elders, afraid for their lives, wrote back, declaring themselves his servants, ready to do anything that he would command. Jehu sent them instructions to cut the heads of all the seventy sons of Ahab. The elders killed the princes, put their heads in baskets, and sent them to Jezreel to Jehu.

Jehu went to Samaria and saw a group of people on the way. He asked who they were, and, when told that they were the brothers of Ahaziah, king of Judah, who had come to salute the children of the king of Israel, he had them killed.

His next target was the followers of Baal, the Phoenician god brought to Israel by Jezebel. He asked Jehonadab, son of Rechab, the leader of an ascetic sect, to help him in his mission. When Jehonadab said yes, Jehu pulled him up into his chariot and took him to Samaria, where Jehu killed all the surviving relatives of King Ahab of Israel.

Jehu told the followers of Baal that he wanted to offer a sacrifice to their god, and that they should all gather in a solemn assembly inside their Temple. When they were all inside, Jehu and Jehonadab entered the Temple and told the followers of Baal to make sure that only they were inside the Temple. Then, Jehu gave instructions to the army to kill them all, and let no one escape, to destroy the image of Baal, and to tear down the Temple of the idol.

Jehu earned the hostility of Judah and Phoenicia by his murderous actions, and he found himself in political isolation. He did not have any allies to help him defend against Aram's pressure on Israel's north-eastern border. This caused him to lose the territories east of the Jordan River to the Arameans. His attempt to buy the king of Assyria's protection by paying him tribute did not help him, and at the end of his reign, his kingdom had shrunk to just the territory of Ephraim. After reigning for twenty-eight years, he died and was succeeded by his son Jehoahaz, also called Joahaz.

Note: According to the first book of Kings, the father of Jehu was Nimshi (1 Kings 19:16). However, the second book of Kings states that his father was Jehoshaphat, and Nimshi was his grandfather (2 Kings 9:2).

3. (1 Chronicles 2:38). Unspecified date. Jehu, son of Obed and father of Azariah, was a descendant of Jarha, an Egyptian servant who married the daughter of his master Sheshan. Jehu's grandson was called Helez.

4. (1 Chronicles 4:35). 8th century B.C. Jehu, the son of Josibiah, was one of the leaders of the tribe of Simeon who went to the fertile valley of Gedor in search of pasture for their flocks, during the reign of Hezekiah, king of Judah.

The Simeonites destroyed the tents of the people—descendants of Ham—who lived there, wiped them out forever, and settled in their place.

5. (1 Chronicles 12:3).11th century B.C. Jehu, the Antothite, was one of a group of Benjamites, commanded by Ahiezer, who deserted King Saul's army and joined David's band at Ziklag. These men were skilled warriors who could use both their right and left hands to shoot arrows and sling stones.

Jehubbah

(Hebrew origin: *Hidden*)

(1 Chronicles 7:34). Unspecified date. Jehubbah, son of Shamer, of the tribe of Asher, was a chief of his clan. His brothers were Ahi, Rohgah, and Aram.

Jehucal

(Hebrew origin: *Potent*)

(Jeremiah 37:3). 6th century B.C. Jehucal—also called Jucal (Jeremiah 38:1)—son of Shelemiah, was an official in the court of King Zedekiah.

He and Zephaniah, the son of Maaseiah, were sent to Jeremiah by the king, to ask the prophet to pray for the king, who was threatened by the Babylonian army.

Later, when Jehucal heard that Jeremiah was preaching surrender, he went with some other officials to King Zedekiah, accused Jeremiah of weakening the will of the people, with his defeatist talk, and asked that the prophet should be put to death.

Zedekiah turned Jeremiah to Jehucal and his companions, who cast the prophet into the dungeon of Malchiah, which was in the court of the prison.

Jehudi

(Hebrew origin: *Descendant of Judah*)

(Jeremiah 36:14). 7th century B.C. Jehudi, son of Nethaniah, was an official in the court of King Jehoiakim. His fellow officials sent him to bring Baruch, Jeremiah's trusted companion, to the palace to read aloud the scroll dictated by the prophet. Baruch read them the scroll in the chamber of the scribe Elishama.

When the king heard about the content of the roll, he sent Jehudi to bring it to him. Jehudi returned with the roll and read it to the king, who was warming himself with a fire burning in a brazier next to him. After Jehudi had read three or four columns, the king would cut that segment with a knife and throw it into the fire, until the entire scroll was consumed by the fire.

Jehudijah

(Hebrew origin: *Woman descendant of Judah*)

(1 Chronicles 4:18). Unspecified date. Jehudijah—probably not a name but an indication of her tribal origin—was one of the two wives of Mered, a descendant of Judah, whose other wife was Bithiah, the daughter of the

Pharaoh. Jehudijah was the mother of Jered, Heber, and Jekuthiel.

Jehush

(Hebrew origin: *Hasty*)

(1 Chronicles 8:39). Unspecified date. Jehush, the second son of Eshek of the tribe of Benjamin, was a descendant of Jonathan, the son of King Saul. His brothers were Ulam and Eliphelet.

Jeiel

(Hebrew origin: *Carried away of God*)

1. (1 Chronicles 5:7). Unspecified date. Jeiel was the leader of a clan of the tribe of Reuben.
2. (1 Chronicles 15:18). 10th century B.C. Jeiel—also called Jehiah (1 Chronicles 15:24)—was a gatekeeper and Levite of the second rank. He was one of the Levites chosen, by the chief of the Levites, to sing and play musical instruments in front of the Ark of the Covenant, when it was carried from the house of Obededom to its resting place in Jerusalem, as commanded by David.
3. (2 Chronicles 20:14). Unspecified date. Jeiel, a descendant of Asaph, was an ancestor of Jahaziel, the Levite who prophesied to King Jehoshaphat that he would not have to fight against a great army of Moabites and Ammonites who were coming against him, because God would win the battle. The prophecy came true, when the invaders fought among themselves and annihilated each other.
4. (2 Chronicles 26:11). 8th century B.C. Jeiel, a scribe in the court of King Uzziah, was in charge of the records concerning the number of soldiers in the army of Judah. He and Maaseiah worked under the supervision of Hananiah, one of the king's officials.
5. (2 Chronicles 29:13). 8th century B.C. Jeiel and Shimri, descendants of Elizaphan, were among the Levites who assembled all the other Levites to make themselves ritually clean, and to purify the Temple, during the reign of King Hezekiah of Judah.
6. (2 Chronicles 35:9). 7th century B.C. Jeiel was one of the Levites who donated cattle and oxen for the Passover offerings, during the reign of King Josiah.
7. (Ezra 8:13). 5th century B.C. Jeiel was a descendant of Adonikam. He, together with his brothers Eliphelet and Shemaiah, and another sixty males, returned with Ezra to Jerusalem from the Babylonian Exile, during the reign of King Artaxerxes.
8. (Ezra 10:43). 5th century B.C. Jeiel, a descendant of Nebo, divorced his foreign wife, during the days of Ezra.

Jekameam

(Hebrew origin: *The people will rise*)

(1 Chronicles 23:19). Unspecified date. Jekameam was a Levite descendant of Hebron, the son of Kohath and grandson of Levi.

Jekamiah

(Hebrew origin: *God will rise*)

(1 Chronicles 2:41). Unspecified date. Jekamiah was the son of Shallum and the father of Elishama.

Jekuthiel

(Hebrew origin: *Obedience of God*)

(1 Chronicles 4:18). Unspecified date. Jekuthiel, a descendant of Judah, was the son of Mered and Jehudijah. His brothers were Jered and Heber. Jekuthiel was the founder of Zanoah.

Jemima

(Hebrew origin: *Warm, affectionate* [hence, *Dove*])

(Job 42:14). Unspecified date. Jemima was one of the three beautiful daughters born to Job, after he recuperated his health and his wealth. The other two daughters were Kezia and Kerenhappuch.

The three girls shared their father's inheritance with their brothers.

Jemuel

(Hebrew origin: *Day of God*).

(Genesis 46:10). 17th century B.C. Jemuel, son of Simeon and grandson of Jacob, was one of the seventy Israelites who immigrated to Egypt, together with his brothers—Jamin, Ohad, Jachin, Zohar, and Shaul—the last of whom was the son of a Canaanite woman.

Jemuel is called Nemuel in the book of Numbers (Numbers 26:12), where he is mentioned as being the ancestor of the clan of the Nemuelites.

Jephthae

(Hebrew origin: *He will open*)

(Hebrew 11:32). 12th century B.C. Jephthae is an alternative spelling of the name Jephthah.

Jephthah

(Hebrew origin: *He will open*)

(Judges 11:1). 12th century B.C. Jephthah, a man who became renowned for his bravery, was born in the region of Gilead. His father was Gilead, and his mother was a harlot.

His half brothers, sons of their father's legitimate wife, fearful that Jephthah would share in their inheritance, expelled him from the family's home, when he grew up. Jephthah fled to the land of Tob, where he surrounded himself with a band of men of low character.

When the Israelites felt threatened by the Ammonites, the elders of Gilead went to the land of Tob and asked Jephthah to lead their army against the Ammonites.

Jephthah asked them, "You rejected me and drove me out of my father's house. How can you now come to me and ask for help?"

"If you agree to lead the fight against the Ammonites, we would recognize you as the leader in Gilead", said the elders.

Jephthah accepted the offer, returned with the elders to Gilead, and assumed the command of the army in Mizpeh.

He first tried to solve the crisis peacefully, by diplomatic means. He sent messengers to the Ammonite king, asking him why he was attacking them. The king replied that Israel was occupying his land, and he demanded that it should be returned to him.

Jephthah sent his messengers back to Ammon to explain that the Israelites, when they came out of Egypt, had not taken any land from Moab or Ammon. They had not even entered the territory of Moab, but they had fought against Sihon, king of the Amorites, and, after defeating him, had taken possession of the territory of the Amorites. Since then, three hundred years ago, the Israelites had inhabited the land and, not once, during this whole period, had the Ammonites tried to recover it. Therefore, he could not see any justification for Ammon's demands.

The king of Ammon rejected these arguments and continued his aggression. Seeing that the crisis could not be solved by peaceful means, Jephthah marched with his army toward the Ammonites. Before engaging in battle, Jephthah made a vow to God, saying, "If God delivers the Ammonites into my hands, then whatever comes out of my house to meet me on my return, shall be offered by me as a sacrifice to God". The Ammonites were routed, and Jephthah returned victorious to his house in Mizpeh.

His daughter, an only child, came out of the house to welcome him with timbrels and dances. Jephthah, horrified, rented his clothes and cried that he could not take back his vow. The daughter accepted her fate with resignation, but she asked that she should be given two months to go to the hills, with her companions, and lament her virginity. When she returned, Jephthah carried out the vow. This tragedy originated the custom for young girls in Israel to express their sorrow for the daughter of Jephthah, during four days every year.

The tribe of Ephraim complained to Jephthah that he had not asked them to help him against the Ammonites, and they threatened to burn down his house. Jephthah replied that he had summoned them, but they had not reacted. Jephthah gathered an army of Gileadites and defeated the Ephraimites.

The Ephraimites tried to escape by crossing

the river. The Gileadites, who controlled the approaches to the Jordan River, asked each one of the survivors if he was an Ephraimite. If the man denied it, he was asked to say "Shibboleth", a word which the Ephraimites pronounced as "Sibboleth". If he didn't pronounce the word correctly, the Gileadites killed him. Forty-two thousand Ephraimites were, thus, massacred.

Jephthah judged Israel for six years, until his death. He was buried in one of the cities of Gilead.

Note: In the book of Judges, a judge is a ruler or governor of territory or a military leader in pre-monarchical Israel. Later, during the monarchy, the king served in this role and judges were more like the judicial officers that we know today.

Jephunneh

(Hebrew origin: *He will prepared*)

1. (Numbers 13:6) 14th century B.C. His son Caleb was one of the twelve men sent by Moses to Canaan to spy on the land. When the men returned and gave their report, Caleb and Joshua were the only spies who believed that the Israelites were strong enough to attack at once and conquer the land. The other ten expressed fear and defeatism and discouraged the people.

   The genealogical lists mention a Caleb, son of Hezron (1 Chronicles 2:18). If the references are to the same person, then Jephunneh was also called Hezron.

2. (1 Chronicles 7:38). Unspecified date. Jephunneh, son of Jether, was a brave warrior and leader of a clan of the tribe of Asher. His brothers were Ara and Pispah.

Jerah

(Hebrew origin: *Moon*)

(Genesis 10:26). Unspecified date. Jerah was the son of Joktan, descendant of Noah through Shem, Noah's second son. His brothers were Sheleph, Hazarmaveth, Almodad, Hadoram, Uzal, Diklah, Ebal, Abimael, Sheba, Ophir, Havilah, and Jobab.

Jerahmeel

(Hebrew origin: *God will be compassionate*)

1. (1 Chronicles 2:9). Unspecified date. Jerahmeel, the eldest son of Hezron, a descendant of Judah, was the brother of Chelubai—also called Caleb—and Ram, the ancestor of King David. His sons were Ram, Bunah, Oren, Ozem, and Ahijah. Jerahmeel had another wife called Atarah, with whom he had a son called Onam.

2. (1 Chronicles 24:29). 10th century B.C. Jerahmeel, son of Kish, was a Levite who served in the Tabernacle, during the reign of King David.

3. (Jeremiah 36:26). 7th century B.C. Jerahmeel, son of Hammelech, was one of the court officials—the others were Seraiah, son of Azriel, and Shelemiah, son of Abdeel—commanded by King Jehoiakim to arrest the prophet Jeremiah and Baruch, his trusted companion. They failed in their mission, because Jeremiah and Baruch had gone into hiding.

   His brother Malchiah was the owner of a dungeon, situated in the court of the prison, where Jeremiah was kept for a while.

   Note: Some scholars believe that Hammelech—translated as *The King*—is not a given name but a title, in which case, Jerahmeel was a royal prince, son of a king, either King Josiah or King Jehoiakim.

Jered

(Hebrew origin: *Descent*)

1. (1 Chronicles 1:2). Unspecified date. Jered—also spelled Jared—was the grandfather of Methuselah and the ancestor of Noah. (Please see the entry for Jared [Genesis 5:15].)

2. (1 Chronicles 4:18). Unspecified date. Jered, a descendant of Judah, was the son of Jehudijah. He was the founder of Gedor and the brother of Heber and Jekuthiel.

Jeremai

(Hebrew origin: *Elevated*)

(Ezra 10:33). 5th century B.C. Jeremai, a descendant of Hashum, divorced his foreign wife, during the days of Ezra.

Jeremiah

(Hebrew origin: *God will rise*)

1. (2 Kings 23:31). 7th century B.C. Jeremiah of Libnah was the grandfather of two kings, Jehoahaz and Zedekiah, through his daughter Hamutal who married King Josiah.

2. (1 Chronicles 5:24). Unspecified date. Jeremiah, of the half tribe of Manasseh, who had settled east of the Jordan River, was a mighty warrior and leader of his clan. His tribe was deported from their land by the Assyrians and forcibly settled in the region of the river Gozan, where it eventually assimilated into the local population and disappeared from history, being remembered today as one of the "ten lost tribes".

3. (1 Chronicles 12:4). 11th century B.C. Jeremiah was one of the Benjamites who deserted King Saul's army and joined David's band at Ziklag. These men were skilled warriors who could use both their right and left hands to shoot arrows and sling stones.

4. (1 Chronicles 12:10 and 1 Chronicles 12:13). 11th century B.C. They were two Gadites by the name of Jeremiah, both of them captains of the army and very brave men; they joined David at Ziklag, while he was still hiding from King Saul.

5. (Nehemiah 10:2). 5th century B.C. Jeremiah was one of the priests who signed Nehemiah's solemn agreement to separate themselves from the foreigners living in the land, to refrain from intermarrying with them, and to dedicate their firstborn to God, among other obligations.

6. (Nehemiah 12:1). 6th century B.C. Jeremiah was one of the priests who returned with Zerubbabel from the Babylonian Exile and became ancestor of a priestly clan, called by his name. The leader of the clan, during the days of Nehemiah and the High Priest Joiakim, was Hananiah.

7. (Nehemiah 12:34). 5th century B.C. Jeremiah was one of the leaders of the people who marched in the joyful procession, which celebrated the dedication of the rebuilt walls of Jerusalem, during the days of Nehemiah.

8. (Jeremiah 1:1). 7th and 6th century B.C. Jeremiah, son of Hilkiah, a descendant of a priestly family, was born around the middle of the 7th century B.C. in Anathoth, a village in the Benjamin region, not far from Jerusalem.

The book called by his name comprises his prophesies, from the thirteenth year of the reign of Josiah—latter part of the 7th century B.C.—until after the destruction of the kingdom of Judah by the Babylonians, at the beginning of the 6th century B.C. The book also contains biographical and autobiographical narratives concerning the prophet and his activities, as well as historical records of the destruction of Jerusalem, and of the subsequent events, which took place in Judah and in Egypt.

Jeremiah, who never married, was wholly dedicated to his mission, which was to warn the people of the catastrophe that was to fall upon the nation because of their idolatry and sin. He lived to see his predictions come true with the fall of Jerusalem to Nebuchadnezzar, the Babylonian king, the destruction of the city and the Temple, and the exile to Babylonia of the king of Judah, and many of the inhabitants of Jerusalem.

He also foretold, but did not live to see, the eventual return of the people from the Babylonian Exile, and the restoration of the nation.

Jeremiah, horrified and shocked at the prevailing apostasy, began to preach as a young man. He went to the court of the Temple, thundered against sin, warned of its terrible consequences, and predicted that God would bring a disaster upon Jerusalem. Pashur, son of Immer, the priest in charge of the Temple, heard him, had him flogged, and put him in a cell at the Upper Benjamin Gate in the Temple.

The next day, Jeremiah was brought to Pashur's presence to be released. He prophesied to Pashur that he and his family would be taken into captivity and would die and be buried in Babylon.

During the first year of King Jehoiakim's reign, Jeremiah went to the Temple and told the priests and the people that, if they would not repent, the Temple and Jerusalem would become a curse to all nations. The mob crowded around him and threatened to kill him.

The palace officials heard the shouts and rushed to the Temple to inquire what was going on. The priests told them that Jeremiah deserved to die for having dared to prophesy against the city. Jeremiah defended himself, saying that it was God who had sent him to prophesy. The officials told the priests that Jeremiah was innocent.

During that time, a prophet, Urijah, son of Shemaiah, who had prophesied that Jerusalem was doomed, fled for his life to Egypt to escape the murderous wrath of the king. Jehoiakim sent a group of men to Egypt, led by Elnathan, son of Achbor, to capture Urijah and bring him back to Jerusalem. The prophet was brought to the presence of the king, who killed him with his sword.

Jeremiah was not persecuted at that time, because he enjoyed the protection of Ahikam, son of Shaphan, an influential member of the royal court.

Several members of the clan of the Rechabites were brought by the prophet Jeremiah to one of the chambers of the Temple, where he offered them wine. They refused to drink, because their ancestor Jonadab, son of Rechab, had forbidden them to drink wine. Jeremiah praised the Rechabites to the men of Jerusalem as an example to follow of people who keep their commandments and principles.

Baruch, son of Neriah and grandson of Maaseiah, was the scribe of Jeremiah and his constant companion. Jeremiah dictated his prophecies to Baruch who wrote them in a scroll.

The prophet, forbidden to go to the Temple and forced to be in hiding, instructed Baruch to go to the Temple on a fast day and read aloud the scroll, with the hope that the listeners would repent from their evil ways.

Michaiah, son of Gemariah, heard the reading and reported it to the officials of the court. Jehudi, son of Nethaniah, was sent to bring Baruch to the palace. Baruch was brought and ordered to sit and read the scroll.

Troubled by what the scroll said, the officials decided to tell the king and, at the same time, advised Baruch that he and Jeremiah should hide.

King Jehoiakim had the scroll read to him aloud, burned it, and commanded his officials—Jerahmeel, Seraiah, and Shelemiah—to arrest Jeremiah and Baruch, but they could not find them. When Jeremiah heard that the king had burned the roll, he again dictated his prophecies to Baruch, adding even more dire predictions.

King Jehoiakim died and was succeeded by his son Jehoiachin, who, after a reign of only three months, was deposed by Nebuchadnezzar, king of Babylon, and was exiled to Babylon, together with many members of the upper classes. Nebuchadnezzar chose Mattaniah, an uncle of King Jehoiachin, to be the new king, under the name of Zedekiah.

In the fourth year of the reign of Zedekiah, the king paid a royal visit to Babylon. Seraiah, brother of Baruch and an official of the court, accompanied the king in his trip, bringing a book given to him by Jeremiah, where the prophet had written all the evil that would befall on Babylon. The prophet instructed Seraiah that upon his arrival in Babylon, he should read the book, and after finishing it, he should tie it to a stone and throw it into the river Euphrates.

Zedekiah paid tribute to Babylon, during the first nine years of his reign.

Then, he rebelled against Nebuchadnezzar, against the advice of Jeremiah, who believed that God was fighting for the Babylonians, and was using them as his instrument to punish Judah and its leaders.

Jeremiah believed that resistance was useless, and that submission to Nebuchadnezzar was the will of God.

The prophet sent a message to the exiles in Babylon, telling them that God was universal and could be worshipped also far from Jerusalem. Even if the exiles could not sacrifice in the Temple, the worship of God could be done through prayer and obedience to his laws. Elasah, son of Shaphan, together with Gemariah, son of Hilkiah, carried Jeremiah's letter to the captives in Babylon, where the prophet encouraged them to live a normal life in Babylon, build homes, plant gardens, marry, and have children. The letter promised that, after seventy years, they would return from the Babylonian Exile.

Jeremiah also accused two of the exiles—Ahab, son of Kolaiah, and Zedekiah, son of Maaseiah—of doing vile things, committing adultery, and prophesying falsehoods. Jeremiah predicted that they would be burned to death at Nebuchadnezzar's command, and that their memory would be mentioned as a curse by the exiled Judean community in Babylon.

Shemaiah, the Nehelamite, an exile, wrote a letter to the priest Zephaniah, son of Maaseiah, where he accused Jeremiah of being a madman. When Zephaniah read this letter to Jeremiah, the prophet told him to write to the exiled community, saying that Shemaiah and his descendants would be punished for their disloyalty to God and would not live to see the good things that God would do for his people.

Early in the reign of King Zedekiah, Hananiah, the son of the prophet Azur, a native of Gibeon, prophesied that it would take only two years for all the exiles to return to Judah. To dramatize his prediction, Hananiah broke the yoke that Jeremiah was wearing in his neck as a symbol of the captivity, and he said, "Thus, will God break the yoke of Nebuchadnezzar, king of Babylon, from the neck of all the nations".

Jeremiah told Hananiah that he was misleading the people, and that God would put an iron yoke upon the neck of all the nations, to replace the wooden yoke broken by Hananiah, so that they may serve Nebuchadnezzar. And as for Hananiah, he would die within the year, punished by God for fomenting rebellion against the Lord. Hananiah died seven months later.

Gedaliah, son of Pashur, heard that Jeremiah was preaching surrender, and he went with some other officials to King Zedekiah to demand that Jeremiah should be put to death for his defeatist talk, which was weakening the will of the people. Zedekiah turned Jeremiah to them. Gedaliah and his companions cast the prophet into the dungeon of Malchiah that was in the court of the prison.

Hanameel, son of Shallum and cousin of the prophet Jeremiah, came to the prison and offered to sell his field in Anathoth to Jeremiah for seventeen pieces of silver. Baruch formally witnessed the purchase and received the Deed of Transfer, which he guarded in an earthen vessel. This transaction proved to Jeremiah that fields and vineyards would again be possessed in Israel.

Ebedmelech, an Ethiopian eunuch in the service of the king, came to the king and told him that Jeremiah might die of hunger in the dungeon. The king gave him permission to pull Jeremiah out of the dungeon. Ebedmelech was rewarded by a prophecy of Jeremiah, stating that he would survive for having trusted God.

When Zedekiah rebelled against Nebuchadrezzar, the king of Babylon came against Judah with a mighty army. King Zedekiah sent Pashur, the son of Melchiah, and Zephaniah, the son of the priest Maaseiah, to Jeremiah to ask him to pray that God would make Nebuchadrezzar withdraw. The prophet told the king that they all would fall into the hands of the

Babylonians and would be killed without pity. He added that only the people who would go over to the Babylonians would survive.

One day, Jeremiah approached the walls of the city with the intention of going to the territory of Benjamin. Irijah, the guard in charge of the Benjamin Gate, accused Jeremiah of trying to defect to the Babylonians. The prophet was arrested and turned over to the authorities. The officials angrily beat Jeremiah and imprisoned him in the house of Jonathan the Scribe, where he remained for many days, until King Zedekiah had him brought secretly to his presence.

The king asked the prophet to speak frankly. Jeremiah said that he was afraid that, if he would do so, the king would kill him. Zedekiah swore an oath that he would not kill him nor would he deliver the prophet into the hands of his enemies. Jeremiah advised the king to surrender and, thus, avoid the destruction of the city and his own death.

Zedekiah answered, "I am worried that the Chaldeans would hand me over to the Jews that have defected to them, and that they would abuse me".

Jeremiah assured him that the Chaldeans would not hand him over. The prophet then asked the king, "How have I offended you or your servants that you have put me in prison? Please, do not send me back to the house of Jonathan, or I would die there".

Zedekiah told him to keep their conversation a secret, or he would have him killed. He instructed Jeremiah that, if he was asked by the officials of the court about their meeting, he should answer that he had asked the king not to be sent back to the house of Jonathan to die there. The king gave orders to commit Jeremiah to the court of the prison, and to give him daily a piece of bread, while bread was still available in the city. Jeremiah was taken back to the prison where he remained, until the fall of Jerusalem.

The city's walls were breached by the Babylonians, in 587 B.C., after a siege, which lasted a year and a half. Zedekiah fled by night, leaving the palace through the garden's gate. The Babylonians pursued him, captured him near Jericho, and brought him before King Nebuchadrezzar at Riblah in the region of Hamath. The king of Babylon had the children of Zedekiah killed before his eyes and slaughtered all the nobles of Judah. Then, the eyes of Zedekiah were put out; the deposed king was bound in chains and brought to Babylon.

Nebuzaradan, the commander of the Babylonian army, burned down the Temple, the royal palace, the houses of the nobles and the wealthy, and tore down the walls of the city. He exiled all the survivors, except for some of the poorest people who were left in the land, and to whom he gave vineyards and fields.

King Nebuchadrezzar sent personal orders to Nebuzaradan concerning Jeremiah, telling him not to harm the prophet and to grant him every wish. Jeremiah was brought out of the prison and committed to the care of Gedaliah, son of Ahikam, whom the Babylonians had named governor of their newly conquered province. The survivors, including the prophet Jeremiah, found refuge with Gedaliah in Mizpah.

Gedaliah told the commanders of the defeated army that all would go well if they would serve the king of Babylon, giving, thus, cause to some of them to consider him a Babylonian collaborator.

Johanan, the son of Kareah, came to Mizpah and told Gedaliah that Baalis, the king of the Ammonites, had instructed Ishmael, a member of the royal family of Judah and a captain of the defeated Judean army, to kill him. Johanan volunteered to kill Ishmael, but Gedaliah accused Johanan of lying.

Two months later, what Johanan had warned came to pass. Ishmael came to Mizpah with ten men and, during dinner, murdered the governor and all the Jews and Babylonians who were with Gedaliah. The surviving Jews, fearing Babylonian vengeance, fled to Egypt, taking the prophet Jeremiah with them.

The fugitives arrived at the Egyptian city of Tahpanhes, where Jeremiah prophesied that Nebuchadrezzar would also conquer Egypt. He preached against the Jews living in Egypt for having abandoned God. When they answered that they would continue to worship the Queen of Heaven, Jeremiah told them that they would all be consumed by the sword and by famine. Sometime later, the unhappy and long suffering prophet died in Egypt.

9. (Jeremiah 35:3). 7th century B.C. Jeremiah, the son of Habaziniah, was the father of Jaazaniah, a member of the clan of the Rechabites.

Jaazaniah and other Rechabites were brought by the prophet Jeremiah to one of the chambers of the Temple and offered wine. They refused, because their ancestor Jonadab, son of Rechab, had forbidden them to drink wine.

The prophet praised the Rechabites to the men of Jerusalem as an example to follow of people who keep their commandments and principles.

Jeremias

(Hebrew origin: *God will rise*)

(Matthew 16:14). 7th and 6th century B.C. Jeremias is an alternative spelling for the name of the prophet Jeremiah (Jeremiah 1:1).

Jeremoth

(Hebrew origin: *Elevations*)

1. (1 Chronicles 8:14). Unspecified date. Jeremoth, son of Elpaal, was a chief of a clan of the tribe of Benjamin.
2. (1 Chronicles 23:23). 10th century B.C. Jeremoth—also spelled Jerimoth (1 Chronicles 24:30)—was a Levite, descendant of Mushi, who served in the Tabernacle, during the reign of King David.

3. (1 Chronicles 25:22). 10th century B.C. Jeremoth—also spelled Jerimoth (1 Chronicles 25:4)—a Levite, member of a family of musicians, was in charge of the fifteenth turn of service that played musical instruments—cymbals, psalteries, and harps—in the House of God, during the reign of David.

He had thirteen brothers and three sisters, all of them trained as skillful musicians by their father, Heman, one of the three leading musicians—the other two were Asaph and Jeduthun—of the period.

4. (Ezra 10:26). 5th century B.C. Jeremoth, a descendant of Elam, was one of the men who divorced their foreign wives, during the days of Ezra.
5. (Ezra 10:27). 5th century B.C. Jeremoth, a descendant of Zattu, was one of the men who divorced their foreign wives, during the days of Ezra.

Jeremy

(Hebrew origin: *God will rise*)

(Matthew 2:17). 7th and 6th century B.C. Jeremy is an alternative spelling for the name of the prophet Jeremiah (Jeremiah 1:1).

Jeriah

(Hebrew origin: *God will throw*)

(1 Chronicles 23:19). Unspecified date. Jeriah, a Levite, was a descendant of Hebron, the son of Kohath.

Jeribai

(Hebrew origin: *My adversary*)

(1 Chronicles 11:46). 10th century B.C. Jeribai and his brother Joshaviah, the sons of Elnaam, were brave warriors in King David's army.

Jeriel

(Hebrew origin: *Thrown by God*)

(1 Chronicles 7:2). Unspecified date. Jeriel, son of Tola, and his brothers—Uzzi, Rephaiah,

Jahmai, Jibsam, and Shemuel—were leaders of the tribe of Issachar.

Jerijah

(Hebrew origin: *God will throw*)

(1 Chronicles 26:31). 10th century B.C. Jerijah was the head of the Hebronites, during the reign of King David.

Jerimoth

(Hebrew origin: *Elevations*)

1. (1 Chronicles 7:7). 16th century B.C. Jerimoth was a son of Bela, the eldest son of Benjamin. His brothers were Uzzi, Uzziel, Ezbon, and Iri, all of them brave leaders of their clans.

    Note: Elsewhere in the first book of Chronicles (1 Chronicles 8:3), Bela has a different list of sons: Addar, Gera, Abihud, Abishua, Naaman, Ahoah, Gera, Shephuphan, and Huram.

2. (1 Chronicles 7:8). 16th century B.C. Jerimoth was a son of Becher and grandson of Benjamin. His brothers were Zemira, Joash, Eliezer, Elioenai, Omri, Abiah, Anathoth, and Alameth.

3. (1 Chronicles 12:5). 11th century B.C. Jerimoth was one of the Benjamites who deserted King Saul's army and joined David's band at Ziklag. These men were skilled warriors who could use both their right and left hands to shoot arrows and sling stones.

4. (1 Chronicles 24:30). 10th century B.C. Jerimoth—also spelled Jeremoth (1 Chronicles 23:23)—was a Levite, descendant of Mushi, who served in the Tabernacle, during the reign of King David.

5. (1 Chronicles 25:4). 10th century B.C. Jerimoth—spelled Jeremoth (1 Chronicles 25:22)—a Levite, member of a family of musicians, was in charge of the fifteenth turn of service that played musical instruments—cymbals, psalteries, and harps—in the House of God, during the reign of David.

    He had thirteen brothers and three sisters, all of them trained as skillful musicians by their father, Heman, one of the three leading musicians—the other two were Asaph and Jeduthun—of the period.

6. (1 Chronicles 27:19). 10th century B.C. Jerimoth, son of Azriel, was the leader of the tribe of Naphtali, during the reign of King David.

7. (2 Chronicles 11:18). 10th century B.C. Jerimoth, one of the sons of King David, married his cousin Abihail, the daughter of Eliab, David's eldest brother. Their daughter Mahalath was one of the eighteen wives of King Rehoboam.

8. (2 Chronicles 31:13). 8th century B.C. Jerimoth was one of the Levites named by King Hezekiah to serve under Cononiah and Shimei, as supervisors of the gifts, tithes, and offerings, brought by the people to the Temple.

Jerioth

(Hebrew origin: *Curtains*)

(1 Chronicles 2:18). Unspecified date. Jerioth was one of the two wives of Caleb, son of Hezron, of the tribe of Judah. After Azubah, the other wife, died, Caleb married Ephrath.

Jeroboam

(Hebrew origin: *People will contend*)

1. (1 Kings 11:26). 10th century B.C. Jeroboam I, born in the town of Zereda, of the tribe of Ephraim, was the first king of Israel, the northern kingdom, after the division of the kingdom.

    His father Nebat died, when he was young, and he was raised by his widowed mother, Zeruah. His bravery and industriousness caught the eye of King Solomon who put him in charge of the labor forces of the Joseph tribes, Ephraim and Manasseh, which had been conscripted to help fortify Jerusalem.

    His work gave him the opportunity to realize that the tribes in the north, jealous of Judah's dominant position, were restless and unhappy with the Jerusalem royal court, because of Solomon's heavy taxes and the compulsory labor burdens, which the king had imposed on the people to carry out his ambitious building projects.

Jeroboam, in one of his journeys outside Jerusalem, met in an isolated road the prophet Ahijah, a priest serving in the sanctuary of Shiloh, in the territory of Ephraim. The prophet rented his coat in twelve pieces and gave ten to Jeroboam, telling him that God was giving him ten tribes and leaving only two to the descendants of King David.

Jeroboam, aided by Ahijah, plotted against the king. When Solomon discovered the conspiracy, he condemned Jeroboam to death. Before the sentence could be carried out, Jeroboam fled to Egypt, where the Pharaoh Shishak gave him political asylum.

When Solomon died, Rehoboam, his son and successor, went to Shechem to be confirmed as king by the ten northern tribes. Jeroboam, who had returned to Israel as soon as he heard that Solomon had died, spoke in the assembly of the people, complaining to Rehoboam about the forced labor and high taxes imposed by his late father, and asked him to lighten the burden of the people.

Rehoboam promised to give his answer in three days, after consultations with his advisers. The elders recommended that he should reach a compromise with his northern subjects concerning their justified complaints. The king rejected their wise advice and consulted with his young advisers, who told him to be firm in his demands.

Rehoboam went back to the people and told them that not only would he not lighten their burden but he would increase it! The reaction of the people should not have come as a surprise to Rehoboam. The northerners, discontented and rebellious, declared that they were seceding, and they stoned Adoram, the official in charge of the forced labor, to death. Rehoboam, fearing that he would also be killed, mounted his chariot and fled to Jerusalem.

The northern tribes established an independent kingdom, called Israel, with Jeroboam as their sovereign. Their new king resided, at first, in Shechem, then for a period, in Penuel, across the Jordan River, and finally, he chose Tirzah, a town about twelve kilometers northeast of Shechem, to be his capital.

Jeroboam's basic policy was to separate completely Israel from Judah. For that reason, he played down the importance of Solomon's Temple and, instead, revived the old sanctuaries at Bethel, in the south of his country, and Dan, in the north, setting up golden calves in them. He expelled the priestly Levites, who were loyal to the kingdom of Judah, and recruited, in their stead, priests from the common people, whom he personally appointed and ordained. There was constant war between the kingdoms of Israel and Judah, during his reign.

Jeroboam proclaimed a religious holiday on the fifteenth day of the eight month. On that day, he would go to Bethel and sacrifice on the altar to the golden calf. On one of those occasions, a prophet of the tribe of Judah saw Jeroboam burning incense in the altar and prophesied that, one day, a king by the name of Josiah would destroy that altar.

Jeroboam pointed with his arm to the man and ordered his men to seize him. His arm became paralyzed, and he could not move it. The altar broke down, and its ashes were spilled. Distraught, the king asked the prophet to pray to God to heal his arm. The prophet did so, and the king was again able to move his arm. Grateful, Jeroboam asked the prophet to come to the palace, have some refreshment, and receive a gift. The prophet refused and left Bethel.

Sometime later, Abijah, the young son of Jeroboam, became very ill. The king sent his wife in disguise to Shiloh to consult with the prophet Ahijah, who was now old and blind, to ask whether the child would recover.

Despite his blindness and the queen's disguise, the old prophet recognized her and told her that the sick child would die, as soon as she would be back in Tirzah, as God's punishment for having sinned and worshipped idols. Ahijah added that Jeroboam's descendants would die and be eaten by dogs and birds.

Iddo, the seer, also had visions against Jeroboam, which he wrote in a book, which has not survived to our days.

Jeroboam died, after reigning for twenty-two years, and was succeeded by his son Nadab, who, two years later, was overthrown and killed by Baasha.

2. (2 Kings 13:13). 8th century B.C. Jeroboam II, son of King Joash of Israel, was the thirteenth king of Israel, after the partition of the United Monarchy, and the fourth and most successful king in the dynasty founded by Jehu.

Jeroboam recovered several cities, such as Hamath and Damascus, which his predecessors had lost, including territories on the other side of the Jordan River, and elevated the kingdom of Israel to the highest political rank in the region.

Although his reign was a time of great economic prosperity, material abundance, religious piety, and security, his contemporary, the prophet Amos, saw the situation differently: prosperity was limited to the wealthy, and it was based on injustice and on the oppression of the poor; religious observance was insincere, and security was more apparent than real. Amos criticized the materialism of the people and spoke against the selfishness of the rich and their lack of concern for the poor.

Amaziah, the priest of Bethel, told King Jeroboam that Amos was conspiring against him by preaching that the sword would kill the king, and that the people of Israel would be led away to captivity. Amaziah advised Amos to flee back to Judah and prophesy there, but Amos answered that it was God who had sent him to prophesy to Israel. Amos' prediction came true, thirty years later, when the Assyrians put an end to the kingdom of Israel.

Jeroboam reigned forty-one years and was succeeded by his son Zachariah, who, six months later, was overthrown and killed by Shallum.

Jeroham

(Hebrew origin: *Compassionate*)

1. (1 Samuel 1:1). 12th century B.C. Jeroham, son of Elihu, was the father of Elkanah and grandfather of Samuel. The first book of Chronicles mentions the name of his father as Eliab (1 Chronicles 6:27) and Eliel (1 Chronicles 6:34).

2. (1 Chronicles 8:27). Unspecified date. His sons were leaders of several clans of the tribe of Benjamin who lived in Jerusalem.

3. (1 Chronicles 9:8). Unspecified date. Jeroham was the father of Ibneiah, the head of a Benjamite clan that lived in Jerusalem.

4. (1 Chronicles 9:12). 5th century B.C. Jeroham was the son of Pashur, or, according to the book of Nehemiah, the son of Pelaliah (Nehemiah 11:12). His son Adaiah was a priest who served in the Temple, after the return from the Babylonian Exile.

5. (1 Chronicles 12:7). 11th century B.C. Jeroham of Gedor was the father of Joelah and Zebadiah, two of the warriors who joined David at Ziklag, while he was still hiding from King Saul. His sons were skilled fighters who could use both their right and left hands to shoot arrows and sling stones.

6. (1 Chronicles 27:22). 11th century B.C. Jeroham was the father of Azareel, the leader of the tribe of Dan, during the reign of King David.

7. (2 Chronicles 23:1). 9th century B.C. Jeroham was the father of Azariah, who, together with other army commanders, joined the conspiracy headed by the priest Jehoiada to overthrow Queen Athaliah and crown Joash as king of Judah.

Jerubbaal

(Hebrew origin: *Baal will contend*)

(Judges 6:32). 12th century B.C. Jerubbaal was the name given to Gideon, after he had destroyed his father's altar to Baal and cut down the sacred grove next to it. From that day on, Gideon was also called Jerubbaal, which means *Let Baal contend with him*. (Please see the entry for Gideon [Judges 6:11].)

Note: The second book of Samuel uses the euphemism Jerubbesheth, *Shame will contend,* instead of Jerubbaal, to replace the suffix "baal" that was considered offensive, because it was the name of the idol worshipped by the Canaanites and Phoenicians.

Jerubbesheth

(Hebrew origin: *The shame will contend*)

(2 Samuel 11:21). 12th century B.C. The name Jerubbesheth in this verse replaces Jerubbaal, the name given to Gideon, after he had destroyed his father's altar to Baal and cut down the sacred grove next to it. (Please see the entry for Gideon [Judges 6:11].)

Note: The Bible uses the suffix "besheth" or "bosheth" as a euphemism to replace the suffix "baal" that was considered offensive, because it was the name of the idol worshipped by the Canaanites and Phoenicians.

Jerusha

(Hebrew origin: *Inheritance*)

(2 Kings 15:33). 8th century B.C. Jerusha, daughter of Zadok, was the wife of King Uzziah of Judah and the mother of King Jotham. Her name is spelled Jerushah in the second book of Chronicles (2 Chronicles 27:1).

Jerushah

(Hebrew origin: *Inheritance*)

(2 Chronicles 27:1). 8th century B.C. Jerushah, daughter of Zadok, was the wife of King Uzziah of Judah and the mother of King Jotham. Her name is spelled Jerusha in the second book of Kings (2 Kings 15:33).

Jesaiah

(Hebrew origin: *God has saved*)

1. (1 Chronicles 3:21). 6th century B.C.

Jesaiah, son of Hananiah and brother of Pelatiah, was a descendant of the royal family of Judah. His grandfather Zerubbabel was the leader of the first group of captives who returned from the Babylonian Exile.

2. (Nehemiah 11:7). Unspecified date. Jesaiah, the father of Ithiel, was an ancestor of Sallu, a Benjamite who settled in Jerusalem, after his return from the Babylonian Exile.

Jeshaiah

(Hebrew origin: *God has saved*)

1. (1 Chronicles 25:3). 10th century B.C. Jeshaiah was one of the sons of Jeduthun, a Levite who was one of the three leading musicians—the other two were Asaph and Heman—during the reign of David. Jeshaiah was in charge of the eighth turn of service to play musical instruments in the House of God.

2. (1 Chronicles 26:25). Unspecified date. Jeshaiah, son of Rehabiah, a descendant of Moses and Zipporah, was the father of Joram.

His descendant Shelomith was the Levite in charge of the gifts, donated to maintain the Tabernacle. The donors were King David and the captains of his army from their spoils of the wars.

3. (Ezra 8:7). 5th century B.C. Jeshaiah, son of Athaliah, a descendant of Elam, returned with Ezra from the Babylonian Exile at the head of a group of seventy men of his clan.

4. (Ezra 8:19). 5th century B.C. Jeshaiah, a Levite of the clan of Merari, was sent by Iddo, head of the community at Casiphia, to join Ezra in his trip to Jerusalem, in response to Ezra's request for people to serve God in the Temple.

Jeshaiah came with two other Levites—Hashabiah and Sherebiah—and a group of their relatives.

Jesharelah

(Hebrew origin: *Straight toward God*)

(1 Chronicles 25:14). 10th century B.C.

Jesharelah—also called Asarelah (1 Chronicles 25:2)—was the son of Asaph, the Levite appointed by King David to be in charge of the singers in the House of the Lord. He and his brothers assisted Asaph in his work, with Jesharelah taking the seventh turn of service.

Jeshebeab

(Hebrew origin: *Father sits*)

(1 Chronicles 24:13). 10th century B.C. During the reign of King David, the priestly service in the Tabernacle was divided by lot into twenty-four turns. Jeshebeab was in charge of the fourteenth turn.

Jesher

(Hebrew origin: *Straight*)

(1 Chronicles 2:18). Unspecified date. Jesher, son of Caleb, the son of Hezron, was a descendant of Judah. His mother was Azubah. His brothers were Ardon and Shobab.

Jeshishai

(Hebrew origin: *Aged*)

(1 Chronicles 5:14). Unspecified date. Jeshishai, of the tribe of Gad, was the father of Michael and the son of Jahdo. His descendants lived in Gilead, on the eastern side of the Jordan River.

Jeshohaiah

(Hebrew origin: *God will empty*)

(1 Chronicles 4:36). 8th century B.C. Jeshohaiah was one of the leaders of the tribe of Simeon who went to the fertile valley of Gedor in search of pasture for their flocks, during the reign of Hezekiah, king of Judah.

The Simeonites destroyed the tents of the people—descendants of Ham—who lived there, wiped them out forever, and settled in their place.

Jeshua

(Hebrew origin: *He will save*)

1. (2 Chronicles 31:15). 8th century B.C. Jeshua was a Levite who worked under Kore, assisting him in registering the priests and the Levites and distributing among the other Levites the gifts offered by the people to God, during the days of Kings Hezekiah.

2. (Ezra 2:2). 6th century B.C. Jeshua was one of the men who returned with Zerubbabel from the Babylonian Exile.

3. (Ezra 2:6). 6th century B.C. Jeshua was the leader of a clan of people, descendants of Pahathmoab, who returned with Zerubbabel from the Babylonian Exile.

4. (Ezra 2:36). Unspecified date. Jeshua was an ancestor of a clan of priests, descendants of Jedaiah, who returned with Zerubbabel from the Babylonian Exile.

5. (Ezra 2:40). Unspecified date. Jeshua was an ancestor of a clan of Levites, who returned with Zerubbabel from the Babylonian Exile.

6. (Ezra 3:2). 6th century B.C. The High Priest Jeshua, son of Jozadak—called Joshua, son of Josedech, in the book of the prophet Haggai (Haggai 1:1)—returned to Jerusalem with Zerubbabel and assisted him in the reconstruction of the Temple.

   He was symbolically crowned with crowns of gold and silver, made—at the suggestion of the prophet Zechariah—by Heldai, Tobijah, and Jedaiah. The crowns remained in the Temple as a memorial to the three donors.

   The Temple was finished, during the sixth year of the reign of King Darius (Ezra 6:15). Jeshua probably had already died by then, because there is no mention of him being present, during the dedication ceremonies of the Temple. His son Joiakim succeeded him as High Priest

   During the days of Ezra, Jeshua's sons divorced their foreign wives and offered a ram from the flock to expiate their transgression (Ezra 10:18).

7. (Ezra 8:33). 5th century B.C. Jeshua was a Levite, son of Kadmiel. His son Jozabad returned with Ezra from the Babylonian

Exile and helped the priest Meremoth, son of Uriah, to count and weigh the silver and gold utensils of the Temple, which Ezra had brought back from Babylon.

His other son, Ezer, ruler of Mizpah, helped to repair the walls of Jerusalem, during the days of Nehemiah (Nehemiah 3:19).

8. (Nehemiah 8:7). 5th century B.C. Jeshua, son of Azaniah, was one of the Levites who explained the Law to the people, after Ezra the Scribe had read it, while standing on a wooden platform, in front of the open space, before the Water Gate.

He was among the Levites who signed Nehemiah's solemn agreement to separate themselves from the foreigners living in the land, to refrain from intermarrying with them, to dedicate their firstborn to God, and other obligations (Nehemiah 10:9).

9. (Nehemiah 8:17). 13th century B.C. Jeshua is an alternative spelling for Joshua, son of Nun.

Jeshuah

(Hebrew origin: *He will save*)

(1 Chronicles 24:11). 10th century B.C. During the reign of King David, the priestly service in the Tabernacle was divided by lot into twenty-four turns. Jeshuah was in charge of the ninth turn.

Jeshurun

(Hebrew origin: *Upright*)

(Deuteronomy 32:15). Jeshurun is a symbolic name for the people and land of Israel. The book of Isaiah spells it Jesurun (Isaiah 44:2).

Jesiah

(Hebrew origin: *God will lend*)

1. (1 Chronicles 12:6). 11th century B.C. Jesiah, a Korhite, was one of the men who deserted King Saul's army and joined David's band at Ziklag. These men were

skilled warriors who could use both their right and left hands to shoot arrows and sling stones.

2. (1 Chronicles 23:20). Unspecified date. Jesiah, a Levite, was a member of a clan that descended from Uzziel.

Jesimiel

(Hebrew origin: *God will place*)

(1 Chronicles 4:36). 8th century B.C. Jesimiel was one of the leaders of the tribe of Simeon who went to the fertile valley of Gedor in search of pasture for their flocks, during the reign of Hezekiah, king of Judah.

The Simeonites destroyed the tents of the people—descendants of Ham—who lived there, wiped them out forever, and settled in their place.

Jesse

(Hebrew origin: *Existing*)

(Ruth 4:17). 11th century B.C. Jesse, of the tribe of Judah, a sheep owner, son of Obed, and grandson of Boaz and Ruth, was a prominent resident of the town of Bethlehem.

The first book of Samuel states that Jesse had eight sons, including David, the youngest (1 Samuel 17:12), but the list in First Chronicles (1 Chronicles 2:15) mentions only seven sons: Eliab, Abinadab, Shimma—called Shammah in the first book of Samuel (1 Samuel 16:9)—Nethaneel, Raddai, Ozem, and David; plus, two daughters: Zeruiah and Abigail. Among his grandchildren were the three sons of Zeruiah: Abishai, Joab, and Asahel.

One day, the prophet Samuel came to Bethlehem, sent by God, to anoint the next king of Israel. Ostensibly, his visit to Bethlehem was to offer a sacrifice to God. He used that excuse, because he was afraid that Saul might kill him if he would suspect the true reason for his coming to Bethlehem.

Samuel offered a sacrifice with Jesse and then went to his house, where he sanctified him and his family. The prophet asked Jesse to present him his sons, and, after looking at them, he realized that God had not chosen any of them.

"Are these all your children?" asked Samuel.

Jesse replied, "There is one more, the youngest. He is out, taking care of the sheep".

"Send somebody to bring him. We will not sit down, until he comes here".

David, a very handsome young man, came in. God told Samuel, "Arise and anoint him, because he is the one". Samuel took the horn of oil, anointed David, and returned to Ramah.

Sometime later, King Saul, who was suffering of depression and melancholy, heard that David played the harp beautifully. The king sent messengers to Jesse, asking him to send David to the palace. Jesse loaded a donkey with bread, a bottle of wine, and a young goat, and he sent David with these gifts to Saul.

Saul was very much taken with David and asked Jesse to let him stay in the court to play music whenever the king was depressed.

In one of his visits to the paternal home, David was sent by Jesse to the Israelite army camp where his three eldest brothers were serving as soldiers, camped across the valley from the Philistines. Jesse told David to take with him corn and bread for his brothers, and a gift of ten cheeses for their captain. This visit led to David's fight against Goliath, and later to his marriage to Michal, Saul's daughter.

Years later, after David had achieved enormous popularity with the people, the jealousy and hate of Saul caused him to flee to the desert where he became an outlaw.

David found refuge in the desert of Judah, in a cave near the town of Adullam. Men who were oppressed, dissatisfied, or in debt, came to him, and soon, David found himself leading a band of more than four hundred outlaws.

David, worried about the safety of his parents, went to Mizpeh of Moab to ask permission from the king of Moab to let his father and mother stay under his royal protection, in the land of Jesse's grandmother Ruth. There, they stayed, until David's fortunes took a turn for the better.

Jesui

(Hebrew origin: *Level*)

(Numbers 26:44). Unspecified date. Jesui was a descendant of Asher and an ancestor of the clan of the Jesuites.

Jesurun

(Hebrew origin: *Upright*)

(Isaiah 44:2). Jesurun is a symbolic name for the people and land of Israel. The book of Deuteronomy spells it Jeshurun (Deuteronomy 32:15).

Jesus

(Greek form of the Hebrew *Jehoshua* [*God saved*])

1. (Matthew 1:1). A.D. 1st century. Jesus, the Messiah, was the son of the Virgin Mary. Jesus is the common Greek form of the Hebrew name Joshua. In the days of Jesus, the name was pronounced "Yeshua", and it was one of the most common of Jewish names. (Please read below a detailed discussion and biographies according to the Gospels.)

2. (Colossians 4:11). A.D. 1st century. Jesus, also called Justus, a Christian of Jewish origin, was mentioned by Paul, in his letter to the Colossians, as being a comfort to him in his prison in Rome, and a fellow worker for the Kingdom of God.

The source for our information about the birth, life, death, and teachings of Jesus of Nazareth are the Gospels, a word that means "good news".

The Gospels are oral traditions put down in writing, several decades, after the death of Jesus. They do not constitute a biography in the modern sense, but are a collection of episodes of his life, with a detailed description of his last days.

The four Gospels together constitute a composite picture of the life of Jesus, although there are discrepancies among them. The biography below is an attempt to integrate the four Gospels into one continuous narrative.

In the town of Nazareth, in the region of Galilee, lived Mary, a young woman who was engaged to be married to Joseph, a carpenter who descended from the royal family of King David.

One day, the angel Gabriel, sent by God, appeared to Mary and greeted her, "Hail Mary, God is with you. You are blessed among women".

Mary, confused by the appearance of the angel and his greeting, did not understand the meaning of his words.

The angel said to her, "God is pleased with you, Mary; do not be afraid. I have come to tell you that you will conceive and give birth to a son, who shall be called Jesus, the Son of the Highest. God will give him the throne of his ancestor David, and he will reign over the descendants of Jacob forever. His kingdom will never end".

Mary asked him, "How can it be, if I have not had relations with any man?"

The angel answered, "The Holy Spirit will come to you, and the power of the Highest shall overshadow you. That is why the holy child to be born will be called the Son of God. Remember your cousin Elisabeth. She was called barren, but is now six months pregnant, although she is very old. Nothing is impossible to God!"

"I am the Lord's servant", said Mary, "let it happen to me according to what you have said". The angel then departed.

A few days later, Mary traveled to the town where her cousin Elisabeth lived with her husband Zacharias. When Elisabeth heard Mary's greeting, and her baby moved inside her, she was filled with the Holy Spirit and said to Mary in a loud voice, "Blessed are you among women, and blessed is the child in your womb. Why should the mother of my Lord come to me?"

Mary stayed with her relatives about three months, and then, she returned to Nazareth.

Her fiancé, Joseph, was a kind and considerate man. When he found out that Mary was pregnant, he considered breaking the engagement discreetly, because he wished to avoid a scandal that would bring shame upon her.

One night, when he had been thinking about this matter, an angel appeared to him in a dream and said, "Do not be afraid to take Mary to be your wife, because she has conceived by the Holy Spirit. Her son will be called Jesus, because he will save his people from their sins".

Joseph woke up and decided to go ahead with the wedding plans. He married Mary, but he did not have sexual relations with her before she gave birth to her son.

The emperor Augustus decreed a census of all the inhabitants of the Roman Empire, each person to be registered in his native city.

Joseph, as a descendant of David, had to be counted in Bethlehem, the hometown of his ancestors. He took with him his wife Mary, who was in the last month of her pregnancy, and traveled from Nazareth to Bethlehem.

When the couple arrived in the town, they found that it was crowded, and the inn was full. The only available resting place that they could find was a manger. There, Mary gave birth to a baby boy.

That night, some shepherds who were tending their flocks in the nearby fields saw an angel of the Lord, and they were terribly afraid.

The angel said to them, "Do not be afraid. I have good news, which will bring joy to all the people. Today, your Savior, Christ the Lord, was born in the City of David. You will find the baby wrapped in clothes, lying in a manger".

Suddenly, a great multitude of angels appeared, praising God, "Glory to God in the highest, and on earth peace and goodwill to men".

After the angels left them and went back to heaven, the shepherds said to one another, "Let's go to Bethlehem, and see what God has told us".

They hurried to the manger, where they found Mary, Joseph, and the baby. The shepherds told them what the angel had said, and all were amazed; Mary remembered their words and thought deeply about them. The shepherds returned to their fields, singing grateful praises to God for all that they had heard and seen, which was exactly what the angel had told them.

The baby was given the name Jesus at his circumcision, as the angel had prophesied to Mary, nine months before. When the time arrived for the customary ceremony of the purification, according to what the Law stipulated for firstborn male children, Joseph and Mary brought the baby to the Temple in Jerusalem, to offer a sacrifice of a pair of doves or two pigeons to the Lord.

Simeon, a devout and just man, was in the Temple at that moment. Days before, the Holy Spirit had promised him, in a vision, that he would not die, before he had seen the Lord Christ. Simeon saw the baby and took him in his arms; he blessed the child and said, "Lord, now let your servant depart in peace, according to your promise, because my eyes have seen the salvation that you have prepared before the people, a light to the Gentiles, and the glory of your people Israel". Then, he blessed Joseph and Mary, who were amazed at the words that Simeon had expressed about their son.

Anna, an elderly widow, and considered by many to be a prophetess, was also in the Temple. She saw the baby and thanked God for having given her the opportunity of seeing Jesus. Later, Anna spoke of him to all the pilgrims who came to Jerusalem seeking redemption.

Astrologers from the east came to Jerusalem and asked, "Where is the baby born to be king of the Jews? We saw his star and we have come to worship him". Their arrival was mentioned to King Herod, who, upset to hear that a future king of the Jews had been born, called the chief priests and the teachers of the Law and asked them, "Where will the Messiah be born?"

"In the town of Bethlehem", they answered.

The visiting astrologers, when brought to Herod's palace for a secret meeting, told the king the exact time that the star had appeared.

The king said to them, "I also want to see the child and worship him. So, go to Bethlehem, search for the child, and, when you find him, inform me where he is".

The astrologers followed the star, until it stopped over the place where the child was. They went into the manger, and, when they saw the child with his mother, Mary, they knelt down, worshipped him, and gave him gifts of gold, frankincense, and myrrh.

They returned directly to their country by another road, without going through Jerusalem, because God had told them in a dream not to go back to Herod.

After the astrologers had left, an angel appeared to Joseph in a dream and said to him, "Herod is looking for the child in order to kill him. You and your family must escape to Egypt and stay there, until I will let you know when it is safe to return". That same night, Joseph and his family left for Egypt.

Herod was so filled with anger, when he realized that the astrologers had tricked him, that he gave orders to kill all the boys in Bethlehem who were two years old and younger.

After the death of Herod, an angel appeared to Joseph in Egypt and told him that they could now return to Israel, where, in the meantime, Archelaus had succeeded his father Herod as king of Judea.

Joseph, fearful of Herod's son, avoided Judea and, having received more instructions in a dream, returned to the Galilee, where the family settled in the town of Nazareth. The boy grew up strong, filled with wisdom, with the grace of God upon him.

It was Joseph and Mary's custom to go every year to Jerusalem for the Passover Festival. When their son was twelve years old, they traveled to Jerusalem to the festival as usual. They stayed for several days, and, when the festival was over, they started on their way back to Nazareth. However, unknown to them, the boy Jesus stayed behind in Jerusalem.

When the couple noticed that their son was not at their side, they were not worried, at first, because they assumed that the boy was somewhere among the many travelers. At the end of the day, when the travelers camped for the night, Joseph and Mary searched for him among their relatives and friends, but they could not find him.

Growing more and more scared and alarmed by the hour, they returned to Jerusalem and searched all over the city for the boy. It was only after three days that they found him in the Temple, sitting with the doctors of the Law, listening to their teaching, and asking them questions. The people around him were spellbound at his understanding and his answers, which showed an intelligence and knowledge way beyond his years.

Mary, amazed, said to him, "Son, why have you done this to us? Your father and I were worried sick trying to find you".

Jesus replied, "Why did you have to search for me? Didn't you know that I would be in my Father's house?"

Jesus returned with his parents to Nazareth, where he grew up in body and in wisdom, and was favored by God and men.

During the fifteenth year of the reign of Emperor Tiberius, when Pontius Pilate was the Roman governor of Judea, and Herod, the son of King Herod the Great, was the tetrarch of Galilee, John—the son of Mary's cousin, Elisabeth—went into the wilderness, by the Jordan River, dressed with clothes made of camel's hair. His food was locusts and wild honey.

There, he preached to the people, "If you repent from your sins and are baptized, God will forgive you!"

Crowds of people came to John to be baptized by him. He would tell them, "Anyone who has two shirts should give one to the man who has none. And anyone who has food must share it".

To the tax collectors, he said, "Don't collect more money than what is legally due".

To the soldiers, he said, "Don't take money from anyone by force, or accuse anyone falsely. Be satisfied with your pay".

The Jewish authorities in Jerusalem, when informed that a preacher was attracting huge crowds near the Jordan, sent a delegation of priests and Levites to investigate what was going on, and to find out who exactly John was, and what he was doing, or trying to do.

They asked him, "Who are you?"

He answered, "I am not the Messiah".

They asked, "So, who are you? Are you Elijah?"

"I am not Elijah", he answered.

"Are you the prophet?" they asked.

"No, I am not", answered John.

"Who are you then? The people who sent us need clear answers. What do you have to say about yourself?"

"I am, as the prophet Isaiah has said, the voice of one who shouts in the desert, 'Make straight the way of the Lord'".

The delegation asked him, "Why then do you baptize, if you are not the Messiah, Elijah or the prophet?"

John replied, "I baptize with water, but there is one standing among you, whom you don't know. He is coming after me, and I am not even worthy to untie his sandals".

Jesus—then about thirty years old—came to the Jordan River and was baptized by John. The Holy Spirit came down upon him in the form of a dove, and a voice from heaven was heard, saying, "You are my own dear Son, and I am pleased with you".

The next day, John, who was standing with two of his disciples, saw Jesus went by, and he said, "Look, there is the Lamb of God who takes away the sin of the world! He is the one that I said is greater than I am; I baptize with water to make him known to the people of Israel. God, who sent me to baptize with water, told me that the one on whom the Spirit descends will baptize with the Holy Spirit, and I saw the

Spirit come down from heaven like a dove and stay on him! I have seen him; he is the Son of God!"

The two disciples heard John say this, and they followed Jesus. Jesus turned, saw them following him, and asked them, "What are you looking for?"

They answered, "Master, where are you staying?"

"Come and see", he replied.

The two men went with him, saw where he lived, and stayed with him the rest of the day. One of the two men was Andrew, the brother of Simon Peter. He went in search of his brother and, when he found him, said to him, "We have found the Messiah!"

Andrew brought Simon to Jesus, who said to him, "You are Simon, the son of Jona. You will be called Cephas, the rock".

Leaving the bank of the river Jordan, Jesus went into the desert, where the devil tempted him for forty days. During all that time, Jesus fasted and did not eat anything.

The devil said to him, "If you are the Son of God, turn this stone into bread".

Jesus answered, "It is written that man does not live by bread alone, but by every word of God".

The devil took him to a high mountain and showed him all the kingdoms of the world. "I will give you all this power and glory if you will worship me".

Jesus replied, "It is written, you shall worship the Lord, your God, and only him shall you serve".

The devil took Jesus to Jerusalem and set him on the highest point of the Temple. He said to Jesus, "If you are the Son of God, throw yourself down from here, and, so the Scriptures say, God will order his angels to take care of you. They will hold you in their hands, and not even your feet will touch the stones".

Jesus told him, "It is written, you shall not tempt the Lord, your God". The defeated devil left him, and Jesus went to the Galilee, where he taught in the synagogues.

One day, while walking along the shore of the Lake of Galilee, he saw two boats on the beach; the fishermen were outside, washing the nets. Jesus climbed into the boat that belonged to the two brothers, Simon and Andrew, and asked them to push off a little from the shore. He sat in the boat and taught the crowd from there. After he finished teaching, he told Simon to push the boat further out and lower the nets for a catch.

Simon said, "Master, although we worked hard the whole night, we didn't catch any fish. But, if you say so, we will lower the nets".

They lowered the nets and caught so many fish that they told their partners in the other boat to come and help them. The other boat came, and between them, they pulled up such a great quantity of fish that the two boats were in danger of sinking.

Simon fell on his knees before Jesus and said, "I am a sinful man, Lord; please don't stay with me".

Jesus told Simon, "Don't be afraid. Come with me, and I will teach you to catch men".

Simon and his partners—James and John, the sons of Zebedee—brought the boats back to the beach. Jesus called them, and they immediately left the boat and their father and went with him.

The next day, Jesus found Philip, a man from Bethsaida, the hometown of Andrew and Simon, and said to him, "Follow me".

Philip went to Nathanael and told him, "We have found the one about whom Moses and the prophets wrote. He is Jesus of Nazareth, the son of Joseph".

Nathanael said, "Can anything good come out of Nazareth?"

"Come and see", answered Philip.

Jesus saw Nathanael coming to him, and he said, "Look, here is a true Israelite. There is nothing false in him".

Nathanael, surprised, asked him, "Do you know me?"

"I saw you, when you were under the fig tree, before Phillip called you".

Nathanael exclaimed, "Master, you are the Son of God! You are the king of Israel!"

"You believe that just because I said that I saw you under the fig tree? You will see much greater things than that! I tell you, you will see the heaven open, and the angels of God ascending and descending upon the Son of man".

Three days later, there was a marriage in the town of Cana, in Galilee. Jesus, his mother, and his disciples were among the guests. When the wine gave out, his mother said to him, "There is no more wine".

Jesus answered, "Woman, what do I have to do with you? My hour has not yet come".

There were, on the side, six jars of stone, each one with a capacity of twenty to thirty gallons of water to be used in the Jewish custom of ritually washing the hands before eating.

His mother said to the servants, "Do whatever he tells you".

Jesus said to them, "Fill these jars with water".

When the servants filled the jars to the brim, Jesus said, "Now, draw some out and take it to the banquet steward".

The steward tasted the wine, without knowing where it came from. It was so good that he called the bridegroom to congratulate him, "Other people serve the good wine at the beginning of the dinner, and, at the end of the evening, when the guests have already drunk a lot, he serves the ordinary wine. But you have kept the best wine, until now!"

This was Jesus' first miracle. After the wedding, they left Cana and went to Capernaum, a town situated on the northern shore of the lake, where they stayed for a few days.

Jesus went all over the Galilee, preaching in the synagogues about the Kingdom of God. A large crowd gathered that included people who had come from as far away as Judea, Syria, and the foreign cities of Tyre and Sidon. Most came to hear him preach, but many also came to be healed from their diseases and freed from evil spirits.

Jesus and his disciples went to the lake, followed by the large multitude. The crowd was so large that Jesus told his disciples to get him a boat to avoid being crushed.

Jesus went up a hill and stayed there, the whole night, praying to God. When day came, he called his disciples and chose twelve of them as his apostles, giving them authority to preach and to drive out evil spirits. They were Simon—whom he called Peter—James and his brother John, Andrew, Philip, Bartholomew, Matthew, Thomas, James—the son of Alphaeus—Thaddaeus, Simon the Canaanite, and Judas Iscariot, who would one day betray Jesus.

Jesus went up a mount and sat down. His disciples gathered around him, and the crowd surrounded them. Jesus then spoke to them:

"Blessed are the poor in spirit, for theirs
    is the kingdom of heaven.
"Blessed are they that mourn, for they
    shall be comforted.
"Blessed are the meek, for they shall
    inherit the earth.
"Blessed are they who hunger and thirst
    after righteousness, for they shall be
    filled.
"Blessed are the merciful, for they shall
    obtain mercy.
"Blessed are the pure in heart, for they
    shall see God.
"Blessed are the peacemakers, for they
    shall be called the children of God.
"Blessed are they who are persecuted for
    righteousness' sake, for theirs is the
    kingdom of heaven.
"Blessed are you, when men shall revile
    you, and persecute you, and shall say
    all manner of evil against you falsely,
    for my sake".

The crowd was awed at the way he taught, and at the authority that he showed. Jesus finished speaking and came down the mount. At the bottom of the hill, he was met by a man suffering a terrible skin disease.

The man knelt down before him and said, "Lord, if you want to, you can make me clean".

Jesus reached out and touched him. "I want to", he said. At once, the man was cured.

Jesus said to him, "Go straight to the priest, and tell him to examine you to prove to everybody that you are cured. Then, offer a sacrifice of thanksgiving".

Jesus went back to Nazareth, his home-town, and on the Sabbath, he went to the synagogue, as he usually did. He stood up to read the Scriptures and was handed the book of the prophet Isaiah.

He unrolled the scroll and read the verses that say: "The Spirit of the Lord is upon me, because he has chosen me to bring good news to the poor. He has sent me to bind up the brokenhearted, to proclaim liberty to the captives, and to free the oppressed" (Isaiah 61:1).

Jesus rolled up the scroll, gave it back to the synagogue attendant, sat down, and said, "The passage of Scripture that you have heard me read, has come true today".

The people in the synagogue, surprised, stared at him, and one asked his neighbor, "Isn't he the son of the carpenter? Isn't Mary his mother?" Another asked, "Aren't James, Joses, Simon, and Judas his brothers?" "Aren't all his sisters living here?" A third one asked, "Where did he get his wisdom? What about his miracles?"

Jesus said to them, "I am quite sure that you will quote to me the proverb that says, 'Doctor, cure yourself', and then, you will tell me to do here what I have done in Capernaum. But, I say to you, no prophet has ever been welcomed in his own country! There were many starving widows, during the great famine in Elijah's days, but Elijah was not sent to any of them; he went to a widow who lived in Sidon. During the days of Elisha, there were many lepers in the country, but he didn't cure any of them; he cured Naaman the Syrian".

The people in the synagogue were furious at what they considered his presumption. They rose up, dragged him out of town to the top of a hill, and tried to throw him down the cliff, but Jesus managed to walk through the middle of the crowd and went away.

Jesus went to Jerusalem for a Jewish festival. One Sabbath, he went by the pool of Bethesda, located near the city's sheep market. The five porches of the pool were, as always, crowded with a great number of invalids, blind, lame, and paralyzed people who hoped that an angel would come down and stir up the water. According to a local tradition, the first sick person who would go into the pool, after it had been stirred by the angel, would be immediately cured from whatever disease he had.

One of the people, lying around the pool, was a man who had been sick for thirty-eight years. Jesus saw him and asked him, "Do you wish to get well?"

The sick man answered, "Sir, I have nobody to help me get into the pool, when the water is stirred. Somebody else always gets in, before I do!"

Jesus told him, "Rise, take your mat, and walk!" The man was immediately cured. He got up, took his mat, and walked away.

Some people who saw the man, walking around with his mat, reproached him, "Today, is the Sabbath, and it is forbidden for you to carry your mat".

The man replied, "The man who cured me told me, 'Take your mat, and walk'".

"Who said that to you?" they asked him.

The man looked around the crowded area, but Jesus had already left. Later that day, Jesus encountered the man in the Temple and told him, "You are cured now. Don't sin anymore, or something worse will happen to you".

The man pointed Jesus out to the Temple authorities and told them that he was the man who had healed him. They asked Jesus, "Why did you heal the man on a Sabbath?"

Jesus answered, "My Father works all the time, and so do I".

Nicodemus, a Pharisee member of the Jewish Council, came to Jesus, during the night, and said to him, "Master, we know that you are a teacher sent by God, because no man can perform the miracles that you do if God is not with him".

Jesus said to him, "I tell you truly, no one can see the Kingdom of God if he is not born again".

"How can a grown-up man be born again? Can he enter again into his mother's womb and be born?" asked Nicodemus.

"I tell you, a man cannot enter the Kingdom of God if he is not born of water and the Spirit. What is born of flesh is flesh, but what is born of the Spirit is spirit. Don't be amazed, when I say that you must be born again".

Nicodemus asked him, "How can this be?"

"You are a teacher in Israel, and you don't know these things? I tell you that we speak what we know and testify what we have seen. If you do not believe me, when I tell you things about this world, how will you believe me, when I speak about heavenly things? No one has ever gone up to heaven, except the Son of man who came down from heaven. God so loves the world that he has given his only Son, so that everyone who believes in him will live eternally. God did not send his Son to condemn the world but to save it".

The following day, Jesus was walking in the Temple, when people surrounded and confronted him. "Are you the Messiah?" they asked.

Jesus answered, "I have already told you, but you would not believe. I give you eternal life, and you shall never die. The Father and I are one".

They told him, "You are only a man, and you are trying to make yourself God". The people picked up stones, to stone him for his blasphemy. They tried to seize Jesus, but he slipped out of their hands.

Early the next day, Jesus went out of the city. People followed him and tried to convince him to stay. But he told them that he had to go to the Galilee to preach in other towns about the Kingdom of God. Jesus and his disciples left Jerusalem and went to the region of Judea, where they stayed for a while.

John, at that time, was baptizing in a place called Aenon, where there was plenty of water. His disciples heard that Jesus was baptizing more disciples than their teacher; actually, it was not Jesus who baptized them, but his disciples.

They went to John and asked him, "Master, do you remember the man that was with you on the other side of the Jordan, the one that you spoke about? He is now also baptizing, and everybody is going to him!"

John answered, "You heard me saying that I am not the Messiah, but that I was sent ahead of him. I am like the friend of the bridegroom, who stands by and listens, and is filled with joy, when he hears the voice of the bridegroom. He will become more important, and I less. He who comes from heaven is above all. The Father loves his Son, and he who believes in the Son has everlasting life".

Jesus and his disciples left Judea and went back to the Galilee. On the way, they stopped on the outskirts of a Samaritan town called Sychar. Tired by his journey, Jesus sat next to Jacob's well, while his disciples went to the town to buy some food. A Samaritan woman came by around noontime to draw water from the well.

Jesus said to her, "Please give me a drink of water".

The woman said to Jesus, "How can it be that you, a Jew, asks me, a Samaritan, for a drink?"

Jesus answered, "If you would know what God gives, and who is the one that is asking you for water, you would ask him, and he would give you living water".

"Sir, how can you give me living water, when the well is deep, and you have nothing to draw water with? Are you saying that you are greater than our father Jacob who gave us this well, and who, he himself, his children, and his cattle, drank from it?"

Jesus said, "Whoever drinks the water of this well will be thirsty again, but whoever drinks the water that I give will never ever thirst again. The water will become in him a spring that will give him eternal life".

The woman said, "Sir, please give me this water, so that I will never thirst again. And then, I will never have to come here again to draw water".

"Go, call your husband, and come back here", said Jesus.

"I have no husband".

"That is true. You already had five husbands, but you are not married to the man with whom you live now".

"Sir, I can see that you are a prophet! My ancestors worshipped God in this mountain, but you, Jews, say that Jerusalem is the place to worship God".

Jesus said, "The time is coming, when God will not be worshipped here or in Jerusalem. You, Samaritans, do not really know what you worship, but we, Jews, do know, because salvation comes from the Jews. The time is already here, when people will worship the Father, who is a Spirit, in spirit and truth".

The woman said, "I know that the Messiah is coming, and when he arrives, he will tell us everything".

Jesus answered, "I am he, the one that is speaking to you".

The disciples arrived, at that moment, and were surprised to find him talking with the woman, but they made no comment. The woman left her water jar near the well, hurried back to the town, and said to the people there, "Come and see a man who has told me everything that I have ever done. Do you think that he might be the Messiah?" The people of the town immediately went to look for Jesus.

In the meantime, by the well, the disciples were urging Jesus to eat something. Jesus refused and said to them, "I have food to eat that you know nothing about".

They asked each other, "Has anybody brought him anything to eat?"

"My food", Jesus explained, "is to do the will of the One that sent me and to finish the work".

The Samaritans arrived to the well and begged him to remain with them in their town for a while. Jesus agreed and stayed in the Samaritan village for two days.

Later, after he had left, many of the people in the town said to the woman, "We believe in him! Not because of what you have told us, but because of what we ourselves have heard him teach. We know that he is the Messiah, the Savior of the world".

Jesus returned to the Galilee and visited again the town of Cana. An important man came to Jesus and asked him to heal his son, who was mortally ill in Capernaum.

Jesus said to him, "None of you will believe unless you see signs and miracles".

The man implored him, "Sir, please come, before my child dies".

Jesus said, "Go, your son will live".

The man believed the words of Jesus and went back to his home. His servants greeted him with great joy. "Your son is out of danger!" they told him.

He asked them, "At what time did he get better?"

"The fever left him around one o'clock in the afternoon", they informed him.

The man realized that it was the precise moment when Jesus had told him that his son would live.

Jesus went to the synagogue and taught the people on the Sabbath, with knowledge and authority. He also exorcised the demon out a man. People were amazed, and his reputation spread.

He left the synagogue and went to the house of Simon Peter, whose mother-in-law was very sick. Jesus stood over her and ordered the fever to leave her, and she was cured.

That evening, people brought him their sick relatives and friends. Jesus laid his hand on every one of them, healed them, and expelled their demons.

One day, several men, carrying a paralyzed man on a bed, approached the house where Jesus was preaching to some Pharisees and doctors of the Law, who had come from as far away as Jerusalem.

The men found it impossible to enter the house by its door, because a great multitude surrounded the house. They managed to climb to the roof of the house and pulled up the bed with the man. Then, they made a hole on the tiles and carefully lowered the bed, with the man on it, down through the opening, until they placed him in front of Jesus.

Jesus saw how great their faith was, and he said to the paralytic, "Man, your sins are forgiven".

The Pharisees and the doctors of the Law said to each other, "Who is this man who speaks such blasphemies? Only God can forgive sins!"

Jesus read their thoughts and said, "Why do you think that? What is easier to say, 'Your sins are forgiven', or to say, 'Get up and walk?' I will prove to you that the Son of man has power on earth to forgive sins".

He turned to the paralytic and said, "Get up, take your bed, and go home".

The man immediately got up, picked up the bed, and returned to his house, singing praises to God. Everybody was amazed and fearful. They praised God and said, "We have seen such strange things today!"

Jesus, walking in the town, saw a tax collector, called Levi, sitting in his office, and told him to follow him. Levi got up, left everything, and followed Jesus.

Levi wanted his friends and former colleagues to meet Jesus. He prepared a feast in his home for Jesus and invited a large number of tax collectors and other people.

Some Pharisees and teachers of the Law, who happened to be present at the banquet, asked the disciples of Jesus, "Why does your master eat and drink with such disreputable people?"

Jesus heard them and answered, "People who are healthy do not need a doctor; only those who are sick need one. I have not come to ask respectable people to repent, but sinners".

The followers of John the Baptist came to Jesus and asked him, "Why do we, the followers of John the Baptist, and the disciples of the Pharisees, fast often and pray all the time, while your disciples eat and drink, and do not fast at all?"

Jesus answered, "The guests at a wedding do not fast, while the bridegroom is with them. But the day will come, when the bridegroom will be taken away from them, and then, they will fast".

Not long afterward, Jesus was walking through some wheat fields on a Sabbath. His disciples, walking beside him, picked grains of wheat and ate them. The Pharisees saw this and were scandalized. They told Jesus, "Picking grain is forbidden in the Sabbath!"

Jesus replied, "Do you recall that in one occasion, when David and his men were hungry, they went into the House of God and ate the dedicated bread that only priests are allowed to eat? The Son of man is the Lord of the Sabbath".

Jesus left the place and went to a synagogue, where there was a man whose hand was paralyzed. Some people watched him to see if he would heal the cripple on the Sabbath day, so that they could accuse him of desecrating the day of Esther

Jesus said to the man, "Come here". And looking at the others, he said, "Is it lawful to do good on the Sabbath, or to do evil? To save a life or to kill?"

When the men didn't answer, Jesus said to the man, "Stretch out your hand". The man did so and was healed.

Some people brought to Jesus a deaf mute possessed by a demon. Jesus drove him out; the man began to speak, and all were amazed. The people commented, "We have never seen anything like this in Israel!" But some of the men present said, "He expels evil spirits by the power that

Beelzebub, the chief of the devils, has given him".

Jesus said to them, "A kingdom divided against itself will fall. How could Satan's kingdom stand if he would be divided against himself? How can Satan drive out Satan? If a family divides itself into groups, which fight each other, that family will fall apart. So if Satan rises up against himself, he becomes divided and will come to an end".

A few days later, Jesus went across the lake, followed by a large crowd of about five thousand men, who had heard of his miraculous cures. Jesus climbed up a hill and sat there with his disciples.

He saw the large crowd around him, and, to test Philip, he asked him, "Where can we buy bread for all these people?"

Philip answered, "It would cost over two hundred coins to buy even a little for each one of them".

Andrew, Simon Peter's brother, said, "Look, there is a boy here who has five loaves of bread and two small fishes. But of course, that is not enough for all these people".

Jesus said to them, "Make them sit down". Over five thousand men sat on the grass.

Jesus took the loaves, expressed thanks to God, and gave the bread to his disciples, who distributed them to the people who were sitting. He did the same thing with the fishes.

Everybody in the crowd ate as much as he wanted. After they were all fully satisfied, so much food was left over that the disciples were able to fill twelve baskets.

The men who witnessed the miracle exclaimed, "He is the prophet that was expected to come into the world!" Jesus, afraid that the multitude would get carried away and proclaim him king, went off to the hills by himself.

When evening came, the disciples entered a boat and sailed toward Capernaum. During the night, a great wind started blowing and stirring the sea.

They rowed for several hours, but only managed to advance about three or four miles, because the wind was blowing against them and preventing them from reaching land. Suddenly, they saw Jesus coming to them, walking over the water, and they were terrified, because they thought that they were seeing a spirit.

"Don't be afraid", said Jesus. "It is I".

Peter answered, "Lord, if it is really you, order me to come out on the water to you".

"Come", ordered Jesus.

Peter got out of the boat and started walking on the water, but when he felt the strong wind, he became afraid and started to sink. "Save me, Lord", he cried.

Jesus reached out and grabbed him. "You have so little faith! Why did you doubt?"

They got into the boat, and immediately, the boat reached land at the place that they had intended.

The next morning, the crowd, who had stayed on the other side of the lake, realized that Jesus had not been aboard the boat with his disciples, when they had departed the previous evening. And that boat had been the only one that sailed, during the night.

The people looked around, and when they didn't see Jesus or his disciples, they entered the boats that had arrived from Tiberias and sailed to Capernaum, to search for Jesus.

They found him teaching in the synagogue and asked him, "Master, how did you get here?"

Jesus answered, "You didn't search for me because you saw the miracle, but because you ate the bread and were filled. You should not work for perishable food, but for food that lasts for eternity, which the Son of man can give you, food, which God the Father has sealed".

They asked him, "What must we do in order to do God's will?"

Jesus replied, "God wants you to believe in the one he sent".

"What sign will you give us so that we can see it and believe in you? What will you do? Our ancestors ate manna that God sent them from heaven".

Jesus said to them, "I will tell you: Moses was not the one that gave you that bread from heaven. It was my Father who gave you the real bread from heaven, the bread, which gives life to the world".

They pleaded, "Lord, give us this bread always".

Jesus said, "I am the bread of life. He that comes to me will never be hungry, and he that believes in me will never be thirsty. But, I tell you, you have seen me and you do not believe. I have come from heaven not to do what I want, but to do what the One who sent me wants. He will give eternal life to everyone who sees the Son and believes in him".

The people muttered, upset because he had said, "I am the bread, which came down from heaven". They asked, "Isn't he Jesus, the son of Joseph? We know his mother and father! How can he say that he came down from heaven?"

Jesus told them, "Don't mutter! I tell you: he that believes in me will have eternal life. I am the bread of life. Your ancestors ate manna in the wilderness, and they are now dead. But I am the living bread, which came down from heaven. If any man eats of this bread, he will live forever. The bread that I will give is my flesh, which I will give for the life of the world".

The people argued among themselves, "How can this man give us his flesh to eat?"

Jesus said, "Whoever eats my flesh and drinks my blood will have eternal life, because my flesh is food, and my blood is drink".

When many of the people who had been following him found these teachings too hard to accept and left him, Jesus asked the twelve apostles, "Will you also go away?"

Simon Peter answered, "Lord, to whom would we go? You have the words of eternal life. We believe with certainty that you are the Messiah, the Son of the living God".

His mother and brothers arrived, and from outside the house, they sent him a message announcing their presence. The people who were sitting with Jesus said, "Your mother and your brothers are outside, and they want you".

Jesus answered, "Who is my mother? Who are my brothers?" He looked at the people, sitting around him, and he said, "Here are my mother and my brothers! Whoever does the will of God, he is my brother, my sister, my mother".

Jesus traveled through towns and villages, preaching with parables the Kingdom of God to the crowds. Some people asked him why he used parables, when he talked to the people.

Jesus replied, "You are fortunate that you have been given the secret of the Kingdom of God, but others are simple people. They look, but they cannot see. They listen, but they cannot understand".

On the evening of that same day, Jesus asked his disciples to take him to the other side of the lake. They all got into a boat, and Jesus, tired, went to sleep. Suddenly, a fierce storm hit the lake, and the boat was in danger of sinking. The disciples, alarmed, woke Jesus up and said, "Master, Master, we are going to die!"

Jesus stood up and ordered the winds and the waves to be still, and there was a great calm.

The disciples, frightened, asked each other, "Who is this man? Even the wind and the waves obey him!"

Jesus asked his disciples, "Where is your faith?" They were amazed and afraid, and they did not answer.

Jesus and his disciples came to the territory of the Gadarenes, on the other side of the lake. There, they met a man who came out of the burial grounds possessed by demons. He terrorized the people in the surrounding villages by his screams and wild behavior.

Jesus asked him, "What is your name?"

The man answered, "My name is Legion, for we are many".

Jesus drove the demons out of the men and into a large herd of pigs feeding nearby.

The whole herd of about two thousand pigs rushed down the side of the cliff, into the lake, and was drowned.

The people in the town, when they heard what happened, came and were surprised to see that the man, who had always behaved wildly, was now clothed, calm, and quiet. Afraid and not knowing what to think, they asked Jesus to leave their territory.

As Jesus was getting into the boat, the healed man begged him to let him come along. Jesus refused and told him to go back to his home and tell his family what God had done for him. The man left and went all through the Decapolis—the ten towns—telling anybody who would listen how Jesus had cured him. And all who heard him were amazed.

When Jesus returned to the other side of the lake, he was met by Jairus, a leader of the town's synagogue, who threw himself down at his feet and begged him, "Please come with me to my house, and cure my daughter!"

On their way to Jairus' house, a woman, who had been treated from bleeding for twelve years by many doctors without success, touched Jesus' cloak, thinking to herself, "If I touch his cloak, I will get well".

Jesus, feeling that power had gone out of him, turned around and asked, "Who has touched my clothes?" The woman, who trembled with fear, knelt at his feet and told him what she had done.

Jesus said to her, "Your faith has cured you", and at that moment, she was healed.

While Jesus was talking to the woman, messengers came from the house of Jairus with the sad news that the girl had died.

Jesus said to Jairus, "Believe, and don't be afraid". Accompanied only by Peter, James, and John, he entered the house and saw that the people there were busy with the preparations for the burial.

He told the funeral musicians, "Get out! The girl is not dead; she is asleep".

All those present left the room, laughing at him and making fun of his words. As soon as the people went out, he went into the girl's room, touched her hand, and said, "Little girl, get up".

The girl got up at once and started walking around. Jesus told her parents to give her something to eat, and he ordered them not to tell anybody what had happened.

Jesus departed from the house, followed by two blind men, who shouted, "Son of David! Have mercy on us!"

He asked them, "Do you really believe that I can do this?"

"Yes, Lord", they answered.

He touched their eyes, and suddenly, they could see. Jesus asked them not to tell the miracle to anybody, but they were so overjoyed that they went around telling how Jesus had cured them.

Jesus came to Capernaum and was met by some Jewish elders who had been sent by a Roman centurion, whose favorite servant was mortally ill. The men told Jesus that the Roman was a good man, who deserved his help, and asked him to go with them to his house. Jesus agreed, and they walked to the centurion's house.

They were getting close to the house, when a friend of the Roman came to them, with a message that said, "Please do not trouble to come yourself to my house, because I am not worthy of your visit. Just give the order, and my servant will get well. I have soldiers under me. When I say to one of them, 'Go', he goes; and when I say to another one, 'Come', he comes; and when I order my servant, 'Do this', he does it".

Jesus, surprised, exclaimed, "I have never seen faith like this, not even in Israel!"

The messengers went back to the Roman's house and found that the servant was cured.

The next day, Jesus and his disciples, followed by a large crowd, went to a town called Nain. They arrived at the gate of the town, at the moment when a funeral procession was coming out.

They asked who had died and were told that the dead man was the only son of a widowed woman.

Jesus felt great pity for the woman and said to her, "Don't cry". Then, he walked over to the coffin, touched it, and said, "Young man, get up". The dead man sat up and began to talk.

The people who saw this were astonished and terrified. They sang praises to God and said, "A great prophet has risen among us! God has visited his people!"

Jesus asked his disciples, "What do people say about the Son of man?"

"Some say you are John the Baptist", they answered, "Others say that you are Elijah, Jeremiah, or some other prophet".

Jesus asked them, "And you, what do you think?"

Peter answered, "You are the Messiah, the Son of God".

Jesus said to him, "Bless you, Simon, son of Jona! This revelation has not come to you from any human being, but it came to you directly from my Father in heaven. You, Peter, are a rock, and upon this rock, I will build my church. I will give you the keys of the kingdom of heaven; what you forbid on earth will be forbidden in heaven, and what you permit on earth will be permitted in heaven".

Then, Jesus ordered his disciples not to say to anyone that he was the Messiah. From that time on, he began to tell them that he would have to go to Jerusalem, suffer at the hand of the elders, the chief priests, and the scribes. He added, "I will be killed, but three days later, I will come back to life".

Peter took him aside and rebuked him, "God forbid it, Lord". He said, "This must never happen to you".

Jesus turned around and exclaimed to Peter, "Get away from me, Satan! Your thoughts offend me, because they come from man, not from God".

Six days later, Jesus took Peter, John, and James with him and went up a high hill, where they were alone. Suddenly, Jesus was transfigured: his face shined like the sun, and his clothes became dazzling white. Next to him stood Moses and the prophet Elijah.

Peter, awed, and not knowing what else to say, said, "It is good that we are here, so that we can make three tents: one for you, one for Moses, and one for Elijah".

A cloud appeared and covered them with its shadow, and a voice from the cloud said, "This is my beloved Son, with whom I am well pleased. Listen to him!"

The disciples, terrified, flung themselves to the ground. They lifted their faces and looked around, and they saw that only Jesus was with them.

Jesus touched them and said, "Get up, don't be afraid".

Going down the hill, Jesus told them, "Do not tell anybody what you have seen, until the Son of man has risen from death".

The disciples asked Jesus, "Why do the teachers of the Law say that Elijah has to come first?"

Jesus answered, "Elijah has to come to get everything ready. But I tell you that Elijah has already come and the people did not recognize him. They maltreated him in the same way that they will maltreat the Son of man".

When they returned to the crowd, a man came to Jesus, knelt before him, and asked him to cure his son, which the disciples had not succeeded in healing. Jesus exorcised the evil spirit from the boy and healed him.

The disciples asked Jesus, "Why didn't we succeed in driving the evil spirit out?"

Jesus answered, "Because you did not have enough faith".

John the Baptist heard about Jesus' miracles and sent two of his disciples to talk with him. They came to Jesus and witnessed how he healed the people, restored sight to the blind, and expelled demons from the possessed.

"Are you the one who is expected to come, or do we have to look for another?" they asked him.

Jesus answered, "Go back and tell John what you have seen and heard. The blind can see, the lame can walk, the lepers are cured, the deaf can hear, the dead are brought back to life, and the gospel is preached to the poor. Blessed is he who finds no offense in me!"

After John's messengers departed, Jesus spoke to the people about John. "What did you expect to see, when you went into the wilderness? Perhaps, a reed shaken by the wind, or a man elegantly dressed? You can find people like that in the courts of kings! What you expected to find was a prophet, but you saw much more than a prophet! John is greater than any man who ever lived, but, I tell you, he who is the least in the Kingdom of God is greater than John!"

A woman of ill repute, who lived in a certain town, heard that Jesus was eating in the house of a Pharisee called Simon. She came to the house uninvited and stood behind Jesus, crying and wetting his feet with her tears. Then, she dried his feet with her hair, kissed them, and poured perfume on them.

The Pharisee saw this and said to himself, "If this man is really a prophet, he would know what kind of a woman she is!"

Jesus read his thoughts and said to him, "Simon, I want to tell you something".

"Yes, Master, please tell me", he replied.

"There were two men who owed money to a money lender. One owed him five hundred coins, and the other owed him only fifty coins. They were unable to pay, and the money lender forgave them both. Tell me, which of the two will love him more?"

Simon answered, "I suppose the one to whom he forgave the most".

Jesus said, "Simon, you are right". Pointing at the woman, he said, "Simon, do you see this woman? I came to your house, and you didn't give me any water for my feet, but she has washed my feet with tears. You didn't salute me with a kiss, but this woman has not ceased to kiss my feet. You didn't anoint my head with oil, but this woman has anointed my feet with perfume. Her sins, which are many, are forgiven, because she has loved much. Those who have been forgiven little, show little love".

And to the woman, he said, "Your sins are forgiven. Your faith has saved you. Go in peace".

The other guests, sitting at the table, asked themselves, "Who is this man who forgives sins?"

Jesus traveled through towns and villages, preaching the Kingdom of God. He was accompanied by his disciples, by several women—including Mary Magdalene, from whom he had driven out seven demons, Joanna, and Susanna—and by others, who used their own money to help him.

The time for the Festival of the Tabernacles was approaching. Jesus decided to stay in the Galilee, because the authorities in Judea wanted to kill him.

His brothers advised him to go to Judea, "You should go there now, so that your disciples may see the works that you do. If you want to be known, don't do these things in secret. You should show yourself to the world!"

Jesus answered, "No, I will not go yet, because my time has not come. You should go, because the world doesn't hate you. It hates me, because I testify that its works are evil".

However, after his brothers had gone to Jerusalem, Jesus also went there secretly. The festival was half over, when Jesus went to the Temple and began to teach. The Jewish authorities, who had been searching for him and asking where he was, heard him teach and were greatly surprised that a man who had never formally studied was so learned.

Jesus explained to them, "What I teach is not my own teaching. It comes from God, who sent me. A person who speaks on his own authority seeks his own glory, but he, who seeks the glory of the One who sent him, is honest, and there is nothing false in him". He added, "Moses gave you the Law, but you do not keep it. Why do you wish to kill me?"

They answered, "Who says that we wish to kill you? You have a demon inside!"

Jesus said, "I performed one miracle, and you were all surprised. Although the Law of Moses allows to circumcise on the Sabbath, you are angry with me, when I healed somebody in the Sabbath".

The people in Jerusalem argued over Jesus, but they didn't speak openly, because they feared the religious authorities. Some said, "He is a good man". Others said, "No, he deceives the people". Some of the people who heard him teach said, "He really is a prophet!" Others said, "He is the Messiah".

Some of them knew that the Messiah had to be a descendant of King David, and to be born in Bethlehem, but they did not know that Jesus had been born in Bethlehem, and so, they asked, "How can the Messiah come from the Galilee?"

Many people who believed in him said, "If the Messiah comes, will he do more miracles than this man has done?"

Those who knew that the authorities wanted to capture Jesus and kill him commented among themselves, "Isn't he the one they want to kill? How can it be that he talks freely in public, and nobody restrains him? Could it be that the authorities know that he is the Messiah? But, it is said, no one knows where the Messiah will come from, and we certainly know where Jesus came from".

Jesus said to the people around him, "You know me, and you know where I am from, but I have not come of my own will. He who sent me is truthful. You do not know him, but I do, because I come from him, and he has sent me".

On the last day of the festival, the most important day, the chief priests, who had heard the people murmuring these things, sent some guards to arrest him.

The guards came to Jesus, and he said to them, "I will be with you a little while longer. Then, I will go to the One who sent me. You will search for me, but you will not find me, because I will be where you cannot go".

The guards had no idea what he meant. They asked each other, "When he says that we will not find him, and that we will not be able to go where he will be, does he mean that he will go to foreign cities and teach the Gentiles?"

Jesus spoke in a loud voice, "If any man is thirsty, let him come to me and drink. The person who believes in me, as the Scriptures have said, will have rivers of living water flowing from his heart".

The guards went back to the chief priests, who, seeing them come without Jesus, asked them, "Why didn't you bring him?"

The guards answered, "This man speaks like no man has ever done".

The authorities said, "Have you also been deceived? Do you know any authority or Pharisee who believes in him? Only those who are ignorant of the Law are, thus, cursed!"

Nicodemus, a Pharisee who on a previous occasion had met Jesus secretly at night, said to his colleagues, "Our Law forbids to judge a person, before hearing him and finding what he has done".

"What?" they exclaimed, "Are you also from the Galilee? Go, study the Scriptures, and you will see that no prophet has ever come from the Galilee!"

Jesus went, that night, to the Mount of Olives and, early next morning, returned to the Temple. He sat down, surrounded by people, and taught them.

The scribes and the Pharisees brought him a woman who had been caught committing adultery. They made her stand up, before the people, and said to Jesus, "Master, this woman was caught in the act of adultery. The Law of Moses commands us to stone such sinners, but we want to know what you have to say about it".

Jesus bent over and wrote something with his finger on the ground, without answering their question.

When they asked him again, he straightened up and said to them, "Let the one among you, who is without sin, throw the first stone". He bent again and wrote on the ground.

One by one, those who had brought the woman departed, the older ones first. Jesus was left alone with the woman. He straightened up and asked her, "Woman, where are your accusers? Is there no one left to condemn you?"

"No one, Lord", answered the woman.

"I don't condemn you either", said Jesus. "Go, and sin no more".

Jesus spoke to the Pharisees in the treasury room of the Temple, "I am the light of the world; he that follows me shall not work in darkness, but shall have the light of life".

The Pharisees answered, "Saying this about yourself proves nothing".

Jesus replied, "It is true that I say this of myself, because I know from where I came, and where I go, but you don't know from where I came and where I will go. You judge the flesh, but I judge no one. But, if I would judge, my judgment would be true, because I am not alone; the Father who sent me is with me. The Law says that you need two witnesses to state the truth. I am one, and my Father that sent me is the other".

They asked him, "Where is your father?"

Jesus answered, "You don't know me or my Father. If you would know me, you would also know my Father. I will go away, and you will search for me, but you will die in your sins. Where I go, you cannot come".

The Jewish authorities said, "He says that we cannot go where he is going. Does that mean that he plans to commit suicide?"

Jesus said to them, "You are from below, I am from above. You are from this world, but I am not. You will die in your sins, because you do not believe that I am he".

"Who are you?" they asked.

"I told you that already", said Jesus, "I have much to say to you, and condemn

you. He that sent me is truthful, and I only speak to the world what I heard from him".

There were now many people listening to him, and he said to them, "If you obey my teachings, you are my true disciples. You will know the truth, and the truth will make you free".

They said to him, "We, the descendants of Abraham, were never slaves. So, how can you say that you will make us free?"

"I tell you", said Jesus, "whoever sins, becomes the slave of sin. A son is always a part of the family, but a slave does not belong forever to it. If the Son sets you free, you shall be truly free. I know that you descend from Abraham, but you want to kill me, because you do not accept my teachings. I speak what my Father has shown me, and you speak what your father has told you".

They answered, "Abraham is our father".

Jesus said, "If you really were the descendants of Abraham, you would do the same things that he did. But you want to kill me for having told you the truth, which I heard from God. Abraham never did such thing. You are doing what your father did!"

"God is our father", they said.

"If God would really be your father, you would love me, because I didn't come from my own will. He sent me. You don't understand what I say, because the devil is your real father. He was a murderer from the beginning, and a liar, the father of all lies. You don't believe me, because I tell the truth. He who comes from God hears God's words. You don't hear them, because you are not from God".

They said, "We were right, when we said that you really are a Samaritan and have a devil inside you!"

Jesus answered, "I don't have a devil inside me. I honor my Father, and you dishonor me. I am telling you truthfully, the man who obeys my teachings will never die".

They said to him, "Now, we are really sure that there is a devil inside you!

Abraham and the prophets are dead, but you say that whoever obeys your teachings will never die. Are you greater than our father Abraham? Who do you think you are?"

Jesus answered, "If I honor myself, that is not worth anything. The One who honors me is my Father, of whom you say that he is your God. You don't know him, but I do. If I would say that I don't know him, I would be a liar like you are. But I know him, and I obey his word. Your father Abraham was full of joy, when he saw my day".

"You aren't even fifty years old, and you say that you have seen Abraham?" they asked him.

Jesus replied, "I truly say to you, I am before Abraham".

The people, shocked at these sayings, picked up stones to throw at him, but Jesus hid himself and left the Temple.

One Sabbath, Jesus saw a man who had been born blind. His disciples asked him, "Did his own sinning cause his blindness, or is he being punished for his parents' sin?"

Jesus answered, "No, his blindness was not caused by his sins or by his parents' sins. He is blind so that God's power might be seen at work in him. I will do the work of him that sent me, while it is day; night is coming, when nobody can work. I am the light of the world, as long as I am here".

Jesus spat on the ground, made some mud with the spittle, and rubbed the mud on the man's eyes. Then, he told the blind man to go to the pool of Siloam and wash his face. The man did as Jesus told him, and suddenly, he could see.

His neighbors could not believe that this was the same man whom they had known. They wondered, "Isn't this man the one who sat and begged for alms?" Some said, "Yes, he is". Others said, "No, he just looks like him". The man himself assured them, "I am the man!"

"How can it be that you can now see?" they asked him.

"A man called Jesus rubbed mud on my eyes, and told me to go to the pool of Siloam and wash my face. I did so, and now I can see".

They asked him, "Where is he now?"

"I don't know", he answered.

The people took the man to the Pharisees, and he was made to tell the story of his cure again. Some of the Pharisees said, "The man who cured him cannot be from God, because he has desecrated the Sabbath". Others argued that a sinner couldn't perform such miracles.

"Tell us", they asked the man who had been blind, "what do you think about the man who cured you?"

"He is a prophet", the man answered without hesitation.

The Jewish authorities were not convinced that the man had once been blind. They called his parents and asked them, "Is this your son? You say that he was born blind, so how can it be that he can now see?"

His parents answered, "We assure you that he is our son, and that he was born blind. But we don't know how he is now able to see, or who cured him of his blindness. Ask him, he is old enough to speak for himself!"

The blind man's parents were afraid to give the impression that they believed that Jesus was the Messiah. They knew that, if they did, they would be expelled from the synagogue.

The Pharisees called the man back and told him, "You should give thanks to God, because we know that the man who cured you is a sinner".

The man answered, "I don't know if he is a sinner or not. The only thing that I know is that I was blind, and now I can see".

They asked him, "What did he do to you? How did he cure your blindness?"

"I already told you", he answered, "and you don't want to listen. Why should I tell you again? Could it be that you want to become his disciples?"

They became very angry and said, "Don't be insolent! You are the one who is his disciple! We are disciples of Moses, and we know that God spoke to Moses. And as for that fellow, we don't even know where he came from".

The man said, "Isn't that odd? You don't know where he came from, but he has cured my blindness. We know that God doesn't listen to sinners, but he listens to the people that worship him and do his will. Nobody ever heard of a man that could cure somebody who was born blind. If this man does not come from God, he wouldn't be able to do anything".

They insulted him, "You were born in sin! How dare you teach us?" And they expelled him from the synagogue.

Jesus heard what had happened, and he searched for the man. When he found him, he asked him, "Do you believe in the Son of God?

"Who is he, Lord, that I might believe in him?"

"You have seen him, and he is now talking with you".

"I believe, Lord", said the man and knelt down before Jesus.

Jesus said, "I have come into this world to judge, so that the blind should see, and those who see should become blind".

Some Pharisees who were nearby asked him, "Are you hinting that we are blind, too?"

Jesus replied, "If you were blind, you would be sinless, but because you claim that you can see, your sin remains".

In the town of Bethany, a short distance from Jerusalem, lived two sisters called Mary and Martha with their brother Lazarus, all three of whom were held by Jesus in great affection. When Lazarus got very sick, and they had almost lost hope, the sisters sent Jesus a message, asking him to come, because their brother was ill.

Jesus told his disciples that he would go back to Judea, because his dear friend Lazarus had died. The disciples feared that, if they would return to Judea, the people would stone them, but Thomas told them, "Let us all go along with the teacher, so that we may die with him".

When Jesus arrived at their house, he found that Lazarus had been buried four days before. The house was full with people who had come to comfort the sisters.

Martha greeted Jesus in tears and told him, "If you had been here, Lazarus would not have died".

Jesus said to her, "Your brother will rise to life".

She answered, "I know he will do so at the end of the days".

"I am the resurrection and the life. Whoever believes in him will live, even though he dies, and whoever believes in me will never die. Do you believe this?" Jesus asked her.

"Yes, Lord", answered Martha, "I believe that you are the Messiah, the Son of God who was to come into the world".

Mary, when told by Martha that Jesus had arrived, went to him and said, as her sister had said before, "Lord, if you had been here, my brother would not have died".

She wept, and so did Jesus. Then, she took him to the tomb, which was a cave with a stone placed at the entrance.

Jesus ordered, "Take the stone away".

Martha warned him, "There will be a bad smell, because Lazarus has been dead already four days".

Jesus called in a loud voice, "Lazarus, come out". The man who had been dead came out wrapped in his funeral cloths, and Jesus said to the people, "Untie him and let him go".

The Pharisees and the chief priests feared his constantly increasing popularity. They gave orders that anybody who knew where Jesus was, should report it, so that they could arrest him. Jesus, in the meantime, stayed in a town called Ephraim, near the desert.

Jesus called the twelve disciples and gave them power and authority to cure diseases, and to drive out demons. Then, he sent them out to preach the Kingdom of God and to heal sick people.

He told them, "Don't take anything with you. No walking stick, no food, no money, not even an extra shirt. If you are welcome in a house, stay there till you depart from that town. And if nobody is willing to receive you, leave that town, and shake the dust from your feet as a warning to them".

The disciples departed to different towns, where they preached the gospel and healed the sick. When they returned, they told Jesus all that they had done and taught.

Some Pharisees and teachers of the Law came from Jerusalem, and they asked Jesus, "The Law commands that we should wash our hands before eating. Why don't your disciples do that?"

Jesus accused them that they emphasized rituals and behaved with hypocrisy, instead of helping the poor. Later, he explained to his disciples that eating without washing one's hands did not make a person ritually unclean. "What goes into a person's mouth doesn't make him unclean. A person is made unclean by the evil that originates in his heart and comes out of his mouth".

Jesus visited a place near the frontier, not far from the cities of Sidon and Tyre. A Canaanite woman, who lived there, asked him to exorcise an evil spirit from her daughter, but Jesus didn't pay any attention to her, until his disciples asked him to send the woman away.

"Please get rid of her; she is making a nuisance of herself, following us everywhere, and making a lot of noise", they said.

Jesus said, "I have been sent only to the lost sheep of the house of Israel".

The woman insisted, "Help me, sir".

Jesus said, "It isn't right to take the children's food and throw it to the dogs".

The woman answered, "That's true, sir, but even the dogs eat the leftovers that fall from the table of their masters".

Jesus, deeply moved by her answer, replied, "You are a woman of great faith. What you want will be done for you". And at that very moment, her daughter was cured.

Jesus left that place and returned to the lake of Galilee. He climbed a hill and sat down; large crowds came to him, bringing people who were lame, blind, crippled, dumb, and sick, and Jesus cured them all.

Three days later, the crowd no longer had any food left, and Jesus felt sorry for them. "I don't want to send them away hungry, because they could faint on their way home. We must feed them", he told the disciples.

The disciples asked him, "But where can we find enough food in this desert to feed this crowd?"

"How much bread do you have?" asked Jesus.

"Seven loaves and a few small fish", they answered.

Jesus ordered the crowd to sit on the ground. Then, he took the seven loaves and the fish, gave thanks to God, broke them, and gave them to his disciples, and the disciples gave them to the people. Over four thousand men, plus women and children, ate and had enough.

Then, Jesus sent the people away, got into a boat, and went to Magdala.

The collectors of the Temple tax came to Peter and asked him, "Does your teacher pay the Temple tax?"

Peter answered, "He certainly does!"

When Peter returned to the house, Jesus asked him, "Who pays taxes: the citizens or the foreigners?"

Peter answered, "The foreigners".

Jesus said, "In that case, we don't owe any taxes, but to avoid offending the collectors, we will pay".

He instructed Peter to go and fish, and he told him that Peter would find a coin in the mouth of the fish, which would be enough to pay for the taxes of both of them.

Some people brought children to Jesus, and they asked him to place his hands on them, but the disciples tried to drive them away.

Jesus called the children to him and said, "Let the children come to me, because the Kingdom of God belongs to them. I tell you, whoever does not receive the Kingdom of God like a little child will never enter it".

When some Pharisees asked him when the Kingdom of God would come, Jesus answered, "The Kingdom of God does not come in such a way as to be seen. No one will say, 'It is here', or, 'It is there'. The Kingdom of God is within you".

As they went on their way, a man remained behind and said to Jesus, "Lord, I will follow you wherever you go".

Jesus told him, "Foxes have holes, and the birds of the air have nests; but the Son of man has no place to lay his head".

To another man, Jesus said, "Follow me".

The man said, "Lord, first let me go to bury my father".

Jesus replied, "Let the dead bury their dead. You go and preach the Kingdom of God".

Another man said, "Lord, I will follow you; but first, let me go and say goodbye to my family".

Jesus said to him, "Any man who has started to plow and looks back is not fit for the Kingdom of God".

Jesus chose seventy-two men from among his followers, and he sent them out, two by two, to go ahead of him to every town and place where he himself was about to go, to heal the sick, and to preach that the Kingdom of God was near.

The seventy-two men came back, full of joy, and told how even the demons had obeyed them, when they commanded them in the name of Jesus.

Jesus admonished them, "Don't be glad because the evil spirits obey you; but rather, be happy that your names are written in heaven".

A teacher of the Law came to Jesus and tried to trap him. "Master", he asked, "What shall I do to merit eternal life?"

Jesus answered him with a question of his own, "What is written in the Law? And how do you interpret it?"

The teacher said, "You shall love the Lord, your God, with all your heart, with all your soul, with all your strength, and with all your mind; and your neighbor as yourself".

Jesus said, "You have answered correctly. Do it and you will live".

"But who is my neighbor?" asked the teacher.

Jesus answered him with a parable. "A man went from Jerusalem to Jericho, and was attacked by thieves who stole his clothing and left him half dead on the road. A priest saw him lying there, and crossed to the other side of the road. A Levite passed by, and did the same. Then, a Samaritan, a foreigner, saw the wounded man, came to him, poured oil and wine on his wounds, helped him to get on his own animal, and brought him to an inn. The next morning, before he departed, the Samaritan took two coins and gave them to the innkeeper, asking him to take care of the wounded man, and promising to repay him on his return if he would spend more".

Jesus concluded, "Who, in your opinion, was the real neighbor to the man who was attacked by the robbers?"

The teacher answered, "The one who showed mercy on him".

Jesus replied, "Go, and do the same".

One Sabbath, Jesus was teaching in a synagogue. A woman, possessed by an evil spirit, had been ill, during eighteen years. She was bent over and could not straighten up. Jesus saw her, placed his hands on her, and said, "Woman, you are freed from your sickness". She immediately straightened up and praised God.

The ruler of the synagogue, outraged that Jesus had healed on the Sabbath day, said to the people, "There are six days in which we should work, and you can come and be healed, but not on the Sabbath day".

Jesus said, "You, hypocrites! Does not each of you on the Sabbath untie your ox or your donkey from the stall, and take him out to drink water? And this woman, a daughter of Abraham, whom Satan has kept in bounds for eighteen years, should not be released from her burden on the Sabbath?"

His answer made his adversaries feel ashamed, while the people rejoiced for all the wonderful things that he had done.

On another Sabbath, Jesus went to eat a meal in the house of one of the leading Pharisees. Seeing there a man who suffered of dropsy, he asked the lawyers and the Pharisees, "Is it lawful to heal on the Sabbath?" When they did not answer, he healed the man and sent him away.

Jesus asked them, "If any of you had a donkey or an ox that fell into a well on a Sabbath, would you not pull him out immediately?"

Again, they did not answer.

Herod, the tetrarch of Galilee, heard confusing rumors about Jesus: Some people were saying that he was John, who had risen from the dead. Others thought that Elijah had returned, or one of the prophets of the old times. The tetrarch told his officials, "He can't be John, because I have beheaded him, so who is this one about whom I am hearing so much? I would like to see him".

Some Pharisees came to him and warned him that Herod wanted to kill him. Jesus said to them, "Go, and tell that fox that today and tomorrow, I will be casting out devils and healing people. I will be on my way the day after tomorrow, because it cannot be that a prophet should die outside of Jerusalem. O Jerusalem, Jerusalem, you kill the prophets, and you stone those that are sent to you! Your Temple will be abandoned. Truly, I say to you, you will not see me, until the day when you will say, 'Blessed is he that comes in the name of the Lord'".

Jesus told the twelve disciples, "Behold, we are going to Jerusalem, and everything that the prophets wrote concerning the Son of man will come true. He will be handed to the Gentiles, who will mock him, insult him, and spit on him. They will whip him and kill him, but he will rise again on the third day".

The mother of James and John, sons of Zebedee, came to Jesus with her two sons and said, "Lord, let my sons be allowed to sit next to you in your glory, one on your right hand, and the other on your left hand."

Jesus replied, "I can't grant your wish, because those places belong to those for whom God has prepared them".

The other disciples, when they heard the request of Zebedee's wife, were very upset with the two brothers.

Jesus called the disciples and said to them, "If any of you wants to be great, he must be the servant of the others, because the Son of man did not come to be served but to serve and to give his life for the redemption of the people".

On their way to Jerusalem, Jesus went along the border between Samaria and Galilee. As he entered into a village, he met ten lepers who shouted from a distance, "Jesus, Master, have mercy on us".

Jesus told them, "Go, and show yourselves to the priests". As they went, they were cured. One of them, a Samaritan, turned back and gave thanks to God in a loud voice. He threw himself at Jesus' feet and thanked him.

Jesus asked his disciples, "There were ten men who were cured; where are the other nine? How can it be that this man, a foreigner, is the only one that came back to thank God?"

To the Samaritan, he said, "Get up, and go. Your faith has cured you".

Jesus came to the region of Judea and crossed the Jordan River. Some Pharisees came to him and asked him if the Law allowed a man to divorce his wife.

Jesus answered with a question, "What does the Law of Moses say about that?"

They answered, "Moses allows a man to divorce his wife".

Jesus said to them, "Moses wrote that law, because you are so hard to teach, but man should not separate what God has joined together".

They came to Jericho. A blind man called Bartimaeus, who was begging by the road, was told that Jesus was passing by, and he cried out, "Jesus, son of David, have mercy on me".

The people around him tried to quiet him, but the blind man kept shouting. Jesus called him to his side and asked him, "What do you want from me?"

The blind man said, "Lord, I wish to receive my sight".

Jesus said to him, "You can see; your faith has saved you".

Bartimaeus immediately recovered his sight, and he followed Jesus, praising God, as did all the people who saw what had happened.

Zacchaeus, the leading tax collector in Jericho and one of the wealthiest men in the town, heard that Jesus was going to enter Jericho by a certain road, and he was eager to see him.

Realizing that the crowd, lining both sides of the road, would make it impossible for a man of his short stature to catch more than a fleeting glance of Jesus, he ran and climbed a sycamore tree, which overlooked the road.

Jesus, passing by the tree, looked up and said, "Zacchaeus, hurry up and come down, because today, I am going to stay in your house".

Zacchaeus joyfully climbed down. The crowd was resentful and murmured, "He is going to be the house guest of a sinner!"

Zacchaeus, hearing this, stood straight in front of Jesus and said, "Listen, Lord, I will give half of what I have to the poor, and if I have taken anything from any man by false pretenses, I will return it fourfold".

Jesus said, "Today, salvation has come to your house, because you are also a descendant of Abraham. The Son of man has come to seek and to save what was lost".

A large crowd followed Jesus and his disciples, when they left Jericho. Two blind men, who were sitting by the road, heard that Jesus was passing by, and they shouted to him to have mercy on them. When Jesus asked them what they wanted, they replied that they wanted him to give them back their sight. Jesus touched their eyes; at once, they could see, and they followed him.

On their way to Jerusalem, where they were going for the Passover Festival, Jesus and his disciples came to Bethany, to the house of Lazarus and his sisters. They all sat for dinner, including Lazarus. While Martha prepared dinner and set the table, her sister Mary sat down at the feet of Jesus and listened to his teaching.

Martha, upset that she alone was doing all the work, complained about her sister to Jesus, "Lord, don't you mind that my sister is letting me serve alone? Please tell her to help me".

Jesus said to her, "Martha, Martha, you are tense and worried over so many things. Mary has chosen the right portion, and it will not be taken away from her".

Martha served, while Mary took a pound of very expensive ointment, poured them on Jesus' feet, and dried them with her hair. The whole house was filled with the perfume of the ointment.

Judas Iscariot, who would soon betray him, protested loudly, "Why wasn't this ointment sold for three hundred coins, and the money given to the poor?" He really didn't care for the poor, but he was in charge of the money bag of the group, and he would steal from it.

Jesus said, "Leave her alone! She has kept this for the day of my burial. You will always have the poor with you, but you will not always have me".

Many people came to the house, not only to see Jesus, but also out of curiosity to meet Lazarus, who had been raised from the dead. The chief priests took notice of this and thought of killing Lazarus, because on his account, many people were rejecting them and believing in Jesus.

Jesus continued on his way to Jerusalem. As he came near the Mount of Olives, he sent two disciples ahead and told them that, in the village ahead, they would find a colt that had never been ridden. They were to untie it and bring it to him.

After the disciples brought the colt back, they threw their cloaks over the animal, and they helped Jesus to get on. As he rode, people spread their cloaks on the road, while others cut branches in the field and spread them on the road. The crowd shouted in a loud voice, "God bless him who comes in the name of the Lord".

Some people asked, "Who is he?" The crowd answered, "He is the prophet Jesus, from Nazareth in the Galilee".

When he came near the city, at the descent from the Mount of Olives, a large crowd of his followers and disciples accompanied him, shouting, joyfully, praises to God for all the great things that they had seen. "Blessed is the King that comes in the name of the Lord", they said, "peace in heaven, and glory in the highest".

Some of the Pharisees in the crowd, scandalized by the shouting, said to Jesus, "Master, rebuke your disciples!"

Jesus replied, "If they would be silent, the stones would shout out".

Coming closer to the city, Jesus wept, knowing that the city would be attacked by enemies and destroyed sometime in the not-too-distant future. Then, Jesus went into the Temple and was shocked to find merchants who sold cattle, sheep, and doves. He also saw money changers sitting at their tables.

He shouted at them, "You have turned the House of God into a den of thieves!"

He made a whip from cords and drove all the animals out; then, he overthrew the tables of the money changers, and he ordered the pigeon sellers to stop making his Father's house a marketplace.

The Jewish authorities came to him and said, "What sign can you show us for doing this?"

Jesus answered, "Tear down this Temple, and I will rebuild it in three days".

"It took forty-six years to build this Temple", they said, "and you say that you can build it again in three days?"

But Jesus was talking about the Temple of his body. When he rose from death, his disciples remembered his words.

The blind and the crippled came to him, and he cured them. When the chief priests and the teachers of the Law saw what Jesus was doing, and heard the children, shouting, "Praise to David's son", they became angry and began to look for a way to kill him.

At the end of the day, Jesus went out of the city to the village of Bethany, where he spent the night. Early the next morning, on his way back to the city, Jesus was hungry. He saw a fig tree by the side of the road and approached it, but he found nothing on it except leaves. So, he said to the tree, "You will never again bear fruit". The tree dried up and died. The disciples saw this and were astounded.

Jesus taught in the Temple, the people crowding around him, not wanting to miss a single word. The chief priests, the teachers of the Law, and the leaders of the people asked him, "What right do you have to speak like that? Who has given you that right?"

Jesus answered, "I want to ask you one question: Did John's right to baptize come from God or from man?"

Jesus' question placed them in a quandary, and they argued among themselves what to answer. If they would say, "From God", Jesus would then ask them, "Why, then, did you not believe John?" And if they would say, "From man", the crowd, who believed that John was a prophet, would stone them.

So they said, "We cannot tell".

Jesus replied, "Then, I will also not tell you by what right I do these things".

Jesus' enemies needed a pretext to arrest him. They instructed some men to go to Jesus and try to trick him into making subversive declarations that would give them a justification to hand him over to the Roman authorities.

The men came to Jesus and asked him, "Is it allowed by our Law to pay taxes to the Romans or not?"

Jesus understood their malicious intention, and he answered, "You are trying to trap me. Bring me a coin, and let me see it!"

They showed him a silver coin. Jesus looked at it and asked them, "Whose face and name appear on the coin?"

"The emperor's", they answered.

Jesus replied, "Give to the emperor what belongs to the emperor, and to God what belongs to God".

Some Sadducees, members of a sect that did not believe in the resurrection of the dead, came to him and asked him, "If a woman had married a man who died, and then subsequently married his six brothers, each of them dying in his turn, whose wife would she be, when they would all rise back to life?"

Jesus answered, "Your question shows that you don't understand the Scriptures or God's power. When the dead rise to life, they will be like the angels in heaven, and will not marry".

A scribe asked Jesus, "Which is the greatest commandment in the Law?"

Jesus answered, "The greatest commandment is, 'Hear, O Israel! The Lord, our God, is one! Love God with all your heart, your soul, your mind, and your strength'. The second most important commandment is to love your neighbor as you love yourself".

The scribe said, "Very well answered, Master! You have said the truth. It is more important to obey these two commandments than to offer animal sacrifices to God on the altar".

Jesus appreciated his wise comment and told him, "You are very close to the Kingdom of God!" After this, nobody dared ask Jesus more questions.

Jesus sat near the Temple treasury and watched the people, as they dropped in their money. A poor widow came along and dropped two little copper coins.

Jesus said to his disciples, "That poor widow put more in the offering box than all the others. The others put what they could spare. She donated all that she had".

Jesus told the people, "Follow everything that the Pharisees and the teachers of the Law preach, but do not imitate their actions, because they do not practice what they preach. They are hypocrites, whitewashed tombs, which look fine on the outside but are full of bones and decaying corpses on the inside".

When some of the disciples spoke with admiration about the Temple, about its beautiful stones, and the gifts offered to God, Jesus told them, "All these things that you see, the day will come and not even one stone will be left upon another. All of this will be thrown down".

The disciples asked him, "Master, when will this happen? What sign will show us that the time has come for it to happen?"

Jesus answered, "Be careful not to be deceived. Many will come in my name, saying, 'I am the Messiah', and, 'the time has come', but don't follow them. There will be wars, earthquakes, famines, and plagues, but before all these, you will be arrested and persecuted, and brought before kings and rulers for my sake. You will be betrayed by your relatives, and some of you will be killed. Jerusalem will be surrounded by armies, and the people will be led away captive to other countries. The Gentiles will trample Jerusalem, until their time is fulfilled. Then, you will see the Son of man coming in a cloud with power and glory. When these things will happen, look up and lift your heads, because your salvation is near".

When he finished saying these things, Jesus told his disciples that in two days would be the Festival of Unleavened Bread, the Passover, and the Son of man would then be handed over to be crucified. At that very moment, the chief priests and the elders were meeting together in the palace of Caiaphas, the High Priest, conspiring to arrest Jesus, and to put him to death.

Judas Iscariot, one of the twelve disciples, decided to betray Jesus. He went to the chief priests and the officers of the Temple guard, and he asked them, "What will you give me if I betray Jesus to you?" They counted thirty silver coins and gave them to him.

On the first day of the Festival of Unleavened Bread, the disciples asked Jesus where did he want to eat the Passover meal. Jesus sent them to a certain man's house, and he instructed them to tell him that he and the disciples would celebrate the Passover in his house. The disciples did as Jesus had instructed, and they prepared the Passover meal.

When it was evening, Jesus came to the house with the twelve disciples, and he sat down to eat. He took a piece of bread, gave a prayer of thanks, broke it, and gave it to his disciples. "Take it and eat it, this is my body", he said. Then, he took a cup, gave thanks to God, and gave it to them. "Drink it, all of you", he said, "this is my blood, which seals God's covenant".

He then rose from the table, took off his outer garment, and tied a towel around his waist. He poured water into a washbasin, began to wash the feet of his disciples, and dried them with the towel. When he came to Peter, Peter asked him, "Lord, why do you wash my feet?"

Jesus answered, "You will understand later why I am doing this".

Peter said, "I refuse to have you wash my feet!"

Jesus said, "If you don't let me wash you, you will no longer be my disciple!"

Peter answered, "Lord, if that is the case, wash not only my feet, but also my hands and my head".

Jesus said, "Anyone who has already bathed himself is perfectly clean, and only has to wash his feet. You are clean, but not all of you". He said this, because he knew who was going to betray him.

After he finished washing their feet, he put on his outer garment, sat down, and asked them, "Do you understand what I have done to you? You rightly call me Master and Lord, because that is who I am. But if I, your Lord and Master, have washed your feet, you should also wash one another's feet. I have given you an example that you should follow. I tell you, the servant is not greater than his master, and the one that was sent is not greater than the one who sent him. If you understand these things, how happy you will be, when you will do them".

He was silent for a moment, and then, with great emotion, he said, "Truly, I tell you, one of you will betray me".

The disciples looked at one another, not knowing whom he meant. One of the disciples, whom Jesus loved very much, was sitting next to him. Simon Peter gestured to him and said, "Ask him about whom is he speaking".

The disciple asked Jesus, "Lord, who is he?"

Jesus answered, "He is the one to whom I will give a piece of bread, after I dip it". He dipped it and gave it to Judas Iscariot. Then, he said to Judas, "Do quickly what you are going to do". Judas got up and left immediately.

The other disciples didn't understand what Jesus had said to Judas. They assumed that Jesus had told him to go and buy what was needed for the Festival, or to donate some alms to the poor.

After Judas left, Jesus said, "Now is the Son of man glorified, and God is glorified in him. My children, I will not be with you much longer. I tell you now what I once told the Jewish authorities, 'Where I go, you will not be able to come'. I am giving you a new commandment: love one another as I have loved you. If you love one another, everybody will know that you are my disciples".

Simon Peter asked him, "Lord, where are you going?"

Jesus answered, "Where I go, you cannot follow me now, but you will follow me later".

"Lord, why can't I follow you now? I am ready to die for you", said Peter.

Jesus said to him, "Are you really ready to die for me? I tell you, you will deny me three times, before the rooster crows!"

And to all of them, he said, "Don't be worried. Believe in God, and believe in me. There are many rooms in my Father's house, and I am going to prepare a place for you. Then, I will come back, and take you to myself, so that you will be where I am. You know the way where I am going".

Thomas said, "Lord, we don't know where you are going. How then can we know the way to get there?"

Jesus answered, "I am the way, the truth, and the life. No man comes to my Father, except by me. Now that you have known me, you have known my Father also. From now on you know him, and you have seen him".

Philip said to him, "Lord, show us the Father. That would satisfy us".

Jesus replied, "After I have been so long with you, you still don't know me, Philip? Whoever has seen me, has seen the Father. How can you now say, 'Show us the Father'? Don't you believe that I am in the Father, and the Father is in me? If you love me, keep my commandments. I will pray to the Father, and he shall give you another Comforter, who will be with you forever. In a little while, the world will not see me anymore, but you will see me, and because I live, you will also live. He who has my commandments and keeps them, loves me, and he that loves me will be loved by my Father, and I will love him, and reveal myself to him".

Judas—not Iscariot, but the other disciple by that name—said, "Lord, how can it be that you reveal yourself to us, but not to the world?"

Jesus answered, "If a man loves me, he will obey my teachings. My Father will love him, and we will come and live with him. He, who doesn't love me, does not obey my teachings. These sayings are not mine, but they are from my Father who sent me. The Comforter, who is the Holy Ghost, whom the Father will send in my name, will teach you all things, and make you remember all that I have said to you. I give you my peace, which is not the peace that the world gives. Don't be afraid, I am going away, but I will return to you. If you love me, you will rejoice, because I am going to the Father, and my Father is greater than I. I will no longer talk much with you, because the ruler of this world is coming. He has no power over me, but I do, as the Father has commanded me, so that the world may know that I love the Father".

Later, he said to his disciples, "In a little while, you will not see me anymore, but then, a little while later, you will see me again".

His disciples asked one another, "What is he talking about? What does a 'little while' mean?"

Jesus said, "You are sad now, but your hearts will be glad, when I see you again. I came from the Father into the world, and now I am leaving the world and going back to the Father".

The disciples answered, "We now understand that you came from God. We are sure that you know everything, and there is no need to question you".

Jesus said to them, "Do you believe now? The hour is coming, when you will be scattered, and I will be left alone. Tonight, all of you will run away and leave me. But after I am raised back to life, I will go to Galilee ahead of you".

Peter said, "I will never leave you, even if the others do".

Jesus said to Peter, "Three times you will say that you do not know me, before the rooster crows tonight".

Peter answered, "I will never say that, even if I have to die with you".

He asked the disciples, "When I sent you to preach to different towns without a purse, bag, or shoes, did you lack anything?

"Nothing", they answered.

"But now, whoever has a purse or a bag, let him take it", said Jesus, "and he that doesn't have a sword let him sell his clothing and buy one".

"Lord, there are two swords", they told him.

"That is enough", said Jesus.

After dinner, they sang a hymn and went out to the Mount of Olives. They came to a place called Gethsemane, and Jesus told them to remain there, while he would pray some distance away. He took with him Peter and the two sons of Zebedee, went a little farther, and fell on his face to the ground.

"Father", he prayed, "All things are possible for you. Take this cup of suffering away from me. But do not do what I want, but what you want".

He went back to the three disciples and found them asleep. He woke them up and told them to watch and pray. Jesus again went away and said the same prayer.

He returned and, again, found the disciples asleep. Once more, Jesus left them and prayed for the third time the same prayer. Then, he returned to the disciples, woke them up, and told them that the man who was betraying him had arrived.

Judas, who knew the place because Jesus had met there many times with his disciples, arrived at that moment, leading an armed group of soldiers and Temple guards, sent by the religious authorities.

Judas had arranged with the soldiers that they should arrest the man that he would kiss. He went straight to Jesus, said, "Master, master", and kissed him.

"Judas, will you betray the Son of Man with a kiss?" Jesus reproached him.

Jesus stepped forward and asked the armed men, "Who are you looking for?'

"Jesus of Nazareth", they answered.

"I am he", said Jesus.

They stepped back, and Jesus asked them again, "Whom do you seek?"

"Jesus of Nazareth", they replied.

"I already told you that I am he. If you want me, let the others go".

Peter drew his sword and struck a slave of the high priest, a man called Malchus, cutting off his right ear.

Jesus rebuked Peter, saying, "Enough of this! Put your sword back in its place! All who take the sword will die by the sword. Do you think that I will not drink the cup of suffering, which my Father has given me?" He touched the man's ear and healed him.

Then, Jesus said to the guards, "Did you have to come with swords and clubs, as though I were a thief? I was with you in the Temple everyday, teaching, and you did not try to arrest me. But the Scriptures must be fulfilled".

The armed men arrested Jesus, tied him up, and took him to the palace of Annas, the previous high priest, and father-in-law of Caiaphas, the current High Priest

The disciples saw that and ran away from the garden. A young man, dressed only in a linen cloth, started to go after Jesus, but when they tried to arrest him too, he ran away naked, leaving his robe behind.

Peter and another disciple followed Jesus and the guards at a distance. Peter stayed by the gate outside the palace of Annas, while the other disciple, who was an acquaintance of the High Priest, went inside the courtyard of the palace. After a while, he came out and spoke to the maid at the gate, who then opened the door and allowed Peter to come inside.

The maid asked Peter, "Are you not one of the man's disciples?"

"Woman, I don't know him", said Peter. He got up and went to warm himself by the fire that the servants and the guards had built in the courtyard.

The men around the fire asked Peter, "Are you not one of his disciples?"

"I am not", answered Peter.

One of the servants, who happened to be a relative of Malchus, the man whose ear Peter had cut off with his sword, said to him, "You must be one of them. You are a Galilean; your accent gives you away".

Peter shouted, "I swear that I don't know the man you are talking about!" While he was speaking, a rooster crowed, and he remembered that Jesus had said to him, "Before the rooster crows, you will deny me three times". Peter went out and wept bitterly.

The guards, who held Jesus, made fun of him and beat him. They blindfolded him, struck him on the face, and played games with him, asking, "Guess, who hit you?" Then, they took him to the Council of the Elders to be interrogated.

The chief priests and the teachers of the Law cross-examined Jesus, but they were unable to find any evidence against him, until some men testified that they had heard him, saying that he could tear down the Temple and rebuild it in three days.

The High Priest asked him, "Is this true?" When Jesus didn't answer, he asked him, "Are you the Messiah, the Son of the Blessed God?"

"I am. You will see the Son of man sitting at the right side of God and coming in the clouds of heaven", Jesus replied.

The High Priest tore his clothes and exclaimed, "Blasphemy! We don't need any more witnesses! We have heard his blasphemy! What do you think?"

The member of the council answered, "He is guilty and must die". Some of them began to spit on him, covered his eyes, and hit him, saying, "Prophesy now!" while the guards slapped him.

Annas said to Jesus, "Tell me about your disciples and about your teachings".

Jesus answered, "I have always spoken publicly, and my teachings were done openly in the synagogues, and in the Temple, never in secret. Why do you question me? Question the people who heard me!"

A guard slapped him and said, "How dare you talk like that to the High Priest!"

Jesus answered, "If I have said anything wrong, tell everyone what I said. But if I am right in what I said, why do you strike me?"

Annas told the guards to take Jesus, who was still tied up, to the house of his son-in-law, Caiaphas, the High Priest

Judas repented of his treason, when he heard that Jesus had been condemned. He went to the chief priests and the elders and tried to return the thirty silver coins. He said to them, "I have sinned by betraying an innocent man to death".

"We don't care about that. It's your business", they answered.

Judas threw down the coins to the ground and departed. The chief priests picked up the coins, and later, they used them to buy a piece of land to be used as a cemetery for foreigners, because it was blood money, and as such it could not be put in the treasury of the Temple. Judas, heartbroken by the terrible consequences of his treason, hanged himself.

Early next morning, the priests and the elders put Jesus in chains and took him from the house of Caiaphas to the palace of Pilate, the Roman governor of Judea. The priests waited outside the palace, because they wanted to keep themselves ritually clean for the Passover celebration.

Pilate came out and asked them, "What is the accusation against this man?"

They answered, "We would not have brought him to you if he had not committed a crime".

Pilate told them, "Then, take him and try him according to your own law".

They replied, "Roman law does not allow us to condemn anyone to death".

Pilate went back into the palace, and he had Jesus brought inside. While Pilate was sitting in the Judgment Hall, his wife sent him a message that said, "Please don't have anything to do with that innocent man. I had a dream about him, which has caused me great suffering".

Pilate asked Jesus, "Are you the king of the Jews?"

Jesus answered, "Is this your own question, or have others told you about me?"

Pilate said, "Do you think I am a Jew? Your own people and the chief priests have handed you over to me. What have you done?"

"My kingdom is not of this world. If it would be, my followers would have fought to keep me from being delivered to the Jewish authorities", said Jesus.

"But are you a king?" asked Pilate.

"You are the one who is saying that I am a king", said Jesus. "I was born to testify about the truth. Whoever belongs to the truth, hears my voice".

"What is truth?" asked Pilate.

Without waiting for an answer, he went outside and told the chief priests and the crowd, "I see no reason to condemn this man".

They insisted, saying, "He has disturbed the peace in Galilee, and is now doing the same thing in Judea".

Pilate asked them, "Is this man a Galilean? Because, if that is the case, he is under the jurisdiction of Herod, the tetrarch of Galilee".

When the accusers confirmed that Jesus was a Galilean, Pilate sent him to Herod, who was visiting Jerusalem at that time. The tetrarch, who had heard so much about Jesus, was very happy to meet him, because he hoped to see him perform a miracle.

Herod questioned him at length, but Jesus remained silent, while the accusers again stated their case in the strongest of terms.

Herod and his men mocked him, dressed him in a gorgeous robe, and sent him back to Pilate. This act ingratiated Herod to Pilate, with whom he had been in unfriendly terms till then.

Pilate called the elders, the chief priests, and the leaders of the people, and he told them, "I have not found any guilt in this man, and neither has Herod. He has done nothing to deserve death. I will have him whipped, and then, I will let him go".

It was customary for the Roman governor to release a prisoner to the crowds in honor of the Passover Festival. One of the prisoners being held by the Romans was Barabbas, a notorious rebel and robber, who was charged with insurrection and murder.

Pilate went out and said to the people, "Look, I am bringing him here to let you know that I find no reason to condemn him".

Jesus was brought out, wearing the crown of thorns, and dressed in a purple robe.

Pilate announced, "Here is the man!"

The chief priests and the authorities saw Jesus and screamed, "Crucify him! Crucify him!"

Pilate said to them, "Then, you take him, and crucify him. I find no reason to condemn him".

They answered, "Our Law says that he has to die, because he claimed to be the Son of God".

Pilate tried to release him, but the Jewish authorities shouted, "If you let this man go, you are not a friend of Caesar. Anyone who claims to be a king is a rebel against Caesar".

Pilate heard this and was afraid. He went back into the palace and asked Jesus, "Where are you from?"

When Jesus didn't answer, Pilate said to him, "You will not speak to me? Don't you know that I have the power to crucify you or let you go?"

Jesus replied, "Your power over me is what you received from above. Therefore, he that handed me to you is the greater sinner".

Pilate took Jesus outside and said to the people, "Behold, your king! Which of the two prisoners do you want me to set free: Barabbas or the king of the Jews?"

The mob, incited by the chief priests and the elders, screamed, "Release Barabbas!"

Pilate asked them, "Shall I crucify your king?"

The chief priests answered, "Caesar is our only king".

Pilate asked the crowd, "What, then, do you want me to do with the one you call king of the Jews?"

"Crucify him! Crucify him!" they shouted.

"What crime has he committed? I haven't found any reason to condemn him to death. I will whip him and let him go".

The crowd shouted again, "Crucify him!"

When Pilate saw that the crowd might riot, he took some water, washed his hands in front of the crowd, and said, "I am not responsible for the death of Jesus".

The crowd answered, "Let the punishment for his death fall on us and on our children!"

Pilate set Barabbas free. He had Jesus whipped and handed him over to his soldiers to be crucified. The soldiers took Jesus into the court of the Governor's Palace, stripped his clothes, and dressed him with a purple robe. They made a crown with thorny branches and placed it on his head. Then, they began to make fun of him, saluting him, "Hail, King of the Jews!" They spat on him and hit him with a stick. Finally they got tired of their game, took his purple robe off, and dressed him again with his own clothes.

The soldiers led Jesus away to the place of the crucifixion. On their way, they met a man named Simon of Cyrene, who was entering the city. They grabbed him and forced him to carry the cross behind Jesus. A large crowd of people followed them, among them some women who were weeping and wailing.

Jesus turned to the women and said, "Daughters of Jerusalem, do not cry for me. Weep for yourselves and your children, because the days will come, when you will say, 'How lucky are the women who never had children, who never bore babies and never nursed them'".

They arrived to the place called the Skull, and there, they crucified Jesus between the two criminals, one on his right and the other one on his left.

Over the cross, they placed a sign that said in Greek, Latin, and Hebrew, "This is the king of the Jews".

The chief priests asked Pilate to change the wording of the title from "King of the Jews" to, "He claimed to be the king of the Jews". Pilate refused, saying, "What I have written remains!"

The four soldiers who had crucified Jesus divided his garments among them. They played dice for the robe, because they didn't want to cut it into pieces.

The people stood there, watching, while the leaders mocked him, "He saved others. If he is the Messiah whom God has chosen, let him now save himself".

The soldiers made fun of him, offered him vinegar, and said, "If you are the king of the Jews, save yourself".

One of the criminals, hanging next to Jesus, screamed at him, "If you are the Messiah, save yourself and save us!"

The other criminal rebuked him, saying, "Don't you fear God? The three of us have received the same sentence; we both deserve it for what we did, but this man has done no wrong". And to Jesus, he said, "Lord, remember me, when you come into your kingdom".

Jesus said to him, "I promise that you will be, today, with me in Paradise". Then, he exclaimed, "Father, forgive them because they don't know what they are doing".

Nearby stood four women: the mother of Jesus, his aunt, Mary, the wife of Cleophas, and Mary Magdalene. Jesus saw that his mother was standing next to the disciple whom he loved, and he said, "Woman, he is your son". And to the disciple, he said, "She is your mother". From that time, the disciple took Mary to live in his house.

Jesus cried with a loud voice, "*Eloi, Eloi, lama sabachtani?*" which means, "My God, my God, why have you forsaken me?"

Some of the people who heard him said, "Listen, he is calling for Elijah". Jesus then said, "I am thirsty". Somebody ran with a sponge soaked in vinegar, put it on the end of a stick, and held it up to Jesus' lips, saying, "Let's see if Elijah will come to take him down from the cross".

Darkness covered the whole country from noon till three o'clock in the afternoon. At that time, the curtain, hanging in the Temple, was torn in two.

Jesus cried out with a loud voice, "Father, into your hands I commend my spirit!" Then, he said, "It is finished", bowed his head, and died.

The centurion, present at the crucifixion, praised God and said, "This was certainly a righteous man". The people who were watching beat their breasts in sorrow and returned to the city. Those who knew him, including the women who had followed him from Galilee, stood at a distance and watched.

The Jewish authorities asked Pilate to give orders to break the legs of those who were still alive, to speed their death, because it was Friday, and they didn't want the bodies to remain on the crosses, during the Sabbath, especially this Sabbath, which was even more sacred because of the Passover Festival.

The soldiers came and broke the legs of the two men who had been crucified next to Jesus. When they came to Jesus, they saw that he was already dead, and there was no need to break his legs. One of the soldiers plunged his spear into Jesus' side, and at once, blood and water poured out.

A rich man from the Judean town of Arimatea came to Pilate and asked to be given the body of Jesus. The man was Joseph, a good and just man who believed in the Kingdom of God. Although he was a member of the council, he had not agreed with their decisions and actions against Jesus.

Pilate was surprised to hear that Jesus was already dead. After having a centurion confirm this information, he allowed Joseph to take the body. Joseph brought a linen sheet and took the body down from the cross.

With the help of Nicodemus, who had brought about one hundred pounds of spices, a mixture of myrrh and aloes, to prepare the body, Joseph wrapped it in the sheet with the spices, according to the Jewish custom of preparing a body for burial.

The two men took the body to a nearby garden and placed it in Joseph's own tomb, which had recently been dug out of solid rock. They rolled a large stone to close the entrance to the tomb and went away.

Mary Magdalene and Mary, the mother of Joses, witnessed the burial and went back to their homes to prepare spices and perfumes for the body. It was Friday afternoon, and the Sabbath, the day of rest, was about to begin.

On the Sabbath, the chief priests and the Pharisees met with Pilate to warn him that Jesus had said that he would come back to life, three days after his death. They suggested that he should place guards outside the tomb, in order to prevent the disciples from stealing the body, and then claiming that Jesus had risen from the dead. Pilate assigned a guard to watch the tomb, and, as an additional precaution, the tomb was made secure by putting a seal on the stone.

The Gospels differ slightly, one from the other, about the events of the Resurrection. **According to Matthew,** early Sunday morning, Mary Magdalene and another woman, also called Mary, came to the tomb. Suddenly, there was an earthquake; an angel appeared, rolled the stone away, and sat on it. His appearance was like lightning and his clothes were white as snow. The terrified guards trembled and then stood as still as dead men.

The angel spoke to the women, "Do not be afraid. I know you are looking for Jesus who was crucified. Go now and tell his disciples that he has been raised from death, and now he is going to Galilee ahead of you; you will see him there".

The women, filled with joy, ran to tell the good news to the disciples. Suddenly, Jesus appeared to them and said, "Peace be with you. Do not be afraid. Go tell my brothers to go to Galilee, and there, they will see me".

According to Mark, when the Sabbath was over, Mary Magdalene, Mary, the mother of James, and Salome bought spices to anoint the body of Jesus. Early Sunday morning, the women went to the tomb, wondering on the way who could roll away the heavy stone from the entrance. When they arrived to the tomb, they saw that the stone had already been rolled back. They entered it and saw a young man, dressed in a white robe, sitting there.

"Don't be afraid", he said. "I know that you are looking for Jesus of Nazareth who was crucified. He is not here, he has been raised! Tell the disciples, including Peter, that he is going to Galilee ahead of you. You will see him there, just as he told you".

The women went out and ran away, terrified. They didn't tell what they had seen to anyone, because they were afraid.

In Luke's account, Mary Magdalene, Joanna, and Mary, the mother of James, came to the tomb, carrying the spices that they had prepared. When they found that the stone had been rolled away from the entrance to the tomb, they went in but did not see the body. They stood there bewildered, when suddenly two men, in bright shining clothes, stood next to them. Frightened, the women bowed to the ground.

The men said to them, "Why are you looking among the dead for one who is alive? He is not here; he has been raised. Remember what he said to you, while he was in Galilee, 'The Son of man must be handed over to sinful men, be crucified, and, three days later, rise to life'".

The women went to the disciples and told them all these things, but the disciples did not believe them.

Peter got up and ran to the sepulcher. He bent down and saw only the linen clothes. He returned to the disciples, wondering what had happened.

In John's version, it was Mary Magdalene alone who went to the tomb and saw that the stone had been rolled away from the entrance. She ran to Peter and the other disciple whom Jesus loved, and she told them, "They have taken the Lord from the tomb, and we don't know where they have put him!"

Peter and the other disciple ran to the tomb. The other disciple arrived first and saw the linen cloth inside the tomb, but he did not enter the tomb. Peter came behind him and went into the tomb, where he saw the linen cloth, laid on the floor, and close to it, the cloth that had been wrapped around Jesus' head. Then, the two men returned to their home.

Mary Magdalene stayed outside the tomb, crying. She looked inside the tomb and saw two angels dressed in white, sitting where the body of Jesus had been, one at the head and the other at the feet.

They asked her, "Why are you crying?"

She answered, "They have taken my Lord away, and I do not know where they have put him".

She turned around and saw Jesus standing there, but she did not recognize him. Jesus asked her, "Why are you crying? Who is it that you are looking for?"

She thought that the man speaking to her was the gardener, and she said to him, "If you took him, please tell me where you have put him, and I will go and get him".

Jesus said to her, "Mary!"

She looked at him and said, "Rabboni", which means *My teacher* in Hebrew.

Jesus told her, "Do not hold on to me, because I have not yet ascended to the Father. Go to my brothers and tell them that I am returning to the One who is my Father and their Father, my God and their God".

Mary Magdalene went and told the disciples that she had seen Jesus, and she related to them what he had said to her.

After either Mary Magdalene alone—or accompanied by two or three other women—left, the soldiers guarding the tomb went back to the city and told the chief priests everything that had happened.

When the priests heard their report, they gave the soldiers a large amount of money and told them to say that the disciples of Jesus had come, during the night, and had stolen the body, while they were asleep. The guards took the money and did as they were told.

The Gospels also differ on their accounts of the appearances of Jesus, after his death. **Matthew** mentions two appearances: the first, noted above, to Mary Magdalene and the other Mary; and the second one, to the eleven disciples, on a hill in Galilee, where Jesus had told them to go. When they saw him, they worshipped him.

Jesus said to them, "All power is given to me in heaven and in earth. Go, therefore, and teach all nations. Baptize them in the name of the Father, and of the Son, and of the Holy Ghost. Teach them to obey everything I have commanded you. And I will be with you always, to the end of the world".

According to Mark, Jesus first appeared to Mary Magdalene, from whom he had expelled seven devils. She went and told his companions, who were mourning and crying, that Jesus was alive, and that she had seen him. They did not believe her.

Jesus then appeared in another form to two of his followers, while they were walking in the country. The two men told the others, but they didn't believe them.

Lastly, he appeared to the eleven disciples as they were eating. Jesus reproached them for their lack of faith, and their stubborn refusal to believe those who had seen him alive.

He ordered them to go through the whole world and preach to all mankind, and he said, "Whoever believes and is baptized will be saved; whoever does not believe will be condemned. Believers will be given the power to perform miracles, to drive out evil spirits in my name; they will speak in strange tongues; if they pick up snakes or drink poison, they will not be harmed; and they will cure sick people, by placing their hands on them".

After Jesus had talked with them, he was taken up to heaven and sat at the right side of God. The disciples went and preached everywhere. The Lord worked with them and proved that their preaching was true by the miracles that were performed.

Luke mentions only two appearances: The first was to two of his followers near Emmaus, and the second to all the disciples in Jerusalem.

On that same Sunday, when Mary Magdalene had found that the tomb was empty, two of his followers were going to a village named Emmaus, about seven miles from Jerusalem. They were talking about all the things that had happened.

Jesus himself drew near and walked along with them, but they did not recognize him. He asked them, "What are you talking about while you walk?"

They stood still, looking sad, and one of them, called Cleopas, said, "Are you the only stranger in Jerusalem that doesn't know the things that have happened these last days?"

"What things?" he asked them.

"The things that happened to Jesus of Nazareth", they answered. "He was a prophet, powerful in word and in deed, before God and the people. The chief priests and our rulers sentenced him to death, and he has been crucified. We hoped that he would have been the redeemer of Israel. All this happened three days ago. Some of the women in our group went early in the morning, to the sepulcher, and came back saying that the body was not there, but they had seen a vision of angels who told them that he is alive. Some of his disciples went to the sepulcher, and verified what the women had said, but they didn't see him".

Jesus said, "O fools! You are so slow to believe what the prophets have spoken. It was necessary for the Messiah to have suffered these things and then to enter his glory!"

He then explained to them what Moses and the prophets had said in the Scriptures about himself.

When they arrived to the village, Jesus acted as if he wanted to continue on his way, but the men held him back, saying, "Stay with us, it is almost night".

He went in with them. When they sat down to eat, Jesus took the bread and said the blessing; then, he broke the bread and gave it to them.

Their eyes were opened at that moment, and they recognized him, but he disappeared from their sight.

They said to each other, "Didn't we feel a fire in our hearts, when he talked to us on the road, and explained the Scriptures?"

They got up at once and went back to Jerusalem, where they found the eleven disciples commenting excitedly, "The Lord has risen! He has appeared to Simon!" The two men told the eleven disciples how they had met Jesus and only recognized him, when he broke the bread.

While the two were speaking, Jesus suddenly appeared among them and said, "Peace be with you". The terrified disciples thought that they were seeing a ghost.

Jesus said to them, "Why are you alarmed? Look at my hands and feet. It is me. Touch me, and you will know, because a ghost has no flesh or bones, which, as you can see, I have". He showed them his hands and feet, and they, filled with joy, still could not quite believe what they were seeing.

Jesus asked them, "Do you have anything to eat?"

They gave him a piece of broiled fish. He took it and ate it in front of them.

He said to them, "These are the words, which I spoke to you, while I was with you, that all that has been written about me in the Law of Moses, the writings of the prophets, and in the Psalms, had to be fulfilled".

He explained to them the Scriptures and said to them, "It is written that the Messiah should suffer, and then rise from death three days later. The message of repentance and the forgiveness of sin must be preached to all nations, beginning in Jerusalem. You are witnesses to these things. I give you my Father's promise to you, but you must wait in Jerusalem, until you receive the power from above".

Then, he led them out of the city as far as Bethany, where he raised his hands and blessed them. As he was blessing them, he departed from them and was taken up into heaven. They worshipped him and returned to Jerusalem, filled with great joy, and they spent all their time in the Temple, giving thanks to God.

According to John, Jesus appeared four times, after his resurrection. The first time, mentioned above, was to Mary Magdalene, when she stood, crying outside the empty tomb, early on Sunday.

The second time was that same Sunday in the evening. The disciples, fearful of the Jewish authorities, had gathered together behind locked doors. All of them were there, except Thomas.

Jesus appeared to them and said, "Peace be with you". The disciples were filled with joy at seeing him.

Jesus said to them again, "Peace be with you. As the Father sent me, so I send you". He breathed on them and said, "Receive the Holy Spirit. If you forgive people's sins, they will be forgiven; if you do not forgive them, they will not be forgiven".

When Thomas came, the other disciples told him that they had seen Jesus.

He answered, "I will only believe it, if I would see the scars of the nails in his hands, touch them, and thrust my hand into his side".

The third appearance of Jesus was a week later, when all the disciples, including Thomas, were gathered in the same place. Although the doors were locked, Jesus came in, stood among them, and said, "Peace be with you".

Then, he said to Thomas, "Put your fingers here, and look at my hands; then, put your hand in my side. Stop your doubting and believe!"

Thomas exclaimed, "My Lord and my God!"

Jesus said to him, "Do you believe because you see me? Happy are those who believe without seeing me!"

Jesus performed many other miracles in his disciples' presence. After this, the fourth and last appearance of Jesus was at the lake of Galilee.

Peter, Nathanael, the sons of Zebedee, and two other disciples had gone fishing that night, but they did not catch any fish. In the morning, they returned and saw a man standing on the shore. He was Jesus, but they did not recognize him.

Jesus asked them, "Have you caught anything?"

"Nothing", they answered.

He said to them, "Throw your net out on the right side of the boat, and you will catch some". They did so and caught many fish.

The disciple whom Jesus loved said to Peter, "It is the Lord!"

When Peter heard this, he jumped into the water. The other disciples came to shore in the boat, pulling the net full of fish.

Jesus, who was standing next to a charcoal fire with fish on it and some bread, told them, "Bring some of the fish that you have caught".

Peter went aboard and dragged the net ashore, full of big fish.

Jesus said to them, "Come and eat".

After they had eaten, Jesus asked Peter, "Do you love me more than these others do?"

Peter answered, "Yes, Lord, you know that I love you".

Jesus asked him two more times the same question, and both times, Peter gave the same answer.

Jesus said to him, "Take care of my sheep". Then, he added, "Follow me".

Jether

(Hebrew origin: *Excels*)

1. (Judges 8:20). 12th century B.C. Jether, the eldest son of Gideon, was ordered by his father to kill Zebah and Zalmunna, the confessed murderers of Gideon's brothers.

The boy, who was young and timid, did not draw his sword. Gideon then killed the two Midianites and took the ornaments that were on their camels' necks.

2. (1 Kings 2:5). 11th century B.C. Jether was the husband of Abigail, King David's sister. Their son Amasa, who had been the commander of Absalom's army, was murdered by Joab.

There is a controversy about his nationality. According to the first book of Chronicles (1 Chronicles 2:17), he was an Ishmaelite, while the second book of Samuel (2 Samuel 17:25) states that he was an Israelite called Ithra.

3. (1 Chronicles 2:32). Unspecified date. Jether, of the tribe of Judah, was the son of Jada and the brother of Jonathan. He died childless.

4. (1 Chronicles 4:17). Unspecified date. Jether, son of Ezra, a descendant of Judah, was the brother of Epher, Mered, and Jalon. His brother Mered married Bithiah, the daughter of the Pharaoh of Egypt.

5. (1 Chronicles 7:38). Unspecified date. His sons Ara, Jephunneh, and Pispah were brave warriors and leaders of clans of the tribe of Asher.

Jetheth

(Uncertain origin and meaning)

(Genesis 36:40). Unspecified date. Jetheth, a descendant of Esau, was the leader of a clan of Edomites.

Jethro

(Hebrew origin: *His excellence*)

(Exodus 3:1). 13th century B.C. Jethro, a priest of Midian, was the leader of the Kenites, a clan of Midianites. Moses, fleeing from Egypt, found refuge with Jethro, married his daughter Zipporah, and worked for him, keeping his flock of sheep.

Years later, when Moses was leading the Israelites through the Sinai desert, Jethro visited him in the wilderness, bringing with him Zipporah and her two sons, Gershom and Eliezer, who had been staying with him.

Moses went out to meet his father-in-law,

bowed before him, and kissed him. They asked about each other's health and then went into Moses' tent.

Moses told Jethro everything that God had done to the Pharaoh and to the Egyptians to rescue the Israelites, the hardships that the people had faced, and how God had saved them.

Jethro, happy to hear these news, blessed God and offered a sacrifice. Later, he, Aaron, and the elders of Israel sat together to share a meal.

The next day, Jethro observed that Moses was busy from morning to night, settling disputes among the people. Jethro told him that he couldn't continue like that and advised him to choose honest and capable men, to whom Moses could delegate some of his responsibilities. Moses took his father-in-law's advice and appointed leaders of the people to serve as judges. Then, Jethro said goodbye to Moses and went back home.

Jethro is also called by other names: Reuel (Exodus 2:18), Raguel (Numbers 10:29), and Hobab (Judges 4:11).

Note: The book of Numbers states that Hobab was not the same person as Raguel, but his son (Numbers 10:29).

Jetur

(Hebrew origin: *Enclosed*)

(Genesis 25:15). 18th century B.C. Jetur, grandson of Abraham and his Egyptian concubine Hagar, was one of the twelve sons of Ishmael.

Jetur's brothers were Nebajoth, Hadad, Mibsam, Mishma, Dumah, Massa, Adbeel, Tema, Kedar, Naphish, and Kedemah, all of them ancestors of great nations. His sister, Mahalath—also called Bashemath—married Esau, the son of Isaac.

Jeuel

(Hebrew origin: *Carried away by God*)

(1 Chronicles 9:6). 6th century B.C. Jeuel, a descendant of Zerah, was the leader of the members of a clan that settled in Jerusalem, after they returned from the Babylonian Exile.

Jeush

(Hebrew origin: *Hasty*)

1. (Genesis 36:5). 18th century B.C. Jeush, Jaalam, and Korah were the three sons who were born to Aholibamah, one of Esau's wives, in Canaan, before the family moved to Edom, where the brothers became heads of clans.

2. (1 Chronicles 7:10). Unspecified date. Jeush, a brave warrior and leader of a clan of Benjamites, was the son of Bilhan and the brother of Ahishahar, Benjamin, Ehud, Zethan, Tharshish, and Chenaanah.

3. (1 Chronicles 23:10). 10th century B.C. Jeush, a Levite, descendant of Shimei, served in the Tabernacle, during the reign of King David. His brothers were Beriah, Zina, and Jahath. Because Jeush did not have many children, the census of the Levites considered him and his brother Beriah as members of a single clan.

4. (2 Chronicles 11:19). 10th century B.C. Jeush, Shamariah and Zaham, were the three sons whom King Rehoboam had with Mahalath, the daughter of Jerimoth, son of King David.

Jeuz

(Hebrew origin: *Advisor*)

(1 Chronicles 8:10). Unspecified date. Jeuz, born in the country of Moab, was one of the seven sons of Shaharaim, of the tribe of Benjamin, and his wife Hodesh.

His brothers—all of them heads of clans—were Zibia, Jobab, Mesha, Malcham, Shachia, and Mirma.

Jezaniah

(Hebrew origin: *Heard of God*)

(Jeremiah 40:8). 6th century B.C. Jezaniah—called Jaazaniah in the second book of Kings—son of Hoshaiah, was an officer of the defeated Judean army. (Please see the entry for Jaazaniah [2 Kings 25:23].)

Jezebel

(Hebrew origin: *Chaste*)

(1 Kings 16:31). 9th century B.C. Jezebel, a Phoenician princess, daughter of Ethbaal, king of Sidon, was a strong-willed woman, resourceful and unscrupulous, who exercised a great deal of influence over her husband, King Ahab of Israel.

She introduced the Phoenician pagan cult of the god Baal in the country, a development, which was bitterly opposed by the prophet Elijah. Ahab tolerated the foreign cult introduced by his wife and cooperated with her, by building a Temple for Baal in Samaria and erecting a sacred post. He also granted her unlimited administrative authority.

Jezebel initiated a murderous persecution against the prophets of the Lord. One hundred of them were hidden in two caves, fifty men in each cave, by Obadiah, the governor of the royal palace.

Elijah requested an encounter with the several hundred prophets of Baal who were under Queen Jezebel's protection, and who ate at her table. King Ahab consented, and the contest took place in Mount Carmel. The foreign priests were confounded and put to death by Elijah. The queen was furious, when she was told that Elijah had killed her prophets, and sent a messenger to Elijah, threatening to kill him. The prophet escaped to Beersheba.

Sometime afterward, Ahab decided that a piece of land, adjacent to the palace, would be the ideal spot for a vegetable garden. He went to talk to the owner of the land, Naboth the Jezreelite, and offered to pay him for the land, or to exchange it for an equivalent plot. Naboth refused to give up his family inheritance, and the king returned to the palace depressed and angry.

Jezebel asked Ahab why he was depressed, and why he refused to eat. He answered that it was because Naboth had refused to sell him his land. Jezebel told him to be cheerful and to leave the matters in her hands. She arranged to have Naboth accused falsely of insulting God. Naboth was tried and executed, and Ahab took possession of the property.

The prophet Elijah went to Naboth's vineyard to confront Ahab. When he was in his presence, the prophet accused the king of murdering the man and taking over his property. Elijah told Ahab that God would punish him for his evil deeds; that dogs would lick his blood in the very place that dogs licked up Naboth's blood; that his family would come to the same bad end as the descendants of King Jeroboam and King Baasha; and that dogs would eat the body of his wife Jezebel.

Ahab died sometime later of a wound received in a battle against the Syrians, and he was succeeded by his son Joram.

Jehu, the commander of the army of Israel, rebelled against Joram and accused Jezebel of whoredoms and witchcraft. He killed Joram and mortally wounded Ahaziah, the king of Judah, who was at the time visiting the king of Israel.

Jehu went to the royal palace, where Jezebel, having heard what had happened, had painted her face. She looked out from the window and greeted Jehu sarcastically as "Zimri the Regicide". Jehu lifted his face to the window and told the eunuchs that were with the queen to throw her down. Her blood sprinkled on the wall, and Jehu trampled her with his horse.

Jehu went into the palace to eat and drink. Afterward, he gave instructions to bury Jezebel, because she was, after all, a king's daughter. His men went to search for her body, but the dogs had eaten her, and they found only her skull, her feet, and the palms of her hands.

Jezer

(Hebrew origin: *Created; formed*)

(Genesis 46:24). 17th century B.C. Jezer, son of Naphtali and grandson of Jacob and Bilhah, was one of the seventy Israelites who immigrated to Egypt. His brothers were Guni, Jahzeel, and Shillem. Jezer was the ancestor of the clan of the Jezerites.

Jeziah

(Hebrew origin: *Sprinkled of God*)

(Ezra 10:25). 5th century B.C. Jeziah, a

descendant of Parosh, divorced his foreign wife, during the days of Ezra.

Jeziel

(Hebrew origin: *Sprinkled by God*)

(1 Chronicles 12:3). 11th century B.C. Jeziel was one of the sons of Azmaveth, one of King David's mighty warriors. Jeziel and his brother Pelet were part of a group of Benjamites, commanded by Ahiezer, who deserted King Saul's army and joined David's band at Ziklag. They were skilled warriors who could use both their right and left hands to shoot arrows and sling stones.

Jezliah

(Hebrew origin: *Draw out*)

(1 Chronicles 8:18). Unspecified date. Jezliah, a Benjamite, son of Elpaal, was the leader of a clan that lived in Jerusalem.

Jezoar

(Hebrew origin: *He will shine*)

(1 Chronicles 4:7). Unspecified date. Jezoar, Zereth, and Ethnan, descendants of Judah, were the sons of Ashur and his wife Helah.

Jezrahiah

(Hebrew origin: *God will shine*)

(Nehemiah 12:42). 5th century B.C. Jezrahiah was in charge of the singers who marched, singing at the top of their voices, in the joyful procession, which celebrated the dedication of the rebuilt walls of Jerusalem, during the days of Nehemiah.

Jezreel

(Hebrew origin: *God will sow*)

1. (1 Chronicles 4:3). Unspecified date. Jezreel, a descendant of Judah, was the son of the founder of Etam and the brother of Ishma, Idbash, and their sister Hazelelponi.
2. (Hosea 1:4). 8th century B.C. Jezreel was one of the three children—the other two

were a boy named Loammi, and a girl called Loruhamah—whom the prophet Hosea had with his wife Gomer, to all of whom he gave symbolic names. Jezreel's name symbolized the destruction that God would bring over the dynasty of Jehu.

Jibsam

(Hebrew origin: *Fragrant*)

(1 Chronicles 7:2). Unspecified date. Jibsam, son of Tola, and his brothers—Uzzi, Rephaiah, Jeriel, Jahmai, and Shemuel—were leaders of the tribe of Issachar.

Jidlaph

(Hebrew origin: *Tearful*)

(Genesis 22:22). 19th century B.C. Jidlaph was one of the eight children born to Milcah, the wife of Nahor, Abraham's brother. His brothers were Huz, Buz, Kemuel, Chesed, Hazo, Pildash, and Bethuel.

Jimna

(Hebrew origin: *Right hand*)

(Numbers 26:44). 17th century B.C. Jimna, one of the sons of Asher, was the ancestor of the clan of the Jimnites. His name is also spelled Imnah (1 Chronicles 7:30), and Jimnah (Genesis 46:17).

Jimna, his father Asher, his sister Serah, and his brothers—Ishuah, Isui, and Beriah—were among the seventy Israelites who immigrated to Egypt.

Jimnah

(Hebrew origin: *Right hand*)

(Genesis 46:17). 17th century B.C. Jimnah, one of the sons of Asher, was the ancestor of the clan of the Jimnites. His name is also spelled Imnah (1 Chronicles 7:30), and Jimna (Numbers 26:44).

Jimnah, his father Asher, his sister Serah, and his brothers—Ishuah, Isui, and Beriah— were among the seventy Israelites who immigrated to Egypt.

Joab

(Hebrew origin: *God is father*)

1. (1 Samuel 26:6). 10th century B.C. Joab was the brave and loyal commander of King David's army. He was also an unscrupulous and ruthless murderer. Although he was completely devoted to the king, he did not hesitate in manipulating him, or speaking bluntly and frankly if the occasion demanded it. He was even ready to disobey the king's orders if he thought that it would be in David's best interests, which was what he did, when he killed Absalom against the king's express orders.

David publicly disapproved of Joab's murders, but never punished him, probably because he considered him very useful for his purposes. It was only when the king was in his deathbed that he gave instructions to his son Solomon to have Joab killed in punishment for the murders of Abner and Amasa, but, interestingly enough, not for the killing of Absalom, which Joab had carried out against the specific orders of the king.

Joab, one of the three sons of Zeruiah, David's sister, was a nephew of the king. His brothers were Abishai, one of the leading officers in the army, and Asahel, also a warrior.

David, after ruling in Hebron for seven years, decided to conquer the city of Jerusalem, which was in the hands of the Jebusites. Their fortress was impregnable, and the Jebusites boasted that the blind and lame were enough to defend it. David announced that the first soldier who would kill a Jebusite would be named commander of the army. Joab crawled up the water conduct that led up to the city, an act which led to the capture of Jerusalem.

David renamed the fortress and called it the City of David. He rebuilt the area around the fortress, and Joab repaired the rest of the city. David named Joab commander of the army as a reward for his deeds of valor, during the conquest of the city of Jerusalem.

Sometime later, Joab and the army, which included his brothers, Asahel and Abishai, met by the pool of Gibeon, the army of Ishbosheth, the son of Saul, which was commanded by Abner. Abner suggested to Joab that twelve men of each side should fight to the death.

After the twenty-four men killed each other, both armies engaged in battle. Abner's army was defeated. Abner, pursued by Asahel, begged him to desist, saying that he could not face Joab, if he was forced to kill Asahel. Asahel refused to stop, and Abner killed him with a backward thrust of his spear.

Joab and his brother Abishai continued to chase after the defeated enemies, until Abner's soldiers climbed a hill and rallied behind their commander. From the top of the hill, Abner shouted to Joab to stop the bloodshed. Joab agreed to cease the fighting and allowed Abner and his army to retreat to the other side of the Jordan. Joab buried his brother Asahel in his father's sepulcher, in Bethlehem, and returned to Hebron.

When Ishbosheth accused Abner of having made love to Rizpah, who had been one of King Saul's concubines, Abner became very angry and decided to transfer his loyalties to David. David demanded, as a condition for receiving Abner, that he should bring back Michal, Saul's daughter, whom Saul had given in marriage to Phaltiel. Abner complied with David's request without any pity for poor Phaltiel.

After Abner had spoken, on behalf of David, to the elders of Israel and to the tribe of Benjamin, King Saul's own tribe, he came to Hebron with twenty men. David received him with great ceremony and a sumptuous feast. The two men came to an agreement, and Abner promised that he would rally the entire nation around David.

Joab, who had been away fighting, was told, on his return to Hebron, that Abner had come to speak with the king. He immediately went to David and warned him that Abner had come to spy.

Without David's knowledge, he lured

Abner back to Hebron and murdered him at the gate of the city, in revenge for the death of his brother Asahel at Abner's hand, in the battle by the pool of Gibeon.

Shocked by this treacherous murder, David buried Abner in Hebron with full honors. He eulogized him and mourned him publicly. Although David cursed Joab and his family, he did not punish him for having murdered Abner, probably because he found him very useful for his purposes. It was only, many years later, on his deathbed, that David instructed his son Solomon to have Joab killed for this and other crimes.

The death of Abner weakened the position of Ishbosheth, who, soon afterward, was murdered by two of his officers. The elders of Israel came to Hebron and anointed David as king over all Israel. Joab became the commander of the united army, and Benaiah, who years later executed Joab, was put in charge of the mercenary divisions of Cherethites and Pelethites.

Joab was sent by David to avenge the humiliation that the king of Ammon had inflicted on the ambassadors who had come to convey David's condolences on the death of the previous king. The Ammonites hired armies of Syrian mercenaries to defend them against Joab's army, but were defeated.

One warm evening, months later, while Joab and the army were besieging Rabbah, the capital of the Ammonite kingdom, King David, who had stayed in Jerusalem, saw from the rooftop of his palace a beautiful woman washing herself. He inquired and was told that the woman was Bathsheba, the wife of Uriah, an officer of the army.

The king had her brought to the palace, made love to her, and then sent her back to her house. When she told David that she was pregnant, the king decided to avoid a scandal by having Uriah return immediately to Jerusalem, with the pretext of bringing a report from Joab about the military campaign. The real reason was that Uriah could have the opportunity of spending a night with his wife.

After Uriah delivered the report, the king told him to go to his house and rest, but Uriah felt that he could not rest in his own home and sleep with his wife, while his soldiers in the field were in the front lines, sleeping in tents. He spent that night, and the following night, sleeping at the entrance of the king's palace with the guards.

David came to the conclusion that the only way to solve his problem and avoid an unpleasant scandal, was to get Uriah killed. He wrote a letter to Joab ordering that Uriah should be sent to the forefront of the battle, and once there, he should be left alone by his fellow soldiers to ensure that the enemy would kill him. The king sealed the letter and told Uriah to carry it back to Joab.

Joab, after reading the king's instructions, fully cooperated in the murder of Uriah by sending him to fight close to the walls of the city, the most dangerous place in the front line. Uriah and a number of other soldiers were killed. Joab then sent a messenger to the king with a report about the casualties that the army had suffered.

He said to the messenger, "If the king becomes angry, when he hears that soldiers died because they got too close to the wall of the city, tell him that Uriah also died".

When David heard from the messenger that the husband of Bathsheba had been killed, he said to the messenger to tell Joab not to be distressed, because the sword always takes its toll, and to continue with all necessary efforts to attack and destroy the city.

Joab captured the water sources of Rabbah and asked David to come and take charge of the siege, so that the glory of capturing the capital city of the Ammonites should belong to the king.

Sometime later, Absalom, David's favorite son, killed his half brother Amnon, who had raped his sister Tamar, and escaped to the kingdom of Geshur. Three years later, Joab noticed that David still longed for Absalom, but his pride would not allow him to allow his son to return to Jerusalem.

Joab found a clever woman in the town of Tekoah. He told her to request an audience with the king and instructed her in detail what she would say. The woman, dressed in mourning, went to David and told him that she, a widow, was the mother of two sons. The two young men had had a terrible fight and one of them had killed the other one. The killer, the last remaining member of her family, had been condemned to death by her clan. The woman asked the king to spare the life of her son.

David, moved by her story, said that he would issue an order on her behalf. The woman requested permission to say another word to the king.

"Speak on", said David.

And the woman said, "Your Majesty condemns himself, if he does not bring back his own banished one".

The king immediately suspected that she had not come to him on her own initiative, and he asked her, "Has Joab instructed you to do this?"

The woman admitted that this was so. David relented and gave Joab permission to go to Geshur and bring Absalom back to Jerusalem. Joab brought the young man back, but the king refused to see him.

Two years later, Absalom decided that the time had come for his father to receive him. The best way to achieve reconciliation with his father was if Joab, his father's closest collaborator, would speak to David on his behalf.

Absalom sent for him, but Joab refused to come. He sent for him a second time, again with no results. Absalom then ordered his servants to burn the fields of Joab.

This drastic step produced the expected result. Joab came immediately to Absalom's house, and demanded to know why had he given orders to set fire to his fields.

Absalom answered, "I ordered my servants to burn your fields because you wouldn't come to me, when I called you. I want you to go to the king and arrange for me to see him".

Joab went to David and convinced him to receive his son. Absalom came to the palace, was taken to the presence of the king, and bowed down to the ground in front of him. When David saw his son, he welcomed him warmly and kissed him.

Absalom took immediate advantage of the reconciliation with his father to increase his popularity with the people, and prepare the grounds for an insurrection. When he thought that the time was ripe, he went to Hebron and proclaimed himself king.

When David saw that Absalom enjoyed the support of the people, he fled from Jerusalem with his household and left ten of his concubines to take care of the palace.

Absalom entered Jerusalem with his army and took possession of the royal palace. Ahithophel, his wisest counselor, asked Absalom to send him immediately, with an army of twelve thousand men, in hot pursuit of David, taking advantage of the fact that the king would be tired and weak handed. However, another counselor, Hushai, who was secretly working for David, succeeded in convincing Absalom that they should wait a while.

This welcome delay gave David time to cross to the other side of the Jordan River. Once there, he reorganized his army, dividing it into three groups: one under the command of Joab, another under the command of Abishai, Joab's brother, and the third under the command of Ittai the Gittite. The kings asked the three commanders, in the hearing of the whole army, to deal gently with Absalom and not to harm him.

The battle was bitterly fought, and thousands of men died. When it became clear to Absalom that his army had been defeated, he fled mounted on a mule. His long hair was caught by the branches of a tree, and he was left suspended in the air, while his mule ran away. A soldier saw him hanging from the tree and told Joab.

Joab asked him, "Why didn't you kill him? I would have given you ten shekels of silver and a belt".

The man answered, "Even for a thousand shekels of silver, I would not harm the king's son. He gave clear instructions to you and the other commanders, in our hearing, not to touch Absalom".

Joab replied, "Then, I will not wait for you".

He took three darts in his hand and drove them into Absalom's chest. Ten soldiers closed in and struck Absalom, until he died.

Joab told a messenger called Cushi to run to the king and report to him what he had seen. Ahimaaz, the son of Zadok, young and eager to serve, said to Joab, "Let me run to the king with the good news that God has saved him from his enemies".

Joab answered, "You shouldn't run to the king this time. Some other time, yes, but not today, because the son of the king was killed".

Then, he told Cushi, "Go to the king and tell him what you saw". Cushi bowed and ran off.

Ahimaaz insisted, "Please, let me run, too, after Cushi".

"Why would you want to do that, my son?" said Joab. "There are no new tidings".

"Anyway, let me run", said Ahimaaz.

"Run, then", said Joab.

Ahimaaz ran as fast as he could, overtook Cushi, and came to David, who was sitting in the entrance of the city. He threw himself down to the ground, before the king, and said, "Blessed be the Lord, your God, who has given you victory against the rebels".

The king asked him, "Is Absalom safe?"

Ahimaaz answered, "When Joab sent me to you with the news, I saw a great commotion, but I don't know what it was".

Cushi arrived at that time and said to the king, "Good news, Your Majesty. Today, the Lord has given you victory against those who rose against you".

The king asked, "Is Absalom safe?"

Cushi, who had not been warned by Joab, said, "I wish that what happened to that young man should happen to all the enemies of my king".

The king broke down, went upstairs to his chambers over the gate, and wept, endlessly repeating, "O my son Absalom, my son, my son Absalom! If only I had died, instead of you! O Absalom, my son, my son!"

Joab was told that the king was weeping and mourning over Absalom. The victory was turned into mourning, because they heard that the king was grieving over his son. The soldiers entered the city in silence.

Joab went to the chamber of the king and spoke to him with brutal frankness, "Today, you have brought shame to all those who serve you, to all those who today have saved your life, and the lives of your sons, daughters, wives, and concubines. You seem to love your enemies and hate your friends. You have made it very clear today that you don't care for your officers and your soldiers, and if Absalom would be alive now and all of us dead, it would have made you very happy. Now, get up, and reassure your men, because, I swear by God, if you don't do so, not one of them will remain with you longer than tonight. And that would be the worse thing that ever happened to you!"

The king got up and went to the gate of the city. The word got immediately around that the king was there, and the people came to him.

A short time later, David named Amasa, who had been the commander of Absalom's army, as the new commander in chief of the army, replacing Joab. The king's magnanimous appointment was done for the sake of national reconciliation, but the inevitable result of that unfortunate decision was the same as if he would have signed Amasa's death warrant. Joab's implacable jealousy was aroused, and he waited for the earliest opportunity to kill Amasa.

Shortly afterward, a Benjamite called Sheba, son of Bichri, rebelled against the king. David considered that this insurrection could be even more dangerous than the rebellion of Absalom. He urged Amasa to organize an army in three days. When Amasa did not report back in the allotted time, the king sent Abishai to pursue the rebels. Amasa caught up with Abishai and Joab near Gibeon.

Joab saluted Amasa, saying, "How are you, brother?" While he was speaking, he took hold of Amasa's beard with his right hand, as if to kiss him, and with his left hand, he drove his sword into Amasa's belly and spilled his bowels to the ground.

Joab and Abishai left Amasa, lying in a puddle of blood in the middle of the road, and went after Sheba. The soldiers were stunned and didn't follow Joab, until one of the officers pushed Amasa's body to the field on the side of the road and covered the corpse with a cloth.

Joab then proceeded to pursue Sheba who found refuge in the town of Abel. When the troops started to batter down the walls of the city, the inhabitants cut off Sheba's head and threw it down to Joab. Joab and his army returned to Jerusalem, and Joab was again named commander of the army.

David put Joab in charge of the census. It took Joab and his men nine months and twenty days to count the people and report to the king that there were eight hundred thousand soldiers in Israel and five hundred thousand in Judah.

Years later, when the sons of David were competing for the succession to the throne, Joab made the mistake of supporting Adonijah's claim to be the next king. When Bathsheba and the prophet Nathan convinced David to name Solomon as his successor, Joab's position became shaky.

David, on his deathbed, instructed his son Solomon to have Joab killed for the murders of Abner and Amasa.

Adonijah, after the death of David, was killed by Benaiah, by Solomon's order. Joab, knowing that his turn was next, fled to the Tent of the Lord and grasped the horns of the altar. Solomon sent Benaiah to kill him. Benaiah went to the Tent and ordered Joab to come out.

Joab refused, saying that he would die there. Benaiah went back to the king and reported what he and Joab had said.

The king told him, "Do as he says. Kill him and bury him, to avenge the innocent blood that he has shed. He killed two men who were better than he, Abner and Amasa, murders, which were committed without my father David's knowledge."

Benaiah went back to the Tent and killed Joab. Solomon then named Benaiah as the new commander of the army. Joab was buried in his own house in the wilderness.

2. (1 Chronicles 4:14). 12th century B.C. Joab was the son of Seraiah and the grandson of Othniel. His descendants became craftsmen.

3. (Ezra 2.6). Unspecified date. Joab was an ancestor of a clan of people, descendants of Pahathmoab that returned with Zerubbabel from the Babylonian Exile.

Joah

(Hebrew origin: *God's brother*)

1. (2 Kings 18:18). 8th century B.C. Joah, son of Asaph, was the recorder of the court, during the reign of King Hezekiah. The king sent Joah, together with Eliakim and Shebna, to talk to the commanders of the Assyrian army, laying siege to Jerusalem.

Rabshakeh, one of the top Assyrian officers, met the delegation outside the walls of the city and spoke to them in Hebrew in a loud voice. Joah and his companions asked the Assyrian to please speak to them in Aramaic, as they did not wish that the people on the wall should hear the threats. Rabshakeh paid no attention to their request and continued shouting at them in Hebrew.

The men remained silent and returned to the king, with their clothes torn, to show the failure of the negotiations. Hezekiah, after receiving their report, sent Eliakim and Shebna, accompanied by the elders of the priests, all of them covered with sackcloth, to speak to the prophet Isaiah.

The king then tore his clothes, covered himself with sackcloth, and went to the Temple. Isaiah told the king's men that they should not be afraid, of what Rabshakeh had said, and assured them that the Assyrian army would withdraw without taking Jerusalem.

2. (1 Chronicles 6:21). 8th century B.C. Joah, a Levite, father of Iddo—also called Eden—was the son of Zimmah, a descendant of Gershom. During the reign of King Hezekiah of Judah, Joah and Iddo were among the Levites who assembled all the other Levites to make themselves ritually clean, and to purify the Temple (2 Chronicles 29:12).

3. (1 Chronicles 26:4). 10th century B.C. Joah, the third son of Obededom, was, like his father and seven brothers, a gatekeeper of the Tabernacle, during the reign of King David. His brothers were Ammiel, Shemaiah, Jehozabad, Sacar, Nethaneel, Issachar, and Peulthai.

4. (2 Chronicles 34:8). 7th century B.C. Joah, son of Joahaz, was the recorder of the court, during the reign of King Josiah. The king sent him, together with Shaphan, the son of Azaliah, and Maaseiah, the governor of the city, to repair the Temple.

Joahaz

(Hebrew origin: *God seized*)

(2 Chronicles 34:8). 8th century B.C. Joahaz was the father of Joah, the recorder of the court, during the reign of King Josiah.

Joanna

(Hebrew origin: *God favored*)

1. (Luke 3:27). Unspecified date. Joanna, son of Rhesa and father of Juda, was an ancestor of Jesus, in the genealogy of Luke.

2. (Luke 8:3). A.D. 1st century. Joanna was the wife of Chuza, Herod Antipas' steward. She, together with Mary Magdalene, Susanna, and other women, accompanied

Jesus and the twelve disciples, when they preached in the Galilean cities and villages, and helped them out of their own money.

Joanna, Mary Magdalene, and Mary, the mother of James, were among the women who saw the empty tomb and told the apostles.

Joash

(Hebrew origin: *Fire of God*)

1. (Judges 6:11). 12th century B.C. Joash, of the clan of Abiezer of the tribe of Manasseh, was the father of Gideon, the judge and military commander who defeated a large army of Midianites and Amalekites.

Joash, who lived in Ophrah, had built an altar to Baal, next to a sacred grove. One night, his son Gideon, following God's orders, destroyed both the altar and the grove.

When the men of the city found that Gideon had destroyed their pagan places, they demanded that Joash should deliver his son to them, to be killed for what he had done. Joash refused and told them that, if Baal was a god, he should plead for himself, and that anybody who would plead for Baal would die.

Since that day Gideon was also called Jerubbaal, which means *Let Baal contend with him.*

2. (1 Kings 22:26). 9th century B.C. Prince Joash was ordered by his father King Ahab to put the prophet Micaiah in prison, for having predicted disaster, and to give him only bread and water, until he, the king, would return safely from their war against Aram. However, the king never returned from the war, because he was mortally wounded in battle.

3. (2 Kings 11:2). 9th century B.C. Joash—also called Jehoash—the seventh king of Judah, after the partition of the United Monarchy, was the son of King Ahaziah of Judah and Zibiah from Beersheba.

When Athaliah, the queen mother, heard that her son, King Ahaziah, had been killed by Jehu, the rebel commander of the Israelite army, she decided to grab power for herself and gave orders to kill all the members of the royal family. Only Joash, who was still a baby, survived hidden by his aunt Jehosheba, sister of Ahaziah and wife of the High Priest Jehoiada.

During her rule, Athaliah promoted the cult of the Phoenician god Baal. This increased the hate of the priests and the people, who saw in Athaliah a foreign usurper and the murderer of the royal Davidic line.

When Joash was seven years old, a coup, led by Jehoiada and several army officers, proclaimed in the Temple that Joash was the legitimate king. The High Priest placed a crown on the boy's head and anointed him, while the crowd shouted, "God save the king".

Athaliah, hearing the shouts of the crowd, rushed to the Temple, screaming, "Treason! Treason!"

The guards seized her and killed her at the Horse Gate of the palace. The crowd assaulted the Temple of Baal, destroyed the building and the idols, and killed Mattan, the High Priest of Baal.

Joash became king, at the age of seven, and reigned for forty years. While the priest Jehoiada was alive, the king closely followed his advice, even to the point of marrying the two wives whom the priest chose for him.

During this period, when Jehoiada was still alive, the Temple was repaired and restored to its former glory. This work was financed by means of contributions solicited from the nation. Jehoiada died at a very old age and was buried in the royal tombs of the City of David, in recognition of the service that he had given to the Temple and to the king.

After Jehoiada's death, the people stopped worshipping in the Temple and reverted to idolatry. Zechariah, son of Jehoiada, opposed this development, and the king had him killed.

When the king of Aram attacked Judah, Joash was forced to pay a heavy tribute, which he took from the Temple treasury. While he was in bed, recuperating from his battle injuries, Jozachar and Jehozabad, two of his servants, killed him to avenge the death of Zechariah.

Joash was buried in the City of David, but not in the royal tombs. His son Amaziah succeeded him to the throne.

4. (2 Kings 13:9). 8th century B.C. Joash—also called Jehoash—the twelfth king of Israel, after the partition of the United Monarchy, succeeded his father Jehoahaz and reigned sixteen years. (Please see the entry for Jehoash [2 Kings 13:10].)

5. (1 Chronicles 4:22). Unspecified date. Joash, son of Shelah, was a descendant of Judah. His brothers were Er, Laadah, Jokim, and Saraph.

6. (1 Chronicles 7:8). 16th century B.C. Joash, the son of Becher and the grandson of Benjamin, was a member of a family of heads of the tribe and brave warriors. His brothers were Zemira, Eliezer, Elioenai, Omri, Jerimoth, Abiah, Anathoth, and Alameth.

7. (1 Chronicles 12:3). 11th century B.C. Joash, son of Shemaah the Gibeathite, and his brother Ahiezer, the commander of a group of Benjamites, deserted King Saul's army and joined David's band at Ziklag. They were skilled warriors who could use both their right and left hands to shoot arrows and sling stones.

8. (1 Chronicles 27:28). 10th century B.C. Joash was in charge of the oil stores, during the reign of King David.

Joatham

(Hebrew origin: *God is perfect*)

(Matthew 1:9). Unspecified date. Joatham is an alternative spelling for King Jotham, son of Uzziah and father of Ahaz, an ancestor of Jesus, in the genealogy of Matthew. (Please see the entry for Jotham [2 Kings 15:5].)

Job

(Hebrew origin: *Howler*)

1. (Genesis 46:13). 17th century B.C. Job—called Jashub in the book of Numbers (Numbers 26:24)—was the third son of Issachar. He and his brothers—Tola, Pua, and Shimron—were among the seventy Israelites who immigrated to Egypt. Job was the ancestor of the clan of the Jashubites.

2. (Job 1:1). Unspecified date. Job is the central character of the book of the same name, which is considered one of the masterpieces of world literature. The book deals with a profound human theme: why do good people suffer if God is in control?

   Job, the father of seven sons and three daughters, was a blameless and upright man who lived in the land of Uz. He was the wealthiest man in the East, owning thousands of sheep and camels, and hundreds of oxen and asses.

   One day, God told Satan that there was no one on earth like Job, a God-fearing man who shunned evil. The Devil answered cynically that it was easy for a rich man to be God fearing, but if he would lose his possessions, he would readily curse God. God agreed that Satan should put Job to the test, provided his person was not touched.

   Shortly afterward, thieves stole Job's oxen, donkeys, and camels; his sheep died in a fire; and all his children were crushed to death, when the house collapsed upon them.

   Job arose, tore his clothes, cut off his hair, and prostrated himself on the ground, saying, "Naked I came out from my mother's womb, and naked shall I return there; the Lord has given, and the Lord has taken away; blessed be the name of the Lord".

   God, seeing that Job did not reproach him, told Satan that Job had been destroyed for no good reason.

   Satan replied, "If Job would suffer on his bones and his flesh, he would surely blaspheme".

   God said to Satan, "Job is in your power, but spare his life".

   Satan departed from the Presence of God and inflicted severe sores on Job, from the sole of his foot to the top of his head.

   Job's wife saw him, sitting in ashes and scratching himself with a potsherd, and said to him, "You still retain your integrity? Curse God and die!"

   Job replied, "You speak like a foolish woman. Should we accept only good from God and not accept evil?"

   Three friends—Eliphaz, Bildad, and Zophar—heard of the tragedies that had happened to Job and came to mourn with him, and to comfort him. When they came to Job, they saw that he was so changed that they could almost not recognize him. They wailed, wept, rented their mantles, and sprinkled dust upon their heads. Then, they sat with Job for seven days and seven nights, without speaking a word, because they saw that Job's grief was great.

   Job finally broke his silence with a bitter diatribe against his life, cursing the day, on which, he was born. This outburst surprised his friends. They had come to commiserate and console, not to participate in a rebellion against God's judgment, and so, they turned from comforters to scolders.

   Eliphaz told Job that he must have sinned, as there was no other way to explain God's treatment. Bildad ascribed the death of Job's children to their sins. Zophar told him that God's punishment was less than what he deserved.

   A younger man, Elihu, the son of Barachel the Buzite, entered the scene and expressed his anger toward Job, because he justified himself, rather than God, and against his three friends, because they had found no answer, and yet, they had condemned Job.

   God then said that they were all wrong, because they were not God to know it all. He rebuked Job's friends for their presumptuous words and ordered them to go to Job, make a sacrifice, and ask Job to pray for them, so that God would not punish them.

God restored Job's fortune, and he was comforted and consoled; he became wealthier than before and was the father of another seven sons and three daughters.

Jobab

(Hebrew origin: *Howler*)

1. (Genesis 10:29). Unspecified date. Jobab, the son of Joktan, was a descendant of Shem. His brothers were Almodad, Sheleph, Hazarmaveth, Jerah, Hadoram, Uzal, Diklah, Obal, Abimael, Sheba, Ophir, and Havilah.
2. (Genesis 36:33). Unspecified date. Jobab, son of Zerah of Bozrah, was one of the kings of Edom, at a time before there was a king in Israel. He succeeded Bela, the son of Beor, and was in turn succeeded by Husham.
3. (Joshua 11:1). 12th century B.C. Jobab, king of Madon, was part of the confederation of armies organized by Jabin, king of Hazor, to fight against the Israelites led by Joshua. The battle took place by the waters of Meron and ended in the complete defeat of the confederate armies.
4. (1 Chronicles 8:9). Unspecified date. Jobab, of the tribe of Benjamin, born in the country of Moab, was one of the seven sons of Shaharaim and his wife Hodesh. His brothers—all of them heads of clans—were Zibia, Jeuz, Mesha, Malcham, Shachia, and Mirma.
5. (1 Chronicles 8:18). Unspecified date. Jobab, a Benjamite, son of Elpaal, was the leader of a clan that lived in Jerusalem.

Jochebed

(Hebrew origin: *God's honor*)

(Exodus 6:20). 14th century B.C. Jochebed, the Egyptian-born daughter of Levi, married her nephew, Amram, son of Kohath, with whom she had three children: Miriam, Aaron, and Moses.

Her youngest son Moses was born, after Pharaoh had given orders to kill every newly born Israelite boy. Jochebed hid the baby for three months, and when she could no longer hide him, she put the child in a basket and placed it among the reeds by the bank of the Nile.

The daughter of Pharaoh came down to bathe in the Nile and saw the basket among the reeds. She sent a slave girl to fetch it. When she opened it, she saw that it was a baby boy crying, took pity on the baby, and said, "This must be a Hebrew child".

Miriam, the baby's sister, who had been watching from a distance, approached and asked the princess if she could get her a Hebrew nurse to suckle the baby. Pharaoh's daughter agreed, and Miriam went and brought Jochebed. The princess hired her to take care of the baby and to nurse him.

Joed

(Hebrew origin: *God is witness*)

(Nehemiah 11:7). Unspecified date. Joed, the father of Meshullam and son of Pedaiah, was an ancestor of Sallu, a Benjamite who settled in Jerusalem, after his return from the Babylonian Exile.

Joel

(Hebrew origin: *God is the Lord*)

1. (1 Samuel 8:2). 11th century B.C. Joel—also called Vashni (1 Chronicles 6:28)—was the eldest son of the prophet Samuel.

Joel and his brother Abiah were judges in the city of Beersheba. Unfortunately, they were corrupt magistrates who took bribes and perverted judgment. Their dishonest and vile behavior drove the elders of Israel to demand from Samuel that he should appoint a king, rather than let his sons rule over Israel.

Joel's son Heman was one of the Levites appointed by King David to be in charge of the singers in the House of the Lord. His descendants, Jehiel and Shimei, were among the Levites who gathered to make themselves ritually clean, and to purify the Temple, during the reign of King Hezekiah of Judah.

2. (1 Chronicles 4:35). 8th century B.C. Joel was one of the leaders of the tribe of Simeon who went to the fertile valley of Gedor in search of pasture for their flocks, during the reign of Hezekiah, king of Judah.

The Simeonites destroyed the tents of the people—descendants of Ham—who lived there, wiped them out forever, and settled in their place.

3. (1 Chronicles 5:4). Unspecified date. Joel, the father of Shemaiah, was an ancestor of Beerah, a leader of the tribe of Reuben who was carried away captive by Tilgathpilneser, king of Assyria.

4. (1 Chronicles 5:8). Unspecified date. Joel, the father of Shema, was an ancestor of Belah, the leader of a clan of Reubenites, who raised cattle and lived in the region east of Gilead. During the days of King Saul, the clan made war against the descendants of Hagar.

5. (1 Chronicles 5:12). Unspecified date. Joel, a leader of the tribe of Gad, lived in the land of Bashan, east of the Jordan River.

6. (1 Chronicles 6:36). Unspecified date. Joel, son of Azariah and father of Elkanah, was an ancestor of the judge Samuel. His descendant Heman was a leading musician, during the reign of King David.

7. (1 Chronicles 7:3). Unspecified date. Joel, son of Izrahiah, a descendant of Tola, was the leader of a clan of the tribe of Issachar. His brothers were Michael, Obadiah, and Ishiah.

8. (1 Chronicles 11:38). 10th century B.C. Joel, the brother of the prophet Nathan, was one of "The Thirty", an elite group in King David's army.

9. (1 Chronicles 15:7). 10th century B.C. Joel, descendant of Laadan, from the clan of the Gershonites, was the leader of a group of one hundred and thirty Levites, during the reign of King David. His brothers were Zetham and Jehiel.

Joel was one of the Levites who were asked by David to sanctify themselves so they could bring the Ark of the Covenant to Jerusalem. Later, Joel and his brother Zetham were put in charge of the treasures of the house of the Lord.

10. (1 Chronicles 27:20). 10th century B.C. Joel, son of Pedaiah, was the leader of half the tribe of Manasseh, during the reign of King David.

11. (2 Chronicles 29:12). 8th century B.C. Joel, son of Azariah, a descendant of Kohath, was one of the Levites who assembled all the other Levites to make themselves ritually clean, and to purify the Temple, during the reign of King Hezekiah of Judah.

12. (Ezra 10:43). 5th century B.C. Joel, a descendant of Nebo, divorced his foreign wife, during the days of Ezra.

13. (Nehemiah 11:9). 5th century B.C. Joel, the son of Zichri, of the tribe of Benjamin, was the supervisor of a group of Benjamites that settled in Jerusalem, after the return from the Babylonian Exile.

14. (Joel 1:1). 5th century B.C. Joel, son of Pethuel, was the author of the book of prophecies called by his name. Little is known about Joel, except his name and that of his father.

Scholars believe that the prophet wrote his book, during the period of the Second Temple, probably in the 5th or 4th century B.C. The prophet describes a terrible invasion of locusts and a devastating drought, seeing in these events the coming Day of God, a time when the Lord will punish those who oppose his will.

The prophet conveys God's call to the people to repent, and his promise of restoration and blessing, if the people turn back to God, who will reward them with salvation, and a fertile land.

The book can be divided in two parts: the first part includes chapters 1 and 2; the second part includes chapters 3 and 4.

The first part describes a terrible plague of locusts, the likes of which had never been seen before. It left in its wake empty fields, deprived the people of food, and the Temple of its wine and grain offerings.

The prophet exhorts the priests, the leaders, and all the people, to plead God's mercy through repentance, fasting, and prayer. He promises that God will have pity and will bring an end to the plague, rains in their season, abundant harvests, and a time of fruitfulness and peace.

The second part is a prophecy of the coming Day of God, when the Spirit of the Lord, the gift of prophecy and vision, will be granted to all the people, men and women, young and old alike. God will gather all the nations in the valley of Jehoshaphat and will deliver judgment on those who drove the people of Israel into exile.

God will restore His exiled people and fructify the land. He will punish Egypt and Edom for having attacked the people of Judah and shed innocent blood.

The book of Joel is one of the twelve books that make up the Minor Prophets— also called the Twelve—a collection of the books of twelve prophets: Hosea, Joel, Amos, Obadiah, Jonah, Micah, Nahum, Habakkuk, Zephaniah, Haggai, Zechariah, and Malachi.

Note: The phrase "Minor Prophets" does not mean that these prophets are less important than Isaiah, Jeremiah, and Ezekiel. It refers only to the fact that the books of these twelve prophets are much shorter than the books of the other three prophets.

Joelah

(Hebrew origin: *Furthermore*)

(1 Chronicles 12:7). 11th century B.C. Joelah and his brother Zebadiah, sons of Jeroham of Gedor, were Benjamite warriors who deserted King Saul's army and joined David at Ziklag, while he was still hiding from King Saul. These men were skilled fighters who could use both their right and left hands to shoot arrows and sling stones.

Joezer

(Hebrew origin: *God helped*)

(1 Chronicles 12:6). 11th century B.C. Joezer, a Korhite, was one of the men who

deserted King Saul's army and joined David's band at Ziklag. These men were skilled warriors who could use both their right and left hands to shoot arrows and sling stones.

Jogli

(Hebrew origin: *Exiled*)

(Numbers 34:22). 14th century B.C. His son Bukki, a leader of the tribe of Dan, was one of the men appointed by Moses to apportion the land of Canaan among the tribes.

Joha

(Hebrew origin: *God revived*)

1. (1 Chronicles 8:16). Unspecified date. Joha, son of Beriah, was a Benjamite, leader of a clan that lived in Jerusalem.

2. (1 Chronicles 11:45). 10th century B.C. Joha, the Tizite, son of Shimri, and his brother Jediael were two of King David's brave warriors.

Johanan

(Hebrew origin: *God favored*)

1. (2 Kings 25:23). 6th century B.C. Johanan and his brother Jonathan, sons of Kareah, were two of the captains of the defeated army of Judah who came to Gedaliah, the Babylonian appointed governor, to be assured by him that everything would be well if they would serve the king of Babylon.

Having learned that Ishmael was plotting to kill Gedaliah, Johanan went secretly to Gedaliah and volunteered to kill Ishmael. Gedaliah refused his offer and accused him of speaking falsely about Ishmael.

After Ishmael murdered Gedaliah, Johanan chased the assassin, fought against him by the waters of Gibeon, and was able to liberate the people whom Ishmael had carried away captive from Mizpah. Ishmael and eight of his followers managed to escape and found refuge with the Ammonites.

Johanan and his co-leader, Azariah, the son of Hoshaiah, asked Jeremiah for advice on whether to stay in Judah or flee to Egypt, and they assured him that they would do whatever Jeremiah prophesied. However, when Jeremiah told them that God wanted them to stay in Judah, they accused the prophet of speaking falsely under the influence of Baruch, the son of Neriah. They disregarded Jeremiah's words and went to Egypt, taking the prophet and the survivors with them, including the daughters of the king.

2. (1 Chronicles 3:15). 7th century B.C. Johanan, the eldest of the four sons of King Josiah, was the only one who did not become king. His three brothers were Shallum, who reigned under the name of Jehoahaz; Eliakim, who reigned under the name Jehoiakim; and Mattaniah, who became King Zedekiah.

3. (1 Chronicles 3:24). Unspecified date. Johanan, son of Elioenai, was a descendant of Jeconiah—also called Jehoiachin—the king of Judah, who was taken to captivity in Babylon. His brothers were Eliashib, Pelaiah, Akkub, Dalaiah, Hodaiah, and Anani.

4. (1 Chronicles 6:9). 10th century B.C. Johanan, son of Azariah, was the father of Azariah, the High Priest, during the reign of Solomon. He was an ancestor of Ezra the Scribe.

6. (1 Chronicles 12:4). 11th century B.C. Johanan was one of the Benjamites who deserted King Saul's army and joined David's band at Ziklag. These men were skilled warriors who could use both their right and left hands to shoot arrows and sling stones.

7. (1 Chronicle 12:12). 11th century B.C. Johanan was a Gadite warrior who joined David at Ziklag, while he was still hiding from King Saul.

8. (2 Chronicles 28:12). 8th century B.C. His son Azariah was one of the leaders of the tribe of Ephraim who supported the prophet Oded in his demand to free the captives captured by King Pekah in his war against King Ahaz, and to return them to Judah.

Azariah and his companions took the captives, gave them clothing and shoes, food and drink, and took them back to the city of Jericho in Judah.

9. (Ezra 8:12). 5th century B.C. Johanan, son of Hakkatan, returned with Ezra to Judah, leading a group of one hundred and ten men.

10. (Ezra 10:6). 5th century B.C. Johanan, son of Eliashib, was one of the leading Levites, during the time of Nehemiah. He had a chamber in the Temple of Jerusalem, where Ezra once fasted for the sins of the people.

11. (Nehemiah 6:18). 5th century B.C. Johanan was the son of Tobiah, Nehemiah's enemy. He was married to the daughter of Meshullam, son of Berechiah.

John

(Hebrew origin: *God favored*)

1. (Matthew 3:1). A.D. 1st century. John, called the Baptist, was the son of an elderly and childless couple who lived in a town in the hill country of Judea, during the days of King Herod. His father, Zacharias, was a priest who served in the Temple in Jerusalem. His mother, Elisabeth, was a descendant of Aaron, the High Priest, and a cousin of Mary, the mother of Jesus.

John's birth had been announced to his father by an angel, who told him that the boy should be given the name of John.

The angel added, "You will be glad and joyful, and many people will rejoice at his birth. He will be a great man in the sight of God, filled with the Holy Spirit from his birth, and will bring many Israelites back to God. He will go before God, strong like the prophet Elijah, and shall not drink wine or strong drinks. He will bring together fathers and children, and will return the disobedient to the way of the just. He will prepare the people for the Lord".

Elisabeth, during her pregnancy, received the visit of her cousin Mary. When

Elisabeth heard Mary's greeting, her baby moved inside her, and she was filled with the Holy Spirit. Mary stayed with her cousin for about three months, and then she returned home.

Elisabeth, in due course, gave birth to a baby boy. Her neighbors and relatives suggested that she should call him Zacharias, like his father.

She said, "No! He will be called John".

They insisted, "No one in your family is called by that name!" By signs, they asked Zacharias by which name he wanted to call the baby.

Zacharias, who had been unable to speak since seeing the vision of the angel, received a writing tablet and wrote, "His name is John". Everybody was surprised, and even more, when he suddenly was able to speak again, praised God, and prophesied that his son would be a prophet.

This news spread all over the hill country of Judea, and everybody asked, "What is this child going to be?"

During the fifteenth year of the reign of Emperor Tiberius, when Pontius Pilate was the Roman governor of Judea, and Herod, son of King Herod the Great, was the tetrarch of Galilee, John, the son of the priest Zacharias, went into the wilderness, by the Jordan River, and preached to the people, telling them that, if they repented from their sins and were baptized, God would forgive them.

Crowds of people came to John to be baptized by him. He would tell them, "Whoever has two shirts, should give one to the man who has none, and whoever has food must share it".

To the tax collectors, he said, "Don't collect more money than what is legally due".

To soldiers, he said, "Don't take money from anyone by force, or accuse anyone falsely. Be satisfied with your pay".

The people wondered if John might be the Messiah, but he told them, "I baptize you with water, but someone is coming who is much greater than I am. I am not worthy to even untie his sandals. He will baptize you with the Holy Spirit and with fire".

The Jewish authorities in Jerusalem heard of him and sent a delegation of priests and Levites to find out who he was.

They asked John, "Who are you?"

He answered, "I am not the Messiah".

They asked, "So, who are you? Are you Elijah?"

"I am not", he answered.

"Are you the prophet?" they asked.

"No, I am not", answered John.

"Who are you then? We need an answer to report back to those who sent us. What do you say about yourself?"

"I am the voice of one who shouts in the desert, 'Make straight the way of the Lord', as the prophet Isaiah has said".

The delegation sent by the Pharisees asked him, "Why then do you baptize, if you are not the Messiah, Elijah, or the prophet?"

John replied, "I baptize with water, but there is one standing among you, whom you don't know. He is coming after me, and I am not worthy to even untie his sandals".

The next day, John saw Jesus coming to him, and he said, "Look, there is the Lamb of God who takes away the sin of the world. He is the one that I mentioned who is greater than I am. I baptize with water to make him known to the people of Israel. I saw the Spirit come down from heaven like a dove and stay on him. He that sent me to baptize with water told me that the one on whom the Spirit descends will baptize with the Holy Spirit. I have seen him; he is the Son of God!"

Jesus was baptized by John in the Jordan River. The Holy Spirit came down upon him in the form of a dove, and a voice from heaven was heard, saying, "You are my own dear Son, and I am pleased with you".

One of John's disciples, Andrew, the brother of Simon Peter, became a disciple of Jesus. When Andrew met Jesus, he went to his brother Simon and told him that the Messiah had been found.

Sometime later, John the Baptist heard about Jesus' miracles and sent two of his disciples to talk with him. John's disciples came to Jesus and witnessed how he healed the people, restored sight to the blind, and expelled demons from the possessed.

"Are you the one that is expected to come, or do we have to look for another?" they asked him.

Jesus answered, "Go back and tell John what you have seen and heard. The blind can see, the lame can walk, the lepers are cured, the deaf can hear, the dead are brought back to life, and the gospel is preached to the poor. Blessed is he who finds no offense in me".

John's messengers departed, and Jesus spoke to the people about John. "When you went to the wilderness, what did you expect to see? A reed shaken by the wind? A man elegantly dressed? You can find people like that in the courts of kings. Did you expect to see a prophet? Yes, but you saw much more than a prophet! John is greater than any man whoever lived. But, he who is the least in the Kingdom of God is greater than John".

After this, Jesus and his disciples went to the region of Judea, where he spent sometime and baptized. John, at that time, was baptizing in a place called Aenon, where there was plenty of water. An argument arose between the disciples of John and some Jews about the purification rituals. They went to John and said to him, "Master, remember the man that was with you on the other side of the Jordan, the one that you spoke about? He is now also baptizing, and everybody is going to him!"

John answered, "No man receives anything, unless he received it from heaven. You heard me saying that I am not the Messiah, but that I was sent ahead of him. The bridegroom has the bride, but the friend of the bridegroom, who stands by and listens, is filled with joy, when he hears the voice of the bridegroom. So am I. He will become more important, and I less. He who comes from heaven is above all. The Father loves his Son, and he who believes in the Son has everlasting life".

Herod the Tetrarch, the second son of Herod the Great, had married Herodias, his brother Philip's wife. John the Baptist denounced this act and was imprisoned by Herod. During a feast honoring Herod's birthday, the daughter of Herodias danced before the king, who, pleased by her, promised to give her whatever she would ask. The girl asked for John's head on a platter. The king reluctantly agreed and gave instructions to behead John. The head of the slain man was brought and given to the girl, who gave it to her mother.

2. (Matthew 4:21). A.D. 1st century. John, the son of Zebedee, was, according to many scholars, "the disciple whom Jesus loved", that is mentioned several times by the gospel according to John, which also states in its last verses that the same John was its author.

John and his brother James were fishermen in partnership with Simon Peter. One day, the two brothers and their father Zebedee were mending the nets in their ship, when Jesus, walking by the shore of the Sea of Galilee, called them. The two brothers immediately left their father and their ship and followed him, becoming, together with Peter, the favorite disciples of Jesus.

The two brothers—whom Jesus surnamed Boanerges, *The sons of thunder,* because of their irate temperament— wanted on one occasion to call down fire from heaven and destroy a Samaritan village, which had not been hospitable to them. Jesus rebuked them, saying that the Son of man had not come to destroy lives but to save them.

The brothers witnessed the miraculous cure of Peter's sick mother, and the resurrection of the dead daughter of Jairus. They were also with Jesus on the top of a high mountain, where they, together with Peter, witnessed his transfiguration and saw Moses and Elias appear and talk with Jesus.

One day, their mother came with them to Jesus and asked that her sons be allowed to sit next to Jesus in his glory, one on his right hand, and the other on the left hand. Jesus replied that it was not in his power to grant her wish, as those places belonged to those for whom God had prepared them. The other disciples, when they heard this, were very upset with the two brothers.

Judas Iscariot, one of the twelve disciples, decided to betray Jesus. He went to the chief priests and the officers of the Temple guard and asked them, "What will you give me if I betray Jesus to you?" They counted thirty silver coins and gave them to him.

The day before the Passover Festival, after they had had dinner, Jesus rose from the table, took off his outer garment, and tied a towel around his waist. He poured water into a washbasin, washed the feet of his disciples, and dried them with the towel.

Jesus said to his disciples, "If any of you wants to be great, he should be a servant to the others. The Son of man did not come to be served but to serve and to give his life for the redemption of the people".

He was silent for a moment, and then, with great emotion, he said, "Truly, I tell you, one of you will betray me".

The disciples looked at one another, not knowing whom he meant. One of the disciples, whom Jesus loved very much, was sitting next to him. Simon Peter gestured to him and said, "Ask him, about whom is he speaking".

The disciple asked Jesus, "Lord, who is he?"

Jesus answered, "He is the one to whom I will give a piece of bread, after I dip it". He dipped it and gave it to Judas Iscariot. Then, he said to Judas, "What you are going to do, do quickly". Judas got up and left immediately.

The others at the table didn't understand what Jesus had said to Judas. They assumed that Jesus had told Judas, the treasurer of the group, to go and buy what was needed for the Festival, or donate some alms to the poor.

Jesus prayed for his disciples to God, and afterward, he went with them across the Cedron Brook, to a garden. Judas Iscariot, who knew the place because Jesus had met there many times with his disciples, led a number of soldiers and Temple guards to the garden.

Jesus stepped forward and asked them, "Who are you looking for?'

They answered, "Jesus of Nazareth".

"I am he", said Jesus.

They stepped back and fell to the ground. Jesus asked them again, "Whom do you seek?"

"Jesus of Nazareth", they replied.

"I already told you that I am he. If you want me, let the others go".

Peter drew his sword and struck a slave of the High Priest, who was called Malchus, cutting off his right ear. Jesus rebuked Peter, saying, "Put your sword back in its place! All who take the sword will die by the sword. Do you think that I will not drink the cup of suffering, which my Father has given me?"

The soldiers and the guards arrested Jesus, tied him up, and took him to the palace of Annas, the previous High Priest and father-in-law of Caiaphas, the current High Priest

Early Sunday morning, the third day after Jesus had been crucified and buried, Mary Magdalene visited the sepulcher and saw that it was empty. She hurried to tell Peter and John. The two disciples ran together. John arrived first to the tomb and verified that Jesus was not there.

This gave rise to a rumor among the followers of Jesus that this disciple would not die, although Jesus had not said so. He was the disciple who wrote the gospel according to John.

Sometime later, Peter, Thomas, Nathanael, and the two sons of Zebedee went fishing in the Lake of Galilee, but did not catch any fish. Early in the morning, they returned. Jesus was standing on the shore, but the disciples didn't recognize him.

Jesus asked them, "Children, do you have any food?"

"No", they answered.

"Throw your net on the other side of the boat", said Jesus.

They threw the net and were unable to pull it back, because it had caught so many fish.

John said to Peter, "He is the Lord".

Hearing this, Peter, who had been naked, put on his clothing and jumped into the sea. The other disciples brought the boat to the shore, pulling the net full of fish.

When they stepped ashore, they saw a charcoal fire there with fish and bread on it. Jesus told them, "Bring the fish that you have caught".

Peter climbed into the boat and dragged the net ashore, full of large fishes. There were one hundred and fifty-three, but the net didn't break.

Jesus said to them, "Come and eat". None of the disciples dared ask him who he was, because they knew that he was the Lord.

Jesus took the bread and gave it to them, and he did the same with the fish. This was the third time that Jesus appeared to his disciples, after his resurrection.

After they had dined, Jesus asked Peter three times if he loved him. Peter answered that he did, and Jesus told him to feed his sheep and to follow him.

Peter turned and saw John, the disciple whom Jesus loved. He asked Jesus, "Lord, what shall this man do?"

"If I want him to live till I come, what is that to you? Follow me!" said Jesus to Peter.

This gave rise to a rumor among the followers of Jesus that John would never die, although Jesus had not said so. That was the last time that Jesus appeared to his disciples.

One day, after they had returned to Jerusalem, Peter and John went to the Temple in the afternoon, the hour for prayer. There, at the Temple Gate, called Beautiful, they saw a man, who was lame from birth, begging money from the passers-by.

When he saw Peter and John going in, he begged them to give him something. The apostles looked at him, and Peter said, "Look at us!" The lame beggar looked at them, hoping to get something.

Peter told him, "I don't have silver or gold, but I will give you what I have: in the name of Jesus, the Messiah of Nazareth, rise up and walk!" He took the beggar by his right hand and helped him to get up.

At once, the beggar's feet and ankles became strong. He jumped up, stood on his feet, and started walking around. Then, he went into the Temple with the apostles, walking and jumping, and praising God. All the people around who knew him were surprised and amazed to see him walking.

Peter saw the people staring at them, and he said to them, "Men of Israel, why are you amazed at this? Why are you staring at us? Do you think that it was by our own power or holiness that we made this man walk? The God of Abraham, Isaac, and Jacob has given divine glory to his servant Jesus. You handed him over to the authorities, and rejected him in Pilate's presence, even after Pilate had decided to set him free. You killed the one who leads to life, but God raised him from death, and we are witnesses to this. It was the power of his name that gave strength to this lame man. What you see and know was done by faith in his name; it was faith in Jesus that has made him well, as you can all see".

Peter told the crowd that what they and their leaders had done to Jesus was due to their ignorance. He exhorted them to repent and turn to God. "Moses, Samuel, and the prophets", he said, "had all predicted what was now happening, that God had chosen his servant to bless every one of you and make you turn away from your sins".

Peter and John were still addressing the crowd, when some priests, the captain of the Temple guards, and several

Sadducees—who were annoyed because the two men were teaching the people that Jesus had risen from the dead, thus, proving that the dead can return to life—arrested them and put them in jail.

The next day, the council of the leaders of the people, the elders, and the teachers of the Law, gathered in Jerusalem. Among the authorities present were the High Priest Annas, Caiaphas, John, Alexander, and many relatives of the High Priest They ordered the apostles brought to their presence and asked them, "By what power or by what name have you done this?"

Peter, inspired by the Holy Spirit, answered, "Leaders of the people, and elders of Israel, if we are today being questioned about the good deed done to the lame man and how he was healed, then you should all know, and all the people in Israel should know, that it was done by the name of Jesus of Nazareth, the Messiah, whom you crucified and whom God raised from the dead. It was written in the Scriptures that Jesus, the stone that the builders despised, turned out to be the most important of all. Salvation is to be found through him alone".

The members of the council were amazed at the self assurance of Peter and John, whom they had considered to be ignorant and unlearned men. They realized that they had been companions of Jesus, but could do nothing, because the healed man was standing there with the apostles as living proof of what Peter and John were saying.

They asked the apostles to leave the room, and then, they started arguing among themselves. "What shall we do with these men?" they asked each other. "As everyone in Jerusalem knows that they have performed a great miracle, there is no way we can deny it. But to keep this matter from spreading any further among the people, let's warn them never again to speak to anyone in the name of Jesus".

Peter and John were called back to the council, and they were ordered to abstain from speaking or teaching in the name of Jesus.

The apostles answered, "The council should judge what is right in the sight of God: to obey you, or to obey God. We cannot stop speaking of what we have seen and heard".

The council felt powerless to punish them, because the people were praising God for the miracle that the apostles had done. The authorities had no choice but to let the apostles go free, after again warning them.

Peter and John returned to the community of believers and told them what the chief priests and the elders had said to them. When the believers heard them, they all joined in praying to God. After they had finished praying, they were all filled with the Holy Spirit and boldly proclaimed God's word.

The apostles did not cease teaching, and they went everyday to the Temple, where they preached that Jesus was the Messiah.

The church leaders in Jerusalem, having heard that many people in Samaria had been baptized, sent Peter and John to them. When the apostles arrived, they prayed that the believers should receive the Holy Spirit. They placed their hands on them, and the believers received the Holy Spirit.

Simon, a believer who had a reputation for performing amazing acts of magic, was astonished, when he saw the wonders and miracles that the apostles were performing. He went to Peter and John, offered them money, and said, "Give me also this power, so that anyone I place my hands on will receive the Holy Spirit".

Peter answered him, "Your money should die with you! You think that you can buy God's gift with money! You are not worthy to share our work, because your heart is not right in God's sight. Repent of this wicked plan, and pray to God that he will forgive your evil purpose, for I see that you are full of bitter envy and are a prisoner of sin".

Simon begged them to pray to God for him, so that nothing of what they had said would happen to him.

Peter and John returned to Jerusalem, preaching the gospel to many Samaritan villages on their way.

John became one of the leaders of the church in Jerusalem. He, together with James and Peter, came to an agreement with Paul that they would preach to the Jews, while Paul and Barnabas would work among the Gentiles.

A tradition says that John, in his old age, lived in Patmos and Ephesus and wrote three letters to churches in Asia.

The first letter of John is very similar in style and content to the gospel according to John, and it is likely that both works were written by the apostle.

However, several scholars believe that the second and third letters of John were not written by the apostle John, but by an elder who also lived in Ephesus and was also called John.

The other book that tradition attributes to him is Revelation, although current scholar opinion maintains that the author of Revelation was a different person (see John #5 below).

3. (Acts of the Apostles 4:6). A.D. 1st century. John, a relative of Annas the High Priest, was present, when the apostles, Peter and John, were brought to the presence of the Jewish Council that warned them not to speak or teach in the name of Jesus.

4. (Acts of the Apostles 12:12). A.D. 1st century. John, surnamed Mark—also called Marcus (Colossians 4:10)—was the son of a woman called Mary, in whose house in Jerusalem people gathered to pray.

John Mark accompanied Saul and Barnabas in their trip through Asia Minor and the Greek islands, preaching the gospel and making new converts everywhere. Later, while staying in Antioch, Saul and Barnabas had a parting of their ways, because Barnabas wanted to take John Mark again with them, but Paul was opposed to this. As they were not able to agree, Barnabas took John Mark and sailed to Cyprus, while Paul took Silas and departed with him from Antioch.

Paul in his second letter to Timothy mentioned that only Luke was with him, and he asked that Mark should be sent to him, as he would be a great help in his ministry.

In his letters to the Colossians and to Philemon, Paul mentioned that Mark was a fellow prisoner in Rome. Some scholars believe that John Mark was the author of the gospel according to Mark.

5. (Revelation 1:1). A.D. 1st century. Tradition attributes the book of Revelation, written around the year 95 A.D., to the apostle John, but current scholar opinion maintains that the author was a different person, one who had dedicated his life to develop seven churches in the Roman territory of Asia, today called Anatolia in Turkey.

This man was exiled from Ephesus to the island of Patmos, at a time when Christians were being persecuted by the emperor Nero.

The writer of Revelation gives his readers hope and encouragement, and he urges them to remain faithful, during those times of suffering and persecution.

Joiada

(Hebrew origin: *God knows*)

(Nehemiah 12:10). 5th century B.C. Joiada was the son of Eliashib, the High Priest, during the days of Nehemiah. One of his sons was married to a daughter of Sanballat, sworn enemy of Nehemiah.

Joiakim

(Hebrew origin: *God will raise*)

(Nehemiah 12:10). 5th century B.C. Joiakim, High Priest, during the days of Nehemiah, was the son of Jeshua and the father of Eliashib.

Joiarib

(Hebrew origin: *God will contend*)

1. (Ezra 8:16). 5th century B.C. Joiarib, a teacher, was sent by Ezra, together with other leaders of the people, to Casiphia to

speak to Iddo and request from him to send Levites to serve in the Temple in Jerusalem.

2. (Nehemiah 11:5). Unspecified date. Joiarib, son of Zechariah and father of Adaiah, was an ancestor of Maaseiah, one of the persons who settled in Jerusalem, after the return from the Babylonian Exile.

3. (Nehemiah 11:10). 6th century B.C. Joiarib—called Jehoiarib in the first book of Chronicles (1 Chronicles 9:10)—father of Jedaiah, was one of the priests who returned to Jerusalem with Zerubbabel and served under the High Priest Jeshua. He was the ancestor of a priestly clan that was led by Mattenai, when Joiakim was the High Priest, during the days of Nehemiah (Nehemiah 12:19).

Jokim

(Hebrew origin: *God will raise*)

(1 Chronicles 4:22). Unspecified date. Jokim was the son of Shelah, the son of Judah. His brothers were Er, Laadah, Joash, and Saraph.

Jokshan

(Hebrew origin: *Insidious*)

(Genesis 25:2). 18th century B.C. Jokshan was a son of Abraham and Keturah, the woman whom Abraham married, after Sarah died. His brothers were Zimran, Medan, Midian, Ishbak, and Shuah. His sons were Sheba and Dedan.

Shortly before Abraham died, he made Isaac his sole heir, and, in order to avoid trouble, he donated gifts to the sons of his second wife and sent them away to the east.

Joktan

(Hebrew origin: *He will be made little*)

(Genesis 10:25). Unspecified date. Joktan was the son of Eber, a descendant of Noah and Shem. His brother's name was Peleg. His sons were Almodad, Sheleph, Hazarmaveth, Jerah, Hadoram, Uzal, Diklah, Obal, Abimael, Sheba, Ophir, Havilah, and Jobab.

Jona

(Hebrew origin: *Dove*)

(John 1:42). A.D. 1st century. Jona—also called Jonas (John 21:15)—was the father of Simon, the apostle whom Jesus called Peter.

Jonadab

(Hebrew origin: *God is generous*)

1. (2 Samuel 13:3). 10th century B.C. Jonadab was the son of Shimeah, the brother of King David. He was, therefore, a first cousin of his close friend, Amnon, the firstborn son of King David.

When Jonadab found out that Amnon desired his half sister Tamar, he suggested to him that he should pretend to be ill and ask David to let Tamar visit him and cook for him.

Amnon followed his advice and then took advantage of being alone with Tamar to rape her. Absalom, Tamar's brother, waited patiently for an opportunity to revenge his sister.

Two years later, Absalom invited King David to a sheep-shearing celebration. The king did not accept the invitation, but, when Absalom pressed him, he allowed Amnon and his other sons to attend the party.

During the feast, Absalom ordered his servants to kill Amnon in revenge for having raped Tamar. The first report that King David received was that Absalom had killed all his sons, but then, Jonadab informed him that only Amnon was dead.

2. (Jeremiah 35:6). 9th century B.C. Jonadab, son of Rechab, was the leader of an ascetic sect, which abstained from wine, did not sow seeds nor plant vineyards, and did not build houses but lived in tents.

Jonadab assisted Jehu, the commander of King Joram's army, to seize the throne of Israel and exterminate the entire house of Omri, and the followers of the Canaanite god Baal.

Centuries later, the prophet Jeremiah praised the sect to the men of Jerusalem as an example to follow of people who kept their commandments and principles.

Jonadab is called Jehonadab in the second book of Kings (2 Kings 10:15).

Jonah

(Hebrew origin: *Dove*)

(2 Kings 14:25). 8th century B.C. Jonah—called Jonas in the New Testament—son of Amittai, was a prophet who lived, during the reign of Jeroboam II of Israel, and prophesied that the king would be successful in his military campaigns.

He is described in the book of Jonah as an intolerant, unwilling servant of God, who tried to evade fulfilling a mission from God.

Jonah was ordered by God to go to Nineveh to warn its inhabitants that it would be destroyed unless they would repent. Jonah did not want to follow God's order and tried to flee by ship from Jaffa to Tarshish, a direction which was opposite to Nineveh.

God sent a great wind and a storm that threatened to sink the ship. When the sailors found out that Jonah was to blame for the storm, the prophet suggested that they should throw him overboard. The sailors cast forth into the sea, and the sea became calm. The sailors, in gratitude, offered sacrifices and made vows to God.

Jonah was swallowed by a great fish. From its inside, the prophet prayed to God. After three days and nights, the fish spewed him out onto dry land. This incident, of a great fish swallowing a person, is similar to stories in other cultures, but here, it has a unique biblical character: the man inside the fish is rescued not by force but by an answered prayer.

God called Jonah a second time and instructed him to deliver a message of doom to Nineveh. Jonah went to the great city of Nineveh and proclaimed that, in forty days, the city would be overthrown. The people of Nineveh, including its king, believed the word of God, proclaimed a fast, and put on sackcloth.

God saw Nineveh's repentance and decided not to carry out the punishment.

Jonah, displeased by God's mercy, complained and said to God that he preferred to die. Meanwhile, he sat outside Nineveh in the shade of a booth, waiting to see what would happen to the city. God caused a plant to grow over Jonah, to provide shade over his head, which made Jonah very happy.

On the following day, God sent a worm, which destroyed the plant, and after this, he also sent a hot wind, so that Jonah became faint and again asked for death.

God said to him, "You care for a plant, for which, you did not work, which appeared in one night and perished overnight. Should I not spare Nineveh, that great city, where there are more than one hundred and twenty thousand persons, who cannot discern between their right hand and their left hand, and also many cattle?"

The book of Jonah is a lesson in divine forgiveness and mercy. It portrays God's absolute sovereignty over his creation and shows that God is full of love and mercy, preferring to forgive and save even the enemies of his people, inhabitants of a hated foreign city, rather than punish and destroy them. The book also teaches that man needs to accept God's commands.

The book of Jonah is one of the twelve books that make up the Minor Prophets—also called the Twelve—a collection of the books of twelve prophets: Hosea, Joel, Amos, Obadiah, Jonah, Micah, Nahum, Habakkuk, Zephaniah, Haggai, Zechariah, and Malachi.

Note: The phrase "Minor Prophets" does not mean that these prophets are less important than Isaiah, Jeremiah, and Ezekiel. It refers only to the fact that the books of these twelve prophets are much shorter than the books of the other three prophets.

Jonan

(Greek version of *Jonah* [*Dove*])

(Luke 3:30). Unspecified date. Jonan, son of Eliakim, was an ancestor of Jesus, according to Luke's genealogy.

Jonas

(Greek version of *Jonah* [*Dove*])

1. (Matthew 12:39). 8th century B.C. Jonas is an alternative spelling of the name of the

prophet Jonah according to the New Testament.

2. (John 21:15). A.D. 1st century. Jonas—also called Jona (John 1:42)—was the father of Simon, the apostle whom Jesus called Peter.

Jonathan

(Hebrew origin: *God gave*)

1. (Judges 18:30). Unspecified date. Jonathan, son of Gershom and grandson of Manasseh, was a priest in charge of the cult to the graven image, set up by the tribe of Dan, in the city of Dan, previously called Laish. His descendants also served as priests, until the destruction of the kingdom of Israel.

   Some Hebrew manuscripts have the letter *nun,* "n" in Manasseh, suspended above, which would indicate an earlier reading of "Moses", in which case, Jonathan would be Moses' grandson.

2. (1 Samuel 13:2). 11th century B.C. Jonathan, the son of King Saul, was a courageous and daring officer in his father's army. In the war against the Philistines, he commanded a third of the Israelite army and performed acts of great valor.

   Unbeknownst to Jonathan, Saul had forbidden his soldiers to eat. Saul found out that Jonathan had eaten some honey and condemned him to die, but relented, when his soldiers pressured him to let Jonathan live.

   When David came to Saul's court, he and Jonathan formed a deep friendship. Saul, who suffered from depression and paranoia, became jealous of David's successes in battle and ordered Jonathan to kill him. Jonathan warned David of his father's murderous intentions and told him to hide.

   Jonathan went to his father and asked him not to harm David, who had done nothing against the king and, to the contrary, had risked his life, fighting against the Philistines. Saul promised that he would not kill David.

   However, sometime later, Saul again tried to kill David, who fled and asked Jonathan why his father was trying to kill him.

Jonathan said, "My father would not do anything without telling me first".

David answered, "It is because your father knows that we are friends that he will not tell you his intentions, to avoid giving you cause for grief. I will not be present tomorrow at the banquet celebrating the festival of the New Moon. If the king notices my absence, and asks for me, tell him that I went to Bethlehem to make the yearly sacrifice with my family".

The two friends arranged to meet three days hence at an agreed spot. The next day, at the banquet, the king noticed that David was not there, but kept silent, thinking that David had kept away, because he was not ritually clean.

On the second day of the festival, David's seat was again empty. Saul asked Jonathan, "Why is the son of Jesse not here with us?"

Jonathan answered, "David went to Bethlehem to offer a sacrifice with his family".

Saul became angry and said to Jonathan, "You will never become king if David remains alive. Bring him to me to have him killed!" Losing all control, Saul threw his spear at Jonathan to strike him down.

Jonathan rose from the table in a rage, because his father had humiliated him publicly. He now realized that the king was determined to kill David and grieved for his friend.

Jonathan met David the next day at the appointed place and told him that he should go away. They kissed each other goodbye, and David fled to the priestly town of Nob.

Jonathan and David saw each other one last time, when Jonathan went to the wilderness of Ziph, to meet David, who had become the chief of an outlaw band. Jonathan told him not to fear, that the hand of Saul would never touch him, and that, one day, David would be king, and Jonathan would be second to him.

Jonathan fought at the side of his father in a battle against the Philistines near Mount Gilboa. He and his brothers Abidanab and Melchishua died fighting, and Saul committed suicide. Jonathan and Saul were mourned by David in a beautiful eulogy.

Jonathan was survived by a five-year-old son, called Mephibosheth, who fell from his nurse's arms and became lame. Years later, when the boy was grown up, David brought him to the court and, for the sake of Jonathan's memory, restored to him the lands of his grandfather Saul.

3. (2 Samuel 15:27). 10th century B.C. Jonathan, son of the priest Abiathar, was the grandson of Ahimelech, the Nob priest who was killed by Saul's order.

He and Ahimaaz, the son of the High Priest Zadok, served as King David's messengers and spies in Jerusalem, during Absalom's revolt, transmitting Hushai's messages to David. On one occasion, the two young men, pursued by Absalom's soldiers, avoided capture by hiding down in a well.

Years later, Jonathan brought the news to Adonijah that David had made Solomon king. Jonathan's brother Ahimelech served as High Priest, together with Zadok, son of Ahitub, during the reign of King David.

4. (2 Samuel 21:21). 10th century B.C. Jonathan was the son of Shimeah, the brother of David. During a battle against the Philistines near Gath, he killed a giant, who had six fingers on each hand and six toes on each foot.

5. (2 Samuel 23:32). 10th century B.C. Jonathan was one of "The Thirty", an elite group in King David's army. His father, according to the first book of Chronicles, was Shage the Hararite (1 Chronicles 11:34).

6. (1 Chronicles 2:32). Unspecified date. Jonathan, of the tribe of Judah, was the son of Jada and the brother of Jether. His sons were Peleth and Zaza.

7. (1 Chronicles 27:32). 10th century B.C. Jonathan, David's uncle, a wise man, was a counselor and a scribe in the court of King David.

8. (Ezra 8:6). 6th century B.C. Jonathan, a descendant of Adin, was the father of Ebed who headed a group of fifty men who returned with Ezra from the Babylonian Exile.

9. (Ezra 10:15). 5th century B.C. Jonathan, the son of Asahel, was one of the two leaders of Judah—the other was Jahaziah, the son of Tikvah—who remained in Jerusalem to represent the people, when Ezra deliberated on the matter of the marriages to foreign women. They were helped by Meshullam and Shabbethai the Levite.

10. (Nehemiah 12:11). 5th century B.C. Jonathan, son of Joiada and father of Jaddua, was a descendant of Jeshua, the High Priest who returned with Zerubbabel from the Babylonian Exile.

11. (Nehemiah 12:14). 5th century B.C. Jonathan was the head of a priestly clan, descended from Melicu, when Joiakim was High Priest, during the time of Nehemiah.

12. (Nehemiah 12:35). 5th century B.C. Jonathan, son of Shemaiah, a descendant of Asaph, was the father of Zechariah, one of the priests who marched with trumpets in the joyful procession, which celebrated the dedication of the rebuilt walls of Jerusalem, during the days of Nehemiah.

13. (Jeremiah 37:15). 6th century B.C. Jonathan the Scribe was the owner of the house where Jeremiah was imprisoned for many days, during the reign of King Zedekiah.

14. (Jeremiah 40:8). 6th century B.C. Jonathan and his brother Johanan, sons of Kareah, were among the captains of the defeated army of Judah who came to Gedaliah, the Babylonian appointed governor, to be assured by him that everything would be well if they would serve the king of Babylon.

Jorah

(Hebrew origin: *Rainy*)

(Ezra 2:18). Unspecified date. Jorah was the ancestor of a family that returned with Zerubbabel from the Babylonian Exile.

Jorai

(Hebrew origin: *Rainy*)

(1 Chronicles 5:13). Unspecified date. Jorai was a leader of the tribe of Gad who lived in the land of Bashan. His brothers were Michael, Meshullam, Sheba, Jachan, Zia, and Heber.

Joram

(Hebrew origin: *God raised*)

1. (2 Samuel 8:10). 10th century B.C. Joram—called Hadoram in the first book of Chronicles (1 Chronicles 18:10)—was the son of Toi, the king of Hamath.

   Joram was sent by his father King Toi to King David with gifts of vessels of brass, silver and gold, to congratulate David on his victory over Hadadezer, king of Zobah, a bitter enemy of Hamath.

2. (2 Kings 8:16). 9th century B.C. Joram—also called Jehoram (2 Kings 1:17)—the ninth king of Israel, after the partition of the United Monarchy, son of Ahab and Jezebel, succeeded to the throne of Israel, when his brother Ahaziah fell from a balcony and died from his injuries, without leaving any sons.

   When the vassal kingdom of Moab rebelled against him and refused to pay him tribute, Joram made an alliance with Jehoshaphat, king of Judah, and with the king of Edom, to go and fight against Moab.

   After the allied army had traveled for seven days, there was no water left for the soldiers and their cattle. The prophet Elisha was called, and, upon his arrival, he told Joram that he would not even deign to look at him if the king of Judah had not been also present. Elisha asked the kings to bring him a musician, and, while the musician played, he told them that God commanded them to dig ditches.

   The next morning, water came rushing from Edom and turned the ditches into pools. Early the next day, the Moabites saw the red reflection of the rising sun on the pools and thought that it was the blood of the kings' armies that had fought between themselves. They attacked the Israelite camp but were repulsed and defeated. In spite of their defeat, the Moabites succeeded in becoming independent from Israelite rule.

   Joram was also in constant war against the Syrians, and, during a battle against them, he was wounded. Joram left the battlefield and went to his winter palace at Jezreel to recover.

   Jehu, the commander of the army, rebelled against Joram, instigated by the prophet Elisha. He mounted his chariot and drove furiously to Jezreel. A lookout, stationed on a tower, reported to the king that Jehu was approaching.

   Joram and King Ahaziah of Judah, who had come to visit the convalescent king, rode in their chariots and went to his encounter. The kings met Jehu at the field of Naboth, and Joram asked him, "Is everything well?"

   Jehu answered, "How can all be well as long as Jezebel, your mother, carries on harlotries and sorceries!"

   Joram shouted to Ahaziah, "Treason, Ahaziah!" He turned his chariot around and fled. Jehu drew his bow and hit Joram between the shoulders. The arrow pierced his heart, and he died. Jehu told Bidkar, one of his officers, "Take the body and throw it in the field of Naboth".

3. (2 Kings 8:21). 9th century B.C. Joram—also called Jehoram—the fifth king of Judah, after the partition of the United Monarchy, was thirty-two years old, when his father Jehoshaphat died, and he ascended to the throne.

   His brothers, as compensation for not being the heirs to the throne, had received from their father Jehoshaphat generous gifts of gold, silver, and fenced cities. When Joram ascended to the throne, he killed all his brothers and several high officials of the kingdom.

   His wife Athaliah, daughter of Omri, king of Israel, introduced the worship of Baal, a foreign pagan cult, in the kingdom.

During Joram's reign, Edom broke away and declared an independent kingdom. Joram led a military expedition against the Edomites but was defeated. Also, during this time, while the king and the army were probably away from Jerusalem, Philistines and Arabs raided the city, looted the royal palace, and absconded with all the king's wives and sons, except for Ahaziah, Joram's youngest son. The raiders killed the captured princes.

Due to these unfortunate events and to the idolatrous activities of his wife Athaliah, Joram was not popular with the people. After ruling for eight years, he died, after a long and painful illness, and nobody mourned him. He was buried in the City of David, but not in the royal tombs. His son Ahaziah succeeded him.

4. (1 Chronicles 26:25). Unspecified date. Joram, the son of Jeshaiah, a descendant of Eliezer, the second son of Moses and Zipporah, was an ancestor of Shelomith, the Levite in charge of the gifts donated by King David and the captains of his army, from the spoils of the wars, to maintain the Tabernacle.

Jorim

(Derived from Hebrew origin: *God raised*)

(Luke 3:29). Unspecified date. Jorim was the son of Matthat and father of Eliezer, in the genealogy of Jesus, according to Luke.

Josabad

(Hebrew origin: *God endowed*)

(1 Chronicles 12:4). 11th century B.C. Josabad the Gederathite was one of the Benjamites who deserted King Saul's army and joined David's band at Ziklag. These men were skilled warriors who could use both their right and left hands to shoot arrows and sling stones.

Josaphat

(Hebrew origin: *God judged*)

(Matthew 1:8). 9th century B.C. Josaphat is

an alternative spelling for King Jehoshaphat of Judah, an ancestor of Jesus, according to Matthew's genealogy.

Jose

(Hebrew origin: *May God add more*)

(Luke 3:29). Unspecified date. Jose was the son of Eliezer and father of Er, in the genealogy of Jesus, according to Luke.

Josedech

(Hebrew origin: *God is right*)

(Haggai 1:1). 6th century B.C. The priest Josedech, son of Seraiah, was carried into captivity, by Nebuchadnezzar, when the Babylonians conquered the kingdom of Judah.

His son, the High Priest Joshua—also called Jeshua—returned with Zerubbabel from the Babylonian Exile.

Josedech was called Jozadak in the book of Ezra (Ezra 3:2), and Jehozadak in the first book of Chronicles (1 Chronicles 6:14).

Joseph

(Hebrew origin: *May God add more*)

1. (Genesis 30:24). 17th century B.C. Joseph, the first son of the patriarch Jacob and his beloved wife Rachel, was born, when his mother had almost given up hope of ever having a child. She named him Joseph, meaning, "The Lord shall add to me another son".

Joseph was the full brother of Benjamin. His half brothers were Judah, Issachar, Reuben, Levi, Simeon, and Zebulun, sons of Leah; Gad and Asher, sons of Zilpah; Dan and Naphtali, sons of Bilhah. His half sister was Dinah, daughter of Leah.

After the birth of Joseph, Jacob returned with his family to the land of Canaan. Rachel died there, giving birth to her second son, whom Jacob named Benjamin.

Jacob loved Joseph more than any of his other sons, and, when the boy became seventeen years old, he gave him a beautiful coat of many colors. This gift made his brothers jealous and envious.

Joseph's habit of going to his father bearing tales of his brothers' misbehaving was also a cause for resentment. But the main reason for their feelings against Joseph was his dreams, where he saw his brothers doing obeisance to him. Joseph didn't care to keep these dreams to himself, but relished telling them to his brothers.

One day, his father sent Joseph to bring him news of his brothers, who were feeding the sheep in Shechem. On the way, Joseph was told by a man that his brothers were now in Dothan, and he went there.

The brothers saw him coming from afar, and they said, "Here comes the dreamer! Let's kill him, and throw his body into a pit. We can tell everybody that a wild animal killed him. Then, we shall see what will become of his dreams!"

Reuben, intending to save Joseph from his brothers' rage, told them, "Don't hurt Joseph; just cast him into a well".

The brothers stripped him of his coat of many colors and lowered him down into a dry well. Then, they sat down to eat.

They lifted their eyes and saw in the distance a caravan of camels approaching. When the caravan got closer, the brothers saw that the men were Ishmaelites that were carrying spices, balm, and myrrh, from Gilead to Egypt, accompanied by some Midianite merchants.

Judah told his brothers, "What can we profit by killing our brother and concealing his blood? Let's sell him to the Ishmaelites. Then, we won't have to hurt him. After all he is our brother, our own flesh".

His brothers liked the idea. They pulled Joseph out of the well. The Ishmaelites paid for him twenty pieces of silver, and they took him with them. When the caravan arrived in Egypt, the Midianite merchants brought him to the slave market.

Reuben, who had not been with them, during their transaction with the Ishmaelites, returned to the well and was dismayed to find that Joseph was not there.

He tore his clothes, went to his brothers, and asked them, "The boy is not there! What shall I do?"

The brothers dipped Joseph's coat into the blood of a goat, which they had just killed, and brought this "evidence" to their father Jacob. They said to him, "This is what we have found. Does it belong to your son?"

"Yes", said Jacob. "It was my son's. A wild animal has killed him. Joseph must be torn to pieces!" He tore his clothes, put on sackcloth, and mourned his son. His children tried to comfort him, but he refused to be consoled and said to them, "I will go down to my grave mourning for my son!"

The Midianites sold Joseph to Potiphar, an official in the court of Pharaoh and captain of his guard. Potiphar very soon found out that he had made an excellent purchase. Joseph was efficient, honest, and loyal.

Potiphar put Joseph in charge of his house and all his possessions. He relied on Joseph for everything, and it could be said that the only thing, with which Potiphar concerned himself, was the food he ate.

Potiphar's wife noticed that Joseph was a very handsome young man, and, one day, she asked him to sleep with her.

Joseph refused, saying to her, "Look, my master has put me in charge of everything he has. Nobody in this house has more authority than I. He has not kept back anything from me except you. How can I repay his trust with this wickedness, which is also a sin against God?"

The woman didn't give up and insisted day after day. One day, when Joseph had come into the house to do his work, and none of the house servants were present, she caught him by his robe and said, "Come to bed with me".

Joseph ran out, leaving his robe in her hand. She shouted for her servants to come immediately, and she told them, "Look, my husband has brought a Hebrew slave to mock us. He came into my room to rape me, and when I screamed as loud as I could, he left his robe and ran away".

She kept the robe next to her, until Potiphar returned home. She said to him, "The Hebrew slave that you brought here, came into my room and mocked me. When I shouted, he left his robe with me, and escaped".

Potiphar was furious, when he heard his wife's tale. He took Joseph and put him in the prison, where the king's prisoners were jailed.

Fortunately for Joseph, the chief jailer liked him and put him in charge of all the prisoners. Joseph earned his trust, and the chief jailer relied on him completely for everything that had to be done in the prison.

Two high officers of the court were brought to the jail: the royal butler and the royal baker, both of whom had displeased Pharaoh, king of Egypt. The chief jailer asked Joseph to take special care to the two men and to serve them.

One night, the men both dreamed vivid and strange dreams, which greatly disturbed them. Joseph came in the morning and noticed that they were sad and depressed. He asked them, "Why do you look so sad?"

They answered, "Each of us dreamed a dream, and nobody here can tell us what it means".

Joseph said, "Interpretations belong to God. Tell me your dreams, please".

The royal butler told his dream to Joseph, "In my dream, there was a vine before me, which had three branches full with ripe grapes. I took the grapes and pressed them into Pharaoh's cup, which was in my hand, and I gave the cup to Pharaoh".

Joseph said, "The meaning of the dream is the following: The three branches are three days. In three days, Pharaoh will pardon you and restore you to your high position". Joseph added, "Please mention me to Pharaoh, so as to free me, because I have been kidnapped from the land of the Hebrews, and have done nothing to deserve being put in prison".

The royal baker, encouraged by the favorable interpretation of the royal butler's dream, told Joseph, "In my dream, I had three white baskets on my head, with all kinds of morsels for the Pharaoh, and birds were eating them".

Joseph answered, "The meaning is this: The three baskets symbolize three days, after which you will be put to death by Pharaoh, and birds will eat your flesh".

Three days later, the butler was restored to his high position, and the baker was hanged. The butler, once freed, completely forgot Joseph and didn't mention him to the Pharaoh.

Two years later, Pharaoh dreamed two dreams, which puzzled and worried him. In the first dream, he saw seven handsome cows come out of the Nile, followed by seven other cows, ugly and gaunt, which ate the seven first cows. In the second dream, he saw seven healthy ears of grain grow on a single stalk. Behind them, he saw seven thin ears appear and swallow the seven healthy ears.

The next morning, he sent for all the magicians and wise men of Egypt, but no one could explain to him the meaning of his dreams.

The royal butler said, "I remember today what I did wrong. Pharaoh was angry with his servants, and sent me and the royal baker to jail. One night, each of us dreamed a dream. There was a young man in that jail, a Hebrew, a servant of the chief jailer. We told him our dreams, and he interpreted them for us. And it turned out exactly as he said, I was restored to my office, and the baker was hanged".

Pharaoh immediately sent for Joseph. The king's guards took him hurriedly out of the jail, made him shave himself, gave him new clothes, and brought him to the presence of Pharaoh.

Pharaoh said to Joseph, "I have dreamed a dream, and nobody can tell me its meaning. But I have been told that you know how to interpret dreams".

Joseph answered, "It is not me who

interprets, but God who shall give Pharaoh an answer of peace".

Pharaoh told Joseph his dreams, and Joseph said, "Both dreams are one. God has shown Pharaoh what he is about to do. The seven handsome cows and seven healthy years are seven years of plenty. The seven ugly cows and the seven thin ears are seven years of famine, which will follow the seven years of plenty. Pharaoh should find a wise man and set him over the land of Egypt to organize the collection and storage of the food, during the seven good years, so that there will be a reserve for the seven years of famine".

The plan pleased Pharaoh, and he said to these officers, "I don't think that we can find a better man than this one, a man who has God's spirit in him". To Joseph, he said, "God has shown you all this, which proves that you are wiser than anybody else. You will preside over Egypt, and rule the people. Your authority will be second only to mine".

Pharaoh placed his ring on Joseph's finger, had him dressed in robes of fine linen, with a gold chain on his neck, and gave him for his own personal use the second royal chariot, with guards who went before him, shouting, "Bow thy knee!" He also gave Joseph the Egyptian name of Zaphnathpaaneah and married him to Asenath, the daughter of Potipherah, the priest of On, with whom he had two sons.

Thirteen years had gone by, since Joseph had been brought to Egypt and sold as a slave. He was now thirty years old. He left Pharaoh's court and went on an inspection trip all over the land.

During the seven years of abundant crops, Joseph gathered all the surplus food and stored it in the cities. His two sons were born at that time. He named the first-born Manasseh, because, he said, "God has made me forget my sufferings and my family". He named his second son Ephraim, because, "God has caused me to be fruitful in the land of my troubles".

When the good years ended, and the seven years of famine arrived, there was nothing to eat in all the surrounding countries, but in Egypt there was food. When the Egyptians started to feel hunger, they asked Pharaoh for food, and he told them, "Go to Joseph, and do what he tells you".

The famine grew worse and spread in the whole region. Joseph opened his store-houses and sold grain to the Egyptians, and to the foreigners who came to Egypt to buy food.

The famine in Canaan was severe. When Jacob heard that it was possible to buy grain in Egypt, he said to his sons, "Why do you just sit there looking at each other? Go to Egypt and buy grain. If not, we will die".

All the brothers of Joseph went to Egypt, except young Benjamin, because his father was afraid that something would happen to him. They arrived in Egypt and were brought to the presence of Joseph, who was personally in charge of selling the grain. They didn't recognize that the powerful Egyptian vizier in front of them was the young brother whom they had last seen over twenty years before. They bowed down before him, with their faces to the ground.

Joseph recognized them, and he vividly remembered his dreams where his family bowed to him. He decided to act as if he didn't know them, and he asked, "Where are you from?"

They answered, "We are from Canaan, and have come to Egypt to buy grain".

Joseph said, "You are spies! You have come to find out the weak spots of our land".

"No, my lord", they answered. We have come to buy grain. We are the sons of the same father, honest men, not spies".

"I say that you have come to find out where we are weak".

"We, your slaves, are twelve brothers, the son of a man who lives in Canaan. Our youngest brother remained with our father; and the other one is no more".

"This confirms what I said, you are spies!" said Joseph. "This is how we will prove it: I swear by Pharaoh's life that you will never leave, if your youngest brother doesn't come here. Send one of you to bring your brother here. In the meantime, you will be kept in prison, until your words have proven to be true. If not, by Pharaoh's life, you are spies!"

He had them confined in prison for three days. On the third day, he said to them, "I am a God-fearing man. I will let you live if you are honest men. One of you will stay in this prison. The rest of you can take grain to your starving families. But you must bring back your youngest brother, so that your words can be verified, and I will not put you to death".

The brothers said to each other, "This is happening to us because of what we did to our brother, when he pleaded with us, and we wouldn't listen".

Reuben said to them, "Didn't I tell you, don't do anything to the boy, and you wouldn't listen? And now we are paying for it".

The brothers had no idea that Joseph understood each word that they said, because he had been talking to them through an interpreter. Joseph turned away from them and wept. Then, he returned to them, took Simeon, and had him tied up in front of them.

Joseph ordered his men to fill the bags of the brothers with grain, and to place each man's money back in his bag. The brothers received provisions for the trip, loaded the donkeys with the grain, and departed.

That night, they rested in an inn on the road. One of the men opened his bag to feed his donkey and found that his money was there.

He said to his brothers, "My money has been returned to me, it is here in my bag!" They all trembled with fear and apprehension, and they asked each other, "What has God done to us?"

When they came back to Canaan, they said to Jacob, "The lord of Egypt spoke harshly to us, and accused us of being spies.

We told him that we are honest men, not spies. That we are twelve brothers, sons of the same father; the youngest stayed in Canaan with our father, and one is no more. The lord told us that we had to prove our honesty by leaving one of us there, take grain to our hungry families, and then return to Egypt with our youngest brother".

They opened their bags, found their money inside, and were dismayed.

Jacob said to them, "You have made me lose my children. Joseph is no more, Simeon is gone, and you want to take Benjamin away? All these things are against me!"

Reuben said to his father, "I authorize you to kill my two sons if I don't bring him back to you! Give him to my care, and I will bring him back!"

Jacob answered, "My son will not go to Egypt with you. His brother is dead, and he is left alone. If something would happen to him on the way, the sorrow would kill me".

The famine got worse, and after some-time, the family finished all the grain that they had brought from Egypt.

Jacob said to his sons, "Go again to Egypt, and buy a small quantity of grain for us".

Judah answered, "The man swore that we would not see his face if we didn't bring our brother with us. If you will send our brother with us, we will go to Egypt and buy grain for you. But, if you don't send him with us, there is no point in us going there, because the man will refuse to see us".

Jacob complained to them, "Why did you cause me so much trouble by telling the man that you had another brother?"

They answered, "The man asked us directly about our family. 'Is your father alive?' he asked. 'Do you have another brother?' How could we guess that he would ask to bring our brother to Egypt?"

Judah said to his father, "Send the boy with me, and we will go immediately. That is the only way that we will live, and not die, all of us: we, you, our children. I will personally guarantee his safety. If I don't bring him back to you, I will assume the blame forever. If we hadn't stayed, we could have been back twice already".

Jacob said to them, "Well, if we have no choice, take with you the best fruits of the land in your packs, and bring the man a gift, a little balm, a little honey, spices, myrrh, nuts, and almonds. This time take twice as much money as the last time, and carry in your hand the money that you found returned in your bags, because it might have been a mistake. Take your brother, get up, and go to the man. Let God Almighty make the man merciful toward you, so that he may release your other brother and Benjamin. If I have to lose my children, so be it".

The men took the gift, the money, and their young brother Benjamin, and returned to Egypt.

When Joseph saw that they had brought Benjamin with them, he told the steward of his house, "Take these men into the house. Slaughter and prepare an animal, for I will dine this noon with them".

The brothers were brought to Joseph's house, where his steward was waiting for them at the entrance. Fearing that it was a trap to enslave them as punishment for not having paid for the grain in their previous visit, they said to the steward, "When we left Egypt with the grain that we had bought, we found our money in the bags, and, therefore, we have brought it back with us".

The steward answered, "Don't worry, because I did receive the payment. The money that you found in the bags must have come from the God of your father".

The men were let into the house and were given water to wash their feet, and food for their asses. They laid out the gifts and waited Joseph's arrival at noon. When Joseph came, they gave him the gifts and bowed low before him, to the ground.

Joseph asked them, "Is your father well, the old man that you mentioned? Is he alive?"

They answered, "Your servant, our father, is alive". They knelt and bowed down before him.

Joseph saw Benjamin, and he asked them, "Is this the young brother that you mentioned? God bless you, my son".

He couldn't contain himself any longer, hurried to another room, and wept. Then, when he calmed down, he washed his face and returned to the dining room. The servants had set three tables: one for Joseph alone, another for his brothers, and the third one for the Egyptians who were present, because the Egyptians considered that eating with Hebrews in the same table would demean them.

The brothers were amazed to see that they had been seated at their table according to their ages, from oldest to youngest. Joseph sent them food from his own table, but the portions of Benjamin were five times larger than the others. They ate and drank, and they enjoyed themselves.

After they finished eating, Joseph took aside his steward and said to him, "Fill the men's bags with food, as much as they can carry, and put every man's money into his bag. And put my cup, the silver one, in the bag of the youngest, together with the money he brought to buy grain".

Next morning, at dawn, the brothers were sent away with their pack animals. When they were not yet too far from the city, Joseph told his steward to hurry after them, stop them, and accuse them of stealing the cup that Joseph used to drink and for divination.

The steward went out immediately, overtook them, and said to them, "Why have you rewarded evil for good? Is this not the cup where my lord drinks and uses for divination? You have committed an evil deed!"

The brothers, astonished, replied, "Why does our lord say these things? God forbid that we should do such a thing! Look, we brought back the money that we found in our bags. Why, then, should we steal silver or gold from your master's house? If any of us is found to have it, let him die, and the rest of us will by your slaves!"

The steward said, "Fine, it will be as you say, but only the one that has the cup will be my slave. The rest of you are innocent".

As fast as they could, they lowered their bags to the ground and opened them. The steward searched the bag of each man, starting from the eldest and finishing with the youngest. The cup was found in the bag of Benjamin. The men, horrified, tore their clothing in sorrow, loaded their donkeys, and were escorted back to the city.

The brothers were brought to the house of Joseph, who was still there. They fell before him on the ground.

Joseph said to them, "What have you done? Don't you know that a man like me could find out what you have done by divination?"

Judah said, "What can we say to my lord? How can we clear ourselves? God has found our guilt, and we are all my lord's slaves, not just the one with whom the cup was found".

Joseph replied, "God forbid that I should do such a thing! Only the man who had the cup will be my slave. The rest of you can return in peace to your father".

Judah approached Joseph and said, "My lord, please let me speak to you, and do not be angry with your servant; you are as great as Pharaoh. You asked us if we have a father or a brother, and we answered that we have a father, an old man, and a young brother, born to him in his old age, whose brother is dead, and he alone is left of his mother's children, and his father loves him. You told us, 'Bring him to me, so that I can see him', and we said to you that the boy cannot leave his father, because if he did, his father would die. You said that, if we didn't bring our young brother, you would never receive us again. We went back to our father, and told him what you had said. He told us to return to Egypt and buy a little food. We told him that the man would not receive us

if we didn't bring our young brother with us. My father said to us, 'You know that my wife gave me two sons. One is no more; he must have been torn in pieces, because I never saw him again. You want to take this one with you too, and, if something happens to him, sorrow would kill me'. If I return without the boy, he will die. I told my father that I would guarantee my brother's safety, and that, if I didn't bring him back, I would assume the blame forever. Therefore, please, let me stay with you as a slave, and allow my brother to return to my father".

Joseph could no longer control himself and asked everybody to go out of the room and leave him alone with the men. His sobs were so loud that the Egyptians in the other rooms could hear, and the news reached Pharaoh's palace.

Joseph told his brothers, "I am Joseph. Is my father still alive?" His brothers, astounded, could not speak. Then, Joseph said, "Come closer, please".

They did, and he said, "I am Joseph, your brother, whom you sold to Egypt. Don't be upset or angry with yourselves, because you sold me. It was God who sent me here to save your lives. This is the second year of the famine. There are still five years more. I am Pharaoh's highest official, and the ruler of Egypt. Hurry up, go to my father, and tell him that God has made me the lord of Egypt; come to me without delay. You will live in the region of Goshen, close to me, you, your children, and your grandchildren, and all your sheep, and animals, and everything that you have. I will take care of you, because there are still five years of famine, and I will not let you be poor. You and Benjamin have seen that it is me, Joseph, who speaks to you. Tell my father of my glory in Egypt, and all that you have seen. Hurry and bring my father here".

He embraced Benjamin, and they both wept. He kissed all his brothers and wept upon them.

Pharaoh, when told that Joseph's

brothers had come, was very pleased with the news. He said to Joseph, "Tell your brothers to load their donkeys, and go immediately to Canaan. They should bring your father and their families, and I will give them the best land in Egypt. Tell them to take wagons from Egypt for their wives and children. Also, they shouldn't worry about their belongings, because the best of the land of Egypt will be theirs".

Joseph gave his brothers wagons and provisions for the journey. To each of them, he gave a change of clothing, but to Benjamin, he gave five changes of clothing and three hundred pieces of silver. To his father, he sent ten male donkeys loaded with the best things of Egypt, and ten female donkeys loaded with grain, bread, and provisions for his father on the journey. As he sent his brothers off on their way, he admonished them not to quarrel among themselves.

The brothers returned to their father Jacob in the land of Canaan and told him, "Joseph lives, and he is the ruler of Egypt!"

At first, Jacob could not believe them, but when he saw the wagons that Joseph had sent to transport him, he exclaimed, "My son Joseph is alive! I must go and see him, before I die!"

The brothers placed their father Jacob, their children, and their wives in the wagons, took along their livestock and their possessions, and went to the land of Goshen in Egypt. On their way, they stopped in Beersheba, where Jacob offered sacrifices to the God of his father Isaac.

That night, God appeared to Jacob in a vision and said to him, "I am God, the God of your father. Do not fear going to Egypt, because there I will make you into a great nation. I will go with you to Egypt, and I will bring you out, too. Joseph's hand shall close your eyes".

The total number of the Israelites who came to Egypt was seventy. The number included Jacob, Joseph, and the two sons of Joseph, who were born in Egypt. The number did not include the wives of Jacob's sons.

They arrived in Goshen, and Joseph came to them in his chariot. He greeted his father, embraced him, and wept for a long time.

Jacob told him, "Now that I have seen your face, and know that you live, I can die".

Joseph then said to his brothers, "I will go now to Pharaoh and tell him that you have arrived. When Pharaoh calls you and asks, 'What is your occupation?' tell him that you are shepherds, and breeders of live-stock. This way you will be able to stay in Goshen, because shepherds are repulsive to Egyptians".

Joseph came to Pharaoh with five of his brothers, and their conversation went as Joseph had predicted. Pharaoh allowed them to settle in Goshen and shepherd their sheep. Joseph then introduced his father Jacob to Pharaoh.

Pharaoh asked Jacob, "How old are you?"

Jacob answered, "One hundred and thirty are the years of my pilgrimage. They have been few and hard, shorter than the life spans of my ancestors". He blessed Pharaoh and departed.

Joseph settled his family in the region of Rameses, as Pharaoh had commanded, and he took care that they were all provided with bread.

During the following years, the famine got worse. The inhabitants of Egypt, having run out of money, gave their cattle and land to Joseph in exchange for grain, until Pharaoh owned all the land in Egypt, except for the land of the priests. The Egyptians became tenant farmers, receiving seed from Joseph with the obligation to deliver to Pharaoh a fifth of their harvest.

Seventeen years later, Jacob, feeling that he would soon die, called Joseph and asked him to promise that he would not be buried in Egypt, but in the cave of Machpelah with Abraham and Isaac. Joseph swore that he would do so.

Shortly afterward, Joseph was told that his father was very ill. He went to see him with his two sons, Manasseh and Ephraim, to be blessed by Jacob. Jacob told him that he was adopting the two boys. He then looked at them and asked who they were.

Joseph answered, "These are my sons that God has given me here". He brought them closer to his father's bed, and Jacob kissed them and embraced them.

Jacob said to Joseph, "I never expected to see you again, and here, God has let me see your children as well".

Joseph placed Manasseh, his firstborn, on the right side of his father, and Ephraim on the left side of his father. Jacob placed his left hand on Manasseh. He stretched his right hand and placed it on Ephraim's head.

Joseph said to Jacob, "Not so, Father. The other one is the firstborn". He tried to remove Jacob's hand from Ephraim's head and place it on Manasseh's head.

Jacob answered, "I know, my son, he also shall become a great people, but his younger brother shall be greater than he", and he blessed the two boys.

The dying Jacob called his sons to bless them and tell them what would happen to them in the future. His last words were to ask them to bury him in the cave of Machpelah, where Abraham, Sarah, Isaac, Rebekah, and Leah were buried. Joseph flung himself over his father's body, and he wept over him and kissed him.

Jacob died at the age of one hundred and forty-seven. Joseph ordered the Egyptian physicians to embalm his father, a process, which took forty days. When the seventy days' period of mourning was over, Joseph asked permission from the Pharaoh to allow him to go to Canaan and bury his father there. Pharaoh gave him permission to go and bury Jacob as he had promised.

Jacob's body was accompanied in his last trip by his sons, their children, flocks and herds, all the officials of Pharaoh and members of his court, chariots and horsemen. Before crossing the Jordan, the funeral procession made a stop and mourned Jacob for seven days. Then, Jacob's sons took him to Canaan and

buried him in the cave of Machpelah.

After burying his father, Joseph returned to Egypt with his brothers and all those who had accompanied him to Canaan. Joseph's brothers feared that, with Jacob now dead, Joseph would pay them back for the wrong that they had done to him.

They sent a message to Joseph, saying that Jacob, before his death, had told them to urge Joseph to forgive them. The brothers came to Joseph, flung themselves before him, and told him that they were prepared to be his slaves.

Joseph answered kindly, "Do not fear! Although you intended me harm, God intended it all for good, to assure the survival of many people. Don't worry; I will take care of you and your children".

Joseph lived to see the grandchildren of his children. When he was on his deathbed, he asked his brothers to carry his bones from Egypt. He died at the age of one hundred and ten, was embalmed, and placed in a coffin.

Many generations later, the children of Israel, when they left Egypt under the guidance of Moses, took the bones of Joseph with them and buried them in Shechem, in a parcel of ground, which Jacob, his father, had bought from the sons of Hamor for one hundred pieces of silver.

2. (Numbers 13:7). 14th century B.C. Joseph, of the tribe of Issachar, was the father of Igal, one of the twelve men sent by Moses to spy the land of Canaan and report back about its cities and its inhabitants, if they were strong or weak, few or many, and to bring back the fruit of the land. The spies, with the exception of Joshua and Caleb, returned discouraged and afraid.

The Israelites, after listening to the spies, started to wail and cry. God punished their cowardice by condemning them to wander forty years in the wilderness, one year for each day that the spies scouted the land. All those who complained against God died in the wilderness, except Caleb and Joshua.

3. (1 Chronicles 25:2). 10th century B.C. Joseph was one of the sons of Asaph, the Levite appointed by King David to be in charge of the singers in the House of the Lord. He and his brothers—Zaccur, Nethaniah, and Asarelah—assisted Asaph in his work, with Joseph taking the first turn of service.

4. (Ezra 10:42). 5th century B.C. Joseph was one of the men who divorced his foreign wife in the time of Ezra.

5. (Nehemiah 12:14). 5th century B.C. Joseph was the head of a priestly clan, descended from Shebaniah, when Joiakim was High Priest, during the time of Nehemiah.

6. (Matthew 1:16). 1st century B.C. Joseph, a carpenter, living in the town of Nazareth, in the Galilee, was a direct descendant of King David. His father's name was Jacob, according to Matthew, or Heli, according to Luke.

Joseph was engaged to be married to a young woman called Mary. Before the wedding took place, he found out that she was pregnant. Being a kind and considerate man who did not wish to make a scandal that would disgrace Mary publicly and bring shame upon her, he decided to break the engagement discreetly.

While he was thinking about this, an angel appeared to him in a dream and told him, "Do not be afraid to take Mary to be your wife, for it was by the Holy Spirit that she has conceived. Her son will be called Jesus, because he will save his people from their sins".

Joseph woke up and married Mary, but did not have sexual relations with her.

The emperor Augustus decreed a census of all the inhabitants of the Roman Empire, each person to be counted in his native city. Joseph, being a descendant of David, had to travel to Bethlehem with Mary, who was in the last month of her pregnancy.

When they arrived in Bethlehem, they found that the town was crowded, and the inn was full, and they had no choice but to rest in a manger. There, Mary gave birth to Jesus.

On the eighth day, Jesus was circumcised, according to Jewish custom. When the time came for Jesus, as a firstborn child, to be redeemed according to the Law (Numbers 18:15), Joseph, his wife, and the baby went to the Temple in Jerusalem, where Joseph sacrificed a pair of doves. The baby was seen in the Temple by Simeon, a devout man, who recognized him as the Messiah. He was also seen by Anna, a prophetess, who thanked God and spoke of Jesus to all the pilgrims who came to Jerusalem.

A short time later, astrologers, who had heard that the king of the Jews had been born, followed a star and came to visit the child. When they saw him, they worshipped him and gave him gifts of gold, frankincense, and myrrh. Then, they returned to their country.

After the astrologers left, an angel appeared to Joseph in a dream and said to him, "King Herod is looking for the child in order to kill him. You and your family must escape to Egypt and stay there, until I will let you know that it is safe to return".

That same night, the holy family left for Egypt. After the death of Herod, the angel appeared to Joseph in Egypt and told him to return to Israel, where, in the meantime, Archelaus had succeeded his father Herod as king of Judea.

Joseph, fearful of Herod's son, avoided Judea and, having received more instructions in a dream, traveled to the Galilee, where the family settled in the town of Nazareth.

When Jesus was twelve years old, the family went to Jerusalem for the feast of the Passover. On their return trip to Nazareth, after a day's journey, Joseph and Mary noticed that the boy was missing. They went back to Jerusalem to search for their son, and, after three days, they found him in the Temple, sitting with the Jewish teachers, listening and asking them questions that amazed all who heard him.

Mary reproached him, for having caused them so much worry.

Jesus answered, "Why did you have to search for me? Didn't you know that I would be in my Father's house?" But they did not understand his answer. Jesus went back with his parents to Nazareth, where he grew up in body and in wisdom.

Joseph is not mentioned again in the Gospels, which means that he probably died, before Jesus started his public ministry.

According to Matthew (Matthew 13:55), Joseph had four other sons—James, Joses, Simon, and Judas—and a number of daughters. Some scholars believe that these were Joseph's children by a previous marriage; others say that the meaning of the words "brothers" and "sisters", in these passages of the Gospels, refer to cousins or other close relatives.

7. (Matthew 27:57). A.D. 1st century. Joseph, from the town of Arimathaea, a rich and respected member of the Jewish Council, was a secret follower of Jesus and a believer in the Kingdom of God.

In the afternoon of the day that Jesus died on the cross, Joseph went to see Pilate, the Roman governor of Judea, and asked to be given the body of Jesus. Pilate ordered that the body should be delivered to Joseph, who wrapped it in a clean linen cloth and laid it in the tomb that he had prepared for himself, a sepulcher which was hewn out of a rock, and he rolled a stone to close the opening of the sepulcher.

8. (Luke 3:24). Unspecified date. Joseph was an ancestor of Jesus, son of Mattathias and father of Janna, according to the genealogy of Luke.

9. (Acts of the Apostles 1:23). A.D. 1st century. Joseph was the first name of Barsabas, also called Justus, one of the two candidates to replace Judas as the twelfth apostle. Matthias, the other candidate, was chosen by lot, instead of Barsabas.

Joses

(of Hebrew origin: *May God add more*)

1. (Matthew 13:55). A.D. 1st century. Joses was mentioned as being one of the brothers

of Jesus by the villagers of Nazareth, who were surprised to hear Jesus preaching in their synagogue, when they had only known him as a humble carpenter.

Some scholars believe that Joses, James, Simon, and Judas were Joseph's children from a previous marriage. Others say that the terms "brothers" and "sisters", in these verses, refer to cousins or other close relatives.

Note: Joses is short for Joseph, the name of Jesus' father. Today, it would be impossible for a Jewish child to be named after his father, if the latter was still living. In ancient times, however, this was a fairly widespread custom.

2. (Matthew 27:56). A.D. 1st century. Joses was the brother of James the Lesser—i.e. the Younger. His mother, Mary, the wife of Cleophas, was one of the women who witnessed the crucifixion of Jesus.

3. (Acts of the Apostles 4:36). A.D. 1st century. Joses, whom the apostles called Barnabas, was a Levite who resided in the island of Cyprus. He became a faithful traveling companion of the apostle Paul and greatly helped him. (For a detailed biography, read the entry for Barnabas [Acts of the Apostles 4:36].)

Joshah

(Hebrew origin: *God set*)

(1 Chronicles 4:34). 8th century B.C. Joshah, son of Amaziah, was one of the leaders of the tribe of Simeon who went to the fertile valley of Gedor in search of pasture for their flocks, during the reign of Hezekiah, king of Judah.

The Simeonites destroyed the tents of the people—descendants of Ham—who lived there, wiped them out forever, and settled in their place.

Joshaphat

(Hebrew origin: *God has judged*)

(1 Chronicles 11:43). 10th century B.C. Joshaphat the Mithnite was one of the brave soldiers in King David's army.

Joshaviah

(Hebrew origin: *God set*)

(1 Chronicles 11:46). 10th century B.C. Joshaviah and his brother Jeribai, the sons of Elnaam, were brave warriors in King David's army.

Joshbekashah

(Hebrew origin: *Hard seat*)

(1 Chronicles 25:4). 10th century B.C. Joshbekashah, a Levite, member of a family of musicians, was in charge of the seventeenth turn of service that played musical instruments in the House of God, during the reign of David.

He had thirteen brothers and three sisters, all of them trained as skillful musicians by their father, Heman, one of the three leading musicians—the other two were Asaph and Jeduthun—of the period.

Joshua

(Hebrew origin: *God saves*)

1. (Exodus 17:9). 13th century B.C. Joshua, son of Nun, of the tribe of Ephraim, was the loyal assistant of Moses, during the wanderings of the Israelite in the wilderness. When Moses died, he succeeded him as leader of the Israelites, defeated the Canaanites, and distributed the conquered land to the twelve tribes.

His original name was Hoshea (Deuteronomy 32:44), which the book of Number spells as Oshea (Numbers 13:8). Moses renamed him Joshua. Alternative spellings of his name are Jehoshua (Numbers 13:16), Jehoshuah (1 Chronicles 7:27), and Jeshua (Nehemiah 8:17).

Joshua first showed his military prowess, when he commanded the Israelite forces that defeated Amalek in a battle that was watched by Moses, Aaron, and Hur, from the top of a hill.

Joshua is next mentioned in the Bible, when he accompanied Moses to Mount Sinai and waited for Moses at the bottom of the mountain, while Moses climbed the mountain to receive from God the commandments.

After forty days and nights, Moses came down from the mountain, carrying two stone tablets with the commandments written on them. The two men went back to the camp.

Joshua heard shouts from far away and said to Moses, "There are noises of battle in the camp".

Moses answered, "The sounds we are hearing are not sounds of war, but of people singing".

When they came close to the camp, Moses saw the people dancing around the image of a bull. Angrily, he threw down the tablets that he had brought from the mountain, destroyed the bull, and ordered the Levites to kill all the idol worshippers.

Sometime later, when Joshua was told that two elders, Eldad and Medad, were prophesying in the camp, he said to Moses, "My lord Moses, forbid them!"

Moses answered, "Are you worried about me? I wish that the Lord would give his Spirit to all his people, and make all of them prophets!"

Joshua was one of the twelve men sent by Moses to spy the land of Canaan and report back about its inhabitants; to find out if they were strong or weak, few or many, and about the land and its cities; and to bring back the fruit of the land.

The spies went and scouted the land, from the wilderness of Zin to Rehob, near the entrance to Hamath. Forty days later, they returned back to the camp, carrying pomegranates, figs, and a branch, which had a bunch of grapes so heavy that it took two men to carry it on a pole between them.

Their report turned out to be disheartening and defeatist. "We came to the land, and it flows with milk and honey, and here is the fruit that we have brought. But the inhabitants are strong; their cities are walled and very large. The Amalekites dwell in the south; the Hittites, the Jebusites, and the Amorites live in the hill country; and the Canaanites dwell by the sea and along the Jordan River. We are not able to go against them. They are too strong for us. That land devours its inhabitants. All the men that we saw are of great stature, and we even saw giants, the sons of Anak. We felt like grasshoppers, and we must have looked like that to them too".

Only Joshua, the son of Nun, and Caleb, the son of Jephunneh, disagreed and said, "The land that we scouted is an excellent land. If God is pleased with us, he will take us there, and deliver to us a land flowing with milk and honey. Do not rebel against the Lord, and don't be afraid of the people who live there, because we can conquer them easily. God is with us; do not fear them!"

The Israelites refused to listen to the encouraging words of Joshua and Caleb, and they started to wail and cry. God punished their cowardice by condemning them to wander forty years in the wilderness, one year for each day that the spies scouted the land, with the exception of Caleb and Joshua, whose bravery was rewarded by being allowed to come into the Promised Land and possess it.

Moses, knowing that his end was approaching, asked God to appoint him a successor. God told him to take Joshua, have him stand before the priest Eleazar and before the whole community, and commission him in their sight. Moses did as God commanded him, and sometime afterward, he died at the age of one hundred and twenty.

After the thirty-day-mourning period ended, Joshua told the people to prepare themselves to cross the Jordan River within three days. To the tribes of Reuben and Gad, and to half the tribe of Manasseh, to whom Moses had assigned land east of the Jordan River, he told that they could leave their wives, children, and livestock, in their land, but every one of their fighting men would also have to cross the river armed, to help the other tribes to take possession of the land, after which, they could return to their own land.

Joshua sent two spies to Jericho, the largest city in the area. The two men went there and stayed overnight in the house of a harlot called Rahab. The king of Jericho, when informed of the presence of the two Israelites, sent guards to Rahab's house with orders to arrest them.

Rahab, who had hid the men in the roof of her house, told the guards that the two spies had fled a short time before, through the gate of the city. The guards rushed out of the city in hot pursuit.

Rahab went to the roof and said to the men that she knew that God had given the country to them. She asked the men to spare the lives of her parents, brothers, and sisters.

The men promised that they would do so if she would not betray them. The men told her to tie a crimson cord to her window so that her house would be recognized and not attacked.

She let them down by a rope through her window—her house was on top of the city walls—and told them to hide in the hills for three days, until the pursuers turned back. The spies returned safely to the Israelite camp and reported all that they had seen to Joshua.

Three days later, the Israelites crossed the Jordan, which had dried up, following the priests bearing the Ark of the Covenant. Joshua chose twelve men, one from each tribe, and told each of them to take a large stone to their encampment, and to keep them as a symbol of the crossing of the Jordan.

These stones, a few days later, were set up in Gilgal, as a memorial. Joshua also had twelve stones placed in the middle of the Jordan.

There, in Gilgal, Joshua had all the Israelites circumcised, because, during the forty years in the wilderness, nobody had been circumcised. They offered the Passover sacrifice on the fourteenth day of the month, and from that moment on, the Israelites did not receive anymore manna from the sky.

Once, when Joshua was near Jericho, he saw a man standing before him with a drawn sword in his hand. Joshua went to him and asked, "Are you one of us or one of our enemies?"

"I am neither", answered the angel. "I am a captain of God's army, and I have come to you now".

Joshua threw himself to the ground and, prostrating himself, asked, "What does my Lord want his servant to do?"

The angel replied, "Remove your sandals. You are standing on holy ground". And Joshua did as he was told.

The Israelites completely encircled the city of Jericho. Nobody could leave or enter. God said to Joshua, "I will deliver the city, its king, and warriors to you. Let all your troops march around the city, and complete one circuit of the city, with seven priests, each carrying a ram's horn, preceding the Ark. They should do this, during six days, and on the seventh day, they should march around the city seven times, with the priests blowing the horns. And when a long blast will be sounded on the horn, all the people should shout mightily together. This will cause the wall to fall".

Joshua followed God's instructions, and the walls of the city collapsed. The Israelites rushed into the city and exterminated everybody with the sword. Only Rahab and her family were saved, by Joshua's orders, by the two men who had spied out the country.

The city was destroyed and burned with everything inside, except the articles that were made of silver and gold, and objects of copper and iron. These were deposited in the treasury of the House of the Lord.

Joshua decided that the city of Ai would be the next to be conquered. He sent spies to Ai who, upon their return, told him that the city was defended by very few men and could be easily taken by two or three thousand fighters.

Joshua sent an army of three thousand men, but, to his dismay, the attack ended in a rout. The men of Ai killed thirty-six Israelites and pursued the others outside the gate.

Joshua, who was filled with shame, tore his clothes. He and the elders of Israel threw themselves to the ground in front of the Ark, and they lay there till the evening. He cried out to God, "Lord God, why did you bring us across the Jordan? To be destroyed by the Amorites? Why didn't we stay on the other side of the Jordan? What can I say after the Israelites have fled from the enemy? When the Canaanites and all the other inhabitants of this land will hear about this, they will come upon us and kill every one of us. Then, what will you do about your great name?"

God replied, "Get up! Why are you lying on the ground like this? Israel has sinned. They have broken the covenant, which I had commanded them to keep. They have even taken the proscribed things, stole them, lied about it, and kept them with their own things. That is why the Israelites couldn't face their enemies, and fled from them. They are cursed, and I will no longer be with you unless you destroy the proscribed things. Get up, go and purify the people. Tell them what I said. In the morning, let them line up by tribes, clans, and families. The guilty one will be burned to death, because he has broken the covenant of the Lord, and brought shame on Israel".

The next day, early in the morning, Joshua had the Israelites come forward by tribes, and the tribe of Judah was picked. He then had the clans of Judah come forward, and the clan of Zerah was picked. Then, he had the clan of Zerah come forward by families, and the family of Zabdi was picked. Finally, he had the family of Zabdi come forward, man by man, and Achan, son of Carmi, son of Zabdi, son of Zerah, of the tribe of Judah, was picked.

Joshua said to Achan, "My son, honor God and confess to him. Tell me what you have done. Don't try to hide it from me".

Achan answered, "Yes, I have sinned against the Lord, God of Israel. This is what I have done. I took a fine Babylonian mantle, two hundred shekels of silver, and a wedge of gold, weighing fifty shekels, all of which, I buried in the ground under my tent".

Joshua sent men to the tent to dig out the buried treasure, and to bring it to him. He, followed by all the Israelites, took Achan, together with his sons and daughters, the stolen goods, and all his property, including his animals and his tent, to the valley of Achor. There, the Israelites stoned them and then burned them to death. They put a huge pile of stones over him and called that place the valley of Achor.

God said, "Don't be afraid or dismayed. Take all your soldiers, and go again against Ai. I will give you victory over its king, people, city, and land. Do to them what you did to Jericho, but this time, you can keep the spoil and the cattle as booty for yourselves. Set an ambush against the city from behind it".

Joshua sent an army of thirty thousand men to Ai, instructing them to lie in ambush, hidden close behind Ai, while he, with an army of five thousand men, camped in front of the walls of the city.

When the king of Ai saw Joshua and his small army, he thought that again he would be able to defeat the Israelites. He rushed with all his army out of the gates of the city to engage the Israelites in battle. Joshua and his men fled away from the city toward the wilderness, drawing behind them all the troops of Ai in hot pursuit. The city was left open, empty of men, and defenseless.

Joshua pointed his spear toward Ai. Seeing the agreed sign, the Israelite soldiers, who were camped on the back of the city, left their hiding place, rushed into the city, captured it, and immediately set fire to it. The men of Ai looked back and saw the smoke of the city, rising to the sky.

Joshua and his men stopped their flight, turned around, and attacked the men of Ai, who were caught between Joshua's men and

the main Israelite army that, having burned down the city, came out against them. All the men of Ai were slaughtered, except for the king who was taken alive and brought to Joshua. The entire population of the city, about twelve thousand men and women, were killed. The Israelites took the cattle and the spoil of the city as their booty. Joshua burned down Ai and hanged the king on a tree, until the evening. At sunset, the corpse was taken down from the tree and thrown down at the entrance to the city gate. Then, they piled a heap of stones over it.

Joshua built in Mount Ebal an altar of unhewn stones, where he made sacrifices to God, and inscribed a copy of the teachings of Moses. All Israel, strangers and citizens alike, stood on either side of the Ark, half of them facing Mount Gerizim, and the other half facing Mount Ebal, while Joshua read them all the words of the Law, the blessings and the curses.

The inhabitants of Gibeon were afraid that they would suffer the fate of Jericho and Ai. Their city, larger than Ai, was located only a few miles away from Joshua's camp in Gilgal.

To avoid being destroyed by the Israelites, they sent a delegation, dressed in old clothes and worn sandals, with provisions of dry and moldy bread, to the Israelite camp.

The delegation met with Joshua and with the leaders of the people and said, "We come from a distant land, and wish to enter into a peace pact with you. We heard about the Lord, your God, what he did for you in Egypt, and how you defeated the kings of Heshbon and Bashan. Our leaders gave us freshly baked bread for our trip, and, look, it is now dry and moldy. Our wineskins were new, now they were torn. Look how worn out are our sandals and clothing".

Their story was believed and a treaty was signed. Three days later, the Israelites learned that the Gibeonites lived nearby and had tricked them into signing a non-aggression pact.

The Israelites were angry that they had been deceived, but could not harm the Gibeonites because of the treaty. However, Joshua told the Gibeonites that, because they had lied to him, they would be hewers of wood and drawers of water for the community, and servants in the House of God.

Adonizedek, king of Jerusalem, heard that Joshua had taken Ai and destroyed it, and that the inhabitants of Gibeon had become Joshua's allies. He made a military alliance—with Hoham, king of Hebron; Piram, king of Jarmuth; Japhia, king of Lachish; and Debir, king of Eglon—to attack Gibeon for having made peace with the people of Israel.

The people of Gibeon appealed to Joshua for help. Joshua came from Gilgal with his army. Joshua prayed to God and said, "Sun, stand still at Gibeon, and you, Moon, in the valley of Ajalon".

The battle took place at Gibeon, and it ended in a great victory for the Israelites. The soldiers who had survived and ran away were killed by hailstones. The five kings fled and hid in a cave at Makkedah, where they were trapped, while Joshua and his army returned to Gilgal.

When Joshua was informed that the kings were hiding in a cave, he gave instructions to roll large rocks to the entrance of the cave and seal it. He also placed guards outside.

After Joshua finished liquidating the enemy survivors, the kings were taken out from the cave, humiliated, and they were killed and hanged on five trees, until the evening, when their corpses were taken down and thrown into the cave, where they had been hiding.

That day, Joshua captured Makkedah, killed the king, and exterminated its inhabitants. After this, Joshua continued his victorious campaign, conquering and destroying Libnah, Lachish, Eglon, Hebron, and Debir.

Jabin, king of Hazor, the most powerful city state in the north of the country, made an alliance with the kings of the neighboring cities of Madon, Shimron, and Achshaph. Joshua engaged them in battle near the waters of Merom and defeated them. He then captured Hazor, killed its king, and burned the city down.

Joshua conquered the whole country, except for the territories of the Philistines and the Geshurites. He then distributed the conquered land of Canaan among the tribes, except for the tribes of Reuben, Gad, and the half tribe of Manasseh, who received land on the east side of the Jordan River. The tribe of Levi was not assigned with land, but received a number of towns to live in. He gave Hebron to Caleb, the man who had been his fellow spy.

When Joshua was old and felt that his end was near, he assembled all the tribes of Israel in Shechem and told the people not to turn to strange gods. The people solemnly promised not to serve other gods.

On that day, Joshua made a covenant with the people and recorded it in a book of divine instruction. He took a great stone and set it up at the foot of the oak by the sanctuary of the Lord, saying to the people, "This stone shall be a witness against you, lest you break faith with God".

Joshua died at the age of one hundred and ten, and he was buried in his own property in Timnathserah, which was in Mount Ephraim, on the north side of the hill of Gaash.

2. (1 Samuel 6:14). 11th century B.C. Joshua, a Bethshemite, was the owner of the field where the cows, pulling the cart sent by the Philistines, carrying the Ark of the Covenant, came to a stop. The lord of the Philistines, who had walked behind the cart, saw this and returned to Ekron.

The men of Bethshemesh split up the wood of the cart, built up a fire, and sacrificed the cows to God. Unfortunately, they looked into the Ark, and for this transgression, over fifty thousand men died.

The Bethshemites asked the inhabitants of Kirjathjearim to come and take the Ark away. This was done, and Eleazar, the son of Abinadab, was appointed to keep the Ark of the Covenant that the men of Kirjathjearim had brought to his father's house.

3. (2 Kings 23:8). 7th century B.C. Joshua was the governor of Jerusalem, during the reign of King Josiah.

4. (Haggai 1:1). 6th century B.C. Joshua—also called Jeshua (Ezra 3:2)—son of Jozadak, was the High Priest who returned to Jerusalem with Zerubbabel and started to rebuild the Temple.

His sons took foreign wives, during the days of Ezra, but they divorced them and offered a ram from the flock to expiate their transgression (Ezra 10:18).

The prophet Zechariah saw Joshua in a vision, dressed in dirty clothing, standing before the angel of the Lord, with Satan standing at his right to accuse him. The Lord rebuked Satan and gave instructions to clothe Joshua in clean robes, and to place a purified diadem on his head.

The prophet Zechariah later suggested to Heldai, Tobijah, and Jedaiah, to make crowns of gold and silver, and to crown Joshua with them. The crowns then remained in the Temple as a memorial to the three donors. Joshua's son Joiakim succeeded him as High Priest

Josiah

(Hebrew origin: *God healed*)

1. (1 Kings 13:2). 7th century B.C. Josiah was the son of King Amon and his wife Jedidah. His birth had been prophesied by a prophet, during the reign of King Jeroboam. He was eight years old, when his father Amon was murdered in a palace revolt. The conspirators were then killed by the people, who proclaimed Josiah king.

Josiah, the fifteenth king of Judah, after the partition of the United Monarchy, reigned for thirty-one years and died at the age of thirty-nine, from wounds received in Megiddo, fighting against Pharaoh Necho.

During the eighteenth year of his reign, Josiah sent Shaphan the Scribe to the Temple with instructions to tell the High Priest Hilkiah to count the silver, which the gate guards had collected from the people, and to give it to the overseers of the workers who were repairing the Temple.

Hilkiah gave Shaphan a scroll that he had found in the Temple. Shaphan took the scroll to the king and read it to him. When the king heard the words of the scroll, he rent his clothes and sent men—Hilkiah; Shaphan; Ahikam, the son of Shaphan; Achbor, the son of Michaiah; and Asahiah, a minister of the king—to consult with the prophetess Huldah. She predicted that God would punish the nation for having forsaken him, but that King Josiah, having humbled himself, would be spared the sight of this evil and would die, before the collective punishment.

Thereafter, his reign was marked by a great national and religious revival. His reputation became very great, "And like him there was no king before him . . . neither after him arose there any like him" (2 Kings 23:25).

Pagan practices were extirpated, the idolatrous priests were killed, the necromancers and the mediums were liquidated, the cult was reformed, worship was centralized in Jerusalem, and the rediscovered Book of the Law, which scholars believe to be Deuteronomy, became the main vehicle of the Jewish religion. This reform revolutionized the Jewish faith.

The abolition of local worship and the fact that, due to distance, the people of other cities could not attend frequently the single sanctuary in Jerusalem, except for the festival pilgrimages, created a vacuum in daily religious life, which was filled with prayer and the reading of the Law.

Judaism was thus transformed, because of Josiah's reforms, from a religion of cult to a religion of prayer and Torah, which, to our own days, is the most important factor in Jewish religious life.

The celebration of the Passover sacrifice was renewed. Never had there been a Passover like that in Israel, since the days of

Samuel. It was celebrated by the priests, the Levites, the inhabitants of the city, and the survivors of the destroyed kingdom of Israel.

During Josiah's reign, the kingdom of Judah was completely independent. The frontiers of the country expanded to include Samaria, Megiddo, Galilee, Ekron, Ashdod, Gaza, and Bethel. The city of Jerusalem also grew acquiring a new outer wall and new quarters.

When Pharaoh Necho of Egypt marched toward Assyria through the ancient road called the Way of the Sea, Josiah tried to stop him at Megiddo and was badly wounded in the battle. The king was brought in his chariot to Jerusalem, where he died and was buried in the tombs of his fathers, mourned by the whole nation. His son Jehoahaz succeeded him.

Twenty-three years later, another one of Josiah's sons, Zedekiah, was deposed by Nebuchadnezzar, blinded, and taken in chains to Babylon where he died in prison. Thus, two decades, after the death of Josiah, ended the existence of Judah as an independent kingdom.

2. (Zechariah 6:10). 6th century B.C. Josiah, son of Zephaniah, was the owner of the house where Heldai, Tobijah, and Jedaiah made crowns of gold and silver to place on the head of the High Priest, Joshua, son of Josedech. The crowns remained in the Temple as a memorial to the three donors.

Josias

(Hebrew origin: *God healed*)

(Matthew 1:10). 7th century B.C. Josias is an alternative spelling for Josiah, the son of King Amon and his wife Jedidah. (Please see the entry for Josiah [2 Kings 13:2].)

Josibiah

(Hebrew origin: *God will settle*)

(1 Chronicles 4:35). 8th century B.C. Josibiah, son of Seraiah, was the father of Jehu, one of the leaders of the tribe of Simeon who

went to the fertile valley of Gedor in search of pasture for their flocks, during the reign of Hezekiah, king of Judah.

The Simeonites destroyed the tents of the people—descendants of Ham—who lived there, wiped them out forever, and settled in their place.

Josiphiah

(Hebrew origin: *God will add*)

(Ezra 8:10). 5th century B.C. His son, a descendant of Shelomith, returned with Ezra from Babylon, at the head of one hundred and sixty males of his clan

Jotham

(Hebrew origin: *God is perfect*)

1. (Judges 9:5). 12th century B.C. Jotham was the youngest son of the judge Gideon. After Gideon died, his son Abimelech went to Shechem and asked his mother's relatives for political support. They gave him seventy pieces of silver from their Temple's treasury, which Abimelech used to hire mercenaries to murder his brothers in order to eliminate them as rivals.

Jotham was the only brother who survived the massacre. He went to the top of Mount Gerizim and gazed down at the plain of the pillar in Shechem. He saw that the men of the city were crowning Abimelech as king, and he shouted to them a parable of the trees whose elected king consumed them by his fire. After prophesying that the men of Shechem and Abimelech would one day destroy each other, Jotham fled to Beer, fearing for his life.

2. (2 Kings 15:5). 8th century B.C. Jotham, the tenth king of Judah, after the partition of the United Monarchy, was the son of King Uzziah and Jerushah. Jotham became regent, when his father was struck with leprosy, and ascended to the throne at the age of twenty-five, when his father died.

Jotham built the high gate of the Temple, fortified Jerusalem and the cities of

Judah, built fortresses, subjugated the Ammonites, and forced them to pay tribute.

After reigning for sixteen years, he died at the age of forty-one and was buried in the City of David. Jotham was succeeded by his son Ahaz.

3. (1 Chronicles 2:47). Unspecified date. Jotham was the son of Jahdai of the tribe of Judah. His brothers were Ephah, Regem, Gesham, Pelet, and Shaaph.

Jozabad

(Hebrew origin: *God has endowed*)

1. (1 Chronicles 12:20). 11th century B.C. Two men of this name, both from the tribe of Manasseh, deserted from Saul's army with their men, joined David at Ziklag, and became captains of his army.
2. (2 Chronicles 31:13). 8th century B.C. Jozabad was one of the Levites named by King Hezekiah and the High Priest Azariah to serve under Cononiah and Shimei, as supervisors of the gifts, tithes, and offerings, brought by the people to the Temple.
3. (2 Chronicles 35:9). 7th century B.C. Jozabad, chief of the Levites, during the reign of King Josiah, was one of the men who donated cattle and oxen for the Passover offerings.
4. (Ezra 8:33). 5th century B.C. Jozabad, a Levite, son of Jeshua, returned with Ezra from the Babylonian Exile and helped Meremoth—the son of Uriah, the priest—count and weigh the silver and gold utensils of the Temple, which Ezra had brought back from Babylon. His brother Ezer, ruler of Mizpah, helped to repair the walls of Jerusalem, during the days of Nehemiah.
5. (Ezra 10:22). 5th century B.C. Jozabad was a priest, descendant of Pashur, who divorced his foreign wife, during the days of Ezra.
6. (Ezra 10:23). 5th century B.C. Jozabad was a Levite who divorced his foreign wife, during the days of Ezra.
7. (Nehemiah 8:7). 5th century B.C. Jozabad was one of the Levites who explained the Law to the people in Jerusalem, after Ezra the Scribe had read it, while standing on a wooden platform, in front of the open space, before the Water Gate. He and Shabbethai, another leading Levite, were in charge of the external work of the Temple.

Jozachar

(Hebrew origin: *God remembered*)

(2 Kings 12:21). 9th century B.C. Jozachar—called Zabad in the second book of Chronicles (2 Chronicles 24:26)—son of Shimeath, was an official in the court of Jehoash, king of Judah.

After the death of the priest Jehoiada, the people stopped worshipping in the Temple and reverted to idolatry. When Zechariah, son of the priest Jehoiada, protested against this, the king had him killed.

Jozachar and a fellow court official, Jehozabad, son of Shomer, decided to avenge the death of Zechariah and killed Jehoash, who was lying in bed, recuperating from injuries received in a battle against the king of Aram.

Amaziah succeeded his father to the throne and put the two murderers to death.

Note: According to the second book of Kings (2 Kings 12:21), Shimeath was the *father* of Jozachar. However, according to the second book of Chronicles (2 Chronicles 24:26), Shimeath, an Ammonitess woman, was his *mother*.

Jozadak

(Hebrew origin: *God is righteous*)

(Ezra 3:2). 6th century B.C. The priest Jozadak, son of Seraiah, was carried into captivity, by Nebuchadnezzar, when the Babylonians conquered the kingdom of Judah.

His son, the High Priest Jeshua—also called Joshua—returned with Zerubbabel from the Babylonian Exile.

Jozadak is called Jehozadak in the first book of Chronicles (1 Chronicles 6:14), and Josedech in the books of Haggai (Haggai 1:1) and Zechariah (Zechariah 6:11).

Jubal

(Hebrew origin: *Stream*)

(Genesis 4:21). Antediluvian. Jubal, the son of Lamech and Adah, was the ancestor of the musicians who played the harp and the organ. His brother Jabal was the ancestor of those who dwelled in tents and raised cattle.

Jucal

(Hebrew origin: *Potent*)

(Jeremiah 38:1). 6th century B.C. Jucal— also called Jehucal—son of Shelemiah, was an official in the court of King Zedekiah. (Please see the entry for Jehucal [Jeremiah 37:3].)

Juda

(Hebrew origin: *Celebrated*)

1. (Mark 6:3). A.D. 1st century. Juda, traditionally considered to be the author of the letter of Jude, was one of the four brothers of Jesus mentioned by the people of Nazareth, when they expressed their surprise and anger against Jesus for preaching in their synagogue. Matthew spells the name as Judas (Matthew 13:55).

   The other brothers of Jesus were James, who became the leader of the early church in Jerusalem, Joses, and Simon.

   Theologians and historians debate if these relatives were full-blooded siblings, half brothers and half sisters, or only cousins. Some scholars believe that these brothers and sisters were Joseph's children by a previous wife.
2. (Luke 3:26). Unspecified date. Juda, son of Joanna and father of Joseph, was an ancestor of Jesus, according to Luke's genealogy.
3. (Luke 3:30). Unspecified date. Juda, son of Joseph and father of Simeon, was an ancestor of Jesus, according to Luke's genealogy.
4. (Luke 3:33). 17th century B.C. Juda is an alternative spelling of Judah, the son of Jacob.

Judah

(Hebrew origin: *Celebrated*)

1. (Genesis 29:35). 17th century B.C. Judah, the ancestor of King David, was the fourth son born to Jacob and Leah, in Paddan-Aram, where Jacob was working for his father-in-law Laban. His mother called him Judah, because she said, "Now, I will praise the Lord".

   Judah was the full brother of Issachar, Reuben, Levi, Simeon, and Zebulun, sons of Leah. His half brothers were Gad and Asher, sons of Zilpah; Dan and Naphtali, sons of Bilhah; and Benjamin and Joseph, sons of Rachel. His sister was Dinah, daughter of Leah.

   Judah became the leader of the family, although he had older brothers. His descendants, the tribe of Judah, gave their name to the southern kingdom.

   After the birth of Joseph, Jacob returned with his family to the land of Canaan. Rachel died there, giving birth to her second son, whom Jacob named Benjamin.

   Joseph's brothers were jealous that he was Jacob's favorite son. They resented him for reporting their misbehaviors to their father, and they hated him more for telling them his dreams where the brothers did obeisance to him.

   One day, his father sent Joseph to bring him news of his brothers who were feeding the sheep in Shechem. Joseph found them in Dothan. The brothers saw him coming from afar and conspired to kill him.

   Reuben told his brothers, "Don't hurt the boy, just cast him into a pit". His intention was to come back later, save Joseph, and return him to his father. The brothers stripped Joseph of his coat of many colors and lowered him down into a dry well. Then, they sat down to a meal. Reuben, instead of staying with them, and keeping a watchful eye on Joseph, went away on some personal errand.

   While the brothers were eating, they saw in the distance a caravan of camels approaching. When it came close, they saw that the men were Ishmaelites, accompanied by some Midianite merchants, who were carrying spices, balm, and myrrh from Gilead to Egypt.

Judah, knowing that his brothers were still determined to kill Joseph, said to them, "There is nothing to gain by killing our brother and concealing his blood. Let's sell him to the Ishmaelites. Then, we won't have to hurt him, because after all, he is our brother, our own flesh".

The brothers, convinced by Judah's argument, pulled Joseph out of the well and sold him to the Ishmaelites for twenty pieces of silver. In Egypt, the Midianite merchants brought him to the slave market, where he was bought by an official of the Pharaoh.

Reuben returned to his brothers, after the caravan had already left with Joseph. He looked down the well and was dismayed to find that Joseph was not there. He tore his clothes, went to his brothers, and, in desperation, asked them, "What shall I do? The boy is not there!"

The brothers concocted a plausible story to tell Jacob. They dipped Joseph's coat into the blood of a goat, which they had just killed, brought this "evidence" to their father, and said to him, "This is what we have found. Does it belong to your son?"

Jacob, recognizing his son's coat, assumed that Joseph had been killed and eaten by a wild animal. He tore his clothes, put on sackcloth, and mourned him. His children tried to comfort him, but he refused to be consoled and said to them, "I will go down to my grave mourning for my son!"

Shortly after these events, Judah left his brothers and camped near a friend of his, an Adullamite called Hirah. There, he met Bathshua, a Canaanite woman, and married her. She gave him three sons: Er, Onan, and Shelah.

Judah married his oldest son, Er, to a girl called Tamar. When Er died young and childless, Judah told his second son, Onan, to marry Tamar and, thus, provide offspring for his dead brother. Onan, unwilling to have his children carry his brother's name, spilled his seed on the ground whenever he made love to Tamar. He also died childless.

Judah, fearful that his youngest son, Shelah, would also go to an early grave if he would marry Tamar, told her to return to her father's house, and to remain there as a widow "until Shelah would grow up". Years went by, Shelah grew up, but Judah didn't marry him to Tamar.

After Judah's wife died, and his mourning period was over, Judah went with his sheepshearers and his friend Hirah to Timnath, near the home of Tamar's parents.

Tamar was told that her father-in-law would be coming for the sheep shearing. She took off her widow's garments, wrapped herself, and, with her face covered by a veil, sat by the side of the road.

Judah saw her and didn't recognize her. He approached her and, assuming that she was a harlot, told her that he wanted to sleep with her.

"What", she asked, "will you pay me to sleep with me?"

"I will send you a young goat from my flock", promised Judah.

Tamar said, "You must leave a pledge with me, until you have sent it".

"What pledge do you want me to give you?"

"Your seal with its cord, and the walking stick that you are carrying", said Tamar.

She received the pledges and slept with him. Then, she went home, took off her veil, and put back her widow's clothing.

Judah, a man of his word, sent his friend Hirah with the young goat to receive his pledges back from the "harlot". Hirah asked some men, "Where is the harlot that sat by the side of the road?"

"There has been no harlot here", they answered.

Unable to find her, Hirah returned to Judah and told him that he couldn't find the harlot.

Judah said, "Let her keep the pledges, or people will laugh at us. I tried to pay her, but you couldn't find her".

Three months later, Judah was told that Tamar was pregnant. Judah, furious, ordered that she should be brought to him and burned.

When Tamar was brought to the presence of Judah, she showed him the pledges and said, "I am pregnant from the man who owns these things. Can you tell to whom do they belong?"

Judah examined them, recognized that they were his, and said, "She is right, because I never gave her my son Shelah". He was never intimate with her again.

Six months later, Tamar gave birth to twins, who were called Pharez and Zarah. During their birth, the midwife, seeing Zarah's hand, tied a scarlet thread on it, but it was his brother Pharez who first came out.

Many years went by, Joseph, after having been the trusted servant in the home of Potiphar, an important Egyptian official, spent years in jail, because of the trumped-up charges of his master's wife, and he had now become, in an astonishing turn of events, the most powerful man in Egypt after Pharaoh.

There was a great famine in Egypt, but Joseph, having foreseen that this would happen, had taken care of storing in warehouses the abundant crops that had been produced in the previous seven years.

The famine in Canaan was also severe. When Jacob heard that it was possible to buy grain in Egypt, he sent there all his sons, except for young Benjamin, because his father was afraid that something would happen to him.

The brothers arrived in Egypt and were brought to the presence of Joseph, who was personally in charge of selling the grain. They didn't recognize that the powerful Egyptian vizier in front of them was the young brother whom they had last seen over twenty years before, but Joseph recognized them immediately and remembered

his dreams where his family bowed to him. He decided to act as if he didn't know them, and he accused them of being spies. The brothers denied this, saying that they were all sons of the same man, and that they had a younger brother at home.

Joseph confined them in prison for three days. On the third day, he told them that they could return to their families with the grain bought in Egypt, but one of them would have to stay in prison to make sure that they would return with their younger brother.

Joseph ordered his men to fill the bags of the brothers with grain, and to place each man's money back in his bag. The brothers received provisions for the trip, loaded the donkeys with the grain, and departed. That night, they rested in an inn on the road. One of the men opened his bag to feed his donkey and was shocked to find that his money was there.

When they came back to Canaan, they told their father every word that the Egyptian vizier had said to them, and his demand that they should bring Benjamin to Egypt. This, Jacob absolutely refused to allow.

Reuben tried to change his father's mind and said, "I authorize you to kill my two sons if I don't bring Benjamin back to you! Give him to my care, and I will bring him back!" Not surprisingly, Jacob was not convinced by this senseless offer to have two of his grandsons killed.

The famine got worse, and, soon enough, the grain that the brothers had brought from Egypt was finished. When Jacob asked his sons to go again to Egypt to buy more grain, Judah answered, "The man swore that we would not see his face if we didn't bring our brother with us. If you will send our brother with us, we will go to Egypt and buy grain for you. But, if you don't send him with us, there is no point in us going there, because the man will refuse to see us".

Jacob complained to them, "Why did you have to tell the man that you had another brother? You have caused me so much trouble!"

They answered, "The man spoke to us about our family. 'Is your father alive?' he asked. 'Do you have another brother?' How could we guess that he would ask us to bring our brother to Egypt?"

Judah said to his father, "Send the boy with me, and we will go immediately. That is the only way that we will live, and not die, all of us: we, you, our children. I will personally guarantee his safety. If I don't bring him back to you, I will assume the blame forever. If we hadn't stayed, we could have been back twice already".

Jacob realized that he had no choice and reluctantly allowed Benjamin to go with his brothers to Egypt.

The brothers arrived in Egypt and were taken to Joseph's house. Joseph saw Benjamin and was unable to control his emotion; he went into another room and wept there. Returning to his brothers, he invited them to stay for dinner, but still did not make himself known to them. To his servant, he gave instructions that Benjamin should receive extra portions.

When the time came for the brothers to return to Canaan, Joseph's steward, on the orders of his master, concealed a silver cup in Benjamin's bag, and, later, he overtook the brothers on their way home, accused Benjamin of theft, and brought them all back.

Joseph said to them, "What have you done? Don't you know that a man like me could find out what you have done by divination?"

Judah said, "What can we say to my lord? How can we clear ourselves? God has found our guilt, and we are all my lord's slaves, not just the one with whom the cup was found".

Joseph replied, "God forbid that I should do such a thing! Only the man who had the cup will be my slave. The rest of you can return in peace to your father".

Judah approached Joseph and said, "My lord, please let me speak to you, and do not be angry with your servant; you are as great as Pharaoh. You asked us if we have a father or a brother, and we answered that we have a father, an old man, and a young brother, born to him in his old age, whose brother is dead, and he alone is left of his mother's children, and his father loves him".

"You told us, 'Bring him to me, so that I can see him', and we said to you that the boy cannot leave his father, because if he did, his father would die. You said that, if we didn't bring our young brother, you would never receive us again. We went back to our father, and told him what you had said. He told us to return to Egypt and buy a little food. We told him that the man would not receive us if we didn't bring our young brother with us.

"My father said to us, 'You know that my wife gave me two sons. One is no more; he must have been torn in pieces, because I never saw him again. You want to take this one with you too, and, if something happens to him, sorrow would kill me'.

"If I return without the boy, my father will die. I told him that I would guarantee my brother's safety, and that, if I didn't bring him back, I would assume the blame forever. Therefore, please, let me stay with you as a slave, and allow my brother to return to my father".

Joseph could no longer control himself and asked everybody to go out of the room and leave him alone with the men. His sobs were so loud that the Egyptians in the other rooms could hear, and the news reached Pharaoh's palace.

Joseph told his brothers, "I am Joseph. Is my father still alive?" His brothers, astounded, could not speak. Then, Joseph said, "Come closer, please".

They did, and he said, "I am Joseph, your brother, whom you sold to Egypt. Don't be upset or angry with yourselves, because you sold me. It was God who sent me here to save your lives. This is the second year of the famine. There are still five years more. I am Pharaoh's highest official, and the ruler of Egypt. Hurry up, go to my father, and tell him that God has made me the lord of Egypt; come to me without delay. You will live in the region of Goshen, close to me, you, your children, and your grandchildren, and all your sheep, and animals, and everything that you have. I will take care of you, because there are still five years of famine, and I will not let you be poor. You and Benjamin have seen that it is me, Joseph, who speaks to you. Tell my father of my glory in Egypt, and all that you have seen. Hurry and bring my father here". He embraced Benjamin, and they both wept. He then kissed all his brothers and wept upon them.

Joseph gave his brothers wagons and provisions for the journey. To each of them, he gave a change of clothing, but to Benjamin, he gave five changes of clothing and three hundred pieces of silver. To his father, he sent ten male donkeys loaded with the best things of Egypt, and ten female donkeys loaded with grain, bread, and provisions for his father on the journey. As he sent his brothers off on their way, he admonished them not to quarrel among themselves.

The brothers returned to their father Jacob in the land of Canaan and told him, "Joseph lives, and he is the ruler of Egypt!"

At first, Jacob could not believe them, until he saw the wagons that Joseph had sent to transport him. Then, he exclaimed, "My son Joseph is alive! I must go and see him, before I die!"

The brothers placed their father Jacob, their children, and their wives in the wagons, took along their livestock and their possessions, and went to the land of Goshen in Egypt. The group included the sons of Judah—Shelah, Pharez, and Zarah—and the two sons of Pharez, Hezron and Hamul.

Seventeen years later, Jacob, feeling that he would soon die, called his sons to bless them and tell them what would happen to them in the future. About Judah, he said, "Your brothers will praise you, and will bow down before you. Judah is like a lion,

killing his victim and returning to his den. He will hold the royal scepter, and his descendants will always rule".

Jacob's last words were to ask them to bury him in the cave of Machpelah, where Abraham, Sarah, Isaac, Rebekah, and Leah were buried. Jacob died at the age of one hundred and forty-seven. Joseph ordered the Egyptian physicians to embalm his father, a process, which took forty days. When the seventy days' period of mourning was over, Joseph asked permission from the Pharaoh to allow him to go to Canaan and bury his father there. Pharaoh gave him permission to go and bury Jacob as he had promised.

Jacob's body was accompanied on his last trip by his sons, their children, flocks and herds, all the officials of Pharaoh and members of his court, chariots and horsemen. Before crossing the Jordan, the funeral procession made a stop and mourned Jacob for seven days. Then, Judah and his brothers took him to Canaan and buried him in the cave of Machpelah.

After burying their father, they all returned to Canaan. Joseph's brothers feared that with Jacob now dead, Joseph would pay them back for the wrong that they had done to him.

They sent a message to Joseph, saying that Jacob, before his death, had told them to urge Joseph to forgive them. Judah and his brothers came to Joseph, flung themselves before him, and told him that they were prepared to be his slaves.

Joseph answered kindly, "Do not fear! Although you intended me harm, God intended it all for good, to assure the survival of many people. Don't worry; I will take care of you and your children".

Centuries later, Moses, in his last speech, said this about the tribe of Judah, "Lord, listen to their cry for help. Unite them again with the other tribes. Fight for them, Lord, and help them against their enemies".

According to the genealogies of Luke and Matthew, Jesus was a direct descendant of Judah.

2. (Ezra 10:23). 5th century B.C. Judah was a Levite who divorced his foreign wife, during the days of Ezra.

3. (Nehemiah 11:9). 5th century B.C. Judah, the son of Senuah, of the tribe of Benjamin, was the second in command of the city, after the return to Jerusalem from the Babylonian Exile.

4. (Nehemiah 12:8). 6th century B.C. Judah was a Levite who returned with Zerubbabel from the Babylonian Exile.

5. (Nehemiah 12:34). 5th century B.C. Judah was one of the leaders of the people who marched in the joyful procession, which celebrated the dedication of the rebuilt walls of Jerusalem, during the days of Nehemiah.

6. (Nehemiah 12:36). 5th century B.C. Judah was one of the priests who marched playing musical instruments behind Ezra the Scribe in the joyful procession, which celebrated the dedication of the rebuilt walls of Jerusalem, during the days of Nehemiah.

Judas

(Hebrew origin: *Celebrated*)

1. (Matthew 1:2). 17th century B.C. Judas is an alternative spelling for Judah, the son of Jacob.

2. (Matthew 10:4). A.D. 1st century. Judas Iscariot, son of Simon, one of the twelve apostles, was the man who betrayed Jesus to his enemies.

He was their treasurer, the man in charge of the group's money. On one occasion, he objected to Mary of Bethany anointing Jesus' feet with an expensive ointment, which, he said, could have been sold, and the proceeds given to the poor.

Judas Iscariot decided to betray Jesus. He went to the chief priests and the officers of the Temple guard, and he asked them, "What will you give me if I betray Jesus to you?" They counted thirty silver coins and gave them to him.

During the Last Supper, after they had had dinner, Jesus rose from the table, took off his outer garment, and tied a towel around his waist. He poured water into a washbasin, washed the feet of his disciples, and dried them with the towel.

Jesus said to his disciples, "If any of you wants to be great, he should be a servant to the others. The Son of man did not come to be served but to serve and to give his life for the redemption of the people".

He was silent for a moment, and then, with great emotion, he said, "Truly, I tell you, one of you will betray me".

The disciples looked at one another, not knowing whom he meant. One of the disciples, whom Jesus loved very much, was sitting next to him. Simon Peter gestured to him and said, "Ask him, about whom is he speaking".

The disciple asked Jesus, "Lord, who is he?"

Jesus answered, "He is the one to whom I will give a piece of bread, after I dip it". He dipped it and gave it to Judas Iscariot.

Judas asked, "Surely you don't mean me?"

Jesus answered, "So you say. Do what you have to do, and do it quickly". Judas got up and left immediately.

The others in the table didn't understand what Jesus had said to Judas. They assumed that Jesus had told Judas, the treasurer of the group, to go and buy what was needed for the Festival, or donate some alms to the poor.

Jesus prayed for his disciples to God, and afterward, he went with them across the Cedron Brook, to a garden. Judas Iscariot led a number of soldiers and Temple guards to the garden.

That night, Jesus and the apostles went to the Mount of Olives. They came to a place called Gethsemane. Jesus went a little farther, fell on his face to the ground, and prayed to God that, if it would be possible, to take away the cup of suffering from him, but to do not what he wanted but what God wanted. Then, he returned to the disciples and woke them up, telling them that the man who was betraying him had arrived.

Jesus was still speaking, when a crowd, armed with swords and staves, arrived led by Judas, who knew the place because Jesus had met there many times with his disciples. The betrayer approached Jesus and kissed him, which was the sign that he had arranged with the chief priests. Jesus said to him, "Judas, do you betray the Son of Man with a kiss?"

Jesus stepped forward and asked the soldiers, "Who are you looking for?'

They answered, "Jesus of Nazareth".

"I am he", said Jesus.

They stepped back and fell to the ground. Jesus asked them again, "Whom do you seek?"

"Jesus of Nazareth", they replied.

"I already told you that I am he. If you want me, let the others go".

Peter drew his sword and struck a slave of the High Priest, who was called Malchus, cutting off his right ear. Jesus rebuked Peter, saying, "Put your sword back in its place! Those who take the sword will die by the sword. Do you think that I will not drink the cup of suffering, which my Father has given me?"

The soldiers and the guards arrested Jesus, tied him up, and took him to the palace of Annas, the previous High Priest and father-in-law of Caiaphas, the current High Priest

When Judas heard that Jesus had been crucified, he repented, went to the chief priests and the elders, and tried to return the thirty silver coins. He said to them, "I have sinned by betraying an innocent man to death".

They answered, "We don't care about that. That is your problem".

Judas threw down the coins, left, and hanged himself. The chief priests picked up the coins and used them to buy a piece of land to be used as a cemetery for foreigners, because, as blood money, it could not be put in the treasury of the Temple.

After the death of Jesus, the disciples chose Matthias by lot to replace Judas.

3. (Matthew 13:55). A.D. 1st century. Judas— Mark spells his name as Juda (Mark 6:3)—was one of the four brothers of Jesus mentioned by the people of Nazareth, when they expressed their surprise and anger against Jesus for preaching in their synagogue. The other brothers were James, who became the leader of the early church in Jerusalem, Joses, and Simon.

Some scholars believe that Joses, James, Simon, and Judas were Joseph's children from a previous marriage. Others say that the terms "brothers" and "sisters", in these verses, refer to cousins or other close relatives.

It is probable that he was the author of the book of Jude.

4. (Luke 6:16). A.D. 1st century. Judas, son of James, was one of the twelve apostles, and, according to some scholars, the author of the book of Jude. Matthew calls him Lebbaeus, surnamed Thaddaeus (Matthew 10:3).

5. (Acts of the Apostles 5:37). A.D. 1st century. Judas of Galilee, according to the report of Gamaliel to the Jewish Council, was the leader of a rebellion against the Romans. He was killed and his followers scattered.

6. (Acts of the Apostles 9:11) A.D. 1st century. Judas, who lived in Straight Street, in the city of Damascus, sheltered in his house the blinded Saul. A Christian called Ananias was instructed by God in a vision to go to the house of Judas and restore Saul's sight by touching him.

7. (Acts of the Apostles 15:22). A.D. 1st century. Judas Barsabas was sent by the Jerusalem church, together with Silas, Paul, and Barnabas, to Antioch, carrying a letter from the Jerusalem church to the Gentile believers in Antioch, Syria, and Cilicia, exonerating them of the need for circumcision, and asking them to abstain from food offered to idols, from blood, from eating strangled animals, and from sexual immorality.

In Antioch, they gathered the congregation and read the letter. Barsabas and Silas, who were themselves prophets, spoke a long time to the believers and gave them encouragement. Barsabas then returned to Jerusalem, but Silas stayed on for a while in Antioch.

Jude

(Hebrew origin: *Celebrated*)

(Jude 1:1). A.D. 1st century. Jude, the author of the book of Jude, is identified by some scholars with the apostle Judas, son of James, whom Matthew calls Lebbaeus, surnamed Thaddaeus (Matthew 10:3).

Note: Other scholars believe that the author of the book was Judas, the brother of Jesus.

Judith

(Hebrew origin: *Jewess*)

(Genesis 26:34). 18th century B.C. Judith, daughter of Beeri, was one of the two Hittite wives of Esau—the other was Bashemath—whom he married, when he was forty years old. Both women made miserable the lives of Isaac and Rebekah.

Julia

(Word of Latin origin)

(Romans 16:15). A.D. 1st century. Julia was a Christian to whom Paul sent greetings in his letter to the Christians in Rome.

The apostle mentioned her in the same verse with four other persons—Philologus, Olympas, Nereus, and his sister—and "all the saints who were with them", which gives grounds to consider the possibility that Julia and her companions might have formed a small separate group within the larger Christian community of Rome.

Julius

(Word of Latin origin)

(Acts of the Apostles 27:1). A.D. 1st century. Julius, a centurion of the Augustus regiment, was in charge of Paul and other pris-oners who were being sent from Caesarea to Rome.

When the ship made a stopover in Sidon, Julius kindly allowed Paul to go ashore and visit his friends.

Later, when the ship was in Crete, the centurion disregarded the peril warnings of Paul and let the captain and the owner of the ship convince him to continue with the trip. A fierce storm threatened to sink the ship, but eventually, the ship ran aground in the island of Melita, today's Malta.

The soldiers wanted to kill the prisoners to thwart their escape. Julius prevented this and instructed all those prisoners who could swim to jump into the sea and swim to the land. Others followed on planks and broken pieces of the ship. Everybody was saved. When they arrived in Rome, their final destination, Julius delivered the prisoners to the captain of the guard.

Junia

(Word of Latin origin)

(Romans 16:7). A.D. 1st century. Junia was a Christian, residing in Rome, to whom Paul sent greetings in his epistle to the Romans.

The fact that Paul mentioned Junia together with Andronicus, calling them his "kinsmen" and his "fellow prisoners" could mean that they were man and wife. Paul added that they had become Christians, before he did.

Note: Some scholars, considering it unlikely that a woman would be among those referred to as apostles, argue that Junia was a male called Junias. However, the female name "Junia" occurs more than 250 times in Greek and Latin inscriptions found in Rome alone, while the male name "Junias" never appears. If the biblical name is indeed Junia, then it provides a direct challenge to the common assumption that women were not included among the apostles in the early church.

Jupiter

(Name of a Roman god, *Zeus* in Greek)

(Acts of the Apostles 14:12). During the

stay of Paul and Barnabas in the city of Lystra, Paul healed a cripple who had never walked in his life. This miracle so impressed the pagans in the city that they excitedly exclaimed that Barnabas was Jupiter, and Paul was Mercurius, who came down to earth in the likeness of men.

The priest of Jupiter brought oxen to sacrifice in front of them. Paul and Barnabas cried out that they were not gods but men, and that the people of the city should turn away from idols and believe in the living God.

Jushabhesed

(Hebrew origin: *Kindness will be returned*)

(1 Chronicles 3:20). 6th century B.C. His father Zerubbabel was the leader of the first group of captives who returned from the Babylonian Exile.

Jushabhesed descended from Jehoiachin, the king of Judah, who was taken to captivity in Babylon, after reigning for only three months.

Justus

(Latin origin: *Just*)

1. (Acts of the Apostles 1:23). A.D. 1st century. Justus, also called Joseph Barsabas, was one of the two candidates to replace Judas as the twelfth apostle. The apostles chose by lot Matthias, the other candidate.

2. (Acts of the Apostles 18:7). A.D. 1st century. Justus, a Corinthian Christian, hosted Paul in his house, which was right next to the synagogue.

3. (Colossians 4:11). A.D. 1st century. Justus, also called Jesus, a Christian of Jewish origin, was mentioned by Paul, in his letter to the Colossians, as a fellow worker for the Kingdom of God who was a comfort to him in his prison in Rome.

Kadmiel

(Hebrew origin: *In front of God*)

1. (Ezra 2:40). Unspecified date. Kadmiel was the ancestor of a clan of Levites who returned with Zerubbabel from the Babylonian Exile.
2. (Ezra 3:9). 6th century B.C. Kadmiel, a descendant of Judah, returned to Jerusalem with Zerubbabel and the High Priest Jeshua. He worked in the rebuilding of the Temple, aided by his sons.
3. (Nehemiah 9:4). 5th century B.C. Kadmiel, a Levite, stood with other Levites—Jeshua, Bani, Hashabniah, Sherebiah, Hodijah, Shebaniah, and Pethahiah—on a raised platform and prayed to God in a loud voice, during an assembly of public confession and fasting in the days of Ezra.

   Kadmiel was also one of the Levites who signed Nehemiah's solemn agreement to separate themselves from the foreigners living in the land, to refrain from intermarrying with them, to dedicate their firstborn to God, and other obligations (Nehemiah 10:9).
4. (Nehemiah 12:24). 6th century B.C. Kadmiel, a Levite, was the father of Jeshua and the grandfather of Jozabad and Ezer.

   His grandson Jozabad returned with Ezra from the Babylonian Exile and helped to count and weigh the silver and gold utensils of the Temple brought back from Babylon.

   His other grandson Ezer, ruler of Mizpah, helped to repair the walls of Jerusalem, during the days of Nehemiah.

Kallai

(Hebrew origin: *Lighthearted*)

(Nehemiah 12:20). 5th century B.C. Kallai was the head of a priestly clan, descended from Sallai, when Joiakim was the High Priest, in the days of Nehemiah.

Kareah

(Hebrew origin: *Bald*)

(Jeremiah 40:8). 7th century B.C. His sons Johanan and Jonathan were two of the captains of the defeated army of Judah, who came to Gedaliah, the Babylonian appointed governor, to be assured by him that everything would be well if they would serve the king of Babylon. His name is spelled Careah in the second book of Kings (2 Kings 25:23).

Kedar

(Hebrew origin: *Dusky*)

(Genesis 25:13). 18th century B.C. Kedar, grandson of Abraham and his Egyptian concubine Hagar, was one of the twelve sons of Ishmael. His eleven brothers were Nebajoth, Hadad, Mibsam, Mishma, Dumah, Massa, Adbeel, Tema, Jetur, Naphish, and Kedemah, all of them ancestors of great nations. His sister, Mahalath—also called Bashemath—married Esau, the son of Isaac.

Kedemah

(Hebrew origin: *Precedence*)

(Genesis 25:15). 18th century B.C. Kedemah, grandson of Abraham and his Egyptian concubine Hagar, was one of the twelve sons of Ishmael. His eleven brothers were Nebajoth, Kedar, Mibsam, Mishma, Dumah, Massa, Adbeel, Hadad, Jetur, Tema, and Naphish, all of them ancestors of great nations. His sister, Mahalath—also called Bashemath—married Esau, the son of Isaac.

Keilah

(Uncertain origin and meaning)

(1 Chronicles 4:19). Unspecified date. Keilah the Garmite was the grandson of Hodiah, the sister of a man named Naham.

Kelaiah

(Hebrew origin: *Insignificance*)

(Ezra 10:23). 5th century B.C. Kelaiah—

also called Kelita—was forced to divorce his foreign wife, during the days of Ezra.

Later, he was among the Levites who explained the Law to the people in Jerusalem, after Ezra the Scribe had read it, while standing on a wooden platform, in front of the open space, before the Water Gate (Nehemiah 8:7).

He was also one of the Levites who signed Nehemiah's solemn agreement to separate themselves from the foreigners living in the land, to refrain from intermarrying with them, to dedicate their firstborn to God, and other obligations (Nehemiah 10:10).

Kelita

(Hebrew origin: *Maiming*)

(Ezra 10:23). 5th century B.C. Kelita—also called Kelaiah—was forced to divorce his foreign wife, during the days of Ezra. (Please see the entry for Kelaiah [Ezra 10:23].)

Kemuel

(Hebrew origin: *Raised by God*)

1. (Genesis 22:21). 19th century B.C. Kemuel, the father of Aram, was one of the eight children born to Milcah, the wife of Nahor, Abraham's brother.
2. (Numbers 34:24). 13th century B.C. Kemuel, son of Shiphtan, leader of the tribe of Ephraim, was one of the men appointed by Moses to apportion the land of Canaan among the tribes.
3. (1 Chronicles 27:17). 10th century B.C. His son Hashabiah was in charge of the Levites, during the reign of King David.

Kenan

(Hebrew origin: *Nest*)

(1 Chronicles 1:2). Unspecified date. Kenan, son of Enosh and grandson of Seth, Adam's third son, was seventy years old, when his son Mahalaleel was born.

Kenan died at the age of nine hundred and ten, after having had more sons and daughters.

In the book of Genesis, he is called Cainan, son of Enos (Genesis 5:9).

Kenaz

(Hebrew origin: *Hunter*)

1. (Genesis 36:11). 16th century B.C. Kenaz, the ancestor of an Edomite clan, was the son of Eliphaz and the grandson of Esau and his wife Adah, daughter of Elon the Hittite. Kenaz' brothers were Gatam, Teman, Zepho, Omar, and Amalek.
2. (Genesis 36:42). Unspecified date. Kenaz was a chief of an Edomite clan.
3. (Joshua 15:17). 13th century B.C. Kenaz, a descendant of Judah, was the younger brother of Caleb and the father of Othniel and Seraiah.
4. (1 Chronicles 4:15). Unspecified date. Kenaz, son of Elah, was a descendant of Judah.

Kerenhappuch

(Hebrew origin: *Horn of cosmetic*)

(Job 42:14). Unspecified date. Kerenhappuch was one of the three beautiful daughters born to Job, after he recuperated his health and his wealth. The other two daughters were Kezia and Jemima. The three girls shared their father's inheritance with their brothers.

Keros

(Hebrew origin: *Ankled*)

(Ezra 2:44). Unspecified date. Keros was the ancestor of a clan of Temple servants that returned with Zerubbabel from the Babylonian Exile.

Keturah

(Hebrew origin: *Perfumed*)

(Genesis 25:1). 19th century B.C. Keturah was the woman whom Abraham married, after the death of Sarah. Some scholars identify her with Hagar, Abraham's concubine.

Abraham and Keturah had six sons: Zimran, Jokshan, Medan, Midian, Ishbak, and Shuah. They received gifts from their father, but Isaac remained his sole heir.

Kezia

(Hebrew origin: *Peeled*)

(Job 42:14). Unspecified date. Kezia was one of the three beautiful daughters born to Job, after he recuperated his health and his wealth. The other two daughters were Kerenhappuch and Jemima. The three girls shared their father's inheritance with their brothers.

Kish

(Hebrew origin: *Bow*)

1. (1 Samuel 9:1). 11th century B.C. Kish, of the tribe of Benjamin, was a wealthy and powerful man in his community.

   One day some of Kish's asses were lost, and he sent his son Saul, a tall and good-looking young man, to search for them. This search led to Saul's meeting with the prophet Samuel, and his anointment as king.

   It is not clear, which was the name of the father of Kish. The first book of Samuel says that it was Abiel (1 Samuel 9:1). The first book of Chronicles calls him Jehiel (1 Chronicles 9:35), and it mentions that he lived in Gibeon with his wife Maachah.

   In a different verse in the same first book of Chronicles (1 Chronicles 8:33), it says that Ner, the son of Jehiel, was the father of Kish.

   Kish is called Cis, in the book of Acts of the Apostles (Acts of the Apostles 1:21).
2. (1 Chronicles 23:21). Unspecified date. Kish, son of Mahli, was a descendant of Merari, the son of Levi. His sons—one of them was Jerahmeel—married the daughters of his brother Eleazar, who had died without sons.
3. (2 Chronicles 29:12). 8th century B.C. Kish, son of Abdi, a descendant of Merari, lived, during the reign of King Hezekiah of Judah. He was one of the Levites who assembled all the other Levites to make themselves ritually clean, and to purify the Temple.
4. (Esther 2:5). Unspecified date. Kish, a Benjamite, was the father of Shimei, and an ancestor of Mordecai and Esther.

Kishi

(Hebrew origin: *My bow*)

(1 Chronicles 6:44). 11th century B.C. Kishi—also called Kushaiah (1 Chronicles 15:17)—was a descendant of Merari.

His son Ethan was one of the Levites appointed by King David to play trumpets and cymbals in the House of the Lord. His descendants were gatekeepers in the Temple.

Kittim

(Hebrew origin: *From Cyprus*)

(Genesis 10:4). Unspecified date. Kittim, the son of Javan, was the brother of Tarshish, Elishah, and Dodanim.

Kohath

(Hebrew origin: *Allied*)

(Genesis 46:11). 17th century B.C. Kohath, one of the three sons of Levi and the ancestor of a clan of Levites, was one of the seventy Israelites who immigrated to Egypt with Jacob.

His brothers were Gershon and Merari. His sons were Izhar, Hebron, Uzziel, and Amram, the father of Moses. His grandson Korah, son of Izhar, was one of the leaders of the rebellion against Moses.

Kohath died at the age of one hundred and thirty. His descendant Uriel was one of the Levites chosen by King David to carry the Ark of the Covenant to Jerusalem, by means of poles upon their shoulders. They were accompanied by singers and musicians.

Kolaiah

(Hebrew origin: *Voice of God*)

1. (Nehemiah 11:7). Unspecified date. Kolaiah, son of Maaseiah and father of Pedaiah, was an ancestor of Sallu, a Benjamite who settled in Jerusalem, after his return from the Babylonian Exile.
2. (Jeremiah 29:21). 7th century B.C. His son Ahab was a false prophet in Babylon, during the days of Jeremiah.

   Ahab and Zedekiah, son of Maaseiah, were accused by the prophet Jeremiah of doing vile things, committing adultery and prophesying falsehoods. Jeremiah predicted that their death, by burning at Nebuchadnezzar's command, would be mentioned as a curse by the exiled Judean community in Babylon.

Korah

(Hebrew origin: *Baldness*)

1. (Genesis 36:5). 18th century B.C. Korah was one of the three sons—the others were Jaalam and Jeush—who were born to Aholibamah, one of Esau's wives, in Canaan, before the family moved to Edom, where the brothers became heads of clans.

2. (Genesis 36:16). 17th century B.C. Korah, an Edomite chieftain, was the son of Eliphaz and the grandson of Esau and Adah.

3. (Exodus 6:21). 13th century B.C. Korah, the ancestor of the Levite clan of the Korhites, was one of the three sons of Izhar. His brothers were Nepheg and Zichri.

His father Izhar—called Amminadab in the first book of Chronicles (1 Chronicles 6:22)—was a younger brother of Amram, Moses' father, thus, making Korah a first cousin of Moses and Aaron.

Korah, together with three members of the tribe of Reuben—the brothers Dathan and Abiram, sons of Eliab, and On, son of Peleth—at the head of a group of two hundred fifty renowned men, accused Moses and Aaron of raising themselves over the rest of the people.

Moses threw himself on the ground and said to the rebels, "Tomorrow, the Lord will show us who belongs to Him, who can come close to him. Take your fire pans, you Korah, and all your followers, and put incense and fire in it, and present them to the Lord tomorrow, and we will see who will the Lord choose to make holy. You have gone too far, sons of Levi! It seems that it is not enough for you that God has set you apart from the community to serve him, and brought you near him. You also want the priesthood? You are not standing

against Aaron, you have banded against the Lord!"

Moses called Dathan and Abiram to talk with them, but they refused to come, saying, "Isn't it enough that you took us out of Egypt, a land that flowed with milk and honey, to kill us in the wilderness, that you also want to lord it over us? Even if you had brought us to a land of milk and honey, and given us possession of fields and vineyards, should you gouge out those men's eyes? We will not come!"

Moses became very angry and said to God, "Don't accept their offerings. I have never hurt any of them, nor have I taken even one of their donkeys!"

The next day, the rebels, with their fire pans, stood in the door of the Tabernacle, with Moses and Aaron, surrounded by the people.

The Presence of God appeared to the whole community, and God said to Moses and Aaron, "Stand apart from this community that I may annihilate them immediately".

Moses and Aaron threw themselves to the ground and said, "O God, do not be angry with the whole community because of the sins of one man".

God said to them, "Tell the community to get away from the tents of Korah, Dathan, and Abiram".

Moses got up and went toward the tents of Dathan and Abiram, followed by the leaders of the people. He then asked the people to stay away from the tents of the rebels, so that they should not also be destroyed.

Dathan and Abiram came out and stood at the entrance of their tents, with their wives, sons, and small children.

Moses then spoke, "This is how you will know that God has sent me to do all these things. They are not done by my own choice. If these men will die of a natural death, then I have not been sent by God, but if God does something never before seen, so that the earth will open and swallow them up with all they own, this will prove that the rebels have offended God".

As soon as he finished speaking, the earth opened, and Korah, his followers, their tents and all their possessions fell inside. The earth closed upon them and they all perished.

Eleazar the Priest took the fire pans of the rebels and made with them broad plates for the covering of the altar, to remind the people that only the descendants of Aaron could offer incense to God.

The sons of Korah, Assir, Elkanah, and Abiasaph, did not take part in the rebellion and were not killed. Their descendants were singers and musicians in the Temple.

4. (1 Chronicles 2:43). Unspecified date. Korah was the son of Hebron, of the tribe of Judah, and brother of Tappuah, Rekem, and Shema.

Kore

(Hebrew origin: *Crier*)

1. (1 Chronicles 9:19). 11th century B.C. Kore, son of Ebiasaph, was the father of Shallum, the Levite in charge of the gate-keepers of the Tabernacle, during the reign of King David.

Kore's grandchildren, also gatekeepers, were Zechariah, Jediael, Zebadiah, Jathniel, Elam, Jehohanan, and Elioenai. His son Shallum was called Meshelemiah in the first book of Chronicles (1 Chronicles 26:1).

2. (2 Chronicles 31:14). 8th century B.C. Kore was one of the Levites chosen by King Hezekiah to distribute the gifts, tithes, and offerings that the people brought to the Temple. His father Imnah was the keeper of the East Gate of the Temple.

Koz

(Hebrew origin: *Thorn*)

1. (Ezra 2:61). Unspecified date. Koz was an ancestor of a family whose members, during the days of Zerubbabel, were rejected as priests, because no proof of their claim was found in the records of the genealogy.

2. (Nehemiah 3:4). 6th century B.C. Koz was the grandfather of Meremoth, son of Urijah, who helped to rebuild the walls of Jerusalem, during the days of Nehemiah.

Kushaiah

(Hebrew origin: *Entrapped of God*)

(1 Chronicles 15:17). 11th century B.C. Kushaiah—also called Kishi (1 Chronicles 6:44)—was a descendant of Merari. His son Ethan was one of the Levites appointed by King David to play trumpets and cymbals in the House of the Lord. His descendants were gatekeepers in the Temple.

Laadah

(Uncertain origin and meaning)

(1 Chronicles 4:21). 17th century B.C. Laadah, one of the sons of Shelah, Judah's youngest son, was the founder of Mareshah. His brothers were Er, Jokim, Joash, and Saraph. His descendants were experts in the production of fine linen.

Laadan

(Hebrew origin: Uncertain meaning)

1. (1 Chronicles 7:26). Unspecified date. Laadan, of the tribe of Ephraim, was a son of Tahan. His son Ammihud was an ancestor of Joshua.

2. (1 Chronicles 23:7). 16th century B.C. Laadan—called Libni in the book of Exodus (Exodus 6:17)—of the clan of the Gershonites, was the father of Jahath (1 Chronicles 6:20), and the brother of Shimei.

   His descendant Asaph was one of the Levites appointed by King David to be in charge of the singers in the House of the Lord. His other descendants—Jehiel, Zetham, and Joel—were Levites who worked in the Tabernacle, during the reign of David.

Laban

(Hebrew origin: *White*)

(Genesis 24:29). 19th century B.C. Laban, a sly and greedy man, was the son of Bethuel, Abraham's nephew who had settled with his family in the town of Haran, situated in the south of today's Turkey.

When Isaac was forty years old and still unmarried, Abraham, who did not want his son to marry any of the local Canaanite girls, sent his trusted servant Eliezer to Haran with instructions to find a bride for Isaac among his relatives.

Eliezer took with him ten loaded camels and set out to Haran. When he arrived to the town, he made the camels kneel down by the well outside the city. He said to himself, "If a girl comes to whom I will say, 'Please, lower your jar that I may drink', and she replies, 'Drink and I will also water your camels', she will be the one that God has chosen for Isaac".

He had scarcely finished speaking his thoughts aloud, when Rebekah, the daughter of Bethuel, came carrying a jar on her shoulder. She descended to the spring, filled her jar and climbed back up. Eliezer ran to her and asked her if he could drink a little water from her jar.

"Drink, my lord", she said.

After he had drunk, she said, "I will also bring water for your camels, until they finish drinking".

Eliezer gazed at her silently, while she gave water to the camels. When she finished, he gave her a gold earring and two gold bracelets, and he asked her, "Whose daughter are you? Is there room in your father's house for us to stay?"

She replied, "I am the daughter of Bethuel. There is plenty of straw and feed at home, and also room to spend the night".

The man bowed low and blessed the Lord for having guided him to the house of his master's kinsmen. Rebekah ran to her mother's house and told her relatives what had happened.

Laban, her brother, saw the earring and the bracelets on his sister's hands and ran to the well to invite the man to come to the house.

Eliezer entered the house, while his camels were unloaded and given straw. Water was brought to bathe Eliezer's feet and the feet of the men with him.

When food was set before him, he refused to eat, until he told them how Abraham had send him to find a bride for his son and heir, and how he had realized that Rebekah was the intended one.

Laban and Bethuel answered, "The matter was decreed by God; we cannot speak to you bad or good. Here is Rebekah, take her with you and go, and let her be a wife to your master's son, as the Lord has spoken".

When Eliezer heard these words, he bowed low to the ground before God. Then, he took out more objects of silver and gold, and clothing, and gave them to Rebekah. He also gave presents to Laban and to his mother. Eliezer and his men ate and drank, and they spent the night.

Early next morning, they announced that they would depart. Rebekah's mother and Laban asked if Rebekah could stay with them for another ten days. Eliezer answered, "Please do not delay our departure".

Many years later, Rebekah, fearing that Esau would kill Jacob for having deceived Isaac into blessing Jacob, decided to send her younger son away to her brother Laban in Haran. She went to Isaac and complained that she was weary of her life because of the Hittite wives of Esau, and if Jacob would also marry one of the local girls, she had no wish to continue living.

Isaac called Jacob, blessed him, and said, "You shall not marry any Canaanite girl. Go to Paddan-Aram, to the house of Bethuel, your mother's father, and marry one of the daughters of your uncle Laban".

Jacob left Beersheba and set out for his uncle's house. Upon arriving to Haran, Jacob saw shepherds next to a well and asked them if they knew Laban. They answered that they did, and they added that Rachel, Laban's daughter, was approaching with her father's sheep. Jacob went to the well, rolled the stone from its opening, watered the sheep, kissed Rachel, and wept, when he told her that he was her relative. She ran home and told her father, who came out to see Jacob, embraced him, and brought him to his house.

Four weeks later, during which time Jacob had fallen in love with his beautiful cousin Rachel, Laban said to Jacob, "You are my relative, but you should not work for me for nothing! What shall your wages be?"

Jacob answered, "I will serve you seven years for your younger daughter Rachel".

"It is better that I should give her to you than to an outsider. Stay with me", said Laban.

The seven years that Jacob worked for Laban seemed to him like only a few days, so great was his love for her. When the seven years were over, Jacob told Laban, "Give me Rachel now, because my time has been fulfilled".

Laban made a wedding feast and invited all the people of the place. After the wedding night, Jacob woke up to find that the woman next to him was not Rachel but her older sister Leah. When he complained that he had been deceived, Laban explained that it was the custom of the land that the elder daughter should be married before the younger, but that he would allow Rachel to marry him, a week later, with the condition that Jacob should work another seven years for Laban.

When the second seven years' period was over, Jacob told Laban, "I wish to return to my own homeland with my wives and children, for whom I have served you".

"I know that God has blessed me for your sake. Name your wages and I will give them to you", said Laban.

"You know how I have served you. You had a small flock, before I came to you, and it has grown tremendously under my care. Now, I have to look out for my own interests", said Jacob.

"What shall I pay you?"

"You don't have to pay me anything. If you agree to my proposal, I will continue to take care of your flock. I will go through all your flock today and remove every speckled, spotted, and brown lamb, and every spotted and speckled goat. That is all the pay I want. In the future, you will easily see if I have been honest. When you come to check my wages, any goat that is not speckled and spotted, and any sheep, which is not brown, you will know that it has been stolen".

"It's a deal", answered Laban. That same day, he removed all the goats that were speckled, spotted, or that had some white on them, and all the brown sheep, and he gave them to his sons. He then went away from Jacob as far as he could travel in three days. Jacob took care of the rest of Laban's flock.

Jacob took some green branches of poplar, hazel, and chestnut trees, and he stripped off some of the bark so that the branches had white stripes on them. He placed these branches in front of the flocks at their drinking troughs, so that they would look at them when they mated, when they came to drink. All the young animals that were born were streaked, speckled, and spotted. In this way, he built up his own flock and became a very wealthy man.

After six years, Jacob, who now owned much cattle, slaves, camels, and donkeys, felt that Laban's sons were jealous of his wealth, and that Laban himself looked at him differently than before. He called his wives, Leah and Rachel, and told them that they would all go to Canaan.

Leah and Rachel answered, "There is nothing left for us to inherit from our father. He treats us like strangers. He sold us and has spent all our money. All this wealth that God has taken from our father belongs to us and to our children. Do whatever God has told you".

Jacob gathered all his possessions and his flocks, put his sons and his wives on the camels, and left Paddan-Aram. Rachel secretly took her father's idols, taking advantage that Laban had gone to shear his sheep.

When Laban discovered that Jacob was gone, he and his men set out in pursuit and caught up with Jacob and his family seven days later, near the hills of Gilead. Laban reproached Jacob for taking away his daughters in secret, without letting him say goodbye, or kiss his grandchildren.

"I understand", he said, "that you wish to return to your home, but why did you have to steal my household gods?"

"I was afraid that you might take your daughters away from me. If you find that anyone here has your gods, that person will be put to death", answered Jacob, not knowing that Rachel had stolen the idols. Laban searched the tents but did not find the idols, because Rachel was sitting upon them.

Jacob and Laban made a covenant between them, which they celebrated by gathering stones into a heap, making a sacrifice, and eating. Then, they parted in peace: Laban returned home, and Jacob continued his voyage to Canaan.

Lael

(Hebrew origin: *Belonging to God*)

(Numbers 3:24). 14th century B.C. Lael was the father of Eliasaph, the head of the Gershonite clan of the Levites. During the wanderings of the Israelites in the wilderness, the clan was responsible for the Tabernacle, the tent, its covering, and the screen for the entrance.

Lahad

(Hebrew origin: *To glow*)

(1 Chronicles 4:2). Unspecified date. Lahad, a descendant of Judah, of the clan of the Zorathites, was the son of Jahath and the brother of Ahumai.

Lahmi

(Hebrew origin: *Foodful*)

(1 Chronicles 20:5). 10th century B.C. Lahmi was a Philistine warrior, brother of Goliath, whose spear had a shaft like a weaver's beam. He was killed in battle by Elhanan, son of Jair.

Laish

(Hebrew origin: *Lion*)

(1 Samuel 25:44). 11th century B.C. His son Phalti—also called Phaltiel (2 Samuel 3:15)—married Michal, King Saul's daughter, after Saul had driven away her husband David.

Years later, when David reigned in Hebron, he forced Ishbosheth, Saul's son, to have Abner bring back Michal to him. Phalti followed her weeping, until Abner abruptly told him to return.

Lamech

(Hebrew origin: Uncertain meaning)

1. (Genesis 4:18). Antediluvian. Lamech, son of Methusael, a descendant of Cain, married two wives: Adah and Zillah.

   Adah was the mother of Jabal, the ancestor of those who lived in tents and raise cattle, and Jubal, the ancestor of the musicians who played the harp and the organ.

Zillah was the mother of Tubalcain, an expert artisan of cooper and iron, and a girl named Naamah.

Lamech boasted to his wives that he had killed two men who had wounded him, saying that, if Cain would be avenged sevenfold, he, Lamech, would be seventy-sevenfold.

2. (Genesis 5:25). Antediluvian. Lamech, son of Methuselah, a descendant of Seth, was the father of Noah. He died at the age of seven hundred and seventy-seven.

Lapidoth

(Hebrew origin: *Torches*)

(Judges 4:4). 12th century B.C. Lapidoth was the husband of Deborah, the judge, prophetess, and leader of Israel. When Jabin, king of Hazor, threatened war, Deborah designated Barak, son of Abinoam, to be the commander of the Israelite army, which was composed of ten thousand men drawn from the tribes of Naphtali and Zebulun.

The army of Jabin was defeated, and its commander, Sisera, was killed by a Kenite woman called Jael, while hiding in her tent from the victorious Israelite army.

Lazarus

(Latin version of the Hebrew *Eleazar* [*God helped*])

1. (Luke 16:20). Lazarus is an imaginary beggar, sick and hungry, mentioned by Jesus in a parable, who was comforted by Abraham, after his death, while the rich man who had despised him suffered the torments of hell.

2. (John 11:1). A.D. 1st century. Lazarus lived in the town of Bethany, about two miles away from Jerusalem, with his two sisters, Mary and Martha, all three of whom were held by Jesus in great affection. One day, he fell gravely ill, and his sisters sent Jesus a message, telling him that their brother was on his deathbed.

Jesus told his disciples, "This illness will not end in death, but in the glory of God, and in the glorification of the Son of God". And he didn't depart from where he was.

Two days later, Jesus said to his disciples, "Let's go back to Judea".

His disciples said to him, "Master, the Jews tried to stone you, and you wish to go there again?"

Jesus said, "Aren't there twelve hours in the day? If a man walks, during the day he will not stumble, because he sees the light of this world. But if he walks, during the night, he will stumble, because there is no light". He added, "Our friend Lazarus is sleeping. I will go and wake him up".

"If he is sleeping, he must be getting well", said his disciples, not understanding that Jesus meant that Lazarus had died.

Jesus said to them plainly, "Lazarus is dead. I am glad for your sakes that I was not there, so that you will believe. Let's go to him".

Thomas, who was also called Didymus, said to the other disciples, "Let us also go, so that we may die with him".

When Jesus arrived, he found that Lazarus had been buried four days before. The sisters' house was full with people who had come to comfort them about their brother's death.

When Martha heard that Jesus was coming, she went out to greet him, while her sister remained inside the house.

Martha said to Jesus, "Lord, if you had been here, my brother would not have died, but, even now, I know that whatever you will ask of God, God will grant it to you".

Jesus answered, "Your brother will come back to life".

"I know he will do that, at the end of the days", said Martha.

Jesus said to her, "I am the Resurrection and the life. Whoever believes in me, will live, even if he dies; and whoever believes in me, will never die. Do you believe this?"

"Yes, Lord", she said, "I believe that you are the Messiah, the Son of God, who has come to the world".

Martha went into the house and said to her sister Mary's ear, "The Master has arrived, and he is calling you". Mary rose and hurried out of the house. The people who had come to console them followed her, thinking that she was going to the grave to weep there.

Mary arrived to where Jesus was. She fell at his feet weeping and repeated what her sister had said, "Lord, if you had been here, my brother would not have died".

Jesus saw her weeping, and he also saw that the people who came with her were crying, and he was deeply moved. He asked them, "Where did you bury him?"

They took him to the grave, which was a cave with its entrance closed by a stone. Jesus looked at it and wept. The people said, "See how he loved him!" Others said, "He restored sight to a blind man. Couldn't he have prevented the death of this man?"

Jesus ordered, "Take away the stone".

Martha said, "Lord, he has been dead already four days. There is bound to be a bad smell".

Jesus replied, "Didn't I say to you that, if you would believe, you would see the glory of God?"

They moved the stone from the entrance to the cave. Jesus lifted up his eyes and said, "Father, thank you for listening to me. I know that you always hear me, but I have said this, because of the people who are standing next to me, so that they should believe that you sent me". Then, in a loud voice, he said, "Lazarus, come out!"

Lazarus came out, with his hands, feet, and face wrapped in his burial clothes. "Untie him", said Jesus, "and let him go".

Many of the people who saw this became believers. Others went to the Pharisees and told them what Jesus had done.

Lazarus was present at the dinner where his sister Mary took a pound of very expensive ointment, poured them on Jesus' feet, and dried them with her hair. The whole house was filled with the perfume of the ointment. This caused Judas Iscariot to protest against what he considered a waste of money, but Jesus told him to leave her alone, because she had kept the ointment for the day of his burial.

Many people came to the house, not only to see Jesus, but also out of curiosity to meet Lazarus, who had been raised from the dead.

The chief priests took notice of this and considered killing Lazarus, because on his account, many people were rejecting them and believing in Jesus.

Leah

(Hebrew origin: *Weary*)

(Genesis 29:16). 18th century B.C. Leah was the eldest daughter of Laban, Jacob's uncle. She was weak eyed and not as pretty as her younger sister Rachel.

Her cousin Jacob, who had recently come to Haran and was staying with them, fell in love with Rachel and agreed to serve Laban seven years for her.

The seven years that Jacob worked for Laban seemed to him like only a few days, so great was his love for her. When the seven years were over, Jacob told Laban, "Give me Rachel now, because my time has been fulfilled".

The day of the wedding, Laban made a great feast, but, instead of Rachel, he sent Leah in her place disguised behind a veil.

After the wedding night, Jacob woke up to find that the woman next to him was not Rachel but her older sister Leah. When he complained that he had been deceived, Laban explained that it was the custom of the land that the elder daughter should be married before the younger, but that he would allow Rachel to marry him, a week later, with the condition that Jacob should work another seven years for Laban.

Jacob did not hide the fact that he loved Rachel and hated Leah, but it was Leah who gave him sons, while Rachel remained barren. Leah called her first son Reuben, *See a son,* thinking that now her husband would love her. She called her second son Simeon, *Has heard,* saying that God had given her that child, because he had heard that she was hated. Her third son was Levi, and her fourth one Judah.

Rachel became envious of her sister and said to Jacob, "Give me children, or I shall die". Jacob was angry and answered, "Can I take the place of God, who has denied you the fruit of your womb?"

Rachel said, "Take my maid Bilhah as a concubine, so that through her, I too may have children". Bilhah had two children, Dan and Naphtali, whom Rachel considered hers.

When Leah saw that she had stopped bearing children, she followed her sister's example and gave her maid Zilpah to Jacob as a concubine. Zilpah gave birth to Gad and Asher, both of whom were born in Paddan-Aram.

One day, Reuben, Leah's oldest son, brought some mandrakes from the field and gave them to his mother.

Rachel saw the mandrakes and said to Leah, "Please give me some of your son's mandrakes".

Leah answered, "Is it not enough that you have taken my husband, that you would also take my son's mandrakes?"

Rachel replied, "If you give me those mandrakes, I promise that Jacob will spend the night with you".

When Jacob came home from the field that evening, Leah went out to meet him and said, "You are to sleep with me, because I have hired you with my son's mandrakes".

That night, Leah conceived, and when the time came, she gave birth to Issachar. Later, she gave birth to another son, Zebulun, and a daughter, Dinah.

Time went by, and Jacob, now a very rich man, owner of many cattle, camels, asses, maids, and servants, felt that Laban's sons were jealous of his wealth, and that Laban himself looked at him differently than before. He decided to return to Canaan with his two wives, his two concubines, and his children.

When Laban discovered that Jacob was gone, he and his relatives set out in pursuit and caught up with Jacob and his family seven days later, overtaking them in the hills of Gilead. That night, Laban dreamed that God told him not to attempt anything with Jacob, good or bad.

The next morning, Laban met Jacob and reproached him for taking away his daughters in secret, without letting him kiss them goodbye. He also accused Jacob of stealing his house idols, which, unbeknownst to Jacob, had been taken by Rachel.

Jacob answered that he had been afraid that Laban would have taken his daughters away by force, and he denied that he had taken the idols, saying that, if Laban would find the idols, the persons that had taken them would die. Laban searched the tents but did not find the idols, because Rachel was sitting upon them.

Jacob and Laban made a covenant of friendship between them, which they celebrated by gathering stones into a heap, making a sacrifice, and eating. Then, they parted in peace: Laban returned home, and Jacob continued his voyage to Canaan.

Jacob sent messengers to his brother Esau, who was living in Edom, announcing that he was returning from his long sojourn with Laban. The messengers returned, saying that Esau was coming to meet him with four hundred men.

Fearing that Esau wanted to revenge himself, Jacob sent servants to Esau with gifts of goats, rams, camels, bulls, asses, and foals. He made his wives, concubines and children cross to the other side of the Jabbok River, and he stayed behind alone. That night, Jacob wrestled with a mysterious stranger until, daybreak. Limping, because the stranger had damaged his hip, Jacob returned to join his family. He put his concubines and their children in the front, followed by Leah and her children, and, at the back, he placed Rachel and her son Joseph.

When he saw Esau approaching with his troop of four hundred men, Jacob bowed to the ground seven times. Esau ran to him and embraced him, and both brothers wept. After Jacob had presented his family to his brother, Esau asked him why Jacob sent him all those animals. Jacob told him that they were a gift to appease him. Esau graciously refused the gift, saying that he had enough, but Jacob insisted and Esau accepted.

Esau invited Jacob and his family to come with him to Seir, but Jacob told him that he should go ahead and that he, Jacob, would follow at a pace suitable to his children and his young animals. Esau returned that day to Seir, but Jacob did not follow, and he settled near Shechem.

When, years later Leah died, Jacob buried her in the cave of Machpelah, where Abraham, Sarah, Isaac, and Rebekah were also buried.

Her son Judah was the ancestor of the tribe of Judah.

Lebana

(Hebrew origin: *White*)

(Nehemiah 7:48). Unspecified date. Lebana, or Lebanah, was the ancestor of a clan of Temple servants that returned with Zerubbabel from the Babylonian Exile.

Lebanah

(Hebrew origin: *White*)

(Ezra 2:45). Unspecified date. Lebanah, or Lebana, was the ancestor of a clan of Temple servants that returned with Zerubbabel from the Babylonian Exile. His name was also spelled Lebana.

Lebbaeus

(Uncertain origin and meaning)

(Matthew 10:3). A.D. 1st century. Lebbaeus, surnamed Thaddaeus, was the name, by which, the evangelist Matthew called the apostle Judas, the son of James (Luke 6:16).

According to some scholars, Lebbaeus was the author of the book of Jude. Other scholars disagree and state that the author of the book was Judas, the brother of Jesus.

Legion

(Latin origin: *A Roman regiment*)

(Mark 5:9). The legion was a standard unit in the Roman army. It had between four thou-

sand to six thousand infantry soldiers supported by a cavalry contingent. It can be considered the tactical ancestor of the modern army division.

When Jesus came to the territory of the Gadarenes, on the other side of the lake, he met a man who came out of the burial grounds possessed by demons.

Jesus asked him, "What is your name?"

The demons in the man answered, "Our name is Legion, for we are many".

Jesus drove the demons out of the men and into a large herd of pigs feeding nearby. The whole herd of about two thousand pigs rushed down the side of the cliff, into the lake, and was drowned.

The people in the town heard this, came, and saw the man who had been possessed now clothed and in his right mind. Afraid, they asked Jesus to leave their territory.

As Jesus was getting into the boat, the healed man begged him to let him come with him. Jesus refused and told him to go back to his home and tell his family what the Lord had done for him. The man left and went all through the Decapolis—the ten towns—telling how Jesus had cured him, and all who heard him were amazed.

Lehabim

(Hebrew origin: *Flames*)

(Genesis 10:13). Unspecified date. Lehabim was the son of Mizraim, *Egypt*, and grandson of Ham.

Lemuel

(Hebrew origin: *Belonging to God*)

(Proverbs 31:1). King Lemuel—identified by some scholars as King Solomon—was advised by his mother not to waste his energy pursuing women, to stay away from wine and strong drink, which perverts sound judgment, to judge righteously, and to defend the poor and the needy.

Letushim

(Hebrew origin: *Oppressed*)

(Genesis 25:3). Unspecified date. Letushim, son of Dedan, was a descendant of Abraham and Keturah, the woman whom Abraham married, after Sarah died.

Letushim's brothers were Asshurim and Leummim.

Leummim

(Hebrew origin: *Communities*)

(Genesis 25:3). Unspecified date. Leummim, son of Dedan, was a descendant of Abraham and Keturah, the woman whom Abraham married, after Sarah died.

Leummim's brothers were Asshurim and Letushim.

Levi

(Hebrew origin: *Attached*)

1. (Genesis 29:34). 17th century B.C. Levi, the third son of Jacob and Leah, was the ancestor of the priests of the Temple—through his son Kohath—and of the Levites, who were servants of the Temple—through his sons Gershon and Merari.

Levi was the full brother of Issachar, Reuben, Judah, Simeon, and Zebulun, sons of Leah. His half brothers were Gad and Asher, sons of Zilpah; Dan and Naphtali, sons of Bilhah; and Benjamin and Joseph, sons of Rachel. His sister was Dinah, daughter of Leah.

After Jacob and his family came to Canaan, and settled near Shechem, Dinah became friendly with the local girls and visited their city.

Shechem, son of Hamor, the Hivite ruler of Shechem, saw her, seized her, and raped her. Afterward, Shechem, having fallen in love with Dinah, asked his father Hamor to speak to Jacob and ask for Dinah's hand.

The sons of Jacob took charge of the negotiations and deceitfully agreed to Hamor's request on condition that Hamor, Shechem, and all the men in their city should first be circumcised. Hamor and his son agreed to this condition, and they, together with all the men in the city, were circumcised.

Simeon and Levi considered that Shechem had treated their sister as a harlot. They took advantage of the weakened condition of the circumcised men to revenge their sister's lost honor; they slaughtered all the men in the city, including Hamor and Shechem, took their sheep, oxen, and all their other possessions, and brought Dinah back to her home.

Jacob, fearing that the actions of his sons had placed them all in great danger, left Shechem and took the family to Hebron.

Levi and his brothers were involved in the events that led to Joseph being taken as a slave to Egypt. (For the detailed story of Joseph and his brothers, please see the entry for Joseph.)

Years later, when there was a famine in the land, he and his brothers were sent by Jacob to Egypt to buy corn. Joseph, who was now the second most powerful man in the country, recognized them, forgave them, and invited them to settle in Egypt.

The brothers placed their father Jacob, their children, and their wives in the wagons; they took along their livestock and their possessions and went to the land of Goshen in Egypt. On their way, they stopped in Beersheba, where Jacob offered sacrifices to the God of his father Isaac.

Levi and his sons—Gershon, Kohath, and Merari—were among the seventy Israelites who immigrated to Egypt. They arrived in Goshen, and Joseph came to them in his chariot. He greeted his father, embraced him, and wept for a long time.

Seventeen years later, Jacob, feeling that he would soon die, called his sons to tell them what would happen to them in the future. He said that Levi and Simeon, for their violence and their cruelty, when they slaughtered the men of Shechem, would be dispersed among the people of Israel.

Jacob's last words were to ask them to bury him in the cave of Machpelah, where

Abraham, Sarah, Isaac, Rebekah and Leah were buried. Jacob died at the age of one hundred and forty-seven. Jacob's body was accompanied in his last trip by his sons, their children, flocks and herds, all the officials of Pharaoh and members of his court, chariots and horsemen. Before crossing the Jordan, the funeral procession made a stop and mourned Jacob for seven days. Then, his sons took him to Canaan and buried him in the cave of Machpelah.

After burying their father, they all returned to Canaan. Joseph's brothers feared that, with Jacob now dead, Joseph would pay them back for the wrong that they had done to him.

They sent a message to Joseph, saying that Jacob, before his death, had told them to urge Joseph to forgive them. Judah and his brothers came to Joseph, flung themselves before him, and told him that they were prepared to be his slaves.

Joseph answered kindly, "Do not fear! Although you intended me harm, God intended it all for good, to assure the survival of many people. Don't worry; I will take care of you and your children".

Levi died at the age of one hundred and thirty-seven. His daughter Jochebed married his grandson, Amram, son of Kohath, and gave birth to Aaron, Miriam, and Moses. His descendants, the Levites, served in the Temple.

Moses, in his farewell speech, praised the tribe of Levi for being faithful to the covenant with God, and for teaching the people to obey the Law.

2. (Mark 2:13). A.D. 1st century. Levi, son of Alphaeus, was the other name of the apostle Matthew.

Levi worked as a tax collector in Capernaum, when Jesus saw him and told him to follow. He didn't hesitate for a second, arose, and followed Jesus. He then made a great feast in his house, in honor of Jesus, to which he invited publicans and other people of bad reputation. The scribes and the Pharisees criticized Jesus for eating and drinking with sinners.

Jesus answered, "Those that are whole do not need a physician, but those who are sick do".

Other references to Matthew are found only within the lists of the apostles. Scholars believe that he probably was the author of the gospel according to Matthew.

3. (Luke 3:24). Unspecified date. Levi, the son of Melchi and father of Matthat, was an ancestor of Jesus, according to Luke's genealogy.

4. (Luke 3:29). Unspecified date. Levi, the son of Simeon and father of Matthat, was an ancestor of Jesus, according to Luke's genealogy.

Leviathan

(Hebrew origin: *Sea monster*)

(Job 41:1). Leviathan was a sea monster, which, according to Isaiah, had the body of a crooked serpent.

Libni

(Hebrew origin: *Whiteness*)

1. (Exodus 6:17). 16th century B.C. Libni—called Laadan in the first book of Chronicles (1 Chronicles 23:7)—a descendant of Levi, was the son of Gershon and the father of Jahath. His brother was called Shimi. Libni was the ancestor of the clan of Libnites.

2. (1 Chronicles 6:29). Unspecified date. Libni, son of Mahli, a descendant of Merari, was the father of Shimei. His descendant Asaiah was a Levite appointed by King David to be in charge of the singers in the House of the Lord, from the time when the Ark came to rest in Jerusalem.

Likhi

(Hebrew origin: *Learned*)

(1 Chronicles 7:19). Unspecified date. Likhi was the son of Shemidah, a descendant of Manasseh. His brothers were Ahian, Shechem, and Aniam.

Linus

(Greek origin: derived from *Flax*)

(2 Timothy 4:21). A.D. 1st century. Linus was one of the four persons—the others were Claudia, Eubulus, and Pudens—who sent greetings to Timothy in the last letter written by Paul.

Loammi

(Hebrew origin: *Not my people*)

(Hosea 1:9). 8th century B.C. Loammi was one of the three children—the other two were a boy named Jezreel, and a girl called Loruhamah—whom the prophet Hosea had with his wife Gomer, to all of whom he gave symbolic names. Loammi's name symbolized that God had rejected the people.

Lois

(Uncertain origin and meaning)

(2 Timothy 1:5). A.D. 1st century. Lois, a Jewish woman who lived in Lystra, was the mother of Eunice and the grandmother of Timothy. The family was probably converted by Paul in his previous visit to Lystra.

Timothy, whose father was Greek, was circumcised by Paul, who then took him as a travel companion.

Loruhamah

(Hebrew origin: *Not pitied*)

(Hosea 1:6). 8th century B.C. Loruhamah was one of the three children—the others were two boys named Jezreel and Loammi—whom the prophet Hosea had with his wife Gomer, to all of whom he gave symbolic names. Loruhamah's name symbolized that God would exile the people and show them no pity.

Lot

(Hebrew origin: *A covering*)

(Genesis 11:27). 19th century B.C. Lot, son of Haran, grandson of Terah, and nephew of Abraham, was born in Ur of the Chaldeans, a Sumerian city in the Euphrates valley, near the head of the Persian Gulf. He was the eleventh generation from Noah, through the line of Shem.

When Haran died, Terah took his son Abram, his daughter-in-law Sarai, and his grandson Lot, the son of Haran, and traveled to the city of Haran, which lay between the Euphrates and the Tigris in northern Aram, near the modern frontier between Syria and Turkey.

When Terah died at the age of two hundred and five, his son Abram took his wife Sarai and his nephew Lot, to the land of Canaan. Both men became very wealthy and owned flocks, herds, and tents.

Years went by, and Lot, by this time also a wealthy man owning flocks, herds, and tents, continued to live with his uncle Abram. Their proximity caused problem between their respective herdsmen, who started arguing and fighting over the limited grazing area that was available for their animals.

Abram, trying to find a solution to this problem, proposed to Lot that they should separate amicably, and Lot, given first choice by Abram, settled in the well-watered valley of the Jordan, near the cities of Sodom and Gomorrah, while Abram went to live in the plain of Mamre, near Hebron, and built there an altar to God, who again promised to give all the land that Abram could see to him and his descendants.

Chedorlaomer, king of Elam, was the over-lord of several kingdoms. Bera, king of Sodom, was one of his vassals. After serving him for twelve years, Bera and four other kings rebelled and formed an alliance. Chedorlaomer and his allies—King Amraphel of Shinar, King Arioch of Ellasar, and King Tidal—fought against them in the valley of Sidim, in the region of the Dead Sea, and defeated them.

The victors took a number of prisoners, including Lot, and departed back to their countries, loaded with all the goods from Sodom and Gomorrah that they could carry.

A man, who managed to escape from Chedorlaomer, came to Abram and told him that his nephew Lot had been captured, and was being taken away. Abram armed three hundred and eighteen of his servants and—with his allies Aner, Eshcol, and Mamre—pursued the four kings, until he caught up with them in Daniel. There, he divided his men in groups, attacked the enemy, that night, and defeated them, chasing them back as far as Hobah, near Damascus. He succeeded in recovering all the stolen loot, liberated Lot, and brought him to Sodom with all his possessions, together with the women who had been captured, and other prisoners.

Sometime later, God told Abraham that the sins of Sodom and Gomorrah were very great. Abram—who was now called Abraham, a name given to him by God—argued and bargained with God, trying to convince him not to destroy the city, even if there were only a few innocent people there.

God promised to Abraham that he would not destroy the city if as few as ten innocent men could be found there.

That evening, two angels came to Sodom. Lot, who was sitting in the gate of the city, rose to meet them and invited them to stay at his house. They, at first, refused the invitation but accepted, after Lot insisted.

The visitors dined with Lot and his family, and they were getting ready to go to bed, when the men of Sodom surrounded the house and demanded from Lot that he should hand them the visitors, which they intended to rape. Lot went out of the house, closing the door behind him, and implored them not to commit such a wicked act. He offered to give them his two virgin daughters, so that they could do with them what they wanted.

The men of Sodom screamed that Lot was a foreigner, and had no right to tell them what to do. They pressed against him and tried to break down the door. The visitors pulled Lot inside the house and shut the door. The men outside were stricken with blindness and could not find the entrance.

The visitors told Lot to take all the members of his household out of the city, because God had sent them to destroy it. Lot went to his sons-in-law and told them to leave the city, because God was going to destroy it. The sons-in-law laughed and thought that Lot was joking.

Early next morning, the angels urged Lot to take his wife and his two daughters and flee the city. When he delayed, the men seized his hand, and the hands of his wife and his two daughters, and brought them out of the city, telling them not to look behind them and to escape to the hills.

Lot told them that he wasn't able to get that far, and to allow them to find refuge in a small town nearby. The angel agreed and told him that the little town, called Zoar, would not be destroyed.

The sun was rising, when Lot entered Zoar, and God rained sulfurous fire upon Sodom and Gomorrah, destroying both cities and annihilating their inhabitants. Lot's wife looked back and was turned into a pillar of salt.

Lot, afraid of staying in Zoar, left the town with his two daughters and went to the hills, where they lived in a cave.

The two daughters, believing that no man had been left alive, and anxious to have children, made their father drunk and laid with him. The eldest one gave birth to a son, whom she called Moab, and was the ancestor of the Moabites. The youngest one also had a son, and called him Benammi, the ancestor of the Ammonites.

Lotan

(Hebrew origin: *Covering*)

(Genesis 36:20). Unspecified date. Lotan was one of the sons of Seir the Horite, ancestor of the clans, who settled in the land of Edom. His sons were Hori and Hemam. His brothers were Dishan, Shobal, Zibeon, Dishon, Ezer, and Anah. His sister was Timna.

Lucas

(Latin origin: Uncertain meaning)

(Philemon 1:24). A.D. 1st century. Lucas—also called Luke (Colossians 4:14)—a faithful companion of the apostle Paul, who called him "beloved physician", is acknowledged to be the author of the Third Gospel and the Acts of the Apostles.

Although his name is not mentioned in the

Acts of the Apostles, there are certain sections of the book where he uses the pronoun "we". From these verses, it seems that Lucas accompanied Paul on his second journey across the Aegean from Troas in Asia Minor to Philippi in Greece.

Six years later, on Paul's third journey, he returned with Paul from Philippi to Jerusalem. And, finally, Lucas went with Paul on his last journey, from Caesarea to Rome.

He remained with Paul, throughout his captivity in prison, and was mentioned by the apostle in his letter to Philemon as sending greetings.

Lucifer

(Translated from Hebrew origin: *Shining*)

(Isaiah 14:12). Lucifer was a fallen angel, whom Isaiah calls "son of the morning". The prophet accuses him of having tried to be like God. Lucifer was punished for this sacrilegious ambition by falling from heaven down to hell. It is identified with Satan.

Lucius

(Latin origin: *Illuminative*)

1. (Acts of the Apostles 13:1). A.D. 1st century. Lucius of Cyrene was a prophet and teacher in the Antioch church, who preached and organized the church, during the year that Paul stayed in Antioch. It might be that he was the same person as the Lucius mentioned by Paul in his epistle to the Romans (see below). It was in Antioch that the believers in Jesus were first called Christians.

2. (Romans 16:21). A.D. 1st century. Lucius was a Christian mentioned by Paul, in his epistle to the Romans, as being his kinsman and sending his regards. It might be that he was the same person as Lucius of Cyrene (see above).

Lud

(Hebrew origin: Uncertain meaning)

(Genesis 10:22). Unspecified date. Lud was the son of Shem and grandson of Noah. His

brothers were Elam, Asshur, Arphaxad, Lud, Aram, Uz, Hul, Gether, and Meshech.

Ludim

(Hebrew origin: Uncertain meaning)

(Genesis 10:13). Unspecified date. Ludim was the son of Mizraim, *Egypt*, and grandson of Ham.

Luke

(Latin origin: Uncertain meaning)

(Colossians 4:14). A.D. 1st century. Luke—also called Lucas (Philemon 1:24)—a faithful companion of the apostle Paul, who called him "beloved physician", is acknowledged to be the author of the Third Gospel and the Acts of the Apostles.

Although his name is not mentioned in the Acts of the Apostles, there are certain sections of the book where he uses the pronoun "we". From these verses, it seems that Luke accompanied Paul on his second journey across the Aegean from Troas in Asia Minor to Philippi in Greece.

Six years later, on Paul's third journey, he returned with Paul from Philippi to Jerusalem. And, finally, Luke went with Paul on his last journey, from Caesarea to Rome.

He remained with Paul, throughout his captivity in prison, and was mentioned by the apostle in his letter to Philemon as sending greetings.

Lydia

(Latin origin: Uncertain meaning)

(Acts of the Apostles 16:14). A.D. 1st century. Lydia, of the city of Thyatira, made her living selling purple cloth. One Saturday, when Paul was staying in Philippi, a Roman colony in Macedonia, he and his companion went out of the city to the riverside, where the apostle thought there would be a place where people gathered for prayer.

The apostle preached to the women who were there, one of whom was Lydia. She was converted and was baptized together with the other members of her household. Lydia then convinced Paul to be a guest in her house, during his stay in Philippi.

Lysanias

(Latin origin: Uncertain meaning)

(Luke 3:1). A.D. 1st century. Lysanias was the tetrarch of Abilene, a district situated in what today is Syria, during the period when Pontius Pilate was the Roman governor of Jerusalem.

Lysias

(Latin origin: Uncertain meaning)

(Acts of the Apostles 23:26). A.D. 1st century. Claudius Lysias was the commander of the Antonia fortress, the headquarters of the Roman army in Jerusalem.

Paul, during his last visit to Jerusalem, was in the Temple, when some Jews, who had arrived from the region of Asia, recognized him. They stirred up the crowd and grabbed Paul, shouting, "Men of Israel, help us! This is the man who goes everywhere teaching everyone against the Jews, the Law of Moses, and this Temple. And now he has brought some Gentiles into the Temple and defiled this holy place".

They said that, because they had previously seen Paul walk around in the city with a Greek from Ephesus, called Trophimus, and had assumed that Paul had brought him into an area of the Temple, which was forbidden for foreigners.

The aroused crowd ran to Paul, seized him, and dragged him out of the Temple. At once, the Temple guards shut the gates. The mob was trying to kill Paul, when Claudius Lysias, the commander of the Roman troops, was told that the people of Jerusalem were rioting. He immediately ran toward the crowd with his soldiers and centurions.

When the people saw the soldiers coming, they stopped beating Paul. The commander arrested him and had him bound with two chains; he then asked if somebody knew who the man was and what he had done. Some

people in the crowd shouted one thing, others something else. When the commander saw that he couldn't get a clear answer, he ordered his men to take Paul inside the fortress. The soldiers had to carry him, because the mob had become very violent and threatened Paul's life.

Before entering the fortress, Paul asked the commander if he could have a word with him. Claudius Lysias asked him, "Do you speak Greek? Are you that Egyptian who recently stirred up a revolt and led a band of four thousand murderers out into the desert?"

Paul answered, "I am a Jew, born in Tarsus, a citizen of an important city. Please allow me to speak to the people". The commander gave him permission, so Paul stood on the steps and made gestures with his hands to quiet the people. He told the people that he had once persecuted the Christians, but now, after his conversion, he had been instructed by God to preach to the Gentiles.

The people, who had been listening quietly to Paul, started shouting, "Away with such a fellow from the earth, for he doesn't deserve to live!" They screamed, waved their clothing, and threw dust into the air.

Claudius Lysias ordered his men to take Paul into the fortress, and to whip him in order to find out why the crowd shouted against him.

When he was being tied up, Paul said to the centurion who was standing next to him, "Is it lawful to whip a Roman citizen who has not been condemned?"

The centurion heard this and rushed to his commander, saying, "Be careful of what you do, because this man is a Roman citizen".

The commander came to Paul and asked him, "Are you a Roman citizen?"

When Paul answered, "Yes", Claudius Lysias confided in him, "I became a Roman citizen by paying a lot of money".

Paul answered, "But I am a citizen by birth".

At once, the soldiers who were going to interrogate Paul drew away from him, and Claudius Lysias was frightened, when he realized that he had made a mistake by chaining a Roman citizen.

The next morning, Claudius Lysias, wanting to know the real reason why the Jews were accusing Paul, took his chains off and ordered the chief priests and the whole council to meet. He then brought Paul to the council and made him stand before them.

Paul stared at the council and said, "Brothers, I have lived with a clear conscience before God, until today".

Ananias, the High Priest, ordered those who were standing closest to Paul to hit him on the mouth.

Paul said to him, "God will strike you, you whitewashed wall! You are sitting here to judge me according to the Law, and at the same time, you break the Law by ordering them to hit me".

The men standing close to Paul said, "How dare you insult God's High Priest!"

Paul answered, "Brothers, I didn't know that he was the High Priest, because the Scriptures state, 'Do not speak evil of the ruler of your people'"

Paul noticed that some members of the council were Sadducees, members of a sect, which did not believe in the resurrection of the dead nor in angels, while others were Pharisees, men who believed that the dead would one day live again. He then exclaimed, "Brothers, I am a Pharisee, the son of a Pharisee. I am being questioned here, because of my hope that the dead will rise to life".

Immediately, the Sadducees and the Pharisees started to argue with each other, and the council was divided. Some of the scribes belonging to the Pharisee sect stood up and said, "We find no evil in this man. If a spirit or an angel has spoken to him, we should not fight against God!"

The arguments in the council turned violent, and Claudius Lysias, fearing that Paul would be torn to pieces by his opponents, ordered the soldiers to rescue him, using force if necessary, and to bring him back to the fortress.

That night, God spoke to Paul, "Be of good cheer. You have testified about me in Jerusalem, and now, you must do it also in Rome".

The next day, a group of about forty Jews got together and made a vow that they would not eat nor drink, until they had killed Paul. They went to the chief priests and elders, and they said, "We have taken a solemn vow together that we will abstain from food, until we have killed Paul. We want you and the council to tell the Roman commander to bring Paul back to you tomorrow so that you can interrogate him more closely. We will kill him, before he gets here".

Paul's nephew, the son of his sister, heard that the men were preparing to ambush Paul. He went to the fortress and told Paul about the plot against his life.

Paul called one of the centurions and said, "Take this young man to your commander, for he has something to tell him".

The centurion took the young man to Claudius Lysias and told him that Paul's nephew had something to say to him. Claudius Lysias took him by his hand, away from prying ears, and asked him, "What is it that you want to tell me?"

The young man answered, "The Jews have agreed to ask you to bring Paul tomorrow back to them, pretending that they wish to interrogate him more closely. Don't listen to them, because more than forty men, who have vowed to kill him, will be waiting in ambush".

Claudius Lysias instructed him not to tell anyone what he had told him, and then, he sent the young man away. He called two centurions and said, "Take two hundred soldiers, seventy horsemen, and two hundred spearmen, and get ready to leave for Caesarea tonight at the third hour. Provide some horses for Paul to ride, and convey him safely to Felix, the governor".

He then sat down to write a self-serving letter to the governor, where he shrewdly showed himself in a good light. He wrote:

Claudius Lysias sends greetings to His Excellency, Governor Felix: This man was seized by the Jews who would have killed him if I, having learned that he was a Roman citizen, hadn't come with my soldiers and rescued him.

Wishing to know the accusations against him, I brought him to their council. I found out that the accusations merely referred to questions about their own religious law, and that the man had done nothing deserving of death or jail.

When I was informed that the Jews were planning to ambush him, I sent him to you at once.

I have told his accusers to bring their charges against him before you.

The troop departed the fortress of Antonia, taking Paul with them. That night, they got as far as Antipatris. The next morning, the foot soldiers returned to Jerusalem, and the horsemen proceeded on. They arrived in Caesarea, delivered Claudius Lysias' letter to Felix, and turned Paul over to him.

Maacah

(Hebrew origin: *Depression*)

(2 Samuel 3:3). 10th century B.C. Maacah—called Maachah in the first book of Chronicles (1 Chronicles 3:2)—daughter of Talmai, king of Geshur, a kingdom situated northeast of the Sea of Galilee, was the mother of Absalom, the third son of King David, and Tamar, the girl who was raped by Amnon.

Maachah

(Hebrew origin: *Depression*)

1. (Genesis 22:24). 19th century B.C. Maachah was one of the sons of Nahor, Abraham's brother, and his concubine Reumah. His brothers were Tebah, Gaham, and Thahash.

2. (1 Kings 2:39). 11th century B.C. Maachah—called Maoch in the first book of Samuel (1 Samuel 27:2)—was the father of Achish, king of Gath, the Philistine city to which David fled, when escaping from Saul's persecution.

3. (1 Kings 15:2). 10th century B.C. Maachah, daughter of Abishalom, was the favorite wife of King Rehoboam, who had eighteen wives and sixty concubines. She was the mother of Kings Abijah and Asa.

   It is very likely that Abishalom and Absalom, King David's rebellious son, were the same person. Possible evidence for this is that Abishalom's daughter, Maachah, had the same name as Absalom's mother (1 Chronicles 3:2). However, the second book of Chronicles (2 Chronicles 13:2) states that her name was Michaiah, and her father's name was given as Uriel

   Maachah was stripped of her title of queen mother by her son Asa, because she had made an idol, which Asa destroyed and burned.

4. (1 Chronicles 2:48). Unspecified date. Maachah was a concubine of Caleb, son of Hezron and brother of Jerahmeel, of the tribe of Judah. Her sons were Sheber, Tirhanah, Sheva, and Shaaph.

5. (1 Chronicles 3:2). 10th century B.C. Maachah, daughter of Talmai, king of Geshur, a kingdom situated northeast of the Sea of Galilee, was the mother of Absalom, the third son of King David, and Tamar, the girl who was raped by Amnon. She was called Maacah in the second book of Samuel (2 Samuel 3:3).

6. (1 Chronicles 7:15). 17th century B.C. Maachah was the wife of Machir, the son of Manasseh. She had two sons: Peresh and Sheresh.

7. (1 Chronicles 8:29). 12th century B.C. Maachah was married to Jehiel, of the tribe of Benjamin, the founder of Gibeon.

8. (1 Chronicles 11:43). 11th century B.C. Maachah was the father of Hanan, one of the brave soldiers in the army of King David.

9. (1 Chronicles 27:16). 11th century B.C. Maachah was the father of Shephatiah, ruler of the tribe of Simeon, during the days of King David.

Maadai

(Hebrew origin: *Ornamental*)

(Ezra 10:34). 5th century B.C. Maadai, a descendant of Bani, divorced his foreign wife, during the days of Ezra.

Maadiah

(Hebrew origin: *God's ornament*)

(Nehemiah 12:5). 6th century B.C. Maadiah—also spelled Moadiah (Nehemiah 12:17)—was one of the leading priests who returned with Zerubbabel from the Babylonian Exile.

He was the ancestor of a clan of priests, which, during the days of the High Priest Joiakim, son of Jeshua, was led by Piltai.

Maai

(Hebrew origin: *Sympathetic*)

(Nehemiah 12:36). 5th century B.C. Maai was one of the priests who marched behind Ezra the Scribe, playing musical instruments in the joyful procession, which celebrated the dedication of the rebuilt walls of Jerusalem, during the days of Nehemiah.

Maaseiah

(Hebrew origin: *Work of God*)

1. (1 Chronicles 15:18). 10th century B.C. Maaseiah, a Levite of the second rank, was among those chosen by the chief of the Levites to sing and play musical instruments in front of the Ark of the Covenant, during the reign of King David.

2. (2 Chronicles 23:1). 9th century B.C. Maaseiah, son of Adaiah, was one of the army commanders, who joined the conspiracy headed by Jehoiada the priest to overthrow Queen Athaliah and crown Joash as king of Judah.

3. (2 Chronicles 26:11). 8th century B.C. Maaseiah was the record keeper in King Uzziah's army. He and Jeiel, a scribe, worked under the supervision of Hananiah, one of the king's officials.　　.

4. (2 Chronicles 28:7). 8th century B.C. Maaseiah, son of King Ahaz of Judah, was killed in battle by Zichri, a commander of King Pekah's army, during a war between Judah and Israel.

5. (2 Chronicles 34:8). 7th century B.C. Maaseiah, governor of the city of Jerusalem, was sent by King Josiah, together with Shaphan, the son of Azaliah, and Joah, the son of Joahaz, the recorder, to deliver money to the High Priest Hilkiah for the repairs of the Temple.

6. (Ezra 10:18). 5th century B.C. Maaseiah, son of Jozadak, was one of the priests who divorced his foreign wife, during the days of Ezra, and offered a ram from the flock to expiate his transgression.

7. (Ezra 10:21). 5th century B.C. Maaseiah, a priest, descendant of Harim, divorced his foreign wife, during the days of Ezra.

8. (Ezra 10:22). 5th century B.C. Maaseiah, a priest, descendant of Pashur, divorced his foreign wife, during the days of Ezra.

9. (Ezra 10:30). 5th century B.C. Maaseiah, a descendant of Pahathmoab, divorced his foreign wife, during the days of Ezra.

10. (Nehemiah 3:23). 5th century B.C. Maaseiah, son of Ananiah, was the father of Azariah who, in the days of Nehemiah, repaired the section of the walls of Jerusalem, which was opposite his house.

11. (Nehemiah 8:4). 5th century B.C. Maaseiah was one of the leaders who stood next to Ezra, upon a pulpit of wood, when the scribe read the Law of Moses to the people in the marketplace.

12. (Nehemiah 8:7). 5th century B.C. Maaseiah was one of the Levites who explained the Law to the people, after Ezra the Scribe had read it, while standing on a wooden platform, in front of the open space, before the Water Gate.

13. (Nehemiah 10:25). 5th century B.C. Maaseiah was one of the leaders who signed Nehemiah's solemn agreement to separate themselves from the foreigners living in the land, to refrain from intermarrying with them, and to dedicate their firstborn to God, among other obligations.

14. (Nehemiah 11:5). 5th century B.C. Maaseiah, son of Baruch, a descendant of Perez of the tribe of Judah, lived in Jerusalem, during the days of Nehemiah.

15. (Nehemiah 11:7). Unspecified date. Maaseiah, son of Ithiel and father of Kolaiah, was an ancestor of Sallu, a Benjamite who settled in Jerusalem, after his return from the Babylonian Exile.

16. (Nehemiah 12:41). 5th century B.C. Maaseiah was one of the priests who played the trumpet in the joyful procession, which celebrated the dedication of the rebuilt walls of Jerusalem, during the days of Nehemiah.

17. (Nehemiah 12:42). 5th century B.C. Maaseiah was one of the priests who marched, led by Jezrahiah, their overseer, singing at the top of their voices, in the joyful procession that celebrated the dedi-

cation of the rebuilt walls of Jerusalem, during the days of Nehemiah.

18. (Jeremiah 21:1). 7th century B.C. Maaseiah was the father of Zephaniah, the High Priest, during the reign of King Zedekiah.

19. (Jeremiah 29:21). 7th century B.C. Maaseiah was the father of Zedekiah, a false prophet in Babylon, during the days of Jeremiah. Zedekiah and Ahab, son of Kolaiah, were accused by the prophet Jeremiah of doing vile things, committing adultery and prophesying falsehoods.

Jeremiah predicted that their death by burning, at Nebuchadnezzar's command, would be mentioned as a curse by the exiled Judean community in Babylon.

20. (Jeremiah 32:12). 7th century B.C. Maaseiah, father of Neriah, was the grandfather of Baruch, the trusted companion of Jeremiah, and of Seraiah, who was sent to the Babylonian Exile together with King Zedekiah.

21. (Jeremiah 35:4). 6th century B.C. Maaseiah, son of Shallum, was the keeper of the door in the Temple and had a chamber there.

Maasiai

(Hebrew origin: *Operative*)

(1 Chronicles 9:12). 5th century B.C. Maasiai, son of Adiel, was a priest who served in the Temple, after the return from the Babylonian Exile.

Maath

(Uncertain origin and meaning)

(Luke 3:26). Unspecified date. Maath, son of Mattathias and father of Nagge, was an ancestor of Jesus, according to Luke's genealogy.

Maaz

(Hebrew origin: *Closure*)

(1 Chronicles 2:27). Unspecified date. Maaz, a descendant of Judah, was the son of

Ram, the firstborn son of Jerahmeel. His brothers were Jamin and Eker.

Maaziah

(Hebrew origin: *Fortification of God*)

1. (1 Chronicles 24:18). 10th century B.C. During the reign of King David, the priestly service in the Tabernacle was divided by lot into twenty-four turns. Maaziah was in charge of the twenty-fourth turn.

2. (Nehemiah 10:8). 5th century B.C. Maaziah was one of the priests who signed Nehemiah's solemn agreement to separate themselves from the foreigners living in the land, to refrain from intermarrying with them, and to dedicate their firstborn to God, among other obligations.

Machbanai

(Hebrew origin: *Native of Machbenah*)

(1 Chronicles 12:13). 11th century B.C. Machbanai, a brave Gadite, was one of the captains of Saul's army who defected and joined David at Ziklag.

Machbenah

(Hebrew origin: Uncertain meaning)

(1 Chronicles 2:49). Unspecified date. Machbenah was the son of Sheva, of the tribe of Judah, and grandson of Caleb and his concubine Maachah.

Machi

(Hebrew origin: *Pining*)

(Numbers 13:15). 14th century B.C. His son Geuel, of the tribe of Gad, was one of the twelve men sent by Moses to spy the land of Canaan and report back about its cities and its inhabitants, if they were strong or weak, few or many, and to bring back the fruit of the land. The spies returned and gave a report, which was disheartening and defeatist.

Only two of the spies—Joshua, the son of Nun, and Caleb, the son of Jephunneh—

disagreed and told the people that they should not fear the inhabitants of Canaan.

The Israelites refused to listen to the words of Joshua and Caleb, and they started to wail and cry. God punished their cowardice by condemning them to wander forty years in the wilderness, one year for each day that the spies scouted the land.

Machir

(Hebrew origin: *Salesman*)

1. (Genesis 50:23). 17th century B.C. Machir was the firstborn son of Manasseh and his concubine, an Aramean woman. He was the ancestor of the clans of the Machirites.

   Machir had two sons, Peresh and Sheresh, from his wife Maachah, the sister of Huppim and Shuppim. Another son, Gilead, was the ancestor of the Gileadites. One of his daughters married Hezron, a sixty-year-old man, and gave birth to Segub.

2. (2 Samuel 9:4). 10th century B.C. Machir, son of Ammiel, from Lodebar, was the owner of the house where Mephibosheth, son of Jonathan and grandson of Saul, lived, until King David had him brought to his court.

   Machir showed great kindness to David, when the king was fleeing from Absalom, bringing him utensils and food.

Machnadebai

(Hebrew origin: *What is like a liberal man*)

(Ezra 10:40). 5th century B.C. Machnadebai divorced his foreign wife, during the days of Ezra.

Madai

(Hebrew origin: *A Mede*)

(Genesis 10:2). Unspecified date. Madai was a son of Japheth and a grandson of Noah. His brothers were Gomer, Magog, Javan, Tubal, Meshech, and Tiras.

Magbish

(Hebrew origin: *Stiffening*)

(Ezra 2:30). Unspecified date. Magbish was the ancestor of a group of one hundred and fifty-six Israelites who returned with Zerubbabel from the Babylonian Exile.

Magdalene

(Hebrew origin: *Inhabitant of the town Magdala*)

(Matthew 27:56). A.D. 1st century. Mary, from the town of Magdala, was surnamed Magdalene to differentiate her from the other women called Mary, who are mentioned in the New Testament.

Tradition identifies her with the nameless woman with a sinful past, who went to the house of Simon the Pharisee, where Jesus was eating, and stood behind Jesus, crying and wetting his feet with her tears. Then, she dried his feet with her hair, kissed them, and poured perfume on them.

Jesus said to her, "Your sins are forgiven; your faith has saved you. Go in peace".

After Jesus had driven out the seven devils that had possessed her, Mary Magdalene followed him from Galilee to Jerusalem, and she was among the women who witnessed his crucifixion.

Two days later, early on Sunday morning, Mary Magdalene and another woman, also called Mary, went to the sepulcher where Joseph of Arimathaea had placed Jesus' body. They were worried about not being able to move the heavy stone from the entrance to the tomb, but when they arrived there, they saw that the stone had already been rolled back.

They entered the sepulcher and saw a young man—according to the gospel of John (John 20:17), it was Jesus himself—who told them that Jesus had been raised, and that they should tell Peter and the disciples that Jesus was on his way to Galilee, where they could see him. The women ran away, terrified.

Mary Magdalene went to the disciples and found them mourning and crying. They did not believe her, when she told them that Jesus was alive.

Magdiel

(Hebrew origin: *Preciousness of God*)

(Genesis 36:43). Unspecified date. Magdiel, a ruler of Edom, was a descendant of Esau.

Magog

(Uncertain origin and meaning)

(Genesis 10:2). Unspecified date. Magog was one of the sons of Japheth. His brothers were Gomer, Madai, Javan, Tubal, Meshech, and Tiras.

The book of Revelation (Revelation 20:8) states that Magog, together with Gog and Satan, will be destroyed by fire from heaven, while doing battle against God's people.

Magormissabib

(Hebrew origin: *Terror all around*)

(Jeremiah 20:3). 6th century B.C. This was the name, by which, God would call Pashur, as prophesied by Jeremiah.

Pashur, son of the priest Immer, was in charge of the Temple. Angry against Jeremiah for what he considered his prophecies of defeatism, he inflicted heavy blows on the prophet and put him in the cell that was in the Temple's Gate of Benjamin.

The next morning, when Pashur brought Jeremiah out of the cell, the prophet told him that God would call him Magormissabib, *Terror all around,* because the kingdom of Judah would fall to the king of Babylon; and Pashur, and all his family, would be sent to Babylon, where they would die.

Magpiash

(Hebrew origin: *Moth exterminator*)

(Nehemiah 10:20). 5th century B.C. Magpiash was one of the leaders who signed Nehemiah's solemn agreement to separate themselves from the foreigners living in the land, to refrain from intermarrying with them, and to dedicate their firstborn to God, among other obligations.

Mahalah

(Hebrew origin: *Sickness*)

(1 Chronicles 7:18). Unspecified date. Mahalah, a descendant of Manasseh, was the brother of Abiezer and Ishod. His mother was Hammoleketh, the sister of Gilead.

Mahalaleel

(Hebrew origin: *Praise of God*)

1. (Genesis 5:12). Antediluvian. Mahalaleel—called Maleleel in the gospel according to Luke (Luke 3:37)—was the son of Cainan, born when his father was seventy years old.

   Mahalaleel's firstborn son Jared was born, when he was sixty-five years old. He died at the age of eight hundred and thirty, after having had many other sons and daughters.

2. (Nehemiah 11:4). Unspecified date. Mahalaleel was a descendant of Perez and father of Shephatiah. His descendant Athaiah was a member of the tribe of Judah who settled in Jerusalem, after they returned from the Babylonian Exile.

Mahalath

(Hebrew origin: *Sickness*)

1. (Genesis 28:9). 18th century B.C. Mahalath, one of Esau's wives, was the daughter of Ishmael and the mother of Reuel. She is also called Bashemath (Genesis 36:3).

   Mahalath had twelve brothers: Nebajoth, Kedar, Mibsam, Mishma, Dumah, Massa, Hadad, Tema, Jetur, Naphish, Adbeel, and Kedemah, all of them ancestors of nations.

2. (2 Chronicles 11:18). 10th century B.C. Mahalath was one of the eighteen wives of King Rehoboam. Her father was Jerimoth, a son of King David, and her mother was Abihail, the daughter of Eliab, David's brother. Her children were Jeush, Shamariah, and Zaham.

   Although Mahalath was the first woman whom Rehoboam married, his favorite wife was Maachah, the mother of Abijah, Rehoboam's successor.

Mahali

(Hebrew origin: *Sick*)

(Exodus 6:19). 16th century B.C. Mahali—spelled Mahli in the book of Numbers (Numbers 3:20)—was the son of Merari and the grandson of Levi. His son was Libni, and his brother was called Mushi.

Mahali was the ancestor of a clan of Levites, who were servants of the Temple.

Maharai

(Hebrew origin: *Swift*)

(2 Samuel 23:28). 10th century B.C. Maharai the Netophathite was one of "The Thirty", an elite group in King David's army. He served as captain of the army, during the tenth month of each year, commanding a division of twenty-four thousand soldiers.

Mahath

(Hebrew origin: *Erasure*)

1. (1 Chronicles 6:35). Unspecified date. Mahath was the son of Amasai and the father of Elkanah. His descendant Heman, of the clan of the Kohathites, was one of the Levites appointed by King David to be in charge of the singers in the House of the Lord.

2. (2 Chronicles 29:12). 8th century B.C. Mahath, son of Amasai, was one of the Levites who assembled all the other Levites to make themselves ritually clean, and to purify the Temple, during the reign of King Hezekiah of Judah.

    Mahath was named by King Hezekiah to serve under Cononiah and Shimei, as one of the supervisors of the gifts, tithes, and offerings, brought by the people to the Temple.

Mahazioth

(Hebrew origin: *Visions*)

(1 Chronicles 25:4). 10th century B.C. Mahazioth, a Levite, member of a family of musicians, was in charge of the twenty-third turn of service that played musical instruments—cymbals, psalteries, and harps—in the House of God, during the reign of David.

He had thirteen brothers and three sisters, all of them trained as skillful musicians by their father, Heman, one of the three leading musicians—the other two were Asaph and Jeduthun—during the reign of King David.

Mahershalalhashbaz

(Hebrew origin: *Booty and shame are imminent*)

(Isaiah 8:1). 8th century B.C. Mahershalalhashbaz was one of the two sons whom the prophet Isaiah had with a woman whom he called the prophetess.

The prophet gave his two sons symbolic names: the eldest one was called Shearjashub, *A remainder will return*, and the second one Mahershalalhashbaz, *Booty and shame are imminent.*

Mahlah

(Hebrew origin: *Sickness*)

(Numbers 26:33). 13th century B.C. Mahlah was one of the five daughters of Zelophehad, the son of Hepher, of the tribe of Manasseh.

When Zelophehad died, Mahlah and her sisters—Hoglah, Noah, Milcah, and Tirzah—came to Moses and Eleazar the High Priest, and they requested to inherit from their father, who had died in the wilderness without sons.

Moses, after consulting with God, modified the law to entitle a daughter to inherit from her father, if the man had died without sons, but with the condition that she had to marry within the clan, in order that her inheritance would remain in her tribe.

After the death of Moses, the sisters came to Joshua and demanded, as their right, to receive a portion of the conquered territories, which had been given to the tribe of Manasseh.

Mahli

(Hebrew origin: *Sick*)

1. (Numbers 3:20). 16th century B.C. Mahli—spelled Mahali in the book of

Exodus (Exodus 6:19)—the ancestor of a clan of Levites, who were servants of the Temple, was the son of Merari and the grandson of Levi. His brother Mushi was the son of Mahli #2 (see below). His sons were Libni (1 Chronicles 6:29), Eleazar, and Kish (1 Chronicles 23:21).

2. (1 Chronicles 6:47). 16th century B.C. Mahli, son of Mushi, grandson of Merari, and father of Shamer, was a nephew of Mahli #1. His brothers were Eder and Jeremoth.

His descendant Ethan was one of the Levites appointed by King David to be in charge of the singers in the House of the Lord.

Mahlon

(Hebrew origin: *Sickly*)

(Ruth 1:2). 12th century B.C. Mahlon and his brother Chilion were the sons of Elimelech and Naomi. A famine forced the family to emigrate from their native town of Bethlehem to Moab.

After the death of their father the brothers married Moabite girls: Mahlon married Ruth, and Chilion married Orpah.

About ten years later both men died childless. Mahlon's widow, Ruth, went to Bethlehem with Naomi. There, she married Boaz, an ancestor of King David.

Mahol

(Hebrew origin: *Dancing*)

(1 Kings 4:31). Unspecified date. Mahol was the father of Ethan the Ezrahite, Heman, Chalcol, and Darda. The wisdom of his sons was surpassed only by King Solomon.

Malachi

(Hebrew origin: *My messenger*)

(Malachi 1:1). 5th century B.C. Malachi was the author of the prophetic book of the same name, written at the beginning of the post-Exilic period.

Many scholars believe that the Hebrew word "Malachi", meaning *My messenger*, is probably not a personal name, in which case, the book must be regarded as anonymous.

The book of Malachi has three chapters, with its contents falling into six clearly marked sections, each of them introduced by a statement of God, or of the prophet, which is then challenged by the people, or the priests, and defended by God himself in words of reproach and doom.

The priests, who were neglecting the sacrificial cult, and the people, who were not living according to the divine teachings, are called to renew their faithfulness to their covenant with God.

The three main abuses denounced in the book are the laxity and corruption of the priesthood, intermarriage with foreign women, and the people cheating God by not paying the tithes.

The book closes with an appeal to observe the laws that God gave to Moses, and with the announcement that the prophet Elijah will come, before the threatened judgment.

The book of Malachi is the last of the twelve books that make up the Minor Prophets—also called the Twelve—a collection of the books of twelve prophets: Hoshea, Joel, Amos, Obadiah, Jonah, Micah, Nahum, Habakkuk, Zephaniah, Haggai, Zechariah, and Malachi.

Note: The phrase "Minor Prophets" does not mean that these prophets are less important than Isaiah, Jeremiah, and Ezekiel. It refers only to the fact that the books of these twelve prophets are much shorter than the books of the other three prophets.

Malcham

(Hebrew origin: *Their king*)

1. (1 Chronicles 8:9). Unspecified date. Malcham, born in the country of Moab, was one of the seven sons of Shaharaim, of the tribe of Benjamin, and his wife Hodesh.

His brothers—all of them heads of clans—were Zibia, Jobab, Mesha, Jeuz, Shachia, and Mirma.

2. (Zephaniah 1:5). Malcham—also called Milcom, Moloch, and Molech—was the god of the Ammonites. His worship demanded the sacrifice of children by fire. (Please see the entry for Milcom [1 Kings 11:5].)

Malchiah

(Hebrew origin: *God is my king*)

1. (1 Chronicles 6:40). Unspecified date. Malchiah, son of Ethni and father of Baaseiah, of the clan of the Kohathites, was an ancestor of Asaph, one of the Levites appointed by King David to be in charge of the singers in the House of the Lord.
2. (Ezra 10:25). 5th century B.C. Malchiah, a descendant of Parosh, divorced his foreign wife, during the days of Ezra.
3. (Ezra 10:31). 5th century B.C. Malchiah, a descendant of Harim, divorced his foreign wife, during the days of Ezra.
4. (Nehemiah 3:14). 5th century B.C. Malchiah, son of Rechab, ruler of the Bethhaccerem district, repaired the Dung Gate of Jerusalem, including the doors, locks, and the bars, during the days of Nehemiah.
5. (Nehemiah 3:31). 5th century B.C. Malchiah, the son of a goldsmith, helped to repair the walls of Jerusalem, during the days of Nehemiah.
6. (Nehemiah 8:4). 5th century B.C. Malchiah was one of the leaders who stood next to Ezra, upon a pulpit of wood, when the scribe read the Law of Moses to the people in the marketplace.
7. (Nehemiah 11:12). Unspecified date. Malchiah was an ancestor of the priest Adaiah who worked in the Temple, during the days of Nehemiah.
8. (Jeremiah 38:1). 7th century B.C. Malchiah—also spelled Melchiah (Jeremiah 21:1)—was the father of Pashur, one of the officials in the court of King Zedekiah.
9. (Jeremiah 38:6). 7th century B.C. Malchiah, the son of Hammelech, owned a dungeon in the court of the prison, where Jeremiah was kept for a while.

His brother Jerahmeel, an official of King Jehoiakim, was ordered by the king to arrest the prophet Jeremiah and Baruch, his trusted companion, but was not able to find them.

Note: Some scholars believe that Hammelech—translated as *The King*—is not a given name but a title, in which case, Malchiah was a royal prince, son of a king, either King Josiah or King Jehoiakim.

Malchiel

(Hebrew origin: *God is my king*)

(Genesis 46:17). 16th century B.C. Malchiel was the son of Beriah and grandson of Asher. He and his brother Heber were among the seventy Israelites who immigrated to Egypt.

Malchiel was the ancestor of the clan of the Malchielites.

Malchijah

(Hebrew origin: *God is my king*)

1. (1 Chronicles 9:12). Unspecified date. His descendant, the priest Adaiah, served in the Temple, after the return from the Babylonian Exile.
2. (1 Chronicles 24:9). 10th century B.C. Malchijah was the priest in charge of the fifth turn, out of a total of twenty-four turns, of the priestly service in the Tabernacle, during the reign of King David.
3. (Ezra 10:25). 5th century B.C. Malchijah, a descendant of Parosh, divorced his foreign wife, during the days of Ezra.
4. (Nehemiah 3:11). 5th century B.C. Malchijah, son of Harim, together with Hashub, the son of Pahathmoab, repaired a sector of the walls of Jerusalem and the tower of the furnaces, during the days of Nehemiah.
5. (Nehemiah 10:3). 5th century B.C. Malchijah was one of the priests who signed Nehemiah's solemn agreement to separate themselves from the foreigners living in the land, to refrain from intermarrying with them, and to dedicate their firstborn to God, among other obligations.

6. (Nehemiah 12:42). 5th century B.C. Malchijah was one of the priests, led by Jezrahiah, their overseer, who marched, singing at the top of their voices, in the joyful procession, which celebrated the dedication of the rebuilt walls of Jerusalem, during the days of Nehemiah.

Malchiram

(Hebrew origin: *My king is exalted*)

(1 Chronicles 3:18). 6th century B.C. Malchiram was one of the seven sons of King Jehoiachin, the king who was deposed and taken captive by the Babylonians.

Malchiram's brothers were Salathiel, Hoshama, Pedaiah, Shenazar, Jecamiah, and Nedabiah.

Malchishua

(Hebrew origin: *My king is salvation*)

(1 Chronicles 8:33). 11th century B.C. Malchishua—also spelled Melchishua (1 Samuel 14:49)—son of King Saul, fought with his father against the Philistines in the battle of Mount Gilboa and was killed, together with his brothers Jonathan and Abinadab.

Malchus

(Hebrew origin: Uncertain meaning)

(John 18:10). A.D. 1st century. Malchus, a servant of the High Priest, accompanied the armed Roman soldiers and Temple guards who came to capture Jesus in the garden where he was praying.

Peter drew his sword and struck Malchus, cutting off his right ear. Jesus rebuked Peter, saying, "Put your sword back in its place! Those who take the sword will die by the sword!" Then, he touched Malchus' ear and healed him.

One of Malchus' relatives, a servant in the house of Caiaphas where Jesus was being held, thought that he recognized Peter and asked him if he hadn't seen him in the garden with Jesus. Peter answered, "No". And then, a rooster crowed, according to what Jesus had predicted.

Maleleel

(Hebrew origin: *Praise of God*)

(Luke 3:37). Antediluvian. Maleleel—called Mahalaleel in the book of Genesis (Genesis 5:12)—was the son of Cainan, born when his father was seventy years old.

Mahalaleel was sixty-five years old, when his firstborn son Jared was born. He died at the age of eight hundred and thirty, after having had many other sons and daughters.

Mallothi

(Hebrew origin: *I have talked*)

(1 Chronicles 25:4). 10th century B.C. Mallothi, a Levite, member of a family of musicians, was in charge of the nineteenth turn of service that played musical instruments—cymbals, psalteries, and harps—in the House of God, during the reign of David.

He had thirteen brothers and three sisters, all of them trained as skillful musicians by their father, Heman, one of the three leading musicians—the other two were Asaph and Jeduthun—of the period.

Malluch

(Hebrew origin: *Ruling*)

1. (1 Chronicles 6:44). Unspecified date. Malluch, son of Hashabiah, was a descendant of Merari. His descendant Ethan, son of Kishi, was one of the Levites appointed by King David to be in charge of the singers in the House of the Lord.

2. (Ezra 10:29). 5th century B.C. Malluch, a descendant of Bani, divorced his foreign wife, during the time of Ezra.

3. (Ezra 10:32). 5th century B.C. Malluch, a descendant of Harim, divorced his foreign wife, during the time of Ezra.

4. (Nehemiah 10:4). 5th century B.C. Malluch was one of the priests who signed Nehemiah's solemn agreement to separate themselves from the foreigners living in the land, to refrain from intermarrying with them, and to dedicate their firstborn to God, among other obligations.

5. (Nehemiah 10:27). 5th century B.C. Malluch was one of the leaders of the people who signed with Nehemiah a solemn agreement to separate themselves from the foreigners living in the land, to refrain from intermarrying with them, and to dedicate their firstborn to God, among other obligations.

6. (Nehemiah 12:2). 6th century B.C. Malluch was one of the priests who returned from the Babylonian Exile with Zerubbabel and the High Priest Jeshua.

Mamre

(Hebrew origin: *Vigorous*)

(Genesis 14:13). 19th century B.C. Mamre, an Amorite, gave his name to the plain where Abraham lived, near Hebron.

Mamre and his two brothers, Aner and Eshcol, joined Abraham in his pursuit of the kings who had taken Lot captive. Abraham overtook the kings, defeated them, and brought back the captives and the stolen booty.

The king of Sodom offered to reward him, but he declined, suggesting instead that the reward should be given to Mamre and his brothers.

Manaen

(Uncertain origin and meaning)

(Acts of the Apostles 13:1). A.D. 1st century. Manaen, who had been brought up with Herod the Tetrarch, was one of the prophets and teachers active in the Antioch church, preaching and organizing the church, during the year that Paul stayed in Antioch.

It was in Antioch that the believers in Jesus were first called Christians.

Manahath

(Hebrew origin: *Rest*)

(Genesis 36:23). Unspecified date. Manahath was the son of Shobal, a descendant of Seir the Horite. His brothers were Alian, Ebal, Shephi, and Onam.

Manasseh

(Hebrew origin: *Causing to forget*)

1. (Genesis 41:51). 17th century B.C. Manasseh, the ancestor of the tribe of Manasseh, was the firstborn son of Joseph and his wife Asenath, daughter of an Egyptian priest His father called him Manasseh, because, he said, "God had made me forget all my toil and my father's house".

Years later, after Joseph's brothers and father had settled in Egypt, Joseph was informed that his father Jacob was dying. He took with him his two sons, Manasseh and Ephraim, to be blessed by his father. Jacob told him that he was adopting the two boys.

Joseph placed Ephraim on the left side of his father, and Manasseh on the right hand of his father, but Jacob placed his right hand on Ephraim, the younger son, and his left hand on Manasseh. Joseph tried to remove Jacob's hand from Ephraim's head and place it on Manasseh's head, telling his father that Manasseh was the firstborn.

Jacob refused and said that both brothers would be the ancestors of tribes, but the younger brother's descendants would be more numerous.

Manasseh had two sons, Machir and Ashriel, with his Aramean concubine.

2. (Judges 18:30). Unspecified date. Manasseh, father of Gershom, was the grandfather of Jonathan, the priest in charge of the worship to the graven image set up by the tribe of Dan, in the city of Dan, previously called Laish.

Some Hebrew manuscripts have the letter *nun* in Manasseh suspended above, which would indicate an earlier reading of "Moses", instead of Manasseh.

3. (2 Kings 20:21). 7th century B.C. Manasseh, the son of King Hezekiah and his wife Hephzibah, was twelve years old, when he ascended to the throne, and became the thirteenth king of Judah, after the partition of the United Monarchy. He reigned for forty-five years and died at the

age of fifty-seven. The name of his wife was Meshullemeth.

Manasseh abolished the religious reforms of his father, introduced pagan rites and idols into the Temple, and even sacrificed his own son by fire to pagan gods.

Although he fortified Jerusalem, Judah, during his reign, was a submissive vassal of Assyria.

When he died, he was buried in the garden of the palace. His son Amon succeeded him.

4. (Ezra 10:30). 5th century B.C. Manasseh, a descendant of Pahathmoab, divorced his foreign wife, during the days of Ezra.

5. (Ezra 10:33). 5th century B.C. Manasseh, a descendant of Hashum, divorced his foreign wife, during the days of Ezra.

Manasses

(Hebrew origin: *Causing to forget*)

(Matthew 1:10). 7th century B.C. Manasses is an alternative spelling for Manasseh, king of Judah, and ancestor of Jesus. (See the entry for Manasseh [2 Kings 20:21].)

Manoah

(Hebrew origin: *Rest*)

(Judges 13:2). 12th century B.C. At a time when the Israelites lived under the domination of the Philistines, there lived in the town of Zorah a childless couple. The name of the husband was Manoah, and he belonged to the tribe of Dan.

One day, an angel appeared to the woman and announced to her, "You are now childless, but you will have a son. Listen carefully: You have to abstain from drinking alcoholic drinks and from eating unclean food. The son that you will have will free Israel from the hands of the Philistines. He will be dedicated to God from his birth, and no razor shall touch his head".

The woman went to her husband and told him what had happened. Manoah prayed to God to send them once more his messenger to teach them how to raise their future son.

When the angel again appeared to the woman, when she was alone in the field, she ran to her husband and said, "Look, that strange man that appeared to me the other day has come again".

Manoah got up and followed his wife. When they came to the place where the man was, Manoah asked him, "Are you the man who spoke to my wife?"

The angel answered, "I am".

Manoah said, "If what you predict will come true, how shall we raise the child?"

The angel explained, "Your wife should take care not to drink wine or any other alcoholic drink, nor should she eat unclean food".

"Please stay with us, while I prepare you a young goat to eat", said Manoah, not knowing that he was speaking to an angel.

The angel said, "Even if you keep me here, I will not eat your food. If you wish to make a sacrifice, offer it to God".

Manoah asked him, "Please tell us your name, so that, when your predictions come true, we will know whom should we thank".

The angel said, "You should not ask my name, because it is a secret".

Manoah took the young goat and the meal offering, and he offered them on a rock to God. While the flames of the altar flew upward, the angel ascended to the sky inside the flames. Manoah and his wife, seeing this, flung themselves on their faces to the ground.

When they didn't see the angel anymore, Manoah realized that the being, whom he had thought to be a man, was an angel.

Worried, he said to his wife, "We shall surely die, because we have seen God".

She calmed him, saying, "If God would have wanted to kill us, he would not have accepted the sacrifice that we offered, nor would he have shown us these things, or predicted what will happen".

The woman in due time had a son, and they called him Samson, who grew up to be a leader of his people in their fight against the Philistines.

One day, Samson saw a Philistine girl in Timnath whom he liked. He went to his parents and told them, "I have met a Philistine girl, and I want to marry her!"

Manoah and his wife said to Samson, "Can't you find any girl among your own clan, or among all our people, that you have to go and get a wife from those uncircumcised Philistines?"

Samson answered, "That's the one I like. Get her for me!"

Samson went to Timnath with his father and mother. On the way, he killed a lion with his bare hands, but didn't tell his parents. He later found a swarm of bees and honey inside the dead body of the lion. He took the honey and gave some of it to his parents, without again telling them anything.

When the wedding day arrived, Manoah went to the girl's house where Samson offered a banquet.

Manoah died, sometime later, and was buried between Zorah and Eshtaol, in the same grave where his son Samson was also buried several years afterward.

Maoch

(Hebrew origin: *Oppressed*)

(1 Samuel 27:2). 11th century B.C. Maoch—called Maachah in the first book of Kings (1 Kings 2:39)—was the father of Achish, king of Gath, the Philistine city to which David fled, when escaping from Saul's persecution.

Maon

(Hebrew origin: *Residence*)

(1 Chronicles 2:45). Unspecified date. Maon, a descendant of Caleb, was the son of Shammai and the founder of Bethzur.

Mara

(Hebrew origin: *Bitter*)

(Ruth 1:20). 12th century B.C. This is the name that Naomi told the people of Bethlehem to call her, when she returned from Moab with Ruth, after having lost her husband and her two sons.

She said, "God has dealt bitterly with me. I went away full, and God has brought me back empty".

Marcus

(Latin origin: Uncertain meaning).

(Colossians 4:10). A.D. 1st century. Marcus, a close relative of Barnabas, is believed by scholars to be the John Mark who traveled with Barnabas and Paul through Asia Minor and the Greek islands, preaching the gospel and making new converts.

John Mark was the son of a woman called Mary, in whose house in Jerusalem people gathered to pray.

For some unexplained reason, Paul refused to allow John Mark to continue traveling with him. This refusal caused Barnabas and Mark to leave Antioch and sail to Cyprus.

In spite of this incident, Paul continued having a very high opinion of Mark. In his second letter to Timothy, Paul asked that Mark should be sent to him, as he would be a great help in his ministry. In his letters to the Colossians and to Philemon, Paul mentioned that Mark was a fellow prisoner in Rome.

Some scholars believe that John Mark was the author of the gospel according to Mark.

Mareshah

(Hebrew origin: *Summit*)

(1 Chronicles 2:42). Unspecified date. Mareshah, a descendant of Caleb, was the father of Hebron and the grandfather of Korah, Tappuah, Rekem, and Shema.

Mark

(Latin origin: Uncertain meaning)

(Acts of the Apostles 12:12). A.D. 1st century. Mark was the surname of John—also called Marcus (Colossians 4:10)—who is believed by some scholars to be the author of the gospel according to Mark.

His mother, a woman called Mary, owned the house in Jerusalem where the believers gathered to pray.

Mark traveled with Barnabas, who was his close relative, and Paul through Asia Minor and the Greek islands, preaching the gospel and making new converts. For some unexplained reason, Paul refused at one point to continue taking John Mark with him in his travels. This refusal caused Barnabas and Mark to leave Antioch and sail for Cyprus.

In spite of this incident, Paul continued having a very high opinion of Mark. In his second letter to Timothy, Paul asked that Mark should be sent to him, as he would be a great help in his ministry. In his letters to the Colossians and to Philemon, Paul mentioned that Mark was a fellow prisoner in Rome.

Marsena

(Persian origin: Uncertain meaning)

(Esther 1:14). 5th century B.C. Marsena was one of the seven high officials of Persia and Media—the others were Shethar, Carshena, Tarshish, Meres, Admatha, and Memucan— whom King Ahasuerus consulted about the punishment to be imposed on Queen Vashti for disobeying his command to appear before him.

Martha

(Chaldean: *Mistress*)

(Luke 10:38). A.D. 1st century. Martha lived in the town of Bethany, about two miles away from Jerusalem, with her sister Mary and her brother Lazarus, all three of whom were held by Jesus in great affection.

Jesus and his disciples came to their village, and Martha welcomed them in their home. While she prepared dinner and set the table, her sister Mary sat down at the feet of Jesus and listened to his teaching.

Martha complained that her sister had left her to do all the work, and she asked Jesus to tell Mary to come and help her. Jesus answered that Mary had chosen the right thing.

Sometime later, the sisters sent Jesus a message, telling him that their brother Lazarus was very ill. Jesus told his disciples that he would go back to Judea, because his dear friend Lazarus had died.

The disciples feared that, if they would return to Judea, the people would stone them, but Thomas told them, "Let us all go along with the teacher, so that we may die with him".

When Jesus arrived, he found that Lazarus had been buried four days before. The house was full with people who had come to comfort the sisters for their brother's death.

When Martha heard that Jesus was coming, she went out to greet him, while her sister remained inside the house.

Martha said to Jesus, "Lord, if you had been here, my brother would not have died, but, even now, I know that whatever you will ask of God, God will grant it to you".

Jesus answered, "Your brother will come back to life".

"I know he will do that, at the end of the days", said Martha.

Jesus said to her, "I am the Resurrection and the life. Whoever believes in him, will live, even if he dies; and whoever believes in me, will never die. Do you believe this?"

"Yes, Lord", she said, "I believe that you are the Messiah, the Son of God, who has come to the world".

Martha went into the house and said into her sister Mary's ear, "The Master has arrived, and he is calling you".

Mary rose and hurried out of the house to meet Jesus. The people who had come to console them followed her, thinking that she was going to the grave to weep there. They took him to the grave, which was a cave with its entrance closed by a stone. Jesus looked at it and wept.

The people said, "See how he loved him!"

Others said, "He restored sight to a blind man. Couldn't he have prevented the death of this man?"

Jesus ordered, "Take away the stone".

Martha said, "Lord, he has been dead already four days. There is bound to be a bad smell".

Jesus replied, "Didn't I say to you that, if you would believe, you would see the glory of God?"

They moved the stone from the entrance to the cave. Jesus lifted up his eyes and said, "Father, thank you for listening to me. I know that you always hear me, but I have said this, because of the people who are standing next to me, so that they should believe that you sent me". Then, in a loud voice, he said, "Lazarus, come out!"

Lazarus came out, with his hands, feet, and face wrapped in his burial clothes. "Untie him", said Jesus, "and let him go".

Many of the people who saw this became believers. Others went to the Pharisees and told them what Jesus had done.

Six days before the Passover, Jesus returned to Bethany. Martha prepared a dinner for Jesus and his disciples and served it.

While Jesus was eating, her sister Mary poured an expensive perfume on his feet and wiped them with her hair. Judas Iscariot protested that it was a waste of money, because the perfume could have been sold for three hundred silver coins, and the proceeds given to the poor. Jesus told them to leave her alone, and to let her keep what she had for the day of his burial, and that they would always have the poor with them, but they would not always have Jesus.

Mary

(From the Hebrew *Miriam* [*Rebellious*])

1. (Matthew 1:16). A.D. 1st century. Mary, a young woman living in Nazareth, was engaged to Joseph, a carpenter who descended from the royal line of King David.

   One day, the angel Gabriel appeared to her and announced that she would become pregnant and give birth to a son, whom she would call Jesus, who would be a king with a kingdom that would never end.

   Mary asked the angel, "I am a virgin. How can this be?"

   The angel answered, "The Holy Spirit will come on you, and for this reason, the holy child will be called the Son of God".

   The angel added that Elisabeth, her relative, was six months pregnant, although she was an old woman.

   "I am the Lord's servant, may it happen to me as you have said", answered Mary, and the angel departed.

   Soon afterward, Mary traveled to the town in Judea, where Elizabeth lived with her husband Zacharias. When Elisabeth saw Mary, she blessed her and the fruit of her womb. Mary stayed with her relatives for three months and then returned to her own house.

   Joseph found out that she was pregnant, and being a kind and considerate man who did not wish to make a scandal that would disgrace Mary publicly and bring shame upon her, he made plans to break the engagement privately. While he was thinking about this, an angel appeared to him in a dream and told him, "Do not be afraid to take Mary to be your wife, for it was by the Holy Spirit that she has conceived. Her son will be called Jesus, because he will save his people from their sins". Joseph woke up and married Mary, but did not have sexual relations with her.

   The emperor Augustus decreed a census of all the inhabitants of the Roman Empire, each person to be counted in his own city. Joseph, being a descendant of David, had to travel to Bethlehem with Mary, who was in the last month of her pregnancy.

   When they arrived in Bethlehem, they found that the city was crowded, and the inn was full. They had no choice but to rest in a manger. There, Mary gave birth to Jesus. On the eighth day, Jesus was circumcised, according to Jewish custom.

   When the time came for Jesus, as a first-born child, to be redeemed according to the Law (Numbers 18:15), Joseph, his wife, and the baby went to the Temple in Jerusalem, where Joseph sacrificed a pair of doves. The baby was seen and recognized as the Messiah by Simeon, a devout man, and also by Anna, a prophetess, who thanked God and spoke of Jesus to all the pilgrims who came to Jerusalem.

   A short time later, astrologers, who had heard that the king of the Jews had been born, followed a star, which guided them to Bethlehem. They saw the baby, worshipped him, and gave him gifts of gold, frankincense, and myrrh. Then, they returned to their country.

After the astrologers left, an angel appeared to Joseph in a dream and said to him, "Herod is searching for the child in order to kill him. You and your family should escape to Egypt and stay there, until I will let you know when it is safe to return". That same night, Joseph and his family left for Egypt.

After the death of Herod, an angel appeared to Joseph in Egypt and told him to return to Israel, where, in the meantime, Archelaus had succeeded his father Herod as king of Judea.

Joseph, fearful of Herod's son, avoided Judea and, having received more instructions in a dream, traveled to the Galilee, where the family settled in the town of Nazareth.

When Jesus was twelve years old, the family went to Jerusalem for the feast of the Passover. On their return trip to Nazareth, Joseph and Mary noticed, after a day's journey, that the boy was missing.

They went back to Jerusalem to search for their son, and, after three days, they found him in the Temple, sitting with the Jewish teachers, listening and asking them questions that amazed all who heard him. Mary reproached him, for having caused them so much worry.

Jesus answered, "Why did you have to search for me? Didn't you know that I would be in my Father's house?"

They did not understand his answer. Jesus went back with his parents to Nazareth, where he grew up in body and in wisdom.

Joseph is not mentioned again in the Gospels, which means that he probably died before Jesus started his public ministry.

Mary was present the first time that her son Jesus made a miracle. This happened at a wedding in the town of Cana, where Mary, Jesus, and his disciples had been invited.

Mary noticed that there was no more wine left and mentioned it to her son. Jesus told the servants to fill with water six stone water jars that were there.

After they filled them to the top, he told them to draw some water out and take it to the man in charge of the feast. The water had turned to wine.

When the man tasted it, he said to the bridegroom, "Everyone serves the best wine first, and at the end he serves the ordinary wine, but you have saved the best wine, until now!"

One day, sometime later, when Jesus was preaching near the lake of Galilee, someone told him that his mother and brothers had arrived and were standing outside, waiting to speak with him.

Jesus answered, "My disciples are my mother and my brothers. Anybody who does what God wants him to do is my brother, my sister, and my mother".

Mary was present at the crucifixion of her son, together with other women. Jesus saw his mother and the disciple he loved standing there, and he said to his mother, "He is your son", and to the disciple, he said, "She is your mother". From that time, the disciple took her to live in his home.

The last mention of Mary in the Bible states that she frequently met with the disciples to pray as a group (Acts of the Apostles 1:14).

Note: According to Matthew (Matthew 13:55), Jesus had four brothers—James, Joses, Simon, and Judas—and an unspecified number of sisters. Some scholars believe that these were Joseph's children by a previous marriage; others say that the meaning of the words "brothers" and "sisters", in these passages of the Gospels, refer to cousins or other close relatives.

2. (Matthew 27:56). A.D. 1st century. Mary, from the town of Magdala, was called Magdalene to differentiate her from the other women called Mary in the Bible.

Tradition identifies her with the nameless woman, with a sinful past, who went to the house of Simon the Pharisee, where Jesus was eating, and stood behind Jesus, crying and wetting his feet with her tears. Then, she dried his feet with her hair, kissed them, and poured perfume on them.

Jesus said to her, "Your sins are forgiven; your faith has saved you; go in peace".

After Jesus had driven out the seven devils that had possessed her, Mary Magdalene followed him from Galilee to Jerusalem, and she was among the women who witnessed his crucifixion.

Two days later, early on Sunday morning, Mary Magdalene and another woman, also called Mary, went to the sepulcher where Joseph of Arimathaea had placed Jesus' body.

They were worried about not being able to move the heavy stone from the entrance to the tomb, but when they arrived there, they saw that the stone had already been rolled back.

They entered the sepulcher and saw a young man—according to the gospel of John (John 20:17), it was Jesus himself—who told them that Jesus had been raised, and that they should tell Peter and the disciples that Jesus was on his way to Galilee, where they could see him. The women ran away, terrified.

Mary Magdalene went to the disciples and found them mourning and crying. They did not believe her, when she told them that Jesus was alive.

3. (Matthew 27:56). A.D. 1st century. Mary, wife of Cleophas and the mother of James the Younger and Joses, was among the women who witnessed Jesus' crucifixion.

Two days later, early on Sunday morning, Mary and Mary Magdalene went to the sepulcher where Joseph of Arimathaea had placed Jesus' body.

They were worried about not being able to move the heavy stone from the entrance to the tomb, but when they arrived there, they saw that the stone had already been rolled back.

They entered the sepulcher, and saw a young man—according to the gospel of John (John 20:17), it was Jesus himself—who told them that Jesus had been raised, and that they should tell Peter and the disciples that Jesus was on his way to Galilee, where they could see him. The women ran away, terrified.

4. (Luke 10:39). A.D. 1st century. Mary lived in the town of Bethany, about two miles away from Jerusalem, with her sister Martha and her brother Lazarus, all three of whom were held by Jesus in great affection.

Jesus and his disciples came to their village, and Martha welcomed them in their home. While she prepared dinner and set the table, Mary sat down at the feet of Jesus and listened to his teaching.

Martha complained that Mary had left her to do all the work, and she asked Jesus to tell her sister to come and help her. Jesus answered that Mary had chosen the right thing.

Sometime later, the sisters sent Jesus a message, telling him that their brother Lazarus was very ill. Jesus told his disciples that he would go back to Judea, because his dear friend Lazarus had died.

The disciples feared that, if they would return to Judea, the people would stone them, but Thomas told them, "Let us all go along with the teacher, so that we may die with him".

When Jesus arrived, he found that Lazarus had been buried four days before. The house was full with people who had come to comfort the sisters for their brother's death.

When Martha heard that Jesus was coming, she went out to greet him, while Mary remained inside the house.

Martha said to Jesus, "Lord, if you had been here, my brother would not have died, but, even now, I know that whatever you will ask of God, God will grant it to you".

Jesus answered, "Your brother will come back to life".

"I know he will do that, at the end of the days", said Martha.

Jesus said to her, "I am the Resurrection and the life. Whoever believes in me, will live, even if he dies; and whoever believes in me, will never die. Do you believe this?"

"Yes, Lord", she said, "I believe that you are the Messiah, the Son of God, who has come to the world".

Martha went into the house and said

into Mary's ear, "The Master has arrived, and he is calling you".

Mary rose and hurried out of the house to meet Jesus. The people who had come to console them followed her, thinking that she was going to the grave to weep there. They took him to the grave, which was a cave with its entrance closed by a stone. Jesus looked at it and wept.

The people said, "See how he loved him!"

Others said, "He restored sight to a blind man. Couldn't he have prevented the death of this man?"

Jesus ordered, "Take away the stone".

Martha said, "Lord, he has been dead already four days. There is bound to be a bad smell".

Jesus replied, "Didn't I say to you that, if you would believe, you would see the glory of God?"

They moved the stone from the entrance to the cave. Jesus lifted up his eyes and said, "Father, thank you for listening to me. I know that you always hear me, but I have said this, because of the people who are standing next to me, so that, they should believe that you sent me". Then, in a loud voice, he said, "Lazarus, come out!"

Lazarus came out, with his hands, feet, and face wrapped in his burial clothes. "Untie him", said Jesus, "and let him go".

Many of the people who saw this became believers. Others went to the Pharisees and told them what Jesus had done.

Six days before the Passover, Jesus returned to Bethany. Martha prepared a dinner for Jesus and his disciples and served it.

While Jesus was eating, Mary poured an expensive perfume on his feet and wiped them with her hair. Judas Iscariot protested that it was a waste of money, because the perfume could have been sold for three hundred silver coins, and the proceeds given to the poor. Jesus told them to leave her alone, and to let her keep what she had

for the day of his burial, and that they would always have the poor with them, but they would not always have Jesus.

5. (Acts of the Apostles 12:12). A.D. 1st century. Mary, a relative of Barnabas, was a Christian woman, owner of a house in Jerusalem where people gathered to pray. It was in her house that Peter found refuge, when he escaped, with the help of an angel, from Herod's prison.

Her son John, surnamed Mark, accompanied Saul and Barnabas in their trip through Asia Minor and the Greek islands, preaching the gospel and making new converts.

6. (Romans 16:6). A.D. 1st century. Mary was a Christian woman to whom Paul sent greetings in his letter to the Christians in Rome, adding that she had worked hard for the church.

Note: All the women named Mary in the New Testament were called Miriam in Hebrew, including the Virgin Mary.

Mash

(Uncertain origin and meaning)

(Genesis 10:23). Unspecified date. Mash was a son of Aram and a grandson of Shem, the son of Noah. His brothers were Uz, Gether, Gether and Hul.

The first book of Chronicles calls him Meshech and states that he was the brother of Aram, and the son of Shem (1 Chronicles 1:17).

Massa

(Hebrew origin: *Burden*)

(Genesis 25:14). 18th century B.C. Massa, grandson of Abraham and his Egyptian concubine Hagar, was one of the twelve sons of Ishmael.

Massa's brothers were Nebajoth, Hadad, Mibsam, Mishma, Jetur, Dumah, Adbeel, Tema, Kedar, Naphish, and Kedemah, all of them ancestors of great nations. His sister, Mahalath—also called Bashemath—married Esau, the son of Isaac.

Mathusala

(Hebrew origin: *Man of a dart*)

(Luke 3:37). Antediluvian. Mathusala—also spelled Methuselah (Genesis 5:21)—was a son of Enoch and the grandfather of Noah.

He was one hundred and eighty-seven years old, when Lamech, his first son, was born. Mathusala died at the age of nine hundred and sixty-nine, the longest life span mentioned in the Bible.

Matred

(Hebrew origin: *Propulsive*)

(Genesis 36:39). Unspecified date. Matred, the daughter of Mezahab, was the mother of Mehetabel, the wife of Hadar, an Edomite king.

Matri

(Hebrew origin: *Rainy*)

(1 Samuel 10:21). Unspecified date. Matri was an ancestor of the clan of the tribe of Benjamin, to which the family of King Saul belonged.

Mattan

(Hebrew origin: *Gift*)

1. (2 Kings 11:18). 9th century B.C. Mattan was the High Priest in the Temple of Baal in Jerusalem, during the reign of Queen Athaliah.

   A coup led by the priest Jehoiada and several army officers proclaimed in the Temple the seven-year-old Joash as the legitimate king. They put a crown on the boy and anointed him, while everybody shouted, "God save the king".

   Athaliah, hearing the shouts of the crowd, rushed to the Temple, screaming, "Treason! Treason!"

   The guards seized her and killed her at the Horse Gate of the palace. The crowd assaulted the Temple of Baal, destroyed the building and the idols, and killed Mattan.

2. (Jeremiah 38:1). 7th century B.C. His son Shephatiah, an official in the court of King Zedekiah—together with Jucal, son of Shelemiah; Gedaliah, son of Pashur; and Pashur, son of Malchiah—asked the king to put Jeremiah to death for preaching surrender and undermining the courage of the soldiers.

   King Zedekiah told them that they could do with Jeremiah whatever they wanted. Shephatiah and his fellow court officials cast the prophet into the dungeon of Malchiah, which was in the court of the prison.

Mattaniah

(Hebrew origin: *God's gift*)

1. (2 Kings 24:17). 6th century B.C. Mattaniah was the original name of Zedekiah, the last king of Judah, son of King Josiah and Hamutal. His brothers were Johanan, the firstborn; Eliakim, who reigned under the name Jehoiakim; and Shallum, who reigned under the name Jehoahaz.

   Mattaniah was twenty-one years old, when Nebuchadnezzar, king of Babylon, deposed his nephew Jehoiachin—who had reigned for only three months—made him king, and gave him the name of Zedekiah.

   After nine years of being a puppet king, Mattaniah made an alliance with several neighboring kingdoms and rebelled against the Babylonians, against the advice of the prophet Jeremiah.

   Nebuchadnezzar invaded Judah with a powerful army and laid siege to Jerusalem. The city defended itself heroically, during two years, until finally, in the year 587 B.C., in the middle of the summer, the Babylonian army broke through the northern wall. Further resistance became hopeless.

   King Zedekiah and some of his soldiers escaped from the city and fled eastwards, toward the Jordan River, but they were captured near Jericho. Zedekiah was brought before Nebuchadnezzar and was forced to see the slaying of his children. He was then blinded and taken in chains to Babylon, where he died in prison.

Jerusalem was sacked, the Temple destroyed, and most of the inhabitants were taken off to Babylon into captivity. Thus ended the kingdom of Judah, which had lasted three hundred forty years, from the days of Rehoboam till the destruction of the Temple that had been built by King Solomon.

2. (1 Chronicles 9:15). 6th century B.C. Mattaniah, son of Micah, a Levite, was among the first to settle in the land of Judah, after the return from the Babylonian Exile.

3. (1 Chronicles 25:4). 10th century B.C. Mattaniah, son of Heman, a Levite, member of a family of musicians, was in charge of the ninth turn of service that played musical instruments—cymbals, psalteries, and harps—in the House of God, during the reign of David.

He had thirteen brothers and three sisters, all of them trained as skillful musicians by their father, Heman, one of the three leading musicians—the other two were Asaph and Jeduthun—of the period.

4. (2 Chronicles 20:14). Unspecified date. Mattaniah, a Levite descendant of Asaph, was an ancestor of Jahaziel, the prophet who predicted victory for King Jehoshaphat of Judah in his war against the armies of Ammon and Moab.

5. (2 Chronicles 29:13). 8th century B.C. Mattaniah, a descendant of Asaph, was one of the Levites who assembled all the other Levites to make themselves ritually clean, and to purify the Temple, during the reign of King Hezekiah of Judah.

6. (Ezra 10:26). 5th century B.C. Mattaniah, a descendant of Elam, divorced his foreign wife, during the days of Ezra.

7. (Ezra 10:27). 5th century B.C. Mattaniah, a descendant of Zattu, divorced his foreign wife, during the days of Ezra.

8. (Ezra 10:30). 5th century B.C. Mattaniah, a descendant of Pahathmoab, divorced his foreign wife, during the days of Ezra.

9. (Ezra 10:37). 5th century B.C. Mattaniah, a descendant of Bani, divorced his foreign wife, during the days of Ezra.

10. (Nehemiah 11:17). 5th century B.C.

Mattaniah, son of Micha, was a Levite who lived in Jerusalem, during the days of Nehemiah, and was in charge of leading the thanksgiving prayers.

11. (Nehemiah 11:22). Unspecified date. Mattaniah, son of Micha, was the ancestor of Uzzi, son of Bani, the overseer of the Levites in Jerusalem, during the days of Nehemiah.

12. (Nehemiah 12:25). 5th century B.C. Mattaniah was a gatekeeper, during the days of Nehemiah.

13. (Nehemiah 12:35). Unspecified date. Mattaniah, son of Michaiah, was an ancestor of the priest Zechariah who played the trumpet in the joyful procession, which celebrated the dedication of the rebuilt walls of Jerusalem, during the days of Nehemiah.

14. (Nehemiah 13:13). 6th century B.C. Mattaniah was the father of Zaccur. His grandson Hanan was one of the four persons designated by Nehemiah to supervise the treasuries of the Temple, and to distribute the offerings among the Levites and the priests.

Mattatha

(Hebrew origin: *Gift of God*)

(Luke 3:31). 10th century B.C. Mattatha, an ancestor of Jesus in Luke's genealogy, was the son of Nathan and a grandson of King David. His son was called Menan.

Mattathah

(Hebrew origin: *Gift of God*)

(Ezra 10:33). 5th century B.C. Mattathah, a descendant of Hashum, divorced his foreign wife, during the days of Ezra.

Mattathias

(Hebrew origin: *Gift of God*)

1. (Luke 3:25). Unspecified date. Mattathias, son of Amos and father of Joseph, was an ancestor of Jesus, according to Luke's genealogy.

2. (Luke 3:26). Unspecified date. Mattathias, son of Semei and father of Maath, was an ancestor of Jesus, according to Luke's genealogy.

Mattenai

(Hebrew origin: *Liberal*)

1. (Ezra 10:33). 5th century B.C. Mattenai, a descendant of Hashum, divorced his foreign wife, during the days of Ezra.

2. (Ezra 10:37). 5th century B.C. Mattenai, a descendant of Bani, divorced his foreign wife, during the days of Ezra.

3. (Nehemiah 12:19). 5th century B.C. Mattenai was the leader of a clan of priests who descended from Joiarib, during the days of the High Priest Joiakim and Nehemiah.

Matthan

(Hebrew origin: *Present*)

(Matthew 1:15). Unspecified date. Matthan, son of Eleazar and father of Jacob, was an ancestor or Jesus, according to Matthew's genealogy.

Matthat

(Hebrew origin: *Gift of God*)

1. (Luke 3:24). Unspecified date. Matthat, son of Levi and father of Heli, was an ancestor of Jesus, according to Luke's genealogy.

2. (Luke 3:29). Unspecified date. Matthat, son of Levi and father of Jorim, was an ancestor of Jesus, according to Luke's genealogy.

Matthew

(Greek form of the Hebrew origin: *Gift of God*)

(Matthew 9:9). A.D. 1st century. Matthew, also called Levi, son of Alphaeus (Mark 2:13), worked as a tax collector in Capernaum, when Jesus saw him and told him to follow. He didn't hesitate for a second, got up, and followed Jesus.

Matthew made a great feast in his house, in honor of Jesus, to which he invited publicans and other people of bad reputation. This gave grounds to the scribes and the Pharisees to criticize Jesus for eating and drinking with sinners.

Jesus answered, "Healthy people do not need a physician, but those who are sick do".

Other references to Matthew are found only within the lists of the apostles. Scholars believe that he probably was the author of the gospel according to Matthew.

Matthias

(From the Hebrew origin: *Gift of God*)

(Acts of the Apostles 1:23). A.D. 1st century. Matthias and Barsabas were candidates to replace Judas Iscariot as the twelfth apostle. The apostles chose Matthias by lot.

Mattithiah

(Hebrew origin: *Gift of God*)

1. (1 Chronicles 9:31). 6th century B.C. Mattithiah, a Levite, eldest son of Shallum, a descendant of Korah, returned from the Babylonian Exile and settled in Jerusalem, where he was responsible for the baked offerings cooked in flat pans.

2. (1 Chronicles 15:18). 10th century B.C. Mattithiah, a Levite of the second rank, was among those chosen by the chief of the Levites to sing and play musical instruments in front of the Ark of the Covenant, when it was carried from the house of Obededom to its resting place in Jerusalem, during the reign of King David.

When his father Jeduthun was appointed by King David to play the harp in the House of the Lord, Mattithiah and his brothers assisted their father in his work. Mattithiah was in charge of the fourteenth turn of service to play musical instruments in the House of God.

3. (Ezra 10:43). 5th century B.C. Mattithiah, a descendant of Nebo, divorced his foreign wife, during the days of Ezra.

4. (Nehemiah 8:4). 5th century B.C. Mattithiah was one of the leaders who

stood next to Ezra, upon a pulpit of wood, when the scribe read the Law of Moses to the people in the marketplace in Jerusalem.

Mebunnai

(Hebrew origin: *Built up*)

(2 Samuel 23:27). 10th century B.C. Mebunnai, the Hushathite—called Sibbecai in the first book of Chronicles (1 Chronicles 11:29), and Sibbechai in the second book of Samuel (2 Samuel 21:18)—was one of "The Thirty", an elite group in King David's army and the commander of a division of twenty-four thousand men. He was in charge of everything related to the army, during the eighth month of each year.

In a battle against the Philistines, Mebunnai killed Saph—also called Sippai—a descendant of a tribe of giants.

Medad

(Hebrew origin: *Affectionate*)

(Numbers 11:26). 13th century B.C. Medad and Eldad were two of the elders to whom God gave some of the spirit of Moses, so that they could help him by sharing his leadership tasks.

Moses, overwhelmed by his responsibilities, had spoken to God in his distress, "Why have you treated me so badly, laying the burden of this people on me? Did I conceive them? Did I bring them to birth? I cannot be responsible for all these people by myself; it is too much for me. If you deal, thus, with me, I prefer that you kill me, and let me see no more of my misery".

God answered, "Bring seventy elders of the people, that you know are respected leaders, to the Tent, and let them stand next to you. I will come down and speak with you there, and I will take from the spirit, which is on you, and will put it on them, and they will share your burden".

Moses brought the elders to the Tent and placed them around it. God came down in a cloud, spoke to Moses, took from his spirit, and gave it to the elders, who started to prophesy.

Two of the elders, Medad and Eldad, had remained in the camp, but they also received the spirit and prophesied inside the camp.

A young man came running and complained to Moses, "Eldad and Medad are acting like prophets in the camp".

Joshua heard this and said, "My lord Moses, forbid them!"

Moses answered, "Are you worried about me? I wish that the Lord would give his Spirit to all his people, and make all of them prophets!"

Medan

(Hebrew origin: *Discord*)

(Genesis 25:2). 19th century B.C. Medan was one of the six sons of Keturah, the woman whom Abraham married, after the death of Sarah. His brothers were Zimran, Jokshan, Ishbak, Midian, and Shuah.

Shortly before Abraham died, he made Isaac his sole heir, and, in order to avoid trouble, he donated gifts to the sons of his second marriage and sent them away to the east.

Mehetabeel

(Hebrew origin: *Improved by God*)

(Nehemiah 6:10). 6th century B.C. Mehetabeel was the father of Delaiah and the grandfather of Shemaiah.

His grandson Shemaiah was hired by Tobiah and Sanballat, Nehemiah's enemies, to convince Nehemiah that he should hide in the Temple. He didn't succeed, because Nehemiah realized that his enemies were setting a trap for him, to induce him to sin, and then report it.

Mehetabel

(Hebrew origin: *Improved by God*)

(Genesis 36:39). Unspecified date. Mehetabel, daughter of Matred and granddaughter of Mezahab, was the wife of Hadar, the king of Edom, who reigned in the city of Pau.

Mehida

(Hebrew origin: *Junction*)

(Ezra 2:52). Unspecified date. Mehida was the ancestor of a clan of Temple servants that returned with Zerubbabel from the Babylonian Exile.

Mehir

(Hebrew origin: *Price*)

(1 Chronicles 4:11). Unspecified date. Mehir, a descendant of Judah, was the son of Chelub and the nephew of Shuah. His son was called Eshton. His grandchildren were Bethrapha, Paseah, and Tehinnah.

Mehujael

(Hebrew origin: *Smitten of God*)

(Genesis 4:18). Antediluvian. Mehujael was the son of Irad and the father of Methusael.

Mehuman

(Persian origin: Uncertain meaning)

(Esther 1:10). 5th century B.C. Mehuman was one of the seven eunuchs who served in the court of Ahasuerus, the king of Persia, usually identified by historians as King Xerxes I of Persia, son and successor of Darius I.

The other six eunuchs who served the king were Harbona, Abagtha, Biztha, Bigtha, Zethar, and Carcas.

In the third year of his reign, the king gave a banquet for all his princes and administrators to show off his wealth. The great celebration lasted one hundred and eighty days.

When the festivities for the nobles ended, the king gave a banquet in the garden of his palace for the common people of Shushan. During seven days, everybody, rich and poor, drank as much as he wanted. At the same time, Vashti, his queen, gave a banquet for the women inside the palace.

On the seventh day of the celebration, the drunken Ahasuerus ordered Mehuman and the other six eunuchs who served the king to fetch Queen Vashti, and to make sure that she was wearing her royal crown. She was a beautiful woman, and the king wanted everybody to see her. The eunuchs returned and told the king that the queen refused to come.

Mehunim

(Hebrew origin: *Residents*)

(Ezra 2:50). Unspecified date. Mehunim—also spelled Meunim (Nehemiah 7:52)—was the ancestor of a clan of Temple servants that returned with Zerubbabel from the Babylonian Exile.

Melatiah

(Hebrew origin: *God has delivered*)

(Nehemiah 3:7). 5th century B.C. Melatiah, the Gibeonite, helped to repair the walls of Jerusalem, during the days of Nehemiah.

Melchi

(Hebrew origin: *My king*)

1. (Luke 3:24). Unspecified date. Melchi was the son of Janna and the father of Levi, according to Luke's genealogy of Jesus.
2. (Luke 3:28). Unspecified date. Melchi was the son of Addi and the father of Neri, according to Luke's genealogy of Jesus.

Melchiah

(Hebrew origin: *God is my king*)

(Jeremiah 21:1). 7th century B.C. Melchiah—also spelled Malchiah (Jeremiah 38:1)—was the father of Pashur, one of the officials in the court of King Zedekiah.

Melchisedec

(Hebrew origin: *King of righteousness*)

(Hebrews 5:6). 19th century B.C. Melchisedec is the New Testament's spelling of Melchizedek, the priest-king of Salem, a city kingdom, which scholars identify with Jerusalem.

When Abraham returned victorious, after having defeated Chedorlaomer and his three allied kings, and having rescued his nephew Lot, Melchizedek received him with bread and wine and blessed him. Abraham gave him a tenth of all the booty that he had recovered.

The epistle to the Hebrews mentions him repeatedly as a High Priest who did not descend from Aaron, but was the founder of an order called by his name, to prove that Jesus, who was not a descendent from the priestly caste, had been made by God an eternal priest, superior to the priests who descend from Aaron.

Melchishua

(Hebrew origin: *My king is salvation*)

(1 Samuel 14:49). 11th century B.C. Melchishua, son of King Saul, fought with his father, against the Philistines in the battle of Mount Gilboa, and was killed, together with his brothers Jonathan and Abinadab. His name is also spelled Malchishua (1 Chronicles 8:33).

Melchizedek

(Hebrew origin: *King of righteousness*)

(Genesis 14:18). 19th century B.C. Melchizedek was the priest-king of Salem, a city kingdom, which scholars identify with Jerusalem.

When Abraham returned victorious, after having defeated Chedorlaomer and his three allied kings, and having rescued his nephew Lot, Melchizedek received him with bread and wine and blessed him. Abraham gave him a tenth of all the booty that he had recovered.

The New Testament spells his name Melchisedec.

(Hebrew 5:6). The epistle to the Hebrews mentions him repeatedly as a High Priest who did not descend from Aaron, but was the founder of an order called by his name, to prove that Jesus, who was not a descendent from the priestly caste, had been made by God an eternal priest, superior to the priests who descend from Aaron.

Melea

(Uncertain origin and meaning)

(Luke 3:31). Unspecified date. Melea, son of Menan and father of Eliakim, was an ancestor of Jesus, according to Luke's genealogy.

Melech

(Hebrew origin: *King*)

(1 Chronicles 8:35). Unspecified date. Melech, son of Micah, was a descendant of King Saul. His brothers were Pithon, Tarea, and Ahaz.

Melicu

(Hebrew origin: *Regnant*)

(Nehemiah 12:14). Unspecified date. His descendant Jonathan was the head of a priestly clan, when Joiakim was High Priest, during the time of Nehemiah.

Melzar

(Hebrew origin: *Butler*)

(Daniel 1:11). 6th century B.C. Melzar, an official of the Babylonian court, was placed by King Nebuchadnezzar in charge of four Jewish boys—Daniel, Hananiah, Mishael, and Azariah—who were being educated for service in the Babylonian royal court.

In order not to transgress by eating and drinking ritually forbidden food and wine, Daniel asked permission from Melzar to eat only legumes and drink only water.

Melzar feared that this diet might endanger their health, but Daniel asked him to let him try it for ten days. When the ten days were over, the four Jewish boys looked better and healthier than the boys who had eaten of the king's food.

Memucan

(Persian origin: Uncertain meaning)

(Esther 1:14). 5th century B.C. Memucan was one of the seven high officials of Persia and Media—the others were Tarshish, Carshena,

Admatha, Meres, Shethar, and Marsena—whom King Ahasuerus consulted about the punishment due to Queen Vashti for disobeying his command to appear before him.

Memucan, speaking on behalf of the seven advisers, told the king that he should divorce the queen and marry another woman worthier than Vashti, in order to prevent the women in the kingdom from following Vashti's rebellious example, thus, assuring that all wives would treat their husbands with respect. The king accepted his advice and did accordingly.

Menahem

(Hebrew origin: *Comforter*)

(2 Kings 15:14). 8th century B.C. Menahem, son of Gadi, rebelled in Tirzah against Shallum, the man who, a month before, had killed Zachariah, the son of King Jeroboam II, and usurped the throne of the kingdom of Israel.

Menahem marched to Samaria, killed Shallum, and proclaimed himself king, the sixteenth king of Israel, since the partition. The inhabitants of Tiphsah, a town which had refused to surrender, were killed and the pregnant women were ripped open.

When the king of Assyria, Tiglathpileser—also spelled Tilgathpilneser, (1 Chronicles 5:6), and called Pul in another verse (2 Kings 15:19)—invaded Israel, Menahem succeeded in turning him back by paying the Assyrian a tribute of one thousand talents of silver, a sum, which he got by taxing every rich man in the kingdom fifty shekels of silver.

Menahem died, after reigning for ten years, and was succeeded by his son Pekahiah.

Menan

(Uncertain origin and meaning)

(Luke 3:31). Unspecified date. Menan, son of Mattatha and father of Melea, was an ancestor of Jesus, according to Luke's genealogy.

Meonothai

(Hebrew origin: *My dwellings*)

(1 Chronicles 4:14). 12th century B.C. Meonothai, son of Othniel, a descendant of Judah, was the father of Ophrah. His father Othniel liberated the Israelites from the oppression of Chushanrishathaim, king of Mesopotamia.

Mephibosheth

(Hebrew origin: *Dispeller of shame*)

1. (2 Samuel 4:4). 10th century B.C. Mephibosheth was the son of Jonathan, David's great friend. His real name was Meribbaal (1 Chronicles 8:34), *Quarreler of Baal*. (See note below.)

   Mephibosheth was five years old, when his nurse, having heard that Saul and Jonathan had been killed fighting against the Philistines, fled in panic, carrying the child. The boy fell from his nurse's arms and became lame in both feet.

   Mephibosheth grew up in Lodebar, in the house of Machir, the son of Ammiel. Years later, David, for the sake of his dead friend Jonathan, inquired if there were any survivors of Saul's family.

   Ziba, a man who had been one of Saul's servants, was summoned to the court and informed David that there was one survivor, Mephibosheth, a cripple, who lived in the house of Machir in Lodebar.

   King David had Mephibosheth brought to his presence. When Mephibosheth saw David, he flung himself on his face and prostrated himself. David told him not to be afraid, that his grandfather's land would be returned to him, for the sake of Jonathan's memory, and that he would always eat at the king's table.

   The king told Ziba that he was giving to Mephibosheth everything that had belonged to Saul, and that he, Ziba, his fifteen sons, and his twenty slaves would farm the land for Mephibosheth to provide food for his master's grandson. Mephibosheth stayed in Jerusalem with his young son Micha.

During Absalom's rebellion, when David was fleeing from Jerusalem, Ziba came to him with two asses, carrying two hundred loaves of bread, a hundred bunches of raisins, a hundred summer fruits, and a bottle of wine, and told the king that the asses were for the king's family, the food for his attendants, and the wine for those who were exhausted.

The king asked him, "Where is Mephibosheth?"

Ziba replied, "He has stayed behind in Jerusalem, hoping that the people of Israel would crown him king".

David said to Ziba, "Everything that had belonged to Mephibosheth is now yours". Ziba bowed low and thanked him.

When Absalom was defeated and David returned to Jerusalem, Mephibosheth was one of the men who came down to meet the king. He had not pared his toenails, or trimmed his beard, nor washed his clothes from the day that the king had departed, until the day he returned safe.

The king asked him, "Why didn't you come with me?"

Mephibosheth answered, "I am lame. I intended to saddle my donkey and join the king, but Ziba deceived me and slandered me. My lord, the king is like an angel of God, so do whatever seems right to you. All my family deserved to be put to death, but you gave me the right to eat at your table. I have no right to appeal to you".

David said, "Let's not speak more about this matter. You and Ziba will divide Saul's property".

Mephibosheth answered, "Let him take all. It is enough for me that Your Majesty has returned home safely".

Mephibosheth had a son called Micah—also spelled Micha—who gave him four grandsons: Pithon, Melech, Tarea, and Ahaz.

2. (2 Samuel 21:8). 10th century B.C. Mephibosheth was the son of King Saul and his concubine Rizpah. Mephibosheth, his brother Armoni, and their five nephews were delivered by King David to the Gibeonites, who hanged them on a hill, to avenge Saul's massacre.

His mother Rizpah placed sackcloth on a rock and sat on it to guard the bodies against the birds and the beasts of the field, from the beginning of the harvest season, until the rains came, months later.

Note: The word "Baal", which means *Master* or *Lord* in Hebrew, was originally a title of dignity. Eventually it became associated to a Canaanite god, causing the ancient Hebrew editors of the Bible to substitute the word "Bosheth", meaning *Shame*, for "Baal".

Merab

(Hebrew origin: *Increasing*)

(1 Samuel 14:49). 10th century B.C. Merab was the eldest of the two daughters—the other one was Michal—of King Saul and his wife Ahinoam.

Saul, jealous of David's victories and popularity, devised a plan to get rid of him by offering him Merab in marriage, if he would fight against the Philistines, secretly hoping that David would be killed in battle. However, when the time came, instead of giving Merab to David, he married her to Adriel, the son of Barzillai the Meholathite.

The couple had five sons who, many years later, together with Mephibosheth and Armoni, sons of King Saul and his concubine Rizpah, were delivered by King David to the Gibeonites, who hanged them on a hill to avenge Saul's massacre.

Meraiah

(Hebrew origin: *Rebellion*)

(Nehemiah 12:12). 5th century B.C. Meraiah was the head of a priestly clan descended from Seraiah, during the days of the High Priest Joiakim.

Meraioth

(Hebrew origin: *Rebellious*)

1. (1 Chronicles 6:6). 12th century B.C. Meraioth, son of Zerahiah and father of

Amariah, was an ancestor of Zadok, King David's High Priest

2. (1 Chronicles 9:11). Unspecified date. Meraioth, son of Ahitub and father of Zadok, was an ancestor of Azariah, who was a High Priest, after the return from Babylon.

3. (Ezra 7:3). Unspecified date. Meraioth, son of Zerahiah and father of Azariah, was a descendant of Aaron and an ancestor of Ezra the Scribe.

4. (Nehemiah 12:15). Unspecified date. Meraioth was the ancestor of a priestly clan, whose leader was Helkai, when Joiakim was High Priest, during the time of Nehemiah.

Merari

(Hebrew origin: *Bitter*)

(Genesis 46:11). 17th century B.C. Merari, one of the three sons of Levi and the ancestor of a clan of Levites, was one of the seventy Israelites who immigrated to Egypt.

His brothers were Kohath and Gershon. His sons were Mahali and Mushi.

His grandsons—from Mahali—were Eleazar and Kish, and—from Mushi—were Mahli, Eder, and Jeremoth.

Mercurius

(Name of Roman god)

(Acts of the Apostles 14:12). During the stay of Paul and Barnabas in the city of Lystra, Paul healed a cripple who had never walked in his life. This miracle so impressed the pagans in the city that they excitedly exclaimed that Barnabas was Jupiter, and Paul, Mercurius, who came down to earth in the likeness of men.

The priest of Jupiter brought oxen to sacrifice in front of them. Paul and Barnabas cried out that they were not gods but men, and that the people of the city should turn away from idols and believe in the living God.

Mered

(Hebrew origin: *Revolt*)

(1 Chronicles 4:17). Unspecified date.

Mered, a descendant of Judah, was the son of a man named Ezra. He married Bithiah, the daughter of the Pharaoh of Egypt.

Meremoth

(Hebrew origin: *Heights*)

1. (Ezra 8:33). 5th century B.C. Meremoth, the son of the priest Uriah, counted and weighed the silver and gold utensils of the Temple, which Ezra had brought back from the Babylonian Exile.

   He was helped in his task by three Levites: Eleazar, son of Phinehas, Jozabad, son of Jeshua, and Noadiah, son of Binnui.

2. (Ezra 10:36). 5th century B.C. Meremoth, a descendant of Bani, divorced his foreign wife, during the days of Ezra.

3. (Nehemiah 3:4). 5th century B.C. Meremoth, son of Urijah and grandson of Koz, helped to repair the walls of Jerusalem, during the days of Nehemiah.

4. (Nehemiah 10:5). 5th century B.C. Meremoth was one of the priests who signed Nehemiah's solemn agreement to separate themselves from the foreigners living in the land, to refrain from intermarrying with them, and to dedicate their firstborn to God, among other obligations.

5. (Nehemiah 12:3). 6th century B.C. Meremoth was a priest who returned with Zerubbabel from the Babylonian Exile.

Meres

(Persian origin: Uncertain meaning)

(Esther 1:14). 5th century B.C. Meres was one of the seven high officials of Persia and Media—the others were Shethar, Admatha, Tarshish, Carshena, Marsena, and Memucan—whom King Ahasuerus consulted about the punishment to be imposed on Queen Vashti for disobeying his command to appear before him.

Meribbaal

(Hebrew origin: *Quarreler of the god Baal*)

(1 Chronicles 8:34). 10th century B.C.

Meribbaal—called Mephibosheth elsewhere in the Bible—was the son of Jonathan, David's great friend. (Please see the entry for Mephibosheth [2 Samuel 4:4].)

Note: The word "Baal", which means *Master* or *Lord* in Hebrew, was originally a title of dignity. Eventually, it became associated to a Canaanite god, causing the ancient Hebrew editors of the Bible to substitute the word "Bosheth", meaning *Shame* for "Baal".

Merodach

(Name of a pagan god)

(Jeremiah 50:2). Merodach was a Babylonian idol.

Merodachbaladan

(Uncertain origin and meaning)

(Isaiah 39:1). 8th century B.C. Merodachbaladan—called Berodachbaladan in the second book of Kings (2 Kings 20:12)—was the king of Babylon, during the reign of Hezekiah.

Having heard that the king of Judah was very sick, he sent messengers to Jerusalem with letters and gifts to King Hezekiah, to wish him a speedy recovery.

Hezekiah naively gave the Babylonian ambassadors a tour of his palace and the treasure house. He showed them all his treasures, disregarding the Babylonians as a possible threat, because, to him, Babylon was a far-away country.

The prophet Isaiah berated the king, saying that, one day, the Babylonians would destroy Judah, and all the treasures in the palace would be carried off to Babylon.

Mesha

(Hebrew origin: *Departure*)

1. (2 Kings 3:4). 9th century B.C. King Mesha of Moab, a vassal of Israel, paid a tribute to King Ahab of one hundred thousand lambs and one hundred thousand rams with their wool.

When Jehoram became king of Israel, after the accidental death of his brother Ahaziah, Mesha rebelled and refused to continue paying the tribute.

Jehoram entered into an alliance with King Jehoshaphat of Judah and with the king of Edom to go and fight against Moab. After the allied army had traveled for seven days, there was no water left for the soldiers and their cattle.

The prophet Elisha was called. Upon his arrival, he told the king of Israel that he would not have even looked at him if the king of Judah had not also been present. Elisha asked them to bring a musician, and while the musician played, he told them that God commanded them to dig ditches.

Before dawn water came rushing from Edom and turned the ditches into pools. Early the next day the Moabites, thought that the red reflection of the rising sun on the pools was the blood of the kings' armies that, they believed, had fought between themselves.

The Moabites attacked the allied camp but were repulsed and defeated. In spite of its defeat, Moab succeeded in becoming independent from Israelite rule.

2. (1 Chronicles 2:42). Unspecified date. Mesha was the firstborn son of Caleb, nephew of Jerahmeel, and father of Ziph.

3. (1 Chronicles 8:9). Unspecified date. Mesha, born in the country of Moab, was one of the seven sons of Shaharaim, of the tribe of Benjamin, and his wife Hodesh. His brothers—all of them heads of clans—were Zibia, Jobab, Jeuz, Malcham, Shachia, and Mirma.

Meshach

(Uncertain origin and meaning)

(Daniel 1:7). 6th century B.C. Meshach was the Babylonian name that the chief of the eunuchs of King Nebuchadnezzar gave to Mishael, a young boy from a noble Jewish family that resided in Babylon.

Mishael was chosen, together with Daniel and two other young men, Hananiah and Azariah, to receive an education that would allow them to become officials of the king's court.

Years later, at the request of Daniel, the king appointed Mishael and his friends, Hananiah and Azariah, to be in charge over the affairs of the province of Babylon.

When the three men refused to serve the Babylonian gods, or worship the golden idol that the king had set up, they were thrown into a burning furnace. An angel saved them, and the men survived the fire, without even one hair of their heads being singed.

Nebuchadnezzar was so impressed by this miracle, that he blessed God and decreed that anyone who would speak against God would be cut in pieces and his house would be turned into a dunghill.

Meshech

(Hebrew origin: *Drawn out*)

1. (Genesis 10:2). Unspecified date. Meshech, the son of Japheth and grandson of Noah, was the brother of Gomer, Magog, Madai, Javan, Tubal, and Tiras.

    The prophet Ezekiel mentioned that the uncircumcised descendants of Meshech trafficked in human beings and copper utensils.

2. (1 Chronicles 1:17). Unspecified date. Meshech, the son of Shem and grandson of Noah, was the brother of Elam, Asshur, Arphaxad, Lud, Aram, Uz, Hul, and Gether.

    The book of Genesis calls him Mash and states that he was the son of Aram and the grandson of Shem (Genesis 10:23).

Meshelemiah

(Hebrew origin: *Allied of God*)

(1 Chronicles 9:21). 10th century B.C. Meshelemiah—also called Shallum (1 Chronicles 9:17), and Shelemiah (1 Chronicles 26:14)—son of Kore, a descendant of Asaph, was the head of all the gatekeepers of the Tabernacle, during the reign of King David. He was chosen by lot to be in charge of the East Gate

His son Zechariah, who had a reputation as a wise counselor, was chosen to be the gatekeeper of the North Gate.

His other sons were Jediael, Zebadiah, Jathniel, Elam, Jehohanan, and Elioenai.

Meshelemiah was the ancestor of a clan of gatekeepers who returned with Zerubbabel from the Babylonian Exile (Ezra 2:42).

Meshezabeel

(Hebrew origin: *Delivered of God*)

1. (Nehemiah 3:4). 6th century B.C. Meshezabeel was the father of Berechiah. His grandson Meshullam, who was related by marriage to Tobiah, Nehemiah's enemy, helped to repair the walls of Jerusalem.

2. (Nehemiah 10:21). 5th century B.C. Meshezabeel was one of the leaders who signed Nehemiah's solemn agreement to separate themselves from the foreigners living in the land, to refrain from inter-marrying with them, and to dedicate their firstborn to God, among other obligations.

3. (Nehemiah 11:24). 5th century B.C. Meshezabeel, a descendant of Judah, was the father of Pethahiah, the adviser to the king of Persia.

Meshillemith

(Hebrew origin: *Reconciliation*)

(1 Chronicles 9:12). Unspecified date. Meshillemith, son of Immer and father of Meshullam, was an ancestor of Maasiai, a priest who served in the Temple, after the return from the Babylonian Exile.

Meshillemoth

(Hebrew origin: *Reconciliations*)

1. (2 Chronicles 28:12). 8th century B.C. Meshillemoth was the father of Berechiah, a leader of the tribe of Ephraim, during the reign of King Pekah of Israel who protested against the king's intention to turn the captured Judahite prisoners of war into slaves.

2. (Nehemiah 11:13). Unspecified date. Meshillemoth, son of Immer and father of Ahasai, was an ancestor of Amashai, a priest who settled in Jerusalem, after the return from the Babylonian Exile.

Meshobab

(Hebrew origin: *Returned*)

(1 Chronicles 4:34). 8th century B.C. Meshobab was one of the leaders of the tribe of Simeon who went to the fertile valley of Gedor in search of pasture for their flocks, during the reign of Hezekiah, king of Judah.

The Simeonites destroyed the tents of the people—descendants of Ham—who lived there, wiped them out forever, and settled in their place.

Meshullam

(Hebrew origin: *Rewarded*)

1. (2 Kings 22:3). 8th century B.C. Meshullam was the grandfather of Shaphan, the court's scribe who brought to King Josiah the Book of the Law, which had been found by the High Priest Hilkiah, while repairing the Temple.

2. (1 Chronicles 3:19). 6th century B.C. Meshullam was a descendant of the royal family of Judah. His father Zerubbabel was the leader of the first group of captives who returned from the Babylonian Exile.

3. (1 Chronicles 5:13). Unspecified date. Meshullam was a leader of the tribe of Gad who lived in the land of Bashan. His brothers were Michael, Jorai, Sheba, Jachan, Zia, and Heber.

4. (1 Chronicles 8:17). Unspecified date. Meshullam, son of Elpaal, a Benjamite, was the leader of a clan that lived in Jerusalem.

5. (1 Chronicles 9:7). 6th century B.C. Meshullam was the son of Hodaviah and the grandson of Hasenuah, of the tribe of Benjamin. His son Sallu was one of the first captives who returned from the Babylonian Exile and settled in Jerusalem.

6. (1 Chronicles 9:8). Unspecified date. Meshullam, the son of Shephathiah, was the head of a Benjamite clan that lived in Jerusalem.

7. (1 Chronicles 9:11). 7th century B.C. Meshullam, son of Zadok and father of Hilkiah, was the grandfather of Azariah, also called Seraiah, a High Priest in the days of Nehemiah.

Meshullam is called Shallum in another chapter of First Chronicles (1 Chronicles 6:12), where he is mentioned as being an ancestor of Jehozadak, the High Priest exiled by Nebuchadnezzar, when the Babylonians captured Jerusalem.

8. (1 Chronicles 9:12). Unspecified date. Meshullam, son of Meshillemith and father of Jahzerah, was an ancestor of Maasiai, a priest who served in the Temple, after the return from the Babylonian Exile.

9. (2 Chronicles 34:12). 7th century B.C. Meshullam, a Levite, of the clan of the Kohathites, was one of the four overseers of the repairs done in the Temple, during the reign of King Josiah. The other overseers were Obadiah and Jahath, descendants of Merari, and Zechariah of the clan of the Kohathites.

10. (Ezra 8:16). 5th century B.C. Meshullam was one of the leaders of Judah who was sent by Ezra to Casiphia, to speak to Iddo and request from him to send Levites to serve in the Temple in Jerusalem.

11. (Ezra 10:15). 5th century B.C. Meshullam and Shabbethai, two Levites, participated with Jonathan and Jahaziah, two leaders of Judah, in the deliberations led by Ezra, concerning the matter of the marriages to foreign women.

12. (Ezra 10:29). 5th century B.C. Meshullam, a descendant of Bani, divorced his foreign wife, during the time of Ezra.

13. (Nehemiah 3:4). 5th century B.C. Meshullam, son of Berechiah, helped to repair the walls of Jerusalem, during the days of Nehemiah. His daughter married Johanan, the son of Tobiah, Nehemiah's enemy.

14. (Nehemiah 3:6). 5th century B.C. Meshullam, son of Besodeiah, together with Jehoiada, son of Paseah, repaired the

old gate of the walls of Jerusalem, including the doors, locks, and bars, in the days of Nehemiah.

15. (Nehemiah 8:4). 5th century B.C. Meshullam was one of the leaders who stood next to Ezra, upon a pulpit of wood, when the scribe read the Law of Moses to the people in the marketplace.

16. (Nehemiah 10:7). 5th century B.C. Meshullam was one of the priests who signed with Nehemiah a solemn agreement to separate themselves from the foreigners living in the land, to refrain from intermarrying with them, and to dedicate their firstborn to God, among other obligations.

17. (Nehemiah 10:20). 5th century B.C. Meshullam was one of the leaders who signed Nehemiah's solemn agreement to separate themselves from the foreigners living in the land, to refrain from intermarrying with them, and to dedicate their firstborn to God, among other obligations. He marched in the joyful procession, which celebrated the dedication of the rebuilt walls of Jerusalem (Nehemiah 12:33).

18. (Nehemiah 11:7). Unspecified date. Meshullam, the son of Joed and grandson of Pedaiah, was the father of Sallu, a Benjamite who settled in Jerusalem, after his return from the Babylonian Exile.

19. (Nehemiah 12:13). 5th century B.C. Meshullam, of the Ezra clan, was one of the chief priests in Jerusalem under the High Priest Joiakim, in the days of Nehemiah.

20. (Nehemiah 12:16). 5th century B.C. Meshullam was the head of a priestly clan, descended from Ginnethon, when Joiakim was High Priest, during the time of Nehemiah.

21. (Nehemiah 12:25). 5th century B.C. Meshullam was a gatekeeper in the days of Nehemiah.

Meshullemeth

(Hebrew origin: *Rewarded*)

(2 Kings 21:19). 7th century B.C. Meshullemeth, the wife of King Manasseh, was

the daughter of Haruz of Jotbah and the mother of King Amon.

Methusael

(Hebrew origin: *Man who is from God*)

(Genesis 4:18). Antediluvian. Methusael, the son of Mehujael, was the father of Lamech.

Methuselah

(Hebrew origin: *Man of a dart*)

(Genesis 5:21). Antediluvian. Methuselah—also spelled Mathusala (Luke 3:37)—son of Enoch, was the grandfather of Noah.

He was one hundred and eighty-seven years old, when his son Lamech was born. Afterward, he had other sons and daughters.

Methuselah died at the age of nine hundred and sixty-nine, the longest life span mentioned in the Bible.

Meunim

(Hebrew origin: *Residences*)

(Nehemiah 7:52). Unspecified date. Meunim—also spelled Mehunim (Ezra 2:50)—was the ancestor of a clan of Temple servants that returned with Zerubbabel from the Babylonian Exile.

Mezahab

(Hebrew origin: *Water of gold*)

(Genesis 36:39). Unspecified date. Mezahab was the mother of Matred. Her granddaughter Mehetabel was the wife of Hadar, an Edomite king.

Miamin

(Hebrew origin: *From the right*)

1. (Ezra 10:25). 5th century B.C. Miamin, a descendant of Parosh, divorced his foreign wife, during the days of Ezra.

2. (Nehemiah 12:5). 6th century B.C. Miamin was one of the leading priests who returned with Zerubbabel from the Babylonian Exile.

Mibhar

(Hebrew origin: *Selected*)

(1 Chronicles 11:38). 10th century B.C. Mibhar, son of Haggeri, was one of King David's brave soldiers.

Mibsam

(Hebrew origin: *Fragrant*)

1. (Genesis 25:13). 18th century B.C. Mibsam, grandson of Abraham and his Egyptian concubine Hagar, was one of the twelve sons of Ishmael.

   His brothers were Nebajoth, Hadad, Adbeel, Mishma, Dumah, Massa, Jetur, Tema, Kedar, Naphish, and Kedemah, all of them ancestors of great nations. His sister, Mahalath—also called Bashemath—married Esau, the son of Isaac.

2. (1 Chronicles 4:25). Unspecified date. Mibsam, a descendant of Simeon, was the son of Shallum and the father of Mishma.

Mibzar

(Hebrew origin: *Fortification*)

(Genesis 36:42). Unspecified date. Mibzar was a chief of an Edomite clan.

Micah

(Hebrew origin: *Who is like*)

1. (Judges 17:1). 12th century B.C. Micah, a man* who lived in the hilly country of Ephraim, had a shrine in his house, where he had placed an ephod and several teraphim. He consecrated one of his sons to serve as his priest

   One day, he took from his mother, without her knowledge, eleven hundred shekels of silver. When the woman saw that the silver was missing, she cursed, in the hearing of her son, whoever knew where the silver was and did not disclose it.

   Micah confessed to his mother that the silver was in his possession, and he returned it to her. She said to her son that God should bless him, took two hundred shekels of silver, and gave it to a silversmith, with instructions to make two idols, one sculptured and the other molten.

   A young Levite from Bethlehem came to Micah's house, searching for a place where he could take up residence.

   Micah said to him, "Stay with me as a father and a priest. I will pay you ten shekels of silver a year; give you an allowance of clothing, and food." The Levite agreed to stay with Micah and became his priest. Micah was very happy with the arrangement and treated the young Levite as one of his sons.

   In those days, the tribe of Dan did not yet have a territory of its own. The Danites, wishing to find where to settle, sent five of their men to spy the land and explore it. When they were near the house of Micah, they met the Levite and asked him, "What are you doing in this place?"

   The Levite answered, "Micah hired me to be the priest of his shrine".

   They said, "Please inquire from God if our mission will be successful".

   The Levite assured them, "Go in peace. God views with favor your mission".

   The five men departed and went to the city of Laish. They saw that its inhabitants were easy going, peaceful, and unsuspecting. The location of the city, far away from the Sidonians, was also excellent. The five men returned to Zorah and Eshtaol and told their fellow tribesmen that they should go and take possession of the city.

   Six hundred armed Danites set out to conquer Laish. On their way, they stopped near the house of Micah. The five men who had spied Laish told their companions, "Do you know that, in this house, they have an ephod, teraphim, and two idols, one sculptured, and the other one molten?"

   The six hundred men stood by the gate, while the five spies entered the shrine and took all the idols. The Levite, surprised to see them, asked, "What are you doing?"

   They answered, "Be silent! Come with us, and be our father and our priest. Isn't it much better for you to be the priest of a whole tribe than the priest of a single household?"

The Levite was delighted. He took the idols and left with the Danites. Micah and his neighbors pursued and overtook them.

They called out to the Danites, who turned around and said to Micah, "What is the matter with you that you come with so many people?"

Micah answered, "You have taken my priest and the gods that I made. What do I have left? And you ask me, 'What is the matter'!"

The Danites said, "Don't shout. Some people here might get angry and kill you and your family." Micah, realizing that he was outnumbered, returned to his home.

The Danites went on their way, taking with them the priest and the idols. They conquered Laish, killed the people, and burned down the town. They rebuilt the town and called it Daniel.

Jonathan, son of Gershom and grandson of Manasseh, was their priest in charge of the cult to the graven image, set up by the tribe of Dan, in the city of Dan, previously called Laish. His descendants also served as priests, until the destruction of the kingdom of Israel.

Note: Some Hebrew manuscripts have the letter *nun*, "n" in Manasseh, suspended above, which would indicate an earlier reading of "Moses", in which case, Jonathan would be Moses' grandson.

2. (1 Chronicles 5:5). Unspecified date. Micah, son of Shimei and father of Reaia, was an ancestor of Beerah, a leader of the tribe of Reuben who was carried away captive by Tilgathpilneser, king of Assyria.

3. (1 Chronicles 8:34). 10th century B.C. Micah—called Micha in the second book of Samuel (2 Samuel 9:12)—was the son of Mephibosheth, a descendant of King Saul. His sons were Pithon, Melech, Tarea, and Ahaz.

4. (1 Chronicles 9:15). Unspecified date. Micah, son of Zichri, was the father of Mattaniah, a Levite who settled in Jerusalem, after he returned from the Babylonian Exile.

5. (1 Chronicles 23:20). 10th century B.C. Micah—also spelled Michah (1 Chronicles 24:24)—a Levite descendant from Uzziel, served in the Tabernacle, during the reign of King David. His brother was called Isshiah, and his son was Shamir.

6. (2 Chronicles 34:20). 7th century B.C. His son Abdon—elsewhere called Achbor—was sent by King Josiah with two other court officials to consult with Huldah, the prophetess, concerning the Book of the Law that had been found in the Temple, while it was being repaired. He is called Michaiah in the second book of Kings (2 Kings 22:12).

7. (Micah 1:1). 8th century B.C. The prophet Micah, the Morasthite, preached in Judah, during the reigns of the kings Jotham, Ahaz, and Hezekiah.

Micah, a contemporary of the prophet Isaiah—last half of the 8th century B.C.—was born in the village of Moreshetgath, near the city of Lachish, in the kingdom of Judah.

In contrast to Isaiah, he does not express an explicit love for Jerusalem, probably because he was a man of the country.

Although for him there was only one king of Israel, God, he also considered that the people should unite around the royal dynasty of David, which was a guarantee of the nation's hope.

Micah was convinced that Judah was about to face the same kind of national catastrophe that Amos had predicted for the northern kingdom of Israel, because God would punish the hateful injustice of the Jerusalem leaders and magistrates, who ignored the law and fought with each other, causing suffering among the people.

When he prophesied in the days of Hezekiah that Zion would be plowed like a field, and Jerusalem would become heaps, the king, instead of getting angry with the prophet, and putting him to death, repented. This tolerant behavior was quoted as a precedent by the people who defended Jeremiah and did not want him to be killed for speaking what many considered defeatist talk (Jeremiah 26:18).

The book of Micah can be divided in three sections. The first part of the book, chapter 1 to chapter 3, speak of condemnation and judgment on Israel and Judah, placing direct guilt on Samaria and Jerusalem, the capital cities, and predicting their destruction. The prophet attacks those who lie awake and plan evil: the rulers who govern for bribes, the priests who interpret the religious law for pay, and the false prophets who give their revelations for money, claiming that God is with them.

The second part of the book, chapters 4 and 5, speak of consolation, restoration, and peace. Here Micah states that, in the future, nations will come to the Temple, to the hill of the Lord, and God would teach them to walk in His paths. Nations will no longer go to war, and everyone will live in peace. The people will be brought from the Babylonian Exile, Jerusalem will become strong, and the nation will be united in safety under a ruler of the David dynasty. Assyria would be destroyed, and Israel will conquer her enemies.

The last part of the book, chapters 6 and 7, is a message of warning and hope, mixing condemnation and consolation.

The book of Micah is one of the twelve books that make up the Minor Prophets—also called the Twelve—a collection of the books of twelve prophets: Hosea, Joel, Amos, Obadiah, Jonah, Micah, Nahum, Habakkuk, Zephaniah, Haggai, Zechariah, and Malachi.

Note: The phrase "Minor Prophets" does not mean that these prophets are less important than Isaiah, Jeremiah, and Ezekiel. It refers only to the fact that the books of these twelve prophets are much shorter than the books of the other three prophets.

Micaiah

(Hebrew origin: *Who is like God*)

(1 Kings 22:8). 9th century B.C. Micaiah, son of Imlah, was a frank and outspoken prophet, traits, which compelled him to always express the truth. King Ahab of Israel intensely disliked him for prophesying only what the king considered evil.

King Ahab, on the eve of going to war against the Syrians, gathered about four hundred prophets on the threshing floor at the entrance of the gate of Samaria, and he asked them, "Shall I go and do battle against Ramothgilead?"

They unanimously declared, "Go, and God will deliver it into the hands of the king".

His ally, King Jehoshaphat of Judah, not yet convinced, asked, "Isn't there another prophet of the Lord through whom we can inquire?"

Ahab answered, "Yes, there is one, Micaiah, son of Imlah, but I hate him, because he never prophesies anything good for me, only misfortune".

"The king shouldn't say that", admonished Jehoshaphat.

Ahab sent an official to bring Micaiah to their presence. The man who brought Micaiah advised him on the way to tell the kings only good tidings, as the other prophets had.

Micaiah rejected his advice, saying, "I will say whatever God would tell me to say".

The kings, dressed in their royal robes, received Micaiah near the gate of the city of Samaria.

Ahab asked him, "Micaiah, shall we go against Ramothgilead and fight?"

Micaiah answered, "Go, and prosper, for God will deliver it into the hands of the king".

Ahab sensed a mocking tone in the prophet's words and said to him, "How many times have I asked you to tell me nothing but what is true in the name of the Lord?"

Micaiah answered, "I saw Israel scattered upon the hills, as sheep without a shepherd".

Ahab turned to Jehoshaphat and said to him, "Didn't I tell you that he would only prophesy evil?"

Micaiah added, "I had a vision where I saw God sitting on his throne, with the angels around him. God asked them, 'Who shall persuade Ahab to go to Ramothgilead and fall there?' A spirit came forth and said to God, 'I will persuade him by being a lying spirit in the mouth of all his prophets'".

Zedekiah, the son of Chenaanah, one of the prophets who had predicted victory, went to Micaiah, slapped him on the face, and asked, "How did the spirit go from me to speak to you?"

Micaiah answered, "You shall see it on that day when you go into an inner chamber to hide yourself".

Ahab ordered his guards to seize Micaiah, and to take him to Amon, the governor of the city, and to Joash, the king's son, with instructions to put the prophet in prison, and to give him only some bread and water, until the king would return in peace.

Micaiah's last words to Ahab were "If you return in peace, the Lord has not spoken by me".

Ahab went to war, the Israelites were defeated, and the king was killed in the battle.

Micha

(Hebrew origin: *Who is like*)

(2 Samuel 9:12). 10th century B.C. Micha—called Micah in the first book of Chronicles (1 Chronicles 8:34)—was a descendant of King Saul. His father was Mephibosheth, also called Meribbaal. Micha's sons were Pithon, Melech, Tarea, and Ahaz.

(Nehemiah 10.11). 5th century B.C. Micha was one of the Levites who signed Nehemiah's solemn agreement to separate themselves from the foreigners living in the land, to refrain from intermarrying with them, and to dedicate their firstborn to God, among other obligations.

(Nehemiah 11:17). 5th century B.C. Micha, son of Zabdi, was the father of Mattaniah, a Levite who lived in Jerusalem, during the days of Nehemiah, and was in charge of leading the thanksgiving prayers.

(Nehemiah 11:22). Unspecified date. Micha, father of Mattaniah, was the ancestor of Uzzi, the overseer of the Levites in Jerusalem, during the days of Nehemiah.

Michael

(Hebrew origin: *Who is like God*)
1. (Numbers 13:13). 14th century B.C. His

son Sethur, of the tribe of Asher, was one of the twelve men sent by Moses to spy the land of Canaan and report back about its cities and its inhabitants, if they were strong or weak, few or many, and to bring back the fruit of the land.

The spies returned and gave a report, which was disheartening and defeatist. Only two of the spies—Joshua, the son of Nun, and Caleb, the son of Jephunneh—disagreed and told the people that they should not fear the inhabitants of Canaan.

The Israelites refused to listen to the words of Joshua and Caleb, and they started to wail and cry. God punished their cowardice by condemning them to wander forty years in the wilderness, one year for each day that the spies scouted the land.

2. (1 Chronicles 5:13). Unspecified date. Michael was a leader of the tribe of Gad who lived in the land of Bashan. His brothers were Heber, Meshullam, Sheba, Jorai, Zia, and Jachan.

3. (1 Chronicles 5:14). Unspecified date. Michael was the son of Jeshishai and the father of Gilead, of the tribe of Gad. His descendants lived in the region of Gilead, on the eastern side of the Jordan River.

4. (1 Chronicles 6:40). Unspecified date. Michael, son of Baaseiah and father of Shimea, of the clan of the Kohathites, was an ancestor of Asaph, one of the Levites appointed by King David to be in charge of the singers in the House of the Lord.

5. (1 Chronicles 7:3). Unspecified date. Michael, son of Izrahiah, a descendant of Tola, was the leader of a clan of the tribe of Issachar. His brothers were Ishiah, Obadiah, and Joel.

6. (1 Chronicles 8:16). Unspecified date. Michael, son of Beriah, a Benjamite, was the leader of a clan, who lived in Jerusalem.

7. (1 Chronicles 12:20). 11th century B.C. Michael, from the tribe of Manasseh, deserted Saul's army with his men, joined David at Ziklag, and became a captain of his army.

8. (2 Chronicles 21:2). 9th century B.C. Michael, a son of King Jehoshaphat,

received from his father great gifts of gold, silver, and fenced cities. When Jehoshaphat died, his firstborn son Jehoram ascended to the throne and killed Michael and all his other brothers.

9. (1 Chronicles 27:18). 11th century B.C. Michael was the father of Omri, the leader of the tribe of Issachar, during the reign of King David.

10. (Ezra 8:8). 5th century B.C. His son Zebadiah, a descendant of Shephatiah, returned with Ezra from Babylon, leading eighty males of his clan

11. (Daniel 10:13). 6th century B.C. Michael, in the visions that Daniel had, during the reign of Cyrus of Persia, was a prince of the highest rank, who was mentioned by a mysterious figure that appeared to Daniel and told him, "Do not fear. A Persian prince has opposed me for twenty-one days, but Michael, a prince of the highest rank, has come to my aid".

The man in the vision added that he would show Daniel the future of his people, that he was going back to fight the prince of Persia, and the prince of Greece would now come in, and that the only one helping him against them was the prince Michael, who in a future troubled time would stand beside the sons of Daniel's people, and the people would be saved.

The letter from Jude (Jude 1:9) mentions that the archangel Michael quarreled with the Devil for the body of Moses, that he did not dare condemn the Devil with insulting words, but told him that God would rebuke him. In the book of Revelation (Revelation 12:7), Michael and his angels fought against the dragon Satan, who fought back with his angels. Satan was defeated, and he and his angels were not allowed to stay in heaven any longer and were thrown down to earth.

Michah

(Hebrew origin: *Who is like*)

(1 Chronicles 24:24). 10th century B.C. Michah—also spelled Micah (1 Chronicles

23:20)—a Levite descendant from Uzziel, served in the Tabernacle, during the reign of King David. His brother was called Isshiah, and his son was Shamir.

Michaiah

(Hebrew origin: *Who is like God*)

1. (2 Kings 22:12). 7th century B.C. His son Achbor—elsewhere called Abdon—was sent by King Josiah with two other officials of the court to consult with Huldah, the prophetess, concerning the Book of the Law that had been found in the Temple, while it was being repaired.

   He is called Micah in the second book of Chronicles (2 Chronicles 34:20).

2. (2 Chronicles 13:2). 10th century B.C. Michaiah, daughter of Uriel of Gibeah, was the favorite wife of King Rehoboam and the mother of King Abijah. She is also called Maachah, daughter of Abishalom. (Please see the entry for Maachah [1 Kings 15:2].)

3. (2 Chronicles 17:7). 9th century B.C. Michaiah, an official in the court of King Jehoshaphat, was sent by the king, during the third year of his reign, together with other officials, Levites and priests, to teach the laws of God in the cities of Judah.

4. (Nehemiah 12:35). Unspecified date. Michaiah, son of Zaccur, was an ancestor of the priest Zechariah who played the trumpet in the joyful procession, which celebrated the dedication of the rebuilt walls of Jerusalem, during the days of Nehemiah.

5. (Nehemiah 12:41). 5th century B.C. Michaiah was one of the priests who played the trumpet in the joyful procession, which celebrated the dedication of the rebuilt walls of Jerusalem, during the days of Nehemiah.

6. (Jeremiah 36:11). 6th century B.C. Michaiah, a court official in the court of King Jehoiakim, was in the chamber of his father Gemariah, in the Temple, when Baruch, Jeremiah's trusted companion, read aloud the prophet's words.

Immediately, Michaiah went to the king's palace, to the chamber of Elishama the Scribe, and reported to his father Gemariah and to the other assembled officials what Baruch had read.

Baruch was brought to the palace and was asked to read aloud the scroll where he had written Jeremiah's words. When Baruch finished, the officials, terrified at what they had heard, told Baruch that he and Jeremiah should hide.

Baruch's scroll was brought to King Jehoiakim and was read to him. As soon as a couple of leaves of the scroll had been read, the king would cut them with a knife and throw them into the fireplace.

Michal

(Hebrew origin: *Who is like God*)

(1 Samuel 14:49). 10th century B.C. Michal was the youngest of the two daughters of King Saul and his wife Ahinoam. Her older sister was called Merab.

Saul, jealous of David's victories and popularity, devised a plan to get rid of his widely admired army officer. He offered him Merab in marriage, if David would fight against the Philistines, secretly hoping that he would be killed in battle.

David fought successfully against the Philistines, but Saul didn't honor his promise. Instead of giving Merab to David, he married her to Adriel, the son of Barzillai the Meholathite.

Saul was very pleased, when he found that Michal, his youngest daughter, loved David, because he saw a way to use her as a snare. The king sent a message to David, offering him his daughter in marriage, and asked for no dowry, except for the foreskins of a hundred Philistines, still hoping that David would be killed by them.

David went, fought against the Philistines, and slew two hundred of them, twice as many as Saul had demanded for his daughter's hand. He brought their foreskins to the king, who had no choice but to allow him to marry Michal.

Saul grew more and more distrustful and afraid of David, and he asked his son Jonathan to kill David. Jonathan went to David and advised him to hide, while he would try to convince his father not to kill him.

Saul listened to Jonathan's good words about David and agreed not to kill him. However, a short time later, while David was playing music for him, Saul attempted to kill David with his spear. It struck the wall, and David fled to his house.

That same night, helped by his wife Michal, David went out of his house, through a window, and escaped. Michal placed a man-sized idol on David's bed, covered it with a cloth, and put a pillow, made of goat's hair, at its head.

When Saul's guards came to arrest David, she told them that her husband was sick in bed. Saul sent his guards again with order to carry David, in his bed if this was needed, to the palace. The guards entered the bedroom and, finding that the figure in the bed under the covers was an idol, took Michal with them back to the palace, to Saul's presence.

Saul asked her, "Why did you deceive me, and let my enemy escape?"

Michal answered, "I had no choice. David threatened to kill me if I wouldn't help him".

Saul didn't punish his daughter, but gave her to Phaltiel, son of Laish, to be his wife.

Many years went by, David, from first being an outlaw, and then a mercenary at the service of the Philistines, was now the king of the tribe of Judah, with his capital in Hebron.

Ishbosheth, the son of Saul, was now the figurehead king of Israel, with the real power held by Abner, the general of his army.

One day, Ishbosheth committed the fatal mistake of accusing Abner of having made illicit love to Rizpah, one of King Saul's concubines. Abner became very angry and decided to transfer his loyalties to David.

David set as a condition for receiving Abner that he should bring him back Michal, Saul's daughter, now happily married to Phaltiel. David sent messengers to Ishbosheth, requesting that Michal should be delivered to him. Ishbosheth took her from her husband,

and Abner brought her to David. Phaltiel followed them, crying, until Abner abruptly ordered him to turn back.

After David had conquered Jerusalem and made it his capital, he decided to have the Ark brought to the city. This was done with a great celebration, with shouts of joy and sounds of trumpets. David danced with all his might in front of the procession.

Michal looked out of the window and saw David dancing and jumping, and she was disgusted by his behavior.

When the king returned to greet his household, Michal came out to him and said with scorn, "How glorious was the king of Israel today, showing off himself in the sight of the slave girls of his servants, as one of the rabble might do!"

David replied, "I danced before the Lord who chose me, instead of your father and all his family, and appointed me ruler over his people Israel! I will again dance before God, and disgrace myself even more, and be low in my own sight, but among the slave girls that you mention I will be honored!"

He never again came near Michal, and she, the only woman reported by the Bible as being in love with a man, died unloved, childless, and full of hate and contempt toward David, the love of her youth.

Michri

(Hebrew origin: *Salesman*)

(1 Chronicles 9:8). Unspecified date. Michri, father of Uzzi, was the grandfather of Elah, the head of a Benjamite clan that lived in Jerusalem.

Midian

(Hebrew origin: *Quarrel*)

(Genesis 25:2). 19th century B.C. Midian was the ancestor of the Midianites, a desert tribe that constantly fought against the Israelites.

Midian was one of the six sons of Keturah, the woman whom Abraham married, after the death of Sarah. His brothers were Zimran,

Jokshan, Medan, Ishbak, and Shuah. His sons were Ephah, Epher, Hanoch, and Eldaah.

Shortly before Abraham died, he made Isaac his sole heir, and, in order to avoid trouble, he donated gifts to the sons of his second marriage and sent them away to the east.

Mijamin

(Hebrew origin: *From the right*)

1. (1 Chronicles 24:9). 10th century B.C. Mijamin was the priest in charge of the sixth turn, out of a total of twenty-four turns, of the priestly service in the Tabernacle, during the reign of King David.

2. (Nehemiah 10:7). 5th century B.C. Mijamin was one of the priests who signed with Nehemiah a solemn agreement to separate themselves from the foreigners living in the land, to refrain from intermarrying with them, and to dedicate their firstborn to God, among other obligations.

Mikloth

(Hebrew origin: *Rod*)

1. (1 Chronicles 8:32). Unspecified date. Mikloth, father of Shimeah—also called Shimeam (1 Chronicles 9:38)—lived in Jerusalem.

2. (1 Chronicles 27:4). 10th century B.C. Mikloth was the chief officer of Dodai the Ahohite, one of the twelve commanders of King David's army, with twenty-four thousand men under him.

Mikneiah

(Hebrew origin: *Possessed by God*)

(1 Chronicles 15:18). 10th century B.C. Mikneiah, a Levite of the second rank, was one of the men chosen by the chief of the Levites to sing and play musical instruments in front of the Ark of the Covenant, when it was carried from the house of Obededom to its resting place in Jerusalem, as commanded by King David.

Milalai

(Hebrew origin: *Talkative*)

(Nehemiah 12:36). 5th century B.C. Milalai was one of the priests who played musical instruments, marching behind Ezra the Scribe, in the joyful procession, which celebrated the dedication of the rebuilt walls of Jerusalem, during the days of Nehemiah.

Milcah

(Hebrew origin: *Queen*)

1. (Genesis 11:29). 19th century B.C. Milcah was a daughter of Haran, the brother of Abram and Nahor. Her brother was Lot, and her sister was Iscah.

    She married her uncle Nahor, to whom she gave eight sons: Huz, Buz, Kemuel, Chesed, Hazo, Pildash, Jidlaph, and Bethuel. Her granddaughter Rebekah married Isaac, the son of Abraham.

2. (Numbers 26:33). 13th century B.C. Milcah was one of the five daughters of Zelophehad, the son of Hepher, of the tribe of Manasseh.

    When Zelophehad died, Milcah and her sisters—Hoglah, Noah, Mahlah, and Tirzah—came to Moses and Eleazar the High Priest, asking to inherit from their father, who had died in the wilderness without sons.

    Moses, after consulting with God, modified the law to entitle a daughter to inherit from her father, if the man did not have any sons, but with the condition that she had to marry within the clan, in order that her inheritance would remain in her tribe.

    After the death of Moses, the sisters came to Joshua and demanded, as their right, to receive a portion of the conquered territories, which had been given to the tribe of Manasseh.

Milcom

(Hebrew origin: *King*)

(1 Kings 11:5). Milcom—also called Moloch (Amos 5:26), Molech (Leviticus 18:21), and Malcham (Zephaniah 1:5)—was the god of the Ammonites. His worship demanded the sacrifice of children by fire.

Milcom was one of the pagan gods, for which King Solomon, influenced by his foreign wives, built a shrine in the outskirts of Jerusalem. This shrine, called Topheth, was destroyed centuries later by King Josiah, who desecrated it with human bones, so that it would no longer be suitable for any worshipper to make his son or daughter pass through fire.

Miniamin

(Hebrew origin: *From the right*)

1. (2 Chronicles 31:15). 8th century B.C. Miniamin, a Levite, worked under Kore, assisting him to register the priests and the Levites, and to distribute among the other Levites the gifts offered by the people to God, during the days of Kings Hezekiah.

2. (Nehemiah 12:17). Unspecified date. Miniamin was the ancestor of a clan of priests who lived in Jerusalem, during the days of the High Priest Joiakim, son of Jeshua.

3. (Nehemiah 12:41). 5th century B.C. Miniamin was one of the priests who played the trumpet in the joyful procession, which celebrated the dedication of the rebuilt walls of Jerusalem, during the days of Nehemiah.

Miriam

(Hebrew origin: *Rebellious*)

1. (Exodus 15:20). 13th century B.C. Miriam, the daughter of Amram and Jochebed, and the older sister of Aaron and Moses, is one of the few women that the Bible calls prophetess.

    Her mother gave birth to Moses, after Pharaoh had given orders to kill every newly born Israelite boy. Jochebed hid the baby for three months, and, when she could no longer hide him, she put the child in a basket and placed it among the reeds by the bank of the Nile.

    Miriam stationed herself at a distance to see what would befall the baby. The daughter of Pharaoh came down to bathe in the Nile, saw the basket among the reeds, and sent a slave girl to fetch it. When she opened the basket, she saw inside a baby boy crying.

The princess took pity on the baby and said, "This must be a Hebrew child".

Miriam approached and asked her if she could get her a Hebrew nurse to suckle the baby. When the daughter of Pharaoh agreed, Miriam went and brought Jochebed, who was hired on the spot by the princess to take care of the baby and to nurse him.

Years later, when the Israelites left Egypt and crossed the Red Sea, Miriam took a timbrel in her hand and led the women in a triumphal procession, singing and dancing.

Later, when the Israelites were camping in Hazeroth, Miriam and Aaron made known their displeasure with the Ethiopian woman whom Moses had married. They also expressed their dissatisfaction with Moses himself, saying that God did not speak only through Moses, but also through them.

Moses, a very humble and long-suffering man, did not react to their criticisms, but God called the three siblings to the Tabernacle. The Lord came down in a pillar of cloud, stopped at the entrance of the Tabernacle, and ordered Aaron and Miriam to come out.

God told them, "I appear in dreams and in visions to any prophet, but only to Moses do I speak personally, directly and plainly. How dare you speak against my servant Moses?"

Angry with them, the Lord departed. When the cloud rose from the Tabernacle, Miriam had become a leprous, white as snow.

Aaron looked at her, and turning to Moses, asked for forgiveness, and begged him to restore Miriam's health.

Moses prayed to God to heal Miriam, and God answered that Miriam should be kept out of the camp for seven days, and then should be allowed back.

Miriam was shut out of the camp for seven days. The people waited and did not renew their march, until Miriam was read-mitted. She died sometime later in Kadesh and was buried there.

2. (1 Chronicles 4:17). Unspecified date. Miriam, daughter of Mered, a descendant of Judah, was the sister of Shammai and Ishbah, and, through her mother Bithiah, the granddaughter of an Egyptian Pharaoh.

Note: All the women named Mary in the New Testament were called Miriam in Hebrew, including the Virgin Mary.

Mirma

(Hebrew origin: *Fraud*)

(1 Chronicles 8:10). Unspecified date. Mirma, born in the country of Moab, was one of the seven sons of Shaharaim, of the tribe of Benjamin, and his wife Hodesh. His brothers— all of them heads of clans—were Zibia, Jobab, Mesha, Jeuz, Shachia, and Malcham.

Mishael

(Hebrew origin: *Who is God's*)

1. (Exodus 6:22). 13th century B.C. Mishael, son of Uzziel, a descendant of Levi, was a first cousin of Moses and Aaron. His brothers were Elzaphan and Zithri.

When Abihu and Nadab, the sons of Aaron, burned forbidden incense and were killed by a fire from the Lord, Moses told Mishael and Elzaphan to take out the two bodies from the sanctuary and to carry them to a place outside the camp.

2. (Nehemiah 8:4). 5th century B.C. Mishael was one of the leaders who stood next to Ezra, upon a pulpit of wood, when the scribe read the Law of Moses to the people in the marketplace.

3. (Daniel 1:6). 6th century B.C. Mishael was a young boy from a noble Jewish family in Babylon, who was chosen—together with his companions Daniel, Hananiah, and Azariah—to receive an education that would allow them to become officials of the king's court.

Mishael was given the Babylonian name of Meshach by the chief of the eunuchs of King Nebuchadnezzar.

In order not to transgress by eating and drinking ritually forbidden food and wine, Daniel asked permission from Melzar, the man who had been placed in charge of them, to eat only legumes and drink only water. Melzar feared that this diet might endanger their health, but Daniel asked him to let them try it for ten days. When the ten days were over, the four Jewish boys looked better and healthier than the boys who had eaten of the king's food.

During the three following years, the four boys acquired knowledge and skill, and Daniel learned to interpret the significance of visions and dreams.

Years later, after ending their studies, the king, at the request of Daniel, appointed Mishael and his companions Azariah and Hananiah to be in charge over the affairs of the province of Babylon.

The king set up a golden idol and decreed that everybody in the kingdom should worship it. When the king was informed that Hananiah, Azariah, and Mishael refused to worship the golden idol and did not serve the Babylonian gods, he gave orders to throw them into a burning furnace.

The three men were saved by an angel and survived, without even one hair of their heads being singed. Nebuchadnezzar was so impressed by their miraculous survival that he blessed God and decreed that, from that moment on, anyone in the Babylonian Empire who would dare speak against God would be cut in pieces, and his house would be turned into a dunghill.

Misham

(Hebrew origin: *Inspection*)

(1 Chronicles 8:12). Unspecified date. Misham was a Benjamite, son of Elpaal, leader of a clan, who lived in Jerusalem.

Mishma

(Hebrew origin: *Heard*)

1. (Genesis 25:14). 18th century B.C. Mishma, grandson of Abraham and his Egyptian concubine Hagar, was one of the twelve sons of Ishmael. His brothers were Nebajoth, Hadad, Adbeel, Mibsam, Dumah, Massa, Jetur, Tema, Kedar, Naphish, and Kedemah, all of them ancestors of great nations. His sister, Mahalath—also called Bashemath—married Esau, the son of Isaac.

2. (1 Chronicles 4:25). Unspecified date. Mishma, a descendant of Simeon, was the son of Mibsam. His son was called Hamuel, and his grandson Zacchur.

Although most families of the tribe of Simeon didn't have many children, his descendant Shimei had sixteen sons and six daughters.

Mishmannah

(Hebrew origin: *Fatness*)

(1 Chronicles 12:10). 11th century B.C. Mishmannah, a brave Gadite, captain of Saul's army, joined David's band at Ziklag.

Mispereth

(Hebrew origin: *Enumeration*)

(Nehemiah 7:7). 6th century B.C. Mispereth—also called Mizpar (Ezra 2:2)—was one of the men who returned with Zerubbabel from the Babylonian Exile.

Mithredath

(Persian origin: Uncertain meaning)

1. (Ezra 1:8). 6th century B.C. Mithredath, the treasurer of King Cyrus of Persia, delivered to Sheshbazzar, a prince of Judah, the vessels that the Babylonians had taken from the Temple.

2. (Ezra 4:7). 6th century B.C. Mithredath, Tabeel, and Bishlam, non-Jews who lived in the land of Israel, offered to help the returnees from Babylon in the reconstruction of the Temple. When their offer was

rejected, they became offended and angry. As an act of revenge, they wrote a letter in Syrian to Artaxerxes, king of Persia, asking the king to stop the work in the Temple.

Mizpar

(Hebrew origin: *Number*)

(Ezra 2:2). 6th century B.C. Mizpar—called Mispereth in the book of Nehemiah (Nehemiah 7:7)—was one of the men who returned with Zerubbabel from the Babylonian Exile.

Mizraim

(Hebrew origin: *Egypt*)

(Genesis 10:6). Unspecified date. Mizraim, *Egypt*, son of Ham and grandson of Noah, was the father of Ludim, Anamim, Lehabim, Naphtuhim, Pathrusim, Caphtorim, and Casluhim. His brothers were Cush, Phut, and Canaan, ancestors of their respective nations.

Mizzah

(Hebrew origin: *Faint*)

(Genesis 36:13). 17th century B.C. Mizzah, son of Reuel, was the grandson of Esau and Bashemath, the daughter of Ishmael. Mizzah's brothers were Nahath, Zerah, and Shammah. They were also ancestors of Edomite clans.

Mnason

(Uncertain origin and meaning)

(Acts of the Apostles 21:16). A.D. 1st century. Mnason, born in Cyprus, was one of the first Christian converts. Paul and some of his disciples from Caesarea stayed in his house, when the apostle returned to Jerusalem from his third journey.

Moab

(Hebrew origin: *From the father*)

(Genesis 19:37). 19th century B.C. Moab, ancestor of the Moabites, was the son of the incestuous relationship between Lot and his

older daughter. His descendant Ruth was an ancestor of King David.

Moadiah

(Hebrew origin: *Assembly of God*)

(Nehemiah 12:17). 6th century B.C. Moadiah—also spelled Maadiah (Nehemiah 12:5)—was one of the priests who returned from the Babylonian Exile with Zerubbabel.

He was the ancestor of a clan of priests, which, during the days of the High Priest Joiakim, son of Jeshua, was led by Piltai.

Molech

(Hebrew origin: *King*)

(Leviticus 18:21). Molech—also called Moloch (Amos 5:26), and Milcom (1 Kings 11:5)—was the god of the Ammonites. His worship demanded the sacrifice of children by fire.

Molech was one of the pagan gods, for which King Solomon, influenced by his foreign wives, built a shrine in the outskirts of Jerusalem.

This shrine, called Topheth, was destroyed centuries later by King Josiah, and desecrated with human bones, so that it would no longer be suitable for any worshipper to make his son or daughter pass through fire.

Molid

(Hebrew origin: *Genitor*)

(1 Chronicles 2:29). Unspecified date. Molid, a descendant of Judah, was the son of Abishur and Abihail. His brother was called Ahban.

Moloch

(Hebrew origin: *King*)

(Amos 5:26). Moloch—also called Molech (Leviticus 18:21), and Milcom (1 Kings 11:5)—was the god of the Ammonites. His worship demanded the sacrifice of children by fire.

Moloch was one of the pagan gods, for which King Solomon, influenced by his foreign wives, built a shrine in the outskirts of Jerusalem.

This shrine, called Topheth, was destroyed centuries later by King Josiah, and desecrated with human bones, so that it would no longer be suitable for any worshipper to make his son or daughter pass through fire.

Mordecai

(Hebrew origin: *Belonging to Merodach, a Babylonian god*)

1. (Ezra 2:2). 6th century B.C. Mordecai was one of the leaders who returned to Jerusalem with Zerubbabel from the Babylonian Exile.

2. (Esther 2:5). 5th century B.C. Mordecai, son of Jair, a descendant of the family of King Saul, lived in Shushan, the capital of the Persian Empire, with Esther, a young cousin, whom he had brought up, when she became an orphan. His great grandfather Kish, a Benjamite, had been exiled from Jerusalem together with King Jeconiah of Judah.

Years later, after King Ahasuerus got rid of his rebellious wife Vashti, there was a countrywide search for a new queen, and Esther was chosen. She, advised by Mordecai, didn't tell anybody that she was Jewish.

One day, Mordecai, sitting, as was his custom, in the palace gate, overheard two of the king's guards plotting against Ahasuerus' life. He told this to Esther, and she reported it to the king in Mordecai's name. The matter was investigated and verified, and the two men were executed. The king ordered to write an account of the matter in the official records of the empire.

Sometime later, the king promoted a man named Haman to the position of vizier, making him the most powerful man in the country after the king himself. The king also ordered all the officials in his service to show their respect for Haman by kneeling and bowing to him.

Mordecai refused to kneel or bow, explaining that, as a Jew, he only kneeled and bowed to God.

Haman, offended by Mordecai's refusal, decided that punishing Mordecai alone was not enough; all the Jews in the empire had to be exterminated.

Haman went to the king and denounced the Jews as a people with different customs who did not obey the king's laws. He added that, if the king would issue the death decree against the Jews, Haman would pay ten thousand talents of silver to the royal treasury.

The king took off the ring from his hand and gave it to Haman, saying, "The silver and the people are yours to do with them as you see fit".

The king's scribes were called, and Haman dictated letters proclaiming that all Jews, young and old, women and children, would be killed on the thirteenth day of the month of Adar. These letters, sealed with the king's ring, were sent to all the governors of the provinces. Having taken care of this business, the king and Haman sat down to drink.

When Mordecai learned of the death decree, he tore his clothes, dressed in sackcloth, covered his head with ashes, and walked through the city, crying out loudly and bitterly. The Jews in the provinces fasted, wept, wailed, and put on sackcloth.

Mordecai sent a message to Esther, explaining the gravity of the situation, and asking her to plead with the king to have mercy on her people.

Esther sent a message back to Mordecai, saying that according to the law, she would be put to death if she would go to the king without being summoned, unless the king would extend his golden scepter to her.

Mordecai replied, "Do you think that you are safer than other Jews, because you are in the palace?"

Esther answered, "Tell the Jews in Shushan to fast on my behalf for three days. I will also fast, and then I will go to the king, even if I have had to die for doing so".

On the third day, Esther put on her royal garments and stood in the inner court of the king's palace, facing the throne room, in front of the king who was sitting on his throne, facing the entrance

The king was pleased to see her. He extended to Esther the golden scepter, which he had in his hand. She approached and touched the tip of the scepter.

"What do you wish, Queen Esther?" the king asked. "Tell me and you shall have it, even if it is half my empire".

Esther replied, "I would like Your Majesty and Haman to come to a banquet tonight".

That night, the king and Haman went to the queen's banquet. After they ate and drank, the king again asked Esther, "What is your wish? And what is your request? I will grant it even if it is half my empire".

Esther answered, "I would like Your Majesty and Haman to be again my guests tomorrow at another banquet".

Haman left the banquet in a great mood, but his happiness was marred, when he went through the palace gate, and Mordecai, sitting there as usual, did not kneel or bow to him. Haman became furious, but was able to control himself, and went out.

Once back in his home, Haman invited his friends and his wife to join him. He boasted to them about his great wealth, his many sons, his high position in court, and how he and the king were the only guests at a banquet given by Queen Esther.

"But", he said, "all that means nothing to me, when I saw the Jew Mordecai sitting in the palace gate".

His wife and friends tried to console him and make him feel better, by advising him to build a gallows, and to ask the king to have Mordecai hanged on it. Haman liked the idea, and he had the gallows built.

That night, the king was unable to fall asleep. To pass the time, he ordered that the official records of the empire should be brought and read to him, including the account of how Mordecai had uncovered a plot to assassinate him.

The king inquired, "Has Mordecai been honored and rewarded for his deed?"

His servants answered, "Nothing has been done for him".

The king asked, "Is any of my government officials in the palace?"

The servants went out to search for an official and saw Haman entering the courtyard of the palace. He had come to ask the king for permission to hang Mordecai. The servants brought him to the presence of the king.

The king said to Haman, "I want to honor a certain man. What do you suggest we should do?"

Haman, assuming that the king was referring to him, said, "The man to be honored should be dressed in royal robes and set upon the king's horse. Then, he should be led through the city square by one of the highest noblemen, who will announce as they go, 'See how the king rewards a man he wishes to honor'".

The king told Haman, "Hurry, get the robes and the horse, and do to Mordecai the Jew all the honors that you have proposed".

Haman did everything that the king had ordered him. Afterward, he hurried home, deeply distressed. His despondency deepened, when his wife and friends, after listening to his tale, predicted that Mordecai would defeat him. Their conversation ended, when the palace eunuchs arrived to take Haman to Esther's banquet.

Over the wine, the king asked her again, "What is your wish, Queen Esther? I'll even give you half the empire".

Esther answered, "My wish is that I and my people may live, because we are about to be destroyed and exterminated".

King Ahasuerus asked Esther, "Who dares to do such a thing? Where is this man?"

Esther answered, "Our enemy, our persecutor, is this evil Haman!"

Haman cringed in terror. The king got up in a fury, left the room, and went outside to the palace gardens, while Haman stayed behind, begging Queen Esther for his life. He threw himself down on Esther's couch, pleading for mercy, when the king came back from the palace garden to the banquet room.

Seeing Haman on the queen's couch, the king shouted, "Is this man going to rape the queen right here in front of me, in my own palace?"

The eunuchs immediately gripped Haman, and one of them, named Harbonah, said that Haman had built a gallows at his house to hang Mordecai.

The king commanded, "Hang Haman on it!"

Haman was hanged and the king's anger calmed down. That same day, King Ahasuerus gave Haman's property to Esther, and he was told by the queen that Mordecai was her relative. The king took off his ring, which he had taken back from Haman, and gave it to Mordecai.

Esther spoke to the king again, falling at his feet, crying and asking him to stop the evil plot that Haman had made against the Jews. The king extended the golden scepter to Esther.

She stood up and said, "Please issue a proclamation revoking the orders that Haman gave for the destruction of the Jews in the empire".

The king told Esther and Mordecai that proclamations issued in the king's name and stamped with the royal seal could not be revoked, but that they could write to the Jews whatever they liked, in the king's name, and stamp it with the royal seal.

Mordecai dictated letters in the name of King Ahasuerus, stamped them with the royal seal, and sent them with couriers, mounted on fast horses from the royal stables. The letters stated that the Jews were authorized by the king to organize for self-defense, fight back if attacked, destroy their enemies along with their wives and children and take their possessions.

Mordecai left the palace, wearing royal robes of blue and white, a cloak of fine purple linen, and a magnificent crown of gold.

The thirteenth day of the month of Adar came, the day, on which, the enemies of the Jews had planned to destroy them. Instead, the Jews attacked them with swords and slaughtered them, including the ten sons of Haman.

When the number of those killed in Shushan was reported to the king, Ahasuerus said to Esther, "In Shushan alone, the Jews have killed five hundred people. What must they have done in the provinces?! What do you want now? You shall have it".

Esther answered, "Let the Jews in Shushan be allowed to do again tomorrow what they were allowed to do today; and let Haman's ten sons hang on the gallows".

The king ordered this to be done. The bodies of Haman's ten sons were publicly displayed, and the next day, the Jews of Shushan killed three hundred more of their enemies. Esther and Mordecai wrote a letter to all the Jews, wishing them peace and security, and instructed them and their descendants to celebrate Purim.

King Ahasuerus imposed tribute on the mainland and the islands, and he promoted Mordecai to a position second in rank only to the king.

Moses

(Hebrew origin: *Drawing out*)

(Exodus 2:10). 13th century B.C. Moses is the leading figure in the Old Testament. Religious tradition considers him to be the author of the Pentateuch, the first five books of the Bible.

Moses, the man who freed his people from slavery and led them to freedom, was a unique leader, founder of the community, organizer, legislator, and intercessor for the people. One of his most remarkable characteristics was his solicitude for his people, in spite of their obstinate and contentious ways.

He was the greatest of prophets, the only person in the Old Testament to whom God spoke personally, face to face, in contrast to other prophets to whom God spoke only in visions and dreams.

The nation that he molded has now survived for over three millenniums, based on his teachings.

Four hundred years had passed, since Joseph settled his father Jacob and his brothers in the fertile land of Goshen. The small group of seventy Israelites who immigrated to Egypt had now grown to many thousands, living in peace and prosperity all over the land.

A new Pharaoh came to the throne who didn't know who Joseph had been or what he had done for Egypt. Alarmed that the Israelite population had grown so large, he feared that if there would be a war, they would join his enemies, fight against the Egyptians, and escape from the country.

To prevent the Israelites from becoming even more numerous, he enslaved them and compelled them to build the store-cities of Pithom and Raamses. The Egyptians lived in fear of the Israelites and made their lives wretched, by forcing them to work harder and harder. But the more the Egyptians oppressed the Israelites, the more their numbers increased, and the more they spread through the land.

Pharaoh, to control the growth of the Israelite population, instructed the two Hebrew midwives, Puah and Shiphrah, to kill all the Israelite male babies, but to allow the female babies to live. The two women did not carry out the command of the Pharaoh, because they were God fearing.

The midwives were called to the presence of the sovereign, who asked them, "Why are you letting the baby boys live?"

The midwives answered, "The Hebrew women are not like the Egyptian women. They are so hale and hearty that they deliver their babies, before we arrive".

God rewarded the two women and gave them families of their own.

Around that time, Jochebed, an Israelite woman who was married to her nephew, Amram, son of Kohath and grandson of Levi, gave birth to a baby boy. The couple already had two children: Miriam, a young girl, and Aaron, a three-year-old boy.

Jochebed hid the baby in her home for three months. When she realized that she could no longer hide him, she put the child in a basket and went with Miriam to the bank of the Nile. She placed the basket in the water among the reeds, left it there, and returned to her home. Her daughter Miriam stayed behind, at a distance from the basket, and waited to see what would happen to the baby.

The daughter of Pharaoh came down to bathe in the Nile, saw the basket among the reeds, and sent a slave girl to fetch it. When she opened the basket, she saw inside a baby boy crying.

The princess took pity on the baby and said, "This must be a Hebrew child".

Miriam approached and asked her, "Shall I go and get a Hebrew woman to breast-feed the baby for you?"

The daughter of Pharaoh answered, "Please do".

Miriam went and brought Jochebed, who was hired on the spot by the princess to take care of the baby and to nurse him.

When the child was no longer a baby, Jochebed brought him to Pharaoh's daughter, who adopted him as her own son. She named him Moses, because, as she is quoted in the Bible, "she had pulled him out of the water".

The Bible does not give any information about his young years, but it is evident from his accomplishments that Moses was brought up in the Egyptian court, as a royal prince, and received the best education available at the time.

Having somehow learned that he was an Israelite, he visited his people, out of concern and curiosity, and saw the oppressive measures under which they labored. He saw an Egyptian taskmaster cruelly beating an Israelite laborer, and he couldn't control his sense of justice any longer. After looking around to make sure that no one was in sight, he killed the Egyptian and buried his body in the sand.

The next day, Moses returned to the same place and saw two Israelites fighting. He separated them and, wishing to mediate the disagreement, asked the offender, "Why are you beating a fellow Hebrew?"

He was shocked, when the Israelite asked him, "Who made you a prince and a judge over us? Do you intend to kill me as you killed the Egyptian?"

Fearing that his deed would be soon known by the Pharaoh, and that he would be punished, Moses fled to the land of Midian, a territory on the northwest of today's Saudi Arabia, near the Gulf of Aqabah.

Moses arrived in Midian and sat down by a well. While he was resting, the seven daughters of a local priest called Reuel came to water their father's flocks. Other shepherds arrived and drove the girls away in order to water their own flocks first. Moses, fearlessly, took on the shepherds and drove them away.

When the girls returned home, their father Reuel asked them, "Why are you back so early today?" The girls answered, "An Egyptian rescued us from the shepherds, drew water for us, and watered the animals".

"Where is he?" Reuel asked them. "Why did you leave him? Call him and invite him to eat with us".

Moses stayed to live with the Midianite priest and his family. Reuel gave him his daughter Zipporah in marriage, and, in due time, she gave birth to Gershom and later to Eliezer.

One day, Moses took his father-in-law's flock to graze near the mountain of Horeb. Suddenly, an angel of God appeared to him in a blazing fire out of a bush. Moses looked and saw that the bush burned, but was not consumed.

He came closer to investigate the strange sight and heard the voice of God calling him from the middle of the bush, "Moses, Moses".

Moses answered, "Here I am".

God warned him, "Don't get any closer. Remover your sandals, because you are standing on holy ground. I am the God of your father, the God of Abraham, the God of Isaac, and the God of Jacob. I have seen the affliction of my people in Egypt, and have come down to rescue them from the Egyptians and to bring them to a land flowing with milk and honey. I will send you to Pharaoh, and you shall free my people, the Israelites, from Egypt. And when you have freed the people, you shall worship God at this mountain".

Moses asked God, "When I come to the Israelites and tell them that the God of their fathers has sent me, they will ask me, 'what is his name?' What shall I tell them?"

God answered, "I am that I am. Tell the elders of Israel that the God of their ancestors will take them out of the oppression of Egypt to a land flowing with milk and honey".

Moses asked, "What if they don't believe that God appeared to me?"

God said, "What do you have in your hand?"

"A walking stick", answered Moses.

God told him, "Throw it to the ground!"

Moses threw the stick to the ground. It became a snake, and Moses, startled, jumped back.

God said to Moses, "Pick it up by its tail".

Moses did so, and the snake turned back into a walking stick.

"Now, put your hand into your bosom", said God.

Moses put his hand into his bosom, and, when he took it out, his hand was leprous.

"Put again your hand into your bosom!"

Again Moses put his hand into his bosom, and, this time, when he took it out, the hand was healthy.

God told him, "If they do not believe the first sign, they will believe the second; and if they don't believe the second sign, then take some water from the Nile and pour it on the ground. It will turn to blood".

Moses, still reluctant to accept his mission, said, "I am a stammerer, not a man of words".

God answered, "I will accompany you, and will tell you what to say".

Moses insisted, "Please send somebody else".

God, now angry with Moses, told him, "Your brother, Aaron, is a born speaker. He will go with you, and will be your spokesman".

Moses went back to his father-in-law and asked his permission to visit his relatives in Egypt, without disclosing that God had given him a mission.

After all the men in Egypt who had sought his death had died, God commanded Moses to return to Egypt. Moses took his wife and sons and started his journey back to Egypt. On the road, they stayed in an inn, and a mysterious incident took place. God, states the Bible, came and sought to kill Moses. Zipporah quickly circumcised Gershom with a sharp stone and touched Moses' legs with it, saying, "You are truly a bridegroom of blood to me".

After that event, Moses sent Zipporah and the children back to her father Jethro in Midian, and he continued alone to Egypt. He was met by Aaron, who had been ordered by God to go to the desert to welcome his brother. The two brothers kissed, and then, Moses told Aaron everything that God had said to him, and the miracles that he had been ordered to do.

The brothers gathered all the elders of the Israelites, and Aaron said to them, "God has visited you, and has seen your affliction". He told them what God had said to Moses, and then, Moses proved the truth of their words by performing miracles in front of the people. The elders, deeply moved, bowed down and worshipped.

The two old men—Moses was eighty years old at the time, and Aaron was eighty-three—went to Pharaoh and told him, "The Lord, God of Israel, has said, 'Let my people go, that they may hold a festival in the desert to honor me'".

Pharaoh answered, "Who is the Lord that I should obey his command to let Israel go? I do not know him, and I will not let Israel go!"

They said, "The God of the Hebrews has met with us. Let us travel three days into the desert and offer sacrifices to the Lord, our God. If we don't do so, he will kill us with disease, or with the sword".

Pharaoh said to them, "Moses and Aaron, why do you take the people away from their work? They have now become numerous, and you want them to stop working!"

That same day, Pharaoh commanded the taskmasters and the foremen to stop providing the Israelites with straw binder for making bricks. From then on, the slaves had to go and gather straw for themselves, but they would still be required to produce the same quota of bricks everyday.

"The problem is that these men don't have enough work", said Pharaoh. "That is why they ask me to let them go and offer sacrifices to their God. If you make them work harder, they will be too busy to listen to lying words".

The Israelites spent a lot of time looking for straw, but the taskmasters still expected them to make the same daily number of bricks as they had done before. When the production went down, the taskmasters beat the Israelite foremen and asked them, "Why aren't you making the same number of bricks as you made before?"

The Israelite foremen went to Pharaoh and complained to him, "Why do you deal like this with us? We are not given straw, but we are still expected to produce as many bricks as before. And then they beat us, when it is not our fault!"

Pharaoh answered, "You are lazy, and don't want to work. That is why you ask me to let you go and offer sacrifices to your God. Now, go back to work! You will not receive any straw, but you must still make the same number of bricks".

The foremen went out, dispirited. They saw, outside, Moses and Aaron, who were waiting for them, and said, "God has seen what you have done, and will judge you, because you have made Pharaoh and his officials loathe us so much that they will kill us".

Moses turned to God and asked, "Lord, why have you done evil to this people? Why did you ever send me? Since I came to Pharaoh to speak in your name, he has treated them even worse. And you have not helped them at all!"

God answered, "Now, you shall see what I will do to Pharaoh. He will let them go. He will even drive them out of his land".

Moses asked God, "How can I, a lousy speaker, make Pharaoh listen to me?"

God answered, "I will make you like a god to Pharaoh, and Aaron, your brother, will be your prophet. You will tell Aaron everything that I say to you, and he will tell Pharaoh to let the people of Israel leave his country. But I will harden Pharaoh's heart, and although I will multiply my signs and my wonders in the land of Egypt, Pharaoh will not listen to you, until I lay my hand upon Egypt and bring the Israelites out of the land. The Egyptian will know that I am the Lord, when I raise my hands against them, and bring the Israelites out of their country".

The two brothers went back to Pharaoh. Aaron threw his walking stick to the ground, and it turned into a snake. Pharaoh told his magicians to throw their sticks, and these also turned into serpents. Although the magicians' snakes were eaten by Aaron's, Pharaoh was not impressed and refused to let the people go.

God instructed Moses and Aaron to go early the next morning to the place in the river, where Pharaoh bathed, and to strike the water with the walking stick at the moment when the king would come out of the water. The water would then turn into blood, it would stink, and the fish in the Nile would all die.

Moses and Aaron did what God commanded. The water turned into blood. However, when the Egyptian magicians were able to do the same miracle, Pharaoh turned his back to Moses and Aaron, and he returned to his palace, without paying them any attention.

Seven days later, God told Moses to go again to Pharaoh and request him to let the people go. If he would refuse, the whole country would be plagued with frogs.

Pharaoh refused, and Aaron, following God's instructions, held his walking stick over the rivers, the canals, and the pools. Frogs came up and covered the land of Egypt. Again, the Egyptian magicians showed that they could do the same, and they made frogs come up on the land.

Pharaoh told Moses and Aaron, "Pray to God to take away the frogs, and I will let the Israelites go to offer sacrifices to the Lord".

Moses answered, "I will be pleased to do so. When would you like me to pray?"

"Tomorrow", replied Pharaoh.

Moses and Aaron left Pharaoh, and Moses, the next day, prayed to God to take away the frogs.

The frogs died everywhere. The Egyptians piled them up in heaps, which stank terribly. But Pharaoh, once he saw that the frogs were no longer a nuisance, reneged once again on his promise.

God then said to Moses, "Tell Aaron to strike the ground with his stick, and the dust will change into gnats all over the land of Egypt".

Aaron struck the ground with his stick, and all the dust in Egypt turned into gnats, which covered the people and the animals. The magicians tried to emulate Aaron's miracle, but this time, they failed.

The magicians went to Pharaoh and said, "This is God's doing!" Pharaoh did not believe them.

Early the next morning, Moses, following God's instructions, went to Pharaoh, as the king was going to the river, and said to him, "God has said, 'Let my people go, so that they may worship me. If you do not let my people go, I will send swarms of flies on you, your servants, and your people. The houses of the Egyptians will be covered with flies, and also the ground. Only in the region of Goshen, where my people live, there will be no flies. This will happen tomorrow'".

The next day, God sent swarms of flies to Pharaoh's palace and to the houses of his servants. The whole land of Egypt was ruined by the flies.

Pharaoh called Moses and Aaron and said to them, "You can sacrifice to your God here in this country".

Moses replied, "That would not be the right thing to do, because the Egyptians will be offended by the sight of our sacrifices, and they would stone us. We must travel three days into the desert to offer sacrifices to the Lord, our God, as he has commanded us".

Pharaoh said, "I will let you go to sacrifice to God in the desert, but don't go very far, and pray for me".

Moses answered, "As soon as I leave, I will pray to God that the flies should leave you tomorrow, but do not deceive us again and prevent the people from going to sacrifice to God".

Moses left, prayed to God, and God removed the flies, but Pharaoh again did not let the people go.

God told Moses, "Go to Pharaoh, and tell him that the Lord, the God of the Hebrews, says, 'Let my people go, so that they may worship me. If you again refuse, a terrible sickness will kill your animals, your horses, your donkeys, camels, cattle, sheep, and goats. But the animals of the Israelites will not die. This will happen tomorrow'".

The next day, God did as he had said. All the animals of the Egyptians died, but not one single animal of the Israelites died. Still, the Pharaoh did not allow the Israelites to go.

God told Moses, "Get a few handfuls of ashes from a furnace, and throw into the air in front of the Pharaoh".

Moses did so, and the ashes spread out like fine dust all over Egypt, producing boils that became open sores on the people and the animals. The magicians did not come forward to confront Moses, because they were covered with boils, as were all the other Egyptians. The stubborn Pharaoh again refused to listen to Moses and Aaron.

God told Moses, "Tomorrow, rise up early in the morning, and tell Pharaoh that the Lord, the God of the Hebrews, says, 'Let my people go, so that they may worship me. This time, I will strike you, your servants, and your people, that you may know that there is none like me in the entire world. I could have completely destroyed you with disease, but I have let you live to show you my power. Tomorrow, I will cause the heaviest hail ever seen to fall on Egypt. Get your cattle under safe shelter, because any person or animal left outside unprotected will die'".

Some of the officials in the court of Pharaoh feared what God had said and brought their slaves and animals indoors for shelter. Others did not believe in the warning and left them outside.

God told Moses, "Raise your hand toward the sky and hail will fall". Moses raised his stick toward the sky, and God sent thunder, lightning, and the heaviest hail that Egypt had ever known. It killed people and animals, and it broke all the trees. The only place in Egypt where hail didn't fall was in the region of Goshen, where the Israelites lived.

Pharaoh sent for Moses and Aaron and said, "This time, I have sinned. God is right, and my people and I are wrong. We have had enough of thunder and hail. I will let you go; you don't have to stay here any longer".

Moses said to him, "As soon as I am out of the city, I shall raise my hands to God; the thunder and the hail will cease. But I know that you and your officials do not yet fear the Lord".

When Pharaoh saw that the thunder and the hail had ceased, he again changed his mind and did not let the Israelites go.

Moses and Aaron returned to the Pharaoh and said to him, "The Lord, God of the Hebrews, asks, 'How long will you refuse to humble yourself before me? Let my people go that they may worship me. If you refuse, I will bring locusts to Egypt, which will cover the whole land, and eat all the plants and trees that survived the hail. The locusts will fill your palaces and all the houses, something that your ancestors never saw'". Moses, when finished speaking, turned and left Pharaoh's presence, without waiting for an answer.

Pharaoh's court officials, worried, spoke to him, "How long will this man continue to be a snare to us? Let them go to worship their God. Don't you realize that Egypt is ruined?"

Moses and Aaron were brought back to the palace. Pharaoh said to them, "Go, worship the Lord, your God, but, tell me, who will go?"

Moses replied, "We will all go, young and old, with our sons and daughters, with our flocks and our herds, for we must all observe the Lord's festival".

"Oh, no!" said Pharaoh. "The men can go with you, because that is what you wish, but I will not let your children go! It is clear that you are planning something evil". And he had them expelled from his presence.

God told Moses to stretch his hand over the land of Egypt. An east wind blew that day and night, bringing the locusts with it. They came in a thick mass darkening the sky and covering the land. Never before had there been so many, and never again would they come in such numbers. They ate all the grass, plants, and trees that had survived the hail. Nothing green was left in the fields and gardens of Egypt.

Pharaoh had Moses and Aaron brought urgently to him, and he said, "I have sinned against the Lord, your God, and against you. Please forgive me this once, and plead with the Lord, your God, to take this death away from me".

God sent a west wind, which lifted all the locusts and threw them into the Red Sea. Not a single locust remained in Egypt. But God hardened Pharaoh's heart, and he would not let the Israelites go.

Then, God said to Moses, "Hold out your arm toward the sky, and there will be darkness over the land. A darkness so thick that it can even be felt". The darkness came and lasted three days. People could not see one another, and they stayed home, but the Israelites enjoyed light in their dwellings.

Pharaoh summoned Moses and said, "Go, worship the Lord! You can even take your children with you. But you must leave behind your flocks and your herds".

Moses answered, "You must provide us with sacrifices and burnt offerings to offer up to the Lord, our God. Our cattle will go with us, not one will be left back, because we do not know with what we are to worship the Lord, until we get there".

God stiffened Pharaoh's heart, and he said to Moses, "Go away from me, and take care never to see me again, because the moment that you will look upon my face you shall die".

Moses replied, "You have spoken rightly. I shall not see your face again".

God said to him, "I will bring one more plague upon Pharaoh and upon Egypt. After that he shall let you go; even more, he will drive out all of you. Tell the people to borrow jewels of silver and gold from their neighbors".

Moses announced, "Thus, says the Lord: 'Toward midnight, I will go forth among the Egyptians, and every firstborn in the land of Egypt shall die, from the firstborn of the Pharaoh who sits on his throne, to the firstborn of the slave girl who is behind the mill, and all the firstborn of the cattle'". And Moses continued, "And there shall be a great cry in all the land of Egypt, such has never been or will

ever be again. But not a dog will move his tongue against the Israelites or their animals, so that you will know that the Lord differentiates between the Egyptians and the Israelites. Then, your servants will come down to me, and bow low, and beg us to depart. After that I will depart". And he left Pharaoh's presence in hot anger.

God instructed Moses and Aaron to tell the Israelites that each family, on the tenth of that month, should take a lamb, a yearling without blemish, and slaughter it on the fourteenth of the month, at twilight. They should take some of the blood of the animal and put it on the two doorposts and the lintel of the houses, in which they are to eat it. Then, they should roast the lamb over fire and eat that same night, with unleavened bread and with bitter herbs. Whatever would be left, until the morning, should be burned.

God added, "You shall eat hurriedly, with sandals on your feet, and your staff in your hand. It is a Passover offering to the Lord. For that night, I will go through the land of Egypt and strike down every firstborn in the land of Egypt, both men and beast, and I will punish all the gods of Egypt. And the blood on the houses where you are staying shall be a sign for you, when I see the blood I will pass over you, so that no plague will destroy you when I strike the land of Egypt. This day shall be to you one of remembrance; you shall celebrate it as a festival to the Lord through the ages. Seven days you shall eat unleavened bread. On the first day, you should remove leaven from your house, for whoever eats leavened bread from the first day to the seventh day, that person shall be cut off from Israel".

Moses summoned all the elders of Israel and told them what God had said to him. The people bowed low in homage, and then, they went and carried out the instructions.

In the middle of the night, God struck down all the firstborn of Egypt. Pharaoh and his people rose up in the night, and there was a loud cry in Egypt, because there was not a single house where there was not someone dead.

Pharaoh called Moses and Aaron that same night and told them, "Rise, depart from among my people, you and the Israelites with you! Go; worship the Lord as you said. Take all your cattle, and be gone! And pray for a blessing for me!"

The Egyptians, fearing that they would all die, urged the Israelites on, impatient to have them leave the country immediately. The Israelites took their unleavened dough, and all the objects of gold and silver that they had borrowed from the Egyptians, according to Moses' instructions, and journeyed on foot from Rameses to Succoth.

Four hundred and thirty years after Jacob and his family had arrived in Egypt, their descendants, about six hundred thousand men, beside children, left the country, with flocks and herds, accompanied by a mixed multitude of foreigners. Moses took with him the bones of Joseph, who had requested in his deathbed that the Israelites should not leave his bones in Egypt (Genesis 50:25).

The shortest way from Egypt to Canaan passed through the land of the Philistines, but God, to prevent the people from changing their minds and turning back if they would encounter armed opposition, led the Israelites roundabout by way of the wilderness of the Red Sea.

The Israelites left Succoth and encamped in Etham, in the edge of the wilderness. God went before them, in a pillar of a cloud by day, to lead them on the way, and in a pillar of fire by night, to give them light, so that they could travel day and night.

God spoke to Moses, "Tell the Israelites to turn back and encamp before Pihahiroth, between Migdol and the sea, before Baalzephon, facing the sea. Pharaoh will say that the Israelites are astray in the land, enclosed by the wilderness. I will harden his heart, and he will follow after you".

Pharaoh and his court officials, when informed that the Israelites had fled, regretted having let them go and asked themselves, "Why have we done this? Why have we released Israel from serving us?"

They decided to pursue the Israelites with an army that included six hundred chosen chariots, and the rest of the chariots of Egypt, with officers in each of them.

The Israelites saw the Egyptian army approaching. Terrified, they asked Moses, "Was there a lack of graves in Egypt that you have brought us to die in the wilderness? We told you in Egypt to leave us alone, so that we could serve them, because that would be better for us than to die in the wilderness".

Moses answered, "Don't be afraid. Stand by, and witness how God will save you today. The Egyptians that you see today, you will never see again! God will fight for you".

God said to Moses, "Why do you cry out to me? Tell the Israelites to go forward. Lift your stick, and hold your hand over the sea. It will split, and the Israelites will march on dry ground through the sea. I will harden the hearts of the Egyptians, and they will follow you; and I will gain glory by my victory over Pharaoh, his army, his chariots, and his horsemen".

The angel of God, who had been going ahead of the Israelites, now moved behind them. The pillar of cloud also moved to the back of the Israelites, between them and the Egyptians.

Moses held out his arm over the sea, and God sent a strong wind from the east that blew, during the whole night, and split the waters. The Israelites walked into the sea, on dry ground, with great walls of water to their right and to their left. The whole Egyptian army pursued them into the sea.

At dawn, the Egyptians were thrown into a panic, when they saw the pillar of fire. At the same time, the wheels of their chariots got stuck and moved with difficulty. They exclaimed, "Let us flee from the Israelites, for God is fighting for them against Egypt".

God told Moses to hold his hand over the sea. The sea returned to its normal state, and the waters covered the Egyptians, drowning all of them, while the Israelites continued marching through dry ground, till they reached the other side.

The Israelites, safe on the other side, celebrated their escape with a song of praise to God. Moses led the men, and Miriam, his sister, sang and danced with the women.

They continued on their way through the wilderness of Shur, and, during three days, they could not find water, until they arrived in Marah, but to their great disappointment, the water was bitter.

The people complained to Moses and asked them, "What will we drink?" God showed Moses a tree, which he threw into the water, and the water became sweet.

From Marah, they continued to Elim, an oasis, which had twelve water wells and seventy palm trees. They encamped beside the water.

From Elim, they went to the wilderness of Sin, where the people started to grumble against Moses and Aaron. They said, "We wish God would have killed us in Egypt, when we sat by the flesh pots, and were full with bread. You have brought us here to die of hunger!"

God told Moses, "I will rain down bread from the sky, and the people shall go out and gather everyday a daily portion. On the sixth day, they will gather a double portion".

Moses and Aaron told the Israelites, "This evening, you will know that it was God who brought you out of Egypt. And in the morning, you shall see the glory of the Lord, because God has heard your grumbling, which is against him, not against us".

Then, Moses said to Aaron, "Tell the congregation to approach toward God, because He has heard their grumblings".

While Aaron spoke to the Israelites, they turned toward the wilderness and saw the glory of God in a cloud.

God spoke to Moses and said, "I have heard the grumblings of the Israelites. Tell them: 'In the evening, you will eat meat, and in the morning, you will be filled with bread, and you will know that I am the Lord, your God'".

That evening, quails came and covered the camp, and in the morning, dew lay on the ground. When the dew had evaporated, it left a substance, which, the Israelites, not knowing what it was, called manna. It resembled coriander seed, its color was white, and its taste was similar to that of wafers made with honey.

Moses told them, "This is the bread that the Lord has given you to eat, about, which God commanded: Every man should gather as much as he needs, the measure of an omer for every person in his tent".

Some Israelites gathered more, others less, but, when they measured it by the omer, they all had what they needed, neither more nor less. Although Moses told them not to leave any of it till morning, some of them did, and it became infested with worms, and it stank, which made Moses very angry with them.

The Israelites gathered manna, each as much as he needed to eat, early in the morning, because when the sun grew hot, it would melt. On the sixth day, they gathered twice as much, two omers each. The leaders of the congregation came to Moses for an explanation.

He said to them, "This is what God has said: Tomorrow is a day of rest, a holy Sabbath of the Lord. Bake and boil what you need, and what is left save it till tomorrow". They did so, and it did not turn foul nor were there worms in it.

Moses told Aaron to keep an omer of manna in a jar and place before the Lord, so that future generations could see the bread that God fed the people in the wilderness. The Israelites ate manna, during the forty years that they spent in the wilderness.

From the wilderness of Sin, the people continued to Rephidim, where they pitched their tents. The place had no water, and the people again grumbled against Moses.

They said, "Why did you bring us out of Egypt to kill us and our children and our cattle with thirst?"

Moses cried out to God, "What shall I do with this people? They are ready to stone me!"

God answered, "Pass before the people, and take with you some of the elders. Carry the stick that you used to strike the river, and go. I will be standing before you on the rock at Horeb. You will strike the rock and water will flow from it, so that people may drink". Moses did so in the sight of the elders of Israel.

While the Israelites were still in Rephidim, the Amalekites came and attacked them. Moses told Joshua, "Choose men, and go and fight Amalek. Tomorrow, I will stand on the top of the hill with the rod of God in my hand".

Joshua went and fought with Amalek, while Moses, Aaron, and Hur climbed to the top of the hill. When Moses held up his hand, the Israelites would prevail, but when he lowered his hand, Amalek would prevail. Moses grew tired, and his hands felt heavy. Aaron and Hur took a stone, and Moses sat on it. Aaron and Hur supported his hands, one on each side; thus, his hands remained steady, until sunset, and Joshua defeated Amalek with his sword.

Moses built an altar and called it Jehovahnissi, meaning that God would be at war with Amalek in each generation.

Jethro, Moses' father-in-law, came to the Israelite camp, bringing with him Moses' wife Zipporah and her two sons, Gershom and Eliezer, who had been staying with him. Moses went out to meet his father-in-law, bowed before him, and kissed him. They asked about each other's health and then went into Moses' tent.

Moses told Jethro everything that God had done to the Pharaoh and to the Egyptians to rescue the Israelites: the hardships that the people had faced, and how God had saved them. Jethro, happy to hear these news, blessed God and offered a sacrifice. Later, they, together with Aaron, and the elders of Israel, sat to share a meal.

The next day, Jethro observed that Moses was busy from morning to night, settling disputes among the people.

Jethro said to him, "You can't continue like this. It's too much for you! Choose honest and capable men, and delegate to them some of your responsibilities".

Moses took his father-in-law's advice and appointed leaders of the people to serve as judges. Then, Jethro said goodbye to Moses and went back home.

The Israelites left Rephidim and entered the desert of Sinai. Three months had passed, since they had departed from Egypt. They camped in front of a mountain, and Moses climbed up it to hear the word of God.

God said to Moses, "If the Israelites will obey me, and keep my covenant, I will make them my treasured possession, a kingdom of priests, and a holy nation".

Moses returned to the camp and told the elders of the people what the Lord had said.

The elders answered, "We will do all that the Lord has spoken".

Moses climbed again the mountain to bring the people's answer to God.

God said to Moses, "Tell the people to sanctify themselves today and tomorrow, to wash their clothes, and to be ready for the third day, because on the third day, I will come down, in the sight of all the people, on Mount Sinai. The people should not go up the mountain or touch its border; whoever does it will be put to death. Only when the trumpet sounds a long blast, they may go up the mountain".

On the morning of the third day, there was a fierce storm, with lightning and deafening thunder. The mountain was all in smoke, its top was covered by a thick cloud, and it shook violently with earthquakes. A trumpet sounded louder and louder. The people who were in the camp trembled with fear.

Moses spoke, and God answered with thunder. The Lord called Moses to come to him. Moses went up, and God told him to go down and return with Aaron, but to tell the people and the priests not to cross the boundary of the mountain.

Moses went down and told the people what God had said.

God now spoke to the people and said the Ten Commandments:

"I am the Lord, your God, who brought you out of Egypt where you were slaves. You shall have no other gods besides me.

"You shall not make for yourself sculptured images of anything in heaven, in earth or in the water under the earth. You shall not bow to them or serve them. For I, the LORD your God, am a jealous God, visiting the iniquity of the fathers upon the children unto the third and fourth generation of those that hate me, but showing mercy to thousands of generations of those that love me, and keep my commandments.

"You shall not take the name of the Lord thy God in vain; for the Lord will not hold him guiltless that takes his name in vain.

"Observe the Sabbath day, to keep it holy. Six days shall you labor, and do all your work, but the seventh day is the Sabbath of the Lord, your God; in it you shall not do any work, you, nor your son, nor your daughter, your servants, nor your animals, nor any foreigner who is within your gates. For in six days, the Lord made heaven and earth, the sea, and all that is in them, and rested on the seventh day. Therefore, the Lord blessed the Sabbath day, and made it holy.

"Honor your father and your mother that you may long endure on the land that I am giving you.

"You shall not kill.

"You shall not commit adultery.

"You shall not steal.

"You shall not bear false witness against your neighbor.

"You shall not desire your neighbor's house, nor his wife, nor his slaves, nor his animals, nor anything that belongs to him".

The terrified people pleaded with Moses, "If you speak to us, we will listen, but, please, don't let God speak to us, because we will die".

Moses replied, "Don't be afraid. God has come only to test you, and make you obey him so that you will not sin".

Moses went into the thick cloud, where God was. The Lord instructed him to make an altar of stone, and told him his laws and instructions.

God promised to Moses, "I will send an angel before the people to guard them on their way and to bring them to the place, which I have prepared, to the land of other nations. The people should not worship their gods or follow their practices. All those nations will be gradually driven out, and the borders of the land will be from the Red Sea to the sea of the Philistines, and from the desert to the river".

God added, "Come back up to the mountain, bringing with you Aaron, with his sons Nadab and Abihu, and seventy elders of the people".

Moses went down and told the people what God had said to him. They answered with one voice, "We will do all that God has commanded".

Early next morning, Moses set an altar at the foot of the mountain and erected twelve pillars, one for each of the twelve tribes of Israel. After they had offered sacrifices on the altar, Moses went up the mountain with Aaron, Nadab, Abihu, and the seventy elders. There, they saw God standing on a pavement of a clear as heaven sapphire stone.

God said to Moses, "Climb up to the top of the mountain, and you will receive the stone tablets with the inscribed laws and commandments".

Moses rose, accompanied by Joshua, and told the elders, "Stay and wait for me. If, in my absence, there is any matter that must be settled, consult with Aaron and Hur".

Moses went up the mountain, which was covered with a cloud. During six days, the Presence of the Lord was on Mount Sinai, hidden by the cloud, but it was seen by the Israelites below as a fire burning on top of the mountain. On the seventh day, God called Moses from inside the cloud. Moses went into the cloud, and he stayed there for forty days and nights, while God gave him detailed instructions about the construction of the sacred Tent and the Ark of the Covenant.

God also said to Moses, "Aaron and his sons—Nadab, Abihu, Eleazar, and Ithamar—shall be anointed, ordained, and consecrated to serve me as priests. They should wear holy garments by skilled craftsmen, which will include a breast piece, an ephod, a robe, a tunic, a headdress, and a sash, that will provide them with dignity and beauty.

"Make a bronze basin with a bronze base, and pour water in it, that Aaron and his sons will use to wash their hands and feet, before entering the sacred Tent or approach the altar to make a sacrifice.

"I have chosen Bezaleel, the son of Uri of the tribe of Judah, and Aholiab, the son of Ahisamach of the tribe of Dan, two gifted craftsmen, expert in working in gold, silver, brass, wood, and embroidering, to design and carry out the work for the sacred Tent, the Ark, the furniture, and the altar".

God finished speaking to Moses and gave him two stone tablets, on which he had written the commandments with His finger.

In the meantime, the people, seeing that many days had gone by, and that Moses had not come down from the mountain, gathered around Aaron and said to him, "We do not know what has happened to Moses, the man who brought us out of Egypt. So make us gods, which shall go before us".

Aaron said to them, "Take off the gold earrings that your wives, sons, and daughters are wearing and bring them to me".

Aaron received the earrings, melted them, poured the metal into a mold, and made a golden idol in the shape of a bull.

The people saw it and exclaimed, "Israel, this is your god, who brought you out of Egypt!"

Aaron, seeing their enthusiasm, built an altar and told the people, "Tomorrow, we shall celebrate a festival to honor the Lord".

Early the next day, the people brought animals to sacrifice and celebrated a great feast. They sat down to eat and drink, and then they rose to dance, surrendering all inhibitions.

God told Moses, "The people have corrupted themselves and are worshipping and sacrificing to an idol. I see that this people are stiff necked. Now, let me be, I am angry with them; I will destroy them, and I will make of your descendants a great nation".

Moses pleaded with God, saying, "Why should you be angry with this people, whom you have rescued from Egypt with great power and a mighty hand? The Egyptians will say, he brought them out with an evil purpose, to kill them in the mountains, and to completely destroy them. Do not be angry, and do not bring this disaster against your people. Remember Abraham, Isaac, and Israel, your servants, to whom you swore by yourself, and said to them, I will multiply your seed as the stars of heaven, and all this land that I have spoken of will I give to your seed, and they shall inherit it forever".

God changed His mind and did not punish the people. Moses went down the mountain, carrying the two stone tablets where God had written the commandments, and was met on the way by Joshua.

When they were near the camp, Joshua said to Moses, "I hear sounds of war coming from the camp".

Moses answered, "Those are not cries of victory or defeat. What we are hearing are sounds of singing".

As soon as Moses was close enough to see the idol and the dancing, he became furious. He threw down the stone tablets and broke them. He took the idol, melted it, ground it into fine powder, and mixed it with water. Then, he forced the Israelites to drink it.

Moses asked Aaron, "What did these people do to you that you allowed them to commit such a terrible sin?"

Aaron answered, "Let not my lord be angry. You know that this people are determined to do evil. They said to me, 'We do not know what has happened to Moses, the man who brought us out of Egypt. So make us gods, which shall go before us'. I told them to bring me their gold, threw the gold into the fire, and out came this bull!"

Moses stood in the gate of the camp and saw that Aaron had let the people get out of control. He shouted, "Whoever is on the side of the Lord, come to me!"

The Levites gathered around him, and he said to them, "The Lord, God of Israel, commands that you put on your sword, and you go throughout the camp, from one gate to the other, and kill your brothers, your friends, and your neighbors".

The Levites carried out the order, and that day, they killed about three thousand men.

Moses told them, "Consecrate yourselves today to the Lord, for each of you has been against son and brother, that God may bless you today".

The next day, Moses told the people, "You have committed a terrible sin. I will go up the mountain to speak to God, and perhaps, I will obtain His forgiveness for your sin".

Moses went back to God and said, "The people have committed a great sin by making an idol of gold. Please forgive their sin, and if not, erase me from your book".

God answered, "I will erase from my book only those who have sinned against me. Go now; lead the people to the place I told you. My angel shall go before you. When the time comes, I will punish the people for their sin".

Soon afterward, God sent a plague to the people for having forced Aaron to make the idol.

God said to Moses, "Depart, leave this place, you and the people, which you have brought out of Egypt, and go to the land, which I swore to Abraham, Isaac, and Jacob, that I would give it to their descendants, a land flowing with milk and honey. I will send an angel before you, and I will drive out the Canaanite, the Amorite, the Hittite, the Perizzite, the Hivite, and the Jebusite. But I will not go in your midst, since you are a stiff-necked people, and I might destroy you on the way".

Wherever the people set camp, Moses would take the sacred Tent—called the Tent of the Congregation—and erect it outside the camp, at some distance from it. Anyone who wanted to consult the Lord would come to it.

When Moses would go to the Tent, every man would rise and stand, each at the entrance of his tent, and watch Moses, until he entered the Tent. Then, the pillar of cloud would descend and stand at the entrance of the Tent, while God spoke with Moses face to face, as a man speaks to his friend. The people, seeing the pillar of cloud at the door of the tent, would bow down. When Moses would return to the camp, Joshua, the son of Nun, his helper, would stay in the Tent.

Moses asked God, "Please let me see your Presence."

God answered, "Stand on the rock. I will put you on a cleft of the rock and cover you with my hand, until I have passed by. Then, I will take my hand away, and you will see my back but not my face, because no man can see me and live".

God told Moses, "Cut two stone tablets like the first ones, and I will write on them the same words that were on the first tables, which you broke. Come to me in the morning to Mount Sinai, and meet me there at the top. No one should come up with you; nobody should be seen on the mountain, and no animals should graze at the foot of the mountain".

Moses cut two tablets of stone, similar to the first set, rose early the next morning, and climbed Mount Sinai, carrying the two tablets with him. God came down in a cloud, and Moses bowed down to the ground and worshipped.

God instructed him on the laws and commandments and told him, "Write down these commandments, because, on the basis of these commandments, I am making a covenant with you and with Israel".

Moses stayed with God forty days and forty nights, writing the Ten Commandments on the tablets, without drinking or eating.

When he came down from the mountain, Aaron and the people of Israel were afraid to come near him, because his face was shining. Moses called Aaron and the rulers of the people, and Moses talked with them. Then, the Israelites approached, and Moses told them all the laws that God had given him. When he finished speaking, he covered his face with a veil, which, from that moment, he kept on all the time, except when he was in the Tent speaking with God.

Moses asked the people to contribute with gifts of precious metals, yarns, skins, and oil, to beautify the Tent. He also asked those who were craftsmen and skilled workmen to come and work in the Tent, explaining to them that the work would be directed by Bezaleel and Aholiab.

The Tent was finished in the first month of the second year after the departure from Egypt, and the Ark of the Covenant was placed inside. The cloud covered the Tent of the Congregation and the Presence of the Lord filled it.

The Israelites would move their camp to another place, only when the cloud lifted from the Tent. If the cloud stayed there, they would remain in the same place. During all their wanderings, they could see the cloud of the Lord's Presence over the Tent at daytime, and a fire burning above it at night.

God ordered Moses to anoint Aaron and his sons as priests. The whole community gathered near the door of the Tent of the Congregation to see the ceremony. Moses brought Aaron and his sons and washed them with water. He put the garment on Aaron, girded him with the sash, clothed him with the robe, and placed the ephod on him.

Moses put the breast piece on Aaron, and on it, he placed the Urim and the Thummim. Then, he put the headdress on Aaron's head, and over it the gold frontlet, the holy crown, as God had commanded him.

He took the anointing oil and anointed the Tent and all that was inside, and he consecrated it. He then sprinkled the oil seven times upon the altar and poured the anointing oil on Aaron's head to consecrate him.

Next, Moses brought the sons of Aaron forward and put robes on them, sashed around their waists, and head coverings on their heads. Then, he sacrificed a bull and two rams and put blood on the horns of the altar, and on the base of the altar. He took some of the blood and put it on the lobe of Aaron's ear, on the thumb of his right hand, and on the big toe of his right foot. He did the same to the sons of Aaron. Then, he poured the rest of the blood on all four sides of the altar.

Moses commanded Aaron and his sons to take the meat of the sacrifice to the entrance of the Tent, and to eat it there with the consecrated bread. Any bread or meat left over would have to be burned. To complete their ordination rites, Aaron and his sons stayed at the entrance of the Tent for seven days and seven nights.

Aaron's two eldest sons, Nadab and Abihu, took their fire pans, put incense and fire on them, and presented these fires to the Lord, an act which God had not commanded them to do. Suddenly, a fire came from God and burned them to death.

Moses told Aaron, "This is what the Lord meant when he said, 'All who serve me must respect my holiness'". Aaron remained silent and didn't reply.

Moses called Mishael and Elzaphan, the sons of his uncle Uzziel, and said to them, "Carry your cousins' bodies away from the Tent, and take them outside of the camp".

To Aaron and his remaining sons, he said, "Do not show any signs of mourning. If you do so, you will die, and anger will strike the whole community. Do not leave the entrance of the Tent or you will die, because the Lord's anointing oil is upon you. But your relatives and the whole community may bewail the burning that the Lord has sent".

Moses told Aaron and his two sons to take the grain offering that was left from the sacrifices, make unleavened bread with it, and eat it in the sacred precinct.

He then asked them, "What about the goat for the sin offering?"

The two sons of Aaron answered, "It has already been burned".

Angrily, he asked Eleazar and Ithamar, "Why didn't you eat the sin offering in a sacred place? It is holy, and God gave it to you to remove the guilt of the community and to expiate for their sins. Since its blood was not brought into the sacred precinct, you should have eaten it there as I commanded".

Aaron replied, "Today, they sacrificed to the Lord, and these things have befallen me! Had I eaten the sin offering today, would God have approved?"

When Moses heard Aaron's answer, he was satisfied.

God said to Moses, "Aaron may enter the sacred precinct only if he has first washed himself with water, and then put on his priestly garments. He should bring with him a bull and sacrifice it to make expiation for himself and for his household. Then, he should take two goats and let them stand before me at the entrance to the Tent. There, he should place lots upon the two goats, one goat marked for the Lord, which would be offered in sacrifice, and the other goat to be the scapegoat, upon which Aaron should lay his hand and confess over it all the sins and transgressions of the people. Then, a man appointed for this task should take the goat to the desert, and set it free, carrying all the sins of the community to an uninhabited land".

On the first day of the second month, in the second year following the departure from Egypt, God commanded Moses to take a census of the whole community by tribes, clans, and families, listing the names of all the men twenty years old or older who were fit for military service. The census counted six hundred three thousand and five hundred such men, a number which did not include the Levites, because their role was to care for the Tent and to serve the priests.

Later, the Levites were also counted, and their total number of males, one month old and older, was found to be twenty-two thousand. Only the Levites between the ages of thirty and fifty were qualified to work in the Tent; their number was eight thousand five hundred and eighty.

On the twentieth day of the second month, in the second year, the cloud lifted from the Tent, and the Israelites started on their journey out of the Sinai desert toward the wilderness of Paran.

The people started again to complain. God, in his anger, sent a fire, which consumed part of the camp, and only died, when Moses prayed.

The foreigners among the Israelites expressed a strong desire for meat, and even the Israelites wept and said, "If only we had meat to eat! We remember the fish that we used to eat free in Egypt, the cucumbers, the melons, the leeks, the onions, the garlic! Now, all we have is this manna!"

Moses heard them weep as they stood outside their tents, and he spoke to God in his distress, "Why have you treated me so badly laying the burden of this people on me? Did I conceive them? Did I bring them to birth? Where can I get meat for them, when they whine before me and beg me for meat? I cannot be responsible for all these people by myself; it is too much for me! If you deal, thus, with me, it is better if you kill me and end my misery!"

God answered, "Bring seventy elders of the people, whom you know to be respected leaders, to the Tent, and let them stand next to you. I will come down and speak with you there, and I will take from your spirit, and put it on them, and they will share your burden. Tell the people that they should purify themselves tomorrow, because they will have meat to eat. I have heard their whining for meat, and I will give you meat, and you will eat it, not one day, not two days, not five or ten or twenty days, but a whole month, until it comes out of

your nostrils and becomes loathsome to you; because you have despised the LORD who is among you, and have complained that you should have never left Egypt".

Moses, puzzled, asked God, "There are six hundred thousand men with me, and you say that you will give them enough meat for a whole month? Can there be enough cattle and sheep to satisfy them? Are all the fish in the sea enough for them?"

God answered, "Is there a limit to God's power? You will soon see if what I have said will happen or not".

Moses told the people what God had said. Then, he brought the seventy elders to the Tent and placed them around it. God came down in a cloud, spoke to Moses, and took from his spirit and gave it to the seventy elders, who started to prophesy.

Two men, Eldad and Medad, had remained in the camp, but they also received the spirit and prophesied inside the camp. A young man came running and reported it to Moses. Joshua heard this and asked Moses to stop them.

Moses answered, "Are you worried about me? I wish that the Lord would give his spirit to all his people, and make all of them prophets!"

A wind from God that started up swept quail from the sea, which settled on the camp, and all around it, for several miles in every direction. The people gathered quail all that day, and all that night, and also the next day. While they were still chewing the meat, the anger of God blazed forth against the people and caused an epidemic to break out among them. The place was named Kibrothhattaavah, *Graves of craving*, because the people who had lusted for meat were buried there.

From Kibrothhattaavah the Israelites journeyed to Hazeroth, where they set camp. There, Miriam and Aaron spoke against Moses, criticizing him, because of the Ethiopian woman whom he had married. They also claimed that God spoke, not only through Moses, but also through them. Moses did not react, because he was a meek and humble man. Suddenly, God called Moses, Aaron, and Miriam to come to the Tent.

The Lord came down in a pillar of cloud, stood at the entrance to the Tent, and told Aaron and Miriam to come forth.

They did so, and God said to them, "Hear my words! I make myself known to the prophets in visions, and I speak to them in dreams. But only to Moses I speak face to face, plainly, and not in riddles. He has even seen my likeness! How could you not be afraid of speaking against my servant Moses?" God departed, angry with them. When the cloud rose from the Tent, Miriam's skin had become leprous, white as snow.

Aaron looked at her, turned to Moses, and said, "My lord, I beg you, please forgive us for the sin that we have foolishly committed. Don't let her be as someone born dead, with his flesh half consumed, when he emerges from his mother's womb".

Moses prayed to God, "O God, please heal her now!"

God replied, "If her father had spit in her face, would she not bear her shame for seven days? Let her be shut out of the camp for seven days, and after that, she can be received back".

Miriam was not allowed inside the camp for seven days. When she returned to the camp, cured, the Israelites left Hazeroth and set camp in the wilderness of Paran.

God told Moses to send twelve men, one from each tribe, to scout the land of Canaan and report back about its cities and its inhabitants, to find out if they were strong or weak, few or many, and to bring back the fruit of the land.

The spies went and scouted the land, from the wilderness of Zin to Rehob, near the entrance to Hamath. Forty days later, they returned back to the camp, carrying pomegranates, figs, and a branch, which had a bunch of grapes so heavy that it took two men to carry it on a pole between them.

Their report turned out to be disheartening and defeatist. "We came to the land and saw that it flows with milk and honey, and here is the fruit that we have brought. But the inhabitants are strong; their cities are walled and very large. The Amalekites dwell in the south; the Hittites, the Jebusites, and the Amorites live in the hill country; and the Canaanites dwell by the sea and along the Jordan River".

Caleb, the son of Jephunneh, the scout from the tribe of Judah, interrupted them, "We can overcome them. Let us go up at once, and possess the land".

But the others insisted, "We are not able to go against them. They are too strong for us. That land devours its inhabitants. All the men that we saw are of great stature, and we even saw giants, the sons of Anak. We felt like grasshoppers, and we must have looked like that to them too." Hearing this frightening report, the congregation murmured against Moses and Aaron and said to them, "We wish that we had died in Egypt or in this wilderness! Why did God bring us to this land, to die by the sword? Should our wives and children be captured? Wouldn't it be better for us to return to Egypt?" And they said to one another, "Let's choose a leader and go back to Egypt".

Only Joshua, the son of Nun, and Caleb, the son of Jephunneh, disagreed and said, "The land that we scouted is an excellent land. If God is pleased with us, he will take us there, and deliver to us a land flowing with milk and honey. Do not rebel against the Lord, and don't be afraid of the people who live there, because we can conquer them easily. God is with us; do not fear them!"

The congregation threatened to stone them to death, when, suddenly, the Presence of the Lord appeared in the Tent before all the Israelites.

God said to Moses, "How long will this people reject me? How long will they refuse to believe in me despite all the miracles that I have performed among them? I will strike them with pestilence and disown them, and I will make you the father of a nation more numerous and more powerful than they are!"

Moses said to God, "The Egyptians will hear that you have done that, and will tell it to the inhabitants of the land, and the nations who have heard your fame will say that God was unable to bring his people into the land, which he had promised to them, and, therefore, he killed them in the wilderness. Please forgive this people, as you have done till now".

God said, "I will pardon them, as you asked. But none of these men who have seen my Presence, and the miracles, which I performed in Egypt and in the wilderness, and who have provoked me ten times, and have not listened to my voice, will ever see the land, which I promised to your ancestors!. But I will bring my servant Caleb into the land, and his descendants will possess it. He has a different spirit in him, and has remained loyal to me. Turn back tomorrow and go into the wilderness by the way of the Red Sea. You will wander forty years in the wilderness, one year for each of the days that your spies scouted the land. All those who complained against me will die in the wilderness. No one of you over the age of twenty will enter that land, except Caleb and Joshua!"

When Moses told the Israelites what the Lord had said, they were overcome with grief and told Moses, "We were wrong. We are now ready to go to the place that God has told us about".

Moses told them, "Don't do that. God is not with you, and your enemies will defeat you".

They refused to listen to Moses. They left him in the camp with the Ark of the Covenant and went to the hill country, where the Amalekites and the Canaanites that lived in that region attacked and defeated them.

Sometime later, an Israelite was found gathering wood on the Sabbath. The people were not sure what to do with him, so they brought him to the presence of Moses and Aaron.

Moses consulted with God, and God commanded that the man should be put to death. The people took the man outside the camp and stoned him to death.

Korah was a first cousin of Moses, his father being Izhar, a younger brother of Amram. Together with three other men—Dathan, Abiram, and On—Korah, at the head of a group of two hundred fifty well-known men, accused Moses and Aaron of raising themselves over the rest of the people. Moses heard this and flung himself on the ground. Then, he said to Korah, "Tomorrow you and your followers will take your censers, put fire and incense inside on them before the Lord, and the man that the Lord will choose, will be the holy one".

The next day, the rebels, with their censers, stood in the door of the Tent with Moses and Aaron, surrounded by the people. Moses asked the people to depart from there, and also to stay away from the tents of the rebels, lest they be also consumed together.

Moses then spoke, "If these men will die of a natural death, then I have not been sent by God, but if the earth will open and swallow them up, this will prove that the rebels have offended God".

As soon as he finished speaking, the earth opened, and Korah, his followers, their tents, and all their goods fell inside. The earth closed upon them, and they all perished. Eleazar the Priest took the censers of the rebels and made with them broad plates for the covering of the altar, to remind the people that only the descendants of Aaron could offer incense to God.

The next day, the whole community complained against Moses and Aaron, accusing them of having killed the people of the Lord. They looked toward the Tent and saw that the cloud was covering it, which meant that the Presence of the Lord had appeared.

When Moses and Aaron reached the Tent, God spoke to Moses and said, "Move back from these people so that I can destroy them in this instant".

Moses and Aaron fell on their faces, and Moses said to Aaron, "Quickly, take a censer and put there incense and fire from the altar. Go to the congregation, and make expiation for them, because the anger of God has brought the plague".

Aaron did as Moses had ordered, and he ran into the congregation, where the plague had already begun. He put on the incense and made expiation for the people, until the plague ended, after killing fourteen thousand seven hundred, not counting those who had died with Korah.

God told Moses, "Tell the people to bring you twelve walking sticks, one from the leader of each tribe. Write each man's name on his stick, and then write Aaron's name on the stick representing the tribe of Levi. Place the sticks inside the Tent, in front of the Ark of the Covenant. The stick of the man that I have chosen will sprout".

Moses did as God told him. The next day, when Moses went into the Tent, he saw that Aaron's stick had budded, blossomed, and produced almonds. He took the sticks out, and each leader took his own stick back.

God told Moses, "Put Aaron's stick back in front of the Ark, to serve as a remainder and a warning to the rebel Israelites that they will die if they don't stop complaining".

In their wanderings, the Israelites came to the wilderness of Zin and camped in Kadesh, where Miriam, Moses and Aaron's sister, died and was buried.

When the people complained that there was no water, and that they would die of thirst, God said to Moses, "Take the stick that is in front of the Ark, and assemble the community, and in front of them speak to the rock and water will flow from it".

Moses and Aaron assembled the whole community in front of the rock. This time, Moses' anger and frustration with the constantly complaining Israelites caused him to lose his patience, and he shouted, "Listen, you rebels! Shall we get water for you out of this rock?"

He then raised the stick and struck the rock twice with it. Out came a great stream of water, and the people and the animals drank.

God reproved Moses and Aaron, "Because you did not believe in me enough to affirm my sanctity in the eyes of the Israelites, you will not bring this congregation into the land, which I have given them". They called the place Meribah, because the Israelites quarreled there with God.

Moses sent messengers to the king of Edom, asking him to allow the Israelites to pass peacefully through his land, promising that they would stay on the main road. The Edomites refused the request, and the Israelites had to take another road.

The Israelites left Kadesh and arrived at Mount Hor, near the border of Edom. There,

God announced to Moses and Aaron that Aaron would not enter the Promised Land; he would die, because of their behavior at Meribah.

Moses, following God's instructions, took Aaron and his son Eleazar up Mount Hor, watched by the whole congregation. When they arrived to the top of the mountain, Moses removed Aaron's priestly garments and put them on Eleazar. When Moses and Eleazar came down the mountain, the whole community understood that Aaron had died, and they mourned him for thirty days.

Arad, the king of a southern Canaanite kingdom, heard that the Israelites were coming. He attacked them with his army and took some of them captive. The Israelites vowed to God that, if he would deliver the Canaanites into their hands, they would utterly destroy their towns. The Israelites defeated Arad and destroyed his city, to such an extent that, from then on, the place was called Hormah, *Complete ruin.*

The Israelites left the region of Mount Hor and continued along the Red Sea, skirting the territory of Edom. Once again, the people started to complain against God and Moses, "Why did you bring us out of Egypt to die in the wilderness? We have no bread and no water".

God sent them poisonous serpents, which bit the people, and many died. The Israelites came to Moses and asked him to pray to God to take the serpents away. Moses prayed for the people, and God answered, "Make a brass serpent and place it on a pole. Anybody who is bitten will be cured if he looks at it". Moses did as he was told.

The Israelites continued their journey to Oboth, from there to Ijeabarim, near the territory of Moab, and from there to the valley of Zared. They crossed the river Arnon and camped on the other side. From there, they went to Beer, Mattanah, and Nahaliel, until they reached Bamoth, at the foot of Mount Pisgah.

The Israelites sent messengers to Sihon, king of the Amorites, who requested permission to cross his territory and promised that the Israelites would not disturb the wells, and would stay in the main roads.

Sihon's response was to gather an army and march against the Israelites. The battle took place in Jahaz, and the Israelites utterly defeated the Amorites, occupying their land from the Arnon to the Jabbok, which was their border with the Ammonites. After Moses sent men to spy the city of Jaazer, the Israelites conquered it and drove out the Amorites that lived there.

Their next battle was at Edrei, against the army of Og, the king of Bashan. The Israelites again triumphed. King Og, his sons, and all his people perished in the battle. The Israelites killed all the survivors and took over their land.

The Israelites moved on and camped in the plains of Moab, on the east side of the river Jordan, opposite the city of Jericho.

Balak, the son of Zippor, was the king of Moab at that time. He was terrified that the people of Israel, who had recently defeated the Amorites, would do the same to Moab, because the Israelites vastly outnumbered his own people. The solution that he found was to get the seer Balaam to come from his home in Aram and curse the people of Israel.

Balak took Balaam to a high mountain from where they could see the people of Israel. On Balaam's instructions, seven altars were built, and a bull and a ram were sacrificed in each of them. However, to Balak's surprise, Balaam uttered blessings for Israel, instead of curses. This same turn of events happened two more times, on the top of Pisgah, and at the peak of Peor.

Balak, angry and disappointed, told Balaam to flee back to his land. Balaam then prophesied that Israel one day would triumph over Moab.

The Israelites camped in a place called Shittim, where they were seduced by Moabite women, who incited them to participate in the licentious worship of their god Baalpeor.

God, furious with the people, sent a plague, which killed twenty-four thousand persons, and ordered Moses to hang the leaders. Moses then gave instructions to his officials to kill all the men who had worshipped Baalpeor.

At that moment, Zimri, son of Salu, of the tribe of Simeon, brought into his tent a woman called Cozbi, the daughter of Zur, a Midianite prince. Phinehas—the grandson of Aaron, the priest—saw that, took a javelin in his hand, went into the tent, and killed the couple.

God was appeased by this act and rewarded Phinehas, by making with him and his descendants a covenant of an everlasting priesthood.

When the plague was over, God ordered Moses and Eleazar to take a new census and count all the men twenty years and older, who were fit for military service. It was found that there were 601,730 potential soldiers.

The Levites, one month old or older, who were counted separately, were twenty-three thousand.

The five daughters of a man called Zelophehad, of the tribe of Manasseh, came to Moses and Eleazar the High Priest, asking to inherit from their father, who had died in the wilderness. Moses, after consulting with God, modified the law to entitle a daughter to inherit from her father if he did not have any sons, but with the condition that she had to marry within the clan, in order that her inheritance would remain in her tribe.

God said to Moses, "Go up to Mount Abarim, and look out over the land that I am giving to the Israelites. After you have seen it, you will die, because of your behavior at Meribah".

Moses said, "Lord God, please appoint a man who can lead the people, and command them in battle, so that your community will not be like sheep without a shepherd".

God answered, "Take Joshua, son of Nun, a capable man, and lay your hand upon him. Have him stand before Eleazar the Priest and the whole community, and proclaim him as your successor. Delegate on him some of your authority, so that the whole community of Israelites shall obey him. He shall present himself to Eleazar the Priest, who shall on his behalf seek the decision of the Urim before the Lord". Moses did as the Lord had commanded him.

God told Moses, "Punish the Midianites for what they did to the people of Israel. And after you have done so, you will die".

Moses sent an army of twelve thousand men, a thousand warriors from each tribe, against the Midianites. Phinehas, equipped with the sacred utensils and the trumpets for sounding the blast, accompanied the army. The army attacked Midian and killed all the men, including their five kings, and also Balaam, the seer, who had been with them. The Midianite women, the children, and the cattle were captured and brought to the camp.

Moses, Eleazar, and the leaders of the community went outside the camp to meet the returning warriors. When Moses saw the women, he angrily rebuked the commanders of the army for having brought the women who had seduced the men into worshipping Baalpeor. He then ordered to kill all the male children, and all the women, sparing only the virgins.

The tribes of Reuben and Gad wished to settle in the east bank of the river Jordan, in the regions of Jazer and Gilead, because the pastures in those regions were very suitable for their large number of cattle. They came to Moses and Eleazar and asked permission to settle there.

Moses asked them, "Shall your brothers go to war while you stay here? How can you discourage the people of Israel from crossing the river to the land that God has given them? This is exactly what your fathers did when I sent them to scout the land! If you turn away from him, he will once again abandon all the people in the wilderness, and you will be responsible for their calamity".

They answered, "We will build sheepfolds for our cattle, and fortified towns for our children, and then we ourselves will go armed in the forefront of the army, and will not return, until all the other Israelites have taken possession of the land assigned to them".

Moses replied, "If you do this, you shall be clear before the Lord and before Israel, and the land east of the Jordan will be yours".

God told Moses that Eleazar the Priest and Joshua, with the help of one leader from each tribe, would apportion the land of Canaan for the people. Each tribe would receive an assigned territory, except for the tribe of Levi, which would not receive any land, but would live on the offerings and sacrifices given to the Lord.

Moses put in writing the words of the Teaching, and he gave the roll to the Levites who carried the Ark of the Covenant with instructions to place it beside the Ark.

That same day, God said to Moses, "Go to the Abarim mountains in the land of Moab, opposite the city of Jericho; climb Mount Nebo, and look at the land of Canaan that I am about to give to the people of Israel. You will die on that mountain, as your brother Aaron died on Mount Hor, because at the waters of Meribah, you failed to uphold my sanctity. You may look at the land from a distance, but you will not enter it".

Moses, before he died, blessed the people of Israel, with a blessing for each tribe. Then, he climbed Mount Nebo, to the top of Mount Pisgah, opposite Jericho, and the Lord showed him all the land.

Moses died at the age of one hundred and twenty in possession of all his faculties. God buried him in a valley in the land of Moab, near Bethpeor, in an unknown grave, and the Israelites mourned him for thirty days.

Moza

(Hebrew origin: *Exit*)

1. (1 Chronicles 2:46). Unspecified date. Moza, of the tribe of Judah, was a descendant of Hezron. His parents were Caleb and his concubine Ephah. His brothers were Haran and Gazez.

2. (1 Chronicles 8:36). Unspecified date. Moza, of the tribe of Benjamin, a descendant of King Saul, was the son of Zimri and the grandson of Jehoadah. His son was called Binea. His uncles were Alemeth and Azmaveth. His grandfather Jehoadah is called Jarah in First Chronicles (1 Chronicles 9:42).

Muppim

(Hebrew origin: *Wavings*)

(Genesis 46:21). 17th century B.C. Muppim was one of the ten sons of Benjamin according to the list in Genesis, which also includes Belah, Becher, Ashbel, Gera, Naaman, Ehi, Rosh, Huppim, and Ard. He was one of the seventy Israelites who immigrated to Egypt.

The other lists of the sons of Benjamin in the Bible do not include Muppim: Numbers 26:38, 1 Chronicles 7:6, and 1 Chronicles 8:1.

Mushi

(Hebrew origin: *Sensitive*)

(Exodus 6:19). 16th century B.C. Mushi, son of Merari, grandson of Levi, and brother of Mahli, was the ancestor of a clan of Levites, who were servants of the Temple. His sons were Mahli, Eder, and Jeremoth.

Naam

(Hebrew origin: *Pleasant*)

(1 Chronicles 4:15). 12th century B.C. Naam was one of the sons of Caleb. His grandfather was Jephunneh, a descendant of Judah. Naam's brothers were Iru and Elah.

Naamah

(Hebrew origin: *Pleasantness*)

1. (Genesis 4:22). Antediluvian. Naamah was the daughter of Lamech, a descendant of Cain, and his wife Zillah. Her brother was Tubalcain, an expert artisan of cooper and iron. Her half brothers—the sons of Adah, Lamech's other wife—were Jabal and Jubal.
2. (1 Kings 14:21). 10th century B.C. Naamah, an Ammonitess, was the wife of King Solomon and the mother of King Rehoboam.

Naaman

(Hebrew origin: *Pleasing*)

1. (Genesis 46:21). 17th century B.C. Naaman, son of Benjamin and grandson of Jacob, was one of the seventy Israelites who immigrated to Egypt. His brothers, according to the Genesis' list, were Belah, Becher, Ashbel, Gera, Ehi, Rosh, Muppim, Huppim, and Ard.

    Note: Naaman is not mentioned in any of the other three lists of the sons of Benjamin: Numbers 26:38, 1 Chronicles 7:6, and 1 Chronicles 8:1.
2. (Numbers 26:40). 16th century B.C. Naaman, ancestor of the clan of the Naamites, was a son of Bela and a grandson of Benjamin.
3. (2 Kings 5:1). 9th century B.C. Naaman, the commander of the Syrian army, was a leper. His wife's maid, an Israelite girl who had been captured by the Syrians in one of their army's incursions in Israel, told her

mistress that she wished that Naaman would go to the prophet in Samaria, because he would certainly cure him of his sickness.

The king of Syria must have heard a garbled version of the Israelite girl's suggestion, because he assumed that the person with the power to cure his commandment was the king of Israel. He immediately sat down to write a letter to the Israelite ruler, telling him that he was sending Naaman to Israel, and that he expected the king to cure his commander from his leprosy. A messenger took the letter to Israel, together with ten talents of silver, six thousand pieces of gold, and ten changes of clothing.

The king of Israel was flabbergasted, when he read the letter with its unusual request. The only conclusion that he could reach was that the Syrian king was looking for a pretext to provoke a quarrel between the two countries. He informed his advisers of his fears and rented his clothes.

When the prophet Elisha heard about this matter, he sent a message to the king that said, "Why did you rent your clothes? Tell Naaman to come to me, and I will show him that there is a prophet in Israel".

Naaman came to the house of Elisha, with his horses and chariot, and waited outside, while his presence was announced to the prophet. Elisha didn't come out, but sent word to the Syrian that, if he wished to be cured, he should go to the Jordan River and wash seven times. Naaman was offended and disappointed; he had expected that Elisha would personally receive him and cure him by praying to God, while touching him with his hand.

He commented angrily, "Are not Abana and Pharpar, the rivers of Damascus, better than all the waters in Israel? Can I not be clean by washing in them?" He turned away in a rage and left.

However, on his way back to Syria, his servants convinced him that he should try Elisha's advice. What could he lose?

Naaman went to the Jordan, bathed seven times, and was completely cured.

Naaman went back to Elisha's house to thank the prophet and offered him a gift in appreciation, which Elisha refused to receive.

He then said to Elisha, "I recognize that God is the true God. I want to take back with me two mules, loaded with Israelite earth, so that, in the future, I will only pray and sacrifice to God. However, if there are occasions in the future where I will have to accompany my master, the king of Syria, to the Temple of the god Rimmon, I ask God to pardon me in advance if I bow to the idol Rimmon".

Naaman again expressed his thanks to Elisha and departed. Gehazi, the prophet's servant, greedy to gain some benefit from Naaman's cure, ran after the Syrian. Naaman saw Gehazi, stopped his chariot, alighted, and asked him if everything was well.

Gehazi answered, "My master Elisha has sent me to request from you two changes of clothing and a talent of silver for two young prophets who have come to visit him." Naaman, happy that he was able to show his gratitude to the prophet, gave him the two changes of clothing and the two talents of silver.

Gehazi returned to his master's house, and Elisha asked him, "Where did you go?"

Gehazi replied, "I didn't go out".

Elisha said to him, "In punishment for having received money from Naaman, the Syrian's leprosy would cling to you and your posterity forever!"

4. (1 Chronicles 8:7). Unspecified date. Naaman was one of the descendants of Ehud of the tribe of Benjamin, who were leaders of clans expelled from Geba to Manahath.

Naarah

(Hebrew origin: *Young girl*)

(1 Chronicles 4:5). Unspecified date. Naarah was one of the two wives—the other one was Helah—of Ashur, the founder of Tekoa, with whom she had four sons: Ahuzam, Hepher, Temeni, and Haahashtari.

Naarai

(Hebrew origin: *Youthful*)

(1 Chronicles 11:37). 10th century B.C. Naarai, the son of Ezbai, was one of "The Thirty", an elite group in King David's army. He is called Paarai the Arbite in the second book of Samuel (2 Samuel 23:35).

Naashon

(Hebrew origin: *Snake enchanter*)

(Exodus 6:23). 13th century B.C. Naashon, the son of Amminadab, an ancestor of King David, was the father of Salmon and the brother of Elisheba, the wife of Aaron. He commanded the tribe of Judah, during the Israelites' sojourn in the Sinai desert, and was one of the twelve Israelite leaders who donated gifts of silver and gold, bulls, rams, goats, and lambs for the dedication of the altar.

He is also called Naasson (Matthew 1:4), and Nahshon (Numbers 1:7).

Naasson

(Hebrew origin: *Snake enchanter*)

(Matthew 1:4). 13th century B.C. Naasson is an alternative spelling for Naashon. (Please see the entry for Naashon [Exodus 6:23].)

Nabal

(Hebrew origin: *Fool*)

(1 Samuel 25:3). 11th century B.C. Nabal, a descendant of Caleb, was a wealthy man—he owned over three thousand sheep and a thousand goats—who lived in Carmel, near the city of Hebron. Although he was a most disagreeable person, churlish, and an evildoer, he had the fortune of being married to Abigail, a beautiful and intelligent woman.

David, at that time, led a band of outcasts that made their living from the contributions that they requested from the rich people who lived in the surrounding area. Hearing that Nabal was shearing his sheep, he sent ten of his men to request from Nabal to give them whatever he could. Nabal treated them insultingly and refused to give them anything.

His wife Abigail realized that David would come to punish Nabal. To prevent this, she loaded several asses with food and wine, and, without telling her husband, she went to intercept David. When she met David, who was on his way to Nabal's house, she apologized for her husband's bad manners and convinced him not to take revenge against Nabal.

Abigail returned home and, seeing that Nabal was drunk, waited till the next morning to tell him how she had saved his life. Nabal's shock, when he heard of his close escape, was too much; he suffered a stroke and died ten days later.

When David heard that Nabal had died, he asked Abigail to marry him, and she agreed.

Naboth

(Hebrew origin: *Fruits*)

(1 Kings 21:1). 9th century B.C. Naboth the Jezreelite owned a vineyard in the city of Jezreel, which, to his bad fortune, was situated next to the palace of King Ahab of Israel.

The king considered that the vineyard could be converted into a great vegetable garden for the palace. He went to Naboth and offered to buy the vineyard, or exchange it for a similar vineyard in another neighborhood.

Naboth told him, "God forbid that I should give you the land that I have inherited from my fathers!"

Ahab went back to the palace, depressed and angry. He lay down on his bed, with his face turned to the wall, and would not eat.

His wife Jezebel asked him, "Why are you so sad? And why do you refuse to eat?"

The king answered, "I want to buy Naboth's vineyard, but he will not give it to me".

Jezebel told him, "Aren't you the king of Israel? Get up, eat something, and be cheerful! I will get Naboth's vineyard for you".

She wrote letters in Ahab's name, sealed them with the royal seal, and sent them to the elders and nobles who lived in Naboth's town. She wrote to them, "Proclaim a fast and sit Naboth at the front of the assembly, and then sit two scoundrels opposite him and let them give false testimony that Naboth has blasphemed against God and king. Then, take him out and stone him to death".

The mock trial was carried out as planned; Naboth was found guilty of blasphemy, taken outside the city, and was stoned, until he died.

As soon as Jezebel heard that Naboth had been killed, she told Ahab that he could now go and take possession of the vineyard, because Naboth was dead.

The prophet Elijah went to Naboth's vineyard, where the king was looking at his new property. He confronted the king and accused him of murdering the man and taking over his land.

The prophet told the king, "God will punish you for your evil deeds; dogs will lick your blood in the very place that dogs have licked Naboth's blood; your family will come to the same bad end as the descendants of King Jeroboam and King Baasha; and dogs will eat the body of your wife Jezebel".

When Elijah finished speaking, Ahab tore his clothes, took them off, and put on sackcloth. He fasted, slept in the sackcloth, and walked about gloomy and depressed. Ahab's humble behavior made God relent and postpone the prophesied disaster to his son's reign, after Ahab's death.

Nachon

(Hebrew origin: *Prepared*)

(2 Samuel 6:6). 10th century B.C. Nachon—also called Chidon (1 Chronicles 13:9)—was the owner of the threshing floor where Uzza died, when he accidentally touched the Ark, while it was being brought to Jerusalem.

Nachor

(Hebrew origin: *Snorer*)

(Joshua 24:2). 20th century B.C. Nachor—also called Nahor—born in the city of Ur, was the son of Terah and the brother of Abram and Haran. (Please see the entry for Nahor [Genesis 11:26].)

Nadab

(Hebrew origin: *Generous*)

1. (Exodus 6:23). 13th century B.C. Nadab was the eldest son of the High Priest Aaron and his wife Elisheba. He and Abihu, his younger brother, accompanied Moses, and seventy elders, up Mount Sinai, where they saw God standing on a pavement of sapphire stone, clear as heaven.

   Nadab and Abihu were burned to death by a fire sent by God, in punishment for having burned forbidden incense before the Lord.

   Moses forbade Aaron and his two youngest sons, Eleazar and Ithamar, to show the traditional signs of mourning, which were the uncovering of the head and the rending of the clothes.

   As Nadab and Abihu both died childless, the priestly line was continued through Eleazar and Ithamar.

2. (1 Kings 14:20). 10th century B.C. Nadab, son of Jeroboam, was the second king of Israel, after the secession of the northern tribes. He was a contemporary of Asa, king of Judah, with whom he was constantly in war. While fighting in Gibbethon against the Philistines, Nadab was overthrown by Baasha, who killed him and all his family.

3. (1 Chronicles 2:28). Unspecified date. Nadab was the son of Shammai and the brother of Abishur. His sons were Seled, who died childless, and Appaim.

4. (1 Chronicles 8:30). 11th century B.C. Nadab, a Benjamite, was the son of Jehiel, the founder of Gibeon, and Maachah.

Nagge

(Uncertain origin and meaning)

(Luke 3:25). Unspecified date. Nagge, the son of Maath and the father of Esli, was an ancestor of Jesus, according to Luke's genealogy.

Naham

(Hebrew origin: *Comforter*)

(1 Chronicles 4:19). Unspecified date. Naham was the brother of a woman called Hodiah. His nephews were the fathers of Keilah the Garmite and Eshtemoah the Maachathite.

Nahamani

(Hebrew origin: *Consolatory*)

(Nehemiah 7:7). 6th century B.C. Nahamani was one of the men who returned with Zerubbabel from the Babylonian Exile.

Naharai

(Hebrew origin: *Snorer*)

(1 Chronicles 11:39). 10th century B.C. Naharai the Beerothite—also called Nahari (2 Samuel 23:37)—was one of "The Thirty", an elite group in King David's army. He served as the armor bearer of Joab.

Nahari

(Hebrew origin: *Snorer*)

(2 Samuel 23:37). 10th century B.C. Nahari the Berothite—also called Naharai (1 Chronicles 11:39)—was one of "The Thirty", an elite group in King David's army. He served as the armor bearer of Joab.

Nahash

(Hebrew origin: *Snake*)

(1 Samuel 11:1). 11th century B.C. Nahash, king of Ammon, laid siege to the town of Jabeshgilead. His condition for accepting the surrender of the town was that all the men had to take out their right eyes.

The elders of Jabesh asked Nahash to give them a waiting period of seven days, after which, if nobody from Israel would come to their rescue, they would accept Nahash's cruel demand. They sent messengers to Gibeah to tell what was happening. The people heard the terrible news and wept.

Saul, returning from the field, asked, "Why are the people crying?" When he was told on the tidings of Jabesh, Saul became very angry. He took a yoke of oxen, cut them in pieces, and sent them throughout all the territory of

Israel, saying, "This is what will be done to the oxen of whoever does not come after Saul and Samuel!"

The response of the people was immediate. They gathered in Bezek, three hundred thousand men of Israel and thirty thousand of Judah, and sent word to the people of Jabesh that the next day they would be saved. Saul divided his army in three companies, attacked the Ammonites, and routed them.

Many years later, when Nahash died and was succeeded by his son Hanun, King David sent messengers to Ammon, bearing condolences. Hanun, ill advised, treated them as spies; he humiliated them and expelled them from his country, thus, provoking a war with Israel, which resulted in his defeat.

Note: The second book of Samuel (2 Samuel 17:25) states that Nahash was the father of Abigail, David's sister, in which case, David and his sister had the same mother but not the same father. This family relationship would explain why Nahash, previously a bitter enemy of Israel, showed great friendliness toward David, and why Shobi, one of the sons of Nahash, gave support to David, during his flight from Absalom.

Nahath

(Hebrew origin: *Quiet*)

1. (Genesis 36:13). 17th century B.C. Nahath, son of Reuel, was the grandson of Esau and Bashemath, the daughter of Ishmael. Nahath's brothers were Mizzah, Zerah, and Shammah. They were all ancestors of Edomite clans.
2. (1 Chronicles 6:26). 12th century B.C. Nahath—also called Toah (1 Chronicles 6:34), and Tohu (1 Samuel 1:1)—was the son of Zophai and the father of Eliab—also called Elihu and Eliel—an ancestor of Samuel. His descendants served in the Tabernacle, during the reign of King David.
3. (2 Chronicles 31:13). 8th century B.C. Nahath was one of the Levites who were named by King Hezekiah to serve under Cononiah and Shimei, as supervisors of the gifts, tithes, and offerings, brought by the people to the Temple.

Nahbi

(Hebrew origin: *Occult*)

(Numbers 13:14). 13th century B.C. Nahbi, son of Vophsi, of the tribe of Naphtali, was one of the twelve spies sent by Moses to Canaan, to scout the land, its cities, and its inhabitants; to find out if they were strong or weak, few or many; and to bring back the fruit of the land. The spies came back, frightened and disheartened, and told the Israelites that the Canaanites were too big and too strong to be defeated.

Two of the spies—Joshua, the son of Nun, and Caleb, the son of Jephunneh—disagreed and told the people not to fear.

The Israelites refused to listen to the encouraging words of Joshua and Caleb, and they started to wail and cry. God punished their cowardice by condemning them to wander forty years in the wilderness, one year for each day that the spies scouted the land. All those who complained against God, including Nahbi, died in the wilderness, except Caleb and Joshua.

(For more detailed information about the twelve spies, please see the entry for Joshua.)

Nahor

(Hebrew origin: *Snorer*)

1. (Genesis 11:22). 21st century B.C. Nahor, son of Serug, was twenty-nine years old, when his firstborn son Terah was born. He died at the age of one hundred and nineteen, after having had more sons and daughters. He was the grandfather of Nahor #2.
2. (Genesis 11:26). 20th century B.C. Nahor—also called Nachor (Joshua 24:2)—born in the city of Ur, was the son of Terah and the brother of Abram and Haran. He was the grandson of Nahor #1. He married Milcah, his niece, the daughter of his brother Haran, and also had a concubine, called Reumah.

The sons of Milcah were Uz—his first-born—Buz, Kemuel, Chesed, Hazo, Pildash, Jidlaph, and Bethuel. The sons of Reumah were Tebah, Gaham, Thahash, and Maachah.

His granddaughter Rebekah, daughter of Bethuel, married Isaac, Abraham's son. His grandson Laban, son of Bethuel, was the father of Leah and Rachel, Jacob's wives.

Nahshon

(Hebrew origin: *Snake enchanter*)

(Numbers 1:7). 13th century B.C. Nahshon—also called Naasson (Matthew 1:4), and Naashon (Exodus 6:23)—the son of Amminadab, was the father of Salma—also called Salmon—and the brother of Elisheba, the wife of Aaron. His grandson Boaz married Ruth and was the great-grandfather of David.

Nahshon commanded the tribe of Judah, during the Israelites' sojourn in the Sinai desert, and was one of the twelve Israelite leaders who donated gifts of silver and gold, bulls, rams, goats, and lambs for the dedication of the altar.

Nahum

(Hebrew origin: *Comforted*)

(Nahum 1:1). 7th century B.C. The prophet Nahum, author of the book of his name, was born in Elkosh. There are different theories about the location of this town. Some scholars believe that it was near Nineveh, in today's Iraq; others say that it was near Lachish, Israel, or that it was another name for Capernaum, *Town of Nahum*, in the Galilee.

The book of Nahum, a masterful poem in three chapters written in forceful and vivid language, celebrates the fall of Nineveh, the capital city of the mighty Assyrian Empire, the cruel and oppressive enemy, which had destroyed the northern kingdom of Israel and exiled all its inhabitants.

Historians believe that the book was written in the year 612 B.C., when Nineveh was captured and razed by the Babylonians and the Medes. Some scholars say that the book is a prophecy of doom against Nineveh, written very shortly before the fall of the city, while others maintain that it is an expression of joy, celebrating the recent destruction of the hateful enemy.

The book of Nahum is one of the twelve books that make up the Minor Prophets—also called the Twelve—a collection of the books of twelve prophets: Hosea, Joel, Amos, Obadiah, Jonah, Micah, Nahum, Habakkuk, Zephaniah, Haggai, Zechariah, and Malachi.

Note: The phrase "Minor Prophets" does not mean that these prophets are less important than Isaiah, Jeremiah, and Ezekiel. It refers only to the fact that the books of these twelve prophets are much shorter than the books of the other three prophets.

Naomi

(Hebrew origin: *Pleasant*)

(Ruth 1:2). 12th century B.C. Naomi, the wife of Elimelech the Ephrathite, had two sons, Mahlon and Chilion. The family was forced to emigrate from Bethlehem in Judah to Moab, on the eastern side of the river Jordan, because of a great famine in the land.

After the death of Elimelech, the brothers married two Moabite girls, Ruth and Orpah, and, about ten years later, both of them died childless. Naomi, having lost her husband and her sons, decided to return to Bethlehem. Her two daughters-in-law expressed their wish to go with her.

Naomi said to them, "Stay in Moab with your parents. I am too old to have sons that would marry you, and even if I had new sons, you would have to wait too many years for them to grow up".

The girls wept; Orpah kissed her mother-in-law and went back to her parents' home, but Ruth stayed with Naomi.

Naomi said, "Ruth, go back with your sister-in-law".

Ruth answered, "Do not ask me to leave you; wherever you go, I will go, and where you live, I will live; your people shall be my people; and your God my God; where you die, I will die, and there, I will be buried; and God should punish me if anything else than death would make me part from you".

Naomi saw that Ruth's mind was made up, and she said no more.

The two women walked on, until they came to Bethlehem. The people in the town, surprised to see them, asked each other, "Is this Naomi?"

Naomi said to them, "Do not call me Naomi, call me Mara, because God has dealt bitterly with me. I went away full, and God has brought me back empty".

The two women had arrived at the beginning of the barley harvest. As they didn't have anything to eat, nor money, with which, to buy food, Ruth told Naomi that she would like to go to the fields and glean among the ears of grain, behind someone who may show her kindness.

Naomi said, "Yes, my daughter, go".

Ruth went to a certain field, which belonged to Boaz, a wealthy relative of Naomi's dead husband, and gleaned behind the reapers.

Boaz saw her and asked his overseer, "Who is that girl?"

His servant answered, "She is the Moabite maiden who came with Naomi. She came early in the morning and asked me for permission to gather the sheaves after the reapers. Since then, she has not rested even for one moment!"

Boaz went to Ruth and said, "You can continue to glean. I have ordered my workers not to bother you, and, if you are thirsty, to give you water".

Ruth answered, "Why are you doing this kindness to me when I am a foreigner?"

Boaz replied, "I have been told everything that you have done for your mother-in-law, since the death of your husband; how you left your parents and your native land, and came to a people that are strange to you".

That evening, when Ruth returned home, she told Naomi that she had worked in the field of a man named Boaz.

Naomi said to her, "Boaz is a close relative. Tomorrow, dress in your best clothes and anoint yourself, but make sure that Boaz should not see you, until he has finished eating

and drinking. Then, when he has lied down for the night, uncover his feet and lie down next to him". Ruth did what her mother-in-law told her to do.

Boaz woke up in the middle of the night and was surprised to see that there was a woman lying at his feet. When he saw that the woman was Ruth, he said to her, "I am grateful that you have chosen me, and not a younger man. Tomorrow, I will go to a man who is a closer blood relative to Naomi than myself, and if that man refuses to act as a redeemer for you, I will then do it personally".

The next morning, Boaz went to the gate of the town, and there, in the presence of ten elders, he spoke to his kinsman, "Naomi, who has returned now from Moab, must sell the piece of land, which belonged to our kinsman Elimelech. If you are willing to buy it and redeem it, do so. If not, I will do it".

The kinsman replied, "I am willing to redeem it".

Boaz then said, "Don't forget that, when you buy the property from Naomi, you must also acquire Ruth the Moabite, so as to perpetuate the name of the deceased upon his estate".

The man said, "This I cannot do. You take over my right of redemption, because I am unable to exercise it". To confirm what he had said, he took off his sandal, according to the custom of the time, and gave it to Boaz.

Boaz said to the elders and to the people gathered at the gate, "You are witnesses today that I have acquired from Naomi all that belonged to Elimelech and to his sons, including Ruth the Moabite as my wife, so as to perpetuate the name of the deceased upon his estate".

Boaz and Ruth got married and had a son called Obed. Naomi took the child, held him to her bosom, and raised him. Obed, when he grew up and married, became the father of Jesse, the father of David.

The women of the town congratulated Naomi for having such a loving daughter-in-law, and a redeemer who would renew her life and become the support of her old age.

Naphish

(Hebrew origin: *Refreshed*)

(Genesis 25:15). 18th century B.C. Naphish—also called Nephish (1 Chronicles 5:19)—was one of the twelve sons of Ishmael and the grandson of Abraham and his Egyptian concubine Hagar.

The eleven brothers of Naphish were Nebajoth, Kedar, Mibsam, Mishma, Dumah, Massa, Adbeel, Hadad, Jetur, Tema, and Kedemah, all of them ancestors of great nations. His sister, Mahalath—also called Bashemath—married Esau, the son of Isaac.

Naphtali

(Hebrew origin: *My wrestling*)

(Genesis 30:8). 17th century B.C. Naphtali, the ancestor of the tribe of Naphtali, was the youngest of the two sons whom Bilhah, Rachel's maid, had with Jacob; the other was Daniel. His mother had been given as a wedding gift by Laban to his daughter Rachel, when she married Jacob. When Rachel was unable to get pregnant, she gave Bilhah to Jacob, so that, according to the custom of the time, any children who would be born from her maid would be considered Rachel's.

Naphtali was born in Paddan-Aram, where Jacob was working for his father-in-law Laban. Rachel gave him that name, because, she said, "I have fought a hard fight with my sister, but I won".

Naphtali was the full brother of Daniel. His half brothers were Zebulun, Issachar, Reuben, Levi, Judah, and Simeon, sons of Leah; Gad and Asher, sons of Zilpah; and Benjamin and Joseph, sons of Rachel. His half sister was Dinah, daughter of Leah.

Naphtali and his brothers were involved in the events that led to Joseph being taken as a slave to Egypt. (For the detailed story of Joseph and his brothers, please see the entry for Joseph.)

Years later, when there was a famine in Canaan, Naphtali and his brothers were sent by Jacob to Egypt to buy corn. Joseph, who was now the second most powerful man in the country, recognized them, forgave them, and invited them to settle in Egypt.

Naphtali and his sons—Jahzeel, Guni, Jezer, and Shillem—were among the seventy Israelites who immigrated to Egypt. They arrived in Goshen, and Joseph came to them in his chariot. He greeted his father, embraced him, and wept for a long time.

Seventeen years later, Jacob, feeling that he would soon die, called his sons to bless them and compared Naphtali to a deer that ran free.

Jacob's last words were to ask them to bury him in the cave of Machpelah, where Abraham, Sarah, Isaac, Rebekah, and Leah were buried. Jacob's body was accompanied in his last trip by his sons, their children, flocks and herds, all the officials of Pharaoh and members of his court, chariots and horsemen. Before crossing the Jordan, the funeral procession made a stop and mourned Jacob for seven days. Then, Judah and his brothers took him to Canaan and buried him in the cave of Machpelah.

After burying their father, they all returned to Canaan. Joseph's brothers feared that, with Jacob now dead, Joseph would pay them back for the wrong that they had done to him.

They sent a message to Joseph, saying that Jacob, before his death, had told them to urge Joseph to forgive them. Judah and his brothers came to Joseph, flung themselves before him, and told him that they were prepared to be his slaves.

Joseph answered kindly, "Do not fear! Although you intended me harm, God intended it all for good, to assure the survival of many people. Don't worry; I will take care of you and your children".

Centuries later, Moses, in his farewell blessings to the tribes, said that Naphtali was full of the Lord's blessing.

When Joshua conquered Canaan, the tribe of Naphtali settled in the Galilee, on the west side of the Jordan. The Assyrians exiled them in the 8th century B.C., and they disappeared from history, being known since then as one of the "ten lost tribes".

Naphtuhim

(Uncertain origin and meaning)

(Genesis 10:13). Unspecified date. Naphtuhim was the son of Mizraim, *Egypt*, and grandson of Ham.

Narcissus

(Greek origin: Name of a flower)

(Romans 16:11). A.D. 1st century. Narcissus was a Christian to whose family Paul sent greetings in his letter to the Christians in Rome.

Nathan

(Hebrew origin: *He gave*)

1. (2 Samuel 5:14). 10th century B.C. Nathan, born in Jerusalem, was one of the four sons of King David and Bathsheba. His brothers were Solomon, Shimea— alternative spelling Shammuah—and Shobab. According to the genealogy of Luke, Nathan was the father of Mattatha, an ancestor of Jesus.

2. (2 Samuel 7:2). 10th century B.C. Nathan, the prophet, was an advisor to King David and a key supporter of Solomon in his successful quest to succeed David. His brother Joel was one of "The Thirty", an elite group in King David's army.

   David told Nathan that he was unhappy with the fact that he lived in a mansion of cedar, while the Ark of the Covenant was in a tent, surrounded only by curtains. Nathan's first reaction was to tell David to do whatever was in his mind, because God was with him; however, that same night, God appeared to Nathan in a vision and told him to say to David that his son would be the one to build the Temple, not David.

   After David sent Uriah to his death, and hastily married his pregnant widow Bathsheba, Nathan came to David and told him a parable of a rich man, who owned many sheep, but took his poor neighbor's lamb, and cooked it to honor a traveler. David, not understanding the allusion, became angry and threatened to punish the rich man for his lack of pity.

   Nathan told him, "You are that man". David then recognized that he had sinned. Nathan told him that he would not die, but the baby would. The baby became seriously ill and died. Later, Bathsheba gave birth to another son, whom they called Solomon, but who was named Jedidiah by Nathan.

   David grew old, and the succession to the throne, after the death of Amnon and Absalom, was disputed between Adonijah, the eldest remaining son, and Solomon, the son of Bathsheba. Joab, the commander of the army, and Abiathar the Priest supported Adonijah, while Nathan, the priest Zadok, Benaiah, and other powerful men wanted Solomon to be king.

   When Nathan realized that Adonijah was getting the upper hand, he instructed Bathsheba to go to the aged and ailing king, and to say to him, "Did you not, O King, swear to me that Solomon would succeed you as king? Then, why has Adonijah become king?" Nathan added that, while she would be speaking with the king, he would come in and confirm her words.

   Their ploy succeeded, and David commanded Nathan and Zadok to take Solomon on the royal mule to the spring of Gihon and anoint him king.

   After the death of David, Solomon placed the sons of Nathan in high positions: Azariah was in charge of the officials responsible for the twelve tax districts, and Zabud became the trusted advisor of the king.

   The Bible (2 Chronicles 9:29) mentions that Nathan wrote a book about the reign of King Solomon, but it has not survived to our days.

3. (2 Samuel 23:36). 11th century B.C. Nathan of Zobah was the father of Igal, a member of King David's elite army group known as The Thirty.

4. (1 Chronicles 2:36). Unspecified date. Nathan was the son of Attai and the father of Zabad. Nathan's grandfather, an Egyptian called Jarha, had married the

daughter of his master Sheshan, a leader of the tribe of Judah.

5. (Ezra 8:16). 5th century B.C. Nathan was one of the leaders of the people who left Babylon with Ezra and was sent by the scribe to Casiphia to speak to Iddo and request from him to send Levites to serve in the Temple in Jerusalem.

6. (Ezra 10:39). 5th century B.C. Nathan, a descendant of Binnui, divorced his foreign wife, during the time of Ezra.

Nathanael

(Hebrew origin: *God gave*)

(John 1:45). A.D. 1st century. Scholars believe that Nathanael, born in Cana, and Bartholomew (Matthew 10:3) were the same person, in which case, the name Bartholomew was Nathanael's patronymic—i.e. a name derived from the name of a person's father or paternal ancestor. The complete name of the apostle would then be Nathanael, son of Tolmai. This assertion is based on the fact that Bartholomew and Nathanael are usually mentioned in the same phrase as Philip, but the two names never appear together.

Philip went to Nathanael and told him, "We have found the one about whom Moses and the prophets wrote. He is Jesus of Nazareth, the son of Joseph".

Nathanael said, "Can anything good come out of Nazareth?"

"Come and see", answered Philip.

Jesus saw Nathanael coming to him and said, "Look, here is a true Israelite. There is nothing false in him".

Nathanael, surprised, asked him, "How do you know me?"

"I saw you when you were under the fig tree, before Phillip called you".

Nathanael exclaimed, "Master, you are the Son of God! You are the king of Israel!"

"You believe that because I said that I saw you under the fig tree? You will see much greater things than that! I tell you, you will see the heaven open, and the angels of God ascending and descending upon the Son of man".

Nathanael followed Jesus and became one of the twelve apostles.

Nathanmelech

(Hebrew origin: *The king gave*)

(2 Kings 23:11). 7th century B.C. Nathanmelech, a high ranking official in the court of King Josiah, had a chamber near to the place in the Temple's courtyard, where previous kings of Judah had placed horses and dedicated them to the worship of the sun. King Josiah, in his fight against pagan idols, destroyed these "chariots of the sun" by fire.

Naum

(Hebrew origin: *Comforted*)

(Luke 3:25). Unspecified date. Naum, son of Esli and father of Amos, was an ancestor of Jesus, according to Luke's genealogy.

Neariah

(Hebrew origin: *Child of God*)

1. (1 Chronicles 3:22). Unspecified date. Neariah, son of Shemaiah, was a descendant of Jehoiachin, the king of Judah, who was taken to captivity in Babylon. Neariah's brothers were Hattush, Igeal, Bariah, and Shaphat, and his sons were Elioenai, Hezekiah, and Azrikam.

2. (1 Chronicles 4:42). 8th century B.C. Neariah, son of Ishi, and his brothers—Pelatiah, Rephaiah, and Uzziel—of the tribe of Simeon, at the head of five hundred men, went to Mount Seir, southeast of the Dead Sea, exterminated the last surviving Amalekites and settled in the region.

Nebai

(Hebrew origin: *Fruitful*)

(Nehemiah 10:19). 5th century B.C. Nebai was one of the leaders who signed Nehemiah's solemn agreement to separate themselves from the foreigners living in the land, to refrain from intermarrying with them, and to dedicate their firstborn to God, among other obligations.

Nebaioth

(Hebrew origin: *Fruitfulness*)

(1 Chronicles 1:29). 18th century B.C. Nebaioth—also called Nebajoth (Genesis 25:13)—was the eldest of the twelve sons of Ishmael, and the grandson of Abraham and his Egyptian concubine Hagar.

His brothers were Hadad, Kedar, Mibsam, Mishma, Dumah, Massa, Adbeel, Tema, Jetur, Naphish, and Kedemah, all of them ancestors of great nations. His sister, Mahalath—also called Bashemath—married Esau, the son of Isaac.

Nebajoth

(Hebrew origin: *Fruitfulness*)

(Genesis 25:13). 18th century B.C. Nebajoth is an alternative spelling for Nebaioth, eldest of the twelve sons of Ishmael. (Please see the entry for Nebaioth [1 Chronicles 1:29].)

Nebat

(Hebrew origin: *Regard*)

(1 Kings 11:26). 10th century B.C. Nebat, an Ephrathite of Zereda, was married to a woman called Zeruah. Nebat died young, and the widow alone raised their son Jeroboam, who, years later, became the first king of the northern kingdom of Israel.

Nebo

(Foreign origin: Name of a pagan god)
1. (Ezra 10:43). Unspecified date. During the days of Ezra, some of his descendants were among those who divorced their foreign wives.
2. (Isaiah 46:1). Nebo was one of the gods of Babylon.

Nebuchadnezzar

(Uncertain origin and meaning)

(2 Kings 24:1). 7th and 6th century B.C. Nebuchadnezzar, king of Babylon—also called Nebuchadrezzar (Jeremiah 21:2)—sent an army against Jerusalem to punish Jehoiakim, king of Judah, who, after three years of paying tribute, had rebelled against him, against the advice of the prophet Jeremiah.

King Jehoiakim died, during the siege of Jerusalem, and was succeeded by his son, the eighteen-year-old Jehoiachin, who surrendered to Nebuchadnezzar, after resisting for three months, and was exiled to Babylon together with his mother, servants, and officials of his court.

Nebuchadnezzar appointed Mattaniah, the twenty-one-year-old uncle of Jehoiachin, to be the new king, and changed his name to Zedekiah.

Zedekiah, in the ninth year of his reign, rebelled against Nebuchadnezzar, who again came against Jerusalem, besieged it, and built towers all around it. After a siege of two years, the wall of the city was breached. Zedekiah escaped from the city through the garden of the palace, but was pursued and captured near Jericho. He was then taken to Riblah, to the presence of Nebuchadnezzar. The Babylonians slaughtered his sons before his eyes, then put his eyes out, chained him in bronze fetters, and took him to Babylon.

Nebuzaradan, captain of the guards of Nebuchadnezzar, came to Jerusalem and burned down the Temple, the king's palace, and all the houses of Jerusalem. The walls of the city were torn down. The survivors, with the exception of the poorest of the land, were taken into exile in Babylon.

Nebuchadnezzar named Gedaliah, son of Ahikam, to be the governor of the conquered kingdom. A few months later, Gedaliah was murdered by one of the captains of the defeated Judean army, called Ishmael, a member of the royal family of Judah.

Nebuchadnezzar gave instructions to select four promising boys from the Israelites exiled in Babylon. The chosen boys—Daniel, Hananiah, Mishael, and Azariah—were given a three-year course of instruction that prepared them for service in the Babylonian royal court. When the three years were over, the king examined them personally and found them to be ten times better than all the magicians and astrologers in the kingdom.

Sometime later, Nebuchadnezzar had a disturbing dream, but could not recall it, when he woke up. He summoned the magicians to his presence and ordered them to tell him the dream and its interpretation.

The magicians replied, "Your Majesty, it is impossible to comply with your request".

The king flew into a rage and ordered Arioch, the captain of the king's guard, to kill all the wise men of Babylon. When Arioch came to kill him, Daniel asked for an explanation, and when he heard the king's demand, he asked to be given some time.

That night, the king's dream was revealed to Daniel in a vision. In the morning, he went to Arioch and said to him, "Do not kill the wise men. Take me to the king, and I will interpret his dream for him".

When brought to the presence of Nebuchadnezzar, Daniel said, "Your Majesty dreamt that he saw a great statue, its head made of gold, its breast and arms of silver, his thighs of brass, his legs of iron, and its feet partly of iron and partly of clay. Suddenly, a thrown stone broke the statue in small pieces, blown away by the wind, and grew into a great mountain that filled the whole earth. The head of gold was Nebuchadnezzar himself, and the rest of the statue, made of different materials, represented successive kingdoms, which would be swept away by the Kingdom of God that would last forever".

The astounded king acknowledged the supremacy of God and rewarded Daniel, by naming him governor of the province of Babylon and head of all the wise men in the kingdom.

Sometime later, the king made a large idol of gold and invited all the princes, governors, and leading personalities of the kingdom to attend the dedication of the image. A herald proclaimed that all should fall down and worship the statue upon hearing the sound of musical instruments.

Hananiah, Mishael, and Azariah refused to worship the golden idol and were denounced to the king. Nebuchadnezzar had the three men brought to him, and he threatened them that, if they would continue in their refusal to worship the idol, he would have them thrown into a burning fiery furnace.

The three men refused, and the king ordered that they should be thrown into the furnace, which was so hot that it burned to death the men who threw them in. An angel came and protected the three men from injury. The amazed Nebuchadnezzar told them to come out, again recognized the supremacy of God, and decreed that nobody should speak against God.

The king had another dream, where he saw a tree of great height with beautiful foliage and abundant fruit; along came a holy man who ordered to cut down the tree, and to leave just the stump of the roots.

Daniel, called to interpret the dream, explained, "Your Majesty, you are the tree, and God will make you eat grass as an animal and live with the beasts of the field".

A year later, while the king was boasting of his prowess, a voice from heaven told him that the kingdom had departed from him, and that he would dwell with the beasts of the field and eat grass as oxen. After sometime, when the king had recovered his sanity and was restored to his former exalted position, he gave praises to God.

According to the Bible, Nebuchadnezzar was succeeded by his son Belshazzar, during whose reign Babylon fell to the Persians.

Nebuchadrezzar

(Uncertain origin and meaning)

(Jeremiah 21:2). 7th and 6th century B.C. Nebuchadrezzar is an alternative spelling for Nebuchadnezzar, the king of Babylon, who conquered the kingdom of Judah and exiled its inhabitants. (Please see the entry for Nebuchadnezzar [2 Kings 24:1].)

Nebushazban

(Uncertain origin and meaning)

(Jeremiah 39:13). 6th century B.C. Nebushazban held the position of "Rabsaris", a high commanding rank in the army of Nebuchadnezzar. He was among the men whom the king of Babylon instructed to take good care of Jeremiah, and to make sure that he would not be harmed. He and other officials took the prophet out of the prison and put him under the protection of the Babylonian appointed governor of Judah, Gedaliah, son of Ahikam.

Nebuzaradan

(Uncertain origin and meaning)

(2 Kings 25:8). 6th century B.C. Nebuzaradan, captain of the guard of King Nebuchadnezzar of Babylon, came to Jerusalem, four weeks after the walls of the city had been breached. He proceeded to tear down the walls of the city, and to burn the Temple, the king's palace, the houses of Jerusalem, and the mansions of the nobles. He also destroyed the bronze columns of the Temple and sent the bronze to Babylon, together with all the gold and silver vessels of the Temple.

Nebuzaradan captured the High Priest Seraiah, his second in command Zephaniah, three gatekeepers of the Temple, a commander of the Judean army, five royal councilors, the scribe of the army commander, and sixty men whom he found inside the city. The prisoners were sent to Riblah, to the king of Babylon, who had them killed.

Nebuzaradan exiled all the inhabitants of Judah to Babylon, with the exception of some poor people who were left to work as vine-dressers and field hands. The prophet Jeremiah was among the captives, but was freed in Ramah, when Nebuzaradan received instructions from King Nebuchadnezzar to take good care of Jeremiah, and to make sure that he should not be harmed.

Nebuzaradan said to the prophet, "The disaster that has fallen on Judah is because the people have sinned against God. Now, I free you from your chains. If you want to come with me to Babylon, I will look after you. If you wish to stay, you can stay. Or, if you prefer, you can go to Gedaliah, whom we have appointed governor of Judah, and stay with him".

Jeremiah chose to go to Gedaliah. Nebuzaradan gave him some food for the trip and allowed him to go.

Necho

(Uncertain origin and meaning)

(2 Kings 23:29). 7th century B.C. Pharaoh Necho of Egypt, wanting to ascertain his supremacy, decided to go to war against Assyria. He marched toward Charchemish through the ancient road called the Way of the Sea, which passed through the kingdom of Judah.

Necho wrote to King Josiah saying, "I have no quarrel with Judah. As I am in a hurry to reach my enemy Assyria, I ask you not to interfere with the advance of his army when we pass through your kingdom".

King Josiah disregarded Necho's request and tried to stop the Egyptian army at Megiddo, but was badly wounded in the subsequent battle. The king was brought in his chariot to Jerusalem, where he died and was buried in the tombs of his fathers, mourned by the whole nation. Josiah was succeeded by his twenty-three-year-old son Jehoahaz.

Three months later, Pharaoh Necho summoned the young king to his headquarters at Riblah in the land of Hamath, Syria. When Jehoahaz arrived, Necho arrested him, put him in chains, and deported him to Egypt, where the deposed king died. Necho fined the kingdom of Judah the sum of one hundred silver talents and one gold talent, and he named Jehoahaz' older brother, Eliakim, as the new king of Judah, giving him the name of Jehoiakim.

Nedabiah

(Hebrew origin: *God is generous*)

(1 Chronicles 3:18). 6th century B.C. Nedabiah was one of the seven sons of King Jehoiachin, the king who was deposed and taken captive by the Babylonians. Nedabiah's brothers were Salathiel, Hoshama, Malchiram, Pedaiah, Jecamiah, and Shenazar.

Nehemiah

(Hebrew origin: *God has consoled*)

1. (Ezra 2.2). 6th century B.C. Nehemiah was one of the men who returned with Zerubbabel from the Babylonian Exile.

2. (Nehemiah 1:1). 5th century B.C. Nehemiah, son of Hachaliah, was the cupbearer of Artaxerxes, the king of Persia, in the city of Shushan. One day, during the twentieth year of the reign of Artaxerxes, Hanani, one of Nehemiah's brothers, came to the palace in Shushan, together with some men from Judah, and told Nehemiah of the dire situation of the survivors in Jerusalem.

Nehemiah was summoned to the presence of the king, to pour him wine. The king saw in Nehemiah's face that something was wrong, and he said to him, "If you are not sick, why are you so sad?"

Nehemiah, although frightened by the king's question, found the courage to say, "Your Majesty, how can I not be sad when the city where my ancestors are buried lies in ruins and its gates have been consumed by fire!"

The king asked him, "What is your request?"

Nehemiah, inwardly praying to God, answered, "Please send me to Judah to rebuild it".

The king asked him, "How long will you be away?"

Nehemiah told the king how long he estimated that he would be away, and he asked him for letters of presentation to the governors of the different provinces, directing them to grant Nehemiah safe passage, until he reached Judah. Nehemiah also asked for a letter to Asaph, the official in charge of the Persian king's forest, requesting that he should provide timber for beams to be used in the reconstruction of the walls of Jerusalem, the palace, and the residence of Nehemiah in Jerusalem. After the king had given him these letters, Nehemiah left for Jerusalem, escorted by army officers and cavalry.

Sanballat the Horonite and Tobiah the Ammonite, who were declared enemies of the Israelites, were greatly displeased, when they heard that somebody was coming to improve the condition of the Israelites.

Nehemiah, three days after having arrived in Jerusalem, went out secretly at night with a small group of men to survey the ruins of the walls of Jerusalem and the burned-down gates of the city. The next day, he ordered to start the reconstruction of the walls. Everybody took part in the rebuilding of the walls, including the High Priest Eliashib, the priests, the Levites, and the leaders of the people.

When Sanballat, who had sneered at the Jews when they started the work, and his allies—Tobiah, the Arabs, the Ammonites, and the Ashdodites—saw that the walls of the city had been repaired, they gathered to conspire to fight against Jerusalem. Nehemiah, when told about their intentions, took preventive measures by placing armed men next to the workers, with half the people doing the work, and the other half carrying weapons.

Nehemiah took note that the poor people had borrowed money from the wealthy to buy food and pay taxes, and that those unlucky enough to be unable to pay back their loans had been forced to pawn their fields, vineyards, and homes. Some debtors had even become slaves to their pitiless lenders. Angered, Nehemiah assembled the nobles and the wealthy families, and he ordered them to return to the poor their fields, vineyards, olive trees, and homes, and to abandon their claims. He summoned the priests to put them under oath. All the assembled men did so, praised God, and kept their promise.

Sanballat and his allies sent a message to Nehemiah, asking him to meet them in one of the villages in the plain of Ono. Nehemiah refused the invitation, saying that he was too busy with his work. After they had sent the message four more times, and always received the same answer from Nehemiah, they sent him a letter accusing him of inciting rebellion and planning to make himself king. Nehemiah answered that those accusations were figments of their imagination.

Tobiah and Sanballat paid Shemaiah, the son of Delaiah, to convince Nehemiah that he should hide in the Temple. Nehemiah saw through Shemaiah's advice that it was a trick, and he refused.

Many nobles related by marriage with Tobiah were in constant correspondence with him, and they informed him of everything that Nehemiah did.

After the walls of the city had been repaired, and the doors had been set up, Nehemiah assigned tasks to the gatekeepers, the singers, and the Levites. He placed his brother Hanani in charge of Jerusalem, together with Hananiah, the ruler of the fortress, and gave them detailed instructions when to open and close the gates of the city.

On the first day of the seventh month, the entire population of the city assembled in the square, before the Water Gate, and Ezra, who had been in Jerusalem already for seven years, stood on a wooden pulpit and read to the people the Book of the Law of Moses, from sunrise till noon, with the priests and the Levites, explaining the teachings to the people. The people wept and cried, until the Levites told them to rejoice and not to be sad, for this was a festive holy day.

The leaders of the people, the priests, and the Levites met with Ezra the next day to study the books of Moses. They read that God had commanded the Israelites to celebrate the Feast of Booths and realized that this had not been done since the days of Joshua. The people immediately went to the fields, brought back branches of trees, and built booths on their roofs, in their courtyards and in many public places.

On the twenty-fourth day of that month, the people assembled, dressed in sackcloth, fasted, and prayed, led by the Levites. After the prayers ended, the priests, the Levites, the leaders of the people, the gatekeepers, the singers, their wives, sons and daughters, and all others, who knew enough to understand the Law, entered into a solemn agreement to separate themselves from the foreigners living in the land, to refrain from intermarrying with them,

and to dedicate their firstborn to God, among other obligations.

After the reconstruction work of the wall had ended, Nehemiah decided to have a joyful celebration with thanksgiving and music. The Levites and the singers were brought to Jerusalem from wherever they lived. The priests and the Levites purified themselves, and then, they purified the people, the wall, and the gates.

Nehemiah organized the people into two processions, one went south by the wall, while the other marched in the opposite direction, led by singers and musicians who blew the trumpets. The two processions met at the Temple, where the people offered sacrifices to God.

It was found that the book of Moses did not allow any Ammonite or Moabite to enter the congregation of God, and in consequence, the mixed multitude was separated from Israel.

After twelve years of staying in Jerusalem, Nehemiah took a leave of absence and went back to Babylon to visit the Persian king. He stayed in the court for sometime and then returned to Jerusalem, where he was surprised to find that, during his absence, the priest Eliashib, who was in charge of the rooms in the Temple, had given a room— which previously had served as a stockroom for the equipment of the Temple, incense, grain, wine, oil, and the gifts of the priests— to Tobiah, Nehemiah's enemy.

Nehemiah, greatly displeased, ordered that all the belongings of Tobiah should be thrown out immediately; the room was purified, and the equipment of the Temple, the incense, and the other items were brought back to the room.

He also discovered that the work in the Temple had been neglected, and that many of the Levites and the singers had left to return to their own towns, because they had not received the portions that were due to them. Nehemiah had them brought back to Jerusalem and installed them again in their posts. He placed new people, whom he considered honest and trustworthy, in charge of the treasures of the Temple: Shelemiah the Priest, Zadok the Scribe, Pedaiah the Levite, and, to assist them, Hanan, the son of Zaccur.

When Nehemiah saw that some people worked on the Sabbath to avoid the profanation, he gave orders that the gates of Jerusalem should be closed at the approach of the Sabbath, and should not be opened, until after the Sabbath. He stationed guards at the gates to prevent goods from entering the city on the Sabbath. He noticed that some merchants spent the night outside Jerusalem and threatened to punish them if they would do it again.

Nehemiah saw that many Jews had married Ashdodites, Ammonite, and Moabite women, and that their children, instead of speaking Hebrew, spoke those foreign languages. He censured them, cursed them, and had them flogged, and he forbade them to give their sons and daughters in marriage to foreigners, reminding them that even the wise King Solomon had sinned because of his foreign wives. When he found that one of the sons of Joiada, son of Eliashib the High Priest, was married to a daughter of Sanballat the Horonite, he had him expelled.

Nehemiah was always careful to avoid being placed in a situation where his enemies could find a pretext to report evil about him. He was proud of his good name and reputation for honesty, declaring that he had never eaten of the governor's food allowance, nor had he in any way profited personally from his position. Most important to him, Nehemiah wanted God to recognize his diligence in restoring the purity of religion, and in preserving the national identity of the Jews. The last words that he wrote in his book were, "O my God, remember it to my credit!"

3. (Nehemiah 3:16). 5th century B.C. Nehemiah, son of Azbuk, was the ruler of half the district of Beth-Zur. He helped to repair the walls of Jerusalem, during the days of Nehemiah, son of Hachaliah, the governor of Jerusalem.

Nehum
(Hebrew origin: *Comforted*)

(Nehemiah 7:7). 6th century B.C. Nehum—also called Rehum (Ezra 2:2)—was one of the men who returned with Zerubbabel from the exile in Babylon.

Nehushta
(Hebrew origin: *Copper*)

(2 Kings 24:8). 7th century B.C. Nehushta, daughter of Elnathan, was the wife of King Jehoiakim. After her husband died, she was taken prisoner by King Nebuchadnezzar and brought to Babylon, together with her young son, King Jehoiachin, his wives, and the nobles of his court.

Nekoda
(Hebrew origin: *Spotted*)

(Ezra 2:48). Unspecified date. Nekoda was the ancestor of a family that returned with Zerubbabel from the Babylonian Exile. The members of this family were dismissed from the priesthood, because they could not prove their genealogy.

Nemuel
(Hebrew origin: transposition of letter "n" for "j" in *Jemuel* [*Day of God*])

1. (Numbers 26:9). 13th century B.C. Nemuel was the son of Eliab, of the tribe of Reuben. Although his brothers Abiram and Dathan were among the leaders of Korah's revolt against Moses, he did not participate in the rebellion.

2. (Numbers 26:12). 17th century B.C. Nemuel—called Jemuel in the book of Genesis (Genesis 46:10)—son of Simeon and grandson of Jacob, was among the seventy Israelites who immigrated to Egypt, together with his brothers Jamin, Jachin, Zerah, and Shaul.

Nepheg

(Hebrew origin: *Sprout*)

1. (Exodus 6:21). 13th century B.C. Nepheg, son of Izhar, was the brother of Korah and Zichri, and a first cousin of Moses, Aaron, and Miriam, the children of Amram, his father's older brother. His brother Korah was the leader of a revolt against Moses, which ended in the death of the rebels, when the earth opened and swallowed them.

    His father was called Amminadab in the first book of Chronicles (1 Chronicles 6:22), and Izehar in the book of Numbers (Numbers 3:19).

2. (2 Samuel 5:15). 10th century B.C. Nepheg was one of the sons of King David who were born in Jerusalem.

Nephish

(Hebrew origin: *Refreshed*)

(1 Chronicles 5:19). 18th century B.C. Nephish—also called Naphish (Genesis 25:15)—grandson of Abraham and his Egyptian concubine Hagar, was one of the twelve sons of Ishmael. His brothers were Nebajoth, Kedar, Mibsam, Mishma, Dumah, Massa, Adbeel, Hadad, Jetur, Tema, and Kedemah, all of them ancestors of great nations. His sister, Mahalath—also called Bashemath—married Esau, the son of Isaac.

Nephishesim

(Hebrew origin: *Scattered*)

(Nehemiah 7:52). Unspecified date. Nephishesim—called Nephusim in the book of Ezra (Ezra 2:50)—was the ancestor of a clan of Temple servants that returned with Zerubbabel from the Babylonian Exile.

Nephthalim

(Hebrew origin: *My wrestlings*)

(Matthew 4:13). 17th century B.C. Nephthalim is an alternative name for Naphtali, the ancestor of the tribe of the same name. (Please see the entry for Naphtali [Genesis 30:8].)

Nephusim

(Hebrew origin: *Expansions*)

(Ezra 2:50). Unspecified date. Nephusim—called Nephishesim in the book of Nehemiah (Nehemiah 7:52)—was the ancestor of a clan of Temple servants that returned with Zerubbabel from the Babylonian Exile.

Ner

(Hebrew origin: *Candle*)

(1 Samuel 14:50). 11th century B.C. Ner, son of Abiel, of the tribe of Benjamin, was the brother of Kish, the father of King Saul. His son was Abner, the commander of the king's army.

Note: The first book of Chronicles (1 Chronicles 9:36) states that Ner—the brother of Kish, Abdon, Zur, Baal, and Nadab—was the son of Jehiel and Maachah. Ner had a son, called Kish, like his brother, who was the father of Saul. This would mean that Ner was not Saul's uncle, but his grandfather (1 Chronicles 9:39).

Nereus

(Greek origin: *Wet*)

(Romans 16:15). A.D. 1st century. Nereus was a Christian to whom Paul sent greetings in his letter to the Christians in Rome. The apostle mentioned him in the same verse with four other persons—Philologus, Julia, Olympas, and Nereus' sister—and "all the saints who were with them". This gives grounds to think that Nereus and his companions formed a small separate group within the larger Christian community of Rome.

Nergal

(Uncertain origin and meaning)

(2 Kings 17:30). Nergal was an idol worshipped by the men of Cuth, a people whom the Assyrians settled in Samaria, after they destroyed it in the 8th century B.C.

Nergalsharezer

(Uncertain origin and meaning)

(Jeremiah 39:3). 6th century B.C. Nergalsharezer was the name of two commanders of King Nebuchadnezzar's army who sat at the Middle Gate of Jerusalem, after the Babylonians had succeeded in breaking through the walls of the city.

One of these two commanders was among the officials whom the king of Babylon instructed to take good care of Jeremiah, and to see that he would not be harmed. The prophet was taken out of the court of the prison and put under the protection of the Babylonian appointed governor of Judah, Gedaliah, son of Ahikam.

Neri

(Hebrew origin: *My light*)

(Luke 3:27). Unspecified date. Neri, the son of Melchi and the father of Salathiel, was an ancestor of Jesus, according to Luke's genealogy.

Neriah

(Hebrew origin: *God is my light*)

(Jeremiah 32:12). 7th century B.C. Neriah, the son of Maaseiah, had two sons. One was Baruch, Jeremiah's scribe and loyal companion. The other one was Seraiah, an official of the court who accompanied King Zedekiah in the royal visit that the king paid to Babylon, during the fourth year of his reign.

Nethaneel

(Hebrew origin: *God gave*)

1. (Numbers 1:8). 13th century B.C. Nethaneel, the son of Zuar, was the leader of the tribe of Issachar in the days of Moses, and one of the twelve Israelite leaders who donated gifts of silver and gold, bulls, rams, goats, and lambs for the dedication of the altar.

2. (1 Chronicles 2:14). 11th century B.C. Nethaneel, son of Jesse, was one of David's six brothers. The other brothers were Eliab, Abinadab, Shimma, Raddai, and Ozem.

3. (1 Chronicles 15:24). 10th century B.C. Nethaneel was one of the priests who blew the trumpets, during the joyful procession led by King David, which brought the Ark of the Covenant to Jerusalem.

4. (1 Chronicles 24:6). 11th century B.C. Nethaneel was the father of Shemaiah, who was the court's scribe, during the reign of King David.

5. (1 Chronicles 26:4). 10th century B.C. Nethaneel, one of the sons of Obededom, was, like his father and seven brothers, a gatekeeper of the Tabernacle, during the reign of King David. His brothers were Ammiel, Shemaiah, Jehozabad, Sacar, Joah, Issachar, and Peulthai.

6. (2 Chronicles 17:7). 9th century B.C. Nethaneel, an official in the court of King Jehoshaphat, was sent by the king, during the third year of his reign, together with other officials, Levites and priests, to teach the laws of God in the cities of Judah.

7. (2 Chronicles 35:9). 7th century B.C. Nethaneel was one of the Levites who, during the reign of King Josiah, gave to the priests the cattle and oxen that had been donated by the princes of the kingdom for the Passover offerings.

8. (Ezra 10:22). 5th century B.C. Nethaneel was a priest, descendant of Pashur, who divorced his foreign wife, during the days of Ezra.

9. (Nehemiah 12:21). 5th century B.C. Nethaneel, during the days of Nehemiah, when Joiakim was the High Priest, was the leader of a clan of priests descended from Jedaiah, a leading priest who had returned to Jerusalem with the High Priest Joshua and Zerubbabel.

10. (Nehemiah 12:36). 5th century B.C. Nethaneel was one of the priests who played musical instruments, marching behind Ezra the Scribe, in the joyful procession, which celebrated the dedication of the rebuilt walls of Jerusalem, during the days of Nehemiah.

Nethaniah

(Hebrew origin: *Given by God*)

1. (2 Kings 25:23). 7th century B.C. Nethaniah, son of Elishama, of the royal family of Judah, was the father of Ishmael the assassin of Gedaliah, the Babylonian appointed governor of Judah.

2. (1 Chronicles 25:2). 10th century B.C. Nethaniah was the son of Asaph, the Levite appointed by King David to be in charge of the singers in the House of the Lord. He and his brothers—Zaccur, Joseph, and Asarelah—assisted their father Asaph in his work, with Nethaniah taking the fifth turn of service.

3. (2 Chronicles 17:8). 9th century B.C. Nethaniah, a Levite, was sent by King Jehoshaphat, in the third year of his reign, to teach the laws of God in the cities of Judah. Nethaniah was accompanied in his mission by other Levites, by the priests Elishama and Jehoram, and by several officials of the court.

4. (Jeremiah 36:14). 7th century B.C. Nethaniah, son of Shelemiah and grandson of Cushi, was the father of Jehudi, a high official in the court of King Jehoiakim.

Neziah

(Hebrew origin: *Conspicuous*)

(Ezra 2:54). Unspecified date. Neziah was an ancestor of a clan of Temple servants that returned with Zerubbabel from the Babylonian Exile.

Nibhaz

(Uncertain origin and meaning)

(2 Kings 17:31). Nibhaz was one of the two idols—the other one was Tartak—worshipped by the Avites, a people whom the Assyrians settled in Samaria, after they destroyed it in the 8th century B.C.

Nicanor

(Greek origin: *Victorious*)

(Acts of the Apostles 6:5). A.D. 1st century.

After the death of Jesus, his Hebrew and Greek followers became known as the Jerusalem church. There was some dissension between the two groups. The Greek converts complained that the Hebrew Christians neglected the Greek widows in the daily distribution of the food.

The twelve apostles summoned all the believers and told them, "It is not right that we should give up preaching the word of God to serve tables. Therefore, brothers, choose from among you seven men, whom we may appoint to this duty, while we devote ourselves to prayer and to the ministry of the word".

The congregation accepted this suggestion, and they chose Nicanor and another six men—Stephen, Philip, Prochorus, Timon, Parmenas, and Nicolas, a proselyte from Antioch—all of them Christians of good reputation, who were respected for their piety and their wisdom, to serve on the tables and distribute food to the needy of the community.

Nicodemus

(Greek origin: *Victorious among his people*)

(John 3:1). A.D. 1st century. Nicodemus, a Pharisee member of the Jewish Council, came to Jesus, during the night, and said to him, "Master, we know that you are a teacher sent by God, because no man can perform the miracles that you do if God is not with him".

Jesus said to him, "Truly, I tell you, no one can see the Kingdom of God if he is not born again".

"How can a grown-up man be born again? Can he enter again into his mother's womb and be born?" asked Nicodemus.

"I tell you, a man cannot enter the Kingdom of God if he is not born of water and the Spirit. What is born of flesh is flesh, but what is born of the Spirit is spirit. Don't be amazed when I say that you must be born again".

Nicodemus asked him, "How can this be?"

"You are a teacher in Israel, and you don't know these things? I tell you that we speak what we know and testify what we have seen. If you do not believe me when I tell you things about this world, how will you believe me when I speak about heavenly things? No one has ever gone up to heaven, except the Son of man who came down from heaven. God so loves the world that he has given his only Son, so that everyone who believes in him will live eternally. God did not send his Son to condemn the world but to save it".

Later, in a meeting of the Jewish Council, when the Pharisees wanted to arrest Jesus, Nicodemus said to his colleagues, "Our Law forbids to judge a person, before hearing him and finding what he has done".

"What?" they exclaimed, "Are you also from the Galilee? Study the Scriptures and you will see that no prophet has ever come from the Galilee".

After Jesus was crucified and his body was given to Joseph of Arimathaea, Nicodemus brought about one hundred pounds of spices, a mixture of myrrh and aloes, to prepare the body for the burial according to Jewish custom. He and Joseph took the body to a nearby garden and placed it in Joseph's tomb, which had recently been dug out of solid rock. The two men rolled a large stone to close the entrance to the tomb and went away.

Nicolas

(Greek origin: *Victorious over the people*)

(Acts of the Apostles 6:5). A.D. 1st century. After the death of Jesus, his Hebrew and Greek followers became known as the Jerusalem church. There was some dissension between the two groups. The Greek converts complained that the Hebrew Christians neglected the Greek widows in the daily distribution of the food.

The twelve apostles summoned all the believers and told them, "It is not right that we should give up preaching the word of God to serve tables. Therefore, brothers, choose from among you seven men, whom we may appoint to this duty, while we devote ourselves to prayer and to the ministry of the word".

The congregation accepted this suggestion, and they chose Nicolas, a proselyte from Antioch, and another six men—Stephen,

Philip, Prochorus, Timon, Parmenas, and Nicanor—all of them Christians of good reputation, who were respected for their piety and their wisdom, to serve on the tables and distribute food to the needy of the community.

Niger

(Latin origin: *Black*)

(Acts of the Apostles 13:1). A.D. 1st century. Niger was the nickname of Simeon, one of the prophets and teachers active in the Antioch church, during the year that Paul stayed in that city, preaching and organizing the church.

Note: It was in Antioch that the believers in Jesus were first called Christians.

Nimrod

(Uncertain origin and meaning)

(Genesis 10:8). Unspecified date. Nimrod, the son of Cush and grandson of Ham, was a powerful man and a mighty hunter, who established a kingdom in the land of Shinar, and founded Nineveh and other cities. His brothers were Seba, Havilah, Sabtah, Raamah, and Sabtechah.

Nimshi

(Hebrew origin: *Extricated*)

(1 Kings 19:16). 9th century B.C. Nimshi was the father of Jehu, the commander of King Joram's army who seized the throne of Israel and established a dynasty, which ruled over Israel for almost one hundred years.

Note: According to the second book of Kings, Nimshi was not the father of Jehu, but—through his son Jehoshaphat—his grandfather (2 Kings 9:2).

Nisroch

(Uncertain origin and meaning)

(2 Kings 19:37). Nisroch was a pagan god worshipped in Assyria. Sennacherib, king of Assyria, was worshipping in the Temple of Nisroch, when his sons Adrammelech and

Sharezer murdered him. The two patricides escaped to Armenia, and their brother Esarhaddon became king of Assyria.

Noadiah

(Hebrew origin: *Revealed by God*)

1. (Ezra 8:33). 5th century B.C. Noadiah, a Levite, son of Binnui, helped Meremoth, son of the priest Uriah, to count and weigh the silver and gold utensils of the Temple that Ezra had brought back from Babylon.

2. (Nehemiah 6:14). 5th century B.C. Noadiah, a prophetess, was thought by Nehemiah to be involved in the conspiracy of his enemies—Tobiah, Sanballat, and others—to set a trap for him, induce him to sin, and then report it.

Noah

(Hebrew origin: *Rest*)

1. (Genesis 5:29). Unspecified date. Noah, the son of Lamech, was a righteous man, a man "who walked with God". He was blameless in a generation whose wickedness and corruption were so great that God had repented that he had created man.

One day, God said to Noah, "I have decided to make an end of all flesh and destroy all living creatures, by bringing a flood of waters upon the earth; but you should build an ark of gopher wood, with inner rooms in three decks, a roof, and a door in the side, and cover it inside and out with pitch. You, your wife, your sons Shem, Ham, and Japheth, and the wives of your sons, will go into the ark, plus two living creatures of every kind, male and female. You will take every sort of food and store it in the ark".

Noah did as he was told and built the ark.

When the ark was finished, God said to Noah, "Go inside, and take with you seven pairs of all the animals that are ritually clean for eating, seven pairs of the birds of the air, and one pair of the animals that are not clean, because in seven days, I will send

rain for forty days and forty nights, and every living thing outside the ark will die".

Noah, his family, and all the living things that he had chosen went into the ark. This happened on the seventeenth day of the second month, at a time when Noah was six hundred years old. The rain continued for forty days, and the waters increased and bore up the ark. Every living creature died, and even the highest mountains were submerged.

After forty days, the rain stopped, and for one hundred and fifty days, the waters receded continually, until the ark came to rest upon the mountains of Ararat, in today's Turkey. Forty days later, Noah opened the window of the ark and sent forth a raven, which went to and fro. Then, he sent a dove, which did not find a place to set its foot and returned to the ark.

Noah waited another seven days, and again, he sent forth the dove. The bird came back in the evening, carrying in its mouth a freshly plucked olive leaf. Noah again waited seven days and sent forth the dove a third time. This time the dove did not return. Noah looked and saw that the surface of the ground was dry.

Several weeks later, when the earth was dry, God told Noah that they should all go out: he, his family, and all the living creatures. Noah built an altar to God and offered a thanksgiving sacrifice.

God said to Noah, "I promise to you and your sons that never again will I send a flood to destroy the earth. The rainbow will be the sign of the covenant that I have now made with all living creatures".

Noah became a tiller of the soil, and he planted a vineyard. He drank the wine that he made from the grapes, until he lay uncovered in his tent, totally intoxicated.

Ham went into the tent and saw his father naked. He went outside and told his brothers; Shem and Japheth took a cloth, and walking backward, entered the tent, and covered their father, taking care to turn their faces the other way so as not to see his nakedness. When Noah woke up and learned that Ham had treated him disrespectfully, he cursed Canaan, Ham's son, condemning him to be a slave to his father's brothers.

Noah lived three hundred and fifty years more, after the flood, and died at the age of nine hundred and fifty.

2. (Numbers 26:33). 13th century B.C. Noah was one of the five daughters of Zelophehad, the son of Hepher, of the tribe of Manasseh. When their father died, Noah and her sisters—Hoglah, Mahlah, Milcah, and Tirzah—came to Moses and Eleazar the High Priest and asked to inherit from their father, who had died in the wilderness without sons.

Moses, after consulting with God, modified the law to entitle a daughter to inherit from her father if he did not have any sons, but with the condition that she had to marry within her clan, in order that her inheritance would remain in her tribe.

After the death of Moses, the sisters came to Joshua and demanded, as their right, to receive a portion of the conquered territories, which had been given to the tribe of Manasseh.

Nobah

(Hebrew origin: *Bark*)

(Numbers 32:42). Unspecified date. Nobah, a leader of the tribe of Manasseh, captured the region of Kenath and changed its name to his own.

Noe

(Hebrew origin: *Rest*)

(Matthew 24:37). Unspecified date. Noe is the New Testament's spelling for Noah. (Please see the entry for Noah [Genesis 5:29].)

Nogah

(Hebrew origin: *Bright*)

(1 Chronicles 3:7). 10th century B.C. Nogah was one of the sons of King David who were born in Jerusalem. He appears in the list of King David's sons in the first book of Chronicles, chapter 3, but not in the list of Second Samuel, chapter 5.

Nohah

(Hebrew origin: *Quietude*)

(1 Chronicles 8:2). 17th century B.C. Nohah was one of the five sons of Benjamin. According to this list, his brothers were Bela, Ashbel, Aharah, and Rapha.

Nohah's name is not mentioned in the other lists of the sons of Benjamin: Genesis 46:21, Numbers 26:38, and 1 Chronicles 7:6.

Non

(Hebrew origin: *Perpetuity*)

(1 Chronicles 7:27). 14th century B.C. Non, of the tribe of Ephraim, was the father of Joshua, Moses' successor as leader of the Israelites. Alternative spelling is Nun (Exodus 33:11).

Nun

(Hebrew origin: *Perpetuity*)

(Exodus 33:11). 14th century B.C. Nun, of the tribe of Ephraim, was the father of Joshua, Moses' successor as leader of the Israelites. Alternative spelling is Non (1 Chronicles 7:27).

Nymphas

(Greek origin: *Nymph given*)

(Colossians 4:15). A.D. 1st century. Nymphas, a Christian who lived in Laodicea, and whose house was used as a church by the believers, was saluted by Paul in his letter to the Colossians.

Obadiah

(Hebrew origin: *Servant of God*)

1. (1 Kings 18:3). 9th century B.C. Obadiah, the governor of the royal palace, during the reign of King Ahab of Israel, risked his life by hiding one hundred prophets of the Lord in two caves, fifty per cave, and providing them with food and drink, to protect them from the murderous rage of Queen Jezebel.

   During a severe famine in Samaria, Obadiah was instructed by King Ahab to search for places where they could find fodder to feed the horses and the mules. Ahab went in one direction and told Obadiah to go in another direction.

   Obadiah was still searching for fodder, when he met Elijah. He recognized the prophet and flung himself on his face, saying, "Is that you, my lord, Elijah?"

   The prophet answered, "Yes, I am Elijah. I want you to go to Ahab and tell him that I am now back in the kingdom".

   Obadiah answered, "I fear for my life if, after having told King Ahab that you have returned, the Spirit of God will take you somewhere else, and then, when the king will not find you, he will surely kill me".

   Elijah assured him that he would appear to Ahab that same day. Obadiah went to the king and informed him that the prophet had returned. Ahab went to meet Elijah, and, when he saw him, he accused the prophet of being a troublemaker.

   Elijah retorted, "You and your father are the real troublemakers for forsaking the true God and worshiping the idols of Baal".

2. (1 Chronicles 3:21). Unspecified date. Obadiah was a descendant of Zerubbabel.

3. (1 Chronicles 7:3). Unspecified date. Obadiah, the son of Izrahiah, was a descendant of Tola. He and his brothers—Michael, Ishiah, and Joel—were leaders of the tribe of Issachar.

4. (1 Chronicles 8:38). Unspecified date. Obadiah was one of the six sons of Azel, son of Eleasah of the tribe of Benjamin, a descendant of King Saul. His brothers were Azrikam, Ishmael, Sheariah, Bocheru, and Hanan.

5. (1 Chronicles 9:16). 5th century B.C. Obadiah, son of Shemaiah, was among the first Levites to settle in the land of Judah, after the return from the Babylonian Exile. He was one of the two hundred eighty-four Levites residing in Jerusalem, during the days of Nehemiah. Obadiah is also called Abda, son of Shammua (Nehemiah 11:17).

6. (1 Chronicles 12:9). 11th century B.C. Obadiah, a Gadite, was one of the men who joined David's band, when he was hiding from Saul.

7. (1 Chronicles 27:19). 10th century B.C. Obadiah was the father of Ishmaiah, the leader of the tribe of Zebulun, during the reign of King David.

8. (2 Chronicles 17:7). 9th century B.C. Obadiah, an official in the court of King Jehoshaphat, was sent by the king, during the third year of his reign, together with other officials, Levites and priests, to teach the laws of God in the cities of Judah.

9. (2 Chronicles 34:12). 7th century B.C. Obadiah, a Levite descendant of Merari, was one of the four overseers of the repairs done in the Temple, during the reign of King Josiah. The other overseers were Jahath—a descendant of Merari—Zechariah, and Meshullam, of the clan of the Kohathites.

10. (Ezra 8:9). 5th century B.C. Obadiah, the son of Jehiel, returned with Ezra from Babylon, leading two hundred and eighteen males of his clan.

11. (Nehemiah 10:5). 5th century B.C. Obadiah was one of the priests who signed Nehemiah's solemn agreement to separate themselves from the foreigners living in the land, to refrain from intermarrying with them, and to dedicate their firstborn to God, among other obligations.

12. (Nehemiah 12:25). 5th century B.C. Obadiah was a gatekeeper in the days of Nehemiah.

13. (Obadiah 1:1). 5th century B.C. The prophet Obadiah wrote his book—the shortest in the Bible, consisting of only one chapter—shortly after the fall of Jerusalem.

The book is a prophecy against the Edomites, chastising them, because they refused to help fight against the invaders who conquered Jerusalem, rejoiced over the fall of Jerusalem, and took advantage of the catastrophe to loot the city and help the invaders.

The book also announces the proximity of the Day of the Lord, when God's power will be manifested: the evil will be punished, and the righteous will be renewed. The final verses prophesy the restoration of Israel.

The book of Obadiah is the fourth of the twelve books that make up the Minor Prophets—also called the Twelve—a collection of the books of twelve prophets: Hosea, Joel, Amos, Obadiah, Jonah, Micah, Nahum, Habakkuk, Zephaniah, Haggai, Zechariah, and Malachi.

Note: The phrase "Minor Prophets" does not mean that these prophets are less important than Isaiah, Jeremiah, and Ezekiel. It refers only to the fact that the books of these twelve prophets are much shorter than the books of the other three prophets.

Obal

(Uncertain origin and meaning)

(Genesis 10:28). Unspecified date. Obal, the son of Joktan—also called Ebal (1 Chronicles 1:22)—was a descendant of Noah through Shem, Noah's second son. His brothers were Almodad, Sheleph, Hazarmaveth, Jerah, Hadoram, Uzal, Diklah, Abimael, Sheba, Ophir, Havilah, and Jobab.

Obed

(Hebrew origin: *Servant*)

1. (Ruth 4:17). 12th century B.C. Obed, the son of Boaz and Ruth, was the father of Jesse and the grandfather of David.

2. (1 Chronicles 2:37). Unspecified date. Obed, the son of Ephlal, was the father of a man called Jehu. His ancestor Jarha was an Egyptian servant who had married the daughter of his master Sheshan, a leader of the tribe of Judah.

3. (1 Chronicles 11:47). 10th century B.C. Obed was one of the brave soldiers in King David's army.

4. (1 Chronicles 26:7). 10th century B.C. Obed, son of Shemaiah and grandson of Obededom, was one of the gatekeepers of the Tabernacle, during the reign of King David. His brothers—all of them brave men and leaders of their clan—were Othni, Rephael, Elihu, Elzabad, and Semachiah.

5. (2 Chronicles 23:1). 9th century B.C. Obed was the father of Azariah, one of the army commanders who joined the conspiracy headed by the priest Jehoiada, which overthrew Queen Athaliah and crowned Joash as king of Judah.

Obededom

(Hebrew origin: *Servant of Edom*)

1. (2 Samuel 6:10). 10th century B.C. Obededom, the Gittite, was the owner of the house where David left the Ark of the Covenant, which previously had been kept, during twenty years by Abinadab in his house in Geba, near the town of Kirjathjearim.

When David was bringing the Ark from Kirjathjearim to Jerusalem, Abinadab's son Uzza died on the road, because he touched the Ark. David decided to leave the Ark for an indefinite time in the house of Obededom. After three months, when David saw that Obededom had been blessed by God, he decided to have the Ark brought to Jerusalem.

2. (1 Chronicles 15:18). 10th century B.C. Obededom, son of Jeduthun, a gatekeeper and Levite of the second rank, was among those chosen by the chief of the Levites to sing and play musical instruments in front of the Ark of the Covenant, when it was carried from the house of Obededom to its

resting place in Jerusalem, as commanded by David.

His sons were Shemaiah, Jehozabad, Joah, Sacar, Nethaneel, Ammiel, Issachar, and Peulthai.

3. (2 Chronicles 25:24). 8th century B.C. Obededom was the custodian of all the gold, silver, and utensils of the Temple, during the reign of King Amaziah of Judah. These valuable items, together with the treasuries of the royal palace, were taken away as booty by King Joash of Israel, when he defeated Amaziah and broke down the walls of Jerusalem.

Obil

(Hebrew origin: *Mournful*)

(1 Chronicles 27:30). 10th century B.C. Obil, the Ishmaelite, was in charge of the king's camels, during the reign of King David.

Ocran

(Hebrew origin: *Disturber*)

(Numbers 1:13). 14th century B.C. His son Pagiel was the leader of the tribe of Asher, during the Exodus from Egypt.

Oded

(Hebrew origin: *Reiteration*)

1. (2 Chronicles 15:1). 9th century B.C. Oded was the father of Azariah, the prophet who told King Asa, when he returned victorious over Zerah the Ethiopian, that God would be with him as long as the king would not forsake God.

2. (2 Chronicles 28:9). 8th century B.C. Oded was a prophet who lived in the northern kingdom of Israel, during the reign of King Pekah.

Pekah went to war against King Ahaz of Judah, defeated him, and brought tens of thousands of captives back to Samaria with the intention of making them slaves.

The prophet Oded demanded that the king free the captives and return them to Judah. Several leaders of Israel donated clothing, shoes, food, and drink to the captives, and they returned them to the city of Jericho in Judah.

Og

(Hebrew origin: *Round*)

(Numbers 21:33). 13th century B.C. Og, king of Bashan, was a man of great height, whose iron bedstead was of an enormous size. He and his people were utterly defeated by the Israelites in a battle in Edrei.

The Israelites took possession of his country and divided it among the tribes of Gad and Reuben, and the half tribe of Manasseh.

Ohad

(Hebrew origin: *Unity*)

(Genesis 46:10). 17th century B.C. Ohad, son of Simeon and grandson of Jacob, was among the seventy Israelites who immigrated to Egypt. His brothers were Jemuel—called Nemuel in 1 Chronicles—Jamin, Jachin—called Jarib in 1 Chronicles—Zohar—called Zerah in the book of Numbers—and Shaul, the son of a Canaanite woman.

Ohel

(Hebrew origin: *Tent*)

(1 Chronicles 3:20). 6th century B.C. Ohel was a descendant of the royal family of Judah. His father Zerubbabel was the leader of the first group of captives who returned from the Babylonian Exile.

Olympas

(Greek origin: *Heavenly*)

(Romans 16:15). A.D. 1st century. Olympas was a Christian to whom Paul sent greetings in his letter to the Christians in Rome. The apostle mentioned him in the same verse with four other persons—Philologus, Julia, Nereus, and his sister—and "all the saints who were with them". This gives grounds to think that Olympas and his companions formed a small separate group within the larger Christian community of Rome.

Omar

(Hebrew origin: *Speaker*)

(Genesis 36:11). 16th century B.C. Omar, the ancestor of an Edomite clan, was the son of Eliphaz, and the grandson of Esau and his wife Adah, the daughter of Elon the Hittite. His brothers were Gatam, Teman, Zepho, Kenaz, and Amalek.

Omri

(Hebrew origin: *Sheaf of corn*)

1. (1 Kings 16:16). 9th century B.C. Omri, the sixth king of Israel, after the partition of the United Monarchy, was one of the ablest and most successful of the Israelite kings. He made such an indelible impression that, even a hundred years later, the kingdom of Israel was mentioned in documents of the neighboring countries as "Beit Omri", the house of Omri, his name having become an established term to indicate the Israelite kings, even after the death of all his descendants.

   Omri had been the commander of the army of Israel. He was encamped in Gibbethon, fighting against the Philistines, when he heard that Zimri, the commander of half the chariots of the army, had seized the throne and killed King Elah and all his family, leaving no survivors of the royal family.

   Omri went immediately with his army to Tirzah, the capital city, and occupied it. Zimri, who had been king for a scant seven days, realized that all was lost and committed suicide by burning down the royal palace with him inside it.

   The death of Zimri was followed by a civil war, where half the people of Israel supported Omri as the next king, and the others wanted Tibni, the son of Ginath, to be their new ruler. Omri triumphed over Tibni, put his defeated rival to death, and proclaimed himself king of Israel, with his capital in Tirzah.

   Six years later, Omri bought a hill from a man named Shemer for two talents of silver. There on the hill, he built a splendid city, worthy of comparison with Jerusalem,

the capital of Judah. He called it Samaria, in honor of the previous owner of the site, and made it his capital.

Omri's first official act was to make peace with Judah, ending the war between the two kingdoms, which had lasted since the death of Solomon. He married his daughter Athaliah—or, as some historians believe, his granddaughter—to Joram, the crown prince of Judah. He made an alliance with the Phoenician kingdoms of Tyre and Sidon, by marrying his son Ahab to Jezebel, the daughter of the king of Zidon. He recovered the lost territory, east of the Jordan River, including the kingdom of Moab, which had managed to become independent twenty years ago, during the reign of King Baasha.

Omri died, after reigning for twelve years, and was succeeded by his son Ahab.

2. (1 Chronicles 7:8). 16th century B.C. Omri, the son of Becher and grandson of Benjamin, was a member of a family of heads of the tribe and brave warriors. His brothers were Zemira, Joash, Eliezer, Elioenai, Alameth, Jerimoth, Anathoth, and Abiah.

3. (1 Chronicles 9:4). Unspecified date. Omri, the son of Imri, was the father of Ammihud. His grandson Uthai was among the first persons who returned from the Babylonian Exile to live in Jerusalem.

   In the book of Nehemiah (Nehemiah 11:4), Omri's son is called Uzziah, and his grandson is called Athaiah.

4. (1 Chronicles 27:18). 10th century B.C. Omri, the son of Michael, was the leader of the tribe of Issachar, during the reign of King David.

On

(Hebrew origin: *Wealth*)

(Numbers 16:1). 13th century B.C. On—the son of Peleth—Dathan, and Abiram were the main supporters of Korah's rebellion against Moses. The four men, at the head of a group of two hundred fifty renowned men, accused Moses and Aaron of raising themselves over the rest of the people.

Moses threw himself on the ground and said to the rebels, "Tomorrow, the Lord will show us who belongs to him, who can come close to him. Take your fire pans, you Korah, and all your followers, and put incense and fire in it, and present them to the Lord tomorrow, and we will see who will the Lord choose to make holy. You have gone too far, sons of Levi! It seems that it is not enough for you that God has set you apart from the community to serve him, and brought you near him. You also want the priesthood? You are not standing against Aaron, you have banded against the Lord!"

Moses became very angry, and he said to God, "Don't accept their offerings. I have never hurt any of them, nor have I taken even one of their donkeys!"

The next day, the rebels, with their fire pans, stood in the door of the Tabernacle, with Moses and Aaron, surrounded by the people.

Moses said to the people, "Depart and stay away from the tents of the rebels, lest they be also consumed together. If those men will die of a natural death, then I have not been sent by God, but if the earth would open and swallow them up, this will prove that the rebels had offended God".

As soon as he finished speaking, the earth opened, and the rebels, their tents, and all their goods fell inside. The earth closed upon them, and they all perished.

Eleazar the Priest took the censers of the rebels and made with them broad plates for the covering of the altar, to remind the people that only the descendants of Aaron could offer incense to God.

Onam

(Hebrew origin: *Strong*)

1. (Genesis 36:23). Unspecified date. Onam was the son of Shobal, a descendant of Seir. His brothers were Manahath, Ebal, Shepho, and Alvan.
2. (1 Chronicles 2:26). Unspecified date. Onam, of the tribe of Judah, was the son of Jerahmeel and Atarah, his second wife. His sons were Shammai and Jada.

Onan

(Hebrew origin: *Strong*)

(Genesis 38:4). 17th century B.C. Onan was the second son of Judah and a Canaanite woman, daughter of a man named Shuah.

His older brother Er had been married to a girl called Tamar. When Er died, Onan was told by his father Judah to marry Tamar and, thus, provide offspring for his dead brother.

Onan, unwilling that his children should carry on his brother's name, would spill his seed on the ground. When he also died, Judah became fearful that his youngest son Shelah would also die if he would marry Tamar. So he told her to return to her father's house and remain a widow "until Shelah would grow up".

Eventually Tamar, by tricking Judah, became pregnant by him and gave birth to twins: Pharez and Zarah.

Onesimus

(Greek origin: *Profitable*).

(Colossians 4:9). A.D. 1st century. Onesimus was an escaped slave whom Paul had met in prison and converted to Christianity. His master was Philemon, a prominent Christian whose house hosted the church in Colossae.

Paul wrote a short letter to Philemon, appealing to him to be reconciled to his slave, whom Paul was sending back to him, and to welcome him not only as a forgiven slave but as a brother in Christ.

Onesiphorus

(Greek origin: *Profit bearer*)

(2 Timothy 1:16). A.D. 1st century. Onesiphorus, a kind Christian, had been a great help to Paul, during the apostle's stay in Ephesus. Years later, Onesiphorus came to Rome and went to great lengths to find Paul. Having learned that the apostle was in prison, he visited him there.

Paul, in his second letter to Timothy, wrote about Onesiphorus, with great appreciation, and sent him regards.

Ophir

(Uncertain origin and meaning)

(Genesis 10:29). Unspecified date. Ophir was the son of Joktan, a descendant of Shem. His brothers were Almodad, Sheleph, Hazarmaveth, Jerah, Hadoram, Uzal, Diklah, Obal, Abimael, Sheba, Havilah, and Jobab.

Ophrah

(Hebrew origin: *Fawn*)

(1 Chronicles 4:14). 12th century B.C. Ophrah, the son of Meonothai and grandson of Othniel, was a descendant of Judah.

Oreb

(Hebrew origin: *Mosquito*)

(Judges 7:25). 12th century B.C. Oreb was one of the two Midianite princes—the other was Zeeb—who were captured and killed by the men of Ephraim.

The Ephraimites brought their heads to Gideon, who was on the other side of the river Jordan, and angrily complained that Gideon had not called them to fight at his side against the Midianites.

Gideon, to assuage them, said that he had done nothing that could compare to their success in capturing Oreb and Zeeb. They were, thus, mollified.

Oren

(Hebrew origin: *Ash tree*)

(1 Chronicles 2:25). Unspecified date. Oren was the son of Jerahmeel, of the clan of the Hezronites of the tribe of Judah. His brothers were Ram, Bunah, Ahijah, and Ozem.

Ornan

(Jebusite: title meaning *The Lord*)

(1 Chronicles 21:15). 10th century B.C. Ornan—called elsewhere Araunah—the Jebusite, owned a threshing floor on Mount Moriah, which he sold to King David. (Please see the entry for Araunah [2 Samuel 24:16].)

Orpah

(Hebrew origin: *Mane*)

(Ruth 1:4). 12th century B.C. Orpah, a Moabite girl, married Chilion, an Israelite from Bethlehem who had been forced by a famine in his native land to immigrate to Moab with his parents, Elimelech and Naomi, and his brother Mahlon.

Mahlon also married a Moabite woman, a local girl called Ruth. Ten years later, after the two brothers had died childless, their mother, Naomi, decided to return to Bethlehem. Her two daughters-in-law wanted to go with her, but Naomi told them to stay with their parents in their own country.

Naomi said, "I am too old to have sons that could marry you; and even if I would have new sons, how could you wait so many years for them to grow up?"

The girls wept; Orpah kissed her mother-in-law and turned back, but Ruth went with Naomi to Bethlehem. There, she married Boaz and had a son, named Obed, who became an ancestor of King David.

Oshea

(Hebrew origin: *Deliverer*)

(Numbers 13:8). 13th century B.C. Oshea was the original name of Joshua, the man who succeeded Moses as the leader of the Israelites. An alternative spelling is Hoshea (Deuteronomy 32:44). (Please see the entry for Joshua [Exodus 17:9].)

Othni

(Hebrew origin: *Force*)

(1 Chronicles 26:7). 10th century B.C. Othni, son of Shemaiah and grandson of Obededom, was one of the gatekeepers of the Tabernacle, during the reign of King David. His brothers—all of them brave men and leaders of their clan—were Rephael, Elihu, Obed, Elzabad, and Semachiah.

Othniel

(Hebrew origin: *Force of God*)

(Joshua 15:17). 12th century B.C. Othniel, a descendant of Judah, was the brother of Seraiah and the son of Kenaz, the younger brother of Caleb.

His uncle Caleb offered to give his daughter Achsah to whoever would conquer the town of Kirjathsepher. Othniel took the town and married Achsah.

After the death of Joshua, Chushanrishathaim, king of Mesopotamia, oppressed the Israelites, during eight years, until Othniel led the Israelites against the foreign tyrant and freed his people. Othniel's sons were Hathath and Meonothai.

Ozem

(Hebrew origin: *Strong*)

1. (1 Chronicles 2:15). 11th century B.C. Ozem, son of Jesse, was one of David's six brothers.
2. (1 Chronicles 2:25). Unspecified date. Ozem was the son of Jerahmeel, of the clan of the Hezronites of the tribe of Judah. His brothers were Ram, Bunah, Ahijah, and Oren.

Ozias

(Hebrew origin: *Strength of God*)

(Matthew 1:8). 8th century B.C. Ozias is an alternative spelling for Uzziah, king of Judah, in Matthew's genealogy of Jesus.

Note: Matthew mentions Joram as the father of Ozias, but elsewhere in the Bible it is stated that Uzziah's father was Amaziah.

Ozni

(Hebrew origin: *Ears*)

(Numbers 26:16). 17th century B.C. Ozni—called Ezbon in the book of Genesis (Genesis 46:16)—a son of Gad, was the ancestor of the clan of the Oznites. His brothers were Zephon, Haggi, Shuni, Eri, Arod, and Areli, all of them ancestors of clans.

Paarai

(Hebrew origin: *Yawning*)

(2 Samuel 23:35). 10th century B.C. Paarai the Arbite was one of "The Thirty", an elite group in King David's army. He is called Naarai, son of Ezbai, in the first book of Chronicles (1 Chronicles 11:37).

Padon

(Hebrew origin: *Ransom*)

(Ezra 2:44). Unspecified date. Padon was the ancestor of a clan of Temple servants that returned with Zerubbabel from the Babylonian Exile.

Pagiel

(Hebrew origin: *Accident of God*)

(Numbers 1:13). 13th century B.C. Pagiel, son of Ocran, was the leader of the tribe of Asher, during the Exodus from Egypt.

Pahathmoab

(Hebrew origin: *Pit of Moab*)

1. (Ezra 2:6). Unspecified date. Pahathmoab was the ancestor of a clan, some of whom returned with Zerubbabel from the Babylonian Exile, and others with Ezra. Several of his descendants were forced to divorce their foreign wives, during the days of Ezra.

2. (Nehemiah 3:11). 5th century B.C. His son Hashub, together with Malchijah, son of Harim, repaired a sector of the walls of Jerusalem and the tower of the furnaces, during the days of Nehemiah.

3. (Nehemiah 10:14). 5th century B.C. Pahathmoab was among the leaders who signed Nehemiah's solemn agreement to separate themselves from the foreigners living in the land, to refrain from inter-marrying with them, and to dedicate

their firstborn to God, among other obligations.

Palal

(Hebrew origin: *Judge*)

(Nehemiah 3:25). 5th century B.C. Palal, the son of Uzai, helped to repair the walls of Jerusalem, during the days of Nehemiah.

Pallu

(Hebrew origin: *Distinguished*)

(Exodus 6:14). 17th century B.C. Pallu—called Phallu in the book of Genesis (Genesis 46:9)—a son of Reuben, was among the seventy Israelites who immigrated to Egypt. He was the ancestor of the clan of the Palluites. His brothers were Hanoch, Hezron, and Carmi.

His son Eliab was the father of Dathan and Abiram, who sided with Korah in his rebellion against Moses and Aaron and were punished by being swallowed by the earth.

Palti

(Hebrew origin: *Delivered*)

(Numbers 13:9). 13th century B.C. Palti, son of Raphu, of the tribe of Benjamin, was one of the twelve spies sent by Moses to Canaan, to scout the land, its cities, and its inhabitants; to find out if they were strong or weak, few or many; and to bring back the fruit of the land. The spies came back, frightened and disheartened, and told the Israelites that the Canaanites were too big and too strong to be defeated.

Two of the spies—Joshua, the son of Nun, and Caleb, the son of Jephunneh—disagreed and told the people not to fear.

The Israelites refused to listen to the encouraging words of Joshua and Caleb, and they started to wail and cry. God punished their cowardice by condemning them to wander forty years in the wilderness, one year for each day that the spies scouted the land. All those who complained against God, including Palti, died in the wilderness, except Caleb and Joshua.

(For more detailed information about the twelve spies, please see the entry for Joshua.)

Paltiel

(Hebrew origin: *Delivered by God*)

(Numbers 34:26). 13th century B.C. Paltiel, the son of Azzan, was the leader of the tribe of Issachar chosen by Moses to help apportion the land of Canaan among the tribes.

Parmashta

(Persian origin: Uncertain meaning)

(Esther 9:9). 5th century B.C. Parmashta was one of the ten sons of Haman, the vizier of Persia who wanted to kill all the Jews in the kingdom. His brothers were Parshandatha, Arisai, Aspatha, Poratha, Adalia, Aridatha, Dalphon, Aridai, and Vajezatha. All of them were executed, when Haman's plot against the Jews backfired.

Parmenas

(Greek origin: *Constant*)

(Acts of the Apostles 6:5). A.D. 1st century. After the death of Jesus, his Hebrew and Greek followers became known as the Jerusalem church. There was some dissension between the two groups. The Greek converts complained that the Hebrew Christians neglected the Greek widows in the daily distribution of the food.

The twelve apostles summoned all the believers and told them, "It is not right that we should give up preaching the word of God to serve tables. Therefore, brothers, choose from among you seven men, whom we may appoint to this duty, while we devote ourselves to prayer and to the ministry of the word".

The congregation accepted this suggestion, and they chose Parmenas and another six men—Stephen, Philip, Prochorus, Timon, Nicanor, and Nicolas, a proselyte from Antioch—all of them Christians of good reputation, who were respected for their piety and their wisdom, to serve on the tables and distribute food to the needy of the community.

Parnach

(Uncertain origin and meaning)

(Numbers 34:25). 14th century B.C. Parnach was the father of Elizaphan, the leader of the tribe of Zebulun, chosen by Moses to help apportion the land of Canaan among the tribes.

Parosh

(Hebrew origin: *Flea*)

1. (Ezra 2:3). Unspecified date. Parosh was the ancestor of a group of men who returned with Zerubbabel from the Babylonian Exile. Some of his descendants were forced to divorce their foreign wives, during the days of Ezra.

2. (Nehemiah 3:25). 5th century B.C. Parosh was one of the leaders who signed Nehemiah's solemn agreement to separate themselves from the foreigners living in the land, to refrain from intermarrying with them, and to dedicate their firstborn to God, among other obligations (Nehemiah 10:14). His son Pedaiah helped to repair the walls of Jerusalem (Nehemiah 3:25).

Parshandatha

(Persian origin: Uncertain meaning)

(Esther 9:7). 5th century B.C. Parshandatha was one of the ten sons of Haman, the vizier of Persia who wanted to kill all the Jews in the kingdom. His brothers were Parmashta, Arisai, Aspatha, Poratha, Adalia, Aridatha, Dalphon, Aridai, and Vajezatha. All of them were executed, when Haman's plot against the Jews backfired.

Paruah

(Hebrew origin: *Blossomed*)

(1 Kings 4:17). 10th century B.C. His son Jehoshaphat, one of the twelve district governors, during the reign of Solomon, was responsible for providing food from his district, the territory of Issachar, for the king and the royal household for one month of each year

Pasach

(Hebrew origin: *Passed over*)

(1 Chronicles 7:33). Unspecified date. Pasach, son of Japhlet, a leader of the tribe of Asher, was the brother of Ashvath and Bimhal.

Paseah

(Hebrew origin: *Limping*)

1. (1 Chronicles 4:12). Unspecified date. Paseah, a descendant of Judah, was the son of Eshton, and the brother of Bethrapha and Tehinnah.
2. (Ezra 2:49). Unspecified date. Paseah was the ancestor of a clan of Temple servants that returned with Zerubbabel from the Babylonian Exile.
3. (Nehemiah 3:6). 5th century B.C. His son Jehoiada, together with Meshullam, son of Besodeiah, repaired the old gate of the walls of Jerusalem, including the doors, locks, and bars, in the days of Nehemiah.

Pashur

(Hebrew origin: *Liberation*)

1. (1 Chronicles 9:12). 6th century B.C. Pashur, the son of Malchijah, was the father of Jeroham. His grandson Adaiah served as a priest in the Temple, after the return from the Babylonian Exile.
2. (Ezra 2:38). Unspecified date. Pashur was the ancestor of a clan of priests who returned with Zerubbabel from the Babylonian Exile. During the days of Ezra, several of his descendants—Elioenai, Maaseiah, Ishmael, Nethaneel, Jozabad, and Elasah—were forced to divorce their foreign wives.
3. (Nehemiah 10:3). 5th century B.C. Pashur was among the priests who signed Nehemiah's solemn agreement to separate themselves from the foreigners living in the land, to refrain from intermarrying with them, and to dedicate their firstborn to God, among other obligations.
4. (Nehemiah 11:12). Unspecified date. Pashur, a priest, the son of Malchiah, was the father of Zechariah. His descendant

Adaiah was a Temple priest, during the days of Nehemiah.

5. (Jeremiah 20:1). 6th century B.C. Pashur, son of Immer, was the priest in charge of the Temple, in the period right before the fall of Jerusalem.

Angry against Jeremiah for what he considered his prophecies of defeatism, he inflicted heavy blows on the prophet and put him in the cell that was in the Temple's Gate of Benjamin. The next morning, when Pashur brought Jeremiah out of the cell, the prophet told him that God would call him Magormissabib, *Terror all around,* because the kingdom of Judah would fall to the king of Babylon, and Pashur and all his family would be sent to Babylon where they would die.

6. (Jeremiah 21:1). 6th century B.C. Pashur, son of Melchiah—also spelled Malchiah— was a high official in the court of King Zedekiah. The king sent him, together with the priest Zephaniah, son of Maaseiah, to inquire from Jeremiah if God would help him against Nebuchadrezzar, king of Babylon.

Later, Pashur—together with his son Gedaliah; Jucal, son of Shelemiah; and Shephatiah, son of Mattan—asked the king to put Jeremiah to death for preaching surrender and undermining the courage of the soldiers.

When King Zedekiah told them that they could do with Jeremiah whatever they wanted, Pashur and his fellow court officials cast the prophet into the dungeon of Malchiah, which was in the court of the prison.

Ebedmelech, an Ethiopian eunuch in the service of the king, told the king that Jeremiah might die of hunger in the dungeon. Zedekiah instructed Ebedmelech to pull Jeremiah out of the dungeon.

Pathrusim

(Hebrew origin: *Inhabitant of Pathros*)

(Genesis 10:14). Unspecified date. Pathrusim was the son of Mizraim and grandson of Ham. His brothers were Ludim, Anamim, Lehabim, Naphtuhim, Casluhim, and Caphtorim.

Patrobas

(Greek origin: *Father's life*)

(Romans 16:14). A.D. 1st century. Patrobas was a Christian to whom Paul sent greetings in his letter to the Christians in Rome.

The apostle mentioned him in the same verse with four other men—Phlegon, Hermas, Asyncritus, and Hermes—and "the brothers who were with them", which gives grounds to think that Patrobas and his companions formed a small separate group within the larger Christian community of Rome.

Paul

(Latin origin: *Pause*)

(Acts of the Apostles 13:9). A.D. 1st century. Paul—whose Hebrew name was Saul (Acts of the Apostles 7:58)—was born in Tarsus, a large city in Cilicia, a region situated in today's Anatolia, Turkey. His family, descendant of the tribe of Benjamin, enjoyed the status of Roman citizenship. To complete his education, Paul moved to Jerusalem where—under the influence of his teacher, Master Gamaliel, a doctor of the law, who enjoyed great renown among the people—he became a Pharisee. He also learned a trade, tent making, which, throughout his life, allowed him to earn a living.

When Christianity started to spread in Jerusalem, Paul became one of its most active and hostile opponents, entering the houses of the believers and dragging them out to prison. He witnessed the stoning of Stephen and did nothing to stop the killing.

Eager to fight against Christianity, Paul requested letters of introduction to the synagogues in Damascus from the High Priest, so that, if he should find there any converts, men or women, he would have the authority to arrest them and bring them back to Jerusalem.

Paul was approaching the city of Damascus, when suddenly a light from heaven flashed around him. He fell to the ground and heard a voice that said, "Saul, Saul, why do you persecute me?"

Paul asked, "Who are you, Lord?"

The voice answered, "I am Jesus, whom you persecute. Get up and go into the city, where you will be told what you must do".

The men who were traveling with Saul stood speechless; they heard the voice but saw no one. Saul got up from the ground and opened his eyes, but he had become blind and could not see. His companions took him by the hand and led him into Damascus. For three days, he was not able to see, and, during that time, he did not eat or drink anything.

Ananias, a Christian who lived in Damascus, was ordered by God in a vision to go to the house of a man called Judas, which was located in the street called Straight. There, he would find the blind Saul immersed in prayer. Ananias protested to God that he had heard of Saul's reputation as a persecutor of Christians. God told him that he had chosen Saul to spread the divine message to the Gentiles, kings, and Jews.

Saul had also received a vision, where he was told that he would recover his sight, when a man called Ananias would touch him. Therefore, when Ananias came to the house and told him that Jesus had sent him, Saul was expecting him. Ananias touched him, and he immediately recovered his eyesight. Paul then arose, ate, recovered his strength, and was baptized.

Years later, at his trial in Jerusalem, Paul recounted the story of his conversion and baptism, and he said that Ananias was "a devout man according to the Law, having a good report of all the Jews, which dwelt there".

Saul stayed in Damascus for a while, preaching in the synagogues that Jesus was the Son of God. All those who heard them could not believe their ears. "Isn't he the man who persecuted the believers in Jerusalem?" they asked. "Didn't he come here to arrest them and take them back to the chief priests?"

Saul's preaching became more and more forceful and eloquent. When the Jews who lived in Damascus found it difficult to refute his arguments that proved that Jesus was the Messiah, they became angry and conspired to kill him. The followers of Saul learned of the plot and helped him to escape, by lowering him in a basket down the wall of the city, because the gates of the city were closely watched day and night by his enemies.

Once back in Jerusalem, Saul tried to join the community of the believers, but they, knowing his past, were afraid of him and could not believe in his sincerity.

Barnabas, a Jewish convert whose deep faith had caused him to sell his land and give the money to the apostles, testified to the leaders of the congregation that Saul had seen the Lord in the road to Damascus, and that, during his stay in that city, he had preached courageously in the name of Jesus.

After Saul was accepted wholeheartedly by the disciples, he dedicated himself to preach in Jerusalem about Jesus, talking and arguing with the Jews, who sought to kill him. To save Saul's life, the believers took him to the port city of Caesarea, and from there, they sent him to Tarsus, his native city.

Barnabas, who had been sent by the Jerusalem church to Antioch, came to Tarsus, seeking Saul, and, when he found him, took him to Antioch. Saul stayed there for a whole year, preaching, and organizing the church of the city. It was there in Antioch that the believers in Jesus were first called Christians.

A prophet named Agabus, who recently arrived from Jerusalem, predicted that a severe famine was about to come over the entire world. The leaders of the Antioch congregation received from the believers as much as they could afford to give help to their brothers in Judea, and they gave the money that was collected to Barnabas and Paul, to take to Jerusalem.

Barnabas and Paul went to Jerusalem, delivered the money, and returned to Antioch, bringing with them a young man called John, whose surname was Mark. The three men stayed for a while, until the leaders of the Christian community sent them off to preach the word of God in other lands.

Paul and his two companions went to Seleucia and sailed from there to the island of Cyprus. They arrived in Salamis and preached the word of God in the synagogues. Then, they went all the way across the island to Paphos, where Sergius Paulus, the Roman proconsul of Cyprus, having learned that Paul was on the island, invited him to his quarters, so that he could hear the word of God from his mouth. Present in that meeting was a sorcerer and false prophet named Barjesus—also called Elymas—who attempted to refute Paul's arguments. The apostle turned to him, cursed him, and told him that he wouldn't be able to see the sun for a season. Barjesus immediately became blind and had to be lead outside by his hand. This event so impressed the proconsul that he became a Christian believer.

From Paphos, the three men sailed to the town of Perga in Pamphylia, in today's Anatolia, Turkey. There, John Mark left his companions and returned to Jerusalem. Paul and Barnabas continued to Antioch in Pisidia. On the Sabbath, they went to the synagogue and sat down. After the public reading of the Law and the prophets, the rulers of the synagogue invited them to speak to the people.

Paul stood up and gave a speech, summarizing the history of the people of Israel from the time that God had freed them from slavery in Egypt, until the death and resurrection of Jesus. He told them that it was through Jesus that sins were forgiven.

When he finished speaking, the people invited them to come back the next Sabbath and tell them more. When the services were over, many Jews and Gentiles who had been converted to Judaism followed Paul and Barnabas, who spoke to them and encouraged them to continue in the grace of God.

The next Sabbath, almost the whole town came to the synagogue to hear the word of God. The Jews saw the multitude and were filled with jealousy. They argued with Paul and insulted him. Paul and Barnabas told them that, because they had rejected the word of God, they would leave them and would go and preach to the Gentiles.

The Gentiles were very happy to hear Paul, and they praised the word of God, which spread throughout the region, and many converted. The Jews incited the city authorities to persecute Paul and Barnabas and expel them from the town. Paul and Barnabas left the city and went to Iconium.

The same thing happened in Iconium; Paul and Barnabas went to the synagogue, preached the word of God, and made many converts of both Jews and Gentiles. The Jews who did not convert stirred up the Gentiles and turned them against the believers. Some of the people of the city who were on the side of the Jews threatened to stone Paul and Barnabas. The two men fled to the city of Lystra, in the region of Lycaonia, where they stayed for sometime and preached the gospel.

One day, in Lystra, Paul noticed a cripple who had never walked in his life. He told the poor man, "Stand upright on your feet". The man jumped up and started walking around. This miracle so impressed the pagans in the city that they shouted in their local Lycaonian language, "The gods have come down to us in the shape of men", and excitedly proclaimed that Barnabas was Jupiter, and Paul, Mercurius. The priest of Jupiter even brought oxen to sacrifice in front of them.

Paul and Barnabas cried out, "We are men, not gods! You should turn away from idols and believe in the living God!"

Some Jews from Antioch and Iconium, who were visiting Lystra, incited the crowd against Paul. The mob stoned Paul and dragged him out of the town, thinking that he was dead. The believers gathered around him and were relieved, when they saw that he managed to get up and return to town. The next day, he and Barnabas went to Derbe, where they preached the gospel and made many new converts. Afterward, they again visited Lystra, Iconium, and Antioch on Pisidia, and they organized the church in each town. They continued to Pamphylia, Perga, and Attalia, and then, they sailed to Antioch, where they stayed for a long time, converting the Gentiles.

Some men who came from Judea to Antioch told the local converts that to be saved they first had to be circumcised according to the Law of Moses. After Paul and Barnabas disagreed and fiercely argued with them, it was decided that Paul, Barnabas, and some of the other leaders of the Antiochian church, including Titus, an uncircumcised Greek convert, should go to Jerusalem and consult with the apostles and the elders about this matter.

Barnabas and Paul went to Jerusalem and took part in the Jerusalem's church debate over the admission of Gentiles to the community of believers. Paul refused to circumcise Titus, who, thus, became a symbol of Paul's determination to receive Gentiles into the church.

On their way, passing through Phoenicia and Samaria, they reported that many Gentiles had been converted, causing great joy to the local believers.

Back in Jerusalem, they were welcomed by the church, the apostles, and the elders, to whom they gave a full report of all their activities. Some believers who belonged to the party of the Pharisees stood up and stated that the Gentiles should be circumcised and told to obey the Law of Moses.

After much discussion, Peter stood up and said, "Brothers, you know that a long time ago God chose me from among you to preach the gospel to the Gentiles, so that they should hear and believe. God has given the Holy Spirit to the Gentiles as he has to us. There is no difference between them and us. Why put God to the test by imposing a burden on the backs of the believers, which neither we nor our ancestors were able to carry? We believe that we shall be saved through the grace of the Lord Jesus, just as they are".

The assembly kept silent, while Paul and Barnabas reported all the miracles and wonders that God had performed through them among the Gentiles. When they had finished speaking, James, the brother of Jesus, stood and said, "Brothers, listen to me! Simon has explained how God showed his care for the Gentiles by taking out of them a people for his name. This agrees with the words of the prophets. Therefore, I suggest that we should not trouble the Gentiles. Instead, we should write to them that they should abstain from eating food, which had been offered to idols, blood or animals, which had been strangled; and also to forbid them to engage in sexual immorality".

The apostles, elders, and the whole congregation chose two men—Judas, also called Barsabas, and Silas—to accompany Paul and Barnabas to Antioch, carrying a letter from the Jerusalem church to the Gentile believers in Antioch, Syria, and Cilicia, exonerating them of the need for circumcision, but asking them to abstain from eating food offered to idols, blood, and strangled animals, and also to avoid sexual immorality. In Antioch, they gathered the congregation and read the letter, and Barsabas and Silas, who were themselves prophets, spoke a long time with the believers and gave them encouragement. Barsabas then returned to Jerusalem, but Silas stayed on for a while.

After sometime, Paul told Barnabas that they should visit again all the cities where they had founded churches to see how they were doing. Barnabas wanted to take John Mark with them, but Paul opposed the idea. They argued and decided to separate. Barnabas and John Mark sailed to Cyprus, while Paul and Silas traveled through Syria and Cilicia, strengthening the local churches.

Paul traveled to Derbe and Lystra, where he met a believer called Timothy—also called Timotheus—the son of a Jewish mother and a Greek father. Paul wanted to take Timothy along with them, so he circumcised him, because the Jews who lived in those places knew that his father was Greek. As they went through the towns, they delivered to the local congregations the rules decreed by the apostles and elders in Jerusalem, and they instructed to carry them out.

Paul and his companions traveled through different regions, until they came to Troas, where a vision appeared to Paul in the night. He saw a man of Macedonia, begging him to come to Macedonia and help them. Paul understood that the vision meant that God wanted them to preach the gospel to the people of Macedonia. They immediately sailed from Troas to Samothracia and continued the next day to Neapolis, and from there to Philippi, a Roman colony, which was the main city of Macedonia.

A few days later, on the Sabbath, they went out of the city to the riverside, where they thought they might find a place for prayer. They sat down and spoke to the women who gathered there. One of them was a woman named Lydia, a seller of purple cloth, originally from the city of Thyatira. She listened with great attention to Paul, became a believer, and was baptized, together with other members of her household. Lydia then convinced Paul to be a guest in her house, during his stay in Philippi.

One day, when Paul and his companions were going to offer prayer, they met a slave girl who was possessed by a spirit that allowed her to predict the future. Her owners earned a lot of money from her fortune telling. She followed Paul and his companions, shouting, "These men are servants of the Most High God, who proclaim to you how you can be saved!" She did this for many days, until Paul became so annoyed that he turned around and said to the spirit, "I command you, in the name of Jesus Christ, to come out of her". And at that moment, the spirit left her.

Her owners were very angry, when they realized that their income from her was gone now that she was no longer able to tell the future. They seized Paul and Silas and dragged them to the marketplace, before the authorities of the city. They complained to the magistrates, saying, "These Jews are disturbing our city by teaching customs that we, as Roman citizens, cannot lawfully accept or practice". The crowd joined in the attack against Paul and Silas, and the authorities tore their clothes and ordered them to be whipped.

Paul and Silas, after being severely beaten, were sent to jail. The jailer threw them into an inner cell and fastened their feet between heavy blocks of wood.

At midnight, Paul and Silas prayed and sang praises to God in a loud voice heard by the other prisoners. Suddenly, there was a great earthquake that shook the foundations of the prison; the doors were thrown open, and the chains fell off all the prisoners.

The jailer woke up and, seeing all the doors open, assumed that the prisoners had escaped. He pulled out his sword and was about to commit suicide, when Paul shouted, "Don't harm yourself! We are all here!"

The jailer called for a light, rushed into the cell, and, trembling, flung himself to the ground in front of Paul and Silas. Then, he brought them out and asked, "Sirs, what must I do to be saved?"

They told him, "Believe in the Lord Jesus Christ, and you and your family will be saved". Then, they preached to him and his family the word of God, and they baptized them that very moment. The jailer, full of joy that he and his family now believed in God, washed their wounds, brought them into his house, and gave them food to eat.

Early the next morning, the authorities sent officials with orders to the jailer to let Paul and Silas go free. The jailer told Paul, "The magistrates have released you. You can now leave. Go in peace".

Paul refused to leave, saying, "Although we are Roman citizens, and have not been condemned, they have publicly beaten us! They threw us in jail, and now, they want to send us away secretly. No, we will not go! Let them come themselves and let us out!"

When the magistrates realized that Paul and Silas were Roman citizens, and that they could get in trouble for having treated them like that, they hurried to the jail and apologized to them. They took Paul and Silas out of prison and asked them to please leave the city. The two men went to Lydia's house, where they met the believers, spoke to them words of encouragement and farewell, and departed from Philippi.

Paul and his companions went to Thessalonica, where they stayed in the house of a man called Jason. According to his usual custom, Paul went on the Sabbath to the synagogue. During three successive Sabbaths, he held discussions with the people and quoted verses of the Scriptures to prove that the Messiah had to suffer and rise from the dead, and that the announced Messiah was Jesus. A number of his Jewish listeners converted, and

so did many of the Greeks who believed in God, including several of the leading women of the city.

Some of the members of the synagogue, upset with Paul's teachings, gathered a mob, with the help of some ruffians, and assaulted the house of Jason, searching for Paul and Silas. When they did not find them in the house, they grabbed Jason and other Christians and took them to the rulers of the city, accusing them of saying that Jesus was their king, not the Roman emperor. The authorities made Jason and the others deposit security and allowed them to go. That same night, the believers sent Paul and Silas to the town of Berea for their safety.

In Berea, they went to the synagogue, where their preaching met with more success than in Thessalonica. Their listeners heard them with open minds and checked the Scriptures to verify if their assertions were true. Many converted, including some Greek men and women of high social standing.

The Jews of Thessalonica, when told that Paul was preaching in Berea, came to the town and incited the crowds against him. The believers immediately sent Paul to Athens, while Silas and Timothy remained in Berea, until Paul, having arrived in Athens, sent them word to come to him.

Paul, while waiting for his companions to arrive, walked around Athens and was shocked to see that the city was full of idols. He held discussions in the synagogue with the Jews and with the Gentiles who believed in God. He also went everyday to the marketplace, where he argued with any person who happened to pass by.

Some of the Epicurean and Stoic philosophers heard Paul talk about Jesus and the Resurrection, and they asked, "What is this babbler talking about?" Others answered, "He seems to be preaching about foreign gods". They took him to the Hill of Mars, where the Areopagus met to debate philosophical issues and legal cases, and asked him to explain his teachings.

Paul stood up and said, "Men of Athens, I can see that you are very religious. You even have an altar with the inscription, 'To the unknown God'. The God that you worship without knowing is the Creator of the world, and the Lord of heaven and earth. He does not reside in man-made temples, nor does he need anything from human hands, since he is the One that gives to all men life, breath, and everything. God is not like a gold, silver, or stone man-made image. God created one man from whom all nations descend, and he has fixed the day, on which, he will judge the world by means of a man he has chosen, and the proof is that he has raised that man from death!"

Some of his listeners, who did not believe in the resurrection of the dead, made fun of him, but many others expressed their willingness to hear him speak again. Paul left the Hill of Mars, accompanied by some people who believed him, among them Dionysius the Areopagite, and a woman named Damaris.

Paul left Athens and went to Corinth, where he stayed in the house of a man named Aquila and his wife Priscilla, a Jewish couple who had been expelled from Rome by the emperor Claudius, together with all the other Jews. In Corinth, they made their living by making tents, which was also Paul's trade.

Paul went to the synagogue every Sabbath and preached to the Jews and the Greeks. When Silas and Timothy arrived from Macedonia, they found him in the synagogue, testifying to the Jews that Jesus was the Messiah. The Jews opposed him and reviled him. Paul shook out his clothing and told them, "I am not responsible if your blood be upon your heads. From now on, I will go to the Gentiles". He moved to a house, right next to the synagogue, which belonged to Justus, a Gentile who worshipped God.

Paul had a vision, in the night, where God told him not to be afraid, and to continue preaching, because many people in the city were believers. Thus, encouraged, Paul stayed in Corinth for over a year and a half, a period, during which Crispus, the leader of the synagogue, converted, together with his whole family. Many Corinthians, hearing this, also converted and were baptized.

When Gallio became the Roman governor of Achaia, the Jews seized Paul and brought him before the tribunal, accusing him of trying to persuade people to worship God in a way that was against the law.

Before Paul could defend himself, Gallio said, "If this would be a matter of a crime or wrongdoing, I would be patient with you, Jews. But since the argument is about words, names, and your own law, you must settle it among yourselves. I will not be a judge of these matters", and he drove them away from the tribunal.

The Greeks who had witnessed the incident grabbed Sosthenes, the leader of the synagogue, and beat him in front of Gallio, who did nothing to stop them.

Paul left Corinth and departed for Syria, taking Aquila and Priscilla with him. Before sailing from Cenchrea, he had his head shaved to comply with a vow he had made. The ship made a stop in Ephesus, and Paul used the time to visit the local synagogue, and to preach there. The people asked him to stay in the city; he declined, but promised that, God willing, he would some day return to them.

When the time came for the ship to continue to Caesarea, Paul boarded the vessel without Aquila and Priscilla, who stayed in Ephesus. From Caesarea, Paul went to Antioch, where he stayed for a while, before going to the regions of Galatia and Phrygia, strengthening and encouraging all the local congregations of believers.

During a visit that Peter made to Antioch, Paul had a confrontation with him. He noticed that, after some men who had been sent by James from Jerusalem arrived in the city, Peter stopped eating with the Gentile converts, afraid that the men from Jerusalem would see him. Other Jewish converts, even Barnabas, also did the same.

Paul was unable to accept that behavior. He reproached Peter publicly, "You are a Jew and you live like a Gentile. How can you force Gentiles to live like Jews? We that were born Jews know that only our faith in Jesus Christ justifies us, and not doing what the Law demands us to do".

In the meantime in Ephesus, Aquila and Priscilla heard a speech about Jesus given in the synagogue by Apollos, an Alexandrian Jew well versed in Hebrew Scripture. They were impressed by his eloquence, but realized that his knowledge of Christianity was limited to John's baptism. They took Apollos under their wing, taught him the Way of God, and sent him to Achaia, carrying with him letters exhorting the local Christian community to receive him.

In Corinth, Apollos proved to be a convincing and effective Christian preacher. He succeeded in converting many Jews by proving and quoting the appropriate Hebrew Scriptures that Jesus was the Messiah.

He became so popular and respected among the Corinthian Christians that at one point there was a real danger that the congregation would become divided into three separate groups: the followers of Paul, the followers of Apollos, and the followers of Cephas, as Peter was called. This prompted Paul to write to the Corinthians that he had planted, and Apollos had watered, but both were servants of God, and that it was God alone who produced the results (1 Corinthians 3:6).

Paul arrived in Ephesus, after Apollos had already left. He met a group of about twelve disciples and asked them, "Did you receive the Holy Spirit when you became believers?"

"We have not even heard that there is a Holy Spirit", they answered.

"What kind of baptism did you receive?" he asked them.

"The baptism of John", they answered.

Paul explained to them that John, who baptized with the baptism of repentance, had taught his listeners that they should believe in the one that was to come after him, that is, in Jesus. The apostle then baptized them in the name of Jesus and placed his hands on them. The Holy Spirit came upon them, and they spoke in tongues and prophesied.

Paul spent the next three months in Ephesus, preaching in the synagogue, arguing and trying to teach the people about the Kingdom of God. When many of his listeners stubbornly rejected his teachings and spoke evil about the Way of God in front of the whole congregation, Paul left the synagogue, took the believers with him, and, for the next two years, taught daily in the hall of a man named Tyrannus.

His reputation as a miracle worker grew. People would take his handkerchiefs and aprons, and they would give them to the sick to cure them, and to expel evil spirits.

Some itinerant Jewish exorcists tried to imitate him. Among these false prophets, there were seven brothers, sons of a High Priest called Sceva. One of them said to a man possessed by an evil spirit, "I command you in the name of Jesus, whom Paul preaches". The evil spirit answered, "I know Jesus, and I know Paul, but who are you?" The man possessed by the evil spirit attacked the brothers with such violence that they ran away, wounded and naked.

This incident became known to all the people living in Ephesus, both Jews and Gentiles, who were filled with awe, and regarded the name of Jesus with greater honor. People came to Paul to confess their sins and bad deeds. Many of those who practiced magic brought their books and burned them publicly. It was calculated that the value of the burned books was around fifty thousand silver coins.

Paul had started thinking about going to Jerusalem, and from there to Rome, but for the time being, he continued to stay in the Roman province of Asia, today's Anatolia in Turkey. In the meantime, he sent two of his helpers, Timothy and Erastus, to preach in Macedonia.

Demetrius, a silversmith who earned his living making and selling silver statues of the goddess Diana, noticed a sharp reduction in the demand for idols. He attributed the decline in his income to Paul's successful missionary activities.

He called a meeting of the people of his craft and said to them, "You know that we make our living through our craft. This Paul has convinced many people, not only in Ephesus but in all the province of Asia, that our handmade gods are not gods. Our trade is in danger of coming into disrepute, and, even worse, the Temple of our great goddess Diana, worshipped by all in Asia and in the world, might come to mean nothing".

His listeners were enraged and shouted, "Great is Diana of Ephesus!"

The riot spread throughout the city. The mob caught two Macedonians, Gaius and Aristarchus, companions of Paul, and dragged them inside the theater. Paul attempted to enter into the theatre, but his disciples, fearful for his life, prevented him from doing so. Some of the authorities of the city, who were his friends, sent him a message, also advising him not to go into the theater.

The theater was a scene of utter confusion: some people shouting one thing, others something else, and most of them with no idea why they were there. Aristarchus and Gaius took advantage of the chaos and managed to escape from the theater.

Alexander, a convert to Christianity, attempted to calm the crowd, but, when he was recognized as a Jew, the people shouted him down, screaming for over two hours without stopping, "Diana of Ephesus is great!"

The town clerk calmed the crowd and said, "Nobody can deny that the Ephesians worship the goddess Diana. The men that you brought here have not robbed the Temple or blasphemed against our goddess. If Demetrius and his fellow craftsmen have a legitimate complaint against anybody, they should press charges in a court of law. We might be accused of unjustified rioting because of what happened today". He then dismissed the assembly.

After the calm had been restored, Paul called the believers, embraced them, and departed for Macedonia. From there, Paul moved to Greece, where he stayed for three months. While he was in Athens, he sent Timothy to Thessalonica to strengthen the faith of the Thessalonians, and to encourage them to endure their persecution. Timothy returned with good news about the faith and the love shown by the Thessalonians.

Paul was ready to go to Syria, but when he discovered that the Jews were plotting against him, he decided to return through Macedonia. He was accompanied on his trip by Sopater of Berea, by the Thessalonians, Aristarchus and Secundus, by Gaius of Derbe, by Timotheus, and by Tychicus and Trophimus of the region of Asia. They went ahead and waited for Paul in Troas.

Paul left Philippi, after the Festival of the Unleavened Bread. After sailing for five days, he arrived in Troas, where he met his companions, and stayed for a week. On Sunday, the day before his departure, his disciples joined him for breakfast; Paul preached to them and kept on speaking till midnight. They were all gathered in an upper floor, in a chamber brightly lighted by many burning lamps. A young man called Eutychus, who was sitting in the windowsill, fell asleep, while Paul preached, lost his equilibrium, and fell to the ground from the third floor. The people in the room looked down from the window and thought that he was dead, but Paul rushed downstairs, checked the boy, and, to everybody's relief, pronounced him alive. Paul then went back upstairs, ate a piece of bread, and resumed his teaching, before leaving in the early hours of the morning.

His companions sailed in the ship to Assos, where Paul, who had come by land, joined them. They continued to Mitylene, Chios, Samos, Trogyllium, until they arrived in Miletus. Paul was in a hurry to get back to Jerusalem by the day of Pentecost.

Paul took advantage of his stay in Miletus to send a message to the elders of the church in Ephesus, asking them to come to him.

When they arrived, he said to them, "I have served God with all humility and many tears, doing my work in spite of the plots of the Jews. I ask the Jews and the Greeks to repent and have faith in Jesus Christ. I am now going to Jerusalem, and don't know what will happen to me there, probably prison and trouble. As I do not expect to see any of you again, I warn you that, after my departure, fierce wolves will attack your flock, and some of your own people will speak perversely to lead astray the believers. I have never sought gold, silver, or clothing, and you yourselves know that I have worked with my own hands to provide anything that my companions and I have needed. I have shown you that by working hard, you should always help the weak. Remember the words of Jesus, 'It is more blessed to give than to receive'".

When Paul finished, he knelt down with them and prayed. Then, they accompanied him to the ship, crying as they hugged him and kissed him, knowing that they would never see him again.

The ship sailed straight to Coos; from there, the next day, they reached Rhodes, and then, they continued to Patara, where they found a ship going to Phoenicia. They passed by Cyprus, on their way to Syria, and landed at Tyre, where the ship unloaded its cargo.

They met believers in Tyre and stayed with them for seven days. These men advised Paul not to go to Jerusalem. When the time came for the ship's departure, the believers—men, women, and children—accompanied Paul to the port, where they all knelt and prayed, and bade one another farewell. Then, Paul and his companions boarded the ship, and the Tyrean believers returned to their homes.

The ship stopped for one day in Ptolemais, which gave Paul the opportunity to greet the believers of the city. The next day, they departed and came to Caesarea, where they stayed in the house of Philip, the evangelist, one of the seven men who had been chosen by the Jerusalem church to serve on the tables and distribute food to the needy of the congregation. He had settled in Caesarea with his four unmarried daughters, who also preached the gospel.

The prophet Agabus, whom Paul had met in Antioch many years before, came to visit them. The prophet took Paul's girdle, tied up his own feet and hands with it, and said, "This is what the Holy Spirit says, 'So shall the Jews at Jerusalem tie the man that owns this girdle, and shall hand him over to the Gentiles'".

Hearing this all those present begged Paul not to go to Jerusalem. He answered, "Why do you cry and break my heart? I am ready not only to be tied, but even to die at Jerusalem for the name of the Lord Jesus".

Seeing that he was adamant in his decision, they said, "The will of the Lord be done".

A few days later, Paul and some of his disciples from Caesarea went to Jerusalem and stayed in the house of Mnason of Cyprus, one of the first Christian converts. That night, many believers came and greeted him warmly. The next day, Paul and his companions went to see James, the brother of Jesus, and the other elders of the church, and told them all that God had done among the Gentiles through his work.

His listeners praised the Lord and said to him, "Brother, you can see that thousands of Jews have become believers, and they are all devoted to the Law. They have been told that you teach the Jews who live among the Gentiles to abandon the Law of Moses, telling them not to circumcise their children or follow the Jewish customs. What should be done? They will certainly hear that you have come. So this is what we want you to do. There are four men here who have taken a vow. Go with them and join them in the ceremony of purification; pay their expenses, so that they will be able to shave their heads. This way, the people will know that the rumors are false and that you yourself live in accordance with the Law of Moses. About the Gentiles, we have sent them a letter telling them not to eat food that had been offered to idols, or any blood, or any animal that has been strangled, and that they should not indulge in sexual immorality".

Paul took the men, and the next day, he performed the ceremony of purification with them. Then, he entered the Temple to give notice of how many days it would be, until the end of the period of purification, when a sacrifice would be offered for each one of them.

When the seven days were almost over, some Jews from the region of Asia, who were visiting Jerusalem, saw him in the Temple. They grabbed Paul and shouted, "Men of Israel, help us! This is the man who goes everywhere, inciting everyone against the Jews, the Law of Moses, and this Temple. And now he has brought some Gentiles into the Temple to defile this holy place!" They said that, because they had previously seen Paul walk around the city with a Gentile, Trophimus of Ephesus, and had assumed that Paul had brought him into the Temple to an area where only Jews were allowed to enter.

The aroused crowd ran to Paul, seized him, and dragged him out of the Temple. At once, the gatekeepers closed the Temple gates. The mob was trying to kill Paul, when Claudius Lysias, the commander of the Roman troops, who was told that the people of Jerusalem were rioting, ran toward the crowd with his soldiers and his centurions. When the people saw the soldiers coming, they stopped beating Paul.

The commander arrested Paul and ordered him to be bound with chains; he then asked the people, "Who is this man? And what has he done?"

Some of the men in the crowd shouted one thing, others something else. When the commander saw that he couldn't get a clear answer, he ordered his men to take Paul inside the fortress. The soldiers had to carry him, because the mob had become violent and threatened Paul's life.

Before entering the fortress, Paul asked the commander if he could have a word with him. Claudius Lysias asked him, "Do you speak Greek? Are you that Egyptian who recently stirred up a revolt and led a band of four thousand murderers in the desert?"

Paul answered, "I am a Jew, born in Tarsus, a citizen of an important city. Please allow me to speak to the people".

The commander gave him permission; Paul stood on the steps and made gestures with his hands to quiet the crowd. When they were silent, Paul spoke to them in Hebrew, saying, "Brothers and fathers, listen to my defense". Hearing him speak in Hebrew, they became even quieter. Paul continued, "I am a Jew, born in Tarsus, a city in Cilicia, but was brought up in Jerusalem, studying under Gamaliel. I was educated strictly according to the Law of our fathers and was as dedicated to God as are all of you now present. I persecuted to the death the people who followed the Way. I arrested men and women and put them in jail. The High Priest and the elders of the council can testify that I received letters from them written to our brothers in Damascus, authorizing me to arrest those people and bring them back in chains to

Jerusalem to be punished. I was almost at the end of my journey, approaching the city of Damascus, when suddenly about noon, a light from heaven flashed around me. I fell to the ground and heard a voice, saying, 'Saul, Saul, why do you persecute me?' I asked, 'Who are you, Lord?' The voice answered, 'I am Jesus, whom you persecute. Get up and go into the city, where you will be told what you must do'.

"The men who were traveling with me heard the voice but didn't see anyone. I had been blinded by the bright light, and so my companions had to take me by the hand and led me into Damascus. For three days, I was not able to see, and, during that time, I did not eat or drink anything.

"In that city, there was a man, called Ananias, a religious man who obeyed our Law, highly respected by all the Jews that lived there. He came to me and told me, 'Brother Paul, you can see again!' I recovered at that moment my sight, got up, and was baptized.

"I returned to Jerusalem, and while I was praying in the Temple, I had a vision, in which Jesus said to me, 'Hurry up, and leave Jerusalem as fast as you can, because the people here will not accept your testimony about me'. And I said, 'They know that I arrested and beat those who believe in you. When your martyr Stephen's blood was shed, I was right there witnessing his murder, and keeping the clothes of those who killed him'. And he said, 'Go, for I will send you far away to the Gentiles'".

The people, who had been listening in silence to Paul, started shouting, "Away with him! He doesn't deserve to live!" They screamed, waved their clothes, and threw dust into the air.

Claudius Lysias ordered his troops to take Paul into the fortress, and to whip him, in order to find out why the crowd shouted against him.

When he was being tied up, Paul said to the centurion that was standing by, "Is it lawful to whip a Roman citizen who has not been condemned?"

The centurion heard this, rushed to his commander, and said, "Be careful of what you do, because this man is a Roman citizen".

Claudius Lysias came to Paul and asked him, "Are you a Roman citizen?"

Paul answered, "Yes".

Claudius Lysias confided in him, "I became a Roman citizen by paying a lot of money".

Paul answered, "But I am a citizen by birth".

At once, the soldiers who were going to interrogate him drew back from him, and Claudius Lysias was frightened, when he realized that he had put a Roman citizen in chains.

The next morning, wanting to know the real reason why the Jews were accusing Paul, the commander took his chains off and ordered the chief priests and the whole Jewish Council to meet. He brought Paul to the council and made him stand before them.

Paul stared at the council members and said, "Brothers, I have lived with a clear conscience before God, until today".

The High Priest Ananias ordered those who were standing closest to Paul to hit him on the mouth.

Paul said to him, "God will strike you, you whitewashed wall! You are sitting here to judge me according to the Law, and at the same time, you break the Law by ordering them to hit me".

The men standing close to Paul said, "How dare you insult God's High Priest!"

Paul answered, "The Scriptures state, 'Do not speak evil of the ruler of your people'. Brothers, I didn't know that he was the High Priest".

Paul noticed that some members of the council were Sadducees, belonging to a sect, which did not believe in the resurrection of the dead nor in angels, while others were Pharisees, men who believed that the dead would one day live again.

He exclaimed, "Brothers, I am a Pharisee, the son of a Pharisee. I am being questioned here, because of my hope that the dead will rise to life!"

Immediately, the Sadducees and the Pharisees started to argue with each other, and the council was divided. Some of the members belonging to the Pharisee sect stood up and said, "We find no evil in this man. If a spirit or an angel has spoken to him, we should not fight against God!"

When the arguments in the council became violent, the commander, fearing that Paul would be torn to pieces by his opponents, ordered his soldiers, "Rescue him! Use force if necessary, and bring him back to the fortress".

That night, God spoke to Paul, "Be of good cheer. You have testified about me in Jerusalem, and now you must do it also in Rome".

The next day, a group of about forty Jews got together and made a vow that they would not eat nor drink, until they had killed Paul. They went to the chief priests and elders and said, "We have taken a solemn vow together that we will abstain from food, until we have killed Paul. We want you and the council to tell the Roman commander to bring Paul back to you tomorrow, so that you can interrogate him more closely. We will kill him, before he gets here".

Paul's nephew, the son of his sister, heard that the men were preparing to ambush Paul. He went to the fortress, where Paul was being held, and told his uncle about the plot against his life.

Paul called one of the centurions and said, "Take this young man to your commander, for he has something to tell him".

Paul's nephew was brought to the presence of Claudius Lysias. The Roman commander took him by the hand, led him aside, away from prying ears, and asked him, "What is it that you want to tell me?"

The young man answered, "The Jews have agreed to ask you to bring Paul tomorrow back to them, pretending that they wish to interrogate him more closely. Don't listen to them, because more than forty men, who have vowed to kill him, will be waiting in ambush".

Claudius Lysias instructed him not to tell anyone what he had told him, and then, he sent the young man away. He called two centurions and said, "Take two hundred soldiers, seventy horsemen, and two hundred spearmen, and get ready to leave for Caesarea tonight at the third hour. Provide a horse for Paul to ride, and convey him safely to Felix, the governor".

Claudius Lysias then sat down to write a self-serving letter to the Roman governor, where he tried to put himself in the best possible light. He wrote:

Claudius Lysias sends greetings to His Excellency, Governor Felix: This man was seized by the Jews who would have killed him if I, having learned that he was a Roman citizen, hadn't come with my soldiers and rescued him.

Wishing to know the accusations against him, I brought him to their council and found that the accusations merely referred to questions about their own religious law, and that the man had done nothing deserving of death or jail.

When I was informed that the Jews were planning to ambush him, I sent him to you at once.

I have told his accusers to personally bring to you their charges against him.

The troop departed Jerusalem, taking Paul with them. That night, they got as far as Antipatris. The next morning, the foot soldiers returned to Jerusalem, and the horsemen proceeded to Caesarea, where they delivered Claudius Lysias' letter to Felix and turned Paul over to him.

Felix read the letter and asked Paul, "From which province are you?"

Paul answered, "I am from Cilicia".

The governor said, "I will give you a hearing when your accusers arrive". Then, he gave orders that, in the meantime, Paul should be kept in Herod's Judgment Hall.

The High Priest Ananias arrived in Caesarea five days later, to present to the governor the charges against Paul. He brought with him several elders, and a spokesman called Tertullus.

Tertullus stood up, before Felix, and said, "First of all, we wish to thank you, Governor Felix, for the peace that we are enjoying, and for the excellent reforms that you have carried out for the good of our country. But I do not wish to take too much of your time; I will be brief. I beg you to be kind and hear my

account. This is a pestilent man; he incites the Jews all over the world to riot, and is one of the ringleaders of the Nazarene sect. We caught him, when he attempted to defile the Temple, and would have judged him according to our Law if the commander Lysias, by violent means, had not taken him away from us, and commanded us to bring charges against him before you. If you examine him yourself, you will verify our accusations".

The Jews joined in the accusation and said that all the charges were true. The governor motioned to Paul to speak in his own defense.

Paul said, "I am glad to defend myself in front of you, because I know that you have been a judge over this nation for many years. As you can easily find out, it was only twelve days ago that I went to Jerusalem to worship. They did not find me in the Temple arguing with any man, or inciting them to riot, either in the synagogues or anywhere else in the city. They cannot prove the charges that they have brought against me.

"I confess to you that, although I worship the God of my ancestors, and fully believe in the Law and the prophets, I do so following the Way, which they consider heretical. I share their hope that all the people, both the good and the bad, will resurrect from death. My conscience, before God and man, is clear. After many years abroad, I have returned to offer sacrifices, bringing donations to my people.

"Some Jews from the region of Asia saw me in the Temple, when I had completed the ceremony of purification. It is not true that there was a crowd with me, nor was there a riot. They themselves should be here before you and personally accuse me if they have anything against me. The real reason why I am being tried by you today is for believing in the resurrection of the dead".

Felix, who was well informed of the Way, declined to make a decision at that moment and said, "I will wait for the Commander Lysias to come here and give me a fuller report". He ordered a centurion to keep Paul under guard, but to give him some freedom and allow his friends to attend to his needs.

A few days later, Felix, with his Jewish wife

Drusilla, spoke to Paul, who told him about his faith in Jesus. When Paul started talking about justice, self-control, and the Judgment Day, Felix became uneasy and cut short the meeting, telling Paul to go away, and that he would call him, when he had the opportunity.

That was the first of many conversations that Felix had with Paul. Actually, his interest was not purely religious; he hoped that Paul would give him money.

Two years later, when Porcius Festus, the new governor, arrived to replace him, Felix, wishing to ingratiate himself with Paul's enemies, put him in jail.

Three days after his arrival, Festus went to Jerusalem and met the High Priest and the leaders of the people. They presented their accusations against Paul and asked Festus, with the secret intention of killing Paul, to have the apostle brought to Jerusalem. Festus refused their request and, instead, asked them to come to Caesarea with him, and to repeat there their charges against Paul.

After staying eight or ten days in Jerusalem, Festus returned to Caesarea. The next day, he ordered that Paul should be brought to the Judgment Hall, where the Jews who had come from Jerusalem made serious charges against him, but were not able to prove them.

Paul said, "I reject all the charges, because I am innocent".

Festus, trying to ingratiate himself with the Jews, asked him, "Are you willing to go to Jerusalem and be judged by me there?"

Paul answered, "If I had broken the law and deserved to die, I would not try to evade my punishment. But if there is no truth in their charges, no one can deliver me to them". Exercising his rights as a Roman citizen, he added, "I appeal to the emperor!"

Festus, after consulting with his advisers, decreed, "You have appealed to the emperor, so to the emperor, you will go".

Sometime later, King Agrippa—Herod Agrippa II—the great grandson of Herod the Great, came to Caesarea with his sister Bernice to visit Festus. After several days of official festivities, Festus consulted the case of Paul with the king.

"There is a man left in jail by Felix", he said, "against whom the chief priests and the elders of the Jews brought charges, during my visit to Jerusalem, and asked me to condemn him. I told them that it was not the custom of the Romans to hand over any accused man, before he has met his accusers face to face and has the opportunity to defend himself. When they came here, I didn't waste any time, and the next day, I sat in the Judgment Hall and ordered the man to be brought in. The accusers stood up but did not bring any charge of evil doings; they just argued certain points about their own religion, and about a man named Jesus, who is dead, but whom Paul claims that is alive. Not being sure of how to proceed, I asked Paul if he would be willing to go to Jerusalem and be tried there on these charges. He demanded to be kept in custody for the decision of the emperor, so I gave orders to hold him, until I could send him to the emperor".

Agrippa said to Festus, "I would like to hear this man myself".

Festus answered, "Tomorrow, you will hear him".

The next morning, King Agrippa and Bernice came to the Governor's Palace with great pomp, accompanied by military commanders and the leading citizens of the city.

When Paul was brought in, Festus spoke to the gathering, "King Agrippa, and all men who are present here, the Jews who live in Caesarea and in Jerusalem have asked me to put to death the man that you see here. I have not found him guilty of any charge deserving death, but, as he has appealed to the emperor, I have decided to send him to Rome. But I have nothing specific to write to my emperor about him. Therefore, I have brought him before this assembly, and especially before you, King Agrippa, so that, after we have interrogated him, I may have something to write. It doesn't seem reasonable to me to send a prisoner without specifying the charges against him".

King Agrippa said to Paul, "You have permission to speak for yourself".

Paul stretched out his hand and said, "I am fortunate, King Agrippa, that today I am able to defend myself before you against all the accusations of the Jews, because you are an expert regarding all the customs and disputes of the Jews. Please listen to me with patience.

"The events of my life, during my youth, among my own nation and at Jerusalem, are known to all the Jews. Those who know me then can testify, if they are willing, that I was a Pharisee, a member of the strictest sect of our religion. I stand now on trial for having hope in the promise that God made to our ancestors, for which our twelve tribes pray to God day and night. Why should it be incredible to you that God can raise the dead?

"I was very active in Jerusalem against the believers in Jesus. I put many of them in prison, and voted for their death penalty. I punished them many times in the synagogues, and tried to make them blaspheme. I was so angry against them that I even went to foreign cities to persecute them.

"That is why I went to Damascus with the full knowledge and authorization of the chief priests. At midday, I saw a light from heaven, brighter than the sun, shining around me and my companions. And when we had fallen to the ground, I heard a voice, saying to me in Hebrew, 'Saul, Saul, why do you persecute me?' I asked, 'Who are you, Lord?' And the voice answered, 'I am Jesus whom you are persecuting. Rise and stand on your feet. I have appeared to you to appoint you to serve me, and to testify of what you have seen, and what I will show you in the future. I will rescue you from the Jews and from the Gentiles, to whom I am now sending you. Open their eyes and turn them from darkness to light, from the power of Satan to God, so that they may have their sins forgiven and find their place among those who are sanctified through their faith in me'.

"King Agrippa, I didn't disobey the vision from heaven. First in Damascus, and then in Jerusalem, and afterward in the whole country of Judea and among the Gentiles, I preached that they must repent and turn to God, and perform deeds proving their repentance.

"It is for this reason that the Jews seized me in the Temple and tried to kill me. I continue to this day, with God's help, to testify to small and great, saying nothing but what the prophets and Moses said would come to pass. That Christ would suffer, that he would be the first to rise from the dead, and proclaim light to the Jews and to the Gentiles".

Festus interrupted him, shouting, "Paul, you are crazy! Too much learning has made you mad!"

Paul said, "I am not mad, most noble Festus. I am speaking the sober truth. The king understands these things, and to him, I speak freely. I am convinced that none of these things has escaped his notice, because all this has not happened away in a corner".

Addressing himself to the king, Paul asked, "King Agrippa, do you believe in the prophets? I know you do".

Agrippa answered, "You think that you can convert me in such a short time?"

Paul replied, "I wish that not only you, but all those that hear me today might become as I am, except for these chains, of course".

The king rose up and brought the proceedings to an end. Festus and Agrippa commented among themselves that Paul was innocent, but acknowledged that they were powerless to help him, because, once the apostle had appealed to Rome for a ruling, the case was out of their jurisdiction.

Paul was handed to Julius, a centurion of the Augustus regiment, who was in charge of the prisoners who were being sent from Caesarea to Rome. Paul was accompanied by Luke and by Aristarchus. When the ship made a stopover in Sidon, Julius kindly permitted Paul to go ashore and visit his friends. The ship then continued to Cyprus, and from there to Myra, a city in Lycia. There, the centurion transferred the prisoners to a ship that was sailing from Alexandria to Italy.

Later, when the ship was near Crete, Paul felt that, due to the weather at that time of the year, it would not be advisable to continue the voyage, because there was great danger that the ship would sink with the loss of the cargo and the drowning of the two hundred and seventy-six persons that were on board. He mentioned his misgivings to the centurion, but Julius disregarded Paul's warnings and allowed the captain and the owner of the ship to continue with the trip.

A fierce storm that lasted many days threatened to sink the ship. Paul encouraged his fellow prisoners to be brave, by telling them that an angel of God had told him in a vision that nobody in the ship would drown. On the fourteenth night, Paul begged them to eat something and again assured them that they would all be saved.

The next morning, the ship ran aground near the shore of an island. The front part of the ship got stuck and could not be moved, and the rear started to break into pieces by the violence of the waves. The soldiers, afraid that the prisoners would take advantage of the situation to jump overboard and swim to freedom, decided to kill them all. Julius stopped them from carrying out their plan. Instead, he ordered all those prisoners who could swim to jump into the sea and swim to the land. The other prisoners followed, holding on to planks and broken pieces of the ship. Everybody was saved.

The people in the island—it was Malta—were very kind to the shipwrecked prisoners. It was very cold, and it started to rain, so they built a fire to warm them. Paul gathered a bundle of sticks and was putting them on the fire, when a snake came out of the heat and fastened itself to his hand. The islanders saw the snake hanging from Paul's hand and said to one another, "This prisoner must be a murderer, because, though he escaped drowning in the sea, fate will not let him live".

Paul shook the snake into the fire, and the islanders waited to see him become swollen and fall down dead. After quite sometime, with Paul not showing any signs of being harmed, they changed their minds and said with awe, "He is a god!"

Publius, the Roman governor of the island, received Paul and his companions kindly and lodged them for three days in the property that he owned near the area where the ship had ran aground. Publius' father was in bed ill with fever and dysentery. Paul went into his room, prayed, placed his hands on him, and healed him. When this was known, all the sick people on the island came and were healed. Full of gratitude, they gave Paul many gifts.

Paul stayed in Malta for three months, and when he sailed, the people put on board all kinds of things that Paul and his companions might need, during the voyage. From Malta, the prisoners were taken to Syracuse in an Alexandrian ship, which flew the flag of the Roman gods Castor and Pollux. The ship made a three-day stop in Syracuse and then continued to Rome, where Paul was greeted by a group of believers, and Julius delivered the prisoners to the captain of the guard.

Paul was allowed to live by himself, guarded by a soldier. After three days, Paul called the leaders of the Jewish community to a meeting. When they had gathered, he told them, "Brothers, though I have done nothing against our people or against the customs of our ancestors, I was taken prisoner in Jerusalem and handed over to the Romans. After they questioned me, the Romans wanted to set me free, because they found that I had done nothing, for which, I deserved to die. But because the Jews opposed this, I had no choice but to appeal to the emperor, even though I have nothing to accuse my own people. That is why I wanted to see you and speak with you, because I am bound with this chain for the sake of him who is the hope of Israel".

They replied, "We have never received any letters from Judea concerning you, and none of the people that have come from there have said anything bad about you. We wish to hear your ideas, because everybody is speaking against your sect".

They arranged a date for their next visit, and many of them came on that day. Paul explained to them, from morning to night, his message about the Kingdom of God, and he tried to convince them about Jesus by quoting from the teachings of Moses and the writings of the prophets. Some of his listeners became believers; others were not convinced. They left, disagreeing among themselves.

As they were leaving, Paul told them that the prophet Isaiah had said, "You will listen, but you will not understand; you will look, but you will not see; because the people have stopped up their ears and closed their eyes". Paul concluded: "God's message of salvation has been sent to the Gentiles. They will listen!"

Paul spent the next two years living in Rome, in a rented house, where he welcomed all those who came to see him. He preached the Kingdom of God and taught about Jesus Christ, speaking openly and freely. During this time, he wrote letters to churches in several cities of the Roman Empire.

Scholars, based on the writings of early church historians, believe that Paul was killed in Rome, during Nero's persecution of the Christians.

Paulus

(Latin origin: *Pause*)

(Acts of the Apostles 13:7). A.D. 1st century. Sergius Paulus was the Roman proconsul in the city of Paphos, in the island of Cyprus. (Please see the entry for Sergius.)

Pedahel

(Hebrew origin: *God has ransomed*)

(Numbers 34:28). 13th century B.C. Pedahel, son of Ammihud, was a leader of the tribe of Naphtali, chosen to help apportion the land of Canaan among the Hebrew tribes.

Pedahzur

(Hebrew origin: *The Rock has ransomed*)

(Numbers 1:10). 14th century B.C. Pedahzur was the father of Gamaliel, the leader of the tribe of Manasseh. His son commanded his tribe's army, during the march in the wilderness, and was one of the twelve Israelite leaders who donated gifts of silver and gold, bulls, rams, goats, and lambs for the dedication of the altar.

Pedaiah

(Hebrew origin: *God has ransomed*)

1. (2 Kings 23:36). 7th century B.C. Pedaiah of Rumah was the father of Zebudah, the wife of King Josiah and the mother of King Jehoiakim.

2. (1 Chronicles 3:18). 6th century B.C. Pedaiah was one of the seven sons of Jehoiachin, the king who was deposed and taken captive by the Babylonians, after reigning for only three months.

Pedaiah's brothers were Salathiel, Hoshama, Malchiram, Shenazar, Jecamiah, and Nedabiah. His sons were Shimei and Zerubbabel, the leader of the first group of exiles that returned from Babylon.

Note: The book of Ezra states that the father of Zerubbabel was not Pedaiah, but Salathiel, although it spells this name as Shealtiel (Ezra 3:2).

3. (1 Chronicles 27:20). 11th century B.C. Pedaiah was the father of Joel, a leader of half the tribe of Manasseh, during the reign of King David.

4. (Nehemiah 3:25). 5th century B.C. Pedaiah, son of Parosh, helped to repair the walls of Jerusalem, during the days of Nehemiah. Pedaiah was among the leaders who stood next to Ezra, upon a pulpit of wood, when the scribe read the Law of Moses to the people in the marketplace (Nehemiah 8:4).

5. (Nehemiah 11:7). Unspecified date. Pedaiah, the son of Kolaiah and father of Joed, was an ancestor of Sallu, a Benjamite who settled in Jerusalem, after his return from the Babylonian Exile.

6. (Nehemiah 13:13). 5th century B.C. Pedaiah, a Levite, was one of the four persons designated by Nehemiah to supervise the treasuries of the Temple, and to distribute the offerings among the Levites and the priests. The other three supervisors were Shelemiah the Priest, Zadok the Scribe, and Hanan.

Pekah

(Hebrew origin: *Observer*)

(2 Kings 15:25). 8th century B.C. Pekah, son of Remaliah, was the commander of the army of King Pekahiah of Israel. He entered into a conspiracy against the king, and at the

head of fifty men of Gilead, Pekah assaulted the royal palace in Samaria, killed Pekahiah and two of his officers, and proclaimed himself king, the eighteenth king of Israel, since the partition.

When the Assyrian Empire threatened his kingdom, he entered into an alliance with Rezin, the king of Syria, against Ahaz, the king of Judah, to force him to join them against the Assyrians.

The two allied kings invaded Judah and besieged Jerusalem. Ahaz, afraid of his impending defeat, reverted to idolatry and sacrificed one of his sons to pagan gods.

The invaders' aim was to depose the king and install a certain son of Tabeal in his place (Isaiah 7:6), but they were unable to capture the city. However, Rezin succeeded in capturing and annexing the Judean port of Elath, in the south of the country.

Pekah defeated the army of Judah, killed over one hundred thousand enemy soldiers, and captured tens of thousands of men, women, and children, whom he brought to Samaria with the intention of using them as slaves.

Oded, a prophet who lived in Israel, was outraged. Supported by several leaders of Israel, he demanded that the king should free the captives immediately and return them to Judah. The captives were given clothing, shoes, food, and drink, and were taken back to the city of Jericho in Judah.

King Ahaz of Judah requested the help of Tiglathpileser, king of Assyria, against Aram and Israel, and sent him the treasuries of the Temple and the royal palace as a tribute.

The king of Assyria attacked Damascus, captured it, and killed King Rezin. He then proceeded to invade Israel. He conquered a large part of its territory, which he annexed to the Assyrian Empire, and deported most of the population to Assyria. The kingdom of Israel was reduced to its capital Samaria and its surrounding areas.

After reigning for twenty years, Pekah was killed by Hoshea, son of Elah, who was the last king to rule Israel, until its final destruction by the Assyrians.

Pekahiah

(Hebrew origin: *God has observed*)

(2 Kings 15:22). 8th century B.C. Pekahiah, the seventeenth king of Israel, since the partition, succeeded his father Menahem and reigned for two years, until his army commander Pekah killed him and proclaimed himself king.

Pelaiah

(Hebrew origin: *God has distinguished*)

1. (1 Chronicles 3:24). Unspecified date. Pelaiah, son of Elioenai, was a descendant of Jeconiah, also called Jehoiachin, the king of Judah, who was taken to captivity in Babylon. Pelaiah's brothers were Eliashib, Akkub, Anani, Johanan, Dalaiah, and Hodaiah.

2. (Nehemiah 8:7). 5th century B.C. Pelaiah was one of the Levites who explained the Law to the people in Jerusalem, after Ezra the Scribe had read it in front of the open space, before the Water Gate.

He was also one of the Levites who signed Nehemiah's solemn agreement to separate themselves from the foreigners living in the land, to refrain from intermarrying with them, to dedicate their firstborn to God, and other obligations (Nehemiah 10:10).

Pelaliah

(Hebrew origin: *God has judged*)

(Nehemiah 11:12). Unspecified date. Pelaliah, son of Amzi and father of Jeroham, was an ancestor of Adaiah, a priest who served in the Temple, during the days of Nehemiah.

Pelatiah

(Hebrew origin: *God has delivered*)

1. (1 Chronicles 3:21). 6th century B.C. Pelatiah, son of Hananiah and brother of Jesaiah, was a descendant of the royal family of Judah. His grandfather Zerubbabel was the leader of the first group of captives who returned from the Babylonian Exile.

2. (1 Chronicles 4:42). 8th century B.C. Pelatiah, son of Ishi, and his brothers—Neariah, Rephaiah, and Uzziel, of the tribe of Simeon—at the head of five hundred men, went to Mount Seir, southeast of the Dead Sea, exterminated the last surviving Amalekites, and settled in the region.

3. (Nehemiah 10:22). 5th century B.C. Pelatiah was among the leaders who signed Nehemiah's solemn agreement to separate themselves from the foreigners living in the land, to refrain from intermarrying with them, and to dedicate their firstborn to God, among other obligations.

4. (Ezekiel 11:1). 6th century B.C. Pelatiah, son of Benaiah, was a leader of the people and a false prophet. The prophet Ezekiel, in a vision, saw Pelatiah standing at the east gate of the Temple, falsely assuring the people that Jerusalem would not be destroyed, and then, suddenly, while Ezekiel prophesied, Pelatiah died.

Peleg

(Hebrew origin: *Divided*)

(Genesis 10:25). Unspecified date. Peleg, a descendant of Noah and Shem, was the son of Eber and the brother of Joktan. He was thirty years old, when his son Reu—called Ragau by Luke (Luke 3:35)—was born. After that, he lived for another two hundred and nine years and had other sons and daughters. His name is spelled Phalec, in Luke's genealogy of Jesus (Luke 3:35).

Pelet

(Hebrew origin: *Escape*)

1. (1 Chronicles 2:47). Unspecified date. Pelet was the son of Jahdai and the brother of Ephah, Regem, Jotham, Gesham, and Shaaph.

2. (1 Chronicles 12:3). 11th century B.C. Pelet was the son of Azmaveth, one of King David's mighty warriors. Pelet and his brother Jeziel were part of a group of Benjamites, commanded by Ahiezer, who deserted King Saul's army and joined

David's band at Ziklag. They were skilled warriors who could use both their right and left hands to shoot arrows and sling stones.

Peleth

(Hebrew origin: *Swiftness*)

1. (Numbers 16:1). 14th century B.C. Peleth was the father of On, one of the leaders of Korah's rebellion against Moses.

2. (1 Chronicles 2:33). Unspecified date. Peleth, son of Jonathan, of the tribe of Judah, was the brother of Zaza.

Peninnah

(Hebrew origin: *Pearl*)

(1 Samuel 1:2). 11th century B.C. Peninnah was one of the two wives—the other was Hannah—of a man named Elkanah, who lived in Ramathaimzophim. Peninnah, who had several children, was jealous that Elkanah loved Hannah more, and she constantly provoked her, because Hannah was barren and desperate to have a child.

Penuel

(Hebrew origin: *Face of God*)

1. (1 Chronicles 4:4). Unspecified date. Penuel, son of Hur, of the tribe of Judah, was the father of Gedor and the brother of Ezer.

2. (1 Chronicles 8:25). Unspecified date. Penuel, son of Shashak, was a leader of the tribe of Benjamin who lived in Jerusalem.

Peor

(Hebrew origin: *A gap*)

(Numbers 25:18). Peor was a pagan deity worshipped by the Midianites on the mountain of the same name. (Please see the entry for Baalpeor [Numbers 25:3].)

Peresh

(Hebrew origin: *Dung*)

(1 Chronicles 7:16). 16th century B.C.

Peresh, a descendant of Manasseh, was the son of Machir and his wife Maachah. His brother was Sheresh, and his sons were Ulam and Rakem. His mother Maachah was the sister of Huppim and Shuppim.

Perez

(Hebrew origin: *Breach*)

(1 Chronicles 27:3). 17th century B.C. Perez—also called Phares (Matthew 1:3), and Pharez (Genesis 38:29)—son of Judah, and his daughter-in-law, Tamar, was one of the seventy Israelites who immigrated to Egypt.

His mother Tamar had been first married to Er, and then to Onan, the two eldest sons of Judah. Both her husbands died young and childless. Tamar expected Judah to give her in marriage to Shelah, his youngest son, but when the boy grew up, and Judah showed no sign of marrying him to Tamar, she tricked Judah into making love to her.

She became pregnant from this encounter and gave birth to twins, Perez and Zarah. During the birth, the midwife saw Zarah's hand and tied a scarlet thread on it, but it was Perez who first came out.

Perez was the ancestor of the clans of the Pharzites. His sons Hezron and Hamul were also ancestors of clans.

Perida

(Hebrew origin: *Dispersion*)

(Nehemiah 7:57). 10th century B.C. Perida—called Peruda in the book of Ezra (Ezra 2:55)—was a servant of Solomon, and the ancestor of a family that returned with Zerubbabel from the Babylonian Exile.

Persis

(Greek origin: *A Persian woman*)

(Romans 16:12). A.D. 1st century. Persis was a Christian woman, very active in the church, for whom Paul felt great affection. The apostle sent her greetings in his letter to the Christians in Rome, calling her "beloved".

Peruda

(Hebrew origin: *Dispersion*)

(Ezra 2:55). 10th century B.C. Peruda—called Perida in the book of Nehemiah (Nehemiah 7:57)—was a servant of Solomon, and the ancestor of a family that returned with Zerubbabel from the Babylonian Exile.

Peter

(Latin origin: *Rock*)

(Matthew 4:18). A.D. 1st century. Peter was the name given by Jesus to his disciple Simon, son of Jonas, to symbolize that he was the "rock", upon which his church would be built. Paul usually called him Cephas, which is the Latinized form of the Greek word for "rock".

Simon Peter and his brother Andrew were born in the town of Bethsaida and lived in Capernaum in the northern shore of the Sea of Galilee, where they earned their living as fishermen.

According to John's gospel, Andrew, the brother of Simon Peter, had been a disciple of John the Baptist. One day, he heard John saying that Jesus was the Lamb of God. After he met Jesus and spent the rest of the day with him, Andrew went in search of his brother and told him, "We have found the Messiah!"

He brought Simon Peter to Jesus, who said to him, "You are Simon, the son of Jona. You will be called Cephas, the rock".

The next time that Simon Peter met Jesus was several weeks later, when Jesus was walking along the shore of the Lake of Galilee. Jesus climbed into the boat that belonged to the two brothers, Simon Peter and Andrew, and asked them to push off a little from the shore. He sat in the boat and taught the crowd from there. After he finished teaching, he told Simon Peter to push the boat further out, and to lower the nets for a catch.

Simon Peter said, "Master, we have worked hard the whole night, and caught nothing, but if you say so, we will let down the nets".

They lowered the nets and caught so many fish that they told their partners in the other boat to come and help them. They came and pulled up such a great quantity of fish that their boats began to sink.

Simon Peter fell on his knees, before Jesus, and said, "Go away from me, Lord, I am a sinful man".

Jesus told Simon Peter, "Don't be afraid. Come with me, and I will teach you to catch men".

Simon Peter and his partners, James and John, the sons of Zebedee, brought the boats back to the beach. Jesus called them, and they immediately left their boat and their father and went with him.

One Sabbath, after Jesus and his disciples had come out of the synagogue, where Jesus had cured a man possessed by an evil spirit, they went to the house of Simon Peter and Andrew. Jesus was told that Simon's mother-in-law was sick with a high fever. He went to her, took her by the hand, and helped her to get up. The fever left her, and she felt so well that she began to wait on them.

On the evening of the day, when Jesus had miraculously fed a great multitude with bread and fishes, and then had gone out to the hills by himself, the disciples entered a boat and sailed toward Capernaum. During the night, a great wind started blowing and stirring the sea. They rowed for several hours, but they only managed to advance about three or four miles, because the wind blowing against them prevented them from reaching land. Suddenly, they saw Jesus coming to them, walking over the water, and they were terrified, because they thought that they were seeing a spirit.

"Don't be afraid", said Jesus. "It is I".

Simon Peter answered, "Lord, if it is really you, order me to come out on the water to you".

"Come", answered Jesus.

Simon Peter got out of the boat and started walking on the water, but when he noticed the strong wind, he became afraid and started to sink. "Save me, Lord", he cried.

Jesus reached out and grabbed him. "You have so little faith! Why did you doubt?"

They got into the boat, and immediately, the boat reached land at the place that they had intended.

On one occasion, Jesus asked his disciples, "What do people say about the Son of man?"

"Some say you are John the Baptist", they answered, "Others say that you are Elijah, Jeremiah, or some other prophet".

Jesus asked them, "And you, what do you think?"

Simon Peter answered, "You are the Messiah, the Son of God".

Jesus said to him, "Bless you, Simon, son of Jona! This revelation has not come to you from any human being, but it came to you directly from my Father in heaven. You, Peter, are a rock, and upon this rock, I will build my church. I will give you the keys of the kingdom of heaven; what you prohibit on earth will be prohibited in heaven, and what you permit on earth will be permitted in heaven".

Then, Jesus ordered his disciples not to say to anyone that he was the Messiah, and from that time on, he began to tell them that he would have to go to Jerusalem, to suffer at the hand of the elders, the chief priests, and the scribes. He added, "I will be killed, but three days later, I will come back to life".

Simon Peter took him aside and rebuked him. "God forbid it, Lord", he said, "This must never happen to you".

Jesus turned around and exclaimed to Simon Peter, "Get away from me, Satan! You are an offence to me, because these thoughts of yours come from man, not from God".

Six days later, Jesus took Simon Peter, John, and James with him and went up a high hill, where they were alone. Suddenly, Jesus was transfigured: his face shined like the sun, and his clothes became dazzling white. Next to him stood Moses and the prophet Elijah.

Simon Peter said, "It is good that we are here, so that we can make three tents: one for you, one for Moses, and one for Elijah".

A cloud appeared and covered them with its shadow, and a voice from the cloud said, "This is my beloved Son, with whom I am well pleased. Listen to him!"

The disciples, terrified, flung themselves to the ground. As they came down the mountain, Jesus asked them not to tell anyone about their vision.

Jesus touched them and said, "Get up, don't be afraid".

They lifted their faces and looked around, and they saw that only Jesus was with them. Going down the hill, Jesus told them, "Do not tell anybody what you have seen, until the Son of man has risen from death".

When they returned to Capernaum, the tax collectors came to Simon Peter and asked him, "Does your master pay the tax?"

"Yes", answered Simon Peter.

When he entered the house, Jesus asked him, "Simon, what do you think? From whom do the kings collect taxes: from their own subjects or from foreigners?

Simon Peter answered, "From foreigners".

Jesus replied, "That means that the subjects do not have to pay. But we have no intention to offend these people. Go to the sea and drop in a line. Pull up the first fish that you catch, and you will find a coin in its mouth. Take it and pay them your taxes and mine".

Simon Peter came to Jesus and asked, "Lord, if my brother keeps sinning against me, how many times shall I forgive him? Seven times?" Jesus answered, "No, not seven times, but seventy-seven".

Simon Peter said to Jesus, "Your disciples have left everything to follow you. What will we have?"

Jesus assured them that when the Son of man would sit on his glorious throne, the twelve disciples would also sit on thrones, to judge the twelve tribes of Israel.

Jesus and his disciples came to Jerusalem for the Festival of Unleavened Bread. Jesus sent Simon Peter and John to get the Passover meal ready for them. He instructed them to follow a man carrying a jar of water into the house that he would enter, and then to ask the owner of the house to show them the room where they would eat the meal. The disciples did as Jesus had instructed, and they prepared the Passover meal.

When it was evening, Jesus came to the house with the twelve disciples and sat down to eat. Jesus took a piece of bread, gave a prayer of thanks, broke it, and gave it to his disciples. "Take it and eat it; this is my body", he said. Then, he took a cup, gave thanks to God, and gave it to them. "Drink it, all of you", he said, "this is my blood, which seals God's covenant".

He then rose from the table, took off his outer garment, and tied a towel around his waist. He poured water into a washbasin, began to wash the feet of his disciples, and dried them with the towel. When he came to Peter, Peter asked him, "Lord, why do you wash my feet?"

Jesus answered, "You don't understand now what I am doing, but you will understand it later".

Simon Peter said, "I refuse to have you wash my feet!"

Jesus said, "If you don't let me wash you, you will no longer be my disciple!"

Simon Peter answered, "Lord, if that is the case, wash not only my feet, but also my hands and my head".

Jesus said, "Anyone who has already bathed himself is perfectly clean, and only has to wash his feet. You are clean, but not all of you". He said this, because he knew who was going to betray him.

After he finished washing their feet, he put on his outer garment, sat down, and asked them, "Do you understand what I have done to you? You rightly call me Master and Lord. If, I, your Master and Lord, have washed your feet, you, then, should wash one another's feet. No slave is greater than his master, and no messenger is greater than the one who sent him".

He was silent for a moment, and then, with great emotion, he said, "Truly, I tell you, one of you will betray me".

The disciples looked at one another, not knowing whom he meant. One of the disciples, whom Jesus loved very much, was sitting next to him. Simon Peter gestured to him and said, "Ask him about whom is he speaking".

The disciple asked Jesus, "Lord, who is he?"

Jesus answered, "He is the one to whom I will give a piece of bread, after I dip it". He dipped it and gave it to Judas Iscariot. Then, he said to Judas, "Do quickly what you are going to do". Judas got up and left immediately. The other disciples thought that Jesus had sent him to buy something.

After they had dined, Jesus took his disciples to the Mount of Olives and told them, "Tonight you will all run away and leave me alone. But after I come back to life, I will go to Galilee ahead of you".

Peter spoke up and said to Jesus, "Even if all the others leave you, I will not do so!"

Jesus said, "I tell you that, before the rooster crows tonight, you will deny three times knowing me".

Peter answered, "I will never deny you, even if I have to die with you". And all the other disciples said the same thing.

Then, Jesus came with them to a place called Gethsemane and told his disciples to wait there, while he would go and pray a little distance away. He took with him Simon Peter and the two sons of Zebedee. Grief and anguish came over him, and he said to them, "The sorrow in my heart is very great. Stay here and keep watch with me".

He went a little farther, fell on his face, and prayed. He returned to the three disciples, and when he found them asleep, he said to Simon Peter, "Could you not watch with me for even one hour?"

He again went away to pray, and when he returned, he saw that the disciples could not keep their eyes open. He left them a third time, returned, and told the three, "Get up, look, here is the man who is betraying me".

Jesus was still speaking, when Judas arrived with a large crowd, armed with swords and clubs. Among them was Malchus, a servant of the High Priest. Simon Peter drew his sword and struck Malchus, cutting off his right ear.

Jesus rebuked Simon Peter, saying, "Put your sword back in its place. Those who take the sword will die by the sword!" Then, he touched Malchus' ear and healed him.

The armed men who had arrested Jesus led him away to Caiaphas the High Priest, where the scribes and the elders were assembled. Simon Peter and another disciple followed Jesus and the guards at a distance. Peter stayed by the gate outside the house, while the other disciple, who was an acquaintance of the High Priest, went inside the courtyard of the palace; after a while, he came out and spoke to the maid at the gate, who opened the door to allow Peter to come inside.

The maid asked Peter, "Are you not one of the man's disciples?"

"Woman, I don't know him", said Peter. He got up and went to warm himself by the fire that the servants and the guards had built in the courtyard.

The men around the fire asked Peter, "Are you not one of his disciples?"

"I am not", answered Peter.

One of the servants, who happened to be a relative of Malchus, the man whose ear Peter had cut off with his sword, said to him, "You must be one of them. You are a Galilean; your accent gives you away".

Peter shouted, "I swear that I don't know the man you are talking about!" While he was speaking, a rooster crowed, and he remembered what Jesus had said to him: "Before the rooster crows, you will deny me three times". Peter went out and wept bitterly.

Two days after the crucifixion of Jesus, several women—including Mary Magdalene, Joanna, and Mary, the mother of James—went to the tomb, carrying the spices they had prepared. They found the stone rolled away from the entrance. They went into the tomb, but they did not find the body of Jesus. Suddenly, two men in bright shining clothes stood by them and told them, "Why are you looking among the dead for one who is alive? He is not here; he has been raised. Remember that he said that the Son of man would be crucified, and three days later rise to life".

The women went to the eleven apostles and told them what they had seen and heard, but they did not believe them. But Simon Peter got up and ran to the tomb; he saw that it was empty, and he went back home, amazed at what had happened.

Jesus appeared several times to his disciples, who were filled with joy at seeing the Lord. The last time that Jesus appeared to his disciples was at the Sea of Galilee. Simon Peter and a few other disciples had gone out in a boat to fish, but all that night, they did not catch anything. As the sun was rising, Jesus stood on the shore, but the disciples did not recognize him. He asked them, "Have you caught anything?" "Nothing", they answered. He said to them, "Throw your net out on the right side of the boat, and you will catch some". They threw the net but could not pull it back, because they had caught so many fish.

One of the disciples said to Simon Peter, "It is the Lord!"

Simon Peter, who was naked, put on his garment and jumped to the water. The other disciples came to shore in the boat, pulling the net full of fish. When they stepped ashore, they saw a fire with fish on it and some bread. Jesus said to them, "Bring some of the fish you have caught".

Simon Peter went aboard and dragged the net ashore, full of big fish, a hundred and fifty-three in all. The net did not break, even though there were so many fish.

Jesus said to them, "Come and eat". None of the disciples dare to ask him who he was, because they knew it was the Lord.

After they had eaten, Jesus asked Peter, "Simon, son of Jonas, do you love me more than these others do?"

"Yes", answered Peter, "you know that I love you". Jesus said to him, "Take care of my lambs".

Jesus asked Peter a second time, "Simon, son of Jonas, do you love me?" and again Peter answered, "Yes, Lord, you know that I love you". Jesus said to him, "Take care of my sheep".

A third time, Jesus asked Peter the same question, which made Peter sad. He answered, "Lord, you know all things; you know that I love you".

Jesus repeated, "Take care of my sheep. When you were young, you would go anywhere you wanted to; but when you are old, you will stretch out your hands, and someone else will tie you up and take you where you don't want to go".

The apostles witnessed the ascension of Jesus to heaven, and they returned from the Mount of Olives to Jerusalem. From then on, they gathered frequently to pray as a group, together with the women, with Mary, the mother of Jesus, and with his brothers.

A few days later, there was a meeting of the believers, about a hundred and twenty in all, and Simon Peter stood up to speak. "My brothers", he said, "the Scripture, in which the Holy Spirit, speaking through David, said that Judas would guide the men who arrested Jesus, has come true. Judas was one of us, and someone must now take his place as a witness to the resurrection of Jesus. He must be one of the men who were in our group, during the whole time that Jesus traveled with us".

The believers proposed two candidates to replace Judas as the twelfth apostle: Joseph, who was called Barsabas, also called Justus, and Matthias. They prayed and drew lots. Matthias was chosen to be the twelfth apostle.

When the day of Pentecost came, the believers got together in one place in the city. Suddenly, there was a strong noise from the sky, and they saw tongues of fire, which touched each person there. They were all filled with the Holy Spirit, and they began to talk in other languages.

A large crowd of Jerusalemites and pilgrims from other countries gathered and were amazed that each one of them heard the believers talking in his own native language. Others mocked, saying, "These people are drunk".

Simon Peter stood up, with the other eleven apostles, and spoke in a loud voice to the crowd. "Jews", he said, "and all of you who live in Jerusalem, listen to me, and I will explain what this means. These people are not drunk, as you may think; it is only early morning. This was predicted by the prophet Joel. Men of Israel, listen to these words! Jesus of Nazareth was send by God, as proved by the miracles and wonders, which God performed through him, as you yourselves know. In accordance to God's plan, he was handed over to you, and wicked men crucified him. But God raised him from death, because it was impossible that death should hold him. David spoke about him. Brothers, let me speak frankly about David, who is dead and buried, and his grave is still with us. He was a prophet, and he knew that God had vowed to make one of David's descendants king. David spoke about the resurrection of the Messiah, that his soul would not be left in hell, and his body would not be corrupted. God has raised Jesus, and we are all witnesses. All the people of Israel should know that this Jesus, whom you crucified, is the one that God has made Lord and Messiah".

The people, hearing this, were very troubled and asked Peter and the other apostles, "Brothers, what shall we do?"

Peter answered, "Each one of you should repent and be baptized in the name of Jesus, the Messiah, so that your sins should be forgiven, and you will receive the gift of the Holy Spirit".

Many in the crowd believed Peter, and over three thousand people were baptized that day and joined the group of the believers, learning from the apostles, and sharing in their meals and prayers.

The believers sold their property and their possessions, and they distributed the money among all, according to what each one needed. Everyday, the number of the believers grew.

One day, Peter and John went to the Temple in the afternoon, the hour for prayer. There, at the Temple Gate, the one called Beautiful, they saw a man who was lame from birth, begging money from the passers-by. When he saw Peter and John going in, he begged them to give him something. Peter said to him, "Look at us!" The lame beggar looked at them, hoping to get something.

Peter told him, "I don't have silver or gold, but I will give you what I have: in the name of Jesus, the Messiah of Nazareth, rise up and walk!"

He took the beggar by his right hand and helped him up. At once, the beggar's feet and ankles became strong; he jumped up, stood on his feet, and started walking around. Then, he went into the Temple with the apostles, walking and jumping, and praising God. All those around who knew him were surprised and amazed to see him walking.

When Peter saw the people staring at them, he said, "Men of Israel, why are you amazed at this? Why are you staring at us? Do you think that it was by our own power or holiness that we made this man walk? The God of Abraham,

Isaac, and Jacob has given divine glory to his servant Jesus. You handed him over to the authorities, and rejected him in Pilate's presence, even after Pilate had decided to set him free. You killed the one who leads to life, but God raised him from death, and we are witnesses to this ".

"It was the power of his name", he explained, "that gave strength to this lame man. What you see and know was done by faith in his name; it was faith in Jesus that has made him well, as you can all see. What you and your leaders did to Jesus is because of your ignorance. Repent, turn to God! Moses, Samuel, and all the prophets predicted what is now happening, that God has chosen his servant to bless every one of you and make you turn away from your sins".

Some priests, the captain of the Temple guards, and several Sadducees, who were listening to Simon Peter, became upset, because the two apostles were teaching the people that Jesus had risen from the dead, thus, proving that the dead can return to life. They arrested them and put them in jail. However, many of those who heard Peter converted, and the number of believers grew to about five thousand.

The next day, the council of the leaders of the people, the elders, and the teachers of the Law gathered in Jerusalem. Among those present were the High Priest Annas, Caiaphas, John, Alexander, and many relatives of the High Priest

When the apostles were brought to their presence, they asked them, "By what power or by what name have you done this?"

Simon Peter, inspired by the Holy Spirit, answered, "Leaders of the people, and elders of Israel, if we are today being questioned about the good deed done to the lame man and how he was healed, then you should all know, and all the people in Israel should know, that it was done by the name of Jesus of Nazareth, the Messiah, whom you crucified and whom God has raised from the dead. It was written in the Scriptures that Jesus, the stone that the builders despised, turned out to be the most important of all. Salvation is to be found through him alone!"

The members of the council were amazed at the self assurance of Simon Peter and John, whom they had considered to be ignorant and unlearned men. They realized that the healed man who was standing in front of them was living proof of what Simon Peter and John were saying. They asked the apostles to leave the room, and then, they started discussing among themselves.

"What shall we do with these men?" they asked each other. "As everyone in Jerusalem knows that they have performed a great miracle, there is no way we can deny it. But to keep this matter from spreading any further among the people, let's warn them never again to speak to anyone in the name of Jesus".

Simon Peter and John were called back to the council, and they were ordered to abstain from speaking or teaching in the name of Jesus.

Peter answered, "The council should judge what is right in the sight of God: to obey you or to obey God?" "We", they said, "cannot stop speaking of what we have seen and heard".

The council felt powerless to punish them, because the people were all praising God for the miracle, and so they had no choice but to let the apostles go free, after again warning them.

Simon Peter and John returned to the community of believers and told them what the chief priests and the elders had said to them. Then, all of them prayed to God, were filled with the Holy Spirit, and boldly proclaimed God's word.

The community of believers was united in heart and soul. They owned all their possessions in common. No one in the group was in need, because those believers who owned fields or houses sold them and gave the money to the apostles, who distributed to each one according to his or her need.

One couple, Ananias and his wife Sapphira, behaved differently, motivated by greed. They sold their property but, instead of giving all the money to the apostles, connived to keep part of it for themselves.

Peter, when told of their unchristian behavior, went to Ananias' house and found him there alone—his wife Sapphira had gone out—and he said to him, "Ananias, why did you let Satan fill your heart and make you lie to the Holy Spirit by keeping part of the money that you received for the property? The property, before you sold it, belonged to you, but after you sold it, the money was ours. You have not lied to men; you have lied to God!"

Ananias, upon hearing these words, fell down and died. Several young men of the congregation came in, carried the body out, and buried him.

Three hours later, Sapphira returned to her home, not yet knowing what had happened to her husband. She was confronted by Peter, who showed her the money and asked, "Is this the full amount you and your husband received for your property?"

"Yes", she answered, "it is the full amount".

Peter asked her, "Why did you and your husband put the Spirit of the Lord to the test? The men who buried your husband are outside the door, and they will carry you out, too!"

And, at that moment, Sapphira fell down at his feet and died. The young men came in, carried her out, and buried her next to her husband. The believers and all others who heard of this were terrified.

The number of the believers kept growing. Many people placed their sick relatives and friends in beds and couches in the street near the house of Simon, hoping that Peter's shadow might fall on some of them as he passed by. Crowds of people came from the towns outside Jerusalem, bringing the sick and those who had evil spirits in them, and they were all healed.

The High Priest and his companions, members of the Sadducee party, became very jealous of the popularity and success of the apostles, and they decided to take action. They arrested the apostles and put them in the public jail. That night, an angel of the Lord opened the doors of the prison. The apostles came out, and the angel said to them, "Go and stand in the Temple, and tell the people about this life". The apostles entered the Temple early in the morning and started teaching.

The High Priest and his companions

summoned the elders for a special meeting of the council, and they sent officials to the prison to have the apostles brought before them. The officials returned empty handed and reported that there was no one inside the jail. At that moment, a man came and told the council that the men that they had jailed were in the Temple, teaching the people.

The officer went with his soldiers to the Temple and gently persuaded the apostles to come to the council with them, afraid that if they would use violence, the people might stone them.

Once Peter and his companions were in front of him, the High Priest said, "We gave you strict orders not to teach in the name of this man, but you have filled Jerusalem with your teachings, and accuse us of being responsible for his death!"

Peter and the apostles answered, "We must obey God, not men. The God of our fathers raised Jesus from death, after you crucified him. God raised him to his right hand as Leader and Savior to make people repent and forgive their sins. We are witnesses to this thing, and so is the Holy Spirit, who is God's gift to those who obey them".

Peter's answer angered the members of the council. Their fury was so great that they wanted to have the apostles killed. But one of them, a Pharisee called Gamaliel, a teacher of the Law who enjoyed great renown among the people and who had been Paul's teacher before his conversion, stood up and said, "We should not kill these men, because if their acts are not directed by God, they have no meaning; but if they are directed by God, to oppose them means fighting the will of God".

The council members were convinced by Gamaliel's arguments, and they contented themselves with having the apostles beaten. They warned them again not to speak in the name of Jesus, and then, they let them go.

The apostles left the council joyful, because God had considered them worthy to suffer disgrace for the sake of Jesus. They did not cease teaching and went everyday to the Temple, where they preached that Jesus was the Messiah.

The church in Jerusalem, having heard that many people in Samaria had been baptized, sent Peter and John to that region. When the apostles arrived, they gathered the converts, placed their hands on them, and prayed that the believers should receive the Holy Spirit, and so it happened.

Simon, a recent convert who had a reputation for performing amazing acts of magic, was astonished, when he saw the wonders and miracles that the apostles were performing. He went to Peter and John, offered them money, and said, "Give me also this power, so that anyone I place my hands on will receive the Holy Spirit".

Simon Peter answered him, "Your money should die with you! You think that you can buy God's gift with money! You are not worthy to share our work, because your heart is not right in God's sight. Repent of this wicked plan, and pray to God that he will forgive your evil purpose, for I see that you are full of bitter envy and are a prisoner of sin".

Simon, ashamed, begged them to pray to God for him, so that nothing of what they had said would happen to him. After this, Simon Peter and John returned to Jerusalem, preaching the gospel to many Samaritan villages in their way.

In one of his many travels, Simon Peter visited the community of believers in Lydda, where he met Aeneas, a man who was paralyzed and had been confined to his bed for eight years.

Simon Peter said to him, "Jesus, the Messiah, makes you well. Get up and make your bed". Immediately, Aeneas got up.

Tabitha—called Dorcas in Greek—was a Christian convert, known for her charity and good deeds, who lived in Joppa. When she got sick and died, her friends sent two messengers to Lydda to ask Simon Peter to come to Joppa immediately. The moment he arrived, he went straight to Dorcas' room in the upper floor. A number of widows were there, crying and wailing, looking at Tabitha's coats and garments.

Simon Peter asked them to leave the room. He knelt and prayed, and he said, "Tabitha, arise". She opened her eyes and sat up. He gave her his hand and helped her to get up. The news spread in Joppa, and many people converted.

Cornelius, a centurion of the Italian regiment stationed in Caesarea, was a just, devout, and charitable man; he had a vision where an angel told him to send men to Joppa and fetch Simon Peter, who was staying there in the house of Simon the Tanner. Cornelius sent two of his servants, accompanied by a soldier, to Joppa.

That night, Simon Peter had a vision where God told him that he was allowed to eat anything, including food that was ritually forbidden to Jews. The envoys arrived to the house and inquired if Simon Peter was lodged there. At that very moment, the apostle was being told by the Spirit that three men were seeking him, and that he should go with them.

The next day, Simon Peter, together with some of his Joppa disciples, went to Caesarea. Cornelius was waiting for him with his relatives and friends. Upon seeing Simon Peter, Cornelius fell down at his feet. Simon Peter told him, "Please stand up; I am also a man".

Simon Peter then understood that the meaning of his vision was that God had told him that no man was unclean, even if he belonged to a different nation.

Cornelius told Simon Peter of his vision, and then, he and his friends started to speak in tongues and magnify God. Peter, seeing this, baptized them in the name of the Lord.

After Simon Peter stayed a few days in Caesarea, he returned to Jerusalem, where the believers who were circumcised asked him, "Why did you stay in the home of uncircumcised Gentiles, and even ate with them?"

Simon Peter told them that, when he was in Joppa, he had a vision where he was told three times by God that he could eat forbidden food, and at that very moment, three men arrived from Caesarea to take him there. When he, accompanied by six believers, entered the man's house, the centurion told them that an angel had instructed him to send men to Joppa to bring Simon called Peter, who would give him a message, by which the man and all his family would be saved. "Then", Peter said, "I remembered what Jesus said, 'John baptized with water, but you shall be baptized with the Holy Spirit'. If God gave them the same gift that he gave to us when we believed in Jesus Christ, who was I, then, to try to oppose God?"

When his listeners heard this, they didn't criticize Simon Peter anymore. They praised God and said, "Then, God has also given to the Gentiles the opportunity to repent and live!"

About this time, King Herod—Herod Agrippa I—began to persecute the Christians. He killed James, the brother of John, with the sword, and had Simon Peter arrested, during the Passover Festival.

Simon Peter was taken to prison to be guarded by four squads of soldiers, until the day, after the Passover, when Herod planned to put him on public trial. In the meantime, the congregation of believers prayed fervently for him.

The night before the intended trial, Simon Peter, tied with two chains, was sleeping between two guards. There were also other guards on duty at the entrance of the prison. Suddenly, an angel of the Lord appeared, and a bright light shined in the cell. The angel shook Simon Peter and told him, "Get up quickly". At once, the chains fell from his hands. The angel said, "Tighten your belt and put on your sandals". Simon Peter did so, and the angel said, "Wrap your cloak around you and follow me". Simon Peter followed the angel out of the prison, passing by the first and second guard station, until they came to the prison's iron gate, which opened for them by itself. They went out to the street, and suddenly, Simon Peter found himself alone.

Simon Peter realized what had happened to him and said, "Now, I am sure that the Lord sent his angel to save me from the hand of Herod, and from everything the Jews wanted that should happen to me".

He went to the house of Mary, the mother of John Mark, where many believers had gathered to pray, and knocked on the door. Rhoda, the servant girl, approached the door and heard Simon Peter's voice asking her to open. She was so overwhelmed with joy that, instead of opening the door, she ran back inside the house and told all those present that Simon Peter was outside the gate.

"You are crazy!" they told her.

When she insisted that Peter was outside, they retorted, "It must be his angel". Peter continued knocking. Finally, they opened the door and were astonished to see him safe and sound. They were filled with joy, and it took quite a while for Simon Peter to be able to calm them, and to tell them how God had freed him. He asked them to tell it also to James and to the other believers; then, he departed and went somewhere else.

The next morning, the prison guards discovered that Simon Peter had escaped, during the night. Herod gave orders to search for him, but Simon Peter was not found. The king, after interrogating the guards, had them put to death.

A short time later, the king died suddenly, during a reception to the ambassadors of Tyre and Sidon in Caesarea.

Simon Peter was present in the assembly of the believers in Jerusalem, when Paul and Barnabas gave their report about the many Gentiles that they had converted. Some believers, who belonged to the party of the Pharisees, stood up and stated that the Gentiles should be circumcised and instructed to obey the Law of Moses.

After much discussion, Simon Peter stood up and said, "Brothers, you know that a long time ago, God chose me from among you to preach the gospel to the Gentiles, so that they should hear and believe. God has given the Holy Spirit to the Gentiles, as he had to us. There is no difference between them and us. Why put God to the test by imposing a burden on the backs of the believers, which neither we nor our ancestors were able to carry? We believe that we shall be saved through the grace of the Lord Jesus, just as they are".

The assembly kept silent, while Paul and Barnabas reported all the miracles and wonders that God had performed through them among the Gentiles. When they had finished

speaking, James, the brother of Jesus, stood and said, "Brothers, listen to me! Simon has explained how God showed his care for the Gentiles, by taking out of them a people for his name. This agrees with the words of the prophets. Therefore, I suggest that we should not trouble the Gentiles. Instead, we should write to them that they should abstain from eating food, which had been offered to idols, blood or animals, which had been strangled, and also to forbid them to engage in sexual immorality".

Simon Peter visited Paul in Antioch, where he, according to Paul's letter to the Galatians (Galatians 2:11), avoided all contact with the Gentile converts, afraid that this might antagonize the Jewish converts.

Paul confronted Simon Peter publicly and asked him, "If you, a Jew, live like a Gentile, why should you compel the Gentiles to live as Jews? A man is not justified by doing what the Law demands, but by having faith in Jesus Christ".

Scholars, based on the writings of early church historians, believe that Peter was crucified, head downwards, in Rome, during Nero's persecution of the Christians.

Pethahiah

(Hebrew origin: *God has opened*)

1. (1 Chronicles 24:16). 10th century B.C. During the reign of King David, the priestly service in the Tabernacle was divided by lot into twenty-four turns. Pethahiah was in charge of the nineteenth turn.

2. (Ezra 10:23). 5th century B.C. Pethahiah, a Levite, was forced to divorce his foreign wife, during the days of Ezra. Later, during an assembly of public confession and fasting in the days of Ezra, Pethahiah stood with other Levites—Jeshua, Bani, Hashabniah, Sherebiah, Hodijah, Shebaniah, and Kadmiel—on a raised platform and prayed to God in a loud voice (Nehemiah 9:5).

3. (Nehemiah 11:24). 5th century B.C. Pethahiah, son of Meshezabeel, a descen-

dant of Zerah, was an adviser to the king of Persia.

Pethuel

(Hebrew origin: *Enlarged by God*)

(Joel 1:1). 5th century B.C. Pethuel was the father of the prophet Joel.

Peulthai

(Hebrew origin: *Laborious*)

(1 Chronicles 26:5). 10th century B.C. Peulthai, the eighth son of Obededom, was, like his father and brothers, a gatekeeper of the Tabernacle, during the reign of King David. His brothers were Ammiel, Shemaiah, Jehozabad, Joah, Sacar, Nethaneel, and Issachar.

Phalec

(Hebrew origin: *Divided*)

(Luke 3:35). Unspecified date. Phalec—called Peleg in Genesis (Genesis 10:25)—a descendant of Noah and Shem, was the son of Heber, spelled Eber in Genesis (Genesis 10:21).

Phalec was thirty years old, when his son Reu—called Ragau by Luke (Luke 3:35)—was born. After that, he lived for another two hundred and nine years and had other sons and daughters.

Phallu

(Hebrew origin: *Distinguished*)

(Genesis 46:9). 17th century B.C. Phallu—called Pallu in the book of Exodus (Exodus 6:14)—son of Reuben and grandson of Jacob, was among the seventy Israelites who immigrated to Egypt. He was the ancestor of the clan of the Palluites. His brothers were Hanoch, Hezron, and Carmi.

His son Eliab was the father of Dathan and Abiram, who rebelled with Korah against Moses and Aaron, and who were punished by being swallowed by the earth.

Phalti

(Hebrew origin: *Delivered*)

(1 Samuel 25:44). 10th century B.C. Phalti—also called Phaltiel (2 Samuel 3:15)—was the second husband of Michal, the daughter of King Saul. After David—with Michal's help—fled from Saul and became an outlaw, Saul married Michal to Phalti, the son of Laish.

Years later, when David was king in Hebron, Ishbosheth, Saul's son, accused his general, Abner, of having made love to Rizpah, who had been one of King Saul's concubines.

Abner, furious at Ishbosheth, decided to transfer his loyalties to David. He contacted David and told him that he could convince the heads of the tribes to recognize him as king.

David told Abner that he was willing to receive him, on condition that Michal, Saul's daughter, who had been his first wife, should be returned to him. She was forcefully taken away from her husband, Phalti, who followed them as far as Bahurim, crying silently, until Abner ordered him to turn back.

Phaltiel

(Hebrew origin: *Delivered by God*)

(2 Samuel 3:15). 10th century B.C. Phaltiel—also called Phalti—was the second husband of Michal, the daughter of King Saul. (Please see the entry for Phalti [1 Samuel 25:44].)

Phanuel

(Hebrew origin: *Face of God*)

(Luke 2:36). A.D. 1st century. Phanuel was the father of Anna, a prophetess, who, in her old age, was present, when Joseph and Mary brought the child Jesus to the Temple to sacrifice in his behalf, according to the custom for firstborn male children.

Pharaoh

(Egyptian origin: Title of the Egyptian kings)

1. (Genesis 12:15). 19th century B.C. Unspecified name. This Pharaoh met

Abram, when the patriarch came to Egypt, because in a famine in Canaan. Abram, fearing for his life, instructed Sarai to say that she was not his wife but his sister. Pharaoh, having heard that Sarai was beautiful, brought her to the palace and gave generous gifts of sheep, oxen, asses, camels, and slaves to her "brother".

Pharaoh realized that he had been deceived, when God punished him and his house with great plagues because of Abram's wife. Pharaoh called Abram, returned Sarai to him, and expelled them from Egypt. Abram returned to Canaan, with his wife and his nephew Lot, rich in cattle, silver and gold.

2. (Genesis 37:36). 17th century B.C. Unspecified name. This is the Pharaoh who was so pleased and impressed by Joseph's interpretation of his dreams that he, on the spot, named Joseph to be his second in command. When Jacob and his family came to Egypt, Pharaoh received them kindly and allowed them to settle in the region of Goshen.

3. (Exodus 1:11). 14th century B.C. Unspecified name. Several hundred years later, a new Pharaoh, "who did not know Joseph", came to power in Egypt. Alarmed by the growth of the Israelite population in Egypt, he made them work as slaves and ordered the death of all new-born Israelite males. The baby boy whom his daughter found in a basket, floating in the Nile, to whom she gave the name of Moses, and who was brought up in his court, became the liberator of the enslaved Israelites.

4. (Exodus 3:10). 13th century B.C. Unspecified name. Moses was eighty years old (Exodus 7:7), when he returned to Egypt and requested the currently reigning Pharaoh to let his people go. The Egyptians had to endure the punishment and suffering of the ten plagues, including the death of their firstborn sons, before Pharaoh allowed the Israelites to leave his country. But Pharaoh soon regretted the loss of his slaves, and he pursued the fugitives with his army. The waters of the sea

miraculously parted, and the Israelites were able to cross the sea, but Pharaoh and his army were drowned by the returning waters.

5. (1 Kings 3:1). 10th century B.C. Unspecified name. This Pharaoh entered into an alliance with King Solomon and gave him his daughter in marriage, with the city of Gezer as her dowry. She remained a pagan, and Solomon had to build a palace for her, outside the City of David, because he didn't want her to live in a place made holy by the ark of God.

6. (1 Kings 11:40). 10th century B.C. Shishak is the first Pharaoh mentioned by name in the Bible. He gave political asylum to Jeroboam, who had been condemned to death by King Solomon for conspiring against him. Although his name is not specified, Shishak is probably the Pharaoh who received warmly, in his court, an Edomite of royal blood, Hadad, who had survived Joab's massacre of the Edomite males (1 Kings 11:18). He gave him land and a house, and he married him to the sister of his wife Tahpenes.

During the fifth year of King Rehoboam's reign, Shishak attacked Jerusalem and carried away the treasures of the palace and the Temple.

7. (2 Kings 17:4). 8th century B.C. King So of Egypt was asked by King Hoshea of Israel to come to his aid against Shalmaneser, the Assyrian king who had attacked Samaria. After a siege, which lasted three years, the Assyrians took Hoshea prisoner and destroyed Samaria. This final defeat marked the end of the northern kingdom of Israel, which had been in existence for over two hundred years.

8. (2 Kings 19:9). 8th century B.C. Tirhakah, king of Ethiopia, went to fight against Sennacherib, king of Assyria, who had invaded Judah. When Sennacherib heard that Tirhakah was coming with his army, he sent a message to King Hezekiah, telling him that he should not hope that God would prevent Jerusalem from falling into the hands of the Assyrians. Hezekiah read

the message and went to the Temple to pray to God to save him from Sennacherib.

The great prophet-statesman Isaiah came to the king and told him that God had heard his prayer. That night, over one hundred and eighty-five thousand Assyrian soldiers died suddenly. Sennacherib, having failed in his purpose to capture Jerusalem, returned to Assyria, to his capital Nineveh. There, while praying in the Temple of the god Nisroch, his sons Adrammelech and Sharezer murdered him.

9. (2 Kings 23:29). 7th century B.C. Pharaoh Necho of Egypt, wanting to ascertain his supremacy, decided to go to war against Assyria. He marched toward Charchemish through the ancient road called the Way of the Sea, which went through Judah.

Necho wrote to King Josiah, saying that he had no quarrel with Judah, and asked him not to interfere with the advance of his army, as he was in haste to reach his enemy Assyria. However, King Josiah tried to stop him at Megiddo and was badly wounded in the battle. The king was brought in his chariot to Jerusalem, where he died and was buried in the tombs of his fathers, mourned by the whole nation. Josiah was succeeded by his twenty-three-year-old son Jehoahaz.

Three months later, Pharaoh Necho summoned the young king to his head-quarters at Riblah in the land of Hamath, Syria. When Jehoahaz arrived, he was arrested, put in chains, and deported to Egypt, where he died. Judah was fined one hundred silver talents and one gold talent. Necho made Jehoahaz' older brother Eliakim the puppet king of Israel, giving him the name of Jehoiakim.

10. (1 Chronicles 4:18). Unspecified date. This Pharaoh, whose name is not mentioned, was the father of a woman called Bithiah, the wife of Mered, a descendant of Judah.

11. (Jeremiah 44:30). 6th century B.C. King Hophra of Egypt, a contemporary of King Zedekiah of Judah, was prophesied by Jeremiah with defeat and death at the hand of his enemies.

Phares
(Hebrew origin: *Breach*)

(Matthew 1:3). 17th century B.C. Phares—also called Perez and Pharez—son of Judah and his daughter-in-law Tamar, was an ancestor of King David and Jesus, in the genealogy of Matthew. (Please see the entry for Perez [1 Chronicles 27:3].)

Pharez
(Hebrew origin: *Breach*)

(Genesis 38:29). 17th century B.C. Pharez—also called Perez and Phares—son of Judah and his daughter-in-law Tamar, was an ancestor of King David. (Please see the entry for Perez [1 Chronicles 27:3].)

Pharosh
(Hebrew origin: *Flea*)

(Ezra 8:3). Unspecified date. His descendant Zechariah returned with Ezra from Babylon, leading one hundred and fifty men.

Phaseah
(Hebrew origin: *Limping*)

(Nehemiah 7:51). Unspecified date. Phaseah was the ancestor of a clan of Temple servants that returned with Zerubbabel from the Babylonian Exile.

Phebe
(Greek origin: *Bright*)

(Romans 16:1). A.D. 1st century. Phebe, a Christian woman leader in the church at Cenchrea, near Corinth, carried Paul's letter to the Christian community in Rome. In his letter, the apostle asked the Roman Christians to help Phebe in whatever she needed, called her "our sister", and mentioned that she had been a great help to him personally and to the church in general.

Phichol

(Hebrew origin: *Mouth of all*)

(Genesis 21:22). 19th century B.C. Phichol, captain of the army of Abimelech, the Philistine king of Gerar, was present, together with Ahuzzath, a friend of the king, when Abimelech met Isaac and made a peace covenant with him.

Philemon

(Greek origin: *Friendly*)

(Philemon 1:1). A.D. 1st century. Philemon was a prominent Christian whose house hosted the church in Colossae. Scholars believe that he was married to Apphia, and that Archippus was their son.

Paul wrote a short letter to Philemon about Onesimus, an escaped slave whom Paul had met in prison and converted to Christianity. Paul, in his letter, appealed to Philemon to be reconciled to his slave, whom Paul was sending back to him, and to welcome him, not only as a forgiven slave, but as a brother in Christ.

Philetus

(Greek origin: *Amiable*)

(2 Timothy 2:17). A.D. 1st century. Philetus was an apostate about whom Paul complained that he and Hymenaeus were teaching falsehoods about the Resurrection.

Philip

(Greek origin: *Fond of horses*)

1. (Matthew 10:3). A.D. 1st century. Philip, one of the twelve apostles, came from Bethsaida, the same town where Andrew and Simon lived. Jesus saw him and said to him, "Follow me".

Philip went to Nathanael and told him, "We have found the one about whom Moses and the prophets wrote. He is Jesus of Nazareth, the son of Joseph".

Nathanael said, "Can anything good come out of Nazareth?"

"Come and see", answered Philip.

Jesus saw Nathanael coming to him, and he said, "Look, here is a true Israelite. There is nothing false in him".

Nathanael, surprised, asked him, "How do you know me?"

"I saw you when you were under the fig tree, before Phillip called you".

Nathanael exclaimed, "Master, you are the Son of God! You are the king of Israel!"

Philip was the disciple responsible for the provisions for Jesus and his followers. On one occasion, Jesus went across the lake, followed by a large crowd of about five thousand men, who had heard of his miraculous cures. Jesus climbed up a hill and sat there with his disciples.

He saw the large crowd around him, and he asked Philip to test him, "Where can we buy bread for all these people?"

Philip answered, "It will cost over two hundred coins to buy even a little for each one of them".

Another of his disciples, Andrew, Simon Peter's brother, said, "There is a boy here who has five loaves of bread and two small fishes. But that is not enough for all these people".

Jesus said to them, "Make them sit down". Over five thousand men sat on the grass.

Jesus took the loaves, gave thanks to God, and gave the bread to his disciples, who distributed them to the people who were sitting. The same thing was done with the fishes.

After everybody ate as much as he wanted, so much food was left over that they were able to fill twelve baskets.

Philip was also responsible for the group's contacts with the "outside" world, as shown in the incident, when a group of Greeks, during Jesus' last visit to Jerusalem, approached Philip and asked him to arrange for them a meeting with Jesus.

During the Last Supper, Jesus said, "I am the way, the truth, and the life. No man comes to my Father, except by me. Now that you have known me, you have known my Father also. From now on, you know him, and you have seen him".

Philip said to him, "Lord, show us the Father. That would satisfy us".

Jesus replied to him, "I have been so long with you, and you still don't know me, Philip? Whoever has seen me, has seen the Father. How can you now say, 'Show us the Father'? Don't you believe that I am in the Father, and the Father is in me?"

2. (Matthew 14:3). A.D. 1st century. Philip, tetrarch of Ituraea and of the region of Trachonitis, was the youngest son of Herod the Great, and the first husband of Herodias, who afterward married her brother-in-law, Herod the Tetrarch. John the Baptist denounced this marriage, an act, for which, he paid with his life.

3. (Acts of the Apostles 6:5). A.D. 1st century. After the death of Jesus, his followers, Hebrew and Greek Christians, became known as the Jerusalem church. The Greek converts complained that the Hebrew Christians neglected the Greek widows in the daily distribution of the food.

The twelve apostles summoned all the believers and told them, "It is not right that we should give up preaching the word of God to serve tables. Therefore, brothers, choose from among you seven men, whom we may appoint to this duty, while we devote ourselves to prayer and to the ministry of the word".

The congregation accepted this suggestion and chose Philip, a Christian convert of good reputation, who were respected for his piety and his wisdom, together with another six men—Stephen, Nicanor, Prochorus, Timon, Parmenas, and Nicolas a proselyte from Antioch—to serve on the tables and distribute food to the needy of the congregation.

Philip, who became known as the evangelist, later went to Samaria, where he preached and converted many people, including Simon, a magician and sorcerer. An angel of the Lord told Philip to go to Gaza. On the road, he saw a man sitting in a chariot. This man, a eunuch, was the treasurer of Candace, the queen of Ethiopia.

Philip approached the chariot, where the man was reading in a loud voice, "Although he was oppressed, and afflicted, he did not open his mouth; he was brought as a lamb to the slaughter, and, as a sheep is dumb in front of its shearers, he did not open his mouth" (Isaiah 53:7).

Philip asked him, "Do you understand what you are reading?"

The man answered, "No, I don't. Please sit with me, and explain to me the meaning of the verse. Was the prophet speaking about himself, or about some other man?"

Philip explained to the eunuch that the verse referred to Jesus. They continued on their way, and when they approached a body of water, the eunuch said, "Here is water. Does anything prevent me from being baptized?"

Philip answered, "If you believe with all your heart, you may be baptized".

The eunuch replied, "I believe that Jesus Christ is the Son of God", and ordered to stop the chariot.

Both men went to the water, and Philip baptized him. Philip departed, and the eunuch continued on his way, full of joy.

Philip continued to Caesarea, preaching in all the cities on the way. He settled in Caesarea with his four daughters, who also preached the gospel.

Years later, Paul stayed in his house, and, during that visit, the prophet Agabus came and prophesied that Paul would be arrested in Jerusalem (Acts of the Apostles 21:10).

Philologus

(Greek origin: *Talkative*)

(Romans 16:15). A.D. 1st century. Philologus was a Christian to whom Paul sent greetings in his letter to the Christians in Rome. The apostle mentioned him in the same verse with four other persons—Julia, Nereus, his sister, and Olympas—and "all the saints who were with them", which gives grounds to think that Philologus and his companions formed a small separate group within the larger Christian community of Rome.

Phinehas

(Hebrew origin: *Mouth of a serpent*)

1. (Exodus 6:25). 13th century B.C. Phinehas was the son of the High Priest Eleazar, and the grandson of Aaron. His son was called Abishua.

   At a time when the people were suffering from a plague sent by God to punish them for their immoral behavior with the daughters of Moab and their sacrifices to the pagan god Baalpeor, Phinehas saw Zimri, of the tribe of Simeon, take Cozbi, daughter of a Midianite prince called Zur, into his tent.

   Phinehas didn't hesitate; he took a javelin in his hand, went into the tent, and killed the couple. God, appeased by this act, lifted the plague and told Moses that he would make a covenant with Phinehas for all time. He and his descendants would be permanently established as priests.

   Phinehas was sent by Moses with an army of twelve thousand men, a thousand warriors from each tribe, against the Midianites, equipped with the sacred utensils and the trumpets for sounding the blast. The army attacked Midian and killed all the men, including their five kings, and also Balaam, the seer.

   During the conquest of Canaan, a report reached the Israelites that the tribe of Reuben, Gad, and the half tribe of Manasseh had built an altar in the east bank of the Jordan. The Israelites gathered at Shiloh and decided to go to war against them, but, before that, they sent Phinehas, who was by now the High Priest, accompanied by ten leaders, to speak to them.

   Phinehas and his companions crossed the Jordan, met with the representatives of the two and a half tribes, and accused them of rebellion against God. The two and a half tribes replied that the altar they had built was intended to present sacrifices to God, in case that, in the future, the descendants of the Israelites would prevent their own descendants from worshipping the Lord. Phinehas accepted their explanation and returned to Shiloh.

2. (1 Samuel 1:3). 11th century B.C. Phinehas and his brother Hophni were the sons of Eli, the priest of Shiloh. Unfortunately, they were wicked and corrupt.

   A man of God came to Eli and charged him with honoring his sons more than he honored God, and that his punishment would be that his two sons would both die on the same day, that his descendants would no longer be the leading priestly family, and that his survivors would be reduced to beg the new High Priest for money and food.

   In a battle with the Philistines, the Israelites suffered a heavy defeat; the Ark of the Covenant was captured, and over thirty thousand men, including the sons of Eli, were killed. When Eli, who was ninety-eight years old, was told about the news, he fell from his seat and broke his neck.

   When the pregnant wife of Phinehas heard that the Ark of the Covenant had been captured, and that her father-in-law and her husband were both dead, she was seized with labor pains and gave birth prematurely. As she lay dying, the woman attending her said, "Do not be afraid, for you have borne a son". When Phinehas' wife did not respond, the woman named the boy Ichabod, saying, "The glory of God has departed".

3. (Ezra 8:33). 5th century B.C. His son Eleazar, a Levite, was one of the men who helped the priest Meremoth, son of Uriah, to weigh the silver and gold vessels of the Temple, brought by Ezra from the Babylonian Exile.

Phlegon

(Greek origin: *Blazing*)

(Romans 16:14). A.D. 1st century. Phlegon was a Christian to whom Paul sent greetings in his letter to the church in Rome. The apostle mentioned him in the same verse with four other men—Hermas, Asyncritus, Patrobas, and Hermes—and "the brothers who were with them", which gives grounds to think that Hermas and his companions formed a small separate group within the larger Christian community of Rome.

Phurah

(Hebrew origin: *Foliage*)

(Judges 7:10). 12th century B.C. Phurah was the servant of Gideon. He went with his master, one night, to the camp of the Midianites and Amalekites, and heard one of the enemy soldiers, saying, "I dreamed that a cake of bread fell into their camp and destroyed a tent".

Another soldier said, "Your dream means that Gideon will defeat Midian".

Gideon, encouraged by the defeatism of the Midianites, attacked with his troops, and the enemy fled in panic, pursued by the Israelites.

Phut

(Uncertain origin and meaning)

(Genesis 10:6). Unspecified date. Phut and his brothers Canaan, Cush—*Ethiopia*—and Mizraim—*Egypt*—were sons of Ham and ancestors of their respective nations. The first book of Chronicles calls him Put (1 Chronicles 1:8).

Phuvah

(Hebrew origin: *Blast*)

(Genesis 46:13). 17th century B.C. Phuvah—called Puah in the first book of Chronicles (1 Chronicles 7:1), and Pua in Numbers (Numbers 26:23)—son of Issachar and grandson of Jacob, was among the seventy Israelites who immigrated to Egypt. His brothers were Tola, Shimrom—called Shimron in Genesis—and Job—called Jashub in the book of Numbers (Numbers 26:24). Phuvah was the ancestor of the clan of the Punites.

Phygellus

(Greek origin: *Fugitive*)

(2 Timothy 1:15). A.D. 1st century. Phygellus was an apostate Christian, living in Asia, who, together with Hermogenes and others, turned against the apostle Paul.

Pilate

(Latin origin: *Firm*)

(Matthew 27:2). A.D. 1st century. Pontius Pilate was the Roman governor of Judea at the time when Jesus preached the Kingdom of God, during the reign of Tiberius Caesar. Although he had a weak character, and was easily swayed by the mob, he governed Judea with a cruel and sadistic hand, an example of which was an event where he killed several Galileans and mixed their blood with their sacrifices to God (Luke 13:1).

Early in the morning, the day after Jesus had been arrested, the priests and the elders put Jesus in chains and took him from the house of Caiaphas to the palace of Pilate, the Roman governor of Judea. The priests waited outside the palace, because they wanted to keep themselves ritually clean for the Passover celebration.

Pilate came out and asked them, "What accusation are you bringing against this man?"

They answered, "We would not have brought him to you if he had not committed a crime".

Pilate told them, "Then, take him and try him according to your own law".

They replied, "Roman law does not allow us to condemn anyone to death".

Pilate went back into the palace and had Jesus brought inside. While Pilate was sitting in the Judgment Hall, his wife sent him a message, asking him to have nothing to do with the innocent man, because she had greatly suffered that day in a dream on account of him.

Pilate asked Jesus, "Are you the king of the Jews?"

Jesus answered, "Is this your own question, or others have told you about me?"

Pilate said, "Do you think I am a Jew? Your own people and the chief priests have handed you over to me. What have you done?"

"My kingdom is not of this world. If it would be, my followers would have fought to keep me from being delivered to the Jewish authorities", said Jesus.

"But are you a king?" asked Pilate.

"You are the one who is saying that I am a king", said Jesus. "I was born to testify about the truth. Whoever belongs to the truth, hears my voice".

"What is truth?" asked Pilate.

Without waiting for an answer, he went outside and told the chief priests and the crowd, "I see no reason to condemn this man".

They insisted, saying, "He has disturbed the peace in Galilee, and is now doing the same in Judea".

Pilate, hearing this, asked if the man was a Galilean, because in that case, he would be under the jurisdiction of Herod, the tetrarch of Galilee.

When the accusers confirmed that Jesus was a Galilean, Pilate sent him to Herod, who was visiting Jerusalem at that time. The tetrarch, who had heard so much about Jesus, was very happy to meet him, and he hoped to see him perform a miracle.

Herod questioned him at length, but Jesus remained silent, while the accusers again stated their case in the strongest of terms.

Herod and his men mocked him, dressed him in a gorgeous robe, and sent him back to Pilate. This act ingratiated Herod to Pilate, with whom he had been till then on unfriendly terms.

Pilate called the elders, the chief priests, and the leaders of the people, and he said to them, "I have not found any guilt in this man, and neither has Herod. He has done nothing to deserve death. I will have him whipped, and then I will let him go".

It was customary for the Roman governor to release a prisoner to the crowds in honor of the Passover Festival. One of the prisoners being held by the Romans was Barabbas, a notorious rebel and robber, who was charged with insurrection and murder.

Pilate went out and said to the people, "Behold, I am bringing him here to let you know that I find no reason to condemn him".

Jesus was brought out, wearing the crown of thorns, and dressed in a purple robe.

Pilate announced, "Behold the man!"

The chief priests and the authorities saw Jesus and screamed, "Crucify him! Crucify him!"

Pilate said to them, "Then, you take him,

and crucify him. I find no reason to condemn him".

They answered, "Our Law says that he has to die, because he claimed to be the Son of God".

Pilate tried to release him, but the Jewish authorities shouted, "If you let this man go, you are not a friend of Caesar. Anyone who claims to be a king is a rebel against Caesar".

Pilate heard this and was afraid. He went back into the palace and asked Jesus, "Where are you from?" When Jesus didn't answer, Pilate said to him, "You will not speak to me? Don't you know that I have the power to crucify you or let you go?"

Jesus replied, "Your power over me is what you received from above. Therefore, he that handed me to you is the greater sinner".

Pilate took Jesus outside and said to the people, "Behold, your king! Which of the two prisoners do you want me to set free: Barabbas or the king of the Jews?"

The mob, incited by the chief priests and the elders, screamed, "Release Barabbas!"

Pilate asked them, "Shall I crucify your king?"

The chief priests answered, "Caesar is our only king".

Pilate asked the crowd, "What, then, do you want me to do with the one you call king of the Jews?"

"Crucify him! Crucify him!" they shouted.

"What crime has he committed? I haven't found any reason to condemn him to death. I will whip him and let him go".

The crowd shouted again, "Crucify him!"

When Pilate saw that the crowd might riot, he took some water, washed his hands in front of the crowd, and said, "I am not responsible for the death of Jesus".

The crowd answered, "Let the punishment for his death fall on us and on our children!"

Pilate set Barabbas free. He had Jesus whipped and handed him over to his soldiers to be crucified. The soldiers, after mocking Jesus, led him away to the place of the crucifixion. When they arrived at the place called the Skull, they crucified Jesus between two criminals, one on his right and the other one on his left.

Over the cross, they placed a sign that said in Greek, Latin, and Hebrew, "This is the king of the Jews".

The chief priests asked Pilate to change the wording of the title from "King of the Jews" to, "He claimed to be the king of the Jews".

Pilate refused, saying, "What I have written remains!"

Darkness covered the whole country from noon till three o'clock in the afternoon. At that time, the curtain, hanging in the Temple, was torn in two.

Jesus cried out with a loud voice, "Father, into your hands I commend my spirit!" Then, he said, "It is finished", bowed his head, and died.

The Jewish authorities asked Pilate to give orders to break the legs of those who were still alive, to speed their death, because it was Friday, and they didn't want the bodies to remain on the crosses, during the Sabbath, especially this Sabbath, which was even more special because of the Passover Festival.

The soldiers came and broke the legs of the two men who had been crucified next to Jesus. When they came to Jesus, they saw that he was already dead, and there was no need to break his legs. One of the soldiers plunged his spear into Jesus' side, and at once, blood and water poured out.

A rich man from the Judean town of Arimathaea came to Pilate and asked to be given the body of Jesus. The man was Joseph, a good and just man who believed in the Kingdom of God. Although he was a member of the council, he had not agreed with their decisions and actions against Jesus.

Pilate was surprised to hear that Jesus was already dead. After having a centurion confirm this information, he told Joseph that he could take the body. Joseph brought a linen sheet and took the body down from the cross.

With the help of Nicodemus, who had brought about one hundred pounds of spices, a mixture of myrrh and aloes, to prepare the body, he wrapped it in the sheet, with the spices according to the Jewish custom of preparing a body for burial. They took the body and placed it in Joseph's own tomb, which had recently been dug out of solid rock. Then, Joseph rolled a large stone to close the entrance to the tomb and went away.

On the next day, which was a Sabbath, the chief priests and the Pharisees met with Pilate to remind him that Jesus had said that he would rise back to life, three days after his death. They advised him to give orders to guard the tomb, to prevent the disciples from stealing the body and then claiming that Jesus had risen from the dead. Pilate gave them a guard to watch the tomb, and the stone on its entrance was sealed.

Early Sunday morning, Mary Magdalene and the other Mary went to look at the tomb. Suddenly, there was an earthquake; an angel appeared, rolled the stone away, and sat on it. His appearance was like lightning, and his clothes were white as snow. The terrified guards trembled and then stood as still as dead men. The angel spoke to the women, "Do not be afraid. I know you are looking for Jesus who was crucified. Go now and tell his disciples that he has been raised from death, and now, he is going to Galilee ahead of you; there, you will see him".

Pildash

(Uncertain origin and meaning)

(Genesis 22:22). 19th century B.C. Pildash was one of the eight children born to Milcah, the wife of Nahor, Abraham's brother.

His brothers were Huz, Buz, Kemuel, Chesed, Hazo, Jidlaph, and Bethuel.

Pileha

(Hebrew origin: *Slicing*)

(Nehemiah 10:24). 5th century B.C. Pileha was one of the leaders who signed Nehemiah's solemn agreement to separate themselves from the foreigners living in the land, to refrain from intermarrying with them, and to dedicate their firstborn to God, among other obligations.

Piltai

(Hebrew origin: *Delivered*)

(Nehemiah 12:17). 5th century B.C. Piltai was the head of a priestly clan, descended from Moadiah, when Joiakim was the High Priest, in the days of Nehemiah.

Pinon

(Hebrew origin: *Perplexity*)

(Genesis 36:41). Unspecified date. Pinon, head of an Edomite clan, was a descendant of Esau.

Piram

(Hebrew origin: *Wildly*)

(Joshua 10:3). 12th century B.C. Piram, the king of Jarmuth, was asked by Adonizedek, the king of Jerusalem, to join him and several other kings—Hoham, the king of Hebron; Debir, the king of Eglon; and Japhia, the king of Lachish—in a military alliance against the city of Gibeon, to punish the Gibeonites for having made peace with the people of Israel. The people of Gibeon appealed to Joshua for help.

Joshua—after ordering the sun to stand still over Gibeon, and the moon over the valley of Ajalon—fought against the five kings and defeated them. Their armies ran away, during a storm of hailstones, which killed many of their soldiers, even more than those who had been killed in the fighting.

The five kings fled and hid in a cave at Makkedah, where they were trapped. After Joshua had liquidated all the surviving enemies, he ordered that the kings should be taken out from the cave.

Piram, Japhia, Debir, Adonizedek, and Hoham, after being humiliated, were killed and hanged on five trees, until the evening. At sunset, their corpses were taken down and thrown into the cave, where they had been hiding, and large stones were placed over the entrance to the cave.

Pispah

(Hebrew origin: *Dispersion*)

(1 Chronicles 7:38). Unspecified date.

Pispah, son of Jether, was a brave warrior and leader of a clan of the tribe of Asher. His brothers were Jephunneh and Ara.

Pithon

(Hebrew origin: *Expansive*)

(1 Chronicles 8:35). Unspecified date. Pithon, son of Micah, was a descendant of King Saul. His brothers were, Ahaz, Melech, and Tarea.

Pochereth

(Hebrew origin: *Trapper*)

(Ezra 2:57). 10th century B.C. Pochereth, a servant of Solomon, was the ancestor of a family that returned with Zerubbabel from the Babylonian Exile.

Pollux

(Latin origin: Uncertain meaning)

(Acts of the Apostles 28:11). Pollux and his twin Castor were Roman deities depicted on a sign on the Alexandrian ship that took the apostle Paul from the island of Melita—today called Malta—to Syracuse.

The Romans used to offer sacrifices to the two deities asking for favorable winds, and help for shipwrecked sailors.

Pontius

(Latin origin: *Bridge*)

(Matthew 27:2). A.D. 1st century. Pontius was the first name of Pilate, the Roman governor of Judea, who interrogated Jesus, when the priests and the elders, who brought him, accused him of claiming to be king of the Jews. (Please see the entry for Pilate.)

Poratha

(Persian origin: Unknown meaning)

(Esther 9:8). 5th century B.C. Poratha was one of the ten sons of Haman, the vizier of Persia who wanted to kill all the Jews in the kingdom. His brothers were Parmashta, Arisai,

Aspatha, Parshandatha, Adalia, Aridatha, Dalphon, Aridai, and Vajezatha. All of them were executed, when Haman's plot against the Jews backfired.

Porcius

(Latin origin: *Swinish*)

(Acts of the Apostles 24:27). A.D. 1st century. Porcius was the first name of Festus, the Roman official who replaced Felix as governor of Judea.

He interrogated Paul, who was imprisoned in Caesarea at that time, and then sent him to Rome, because the apostle had appealed to the emperor. (Please see the entry for Festus.)

Potiphar

(Egyptian origin: Unknown meaning)

(Genesis 37:36). 17th century B.C. Potiphar, an official in the court of Pharaoh and captain of his guard, bought Joseph from the Midianites who had brought him to Egypt. Joseph proved to be a loyal and efficient servant to his master, who put him in charge of his household.

Potiphar's wife noticed that Joseph was a very handsome young man, and she tried to seduce him. Joseph refused her advances and fled from the room, leaving his garments in her hand. The woman told her servants that Joseph had tried to rape her and had run away, when she screamed. Potiphar, when he heard this, was furious and sent Joseph to prison.

Potipherah

(Egyptian origin: Unknown meaning)

(Genesis 41:45). 17th century B.C. Potipherah, a priest of On, was the father of Asenath, the woman whom Pharaoh gave to Joseph as a wife. His grandchildren Manasseh and Ephraim were the ancestors of two Israelite tribes.

Prisca

(Latin origin: *Ancient*)

(2 Timothy 4:19). A.D. 1st century. Prisca is another name for Priscilla, Aquila's wife. (Please see the entry for Priscilla [Acts of the Apostles 18:2].)

Priscilla

(Latin origin: *Little Prisca*)

(Acts of the Apostles 18:2). A.D. 1st century. Priscilla was the wife of Aquila, a Jew born in Pontus, a city situated in Asia Minor. The couple, who had been residing in Rome, moved to Corinth, when the emperor Claudius expelled all the Jews from Rome.

In Corinth, Priscilla and Aquila earned their living by making tents, which was also Paul's trade. When Paul came to Corinth, he stayed with Aquila and Priscilla, most likely earning his living by working with them. The apostle took the couple with him, when he left Corinth, and, on his way to Antioch, left them in Ephesus.

There, Aquila and Priscilla heard Apollos, an Alexandrian Jew, well versed in Hebrew Scripture, give a lecture about Jesus in the synagogue. They were impressed by his eloquence but realized that his knowledge of Christianity was limited. They took Apollos under their wing, taught him the Way of God, and sent him to Corinth, carrying letters exhorting the local Christian community to receive him.

Later, after Claudius' death, when the expulsion edict was no longer in force, they returned to Rome, and Paul, in his letter to the Romans, sent them greetings, adding that they had risked their necks to save his life.

It seems—according to the greetings that Paul sent them in his second letter to Timothy, where he calls her Prisca (2 Timothy 4:19)— that the couple went back to Ephesus.

Prochorus

(Greek origin: *Before the dance*)

(Acts of the Apostles 6:5). A.D. 1st century. After the death of Jesus, his Hebrew and Greek followers became known as the Jerusalem church. There was some dissension between the two groups. The Greek converts complained that the Hebrew Christians neglected the Greek widows in the daily distribution of the food.

The twelve apostles summoned all the believers and told them, "It is not right that we should give up preaching the word of God to serve tables. Therefore, brothers, choose from among you seven men, whom we may appoint to this duty, while we devote ourselves to prayer and to the ministry of the word".

The congregation accepted this suggestion, and they chose Prochorus and another six men—Stephen, Philip, Nicanor, Timon, Parmenas, and Nicolas, a proselyte from Antioch—all of them Christians of good reputation, who were respected for their piety and their wisdom, to serve on the tables and distribute food to the needy of the community.

Pua

(Hebrew origin: *Blast*)

(Numbers 26:23). 17th century B.C. Pua, son of Issachar and grandson of Jacob, was among the seventy Israelites who immigrated to Egypt. His brothers were Tola, Shimrom—called Shimron in Genesis—and Job—called Jashub in the book of Numbers (Numbers 26:24). He was called Puah in the first book of Chronicles (1 Chronicles 7:1), and Phuvah in the book of Genesis (Genesis 46:13). He was the ancestor of the clan of the Punites.

Puah

(Hebrew origin: *Brilliancy*)

1. (Exodus 1:15). 14th century. Puah and Shiphrah, two Hebrew midwives, were instructed by the Pharaoh of Egypt to kill all the Israelite male babies, but to allow the females babies to live. The two women were God fearing, and they did not carry out the command of the Pharaoh. They were called to the presence of the sovereign, who asked them why they were letting the boys live.

   The midwives answered, "The Hebrew women are not like the Egyptian women. They are so vigorous that they deliver their babies, before we arrive".

God rewarded the two women and gave them families of their own.

2. (Judges 10:1). 12th century B.C. Puah, son of Dodo of the tribe of Issachar, was the father of Tola, the man who judged Israel, after the death of Abimelech.

3. (1 Chronicles 7:1). 17th century B.C. Puah, son of Issachar and grandson of Jacob, was among the seventy Israelites who immigrated to Egypt. His brothers were Tola, Shimrom—called Shimron in Genesis—and Jashub, called Job in Genesis. Puah was called Phuvah in the book of Genesis (Genesis 46:13), and Pua in the book of Numbers (Numbers 26:23). He was the ancestor of the clan of the Punites.

Publius

(Latin origin: *Popular*)

(Acts of the Apostles 28:7). A.D. 1st century. Publius, the Roman governor of the island of Melita—today called Malta—owned some fields near the area where the ship, taking Paul and other prisoners from Caesarea to Rome, ran aground.

Publius received Paul and his companions kindly and lodged them for three days. Publius' father was in bed, ill with fever and dysentery. Paul went into his room, prayed, placed his hands on him, and healed him. When this happened, all the sick people on the island came and were healed. They gave Paul many gifts, and when he sailed, the people put on board what Paul and his companions needed for the voyage.

Pudens

(Latin origin: *Modest*)

(2 Timothy 4:21). A.D. 1st century. Pudens was one of the four persons—the others were Claudia, Eubulus, and Linus—who sent greetings to Timothy in the last letter written by Paul.

Pul

(Uncertain meaning)

(2 Kings 15:19). 8th century B.C. The king of Assyria, Tiglathpileser—also spelled Tilgathpilneser, (1 Chronicles 5:6), and called Pul in this verse—invaded Israel, and was paid one thousand talents of silver by King Menahem to turn back. (Please see the entry for Tilgathpilneser.)

Put

(Uncertain origin and meaning)

(1 Chronicles 1:8). Unspecified date. Put and his brothers—Canaan; Cush, *Ethiopia*; and Mizraim, *Egypt*—were sons of Ham and ancestors of their respective nations. The book of Genesis calls him Phut (Genesis 10:6).

Putiel

(Hebrew origin: *Contempt of God*)

(Exodus 6:25). 13th century B.C. Putiel was the father-in-law of Eleazar, the third son of the High Priest Aaron and his wife Elisheba. Putiel's grandson, Phinehas, was the High Priest in the days of Joshua.

Quartus

(Latin origin: *Fourth*)

(Romans 16:23). A.D. 1st century. Quartus was a Christian who, together with Gaius and Erastus, chamberlain of the city of Corinth, sent greetings to the church in Rome, through Paul's letter.

Raamah

(Hebrew origin: *Thunder*)

(Genesis 10:7). Unspecified date. Raamah was the son of Cush and grandson of Ham. His brothers were Seba, Havilah, Sabtah, and Sabtechah. Raamah's sons were Sheba and Dedan.

Later, his father Cush had another son, Nimrod, a powerful man and a mighty hunter, who established a kingdom in the land of Shinar and founded Nineveh and other cities.

Raamiah

(Hebrew origin: *God has shaken*)

(Nehemiah 7:7). 6th century B.C. Raamiah—also called Reelaiah (Ezra 2:2)—was one of the men who returned with Zerubbabel from the Babylonian Exile.

Rabmag

(Babylonian origin: Unknown meaning)

(Jeremiah 39:3). 6th century B.C. Rabmag was one of the commanders of King Nebuchadnezzar's army who sat in the Middle Gate of Jerusalem, after the Babylonians had succeeded in breaking through the walls of the city.

King Zedekiah fled that night, leaving the palace by the garden's gate, but was later captured, taken to the presence of Nebuchadnezzar, and blinded.

Rabmag was one of the officials whom the king of Babylon instructed to take good care of Jeremiah, and to see that he would not be harmed. The officials took the prophet out of the court of the prison and put him under the protection of the newly appointed governor of Judah, Gedaliah, son of Ahikam.

Rabsaris

(Babylonian origin: *Chief of the eunuchs*)

1. (2 Kings 18:17). 8th century B.C. Rabsaris, a high ranking officer in the Assyrian army, marched from Lachish to Jerusalem at the head of a great army, accompanied by two other officers, Tartan and Rabshakeh.

   King Sennacherib, who had just conquered the city of Lachish, had sent them to demand from King Hezekiah of Judah an unconditional surrender.

   A plague on the Assyrian camp wiped out the invaders, and Jerusalem was thus saved. However, the result of the war was that Judah reverted to its vassal status and continued to pay tribute.

2. (Jeremiah 39:3). 6th century B.C. Rabsaris was one of the commanders of King Nebuchadnezzar's army who sat in the Middle Gate of Jerusalem, after the Babylonians had succeeded in breaking through the walls of the city.

   King Zedekiah fled that night, leaving the palace by the garden's gate, but was later captured, taken to the presence of Nebuchadnezzar, and blinded.

   Rabsaris was one of the officials whom the king of Babylon instructed to take good care of Jeremiah, and to make sure that he would not be harmed. The officials took the prophet out of the court of the prison and put him under the protection of the newly appointed governor of Judah, Gedaliah, son of Ahikam.

Rabshakeh

(Assyrian origin: *Chief Butler*)

(2 Kings 18:17). 8th century B.C. Rabshakeh, a high ranking officer in the Assyrian army, marched from Lachish to Jerusalem at the head of a great army, accompanied by two other officers, Tartan and Rabsaris. King Sennacherib, who had just conquered the city of Lachish, had sent them to demand from King Hezekiah of Judah an unconditional surrender.

The Assyrians camped next to the walls of the city and called for the king to come out.

Hezekiah sent Eliakim—son of Hilkiah, head of the palace—Shebna the Scribe, and Joah—son of Asaph, the records keeper—to meet with the Assyrians.

Rabshakeh met them outside the walls of the city and spoke to them in Hebrew in a loud voice, "Hezekiah has no reason to feel confident, because he cannot rely on receiving help from Egypt, or from God".

Eliakim and his companions pleaded with the Assyrian, "Please speak to us in Aramaic! We do not wish that the people on the wall should understand your threats".

Rabshakeh paid no attention to their request, and he continued to shout in Hebrew, "Don't allow Hezekiah to deceive you!"

Eliakim and his companions didn't reply, and they returned to the king, with their clothes torn, to inform him of the failure of the negotiations.

Rabshakeh, when informed that the Assyrian king was now fighting against the city of Libnah, went to Sennacherib to give him his report.

During the siege of Jerusalem, Hezekiah received powerful moral backing from the great prophet-statesman Isaiah. A plague on the Assyrian camp wiped out the invaders, and Jerusalem was thus saved. However, the result of the war was that Judah reverted to its vassal status and continued to pay tribute.

The fact that Rabshakeh spoke perfect Hebrew indicates a strong probability that he was a member of "the ten lost tribes", the Israelites of the northern kingdom of Israel that were exiled years before by the conquering Assyrians to other regions of their empire, where they became "Assyrianized" and lost their previous national identity and religion.

Rachab

(Hebrew origin: *Wide*)

(Matthew 1:5). Unspecified date. Rachab was the wife of Salmon and the mother of Booz, an ancestor of Jesus, according to Matthew's genealogy.

Rachel

(Hebrew origin: *Ewe*)

(Genesis 29:6). 18th century B.C. Rachel, the daughter of Laban, was one of the two wives of her cousin Jacob, the love of his life, and the mother of his sons Joseph and Benjamin.

Jacob, aided by his mother, had tricked his blind father Isaac into giving him the blessing that was designed for Esau, his older brother. Furious at Jacob's trickery, Esau made a vow to kill Jacob, as soon as Isaac passed away. Rebekah, to protect Jacob from Esau's revenge, decided to send him away to her brother Laban in Haran.

She went to Isaac and complained, "The Hittite wives of Esau have made my life miserable. If Jacob would also marry a local girl, I wouldn't wish to continue living!"

Isaac called Jacob, blessed him, and said, "You shall not marry any Canaanite girl. Go to Paddan-Aram, to the house of Bethuel, your mother's father, and marry one of the daughters of your uncle Laban".

Upon arriving in Haran, Jacob saw shepherds next to a well, and he asked them, "Do you know Laban?"

They answered, "We do, and here is Rachel, his daughter, approaching with her father's sheep".

Jacob went to the well, rolled the stone from the opening, watered the sheep, kissed Rachel, and wept when he told her that he was the son of Rebekah, her father's sister.

Rachel ran home and told her father that a relative had arrived. Laban came out to see Jacob, embraced him, and brought him to his house.

Jacob fell in love with his beautiful cousin Rachel, and he told Laban that he would work for him seven years if he would let him marry his daughter. At the end of the seven years, Laban made a wedding feast.

The next morning, after the wedding night, Jacob woke up to find that the woman next to him was not Rachel but her older weak-eyed sister Leah. He immediately went to Laban to complain.

"It is the custom of this land", Laban explained, "that the elder daughter should be married before the younger. However, I will allow Rachel to marry you, a week from now, with the condition that you should work another seven years for me".

Jacob, when the week was over, married Rachel, and Laban gave her, as a wedding gift, his maid Bilhah to be her servant.

Jacob did not hide the fact that he loved Rachel and hated Leah, but it was Leah who gave him sons, while Rachel remained barren and envied her sister.

She said to Jacob, "If you don't give me children, I will die".

Jacob, angry with Rachel, answered, "Can I take the place of God? He is the one who keeps you from having children".

Rachel said, "Take my maid Bilhah and sleep with her, so that she can have a child for me".

Jacob took Bilhah as a concubine; she became pregnant and gave birth to a baby boy to whom Rachel gave the name of Daniel. Bilhah became pregnant a second time, and she had another boy, whom Rachel named Naphtali.

One day, Reuben, Leah's eldest son, brought some mandrakes from the field and gave them to his mother. Rachel saw the mandrakes and said to Leah, "Please give me some of your son's mandrakes".

Leah answered, "Is it not enough that you have taken my husband? You also want to take my son's mandrakes?"

Rachel replied, "He will lie with you tonight, in return for your son's mandrakes".

That evening, when Jacob returned from working in the field, Leah told him, "You are to come with me tonight, because I have hired you with my son's mandrakes". That night, Leah conceived, and when the time came, she gave birth to Issachar.

Rachel eventually also became pregnant and gave birth to a son, whom she called Joseph.

When the second seven years' period of laboring for his father-in-law had ended, Jacob told Laban that he would continue to work for him, but from then on, as payment for his work, he wanted to keep for himself all the speckled and spotted goats, and also all the brown-colored sheep. Laban agreed to those terms.

Six more years passed. Jacob had in the meantime become a very rich man, and he owned many cattle, camels, asses, maids, and servants. He felt that Laban's sons were jealous of his wealth, and that even Laban himself looked at him differently than before. So, he decided to return to Canaan with his two wives, his two concubines—Bilhah and Zilpah, who were the maids of Leah and Rachel—and his children.

When Laban discovered that Jacob was gone, he and his relatives set out in pursuit, and they caught up with Jacob and his family, seven days later, near the hills of Gilead.

"Why did you take away my daughters in secret, without letting me say goodbye?" complained Laban to Jacob. He then accused him of stealing his house idols, which, unbeknownst to Jacob, had been taken by Rachel.

"I was afraid that you would have taken your daughters from me by force. And with respect to your idols, I did not take them. You can search the tents, and if you find them, the person who took them will die".

Laban searched the tents, including Rachel's tent, but did not find the idols, because Rachel was sitting upon them. "I am sorry, Father, that I cannot get up to greet you, but I am having my monthly period", apologized Rachel.

Jacob and Laban made a covenant between them, which they celebrated by gathering stones into a heap, making a sacrifice, and eating. Then, they parted in peace: Laban returned home, and Jacob continued his voyage to Canaan.

On the way, Jacob and his family met Esau, who came to him with a troop of four hundred men. The two brothers embraced and wept. Esau invited Jacob and his family to come with him to Seir, but Jacob told him that Esau should go ahead, and that he, Jacob, would follow at a pace suitable to his children and his young animals. Esau returned that day to Seir, but Jacob did not follow, and they settled near Shechem.

Sometime later, the family traveled from Bethel to Ephrath. Rachel, who was again pregnant, gave birth to a boy, whom she called Benoni, *Son of my suffering*, but Jacob called him Benjamin, *Son of the south*, probably because he was the only one of his children who was born in the south, that is in Canaan; all the others—including Joseph, Benjamin's full brother—were born in Aram-Naharaim.

Rachel died giving birth to Benjamin, and she was buried on the way to Ephrath. Jacob set a pillar upon her grave.

Raddai

(Hebrew origin: *Domineering*)

(1 Chronicles 2:14). 11th century B.C. Raddai, son of Jesse, was one of David's six brothers.

Ragau

(Hebrew origin: *Friend*)

(Luke 3:35). Unspecified date. Ragau—called Reu in the book of Genesis (Genesis 11:18)—was the son of Phalec—called Peleg in Genesis (Genesis 10:25)—a descendant of Noah and Shem.

Ragau was thirty-two years old, when his son Saruch—called Serug in the book of Genesis (Genesis 11:20)—was born. Later, he had other sons and daughters, and he died at the age of two hundred and thirty-nine.

Raguel

(Hebrew origin: *Friend of God*)

(Numbers 10:29). 13th century B.C. Raguel the Midianite, the father-in-law of Moses, was the father of Hobab. He was also called Jethro and Reuel. (Please see the entry for Jethro [Exodus 3:1].)

Rahab

(Hebrew origin: *Wide*)

(Joshua 2:1). 12th century B.C. Rahab, a Canaanite harlot, lived in Jericho, in a house upon the wall of the city, where she rented rooms to travelers and visitors to the city.

Joshua sent two spies to Jericho, who found lodging in the house of Rahab. The king of Jericho, having heard that the two men were staying with Rahab, sent guards to capture them.

Rahab, who had hidden the spies in her roof, told the king's guards, "The two Israelites left just a little while ago. They went out through the gate of the city, under the cover of darkness. If you hurry, you might be able to catch them". The guards left immediately to pursue the men, in the direction of the river Jordan.

Rahab went to the roof and said to the men, "I know that God has delivered this country to the Israelites. I ask you to swear by God that you will spare my life and the life of my family".

The men promised her, "If you do not betray us, we will show you true loyalty when we capture the city".

"Hide for three days in the hills, until your pursuers give up and return to the city", said Rahab.

"Bring all your relatives to your house, and tie a crimson cord to the window, so that our men will recognize your house, and refrain from doing any injury to the people inside", the spies told her.

Rahab let them down by a rope through the window, and the two men made their way safely back to the Israelite camp, where they reported what they had seen to Joshua.

The Israelites captured the city, burned it down, and killed everybody with the sword, except for Rahab, her parents and brothers, whose lives and belongings were spared by orders of Joshua, according to the promise made to her by the spies. She lived the rest of her life among the Israelites.

Raham

(Hebrew origin: *Pity*)

(1 Chronicles 2:44). Unspecified date. Raham, of the tribe of Judah, was the son of Shema, and the father of Jorkoam.

Rahel

(Hebrew origin: *Ewe*)

(Jeremiah 31:15). 18th century B.C. Rahel is an alternative spelling of the name Rachel. The prophet Jeremiah wrote that the voice of Rahel was heard in Ramah, bitterly weeping and lamenting the exile of her children. (See the entry for Rachel [Genesis 29:6].)

Rakem

(Hebrew origin: *Embroidery*)

(1 Chronicles 7:16). 16th century B.C. Rakem, son of Peresh, a descendant of Machir, of the tribe of Manasseh, was the brother of Ulam.

Ram

(Hebrew origin: *High*)

1. (1 Chronicles 2:9). Unspecified date. Ram was the son of Hezron, of the tribe of Judah. His brothers were Jerahmeel and Chelubai, also called Caleb. His son was Amminadab, father of Nahshon, an ancestor of King David.
2. (1 Chronicles 2:25). Unspecified date. Ram was the son of Jerahmeel, the firstborn of Hezron. His brothers were Bunah, Oren, Ozem, and Ahijah. Ram's sons were Maaz, Jamin, and Eker.
3. (Job 32:2). Unspecified date. His descendant Elihu, son of Barachel the Buzite, was the youngest of Job's friends.

Ramiah

(Hebrew origin: *God has raised*)

(Ezra 10:25). 5th century B.C. Ramiah, a descendant of Parosh, divorced his foreign wife, during the days of Ezra.

Ramoth

(Hebrew origin: *Heights*)

(Ezra 10:29). 5th century B.C. Ramoth, a descendant of Bani, divorced his foreign wife, during the time of Ezra.

Rapha

(Hebrew origin: *Giant*)

1. (1 Chronicles 8:2). 17th century B.C. Rapha was the youngest of the five sons of Benjamin. The other sons, according to this list were Bela, Ashbel, Aharah, and Nohah. However, Rapha's name is not mentioned in the other lists of the sons of Benjamin: Genesis 46:21, Numbers 26:38, and 1 Chronicles 7:6.
2. (1 Chronicles 8:37). Unspecified date. Rapha—also called Rephaiah (1 Chronicles 9:43)—the son of Binea, a Benjamite, was a descendant of Jonathan, King Saul's son. His son was Eleasah.

Raphu

(Hebrew origin: *Cured*)

(Numbers 13:9). 14th century B.C. His son Palti, of the tribe of Benjamin, was one of the twelve men sent by Moses to spy the land of Canaan and report back about its cities and its inhabitants, if they were strong or weak, few or many, and to bring back the fruit of the land. The spies returned and gave a report, which was disheartening and defeatist.

Only two of the spies—Joshua, the son of Nun, and Caleb, the son of Jephunneh—disagreed and told the people that they should not fear the inhabitants of Canaan.

The Israelites refused to listen to the words of Joshua and Caleb, and they started to wail and cry. God punished their cowardice by condemning them to wander forty years in the wilderness, one year for each day that the spies scouted the land.

Reaia

(Hebrew origin: *Seen by God*)

(1 Chronicles 5:5). Unspecified date. Reaia, son of Micah and father of Baal, was the grandfather of Beerah, a leader of the tribe of Reuben who was taken to captivity by Tilgathpilneser, king of Assyria.

Reaiah

(Hebrew origin: *Seen by God*)

1. (1 Chronicles 4:2). Unspecified date. Reaiah, descendant of Judah, was the son of Shobal and the father of Jahath. His grandchildren were Ahumai and Lahad.
2. (Ezra 2:47). Unspecified date. Reaiah was the ancestor of a clan of Temple servants that returned with Zerubbabel from the Babylonian Exile.

Reba

(Hebrew origin: *Fourth*)

(Numbers 31:8). 13th century B.C. Reba was one of the five kings of Midian—the others were Rekem, Zur, Hur, and Evi—who were killed in battle by the Israelites, under the command of Phinehas, the son of Eleazar the Priest. Sihon, king of the Amorites, and the seer Balaam were also killed in the same battle.

Rebecca

(Hebrew origin: Uncertain meaning)

(Romans 9:10). 19th century B.C. Rebecca is an alternative spelling for Rebekah, the wife of Isaac. (Please see the entry for Rebekah [Genesis 22:23].)

Rebekah

(Hebrew origin: Uncertain meaning)

(Genesis 22:23). 19th century B.C. Rebekah, the daughter of Bethuel, Abraham's nephew, was the wife of Isaac and the mother of the twins Esau and Jacob.

Isaac was forty years old and still unmarried, when his mother Sarah died. Abraham, who did not want his son to marry any of the local Canaanite girls, sent his trusted servant Eliezer to his relatives in Haran, Mesopotamia, with instructions to bring back a bride for Isaac.

Eliezer took with him ten loaded camels, and he set out for the city of Nahor. When he arrived there, he made the camels kneel down by the well outside the city, and he said to himself, "If a girl comes to whom I will say, 'Please, lower your jar that I may drink', and she replies, 'Drink and I will also water your camels', she will be the one that God has chosen for Isaac".

He had scarcely finished speaking, when Rebekah came, carrying a jar on her shoulder. She went down to the spring, filled her jar, and came up.

Eliezer ran to her and asked, "May I drink a little water from your jar?"

"Drink, my lord", she said. After he had drunk, she said, "I will also bring water for your camels, until they finish drinking".

Eliezer gazed at her silently, while she gave water to the camels. When she finished, he took a gold earring and two gold bracelets, and he asked her, "Whose daughter are you? Is there room in your father's house for us to stay?"

She replied, "I am the daughter of Bethuel. There is plenty of straw and feed at home, and also room to spend the night".

Abraham's servant bowed low and blessed the Lord for having guided him to the house of his master's kinsmen. Rebekah ran to her mother's house and told her relatives what had happened. When her brother Laban saw the earring and the bracelets on his sister's hands, he ran to the well to invite the man to come to the house.

Eliezer entered the house, and the camels were unloaded and given straw. Water was brought to bathe the feet of the guests. When food was set before Eliezer, he refused to eat, until he told them how Abraham had sent him to find a bride for his son and heir, and how he realized that Rebekah was the intended one.

Laban and Bethuel answered, "The matter was decreed by God; we cannot speak to you bad or good. Here is Rebekah, take her with you and go, and let her be a wife to your master's son, as the Lord has spoken".

When Eliezer heard these words, he bowed low to the ground before God. Then, he brought out objects of silver and gold, and clothing, and gave them to Rebekah. He also gave presents to Laban and to his mother.

Eliezer and his men ate and drank, and they spent that night in Bethuel's house. Early next morning, they told their hosts that they were ready to depart.

Rebekah's mother and Laban asked, "May Rebekah stay with us for another ten days?"

Eliezer answered, "Please do not delay our departure".

They called Rebekah and asked her, "Will you go with this man?"

Rebekah answered, "I will". Then, the young woman, her nurse Deborah, and her maids arose, mounted the camels, and followed Eliezer, while her relatives blessed her.

Isaac was strolling in the field toward evening, when he saw camels approaching. Rebekah raised her eyes and saw Isaac. She alighted from the camel and asked Eliezer, "Who is that man walking in the field toward us?"

Eliezer answered, "That's my master".

Rebekah took her veil and covered herself. Isaac brought her into the tent of his mother Sarah. They married, and Rebekah became a great comfort to Isaac, after the death of his mother.

For twenty years, Rebekah was not able to conceive, until Isaac, then sixty years old, prayed to God on her behalf. During Rebekah's pregnancy, she felt the babies struggling in her womb, and she was told by the Lord that each of the boys would become the progenitor of a nation, but that the older would serve the younger. Esau was born first, red and hairy. Moments later, Jacob came out, holding Esau's heel.

Esau, his father's favorite, grew up to be a skilled hunter, a simple fellow, an outdoor man, impetuous, impatient, and easily manipulated by his shrewd brother. Jacob, his mother's favorite, was completely his opposite: a patient, thoughtful, stay-at-home type.

The family went to live in Gerar, a city ruled by Abimelech, king of the Philistines, because there was a famine in Canaan. As Abraham, his father, had done many years ago in similar circumstances, Isaac presented Rebekah as his sister, because he was afraid that, if the men of Gerar would know that he was her husband, they would kill him to get rid of him.

When Abimelech, looking through a window, saw Isaac and Rebekah making love, the king reproached Isaac and told him that his deception could have caused people to sin with Rebekah. Abimelech forbade his people to take any action against Isaac or Rebekah, under penalty of death.

Isaac remained in Gerar and prospered. His wealth made him the target of envy by the people of Gerar, who fought with Isaac's herdsmen for the water wells. Abimelech then asked him to leave his kingdom, and Isaac moved back to Beersheba, where Abimelech visited him and signed a peace treaty with him.

Their two sons grew up. Esau married two Hittite women, Judith and Bashemath, who made Rebekah and Isaac's lives miserable. Jacob remained unmarried, for the time being.

Isaac, who had become blind in his old age, decided to bless his eldest son. He called Esau, told him to go out to the field to hunt, bring back venison, and prepare him his favorite food. This was overheard by Rebekah.

When Esau went out to hunt, she said to Jacob, "I have just heard your father saying to Esau that he will bless him, after he brings him something to eat. Now, do what I tell you: Go to the flock and bring me two young goats, and I will cook them the way your father likes so much. You will take it to your father, so that he will eat it, and bless you, before he dies".

"But mother, Esau is a hairy man, and my skin is smooth", protested Jacob. "If my father will touch me", he added, "he will realize that I am deceiving him, and will curse me, instead of blessing me!"

Rebekah said to her son, "Don't worry, your curse will be upon me, my son. Just do what I tell you, and go bring me the young goats".

Jacob brought the goats to his mother, who cooked them the way Isaac liked it. Rebekah then took some of Esau's clothing and put them on Jacob. She put goat's skin over his hands and neck, gave him the food, and sent him to Isaac.

Jacob succeeded in convincing his father that he was Esau, and the deceived old man bestowed his blessing on Jacob.

When Esau returned and discovered the deception, he implored his father to also give him a blessing. Isaac replied that Esau would live by the sword and serve his brother. Furious at Jacob's trickery, Esau decided to kill Jacob, as soon as Isaac passed away.

Rebekah, to protect Jacob from Esau's revenge, decided to send him away to her brother Laban in Haran. She went to Isaac and complained, "The Hittite wives of Esau have made my life miserable. If Jacob would also marry a local girl, I wouldn't wish to continue living!"

Isaac called Jacob, blessed him, and said, "You shall not marry any Canaanite girl. Go to Paddan-Aram, to the house of Bethuel, your mother's father, and marry one of the daughters of your uncle Laban".

Years passed, Deborah, Rebekah's nurse, died, and was buried near Bethel under an oak. Rebekah died and was buried in the cave of Machpelah, where Abraham and Sarah were buried, and where Esau and Jacob buried Isaac, when he died at the age of one hundred and eighty.

Rechab

(Hebrew origin: *Rider*)

1. (2 Samuel 4:2). 11th century B.C. Rechab and his brother Baanah, of the tribe of Benjamin, sons of Rimmon from Beeroth, were captains in the army of King Ishbosheth, the son and heir of King Saul.

   The two brothers came to the royal palace one day at noontime, found Ishbosheth lying on his bed, beheaded him, and brought his head to David in Hebron, expecting to be handsomely rewarded.

   David's reaction was not what the two murderers had expected. He said to them, "The man who told me that Saul was dead thought that he was bringing me good news. Instead of rewarding him, I had him killed. How much more then, when wicked men have killed a blameless man in bed in his own house?! I will avenge his blood on you, and I will rid the earth of you!"

   The king ordered his men to kill the murderers, cut off their hands and feet, and hang them up by the pool in Hebron. The head of Ishbosheth was buried in the sepulcher of Abner in Hebron.

2. (2 Kings 10:15). 9th century B.C. Rechab was a descendant of the Kenite tribe, to which Hobab, Moses' father-in-law, had belonged. His son Jehonadab—called Jonadab in the book of Jeremiah (Jeremiah 35:6)—was the leader of an ascetic sect, which abstained from wine, did not sow seeds nor plant vineyards, and did not build houses but lived in tents.

3. (Nehemiah 3:14). 5th century B.C. His son Malchiah, ruler of the Bethhaccerem district, repaired the Dung Gate of Jerusalem, including the doors, locks, and the bars, during the days of Nehemiah.

Reelaiah

(Hebrew origin: *Trembling before God*)

(Ezra 2:2). 6th century B.C. Reelaiah—also called Raamiah (Nehemiah 7:7)—was one of the men who returned with Zerubbabel from the Babylonian Exile

Regem

(Hebrew origin: *Stone heap*)

(1 Chronicles 2:47). Unspecified date. Regem was the son of Jahdai, of the tribe of Judah. His brothers were Jotham, Gesham, Pelet, Ephah, and Shaaph.

Regemmelech

(Hebrew origin: *King's heap*)

(Zechariah 7:2). 6th century B.C. Regemmelech and Sherezer, in the fourth year of the reign of King Darius, during the days of the prophet Zechariah, headed a delegation sent from the Jewish community in Persia to the priests in the Temple in Jerusalem. Regemmelech and his companions were instructed to inquire whether the custom of mourning the destruction of the Temple should be continued, taking into account that the Temple had been rebuilt.

Rehabiah

(Hebrew origin: *God has widened*)

(1 Chronicles 23:17). 13th century B.C. Rehabiah, the only son of Eliezer, the second son of Moses and Zipporah, was blessed with many children. Among his descendants were Isshiah, a Levite in the service of the Tabernacle, during the reign of King David. Another descendant was Shelomith, who was in charge of the treasury of the Tabernacle, during the same period.

Rehob

(Hebrew origin: *Street*)

1. (2 Samuel 8:3). 11th century B.C. His son Hadadezer, king of Zobah, a Syrian kingdom near the river Euphrates, was defeated by King David who made him his vassal.

2. (Nehemiah 10:11). 5th century B.C. Rehob was one of the Levites who signed Nehemiah's solemn agreement to separate themselves from the foreigners living in the land, to refrain from intermarrying with them, and to dedicate their firstborn to God, among other obligations.

Rehoboam

(Hebrew origin: *The people have increased*)

(1 Kings 11:43). 10th century B.C. Rehoboam, the son of King Solomon and Naamah the Ammonitess, was forty one years old, when he ascended to the throne of Judah.

After being proclaimed king in Jerusalem, Rehoboam went to Shechem to be confirmed as king by the northern tribes.

Jeroboam, who had found refuge in Egypt from Solomon's persecution, upon hearing of Solomon's death, returned to Shechem at that time and headed the delegation, which met with Rehoboam. The leaders of the northern tribes asked the king to lighten the heavy taxes and the forced labor that Solomon had imposed on them.

Rehoboam said to them, "Come back to me in three days, and you will receive my answer".

King Rehoboam consulted with the elders who had served his father Solomon, during his lifetime. He asked them, "What answer do you advise me to give to this people?"

The elders said to him, "If you will be a servant to those people today and serve them, and if you respond to them with kind words, they will be your servants always".

He ignored their advice and consulted with the younger people, who had grown up with him, and now served him. The young men told him, "You should make it clear to the people that not only you will not lighten their burden, but, to the contrary, you will increase it".

Jeroboam and the delegation of the northern tribes went to see Rehoboam on the third day. The king spoke to them harshly, following the young men's advice, "My father made your yoke heavy, and I will add to it. He flogged you with whips, but I will flog you with scorpions".

The reaction of the people was not surprising. They screamed, "We have no portion in David, no share in Jesse's son!"

Adoram, the officer in charge of the forced labor, was sent to face the discontented and rebellious assembly at Shechem. The people stoned him to death. Rehoboam saved his own life by hurriedly mounting his chariot, and fleeing to Jerusalem. The northern tribes then decided to secede and proclaimed that they were now a new kingdom, to be called Israel. Jeroboam was chosen as their king.

Upon his return to Jerusalem, Rehoboam raised a large army from the tribes of Judah and Benjamin to fight against the rebels. Shemaiah, a prophet, dissuaded Rehoboam from going to war against Jeroboam, saying, "God has willed it to be so".

Jeroboam wished to make Israel completely independent from Judah. To play down the importance of Solomon's Temple, he revived the sanctuaries at Bethel in the south of his country, and Dan in the north, setting up golden calves in each of them.

Rehoboam was left with a small kingdom, called Judah, which included the territories of the tribes of Judah, Simeon, and Benjamin. He also controlled the vassal kingdom of Edom and the Shephelah region. He refused to regard the division as a *fait accompli,* and he waged constant war against the northern kingdom.

Five years later, Pharaoh Shishak invaded the country with a powerful army of one thousand two hundred chariots, and sixty thousand horsemen. The Egyptians forced Rehoboam to give them the treasures of the Temple and the palace, including the shields of gold, which Solomon had made. Rehoboam had them replaced with bronze shields, which were kept in the armory and were brought out only when the king visited the Temple.

To defend the country from future invasions, Rehoboam established in his southern frontier a chain of garrisoned cities along the edge of the hills, and he placed his sons in fortified towns throughout the kingdom. He did not build any fortifications in the northern frontier, because he was still hopeful of reuniting the kingdom.

Rehoboam had eighteen wives and sixty concubines. Among his wives were Mahalath, the daughter of Jerimoth, the son of King David, and Abihail, the daughter of Eliab, King David's brother. His favorite wife was Maachah, the daughter of Absalom, who bore him four sons: Abijah, Attai, Ziza, and Shelomith.

Rehoboam reigned seventeen years. When he died, he was buried in the royal tombs in the City of David, and his son Abijah succeeded him.

Rehum
(Hebrew origin: *Compassionate*)

1. (Ezra 2:2). 6th century B.C. Rehum—also called Nehum (Nehemiah 7:7)—was one of the men who returned with Zerubbabel from the Babylonian Exile.
2. (Ezra 4:8). 5th century B.C. Rehum was the Persian commissioner in Samaria. The foreign settlers that the Assyrians had brought to Samaria asked him and Shimshai the Scribe to send a letter, written in Aramaic, to King Artaxerxes, accusing the Jews of rebuilding the walls of Jerusalem with the intention to rebel.

The king, who was persuaded that the rebuilding constituted a threat to his authority, immediately wrote back, ordering the work to stop, and decreeing that the city should not be rebuilt unless explicitly allowed by him. Rehum and Shimshai received the letter, hurried to Jerusalem, and forced the Jews to stop the work. The rebuilding of Jerusalem was not renewed, until the second year of the reign of King Darius.

3. (Nehemiah 3:17). 5th century B.C. Rehum, son of Bani, was one of the Levites who helped to repair the walls of Jerusalem.
4. (Nehemiah 10:25). 5th century B.C. Rehum was among the leaders who signed Nehemiah's solemn agreement to separate themselves from the foreigners living in the land, to refrain from intermarrying with them, and to dedicate their firstborn to God, among other obligations.
5. (Nehemiah 12:3). 6th century B.C. Rehum was a priest who returned with Zerubbabel from the Babylonian Exile.

Rei
(Hebrew origin: *Sociable*)

(1 Kings 1:8). 10th century B.C. Rei was one of the leading officials in David's court who supported Solomon as heir of the throne against Adonijah. The other supporters of Solomon were Zadok the Priest; Benaiah, the son of Jehoiada; Nathan, the prophet; and Shimei.

Rekem
(Hebrew origin: *Embroidery*)

1. (Numbers 31:8). 13th century B.C. Rekem was one of the five kings of Midian—the others were Reba, Zur, Hur, and Evi—who were killed in battle by the Israelites under the command of Phinehas, the son of Eleazar the Priest. Sihon, king of the Amorites, and the seer Balaam were also killed in the same battle.
2. (1 Chronicles 2:43). Unspecified date. Rekem was the son of Hebron, of the tribe

of Judah, and brother of Tappuah, Korah, and Shema.

Remaliah

(Hebrew origin: *God has bedecked*)

(2 Kings 15:25). 8th century B.C. Remaliah was the father of Pekah, the army commander who killed King Pekahiah of Israel and proclaimed himself king.

Remphan

(Uncertain origin and meaning)

(Acts of the Apostles 7:43). Remphan was a heathen idol. The prophet Amos called it Chiun (Amos 5:26).

Rephael

(Hebrew origin: *God has healed*)

(1 Chronicles 26:7). 10th century B.C. Rephael, son of Shemaiah and grandson of Obededom, was one of the gatekeepers of the Tabernacle, during the reign of King David. His brothers—all of them brave men and leaders of their clan—were Othni, Elihu, Obed, Elzabad, and Semachiah.

Rephah

(Hebrew origin: *Supports*)

(1 Chronicles 7:25). Unspecified date. Rephah was a descendant of Ephraim and an ancestor of Joshua.

Rephaiah

(Hebrew origin: *Healed by God*)

1. (1 Chronicles 3:21). Unspecified date. Rephaiah descended from King David through Zerubbabel.
2. (1 Chronicles 4:42). 8th century B.C. Rephaiah, son of Ishi, and his brothers—Neariah, Pelatiah, and Uzziel, of the tribe of Simeon—at the head of five hundred men, went to Mount Seir, southeast of the Dead Sea, exterminated the last surviving Amalekites, and settled in the region.

3. (1 Chronicles 7:2). Unspecified date. Rephaiah, son of Tola, and his brothers—Uzzi, Jeriel, Jahmai, Jibsam, and Shemuel—were leaders of the tribe of Issachar.
4. (1 Chronicles 9:43). Unspecified date. Rephaiah—also called Rapha (1 Chronicles 8:37)—son of Binea, a Benjamite, was a descendant of Jonathan, King Saul's son. His son was Eleasah.
5. (Nehemiah 3:9). 5th century B.C. Rephaiah, son of Hur, ruler of half of Jerusalem, helped to repair the walls of the city, during the days of Nehemiah.

Resheph

(Hebrew origin: *Live coal*)

(1 Chronicles 7:25). Unspecified date. Resheph was a descendant of Ephraim and an ancestor of Joshua.

Reu

(Hebrew origin: *Friend*)

(Genesis 11:18). Unspecified date. Reu—called Ragau by Luke (Luke 3:35)—was the son of Peleg—called Phalec by Luke—a descendant of Noah and Shem. Reu was thirty-two years old, when his son Serug—called Saruch, in Luke's genealogy of Jesus—was born. Later, he had other sons and daughters, and he died at the age of two hundred and thirty-nine.

Reuben

(Hebrew origin: *See a son*)

(Genesis 29:32). 17th century B.C. Reuben was the firstborn son of Jacob and Leah. She gave him the name Reuben, *See a son*, hoping that now Jacob would love her, but this did not happen.

Reuben was the oldest brother, but, because he was ineffective and not too bright, the leadership of the family fell on the shoulders of his younger brother Judah. The first mention of Reuben, after his birth, is when he brought some mandrakes from the field and gave them to his mother. Rachel felt a craving for them and told her sister Leah that she could spend the night with Jacob, if she would give her some mandrakes. That night, Leah conceived, and, when the time came, she gave birth to Issachar.

Some years later, Reuben went to bed with Bilhah, his father's concubine, thus, showing a lack of filial respect and a mindless disregard of the possible consequences of his act. Jacob found out what Reuben had done, but he did not say anything at the time.

Reuben and his brothers were jealous that their young brother Joseph was Jacob's favorite son. They resented him for reporting their misbehaviors to their father; and they hated him more for telling them his dreams, where the brothers did obeisance to him.

One day, his father sent Joseph to bring him news of his brothers who were feeding the sheep in Shechem. Joseph found them in Dothan. The brothers saw him coming from afar and conspired to kill him.

Reuben told his brothers, "Don't hurt the boy, just cast him into a pit". His intention was to come back later, save Joseph, and return him to his father. The brothers stripped Joseph of his coat of many colors, and they lowered him down into a dry well. Then, they sat down to a meal. Reuben, instead of staying with them, and keeping a watchful eye on Joseph, went away in some personal errand.

While the brothers were eating, they saw in the distance a caravan of camels approaching. When it came close, they saw that the men were Ishmaelites, accompanied by some Midianite merchants, who were carrying spices, balm, and myrrh from Gilead to Egypt.

Judah, knowing that his brothers were still determined to kill Joseph, said to them, "There is nothing to gain by killing our brother and concealing his blood. Let's sell him to the Ishmaelites. Then, we won't have to hurt him, because after all, he is our brother, our own flesh".

The brothers, who were convinced by Judah's argument, pulled Joseph out of the well and sold him to the Ishmaelites for twenty pieces of silver. In Egypt, the Midianite

merchants brought him to the slave market, where he was bought by an official of the Pharaoh.

Reuben returned to his brothers, after the caravan had already left with Joseph. He looked down the well and was dismayed to find that Joseph was not there. He tore his clothes, went to his brothers, and, in desperation, asked them, "What shall I do? The boy is not there!"

The brothers concocted a plausible story to tell Jacob. They dipped Joseph's coat into the blood of a goat that they had just killed, brought this "evidence" to their father, and said to him, "This is what we have found. Does it belong to your son?"

Jacob, recognizing his son's coat, assumed that Joseph had been killed and eaten by a wild animal. He tore his clothes, put on sackcloth, and mourned him. His children tried to comfort him, but he refused to be consoled, and he said to them, "I will go down to my grave mourning for my son!"

Many years went by, Joseph, after having been the trusted servant in the home of an important Egyptian official, spent years in jail, because of the trumped-up charges of his master's wife, and had now become, in an astonishing turn of events, the most powerful man in Egypt after Pharaoh.

There was a great famine in Egypt, but Joseph, having foreseen that this would happen, had taken care of storing in warehouses the abundant crops that had been produced in the previous seven years.

The famine in Canaan was also severe. When Jacob heard that it was possible to buy grain in Egypt, he sent there all his sons, except for young Benjamin, because his father was afraid that something would happen to him.

The brothers arrived in Egypt and were brought to the presence of Joseph, who was personally in charge of selling the grain. They didn't recognize that the powerful Egyptian vizier in front of them was the young brother whom they had last seen over twenty years before, but Joseph recognized them immediately and remembered his dreams where his family bowed to him. He decided to act as if he didn't know them and accused them of being spies. The brothers denied this, saying that they were all sons of the same man, and that they had a younger brother at home.

He had them confined then in prison for three days. On the third day, he said to them, "I am a God-fearing man. I will let you live if you are honest men. One of you will stay in this prison. The rest of you can take grain to your starving families. But you must bring back your youngest brother, so that your words can be verified, and I will not put you to death".

The brothers said to each other, "This is happening to us because of what we did to our brother, when he pleaded with us, and we wouldn't listen".

Reuben said to them, "Didn't I tell you, don't do anything to the boy, and you wouldn't listen? And now we are paying for it".

The brothers had no idea that Joseph understood each word that they said, because he had been talking to them through an interpreter. Joseph turned away from them and wept. Then, he returned to them, took Simeon, and had him tied up in front of them.

Joseph ordered his men to fill the bags of the brothers with grain, and to place each man's money back in his bag. The brothers received provisions for the trip, loaded the donkeys with the grain, and departed. That night, they rested in an inn on the road. One of the men opened his bag to feed his donkey, and he was shocked to find that his money was there.

When they came back to Canaan, they told their father every word that the Egyptian vizier had said to them, and his demand that they should bring Benjamin to Egypt. This, Jacob absolutely refused to allow.

Reuben tried to change his father's mind and said, "I authorize you to kill my two sons if I don't bring Benjamin back to you! Give him to my care, and I will bring him back!" Not surprisingly, Jacob was not convinced by this senseless offer to have two of his grandsons killed.

The famine got worse, and, soon enough, the grain that the brothers had brought from Egypt was finished. Judah asked his father to let Benjamin go with them to Egypt, and he assured Jacob that he would be personally responsible for his young brother's safe return to Canaan. Jacob, seeing that he had no choice, reluctantly allowed Benjamin to go with his brothers to Egypt.

The brothers took Benjamin with them and returned to Egypt, bearing gifts for the vizier. This time Joseph made himself known to his brothers, forgave them, and told them to bring Jacob and their families to Egypt, and to settle in the fertile land of Goshen.

Joseph gave his brothers wagons and provisions for the journey. To each of them, he gave a change of clothing, but to Benjamin, he gave five changes of clothing and three hundred pieces of silver. To his father, he sent ten male donkeys loaded with the best things of Egypt, and ten female donkeys loaded with grain, bread, and provisions for his father on the journey. As he sent his brothers off on their way, he admonished them not to quarrel among themselves.

The brothers returned to their father Jacob in the land of Canaan, and they told him "Joseph lives, and he is the ruler of Egypt!"

At first, Jacob could not believe them, until he saw the wagons that Joseph had sent to transport him. Then, he exclaimed, "My son Joseph is alive! I must go and see him, before I die!" The brothers placed their father Jacob, their children, and their wives in the wagons, and, taking along their livestock and their possessions, went to the land of Goshen in Egypt. Reuben's sons—Hanoch, Phallu, Hezron, and Carmi—were among those who immigrated to Egypt.

Many years later, when Jacob was on his deathbed, he spoke to his sons. To Reuben, he said that, although he was his firstborn, he would excel no longer, because he had defiled his father's bed, referring to the sexual relationship that Reuben had once had with Bilhah, his father's concubine.

Jacob's last words were to ask his sons to bury him in the cave of Machpelah, where his parents, grandparents, and his wife Leah were buried.

When the seventy days' period of mourning for his father was over, Joseph asked permission from the Pharaoh to allow him to go to Canaan and bury his father there. With Pharaoh's approval, Joseph, accompanied by his brothers, the court officials, Egyptian dignitaries, and a large troop of chariots and horsemen, took Jacob's body to Canaan, and they buried him in the cave of the field of Machpelah.

Reuben and his brothers feared that now that Jacob was dead, Joseph would take revenge for the wrong that they had done to him. They sent a message to Joseph, saying that Jacob, before his death, had told them to urge Joseph to forgive them. Then, they went to Joseph, flung themselves before him, and told him that they were prepared to be his slaves.

Joseph said to them, "Don't worry. God intended it all for the good, for the survival of many people".

Centuries later, Moses blessed the tribes in his farewell speech. About the tribe of Reuben, he said, "They are very few. I hope they never die out".

The tribe that descended from Reuben settled on the east side of the Jordan, after the conquest of Canaan. It was small, unremarkable, and it eventually disappeared from history as one of the "ten lost tribes".

(For a detailed story of Joseph and his brothers, please see the entry for Joseph.)

Reuel

(Hebrew origin: *God is my friend*)

1. (Genesis 36:4). 18th century B.C. Reuel was the son of Esau and his wife Bashemath, the daughter of Ishmael.
2. (Exodus 2:18). 13th century B.C. Reuel the Midianite was the father-in-law of Moses. He was also called Jethro, Raguel, and Hobab. (Please see the entry for Jethro [Exodus 3:1].)
3. (Numbers 2:14). 14th century B.C. His son Eliasaph was the leader of the tribe of Gad, during the Exodus from Egypt. His name is spelled Deuel in the book of Numbers (Numbers 1:14).

4. (1 Chronicles 9:8). Unspecified date. Reuel, the son of Ibnijah, was the father of Shephathiah. His grandson Meshullam was the head of a Benjamite clan that lived in Jerusalem.

Reumah

(Hebrew origin: *Raised*)

(Genesis 22:24). 20th century B.C. Reumah was the concubine of Nahor, Abraham's brother. Her sons were Gaham, Tebah, Thahash, and Maachah.

Rezia

(Hebrew origin: *Delight*)

(1 Chronicles 7:39). Unspecified date. Rezia, son of Ulla, was a brave warrior, and the leader of a clan of the tribe of Asher. His brothers were Arah and Haniel.

Rezin

(Hebrew origin: *Delight*)

1. (2 Kings 15:37). 8th century B.C. Rezin, king of Syria, entered into an alliance with King Pekah of Israel against King Ahaz of Judah, to force him to join them in their fight against Assyria. The allied armies invaded Judah and besieged Jerusalem, with the intention to depose the king and install a certain son of Tabeal in his place (Isaiah 7:6). Rezin did not succeed in capturing the city, but he was able to take Elath away from Judah.

Ahaz asked Tiglathpileser, king of Assyria, for help against Aram and Israel, and he sent him, as tribute, the treasuries of the Temple and the palace. The king of Assyria attacked Damascus, captured it, and killed King Rezin.
2. (Ezra 2:48). Unspecified date. Rezin was the ancestor of a clan of Temple servants that returned with Zerubbabel from the Babylonian Exile.

Rezon

(Hebrew origin: *Prince*)

(1 Kings 11:23). 10th century B.C. Rezon, son of Eliadah, was an officer in the army of Hadadezer, king of Zobah. When David conquered Zobah, Rezon and a band of his soldiers fled to Damascus, and they settled there. Eventually, he took over the country and proclaimed himself king of Syria. Rezon remained a bitter enemy of Israel, during all the days of Solomon.

Rhesa

(Hebrew origin: *God has cured*)

(Luke 3:27). Unspecified date. Rhesa, son of Zorobabel and father of Joanna, was an ancestor of Jesus, in the genealogy of Luke.

Rhoda

(Greek origin: *Rose*)

(Acts of the Apostles 12:13). A.D. 1st century. Rhoda was the servant girl of the mother of John Mark, Mary, in whose house the believers gathered to pray in Jerusalem.

Peter, after escaping from Herod's prison with the help of an angel, came to the house of Mary and knocked on the door. Rhoda approached the door and heard Peter's voice asking her to open it. She was so overwhelmed with joy that, instead of letting him in, she ran back inside the house and told all those present that Peter was outside the gate.

"You are crazy!" they told her.

When she insisted that Peter was outside, they retorted, "It must be his angel".

Peter continued knocking. Finally, they opened the door and were astonished to see him safe and sound. They were filled with joy, and it took quite a while for Simon Peter to be able to calm them, and to tell them how God had freed him. He asked them to tell it also to James and to the other believers; then, he departed, and went somewhere else.

Ribai

(Hebrew origin: *Contentious*)

(2 Samuel 23:29). 11th century B.C. Ribai of Gibeah, a Benjamite, was the father of Ittai, a member of King David's elite army group known as The Thirty.

Rimmon

(Hebrew origin: *Pomegranate*)

1. (2 Samuel 4:2). 11th century B.C. Rimmon, a Beerothite of the tribe of Benjamin, was the father of Baanah and Rechab, the murderers of King Ishbosheth. The two brothers brought the head of the murdered man to David in Hebron, expecting a reward, but, instead, were executed for their crime.

2. (2 Kings 5:18). Rimmon, the god of Syria, had a Temple in Damascus, where the king of Syria would come to worship, accompanied by his courtiers and army commanders. Naaman, the commander of the Syrian army, who had become a believer in God, after being cured of his leprosy, asked God to forgive him if he would bow in front of the idol, when carrying out his obligation to accompany the king to the Temple of Rimmon.

Rinnah

(Hebrew origin: *Song*)

(1 Chronicles 4:20). Unspecified date. Rinnah, son of Shimon, was a descendant of Judah. His brothers were Amnon, Benhanan, and Tilon.

Riphath

(Uncertain origin and meaning)

(Genesis 10:3). Unspecified date. Riphath, son of Gomer, was a grandson of Japheth. His brothers were Togarmah and Ashkenaz.

Rizpah

(Hebrew origin: *Pavement*)

(2 Samuel 3:7). 10th century B.C. Rizpah, the daughter of Aiah, had been a concubine of King Saul, to whom she bore two sons, Armoni and Mephibosheth. After Saul died in battle, Rizpah went to Mahanaim where Abner had placed Ishbosheth, King Saul's sole surviving son, as king over all the tribes, with the exception of the tribe of Judah, which recognized David as its ruler.

It was because of Rizpah that Abner switched his loyalties from Ishbosheth to David. Ishbosheth, without foreseeing the consequences, had made the fatal error of accusing Abner of having made love to Rizpah.*

Abner became very angry and swore that he would make David king over Israel and Judah. He went with twenty men to meet David in Hebron; there, Abner promised that he would rally the entire nation around David. David and Abner reached an agreement, but Abner was murdered by Joab, at the city's gate, in revenge for the death of Asahel. Shortly afterward Ishbosheth was also murdered.

Years later, the people of Gibeon demanded revenge against King Saul's family, because he had tried to wipe them out. The two sons of Rizpah—Armoni and Mephibosheth—and their five nephews were delivered by King David to the Gibeonites, who hanged them on a hill.

Rizpah took sackcloth, sat on it upon a rock, and guarded the bodies against the birds and the beasts of the field, from the beginning of the harvest season until, months later, the rains came.

*Note: Making love to the present or past concubine of a king was interpreted in ancient Israel as a symbolic attempt to usurp power, reminiscent of the episode, when Absalom made love to the ten concubines whom David, in his flight from Jerusalem, had left behind to take care of the palace.

Rohgah

(Hebrew origin: *Outcry*)

(1 Chronicles 7:34). Unspecified date. Rohgah was the son of Shamer, of the tribe of Asher. His brothers were Ahi, Jehubbah, and Aram.

Romamtiezer

(Hebrew origin: *I have raised help*)

(1 Chronicles 25:4). 10th century B.C. Romamtiezer, a Levite, member of a family of musicians, was in charge of the twenty-fourth turn of service that played musical instruments—cymbals, psalteries, and harps—in the House of God, during the reign of David.

He had thirteen brothers and three sisters, all of them trained to be skillful musicians by their father Heman, one of the kingdom's three leading musicians; the other two were Asaph and Jeduthun.

Rosh

(Hebrew origin: *Head*)

(Genesis 46:21). 17th century B.C. Rosh, one of the ten sons of Benjamin, was among the seventy Israelites who immigrated to Egypt.

According to the list in Genesis, his brothers were Becher, Ashbel, Gera, Naaman, Ehi, Muppim, Huppim, Belah, and Ard.

Rosh is not mentioned in the other three lists of the sons of Benjamin: Numbers 26:38, 1 Chronicles 7:6, and 1 Chronicles 8:1.

Rufus

(Latin origin: *Red*)

1. (Mark 15:21). A.D. 1st century. Rufus and his brother Alexander were the sons of Simon, a Cyrenian who was compelled by the Roman soldiers to carry Jesus' cross on his way to Calvary.

2. (Romans 16:13). A.D. 1st century. Rufus was a Christian to whom Paul sent greetings in his letter to the Christians in Rome. The apostle calls him "chosen in the Lord" and also salutes Rufus' mother, whom he considers as his own.

Some scholars believe that this Rufus might be the son of Simon, the Cyrenian (see the above entry). If this is so, it would mean that Simon and his family, or at least his wife and his son, had converted to Christianity.

Ruhamah

(Hebrew origin: *Pity*)

(Hosea 2:1). 8th century B.C. Ruhamah was the third child whom the prophet Hosea had with his wife Gomer. The complete name of Ruhamah—Loruhamah, *Without pity* (Hosea 1:6)—symbolizes that God would exile the people of Israel without pity. Later, the prophet expressed hope that, one day, Judah and Israel would be reunited together, and then his daughter Loruhamah would be called Ruhamah, *Pity*.

Her brothers were called Jezreel—a name that symbolized the destruction that God would bring over the dynasty of Jehu—and Loammi, *Not my people*.

Ruth

(Hebrew origin: *Friend*)

(Ruth 1:4). 12th century B.C. Ruth, a Moabite girl, married Mahlon, an Israelite son of Elimelech and Naomi, and brother of Chilion. Her husband and his family had lived in Bethlehem in Judah, but a great famine forced them to immigrate to Moab, on the eastern side of the river Jordan. Elimelech died shortly afterward.

After ten years of marriage, when Ruth's husband and her brother-in-law also died, their bereaved mother Naomi decided to return to her native country. Her two daughters-in-law expressed their wish to go with her.

Naomi said to them, "Stay in Moab with your parents. I am too old to have sons that would marry you, and even if I had new sons, you would have to wait too many years for them to grow up".

The girls wept; Orpah kissed her mother-in-law and went back to her parents' home, but Ruth stayed with Naomi.

Naomi said, "Ruth, go back with your sister-in-law".

Ruth answered, "Do not ask me to leave you; wherever you go, I will go, and where you live, I will live; your people shall be my people; and your God, my God; where you die, I will die, and there, I will be buried; and God should punish me if anything else than death would make me part from you".

Naomi saw that Ruth's mind was made up, and she said no more.

The two women walked on, until they came to Bethlehem. The people in the town, surprised to see them, asked each other, "Is this Naomi?"

Naomi said to them, "Do not call me Naomi, call me Mara, because God has dealt bitterly with me. I went away full, and God has brought me back empty".

The two women had arrived at the beginning of the barley harvest. As they didn't have anything to eat, nor money, with which, to buy food, Ruth told Naomi that she would like to go to the fields and glean among the ears of grain, behind someone who may show her kindness.

Naomi said, "Yes, my daughter, go".

Ruth went to a certain field, which belonged to Boaz, a wealthy relative of Naomi's dead husband, and gleaned behind the reapers.

Boaz saw her and asked his overseer, "Who is that girl?"

His servant answered, "She is the Moabite maiden who came with Naomi. She came early in the morning and asked me for permission to gather the sheaves after the reapers. Since then, she has not rested even for one moment!"

Boaz went to Ruth and said, "You can continue to glean. I have ordered my workers not to bother you, and, if you are thirsty, to give you water".

Ruth answered, "Why are you doing this kindness to me when I am a foreigner?"

Boaz replied, "I have been told everything that you have done for your mother-in-law, since the death of your husband; how you left your parents and your native land, and came to a people that are strange to you".

That evening, when Ruth returned home, she told Naomi that she had worked in the field of a man named Boaz.

Naomi said to her, "Boaz is a close relative.

Tomorrow, dress in your best clothes and anoint yourself, but make sure that Boaz should not see you, until he has finished eating and drinking. Then, when he has lied down for the night, uncover his feet and lie down next to him". Ruth did what her mother-in-law told her to do.

Boaz woke up in the middle of the night and was surprised to see that there was a woman lying at his feet. When he saw that the woman was Ruth, he said to her, "I am grateful that you have chosen me, and not a younger man. Tomorrow, I will go to a man who is a closer blood relative to Naomi than myself, and if that man refuses to act as a redeemer for you, I will then do it personally".

The next morning, Boaz went to the gate of the town, and there, in the presence of ten elders, he spoke to his kinsman, "Naomi, who has returned now from Moab, must sell the piece of land, which belonged to our kinsman Elimelech. If you are willing to buy it and redeem it, do so. If not, I will do it".

The kinsman replied, "I am willing to redeem it".

Boaz then said, "Don't forget that, when you buy the property from Naomi, you must also acquire Ruth the Moabite, so as to perpetuate the name of the deceased upon his estate".

The man said, "This I cannot do. You take over my right of redemption, because I am unable to exercise it". To confirm what he had said, he took off his sandal, according to the custom of the time, and gave it to Boaz.

Boaz said to the elders and to the people gathered at the gate, "You are witnesses today that I have acquired from Naomi all that belonged to Elimelech and to his sons, including Ruth the Moabite as my wife, so as to perpetuate the name of the deceased upon his estate".

Boaz and Ruth got married and had a baby called Obed. Naomi took the child, held him to her bosom, and raised him. Obed, when he grew up and married, became the father of Jesse, the father of David.

Sabta

(Uncertain origin and meaning)

(1 Chronicles 1:9). Unspecified date. Sabta—called Sabtah in the book of Genesis (Genesis 10:7)—was the son of Cush and grandson of Ham. His brothers were Seba, Havilah, Raamah, and Sabtechah.

Later, Cush had another son, Nimrod, a powerful man and a mighty hunter, who established a kingdom in the land of Shinar and founded Nineveh and other cities.

Sabtah

(Uncertain origin and meaning)

(Genesis 10:7). Unspecified date. Sabtah—called Sabta in the first book of Chronicles (1 Chronicles 1:9)—was the son of Cush and grandson of Ham. His brothers were Seba, Havilah, Raamah, and Sabtechah.

Later, Cush had another son, Nimrod, a powerful man and a mighty hunter, who established a kingdom in the land of Shinar and founded Nineveh and other cities.

Sabtecha

(Uncertain origin and meaning)

(1 Chronicles 1:9). Unspecified date. Sabtecha—called Sabtechah in the book of Genesis (Genesis 10:7)—was the son of Cush and grandson of Ham. His brothers were Seba, Havilah, Raamah, and Sabta.

Later, Cush had another son, Nimrod, a powerful man and a mighty hunter, who established a kingdom in the land of Shinar and founded Nineveh and other cities.

Sabtechah

(Uncertain origin and meaning)

(Genesis 10:7). Unspecified date. Sabtechah—called Sabtecha in the first book of Chronicles (1 Chronicles 1:9)—was the son

of Cush and grandson of Ham. His brothers were Seba, Havilah, Raamah, and Sabtah.

Later, Cush had another son, Nimrod, a powerful man and a mighty hunter, who established a kingdom in the land of Shinar and founded Nineveh and other cities.

Sacar

(Hebrew origin: *Reward*)

1. (1 Chronicles 11:35). 11th century B.C. Sacar the Hararite—also called Sharar (2 Samuel 23:33)—was the father of Ahiam, a member of King David's elite army group known as The Thirty.

2. (1 Chronicles 26:4). 10th century B.C. Sacar, the fourth son of Obededom, was, like his father and seven brothers, a gatekeeper of the Tabernacle, during the reign of King David. His brothers were Ammiel, Shemaiah, Jehozabad, Joah, Nethaneel, Issachar, and Peulthai.

Sadoc

(Hebrew origin: *Just*)

(Matthew 1:14). Unspecified date. Sadoc, son of Azor, a descendant of Zorobabel, was the father of Achim, an ancestor of Jesus, in Matthew's genealogy.

Sala

(Hebrew origin: *Branch*)

(Luke 3:35). Unspecified date. Sala, a descendant of Sem, was the father of Heber, also spelled Eber (Genesis 10:21).

According to Luke, Sala was the son of Cainan and the grandson of Arphaxad. However, the book of Genesis (Genesis 10:24), where he is called Salah, and the first book of Chronicles (1 Chronicles 1:18), where he is called Shelah, both state that he was the son of Arphaxad.

Salah

(Hebrew origin: *Branch*)

(Genesis 10:24). Unspecified date. Salah—

called Shelah in First Chronicles (1 Chronicles 1:18)—was the son of Arphaxad, a descendant of Noah.

Salah was born, when his father was thirty-five years old, thirty-seven years after the flood. His first son, Eber, was born, when he was thirty years old. He died at the age of four hundred and thirty-three, having fathered other sons and daughters.

According to Luke, who calls him Sala, he was the son of Cainan and the grandson of Arphaxad (Luke 3:35).

Salathiel

(Hebrew origin: *I have asked God*)

(1 Chronicles 3:17). 6th century B.C. Salathiel was one of the seven sons of King Jehoiachin, the king who was deposed and taken captive by the Babylonians. Salathiel's brothers were Hoshama, Malchiram, Pedaiah, Shenazar, Jecamiah, and Nedabiah.

According to the book of Ezra, where his name is spelled Shealtiel, he was the father of Zerubbabel, the leader of the first group of captives who returned from the Babylonian Exile (Ezra 3:2).

The first book of Chronicles, on the other hand, states that Salathiel was not the father of Zerubbabel, but his uncle, and that the father of the governor of the Persian province of Judah was Pedaiah (1 Chronicles 3:19).

Sallai

(Hebrew origin: *Weighed*)

1. (Nehemiah 11:8). 5th century B.C. Sallai, of the tribe of Benjamin, was one of the men who settled in Jerusalem, after their return from the exile in Babylon.
2. (Nehemiah 12:20). Unspecified date. Sallai was the ancestor of a priestly clan, headed by Kallai, when Joiakim was the High Priest, in the days of Nehemiah.

Sallu

(Hebrew origin: *Weighed*)

1. (1 Chronicles 9:7). Unspecified date. Sallu,

son of Meshullam and grandson of Hodaviah, was one of the first captives who returned from the Babylonian Exile and settled in Jerusalem.
2. (Nehemiah 11:7). 5th century B.C. Sallu, the son of Meshullam and grandson of Joed, was a Benjamite who settled in Jerusalem, after he returned from the exile in Babylon.
3. (Nehemiah 12:7). 6th century B.C. Sallu was the head of a family of priests who returned with Zerubbabel from the Babylonian Exile, when Jeshua was the High Priest

Salma

(Hebrew origin: *Peace*)

(1 Chronicles 2:11). 12th century B.C. Salma—called Salmon in the book of Ruth (Ruth 4:20)—the son of Nahshon, was the father of Boaz, and an ancestor of King David. He was the founder of the town of Bethlehem (1 Chronicles 2:51).

Salmon

(Hebrew origin: *Peaceable*)

(Ruth 4:20). 12th century B.C. Salmon—called Salma in the first book of Chronicles (1 Chronicles 2:11)—the son of Nahshon, was the father of Boaz, and an ancestor of King David. He was the founder of the town of Bethlehem (1 Chronicles 2:51).

Salome

(Hebrew origin: *Peaceable*)

1. (Mark 15:40). A.D. 1st century. Salome was one of the women who, together with Mary Magdalene and Mary, the mother of Joses, witnessed the crucifixion of Jesus from afar, according to Mark's gospel. On the Sunday, after the Crucifixion, early in the morning, she went with the other two women to the tomb of Jesus, bringing sweet spices to anoint the body.

According to scholars, it is very probable that Salome was the wife of the fisherman Zebedee, and the mother of the apostles James and John. They base this belief on the fact that, when Matthew writes that Mary Magdalene and Mary, the mother of Joses, witnessed the crucifixion of Jesus, instead of mentioning "Salome" as the third woman, he writes "the mother of Zebedee's children" (Matthew 27:56).

If Salome was the mother of James and John, she was most ambitious for her children. On one occasion, she asked Jesus that her sons should be allowed to sit in heaven next to him, one at his right hand, and the other at his left hand. Jesus replied that it was not in his power to grant her wish, as those places belonged to those for whom God had prepared them.

2. (Matthew 14:6). A.D. 1st century. Salome—the Scriptures do not specify her name, but the historian Josephus does— was the daughter of Herodias, who, after having been married to Philip, married her brother-in-law, Herod the Tetrarch, the second son of Herod the Great.

John the Baptist denounced this act and was imprisoned by Herod. During a feast honoring Herod's birthday, the daughter of Herodias danced before the king, who, pleased, promised to give her whatever she would ask. The girl asked for John's head on a platter. The king reluctantly agreed and gave instructions to behead John. The head of the slain man was brought and given to the girl, who gave it to her mother.

Salu

(Hebrew origin: *Weighed*)

(Numbers 25:14). 13th century B.C. Salu, a leader of the tribe of Simeon, was the father of Zimri. His son brought Cozbi, a Midianite woman, to his tent, while the people were suffering from a plague sent by God to punish their immoral behavior with the Moabite women, and for having sacrificed to the pagan god Baalpeor.

Zimri's brazenfaced behavior so enraged Phinehas, the grandson of Aaron the Priest, that he took a javelin in his hand, went into the tent, and killed the couple. God was appeased by this act and lifted the plague.

Samgarnebo

(Uncertain origin and meaning)

(Jeremiah 39:3). 6th century B.C. Samgarnebo was one of the commanders of King Nebuchadnezzar's army who sat in the Middle Gate of Jerusalem, after the Babylonians had succeeded in breaking through the walls of the city.

Samlah

(Hebrew origin: *Dress*)

(Genesis 36:36). Unspecified date. Samlah of Masrekah succeeded Hadad as king of Edom. When he died, Saul, of Rehoboth by the river, ascended to the throne.

Samson

(Hebrew origin: *Sunlight*)

(Judges 13:24). 12th century B.C. Samson, of the tribe of Dan, who lived, during the period of the Judges, was a *sui generis* hero, completely different from any other Israelite leader mentioned in the Bible. He fought his enemies, the Philistines, individually, never at the head of an army, and relied more on his own strength than on his faith.

Although he had been dedicated to God from his birth, his character was flawed. He was a womanizer, was easily manipulated by nagging women, preferred Philistine women over women from his own people, and liked to socialize with the Philistines, the enemies of his people.

His parents lived in the town of Zorah. One day, an angel appeared to the woman and announced to her, "You are now childless, but you will have a son. Listen carefully: you have to abstain from drinking alcoholic drinks and from eating unclean food. The son that you will have will free Israel from the hands of the Philistines. He will be dedicated to God from his birth, and no razor shall touch his head".

The woman went to her husband, a man called Manoah, and told him what had happened. Manoah prayed to God to send them once more his messenger to teach them how to raise their future son.

When the angel again appeared to the woman, when she was alone in the field, she ran to her husband and said, "Look, that strange man that appeared to me the other day has come again".

Manoah got up and followed his wife. When they came to the place where the man was, Manoah asked him, "Are you the man who spoke to my wife?"

The angel answered, "I am".

Manoah said, "If what you predict will come true, how shall we raise the child?"

The angel explained, "Your wife should take care not to drink wine or any other alcoholic drink, nor should she eat unclean food".

"Please stay with us, while I prepare you a young goat to eat", said Manoah, not knowing that he was speaking to an angel.

The angel said, "Even if you keep me here, I will not eat your food. If you wish to make a sacrifice, offer it to God".

Manoah asked him, "Please tell us your name, so that, when your predictions come true, we will know whom we should thank".

The angel said, "You should not ask my name, because it is a secret".

Manoah took the young goat and the meal offering, and he offered them on a rock to God. While the flames of the altar flew upward, the angel ascended to the sky inside the flames. Manoah and his wife, seeing this, flung themselves on their faces to the ground.

When they didn't see the angel anymore, Manoah realized that the being, whom he had thought to be a man, was an angel.

Worried, he said to his wife, "We shall surely die, because we have seen God".

She calmed him, saying, "If God would have wanted to kill us, he would not have accepted the sacrifice that we offered, nor would he have shown us these things, or predicted what will happen".

The woman in due time had a son, and they called him Samson, who grew up to be a leader of his people in their fight against the Philistines.

One day, Samson saw a Philistine girl in Timnath, whom he liked. He went to his parents and told them, "I have met a Philistine girl, and I want to marry her!"

Manoah and his wife said to Samson, "Why would you want to marry out of our faith? Can't you get a girl from our own people?"

Samson answered, "That's the one I like. Get her for me!"

Samson went to Timnath with his parents. On the way, he killed a lion with his bare hands, but he didn't tell his parents. Samson entered the town and talked with the girl. He liked her, and they arranged to get married in the near future.

When the time came for the wedding, Samson again went to Timnath. On the way, he left the road to look at the lion he had killed, and he found a swarm of bees and some honey in the body of the lion. He took in his hands the honey and ate it while walking. He gave his parents some of the honey but did not tell them where he got it.

His father came to the girl's house, and Samson offered a banquet there, according to the young men's custom. The Philistines had brought thirty guests to be with him.

Samson told them, "Let's make a bet. I will tell you a riddle. If you give me the right answer, before the seven days of the wedding festivities are over, I will give each of you a linen tunic and a set of clothing; but, if you don't solve the riddle, you will give me thirty linen tunics and thirty sets of clothing".

They accepted his challenge and said, "It's a deal. Tell us your riddle, so we can hear it".

Samson said, "Out of the eater came something to eat; out of the strong came something sweet".

For several days, they couldn't figure out the riddle, and so they went to Samson's wife and said to her, "Get your husband to tell us the answer to the riddle. If not, we will burn down your father's house with you inside. You probably invited us to the wedding only to rob us".

She went, crying to Samson, and said, "You hate me, you don't love me! You told my friends a riddle, and you didn't tell me, your wife, the answer!"

Samson answered, "Look, I haven't even told my parents. Why should I tell you?"

She wept, during the whole seven days that the wedding festivities lasted. Finally, on the seventh day, he couldn't stand her nagging anymore, and he told her the meaning of the riddle. She immediately told it to the Philistines.

That evening, the Philistines told Samson, "What can be sweeter than honey? What can be stronger than a lion?"

"If you hadn't been plowing with my cow, you wouldn't know the answer to my riddle", he answered.

Samson felt the strength of God in him and went down to the Philistine city of Ashkelon, where he killed thirty men, took their garments and gave them to the men who had answered the riddle. Still, full of anger, instead of going back to his wife, he returned to his parent's house. His wife was given to the man who had been his best man at the wedding.

Sometime later, during the wheat harvest, Samson went to visit his wife, bringing with him a young goat as a gift. Her father opened the door, and Samson told him, "I want to go to my wife's room".

Her father refused to let him come into the house, and he said to Samson, "Sorry, I thought that you hated her, and gave her to your friend. Anyway, her sister is even prettier. Take her, instead".

Samson said, "This time I am not going to be blamed for what I will do to the Philistines". He went and caught three hundred foxes, tied them two by two, and put torches in their tails. He set fire to the torches and let loose the foxes in the Philistine fields. The fire burned the wheat that had been harvested, the wheat still in the fields, the vineyards and the olive trees.

The Philistines asked who had done that damage and why. They learned that it had been Samson, angry because his father-in-law had taken away his wife and given her to another man. The Philistines went to the woman's house and burned it to the ground with her and her father inside.

Samson said to them, "If this is the way you act, I will not stop, until I pay you back". He attacked them and killed many of them. Then, he went and stayed in a cave on top of the rock of Etam.

The Philistines came, camped in Judah, and surrounded the town of Lehi. The men of Judah asked them, "Why are you attacking us?"

They answered, "We have come to capture Samson, and to do to him what he has done to us".

Three thousand men of Judah went to the rock of Etam, and they said to Samson, "Don't you know that the Philistines are our rulers? What have you done to us?"

He answered, "I paid them back for what they did to me".

The men of Judah said, "We have come to tie you up, so that we can hand you over to the Philistines". Samson replied, "Swear that you will not kill me".

"We promise that we will not kill you; we will only tie you and hand you to the Philistines".

They tied him with two new ropes and took him down from the rock, without any resistance on his part.

When the Philistines saw that the men of Judah had brought Samson to Lehi, they ran to him shouting curses and insults. Samson felt the strength of God in him, easily broke the ropes, grabbed the jawbone of a dead donkey that he found on the ground, and killed a thousand men with it. Then, he threw the jawbone away.

He felt very thirsty, after his exertions, and said to God, "You gave me this great victory. Should I now die of thirst and be captured by the Philistines?" God opened a hollow place in Lehi and water came gushing out. Samson drank it, and he felt strong again.

One day, Samson went to the Philistine city of Gaza, where he spent the night with a prostitute. When word got around that Samson was in the city, the people of Gaza silently surrounded the place and waited for him the whole night at the city gate. They said to each other, "We will kill him when daylight comes".

Samson left the prostitute's house around midnight, went to the city gate and pulled out the doors with their posts and lock. He put them on his shoulders and carried them far off, to the top of a hill near Hebron.

After that, Samson again fell in love with a Philistine woman, called Delilah, who lived in the valley of Sorek.

The leaders of the Philistines came to her and said, "If you can find for us the secret of his strength, we will pay you eleven hundred pieces of silver, each one of us".

Delilah said to Samson, "Please tell me what makes you so strong. If someone would want you to be helpless, how should he tie you up?"

Samson answered, "If they tie me up with seven new bowstrings, which are not yet dry, I will be as weak as any other man".

The Philistine brought her the seven bowstrings, and that night, she tied him up, while some men waited in another room. Then, she called out in a loud voice, "Samson! The Philistines are upon you!" He easily broke the bowstrings.

Delilah said to him, "Samson, you are telling me lies and making fun of me! Tell me, please, how somebody could tie you up!"

He answered, "If they tie me up with new ropes that have never been used, I will be as weak as any other man".

Delilah got some new ropes and tied Samson with them, while some men waited in the other room. Then, she cried out, "Samson! The Philistines are upon you!" He easily broke the ropes.

Delilah again complained, "You are still telling me lies and mocking me. Tell me how you can be tied up!"

He replied, "If you weave seven locks of hair into a web and make them tight with a pin, I will be as weak as any other man".

That night, while he slept, she wove the seven locks of his hair into a web, and she tightened it with a pin. Then, she shouted, "Samson! The Philistines are upon you!" He woke up and pulled his hair loose from the web.

She told him, "How can you say that you love me, when your heart is not with me? Three times you have made a fool of me, and you still have not told me the secret of your great strength".

Her daily nagging wore him down, and finally, he told her the truth, "My hair has never been cut, because I am a Nazarite, and have been dedicated to God, since my birth. If my head would be shaved, I will be as weak as any other man".

Delilah sensed that this time Samson had told her the truth. She sent a message to the leaders of the Philistines, which said, "Come back, once more. This time he has told me everything".

They came and brought her the promised money. That night, Delilah, after Samson had fallen asleep on her lap, called a man to shave the seven locks of his hair. Then, she shouted, "Samson! The Philistines are upon you!"

He woke up thinking that again this time he would get loose and go free, but he didn't know that God had left him. The Philistine seized him and gouged his eyes out. He was then taken to Gaza, chained with bronze chains, and put to work, grinding at the mill in the prison. Slowly, his hair grew back.

The Philistines gathered to offer a sacrifice of thanks to the god Dagon, for having delivered Samson, their enemy, into their hands. The Temple was full, with over three thousand men and women standing on the roof. They prayed, sang, and thoroughly enjoyed themselves. Then, they decided to bring out Samson to make fun of him.

Samson was brought from the prison and placed between two columns. He asked the boy who was leading him by the hand, "Let me touch the columns that support this building. I want to lean on them".

Samson prayed to God, "O Lord, please remember me only this once, so that I can get revenge from the Philistines for having taken out my two eyes". He put one hand on each column and screamed, "Let me die with the Philistines", and he pushed with all his might.

The Temple came crashing down on the Philistine leaders and on the crowd. Thousands were killed as he died, more than he had killed, during his whole life.

His brothers and the rest of his family came to Gaza to recuperate his body. They buried him between Zorah and Eshtaol, in the tomb of his father Manoah. Samson had been the leader of Israel for twenty years.

Samuel

(Hebrew origin: *God heard*)

(1 Samuel 1:20). 11th century B.C. Samuel—called Shemuel in the first book of Chronicles, (1 Chronicles 6:33)—a prophet and seer, was the last and greatest of the "Judges" Israelite leaders who were chosen by God to rule over the people, and to save them in time of war and oppression.

Note: In the book of Judges, a judge is a ruler or governor of territory or a military leader in pre-monarchical Israel. Later, during the monarchy, the king served in this role and judges were more like the judicial officers that we know today.

His mother Hannah was one of the two wives—the other was Peninnah—of a man named Elkanah, of the clan of the Kohathites, who lived in Ramathaimzophim.

Hannah, who was barren and desperate to have a child, was constantly provoked by Peninnah who had several children. She would weep and fast, and Elkanah, who loved her very much, would try to console her, saying that he was better to her than ten sons.

In one of the family's yearly pilgrimages to Shiloh to worship and sacrifice to the Lord, Hannah prayed silently and bitterly to God, asking for a son.

Eli, the Shiloh priest, saw that her lips moved but heard no sound. He thought that she was drunk, and he advised her to stop drinking.

Hannah said, "Oh no, my lord! I have not drunk wine. I am a very unhappy woman, and have been pouring my heart to God".

"Go away in peace. God will grant your wish", said Eli.

The family returned home, and Hannah conceived and, in due time, gave birth to Samuel. When the boy was weaned, she brought him to Shiloh and left him with the priest Eli, who brought him up to follow in his footsteps and serve God. Every year, Hannah would make a little coat for Samuel and bring it to him, during the family's annual pilgrimages to Shiloh. Eli would bless her and her husband, saying, "May God grant you children by this woman to replace the loan she has made to the Lord". Elkanah and Hannah had five more children: three boys and two girls.

Eli's own sons, Hophni and Phinehas, were scoundrels, wicked and corrupt. Eli pleaded with them to mend their ways and sin no more, but they ignored his supplications. Samuel, meanwhile, grew up to be a young man esteemed by God and men.

A man of God came to Eli and bluntly told him, "You honor your sons more than you honor God. Your punishment will be that your two sons will both die on the same day; your descendants will no longer be the leading priestly family; and their survivors will be reduced to beg the High Priest for money and food".

One night, while both Eli and Samuel were asleep, Eli in his usual place and Samuel in the Tabernacle, next to the Ark of the Covenant, Samuel heard a voice calling him.

He answered, "I am coming", and ran to Eli, saying, "You called me; here I am".

Eli told him, "I didn't call you; go back to sleep".

The same thing happened again twice that night, until Eli understood that it was God who was calling the boy.

He said to Samuel, "Go to your bed. If you are called again, answer, 'Speak, Lord, for your servant is listening'".

Samuel returned to the Tabernacle and lay down.

God called him as before, "Samuel, Samuel".

This time, Samuel answered, "Speak, Lord, for your servant is listening".

God said, "I am going to do in Israel something that will tingle the ears of anyone who hears about it. In that day, I will fulfill against Eli everything that I have spoken concerning his family, from beginning to end. I told them that I will judge his house for the sins of his sons, and him for not having restrained them. I swear that the iniquity of the house of Eli will not be expiated by sacrifice or offering".

Samuel couldn't sleep the rest of the night, afraid to report his vision to Eli. Early in the morning, when he opened the doors of the Tabernacle, Eli came to him and asked him, "What did God say to you? Tell me all!" Samuel told him what God had said to him, and Eli replied, "God will do according to his will". The years passed, and Samuel became known all over the country as a prophet.

When Eli was ninety-eight years old, and had already been a judge for forty years, the Philistines attacked Israel and inflicted a heavy defeat on the Israelites. The Philistines captured the Ark of the Covenant, and they killed over thirty thousand men, including the sons of Eli. Eli, hearing the news, fell from his chair and broke his neck. Samuel succeeded him as judge.

The Ark of the Covenant, which was captured by the Philistines, was brought to the Temple of Dagon in Ashdod and placed in front of the statue of the god. The next morning, the statue was found fallen on the ground, with its head and hands cut off.

This incident, plus a plague of hemorrhoids, convinced the Philistines to send the Ark back to Israel in a cart pulled by two cows, carrying also five golden mice and five golden figures representing the hemorrhoids. When the cart came to a stop in a field, the Israelites dismantled it and used its wood to make a fire, where they sacrificed the two cows to God. Unfortunately, they couldn't resist the temptation and looked inside the Ark. God sent a plague in punishment that killed thousands of men.

The scared survivors sent the Ark to the house of Abinadab, situated on a hill near the town of Kirjathjearim, where it was kept for many years under the supervision of Eleazar, the son of Abinadab.

Twenty years later, the people of Israel lapsed into idolatry. Samuel exhorted them to get rid of their idols and return to God with all their hearts, so that God would deliver them from the hands of the Philistines. He convened an assembly of the Israelites in Mizpeh, where they poured water before God, fasted, and confessed their sins, under Samuel's guidance.

The Philistines, hearing that the Israelites had gathered in Mizpeh, decided to go to war against them. The frightened Israelites asked Samuel to pray to God to save them from the hands of the Philistines.

Samuel took a young lamb and sacrificed it to the Lord. While Samuel was praying to God, the Philistines drew near, but when God thundered mightily, they were thrown into confusion and fled the field. The Israelites pursued them, striking them down near Bethcar, and recovered the towns that had been taken by the Philistines. In commemoration of the victory, Samuel erected a stone, which he called Ebenezer, *The Stone of Help.*

Samuel judged Israel as long as he lived. Each year, he would make the rounds of Bethel, Gilgal, and Mizpeh, and judge in each of those places. Then, he would return to his hometown of Ramah, where he had built an altar to God, and there, too, he would judge Israel.

Samuel, in his old age, made his sons Joel and Abiah judges in the city of Beersheba. Unfortunately, they turned out to be as bad as the sons of Eli, greedy and corrupt, eager to receive bribes and subvert justice.

The elders of Israel came to Samuel in Ramah, and they said to him, "Samuel, you are now an old man, and your sons are not fit to be leaders. We want you to appoint a king that will govern us, like all other nations".

Samuel, displeased by their request, prayed to God. God told him, "Listen to the voice of the people in all that they tell you. They have rejected me as king, not you. Listen to them, but also warn them solemnly about the practices of any king that will rule over them".

Samuel told the people what God had said to him, and he added, "The king will take your sons and appoint them as his charioteers and horsemen. He will appoint them as commanders of thousands and captains of fifties. He will make them work in his fields, reap his harvests, make his weapons and the equipment for his chariots. He will take your daughters and employ them as perfumers, cooks and bakers. He will take away your best fields, your vineyards, and your olive yards, and give them to his officials. He will take your male and female servants, and your donkeys. He will take a tenth of your sheep, and you shall be his servants. You will cry that day because of the king that you had chosen, but God will not listen to you".

The people refused to be persuaded by Samuel's warnings, and they insisted, "We want to be like other nations. We want a king to rule us and to fight our battles".

Samuel again prayed to God, and God told him, "Heed their demands and appoint a king for them". Samuel then said to the people, "Go home all of you".

Sometime later, Samuel was in the region of Zuph, when God spoke to him, "Tomorrow, at this time, I will send to you a man from the land of Benjamin, and you will anoint him ruler over my people Israel. He will free the nation from the Philistines".

The next day, while Samuel was going up to the town's shrine, he encountered a young man, called Saul, son of Kish, who was searching for his father's lost donkeys. As soon as Samuel saw Saul, God said to him, "This is the man I told you about. He will rule my people".

Saul, who did not recognize Samuel, asked him, "Please tell me where is the house of the seer".

Samuel answered, "I am the seer. Go up ahead of me to the shrine, for you will eat with me today. Tomorrow, I will let you go, after telling you all that is in your heart. Don't worry about the lost donkeys; they have been found. Israel is yearning for you and for your father's house!"

Saul, bewildered, answered, "Why do you say these things to me? I am a Benjamite, from the smallest tribe in Israel, and my family is the least of all the families of my tribe".

Samuel took Saul and his servant into the dining hall, where, already, about thirty guests were seating. He made him sit at the head of the table and instructed the cook to bring the food that had been reserved, and to serve it to Saul. After they dined, they went down from the place of the shrine to the town, to Samuel's house, where they spent some hours speaking on the roof of the house.

The next morning, Samuel woke Saul up, and they walked out of the town together. Samuel told Saul to let his servant walk ahead. Then, he took a flask of oil and poured it upon Saul's head, kissed him, and said, "The Lord anoints you ruler over his people. When you leave me today you will find two men by the tomb of Rachel who will tell you that the asses have been found, and that your father is worried about you. Then, you will continue to the plain of Tabor, where you will meet three men going to the shrine in Bethel, one of them carrying three young goats, another three loaves of bread, and the third one a bottle of wine. They will salute you and give you two loaves of bread. Receive them. After that, you will come to the hill of God, where there is a Philistine garrison. There, you will meet a group of prophets, coming down from the shrine with musical instruments, prophesying. The spirit of God will come upon you; you will prophesy, and become another man. After that, go to Gilgal, and wait there seven days for me. I will come to present burn offerings and sacrifice to God".

Samuel assembled the people in Mizpeh and told them to arrange themselves by their tribes and families. The tribe of Benjamin was chosen and told to step forward. From them, the family of Matri was chosen, and from them, Saul, the son of Kish, was indicated.

The people called for Saul, but they couldn't find him. After searching all over, he was found hiding among the baggage. They brought him to the presence of Samuel, and, when he stood among the people, everybody could see that he was a head taller than anybody else.

Samuel said to the people, "Do you see the one chosen by God? There is none like him among the people!"

All the people acclaimed him, shouting, "Long live the king!" Samuel explained to the people the rules of the monarchy, and he wrote them in a document, which he deposited before God. Then, he sent the people back to their homes.

Nahash, the king of Ammon, besieged Jabeshgilead, and threatened to take out the right eye of everyone in the city. Saul rallied the Israelites, attacked the Ammonites, and defeated them.

Samuel gathered the people in Gilgal, and he officially anointed Saul as king of Israel. The people offered sacrifices to God, and held a joyful celebration.

Samuel spoke to the people, saying, "I have listened to you, and set a king over you. From now on, he will lead you. I am now old and gray headed, but my sons are still with you, and I have served you from my childhood to this day.

"I am here, and you can now testify against me in front of God and his anointed if I have taken somebody's ox or donkey; if I have defrauded or oppressed; if I have received a bribe to make me turn a blind eye! If I have done any of these things, I will return it to you!"

The people exclaimed, "You have not defrauded us or oppressed us. You have not taken anything from anybody".

Samuel said, "The Lord and his anointed are witnesses to what you declared today, that you have found nothing in my possession".

Samuel added, "Here is the king that the Lord has set over you. Fear God, serve him, and obey his voice, and do not reject his commandments. If not, the hand of God will be against you, as it was against your ancestors".

To enforce his words, he prayed to God to send thunder and rain, in spite of it being the dry season of wheat harvest. It rained and thundered, and the people greatly feared God and Samuel.

Two years later, Jonathan, Saul's son, with an army of one thousand men struck down the Philistine garrison in Geba. The Philistines, hungry for revenge, put together a great army, which included thirty thousand chariots, six thousand horsemen, and countless soldiers. They marched and camped in Michmash, to the east of Bethaven. Saul and his army waited in Gilgal for Samuel, who had told the king that he would be there in seven days.

When the seven days were over, and Samuel had still not arrived, Saul, seeing that his army was starting to scatter, offered a sacri-

fice to God. At that moment, Samuel arrived and asked him, "What have you done?"

Saul answered, "Seeing that you had not arrived, that the army was scattering, and that the Philistines had gathered at Michmash, I decided to make a sacrifice to God".

Samuel told him, "You have behaved foolishly in not keeping God's command. God would have established your dynasty over Israel forever, but, because you didn't keep God's command, God will find another man, and appoint him to rule over his people". Samuel got up, left Gilgal, and went to Gibeah of Benjamin.

Saul was left with only six hundred soldiers in his army, unarmed, except for Saul and Jonathan, who had swords and spears. However, thanks to the heroic acts of Jonathan and his armor bearer, the Philistines fled in panic and confusion.

Sometime later, Samuel said to Saul, "I am the one that God sent to anoint you as king over Israel. Therefore, listen to what God says, 'I remember what Amalek did to Israel, how they ambushed Israel when the people came out from Egypt'. Now, go, attack Amalek, and wipe them out. Spare no one, kill them all: men, women, children and babies, oxen and sheep, camels and donkeys".

Saul gathered a huge army of over two hundred thousand soldiers, marched to the city of Amalek, and waited in the valley. Before attacking, he warned the Kenite tribe, a people who had been kind to the Israelites, when they left Egypt, to depart from Amalek, so that they would not also be destroyed. The Kenites withdrew, and Saul slaughtered the Amalekites, except for Agag, the king of Amalek, whom he captured alive, together with a number of sheep, oxen, and lambs.

God said to Samuel, "I regret that I chose Saul to be king, because he has not carried out my commands".

Samuel grieved, when he heard these words, and cried the whole night. Then, he went to Saul and found him in Gilgal.

Saul greeted him, "Blessed are you of the Lord! I have done what the Lord commanded me".

Samuel asked, "What then is this bleating of sheep in my ears, and the mooing of oxen that I hear?"

Saul answered, "The troops spared the best of the sheep and oxen of the Amalekites, and brought them to offer them in sacrifice to the Lord, your God. The rest we have destroyed".

Samuel said to Saul, "Wait, I will tell you what God said to me tonight".

"Say it", Saul replied.

Samuel said, "When you were insignificant in your own sight, didn't God make you king over Israel? God sent you to destroy the Amalekites, and exterminate them. Why did you disobey God in keeping the spoil?"

Saul protested, "But I did obey the voice of God. I exterminated the Amalekites, and captured Agag, their king. The soldiers kept the best sheep and oxen only to sacrifice them to the Lord, your God, in Gilgal".

Samuel reproved him, "To obey is better than to offer sacrifices. Rebellion is like the sin of witchcraft. Because you rejected the command of God, he has rejected you as king".

Saul said, "I have sinned against God, because I feared the people, and did what they wanted me to do. Please forgive me and come back with me, and I will worship the Lord".

Samuel said, "I will not go back with you, because you have rejected God, and God has rejected you as king of Israel".

As Samuel turned to leave, Saul seized his robe and it tore. Samuel said to him, "God has torn today the kingdom from you and given it to somebody else who is worthier than you. God does not lie or change his mind as humans do".

Saul insisted, "I have sinned, but, please, do me the honor of your presence, before the elders and before the people, and come back with me, so that I may worship the Lord, your God".

Samuel went back with him, and Saul worshipped God.

Samuel said, "Bring me Agag, the king of the Amalekites".

Agag came walking hesitantly, and said, "Surely the bitterness of death is past".

Samuel said, "As your sword has made women childless, so shall your mother be childless among women" and he hacked Agag in pieces.

Samuel then returned to Ramah, and Saul went back to his house in Gibeah. Samuel, for the rest of his life, never saw Saul again and grieved over Saul, because God regretted that he had made him king over Israel.

God said to Samuel, "How long will you grieve for Saul? Fill your horn with oil and set out. I am sending you to Bethlehem, to the house of Jesse, because I have chosen one of his sons to be king".

Samuel asked, "How can I do that? If Saul hears of it, he will kill me".

God told him, "Take a calf with you, and say that you have come to offer a sacrifice to the Lord. Call Jesse to the sacrifice, and I will tell you what to do. You will anoint the one I point out to you".

Samuel did what God had told him, and he came to Bethlehem. The elders of the town asked him in alarm, "Have you come in peace?"

"Yes", he replied, "I have come to sacrifice to the Lord. Purify yourselves, and come with me to the sacrifice". He also instructed Jesse and his sons to purify themselves and to attend the sacrifice.

Samuel saw Eliab, the eldest son of Jesse, and said to himself, "Surely he must be the one that will be anointed". But God said to Samuel, "Don't pay attention to his appearance or stature, because I have not chosen him. God sees not as man sees; man sees the outward appearance, but God looks into the heart".

After Jesse had made seven of his sons pass in front of Samuel, Samuel said to him, "The Lord has not chosen any of these boys. Are these all your children?"

Jesse answered, "There is one more, the youngest. He is out, taking care of the sheep".

Samuel told him, "Send somebody to bring him here, because we will not sit down till he arrives".

David, a ruddy and handsome boy, was brought in from the field. God said to Samuel, "Arise and anoint him, because this is the one". Samuel took the horn of oil and anointed him in the presence of his brothers. And then, he returned to Ramah.

Years went by, Samuel remained in Ramah. David in the meantime had risen in Saul's court, married the king's daughter, befriended Jonathan, and incurred the enemy of the king. To save his life, David escaped from the murderous wrath of Saul, came to Samuel at Ramah, and told him all that Saul had done to him. Both men decided that it would be safer if they would go to Naioth.

Saul, when told that David was in Naioth, sent messengers to seize him. When the men arrived in Naioth, they saw Samuel at the head of a group of prophets prophesying, and they too began to prophesy. Saul sent a second, and then a third, group of messengers to capture David, but the same thing happened to them; they also began to prophesy. Finally, Saul himself came to Naioth; there, he took off his clothes, began to prophesy, and lay down naked all that day and all night.

Several years later, after Samuel had died and was buried in Ramah, mourned by all of Israel, a great army of the Philistines marched against Israel. Saul gathered his army near the hills of Gilboa, but when he saw the Philistine forces, his heart was filled with fear. He tried to consult God through oracles, but God didn't answer.

Saul ordered his officials to search for a medium, which he could consult. They told him that there was a woman in Endor, which could conjure ghosts. Saul disguised himself, put on different clothes, and, accompanied by two men, went that night to the woman.

He asked her, "Consult the spirits for me. Bring up for me the one I shall name".

The woman was distrustful. "You know that King Saul has forbidden the practice of mediums and wizards in the land", she said, "You want me killed?"

Saul swore to her, "As God lives, nothing will happen to you over this".

The woman asked him, "Whom do you want me to bring?"

Saul answered, "Bring me Samuel".

When the woman saw the ghost of Samuel, she screamed, "Why have you deceived me? You are Saul!"

Saul said, "Don't be afraid. What do you see?"

The woman answered, "I see a spirit coming up from the earth".

"What does he look like?" he asked.

She said, "He looks like an old man covered with a mantle". Then, Saul knew that it was Samuel, and he bowed low with his face to the ground.

The ghost of Samuel asked, "Why have you disturbed me, and brought me up?"

Saul answered, "I am in great trouble. The Philistines are making war against me. God is no longer with me and does not answer, either by prophets or in dreams. That is why I called you. I need you to tell me what I must do".

"Why do you ask me, seeing that God has left you and become your enemy?" said the ghost of Samuel. "God has taken the kingdom from you and given it to David, because you did not obey him, and did not carry out his wrathful commands against the Amalekites. The Lord will deliver you and all of Israel to the hands of the Philistines, and tomorrow, you and your sons will be with me".

Saul, terrified by the words of the ghost, and weak, because he had not eaten anything, during the last twenty-four hours, flung himself to the ground.

The next day, the Israelite army was defeated by the Philistines, and Saul and his sons were killed.

Samuel's grandson, Heman, the son of Joel, was one of the Levites appointed by King David to be in charge of the singers in the House of the Lord. His descendants, Jehiel and Shimei, were among the Levites who gathered to make themselves ritually clean, and to purify the Temple, during the reign of King Hezekiah of Judah.

Sanballat

(Uncertain origin and meaning)

(Nehemiah 2:10). 5th century B.C. Sanballat the Horonite was one of the three sworn enemies of Nehemiah; the others were Tobiah the Ammonite and Geshem the Arab.

Although Sanballat was related by marriage

to the High Priest Eliashib—his daughter was the wife of Joiada, one of the sons of Eliashib—he was greatly disturbed, when he learned that the king of Persia had sent Nehemiah to Jerusalem to improve the situation of the Israelites.

Sanballat and his allies reacted with scorn and contempt, when Nehemiah started to rebuild the walls of Jerusalem. Trying to prevent this, they accused him of planning a rebellion against the Persian king.

The accusation was disregarded, and the work in Jerusalem proceeded. Sanballat became angry, and he complained to his brothers and to the Samaritans, "What are these weak Jews doing? Are they trying to fortify themselves, to offer sacrifices, to do it all in one day? Can they take these burned stones from the rubbish and use them again?"

Sanballat and Geshem decided to capture Nehemiah. They sent him an invitation to meet with them in one of the villages in the plain of Ono. Nehemiah, rightly suspecting that it was a trap, refused to go, giving as an excuse that he was too busy with his work. The two men sent the invitation four more times, and each time, Nehemiah gave them the same answer. The fifth time, they included a letter accusing him of inciting rebellion and planning to make himself king. Nehemiah answered that those accusations were figments of their imagination.

One of the last efforts by Sanballat and Tobiah to discredit Nehemiah was the hiring of Shemaiah, the son of Delaiah, to convince Nehemiah that he should hide in the Temple. That plot also failed.

Saph

(Hebrew origin: *Limit*)

(2 Samuel 21:18). 10th century B.C. Saph—called Sippai in the first book of Chronicles (1 Chronicles 20:4)—descended from a tribe of giants. He was killed by Sibbechai the Hushathite, during a battle between King David's army and the Philistines.

Sapphira

(Hebrew origin: Name of a gem)

(Acts of the Apostles 5:1). A.D. 1st century. Sapphira was the wife of Ananias, a couple who had converted to Christianity and lived in Jerusalem. At that time, it was the custom in the community of believers to own all their belongings in common. The members of the community, who had owned fields or houses, sold their possessions and gave the money to the apostles, who distributed it to each one according to his or her need.

One couple, Ananias and his wife Sapphira, behaved differently, motivated by greed. They sold their property but, instead of turning all the money over to the apostles, connived to keep part of it for themselves.

Peter, when told of their unchristian behavior, went to Ananias' house and said to him, "Ananias, why did you let Satan fill your heart and make you lie to the Holy Spirit by keeping part of the money you received for the property? The property, before you sold it, belonged to you, but after you sold it, the money was ours. You have not lied to men; you have lied to God!"

Ananias, upon hearing these words, fell down and died. Several young men of the congregation came in, carried the body out, and buried him. Three hours later, Sapphira, who had been out, returned to her home, not yet knowing what had happened to her husband.

She was confronted by Peter, who showed her the money and asked, "Is this the full amount you and your husband received for your property?"

"Yes", she answered, "it is the full amount".

Peter asked her, "Why did you and your husband put the Spirit of the Lord to the test? The men who buried your husband are outside the door, and they will carry you out too!"

At that moment, Sapphira fell down at his feet and died. The young men came in, carried her out, and buried her next to her husband. The believers and all others who heard what happened were terrified.

Sara

(Hebrew origin: *Princess*)

(Hebrew 11:11). 19th century B.C. Sara is an alternative spelling for Sarah, Abraham's wife. (Please see the entry for Sarah [Genesis 17:15].)

Sarah

(Hebrew origin: *Princess*)

(Genesis 17:15). 19th century B.C. Sarah-originally called Sarai, until God changed her name-was born in Ur of the Chaldeans. She was married to the patriarch Abraham-then called Abram-ancestor of the Hebrews and many other nations, to whom, in her old age, she bore a son, Isaac. Terah, her father-in-law, took his son Abram, Sarai, and his grandson Lot, to the city of Haran, which is situated between the Euphrates and the Tigris in northern Aram, in today's Turkey, near its frontier with Syria. When Terah died in Haran at the age of two hundred and five, Abram traveled with Sarai, and his nephew Lot, to the land of Canaan, which, God told him, would be given to him and his descendants. Sometime after the family settled in Canaan, there was a famine in the land, and Abram was forced to take the family to Egypt.

Abram feared that the Egyptians, when they would see his beautiful wife Sarai, would kill him to get her. To save his life, he instructed Sarai to say that she was his sister, not his wife.

The Egyptians who saw her admired her beauty and praised her to Pharaoh. He had her brought to the palace and gave generous gifts to her "brother" of sheep, oxen, asses, camels, and slaves. Pharaoh found out the deception, when God punished him and his house with great plagues because of Abram's wife. He immediately called Abram, returned Sarai to him, and expelled the couple and their nephew Lot from Egypt. Abram—now rich in cattle, silver, and gold—returned to Canaan and settled near Bethel. Years went by, and Sarai, no longer a young woman, was still childless. Eager to have a child, she gave Hagar, her Egyptian slave girl, to Abram as a concubine, so that she could have

her husband's child through her maid, according to the custom of the time.

Hagar conceived, and, from the day that she knew she was pregnant, she treated Sarai with insolence. Sarai, unwilling to tolerate her behavior, complained to Abram.

Abram said to her, "She is your slave, and you can do with her whatever you want".

Sarai's subsequent harsh treatment made Hagar run away to the desert. An angel found her at a spring in the desert, and said, "Return to Sarai. You will have a son whom you will name Ishmael, and his descendants will be without number".

Hagar returned and, in due course, gave birth to Ishmael. Abram was eighty-six years old at the time. Thirteen years later, when Abram was ninety-nine years old, God appeared to Abram and told him that his name would no longer be Abram but Abraham, because he would be the father of many nations. God made a covenant with Abram, promising the land of Canaan to him and his descendants. Abram, on his part, as a sign of the covenant, would circumcise himself, and, from then on, every male child born in his house or bought from any stranger would be circumcised, when the baby would be eight days old.

Sarai

(Hebrew origin: *Princess*)

(Genesis 11:29). 19th century B.C. Sarai was the original name of Sarah, the wife of the patriarch Abraham. (Please see the entry for Sarah [Genesis 17:15].)

Saraph

(Hebrew origin: *Burning*)

(1 Chronicles 4:22). 17th century B.C. Saraph was one of the sons of Shelah, Judah's youngest son. His brothers were Laadah, Jokim, Joash, and Er.

Sargon

(Uncertain origin and meaning)

(Isaiah 20:1). 8th century B.C. Sargon, king

of Assyria, sent his army, under the command of Tartan, to capture Ashdod, during the days of the prophet Isaiah.

Sarsechim

(Uncertain origin and meaning)

(Jeremiah 39:3). 6th century B.C. Sarsechim was one of the commanders of King Nebuchadnezzar's army who sat in the Middle Gate of Jerusalem, after the Babylonians had succeeded in breaking through the walls of the city.

King Zedekiah fled that night, leaving the palace by the garden's gate, but was later captured, taken to the presence of Nebuchadnezzar, and blinded.

Saruch

(Hebrew origin: *Tendril*)

(Luke 3:35). Unspecified date. Saruch, the son of Ragau and the father of Nachor, was an ancestor of Abraham, according to the genealogy of Luke. He is called Serug in the book of Genesis (Genesis 11:20).

Satan

(Hebrew origin: *Opponent*)

(1 Chronicles 21:1). The original meaning of the word "Satan" refers to an antagonist who accuses, opposes, and obstructs. The word is used in the Hebrew Bible to refer to both human and angelical adversaries.

In the first book of Chronicles, the word "Satan" is the name of a member of the celestial court who induced David to take a census in Israel, an act that God punished with an epidemic that killed seventy thousand people.

In the book of Job, Satan is an angel, clearly subordinate to God, who acts only through his permission. When God told him that Job was perfect and upright, Satan replied that, if Job's family and possessions would be taken away, he would curse God. God accepted the challenge and told Satan that everything that Job had was in his power, but that he should not lay a hand on him.

A short time later, thieves stole Job's oxen, donkeys, and camels; his sheep died in a fire; and all his children were crushed to death, when the house collapsed upon them.

Job arose, tore his clothes, cut off his hair, and prostrated himself on the ground, saying, "Naked I came out from my mother's womb, and naked shall I return there; the Lord has given, and the Lord has taken away; blessed be the name of the Lord".

God, seeing that Job did not reproach him, said to Satan that Job had been destroyed for no good reason.

Satan replied, "If Job would suffer on his bones and his flesh, he would surely blaspheme".

God said to Satan, "Job is in your power, but spare his life".

Satan departed from the Presence of God and inflicted severe sores on Job, from the sole of his foot to the top of his head. After this, Satan is no longer mentioned in the book of Job.

The prophet Isaiah calls him Lucifer, *Son of the morning* (Isaiah 14:12), a fallen angel, whom the prophet accuses of having tried to be like God. Lucifer was punished for this sacrilegious ambition, by falling from heaven down to hell.

Satan is seen by the prophet Zechariah in a vision, acting as a prosecutor in the Heavenly Court. He stands next to the High Priest Joshua, ready to accuse him, until he is rebuked by the Lord.

The New Testament identifies Satan with the Devil and describes him as being the enemy of God, and the deceiver of the world. Satan tempts Jesus in the desert, induces Judas to betray Jesus, and fills the heart of Ananias with greed.

The book of Revelation depicts a war between God and Satan and calls him "the great dragon" and "that old serpent". An angel from heaven seizes Satan and bounds him for a thousand years, after which, he is let out of his prison to deceive the nations of Gog and Magog, and to gather them together for battle. Fire from heaven will consume them, and Satan will be cast into a lake of fire and brimstone, where he shall be tormented for eternity.

Saul

(Hebrew origin: *Asked*)

1. (Genesis 36:37). Unspecified date. Saul, of Rehoboth by the river, ascended to the throne of Edom, when Samlah died. Saul was succeeded by Baalhanan, the son of Achbor. He was called Shaul in the first book of Chronicles (1 Chronicles 1:48).

2. (1 Samuel 9:2). 11th century B.C. Saul, the first king of the Israelites, was the son of a Benjamite called Kish, a man of substance with a reputation for being a mighty man of valor. The name of his wife was Ahinoam, daughter of Ahimaaz.

Saul is described by the Bible as being tall and handsome. He started as a shy young man, modest and humble, unable to bear a grudge against those who opposed his election as king. Soon enough, he became a brave and decisive leader, who showed his mettle in battle. However, in his later years, he became subject to fits of depression, paranoia, and obsession. His mental illness changed his character, and it drove him to violent acts, bordering on madness, such as hurling his spear at his son Jonathan, or killing the priests of Nob, believing that they had conspired with David against him.

The Bible first mentions him as searching for some lost donkeys that belonged to his father. This was at a time when the Israelites wanted to replace the rule of the Judges by a strong, central authority, under which the loose confederation of tribes could unite against the pressure of the surrounding nations, and especially get rid of the domination of the Philistines.

Saul and his servant, after searching for the lost animals without any success, arrived in the region of Zuph. Saul said to his servant, "Let's go home. My father might stop worrying about the donkeys, and start worrying about us".

The servant suggested, "There is a man of God in this region, with an excellent reputation. Everything that he says comes true. Let's speak to him about this matter; he might be able to help us".

Saul replied, "If we go to him, what gift can we give him"?

The servant said, "I have here a quarter of a silver shekel. We can give that to the man of God".

"That is fine, let's go", said Saul, and they went to the town where the man of God was. On their way, they saw some girls and asked them, "Is the seer here?"

"Yes, he is", they answered. "Hurry, because there will be a sacrifice in the shrine today. As soon as you enter the town, you will find him, before he goes up to the shrine to eat. The people will not eat, until he blesses the sacrifice".

As they were entering the town, they met Samuel, who was on his way up to the shrine, the day before God had told Samuel that, the next day, he would meet a man that would save the people from the hands of the Philistines. As soon as Samuel saw Saul, God said to him, "This is the man I told you about. He will rule my people".

Saul, who did not recognize Samuel, asked him, "Please tell me, where is the house of the seer?"

Samuel answered, "I am the seer. Go up ahead of me to the shrine, for you will eat with me today. Tomorrow, I will let you go, after telling you all that is in your heart. Don't worry about the lost donkeys; they have been found. Israel is yearning for you and for your father's house!"

Saul, bewildered, answered, "Why do you say these things to me? I am a Benjamite, from the smallest tribe in Israel, and my family is the least of all the families of my tribe".

Samuel took Saul and his servant into the dining hall, where, already, about thirty guests were seated. He made him sit at the head of the table, and instructed the cook to bring the food that had been reserved, and serve it to Saul. After they dined, they went down from the place of the shrine to the town, to Samuel's house, where they spent some hours speaking on the roof of the house.

The next morning, Samuel woke up

Saul, and they walked out of the town together. Samuel told Saul to let his servant walk ahead. Then, he took a flask of oil and poured it upon Saul's head, kissed him, and said, "The Lord anoints you ruler over his people. When you leave me today you will find two men by the tomb of Rachel who will tell you that the asses have been found, and that your father is worried about you. Then, you will continue to the plain of Tabor, where you will meet three men going to the shrine in Bethel, one of them carrying three young goats, another three loaves of bread, and the third one a bottle of wine. They will salute you and give you two loaves of bread. Receive them. After that, you will come to the hill of God, where there is a Philistine garrison. There, you will meet a group of prophets, coming down from the shrine with musical instruments, prophesying. The spirit of God will come upon you; you will prophesy, and become another man. After that, go to Gilgal, and wait there seven days for me. I will come to present burnt offerings and sacrifice to God".

On his way back to Gibeah, Saul encountered a group of ecstatic prophets. He was then seized by the spirit of God, and he prophesied among them. The people who saw him were amazed and asked each other, "What has happened to the son of Kish? Is he also a prophet?"

His uncle met him and asked, "Where did you go?"

Saul answered, "We were looking for the donkeys, and when we couldn't find them, we went to Samuel".

"So, tell me, what did Samuel say to you?" asked his uncle.

"He told us that the donkeys had been found", replied Saul and kept to himself what Samuel had told him about the kingship.

Samuel assembled the people in Mizpeh and told them to arrange themselves by their tribes and families. The tribe of Benjamin was chosen and told to step forward. From them, the family of Matri was chosen, and from them, Saul, the son of Kish, was indicated.

The people called for Saul, but they couldn't find him. After searching all over, he was found hiding among the baggage. They brought him to the presence of Samuel, and, when he stood among the people, everybody could see that he was a head taller than anybody else.

Samuel said to the people, "Do you see the one chosen by God? There is none like him among the people!"

All the people acclaimed him, shouting, "Long live the king!" Samuel explained to the people the rules of the monarchy, and he wrote them in a document, which he deposited before God. Then, he sent the people back to their homes. Saul heard some people making scornful comments against him. "How can this man save us?" they said. Saul didn't pay them any attention, and he returned to his house in Gibeah, accompanied by a band of brave men.

Nahash, the king of Ammon, laid siege to the town of Jabeshgilead. His condition for accepting the surrender of the town was that all the men had to take out their right eyes.

The elders of Jabesh asked Nahash to give them a waiting period of seven days, after which, if nobody from Israel would come to their rescue, they would accept Nahash's cruel demand. They sent messengers to Gibeah to tell what was happening. The people heard the terrible news and wept.

Saul, returning from the field, asked, "Why are the people crying?" When he was told on the tidings of Jabesh, Saul became very angry. He took a yoke of oxen, cut them in pieces, and sent them throughout all the territory of Israel, saying, "This is what will be done to the oxen of anybody who will not follow Saul and Samuel!"

The response of the people was immediate. Three hundred thousand men of Israel and thirty thousand of Judah gathered in Bezek, and they sent word to the people of Jabesh that the next day, they would save them. Saul divided his army in three companies, attacked the Ammonites, and routed them.

The people then remembered those who had treated Saul with contempt, and they said to Samuel, "Give us the men that spoke against Saul, so that we can kill them". Saul calmed them down, "Nobody will be killed today when God has given us victory!"

To celebrate the great victory, Samuel gathered the people in Gilgal, and he officially anointed Saul as king of Israel. The people offered sacrifices to God and held a joyful celebration. Samuel then spoke to the people, and he told them that, from then on, the king would be their leader. As for him, he would continue praying for the nation, and teaching them the good and right way. He ended his speech by saying, "Here is the king that the Lord has set over you. Fear God, serve him, and obey his voice, and do not reject his commandments. If not, the hand of God will be against you, as it was against your ancestors".

To enforce his words, he prayed to God to send thunder and rain, in spite of it being the dry season of wheat harvest. It rained and thundered, and the people greatly feared God and Samuel.

Saul, during his second year as king, established a standing army of three thousand soldiers: two thousand under his direct command and one thousand under his son Jonathan.

Jonathan made a successful raid against the Philistines and destroyed their garrison in Geba. The Philistines, to avenge their defeat, organized an army of thirty thousand chariots, six thousand horsemen, and troops as numerous as the sand of the seashore, and marched against Israel, encamping in Michmash. The Israelites were afraid and hid themselves in caves and in pits, and some of them fled to the other side of the Jordan. Saul, in the meantime, stayed in Gilgal, having been told by Samuel to wait there for seven days.

When the seven days were over, and Samuel had still not arrived, Saul, seeing that his army was starting to scatter, offered a sacrifice to God. At that moment, Samuel arrived and asked him, "What have you done?"

Saul answered, "Seeing that you had not arrived, that the army was scattering, and that the Philistines had gathered at Michmash, I decided to make a sacrifice to God".

Samuel told him, "You have behaved foolishly in not keeping God's command. God would have established your dynasty over Israel forever, but, because you didn't keep God's command, God will find another man, and appoint him to rule over his people". Samuel got up, left Gilgal, and went to Gibeah of Benjamin.

Saul was left with only six hundred soldiers in his army, unarmed, except for Saul and Jonathan, who had swords and spears. The day was saved by Jonathan who, with his armor bearer, bravely climbed a hill, surprised and killed a group of twenty Philistine soldiers. This caused the Philistine army to flee full of panic, pursued by the Israelites who came out of hiding.

Unbeknownst to Jonathan, Saul had forbidden his troops to eat anything before nightfall. Jonathan, seeing a beehive with honey, dipped a stick in it and brought it to his mouth.

One of the soldiers said to him, "Your father has cursed the man who eats anything today. And the troops are now feeling weak because of their hunger".

Jonathan replied, "My father has made a terrible mistake. If the soldiers had eaten the food captured from the enemy, they would have killed even more Philistines!"

That day, the soldiers fought against the Philistines from Michmash to Aijalon. Although they were famished, they fought bravely and defeated the enemy. They were so hungry that, when they saw the sheep and oxen captured from the Philistines, they slew them on the spot and ate them with the blood.

Saul, when told that the people were sinning by eating flesh with blood, gave orders that the soldiers should bring their animals to a certain spot, slaughter them there, and eat them without the blood. Saul then built an altar to the Lord, the first altar that he ever erected.

The king decided to attack the Philistines, during that night, and annihilate all of them. The soldiers agreed, but the priest who accompanied the army suggested that they should first consult with God. Saul inquired of God, "Shall we pursue the Philistines? Will you deliver them into our hands?" But God didn't answer.

Saul said to the troops, "Come forward, all chief commanders, and we will find out who committed the sin today. Even if the guilty one is my son Jonathan, he will die!"

When no one came forward and no one answered, Saul said, "You stand on one side, and my son Jonathan and I will stand on the other".

The soldiers replied, "Do as you think best".

Saul asked from God to indicate the guilty party. Saul and Jonathan were indicated by lot, and the troops were cleared. Saul then said, "Cast the lots between me and my son", and Jonathan was indicated.

"Tell me what you have done", said Saul to Jonathan.

"All I did was take a little honey with a stick and taste it, but I am ready to die".

"Yes, you will surely die, Jonathan", said Saul.

The soldiers defended Jonathan, "Shall Jonathan die after bringing us this great victory? Never! We will not allow even one hair of his head to fall on the ground. What he did today was with God's help!" Thus, the troops saved Jonathan's life. After that, Saul stopped pursuing the Philistines, and they went back to their own country.

Saul fought against his enemies on all sides of the country—against Moab, Ammon, Edom, Zobah, Philistia, and Amalek—and defeated all of them.

Sometime later, Samuel said to Saul, "I am the one that God sent to anoint you as king over Israel. Therefore, listen to what God says, 'I remember what Amalek did to Israel, how they ambushed Israel when the people came out from Egypt'. Now, go, attack Amalek, and annihilate them. Spare no one, kill them all: men, women, children and babies, oxen and sheep, camels and donkeys".

Saul gathered a huge army of over two hundred thousand soldiers, marched to the city of Amalek, and waited in the valley. Before attacking, he warned the Kenite tribe, a people who had been kind to the Israelites, when they left Egypt, to depart from Amalek, so that they would not also be destroyed. The Kenites withdrew, and Saul slaughtered the Amalekites, except for Agag, the king of Amalek, whom he captured alive, together with a number of sheep, oxen, and lambs.

God said to Samuel, "I regret that I chose Saul to be king, because he has not carried out my commands".

Samuel grieved, when he heard these words, and cried the whole night. Then, he went to Saul and found him in Gilgal.

Saul greeted him, "Blessed are you of the Lord! I have done what the Lord commanded me".

Samuel asked, "What then is this bleating of sheep in my ears, and the mooing of oxen that I hear?"

Saul answered, "The troops spared the best of the sheep and oxen of the Amalekites, and brought them to offer them in sacrifice to the Lord, your God. The rest, we have destroyed".

Samuel said to Saul, "Wait, I will tell you what God said to me tonight".

"Say it", Saul replied.

Samuel said, "When you were insignificant in your own sight, didn't God make you king over Israel? God sent you to destroy the Amalekites, and exterminate them. Why did you disobey God in keeping the spoil?"

Saul protested, "But I did obey the voice of God. I exterminated the

Amalekites, and captured Agag, their king. The soldiers kept the best sheep and oxen only to sacrifice them to the Lord, your God, in Gilgal".

Samuel reproved him, "To obey is better than to offer sacrifices. Rebellion is like the sin of witchcraft. Because you rejected the command of God, he has rejected you as king".

Saul said, "I have sinned against God, because I feared the people, and did what they wanted me to do. Please forgive me and come back with me, and I will worship the Lord".

Samuel said, "I will not go back with you, because you have rejected God, and God has rejected you as king of Israel".

As Samuel turned to leave, Saul seized his robe, and it tore. Samuel said to him, "God has torn today the kingdom from you and given it to somebody else who is worthier than you. God does not lie or change his mind as humans do".

Saul insisted, "I have sinned, but, please, do me the honor of your presence, before the elders and before the people, and come back with me, so that I may worship the Lord, your God".

Samuel went back with him, and Saul worshipped God.

Samuel said, "Bring me Agag, the king of the Amalekites".

Agag came, walking hesitantly, and said, "Surely the bitterness of death is past".

Samuel said, "As your sword has made women childless, so shall your mother be childless among women", and he hacked Agag in pieces.

Samuel then returned to Ramah, and Saul went back to his house in Gibeah. Samuel, for the rest of his life, never saw Saul again, and he grieved over Saul, because God regretted that he had made him king over Israel.

King Saul, after his final break with Samuel, became increasingly subject to fits of depression. His worried servants felt that music might make the king feel better, and, when somebody recommended David as a

skilled musician, the king asked that he be brought to him.

David came to the palace at Gibeah, carrying the gifts of bread, wine, and a young goat that his father Jesse had sent to the king. Saul was charmed by David, and from then on, whenever Saul would fall into one of his black moods, David would play music for him on his harp.

Sometime later, the Philistines gathered for battle on a hill, and the Israelites, led by Saul, lined on another hill, with a valley between the two armies. A nine feet tall giant, called Goliath, wearing heavy bronze armor, came out from the Philistine camp everyday and shouted a challenge to the Israelite army, saying that he was ready to fight any of them. Goliath did this every morning and evening for forty days.

David was in Bethlehem at that time, helping his father Jesse take care of the sheep. His three eldest brothers—Eliab, Abinadab, and Shammah—served in King Saul's army. Jesse, wanting to know how his sons were getting along, sent David to the army camp to find out, carrying with him ten loaves of bread for his brothers, and a gift of ten cheeses for their commanding officer.

David's arrival at the camp coincided with the moment when Goliath came forward to challenge the Israelites. David heard from the terrified soldiers that King Saul had promised great rewards to the man who would kill the giant. The king would give his daughter in marriage to this man, and he would free the man's family from the obligation of paying taxes.

David told Saul, "Your servant will go and fight that Philistine!" When the king expressed his doubts that he, a mere boy, could fight against the experienced Philistine warrior, David assured him that he had killed lions and bears. "God, who saved me from lion and bear will also save me from that Philistine", said David. "Then, go", Saul said to David, "and may the Lord be with you!"

Saul gave him his armor to wear, but David, not used to it, took it off, picked up five smooth stones, and, with his sling ready in his hand, went to meet Goliath. The giant, seeing a young boy coming against him, called down curses on him. David told him, "You come against me with sword, spear, and javelin, but I come against you in the name of the Lord".

Goliath started walking ponderously toward David, who ran quickly toward the Philistine, took out a stone from his bag, and slung it at Goliath. The stone hit the giant on the forehead and made him fall to the ground. Goliath tried to get up but was unable to do so.

David ran to him, stood over the fallen giant, took his sword, and cut off his head. The Philistines, in shock, ran away, and the Israelites pursued them all the way up to the gates of their cities.

Saul appointed David as an officer in the army and did not allow him to go back to his father's home in Bethlehem. From that day on, the king kept David next to him. And Jonathan, Saul's son, became David's best friend.

David was successful in all his military missions, and he became very popular with the people. The women sang, "Saul has killed thousands, but David has killed tens of thousands". Saul became jealous and angry, and, suffering with depressive paranoia, he started to suspect that David planned to seize the throne. During one of his fits of depression, Saul tried to kill David with his spear, but it missed.

Saul considered that God was now with David and became afraid of him. He removed David from his daily sight, by appointing him captain of a company of a thousand soldiers, and devised a plan to get rid of him, by offering him his eldest daughter Merab in marriage, if he would fight against the Philistines, secretly hoping that David would be killed in battle.

When the time came to fulfill his promise, Saul, instead of giving Merab to David, married her to Adriel, the son of Barzillai the Meholathite. However, Michal, Saul's youngest daughter, loved David, which pleased Saul, as he saw a way to use her as a snare. He sent a message to David, offering him his daughter in marriage, and asked for a peculiar dowry, the foreskins of a hundred Philistines, still hoping that David would be killed by them.

David went and slew not one hundred Philistines but two hundred, and he brought their foreskins to the king. Saul, this time, did as he had promised and gave him Michal, his daughter, for a wife.

Saul grew more and more afraid of David. He even asked Jonathan, David's devoted friend, to kill him, but Jonathan advised David to hide, while he tried to convince his father not to kill him.

Saul listened to Jonathan's good words about David and agreed that he would not try to kill him, or hurt him. This did not last long, and, soon afterward, while David was playing the harp for him, Saul once more attempted to kill David with his spear. The weapon struck the wall, and David fled to his house.

That same night, helped by his wife Michal, David escaped through a window. Saul's envoys brought Michal to the palace, where her father asked her why she helped his enemy to escape. Michal answered that she had done so only because David had threatened to kill her.

Saul, having heard that David had found refuge with Samuel in the town of Naioth in Ramah, sent soldiers to capture him. The men came to the town, but, instead of arresting David, joined a company of prophets, and started to prophesy. Twice again, Saul sent men to Naioth, both times with the same result. Finally, the king decided to go himself in search of David, but, when he came to Naioth, he took off his clothes, lay down naked on the ground, all that day and all that night, and prophesied.

David fled from Naioth and went to see Jonathan, to find out from him why Saul hated him with such a murderous rage. He arrived the day before a banquet that Saul was giving in honor of the New Moon Festival. David told Jonathan that he would not take the risk of attending the king's banquet, and that Jonathan should explain his absence from the celebrations, by saying that David had gone to Bethlehem for the yearly family sacrifice. David instructed Jonathan to watch for Saul's reaction.

The two friends arranged that David should go away for three days, and then return and hide in a field. Jonathan would come to that place, under the pretext of shooting arrows, but in truth to inform David, by a prearranged code, whether it was safe to return to the royal court or not.

The next day, during the banquet, Saul noticed David's absence, but he attributed it to a possible illness. The following day, noticing that David was still absent, Saul asked Jonathan, "Why isn't David here at the banquet?"

Jonathan answered, "He went to Bethlehem to participate in a family sacrifice".

Saul, furious, screamed, "Jonathan, you are a fool! Don't you realize that, as long as David is alive, you will never be king?"

"Why should he be killed? What has he done?" asked Jonathan.

His father, losing all control, raised his spear to strike him. Jonathan arose from the table and left the hall, angry and humiliated. The next day, Jonathan went to the field where he had arranged to meet David. They embraced and wept, and David fled to Nob, where he tricked the priest Ahimelech into giving him bread and the sword of Goliath, which had been kept there.

Unbeknownst to David, his meeting with Ahimelech had been witnessed by Doeg the Edomite, the head of the king's herdsmen. Doeg rushed back to Saul and reported what he had seen. The king had Ahimelech and all the other priests of Nob brought to his presence, and he accused them of conspiring with David against him, and of encouraging him to rebel against the king, by giving him food and a weapon.

Ahimelech denied any wrongdoing, saying that David, the king's son-in-law, was known to be a faithful servant to the king. Saul would not accept any explanations and condemned him to die. The king ordered the soldiers who were guarding the priests to kill them. Appalled, the servants did not move, and the king ordered Doeg to slay them, which he readily did, killing that day eighty-five priests. Then, he massacred all the people in Nob, including the women and the children, and even their animals. Abiathar, son of Ahimelech, the only survivor of King Saul's slaughter, managed to escape and told David about the mass murder. David, feeling that he was the cause of the death of Abiathar's father, asked him to remain with him.

Saul was told that David had come to Keilah, and he rejoiced, thinking that David had shut himself in by entering a town with gates and bars. He summoned his army, to go to Keilah, and to besiege David and his men. David again consulted the oracle of God, through the ephod that the priest Abiathar had brought with him, "Saul intends to come to Keilah and destroy the town because of me. Will the citizens of the town deliver me into his hands?" God, through the oracle, answered, "They will". David and his men left Keilah immediately, and Saul desisted from his intention to besiege the town.

David returned to the desert, moving from place to place, constantly pursued by Saul. Once, while David was in Horesh in the wilderness of Ziph, Jonathan came to him in secret and told him, "Do not be afraid. You are going to be king over Israel, and I shall be second to you; and even my father Saul knows this is so". They never saw each other again.

David went from there and stayed in the wilderness of Engedi, near the Dead Sea. Saul took three thousand men and went in search of David and his men. There was a cave, and Saul went in to relieve himself. David and his men were hiding in the back of the cave. His men told him,

"God has delivered your enemy into your hands; you can do with him as you please". David went and surreptitiously cut off the corner of Saul's cloak. He went back to his men and told them, "God forbid that I should raise my hand against the Lord's anointed". Later, he even felt remorse for cutting off a piece of Saul's cloak.

Saul left the cave and started back to his army's camp. Then, David went out of the cave and called after Saul, "My lord king!" Saul turned around and David bowed low in homage, with his face to the ground, and said, "Why do you listen to people who say that I wish to do you harm? You can see for yourself that the Lord had delivered you into my hands in the cave today. Though I was urged to kill you, I did not raise a hand against you, because you are the Lord's anointed. My father, look at this piece of your cloak in my hand. When I cut it, I did not kill you. You can see that I have not done anything evil or rebellious. My hand will never touch you. Against whom has the king of Israel come out? A dead dog? A single flea?"

Saul asked, "Is that your voice, my son David?" The king broke down, wept, and said, "You are right, not I. I now know that you will become king. So swear to me by the Lord that you will not destroy my descendants or wipe out my name from my father's house". David swore to Saul. The king went home, and David and his men went up to the strongholds.

Saul, when told that David was hiding in the wilderness of Ziph, took with him three thousand chosen men, and they went in search of David. David came to the place where Saul and his army commander, Abner, lay asleep, with troops around them. David asked Ahimelech the Hittite and Abishai, the brother of Joab, to go with him to the king's camp. Abishai answered, "I will go with you". The two men approached the camp by night and found Saul asleep, his spear stuck in the ground near his head, and Abner and the troops sleeping around him. Abishai whispered to David, "God has delivered your enemy into your hands. Let me pin him to the ground with a single thrust of his spear. I will not have to strike him twice!" David rebuked him, "Don't kill him! No one can lay hands on the Lord's anointed with impunity. God himself will strike him down, or his time will come, and he will die, or he will fight in a battle and be killed. Just take the spear and the water jar at this head, and let's get out!" They left without being noticed, or waking anybody up.

David crossed over to the other side, stood on top of a hill, quite a distance away from the king's camp, and started shouting, "Abner, aren't you going to answer?" Abner shouted back, "Who are you to shout at the king?" David answered, "Aren't you a brave man? There is nobody like you in Israel. So why didn't you watch over your lord, the king? One of my men came to kill your master. You failed in your duty! You deserve to die for not protecting your master, the Lord's anointed. Look around, where are the king's spear and the water jar that were right by his head?

Saul recognized David's voice, and he said, "Is this your voice, David, my son?" David replied, "It is, my lord king. Why does my lord continue to pursue his servant? What have I done? Of what wrong am I guilty? If God has incited you against me, I will make an offering to him, but if men have turned you against me, God should curse them, for they have driven me out of God's land to a foreign country and told me to worship foreign gods. Don't let me be killed away from the presence of the Lord. The king of Israel has come to out to seek a single flea, as if he were hunting a partridge in the hills".

Saul answered, "I am wrong. Come back, David, my son. I will do no more harm to you, because you have spared my life tonight. I have been a fool, and I have made so many mistakes!" David said, "Here is the king's spear. Let one of the young men come over and get it. Today, I spared your life. May the Lord do the same to me and free me from all my troubles!" Saul said to David, "God bless you, my son! You will succeed in everything you do!" David then went his way, and Saul returned home.

David knew that Saul would not keep his promise, and that he would soon again try to capture and kill him. So, he went with his wives, Abigail and Ahinoam, and his six hundred men to the Philistine city of Gath. Saul, when informed that David had fled to Gath, stopped pursuing him.

Several years later, after Samuel had died and was buried in Ramah, mourned by all of Israel, a great army of the Philistines marched against Israel. Saul gathered his army near the hills of Gilboa, but when he saw the Philistine forces, his heart was filled with fear. He tried to consult God through oracles, but God didn't answer.

Saul ordered his officials to search for a medium, which he could consult. They told him that there was a woman in Endor, who could conjure ghosts. Saul disguised himself, put on different clothes, and, accompanied by two men, went that night to the woman.

He asked her, "Consult the spirits for me. Bring up for me the one I shall name".

The woman was distrustful. "You know that King Saul has forbidden the practice of mediums and wizards in the land", she said, "You want me killed?"

Saul swore to her, "As God lives, nothing will happen to you over this".

The woman asked him, "Whom do you want me to bring?"

Saul answered, "Bring me Samuel".

When the woman saw the ghost of Samuel, she screamed, "Why have you deceived me? You are Saul!"

Saul said, "Don't be afraid. What do you see?"

The woman answered, "I see a spirit coming up from the earth".

"What does he look like?" he asked.

She said, "He looks like an old man covered with a mantle". Then, Saul knew that it was Samuel, and he bowed low with his face to the ground.

The ghost of Samuel asked, "Why have you disturbed me and brought me up?"

Saul answered, "I am in great trouble. The Philistines are making war against me. God is no longer with me and does not answer, either by prophets or in dreams. That is why I called you. I need you to tell me what I must do".

"Why do you ask me, seeing that God has left you and become your enemy?" said the ghost of Samuel. "God has taken the kingdom from you and given it to David, because you did not obey him, and did not carry out his wrathful commands against the Amalekites. The Lord will deliver you and all of Israel to the hands of the Philistines, and tomorrow, you and your sons will be with me".

Saul, terrified by the words of the ghost, and weak, because he had not eaten anything, during the last twenty-four hours, flung himself to the ground.

The battle took place the next day on the Mount of Gilboa. The Philistines crushed the Israelites and killed many of them, including the sons of Saul: Jonathan, Abinadab, and Melchishua.

Saul, badly wounded by an arrow, begged his arms bearer, "Draw your sword and kill me, so that these uncircumcised may not mock me and kill me".

The young man was too terrified to do it. Saul took his own sword and threw himself on it. When the arms bearer saw that Saul was dead, he also killed himself with his sword.

The populations of the towns close to Gilboa, when they heard that the Israelite army had been defeated, and that Saul was dead, abandoned their towns and fled; the Philistines then came and occupied them.

The next day, the Philistines came to strip the corpses and found the bodies of Saul and his three sons lying on Mount Gilboa. They cut off his head and took off his armor, and they sent them throughout their land to spread the news among their people. Then, they put his armor in the

Temple of Ashtaroth and nailed his body to the wall of Bethshean.

A group of brave men from Jabeshgilead, having heard what the Philistines had done to Saul, marched, during the night to Bethshean, removed the bodies of Saul and his sons, and brought them to Jabesh. They burned them and buried the remains under a tree, and then, they fasted seven days. Jonathan and Saul were mourned by David in a beautiful elegy.

Years later, King David took the bones of Saul and Jonathan from Jabeshgilead, and he had them buried in the country of Benjamin in Zelah, in the sepulcher of Kish, Saul's father.

3. (Acts of the Apostles 7:58). A.D. 1st century. Saul was the Hebrew name of Paul, the apostle to the Gentiles. (Please see the entry for Paul [Acts of the Apostle 13:9].)

Sceva

(Latin origin: *Left handed*)

(Acts of the Apostles 19:14). A.D. 1st century. Sceva, a High Priest, was the father of seven brothers who attempted to exorcise evil spirits in the name of Jesus, saying, "I command you in the name of Jesus, whom Paul preaches".

The evil spirit answered, "I know Jesus, and I know Paul, but who are you?"

The possessed man attacked his would-be exorcisers with such violence that they ran away, bloodied and naked.

Seba

(Uncertain origin and meaning)

(Genesis 10:7). Unspecified date. Seba was the son of Cush and grandson of Ham. His brothers were Sabtah, Havilah, Raamah, and Sabtechah. Later, Cush had another son, Nimrod, a powerful man and a mighty hunter, who established a kingdom in the land of Shinar and founded Nineveh and other cities.

Secundus

(Latin origin: *Second*)

(Acts of the Apostles 20:4). A.D. 1st century. Secundus was one of the companions of Paul in his final trip from Greece to Jerusalem. The apostle's other companions in that trip were Aristarchus—a fellow Thessalonian—Sopater of Berea, Gaius of Derbe, Timotheus, Tychicus, and Trophimus.

Segub

(Hebrew origin: *Aloft*)

1. (1 Kings 16:34). 9th century B.C. Segub, son of Hiel the Bethelite, and his brother Abiram lost their lives, when their father rebuilt Jericho, during the reign of Ahab, thus, fulfilling Joshua's curse (Joshua 6:26).

2. (1 Chronicles 2:21). 17th century B.C. Segub, a descendant of Judah, was the son of Hezron and his wife Abiah, daughter of Machir. His son Jair had twenty-three cities in the region of Gilead.

Seir

(Hebrew origin: *Shaggy*)

(Genesis 36:20). Unspecified date. Seir, the Horite, gave his name to the region, south of the Dead Sea, where he lived. Later, when Esau and his descendants settled there, the land became known as Edom. Seir's sons, chiefs of clans, were Lotan, Shobal, Zibeon, Anah, Dishon, Ezer, and Dishan. His daughter was called Timna.

Seled

(Hebrew origin: *Exultation*)

(1 Chronicles 2:30). Unspecified date. Seled, who died childless, was the son of Nadab, a descendant of Judah, and the brother of Appaim.

Sem

(Hebrew origin: *Name*)

(Luke 3:36). Unspecified date. Sem is an alternative spelling for Shem, the son of Noe.

Semachiah

(Hebrew origin: *God supported*)

(1 Chronicles 26:7). 10th century B.C. Semachiah, son of Shemaiah and grandson of Obededom, was one of the gatekeepers of the Tabernacle in Jerusalem, during the reign of King David. His brothers—all of them brave men and leaders of their clan—were Othni, Rephael, Elihu, Elzabad, and Obed.

Semei

(Hebrew origin: *Famous*)

(Luke 3:26). Unspecified date. Semei, son of Joseph and father of Mattathias, was an ancestor of Jesus, according to Luke's genealogy.

Senaah

(Hebrew origin: *Thorny*)

(Ezra 2:35). Unspecified date. Senaah—also called Hassenaah—was the ancestor of a family that returned with Zerubbabel from the Babylonian Exile. (Please see the entry for Hassenaah [Nehemiah 3:3].)

Sennacherib

(Uncertain origin and meaning)

(2 Kings 18:13). 8th century B.C. Sennacherib, the king of Assyria, invaded Judah, during the fourteenth year of King Hezekiah's reign, and conquered most of the walled cities, including the large city of Lachish, where he established his headquarters. King Hezekiah offered to pay tribute to Sennacherib, who imposed on him the payment of three hundred talents of silver and thirty talents of gold.

Sennacherib decided to demand the unconditional surrender of Hezekiah, and he sent a large Assyrian army from Lachish to Jerusalem, under the command of Rabshakeh, a high ranking officer in the Assyrian army, accompanied by two other officers, Tartan and Rabsaris.

During the siege of Jerusalem, Hezekiah prayed to God to save him from Sennacherib.

The great prophet-statesman Isaiah came to the king and told him that God had heard his prayer. That night, over one hundred and eighty-five thousand Assyrian soldiers died suddenly.

Sennacherib, having failed in his purpose to capture Jerusalem, returned to Assyria, to his capital Nineveh. There, while praying in the Temple of the god Nisroch, his sons Adrammelech and Sharezer murdered him and escaped to Armenia. His son Esarhaddon succeeded him to the throne.

Senuah

(Hebrew origin: *Pointed*)

(Nehemiah 11:9). 5th century B.C. His son Judah, of the tribe of Benjamin, was second in command in the city of Jerusalem, after the return from the Babylonian Exile.

Seorim

(Hebrew origin: *Barley*)

(1 Chronicles 24:8). 10th century B.C. During the reign of King David, the priestly service in the Tabernacle was divided by lot into twenty-four turns. Seorim was in charge of the fourth turn.

Serah

(Hebrew origin: *Superfluity*)

(Genesis 46:17). 17th century. Serah, daughter of Asher and granddaughter of Jacob, was one of the seventy Israelites who immigrated to Egypt. This number includes her father Asher; her brothers Jimnah, Ishuah, Isui, and Beriah; and her nephews, Heber and Malchiel, sons of Beriah.

Seraiah

(Hebrew origin: *God has prevailed*)

1. (2 Samuel 8:17). 10th century B.C. Seraiah—also called Sheva (2 Samuel 20:25), Shavsha (1 Chronicles 18:16), and Shisha (1 Kings 4:3)—was the scribe in the court of King David. His sons, Elihoreph and Ahiah,

followed in his footsteps and became the scribes in the court of King Solomon.

2. (2 Kings 25:18). 6th century B.C. Seraiah, the son of Azariah, was the High Priest of the Temple, when the Babylonians captured Jerusalem. He and Zephaniah—the priest next in rank—together with three Temple gatekeepers, several officials of the court, and sixty men of the common people who were inside the city, were taken by Nebuzaradan, the commander of the Babylonian army, to King Nebuchadnezzar who was in Riblah. There, the king had them beaten and put to death.

Seraiah's son Jehozadak was carried into captivity, by Nebuchadnezzar, when the Babylonians conquered the kingdom of Judah.

His grandson the High Priest Jeshua—also called Joshua—returned with Zerubbabel from the Babylonian Exile.

3. (2 Kings 25:23). 6th century B.C. Seraiah, son of Tanhumeth the Netophathite, was an officer of the defeated Judean army. He came with a group of other commanders and their men to the city of Mizpah to meet with Gedaliah, son of Ahikam, who had been appointed governor of Judah by the Babylonians. Gedaliah told them that everything would be well with them, if they would serve the king of Babylon. Sometime later, Ishmael, another officer of the army, murdered Gedaliah.

4. (1 Chronicles 4:13). 12th century B.C. Seraiah, a descendant of Judah, was the son of Kenaz, the younger brother of Caleb. His son Joab settled in the valley of Charashim, where all the people were craftsmen. His brother was called Othniel.

5. (1 Chronicles 4:35). 9th century B.C. Seraiah, the son of Asiel, was the father of Josibiah. His grandson Jehu was one of the leaders of the tribe of Simeon who went to the fertile valley of Gedor in search of pasture for their flocks, during the reign of Hezekiah, king of Judah. The Simeonites destroyed the tents of the people—descendants of Ham—who lived there, wiped them out forever, and settled in their place.

6. (Ezra 2:2). 6th century B.C. Seraiah—called Azariah in the book of Nehemiah, (Nehemiah 7:7)—was one of the men who returned with Zerubbabel from the Babylonian Exile.

7. (Ezra 7:1). 5th century B.C. Seraiah, the son of Azariah and grandson of Hilkiah, was a descendant of Eleazar, the son of Aaron. His son, Ezra the Scribe, a priest and a scholar, became one of the most influential religious leaders in the history of the Jewish people.

8. (Nehemiah 10:2). 5th century B.C. Seraiah was one of the priests who signed Nehemiah's solemn agreement to separate themselves from the foreigners living in the land, to refrain from intermarrying with them, and to dedicate their firstborn to God, among other obligations.

9. (Nehemiah 11:11). 5th century B.C. Seraiah, son of Hilkiah, a descendant of Ahitub, was the priest in charge of the Temple in the days of Nehemiah. He is called Azariah in the first book of Chronicles (1 Chronicles 9:11).

10. (Nehemiah 12:12). Unspecified date. Seraiah was the ancestor of a priestly clan that was headed by Meraiah, during the days of the High Priest Joiakim.

11. (Jeremiah 36:26). 7th century B.C. Seraiah, the son of Azriel, and two other court officials—Jerahmeel, son of Hammelech, and Shelemiah, the son of Abdeel—were ordered by King Jehoiakim to arrest the prophet Jeremiah and his trusted companion, Baruch the Scribe. The men failed in their mission, because Jeremiah and Baruch had gone into hiding.

12. (Jeremiah 51:59). 6th century B.C. Seraiah, son of Neriah and brother of Baruch—Jeremiah's trusted companion—was a high official of the court, during the reign of King Zedekiah. He accompanied the king in the royal visit that Zedekiah made to Babylon in the fourth year of his reign. Seraiah took with him a scroll where the prophet Jeremiah had written all the disasters that would befall upon Babylon,

with instructions that, after he had finished reading the scroll in Babylon, he should tie a stone to it and throw it into the river Euphrates, to symbolize that Babylon would sink and never rise again.

Seraphims

(Hebrew origin: *Burning*)

(Isaiah 6:2). Seraphims are heavenly beings, which the prophet Isaiah saw in a vision standing above the throne of God. These beings had six wings: two of these wings covered their face, another two covered their feet, and the other two were used for flying. They cried to each other, "Holy, holy, holy is the Lord of hosts: the whole earth is full of his glory".

When the prophet Isaiah said that he was a man of unclean lips, living in the midst of a people of unclean lips, one of the seraphim flew to him and touched his lips with a live coal, which it had taken with tongs from the altar.

Sered

(Hebrew origin: *Trembling*)

(Genesis 46:14). 17th century B.C. Sered, son of Zebulun, was the grandson of Jacob and Leah, and the ancestor of the clan of the Sardites (Numbers 26:26). His brothers were Elon and Jahleel. Sered was one of the seventy Israelites who immigrated to Egypt.

Sergius

(Latin origin: Uncertain meaning)

(Acts of the Apostles 13:7). A.D. 1st century. Sergius Paulus was the Roman proconsul in the city of Paphos, on the island of Cyprus.

Having learned that Paul was in the island, Sergius Paulus invited him to his quarters so that he could hear the word of God from his mouth. Present in that meeting was a sorcerer and false prophet named Barjesus—also called Elymas—who attempted to refute Paul's arguments.

The apostle turned to Barjesus, cursed him, and told him that he wouldn't be able to see the sun for a season. Barjesus immediately became blind, and he had to be led outside by his hand. This event so impressed the proconsul that he became a Christian believer.

Serug

(Hebrew origin: *Tendril*)

(Genesis 11:20). Unspecified date. Serug—called Saruch by Luke (Luke 3:35)—was the son of Reu. He was thirty years old, when his son Nachor, an ancestor of Abraham, was born. After that, he lived for another two hundred years and had other sons and daughters.

Seth

(Hebrew origin: *Substituted*)

(Genesis 4:25). Antediluvian. Seth—called Sheth in the first book of Chronicles (1 Chronicles 1:1)—was the third son of Adam and Eve, born after the death of Abel, when his father Adam was one hundred and thirty years old.

Seth himself was one hundred and five years old, when his son Enos was born. He later had many other sons and daughters, and he died at the age of nine hundred and twelve.

Sethur

(Hebrew origin: *Hidden*)

(Numbers 13:13). 13th century B.C. Sethur, son of Michael, of the tribe of Asher, was one of the twelve spies sent by Moses to Canaan, to scout the land, its cities, and its inhabitants; to find out if they were strong or weak, few or many; and to bring back the fruit of the land. The spies came back, frightened and disheartened, and told the Israelites that the Canaanites were too big and too strong to be defeated.

Two of the spies—Joshua, the son of Nun, and Caleb, the son of Jephunneh—disagreed and told the people not to fear.

The Israelites refused to listen to the

encouraging words of Joshua and Caleb, and they started to wail and cry. God punished their cowardice by condemning them to wander forty years in the wilderness, one year for each day that the spies scouted the land. All those who complained against God, including Sethur, died in the wilderness, except Caleb and Joshua.

(For more detailed information about the twelve spies, please see the entry for Joshua.)

Shaaph

(Hebrew origin: *Fluctuation*)

1. (1 Chronicles 2:47). Unspecified date. Shaaph was the son of Jahdai of the tribe of Judah. His brothers were Regem, Jotham, Gesham, Pelet, and Ephah.
2. (1 Chronicles 2:49). Unspecified date. Shaaph, the founder of Madmannah, was the son of Caleb—also called Chelubai—and his concubine Maachah. His brothers were Sheber, Sheva, and Tirhanah.

Shaashgaz

(Persian origin: Uncertain meaning)

(Esther 2:14). 5th century B.C. Shaashgaz was the eunuch in charge of King Ahasuerus' second harem, the one where the women who had already spent one night with the king were kept. These women remained in the harem, and they never saw the king again, except when he specifically summoned one of them by her name.

Shabbethai

(Hebrew origin: *Restful*)

(Ezra 10:15). 5th century B.C. Shabbethai was a leading Levite in Jerusalem, during the time of Ezra and Nehemiah. He was in charge, together with another Levite called Jozabad, of the external work of the Temple.

He and another Levite called Meshullam, helped Jonathan and Jahaziah, two leaders of Judah who remained in Jerusalem, to represent the people, when Ezra deliberated on the matter of the marriages to foreign women.

Shabbethai was among the Levites who explained the Law to the people in Jerusalem, after Ezra the Scribe had read it, while standing on a wooden platform, in front of the open space, before the Water Gate.

Shachia

(Hebrew origin: *Captivation*)

(1 Chronicles 8:10). Unspecified date. Shachia, of the tribe of Benjamin, born in the country of Moab, was one of the seven sons of Shaharaim and his wife Hodesh. His brothers—all of them heads of clans—were Zibia, Jobab, Mesha, Jeuz, Malcham, and Mirma.

Shadrach

(Uncertain origin and meaning)

(Daniel 1:7). 6th century B.C. Shadrach was the Babylonian name given by the chief of the eunuchs of King Nebuchadnezzar to Hananiah, a young boy from a noble Jewish family in Babylon.

Hananiah was chosen—together with his companions Daniel, Azariah, and Mishael—to receive an education that would allow them to become officials of the king's court.

In order not to transgress by eating and drinking ritually forbidden food and wine, Daniel asked permission from Melzar, the man who had been placed in charge of them, to eat only legumes and drink only water. Melzar feared that this diet might endanger their health, but Daniel asked him to let them try it for ten days. When the ten days were over, the four Jewish boys looked better and healthier than the boys who had eaten of the king's food.

During the three following years, the four boys acquired knowledge and skill, and Daniel learned to interpret the significance of visions and dreams.

Years later, at the request of Daniel, the king appointed Hananiah, Mishael, and Azariah to be in charge over the affairs of the province of Babylon. When the three men refused to serve the Babylonian gods or worship the golden idol that the king had set up, they were thrown into a burning furnace but were saved by an angel.

Nebuchadnezzar was so impressed that the three men had been able to survive the fire without even one hair of their heads singed, that he blessed God, and decreed that anyone who would speak against God would be cut in pieces, and his house would be turned into a dunghill.

Shage

(Hebrew origin: *Erring*)

(1 Chronicles 11:34). 11th century B.C. Shage the Hararite was the father of Jonathan, a member of King David's elite army group known as The Thirty.

Shaharaim

(Hebrew origin: *Double dawn*)

(1 Chronicles 8:8). Unspecified date. Shaharaim, a descendant of Benjamin, had two wives: Hushim—the mother of his sons, Abitub and Elpaal—and Baara.

After sending the two women away, he settled in the land of Moab, east of the river Jordan. There, he married Hodesh with whom he had seven children: Jobab, Zibia, Mesha, Malcham, Jeuz, Shachia, and Mirma.

Shallum

(Hebrew origin: *Reward*)

1. (2 Kings 15:10). 8th century B.C. Shallum, son of Jabesh, killed King Zachariah of Israel and usurped the throne, thus, putting an end to the Jehu dynasty, which had lasted for one hundred years. His reign, as the fifteenth king of Israel, after the partition of the United Monarchy, lasted only one month, until Menahem, son of Gadi, rebelled in Tirzah, marched to Samaria, killed Shallum, and proclaimed himself king.

2. (2 Kings 22:14). 7th century B.C. Shallum, son of Tikvah and grandson of Harhas, was the keeper of the royal wardrobe in the court of King Josiah. His wife was the prophetess Huldah.

3. (1 Chronicles 2:40). Unspecified date. Shallum was the son of Sisamai and the father of Jekamiah.

4. (1 Chronicles 3:15). 7th century B.C. Shallum, who reigned under the name Jehoahaz, was the sixteenth king of Judah, after the partition of the United Monarchy. (Please see the entry for Jehoahaz [2 Kings 23:30].)

5. (1 Chronicles 4:25). Unspecified date. Shallum, a descendant of Simeon, was the son of a man named Shaul, and the father of Mibsam.

6. (1 Chronicles 6:12). 7th century B.C. Shallum, the son of Zadok, was the father of Hilkiah. He was an ancestor of Jehozadak, the High Priest exiled by Nebuchadnezzar, when the Babylonians captured Jerusalem; and he was also an ancestor of Ezra the Scribe.

Shallum is called Meshullam in another chapter of First Chronicles (1 Chronicles 9:11), where he is mentioned as being the grandfather of Azariah, one of the Temple priests in the days of Nehemiah.

7. (1 Chronicles 7:13). 17th century B.C. Shallum—called Shillem in the book of Genesis (Genesis 46:24)—son of Naphtali and grandson of Jacob and Bilhah, was one of the seventy Israelites who immigrated to Egypt. His brothers were Jahziel, Jezer, and Guni.

8. (1 Chronicles 9:17). 10th century B.C. Shallum—also called Meshelemiah (1 Chronicles 9:21), and Shelemiah (1 Chronicles 26:14)—the son of Kore, a descendant of Korah, was chosen by lot to be in charge of the East Gate of the Tabernacle, during the reign of King David. His son Zechariah, who had a reputation of being a wise counselor, was chosen to be the gatekeeper of the North Gate.

Shallum was the head of all the gatekeepers, and the ancestor of a clan of gatekeepers who returned with Zerubbabel from the Babylonian Exile (Ezra 2:42).

His sons were Zechariah, Jediael, Zebadiah, Jathniel, Elam, Jehohanan, and Elioenai.

9. (1 Chronicles 9:31). 6th century B.C. Shallum, a descendant of Korah, was the father of Mattithiah, a Levite who returned from the Babylonian Exile, settled in Jerusalem, and was responsible for the baked offerings cooked in flat pans.

(2 Chronicles 28:12). 8th century B.C. Shallum was the father of Jehizkiah, a leader of the tribe of Ephraim, during the reign of King Pekah of Israel.

10. (Ezra 10:24). 5th century B.C. Shallum, a Temple gatekeeper, divorced his foreign wife, during the days of Ezra.

11. (Ezra 10:42). 5th century B.C. Shallum was one of the men who divorced his foreign wife in the time of Ezra.

12. (Nehemiah 3:12). 5th century B.C. Shallum, son of Halohesh, was the chief of half the district of Jerusalem, during the days of Nehemiah. He helped to repair the walls of Jerusalem, assisted by his daughters.

13. (Jeremiah 32:7). 7th century B.C. Shallum was an uncle of the prophet Jeremiah. His son Hanameel visited Jeremiah, who was in prison, and sold him his field in Anathoth for seventeen pieces of silver. This transaction was a symbol to Jeremiah that fields and vineyards would again be possessed in Israel.

14. (Jeremiah 35:4). 7th century B.C. Shallum was a Temple gatekeeper, during the reign of King Jehoiakim. His son Maaseiah had a room in the Temple.

Shallun

(Hebrew origin: *Reward*)

(Nehemiah 3:15). 5th century B.C. Shallun, son of Colhozeh, was the ruler of part of the district of Mizpah, during the days of Nehemiah. He repaired the Gate of the Fountain, including the doors, locks, and bars of the gate, and the wall of the pool of Siloah. His brother Baruch was the father of Maaseiah, a man who lived in Jerusalem.

Shalmai

(Hebrew origin: *Clothed*)

(Ezra 2:46). Unspecified date. Shalmai was the ancestor of a clan of Temple servants that returned with Zerubbabel from the Babylonian Exile.

Shalman

(Uncertain origin and meaning)

(Hosea 10:14). 8th century B.C. Shalman—shortened form of Shalmaneser—destroyed the city of Betharbel in a battle, killing people without discrimination, including women and children. (Please see the entry for Shalmaneser [2 Kings 17:3].)

Shalmaneser

(Uncertain origin and meaning)

(2 Kings 17:3). 8th century B.C. King Shalmaneser of Assyria made King Hoshea of Israel his vassal and forced him to pay a yearly tribute.

When Hoshea decided to stop paying the tribute, and sent messengers to King So of Egypt asking for his help, Shalmaneser attacked Samaria, and after a siege, which lasted three years, he took Hoshea prisoner and destroyed the city.

This final defeat marked the end of the northern kingdom of Israel, which had been in existence for over two hundred years. The Assyrians deported most of the inhabitants and forcefully settled them in other regions of their empire, where they eventually assimilated into the local population, and disappeared from history, being remembered today as the "ten lost tribes".

The Assyrians settled the abandoned towns of Israel with foreigners, who adopted the Hebrew religion and eventually became the people known today as the Samaritans.

Shama

(Hebrew origin: *Obedient*)

(1 Chronicles 11:44). 10th century B.C. Shama and his brother Jehiel, sons of Hothan

the Aroerite, were two of King David's brave warriors.

Shamariah

(Hebrew origin: *God guarded*)

(2 Chronicles 11:19). 10th century B.C. Shamariah was one of the three sons whom King Rehoboam had with Mahalath, the daughter of Jerimoth, son of King David. His brothers were Jeush and Zaham.

Shamer

(Hebrew origin: *Preserved*)

1. (1 Chronicles 6:46). Unspecified date. Shamer, a descendant of Merari, was the son of Mahli and the father of Bani. His descendant Ethan was one of the Levites appointed by King David to be in charge of the singers in the House of the Lord.
2. (1 Chronicles 7:34). Unspecified date. Shamer, of the tribe of Asher, was the father of Ahi, Rohgah, Jehubbah, and Aram, all of them chiefs of their clans.

Shamgar

(Uncertain origin and meaning)

(Judges 3:31). 12th century B.C. Shamgar, son of Anath, judged Israel after Ehud. He fought against the Philistines and killed six hundred of them with an ox goad.

During his lifetime, the main roads in the country were unsafe and unused; travelers were forced to use the side roads; and many villages stood abandoned. This situation lasted, until Deborah became judge, and Barak defeated Sisera, the commander of the army of King Jabin of Hazor.

Note: In the book of Judges, a judge is a ruler or governor of territory or a military leader in pre-monarchical Israel. Later, during the monarchy, the king served in this role and judges were more like the judicial officers that we know today.

Shamhuth

(Hebrew origin: *Desolation*)

(1 Chronicles 27:8). 10th century B.C. Shamhuth the Izrahite, one of the three most renowned soldiers in King David's army, was a member of "The Thirty", an elite group in King David's army.

He was also called Shammoth, and Shammah, son of Agee the Hararite. (Please see the entry for Shammoth [1 Chronicles 11:27].)

Shamir

(Hebrew origin: *Observed*)

(1 Chronicles 24:24). 10th century B.C. Shamir, the son of Michah, was a Levite in the service of the Tabernacle, during the reign of King David.

Shamma

(Hebrew origin: *Desolation*)

(1 Chronicles 7:37). Unspecified date. Shamma, son of Zophah, of the tribe of Asher, was a brave warrior and leader of his clan. His brothers were Suah, Harnepher, Shual, Beri, Imrah, Bezer, Hod, Shilshah, Ithran, and Beera.

Shammah

(Hebrew origin: *Ruin*)

1. (Genesis 36:13). 17th century B.C. Shammah, son of Reuel, was the grandson of Esau and Bashemath, the daughter of Ishmael. He and his brothers—Nahath, Zerah, and Mizzah—were ancestors of Edomite clans.
2. (1 Samuel 16:9). 11th century B.C. Shammah—also called Shimma (1 Chronicles 2:13), Shimea (1 Chronicles 20:7), and Shimeah (2 Samuel 13:3)—was one of David's brothers, and the third eldest son of Jesse. He, together with his brothers Eliab and Abinadab, joined Saul's army to fight against the Philistines.

His son Jonadab was a good friend of Amnon, David's eldest son. His other son, Jonathan, was a brave warrior who fought and killed a Philistine giant who had six fingers in each hand, and six toes in every foot.

3. (2 Samuel 23:11). 10th century B.C. Shammah, the son of Agee the Hararite, was one of the three most renowned soldiers in King David's army, and a member of "The Thirty", an elite group in King David's army. He was also called Shammoth and Shamhuth. (Please see the entry for Shammoth [1 Chronicles 11:27].)

Shammai

(Hebrew origin: *Destructive*)

1. (1 Chronicles 2:28). Unspecified date. Shammai, of the tribe of Judah, was the son of Onam and the brother of Jada. His sons were Nadab and Abishur.

2. (1 Chronicles 2:44). Unspecified date. Shammai, a descendant of Caleb, was the son of Rekem and the father of Maon.

3. (1 Chronicles 4:17). Unspecified date. Shammai, son of Mered, a descendant of Judah, was the grandson of an Egyptian Pharaoh, through his mother Bithiah. Shammai was the brother of Miriam and Ishbah.

Shammoth

(Hebrew origin: *Ruins*)

(1 Chronicles 11:27). 10th century B.C. Shammoth the Harorite was one of the three most renowned soldiers in King David's army, and a member of "The Thirty", an elite group in King David's army.

On one occasion, when the Philistines had gathered in a field of lentils, the Israelite soldiers fled, but Shammoth stood his ground and fought against the Philistines, killing many of them.

Shammoth had a division of twenty-four thousand men under his orders, and he was in charge of everything related to the army, during the fifth month of each year.

He was also called Shamhuth (1 Chronicles 27:8), and Shammah, the son of Agee the Hararite (2 Samuel 23:11).

Shammua

(Hebrew origin: *Renowned*)

1. (Numbers 13:4). 13th century B.C. Shammua, son of Zaccur, of the tribe of Reuben, was one of the twelve spies sent by Moses to Canaan, to scout the land, its cities, and its inhabitants; to find out if they were strong or weak, few or many; and to bring back the fruit of the land. The spies came back, frightened and disheartened, and told the Israelites that the Canaanites were too big and too strong to be defeated.

Two of the spies—Joshua, the son of Nun, and Caleb, the son of Jephunneh—disagreed and told the people not to fear.

The Israelites refused to listen to the encouraging words of Joshua and Caleb, and they started to wail and cry. God punished their cowardice by condemning them to wander forty years in the wilderness, one year for each day that the spies scouted the land. All those who complained against God, including Shammua, died in the wilderness, except Caleb and Joshua.

(For more detailed information about the twelve spies, please see the entry for Joshua.)

2. (1 Chronicles 14:4). 10th century B.C. Shammua—also called Shammuah (2 Samuel 5:14), and Shimea (1 Chronicles 3:5)—was a son of King David and Bathshua—better known as Bathsheba. He and his brothers—Solomon, Shobab, and Nathan—were born in Jerusalem.

3. (Nehemiah 11:17). 6th century B.C. Shammua, the son of Galal, a descendant of Jeduthun, was the father of Abda, a Levite who was among the first to settle in Judah, after the return from the Babylonian Exile. Shammua is called Shemaiah in the first book of Chronicles (1 Chronicles 9:16), where Abda is called Obadiah.

4. (Nehemiah 12:18). 5th century B.C. Shammua, during the days of the High Priest Joiakim, was the leader of a clan of priests, descended from Bilgah.

Shammuah

(Hebrew origin: *Renowned*)

(2 Samuel 5:14). 10th century B.C. Shammuah—also called Shammua and Shimea—was a son of King David and Bathshua. (Please see the entry for Shammua [1 Chronicles 14:4].)

Shamsherai

(Hebrew origin: *Sun like*)

(1 Chronicles 8:26). Unspecified date. Shamsherai, son of Jeroham, was a leader of the tribe of Benjamin who lived in Jerusalem.

Shapham

(Hebrew origin: *Baldly*)

(1 Chronicles 5:12). Unspecified date. Shapham was a leader of the tribe of Gad, who lived in the region of Bashan, on the other side of the river Jordan.

Shaphan

(Hebrew origin: *Rabbit*)

(2 Kings 22:3). 7th century B.C. Shaphan, the son of Azaliah, was a member of one of the most prominent and influential noble families in the kingdom, during the reigns of King Josiah and his sons. Shaphan, his son Ahikam, and his grandson Gedaliah played important roles in the historical events of their times.

Shaphan held the position of scribe in the court of King Josiah. In the eighteenth year of King Josiah's reign, the king sent Shaphan to the Temple, to check with the High Priest Hilkiah the amount of money that the gate-keepers of the Temple had received from the people as donations, and to tell him to use the money to pay the workers who were repairing the Temple The king added that there was no need to require the workers to account for the funds, because they were completely honest.

The High Priest Hilkiah told Shaphan that, while supervising the repair work that was being done in the Temple, he had found a Book of the Law. The High Priest gave him the book, and Shaphan read it.

The scribe went back to the king, and, after reporting that the money collected in the Temple had been delivered to the workers, he told Josiah that Hilkiah had given him a book, and he proceeded to read it to the king.

Josiah, realizing with dread that the laws of the Lord were not being carried out, rent his clothes and sent a delegation—composed of Hilkiah, Shaphan, Ahikam, Achbor, and Asahiah—to consult with Huldah, the prophetess. She predicted that God would punish the nation for having forsaken him, but that King Josiah, having humbled himself, would be spared the sight of this evil and would go to his grave, before the collective punishment. The king instructed Hilkiah to take out from the Temple all the utensils made for the pagan god Baal and other idols, to burn them in the fields of Kidron, and to carry the ashes to Bethel.

The Bible mentions four of Shaphan's sons: Ahikam, Elasah, Gemariah, and Jaazaniah. Ahikam, a high court official, protected the life of the prophet Jeremiah, during the reign of King Jehoiakim (Jeremiah 26:24).

Elasah was sent by King Zedekiah—a son of King Josiah, and the last king of Judah—in a mission to King Nebuchadnezzar, carrying a letter by Jeremiah to the captives in Babylon. The letter encouraged them to live a normal life in Babylon, build their homes, plant gardens, marry, and have children. It ended, promising that, after seventy years, they would return from the Babylonian Exile.

Gemariah occupied the chamber in the Temple, where Baruch, Jeremiah's trusted companion, read aloud the prophet's scroll. Gemariah was one of the men who tried unsuccessfully to convince the king not to burn the scroll.

Jaazaniah was one of the seventy elders whom the prophet Ezekiel saw in a vision committing abominations, because they believed that God did not see them, and that God had forsaken the earth (Ezekiel 8:11).

Shaphan's grandson, Gedaliah, the son of Ahikam, is a tragic figure in the history of the Jewish people, who, even today, observe the anniversary of his death as a day of fasting and mourning. Due to his family's well-known policy of moderation and submission to Babylon, Gedaliah was appointed governor of Judah by the Babylonian King Nebuchadnezzar. A few months later, he was murdered by Ishmael, son of Nethaniah, who probably hoped to start an uprise against the Babylonians by his bloody act.

Shaphat

(Hebrew origin: *Judge*)

1. (Numbers 13:5). 13th century B.C. Shaphat, son of Hori, of the tribe of Shimeon, was one of the twelve men sent by Moses to Canaan, to scout the land, its cities, and its inhabitants; to find out if they were strong or weak, few or many; and to bring back the fruit of the land. The spies came back, frightened and disheartened, and told the Israelites that the Canaanites were too big and too strong to be defeated.

   Two of the spies—Joshua, the son of Nun, and Caleb, the son of Jephunneh—disagreed and told the people not to fear.

   The Israelites refused to listen to the encouraging words of Joshua and Caleb, and they started to wail and cry. God punished their cowardice by condemning them to wander forty years in the wilderness, one year for each day that the spies scouted the land. All those who complained against God, including Shaphat, died in the wilderness, except Caleb and Joshua.

   (For more detailed information about the twelve spies, please see the entry for Joshua.)

2. (1 Kings 19:16). 9th century B.C. Shaphat of Abelmeholah was the father of the prophet Elisha, the disciple and successor of the prophet Elijah.

3. (1 Chronicles 3:22). Unspecified date. Shaphat was one of the sons of Shemaiah, a descendant of King Jehoiachin, the king of Judah, who was taken to captivity in Babylon. Shaphat's brothers were Hattush, Igeal, Bariah, and Neariah.

4. (1 Chronicles 5:12). Unspecified date. Shaphat was a leader of the tribe of Gad,

who lived in the region of Bashan, in the other side of the river Jordan.

5. (1 Chronicles 27:29). 10th century B.C. Shaphat, son of Adlai, was the official in charge of the cattle in the valleys, during the reign of King David.

Sharai

(Hebrew origin: *Hostile*)

(Ezra 10:40). 5th century B.C. Sharai divorced his foreign wife, during the days of Ezra.

Sharar

(Hebrew origin: *Hostile*)

(2 Samuel 23:33). 11th Century B.C. Sharar the Hararite—also called Sacar (1 Chronicles 11:35)—was the father of Ahiam, a member of King David's elite army group known as The Thirty.

Sharezer

(Uncertain origin and meaning)

(2 Kings 19:37). 8th century B.C. Sharezer and his brother Adrammelech murdered their father, King Sennacherib of Assyria, while the king was worshipping in the Temple of his god Nisroch. The two patricides escaped to Armenia, and their brother Esarhaddon ascended to the throne.

Shashai

(Hebrew origin: *Whitish*)

(Ezra 10:40). 5th century B.C. Shashai divorced his foreign wife, during the days of Ezra.

Shashak

(Hebrew origin: *Pedestrian*)

(1 Chronicles 8:14). Unspecified date. Shashak was a chief of a clan of the tribe of Benjamin. His sons were leaders of the Benjamites who lived in Jerusalem.

Shaul

(Hebrew origin: *Asked*)

1. (Genesis 46:10). 17th century B.C. Shaul, son of Simeon and a Canaanite woman, was one of the grandsons of Jacob. He was among the seventy Israelites who immigrated to Egypt, together with his brothers Jemuel, Jamin, Ohad, Jachin, and Zohar. His son was called Shallum. Shaul was the ancestor of the clan of the Shaulites.
2. (1 Chronicles 1:48). Unspecified date. Shaul, of Rehoboth by the river, ascended to the throne of Edom, when Samlah died. Shaul was succeeded by Baalhanan, the son of Achbor. He was called Saul in the book of Genesis (Genesis 36:37).
3. (1 Chronicles 6:24). Unspecified date. Shaul, son of Uzziah, was a descendant of Kohath, one of the three sons of Levi.

Shavsha

(Hebrew origin: *Joyful*)

(1 Chronicles 18:16). 10th century B.C. Shavsha was the scribe in the court of King David. His sons, Elihoreph and Ahiah, followed in his footsteps and became the scribes in the court of King Solomon.

He was also called Sheva (2 Samuel 20:25), Shisha (1 Kings 4:3), and Seraiah (2 Samuel 8:17).

Sheal

(Hebrew origin: *Request*)

(Ezra 10:29). 5th century B.C. Sheal, a descendant of Bani, divorced his foreign wife, during the time of Ezra.

Shealtiel

(Hebrew origin: *I asked God*)

(Ezra 3:2). 6th century B.C. Shealtiel—called Salathiel in the first book of Chronicles (1 Chronicles 3:17)—was one of the seven sons of King Jehoiachin, the king who was deposed and taken captive by the Babylonians. Shealtiel's brothers were Hoshama, Malchiram, Pedaiah, Shenazar, Jekamiah, and Nedabiah.

According to the books of Haggai and Ezra, Shealtiel was the father of Zerubbabel, the leader of the first group of captives who returned from the Babylonian Exile.

The first book of Chronicles, on the other hand, considers that Shealtiel was the uncle of Zerubbabel, and that the father of the governor of the Persian province of Judah was Pedaiah (1 Chronicles 3:19).

Sheariah

(Hebrew origin: *God has stormed*)

(1 Chronicles 8:38). Unspecified date. Sheariah was one of the six sons of Azel, son of Eleasah of the tribe of Benjamin, a descendant of King Saul. His brothers were Azrikam, Ishmael, Bocheru, Obadiah, and Hanan.

Shearjashub

(Hebrew origin: *Remnant shall return*)

(Isaiah 7:3). 8th century B.C. Shearjashub, the son of the prophet Isaiah, accompanied his father, when he met King Ahaz, who was threatened by Rezin, king of Aram, and Pekah, king of Israel.

The two kings invaded Judah and besieged Jerusalem but could not capture the city. Their objective was to depose the king and install a certain son of Tabeal in his place (Isaiah 7:6). The prophet Isaiah told King Ahaz not to fear and assured him that the invaders would not succeed.

Sheba

(Hebrew origin: *Seven*)

1. (Genesis 10:7). Unspecified date. Sheba and Dedan were the sons of Raamah, a descendant of Noah through his son Ham.
2. (Genesis 10:28). Unspecified date. Sheba was the son of Joktan, a descendant of Noah through Shem, Noah's second son. His brothers were Almodad, Sheleph, Hazarmaveth, Jerah, Hadoram, Uzal, Diklah, Obal, Abimael, Ophir, Havilah, and Jobab.
3. (Genesis 25:3). 18th century B.C. Sheba

and Dedan were the sons of Jokshan and the grandsons of Abraham and Keturah, the woman whom Abraham married, after Sarah died.

4. (2 Samuel 20:1). 10th century B.C. Sheba, son of Bichri, of the tribe of Benjamin, rebelled against King David, after the defeat of Absalom.

David, believing that this insurrection could be even more dangerous than the rebellion of Absalom, urged Amasa, his newly appointed army commander, to organize an army in three days. When Amasa did not report back in the allotted time, the king sent Abishai to pursue the rebels. Amasa caught up with Abishai and Joab near Gibeon.

Joab saluted Amasa, saying, "How are you, brother?"

While he was speaking, he took hold of Amasa's beard with his right hand as if to kiss him, and with his left hand, he drove his sword into Amasa's belly, killing him.

Joab then proceeded to pursue Sheba, who found refuge in the town of Abel. When the troops started to batter down the walls of the city, a woman shouted from the city that she wanted to speak to Joab.

Joab shouted back, "I have no intention to destroy the town; all we want is that you should hand us the rebel".

The woman answered, "We will throw his head over the wall!"

The woman spoke to the inhabitants of Abel, who killed Sheba, cut off his head, and threw it down to Joab.

5. (1 Chronicles 5:13). Unspecified date. Sheba was a leader of the tribe of Gad who lived in the land of Bashan. His brothers were Michael, Meshullam, Jorai, Jachan, Zia, and Heber.

Shebaniah

(Hebrew origin: *God has grown*)

1. (1 Chronicles 15:24). 10th century B.C. Shebaniah was one of the priests who blew the trumpets, during the joyful procession led by King David that brought the Ark of the Covenant to Jerusalem. He might be the same person as Shebaniah #5 (see below).

2. (Nehemiah 9:4). 5th century B.C. Shebaniah, a Levite, stood with other Levites—Jeshua, Bani, Hashabniah, Sherebiah, Hodijah, Kadmiel, and Pethahiah—on a raised platform, during an assembly of public confession and fasting in the days of Ezra, and prayed to God in a loud voice.

He was also among the Levites who signed Nehemiah's solemn agreement to separate themselves from the foreigners living in the land, to refrain from intermarrying with them, to dedicate their firstborn to God, and other obligations (Nehemiah 10:12).

3. (Nehemiah 10:4). 5th century B.C. Shebaniah was one of the priests who signed Nehemiah's solemn agreement to separate themselves from the foreigners living in the land, to refrain from intermarrying with them, and to dedicate their firstborn to God, among other obligations.

4. (Nehemiah 10:10). 5th century B.C. Shebaniah was a Levite who signed Nehemiah's solemn agreement to separate themselves from the foreigners living in the land, to refrain from intermarrying with them, and to dedicate their firstborn to God, among other obligations.

5. (Nehemiah 12:14). Unspecified date. His descendant Joseph was the head of a priestly clan, when Joiakim was the High Priest, during the time of Nehemiah. This Shebaniah might be the same person as Shebaniah #1 (see above).

Sheber

(Hebrew origin: *Fracture*)

(1 Chronicles 2:48). Unspecified date. Sheber was a son of Caleb—also called Chelubai—and his concubine Maachah. His brothers were Shaaph, Sheva, and Tirhanah.

Shebna

(Hebrew origin: *Growth*)

(2 Kings 18:18). 8th century B.C. Shebna, the court's scribe and the overseer of the royal palace, during the reign of King Hezekiah, prepared for himself a beautiful tomb high on a cliff. For this act, he was harshly criticized by the prophet Isaiah, who told him that, one day, his authority over the palace would be transferred to Eliakim, the son of Hilkiah.

When the Assyrian army laid siege to Jerusalem, and demanded that the king should come out, Hezekiah sent Shebna, Eliakim—who had replaced Shebna as overseer of the palace—and Joah, the records keeper, to meet with the Assyrians.

Rabshakeh, one of the Assyrian commanders, met the delegation outside the walls of the city and spoke to them in Hebrew, in a very loud voice that could be heard by the people standing on top of the walls, "Hezekiah has no reason to feel confident, because he cannot rely on receiving help from Egypt, or from God".

Shebna and his companions pleaded with the Assyrian, "Please speak to us in Aramaic! We do not wish that the people on the wall should understand your threats".

Rabshakeh paid no attention to their request, and he continued shouting in Hebrew, "Don't allow Hezekiah to deceive you!"

Shebna and his companions didn't reply and returned to the king, with their clothes torn, to inform him of the failure of the negotiations.

Hezekiah, after hearing them, sent Shebna and Eliakim, accompanied by the elders of the priests, all of them covered with sackcloth, to speak to the prophet Isaiah. The king then tore his clothes, covered himself with sackcloth, and went to the Temple. Isaiah told the king's men that they should not be afraid, of what Rabshakeh had said, and assured them that the Assyrian army would withdraw without taking Jerusalem.

Shebuel

(Hebrew origin: *God's captive*)

1. (1 Chronicles 23:16). 10th century B.C. Shebuel, a Levite descendant of Gershom, the son of Moses, was in charge of the treasury of the Tabernacle, during the reign of King David.

2. (1 Chronicles 25:4). 10th century B.C. Shebuel—also called Shubael (1 Chronicles 25:20)—a Levite, member of a family of musicians, was in charge of the thirteenth turn of service that played musical instruments—cymbals, psalteries, and harps—in the House of God, during the reign of David.

He had three sisters, and thirteen brothers—Bukkiah, Mattaniah, Uzziel, Jerimoth, Hananiah, Hanani, Eliathah, Giddalti, Romamtiezer, Joshbekashah, Mallothi, Hothir, and Mahazioth—all of them trained to be skillful music players by their father Heman, one of the kingdom's three leading musicians; the other two were Asaph and Jeduthun.

Shecaniah

(Hebrew origin: *God has dwelt*)

1. (1 Chronicles 24:11).10th century B.C. During the reign of King David, the priestly service in the Tabernacle was divided by lot into twenty-four turns. Shecaniah was in charge of the tenth turn.

2. (2 Chronicles 31:15). 8th century B.C. Shecaniah, a Levite, worked under Kore, assisting him in registering the priests and the Levites, and distributing among the other Levites the gifts offered by the people to God, during the reign of King Hezekiah.

Shechaniah

(Hebrew origin: *God has dwelt*)

1. (1 Chronicles 3:21). Unspecified date. Shechaniah was a descendant of King David through Zerubbabel. A group of his descendants returned with Ezra from the Babylonian Exile (Ezra 8:3).

2. (Ezra 8:5). 5th century B.C. Shechaniah, son of Jahaziel, returned with Ezra from the Babylonian Exile at the head of three hundred males. His son Shemaiah helped to repair the walls of Jerusalem, during the days of Nehemiah (Nehemiah 3:29).

3. (Ezra 10:2). 5th century B.C. Shechaniah, son of Jehiel, a descendant of Elam, after hearing Ezra's public prayer of confession, declared that the people had sinned against God and had taken foreign wives, and he proposed that a covenant should be made with God to put away all the foreign wives and the children who had been born to these women.

4. (Nehemiah 6:18). 5th century B.C. Shechaniah, son of Arah, was the father-in-law of Tobiah, Nehemiah's enemy.

5. (Nehemiah 12:3). 6th century B.C. Shechaniah was a priest who returned with Zerubbabel from the Babylonian Exile.

Shechem

(Hebrew origin: *Spur of a hill*)

1. (Genesis 34:2). 17th century B.C. Shechem—called Sychem in the book of Acts of the Apostles (Acts of the Apostles 7:16)—was the son of Hamor the Hivite, the ruler of the city of Shechem, during the days of Jacob.

Jacob and his family came to Canaan and settled outside the city of Shechem, in a field that he bought from Hamor's for a hundred pieces of silver.

One day, Dinah, the daughter of Jacob and Leah, went to the city to visit some Canaanite women. Shechem saw her, grabbed her, and raped her. Afterward, he realized that he had fallen in love with her, and he spoke to her tenderly, saying that he wanted to marry her.

Shechem persuaded his father to go with him to Jacob's camp, to ask him for the hand of his daughter. Jacob had already heard what had happened to Dinah, but didn't react, and waited for his sons to return from the field. His sons, when they came back and heard of their sister's disgrace, became very angry.

"My son Shechem has fallen in love with your sister Dinah, and wants to marry her", he said and added, "You should marry the girls of our city, and our men should marry your daughters, and then, we will all live together in the land".

Shechem pleaded, "Do me this favor, and I will pay you whatever you want. Set a price for the bride as high as you wish, and I will pay you, and I will also give you gifts, if you will please allow me to marry her".

The sons of Jacob agreed deceitfully to allow Dinah to marry Shechem. They said to Hamor and Shechem, "We cannot let our sister marry a man who is not circumcised, because that would be a disgrace for us. We would agree only on condition that you circumcise all the males in your city. Then, we will marry your women, and you will marry ours, and we will all become one happy family. But if you do not accept our terms and be circumcised, we will take her and leave this place".

Hamor and Shechem were very pleased with these words. Shechem, who was greatly respected in the city, was eager to do this immediately, because he wanted Jacob's daughter. Both the father and the son went to the gate of the city and spoke to the men of the city, "These people have peaceful intentions; let them settle among us, for the land is large enough for them. We will marry their daughters, and they will marry ours. But they have set the condition that our men should be circumcised as they are. If we do so, their cattle and possessions will be ours".

The men of the city, convinced by these arguments, were all circumcised, including Hamor and Shechem. On the third day, when they were still weak and in pain, two of Jacob's sons, Simeon and Levi, full brothers of Dinah, came to the city, armed with swords, and killed all the males. They put Hamor and Shechem to the sword, took Dinah from Shechem's house, and went away.

The other sons of Jacob came upon the slain and plundered the city. They seized their flocks, herds, and asses, and all their wealth; and they took their wives and children as captives.

Jacob said to them, "You have gotten me into trouble. The Canaanites and the other people of this land will hate me. If they band together and attack me, our whole family will be destroyed, because I don't have many men to defend us".

The brothers answered, "Should he treat our sister as a harlot?"

Jacob, fearing that the actions of his sons had placed them all in great danger, moved the family to Bethel, and from there to Hebron.

2. (Numbers 26:31). Unspecified date. Shechem, the son of Shemidah, of the tribe of Manasseh, was the ancestor of the clan of Shechemites. His brothers were Ahian, Aniam, and Likhi (1 Chronicles 7:19).

Shedeur

(Hebrew origin: *Spreader of light*)

(Numbers 1:5). 14th century B.C. Shedeur was the father of Elizur, of the tribe of Reuben. His son was the commander of his tribe's army, during the march in the wilderness, and was one of the twelve Israelite leaders who donated gifts of silver and gold, bulls, rams, goats, and lambs for the dedication of the altar.

Shehariah

(Hebrew origin: *God has sought*)

(1 Chronicles 8:26). Unspecified date. Shehariah, son of Jeroham, was a leader of the tribe of Benjamin who lived in Jerusalem.

Shelah

(Hebrew origin: *Prayer*)

1. (Genesis 38:5). 17th century B.C. Shelah was the youngest of the three sons whom Judah, the son of Jacob, had with his wife, the daughter of Shua the Canaanite. He, the ancestor of the clan of the Shelanites, was among the seventy Israelites who immigrated to Egypt.

Er, Judah's firstborn, was married to a girl called Tamar. When he died, Judah told Onan, his second son, to marry Tamar and, thus, provide offspring for his dead brother. Onan was unwilling that his children should carry his brother's name, and to prevent this, he would spill his seed on the ground. After he also died, Judah was left with only one son, Shelah, his youngest.

Judah, afraid that Shelah would also die if he would marry Tamar, told her to return to her father's house, and to remain a widow "until Shelah would grow up". However, years went by, and Judah did not carry out his promise to marry Shelah to Tamar.

Tamar tricked Judah into having a sexual relationship with her; she became pregnant and gave birth to twins, whom Judah recognized as his sons.

As for Shelah, he married another woman, with whom he had five sons: Er, Laadah, Jokim, Joash, and Saraph.

2. (1 Chronicles 1:18). Unspecified date. Shelah, son of Arphaxad and grandson of Shem, was born thirty-seven years after the flood, at a time when his father was thirty-five years old.

Shelah was thirty years old, when his son Eber was born. He died at the age of four hundred and thirty-three, having fathered other sons and daughters. He was called Salah in the book of Genesis (Genesis 10:24), and Sala in the New Testament (Luke 3:35).

Shelemiah

(Hebrew origin: *Thank offering of God*)

1. (1 Chronicles 26:14). 10th century B.C. Shelemiah, the son of Kore, was a Levite of the clan of the Korahites, and head of all the gatekeepers, during the reign of King David. He was chosen by lot to be the gatekeeper of the East Gate of the Tabernacle. His son Zechariah, who had a reputation as a wise counselor, was chosen to be the gatekeeper of the North Gate.

A number of his descendants returned with Zerubbabel from the Babylonian Exile

(Ezra 2:42). His sons were Zechariah, Jediael, Zebadiah, Jathniel, Elam, Jehohanan, and Elioenai.

He was also called Meshelemiah (1 Chronicles 9:21), and Shallum (1 Chronicles 9:17).

2. (Ezra 10:39). 5th century B.C. Shelemiah divorced his foreign wife, during the days of Ezra.

3. (Ezra 10:41). 5th century B.C. Shelemiah divorced his foreign wife, during the days of Ezra.

4. (Nehemiah 3:30). 5th century B.C. His son Hananiah helped to repair the walls of Jerusalem, during the days of Nehemiah. He might be the same person as Shelemiah #2, or Shelemiah #3.

5. (Nehemiah 13:13). 5th century B.C. Shelemiah, a priest, was one of the four persons designated by Nehemiah to supervise the treasuries of the Temple, and to distribute the offerings among the Levites and the priests. The other three were Pedaiah, a Levite; Zadok the Scribe; and Hanan, the son of Zaccur.

6. (Jeremiah 36:14). 7th century B.C. Shelemiah was the son of Cushi and the father of Nethaniah. His grandson Jehudi was the court official sent to tell Baruch, the companion of Jeremiah, to come and read aloud the scroll to several of the court officials.

7. (Jeremiah 36:26). 7th century B.C. Shelemiah, the son of Abdeel, was one of the three court officials who were ordered by King Jehoiakim to arrest the prophet Jeremiah and his companion Baruch the Scribe. The three men—Shelemiah; Jerahmeel, son of Hammelech; and Seraiah, son of Azriel—failed in their mission, because Jeremiah and Baruch had gone into hiding.

8. (Jeremiah 37:3). 6th century B.C. His son Jucal—also called Jehucal—was sent to Jeremiah by King Zedekiah, together with Zephaniah, the son of Maaseiah, to ask the prophet to please pray for the king.

Later, when Jucal heard that Jeremiah was preaching surrender, he went with some other officials to King Zedekiah, and they asked that Jeremiah should be put to death for his defeatist talk, which was weakening the will of the people.

Zedekiah turned Jeremiah to Jucal and his companions, who cast the prophet into the dungeon of Malchiah, inside the court of the prison.

9. (Jeremiah 37:13). 7th century B.C. Shelemiah, son of Hananiah, was the father of Irijah, the guard in charge of the Benjamin Gate, during the siege of Jerusalem. When Jeremiah approached the gate with the intention of going to the territory of Benjamin, Irijah accused Jeremiah of trying to defect to the Babylonians, arrested him, and took him to the authorities. The officials angrily beat Jeremiah and imprisoned him in the house of Jonathan the Scribe.

Sheleph

(Hebrew origin: *Extract*)

(Genesis 10:26). Unspecified date. Sheleph was the son of Joktan, a descendant of Noah and Shem. His brothers were Almodad, Hazarmaveth, Jerah, Hadoram, Uzal, Diklah, Ebal, Abimael, Sheba, Ophir, Havilah, and Jobab.

Shelesh

(Hebrew origin: *Triplet*)

(1 Chronicles 7:35). Unspecified date. Shelesh, a clan chief of the tribe of Asher, was the son of Helem, also called Hotham. His brothers were Zophah, Imna, and Amal.

Shelomi

(Hebrew origin: *My peace*)

(Numbers 34:27). 14th century B.C. His son Ahihud, a leader of the tribe of Asher, was chosen to help apportion the land of Canaan among the Hebrew tribes.

Shelomith
(Hebrew origin: *Peace*)

1. (Leviticus 24:11). 13th century B.C. Shelomith, daughter of Dibri of the tribe of Dan, had a son whose father was an Egyptian. The young man got into a fight with an Israelite, cursed, and blasphemed the name of God. For this sin, the son of Shelomith was taken outside the camp and stoned to death.

2. (1 Chronicles 3:19). 6th century B.C. Shelomith was the daughter of Zerubbabel, a descendant of the royal family of Judah. Her father was the leader of the first group of captives who returned from the Babylonian Exile.

3. (1 Chronicles 23:9). 10th century B.C. Shelomith, son of Shimei, a Levite descendant of Gershon, the son of Levi, served in the House of the Lord, during the reigns of David and Solomon.

4. (1 Chronicles 23:18). 10th century B.C. Shelomith—also called Shelomoth (1 Chronicles 24:22)—a Levite descendant of Izhar, the son of Kohath, served, together with his son Jahath, in the Tabernacle, during the reign of David.

5. (1 Chronicles 26:25). 10th century B.C. Shelomith, a Levite, son of Zichri, was in charge of the Tabernacle treasury, where the dedicated articles and the donations were stored, during the reign of King David. These articles included the booty captured in battle by King David and his officers, which they had dedicated to the Lord, and also items dedicated by Samuel, the seer, King Saul, Abner, and Joab.

6. (2 Chronicles 11:20). 10th century B.C. Shelomith was one of the sons of King Rehoboam and his favorite wife Maachah, the daughter of Absalom. His brothers were Abijah—who succeeded King Rehoboam—Ziza, and Attai.

7. (Ezra 8:10). 5th century B.C. Shelomith, son of Josiphiah, returned from the Babylonian Exile at the head of a group of one hundred and sixty males, during the days of Ezra.

Shelomoth
(Hebrew origin: *Pacifications*)

(1 Chronicles 24:22). 10th century B.C. Shelomoth—also called Shelomith (1 Chronicles 23:18)—a Levite of the clan of the Izharites, served, together with his son Jahath, in the Tabernacle, during the reign of David.

Shelumiel
(Hebrew origin: *God's peace*)

(Numbers 1:6). 13th century B.C. Shelumiel, son of Zurishaddai, of the tribe of Simeon, was the commander of his tribe's army, during the march in the wilderness. He was also one of the twelve Israelite leaders who donated gifts of silver and gold, bulls, rams, goats, and lambs for the dedication of the altar.

Shem
(Hebrew origin: *Name*)

(Genesis 5:32). Unspecified date. Shem was the eldest son of Noah. He—together with his parents, his brothers Ham and Japheth, and their wives—survived the flood in the Ark built by Noah.

Noah, after the flood, planted a vineyard, drank from its wine, and became drunk. Ham entered his father's tent and saw him lying naked and unconscious. Instead of covering him, Ham went out and told Shem and Japheth how he had seen his father.

Shem and Japheth entered Noah's tent, averting their eyes, and covered his nakedness. When Noah woke up and found that his son Ham had not treated him with respect, he cursed Canaan, the son of Ham, and prophesied that he would be a servant to Japheth and Shem.

Shem had numerous sons and daughters, and he was the ancestor of many nations, including the Hebrews. He was six hundred years old at the time of his death.

Shema

(Hebrew origin: *Heard*)

1. (1 Chronicles 2:43). Unspecified date. Shema, son of Hebron of the tribe of Judah, was the brother of Tappuah, Rekem, and Korah. His son was called Raham.

2. (1 Chronicles 5:8). Unspecified date. Shema, the son of Joel, of the tribe of Reuben, was the father of Azaz.

3. (1 Chronicles 8:13). Unspecified date. Shema was the leader of a clan of Benjamites, who settled in the region of Aijalon and drove away the inhabitants of Gath.

4. (Nehemiah 8:4). 5th century B.C. Shema was one of the leaders who stood next to Ezra, upon a pulpit of wood, when the scribe read the Law of Moses to the people in the marketplace.

Shemaah

(Hebrew origin: *Annunciation*)

(1 Chronicles 12:3). 11th century B.C. Shemaah the Gibeathite was the father of Ahiezer and Joash, two Benjamites who deserted King Saul's army and joined David's band at Ziklag. His sons and the men with them could use both their right and left hands to shoot arrows and sling stones.

Shemaiah

(Hebrew origin: *God has heard*)

1. (1 Kings 12:22). 10th century B.C. The prophet Shemaiah lived, during the reign of King Rehoboam, about whom he wrote a book, which is now lost.

When Rehoboam raised a large army from the tribes of Judah and Benjamin, in order to fight against the northern tribes, which had seceded from his kingdom, Shemaiah advised the king not to go to war, and to disband the army, because God had willed it to be so.

When the Pharaoh Shishak invaded Judah, Shemaiah went to the king and his officials, who had gathered in Jerusalem, and told them that God was punishing them, because they had forsaken him. The king and his men humbled themselves and acknowledged that God was right.

God's word then came to Shemaiah, saying, "They have humbled themselves; therefore, I will not destroy them, but they will serve Shishak, and they will, thus, know the difference between serving me and serving the kingdoms of the earth".

2. (1 Chronicles 3:22). 5th century B.C. Shemaiah, son of Shechaniah, a descendant of King Jehoiachin, was the keeper of the East Gate, during the days of Nehemiah (Nehemiah 3:29), and helped to repair the walls of Jerusalem. His sons were Hattush, Igeal, Bariah, Neariah, and Shaphat.

3. (1 Chronicles 4:37). Unspecified date. Shemaiah, the father of Shimri, was an ancestor of Ziza, one of the leaders of the tribe of Simeon who went to the fertile valley of Gedor in search of pasture for their flocks, during the reign of Hezekiah, king of Judah.

The Simeonites destroyed the tents of the people—descendants of Ham—who lived there, wiped them out forever, and settled in their place.

4. (1 Chronicles 5:4). Unspecified date. Shemaiah, son of Joel and father of Gog, was an ancestor of Beerah, a leader of the tribe of Reuben who was carried away captive by Tilgathpilneser, king of Assyria.

5. (1 Chronicles 9:14). 5th century B.C. Shemaiah, son of Hasshub, a Levite descendant of Merari, was among the first to settle in Jerusalem, after the return from the Babylonian Exile.

6. (1 Chronicles 9:16). 5th century B.C. Shemaiah—called Shammua in the book of Nehemiah (Nehemiah 11:17)—son of Galal, a descendant of Jeduthun, was the father of Obadiah—also called Abda—a Levite who was among the first to settle in Judah, after the return from the Babylonian Exile.

7. (1 Chronicles 15:8). 10th century B.C. Shemaiah was the leader of a clan of Levites, descendants from Elizaphan, during the reign of King David. As one of

the leading Levites of the kingdom, he was among those chosen by the king to carry, by means of poles on their shoulders, the Ark of David from the house of Obededom to Jerusalem, accompanied by singers and musicians.

8. (1 Chronicles 24:6). 10th century B.C. Shemaiah the Scribe, a Levite son of Nethaneel, wrote a list of the priests, according to their descent from Eleazar or from Ithamar, the sons of Aaron. The purpose was to determine the priests' turn to do their service in the Tabernacle. The list was written in the presence of King David and the High Priests Zadok and Ahimelech.

9. (1 Chronicles 26:4). 10th century B.C. Shemaiah, the firstborn son of Obededom, was a gatekeeper of the Tabernacle, during the reign of King David. His father and his brothers—Ammiel, Sacar, Jehozabad, Joah, Nethaneel, Issachar, and Peulthai—were also gatekeepers.

The sons of Shemaiah—all of them brave men and leaders of their clan—were Othni, Rephael, Obed, Elzabad, Elihu, and Semachiah.

10. (2 Chronicles 17:8). 9th century B.C. Shemaiah, a Levite, was sent by King Jehoshaphat in the third year of his reign, to teach the laws of God in the cities of Judah. Shemaiah was accompanied in his mission by other Levites, by two priests—Elishama and Jehoram—and by several officials of the court.

11. (2 Chronicles 29:14). 8th century B.C. Shemaiah was one of the Levites who gathered to make themselves ritually clean, and to purify the Temple, during the reign of King Hezekiah of Judah. His ancestor Jeduthun was one of King David's leading musicians.

12. (2 Chronicles 31:15). 8th century B.C. Shemaiah was a Levite who, during the days of King Hezekiah, worked under Kore, assisting him in registering the priests and the Levites, and distributing among the other Levites the gifts offered by the people to God.

13. (2 Chronicles 35:9). 7th century B.C. Shemaiah was one of the Levites who, during the reign of King Josiah, gave to the priests the cattle and oxen, which had been donated by the princes of the kingdom for the Passover offerings.

14. (Ezra 8:13). 5th century B.C. Shemaiah, a descendant of Adonikam, together with his brothers Jeiel and Eliphelet, returned with Ezra to Jerusalem from the Babylonian Exile, at the head of a group of sixty males, during the reign of King Artaxerxes of Persia.

Note: It is possible that this person was the same as Shemaiah #15.

15. (Ezra 8:16). 5th century B.C. Shemaiah was one of the men who were sent by Ezra to Casiphia to speak to Iddo and request from him to send Levites to serve in the Temple in Jerusalem.

Note: It is possible that this person was the same as Shemaiah #14.

16. (Ezra 10:21). 5th century B.C. Shemaiah, a priest descendant of Harim, divorced his foreign wife, during the days of Ezra.

17. (Ezra 10:31). 5th century B.C. Shemaiah, a descendant of Harim, divorced his foreign wife, during the days of Ezra.

18. (Nehemiah 6:10). 5th century B.C. Shemaiah, son of Delaiah, was hired by Tobiah and Sanballat, Nehemiah's enemies, to convince Nehemiah that he should hide in the Temple. He failed, because Nehemiah realized that his enemies were setting a trap for him, to induce him to sin, and would then report it to higher authorities.

19. (Nehemiah 10:8). 5th century B.C. Shemaiah was one of the priests who signed Nehemiah's solemn agreement to separate themselves from the foreigners living in the land, to refrain from intermarrying with them, and to dedicate their firstborn to God, among other obligations.

20. (Nehemiah 11:15). 5th century B.C. Shemaiah, the son of Hashub, a Levite descendant of Merari, was one of the first Levites to settle in Jerusalem, after the return from the Babylonian Exile.

21. (Nehemiah 12:6). 6th century B.C. Shemaiah was one of the leading priests who returned to Jerusalem with Zerubbabel from the Babylonian Exile, when Joshua was the High Priest. He was the ancestor of a clan of priests that was led by Jehonathan, during the days of the High Priest Joiakim (Nehemiah 12:18).

22. (Nehemiah 12:34). 5th century B.C. Shemaiah was one of the leaders of the people who marched in the joyful procession, which celebrated the dedication of the rebuilt walls of Jerusalem, during the days of Nehemiah.

23. (Nehemiah 12:35). 6th century B.C. Shemaiah, son of Mattaniah, was the father of Jonathan. His grandson Zechariah was one of the priests who played the trumpets in the joyful procession, which celebrated the dedication of the rebuilt walls of Jerusalem, during the days of Nehemiah.

24. (Nehemiah 12:36). 5th century B.C. Shemaiah was one of the priests who played musical instruments, and marched behind Ezra the Scribe in the joyful procession, which celebrated the dedication of the rebuilt walls of Jerusalem, during the days of Nehemiah.

25. (Nehemiah 12:42). 5th century B.C. Shemaiah was one of the priests, led by Jezrahiah, their overseer, who marched, singing at the top of their voices, in the joyful procession, which celebrated the dedication of the rebuilt walls of Jerusalem, during the days of Nehemiah.

26. (Jeremiah 26:20). 7th century B.C. Shemaiah of Kirjathjearim was the father of the prophet Urijah, a contemporary of Jeremiah. Urijah displeased King Jehoiakim by uttering prophesies similar to the words of Jeremiah. The king tried to find him and kill him, but Urijah had fled to Egypt. The king then sent Elnathan, son of Achbor, to Egypt with a group of men to fetch Urijah. The prophet was captured and brought back to Judah, to the presence of the king, who killed him with his sword and had his body thrown into a common grave.

27. (Jeremiah 29:24). 6th century B.C. Shemaiah, the Nehelamite, who had been carried away to exile by the Babylonians, sent letters to the people who had been allowed to remain in Jerusalem, to the High Priest Zephaniah, son of Maaseiah, and to other priests.

In his letter to Zephaniah, he wrote: "Now that you are the High Priest, instead of Jehoiada, you have the responsibility of putting in prison madmen and self-styled prophets. So why haven't you done this to Jeremiah of Anathoth who pretends that he is a prophet? He has told the people in Babylon that the exile would last a long time, and that we should build houses, plant gardens, and eat the fruits from the trees that we planted".

Zephaniah went to Jeremiah and read him the letter. Jeremiah then sent a message to the captives in Babylon, where he denounced Shemaiah as a false and rebellious prophet, and he prophesied that neither Shemaiah nor his descendants would live to see the good things that God would do for the people.

28. (Jeremiah 36:12). 7th century B.C. Shemaiah was the father of Delaiah, a high official in the court of King Jehoiakim who was sympathetic to Jeremiah and Baruch.

Shemariah

(Hebrew origin: *Guarded by God*)

1. (1 Chronicles 12:5). 11th century B.C. Shemariah was one of the Benjamites who deserted King Saul's army and joined David's band at Ziklag. They were skilled warriors who could use both their right and left hands to shoot arrows and sling stones.

2. (Ezra 10:32). 5th century B.C. Shemariah, a descendant of Harim, divorced his foreign wife, during the days of Ezra.

3. (Ezra 10:41). 5th century B.C. Shemariah divorced his foreign wife, during the days of Ezra.

Shemeber

(Hebrew origin: *Illustrious*)

(Genesis 14:2). 19th century B.C. Shemeber, king of Zeboiim, was one of the vassals of Chedorlaomer, king of Elam. After serving him for twelve years, Shemeber and four other kings—Shinab, king of Admah; Bera, king of Sodom; Birsha, king of Gomorrah; and the king of Bela—rebelled, formed an alliance, and joined their forces in the valley of Sidim, which is now the Dead Sea.

Chedorlaomer and his allies—King Amraphel of Shinar, King Arioch of Ellasar, and King Tidal—defeated them in battle.

Shemeber, Shinab, and the king of Bela managed to escape to the mountains. Bera and Birsha of Gomorrah ran away from the battle, and they fell into the tar pits of the valley.

Shemer

(Hebrew origin: *Preserved*)

(1 Kings 16:24). 9th century B.C. Shemer was the owner of a hill, which he sold to King Omri of Israel for two talents of silver. The king built a new city on the hill, and he established there his capital. He gave it the name Samaria, in honor of the previous owner of the site.

Samaria became a splendid city, worthy of comparison with Jerusalem, the capital of Judah. About a hundred and fifty years after its foundation, it was destroyed by the Assyrians. It was never rebuilt.

Shemida

(Hebrew origin: *Name of knowing*)

(Numbers 26:32). Unspecified date. Shemida—spelled Shemidah in the first book of Chronicles (1 Chronicles 7:19)—of the tribe of Manasseh, was the ancestor of the clan of the Shemidaites. He had four sons: Ahian, Shechem, Likhi, and Aniam.

Shemidah

(Hebrew origin: *Name of knowing*)

(1 Chronicles 7:19). Unspecified date. Shemidah—spelled Shemida in the book of

Numbers (Numbers 26:32)—a descendant of Manasseh, was the ancestor of the clan of the Shemidaites. He had four sons: Ahian, Shechem, Likhi, and Aniam.

Shemiramoth

(Hebrew origin: *Name of heights*)

1. (1 Chronicles 15:18). 10th century B.C. Shemiramoth, a Levite of the second rank, was among those chosen by the chief of the Levites to sing and play musical instruments in front of the Ark of the Covenant, when it was carried from the house of Obededom to its resting place in Jerusalem, during the reign of King David.

2. (2 Chronicles 17:8). 9th century B.C. Shemiramoth, a Levite, was sent by King Jehoshaphat in the third year of his reign, to teach the laws of God in the cities of Judah. Shemiramoth was accompanied in his mission by other Levites, by two priests—Elishama and Jehoram—and by several officials of the court.

Shemuel

(Hebrew origin: *God heard*)

1. (Numbers 34:20). 13th century B.C. Shemuel, son of Ammihud, leader of the tribe of Simeon, was one of the men appointed by Moses to apportion the land of Canaan among the tribes.

2. (1 Chronicles 6:33). 11th century B.C. Shemuel is an alternative spelling for Samuel, the prophet and seer, last and greatest of the Israelite leaders called Judges who were chosen by God to rule over the people and save them in time of war and oppression. (Please see the entry for Samuel [1 Samuel 1:20].)

3. (1 Chronicles 7:2). Unspecified date. Shemuel, son of Tola, and his brothers—Uzzi, Rephaiah, Jeriel, Jibsam, and Jahmai—were leaders of the tribe of Issachar.

Shenazar

(Uncertain origin and meaning)

(1 Chronicles 3:18). 6th century B.C. Shenazar was one of the seven sons of King Jeconiah—also called Jehoiachin—the king who was deposed and taken captive by the Babylonians. His brothers were Salathiel, Hoshama, Malchiram, Pedaiah, Jecamiah, and Nedabiah.

Many scholars, based on the similarity of the names, identify Shenazar with Sheshbazzar, a member of the royal family of Judah, who was named governor of Judah by King Cyrus of Persia (Ezra 1:8). (Please see the entry for Sheshbazzar [Ezra 1:8].)

Shephathiah

(Hebrew origin: *God judges*)

(1 Chronicles 9:8). Unspecified date. Shephathiah, the son of Reuel, was the father of Meshullam, the leader of a Benjamite clan that lived in Jerusalem.

Shephatiah

(Hebrew origin: *God judges*)

1. (2 Samuel 3:4). 10th century B.C. Shephatiah, born in Hebron, was King David's fifth son. His mother was Abital. He probably died in childhood, because the Bible does not mention him again.
2. (1 Chronicles 12:5). 11th century B.C. Shephatiah the Haruphite was one of the Benjamites who deserted King Saul's army and joined David's band at Ziklag. They were skilled warriors who could use both their right and left hands to shoot arrows and sling stones.
3. (1 Chronicles 27:16). 10th century B.C. Shephatiah, the son of Maachah, was the ruler of the tribe of Simeon, during the days of King David.
4. (2 Chronicles 21:2). 9th century B.C. Shephatiah, a son of King Jehoshaphat, received from his father great gifts of gold, silver, and fenced cities. When Jehoshaphat died, his firstborn son Jehoram ascended to the throne and killed Shephatiah and all his other brothers.
5. (Ezra 2:4). Unspecified date. Shephatiah was the ancestor of a group of men who returned with Zerubbabel from the Babylonian Exile. His descendant Zebadiah returned with Ezra from Babylon, leading eighty males of his clan.
6. (Nehemiah 11:4). Unspecified date. Shephatiah, son of Mahalaleel and father of Amariah, was a descendant of Perez, the son of Judah. He was an ancestor of Athaiah, one of the people of Judah who settled in Jerusalem, after the exile.
7. (Jeremiah 38:1). 6th century B.C. Shephatiah, son of Mattan, was an official in the court of King Zedekiah. He—together with Jucal, son of Shelemiah; Gedaliah, son of Pashur; and Pashur, son of Malchiah—asked the king to put Jeremiah to death for preaching surrender and undermining the courage of the soldiers.

King Zedekiah told them that they could do with Jeremiah whatever they wanted. Shephatiah and his fellow court officials cast the prophet into the dungeon of Malchiah, which was in the court of the prison.

Shephi

(Hebrew origin: *Baldness*)

(1 Chronicles 1:40). Unspecified date. Shephi—also spelled Shepho (Genesis 36:23)—was the son of Shobal, a descendant of Seir. His brothers were Manahath, Ebal, Onam, and Alian.

Shepho

(Hebrew origin: *Baldness*)

(Genesis 36:23). Unspecified date. Shepho—also spelled Shephi (1 Chronicles 1:40)—was the son of Shobal, a descendant of Seir. His brothers were Manahath, Ebal, Onam, and Alvan.

Shephuphan

(Hebrew origin: *Serpent-like*)

(1 Chronicles 8:5). 17th century B.C. Shephuphan was one of the sons of Bela, the firstborn of Benjamin.

Sherah

(Hebrew origin: *Kindred*)

(1 Chronicles 7:24). 17th century B.C. Sherah, a daughter of Ephraim, built the towns of Upper and Lower Bethhoron, and Uzzensherah.

Sherebiah

(Hebrew origin: *God has brought heat*)

(Ezra 8:18). 5th century B.C. Sherebiah, a Levite of the clan of Mahli, was sent by Iddo, head of the Jewish community in Casiphia, to join Ezra in his trip to Jerusalem, in response to Ezra's request for people to serve God in the Temple.

Sherebiah came with two other Levites—Jeshaiah and Hashabiah—and a group of their relatives. Ezra gave him, Hashabiah, and ten others, the responsibility, during the journey, to take care of the precious vessels of the Temple, which were to be delivered to the priests in Jerusalem.

Sherebiah became one of the leading Levites in Jerusalem, during the days of Ezra and Nehemiah. He was among the Levites who explained the Law to the people in Jerusalem, after Ezra the Scribe had read it, while standing on a wooden platform, in front of the open space, before the Water Gate.

He stood with other Levites—Jeshua, Bani, Hashabniah, Shebaniah, Hodijah, Kadmiel, and Pethahiah—on a raised platform, during an assembly of public confession and fasting in the days of Ezra, and prayed to God in a loud voice.

He was also among the Levites who signed Nehemiah's solemn agreement to separate themselves from the foreigners living in the land, to refrain from intermarrying with them, to dedicate their firstborn to God, and other obligations (Nehemiah 10:12).

Sheresh

(Hebrew origin: *Root*)

(1 Chronicles 7:16). 16th century B.C. Sheresh, a descendant of Manasseh, was the son of Machir and his wife Maachah. His brother Peresh was the father of Ulam and Rakem. His mother Maachah was the sister of Huppim and Shuppim.

Sherezer

(Uncertain origin and meaning)

(Zechariah 7:2). 6th century B.C. Sherezer and Regemmelech, in the fourth year of the reign of King Darius, during the days of the prophet Zechariah, headed a delegation sent to the priests in the Temple in Jerusalem.

Sherezer and his companions were instructed to inquire whether the custom of mourning the destruction of the Temple should be continued now that the Temple had been rebuilt.

Sheshai

(Hebrew origin: *Whitish*)

(Numbers 13:22). 13th century B.C. Sheshai, Talmai, and Ahiman were three brothers, sons of Anak, and grandsons of Arba, the founder of the city of Hebron. The three brothers' gigantic height made the spies sent by Moses feel like grasshoppers.

Caleb, the son of Jephunneh, expelled Sheshai and his brothers from Hebron, during the conquest of Canaan. The three giants were later killed by the tribe of Judah.

Sheshan

(Hebrew origin: *Lily*)

(1 Chronicles 2:31). Unspecified date. Sheshan, the son of Ishi, a descendant of Jerahmeel, was a leader of the tribe of Judah. Sheshan married off one of his daughters to Jarha, his Egyptian servant.

Note: Although the Bible mentions in this verse that Sheshan had one son, Ahlai, a few verses later, it states that Sheshan didn't have any sons, only daughters (1 Chronicle 2:34).

This probably means that Ahlai either died young, or that he was born, when his sisters were already grown up and had moved away.

Sheshbazzar

(Uncertain origin and meaning)

(Ezra 1:8). 6th century B.C. Sheshbazzar, a member of the royal family of Judah, was named governor of Judah by King Cyrus of Persia.

He returned from Babylon to Jerusalem, leading a number of people, and carrying with him the five thousand four hundred utensils of gold and silver that the Babylonians had taken from the Temple, and that Mithredath, the treasurer of King Cyrus, had given back to him.

Sheshbazzar, upon his arrival to Jerusalem, started to rebuild the destroyed Temple, with the express authorization of King Cyrus.

The fact that he is not mentioned again in the Scriptures, which, instead, state that Zerubbabel was the governor of Judah, has caused some scholars to identify Sheshbazzar with Zerubbabel.

Other scholars based on the similarities of their names, identify Sheshbazzar with Shenazar, one of the seven sons of Jehoiachin, the king who was taken captive by the Babylonians. In this case, Sheshbazzar would be the uncle of Zerubbabel (1 Chronicles 3:18).

Sheth

(Hebrew origin: *Substituted*)

(1 Chronicles 1:1). Antediluvian. Sheth is an alternative spelling for Seth, the third son of Adam and Eve. (Please see the entry for Seth [Genesis 4:25].)

Shethar

(Uncertain origin and meaning)

(Esther 1:14). 5th century B.C. Shethar was one of the seven high officials of Persia and Media—the others were Tarshish, Carshena, Admatha, Meres, Marsena, and Memucan—

whom King Ahasuerus consulted about the punishment to be imposed on Queen Vashti for disobeying his command to appear before him.

Shetharboznai

(Uncertain origin and meaning)

(Ezra 5:3). 6th century B.C. Shetharboznai was an official working under Tatnai, the Persian governor of Judea. When a report was received that Zerubbabel and the High Priest Jeshua were rebuilding the Temple in Jerusalem, both officials decided to go personally to Jerusalem, and to see for themselves.

As soon as they arrived in the city, they asked the Jews who had given them permission to rebuild, and they requested the names of the men working on the construction.

The Jews gave them the information, but the Persian officials decided not to take any action for the time being, until King Darius would answer the letter that they wrote to him, requesting instructions on how to deal with the reconstruction of the Temple, and asking him to order a search of the government records to verify if King Cyrus had allowed the work.

A search was made, and a scroll was found in a palace in Achmetha, in the province of the Medes, which showed that Cyrus had given his full approval to the rebuilding of the Temple, with specific architectural instructions, and orders that the work should be paid from the royal treasury.

The king wrote back, ordering Tatnai and Shetharboznai to allow the work to proceed, to help the Jews to rebuild, and to refrain from interfering with the construction. Tatnai and his officials fully and speedily complied with the king's commands.

Sheva

(Hebrew origin: *False*)

1. (2 Samuel 20:25). 10th century B.C. Sheva—also called Shavsha (1 Chronicles 18:16), Shisha (1 Kings 4:3), and Seraiah (2 Samuel 8:17)—was the scribe in the court of King David. His sons, Elihoreph and

Ahiah, followed in his footsteps and became the scribes in the court of King Solomon.

2. (1 Chronicles 2:49). Unspecified date. Sheva, the founder of Machbenah and Gibea, was the son of Caleb—also called Chelubai—and his concubine Maachah. His brothers were Shaaph, Sheber, and Tirhanah.

Shilhi

(Hebrew origin: *Armed*)

(1 Kings 22:42). 9th century B.C. His daughter Azubah was the wife of King Asa and the mother of Jehoshaphat, king of Judah.

Shillem

(Hebrew origin: *Paid*)

(Genesis 46:24). 17th century B.C. Shillem, the son of Naphtali and grandson of Jacob, was among the seventy Israelites who immigrated to Egypt. This number included his brothers Jahzeel, Guni, and Jezer. Shillem was the ancestor of the clan of the Shillemites.

Shiloni

(Hebrew origin: *Inhabitant of Shiloh*)

(Nehemiah 11:5) Unspecified date. Shiloni, father of Zechariah, was an ancestor of Maaseiah, one of the men who settled in Jerusalem, after the return from the Babylonian Exile.

Shilshah

(Hebrew origin: *Third*)

(1 Chronicles 7:37). Unspecified date. Shilshah, son of Zophah, was a brave warrior, leader of a clan of the tribe of Asher. His brothers were Suah, Harnepher, Shual, Beri, Imrah, Bezer, Hod, Shamma, Ithran, and Beera.

Shimea

(Hebrew origin: *Hearing*)

1. (1 Chronicles 3:5). 10th century B.C. Shimea—also called Shammua and

Shammuah—was a son of King David and Bathshua, the daughter of Ammiel. (Please see the entry for Shammua [1 Chronicles 14:4].)

2. (1 Chronicles 6:30). 11th century B.C. Shimea, son of Uzza and father of Haggiah, was a Levite descendant of Merari. His grandson Asaiah was appointed by King David to be in charge of the singers in the House of the Lord.

3. (1 Chronicles 6:39). 11th century B.C. Shimea, son of Michael, a Levite of the clan of the Kohathites, was the father of Berachiah. His grandson Asaph was a leading musician, during the reign of King David, appointed by the king to be in charge of the singers in the House of the Lord.

4. (1 Chronicles 20:7). 11th century B.C. Shimea—also called Shammah, Shimma, and Shimeah—was one of David's brothers, and the third eldest son of Jesse. (Please see the entry for Shammah [1 Samuel 16:9].)

Shimeah

(Hebrew origin: *Annunciation*)

1. (2 Samuel 13:3). 11th century B.C. Shimeah—also called Shammah (1 Samuel 16:9), Shimea, and Shimma—was one of David's brothers, and the third eldest son of Jesse. (Please see the entry for Shammah [1 Samuel 16:9].)

2. (1 Chronicles 8:32). Unspecified date. Shimeah—also called Shimeam (1 Chronicles 9:38)—son of Mikloth, lived in Jerusalem.

Shimeam

(Hebrew origin: *Annunciation*)

(1 Chronicles 9:38). Unspecified date. Shimeam—also called Shimeah (1 Chronicles 8:32)—son of Mikloth, lived in Jerusalem.

Shimeath

(Hebrew origin: *Annunciation*)

(2 Kings 12:21). 9th century B.C. Shimeath

was one of the parents of Jozachar—also called Zabad—one of the killers of King Jehoash.

The second book of Kings states that Shimeath was the *father* of Jozachar, but the second book of Chronicles (2 Chronicles 24:26) says that Shimeath was the *mother* of Jozachar.

Shimei

(Hebrew origin: *Famous*)

1. (Numbers 3:18). 16th century B.C. Shimei—called Shimi in the book of Exodus (Exodus 6:17)—the son of Gershon and grandson of Levi, was the ancestor of the clan of the Shimites. His brother was Libni, also called Laadan.

2. (2 Samuel 16:5). 10th century B.C. Shimei, son of Gera, a Benjamite member of Saul's clan, met the king on the road, when David was fleeing from Absalom, cursed him, and threw him stones, shouting, "Get out, get out! You are a bloody man, a criminal! You usurped Saul's kingdom, and God is punishing for murdering Saul's family! God has given the kingdom to your son Absalom because you are a bloody man!"

Abishai, the son of Zeruiah, said to David, "Why should this dog curse my lord, the king? Please let me go over and take off his head!"

David replied, "What have I to do with you, you sons of Zeruiah? Let him curse, because God has said to him, 'Curse David'. Who has the right to ask why he does it? My own son is trying to kill me, so don't be surprised at this Benjamite. Leave him alone, let him curse. Perhaps, God will see my affliction, and will repay his cursing with blessings".

David and his men continued on their way, with Shimei walking on the hillside, cursing him, and throwing stones.

After Absalom's defeat and death, Shimei, accompanied by a thousand men of Benjamin, hurried to meet David, who was still on the other side of the river Jordan. They crossed the river, and, when Shimei was in front of the king, he threw himself to the ground and begged for forgiveness.

Abishai said, "Shimei should be put to death for having cursed God's anointed".

David replied, "What have I to do with you, you sons of Zeruiah? I am the king of Israel now, and no Israelite will be put to death today". And to Shimei, he said, "I swear that you will not be put to death".

Years later, when David was in his deathbed, he said to his son Solomon, "About Shimei, the son of Gera, a Benjamite of Bahurim, he cursed me bitterly when I was on my way to Mahanaim, but, after the battle, he met me at the Jordan River, and I swore to him that I would not kill him. But you must not let him go unpunished. You are a wise man, and will know what to do. Don't let him die peacefully!"

Solomon called Shimei and told him, "Build yourself a house in Jerusalem and live there, and don't leave the city. If you ever leave and go beyond the Kidron brook, you will die, and you will be the only one to blame for it".

Shimei answered, "I will do as the king says".

During the next three years, Shimei did not leave Jerusalem, until two of his slaves ran away to Achish, the king of the city of Gath. Shimei went to Gath and brought back his slaves.

When Solomon heard that Shimei had disobeyed his orders and had gone out of Jerusalem, he had him brought to his presence and said to him, "I told you not to leave Jerusalem, and warned you that, if you ever did, you would die. Why then did you disobey me? You know very well what you did to David, my father, and God will punish you for it". Then, the king gave orders to Benaiah, who went out and killed Shimei.

3. (1 Kings 1:8). 10th century B.C. Shimei was one of the officials in the court of King David who opposed Adonijah's bid for the throne.

4. (1 Kings 4:18). 10th century B.C. Shimei,

son of Elah, was one of King Solomon's twelve district governors. He was responsible for the provision of food from his district, the territory of Benjamin, for the king and the royal household, during one month out of each year.

5. (1 Chronicles 3:19). 6th century B.C. Shimei was the son of Pedaiah and the brother of Zerubbabel. His father Pedaiah was one of the seven sons of Jehoiachin, the king who was deposed and taken captive by the Babylonians.

6. (1 Chronicles 4:26). Unspecified date. Shimei, of the tribe of Simeon, was the son of Zacchur. Although most of the families in the tribe of Simeon had very few children, Shimei had sixteen sons and six daughters.

7. (1 Chronicles 5:4). Unspecified date. Shimei, son of Gog and father of Micah, was an ancestor of Beerah, a leader of the tribe of Reuben who was carried away to captivity by Tilgathpilneser, king of Assyria.

8. (1 Chronicles 6:29). 10th century B.C. Shimei, son of Libni, a descendant of Merari, was the father of Uzza. His descendant Asaiah was a Levite appointed by King David to be in charge of the singers in the House of the Lord, from the time when the Ark came to rest in Jerusalem.

9. (1 Chronicles 6:42). Unspecified date. Shimei, of the clan of Kohathites, was the son of Jahath and the father of Zimmah. His descendant Asaph was one of the Levites appointed by King David to be in charge of the singers in the House of the Lord.

10. (1 Chronicles 25:17). 10th century B.C. Shimei was in charge of the tenth turn of service that played musical instruments—cymbals, psalteries, and harps—in the House of God, during the reign of David.

11. (1 Chronicles 27:27). 10th century B.C. Shimei the Ramathite was in charge of the royal vineyards, during the reign of King David.

12. (2 Chronicles 29:14). 8th century B.C. Shimei was one of the Levites who gathered to make themselves ritually clean, and to purify the Temple, during the reign of King Hezekiah of Judah. His ancestor Heman was one of King David's leading musicians.

13. (2 Chronicles 31:12). 8th century B.C. Shimei, a Levite, was appointed by King Hezekiah to help his brother Cononiah, in the supervision of the gifts, tithes, and offerings, brought by the people to the Temple. The two brothers had a number of overseers under their command.

14. (Ezra 10:23). 5th century B.C. Shimei was one of the Levites who divorced his foreign wife, during the days of Ezra.

15. (Ezra 10:33). 5th century B.C. Shimei, a descendant of Hashum, divorced his foreign wife, during the days of Ezra.

16. (Ezra 10:38). 5th century B.C. Shimei was one of the men who had married foreign women, during the days of Ezra, and were forced to divorce them.

17. (Esther 2:5). 6th century B.C. Shimei, the son of Kish, of the tribe of Benjamin, was the father of Jair and Abihail. Jair became the father of Mordecai, and Abihail the father of Queen Esther.

Shimeon

(Hebrew origin: *Hearing*)

(Ezra 10:31). 5th century B.C. Shimeon, a descendant of Harim, divorced his foreign wife, during the days of Ezra.

Shimhi

(Hebrew origin: *Famous*)

(1 Chronicles 8:21). Unspecified date. Shimhi was the father of several leaders of the tribe of Benjamin who lived in Jerusalem.

Shimi

(Hebrew origin: *Famous*)

(Exodus 6:17). 16th century B.C. Shimi—called Shimei in the book of Numbers (Numbers 3:18)—the son of Gershon and grandson of Levi, was the ancestor of the clan of the Shimites. His brother was Libni, also called Laadan.

Shimma

(Hebrew origin: *Annunciation*)

(1 Chronicles 2:13). 11th century B.C. Shimma—also called Shammah, Shimea, and Shimeah—was one of David's brothers, and the third eldest son of Jesse. (Please see the entry for Shammah [1 Samuel 16:9].)

Shimon

(Hebrew origin: *Wasteland*)

(1 Chronicles 4:20). Unspecified date. Shimon, a descendant of Judah, was the father of Rinnah, Benhanan, Amnon, and Tilon.

Shimrath

(Hebrew origin: *Guardship*)

(1 Chronicles 8:21). Unspecified date. Shimrath, a descendant of Shimhi, was a leader of the tribe of Benjamin who lived in Jerusalem.

Shimri

(Hebrew origin: *Watchful*)

1. (1 Chronicles 4:37). Unspecified date. Shimri, son of Shemaiah, was the father of Jedaiah. His descendant Ziza was one of the leaders of the tribe of Simeon who went to the fertile valley of Gedor in search of pasture for their flocks, during the reign of Hezekiah, king of Judah. The Simeonites destroyed the tents of the people—descendants of Ham—who lived there, wiped them out forever, and settled in their place.
2. (1 Chronicles 11:45). 10th century B.C. Shimri was the father of Jediael and Joha, two of King David's brave warriors.
3. (2 Chronicles 29:13). 8th century B.C. Shimri and Jeiel, descendants of Elizaphan, were among the Levites who gathered to make themselves ritually clean, and to purify the Temple, during the reign of King Hezekiah of Judah.

Shimrith

(Hebrew origin: *Female guard*)

(2 Chronicles 24:26). 8th century B.C. Shimrith, a Moabitess, was the mother of Jehozabad, son of Shomer (2 Kings 12:21). Her son and Jozachar, son of Shimeath, murdered King Jehoash and, for that crime, were executed by his son and successor, King Amaziah.

Shimrom

(Hebrew origin: *Guardianship*)

(1 Chronicles 7:1). 17th century. Shimrom—called Shimron in the book of Genesis (Genesis 46:13)—son of Issachar and grandson of Jacob, was the ancestor of the clan of the Shimronites. He was among the seventy Israelites who immigrated to Egypt. Shimrom's brothers were Tola, Puah—called Phuvah in Genesis, and Pua in Numbers—and Jashub, called Job in Genesis.

Shimron

(Hebrew origin: *Guardianship*)

(Genesis 46:13). 17th century. Shimron—also called Shimrom—son of Issachar and grandson of Jacob, was the ancestor of the clan of the Shimronites. (Please see the entry for Shimrom [1 Chronicles 7:1].)

Shimshai

(Hebrew origin: *Sunny*)

(Ezra 4:8). 5th century B.C. Shimshai was the scribe of Rehum, the Persian commissioner in Samaria. The foreign settlers that the Assyrians had brought to Samaria asked him and Rehum to send a letter, written in Aramaic, to King Artaxerxes, accusing the Jews of rebuilding the walls of Jerusalem with the intention to rebel.

The king, who was persuaded that the rebuilding constituted a threat to his authority, immediately wrote back, ordering the work to stop, and decreeing that the city should not be rebuild unless explicitly allowed by him. Rehum and Shimshai, upon receiving the letter, hurried to Jerusalem and forced the Jews to stop the work. The rebuilding of Jerusalem was not renewed, until the second year of the reign of King Darius.

Shinab

(Hebrew origin: *Father has changed*)

(Genesis 14:2). 19th century B.C. Shinab, king of Admah, was one of the vassals of Chedorlaomer, king of Elam. After serving him for twelve years, Shinab and four other kings—Birsha, king of Gomorrah; Shemeber, king of Zeboiim; Bera, king of Sodom; and the king of Bela—rebelled, formed an alliance, and joined their forces in the valley of Sidim, which is now the Dead Sea.

Chedorlaomer and his allies—King Amraphel of Shinar, King Arioch of Ellasar, and King Tidal—defeated them in battle.

Shinab, Shemeber, and the king of Bela managed to escape to the mountains. Birsha and Bera ran away from the battle, and they fell into the tar pits of the valley.

Shiphi

(Hebrew origin: *Copious*)

(1 Chronicles 4:37). 8th century B.C. Shiphi, the son of Allon, was the father of Ziza, one of the leaders of the tribe of Simeon who went to the fertile valley of Gedor in search of pasture for their flocks, during the reign of Hezekiah, king of Judah.

The Simeonites destroyed the tents of the people—descendants of Ham—who lived there, wiped them out forever, and settled in their place.

Shiphrah

(Hebrew origin: *Brightness*)

(Exodus 1:15). 14th century. Shiphrah and Puah, two Hebrew midwives, were instructed by the Pharaoh of Egypt to kill all the Israelite male babies, but to allow the females babies to live.

The two women were God fearing, and they did not carry out the command of the

Pharaoh. They were called to the presence of the sovereign, who asked them why they were letting the boys live.

The midwives answered, "The Hebrew women are not like the Egyptian women. They are so vigorous that they deliver their babies, before we arrive".

God rewarded the two women and gave them families of their own.

Shiphtan

(Hebrew origin: *Judge-like*)

(Numbers 34:24). 14th century B.C. His son Kemuel, a leader of the tribe of Ephraim, was one of the men appointed by Moses to apportion the land of Canaan among the tribes.

Shisha

(Hebrew origin: *Whiteness*)

(1 Kings 4:3). 10th century B.C. Shisha was the scribe in the court of King David. His sons, Elihoreph and Ahiah, followed in his footsteps and became the scribes in the court of King Solomon. Shisha was also called Sheva (2 Samuel 20:25), Shavsha (1 Chronicles 18:16), and Seraiah (2 Samuel 8:17).

Shishak

(Egyptian origin: Uncertain meaning)

(1 Kings 11:40). 10th century B.C. The Pharaoh Shishak of Egypt was contemporary with King Solomon and his son King Rehoboam. He received Jeroboam in Egypt, when Jeroboam fled Israel, after his conspiracy had been discovered by Solomon, and allowed him to stay in Egypt, until the death of Solomon.

During the fifth year of the reign of Rehoboam, Shishak invaded Judah with twelve hundred chariots, sixty thousand horsemen, and a large army of foot soldiers. The prophet Shemaiah went to the king and his officials, who had gathered in Jerusalem, and told them that God was punishing them, because they had forsaken him. Rehoboam and his men humbled themselves and acknowledged that God was right.

God's word then came to Shemaiah, saying, "They have humbled themselves; therefore, I will not destroy them, but they will serve Shishak, and they will, thus, know the difference between serving me and serving the kingdoms of the earth".

Shishak entered Jerusalem and took away the treasuries of the Temple and the royal palace, including the shields of gold that Solomon had made, which Rehoboam then replaced with shields of brass.

Shitrai

(Hebrew origin: *Magisterial*)

(1 Chronicles 27:29). 10th century B.C. Shitrai the Sharonite was the official in charge of the cattle in the Sharon region, during the reign of King David.

Shiza

(Uncertain origin and meaning)

(1 Chronicles 11:42). 10th century B.C. Shiza was the father of Adina, one of King David's brave warriors and a captain of the Reubenites.

Shobab

(Hebrew origin: *Rebellious*)

1. (2 Samuel 5:14). 10th century B.C. Shobab, born in Jerusalem, was one of the four sons of King David and Bathshua. His brothers were Solomon, Shimea, and Nathan (1 Chronicles 3:5).
2. (1 Chronicles 2:18). Unspecified date. Shobab, of the tribe of Judah, was the son of Caleb and Azubah, and the grandson of Hezron.

Shobach

(Hebrew origin: *Thicket*)

(2 Samuel 10:16). 10th century B.C. Shobach—called Shophach in the first book of Chronicles (1 Chronicles 19:16)—was the

captain of the army of King Hadarezer of Zobah, an Aramean kingdom situated near the river Euphrates. The Ammonites, who were fighting a war against King David, asked for help, and Hadarezer sent them his army, commanded by Shobach.

The Israelites utterly defeated the Arameans in a battle at Helam, and they killed over seven thousand charioteers and forty thousand foot soldiers. Shobach died in the fighting, and King Hadarezer became a vassal of David.

Shobai

(Hebrew origin: *Captor*)

(Ezra 2:42). Unspecified date. Shobai was the ancestor of a clan of gatekeepers that returned with Zerubbabel from the Babylonian Exile.

Shobal

(Hebrew origin: *Overflowing*)

1. (Genesis 36:20). Unspecified date. Shobal was one of the sons of Seir the Horite, ancestor of the clans that settled in the land of Edom. His sons were Alvan, Manahath, Ebal, Shepho, and Onam. His brothers were Dishan, Lotan, Zibeon, Dishon, Ezer, and Anah.
2. (1 Chronicles 2:50). Unspecified date. Shobal, the founder of Kirjathjearim, was a descendant of Caleb, and the ancestor of Haroeh, of half the inhabitants of Manahath, and of several clans who lived in Kirjathjearim.
3. (1 Chronicles 4:1). 17th century B.C. Shobal was the son of Judah and grandson of Jacob. His son was called Reaiah.

Shobek

(Hebrew origin: *Forsaking*)

(Nehemiah 10:24). 5th century B.C. Shobek was one of the leaders who signed Nehemiah's solemn agreement to separate themselves from the foreigners living in the land, to refrain from intermarrying with them, and to dedicate their firstborn to God, among other obligations.

Shobi

(Hebrew origin: *Captor*)

(2 Samuel 17:27). 10th century B.C. Shobi, a son of King Nahash of Ammon, showed great kindness to David, when the king was fleeing from Absalom. He, together with Machir and Barzillai, brought beds, basins, vessels, and food for David and his men.

When his father Nahash, who also had always treated David with warm friendship, died, Shobi's brother Hanun became king of Ammon. Hanun's ill treatment of the messengers who had brought him David's condolences provoked a war with Israel, in which the Ammonites were soundly defeated.

Shoham

(Hebrew origin: Name of a gem)

(1 Chronicles 24:27). 10th century B.C. Shoham, a Levite, son of Jaaziah, a descendant of Merari, served in the Tabernacle, during the reign of David, together with his brothers Beno, Zaccur, and Ibri.

Shomer

(Hebrew origin: *Keeper*)

1. (2 Kings 12:21). 8th century B.C. Shomer and a Moabitess named Shimrith were the parents of Jehozabad, a court official who was one of the murderers of King Jehoash.
2. (1 Chronicles 7:32). Unspecified date. Shomer, of the tribe of Asher, was the son of Heber. His brothers were Japhlet and Hotham, and his sister was Shua.

Shophach

(Hebrew origin: *Poured*)

(1 Chronicles 19:16). 10th century B.C. Shophach—also called Shobach—was the captain of the army of King Hadarezer of Zobah. (Please see the entry for Shobach [2 Samuel 10:16].)

Shua

(Hebrew origin: *Riches*)

1. (1 Chronicles 2:3). 17th century. Shua— also spelled Shuah (Genesis 38:2)—a Canaanite, was the father of Judah's wife, Bathshua, *Daughter of Shua* in Hebrew.
2. (1 Chronicles 7:32). Unspecified date. Shua, of the tribe of Asher, was the daughter of Heber. Her brothers were Japhlet, Shomer, and Hotham.

Shuah

(Hebrew origin: *Humble*)

1. (Genesis 25:2). 17th century B.C. Shuah was one of the sons of Abraham and Keturah, the woman whom Abraham married, after the death of Sarah. Shuah's brothers were Zimran, Jokshan, Medan, Midian, and Ishbak.
2. (Genesis 38:2). 17th century. Shuah—also spelled Shua (1 Chronicles 2:3)—a Canaanite, was the father of Judah's wife, Bathshua, *Daughter of Shua* in Hebrew.
3. (1 Chronicles 4:11). Unspecified date. Shuah, a descendant of Judah, was the brother of Chelub and the uncle of Mehir.

Shual

(Hebrew origin: *Fox*)

(1 Chronicles 7:36). Unspecified date. Shual, son of Zophah, was a brave warrior, leader of a clan of the tribe of Asher.

Shubael

(Hebrew origin: *God's captive*)

1. (1 Chronicles 24:20). 10th century B.C. Shubael—also called Shebuel (1 Chronicles 23:16)—a Levite descendant of Amram, Moses, and Gershom, was in charge of the treasury of the Tabernacle, during the reign of King David.
2. (1 Chronicles 25:20). 10th century B.C. Shubael—also called Shebuel (1 Chronicles 25:4)—a Levite, member of a family of musicians, was in charge of the thirteenth turn of service that played

musical instruments—cymbals, psalteries, and harps—in the House of God, during the reign of David. He had thirteen brothers and three sisters, all of them trained as skillful musicians by their father, Heman, one of the three leading musicians of the period; the other two were Asaph and Jeduthun.

Shuham

(Hebrew origin: *Humbly*)

(Numbers 26:42). 17th century B.C. Shuham—called Hushim in the book of Genesis (Genesis 46:23)—son of Dan and grandson of Jacob, was one of the seventy Israelites who immigrated to Egypt. Shuham was the ancestor of the clan of the Shuhamites.

Shuni

(Hebrew origin: *Resting*)

(Genesis 46:16). 17th century B.C. Shuni, son of Gad and grandson of Jacob and Zilpah, Leah's maid, was one of the seventy Israelites who immigrated to Egypt. Shuni was the ancestor of the clan of the Shunites. His brothers were Ziphion, Haggi, Ezbon, Eri, Arodi, and Areli.

Shupham

(Hebrew origin: *Serpent-like*)

(Numbers 26:39). 17th century B.C. Shupham was a son of Benjamin and an ancestor of the clan of the Shuphamites. He is not mentioned in the other lists of the sons of Benjamin: Genesis 46:21, 1 Chronicles 8:1, and 1 Chronicles 7:6.

Shuppim

(Hebrew origin: *Serpents*)

1. (1 Chronicles 7:12). Unspecified date. Shuppim, a descendant of Benjamin, was the son of Ir and the brother of Huppim. His sister Maachah married Machir.
2. (1 Chronicles 26:16). 10th century B.C. Shuppim was one of the Levites who served

as gatekeepers of the Tabernacle, during the reign of King David. He and Hosah were posted on the western side, near the Shallecheth Gate.

Shuthelah

(Hebrew origin: *Crash of breakage*)

1. (Numbers 26:35). 16th century B.C. Shuthelah, son of Ephraim and grandson of Joseph, was the ancestor of the clan of the Shuthalhites. His son Eran was the ancestor of the clan of the Eranites.
2. (1 Chronicles 7:21). Unspecified date. Shuthelah, son of Zabad, was one of the descendants of Ephraim who were killed by the men of Gath, while trying to steal their cattle.

Sia

(Hebrew origin: *Congregation*)

(Nehemiah 7:47). Unspecified date. Sia—called Siaha in the book of Ezra (Ezra 2:44)—was the ancestor of a clan of Temple servants that returned with Zerubbabel from the Babylonian Exile.

Siaha

(Hebrew origin: *Congregation*)

(Ezra 2:44). Unspecified date. Siaha—called Sia in the book of Nehemiah (Nehemiah 7:47)—was the ancestor of a clan of Temple servants that returned with Zerubbabel from the Babylonian Exile.

Sibbecai

(Hebrew origin: *Copse-like*)

(1 Chronicles 11:29). 10th century B.C. Sibbecai the Hushathite—called Sibbechai and Mebunnai in the second book of Samuel—was one of "The Thirty", an elite group in King David's army. (Please see the entry for Mebunnai [2 Samuel 23:27].)

Sibbechai

(Hebrew origin: *Copse-like*)

(2 Samuel 21:18). 10th century B.C. Sibbechai the Hushathite was one of "The Thirty", an elite group in King David's army. He was called Sibbecai in the first book of Chronicles, and Mebunnai in the second book of Samuel. (Please see the entry for Mebunnai [2 Samuel 23:27].)

Sidon

(Hebrew origin: *Fishery*)

(Genesis 10:15). Unspecified date. Sidon was the firstborn son of Canaan, the son of Ham. His name was also spelled Zidon (1 Chronicles 1:13).

Sihon

(Hebrew origin: *Tempestuous*)

(Numbers 21:21). 13th century B.C. Sihon was the king of the Amorites, a nation that lived on the eastern bank of the river Jordan.

The Israelites asked him for permission to go through his country, and they promised that they would not damage his fields and vineyards, or even drink water from his wells.

Sihon denied their request, gathered an army, and went to fight against the Israelites. The battle took place at Jahaz, and the result was a total defeat of the Amorites, whose lands and cities, including Heshbon, their capital, were taken over by the Israelites. The tribes of Gad and Reuben, and half the tribe of Manasseh, settled in the former Amorite lands.

Silas

(Latin origin: contraction of *Silvanus*)

(Acts of the Apostles 15:22). A.D. 1st century. Silas—also called Silvanus (2 Corinthians 1:19)—a Roman citizen, was a prominent leader of the Christian community in Jerusalem. He was present, when Paul and Barnabas reported to the Jerusalem elders about the results of their mission in Asia Minor, and took part in the debate over the admission of non-Jews to the church.

The Jerusalem Christian community decided to send Silas, Barsabas, Paul, and Barnabas, to Antioch, carrying a letter to the Gentile believers. The letter stated that the Gentile converts were exonerated of the need for circumcision, but they were asked to abstain from sexual immorality, and also from eating food offered to idols, blood, and strangled animals.

In Antioch, the envoys gathered the congregation of believers and read them the letter. Afterward, Silas and Barsabas, who were themselves considered to be prophets, spoke for a long time to the believers and gave them encouragement.

Barsabas returned to Jerusalem, but Silas stayed in Antioch, with Paul and Barnabas for sometime. They continued to teach and preach, until Paul suggested that they should travel and see how the churches that they had founded in their previous trip were doing. Barnabas wanted to take John Mark with them, but Paul opposed to this suggestion. As they were not able to agree, they decided to go their separate ways. Barnabas took John Mark with him, and they sailed to Cyprus, while Paul took Silas and traveled with him through Syria and Cilicia, strengthening the local churches.

In Lystra, they met a believer called Timotheus—also called Timothy—the son of a Jewish mother and a Greek father. Paul wanted to take Timotheus along with him, so he circumcised him, because the Jews who lived in those places knew that his father was Greek. As they traveled through the towns, they delivered to the local congregations the rules decreed by the apostles and elders in Jerusalem, and they told them to carry them out.

After traveling through different cities, they arrived in Philippi, a Roman colony, which was the main city of Macedonia. A few days later, on the Sabbath, they went out of the city to the riverside, where they thought there would be a place for prayer. They sat down and spoke to the women who gathered there. One of them was a woman named Lydia, a seller of purple cloth, originally from the city of Thyatira. She listened with great attention to Paul, became a believer, and was baptized, together with other members of her household. Lydia then convinced Paul to be a guest in her house, during his stay in Philippi.

One day, when Paul and his companions were going to offer prayer, they met a slave girl who was possessed by a spirit that allowed her to predict the future. Her owners earned a lot of money from her fortune telling. She followed Paul and his companions, shouting, "These men are servants of the Most High God, who proclaim to you how you can be saved!" She did this for many days, until Paul became so annoyed that he turned around and said to the spirit, "I command you, in the name of Jesus Christ, to come out of her". And at that moment, the spirit left her.

Her owners were very angry, when they realized that she was no longer able to tell the future, and that their income from her was gone. They seized Paul and Silas and dragged them to the marketplace, before the authorities of the city. They complained to the magistrates, saying, "These Jews are disturbing our city by teaching customs that we, as Roman citizens, cannot lawfully accept or practice". The crowd joined in the attack against Paul and Silas, and the authorities tore their clothes and ordered them to be whipped. After being severely beaten, they were taken to jail. The jailer threw them into an inner cell and fastened their feet between heavy blocks of wood.

At midnight, Paul and Silas prayed and sang praises to God in a loud voice heard by the other prisoners. Suddenly, there was a great earthquake that shook the foundations of the prison; the doors were thrown open, and the chains fell off all the prisoners.

The jailer woke up and, seeing all the doors open, assumed that the prisoners had all escaped. He pulled out his sword and was about to commit suicide, when Paul shouted, "Don't harm yourself! We are all here!" The jailer called for a light and rushed into the cell, and trembling, he fell down in front of Paul and Silas. Then, he brought them out and asked, "Sirs, what must I do to be saved?" They told him, "Believe in the Lord Jesus Christ,

and you and your family will be saved", and they preached to him and his family the word of God. The jailer washed their wounds, and he and his family were baptized that very moment. He then brought them into his house and gave them food to eat; he and his family were full of joy, because they now believed in God.

Early the next morning, the authorities sent officials with orders to the jailer to let Paul and Silas go free. The jailer told Paul, "The magistrates have released you. You can now leave. Go in peace".

Paul refused to leave, saying, "We were not condemned, but they have publicly beaten us, who are Roman citizens! They threw us in jail, and now, they want to send us away secretly. No, we will not go! Let them come themselves and let us out!"

The officials went back to the magistrates and reported Paul's words. They were afraid, when they heard that Paul and Silas were Roman citizens. They went to the jail and apologized to them. They took them out of prison and asked them to please leave the city. Paul and Silas left the prison and went to Lydia's house, where they met the believers, gave them words of encouragement, and departed from Philippi.

Paul and Silas passed through Amphipolis and Apollonia, on their way to Thessalonica, where they stayed in the house of a man called Jason. According to his usual custom, Paul went on the Sabbath to the synagogue. During three Sabbaths, he held discussions with the people, quoting verses of the Scriptures to prove that the Messiah had to suffer and rise from the dead, and that the announced Messiah was Jesus. A number of his Jewish listeners converted, and so did many of the Greeks who believed in God, including several of the leading women of the city.

Some of the members of the synagogue, who did not believe, and who were upset with Paul's teachings, gathered a mob, with the help of some ruffians, and assaulted the house of Jason, searching for Paul and Silas. Not finding them in the house, they grabbed Jason and other Christians, and they took them to the rulers of the city, accusing them of calling Jesus their king, instead of the emperor. The authorities made Jason and the others deposit security, and let them go. The disciples, that same night, sent Paul and Silas to Berea for their safety.

In Berea, they went to the synagogue, where their preaching met with more success than in Thessalonica. Their listeners heard them with open minds and checked the Scriptures to verify if their assertions were true. Many converted, including some Greek men and women of high social standing.

The Jews of Thessalonica, hearing that Paul was preaching in Berea, came to the town, stirring up and inciting the crowds. Then, the believers immediately sent Paul off on his way to the sea, but Silas and Timotheus remained in Berea, until Paul, having arrived in Athens, sent them word to come to him.

Paul, while waiting for his companions to arrive, was greatly shocked to see that the city was full of idols. He held discussions in the synagogue with the Jews and with the Gentiles who believed in God. He also went everyday to the marketplace and argued with any person who happened to pass by.

After this, Paul left Athens and went to Corinth. There, he stayed in the house of Aquila and his wife Priscilla, a Jewish couple originally from Pontus, who had been expelled from Rome by the emperor Claudius, together with all the other Jews. In Corinth, they made their living by making tents, which was also Paul's trade.

Paul went to the synagogue every Sabbath and preached to the Jews and the Greeks. When Silas and Timotheus arrived from Macedonia, they found him fully occupied, testifying to the Jews that Jesus was the Messiah. The Jews opposed him and reviled him. Paul shook out his clothing, and he told them, "I am not responsible if your blood be upon your heads. From now on, I will go to the Gentiles". He moved to the house of Justus, a Gentile who worshipped God, and lived right next to the synagogue.

From Corinth, Silas, together with Paul and Timotheus, wrote two letters to the Thessalonian Christian community. Years later,

Silas assisted Peter, possibly in Rome, to write a letter to the Christian congregations in the northern part of Asia Minor, who were facing persecution and suffering for their faith.

Silvanus

(Latin origin: *A god of forests*)

(2 Corinthians 1:19). A.D. 1st century. Silvanus is an alternative name for Silas, one of the faithful companions and helpers of the apostle Paul. (Please see the entry for Silas [Acts of the Apostles 15:22].)

Simeon

(Hebrew origin: *Hearing*)

1. (Genesis 29:33). 17th century B.C. 17th century. Simeon, the second son of Jacob and Leah, was born in Paddan-Aram, where Jacob was working for his father-in-law Laban. She called him Simeon, because, as she said, "God has given me this son, because he heard that I was not loved".

   Simeon was the full brother of Issachar, Reuben, Levi, Judah, and Zebulun, sons of Leah. His half brothers were Gad and Asher, sons of Zilpah; Dan and Naphtali, sons of Bilhah; and Benjamin and Joseph, sons of Rachel. His sister was Dinah, daughter of Leah.

   After Jacob and his family came to Canaan, and settled near Shechem, Dinah became friendly with the local girls and visited their city.

   Shechem, son of Hamor the Hivite, ruler of Shechem, saw her, seized her, and raped her. Afterward, Shechem, having fallen in love with Dinah, asked his father Hamor to speak to Jacob and ask for Dinah's hand.

   The sons of Jacob took charge of the negotiations and deceitfully agreed to Hamor's request, on condition that Hamor, Shechem, and all the men in their city should first be circumcised. Hamor and his son agreed to this condition, and they, together with all the men in the city, were circumcised.

Simeon and Levy considered that Shechem had treated their sister as a harlot. They took advantage of the weakened condition of the circumcised men to revenge their sister's lost honor; they slaughtered all the men in the city, including Hamor and Shechem, took their sheep, oxen, and all their other possessions, and brought Dinah back to her home.

Jacob, fearing that the actions of his sons had placed them all in great danger, left Shechem and took the family to Hebron.

Simeon and his brothers were involved in the events that led to Joseph being taken as a slave to Egypt. (For the detailed story of Joseph and his brothers, please see the entry for Joseph.)

Many years went by, Joseph, after having been the trusted servant in the home of an important Egyptian official, spent years in jail, because of the trumped-up charges of his master's wife, and had now become, in an astonishing turn of events, the most powerful man in Egypt after Pharaoh.

There was a great famine in Egypt, but Joseph, having foreseen that this would happen, had taken care of storing in warehouses the abundant crops that had been produced in the previous seven years.

The famine in Canaan was also severe. When Jacob heard that it was possible to buy grain in Egypt, he sent there all his sons, except for young Benjamin, because his father was afraid that something would happen to him.

The brothers arrived in Egypt and were brought to the presence of Joseph, who was personally in charge of selling the grain. They didn't recognize that the powerful Egyptian vizier in front of them was the young brother whom they had last seen over twenty years before, but Joseph recognized them immediately and remembered his dreams where his family bowed to him. He decided to act as if he didn't know them and accused them of being spies. The brothers denied this, saying that they were all sons of the same man, and that they had a younger brother at home.

Joseph confined them in prison for three days. On the third day, he told them that they could return to their families with the grain bought in Egypt, but one of them would have to stay in prison to make sure that they would return with their younger brother.

The brothers had no idea that Joseph understood each word that they said, because he had been talking to them through an interpreter. Joseph turned away from them and wept. Then, he returned to them, took Simeon, and had him tied up in front of them.

The other brothers returned to Canaan and told their father that the Egyptian vizier demanded that they should bring Benjamin to Egypt, and that he had kept Simeon as a hostage.

Jacob absolutely refused to allow Benjamin to go to Egypt, but, eventually, when the grain that his sons had brought ran out, he reluctantly agreed, assured by Judah that he assumed the responsibility of bringing Benjamin back.

When Joseph saw Benjamin, he broke down and made himself known to his astonished brothers. He forgave them and invited them to settle in Egypt.

Simeon and his sons Jemuel, Jamin, Ohad, Jachin, Zohar, and Shaul—the son of a Canaanite woman—were among the seventy Israelites who immigrated to Egypt.

They arrived in Goshen, and Joseph came to them in his chariot. He greeted his father, embraced him, and wept for a long time.

Seventeen years later, Jacob, feeling that he would soon die, called his sons to tell them what would happen to them in the future. He said that Simeon and Levi, for their violence and their cruelty, when they slaughtered the men of Shechem, would be dispersed among the people of Israel.

Jacob's last words were to ask them to bury him in the cave of Machpelah, where Abraham, Sarah, Isaac, Rebekah and Leah were buried. Jacob's body was accompanied in his last trip by his sons, their children, flocks and herds, all the officials of Pharaoh and members of his court, chariots and horsemen. Before crossing the Jordan, the funeral procession made a stop, and mourned Jacob for seven days. Then, Judah and his brothers took him to Canaan and buried him in the cave of Machpelah.

After burying their father, they all returned to Canaan. Joseph's brothers feared that, with Jacob now dead, Joseph would pay them back for the wrong that they had done to him.

They sent a message to Joseph, saying that Jacob, before his death, had told them to urge Joseph to forgive them. Judah and his brothers came to Joseph, flung themselves before him, and told him that they were prepared to be his slaves.

Joseph answered kindly, "Do not fear! Although you intended me harm, God intended it all for good, to assure the survival of many people. Don't worry; I will take care of you and your children".

When Joshua conquered Canaan, the tribe of Simeon settled in the Negev desert, in the south of the country. During the period of the monarchy the tribe of Simeon and its territory formed an inextricable part of the kingdom of Judah, and, eventually, its population merged with the tribe of Judah.

2. (Luke 2:25). A.D. 1st century. Simeon, a devout and just man who lived in Jerusalem, had a vision where the Holy Ghost told him that he would not die, before he had seen the Lord's Christ. He was present in the Temple, when Joseph and Mary brought the child Jesus to sacrifice on his behalf according to the custom for firstborn male children. He took the baby in his arms, blessed the child, and said, "Lord, now let your servant depart in peace, according to your promise, because my eyes have seen the salvation that you have prepared before the people, a light to the Gentiles, and the glory of your people Israel". And then, he blessed Joseph and Mary.

3. (Luke 3:30). Unspecified date. Simeon, the son of Juda, and the father of Levi, was an ancestor of Jesus, according to Luke's genealogy.

4. (Acts of the Apostles 13:1). A.D. 1st century. Simeon, nicknamed Niger, was one of the prophets and teachers active in the Antioch church, during the year that Paul stayed in Antioch, preaching and organizing the church. It was in Antioch that the believers in Jesus were first called Christians.

5. (Acts of the Apostles 15:14). A.D. 1st century. Simeon is an alternative spelling for Simon, referring to Peter.

Simon

(Hebrew origin: *Hearing*)

1. (Matthew 4:18). A.D. 1st century. Simon, the son of Jona, a fisherman in the Sea of Galilee, became one of the first disciples of Jesus and the leader of the apostles, after the Crucifixion. Jesus gave him the name of Peter to symbolize that he was the "rock" upon which the church would be built. Paul usually called him Cephas, which is the Latinized form of the Greek translation of the Aramaic word for "rock". (Please see the entry for Peter for a detailed biography.)

2. (Matthew 10:4). A.D. 1st century. Simon, one of the twelve apostles, was called the Canaanite. This Aramaic word means "zealot" a member of a fanatical nationalistic group single minded dedicated to the violent expulsion of the Romans from Judea.

3. (Matthew 13:55). A.D. 1st century. Simon was one of the four brothers of Jesus mentioned by the people of Nazareth, when they expressed their surprise and anger against Jesus for preaching in their synagogue. The other brothers were James—who became the leader of the early church in Jerusalem—Joses, and Judas. Scholars and historians debate if these relatives were full-blooded siblings, half brothers, or only cousins.

4. (Matthew 26:6). A.D. 1st century. Simon, the leper—this word probably means that

he suffered of a skin disease—hosted Jesus in his house in Bethany. During dinner, a woman came to Jesus with an alabaster box of expensive ointment, which she poured on his head. The disciples considered that this was a waste of money, because the ointment could have been sold, and the money given to the poor.

Jesus rebuked them, saying, "Why do you trouble this woman? She has done a good thing for me. The poor you will always have with you, but you will not always have me. She has poured this ointment on my body to prepare it for my burial".

5. (Matthew 27:32). A.D. 1st century. Simon, the father of Alexander and Rufus, was a Jew from Cyrene—a region in the north of Africa—who was visiting Jerusalem. He was standing on one of the streets of the city, when he saw a number of Roman soldiers leading Jesus to his crucifixion. The soldiers noticed Simon and forced him to carry Jesus' cross to Golgotha.

Note: If Simon's son Rufus is the same Rufus to whom Paul sent greetings in his letter to the Christians in Rome—as some scholars believe—this would mean that Simon and his family, or at least his son, converted to Christianity.

6. (Luke 7:40). A.D. 1st century. Simon, a Pharisee, invited Jesus to have dinner with him at his home. A woman of ill repute, who lived in the same town, having heard that Jesus was eating in the Pharisee's house, came to the house and stood behind Jesus, crying and wetting his feet with her tears. Then, she dried his feet with her hair, kissed them, and poured perfume on them.

The Pharisee, seeing this, said to himself, "If this man is really a prophet, he would know what kind of a woman this one is!"

Jesus said to him, "Simon, I have something to tell you".

"Yes, Master, tell me", he replied.

"There were two men who owed money to a money lender. One owed five hundred coins, and the other fifty. They were unable to pay, and the money lender forgave them both. Tell me, which of the two will love him more?"

Simon answered, "I suppose that the one to whom he forgave the most".

Jesus said, "Simon, you are right". Pointing at the woman, he said, "Simon, do you see this woman? I came to your house, and you didn't give me any water for my feet, but she has washed my feet with tears. You didn't salute me with a kiss, but this woman has not ceased to kiss my feet. You didn't anoint my head with oil, but this woman has anointed my feet with perfume. Her sins, which are many, are forgiven, because she has loved much. Those who have been forgiven little, show little love".

And to her, he said, "Your sins are forgiven. Your faith has saved you. Go in peace".

The other guests, sitting at the table, asked themselves, "Who is this man who even forgives sins?"

7. (John 6:71). A.D. 1st century. Simon was the father of Judas Iscariot, the disciple who betrayed Jesus.

8. (Acts of the Apostles 8:9). A.D. 1st century. Simon, a Christian convert who lived in Samaria, enjoyed the reputation of being an amazing magician. When Peter and John, who had been sent by the Christian community in Jerusalem, arrived in Samaria, they prayed that the believers should receive the Holy Spirit.

They placed their hands on the converts, and they received the Holy Spirit. Simon was astonished, when he saw the wonders and miracles that Peter and John were performing. He went to them and offered them money. He said to them, "Give me also this power, so that anyone on whom I place my hands will receive the Holy Spirit".

Peter answered, "Your money should die with you! You think that you can buy God's gift with money! You are not worthy to share our work, because your heart is not right in God's sight. Repent of this wicked plan, and pray to God that he will forgive your evil purpose, for I see that you are full of bitter envy and are a prisoner of sin".

Simon begged them to pray to God for him, so that nothing of what they had said would happen to him.

9. (Acts of the Apostles 9:43). A.D. 1st century. Simon, the tanner, was the owner of the house in Joppa, where Peter stayed on the occasion when he had a vision, in which God told him that he was allowed to eat anything, including food that was ritually forbidden to Jews.

Simri

(Hebrew origin: *Watchful*)

(1 Chronicles 26:10). 10th century B.C. Simri, son of Hosah, a Levite descendant of Merari, was one of the gatekeepers of the Tabernacle, during the reign of King David. His brothers were Hilkiah, Tebaliah, and Zechariah. His father Hosah was posted on the western side of the Tabernacle, near the Shallecheth Gate.

Sippai

(Hebrew origin: *Bason-like*)

(1 Chronicles 20:4). 10th century Sippai—called Saph in the second book of Samuel (2 Samuel 21:18)—a descendant of a tribe of giants, was killed by Sibbechai the Hushathite, during a battle between King David's army and the Philistines.

Sisamai

(Uncertain origin and meaning)

(1 Chronicles 2:40). Unspecified date. Sisamai, son of Eleasah and father of Shallum, of the tribe of Judah, was a descendant of Jarha, an Egyptian servant who married the daughter of his master Sheshan.

Sisera

(Uncertain origin and meaning)

1. (Judges 4:2). 12th century B.C. Sisera, the commander of the army of Hazor, the most powerful city kingdom in Canaan, was sent by King Jabin to fight against the Israelites.

Barak, son of Abinoam, from the town of Kedesh in the Naphtali region, was commanded by the prophetess Deborah to take ten thousand men from the tribes of Naphtali and Zebulun, and to march toward Mount Tabor to fight Sisera. Barak agreed with the condition that Deborah should go with him. Although Sisera had nine hundred iron chariots, Barak defeated him and destroyed his army.

Sisera, fleeing on foot, sought refuge in the tent of Jael, the wife of Heber, a member of the Kenite tribe. Jael allowed him to come into the tent, covered him with a mantle, and brought him some milk. As soon as Sisera fell asleep, Jael killed him by hammering a nail in his head.

When Barak, the Israelite commander, approached the tent, Jael came out to meet him and told him that the man that he was pursuing was dead. The power of King Jabin over the Israelites was thus broken.

2. (Ezra 2:53). Unspecified date. Sisera was the ancestor of a clan of Temple servants that returned with Zerubbabel from the Babylonian Exile.

So

(Egyptian origin: Uncertain meaning)

(2 Kings 17:4). 8th century B.C. King So of Egypt was asked by King Hoshea of Israel to come to his aid against Assyria, whose king, Shalmaneser, had attacked Israel. After a siege, which lasted three years, the Assyrians took Hoshea prisoner and destroyed the city of Samaria. This final defeat marked the end of the northern kingdom of Israel, which had been in existence for over two hundred years.

Sodi

(Hebrew origin: *Secretive*)

(Numbers 13:10) 14th century B.C. His son Gaddiel, of the tribe of Zebulun, was one of the twelve men sent by Moses to spy the land of Canaan and report back about its cities and its inhabitants, if they were strong or weak, few or many, and to bring back the fruit of the land. The spies returned and gave a report, which was disheartening and defeatist.

Only two of the spies—Joshua, the son of Nun, and Caleb, the son of Jephunneh—disagreed and told the people that they should not fear the inhabitants of Canaan.

The Israelites refused to listen to the words of Joshua and Caleb, and they started to wail and cry. God punished their cowardice by condemning them to wander forty years in the wilderness, one year for each day that the spies scouted the land.

Solomon

(Hebrew origin: *Peaceful*)

(2 Samuel 5:14). 10th century B.C. Solomon, son of King David and his favorite wife Bathsheba, succeeded his father in the throne of Israel and reigned for forty years. After his death, the northern tribes seceded and the country was split into two, often hostile, kingdoms: Judah in the south, under King Rehoboam, the son of Solomon; and Israel in the north, whose first king was Jeroboam.

In contrast to his predecessors—Saul and David, who both rose from humble beginnings to kingship and constantly fought wars—Solomon was born and raised as a royal prince and enjoyed a lengthy peace, during his reign.

David and Bathsheba's first son, conceived before their marriage, had died in infancy, as God's punishment for David's sin. Later, the couple had four other sons: Solomon, who was called Jedidiah by the prophet Nathan; Shimea, also called Shammuah; Shobab; and Nathan.

Solomon, through his mother, descended from Ahithophel, one of King David's wisest advisers, his counsel being respected by the king almost as if it were the word of God.

Solomon's accession to the throne was far from being an assured matter, because he had several older half brothers ahead of him in the line for the succession, all of them ambitious to become king. Solomon's chances improved

greatly, when two of his brothers met with violent deaths. Absalom killed Amnon in revenge for the rape of his sister Tamar, and, years later, Absalom, who had rebelled against David, was killed by Joab.

After the death of the two older brothers, the next son in line as heir to the kingdom was Adonijah, the fourth son of King David by his wife Haggith. Joab, the army's commander, and Abiathar, the High Priest, supported him in his bid for the throne, but other influential people in the court opposed him, among them Zadok, the other High Priest, and Nathan, the prophet, who sided with Solomon.

When Adonijah invited his brothers—except Solomon—and the leaders of the tribe of Judah to a sacrificial feast, Nathan realized that the time to act had come. He asked Bathsheba to go to King David, tell him what Adonijah was doing, and remind him that he had promised the throne to Solomon.

Bathsheba went to the king, and while she was still talking with him, Nathan came in and confirmed that David had once promised that Solomon would be his heir.

The king, who was old and sick, ordered that Zadok, Nathan, and Benaiah, an officer in the army, should bring Solomon to Gihon, riding on David's mule, and anoint him there as king. This was done, and the people rejoiced and shouted, "God save King Solomon".

Jonathan, the son of Abiathar, came to Adonijah's feast with the news that Solomon had been proclaimed king. All the guests hurriedly left in fear, and Adonijah sought sanctuary at the altar, where he took hold on the horns of the altar, saying, "Let King Solomon swear today to me that he will not kill me with the sword". Solomon had him brought to him and told him to go back to his house.

From the very start of his reign, Solomon showed himself to be an energetic and decisive king, who took vigorous action against opponents and did not shrink from bloody vengeance.

After the death of King David, Adonijah asked Bathsheba to intercede on his behalf with her son, King Solomon, and get his permission to marry Abishag, the beautiful Shunammite girl who had been brought to King David in his old age to minister to him. This, in Solomon's eyes, was tantamount to Adonijah claiming the throne. He did not hesitate and immediately ordered Benaiah to kill his older brother.

Benaiah also executed Joab, who had opposed Solomon's bid to the throne, and Shimei, who had insulted King David, during his flight from Absalom.

With respect to the priest Abiathar, who had made the mistake of supporting Adonijah's failed bid to succeed King David, Solomon spared his life, only because he had carried the Ark of the Covenant before David, but expelled him from the priesthood, and exiled him from Jerusalem to his estate in Anathoth.

Solomon banished the High Priest Abiathar to his native town of Anathoth for having supported Adonijah in his bid for the throne.

Solomon, following the instructions that David, his father, had given him on his deathbed, sent Benaiah to kill Joab, in punishment for having murdered Abner and Amasa. Solomon rewarded Benaiah's loyalty by making him commander of the army.

After eliminating his opposition, Solomon concentrated in ruling the country, reforming the court, maintaining peaceful relations with his neighbors, promoting international trade, and embarking on an ambitious building plan, which embellished Jerusalem and fortified several cities.

Early in his reign, while staying in Gibeon to make sacrifices and burn incense on the altar of the city, God appeared to Solomon in a dream. The king asked God to give him a wise and understanding heart to judge the people, and to be able to discern between good and bad. God, pleased at his request, granted him his wish.

Solomon became known as one of the wisest, wealthiest, and most powerful kings of the eastern lands. He was the author of three thousand proverbs, and he composed one thousand and five songs.

The Bible states that Solomon is the author of three books: Song of Songs, Proverbs, and Ecclesiastes. Exegetes believe that the first one was written during his youth, the second one when he was a mature man, and the third one in his old age.

The most famous example of Solomon's wisdom, intelligence, and sense of justice was the case of the two harlots disputing a baby. The king determined who the real mother was by the reaction of each woman to the prospect of dividing the child into two halves.

His fame became international, and people came from many countries to hear his wisdom. His most famous visitor was the queen of Sheba, a kingdom situated in the south of the Arabian Peninsula, which was rich in gold, frankincense, and myrrh. Solomon needed her products and her trade routes for his commercial network; she needed his cooperation for marketing her goods in the Mediterranean via Solomon's ports.

The queen came to visit him with a great caravan of camels bearing gifts of spices, gold, and precious stones. The royal visitor, after seeing his palace, his servants, and the Temple, was amazed at his wealth and wisdom, which were much greater than what she had been told.

The kingdom that Solomon inherited from his father extended from the Euphrates to the border of Egypt, although it did not include the land of the Philistines. He had dominion over Syria and Transjordan, which meant that he controlled the caravan routes. This brought to him huge commercial benefits, by allowing him to specialize in international trade, such as buying horses in Anatolia and selling them in Egypt, and importing chariots from Egypt to sell in other countries.

His closest ally was Hiram, king of Tyre, who was both a personal friend and a commercial partner. The two kings had a merchant marine joint venture, in which they used Hiram's ships to import gold, exotic trees, and precious stones from Ophir, and precious metals, ivory, apes, and peacocks from Tarshish.

Solomon launched an ambitious building program, aided by King Hiram, who provided craftsmen, lumber, and gold. Hiram sent cedar trees and workers to Solomon to help him build the Temple, in exchange for wheat and olive oil for his household. King Solomon gave him in payment twenty cities in the Galilee, which were a disappointment to Hiram. Solomon embellished Jerusalem by building the magnificent Temple and the royal palace, thus, enhancing the status of Jerusalem as the political and religious center of the nation. The Temple took seven years to build, and the palace another thirteen years.

When the Temple was finished, Solomon celebrated its inauguration with a great feast. The celebrations lasted fourteen days, during which twenty-two thousand oxen and one hundred and twenty thousand sheep were sacrificed.

Solomon also built fortresses at strategic points along the main highways, which passed through the country, and three regional centers for his chariots, Gezer, Megiddo, and Hazor, where archeologists have uncovered impressive and almost identical four-pillar gateways, evidently built according to a uniform, well-devised, royal plan.

Solomon's extensive building projects required a huge labor force and heavy taxation, which embittered many of his subjects. This was aggravated by the contrast between the heavy burdens imposed on the people on the one hand, and the splendor and luxury of the royal court on the other.

The northern tribes resented the special privileges enjoyed by the tribe of Judah, to which Solomon belonged. Thus, the grounds were laid for a rebellion against the king led by Jeroboam, an Ephraimite, who was in charge of the compulsory labor service of the Joseph tribes. The rebellion failed, and Jeroboam fled to Egypt. There, he remained, until the death of Solomon, when he returned and was chosen by the rebellious tribes of the north to be their king.

Solomon's international importance became so great that the Pharaoh of Egypt gave him one of his daughters in marriage—an event without precedent in Egypt—with the city of Gezer as the dowry. Solomon's relations with other kingdoms were also peaceful, cemented by his marriage to many foreign women: Moabites, Ammonites, Edomites, Sidonians, and Hittites. The Bible mentions that he had seven hundred wives and three hundred concubines.

He reorganized the kingdom into twelve administrative districts, with borders specially drawn not to coincide with the tribal boundaries. He did this in order to weaken the loyalty of the people to the tribes and promote the unity of the realm. The governor of each district was responsible for providing food from his district for the king and the royal household for one month out of each year.

During his old age, Solomon, influenced by his foreign wives, did not remain immune to their idolatrous practices. He died, after reigning forty years, and was succeeded by his son Rehoboam, whose mother was Naamah the Ammonitess.

Rehoboam, shortly after his accession to the throne, went to Nablus to be confirmed as king by the northern tribes. Unfortunately, he was ill advised, and he told the northerners that his taxation and repression policies would be even harsher than his father's.

It would not have come as a surprise to a smarter man than Rehoboam that the northerners immediately rebelled against him, seceded from his kingdom, and chose Jeroboam to be their king. Rehoboam remained as king of his tribe, Judah, which continued to be ruled by his descendants, until, centuries later, Babylon captured Jerusalem, destroyed the Temple, and exiled much of the population.

The two sister kingdoms, Judah and Israel, during the following centuries, sometimes were allies and other times fought fratricidal wars.

Sopater

(Greek origin: *Safe father*)

(Acts of the Apostles 20:4). A.D. 1st century. Sopater of Berea was one of the companions of Paul in his final trip from Greece to Jerusalem. The other companions of the apostle in that trip were Gaius of Derbe, Timotheus, Tychicus and Trophimus, and two Thessalonians, called Secundus and Aristarchus.

Note: Some scholars believe that he is the same person as Sosipater. (Please see the entry for Sosipater [Romans 16:21].)

Sophereth

(Hebrew origin: *Scribe*)

(Ezra 2:55). 10th century B.C. Sophereth, a servant of Solomon, was the ancestor of a family that returned with Zerubbabel from the Babylonian Exile.

Sosipater

(Greek origin: *Safe father*)

(Romans 16:21). A.D. 1st century. Sosipater was a Christian mentioned by Paul, in his epistle to the Romans, as being his kinsman who sends his regards.

Note: Some scholars believe that he is the same person as Sopater. (Please see the entry for Sopater [Acts of the Apostles 20:4].)

Sosthenes

(Greek origin: *Safe strength*)

(Acts of the Apostles 18:17). A.D. 1st century. Sosthenes was the leader of the synagogue in Corinth, during the stay of Paul in the city. The Jews seized Paul and brought him before the tribunal, accusing him of trying to persuade people to worship God in a manner that was against the law.

Before Paul could defend himself, Gallio, the Roman governor, said, "If this would be a matter of a crime or wrongdoing, I would be patient with you, Jews. But since the argument is about words, names, and your own law, you must settle it among yourselves. I will not be a judge of these matters", and he drove them away from the tribunal.

The Greeks, who had witnessed the incident, grabbed Sosthenes and beat him in front of Gallio, who did not raise a finger to stop them.

In spite of his initial opposition to the teachings of Paul, Sosthenes eventually converted to Christianity, following the example of Crispus, a leader of the Corinthian synagogue who had become a believer.

A few years later, Sosthenes wrote down the letter that Paul sent to the Corinthians, in which the apostle calls him "our brother" (1 Corinthians 1:1).

Sotai

(Hebrew origin: *Roving*)

(Ezra 2:55). 10th century B.C. Sotai, a servant of Solomon, was the ancestor of a family that returned with Zerubbabel from the Babylonian Exile.

Stachys

(Greek origin: *Head of grain*)

(Romans 16:9). A.D. 1st century. Stachys was a Christian to whom Paul sent greetings in his letter to the Christians in Rome, calling him his "beloved".

Stephanas

(Greek origin: *Crowned*)

(1 Corinthians 1:16). A.D. 1st century. Stephanas and the members of his household were the only persons whom Paul baptized in Corinth, during his second journey, because as Paul wrote, "Christ sent me here not to baptize, but to preach the gospel".

During his stay in Ephesus, several years later, the apostle wrote that he was very glad that Stephanas and two other men— Fortunatus and Achaicus—had come to visit him.

Stephen

(Greek origin: *Crown*)

(Acts of the Apostles 6:5). A.D. 1st century. After the death of Jesus, his Hebrew and Greek followers became known as the Jerusalem church. There was some dissension between the two groups. The Greek converts complained that the Hebrew Christians neglected the Greek widows in the daily distribution of the food.

The twelve apostles summoned all the believers and told them, "It is not right that we should give up preaching the word of God to serve tables. Therefore, brothers, choose from among you seven men, whom we may appoint to this duty, while we devote ourselves to prayer and to the ministry of the word".

The congregation accepted this suggestion, and they chose Stephen and another six men— Nicanor, Philip, Prochorus, Timon, Parmenas, and Nicolas, a proselyte from Antioch—all of them Christians of good reputation, who were respected for their piety and their wisdom, to serve on the tables and distribute food to the needy of the community.

Stephen soon distinguished himself for his great faith, and for doing wonders and miracles. He was opposed by members of the synagogue of the Freedmen, who argued with him. Such was the wisdom of Stephen, and so great was his debating talent, that his opponents were unable to refute his arguments. Therefore, they bribed some men to circulate rumors that he was speaking blasphemies against Moses and God. Stephen was arrested and brought to the presence of the council.

The bribed men, when brought to the council as witnesses, told lies about him, saying, "We heard him say that Jesus of Nazareth will tear down the Temple and change all the customs, which have come down to us from Moses".

The High Priest asked him, "Is this true?" Stephen defended himself with a long speech, in which he reviewed the history of the people of Israel from the days of Abraham to those of King Solomon. He quoted the prophet Isaiah, "Heaven is my throne, and the earth is my footstool" (Isaiah 66:1), and ended by accusing them of betraying and murdering the "righteous one".

While his listeners stared at him with anger, Stephen said, "I see the heavens opened, and the Son of man standing on the right side of God". When they heard this, the council members covered their ears with their hands.

Then, they all rushed at him at once, took him out of the city, and stoned him. The witnesses to Stephen's death left their clothing in the care of a young man named Saul, later known as Paul, who looked on and did nothing to stop the killing.

Stephen's last words were, "Lord Jesus, receive my spirit. Lord, lay not this sin to their charge".

Suah

(Hebrew origin: *Sweeping*)

(1 Chronicles 7:36). Unspecified date. Suah, son of Zophah, was a brave warrior, leader of a clan of the tribe of Asher.

Succothbenoth

(Hebrew origin: *Booths of the daughters*)

(2 Kings 17:30). Succothbenoth was an idol worshipped by the men of Babylon whom the Assyrians settled in Samaria, after they had destroyed it in 722 B.C. and exiled the population.

Susanna

(Hebrew origin: *Lily*)

(Luke 8:3). A.D. 1st century. Susanna, together with Joanna, Mary Magdalene, and other women, accompanied Jesus and the twelve disciples in his teaching tour of Galilean towns and villages, providing for them out of their means.

Susi

(Hebrew origin: *My horse*)

(Numbers 13:11). 14th century B.C. His son Gaddi, of the tribe of Manasseh, was one of the twelve men sent by Moses to spy the land of Canaan and report back about its cities and its inhabitants if they were strong or weak, few or many, and to bring back the fruit of the land. The spies returned and gave a report, which was disheartening and defeatist.

Only two of the spies—Joshua, the son of Nun, and Caleb, the son of Jephunneh—

disagreed and told the people that they should not fear the inhabitants of Canaan.

The Israelites refused to listen to the words of Joshua and Caleb, and they started to wail and cry. God punished their cowardice by condemning them to wander forty years in the wilderness, one year for each day that the spies scouted the land.

Sychem

(Hebrew origin: *Spur of a hill*)

(Acts of the Apostles 7:16). 17th century B.C. Sychem is an alternative spelling for Shechem, the son of Hamor, the ruler of the city of Shechem. Shechem saw Dinah, the daughter of Jacob, raped her, and then asked for her hand in marriage. He was murdered by Dinah's brothers. (See the entry for Shechem [Genesis 34:2].)

Syntyche

(Greek origin: *Accident*)

(Philippians 4:2). A.D. 1st century. Syntyche, a Christian woman living in Philippi, was involved in a disagreement with another Christian woman called Euodias.

Paul, who was grateful to both women for having helped him and Clement, a fellow worker, to spread the word of God, beseeched them in his letter to the Philippians to put aside their quarrel.

Tabbaoth

(Hebrew origin: *Rings*)

(Ezra 2:43). Unspecified date. Tabbaoth was the ancestor of a clan of Temple servants that returned with Zerubbabel from the Babylonian Exile.

Tabeal

(Hebrew origin: *God is good*)

(Isaiah 7:6). 8th century B.C. Tabeal was the father of a man—whose name is not mentioned in the Bible—whom King Pekah of Israel and King Resin of Syria wanted to place on the throne of Judah, instead of King Ahaz.

Tabeel

(Hebrew origin: *God is good*)

(Ezra 4:7). 6th century B.C. Tabeel, Bishlam, and Mithredath, non-Jews who lived in the land of Israel, offered to help the returnees from Babylon in the reconstruction of the Temple. When their offer was rejected, they became offended and angry. As an act of revenge, they wrote a letter in Syrian to Artaxerxes, king of Persia, asking the king to stop the work in the Temple.

Tabitha

(Chaldean origin: *Gazelle*)

(Acts of the Apostles 9:36). A.D. 1st century. Tabitha—Dorcas in Greek—a Christian convert known for her charity and good deeds, was brought back to life by Peter. (Please see the entry for Dorcas.)

Tabrimon

(Hebrew origin: *Rimon is good*)

(1 Kings 15:18). 10th century B.C. Tabrimon, son of Hezion, was the father of

Benhadad, the Syrian king who was contemporary with King Asa of Judah.

Tahan

(Hebrew origin: *Station*)

1. (Numbers 26:35). 16th century B.C. Tahan, son of Ephraim and grandson of Joseph, was the ancestor of the clan of the Tahanites.
2. (1 Chronicles 7:25). Unspecified date. Tahan, son of Telah, a descendant of Ephraim, was the father of Laadan, and an ancestor of Joshua.

Tahath

(Hebrew origin: *Under*)

1. (1 Chronicles 6:24). Unspecified date. Tahath, son of Assir, was the father of Uriel and Zephaniah. His descendant Heman, of the clan of the Kohathites, was one of the Levites appointed by King David to be in charge of the singers in the House of the Lord.
2. (1 Chronicles 7:20). Unspecified date. Tahath, son of Bered, a descendant of Ephraim, was the father of Eladah and the grandfather of Tahath #3.
3. (1 Chronicles 7:20). Unspecified date. Tahath, son of Eladah, a descendant of Ephraim, was the father of Zabad and the grandson of Tahath #2.

Tahpenes

(Egyptian origin: Uncertain meaning)

(1 Kings 11:19). 10th century B.C. Tahpenes was the wife of the Pharaoh who ruled Egypt, during the days of King Solomon.

Her sister married Hadad, an Edomite prince who had survived Joab's massacre of the Edomite males, and who found refuge in Egypt. Tahpenes raised Genubath, Hadad's son, in the palace, where the boy lived with the sons of Pharaoh.

Tahrea

(Hebrew origin: Uncertain meaning)

(1 Chronicles 9:41). Unspecified date. Tahrea—also spelled Tarea (1 Chronicles 8:35)—son of Micah, was a descendant of King Saul. His brothers were, Ahaz, Melech, and Pithon.

Talmai

(Hebrew origin: *Ridged*)

1. (Numbers 13:22). 13th century B.C. Talmai, Sheshai, and Ahiman were three brothers, sons of Anak, and grandsons of Arba, the founder of the city of Hebron. The three brothers' gigantic height made the spies, whom Moses had sent, like grasshoppers. Caleb, the son of Jephunneh, expelled Talmai and his brothers from Hebron, during the conquest of Canaan. The three giants were later killed by the tribe of Judah.

2. (2 Samuel 3:3). 11th century B.C. Talmai, son of Ammihud, was the king of Geshur, a kingdom situated northeast of the Sea of Galilee, in today's Golan Heights.

   His daughter Maacah, one of the wives of King David, was the mother of Absalom and Tamar, the girl who was raped by her half brother Amnon. Absalom, after Amnon was killed, fled to his grandfather's kingdom and stayed with King Talmai for three years, until David allowed him to return to Jerusalem.

Talmon

(Hebrew origin: *Oppressive*)

1. (1 Chronicles 9:17). 10th century B.C. Talmon, a Levite, was one of the gate-keepers—the others were Akkub and Ahiman—in charge of the East Gate of the Tabernacle, under the supervision of Shallum, during the reign of King David. He was the ancestor of a clan of gatekeepers who returned with Zerubbabel from the Babylonian Exile (Ezra 2:42).

2. (Nehemiah 11:19). 5th century B.C. Talmon was one of the gatekeepers of the Temple, during the days of Nehemiah and the High Priest Joiakim.

Tamah

(Hebrew origin: Uncertain meaning)

(Nehemiah 7:55). Unspecified date. Tamah—also spelled Thamah (Ezra 2:53)—was the ancestor of a clan of Temple servants that returned with Zerubbabel from the Babylonian Exile.

Tamar

(Hebrew origin: *Palm tree*)

1. (Genesis 38:6). 17th century B.C. Tamar, the daughter-in-law of Judah, married Er, Judah's firstborn son. When Er died young and childless, Judah told his second son, Onan, to marry Tamar and, thus, provide offspring for his dead brother. Onan, unwilling to have his children carry his brother's name, spilled his seed on the ground, whenever he made love to Tamar. He also died childless.

   Judah, fearful that his youngest son Shelah would also go to an early grave if he would marry Tamar, told her to return to her father's house, and to remain there as a widow "until Shelah would grow up". Years went by, Shelah grew up, but Judah didn't marry him to Tamar.

   After Judah's wife died, and his mourning period was over, Judah went with his sheepshearers and his friend Hirah to Timnath, near the home of Tamar's parents.

   Tamar was told that her father-in-law would be coming for the sheep shearing. She took off her widow's garments, wrapped herself, and, with her face covered by a veil, sat by the side of the road.

   Judah saw her and didn't recognize her. He approached her and, assuming that she was a harlot, told her that he wanted to sleep with her.

   "What", she asked, "will you pay me to sleep with me?"

   "I will send you a young goat from my flock", promised Judah.

Tamar said, "You must leave a pledge with me, until you have sent it".

"What pledge do you want me to give you?"

"Your seal with its cord, and the walking stick that you are carrying", said Tamar.

She received the pledges and slept with him. Then, she went home, took off her veil, and put back her widow's clothing.

Judah, a man of his word, sent his friend Hirah with the young goat to receive his pledges back from the "harlot". Hirah asked some men, "Where is the harlot that sat by the side of the road?"

"There has been no harlot here", they answered.

Unable to find her, Hirah returned to Judah and told him that he couldn't find the harlot.

Judah said, "Let her keep the pledges, or people will laugh at us. I tried to pay her, but you couldn't find her".

Three months later, Judah was told that Tamar was pregnant. Judah, furious, ordered that she should be brought to him and burned.

When Tamar was brought to the presence of Judah, she showed him the pledges and said, "I am pregnant from the man who owns these things. Can you tell to whom do they belong?"

Judah examined them, recognized that they were his, and said, "She is right, because I never gave her my son Shelah". He was never intimate with her again.

Six months later, Tamar gave birth to twins, who were called Pharez and Zarah. During their birth, the midwife, seeing Zarah's hand, tied a scarlet thread on it, but it was his brother Pharez who first came out.

2. (2 Samuel 13:1). 10th century B.C. Tamar, the beautiful daughter of King David and Maacah, was the granddaughter of Talmai, the king of Geshur, a kingdom situated northeast of the Sea of Galilee.

Amnon, David's firstborn, developed a passion for Tamar, his half sister, and,

following his shrewd cousin Jonadab's advice, convinced his father that he was sick, and that he wished that Tamar should bring him food to his house.

David sent Tamar to Amnon's house, where she baked cakes for him. Amnon told his men to go out and leave Tamar alone with him. After raping her, he couldn't stand her sight and had her thrown out of his house.

Tamar put dust on her head, tore the ornamented tunic she was wearing, and walked away, crying loudly as she went. Absalom met her and asked her, "Was it your brother Amnon who did this to you? For the present, sister, keep quiet about it; he is your brother. Don't brood over this matter".

Absalom gave her refuge in his house. David heard what Amnon had done, and, although he was greatly upset, he did not rebuke his son. Absalom also didn't utter a word to Amnon, but silently hated him, and waited patiently for an opportunity to revenge his sister.

Two years later, Absalom saw his opportunity. He invited his father, King David, to a sheep-shearing celebration. The king did not accept the invitation, but he allowed Amnon and his other sons to attend the party. During the feast, Absalom had his servants kill Amnon to avenge his sister's rape.

3. (2 Samuel 14:27). 10th century B.C. Tamar, the daughter of Absalom, was as beautiful as her namesake, her aunt Tamar, the princess who had been raped by her half brother Amnon. She had three brothers whose names are not mentioned in the Bible.

Tammuz

(Uncertain origin and meaning)

(Ezekiel 8:14). Tammuz was a pagan god whose worship was widespread in Judah. Ezekiel, in his vision of abominations, saw a group of women weeping for Tammuz in the gates of the Temple.

Tanhumeth

(Hebrew origin: *Consolation*)

(2 Kings 25:23). 7th century B.C. Tanhumeth, the Netophathite, was the father of Seraiah, an officer of the defeated Judean army who went with a group of other commanders and their men to the city of Mizpah to meet with Gedaliah, son of Ahikam, the newly appointed governor of the Babylonian province of Judah.

Gedaliah told them that everything would be well with them if they would serve the king of Babylon. Sometime later, Ishmael, another officer of the army, murdered Gedaliah.

Taphath

(Hebrew origin: *Drop*)

(1 Kings 4:11). 10th century B.C. Taphath, one of King Solomon's daughters, married one of the kingdom's twelve district governors, a man—son of Abinadab—whose name is not stated by the Bible.

Her husband was responsible for providing food from his district, the territory of Dor, for the king and the royal household for one month out of each year.

Tappuah

(Hebrew origin: *Apple*)

(1 Chronicles 2:43). Unspecified date. Tappuah was the son of Hebron, of the tribe of Judah, and brother of Rekem, Korah, and Shema.

Tarea

(Hebrew origin: Uncertain meaning)

(1 Chronicles 8:35). Unspecified date. Tarea—also spelled Tahrea (1 Chronicles 9:41)—son of Micah, was a descendant of King Saul. His brothers were, Ahaz, Melech, and Pithon.

Tarshish

(Uncertain origin and meaning)

1. (Genesis 10:4). Unspecified date. Tarshish, the son of Javan, was the brother of Elishah, Kittim, and Dodanim.

2. (Esther 1:14). 5th century B.C. Tarshish was one of the seven high officials of Persia and Media—the others were Shethar, Carshena, Admatha, Meres, Marsena, and Memucan—whom King Ahasuerus consulted about the punishment to be imposed on Queen Vashti for disobeying his command to appear before him.

Tartak

(Uncertain origin and meaning)

(2 Kings 17:31). Tartak and Nibhaz were two idols worshipped by the Avites, a foreign people whom the Assyrians settled in Samaria, after they destroyed it in 722 B.C.

Tartan

(Uncertain origin and meaning)

(2 Kings 18:17). 8th century B.C. Tartan, the army commander of Sargon, king of Assyria, captured the city of Ashdod, during the days of the prophet Isaiah.

Later, he marched, with two other commanders, Rabsaris and Rabshakeh, from Lachish to Jerusalem at the head of a great army. King Sennacherib, who had just conquered the city of Lachish, had sent them to demand an unconditional surrender from King Hezekiah of Judah.

A plague on the Assyrian camp decimated the invaders, and Jerusalem was thus saved, but the result of the war was that Judah reverted to its vassal status and continued to pay tribute.

Tatnai

(Persian origin: Uncertain meaning)

(Ezra 5:3). 6th century B.C. Tatnai was the Persian governor of Judea. He and his subordinate Shetharboznai received a report that Zerubbabel and the High Priest Jeshua were rebuilding the Temple in Jerusalem. The officials decided to go personally to Jerusalem, and to see for themselves.

As soon as they arrived in the city, they

asked the Jews who had given them permission to rebuild, and they requested the names of the men working on the construction.

The Jews gave them the information, but the Persian officials decided not to take any action for the time being, until King Darius would answer the letter that they wrote to him, requesting instructions on how to deal with the reconstruction of the Temple, and asking him to order a search of the government records to verify if King Cyrus had allowed the work.

A search was made, and a scroll was found in a palace in Achmetha, in the province of the Medes, which showed that Cyrus had given his full approval to the rebuilding of the Temple, with specific architectural instructions, and orders that the work should be paid from the royal treasury.

The king wrote back ordering Tatnai and Shetharboznai to allow the work to proceed, to help the Jews to rebuild, and to refrain from interfering with the construction. Tatnai and his officials fully and speedily complied with the king's commands.

Tebah

(Hebrew origin: *Slaughter*)

(Genesis 22:24). 19th century B.C. Tebah was one of the sons of Nahor, Abraham's brother, and his concubine Reumah. His brothers were Gaham, Thahash, and Maachah.

Tebaliah

(Hebrew origin: *God has dipped*)

(1 Chronicles 26:11) 10th century B.C. Tebaliah, son of Hosah, a Levite descendant of Merari, was one of the gatekeepers of the Tabernacle, during the reign of King David. His brothers were Simri, Hilkiah, and Zechariah.

Tehinnah

(Hebrew origin: *Graciousness*)

(1 Chronicles 4:12). Unspecified date. Tehinnah, a descendant of Judah, was the son of Eshton and the brother of Bethrapha and Paseah. He founded the town of Irnahash.

Telah

(Hebrew origin: *Breach*)

(1 Chronicles 7:25). Unspecified date. Telah, son of Resheph, a descendant of Ephraim, was the father of Tahan, and an ancestor of Joshua.

Telem

(Hebrew origin: *Oppression*)

(Ezra 10:24). 5th century B.C. Telem, a gatekeeper of the Temple, divorced his foreign wife, during the days of Ezra.

Tema

(Uncertain origin and meaning)

(Genesis 25:15). 18th century B.C. Tema, grandson of Abraham and his Egyptian concubine Hagar, was one of the twelve sons of Ishmael. His brothers were Nebajoth, Kedar, Mibsam, Mishma, Dumah, Massa, Adbeel, Hadad, Jetur, Naphish, and Kedemah, all of them ancestors of great nations. His sister, Mahalath—also called Bashemath—married Esau, the son of Isaac.

Teman

(Hebrew origin: *South*)

(Genesis 36:11). 16th century B.C. Teman, the ancestor of an Edomite clan, was the son of Eliphaz and the grandson of Esau and his wife Adah. His brothers were Gatam, Omar, Zepho, Kenaz, and Amalek.

Temeni

(Hebrew origin: *Southern* or *From Teman, a region in Edom*)

(1 Chronicles 4:6). Unspecified date. Temeni was a son of Ashur and Naarah. His brothers were Ahuzam, Haahashtari, and Hepher. His father, Ashur, of the tribe of Judah, was the founder of Tekoa.

Terah

(Uncertain origin and meaning)

(Genesis 11:24). 20th century B.C. Terah, son of Nahor, was born in Ur of the Chaldees, when his father was twenty-nine years old. His own sons—Abram, Nahor, and Haran—were born, when he was over seventy years old.

After his son Haran died, Terah took his son Abram, (later to be called Abraham), Sarai—the wife of Abram—and his grandson Lot, son of Haran, and left Ur with the intention of going to the land of Canaan. On the way, they stopped in Haran—in today's southern Turkey—and settled there.

Terah died in Haran at the age of two hundred and five.

Teresh

(Uncertain origin and meaning)

(Esther 2:21). 5th century B.C. Teresh was a gatekeeper in the palace of King Ahasuerus, in the city of Shushan, Persia. He conspired with Bigthan, another palace gatekeeper, to kill the king. Mordecai learned of the plot and told it to Queen Esther, who reported it to the king. An investigation found the two conspirators guilty, and they were hanged from a tree.

Tertius

(Latin: *Third*)

(Romans 16:22). A.D. 1st century. Tertius wrote the letter to the Roman church, which Paul dictated to him, and added his own personal greetings.

Tertullus

(Uncertain origin and meaning)

(Acts of the Apostles 24:1). A.D. 1st century. Tertullus, an eloquent speaker, was brought by the High Priest Ananias to Caesarea to serve as his spokesman, and to present to Felix, the Roman governor, the charges against Paul. These accusations included sedition, incitement, and profanation of the Temple.

Tertullus stood up, before Felix, and said, "First of all we wish to thank you, Governor Felix, for the peace that we are enjoying, and for the excellent reforms that you have carried out for the good of our country. But I do not wish to take too much of your time; I will be brief.

"I beg you to be kind and hear my account. This is a pestilent man; he incites the Jews all over the world to riot, and is one of the ringleaders of the Nazarene sect. We caught him, when he attempted to defile the Temple, and would have judged him according to our Law if the commander Lysias, by violent means, had not taken him away from us, and commanded us to bring charges against him before you. If you examine him yourself, you will verify our accusations".

The Jews joined in the accusation and said that all the charges were true.

Felix, after hearing Paul eloquently deny the charges and state that the real reason why he was being tried was for believing in the resurrection of the dead, decided to await the arrival of Claudius Lysias, the military commander of Jerusalem, to find out from him more detailed information about Paul's activities in Jerusalem. In the meantime, he gave limited liberty to Paul under the supervision of a centurion.

Thaddaeus

(Uncertain origin and meaning)

(Matthew 10:3). A.D. 1st century. Thaddaeus is the name, by which, the evangelists Matthew and Mark call the apostle Judas, the son of James (Luke 6:16).

Thaddaeus, whom Matthew also calls Lebbaeus, was, according to some scholars, the author of the book of Jude, although other scholars believe that the author was Judas, the brother of Jesus.

Thahash

(Uncertain origin and meaning)

(Genesis 22:24). 19th century B.C. Thahash was one of the sons of Nahor, Abraham's brother. His mother was Nahor's concubine Reumah. His brothers were Gaham, Tebah, and Maachah.

Thamah

(Hebrew origin: Uncertain meaning)

(Ezra 2:53). Unspecified date. Thamah—also spelled Tamah (Nehemiah 7:55)—was the ancestor of a clan of Temple servants that returned with Zerubbabel from the Babylonian Exile.

Thamar

(Hebrew origin: *Palm tree*)

(Matthew 1:3). 17th century B.C. Thamar is an alternative spelling for Tamar, the daughter-in-law of Judah, who had been married to his sons Er and Onan. After their death, Tamar, realizing that Judah did not intend her to marry his third son Shelah, tricked him into making her pregnant and, in due time, gave birth to the twins Pharez and Zarah. (Please see the entry for Tamar #1 [Genesis 38:6].)

Thara

(Uncertain origin and meaning)

(Luke 3:34). 20th century B.C. Thara is an alternative spelling for Terah, the father of Abraham. (Please see the entry for Terah [Genesis 11:24].)

Tharshish

(Uncertain origin and meaning)

(1 Chronicles 7:10). Unspecified date. Tharshish, son of Bilhan, was the brother of Jeush, Benjamin, Ehud, Chenaanah, Zethan, and Ahishahar. He was a brave warrior and the leader of a clan of Benjamites.

Theophilus

(Greek: *Friend of God*)

(Luke 1:3). A.D. 1st century. Theophilus was the addressee of the gospel according to Luke and the Acts of the Apostles. He is called Most Excellent by the author of these books, a salutation that indicates that Theophilus was a person of high social standing.

The author also mentions that Theophilus had been instructed in the Christian faith, and states that the two books are intended to improve his understanding and knowledge of the teachings of Jesus, and the events concerning the followers of Christ.

Theudas

(Uncertain origin and meaning)

(Acts of the Apostles 5:36). A.D. 1st century. Theudas, as reported by Gamaliel to the Jewish Council, headed a band of four hundred men who rebelled against the Romans. He was killed and his followers scattered.

Thomas

(Hebrew origin: *Twin*)

(Matthew 10:3). A.D. 1st century. It is possible that the name Thomas, meaning *Twin*, and its Greek translation Didymus, are nicknames of an apostle whose real name is not known.

Thomas was loyal to Jesus to the point that he was ready to die for him and with him (John 11:16), but he did not hesitate to interrupt Jesus by asking him questions if he thought that something was not clear (John 14:5).

He was a practical man who preferred the evidence of his own eyes to the reports of others. When he heard that the other disciples had seen Jesus resurrected, he refused to believe them, until one day, in his presence, Jesus appeared to them and showed them his wounds (John 20:27).

Thomas was together with Peter and several other disciples at the sea of Tiberias during the third and last time that Jesus appeared to them, after he had risen from the dead.

Thomas is last mentioned in the New Testament (Acts of the Apostles 1:13), when the disciples got together in the Upper Room to choose a replacement for Judas.

Tiberius

(Latin origin: *From the river Tiber*)

(Luke 3:1). A.D. 1st century. Tiberius, the successor of Augustus, ruled the Roman Empire, during the years of Jesus' ministry and death. Herod Antipas, to honor the emperor, gave the name of Tiberias to the city that he founded on the shores of the Sea of Galilee.

During the fifteenth year of his reign, John the Baptist started to preach in the wilderness. At that time, Pontius Pilate was the governor of Judea, and Annas and Caiaphas were the High Priests.

Tibni

(Hebrew origin: *Strawy*)

(1 Kings 16:21). 9th century B.C. Tibni, son of Ginath, fought Omri for the throne of Israel, after the suicide of the usurper Zimri. Although his cause was supported by half of the population, Tibni was defeated and killed by Omri.

Tidal

(Hebrew origin: *Fearfulness*)

(Genesis 14:1). 19th century B.C. Tidal, king of nations, made an alliance with Arioch, king of Ellasar; Amraphel, king of Shinar; and Chedorlaomer, king of Elam.

Chedorlaomer, king of Elam—a kingdom in what today is Iran—had been for twelve years the overlord of several kingdoms situated in the Dead Sea region. On the thirteenth year, these kingdoms rebelled.

Tidal and his allies went to war in the valley of Siddim against five Canaanite kings: Bera, king of Sodom; Birsha, king of Gomorrah; Shinab, king of Admah; Shemeber, king of Zeboiim; and the king of Bela.

The allies defeated the five kings, carried away booty, and took with them a number of captives, including Lot, Abraham's nephew.

Abraham pursued them as far as Hobah, near Damascus, rescued the captives, and recuperated the booty.

Tiglathpileser

(Uncertain origin and meaning)

(2 Kings 15:29). 8th century B.C. The king of Assyria, Tiglathpileser—also spelled Tilgathpilneser (1 Chronicles 5:6) and called Pul in another verse (2 Kings 15:19)—was asked by King Ahaz of Judah to help him against King Pekah of Israel and King Rezin of Aram, who had invaded his kingdom and besieged Jerusalem.

Ahaz, to persuade the Assyrian king, sent him the treasuries of the Temple and the royal palaces as tribute.

Tiglathpileser attacked Damascus, captured it, and killed King Rezin. Then, he invaded Israel, conquered the largest part of its territory, and annexed it to the Assyrian Empire. He deported most of the population to Assyria and left Pekah in control only over the city of Samaria and the surrounding areas.

The Assyrian king stayed in Damascus for sometime, where he received the visit of King Ahaz who came to pay him homage.

Tikvah

(Hebrew origin: *Hope*)

1. (2 Kings 22:14). 7th century B.C. Tikvah, son of Harhas—called Tikvath, son of Hasrah, in the second book of Chronicles (2 Chronicles 34:22)—was the father of Shallum. His son, the husband of the prophetess Huldah, was the keeper of the wardrobe, during the reign of King Josiah.

2. (Ezra 10:15). 5th century B.C. His son Jahaziah was one of the two leaders of Judah—the other one was Jonathan, the son of Asahel—who, helped by the Levites Meshullam and Shabbethai, remained in Jerusalem to represent the people, when Ezra deliberated on the matter of the marriages to foreign women.

Tikvath

(Hebrew origin: *Hope*)

(2 Chronicles 34:22). 7th century B.C. Tikvath, son of Hasrah—called Tikvah, son of Harhas, in the second book of Kings (2 Kings

22:14)—was the father of Shallum. His son, the husband of the prophetess Huldah, was the keeper of the wardrobe, during the reign of King Josiah.

Tilgathpilneser

(Uncertain origin and meaning)

(1 Chronicles 5:6). 8th century B.C. The king of Assyria, Tilgathpilneser—also spelled Tiglathpileser and called Pul in another verse (2 Kings 15:19)—came to the help of King Ahaz of Judah against King Pekah of Israel and King Rezin of Aram, who had attacked Judah. (Please see the entry for Tiglathpileser [2 Kings 15:29].)

Tilon

(Hebrew origin: *Suspension*)

(1 Chronicles 4:20). Unspecified date. Tilon, son of Shimon, was a descendant of Judah. His brothers were Rinnah, Benhanan, and Amnon.

Timaeus

(Hebrew origin: *Defiled*)

(Mark 10:46). A.D. 1st century. His son was a blind beggar whose sight was restored by Jesus. (See the entry for Bartimaeus.)

Timna

(Hebrew origin: *Restraint*)

1. (Genesis 36:12). 17th century B.C. Timna, the concubine of Eliphaz, son of Esau, was the mother of Amalek.
2. (Genesis 36:22). Unspecified date. Timna was the daughter of Seir the Horite, ancestor of the clans that settled in the land of Edom. Her brothers were Lotan, Dishan, Shobal, Zibeon, Dishon, Ezer, and Anah.
3. (1 Chronicles 1:36). 17th century B.C. Timna was the son of Eliphaz and the grandson of Esau. His brothers were Teman, Omar, Zephi, Gatam, Kenaz, and Amalek.

Timnah

(Hebrew origin: *Restraint*)

(Genesis 36:40). Unspecified date. Timnah, a descendant of Esau, was the leader of an Edomite clan.

Timon

(Greek origin: *Valuable*)

(Acts of the Apostles 6:5). A.D. 1st century. After the death of Jesus, his Hebrew and Greek followers became known as the Jerusalem church. There was some dissension between the two groups. The Greek converts complained that the Hebrew Christians neglected the Greek widows in the daily distribution of the food.

The twelve apostles summoned all the believers and said to them, "It is not right that we should give up preaching the word of God to serve tables. Therefore, brothers, choose from among you seven men, whom we may appoint to this duty, while we devote ourselves to prayer and to the ministry of the word".

The congregation accepted this suggestion, and they chose Timon and another six men—Stephen, Philip, Prochorus, Nicanor, Parmenas, and Nicolas, a proselyte from Antioch—all of them Christians of good reputation, who were respected for their piety and their wisdom, to serve on the tables and distribute food to the needy of the community.

Timotheus

(Greek: *Dear to God*)

(Acts of the Apostles 16:1). A.D. 1st century. Timotheus—also called Timothy (2 Corinthians 1:1)—was loved by Paul as a son. He was the apostle's companion, fellow worker, invaluable helper, and messenger. (Please read the entry for Timothy [2 Corinthians 1:1].)

Timothy

(Greek: *Dear to God*)

(2 Corinthians 1:1). A.D. 1st century. Timothy—also called Timotheus (Acts of the

Apostles 16:1)—was Paul's companion, fellow worker, invaluable helper, and messenger. But, he was more than that. He was loved by the apostle as the son he never had.

Timothy, the son of a Greek man, whose name is not mentioned, and a Jewish woman called Eunice, daughter of a woman called Lois, was a member of the Christian community of Lystra.

Paul, who was acquainted with Eunice and Lois, heard excellent reports about Timothy, and he decided to take the young man along on his trips, but first, he circumcised him, because the Jews in those places knew that his father was Greek.

Paul, Silas, and Timothy traveled to several cities, with the apostle, preaching and converting many of his listeners. When they arrived in Berea, they went to the synagogue, where their preaching met with much success. Their listeners heard them with open minds and checked the Scriptures to verify if their assertions were true. Many converted, including some Greek men and women of high social standing.

The Jews of Thessalonica, hearing that Paul was preaching in Berea, came to the town, to incite the crowd. The believers immediately sent Paul off to a seaport. Silas and Timothy remained in Berea, until Paul arrived in Athens and sent them word to come to him.

Paul left Athens and went to Corinth. There, he stayed in the house of Aquila and his wife Priscilla, Jewish converts. Paul went to the synagogue every Sabbath and preached to the Jews and the Greeks.

When Silas and Timothy arrived from Macedonia, they found him fully occupied, testifying to the Jews that Jesus was the Messiah.

After visiting other cities and regions, the apostle went to the province of Asia. From there, Paul sent Timothy and Erastus, another of his helpers, to Macedonia, while he stayed for a while longer in Asia.

Sometime later, Paul moved to Greece, where he stayed three months. While he was in Athens, he sent Timothy to Thessalonica to strengthen the faith of the Thessalonians, and

to encourage them to endure their persecution. Timothy returned with good news about the faith and the love shown to him by the Thessalonians.

Paul was ready to go to Syria, when he discovered that the Jews were plotting against him, so he decided to return through Macedonia. Timothy and several other men— Sopater, Aristarchus, Secundus, Gaius, Tychicus, and Trophimus—went ahead and waited for Paul in Troas.

Timothy sent his regards to the Roman church in the letter that Paul dictated to Tertius, where the apostle calls the young man "my fellow worker".

In his first letter to the Corinthian church, Paul tells them that he has sent them Timothy, "my beloved son", to remind them of his teachings, and the principles that rule a Christian life. In the same letter, he asked them to treat Timothy with respect, because he was doing the work of the Lord.

Timothy is mentioned as Paul's coauthor in several of the apostle's letters. In his letter to the Philippians, Paul mentioned that he would shortly send them Timothy, because, "He is the only one who shares my thinking, and who cares for you. Others are concerned with their own affairs, not with those of Jesus. You know his worth, how we have worked together, like father and son, in the service of the gospel".

Paul wrote two letters to Timothy. The first letter, probably written before he was imprisoned in Rome, warns against false teachings in the church and gives instructions about church administration and worship. The apostle also advises Timothy how to serve Jesus, and how to behave toward different groups of believers.

Paul's second letter to Timothy, probably the last one he wrote, consists largely of personal advice to his young companion. Although Paul was writing from prison, and his end was near, the letter is filled with courage and strength. Paul urges Timothy to continue being a faithful witness to Jesus, to remain true to the teachings of the Good News and the Scriptures, to endure in spite of persecution and suffering, and to continue his mission as a teacher and evangelist. Paul ends his letter by cautioning Timothy about the dangers of becoming involved in worthless arguments that can only bring harm to the people who listen to them.

Tiras

(Uncertain origin and meaning)

(Genesis 10:2). Unspecified date. Tiras, son of Japheth and grandson of Noah, was the brother of Magog, Madai, Javan, Tubal, Meshech, and Gomer.

Tirhakah

(Uncertain origin and meaning)

(2 Kings 19:9). 8th century B.C. Tirhakah, king of Ethiopia, was asked by King Hezekiah to come to his help against Sennacherib, king of Assyria, who had invaded Judah.

The Bible does not mention if Tirhakah came to Jerusalem, but Sennacherib returned to Assyria without having captured the city. A short time later, while praying in the Temple of the god Nisroch, in his capital Nineveh, he was murdered by his sons Adrammelech and Sharezer.

Tirhanah

(Uncertain origin and meaning).

(1 Chronicles 2:48). Unspecified date. Tirhanah was a son of Caleb—also called Chelubai—and his concubine Maachah. His brothers were Shaaph, Sheber, and Sheva.

Tiria

(Hebrew origin: *Fearful*)

(1 Chronicles 4:16). Unspecified date. Tiria, son of Jehaleleel, a descendant of Judah, was the brother of Ziph, Ziphah, and Asareel.

Tirshatha

(Persia origin: *Governor*)

(Ezra 2:63). 5th century. Tirshatha, the Persian term for "governor" was used in the Bible to refer to Nehemiah.

Tirzah

(Hebrew origin: *Delightsomeness*)

(Numbers 26:33). 13th century B.C. Tirzah was one of the five daughters of Zelophehad, the son of Hepher, of the tribe of Manasseh.

When their father died, Tirzah and her sisters—Hoglah, Noah, Mahlah, and Milcah—came to Moses and Eleazar the High Priest, and they asked to inherit from their father, who had died without sons.

Moses, after consulting with God, modified the law to entitle a daughter to inherit from her father if he did not have any sons, but with the condition that she had to marry within the clan, in order that her inheritance would remain in her tribe.

After the death of Moses, the sisters came to Joshua and demanded, as their lawful right, a portion of the conquered territories, which had been given to the tribe of Manasseh.

Titus (Latin origin: Uncertain meaning)

(2 Corinthians 2:13). A.D. 1st century. Titus, a Greek convert, was Paul's "partner and fellow helper", a companion in many of his trips, and an addressee of one of his letters.

While Paul was in Antioch, some men who came from Judea told the believers that, to be saved, they had first to be circumcised according to the Law of Moses. Paul and Barnabas disagreed and argued fiercely with them. It was then decided that Paul, Barnabas, and some of the other leaders of the Antiochian church, including Titus, an uncircumcised Greek convert, should go to Jerusalem and consult with the apostles and the elders about this question.

Barnabas, Paul, and Titus traveled to Jerusalem and took part in the Jerusalem's church debate over the admission of Gentiles to the community of believers. Paul's refusal to circumcise Titus became a symbol of his determination to receive Gentiles into the church.

Paul sent Titus on missions to several cities, among them Corinth (2 Corinthians 12:18), Dalmatia (2 Timothy 4:10), and Nicopolis (Titus 3:12).

Titus had a special place in his heart for the Corinthian church, and Paul tells of the great joy that Titus felt, when he heard that some problems that Paul had with the Corinthians were now solved.

The last mission that Titus undertook on Paul's behalf was to organize and oversee the church in Crete.

Toah

(Hebrew origin: *Humble*)

(1 Chronicles 6:34). Unspecified date. Toah, son of Zuph, an Ephratite, was the father of Eliel, an ancestor of the prophet Samuel.

Toah was also called Tohu (1 Samuel 1:1), and Nahath (1 Chronicles 6:26). His father Zuph was also called Zophai. His son Eliel was also called Eliab and Elihu.

Tobadonijah

(Hebrew origin: *The Lord, my God, is good*)

(2 Chronicles 17:8). 9th century B.C. Tobadonijah, a Levite, was sent by King Jehoshaphat in the third year of his reign, to teach the laws of God in the cities of Judah. Tobadonijah was accompanied on his mission by other Levites, by two priests—Elishama and Jehoram—and by several officials of the court.

Tobiah

(Hebrew origin: *God's goodness*)

1. (Ezra 2:60). Unspecified date. Tobiah was the ancestor of a family that returned with Zerubbabel from the Babylonian Exile. The members of this family were dismissed from the priesthood, because they could not prove their genealogy.

2. (Nehemiah 2:10). 5th century B.C. Tobiah, the Ammonite, a sworn enemy of Nehemiah, enjoyed the friendship of many people in Judah, because he was related by marriage to some of the most prominent Jewish families. His father-in-law was Shechaniah, the son of Arah, and his son Johanan had married the daughter of Meshullam, the son of Berechiah.

When Tobiah and his allies, Sanballat the Horonite and Geshem the Arab, first heard that Nehemiah was coming to Jerusalem to work for the welfare of the Jews, they became very upset. The three men ridiculed the efforts of Nehemiah to rebuild the walls of Jerusalem, and they accused him of wanting to rebel against the Persian king.

Tobiah made fun of the construction work, saying, "A fox going up will be enough to break down their stone walls".

Nehemiah didn't pay them any attention, and the work on the walls proceeded, until its completion. When Tobiah, Sanballat, the Arabs, the Ammonites, and the Ashdodites heard that the walls had been finished, their scorn changed to anger, and they conspired to go and fight against Jerusalem.

Sanballat and Geshem decided to capture Nehemiah. They sent him an invitation to meet with them in one of the villages in the plain of Ono. Nehemiah, rightly suspecting that it was a trap, refused to go, giving as an excuse that he was too busy with his work. The two men sent the invitation four more times, and each time, Nehemiah gave them the same answer. The fifth time, they included a letter accusing him of inciting rebellion and planning to make himself king. Nehemiah answered that those accusations were figments of their imagination.

One of the last efforts by Sanballat and Tobiah to discredit Nehemiah was to hire Shemaiah, the son of Delaiah, to convince Nehemiah that he should hide in the Temple. That plot also failed.

After twelve years of staying in Jerusalem, Nehemiah took a leave of absence and returned to Persia to visit the king. When he returned to Jerusalem, he was surprised to find that, during his absence, the priest Eliashib, who was in charge of the rooms in the Temple, had given a chamber—which previously had served as a stockroom for the equipment of the Temple, incense, grain, wine, oil, and the gifts of the priests—to Tobiah, Nehemiah's enemy.

Nehemiah, greatly displeased, ordered to throw out all the belongings of Tobiah, purify the chamber, and bring back to the room the equipment of the Temple, the incense, and the other items, which previously had been kept there.

Tobijah

(Hebrew origin: *God's goodness*)

1. (2 Chronicles 17:8). 9th century B.C. Tobijah, a Levite, was sent by King Jehoshaphat, during the third year of his reign, to teach the laws of God in the cities of Judah. Tobijah was accompanied in his mission by other Levites, by two priests—Elishama and Jehoram—and by several officials of the court.

2. (Zechariah 6:10). 6th century B.C. Tobijah, a returnee from the Babylonian Exile, was taken by the prophet Zechariah, together with two other returnees, Heldai and Jedaiah, to the house of Josiah, son of Zephaniah, where they made crowns of gold and silver, and they placed them on the head of the High Priest Joshua, son of Josedech. The crowns remained in the Temple as a memorial to the three donors.

Togarmah

(Uncertain origin and meaning)

(Genesis 10:3). Unspecified date. Togarmah, son of Gomer, was a grandson of Japheth. His brothers were Riphath and Ashkenaz.

Tohu

(Hebrew origin: *Abasement*)

(1 Samuel 1:1). Unspecified date. Tohu, son of Zuph, an Ephratite, was the father of Elihu, an ancestor of the prophet Samuel.

Tohu was also called Toah (1 Chronicles 6:34), and Nahath (1 Chronicles 6:26). His father Zuph was also called Zophai. His son Elihu was also called Eliab and Eliel.

Toi

(Hebrew origin: *Error*)

(2 Samuel 8:9). 10th century B.C. Toi—called Tou in the first book of Chronicles (1 Chronicles 18:9)—king of Hamath, rejoiced, when he heard that David had defeated the army of Hadadezer, king of Zobah, a neighboring nation against which he had fought many wars.

He sent his son Joram—also called Hadoram (1 Chronicles 18:10)—with gifts of gold, silver, and brass, to salute David and congratulate him.

Tola

(Hebrew origin: *Worm*)

1. (Genesis 46:13). 17th century B.C. Tola, son of Issachar and a grandson of Jacob, was among the seventy Israelites who immigrated to Egypt. His brothers were Phuvah, Job, and Shimron. His sons were Uzzi, Rephaiah, Jeriel, Jahmai, Jibsam, and Shemuel. Tola was the ancestor of the clan of the Tolaites.

2. (Judges 10:1). 12th century B.C. Tola, of the tribe of Issachar, son of Puah and grandson of Dodo, lived in Shamir in the region of Ephraim. After the death of Abimelech, Tola judged Israel, during twenty-three years. When he died, he was buried in Shamir. Jair, the Gileadite, judged Israel after him.

Note: In the book of Judges, a judge is a ruler or governor of territory or a military leader in pre-monarchical Israel. Later, during the monarchy, the king served in this role and judges were more like the judicial officers that we know today.

Tou

(Hebrew origin: *Error*)

(1 Chronicles 18:9). 10th century B.C. Tou—also called Toi in the second book of Samuel (2 Samuel 8:9)—king of Hamath, rejoiced, when he heard that David had defeated the army of Hadadezer, king of Zobah, a neighboring nation against which he had fought many wars.

He sent his son Hadoram—also called Joram (2 Samuel 8:10)—with gifts of gold, silver, and brass, to salute David, and to congratulate him.

Trophimus

(Greek origin: *Nutritive*)

(Acts of the Apostles 20:4). A.D. 1st century. Trophimus of Ephesus, a Gentile convert, was one of Paul's travel companions. In one of their trips, he became sick at Miletum, and Paul was forced to leave him behind.

Trophimus was with Paul in his final trip from Greece to Jerusalem. The other companions of the apostle in that trip were two Thessalonians—called Secundus and Aristarchus—Gaius of Derbe, Timotheus, Tychicus, and Sopater of Berea.

Trophimus was the unwitting cause of Paul's eventual imprisonment and death in Rome. Paul's opponents had seen Trophimus, walking around Jerusalem with Paul, and used this as a pretext to publicly accuse Paul of defiling the Temple by having brought a Gentile, Trophimus, into the holy place.

The aroused crowd ran to Paul, seized him, and dragged him out of the Temple. At once, the guards closed the Temple gates. The mob was trying to kill Paul, when Claudius Lysias, the commander of the Roman troops, was told that the people of Jerusalem were rioting. He immediately ran toward the crowd, with his soldiers and centurions, and took Paul into custody.

Claudius sent Paul to Caesarea, where Felix, the Roman governor, placed him under home arrest. Two years later, Festus, the new governor, sent Paul to Rome, where, years later, he was executed.

Tryphena

(Greek origin: *Luxurious*)

(Romans 16:12). A.D. 1st century. Tryphena and Tryphosa were two Christian women to whom Paul sent greetings in his letter to the Christians in Rome.

Tryphosa

(Greek origin: *Luxuriating*)

(Romans 16:12). A.D. 1st century. Tryphosa and Tryphena were two Christian women to whom Paul sent greetings in his letter to the Christians in Rome.

Tubal

(Hebrew origin: Uncertain meaning)

(Genesis 10:2). Unspecified date. Tubal was the son of Japheth and the grandson of Noah. His brothers were Gomer, Magog, Madai, Javan, Meshech, and Tiras.

Tubalcain

(Hebrew origin: Uncertain meaning)

(Genesis 4:22). Antediluvian. Tubalcain, an expert artisan of cooper and iron, was one of the sons of Lamech, a descendant of Cain. His mother was Zillah, and his sister was Naamah. His half brothers—sons of Adah, Lamech's other wife—were Jabal and Jubal.

Tychicus

(Greek origin: *Fortunate*)

(Acts of the Apostles 20:4). A.D. 1st century. Tychicus of Ephesus was one of Paul's companions and helpers. The apostle called him "a beloved brother and faithful minister in the Lord".

Tychicus was sent by Paul on missions to several cities, including Ephesus and Colossae. In his letter to Titus, Paul wrote that he intended to send either Artemas or Tychicus to Crete, probably to substitute for Titus, whom the apostle wanted to come and spend the winter with him at Nicopolis.

Tychicus traveled to Colossae with Onesimus, an escaped slave whom Paul had converted to Christianity. He carried with him two letters from Paul, one to the Christian community of the city, and the other one to Philemon, Onesimus' master, a prominent Christian whose house hosted the church in Colossae. Paul, in his letter, asked Philemon to be reconciled to his slave, and to welcome him not only as a forgiven slave but as a brother in Christ.

Tychicus was with Paul in his final trip from Greece to Jerusalem. The other companions of the apostle in that trip were two Thessalonians—called Secundus and Aristarchus—Gaius of Derbe, Timotheus, Trophimus, and Sopater of Berea.

Tyrannus

(Greek origin: *Tyrant*)

(Acts of the Apostles 19:9). A.D. 1st century. Tyrannus owned a hall or school in Ephesus. During his stay in Ephesus, Paul preached in the synagogue, arguing and trying to convince the people about the Kingdom of God. Some of them stubbornly rejected the teachings of Paul, and they spoke evil about the Way of God in front of the whole congregation.

Paul ceased to go to that synagogue. He took the believers with him and, for the next two years, held daily discussions in the hall of Tyrannus.

Ucal

(Hebrew origin: *Eaten*)

(Proverbs 30:1). Unspecified date. Ucal was one of the two men—the other was Ithiel—to whom Agur, the son of Jakeh, spoke his proverbs.

Uel

(Hebrew origin: *God's will*)

(Ezra 10:34). 5th century B.C. Uel, a descendant of Bani, divorced his foreign wife, during the days of Ezra.

Ulam

(Hebrew origin: *Solitary*)

1. (1 Chronicles 7:16). 16th century B.C. Ulam, a descendant of Machir, of the tribe of Manasseh, was the father of Bedan and the brother of Rakem.
2. (1 Chronicles 8:39). Unspecified date. Ulam, the firstborn son of Eshek of the tribe of Benjamin, was a descendant of Jonathan, the son of King Saul. His brothers were Jehush and Eliphelet. His descendants were famous for being skillful archers and brave men.

Ulla

(Hebrew origin: *Burden*)

(1 Chronicles 7:39). Unspecified date. Ulla, of the tribe of Asher, was the father of Arah, Haniel, and Rezia. His sons were brave warriors and clan chiefs.

Unni

(Hebrew origin: *Afflicted*)

1. (1 Chronicles 15:18). 10th century B.C. Unni was one of the Levites of the second rank who played musical instruments in front of the Ark of the Covenant, when it was carried from the house of Obededom to its resting place in Jerusalem, during the reign of David.
2. (Nehemiah 12:9). 6th century B.C. Unni was a Levite who returned with Zerubbabel from the Babylonian Exile.

Ur

(Hebrew origin: *Light*)

(1 Chronicles 11:35). 11th century B.C. Ur—also called Ahasbai (2 Samuel 23:34)—was the father of Eliphal—also called Eliphelet—one of King David's brave warriors.

Urbane

(Latin origin: *Of the city*)

(Romans 16:9). A.D. 1st century. Urbane was a Christian to whom Paul sent greetings in his letter to the church in Rome, calling him his "helper in Christ".

Uri

(Hebrew origin: *My Light*)

1. (Exodus 31:2). 14th century B.C. Uri was the son of Hur, of the tribe of Judah. His son Bezaleel—a gifted craftsman, expert in working in gold, silver, brass, wood, and embroidering—was chosen by God to design and carry out the work for the Tabernacle, the Ark, the furniture, and the altar.
2. (1 Kings 4:19). 10th century B.C. His son Geber was one of Solomon's twelve district governors, in charge of the territories of Gilead and Bashan, which once had been ruled by Sihon, king of the Amorites, and Og, king of Bashan. Geber was responsible for providing food from his district for the king and the royal household for one month out of each year.
3. (Ezra 10:24). 5th century B.C. Uri, a Levite gatekeeper of the Temple, divorced his foreign wife, during the days of Ezra.

Uriah

(Hebrew origin: *God is my light*)

1. (2 Samuel 11:3). 10th century B.C. Uriah the Hittite, a member of an elite army group known as The Thirty", was a loyal officer who served under Joab. During a war against the Ammonites, Uriah went with the army to fight against them.

   One warm evening, while the army was in campaign against the Ammonites, King David, who had stayed in Jerusalem, went up to the rooftop of his palace and saw, in one of the neighboring houses, a beautiful woman washing herself. He made some inquiries and was told that the woman was Bathsheba, Uriah's wife. David had her brought to the palace, made love to her, and then sent her back to her house.

   Some weeks later, the king was informed that she was pregnant. In order to avoid a scandal, David ordered that Uriah should return immediately to Jerusalem, ostensibly to report about the war, but in reality to give him the opportunity of spending a night with his wife.

   Uriah came to Jerusalem and was received by the king in the palace. After hearing Uriah's report about the war situation, the king told him to go to his house and rest. However, Uriah did not go to his wife. Instead, he spent that night, and the following night, sleeping at the entrance of the king's palace with the guards.

   David, hiding his annoyance, asked him, "Why didn't you go to your house and sleep there?"

   Uriah answered, "While my army comrades are in the front lines, and sleeping in tents, I will not sleep in my own home and be with my wife".

   David came to the conclusion that only the death of Uriah would prevent a scandal. He wrote a letter to Joab, ordering him to arrange that Uriah should be sent to the forefront of the battle, and there, he should be abandoned by his fellow soldiers to make sure that he would be killed. The king sealed it and gave it to Uriah to carry it to Joab.

   Joab carried David's orders, and Uriah was killed as planned. The king married Bathsheba, as soon as her days of mourning were over, and, when her time was due, she gave birth to a baby boy.

   The prophet Nathan came to David and told him a parable of a rich man who owned many sheep. When a traveler came to his house, the rich man took his poor neighbor's lamb, instead of one of his, and cooked it to serve it to his visitor.

   David, not understanding the allusion, became outraged and threatened to punish the rich man for his lack of pity. Nathan exclaimed, "You are that man". David expressed remorse and recognized that he had sinned. Nathan told him that he would not die, but the baby would. And so, it happened: the baby fell sick and died.

2. (Ezra 8:33). 5th century B.C. Uriah, a priest, was the father of Meremoth, who—with the help of three Levites: Eleazar, son of Phinehas; Jozabad, son of Jeshua; and Noadiah, son of Binnui—counted and weighed the silver and gold utensils of the Temple, which Ezra had brought back from the Babylonian Exile.

3. (Isaiah 8:2). 8th century B.C. Uriah the priest was one of the two witnesses—Zechariah, son of Jeberechiah, was the other—to the prophecies written by Isaiah, concerning the conquests of the king of Assyria.

Urias

(Hebrew origin: *God is my light*)

   (Matthew 1:6). 10th century B.C Urias is an alternative spelling for the name of Uriah, the first husband of Bathsheba. (Please see the entry for Uriah [2 Samuel 11:3].)

Uriel

(Hebrew origin: *God is my light*)

1. (1 Chronicles 6:24). 12th century B.C. Uriel, a Levite of the clan of the Kohathites, was the son of Tahath and the father of Uzziah. His descendant Heman was one of

the Levites appointed by King David to be in charge of the singers in the House of the Lord.

2. (1 Chronicles 15:5). 10th century B.C. Uriel, leader of a clan descendant from Kohath, was one of the Levites chosen by King David to carry the Ark of the Covenant to Jerusalem. The porters, accompanied by singers and musicians, carried the Ark with poles placed upon their shoulders.

3. (2 Chronicles 13:2). 10th century B.C. Uriel of Gibeah was the father of Michaiah, King Abijah's mother. In the first book of Kings (1 Kings 15:2), he is called Abishalom; his daughter is called Maachah; and his grandson is called Abijam.

Urijah

(Hebrew origin: *God's light*)

1. (2 Kings 16:10). 8th century B.C. The High Priest Urijah was instructed by King Ahaz of Judah to build an altar, which should be a faithful copy of the one, which Ahaz had seen in Damascus, and to introduce Aramean cults into the Temple of Jerusalem.

2. (Nehemiah 3:4). 5th century B.C. Urijah, the son of Koz, was the father of Meremoth, one of the men who helped to repair the walls of Jerusalem, during the days of Nehemiah. It is possible that he was the same man as Urijah #3.

3. (Nehemiah 8:4). 5th century B.C. Urijah was one of the leaders who stood next to Ezra, upon a pulpit of wood, when the scribe read the Law of Moses to the people in the marketplace. It is possible that he was the same man as Urijah #2.

4. (Jeremiah 26:20). 7th century B.C. The prophet Urijah, son of Shemaiah of Kirjathjearim, greatly displeased King Jehoiakim, by uttering prophesies similar to those of Jeremiah. The prophet fled to Egypt, when he heard that the king was trying to find him and kill him.

The king didn't give up. He sent Elnathan, son of Achbor, to Egypt with a group of men to seize Urijah. The prophet

was captured and brought back to Judah, to the presence of the king, who killed him with his sword and had his body thrown into a common grave.

Uthai

(Hebrew origin: *Succoring*)

1. (1 Chronicles 9:4). 6th century B.C. Uthai, son of Ammihud, of the tribe of Judah, was the leader of a clan that settled in Jerusalem, after they returned from the Babylonian Exile. The book of Nehemiah calls him Athaiah, son of Uzziah (Nehemiah 11:4).

2. (Ezra 8:14). 5th century B.C. Uthai and Zabbud, descendants of Bigvai, returned with Ezra from the Babylonian Exile, at the head of seventy males.

Uz

(Hebrew origin: *Consultation*)

1. (Genesis 10:23). Unspecified date. Uz was a son of Aram and grandson of Shem. His brothers were Hul, Gether, Gether and Mash.

Note: According to the first book of Chronicles, Uz and his brothers were the sons of Shem, and, thus, they were brothers of Aram, not his sons (1 Chronicles 1:17).

2. (Genesis 36:28). Unspecified date. Uz, son of Dishan and brother of Aran, was a descendant of Seir the Horite, leader of a clan that lived in the land of Edom, south of the Dead Sea.

Uzai

(Hebrew origin: *Strong*)

(Nehemiah 3:25). 5th century B.C. His son Palal helped to repair the walls of Jerusalem, during the days of Nehemiah.

Uzal

(Hebrew origin: Uncertain meaning)

(Genesis 10:27). Unspecified date. Uzal was the son of Joktan, a descendant of Noah and Shem.

Uzza

(Hebrew origin: *Strength*)

1. (2 Kings 21:18). Unspecified date. Uzza was the man who gave his name to the garden in the royal palace where King Manasseh was buried. He might have been the man who originally planted the garden, or the current gardener who took care of it.
2. (1 Chronicles 6:29). Unspecified date. Uzza, son of Shimei, a descendant of Merari, was the father of Shimea. His descendant was Asaiah, a Levite who was appointed by King David to be in charge of the singers in the House of the Lord.
3. (1 Chronicles 8:7). Unspecified date. Uzza, a Benjamite, was the son of Gera and the brother of Ahihud.
4. (1 Chronicles 13:7). 10th century B.C. Uzza—also spelled Uzzah—the son of Abinadab, drove the cart, carrying the Ark of the Covenant from Gibeah to Jerusalem, and was struck dead, when he touched the Ark. (Please see the entry for Uzzah [2 Samuel 6:3].)
5. (Ezra 2:49). Unspecified date. Uzza was the ancestor of a clan of Temple servants, who returned with Zerubbabel from the Babylonian Exile.

Uzzah

(Hebrew origin: *Strength*)

(2 Samuel 6:3). 10th century B.C. Uzzah—also spelled Uzza (1 Chronicles 13:7)—son of Abinadab, drove the cart carrying the Ark of the Covenant from Gibeah to Jerusalem, helped by his brother Ahio, and accompanied by King David and a procession of musicians and singers.

When the cart arrived to the threshing floor of Nachon, the oxen stumbled, and the Ark would have fallen if Uzzah had not steadied it with his hand. As soon as he touched the Ark, Uzzah fell dead to the ground.

David, afraid that the Lord had stricken Uzzah for having touched the Ark, left it in the house of Obededom the Gittite, where it stayed for three months, until David brought it to Jerusalem.

Uzzi

(Hebrew origin: *Forceful*)

1. (1 Chronicles 6:5). Unspecified date. Uzzi, son of Bukki and father of Zerahiah, was a descendant of the priests Eleazar and Aaron, and an ancestor of Ezra the Scribe.
2. (1 Chronicles 7:2). Unspecified date. Uzzi, a son of Tola of the tribe of Issachar, was the brother of Rephaiah, Jeriel, Jahmai, Jibsam, and Shemuel. His son Izrahiah and his grandchildren—Michael, Obadiah, Joel, and Ishiah—were all heads of their clans.
3. (1 Chronicles 7:7). 16th century. Uzzi was one of the sons of Bela, and a grandson of Benjamin. He and his brothers—Ezbon, Uzziel, Jerimoth, and Iri, all of them brave men—were heads of their clans.
4. (1 Chronicles 9:8). Unspecified date. Uzzi, the son of Michri, was the father of Elah, a Benjamite leader of his clan, who lived in Jerusalem.
5. (Nehemiah 11:22). 5th century B.C. Uzzi, the son of Bani, was the overseer of the Levites in Jerusalem, during the days of Nehemiah.
6. (Nehemiah 12:19). 5th century B.C. Uzzi was the leader of a clan of priests, descendants of Jedaiah, when Joiakim was the High Priest, during the days of Nehemiah. He was one of the priests led by Jezrahiah, their overseer, who marched, singing at the top of their voices, in the joyful procession, which celebrated the dedication of the rebuilt walls of Jerusalem, during the days of Nehemiah, (Nehemiah 12:42).

Uzzia

(Hebrew origin: *Strength of God*)

(1 Chronicles 11:44). 10th century B.C. Uzzia the Ashterathite was one of King David's brave warriors.

Uzziah

(Hebrew origin: *Strength of God*)

1. (2 Kings 15:13). 8th century B.C. King Uzziah—also called Azariah—the ninth king of Judah, after the partition of the

United Monarchy, was the son of King Amaziah and his wife Jecholiah. He ruled the kingdom of Judah for fifty-two years, a period which included the years when he was coregent with his father, during his youth, and with his son Jotham, during his old age, when he suffered of leprosy. (Please see the entry for Azariah [2 Kings 14:21].)

2. (1 Chronicles 6:24). 12th century B.C. Uzziah, son of Uriel, a Levite of the clan of the Kohathites, was the father of a man called Shaul. His descendant Heman was one of the Levites appointed by King David to be in charge of the singers in the House of the Lord.

3. (1 Chronicles 27:25). 11th century B.C. His son Jehonathan was in charge of the warehouses in the fields, cities, villages, and citadels, during the reign of King David.

4. (Ezra 10:21). 5th century B.C. Uzziah, a priest descendant of Harim, divorced his foreign wife, during the days of Ezra.

5. (Nehemiah 11:4). 6th century B.C. Uzziah, son of Zechariah, was a descendant of Perez, the son of Judah. His son Athaiah was among the first persons who returned from the Babylonian Exile.

Uzziel

(Hebrew origin: *God is my strength*)

1. (Exodus 6:18). 14th century B.C. Uzziel, son of Kohath, was the ancestor of the Uzzielites, a clan of Levites. His brothers were Izhar, Hebron, and Amram, the father of Moses. His sons were Mishael, Elzaphan, and Zithri. His descendant Amminadab was one of the Levites chosen by King David to carry the Ark of the Covenant to Jerusalem, by means of poles upon their shoulders, accompanied by singers and musicians. Michah, another descendant, served in the Tabernacle, during the reign of King David.

2. (1 Chronicles 4:42). 8th century B.C. During the reign of Hezekiah, king of Judah, Uzziel, son of Ishi, and his brothers—Pelatiah, Rephaiah, and Neariah, of the tribe of Simeon—went to Mount Seir, southeast of the Dead Sea, at the head of five hundred men, exterminated the last surviving Amalekites, and settled in the region.

3. (1 Chronicles 7:7). 16th century. Uzziel was one of the sons of Bela, and a grandson of Benjamin. He and his brothers—Ezbon, Uzzi, Jerimoth, and Iri, all of them brave men—were heads of their clans.

4. (1 Chronicles 25:4). 10th century B.C. Uzziel—called Azareel in another verse (1 Chronicles 25:18)—a Levite, member of a family of musicians, was in charge of the eleventh turn of service that played musical instruments—cymbals, psalteries, and harps—in the House of God, during the reign of David.

He had three sisters, and thirteen brothers—Bukkiah, Mattaniah, Shebuel, Jerimoth, Hananiah, Hanani, Eliathah, Giddalti, Romamtiezer, Joshbekashah, Mallothi, Hothir, and Mahazioth—all of them trained to be skillful music players by their father Heman, one of the kingdom's three leading musicians, during that period; the other two were Asaph and Jeduthun.

5. (2 Chronicles 29:14). 8th century B.C. Uzziel was one of the Levites who gathered together to make themselves ritually clean, and to purify the Temple, during the reign of King Hezekiah of Judah. His ancestor Jeduthun was one of King David's leading musicians.

6. (Nehemiah 3:8). 5th century B.C. Uzziel, son of Harhaiah, a member of the goldsmith guild, helped to repair the walls of Jerusalem, during the days of Nehemiah.

Vajezatha

(Persian origin: Uncertain meaning)

(Esther 9:9). 5th century B.C. Vajezatha was one of the ten sons of Haman, the vizier of Persia who wanted to kill all the Jews in the kingdom. His brothers were Parmashta, Arisai, Aspatha, Parshandatha, Adalia, Aridatha, Dalphon, Aridai, and Poratha. All of them were executed, when Haman's plot against the Jews backfired.

Vaniah

(Hebrew origin: *God has answered*)

(Ezra 10:36). 5th century B.C. Vaniah, a descendant of Bani, divorced his foreign wife, during the days of Ezra.

Vashni

(Hebrew origin: *Weak*)

(1 Chronicles 6:28). 11th century B.C. Vashni—also called Joel (1 Samuel 8:2)—was the eldest son of the prophet Samuel. Vashni and his brother Abiah, judges in Beersheba, were known for taking bribes and perverting judgment. The corrupt and vile behavior of the two brothers caused the elders of Israel to request Samuel to appoint a king, rather than let his sons rule over Israel.

Vashti

(Persian origin: Uncertain meaning)

(Esther 1:9). 5th century B.C. Vashti was the beautiful and independent-minded wife of Ahasuerus, king of Persia, usually identified by historians as King Xerxes I of Persia, son and successor of Darius I, who was defeated by the Greeks at Salamis, and became involved in palace intrigues that ended in his assassination.

The Bible states that he ruled over one hundred and twenty-seven provinces, which extended from India to Cush in Africa.

In the third year of his reign, Ahasuerus gave a banquet for all his princes and administrators, a great celebration lasting one hundred and eighty days, where he showed off his wealth. When that party was over, the king gave a banquet to all the other people in Shushan, the rich and the poor, during seven days, in the garden of the palace, where everybody drank as much as he wanted. At the same time, Vashti, his queen, gave a banquet to the women inside the palace.

On the seventh day, Ahasuerus, drunk, ordered the seven eunuchs who were his personal servants to bring Queen Vashti, wearing her royal crown, so that everybody could see her beauty. The queen refused to come and show herself in front of the drunken guests.

Furious, the king consulted his law experts on how to deal with Vashti's refusal to obey his command.

Memucan, one of his chief advisers, declared, "Queen Vashti has offended not only the king but also his officials and all the people in the empire. Her bad example will make all wives despise their husbands. Therefore, I recommend that the king should issue a royal decree, and make it into a law so that it could never be changed, stating that Vashti should never again appear before the king, and that another worthier woman should be made queen instead".

Memucan added, "When this decree will be known in all the empire, women will then treat their husbands with respect".

The kings and his ministers approved the proposal. Sometime later, when the king's anger had calmed down, beautiful virgins from every province were brought to the harem in Shushan, to spend the night with him, and never again to return to him, unless specifically summoned by name.

Eventually, a girl called Esther, cousin and adopted daughter of a Jew named Mordecai, was brought to the king, who liked her more than any other girl and made her his queen.

The Bible does not mention what happened to Vashti, after she was stripped of her position as queen. It is likely that she was put to death for defying the king.

Vophsi

(Hebrew origin: *Additional*)

(Numbers 13:14). 14th century B.C. His son Nahbi, of the tribe of Naphtali, was one of the twelve men sent by Moses to spy the land of Canaan and report back about its cities and its inhabitants, if they were strong or weak, few or many, and to bring back the fruit of the land. The spies returned and gave a report, which was disheartening and defeatist.

Only two of the spies—Joshua, the son of Nun, and Caleb, the son of Jephunneh—disagreed and told the people that they should not fear the inhabitants of Canaan.

The Israelites refused to listen to the words of Joshua and Caleb, and they started to wail and cry. God punished their cowardice by condemning them to wander forty years in the wilderness, one year for each day that the spies scouted the land.

Zaavan

(Hebrew origin: *Disquiet*)

(Genesis 36:27). Unspecified date. Zaavan—spelled Zavan in the first book of Chronicles (1 Chronicles 1:42)—son of Ezer, a descendant of Seir, was the leader of a clan of Horites, who lived in the land of Edom. His brothers were Jakan and Bilhan.

Zabad

(Hebrew origin: *Giver*)

1. (1 Chronicles 2:36). Unspecified date. Zabad, son of Nathan and father of Ephlal, was a descendant of Jarha, an Egyptian servant who had married a daughter of his master Sheshan, a leader of the tribe of Judah.
2. (1 Chronicles 7:21). Unspecified date. Zabad, son of Tahath, of the tribe of Ephraim, was the father of Shuthelah.
3. (1 Chronicles 11:41). 10th century B.C. Zabad, the son of Ahlai, was one of King David's brave warriors.
4. (2 Chronicles 24:26). 8th century B.C. Zabad—also called Jozachar—together with Jehozabad, son of Shomer, murdered King Jehoash. (Please see the entry for Jozachar [2 Kings 12:21].)
5. (Ezra 10:27). 5th century B.C. Zabad, a descendant of Zattu, divorced his foreign wife, during the days of Ezra.
6. (Ezra 10:33). 5th century B.C. Zabad, a descendant of Hashum, divorced his foreign wife, during the days of Ezra.
7. (Ezra 10:43), 5th century B.C. Zabad, a descendant of Nebo, divorced his foreign wife, during the days of Ezra.

Zabbai

(Hebrew origin: Uncertain meaning)

1. (Ezra 10:28). 5th century B.C. Zabbai, a descendant of Bebai, married a foreign woman, during the time of Ezra, and was forced to divorce her.
2. (Nehemiah 3:20). 5th century B.C. His son Baruch helped to repair the walls of Jerusalem, during the days of Nehemiah.

Zabbud

(Hebrew origin: *Given*)

(Ezra 8:14). 5th century B.C. Zabbud, a descendant of Bigvai, returned with Ezra from the Babylonian Exile, together with Uthai and another seventy males, during the reign of King Artaxerxes.

Zabdi

(Hebrew origin: *Giving*)

1. (Joshua 7:1). 13th century B.C. Zabdi, son of Zerah and father of Carmi, head of the clan of the Zarhites, of the tribe of Judah, was the grandfather of Achan—called Achar in First Chronicles (1 Chronicles 2:7)—the man who paid his sacrilegious transgression with his life and the life of his family.
2. (1 Chronicles 8:19). Unspecified date. Zabdi, a descendant of Shimhi, was a leader of the tribe of Benjamin who lived in Jerusalem.
3. (1 Chronicles 27:27). 10th century B.C. Zabdi, the Shiphmite, was in charge of the vineyards that produced the wine for the wine cellars, during the reign of King David.
4. (Nehemiah 11:17). Unspecified date. Zabdi—called Zichri in the first book of Chronicles (1 Chronicles 9:15)—the son of Asaph and father of Micha, was an ancestor of Mattaniah, a Levite who lived in Jerusalem, during the days of Nehemiah.

Zabdiel

(Hebrew origin: *Gift of God*)

1. (1 Chronicles 27:2). 11th century. Zabdiel, of the clan of Perez, of the tribe of Judah, was the father of Jashobeam, the Hachmonite, one of the twelve commanders of King David's army.

2. (Nehemiah 11:14). 5th century B.C. Zabdiel, a descendant of a leading family, was the overseer of a group of one hundred twenty-eight priests who settled in Jerusalem, during the days of Nehemiah.

Zabud
(Hebrew origin: *Given*)

(1 Kings 4:5). 10th century B.C. Zabud, son of the prophet Nathan, was one of the top officials in the court of King Solomon and the king's closest friend. His brother Azariah, also a member of the court of King Solomon, was in charge of the twelve officials of the king who each provided the food for the king and the royal household for one month out of each year.

Zaccai
(Hebrew origin: *Pure*)

(Ezra 2:9). Unspecified date. Zaccai was the ancestor of a clan of Israelites that returned with Zerubbabel from Babylon.

Zacchaeus
(Hebrew origin: *Pure*)

(Luke 19:2). A.D. 1st century. Zacchaeus, the leading tax collector in Jericho and one of the wealthiest men in the town, heard that Jesus was going to enter Jericho by a certain road, and he was eager to see him.

Realizing that the crowd, lining both sides of the road, would make it impossible for a man of his short stature to catch more than a fleeting glance of Jesus, he ran and climbed a sycamore tree, which overlooked the road.

Jesus, passing by the tree, looked up and said, "Zacchaeus, hurry up and come down, because today I am going to stay in your house".

Zacchaeus joyfully climbed down. The crowd was resentful and murmured, "He is going to be the house guest of a sinner!"

Zacchaeus, hearing this, stood straight in front of Jesus and said, "Listen, Lord, I will give half of what I have to the poor, and if I

have taken anything from any man by false pretenses, I will return it fourfold".

Jesus said, "Today, salvation has come to your house, because you are also a descendant of Abraham. The Son of man has come to seek and to save what was lost".

Zacchur
(Hebrew origin: *Remembered*)

(1 Chronicles 4:26). Unspecified date. Zacchur, son of Hamuel, was a descendant of Simeon. His son Shimei was the father of sixteen boys and six girls, which was unusual for families in the small tribe of Simeon.

Zaccur
(Hebrew origin: *Remembered*)

1. (Numbers 13:4). 14th century B.C. His son Shammua, of the tribe of Reuben, was one of the twelve men sent by Moses to spy the land of Canaan and report back about its cities and its inhabitants, if they were strong or weak, few or many, and to bring back the fruit of the land. The spies returned and gave a report, which was disheartening and defeatist.

Only two of the spies—Joshua, the son of Nun, and Caleb, the son of Jephunneh—disagreed and told the people that they should not fear the inhabitants of Canaan.

The Israelites refused to listen to the words of Joshua and Caleb, and they started to wail and cry. God punished their cowardice by condemning them to wander forty years in the wilderness, one year for each day that the spies scouted the land.

2. (1 Chronicles 24:27). 10th century B.C. Zaccur, a Levite, was the son of Jaaziah, a descendant of Merari, who served in the Tabernacle, during the reign of David together with his brothers Shoham, Beno, and Ibri.

3. (1 Chronicles 25:2). 10th century B.C. Zaccur and his brothers—Joseph, Nethaniah, and Asarelah—assisted their father Asaph in his work with the singers in

the House of the Lord, during the reign of King David. Zaccur was in charge of the third turn of the service.

4. (Nehemiah 3:2). 5th century B.C. Zaccur, son of Imri, helped to rebuild the walls of Jerusalem, during the time of Nehemiah. Zaccur worked next to the men of Jericho.

5. (Nehemiah 10:12). 5th century B.C. Zaccur was one of the Levites who signed Nehemiah's solemn agreement to separate themselves from the foreigners living in the land, to refrain from intermarrying with them, and to dedicate their firstborn to God, among other obligations.

6. (Nehemiah 12:35). Unspecified date. Zaccur, son of Asaph and father of Michaiah, was an ancestor of the priest Zechariah who played the trumpet in the joyful procession, which celebrated the dedication of the rebuilt walls of Jerusalem, during the days of Nehemiah.

7. (Nehemiah 13:13). 5th century B.C. Zaccur, the son of Mattaniah, was the father of Hanan, a Levite who was one of the four persons designated by Nehemiah to supervise the treasuries of the Temple, and to distribute the offerings among the Levites and the priests.

Zachariah

(Hebrew origin: *God remembered*)

1. (2 Kings 14:29). 8th century B.C. Zachariah, the fourteenth king of Israel, after the partition of the United Monarchy, and the last king of the dynasty of Jehu, succeeded his father Jeroboam II as king of Israel. Six months later, Shallum, son of Jabesh, a commander of his army, conspired against him, killed him, and usurped the throne.

2. (2 Kings 18:2). 8th century B.C. His daughter Abi was the wife of King Ahaz of Judah and the mother of King Hezekiah.

Zacharias

(Hebrew origin: *God remembered*)

1. (Matthew 23:35). Unspecified date. Zacharias, a prophet, son of Barachias, was

murdered between the Temple and the altar, according to Jesus.

Note: If Jesus refers to the post-Exilic prophet Zechariah, son of Berechiah and grandson of the prophet Iddo, this murder is not mentioned elsewhere in the Bible. The Bible does mention that a prophet Zechariah was stoned to death in the court of the Temple by the command of King Joash, but the name of this prophet's father was Jehoiada the Priest (2 Chronicles 24:20), not Barachias.

2. (Luke 1:5). 1st century B.C. Zacharias, a priest, was married to Elisabeth, a descendant of Aaron. The elderly couple, who had no children, lived in a town in the hill country of Judah.

One day, when Zacharias went to the Temple to burn incense, an angel appeared to him, standing next to the altar of incense, and said to him, "Do not fear, your prayers have been heard. Your wife Elisabeth will give birth to a son, whom you will call John". Zacharias, overwhelmed by his vision, became a deaf mute.

When Elisabeth was in her sixth month of pregnancy, the angel Gabriel appeared to Mary in Nazareth and told her, "You will become pregnant and will give birth to a son. Elisabeth, your relative, is six months pregnant, although she is an old woman".

After the angel had departed, Mary arose and went to visit her cousin. When Elisabeth saw Mary, she blessed her and the fruit of her womb. Mary stayed with her relatives for three months and then returned to her own house.

In due course, Elisabeth's baby was born. On the eighth day, the neighbors came to circumcise the child. They wanted to call him also Zacharias, but Elisabeth insisted that he should be called John.

The neighbors argued that no relative of the couple was ever called by that name. They turned to Zacharias and, by signs, asked him how the child should be called. Zacharias wrote, "His name is John". In that moment, he recovered the power of speech, praised God, and prophesied that his son would be called the prophet of the Highest.

Zacher

(Hebrew origin: *Commemoration*)

(1 Chronicles 8:31). Unspecified date. Zacher—also called Zechariah (1 Chronicles 9:37)—a Benjamite, brother of an ancestor of King Saul, was one of the sons of Jehiel, the founder of Gibeon, and his wife Maachah.

Zadok

(Hebrew origin: *Just*)

1. (2 Samuel 8:17). 10th century B.C. Zadok, son of Ahitub, was one of the two High Priests—the other was Abiathar—during the reign of King David. When David fled from Jerusalem, during the rebellion of Absalom, Zadok, assisted by Abiathar and the Levites, accompanied the king, carrying the Ark of the Covenant.

King David ordered them to go back to Jerusalem with the Ark, and to take with them Ahimaaz, the son of Zadok, and Jonathan, the son of Abiathar.

During Absalom's stay in Jerusalem, Zadok and Abiathar used their sons as messengers to send to King David all the information that Hushai, David's secret agent, passed to them.

After the defeat of Absalom, Zadok and Abiathar were sent by David to the elders of Judah to ask them why they, belonging to the same tribe as David, were the last ones to call him back.

When David was old and his sons were maneuvering for the succession, Zadok was wise or lucky enough to choose the winning side. He, the prophet Nathan, Benaiah, and the army mercenaries took Solomon, riding upon David's mule, to Gihon, where Zadok anointed Solomon as king.

Abiathar, who had made the mistake of supporting Adonijah's failed bid to succeed King David, was not killed by Solomon,

only because he had carried the Ark of the Covenant before David. However, he was expelled from the priesthood and exiled from Jerusalem to his estate in Anathoth. Solomon named Zadok as sole High Priest, and he gave his son Azariah a high position in his court.

2. (2 Kings 15:33). 8th century B.C. His daughter Jerusha was the wife of King Uzziah of Judah and the mother of King Jotham.

3. (1 Chronicles 6:12). Unspecified date. Zadok, the son of Ahitub and father of Shallum, was an ancestor of Jehozadak, the High Priest who was sent to exile in Babylon by Nebuchadnezzar.

4. (1 Chronicles 9:11). Unspecified date. Zadok, son of Meraioth and father of Meshullam, was an ancestor of Azariah— also called Seraiah—one of the Temple priests in the days of Nehemiah.

5. (1 Chronicles 12:28). 10th century B.C. Zadok, a brave young man, joined David's army in Hebron, at the head of twenty-two men.

6. (Nehemiah 3:4). 5th century B.C. Zadok, son of Baana, helped to repair the walls of Jerusalem, during the days of Nehemiah.

7. (Nehemiah 3:29). 5th century B.C. Zadok, son of Immer, helped to repair the walls of Jerusalem, during the days of Nehemiah.

8. (Nehemiah 10:21). 5th century B.C. Zadok was one of the leaders who signed Nehemiah's solemn agreement to separate themselves from the foreigners living in the land, to refrain from intermarrying with them, and to dedicate their firstborn to God, among other obligations.

9. (Nehemiah 13:13). 5th century B.C. Zadok the Scribe was one of the four persons designated by Nehemiah to supervise the treasuries of the Temple, and to distribute the offerings among the Levites and the priests. The other three were Pedaiah, a Levite; Shelemiah, the priest; and Hanan, the son of Zaccur.

Zaham

(Hebrew origin: *Loathing*)

(2 Chronicles 11:19). 10th century B.C. Zaham was one of the three sons that King Rehoboam had with Mahalath, the daughter of Jerimoth, son of King David, and Abihail, the daughter of Eliab, David's eldest brother. Zaham's brothers were Jeush and Shamariah.

Zalaph

(Hebrew origin: Uncertain meaning)

(Nehemiah 3:30). 5th century B.C. His son Hanun helped to repair the walls of Jerusalem, during the days of Nehemiah.

Zalmon

(Hebrew origin: *Shady*)

(2 Samuel 23:28). 10th century B.C. Zalmon the Ahohite—called Ilai in the first book of Chronicles (1 Chronicles 11:29)—was one of "The Thirty", an elite group in King David's army.

Zalmunna

(Hebrew origin: *Shade has been denied*)

(Judges 8:5). 12th century B.C. Zalmunna and Zebah, two kings of Midian, had been defeated by Gideon in the valley of Jezreel, in a battle where one hundred and twenty thousand Midianites perished. The two kings fled with their remaining army of fifteen thousand soldiers to the other side of the river Jordan, pursued by Gideon and his three hundred exhausted men.

Gideon asked the men of the town of Succoth for loaves of bread to give to his famished men, but they refused and mocked him, saying, "Are Zebah and Zalmunna already in your power that we should give bread to your army?"

Gideon said to them, "When the Lord hands me Zebah and Zalmunna, I will tear your flesh with thorns and briers from the desert".

Gideon continued on his way and made the same request to the people of Penuel. They

also refused and gave the same answer as the men of Succoth. Gideon swore that he would destroy their tower on his return, after capturing the Midianites.

Zebah and Zalmunna camped at Karkor with their army. Gideon attacked them and captured the two kings.

On his way back from the battle, Gideon seized a young man from Succoth and questioned him. The boy gave him a list of the names of seventy-seven of the most prominent men of Succoth.

Gideon went to the town and told them, "You refused to give food to my men, because Zebah and Zalmunna were not in my hands. Well, here are Zebah and Zalmunna now". He took thorns and briers and punished the leaders of the town. Then, he went to Penuel, tore down the tower of the town, and killed its men.

Zebah and Zalmunna confessed to Gideon that they had killed his brothers in Tabor. Gideon ordered his eldest son Jether to kill them, but the boy, who was too young and timid, hesitated and did not draw his sword.

The two Midianites said to Gideon, "Kill us yourself! It is a man's job!"

Gideon killed the two Midianites and took the ornaments that were on their camels' necks.

Zaphnathpaaneah

(Egyptian origin: Uncertain meaning)

(Genesis 41:45). 17th century B.C. This was the Egyptian name that Pharaoh gave to Joseph, when he made him his vizier and married him to Asenath, the daughter of Potipherah, priest of On.

Zara

(Hebrew origin: *Rising light*)

(Matthew 1:3). 17th century B.C. Zara is an alternative spelling for Zarah, one of the twin sons—the other one was Pharez—of Judah and his daughter-in-law Tamar. (Please see the entry for Zarah [Genesis 38:30].)

Zarah

(Hebrew origin: *Rising light*)

(Genesis 38:30). 17th century B.C. Zarah—also called Zerah (Numbers 26:20)—was one of the twin sons of Judah and his daughter-in-law Tamar.

His mother Tamar had been first married to Er, and then to Onan, the two eldest sons of Judah, who, both of them, died young. Tamar expected Judah to give her in marriage to Shelah, his youngest son, but, when time went by and this did not happen, she tricked Judah into making love to her.

She became pregnant and, in due time, gave birth to twins, Pharez and Zarah. During the birth of the twins, the midwife, seeing Zarah's hand, tied a scarlet thread on it, but it was Pharez who first came out.

Zarah was among the seventy Israelites who immigrated to Egypt. His sons were Zimri, Ethan, Heman, Calcol, and Dara. Zarah was the ancestor of the clan of the Zarhites.

His descendant Achan paid with his life and his family's for having transgressed sacrilegiously, by stealing some of the booty taken by Joshua in Jericho.

Another descendant, Jeuel, was the leader of a clan that settled in Jerusalem, after they returned from the Babylonian Exile (1 Chronicles 9:6).

Zatthu

(Uncertain origin and meaning)

(Nehemiah 10:14). 5th century B.C. Zatthu was among the leaders who signed Nehemiah's solemn agreement to separate themselves from the foreigners living in the land, to refrain from intermarrying with them, and to dedicate their firstborn to God, among other obligations.

Zattu

(Uncertain origin and meaning)

(Ezra 2:8). Unspecified date. Zattu was the ancestor of a group of nine hundred forty-five men who returned with Zerubbabel from Babylon. Several of his descendants, including Elioenai, Eliashib, Mattaniah, Jeremoth,

Zabad, and Aziza, divorced their foreign wives, during the days of Ezra.

Zavan

(Hebrew origin: *Disquiet*)

(1 Chronicles 1:42). Unspecified date. Zavan—spelled Zaavan in the book of Genesis (Genesis 36:27)—son of Ezer, a descendant of Seir, was the leader of a clan of Horites that lived in the land of Edom. His brothers were Bilhan and Jakan.

Zaza

(Hebrew origin: *Prominent*)

(1 Chronicles 2:33). Unspecified date. Zaza, son of Jonathan, of the tribe of Judah, was the brother of Peleth.

Zebadiah

(Hebrew origin: *God has given*)

1. (1 Chronicles 8:15). Unspecified date. Zebadiah, son of Beriah, head of a Benjamite clan, lived in Jerusalem.

2. (1 Chronicles 8:17). Unspecified date. Zebadiah, son of Elpaal, head of a Benjamite clan, lived in Jerusalem.

3. (1 Chronicles 12:7). 11th century B.C. Zebadiah and his brother Joelah, sons of Jeroham of Gedor, were Benjamite warriors who deserted King Saul's army and joined David at Ziklag, while he was still hiding from King Saul. These men were skilled fighters who could use both their right and left hands to shoot arrows and sling stones.

4. (1 Chronicles 26:2). 10th century B.C. Zebadiah, son of Meshelemiah, was one of the gatekeepers of the Tabernacle, during the reign of King David. His brothers were Jathniel, Jediael, Zechariah, Elam, Jehohanan, and Elioenai.

   His father Meshelemiah was called Shallum in the first book of Chronicles (1 Chronicles 9:17), and Shelemiah (1 Chronicles 26:14).

5. (1 Chronicles 27:7). 10th century B.C. Zebadiah was the son of Asahel, the

nephew of King David who was killed by Abner in the battle of Gibeon. He succeeded his father as commander of the army, during the fourth month, with twenty-four thousand men under him.

6. (2 Chronicles 17:8). 9th century B.C. Zebadiah, a Levite, was sent by King Jehoshaphat in the third year of his reign, to teach the laws of God in the cities of Judah. Zebadiah was accompanied in his mission by other Levites, by two priests—Elishama and Jehoram—and by several officials of the court.

7. (2 Chronicles 19:11). 9th century B.C. Zebadiah, son of Ishmael, was King Jehoshaphat's official in charge of all the king's matters, including the army and taxes, but excluding religious matters, which were under the jurisdiction of Amariah, the chief priest

8. (Ezra 8:8). 5th century B.C. Zebadiah, son of Michael, a descendant of Shephatiah, returned with Ezra from Babylon, at the head of sixty males of his clan

9. (Ezra 10:20). 5th century B.C. Zebadiah, a priest descendant of Immer, divorced his foreign wife, during the days of Ezra.

Zebah

(Hebrew origin: *Sacrifice*)

(Judges 8:5). 12th century B.C. Zebah and Zalmunna, two kings of Midian, were defeated by Gideon in the valley of Jezreel and were later captured by the Israelite leader.

Gideon ordered his eldest son Jether to kill them, but the boy, who was too young and timid, hesitated and did not draw his sword. The two Midianites said to Gideon, "Kill us yourself! It is a man's job!" Gideon killed the two Midianites and took the ornaments that were on their camels' necks.

(Please see the entry for Zalmunna [Judges 8:5], for more detailed information.)

Zebedee

(Hebrew origin: *Giving*)

(Matthew 4:21). A.D. 1st century. Zebedee,

a prosperous fisherman, plied his trade in the Lake of Galilee, helped by his sons, and by hired workers.

Zebedee's sons, James and John, were among the first disciples of Jesus. They were called Boanerges, *Sons of thunder*, a nickname which probably refers to their irate temperaments.

Zebedee's wife, Salome, wanted the best for her children. On one occasion, she asked Jesus that her sons should be allowed to sit in heaven next to him, one at his right hand, and the other at his left hand.

Jesus replied that it was not in his power to grant her wish, as those places belonged to those for whom God had prepared them.

Zebina

(Hebrew origin: *Gainfulness*)

(Ezra 10:43). 5th century B.C. Zebina, a descendant of Nebo, divorced his foreign wife, during the days of Ezra.

Zebudah

(Hebrew origin: *Gainfulness*)

(2 Kings 23:36). 7th century B.C. Zebudah, the daughter of Pedaiah, was the wife of King Josiah and the mother of King Jehoiakim.

Zebul

(Hebrew origin: *Dwelling*)

(Judges 9:28). 12th century B.C. Zebul was the governor of the city of Shechem, under Abimelech, the son of Gideon.

During the fourth year of Abimelech's rule, a man called Gaal, son of Ebed, incited the men of Shechem to rebel against Abimelech, saying, "Who is Abimelech that we should serve him? If I would rule the city, I would get rid of him".

Zebul sent a secret message to Abimelech, reporting the situation, and advised him to come immediately, and to attack at dawn. Abimelech brought his army to Shechem, during the night, and waited, hidden in the fields outside the city.

Early the next morning, Gaal went out and stood at the entrance to the city. From there, he could see Abimelech and his men approaching, but he did not recognize them.

Gaal told Zebul, "I see men coming down from the hills".

Zebul answered, "You are confusing the shadows of the hills with men".

Gaal insisted, "See, there are people coming down the hills, and another group is approaching by the plain of Meonenim".

Zebul then said to him, "Where is your mouth now? You asked, 'Who is Abimelech that we should serve him?' This is the army that you despised. Go fight them now!"

Gaal and his supporters went to fight against Abimelech, but they were defeated and ran away. Zebul then expelled the rebels from the city. Abimelech punished Shechem, by killing the inhabitants and destroying the city completely.

Zebulun

(Hebrew origin: *Habitation*)

(Genesis 30:20). 17th century B.C. Zebulun, the ancestor of the tribe of Zebulun, was the tenth son of his father Jacob and the sixth son of his mother Leah. He was born in Paddan-Aram where Jacob was working for his father-in-law Laban.

Leah gave him the name Zebulun, because, she said, "God has given me a fine gift. Now, my husband will accept me, because I have borne him six sons".

Zebulun was the full brother of Issachar, Reuben, Levi, Judah, and Simeon, sons of Leah. His half brothers were Gad and Asher, sons of Zilpah; Dan and Naphtali, sons of Bilhah; and Benjamin and Joseph, sons of Rachel. His sister was Dinah, daughter of Leah.

Zebulun, together with his brothers, was involved in the events that led to Joseph being taken as a slave to Egypt. (For the detailed story of Joseph and his brothers, please see the entry for Joseph.)

Years later, when there was a famine in Canaan, Zebulun and his brothers were sent by Jacob to Egypt to buy corn. Joseph, who was now the second most powerful man in the country, recognized them, forgave them, and invited them to settle in Egypt.

Zebulun and his sons—Sered, Elon, and Jahleel—were among the seventy Israelites who immigrated to Egypt. They arrived in Goshen, and Joseph came to them in his chariot. He greeted his father, embraced him, and wept for a long time.

Seventeen years later, Jacob, feeling that he would soon die, called his sons to bless them, and he said about Zebulun, "He will live beside the sea, and his territory will reach as far as Sidon".

Jacob's last words were to ask them to bury him in the cave of Machpelah, where Abraham, Sarah, Isaac, Rebekah, and Leah were buried. Jacob's body was accompanied on his last trip by his sons, their children, flocks and herds, all the officials of Pharaoh and members of his court, chariots and horsemen. Before crossing the Jordan, the funeral procession made a stop and mourned Jacob for seven days. Then, Judah and his brothers took him to Canaan and buried him in the cave of Machpelah.

After burying their father, they all returned to Canaan. Joseph's brothers feared that, with Jacob now dead, Joseph would pay them back for the wrong that they had done to him.

They sent a message to Joseph, saying that Jacob, before his death, had told them to urge Joseph to forgive them. Judah and his brothers came to Joseph, flung themselves before him, and told him that they were prepared to be his slaves.

Joseph answered kindly, "Do not fear! Although you intended me harm, God intended it all for good, to assure the survival of many people. Don't worry; I will take care of you and your children".

Centuries later, Moses, in his farewell blessings to the tribes, said, "May Zebulun be prosperous in their trade on the sea"

When Joshua conquered Canaan, the tribe of Zebulun settled in the Galilee, north of Megiddo. The Assyrians exiled them in the 8th century B.C., and they disappeared from history, being known since then as one of the "ten lost tribes".

Zechariah

(Hebrew origin: *God has remembered*)

1. (1 Chronicles 5:7). Unspecified date. Zechariah, a Reubenite, was related to Jeiel, the leader of his clan.

2. (1 Chronicles 9:21). 10th century B.C. Zechariah, the son of Meshelemiah, a descendant of Korah, was chosen to be the gatekeeper of the North Gate, during the reign of King David. He enjoyed a reputation as a wise counselor.

   His father Meshelemiah—also called Shallum and Shelemiah—was the head of all the gatekeepers and was in charge of the East Gate of the Tabernacle.

   Zechariah's brothers were Jediael, Zebadiah, Jathniel, Elam, Jehohanan, and Elioenai.

3. (1 Chronicles 9:37). Unspecified date. Zechariah—also called Zacher (1 Chronicles 8:31)—a Benjamite, brother of an ancestor of King Saul, was one of the sons of Jehiel, the founder of Gibeon, and his wife Maachah.

4. (1 Chronicles 15:18). 10th century B.C. Zechariah, a Levite of the second rank, was one of the Levites chosen by their chief to sing and play musical instruments in front of the Ark of the Covenant, when it was carried from the house of Obededom to its resting place in Jerusalem, during the reign of King David.

5. (1 Chronicles 15:24). 10th century B.C. Zechariah was one of the priests who blew the trumpets, during the joyful procession, led by King David that brought the Ark of the Covenant to Jerusalem.

6. (1 Chronicles 24:25). 10th century B.C. Zechariah, a Levite, son of Isshiah, a descendant of Rehabiah, served in the Tabernacle, during the reign of David.

7. (1 Chronicles 26:11) 10th century B.C. Zechariah, son of Hosah, a Levite descendant of Merari, was one of the gatekeepers of the Tabernacle, during the reign of King David. His brothers were Simri, Hilkiah, and Tebaliah.

   Hosah, their father, was posted on the western side of the Tabernacle, near the Shallecheth Gate.

8. (1 Chronicles 27:21). 11th century B.C. His son Iddo was the leader of the half tribe of Manasseh that lived in Gilead, during the reign of King David.

9. (2 Chronicles 17:7). 9th century B.C. Zechariah, an official in the court of King Jehoshaphat, was sent by the king, during the third year of his reign, together with other officials, Levites, and priests, to teach the laws of God in the cities of Judah.

10. (2 Chronicles 20:14). 9th century B.C. Zechariah, son of Benaiah, was a Levite descendant of Asaph. His son Jahaziel prophesied to King Jehoshaphat that he would not have to fight against a large army of Moabites and Ammonites that were coming against him, because God would win the battle. The prophecy came true, when the invaders fought among themselves and annihilated each other.

11. (2 Chronicles 21:2). 9th century B.C. Zechariah was one of the sons of King Jehoshaphat. When the king named his firstborn son Jehoram as heir to the throne, he gave to Zechariah and to his other sons generous gifts of gold, silver, and fenced cities, to compensate them. Jehoram, upon ascending to the throne, killed Zechariah and all his other brothers.

12. (2 Chronicles 24:20). 9th century B.C. Zechariah was the son of the High Priest Jehoiada, the man who helped dethrone Athaliah and restored the crown to Jehoash, the legitimate heir to the throne of Judah.

    His father Jehoiada died at a very old age and was buried in the royal tombs of the City of David, in recognition of the service that he had given to the Temple and to the king. After Jehoiada's death the people stopped worshipping in the Temple and reverted to idolatry.

    Zechariah, who had succeeded his father as High Priest, told the people that they were bringing disaster upon themselves for disobeying God's commands. The king became angry and, forgetting the debt of gratitude that he owed to Jehoiada, gave orders to stone Zechariah to death in the courtyard of the Temple. Years later, conspirators killed Jehoash to avenge the death of Zechariah.

13. (2 Chronicles 26:5). 8th century B.C. Zechariah, a man who had understanding in visions of God, instructed King Uzziah of Judah on matters related to worship.

14. (2 Chronicles 29:1). 8th century B.C. His daughter Abijah was the wife of King Ahaz and the mother of King Hezekiah.

15. (2 Chronicles 29:13). 8th century B.C. Zechariah and Mattaniah, descendants of Asaph, were among the Levites who assembled all the other Levites to make themselves ritually clean, and to purify the Temple, during the reign of King Hezekiah of Judah.

16. (2 Chronicles 34:12). 7th century B.C. Zechariah, a Levite of the clan of the Kohathites, was one of the four overseers of the repairs done in the Temple, during the reign of King Josiah. The other overseers were Obadiah, Jahath—both were descendants of Merari—and Meshullam of the clan of the Kohathites.

Zechariah was one of the Levites who gave to the priests, for the Passover offerings, over two thousand small cattle and three hundred oxen, which had been donated by the princes of the kingdom.

17. (2 Chronicles 35:8). 7th century B.C. During the reign of King Josiah, the king and the princes of the kingdom donated thousands of cattle and oxen to be used for the Passover offerings. Zechariah, one of the rulers of the Temple, was among those who donated lambs, goats, and bulls to the priests for the Passover sacrifices.

18. (Ezra 8:3). 5th century B.C. Zechariah, a descendant of Pharosh, returned with Ezra from Babylon, leading one hundred and fifty men.

19. (Ezra 8:11). 5th century B.C. Zechariah, a descendant of Bebai, returned with Ezra from Babylon, leading twenty-eight males.

20. (Ezra 8:16). 5th century B.C. Zechariah was one of the leaders of the people sent by Ezra to Casiphia, to request Iddo to send them a number of Levites to serve in the Temple in Jerusalem.

21. (Ezra 10:26). 5th century B.C. Zechariah, a descendant of Elam, divorced his foreign wife, during the days of Ezra.

22. (Nehemiah 8:4). 5th century B.C. Zechariah was one of the leaders who stood next to Ezra, upon a pulpit of wood, when the scribe read the Law of Moses to the people in the marketplace.

23. (Nehemiah 11:4). Unspecified date. Zechariah, son of Amariah, was the father of Uzziah, of the clan of Perez, of the tribe of Judah. His descendant Athaiah settled in Jerusalem, after the exile.

24. (Nehemiah 11:5). Unspecified date. Zechariah, the son of Shiloni and father of Joiarib, was an ancestor of Maaseiah, one of the persons who settled in Jerusalem, after the return from the Babylonian Exile.

25. (Nehemiah 11:12). Unspecified date. Zechariah, son of Pashur, was the father of Amzi. His descendant Adaiah was a Temple priest, during the days of Nehemiah.

26. (Nehemiah 12:16). 5th century B.C. Zechariah, a descendant from Iddo, was the head of a priestly clan, when Joiakim was High Priest, during the time of Nehemiah. It is possible that he is the same person as Zechariah #29.

27. (Nehemiah 12:35). 5th century B.C. Zechariah, son of Jonathan, was one of the priests who played the trumpet in the joyful procession, which celebrated the dedication of the rebuilt walls of Jerusalem, during the days of Nehemiah.

28. (Isaiah 8:2). 8th century B.C. Zechariah, son of Jeberechiah, was one of the two witnesses—Uriah the Priest was the other—to the prophecies written by Isaiah concerning the conquests of the king of Assyria.

29. (Zechariah 1:1). 6th century B.C. The prophet Zechariah, son of Berechiah, prophesied in Jerusalem, during the days of Zerubbabel, the man who was appointed governor of Judah by Darius I, king of Persia.

According to the book of Zechariah, Berechiah, the father of Zechariah, was the son of Iddo. However, according to the book of Ezra, Iddo was the father of the prophet Zechariah (Ezra 5:1).

Like his contemporary, the prophet Haggai, Zechariah called for the immediate rebuilding of the Temple, but, unlike Haggai, he attributed the destruction of the Temple and the exile to sin, and he demanded repentance before redemption.

Zechariah's book consists of fourteen chapters, which in style and content are clearly separated into two distinct parts: the first part, from chapter 1 to chapter 8, containing a number of visions; and the second part, from chapter 8 to chapter 14, which include a collection of messages from later times, about the ultimate destiny of mankind. This entire second section of the book lacks any mention of the prophet's name and period.

His literary style consists of descriptions of his visions, which are accompanied by explanations made by an angel who speaks to him, and who also transmits prophecies from God to the prophet.

His prophecy is unique, for the unique importance he accords to the High Priest He also mentions an angel who instructs him, but, unlike other prophets, he himself did not see God.

It is interesting to mention that the prophet Zechariah is the only person in the Bible who calls the land of Israel "Holy Land" (Zechariah 2:12).

The book of Zechariah is the eleventh of the twelve books that make up the Minor Prophets—also called the Twelve—a collection of the books of twelve prophets: Hosea, Joel, Amos, Obadiah, Jonah, Micah, Nahum, Habakkuk, Zephaniah, Haggai, Zechariah, and Malachi.

Note: The phrase "Minor Prophets" does not mean that these prophets are less important than Isaiah, Jeremiah, and Ezekiel. It refers only to the fact that the

books of these twelve prophets are much shorter than the books of the other three prophets.

Zedekiah

(Hebrew origin: *God is my righteousness*)

1. (1 Kings 22:11). 9th century B.C. Zedekiah, the son of Chenaanah, was one of the four hundred prophets who predicted victory to the kings Jehoshaphat of Judah and Ahab of Israel in their war against the king of Syria.

Zedekiah showed a pair of iron horns to Ahab and said, "With these horns you will defeat the Syrians!"

King Jehoshaphat, not convinced, asked, "Is there another prophet of God through whom we could inquire?"

Ahab answered, "There is one more, Micaiah, the son of Imlah, but I hate him, because he has never yet prophesied anything good for me, only misfortune".

Jehoshaphat insisted, "Bring him to our presence".

The officer, who was sent to fetch Micaiah, told him that all the other prophets had prophesied victory, and he advised that Micaiah should better do the same.

Micaiah answered, "I will speak only what God will tell me".

When the prophet came before Ahab, the king asked him, "Shall we march against Ramoth or not?"

The prophet answered, "Go and triumph, for the Lord will deliver it into your hands".

Ahab, sensing sarcasm in the prophet's tone, said, "How many times must I ask you to tell me nothing but the truth in the name of the Lord?"

Then, the prophet said, "I can see the army of Israel scattered over the hills like sheep without a shepherd".

Ahab, on an aside, told Jehoshaphat, "Didn't I tell you that he would not prophesy anything good for me, but only misfortune?"

The prophet continued, "I saw God seated upon his throne with all the angels standing around him. And God asked, 'Who will convince Ahab so that he will go and be killed at Ramoth?' A spirit stepped forward and said that he would entice Ahab by making his prophets tell lies, and God told him to go and deceive him". And Micaiah concluded, "God has made your prophets lie to you, for he has decreed disaster upon you".

The prophet Zedekiah went to Micaiah, slapped his face, and asked, "Which way did the Spirit of the Lord pass from me to speak to you?"

Micaiah replied, "You will find out on the day when you try to hide into some back room".

The king ordered to put Micaiah in prison, under the supervision of Amon, the governor of the city, and Prince Joash, and to give him only bread and water, until the king would return safely.

Micaiah's parting words were, "If you return safely, then God has not spoken through me!" Ahab was mortally wounded in the battle and died in the evening.

2. (2 Kings 24:17). 6th century B.C. Zedekiah, the nineteenth king of Judah, after the partition of the United Monarchy—or twentieth king if the usurper Queen Athaliah is included in the list—was the last king of Judah. His parents were King Josiah and Hamutal. His brothers were Johanan, the firstborn; Eliakim, who reigned under the name Jehoiakim; and Shallum, who reigned under the name Jehoahaz.

Zedekiah, whose original name was Mattaniah, was twenty-one years old, when Nebuchadnezzar, king of Babylon, deposed his nephew Jehoiachin, gave him the name of Zedekiah, and made him king.

During the first nine years of his reign, Zedekiah paid tribute to Babylon, until he rebelled against Nebuchadnezzar. The prophet Jeremiah opposed the rebellion, because he believed that God was fighting for the Babylonians, and was using them as

his instrument to punish Judah and its leaders. Jeremiah concluded that, not only resistance was useless, but that submission to Nebuchadnezzar was the will of God.

Nebuchadnezzar invaded Judah with a powerful army, and he laid siege to Jerusalem. Jeremiah, who was suspected of trying to defect to the enemy, was beaten and imprisoned in the house of Jonathan the Scribe, where he remained for many days, until King Zedekiah had him brought secretly to his presence.

The king said to the prophet, "You can speak frankly".

Jeremiah answered, "I am afraid that, if I will do so, you kill me".

When Zedekiah swore an oath that he would neither kill him nor would he deliver the prophet into the hands of his enemies, Jeremiah advised the king to surrender and, thus, avoid the destruction of the city and his own death.

Zedekiah said, "I am worried that the Chaldeans will hand me over to the Jews that have defected to them, and that they would abuse me".

Jeremiah assured him that the Chaldeans would not hand him over. The prophet then asked the king, "How have I offended you or your servants that you have put me in prison? Please, do not send me back to the house of Jonathan, or I would die there".

Zedekiah told him to keep their conversation a secret, or he would have him killed. He instructed Jeremiah, to say, if he was asked by the officials of the court about their meeting, that he had asked the king not to be sent back to the house of Jonathan to die there.

The king gave orders to commit Jeremiah to the court of the prison, and to give him daily a piece of bread, while bread was still available in the city. Jeremiah was taken back to the prison, where he remained, until the fall of Jerusalem.

The city defended itself heroically, during two years, until, finally, in the year 586 B.C., in the middle of the summer, the

Babylonian army broke through the northern wall, and further resistance became hopeless. King Zedekiah and some of his soldiers left the palace through the garden's gate, escaped from the city, and fled eastwards, toward the Jordan River. The Babylonians pursued the king, captured him near Jericho, and brought him before King Nebuchadrezzar at Riblah in the region of Hamath.

The king of Babylon forced him to watch the slaying of his children, and the slaughter of all the nobles of Judah. Then, the eyes of Zedekiah were put out, and the deposed king, bound in chains, was taken to Babylon, where he died in prison.

Nebuzaradan, the commander of the Babylonian army, burned down the Temple, the royal palace, the houses of the nobles and the wealthy, and tore down the walls of the city. He exiled all the survivors, except for some of the poorest people who were left in the land, and to whom he gave vineyards and fields. Thus, ended the kingdom of Judah, which had lasted three hundred forty years, from the days of Rehoboam till the destruction of the Temple built by King Solomon.

3. (Jeremiah 29:21). 6th century B.C. Zedekiah, son of Maaseiah, and Ahab, son of Kolaiah, were two false prophets who lived in Babylon, during the days of Jeremiah.

The prophet Jeremiah accused them of doing vile things, committing adultery and prophesying falsehoods, and predicted that their death by burning at Nebuchadnezzar's command would be mentioned as a curse by the exiled Judean community in Babylon.

4. (Jeremiah 36:12). 6th century B.C. Zedekiah, son of Hananiah, was one of the officials of the court to whom Baruch, Jeremiah's trusted companion, read the scroll, which the prophet had dictated to him.

Zeeb

(Hebrew origin: *Wolf*)

(Judges 7:25). 12th century B.C. Zeeb was one of the two Midianite princes—the other was Oreb—who were captured and killed by the men of Ephraim. The Ephraimites cut off their heads and brought them to Gideon, who was on the other side of the river Jordan. They complained angrily that Gideon had not called them to fight at his side against the Midianites.

Gideon, to assuage them, said, "Whatever I might have done is nothing in comparison to your success in capturing Oreb and Zeeb".

The Ephraimites were mollified.

Zelek

(Hebrew origin: *Fissure*)

(2 Samuel 23:37). 10th century B.C. Zelek the Ammonite was one of "The Thirty", an elite group in King David's army.

Zelophehad

(Hebrew origin: Uncertain meaning)

(Numbers 26:33). 13th century B.C. Zelophehad, the son of Hepher, of the tribe of Manasseh, had five daughters—Tirzah, Hoglah, Noah, Mahlah, and Milcah—but no sons.

When Zelophehad died, his daughters came to Moses and Eleazar the High Priest, asking to inherit from their father. Moses, after consulting with God, modified the law to entitle a daughter to inherit from her father if he did not have any sons, but with the condition that she had to marry within the clan, in order that her inheritance would remain in her tribe.

Zemira

(Hebrew origin: *Song*)

(1 Chronicles 7:8). 16th century B.C. Zemira was the son of Becher and grandson of Benjamin, member of a family of heads of the tribe and brave warriors.

Zenas

(Greek origin: *Given by Jove*)

(Titus 3:13). A.D. 1st century. Zenas, a lawyer, was asked by Paul, in his letter to Titus, to come to Nicopolis, a town situated on the Adriatic coast of Greece, accompanied by Titus and Apollos. The apostle did not mention why he needed a lawyer.

Zephaniah

(Hebrew origin: *God has encoded*)

1. (2 Kings 25:18). 6th century B.C. Zephaniah, son of Maaseiah, was the second ranked priest of the Temple, during the reign of King Zedekiah. He and Pashur, son of Melchiah, an official in the court, were sent by King Zedekiah to Jeremiah to inquire if God would help the king against Nebuchadrezzar, king of Babylon.

On another occasion, King Zedekiah sent Zephaniah—this time with Jehucal, son of Shelemiah—to ask Jeremiah to pray for him.

Later, Zephaniah received a letter from Shemaiah the Nehelamite, who had been sent to exile by the Babylonians. In it, Shemaiah wrote: "Now that you are the High Priest, instead of Jehoiada, you have the responsibility of putting in prison madmen and self-styled prophets. So why haven't you done this to Jeremiah of Anathoth who pretends that he is a prophet? He has told the people in Babylon that the exile would last a long time, and that we should build houses, plant gardens, and eat the fruits from the trees that we planted".

Zephaniah went to Jeremiah and read him the letter. Jeremiah reacted by sending a message to the captives in Babylon, where he denounced Shemaiah as a false and rebellious prophet, and foretold that neither Shemaiah nor his descendants would live to see the good things that God would do for the people.

Zephaniah and the High Priest Seraiah, son of Azariah, were taken prisoners by the Babylonians, during the fall of Jerusalem. The two priests, three Temple gatekeepers,

several officials of the court, and sixty of the common people, who were inside the city, were taken by Nebuzaradan, the commander of the Babylonian army, to King Nebuchadnezzar who was in Riblah. There Zechariah and his companions were beaten and killed.

2. (1 Chronicles 6:36). Unspecified date. Zephaniah, a Levite father of Azariah, was the son of Tahath and the grandson of Assir, a descendant of Kohath. His descendant Heman, of the clan of the Kohathites, was one of the Levites appointed by King David to be in charge of the singers in the House of the Lord.

3. (Zephaniah 1:1). 7th century B.C. The prophet Zephaniah, son of Cushi, a descendant of Hizkiah—alternative transliteration for the name of King Hezekiah—prophesied in Jerusalem, during the reign of Josiah, king of Judah.

His book, characterized by its magnificent poetry, consists of only three chapters. The first chapter of the book is a description of the day of the judgment of the Lord, a day of darkness, gloom, and total destruction. There is not one word of hope. No one will be spared.

The second chapter of the book is a plea for repentance, followed by the threat of doom of the nations around Israel.

The third and concluding chapter begins as a prophecy of woe against Jerusalem and Judah, but becomes a salvation oracle. The prophet ends his book with a joyful and beautiful Zion hymn of a bright and prosperous future.

The book of Zephaniah is the ninth of the twelve books that make up the Minor Prophets—also called the Twelve—a collection of the books of twelve prophets: Hosea, Joel, Amos, Obadiah, Jonah, Micah, Nahum, Habakkuk, Zephaniah, Haggai, Zechariah, and Malachi.

Note: The phrase "Minor Prophets" does not mean that these prophets are less important than Isaiah, Jeremiah, and Ezekiel. It refers only to the fact that the books of these twelve prophets are much shorter than the books of the other three prophets.

4. (Zechariah 6:10). 6th century B.C. Zephaniah was the father of Josiah and Hen. His son Josiah was the owner of the house where three returnees from the Babylonian Exile, Heldai—also called Helem—Tobijah, and Jedaiah made crowns of gold and silver to place on the head of the High Priest, Joshua, son of Josedech. The crowns remained in the Temple as a memorial to the three donors.

His other son, Hen, was memorialized in the Temple by the crowns of gold and silver, which Helem, Tobijah, and Jedaiah, as instructed by the prophet Zechariah, had placed on the head of the High Priest, Joshua, son of Josedech, and donated to the Temple.

Zephi

(Hebrew origin: *Observant*)

(1 Chronicles 1:36). 16th century B.C. Zephi—also called Zepho (Genesis 36:11)—the ancestor of an Edomite clan, was the son of Eliphaz and the grandson of Esau and his wife Adah, the daughter of Elon the Hittite. His brothers were Gatam, Teman, Kenaz, Omar, and Amalek.

Zepho

(Hebrew origin: *Observant*)

(Genesis 36:11). 16th century B.C. Zepho—also called Zephi (1 Chronicles 1:36)—the ancestor of an Edomite clan, was the son of Eliphaz and the grandson of Esau and his wife Adah, the daughter of Elon the Hittite. His brothers were Gatam, Teman, Kenaz, Omar, and Amalek.

Zephon

(Hebrews origin: *Watchman*)

(Numbers 26:15). 17th century B.C. Zephon—called Ziphion in the book of Genesis (Genesis 46:16)—son of Gad and grandson of Jacob, was the ancestor of the clan

of the Zephonites. He and his brothers—Haggi, Shuni, Ezbon, Eri, Arodi, and Areli—were among the seventy Israelites who immigrated to Egypt.

Zerah

(Hebrew origin: *Rising light*)

1. (Genesis 36:13). 17th century B.C. Zerah, son of Reuel, was the grandson of Esau and Bashemath, the daughter of Ishmael. Zerah's brothers were Mizzah, Nahath, and Shammah. They were all ancestors of Edomite clans.

2. (Genesis 36:33). Unspecified date. Zerah of Bozrah was the father of Jobab, a king of Edom, who reigned at a time before there was a king in Israel.

3. (Numbers 26:13). 17th century B.C. Zerah—called Zohar in the book of Genesis (Genesis 46:10)—son of Simeon and grandson of Jacob, was one of the seventy Israelites who immigrated to Egypt, and the ancestor of the clan of the Zarhite.

His brothers were Jemuel, called Nemuel in First Chronicles; Ohad, not listed in First Chronicles; Jachin, called Jarib in First Chronicles; Jamin; and Shaul.

4. (Numbers 26:20). 17th century B.C. Zerah, also called Zarah, was one of the twin sons of Judah and his daughter-in-law Tamar. (Please see the entry for Zarah [Genesis 38:30].)

5. (1 Chronicles 6:21). 7th century B.C. Zerah, son of Iddo and father of Jeaterai, was a Levite descendant of Gershom.

6. (1 Chronicles 6:41). Unspecified date. Zerah, son of Adaiah and father of Ethni, of the clan of the Kohathites, was an ancestor of Asaph, the Levite appointed by King David to be in charge of the musicians in the House of the Lord.

7. (2 Chronicles 14:9). 9th century B.C. Zerah, the Ethiopian, invaded Judah with a huge army of foot soldiers and three hundred chariots, and he fought against King Asa in the valley of Zephathah at Mareshah. Zerah was badly defeated, and he fled with the survivors of his army.

Zerahiah

(Hebrew origin: *Rising of God*)

1. (1 Chronicles 6:6). 12th century B.C. Zerahiah, son of Uzzi and father of Meraioth, was an ancestor of Zadok, King David's High Priest
2. (Ezra 8:4). 5th century B.C. Zerahiah, a descendant of Pahathmoab, was the father of Elihoenai, who returned with Ezra from Babylon, leading two hundred men.

Zeresh

(Persian origin: Uncertain meaning)

(Esther 5:10). 5th century B.C. Zeresh was the wife of Haman, the vizier of King Ahasuerus. When her husband told her and their friends that Mordecai's lack of respect marred his happiness, she advised him to build a gallows and to ask the king to have Mordecai hanged on it.

Later, after the king had made Haman honor Mordecai through the streets of the city, Zeresh told him that Mordecai would defeat him.

Her husband and her ten sons were hanged in the gallows, when Haman's plot against the Jews backfired.

Zereth

(Hebrew origin: *Splendor*)

(1 Chronicles 4:7). Unspecified date. Zereth, a descendant of Judah, was the son of Ashur and his wife Helah. His brothers were Jezoar and Ethnan.

Zeri

(Hebrew origin: *Balsam*)

(1 Chronicles 25:3). 10th century B.C. Zeri—called Izri in the first book of Chronicles (1 Chronicles 25:11)—was one of the sons of Jeduthun, a Levite who was one of the three leading musicians—the other two were Asaph and Heman—during the reign of David.

Zeri was in charge of the fourth turn of service to play musical instruments in the House of God.

Zeror

(Hebrew origin: *A parcel*)

(1 Samuel 9:1). 12th century B.C. Zeror, a Benjamite, son of Bechorath and father of Abiel, was an ancestor of King Saul.

Zeruah

(Hebrew origin: *Leprous*)

(1 Kings 11:26). 10th century B.C. Zeruah, the widow of a man named Nebat, of the tribe of Ephraim, was the mother of Jeroboam, the first king of the northern kingdom of Israel.

Zerubbabel

(Hebrew origin: *Descended of Babel*)

(1 Chronicles 3:19). 6th century B.C. Zerubbabel, the son of Pedaiah—or of Shealtiel, according to the book of Ezra (Ezra 3:2)—was the grandson of the exiled king Jehoiachin.

Sheshbazzar, a member of the royal family of Judah, had been named governor of Judah by King Cyrus of Persia (Ezra 1:8). The Bible mentions that he returned from Babylon to Jerusalem, leading a number of people, and carrying with him the five thousand four hundred utensils of gold and silver that the Babylonians had taken from the Temple, and that Mithredath, the treasurer of King Cyrus, had given back to him.

There is no further mention of Sheshbazzar in the Scriptures, which, instead, present Zerubbabel as the governor of Judah. This has caused some scholars to identify Sheshbazzar with Zerubbabel.

Whatever the case may be, Zerubbabel and the High Priest Jeshua, son of Jozadak, became the leaders of the first group of returnees, and he directed the reconstruction of the Temple, encouraged by the prophets Haggai and Zechariah. The foreign settlers that the Assyrians had brought to Samaria came to Zerubbabel, and they offered to participate in the reconstruction of the Temple. When Zerubbabel rejected their offer, the Samaritans made every effort to bring a halt to the building of the Temple, and the work did not resume, until several years later.

The foreign settlers that the Assyrians had brought to Samaria went to Rehum, the Persian governor of Samaria, and asked him and Shimshai the Scribe to send a letter, written in Aramaic, to King Artaxerxes, accusing the Jews of rebuilding the walls of Jerusalem with the intention to rebel.

The king, who was persuaded that the rebuilding constituted a threat to his authority, immediately wrote back, ordering the work to stop, and decreeing that the city should not be rebuild unless explicitly allowed by him.

Rehum and Shimshai received the letter, hurried to Jerusalem, and forced the Jews to stop the work. The rebuilding of Jerusalem was not renewed, until the second year of the reign of King Darius.

Tatnai, the Persian governor of Judea, received a report that Zerubbabel and the High Priest Jeshua were rebuilding the Temple in Jerusalem. The official decided to go to Jerusalem, and to see for himself.

When he arrived in the city, he asked the Jews, "Who has given you permission to rebuild?" He also requested the names of the men working on the construction. The Persian official decided not to take any action for the time being, until King Darius would answer the letter that he had written, asking for instructions on how to deal with the matter.

His letter informed the king that the Jews were rebuilding the Temple, and he requested to have a search made in the records in order to verify if King Cyrus had allowed the rebuilding work to be done.

The Persians searched their records, and they found a scroll in a palace in Achmetha, in the province of the Medes, which showed that Cyrus had given his full approval to the rebuilding of the Temple, with specific architectural instructions, and orders that the work should be paid from the royal treasury.

The king wrote back to Tatnai, ordering to allow the work to proceed, to help the Jews to rebuild, and to refrain from interfering with the construction. Tatnai and his officials fully and speedily complied with the king's commands.

Zerubbabel and Jeshua probably died, while the Temple was still being rebuilt, because there is no mention of them being present, during the dedication ceremonies of the Temple, which took place, during the sixth year of the reign of King Darius (Ezra 6:15).

Zeruiah

(Hebrew origin: *Balsam*)

(1 Samuel 26:6). 10th century B.C. Zeruiah, King David's sister, was the mother of Abishai, Joab, and Asahel. The three brothers were brave and loyal warriors of King David. (Please see the entries for each one of them.)

Zetham

(Hebrew origin: *Olive grove*)

(1 Chronicles 23:8). 10th century B.C. Zetham, a descendant of Laadan of the clan of the Gershonites, was a Levite who worked in the Tabernacle, during the reign of David. He and Joel, another Levite, were in charge of the treasures of the house of the Lord.

Zethan

(Hebrew origin: *Olive grove*)

(1 Chronicles 7:10). Unspecified date. Zethan, a brave warrior and leader of a clan of Benjamites, was the son of Bilhan and the brother of Jeush, Benjamin, Ehud, Chenaanah, Tharshish, and Ahishahar

Zethar

(Persian origin: Uncertain meaning)

(Esther 1:10). 5th century B.C. Zethar was one of the seven eunuchs who served in the court of Ahasuerus, the king of Persia, and were ordered by him to fetch Queen Vashti, so that he could show her beauty to all his guests. Vashti refused to come, and she was stripped of her title and position.

The other six eunuchs who served the king were Harbona, Abagtha, Biztha, Mehuman, Bigtha, and Carcas.

Zia

(Hebrew origin: *Agitation*)

(1 Chronicles 5:13). Unspecified date. Zia was a leader of the tribe of Gad who lived in the land of Bashan. His brothers were Michael, Meshullam, Sheba, Jachan, Jorai, and Heber.

Ziba

(Hebrew origin: *Station*)

(2 Samuel 9:2). 10th century B.C. Ziba, who had been a servant of King Saul, was summoned by King David to the court, and he was asked if there were any survivors of Saul's family.

Ziba informed David that there was one survivor, Mephibosheth, a cripple, who lived in the house of Machir in Lodebar. King David had him brought to his presence. When Mephibosheth saw David, he flung himself on his face and prostrated himself. David told him not to be afraid, that his grandfather's land would be returned to him, for the sake of Jonathan's memory, and that he would always eat at the king's table. Mephibosheth stayed in Jerusalem with his young son Micha.

The king told Ziba that he was giving to Mephibosheth everything that had belonged to Saul, and that he, Ziba, his fifteen sons and his twenty servants would farm the land to provide food for his late master's grandson.

During Absalom's rebellion, when David was fleeing from Jerusalem, Ziba came to him with two donkeys, carrying two hundred loaves of bread, a hundred bunches of raisins, a hundred summer fruits, and a bottle of wine, and told the king that the donkeys were for the king's family, the food for his attendants, and the wine for those who were exhausted.

The king asked him about the whereabouts of Mephibosheth, and Ziba told him that he had stayed behind in Jerusalem, hoping that the people of Israel would crown him king. David told Ziba that everything that had belonged to Mephibosheth was now his. Ziba bowed low and thanked him.

When Absalom was defeated and David returned to Jerusalem, Mephibosheth was one of the first who came down to meet the king.

He had an unkempt appearance, because he had not pared his toenails, or trimmed his beard, nor washed his clothes, from the day that the king had fled.

The king asked him, "Why didn't you come with me?"

Mephibosheth told David that he had intended to saddle his donkey and join the king, but Ziba had deceived him and slandered him. He added that he was grateful to David for all that the king had done for him, and that he had no right to appeal to him.

The king said, "You don't have to explain anything more. The property will be divided between you and Ziba".

Mephibosheth answered, "Ziba can take it all as long as Your Majesty has returned home safe".

Zibeon

(Hebrew origin: *Variegated*)

(Genesis 36:2). 19th century B.C. Zibeon the Hivite was one of the sons of Seir the Horite, ancestor of the clans that settled in the land of Edom.

His sons were Ajah—also called Aiah—and Anah. His brothers were Lotan, Shobal, Anah, Dishon, Ezer, and Dishan, all of them leaders of Horite clans.

His son Anah, the father of Aholibamah, one of the Canaanite wives of Esau, pastured Zibeon's donkeys.

Zibia

(Hebrew origin: *Gazelle*)

(1 Chronicles 8:9). Unspecified date. Zibia, of the tribe of Benjamin, born in the country of Moab, was one of the seven sons of Shaharaim and his wife Hodesh. His brothers—all of them heads of clans—were Jeuz, Jobab, Mesha, Malcham, Shachia, and Mirma.

Zibiah

(Hebrew origin: *Gazelle*)

(2 Kings 12:1). 9th century B.C. Zibiah was the Beersheba-born wife of King Ahaziah of

Judah. She was probably killed, along with all the other members of the royal family, when Athaliah, the mother of King Ahaziah, usurped power.

The only survivor of the massacre was Zibiah's baby son, Jehoash, who was hidden by his aunt Jehosheba, until, seven years later, a coup proclaimed him king.

Zichri

(Hebrew origin: *My memorial*)

1. (Exodus 6:21) 13th century B.C. Zichri, son of Izhar—called Amminadab in the first book of Chronicles (1 Chronicles 6:22)—was the brother of Korah and Nepheg. The three brothers were first cousins of Moses, Aaron, and Miriam, the children of Amram, their father's older brother.

   Korah was the leader of a rebellion against Moses, which ended in the death of the rebels, when the earth opened, and Korah and his followers fell inside.

2. (1 Chronicles 8:19). Unspecified date. Zichri, a descendant of Shimhi, was a leader of the tribe of Benjamin who lived in Jerusalem.

3. (1 Chronicles 8:23). Unspecified date. Zichri, son of Shashak, was a leader of the tribe of Benjamin who lived in Jerusalem.

4. (1 Chronicles 8:27). Unspecified date. Zichri, son of Jeroham, was a leader of the tribe of Benjamin who lived in Jerusalem.

5. (1 Chronicles 9:15). Unspecified date. Zichri—called Zabdi in the book of Nehemiah (Nehemiah 11:17)—son of Asaph and father of Micah, was an ancestor of Mattaniah, a Levite who was among the first to settle in the land of Judah, after the return from the Babylonian Exile.

6. (1 Chronicles 26:25). 11th century B.C. Zichri was the father of Shelomith, the Levite who was in charge of the Tabernacle treasury, where the donated and dedicated articles were stored. These articles included the booty captured in battle by King David and his officers, which they had dedicated to the Lord, and also items dedicated by

Samuel, the seer, King Saul, Abner, and Joab.

7. (1 Chronicles 27:16). 11th century. Zichri was the father of Eliezer, the leader of the tribe of Reuben, during the days of King David.

8. (2 Chronicles 17:16). 9th century B.C. Zichri was the father of Amasiah, one of the commanders of King Jehoshaphat's army, with two hundred thousand men under his command.

9. (2 Chronicles 23:1). 9th century B.C. Zichri was the father of Elishaphat, one of the five army commanders who conspired with the priest Jehoiada to overthrow Queen Athaliah and crown Joash, the legitimate heir to the throne of Judah.

10. (2 Chronicles 28:7). 8th century B.C. Zichri, an Ephraimite, commanded the army of King Pekah of Israel.

    During a war between Judah and Israel, he killed Maaseiah, the son of King Ahaz of Judah; Azrikam, the chief of the palace; and Elkanah, the king's second in command.

    The Israelites captured two hundred thousand Judahites, men, women, and children, and took a large amount of booty, which was brought to Samaria.

11. (Nehemiah 11:9). 5th century B.C. Zichri was the father of Joel, the supervisor of a group of Benjamites who settled in Jerusalem, after the return from the exile.

12. (Nehemiah 12:17). 5th century B.C. Zichri, during the days of the High Priest Joiakim, was the leader of a clan of priests descended from Abijah.

Zidkijah

(Hebrew origin: *God is my righteousness*)

(Nehemiah 10:1). 5th century B.C. Zidkijah was the first of the leaders of the people to sign Nehemiah's solemn agreement to separate themselves from the foreigners living in the land, to refrain from intermarrying with them, and to dedicate their firstborn to God, among other obligations.

Zidon

(Hebrew origin: *Fishery*)

(1 Chronicles 1:13). Unspecified date. Zidon was the firstborn son of Canaan, the son of Ham. His name was also spelled Sidon (Genesis 10:15).

Ziha

(Hebrew origin: *Drought*)

1. (Ezra 2:43). Unspecified date. Ziha was the ancestor of a clan of Temple servants that returned with Zerubbabel from the Babylonian Exile.
2. (Nehemiah 11:21) 5th century B.C. Ziha and Gispa were leaders of the Temple servants, who dwelt in the Jerusalem neighborhood known as Ophel, during the days of Nehemiah.

Zillah

(Hebrew origin: *Shade*)

(Genesis 4:19). Antediluvian. Zillah was one of the two wives of Lamech. Her son Tubalcain was the father of the artisans who worked in brass and iron. She also had a daughter whose name was Naamah.

Her husband Lamech boasted to her and to Adah, his other wife, that he had killed two men who had wounded him. He added that, if Cain would be avenged sevenfold, he, Lamech, would be seventy-sevenfold.

Zilpah

(Hebrew origin: *Fragrant dropping*)

(Genesis 29:24). 18th century B.C. Zilpah was given by Laban to his daughter Leah as a wedding gift.

When Leah thought, erroneously as it turned out to be, that she was unable to have anymore children, she gave Zilpah to her husband Jacob as a concubine. Zilpah gave birth to Gad and Asher, both of whom were born in Paddan-Aram.

Zilthai

(Hebrew origin: *Shady*)

1. (1 Chronicles 8:20). Unspecified date. Zilthai, a descendant of Shimhi, was a leader of the tribe of Benjamin who lived in Jerusalem.
2. (1 Chronicles 12:20). 11th century B.C. Zilthai, from the tribe of Manasseh, deserted Saul's army with his men, joined David at Ziklag, and became a captain of his army.

Zimmah

(Hebrew origin: *Plot*)

1. (1 Chronicles 6:20). 8th century B.C. Zimmah, a Levite, son of Jahath, was a descendant of Gershom according to this verse, or a descendant of Kohath, according to another verse (2 Chronicles 29:12).

   His son Joah and his grandson Iddo—also called Eden—were among the Levites who assembled all the other Levites to make themselves ritually clean, and to purify the Temple, during the reign of King Hezekiah of Judah.
2. (1 Chronicles 6:42). Unspecified date. Zimmah, the son of Shimei and the father of Ethan, was a descendant of Gershom, the son of Levi.

Zimran

(Hebrew origin: *Musical*)

(Genesis 25:2). 19th century B.C. Zimran was one of the six sons of Keturah, the woman whom Abraham married, after the death of Sarah. His brothers were Zimran, Jokshan, Ishbak, Midian, and Shuah.

Shortly before Abraham died, he made Isaac his sole heir, and, in order to avoid trouble, he donated gifts to the sons of his second marriage and sent them away to the east.

Zimri

(Hebrew origin: *Musical*)

1. (Numbers 25:14). 13th century B.C. Zimri, son of Salu, of the tribe of Simeon, brought

into his tent a Midianite woman called Cozbi, while the people were suffering from a plague sent by God to punish them for their immoral behavior with the daughters of Moab and their sacrifices to the pagan god Baalpeor.

Phinehas, the grandson of Aaron the Priest, saw this, took a javelin in his hand, went into the tent, and killed the couple. God was appeased by this act and lifted the plague.

2. (1 Kings 16:9). 9th century B.C. Zimri, the fifth king of Israel, after the partition of the United Monarchy, had been the commander of half the chariots of the Israelite army.

The king, who was visiting Arza, the steward of the royal palace, was in a drunken stupor, when Zimri entered the house and murdered him. Zimri then killed all the other members of the royal family and proclaimed himself king.

Omri, the commander of the army of Israel, was encamped in Gibbethon, fighting against the Philistines, when he heard that Zimri had seized the throne and killed King Elah. He went with his army to Tirzah, the capital city, and occupied it.

Zimri, who had been king for only seven days, realized that all was lost, and he committed suicide by burning down the king's palace with himself inside. This event was followed by a civil war, where half the people of Israel supported Omri as the next king, and the others wanted Tibni, the son of Ginath, to be their new ruler. Omri triumphed, killed his defeated rival, and became king of Israel.

Zimri's name became a byword for traitor in biblical times, as for example in Jezebel's sarcastic greeting to Jehu, "Is all well, Zimri, murderer of your master?" (2 Kings 9:31).

3. (1 Chronicles 2:6). 16th century B.C. Zimri, the son of Zerah, was the grandson of Judah and Tamar. His brothers were Ethan, Heman, Calcol, and Dara.

4. (1 Chronicles 8:36). Unspecified date. Zimri, a son of Jehoadah and the father of

Moza, of the tribe of Benjamin, was a descendant of King Saul. His brothers were Alemeth and Azmaveth #1. His father Jehoadah is called Jarah in First Chronicles (1 Chronicles 9:42).

Zina
(Hebrew origin: *Well fed*)

(1 Chronicles 23:10). 10th century B.C. Zina—also called Zizah (1 Chronicles 23:11)—a Levite, descendant of Shimei, served in the Tabernacle, during the reign of King David. His brothers were Beriah, Jeush, and Jahath.

Ziph
(Hebrew origin: *Flowing*)

1. (1 Chronicles 4:16). Unspecified date. Ziph, son of Jehaleleel, was a descendant of Judah. His brothers were Tiria, Ziphah, and Asareel.

2. (1 Chronicles 2:42). Unspecified date. Ziph was the son of Mesha and the grandson of Caleb.

Ziphah
(Hebrew origin: *Flowing*)

(1 Chronicles 4:16). Unspecified date. Ziphah, son of Jehaleleel, was a descendant of Judah. His brothers were Ziph, Tiria, and Asareel.

Ziphion
(Hebrew origin: *Watchman*)

(Genesis 46:16). 17th century B.C. Ziphion—called Zephon in the book of Numbers (Numbers 26:15)—son of Gad and grandson of Jacob, was the ancestor of the clan of the Zephonites. He and his brothers— Haggi, Shuni, Ezbon, Eri, Arodi, and Areli—were among the seventy Israelites who immigrated to Egypt.

Zippor

(Hebrew origin: *Bird*)

(Numbers 22:2). 14th century B.C. Zippor was the father of Balak, the king of Moab in the days of Moses, who hired the seer Balaam to curse the people of Israel.

Zipporah

(Hebrew origin: *Bird*)

(Exodus 2:21). 13th century B.C. Zipporah, the wife of Moses, was one of the seven daughters of Reuel, a Midianite priest, who was also called Jethro (Exodus 3:1), Raguel (Numbers 10:29), and Hobab (Judges 4:11).

Moses, fleeing from Egypt, arrived in Midian and sat down by a well. Seven girls approached and tried to draw water. Shepherds, who were standing nearby, drove them away. Moses came to their rescue and watered their animals for them.

When the girls returned home, their father Reuel asked them, "Why are you back so early today?"

The girls answered, "An Egyptian rescued us from the shepherds, drew water for us, and watered the animals".

"Where is he?" Reuel asked his daughters. "Why did you leave him? Call him and invite him to eat with us".

Moses stayed to live with the Midianite priest and his family. Reuel gave him his daughter Zipporah in marriage. The couple had two sons: Gershom and Eliezer.

After all the men in Egypt who had sought his death had died, God commanded Moses to return to Egypt. Moses took his wife and sons and started his journey back to Egypt. On the road, they stayed in an inn, and a mysterious incident took place. God came and sought to kill Moses. Zipporah quickly circumcised Gershom with a sharp stone and touched Moses' legs with it, saying, "You are truly a bridegroom of blood to me".

After that event, Moses sent Zipporah and the children back to her father Jethro in Midian, and he continued alone to Egypt.

After Moses succeeded in taking the Israelites out of Egypt, Jethro came to the Hebrew camp in the wilderness, bringing with him Zipporah and her two sons, Gershom and Eliezer, who had been staying with him.

Some scholars identify Zipporah with the Ethiopian woman, whose marriage to Moses was harshly criticized by Miriam and Aaron (Numbers 12:1).

Zithri

(Hebrew origin: *Protective*)

(Exodus 6:22). 13th century B.C. Zithri, son of Uzziel, a descendant of Levi, was a first cousin of Moses and Aaron. His brothers were Elzaphan and Mishael.

Ziza

(Hebrew origin: *Prominence*)

1. (1 Chronicles 4:37). 8th century B.C. Ziza, son of Shiphi, was one of the leaders of the tribe of Simeon who went to the fertile valley of Gedor in search of pasture for their flocks, during the reign of Hezekiah, king of Judah. The Simeonites destroyed the tents of the people—descendants of Ham—who lived there, wiped them out forever, and settled in their place.

2. (2 Chronicles 11:20). 10th century B.C. Ziza was one of the sons of King Rehoboam and his favorite wife Maachah, the daughter of Absalom. His brothers were Abijah—who succeeded King Rehoboam—Attai, and Shelomith.

Zizah

(Hebrew origin: *Prominence*)

(1 Chronicles 23:11). 10th century B.C. Zizah—also called Zina (1 Chronicles 23:10)—a Levite, descendant of Shimei, served in the Tabernacle, during the reign of King David. His brothers were Beriah, Jeush, and Jahath.

Zobebah

(Hebrew origin: *Canopy*)

(1 Chronicles 4:8). Unspecified date.

Zobebah, a descendant of Judah, was the son of Coz.

Zohar

(Hebrew origin: *Whiteness*)

1. (Genesis 23:8). 19th century B.C. Zohar, the Hittite, was the father of Ephron, the man who sold the cave of Machpelah to Abraham.
2. (Genesis 46:10). 17th century B.C. Zohar— was called Zerah in the book of Numbers (Numbers 26:13)—a son of Simeon and grandson of Jacob, was one of the seventy Israelites who immigrated to Egypt, and the ancestor of the clan of the Zarhites.

His brothers were Jemuel, called Nemuel in First Chronicles; Ohad, not listed in First Chronicles; Jachin, called Jarib in First Chronicles; Jamin; and Shaul, the son of a Canaanite woman.

Zoheth

(Hebrew origin: Uncertain meaning)

(1 Chronicles 4:20). Unspecified date. Zoheth, a descendant of Judah, was the son of Ishi. His brother was Benzoheth.

Zophah

(Hebrew origin: *Expand*)

(1 Chronicles 7:35). Unspecified date. Zophah, a clan chief of the tribe of Asher, was the son of Helem, also called Hotham. His brothers were Shelesh, Imna, and Amal. His sons were Suah, Harnepher, Shual, Beri, Imrah, Bezer, Hod, Shamma, Shilshah, Ithran, and Beera.

Zophai

(Hebrew origin: *Honeycomb*)

(1 Chronicles 6:26). Unspecified date. Zophai—also called Zuph (1 Samuel 1:1)— son of Elkanah, was an ancestor of the prophet Samuel and the musician Heman.

His son Nahath was also called Tohu and Toah.

Zophar

(Hebrew origin: *Departing*)

(Job 2:11). Unspecified date. Zophar the Naamathite was one of Job's three friends who came to comfort him. They sat down with him for seven days and nights, without speaking a word, for they saw how great Job's grief was.

After Job broke his silence with a bitter diatribe against his life, his friends were surprised. They had come to commiserate and console, not to participate in a rebellion against God's judgment, and so they turned from comforters to scolds.

Zorobabel

(Hebrew origin: *Descendant of Babel*)

(Matthew 1:12). 6th century B.C. Zorobabel is an alternative spelling for Zerubbabel, the leader of the first group of returnees from the Babylonian Exile. (Please see the entry for Zerubbabel [1 Chronicles 3:19].) In Matthew's genealogy, Zorobabel was the father of Abiud, an ancestor of Jesus.

Zuar

(Hebrew origin: *Small*)

(Numbers 1:8). 14th century B.C. Zuar, of the tribe of Issachar, was the father of Nethaneel, the commander of his tribe's army, during the march in the wilderness. Nethaneel was one of the twelve Israelite leaders who donated gifts of silver and gold, bulls, rams, goats, and lambs for the dedication of the altar.

Zuph

(Hebrew origin: *Honeycomb*)

(1 Samuel 1:1). Unspecified date. Zuph— also called Zophai (1 Chronicles 6:26)—son of Elkanah, was an ancestor of the prophet Samuel and the musician Heman. His son Nahath was also called Tohu and Toah.

Zur

(Hebrew origin: *Rock*)

1. (Numbers 25:15). 13th century B.C. Zur

was one of the five leaders of the Midianites, who were killed fighting against the Israelites. Sihon, the king of the Amorites, and Balaam, the soothsayer, died in the same battle.

Zur's daughter Cozbi was taken by Zimri, the son of Salu, of the tribe of Simeon to his tent, while the people were suffering from a plague sent by God. Phinehas, the grandson of Aaron the Priest, saw this, took a javelin in his hand, went into the tent, and killed the couple.

2. (1 Chronicles 8:30). 11th century B.C. Zur was a Benjamite, son of the founder of Gibeon, and his wife Maachah. His brother Ner (1 Chronicles 9:36) was an ancestor of King Saul.

Zuriel

(Hebrew origin: *Rock of God*)

(Numbers 3:35). 13th century B.C. Zuriel, son of Abihail, was the head of the Levite clan of Merari. The clan was commanded to camp on the northern side of the Tabernacle and was in charge of the boards of the Tabernacle, its bars, pillars, and sockets.

Zurishaddai

(Hebrew origin: *Rock of the Almighty*)

(Numbers 1:6). 14th century B.C. Zurishaddai, of the tribe of Simeon, was the father of Shelumiel, the commander of his tribe's army, during the march in the wilderness.

Bibliography

The following is a list of the books which the author has consulted during the preparation of this book.

Alter, Robert, and Carmode, Frank. *The Literary Guide to the Bible*. Cambridge, Mass. Belknap, 1987.

Alter, Robert. *Genesis: Translation and commentary*. New York. W. W. Norton and Company, 1996.

Alter, Robert. *The Art of Biblical Narrative*. New York. Basic Books, 1981.

Alter, Robert. *The David story: A translation with commentary of 1 and 2 Samuel*. New York. W. W. Norton and Company, 1999.

Anderson, Bernhard W. *Understanding the Old Testament*. Englewood Cliffs, N.J. Prentice-Hall, 1957.

Bimson, John J., editor. *Baker encyclopedia of Bible places*. Michigan, Baker Books, 1995.

Bronner, Leah. *Biblical Personalities and Archeology*. Jerusalem. Keter Publishing, 1974.

Encyclopedia Britannica, 15th edition. Chicago, 1976.

Encyclopedia Judaica. Jerusalem, Keter Publishing House, 1974.

Dothan, Trude, and Dothan, Moshe. *People of the sea – the search for Philistines*. New York, Macmillan Publishing Company, 1992.

Flavius, Josephus. *Complete works*. Michigan, Kregel Publications, 1977.

Flusser, David. *Jesus*. Jerusalem, Israel. The Hebrew University Magnes Press, 2001.

Flusser, David. *Judaism and the origins of Christianity*. Jerusalem, The Hebrew University Magnes Press, 1988.

Friedman, Richard Elliot. *Commentary on the Torah, with a new English translation*. Boston. Little, Brown and Company, 1995.

Friedman, Richard Elliot. *The Disappearance of God*. San Francisco, Harper Collins, 2001.

Friedman, Richard Elliot. *Who wrote the Bible?* San Francisco, Harper Collins, 1997.

Gesenius William, as translated by Edward Robinson. *Hebrew and English Lexicon of he Old Testament*. Oxford. Oxford University Press, 1951.

Grant, Michael. *The History of Ancient Israel*. London, Phoenix, 1997.

Gribetz, Judah, and others. *The Timetable of Jewish History: A Chronology of the Most Important People and Events in Jewish History*. New York. Simon & Schuster, 1993.

Johnson, Paul. *A History of the Jews*. New York, Harper and Row Publishers, 1988.

Josipovici, Gabriel. *The Book of God.* New Haven. Yale University Press, 1988.

Keller, Werner. *The Bible as history.* New York. Bantam Books, 1974.

King, Philip J. and Stager, Lawrence E. *Life in Biblical Israel.* Louisville. Westminster John Knox Press, 2001.

Koehler, Ludwig, and Baumgartner, Walter, translated under the supervision of M.E.J. Richardson. Leiden, Netherlands, Koninklijke Brill, NV, 2001.

Mazar, Benjamin. *Biblical Israel: State and People.* The Hebrew University. Jerusalem, Israel. Magnes Press, 1992.

McKenzie, Steven L. *King David: A biography.* Oxford. University Press, 2000.

Metzger, Bruce M. and Coogan, Michael D, editors. *The Oxford Companion to the Bible.* Oxford, Oxford University Press, 1993.

Miles, Jack. *God: A biography.* New York. Vintage Books, 1996.

Rabbi Gilbert, Arthur, and others. *The Bible Reader.* New York. The Bruce Publishing Co., 1969.

Roberts, J.M. *History of the World.* Oxford, Helicon Publishing, 1992.

Rosenberg, David, Editor. *Congregation: Contemporary Writers Read the Jewish Bible.* New York. Harcourt Brace Jovanovich, Publishers, 1987.

Schonfield, Hugh J. *A History of Biblical Literature.* New York. New American Library, 1962.

Shteinberg, Yehoshua. *Milon haTanakh, (Tanakh dictionary).*Tel Aviv, Israel. Izreel Publishing House, 1960.

Strong, James. *Exhaustive Concordance of the Bible.* Iowa Falls, Ia. World Bible Publishers, Inc. 1989.

Wigoder, Geoffrey, General Editor. *Illustrated Dictionary and Concordance of the Bible.* New York. Macmillan Publishing Company, 1986.

Additional Material

David Mandel studied in the University of Pennsylvania under Dr. Moshe Greenberg, considered to be one of the leading Old Testament scholars of the twentieth century.

Today, Mandel is the CEO of Computronic Corporation, a software development company that specializes in biblical software. Among the products released by Computronic are *The Keys to the Bible, Bible Quiz, The Complete Bible Concordance,* and *Bible in Pictures.*

The Compleat Who's Who in the Bible is the fruit of years of research, using the exhaustive biblical concordance software developed by Computronic Corporation.

The Compleat Who's Who in the Bible, the most thorough, comprehensive, and consummate book of its kind, covers the biographies of all the extraordinary characters who people the Holy Book, presented in a contemporary narrative style.

It is an invaluable and indispensable Bible reference book for families, students, teachers, ministers, religious institutions, colleges, seminaries, religious educators, and participants in Bible study programs. Much of the information and references about the persons named in the Bible are distributed across great stretches of the biblical text, scattered in different books. *The Compleat Who's Who in the Bible* brings together in a narrative format all the elements that relate to each person, and presents his or her biography as a coherent and continuous story, instructive and enjoyable. But, more than anything else, these biographies convey the profound truths of the Bible and give us new insights of examples to be emulated or avoided.

The book is all inclusive—every person named in the Bible is included:

- Over 3,400 entries.

- The biographies are Bible-text based; the information is taken only from the biblical text.

- The entries are arranged in an encyclopedic A-to-Z easy-to-use format.

- Alternative spellings or alternative names, when applicable, are mentioned in the entries.

- Each entry includes, when possible, the meaning of the person's name, the approximate date when the person lived, and the person's first mention in the Scriptures—book, chapter, and verse.

The Compleat Who's Who in the Bible is a wonderful companion book for the Bible itself, and a great reference tool. It is also a great read on its own for those moments we have set aside to relax and enjoy an interesting book. The biographies of the biblical personages are presented in an informative and enjoyable format, written with great clarity of language.